Introduction to CRIMINAL JUSTICE

SIXTH EDITION

SIXTH EDITION

Introduction to CRIMINAL JUSTICE

Joseph J. Senna, M.S.W., J.D.
Northeastern University

Larry J. Siegel, Ph.D.
University of Massachusetts Lowell

WEST PUBLISHING COMPANY
Minneapolis/St. Paul ■ New York ■ Los Angeles ■ San Francisco

Composition Parkwood Composition Services, Inc.
Copyediting Marilynn J. Taylor
Index E. Virginia Hobbs
Cover art *Bramante* by Steven Katz, courtesy of Katharina Rich Perlow Gallery
Design, interior and cover Diane Beasley
Illustrations Academy Artworks, Precision Graphics, Accurate Art

Production, Prepress, Printing and Binding by West Publishing Company.

WEST'S COMMITMENT TO THE ENVIRONMENT

In 1906, West Publishing Company began recycling materials left over from the production of books. This began a tradition of efficient and responsible use of resources. Today, up to 95 percent of our legal books and 70 percent of our college and school texts are printed on recycled, acid-free stock. West also recycles nearly 22 million pounds of scrap paper annually—the equivalent of 181,717 trees. Since the 1960s, West has devised ways to capture and recycle waste inks, solvents, oils, and vapors created in the printing process. We also recycle plastics of all kinds, wood, glass, corrugated cardboard, and batteries, and have eliminated the use of styrofoam book packaging. We at West are proud of the longevity and the scope of our commitment to our environment.

610 Opperman Drive
P.O. Box 64526
St. Paul, MN 55164-0526

Printed in the United States of America

00 99 98 97 96 95 94 93 8 7 6 5 4 3 2 1 0

Library of Congress Cataloging-in-Publication Data
Senna, Joseph J.
Introduction to criminal justice / Joseph J. Senna, Larry J. Siegel.—6th ed.
p. cm.
Includes bibliographical references and indexes.
ISBN 0-314-01145-5 (hard)
1. Criminal justice, Administration of—United States. 2. Criminal law—United States. 3. Criminal procedure—United States. I. Siegel, Larry J. II. Title.
IN PROCESS (COPIED)
345.73'05—dc20
[347.3055] 92–23795
CIP 

PHOTO CREDITS

2 Ruby Grady, *Crime and Victim*, ©1982 West Publishing Company; **4** AP/Wide World Photos; **6** ©1992 John W. Emmons/Impact Visuals; **10** ©L. Migdale/Stock, Boston; **21** ©1990 Jeffry Scott/Impact Visuals; **30** ©Brad Markel/Gamma-Liaison; **47** Janet Sawyer, *Hurrying Home*, ©1989 West Publishing Company; **49** ©Ellis Herwig/Stock, Boston; **53** ©Harry Gustafson; **66** ©Bob Daemmrich/Stock, Boston; **72** ©1992 Bill Biggart/Impact Visuals; **74** ©Utsumi/Gamma-Liaison; **82** Harvey Dinnerstein; *Raped*, ©1983 West Publishing Company; **89** Reprinted by permission from p. 89 of *Fundamentals of Physiology*, by Sherwood. ©1991 West Publishing Company, all rights reserved. **94** ©Gamma-Liaison; **101** ©Andrew Lichtenstern/Impact Visuals; **114** ©Stephen Ferry/Liaison; **125** B. H. Armstrong, *Webster*, ©1983 West Publishing Company; **128** The Granger Collection; **140** ©M. Gubin/Gamma-Liaison; **155** AP/Wide World Photos; **160** ©Harry Gustafson; **162** ©Harry Gustafson; **171** Photograph by Joseph H. Bailey and Larry D. Kinney. Copyright. National Geographic Society; **175** David French, *The Opium Dealer*, ©1988 West Publishing Company; **178** ©Bob Daemmrich/Stock, Boston; **183** AP/Wide World Photos; **187** ©L. Migdale/Stock, Boston; **189** ©Chris Brown/Stock, Boston; **197** ©Jon Levy/Gamma-Liaison; **210** Joseph Hirsch, *Motards*, ©1980 West Publishing Company; **213** ©Robert Fox/Impact Visuals; **214** Historical Pictures Service; **216** J. D. Stinchcomb; **219** ©Harry Gustafson; **221** AP/Wide World Photos; **229** photo courtesy of Visatex Corporation; **231** photo courtesy of Printrak International, Inc., Anaheim, CA 92807; **237** Reprinted with permission from Pinkerton Security and Investigation Services; Pinkerton's, Inc., Van Nuys, CA 91406; **240** James Doolin, *Highway Patrol*, ©1988 West Publishing Company; **246** ©Bob Daemmrich/Stock, Boston; **248** ©Bob Riha/The Gamma-Liaison Network; **253** photo courtesy of Sirchie Fingerprint Laboratories, Inc.; **258** ©Brent Jones 1991; **267** ©AP/Wide World Photos; **275** Joe Jaqua, *The Park*, ©1990 West Publishing Company; **278** ©Don Jones/Gamma-Liaison; **282** AP/Wide World Photos; **298** AP/Wide World Photos; **301** ©Ted Soqui/Impact Visuals; **318** Barbara D. Hultmann, *The Professionals and the Law*, ©1986 West Publishing Company; **320** ©Rick Gerharter/Impact Visuals; **330** ©1989 Jeffry Scott/Impact Visuals; **337** AP/Wide World Photos; **349** ©John Running/Stock, Boston; **354** Frje Echeverria, *Franklin County Courthouse, Iowa*, ©1981 West Publishing Company; **356** ©Bill Pierce/Sygma; **359** ©Bill Pierce/Sygma; **369** ©John Running/Stock, Boston; **376** ©John Maher/Stock, Boston; **381** Sally Storch, *The Heart of the Matter*, ©1983 West Publishing Company; **383** ©Harry Gustafson; **388** ©Billy Barnes/Stock, Boston; **401** ©Christopher Brown/Stock, Boston; **412** AP/Wide World Photos; **418** Arnold Singer, *Justice*, ©1982 West Publishing Company; **434** ©Dagmar Fabricius/Stock, Boston; **436** ©Harry Gustafson; **441** ©Bob Daemmrich/Stock, Boston; **445** ©Dawson Jones/Stock, Boston; **453** R. C. Rothchild *The Lawyer*, ©1979 West Publishing Company; **456** AP/Wide World

Photo Credits continue following index

ABOUT THE AUTHORS

Joseph J. Senna was born in Brooklyn, New York. He graduated from Brooklyn College, Fordham University Graduate School of Social Service, and Suffolk University Law School. Mr. Senna has spent over fourteen years teaching law and justice courses at Northeastern University. In addition, he has served as an Assistant District Attorney, Director of Harvard Law School Prosecutorial Program, and consultant to numerous criminal justice organizations. His academic specialties include the areas of Criminal Law, Constitutional Due Process, Criminal Justice and Juvenile Law.

Mr. Senna lives with his wife and sons outside of Boston. He is currently working on a criminal law textbook.

Larry J. Siegel was born in the Bronx in 1947. While attending City College of New York in the 1960s he was introduced to the study of crime and justice in courses taught by sociologist Charles Winick. After graduation he attended the newly opened program in criminal justice at the State University of New York at Albany, where he earned both his MA and Ph.D. and studied with famed scholars such as Michael Hindelang, Gilbert Geis, and Donald Newman. After completing his graduate work, Dr. Siegel began his teaching career at Northeastern University, where he worked closely with colleague Joseph Senna on a number of texts and research projects. After leaving Northeastern, he held teaching positions at the University of Nebraska-Omaha and Saint Anselm College in New Hampshire. He is currently a professor at the University of Massachusetts-Lowell.

Dr. Siegel has written extensively in the area of crime and justice, including books on juvenile law, delinquency, criminology and criminal procedure. He is a court certified expert on police conduct and currently heads the graduate program in criminal justice at the University of Massachusetts-Lowell. He resides in Bedford, New Hampshire with his wife Therese J. Libby, Esq. and their children.

CONTENTS

CHAPTER 7 The Police: Organization, Role, and Function 239

CHAPTER 8 Issues in Policing 275

CHAPTER 9 Police and the Rule of Law 318

PART THREE COURTS AND ADJUDICATION 353

CHAPTER 10 Courts and the Judiciary 355

CHAPTER 11 The Prosecution and the Defense 381

CHAPTER 12 Pretrial Procedures 418

CHAPTER 13 The Criminal Trial 453

CHAPTER 14 Punishment and Sentencing 483

PART FOUR CORRECTIONS 525

PREFACE

The events of the past few years have appreciably heightened interest in criminal justice studies. Highly publicized rape trials involving socialite William Kennedy Smith and heavyweight boxer Mike Tyson focused the nation's attention on intimate violence. The Rodney King police brutality case and the subsequent Los Angeles riots, during which more than fifty people were killed, directed public concern toward the problems of the inner city and the conflict between police and minority communities. The former cases show that the criminal justice system must be capable of confronting the crimes of the wealthy and powerful, while the latter demonstrates that it must deal effectively with the consequences of poverty and urban conflict.

Because the study of criminal justice is a dynamic, ever-changing field of scientific inquiry and the concepts and processes of justice are constantly evolving, we have updated *Introduction to Criminal Justice* to reflect recent structural and procedural changes in the criminal justice system. The sixth edition includes the most critical legal cases, research studies, and policy initiatives of the past three years. It provides a groundwork for the study of criminal justice by analyzing and describing the agencies of justice and the procedures they use to identify and treat criminal offenders. It covers what most experts believe are the critical issues in criminal justice and analyzes their impact on the justice system. This edition focuses on critical criminal justice policy issues, including preventive detention, shock incarceration, community policing, alternative sentencing, gun control, the war on drugs, and the death penalty.

Our primary goals in writing this sixth edition remain as they have been for the previous five:

1. To provide students with a thorough knowledge of the criminal justice system.
2. To be as thorough and up-to-date as possible.
3. To be objective and unbiased.
4. To describe current methods of social control and analyze their strengths and weaknesses.

We have tried to provide a text that is both scholarly and informative, comprehensive and interesting, and well organized and objective, while being provocative and thought provoking.

Organization of the Text

Part One gives the student a basic introduction to crime, law, and justice. The first chapter covers the problem of crime in the United States, agencies of justice, and the formal justice process, and introduces students to the concept of the informal justice system, which involves discretion, deal making, and plea bargains. Also included is material on career opportunities in criminal justice. Chapter Two discusses the nature and extent of crime and victimization: how crime is measured, where and when it occurs, who commits crime and who are its victims, and what social factors influence the crime rate. Chapter Three covers theoretical issues: why people commit crime, and why some people become the victims of criminal acts. Chapter Four discusses the criminal law and its relationship to criminal justice. It covers the legal definition of crime, the defenses to crime, changes in the insanity defense, the Federal Criminal Code, and issues in procedural law. Finally, Chapter Five reviews the major theoretical perspectives on justice and the dominant issues of gun control, drugs, victims' rights and concern for privacy.

Part Two provides an overview of the law enforcement field. Four chapters cover the history and development of criminal justice organizations, the functions of police in modern society, issues in policing, and the police and the rule of law. Community policing and crime prevention are emphasized, along with private security and other current issues.

Part Three is devoted to the adjudication process, from pretrial indictment to the sentencing of criminal offenders. Chapters ten through fourteen focus on the organization of the court system, the prosecution and defense function, pretrial procedures, the criminal trial, and sentencing. Topics covered include bail reform, court reorganization, sentencing policy, and capital punishment. There are also sections on the processing of felony cases, indigent defense systems, attorney competence, legal ethics, pretrial services, bail reform, preventive detention, plea bargaining, the jury trial, courtroom work groups, appellate caseloads, death-qualified juries, and extralegal factors in sentencing.

Part Five focuses on the correctional system, including probation and the intermediate sanctions of house arrest, intensive supervision, and electronic monitoring. The traditional correctional system of jails, prisons, community-based corrections, and parole are also discussed at length.

Among the issues discussed are the prison and jail overcrowding crisis, house arrest, private corrections, correctional workers, private industry in prison, suing the parole board, parole guidelines, and parole effectiveness.

Part Seven explores the juvenile justice system. There is new information on school searches, preventive detention of youth, waiving youth to the adult court, and the death penalty for children.

Great care has been taken to organize the text to reflect the structure and process of justice. Each chapter attempts to be comprehensive, self-contained, and orderly.

New Features

To keep up with the changes in the criminal justice system, *Introduction to Criminal Justice* has been thoroughly revised and renewed in this sixth edition. The evolution of crime control policy has been followed by updating the discussion of the criminal justice system with recent court decisions, legislative changes, and theoretical concepts. A major effort has been made to cover international crime and justice issues and to provide cross-national data on crime rates, as well as police, court, and correctional practices. A new boxed feature, Analyzing Criminal Justice Issues, helps students to think critically about justice issues. The sixth edition also makes extensive use of figures and art work, now in full color, which help students organize and conceptualize material. In addition, some significant changes have been made in the substance of the text:

1. Chapter One now contains a detailed description of the major crime problems facing the justice system.
2. Chapter Two covers the social factors that influence crime rates and includes international crime rates.
3. Chapter Three contains material on theories of victimization.
4. Chapter Five includes a detailed discussion on gun control and white-collar law enforcement.
5. Chapter Six contains a more detailed analysis of the technological changes that are influencing police work.
6. Chapter Seven includes a major section on community and problem-oriented police work.
7. Chapter Thirteen now contains sections on the confrontation clause, high-profile trials, and court TV.

Learning Tools

The text contains the following features designed to help students learn and comprehend the material:

1. Each chapter begins with an outline and a list of key terms used in the chapter. Every effort has been made to include the key terms within the glossary, which concludes the book.
2. The book contains more than two hundred photos, tables, and charts that help students visualize the events and processes of the criminal justice system. The text is now in full color, so the many photos and graphics are even more effective than in previous editions.
3. Every chapter contains boxed features on intriguing issues concerning criminal justice policy or processes. Within these Analyzing Criminal Justice Issues boxes are critical thinking sections that help students conceptualize problems of the criminal justice system.
4. As in previous editions, the major Supreme Court cases that influence and control the justice system are evaluated in some detail in the Law in Review features. Cases include *Burns v. Reed*, on government immunity, and *Batson v. Kentucky*, on the use of the peremptory challenge.
5. A glossary defines key terms used in the text.

Acknowledgments

The preparation of this text would not have been possible without the aid of our colleagues who helped by reviewing the text and giving us material to use in its preparation. These include:

Jerry Armor	Robert Culbertson
William Ashlen	Robert Doyle
David Barger	Gerhard Falk
Cathy C. Brown	Irwin Flack
Steve Brown	Lorie Fridell
George S. Burbridge	Patrick Gartin
Nicholas Carimi, Jr.	Steven Gilham
Kathy Lynn Cook	Kathryn Golden
Steven G. Cox	Peter Grimes

Ed Grosskopf
Earl Hamb
John P. Harlan
Donald Harrelson
William Hobbs
Robert G. Huckabee
Barton Ingraham
Michael Israel
Dorothy K. Kagehiro
John Klofas
James M. Knight, Sr.
Robert Lockwood
Thomas McAninch
John Mezhir
Tom Mieczowski
Frank Morn
Anthony T. Muratore
Michael Neustrom
Robert Page
Helen S. Ridley
Ronald Robinson
Rudy SanFillipo
John Sargent
William Selke
Gayle Shuman
Mark Tezak
Howard Timm
Donald Torres
Laurin A. Wollan, Jr.
Kevin Wright

In addition, important information was provided by: Eve Buzawa, Marv Zalman, John Laub, Sam Walker, Larry Sherman, James A. Fox, Jack McDevitt, Alan Lincoln, Jack Greene, John Goldkamp, Bob Langworthy, Chuck Fenwick, Lee Ellis, Marty Schwartz; the staff at the Institute for Social Research at the University of Michigan, the National Center for State Courts, the Police Foundation, and the Sentencing Project; Kathleen Maguire and the staff of the Hindelang Research Center at the State University of New York-Albany; James Byrne of the Criminal Justice Research Center at the University of Massachussetts-Lowell; and Kristina Rose and Janet Rosenbaum of the National Criminal Justice Reference Service.

And, of course, our colleagues at West Publishing did their usual outstanding job of aiding us in the preparation of the text. Mary Schiller, our senior executive editor, whom we consider a nonattributed co-author, did her usually superb job of guiding us through another edition. Emily Autumn, our production editor, was patient and understanding, as well as thoroughly professional and creative. This beautifully produced text is a result of their efforts.

PART ONE

THE NATURE OF CRIME, LAW, AND CRIMINAL JUSTICE

CHAPTER 1

Crime and Criminal Justice

CHAPTER 2

The Nature of Crime and Victimization

CHAPTER 3

Understanding Crime and Victimization

CHAPTER 4

Criminal Law: Substance and Procedure

CHAPTER 5

Confronting Crime

CHAPTER 1

Crime and Criminal Justice

OUTLINE

KEY TERMS

criminal justice system
predatory criminals
cult killings
intimate violence
child abuse
neglect
sexual abuse
spouse abuse
date rape
shield laws
marital exemption
insider trading
Housing and Urban Development (HUD)
alien conspiracy theory
enterprise groups
power groups
Law Enforcement Assistance Administration (LEAA)
adversary system
probation
intermediate sanctions
jail
classification center
process
probable cause
in-presence requirement
lineup
bill of indictment
information
arraigned
appeal
nolle prosequi
courtroom work group
pro bono

On October 16, 1991, George Hennard, a deranged Texas man, smashed his truck through a plate glass window in a cafeteria in Killeen, Texas, got out, and systematically shot and killed twenty-two people before committing suicide as police closed in.[1] The Killeen massacre was a shocking reminder of the violence that undercuts American life.

Incidents such as the Killeen massacre, though well publicized, make up only a small segment of the overall crime problem. As the 1990s unfold, the U.S. public finds itself constantly bombarded by media crime stories that involve every element of society: wealthy socialites and champion boxers being charged with date rape; drive-by shootings by heavily armed inner-city gang youth; government corruption and graft; Wall Street insider trading scandals. Many Americans have learned to fear predatory criminals and routinely arm themselves with handguns to protect themselves and their property. Public opinion surveys show that 33 percent of the general public considers crime and drug abuse to be the most important national problems.[2] The general public has also grown skeptical of those in political and economic power, questioning the integrity of elected and appointed officials and business leaders: less than 20 percent of the public has a great deal of confidence in the U.S. Congress and state and local governments.[3]

Forming a buffer between the public and the lawbreakers it fears is the **criminal justice system.** This loosely organized collection of agencies is charged with, among other matters, protecting the public, maintaining order, enforcing the law, identifying transgressors, bringing the guilty to justice, and treating criminal behavior. The public depends on this vast system, which employs more than 1 million people and costs taxpayers more than $60 billion a year, to protect them from evil doers and restore justice to their lives.

This text serves as an introduction to the study of criminal justice. The first chapter introduces some basic issues. It begins with an overview of the crime problem, then turns to a definition of the concept and the study of criminal justice. The chapter introduces the major components and processes of the criminal justice system so that students can develop an overview of how the system functions. Finally, careers in criminal justice are discussed to connect the study of criminal justice to future professional employment choices.

Crime in the United States

We live in a country in which crime is an ever-present facet of life. Crime touches upon all segments of society. Both the poor and the affluent engage in criminal activity. Crime cuts across racial, class, and gender lines. It involves some acts that shock the conscience and others that may seem to be relatively harmless human foibles.

Criminal acts may be the work of strangers, so called **predatory criminals** who care little for the lives of their victims. News accounts have focused on "thrill killings," impulsive acts of violence in which a stranger is killed as an act of "daring" or recklessness; adolescents who throw a boulder from a highway overpass onto an oncoming car may be out for thrills or kicks. There have also been reports of **cult killings** involving members of devil-worshipping groups who conduct the "black mass" and are ordered to kill nonbelievers by their leaders.[4] In contrast, many crimes involve friends and family members, including date rape, spouse abuse, child abuse, elderly abuse, and sexual abuse; as a group, these acts are referred to as **intimate violence.**

Regardless of whether crime is the work of strangers or trusted associates, most people view it as a major social problem. Public opinion polls indicate that a majority of citizens believe that too little money is currently being spent on solving the crime problem; about 30 percent of Americans over age eighteen own firearms and 69 percent of these answer "yes" when asked if they would use them against a burglar in their home; about 40 percent believe it is not safe to walk at night in their own neighborhood.[5]

Considering these trends, what are some of the crime patterns that most disturb Americans?

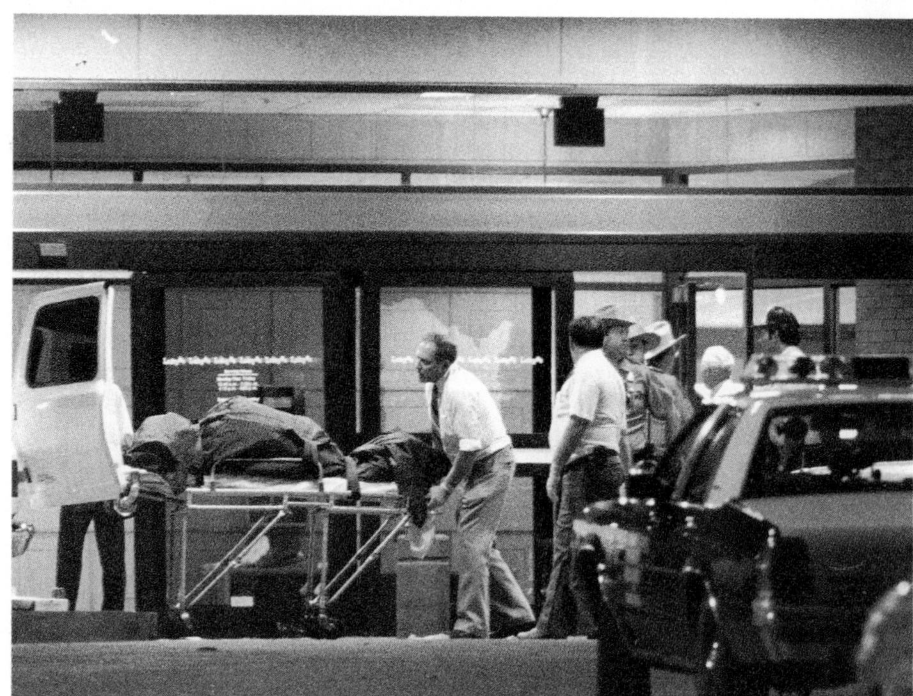

On October 16, 1991 George Hennard killed twenty-two people in Killeen, Texas, the worst mass murder in U.S. history. Here the bodies are being brought out from Luby's cafeteria where the massacre took place.

Gang Violence

After being dormant for many years, organized youth gangs today terrorize neighborhoods in urban communities around the United States. From Boston to Los Angeles, gangs have become actively involved in drug distribution, extortion, and violence.[6]

While youth gangs once relied on group loyalty and emotional involvement with neighborhood turf to encourage membership, modern gangs seem more motivated by the quest for drug profits and street power. The money-making potential of cocaine and crack sales is so great that gangs have become similar in function and structure to traditional organized crime families. Ironically, the decline of the "mob," spurred by federal and state law enforcement crackdowns, has actually aided younger and more violent groups to enter and in some cases dominate the drug trade. The traditional weapons of gangs—chains, knives, and homemade guns—have been replaced by the "heavy artillery" drug money can buy: Uzi and AK-47 automatic weapons. Gang boys rely on secrecy and tight security, and some have eliminated the traditional gang outfit or "colors," which boldly proclaimed membership. Some gangs are now attracting middle-class recruits, lured by the promise of quick drug profits. The number of independent female gangs whose members are as well armed as their male peers has also increased.

To add to their power, some gangs have nationalized their activities by sending out representatives to organize groups in other cities. At one time, gang activity was restricted to the nation's largest cities, especially Philadelphia, New York, Detroit, Los Angeles, and Chicago. Today, these cities still have large gang populations. For example, authorities in Los Angeles claim that there are 600 gangs in operation containing approximately 70,000 members in Los Angeles County alone. Many of these gangs are loosely incorporated into two huge gangs, the Bloods and the Crips, which control a significant portion of the drug trade. Some experts believe that these warring gangs will find common ground and join together to oppose the LA police in the aftermath of the 1992 rioting in South Central Los Angeles. In Chicago, police estimates indicate 135 gangs with over 14,000 members. However, today even smaller cities, such as Cleveland and Columbus, Ohio, and Milwaukee, Wisconsin, which had not experienced serious gang problems, have been the scenes of gang activity.

Serial and Mass Murder

Violent teenage gangs are not the only source of fear in urban United States. Mass murders and serial killings have also become all too familiar occurrences.[7] The threat of the unknown, random, and deranged assailant is a source of constant horror, inspiring such popular films as *Silence of the Lambs*, whose fictional main characters, Hannibal "the Cannibal" Lechter and serial killer James "Buffalo Bill" Gumb, seemed all too genuine when the activities of Milwaukee cannibal Jeffrey Dahmer, killer of fifteen young men, were exposed.

Serial killers operate over a long period of time, sometimes in many different locales. Some, such as Theodore Bundy, roam the country killing a particular type of victim; in Bundy's case, young women. Others terrorize a city, such as Richard Ramirez, the satan-worshipping Los Angeles "Night Stalker," and the unidentified "Green River Killer(s)" believed to have slain more than four dozen

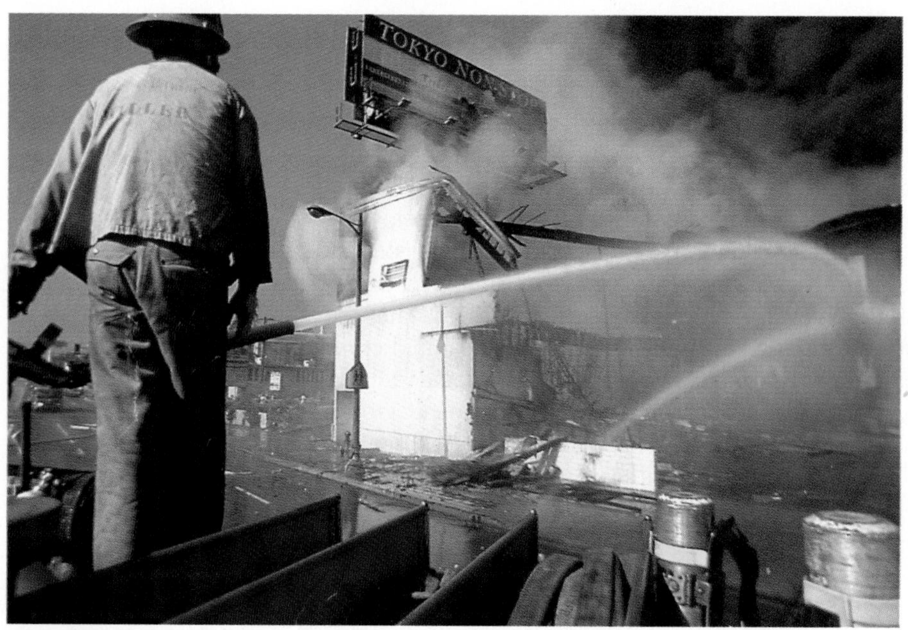

The Los Angeles riot cost hundreds of millions of dollars in damage and resulted in more than fifty deaths. After the riot, warring gangs pledged cooperation to fight the police.

young women in Seattle. A third type of serial murderer, such as hospital orderly Donald Harvey who murdered fifty-four patients, kills so cunningly that many victims are dispatched before the authorities even realize the deaths can be attributed to a single perpetrator.

Mass murderers are those who kill many victims in a single, violent outburst. For example, James Huberty killed twenty-one bystanders in a MacDonald's in San Ysidro, California, in 1984; Michael Ryan, a twenty-five-year-old British gun enthusiast, killed fourteen people in a random shooting spree on August 20, 1987; George Hennard left twenty-two dead in Killeen, Texas.

There is no one type of serial killer. Some seem to be monsters—such as Edmund Kemper, who, in addition to killing six young female hitchhikers, killed his mother, cut off her head, and used it as a dartboard. Others, like the "Hillside Stranglers" Kenneth Bianchi and Angelo Buono, fancied themselves lady's men whose murderous actions surprised even close friends.

Nor is there any one cause of serial and mass murder. Such widely disparate factors as mental illness, sexual frustration, neurological damage, child abuse and neglect, smothering maternal relationships, and childhood anxiety have been suggested as possible causes. However, most experts view the serial killers as sociopaths who from early childhood demonstrated bizarre behavior (such as torturing animals), enjoy killing, are immune to their victims' suffering, and bask in the media limelight when caught.[8]

Intimate Violence

While the violent attacks of strangers produce the most fear and create the graphic headlines, Americans actually face greater physical danger from people with whom they are in close and intimate contact: family members, relatives, spouses, and dating partners.

One area of intimate violence that has received a great deal of media attention is **child abuse.** This term describes any physical or emotional trauma to the child for which no reasonable explanation, such as an accident or ordinary disciplinary practices, can be found. Child abuse can result from actual physical beatings administered to a child by hands, feet, weapons, belts, sticks, and burnings. Another form of abuse results from **neglect**—not providing a child with adequate care and shelter. Another aspect of the abuse syndrome is **sexual abuse**—the exploitation of children through rape, incest, and molestation by parents and guardians. While the actual number of child abuse cases is unknown because so many incidents are never reported to the police, it is estimated that over 1 million children in the United States are subject in a given year to physical abuse from their parents.[9] Though it is even more difficult to estimate the incidence of sexual abuse, Diana Russell's survey of women in the San Francisco area found that 38 percent had experienced intra- or extrafamilial sexual abuse by the time they reached eighteen.[10]

Intimate violence also involves **spouse abuse,** the physical assault of a wife by a husband (though husband abuse is not unknown). In their national survey of family violence, Richard Gelles and Murray Straus found that 16 percent of surveyed families had experienced such assaults.[11] In police departments around the country, 60 to 70 percent of evening calls involve domestic violence.

Date Rape. The nationally publicized William Kennedy Smith and Mike Tyson cases have introduced the public to another element of intimate violence: **date rape** and date battering. Despite their prevalence, less than one in ten date rapes may be reported to police. Some victims fail to report date rapes because they do not view their experiences as a "real rape," which they believe involves a strange man jumping out of the bushes; others are embarrassed and frightened.

Many date rapes occur on college campuses, in dormitories and fraternity houses. Peggy Reeves Sanday has described how the culture of the college fraternity, which encompasses demeaning hazing rituals and antifemale attitudes, supports a climate in which date rape and gang rape is common.[12] To fight back, some campus women's groups have taken to writing the names of men accused of date rape and sexual assault on bathroom walls so that coeds can avoid these predators. Administration officials labeled it "libel and harassment" when such a wall-writing campaign listed the names of fifteen suspected rapists at Rhode Island's Brown University. Brown women countered that it was the only way to alert potential victims to the danger they faced from men who they might have considered trustworthy friends.[13]

Agents of the criminal justice system have not responded to sexual assaults between acquaintances as they have to stranger assaults. To break this pattern and ease prosecution of these cases, some important legal changes have been made. Some states have replaced rape laws with gender-neutral **sexual assault** laws that also protect males from sexual abuse. Other jurisdictions have implemented **shield laws** that protect victims from being questioned about their sexual history unless it can be proven to be relevant to the case at hand. Another change has been to remove the **marital exemption** that had prevented husbands from being charged with raping their wives.[14] In addition, rape crisis centers have been established around the country to help victims deal with the trauma of rape.[15]

Substance Abuse

The United States is currently in a "war against drugs." The public has been bombarded with news reports of the latest seizure of narcotics, the latest shootout involving drug dealers, and the latest death of an entertainer or athlete from a drug overdose.

The most commonly used substance of abuse is alcohol, easily obtained and suspected of being involved in half of all U.S. murders, suicides, and accidental deaths.[16] Alcohol-related deaths number one hundred thousand a year, far more than that taken by all other illegal drugs combined. The economic cost of the nation's drinking problem is equally staggering. An estimated $117 billion is lost each year, including $18 billion from premature deaths, $66 billion in reduced productivity, and $13 billion for treatment efforts.[17]

Equally vexing is the use of cocaine and its derivative crack, which can be smoked in order to give the user an inexpensive and powerful high. An estimated half a million Americans are addicted to heroin and other narcotics. U.S. teenagers and young adults have also been turning to laboratory-created drugs, such as the hallucinogen LSD and meta-amphetamines such as Methedrine, known as "meth," "speed," "crystal meth," or "ice."

Research suggests that many criminal offenders have extensive experience with drug use, and drug users do in fact commit an enormous amount of crime.[18] However, a causal connection between drug use and crime has not been definitively established since many users had a history of early criminal activity before they began to abuse drugs and alcohol. Even if it cannot be shown conclusively that drug use causes otherwise lay-abiding citizens to become criminals, substance abuse certainly seems to magnify the frequency and extent of criminal activity. Research shows that a significant number of arrested criminals test positively for drug use and that as use levels increase, so too do the frequency and seriousness of criminality.[19] Figure 1.1 shows the percentage of people who tested positively for drugs in samples of male and female arrestees drawn from major cities across the nation. This federally sponsored survey finds that the relationship between drug use and crime cuts across age, race, and gender. Nationally, more than 50 percent of all apprehended offenders test positively for at least one drug![20]

White-Collar Crime

As events in the past decade have shown, some of the most costly and damaging crimes are not the violent acts of inner-city gang youth or deranged serial killers but the white-collar crimes of upper-class bankers, brokers, corporate officials, and government officials.

One of the most devastating examples of white-collar criminality involved the looting of the savings and loan industry. During a period of ten or more years, the owners and managers of some of the nation's largest savings and loan banks defrauded investors, depositors, and the general public out of billions of dollars. It has been conservatively estimated that over the next forty years, the cost of rectifying savings and loan fraud cases could total $500 billion, a number almost too staggering to imagine. It is possible that seventeen hundred banks, about one half of the industry, may eventually collapse. Government reports indicate that criminal activity is a central factor in 70 to 80 percent of all these cases.[21]

Another scandal that shook the public's faith in business institutions involved illegal **insider trading,** which rocked Wall Street. Members of distinguished investment firms such as Drexel Burnham Lambert Inc. used their direct knowledge of sensitive market information for their own benefit. **Ivan Boesky,** one of the most prominent and wealthiest investors in the United States, used inside information for which he paid investment bankers in order to profit on the merger

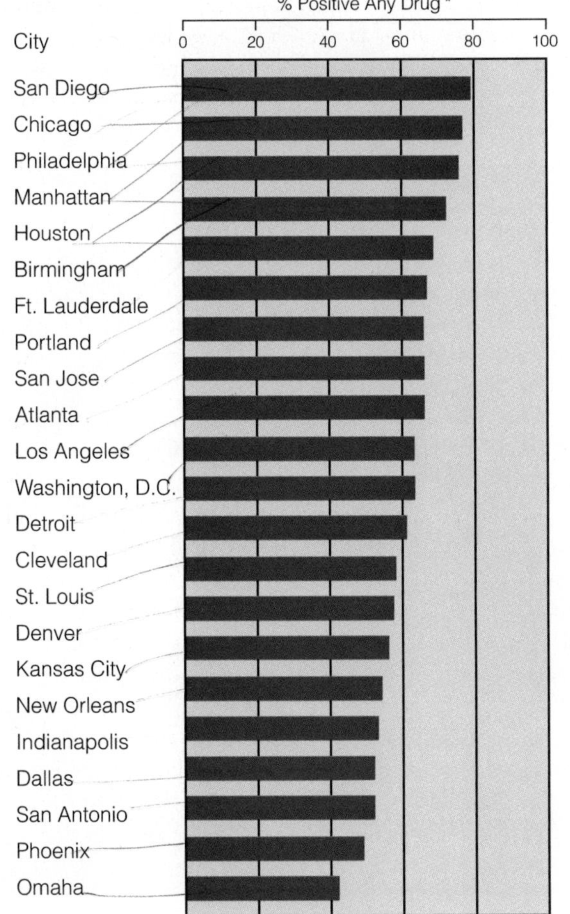

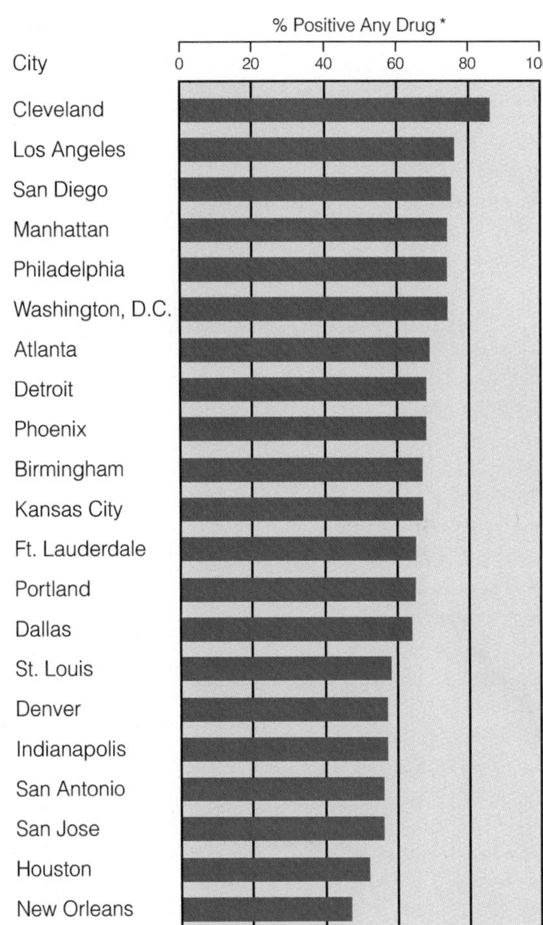

FIGURE 1.1
Drug Use by Arrestees in Large Cities: Percent of Male and Female Offenders Who Tested Positively for Drugs

SOURCE: National Institute of Justice/Drug Use Forecasting Program, 1991.

negotiations between such firms as International Telephone and Telegraph and Sperry Corporation. Facing a long jail sentence, Boesky implicated others, including billionaire junk bond king Michael Milken, who had provided Boesky with inside information. In return for his cooperation, Boesky received a three-year prison sentence. When Milken pleaded guilty to six relatively minor counts of securities fraud, thereby avoiding having to defend against more serious charges of insider trading and racketeering, he received a surprisingly harsh ten-year prison sentence.[22]

Even more shocking and disturbing to the U.S. public have been revelations that government officials used their positions of influence to loot billions of tax dollars. One of the most disturbing scandals concerned the channeling of funds targeted for the poor into the hands of wealthy developers and consultants by officials in the office of **Housing and Urban Development (HUD).** One national magazine branded the conspirators "poverty pimps" who got rich and powerful

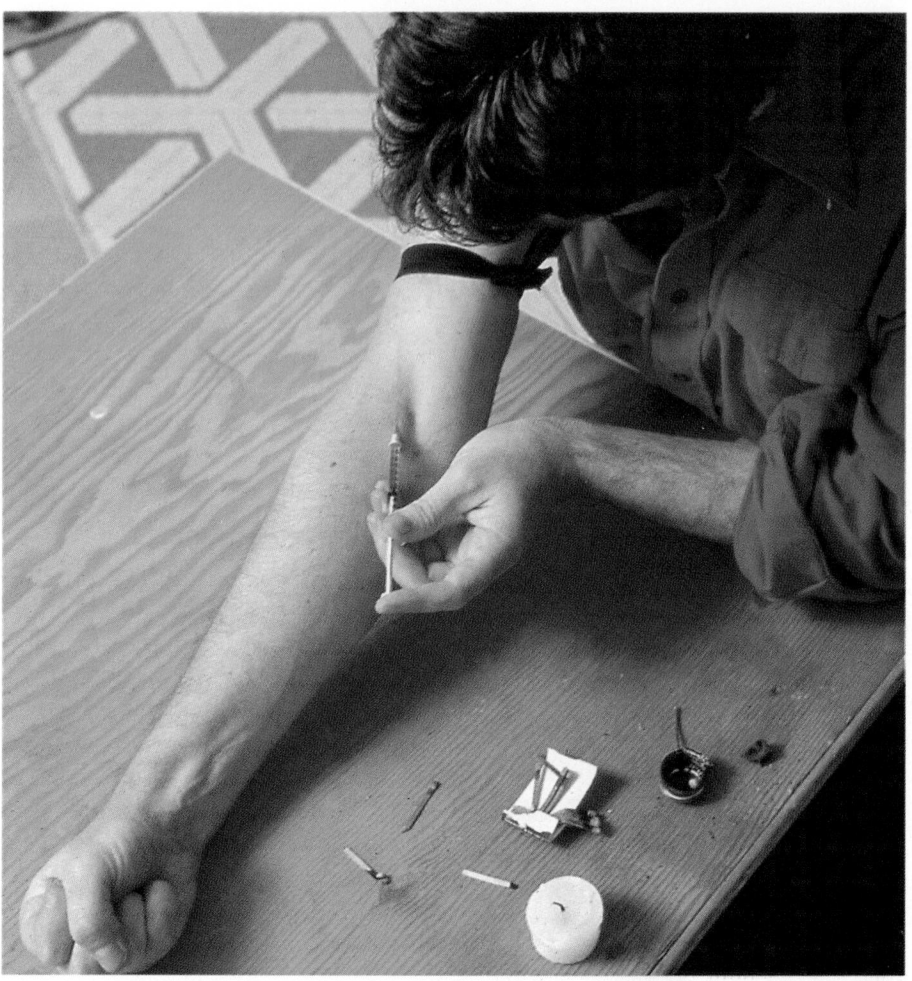

Research indicates that drug users commit an enormous amount of crime, and most criminal offenders have had experience with substance abuse.

by subverting programs intended to help the poor.[23] Over a period of eight years, developers used political influence to drain billions of dollars into questionable enterprises. Even more disturbing were the activities of former HUD officials as consultants and lobbyists who used their personal relationships to obtain cash for the profiteering builders.

The motives for white-collar crimes seem mystifying. Why would otherwise respected and often wealthy business executives and government officials risk all in order to secure illegal payments and profits? Some experts view their actions as a function of an organizational climate in which senior managers wink at behaviors that violate business regulations but make a profit and believe that the end always justifies the means.[24] Another view is that white-collar criminals are simply greedy people who impulsively break the law in order to make a lot of money.[25]

Organized Crime

Organized crime involves the criminal activity of people and organizations whose acknowledged purpose is economic gain through illegal enterprise.[26] These criminal cartels provide those outlawed goods and services demanded by the general public: prostitution, narcotics, gambling, loan sharking, pornography, and untaxed liquor and cigarettes. In addition, organized criminals infiltrate legitimate organizations, such as unions, to drain off their funds and profits for illegal purposes.

For a long time, criminal justice agencies and the general public equated organized crime with the secret activities of close-knit groups of Italians variously called the Mafia or La Cosa Nostra. Many law enforcement officials still focus their attention on so-called crime families in large cities such as New York, Chicago, and Cleveland. Criminologists refer to this view of organized crime as the **alien conspiracy theory.** Another view is that organized crime is not headed by an all-powerful group or syndicate that oversees its operations and settles its disputes; instead, it is a series of groups made up of members of different ethnic and racial backgrounds, including Asians, Jamaicans, Latinos, African-Americans, and Anglos of various ethnic origin, competing with each other for power and profit.

Some organized gangs are **enterprise groups,** which provide illegal goods and services such as prostitution, gambling, and pornography. Others are organized as **power groups,** which provide no tangible goods or services but instead prey upon the public and also upon other criminals through fear, violence, and extortion. Power groups sell protection, demand a percentage of the profits of legitimate businesses, muscle in on unions and other organizations, and carry out large-scale burglaries and robberies.[27]

Federal and state agencies have been dedicated to wiping out organized crime, and some well-publicized arrests have resulted in the imprisonment of important leaders including John Gotti, considered the kingpin of organized crime in New York city. It is estimated that the membership of the traditional crime families is down 50 percent in the past twenty years.[28] Yet, it seems unlikely that the organized crime problem will ever be eradicated. As long as profits can be made from narcotics, prostitution, pornography, gambling, and other illegal enterprises, people will be willing to risk becoming involved in them. And though many of the leaders of "traditional" ethnic crime organizations have been given long prison sentences, new groups including Asian, Hispanic, and black gangs, have filled the vacuum created by federal prosecutors. Organized crime has become more disorganized.

Is Crime a Recent Development?

While we often hear older people say "crime is getting worse every day" and "I can remember when it was safe to walk the streets at night," their memories may be colored by wishful thinking: crime and violence have existed in this country for more than two hundred years.

Crime and violence were not unknown when the nation was first formed.[29] Guerilla activity was common before, during, and after the Revolutionary War. Bands supporting the British (Tories) and the American revolutionaries engaged in savage attacks on each other using hit-and-run tactics, burning, and looting.

The struggle over slavery during the mid-nineteenth century begat decades of conflict, crimes, and violence, including a civil war. After the war, night riders and Ku Klux Klan members were active in the South, using vigilante methods to maintain the status quo and terrorize former slaves. The violence also spilled over into bloody local feuds in the hill country of southern Appalachia. Factional hatreds, magnified by the lack of formal law enforcement and grinding poverty, gave rise to violent attacks and family feuding. Some former Union and Confederate soldiers, heading west with the dream of finding gold or starting a cattle ranch, resorted to theft and robbery. Train robbery was popularized by the Reno Brothers of Indiana and bank robbery by the James-Younger gang of Missouri.

While the Civil War generated criminal gangs, it also produced widespread business crime. The great robber barons bribed government officials and intrigued to corner markets and obtain concessions for railroads, favorable land deals, and mining and mineral rights on government land. The administration of President Ulysses Grant was tainted by numerous corruption scandals.

From 1900 to 1935, the nation experienced a sustained increase in criminal activity. This period was dominated by Depression-era outlaws who became mythic figures. Charles "Pretty Boy" Floyd was a folk hero among the sharecroppers of Eastern Oklahoma, while the nation eagerly followed the exploits of its premier bank robber, John Dillinger, until he was killed in front of a Chicago movie house. The infamous "Ma" Barker and her sons Lloyd, Herman, Fred, and Arthur are credited with killing more than ten people, while Bonnie Parker and Clyde Barrow killed more than thirteen before they were slain in a shootout with federal agents.

While these relatively small and mobile outlaw gangs were operating in the Midwest, more organized gangs flourished in the nation's largest cities. The first criminal gangs formed before the Civil War in urban slums such as the Five Points and Bowery neighborhoods in New York City. Though they sported colorful names, such as the Plug Uglies, the Hudson Dusters, and the Dead Rabbits, they engaged in mayhem, murder, and extortion. These gangs were the forerunners of the organized crime families that developed in New York and spread to Philadelphia, Chicago, New Orleans, and other major urban areas.

The crime problem in the United States has been evolving along with the nation itself. Crime has provided a mechanism for the frustrated to vent their anger, for business leaders to maintain their position of wealth and power, and for those outside the economic mainstream to take a shortcut to the "American Dream." To protect itself from this ongoing assault, the public has supported development of a great array of government agencies whose stated purpose is to control and prevent crime; identify, apprehend, and bring to trial those who choose to violate the law; and devise effective methods of criminal correction. These agencies make up what is commonly referred to today as the *criminal justice system*, and it is to their nature and development we now turn our attention.

The Concept of Criminal Justice

Since concern about crime is not a recent phenomenon, it comes as no surprise that considerable thought has been given to the goal of effective crime control. A sustained effort has been made to create agencies of government whose mission is identifying criminal suspects, providing them with a fair hearing on the charges against them, and, in the event they are found guilty as charged, furnishing them with fair and effective correctional treatment.

The debate over the proper course for effective crime control can be traced back to the publication in 1764 of Italian social thinker Cesare Beccaria's famous treatise *On Crime and Punishment*. Beccaria, an Italian social philosopher, made a convincing argument against the use of torture and capital punishment, common practices in the eighteenth century. He persuasively argued that only the minimum amount of punishment was needed to control crime if criminals could be convinced that their law violations were certain to be discovered and swiftly punished.[30]

Ever since Beccaria's momentous work was brought to the public's attention, experts have sought the formula for a social policy that would effectively control crime, treat criminals, protect victims, and benefit society as a whole. Within fifty years of its publication, the first police agency, the London Metropolitan Police, was developed to keep the peace and identify criminal suspects, and the first prisons were created to provide nonphysical correctional treatment. Nonetheless, there was little recognition that these fledgling agencies of justice worked together in a systematic fashion. In fact, it was not until 1919 that the concept of a *criminal justice system* began to be recognized. It was in that year that the *Chicago Crime Commission*, a professional association funded by private contributions, was created.[31] This organization acted as a citizen's advocate group and kept track of the activities of local justice agencies. The commission still carries out its work today.

The pioneering work of the Chicago group was soon copied in a number of other jurisdictions. In 1922, the Cleveland Crime Commission provided a detailed analysis of local criminal justice policy and uncovered the widespread use of discretion, plea bargaining, and other practices unknown to the public. Some commentators view the Cleveland survey as the first that treats criminal justice as a people-processing system, a view still widely held today.[32] Similar projects were conducted by the Missouri Crime Survey (1926) and the Illinois Crime Survey (1929).

In 1931, President Herbert Hoover appointed the National Commission of Law Observance and Enforcement, which is commonly known today as the *Wickersham Commission*. This national study group made a detailed analysis of the U.S. justice system and helped usher in the era of treatment and rehabilitation. It showed in great detail the variety of rules and regulations that govern the system and exposed how difficult it was for justice personnel to keep track of the system's legal and administrative complexity.[33]

The Modern Era

The modern era of criminal justice began in 1967, when the President's Commission on Law Enforcement and Administration of Justice (the "*Crime Commission*"), which had been appointed by President Lyndon Johnson, published its final report entitled *The Challenge of Crime in a Free Society*.[34] This group of practitioners, educators, and attorneys was charged with creating a comprehensive view of the criminal justice process and recommending reforms. Concomitantly, Congress passed the Safe Streets and Crime Control Act of 1968, providing for the expenditure of federal funds for state and local crime-control efforts.[35] This act helped launch a massive campaign to restructure the justice system by funding the **Law Enforcement Assistance Administration (LEAA),** which provided hundreds of millions of dollars in aid to local and state justice agencies.

Throughout its fourteen-year history, the LEAA was the agency that provided the majority of federal funds to states for criminal justice activities. It required states to establish a state criminal justice planning agency responsible for developing an annual comprehensive criminal justice plan and then funneled development and operating funds to the states for law enforcement purposes. From 1969 to 1980, the LEAA gave over $7.7 billion to state and local criminal justice agencies. On April 15, 1982, the program came to an end when Congress ceased funding it.

During its lifetime, the LEAA received widespread and valid criticism for providing insufficient funds to have a substantial impact on rising crime rates and for allowing political pressure from the White House and Congress to influence its policies. High staff turnover, lack of leadership, and shifting priorities also contributed to negative public opinion about the LEAA.

Despite its well-documented failures, the LEAA helped "invent" the field of criminal justice. Federal funds inspired institutions of higher education to develop academic programs in criminal justice. The LEAA provided millions of dollars in scholarship money for the education of police officers and other criminal justice personnel. Without federal money, the most important graduate programs in criminal justice would probably not have been implemented and many of the professors teaching this course today might have gone into other fields of study. In addition, federal money helped fund some of the most important research and demonstration projects of the 1960s and 1970s, which are mentioned throughout the text. Even though the LEAA is gone, however, the federal government continues to fund the National Institute of Justice (NIJ) and the Bureau of Justice Statistics (BJS), which carry out a more limited role in supporting criminal justice research and development and publishing extremely valuable data and research findings.

The criminal justice system has become a fixture of U.S. life. Numerous public and private groups have attempted to influence its direction by formulating standards for its operations and objectives.[36] Academic programs have been devised to educate students on the intricacies of the legal process. Major research efforts have been aimed at developing a better understanding of criminal justice processes. These efforts have generated widespread interest in the study and understanding of criminal justice.

The Study of Criminal Justice

The term *criminal justice* refers to an area of knowledge devoted to controlling crime through the scientific administration of police, court, and correctional agencies. It is an interdisciplinary field making use of the knowledge bases of sociology, psychology, law, public policy, and other related fields.

Criminal justice is essentially an agency of social control: society considers some behaviors so dangerous and destructive that it chooses to either strictly control their occurrence or outlaw them outright. It is the job of the agencies of justice to prevent these behaviors by apprehending and punishing transgressors or deterring their future occurrence. While society maintains other forms of social control, such as parental and school-based discipline, they are designed to deal with moral and not legal misbehavior. Only the criminal justice system maintains the power to control crime and punish criminals.

As a result of these efforts, an interdisciplinary field of criminal justice has come into being. Nearly every federal, state, and local crime-control program began to use the term *criminal justice system* in one way or another. Rather than viewing police, court, and correctional agencies as thousands of independent institutions, it has become common to view them as components in a large, integrated "people-processing system" that manages law violators from the time of their arrest through trial, punishment, and release. To study criminal justice and train students for management roles in justice-related agencies, more than six hundred departments or colleges of criminal justice were developed in institutions of higher education. Academic institutions have become a major resource for those trying to find solutions to the crime problem; university involvement in problems of criminal justice has provided needed resources and authenticity to a relatively new field.

Criminal justice is truly an interdisciplinary field. A number of academic disciplines have been drawn upon to develop insights into the causes and prevention of criminal behavior. Sociologists have long studied the social and environmental factors associated with crime and delinquency. Psychologists have sought to determine if the typical offender's criminal behavior is symptomatic of some emotional or mental health problem. Legal scholars have focused on such issues as the effect of legal rule changes on the justice process and the relationship between social control and civil liberties, considering such questions as what is the effect on police behavior of a Supreme Court decision prohibiting the police from shooting unarmed suspects who are fleeing arrest?[37]

The field of criminal justice is also aided by a variety of other disciplines. Historians have developed an understanding of the historical context of the law and the development of early justice agencies. Political scientists explore the roles of federal and state governments, political parties, and pressure groups in relation to urban problems, examine legislation, and study how government influences the justice system. Some economists have applied economic theory to crime, suggesting that people commit crime after conducting a cost-benefit analysis of the gains they may make from a criminal act compared to the losses they may suffer if apprehended by the police.

Even members of the physical sciences have become active in criminal justice. For example, forensic chemists work closely with police agencies in the development of scientific techniques for analyzing evidence. Biologists and medical doctors have conducted studies on the biochemical and physical bases of criminal behavior and the effect of diet and medication on the treatment of known offenders, finding indications that improving diets can affect behavior positively.[38]

What exists, then, is a great deal of information taken from various disciplines and consolidated as the knowledge base for a new area of study. Understanding what knowledge is represented in this field helps us to reach a working definition of criminal justice study:

> The study of criminal justice may be defined as the use of the scientific method to understand the administration, procedures, and policies of those agencies of government charged with enforcing the law, adjudicating crime, and correcting criminal conduct. The study of criminal justice involves analyzing how these institutions influence human behavior and how they are in turn influenced by law and society.

Note how this definition recognizes that criminal justice is essentially a social institution. Its study involves analyzing how the justice system responds to social norms and trends and how its operations have a reciprocal relationship to societal behavior and values: the justice system responds to social values and behavior; social values and behavior are influenced by the justice system.

As social scientists, criminal justice experts try to bring carefully controlled scientific methods, such as surveys and experiments, to bear on their subject matter whenever possible. Using these methods, they focus their attention on the inner processes of the agencies of justice: police and law enforcement organizations; courts and related institutions, such as the district attorney's office; and correctional agencies, such as jails, prisons, and parole authorities. Criminal justice, then, is a field of study that deals with the nature of crime in society, as well as analyzing the formal processes and social agencies that have been established for crime control.

Governmental Structure and Criminal Justice

Before describing the criminal justice system and its component parts, it is essential to establish an understanding of how the criminal justice system is situated within our governmental structure.

The basic framework of the U.S. criminal justice system is found in the legislative, judicial, and executive branches of the government. Legal authority to establish crime-control programs rests initially within this structure. The legislature defines the law by determining what conduct is prohibited and establishes criminal penalties for those who violate the law; the appellate courts interpret the law and determine whether it meets constitutional requirements; the executive branch plans programs, appoints personnel, and exercises administrative responsibility for criminal justice agencies (See Figure 1.2).

Criminal justice agencies can be created by legislative acts, by executive orders, or by constitutional requirements. The authority and discretion of administrative organizations, such as a state corrections department are set and controlled by the legislature; others, such as local police departments, fall under the authority of locally elected officials, such as the mayor and/or the city council. Some agencies, such as parole boards, often have broad discretion and delegated authority to provide services for convicted offenders; parole board decision making is rarely subject to review or appeal. Other agencies, such as trial courts, are generally given greater legislative direction. Nonetheless, all criminal justice agencies have authority within the law to develop rules and regulations that control operational policies and procedures.

The legislature is often seen as having the most important role of the three branches of government because it defines criminal behavior, while the judicial and executive branches appear to be secondary sources of crime-control authority. This perception of the criminal justice power structure is not entirely correct. All three branches and the governmental bureaucracy generally work together to influence the operation of the criminal justice system. The legislature is not totally independent of the executive branch, nor is the judiciary independent of the other two branches of government. For example, when the legislature passes a criminal statute setting a mandatory one-year sentence for possession of a handgun, both the judicial and executive branches share in its implementation and effect on the criminal justice system. Such a law may have been a product of the executive branch, requiring legislative approval and judicial review. The trend toward court intervention in the operational procedures of police agencies is another example of the interrelationship of the legislative, judicial, and executive functions, as are the constitutional safeguards established by the courts. Similarly, the sentencing process is based on the operations and functions of the three branches of government: Criminal sanctions are created by legislators, imposed by the judiciary, and carried out by the executive branch of government. To recognize how criminal justice works, one must examine the legislative, judicial, and executive systems, as well as the administrative agencies, which are often collectively referred to as the fourth branch of government.

Legislature

Federal and state constitutions grant authority for legislatures to pass laws. The primary responsibility of legislatures in the justice system is to define criminal

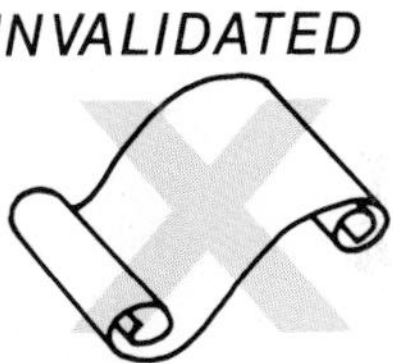

FIGURE 1.2

Creating Law: The Interrelationship between the Branches of the Federal Government This diagram illustrates the long process by which a bill becomes law.

SOURCE: The United States Government Manual 1981/82 and/or 1982/83.

behavior and establish criminal penalties. Legislatures throughout the nation consider thousands of bills each year, many involving the criminal justice system. Only a small number of bills, however, actually become laws. This lawmaking function involves not only passing bills but also modifying and rejecting them.

When a criminal statute is passed, the courts require that it be sufficiently definite and clear. Vague laws, such as those relating to disorderly conduct, juvenile delinquency, and morality crimes involving drunkenness, gambling, obscenity, and sexual misconduct, create uncertainty in police and judicial enforcement practices. Laws prescribing substantive crimes must be clearly stated.

In addition to establishing definitions of crimes, legislatures also pass laws governing criminal justice procedures. These include rules and regulations involving the laws of arrest, search warrants, bail, trial court proceedings, and sentencing. And although much criminal procedure in recent years has resulted from leading constitutional cases relating to the investigation and prosecution of crime, such rules are often enacted into statutory form.

The initiative to pass a law may come from a legislator, a criminal justice agency, a public official, or a group of citizens. The issue is first studied by a legislative committee. Lobbyists and interest groups add their influence and knowledge to the discussion and contents of the proposed bill. The respective legislative houses are subsequently given the bill for a vote. In Congress and bicameral state legislatures, if the legislation is not passed in its initial form by both the House of Representatives and the Senate, it is given to a joint legislative committee of both houses to work out a compromise. A compromise bill is eventually voted on by both bodies. When the bill has been passed, it is given to the chief executive for his or her signature. If signed, the bill becomes a law. If vetoed, the bill may be dropped or referred back to the legislature for reconsideration.

Besides defining crimes and fixing sentences, the legislature also provides financial support for crime-control programs. Availability of funds for such programs remains one of the major concerns of the criminal justice system. Criminal justice agencies often lack financial support for facilities, adequate staff, and programs. In many cases, police, courts, and correctional agencies compete with one another for the same tax dollar.

Other important functions of the legislature include: acting as a forum for the public expression of views on criminal justice issues; investigating possible criminal activity; and working with the executive branch to develop and pass improved legislation.

Judiciary

Although the legislature enacts laws, most criminal procedures are established by the appellate courts. The United States has a dual system of courts. Each state has a court system that deals with the enforcement of its laws, while the federal judiciary enforces federal laws.

Within each system are both trial and appellate courts. Trial courts handle criminal trials and impose sentences on guilty offenders, while appellate courts interpret the law in light of constitutional standards. These courts, the most important of which is the U.S. Supreme Court, decide how laws should be applied. Were it not for the power of judicial review, established within the federal system in the case of *Marbury v. Madison*, the courts would exert only limited influence in the criminal process. In addition, the supremacy clause of the U.S. Constitution allows the Supreme Court to declare state and local laws unconstitutional.[39]

Over the years, the principle of judicial review has been applied both actively and with restraint. Those in favor of judicial activism argue that it is the responsibility of the courts to monitor and control governmental infringement on our civil rights. On the other hand, advocates of judicial restraint suggest that laws should be upheld by the courts unless they clearly violate constitutional provisions. When the Supreme Court was headed by Chief Justice Earl Warren (the *Warren Court*) in the 1960s, it exercised a great deal of judicial leadership by deciding many criminal cases involving the expansion of individual rights. In recent years under the leadership of Chief Justices Warren Burger and William Rehnquist, the Court has taken a more conservative view of criminal justice issues.

ANALYZING CRIMINAL JUSTICE ISSUES

The Costs of Justice

What is the cost of the criminal justice system to the U.S. taxpayer? It is currently estimated that it costs over $60 billion per year to operate the criminal justice system. This figure includes over $27 billion for police and law enforcement services, $13 billion for the courts, and at least $19 billion for the correctional system. (See Figure A and Figure B.) Included within these costs are amounts needed to pay police to investigate crimes and appear in court and public defenders to represent indigent offenders and compensation to judges and juries. Correctional costs include providing inmates with medical care, educational programs, and vocational rehabilitation as well as light, heat, and food. It is not surprising that, as old correctional hands are likely to say, "it costs twice as much to send someone to the state pen than to Penn State." You also must remember that many criminal justice agencies, such as police departments, jails, and prisons, operate around the clock, which requires three shifts of workers.

The costs of justice vary widely between jurisdictions. Nationally, Americans spend about $217 per person on justice expenditures. Expenditures range from $540 per person in Alaska and $398 in New York to less than $100 in Arkansas and West Virginia.

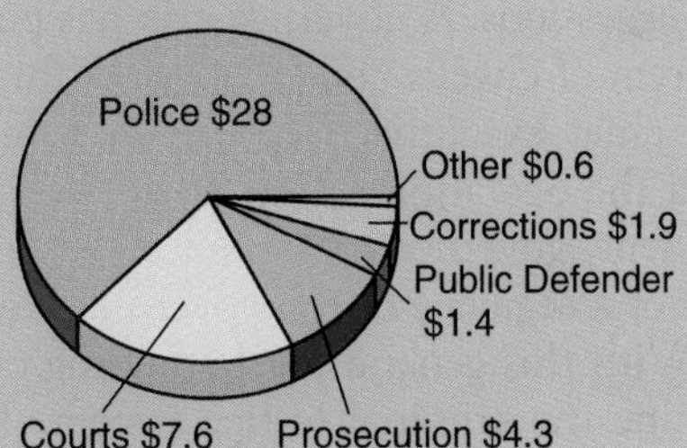

FIGURE A
Costs of Criminal Justice Legal Services in Billions of Dollars

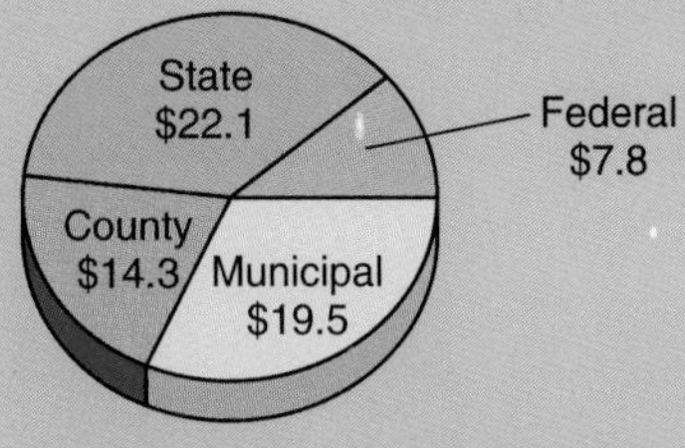

FIGURE B
Costs of Criminal Justice by Level of Government in Billions of Dollars

Critical Thinking Skills

The costs of justice are spiraling (up more than $10 billion since 1985) at a time when large federal and state budget deficits and plans to reduce government spending have already put an overwhelming strain on the criminal justice system. Understaffed police forces, backlogged courts, and overcrowded prisons are the result.

The public seems willing to devote tax dollars to apprehending, trying, and incarcerating criminals while at the same time it calls for cutting spending on welfare and education. Is it fair to argue that if federal, state, and local governments cut back on welfare, medical, and educational programs in order to save tax dollars in the near term, the costs of funding a rapidly expanding justice system will be far greater in the long term? Would an increased commitment to the poor eventually save us billions in tax dollars? In other words, should we pay now or pay later?

SOURCE: Bureau of Justice Statistics, *Report to the Nation on Crime and Justice* (Washington, D.C.: Bureau of Justice Statistics, 1988); Sue Lindgren, *Justice Expenditures and Employment, 1988* (Washington, D.C.: Bureau of Justice Statistics, 1990).

Executive Branch

The third major governmental authority with functions related to criminal justice is the executive branch. Executive power is vested in such public officials as the president, governors, and mayors. Today's officials are often actively involved in criminal justice issues. Many have extensive powers of appointment; they appoint judges and heads of administrative agencies, such as police chiefs, commissioners of corrections, and executive directors of criminal justice planning agencies. They also have the authority to remove administrative personnel. Another important executive function involves the power to grant pardons for crimes. President

Gerald Ford's pardon of Richard Nixon for his involvement in the Watergate scandal is a controversial example of this power.

The elected official also plays an important leadership role in criminal justice matters. For example, through the submission of legislative programs, executive persuasion, and party politics, a governor can influence others to follow his or her suggestions. A governor also has power to veto legislation and thus maintains a system of checks and balances within the governmental structure. In addition, each chief executive has a staff to develop programs and at least theoretically direct the operations of the various criminal justice departments and agencies. A president, governor, or mayor is both a chief executive and the administrative head of a segment of the governmental bureaucracy.

With this general understanding of governmental structure, we can begin to examine the criminal justice system. The following sections set out the system, describe its major component parts, and briefly analyze its most significant processes. In the following chapters, these agencies and procedures will be discussed in more extensive detail.

The Criminal Justice System

The contemporary criminal justice system in the United States is monumental in size. It consists of over 55,000 public agencies, a total annual budget of over $60 billion for police, court, and correctional operations, and a staff of almost 1.4 million people.[40] There are approximately 20,000 police agencies, nearly 17,000 courts, over 8,000 prosecutorial agencies, about 5,700 correctional institutions, and over 3,500 probation and parole departments. The numbers of people processed through these agencies each year are equally enormous. In recent years, the police made over 12 million total arrests annually, including more than 2 million for serious felony offenses.[41] In addition, almost 1 million juveniles were handled by the juvenile courts.[42] The total correctional population is over 4.3 million people, including 1.2 million in correctional facilities, over 2.6 million on probation, and about half a million on parole.[43] It costs about $70,000 to build a prison cell and about $20,000 dollars per year is needed to keep an inmate in prison; juvenile institutions cost about $25,000 per year per resident. The costs of justice are discussed in Analyzing Criminal Justice Issues. The magnitude and complexity of agency services in crime control have led to the development of what experts term the "criminal justice system."

The idea that these agencies of justice actually form a true system is still open to some debate. Theoretically, the term *system* refers to an organized and integrated array of diverse parts or elements that function as an interrelated group or unit. The systems approach to criminal justice presupposes a functional interrelationship among all those agencies concerned with the prevention of crime in our society and assumes that change in one part or agency of the system will effect change in the others. It implies that a closely knit, coordinated structure of organizations exists among the various components of the system. Unfortunately, this approach exists more in theory than in practice. The various elements of the criminal justice system—such as police, courts, and corrections—are all related but only to the degree that they are influenced by the other's policies and practices; they have not yet become so well coordinated that they can be described as operating in unison. Beyond these problems, the justice systems of the various states and federal government do not cooperate as closely as would be desired, nor are their practices and policies closely coordinated or compatible.

Fragmented, divided, and *splintered* continue to be the adjectives most commonly used to describe the U.S. system of criminal justice, prompting one commentator to label it the "criminal justice nonsystem."[44]

Yet, there is enough similarity in the agencies of justice and their operations to make criminal justice a relevant area of study. That is, despite all the apparent organizational differences among the agencies of justice, it has proven possible to develop a body of knowledge that is applicable to criminal justice in jurisdictions across the nation.

Components of Criminal Justice

The control and prevention of criminal activity and the treatment and reform of criminal offenders are carried out by the agencies of government described below.

The Police

Police departments are those public agencies created to maintain order, enforce the criminal law, provide emergency services, keep traffic on streets and highways moving freely, and create a sense of community safety. The system and process of criminal justice depends on effective and efficient police work, particularly when it comes to preventing and detecting crime and apprehending and arresting criminal offenders. As our society becomes more complex, new and additional functions are required of the police officer. Today, police officers work actively with the community to prevent criminal behavior; they help divert members of special needs populations, such as juveniles, alcoholics, and drug addicts, from the criminal justice system; they participate in specialized units such as juvenile and drug prevention squads; they cooperate with public prosecutors to initiate investigations into organized crime and drug trafficking; they resolve neighborhood and family conflicts; and they provide emergency services, such as preserving civil order during strikes and political demonstrations.

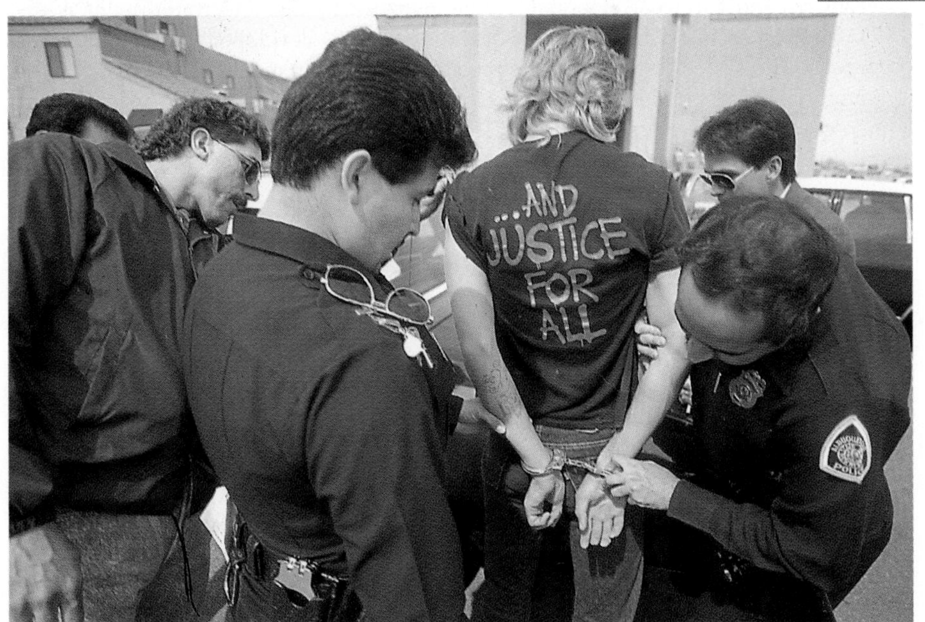

The power to arrest and deprive a person of liberty is one of the most important responsibilities of police officers.

Because of these expanded responsibilities, the role of the police officer has become more professional. The officer must not only be technically competent to investigate crimes but also be aware of the rules and procedures associated with arrest, apprehension, and investigation of criminal activity. The police officer must be aware of the factors involved in the causes of crime in order to screen and divert offenders who might be better handled by other, more appropriate agencies. They must also be part community organizer, social worker, family counselor, dispute resolver, and emergency medical technician.

The police officer's role is established by the boundaries of the criminal law. While the officer sets the criminal justice system in motion by the authority to arrest, and this authority is vested in the law, it is neither final nor absolute. The police officer's duty requires discretion on numerous matters dealing with a variety of situations, victims, criminals, and citizens. The officer must determine when an argument becomes disorderly conduct or criminal assault; whether it is appropriate to arrest a juvenile or refer him or her to a social agency; or when to assume that probable cause exists to arrest a suspect for a crime. Former Chief Justice Warren Burger stressed the importance of individual decision making and discretion when he stated:

> The policeman (or woman) on the beat, or in the patrol car, makes more decisions and exercises broader discretion affecting the daily lives of people every day and to a greater extent, in many respects, than a judge will ordinarily exercise in a week.[45]

Police officers today are required to exercise a great deal of individual discretion in deciding whether to arrest, refer, or simply investigate a situation further; their actions represent the exercise of discretionary justice.

The Courts

The criminal court is considered by many to be the core element in the administration of criminal justice:

> It is [the] part of the system that is the most venerable, the most formally organized, and the most elaborately circumscribed by law and tradition. It is the institution around which the rest of the system has developed and to which the rest of the system is in large measure responsible. It regulates the flow of the criminal process under governance of the law. . . . It is expected to articulate the community's most deeply held, most cherished views about the relationship of individual and society.[46]

The criminal court houses the process by which the criminal responsibility of defendants accused of violating the law is determined. Ideally, the court is expected to convict and sentence those found guilty of crimes while ensuring that the innocent are freed without any consequence or burden. The court system is formally required to seek the truth, to obtain justice for the individual brought before its tribunals, and to maintain the integrity of the government's rule of law. However, overburdened courts are often the scenes of informal bargain justice, which is designed to get the case over with as quickly as possible and at the least possible cost. While the criminal court ideally should hand out fair and evenhanded justice in a forum of strict impartiality and fairness, this standard of justice has not been maintained in millions of cases heard each year in the nation's criminal court system. Instead, a system of "bargain justice" has developed that encourages defendants to plead guilty. This means that most criminal defendants

The defense attorney, on the other hand, is responsible for providing legal defense representation to the defendant. This role involves two major functions:

1. Protecting the constitutional rights of the accused, and
2. Presenting the best possible legal defense for the defendant.

The defense attorney represents a client from initial arrest through the trial stage, during the sentencing hearing, and, if needed, through the process of appeal. The defense attorney is also expected to enter into plea negotiations and obtain for the defendant the most suitable bargain regarding type and length of sentence.

Any person accused of a crime can obtain the services of a private attorney if he or she can afford to do so. One of the most critical questions in the criminal justice system has been whether an indigent (poor) defendant has the right to counsel. The federal court system has long provided counsel to the indigent on the basis of the Sixth Amendment of the U.S. Constitution, which gives the accused the right to have the assistance of defense counsel. Through a series of landmark U.S. Supreme Court decisions, beginning with *Powell v. Alabama* in 1932 and continuing with *Gideon v. Wainwright* in 1963 and *Argersinger v. Hamlin* in 1972, the right of a criminal defendant to have counsel has become fundamental to our system of criminal justice.[47] Today, state courts must provide counsel to indigent defendants who are charged with criminal offenses where the possibility of incarceration exists. Consequently, more than a thousand public defender agencies have been set up around the United States that provide free legal counsel to indigent defendants.

Corrections

Following a criminal trial resulting in conviction and sentencing, the offender enters the correctional system. After many years of indifference, public interest in corrections has grown as a result of well-publicized prison riots, such as that which occurred in New York's Attica facility in 1971, and the alleged inability of the system to rehabilitate offenders.

In the broadest sense, corrections involve community supervision or probation, various types of incarceration (including jails, houses of correction, and state prisons), and parole programs for both juvenile and adult offenders. Corrections ordinarily represent the postadjudicatory care given to offenders when a sentence is imposed by the court and the offender is placed in the hands of the correctional agency.

Complicating this system is the expected dramatic population explosion in the correctional population. As Figure 1.3 shows, the correctional population has increased by over 1 million since 1985.[48] More than thirty states are under court order to reduce prison crowding.[49]

Despite its tremendous size and cost, the correctional system suffers from an extremely poor performance record. It has not been able to offer public protection, nor does it effectively rehabilitate criminal offenders. It is plagued with high recidivism rates (many offenders return to crime shortly after incarceration). High recidivism rates are believed to result from the lack of effective treatment and training programs within incarceration facilities, poor physical environments and health conditions, and the fact that offender populations in many institutions are subjected to violence from other inmates and guards.

FIGURE 1.3

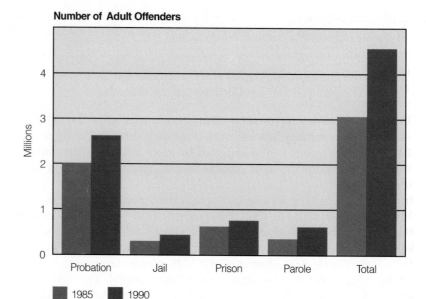

Correctional Populations in the United States, 1985–90 The correctional population is at an all time high!

SOURCE: Louis Jankowski, *Probation and Parole, 1990* (Washington, D.C.: Bureau of Justice Statistics, 1991), p. 1.

Despite these problems, corrections play a critical role in the criminal justice system. By exercising control over those sentenced by the courts to incarceration or community supervision, the system acts as the major sanctioning force of the criminal law. As a result, the system of corrections has many responsibilities, among them protecting society, deterring crime, and—equally important—rehabilitating offenders. The achievement of both proper restraint and effective reform of the offender is the system's most frustrating, yet awesome, goal. Some of the major components of correction are discussed below.

Probation. **Probation** is a judicial action or legal disposition that allows the offender to remain in the community, subject to conditions imposed by court order, under the supervision of a probation officer. It enables the offender to continue working while avoiding the pains of imprisonment.

At the same time, social services are provided to help the offender adjust in the community; counseling, assistance from social workers, and group treatment, as well as the use of community resources to obtain employment, welfare, and housing, are offered to the offender while on probation.

In recent years, the concept of probation has been enhanced with a variety of **intermediate sanctions** that serve as alternatives to incarceration. These typically involve probation plus such additional penalties as house arrest, fines, forfeiture of property, intensive supervision, victim restitution, and even monitoring by computer. Some jurisdictions have instituted nonsecure community-based correctional centers for first-time offenders where they live while holding a job or obtaining an education. Intermediate sanctions hold the promise of being both less costly and intrusive than traditional methods of incarceration and may become the method of choice in offender rehabilitation.

Confinement. The state reserves the right through the criminal law to incarcerate convicted criminals in secure institutions of correction and reform. In the narrow sense, the system of corrections represents the institutional care of offenders brought into the criminal justice system. A person given a sentence involving incarceration ordinarily is confined to a correctional institution for a specified period of time. Different types of institutions are used to hold offenders. First, the **jail** holds offenders convicted of minor offenses or misdemeanors and "detainees"—people awaiting trial or those involved in other proceedings, such as grand jury deliberations, arraignments, or preliminary hearings. The jail is ordinarily operated by local government and is often under the jurisdiction of the county sheriff. Many jails have poor physical conditions, a lack of adequate staff, and a custodial philosophy. Little is done in the way of inmate treatment, principally because the personnel and institutions lack the qualifications, services, and resources.

Prisons or penitentiaries are state-operated facilities that house felony offenders sentenced by the criminal courts.

Most new inmates are first sent to a reception and **classification center,** where they are given a diagnostic evaluation and assigned to an institution that meets individual needs as much as possible within the system's resources. The diagnostic process in the reception center may range from a physical examination and a single interview to an extensive series of psychiatric tests, orientation sessions, and numerous personal interviews. Classification is a way of evaluating inmates and assigning them to appropriate placements and activities within the state institutional system. Classification might mean that instead of residing in a high-security prison, the inmate may be maintained in a halfway house or prerelease center or take part in a work-release and/or home-furlough program. Many convicted offenders do not require maximum security and can be more effectively rehabilitated in community-based facilities. Rather than relegating nondangerous offenders to an impersonal and harsh prison experience for the totality of their sentence, such programs offer them the opportunity to maintain normal family and social relationships while having access to rehabilitative services and resources at lower cost to the taxpayer.

After classification, and depending on their need for treatment and the level of risk they present, inmates are assigned to either minimum-, medium-, or maximum-security institutions. Maximum-security institutions have high walls, barred cells, and careful security measures and house the most dangerous inmate population. Medium-security institutions may physically resemble more guarded institutions, but their inmate population requires less control and therefore can receive more intensive treatment. Minimum-security institutions may have private dorm-like rooms and offer inmates much freedom and good correctional programs.

Parole. Few offenders released from correctional institutions serve their entire sentence behind prison walls. Most early early release because they have accumulated time off for good behavior. About 40 percent reenter the community via the discretionary parole system. Inmates are selected for early release on the condition that they obey a set of restrictive behavioral rules under the supervision of a parole officer. Other ways in which an offender may be released from an institution include mandatory release upon the completion of the sentence less time off for good behavior, completion of the entire sentence without "good time" credit, and pardon—a form of executive clemency.

The main purpose of early-release parole is to help the ex-inmate bridge the gap between institutional confinement and a positive adjustment within the community. After their release, offenders are supervised by parole authorities who help them find employment, deal with family and social difficulties, and gain treatment for emotional or substance abuse problems. If the offender violates conditions of community supervision, parole may be revoked. In that event, the parolee may be sent back to the correctional institution.

The future of discretionary parole is undecided. A number of states have abolished this type of parole and substituted fixed sentencing statutes under which offenders are released after they have served their entire sentence less time off for good behavior. About 40 percent of all inmates today receive mandatory supervised release. Increased public demands for more effective crime control have also resulted in mandatory prison terms for drug offenses and violent crimes without the possibility of parole.

The Formal Criminal Justice Process

Another way of understanding criminal justice is to view it as a **process** that takes an offender through a series of steps beginning with arrest and concluding with reentry into society. The emphasis throughout the process is on the offender and the various sequential stages, or *decision points*, through which he or she passes. At each of these, a determination is made to assign the case to the next stage of the system or to discharge the suspect without further action. This decision making is often a matter of individual *discretion*, based upon a variety of factors and perceptions. Legal factors, including the seriousness of the charges, available evidence, and the suspect's prior record, are usually considered legitimate influences on decision making. Troubling is the fact that such extralegal factors as the suspect's race, gender, class, and age may influence decision outcomes. There is a significant and ongoing debate over the impact of extralegal factors in the decision to arrest, convict, and sentence suspects: critics believe a suspect's race, class, and gender can often determine the direction a case will take, while supporters argue that the system is relatively fair and unbiased.[50]

In reality, few cases actually are processed through the entire formal justice system. Most are handled informally and with dispatch. The system of justice has been roundly criticized for its "backroom deals" and bargain justice. While informality and deal making are in fact the rule, the concept of the formal justice process is important because it implies every criminal defendant charged with a serious crime is entitled to the full range of rights under law. Knowing that every individual is entitled to his or her day in court, to be represented by competent counsel in a fair trial before an impartial jury, with trial procedures subject to review by a higher authority, is central to the American concept of liberty. The kangaroo court and summary punishment are elements of political systems that most Americans fear and despise. The fact that most criminal suspects are actually treated informally may be less important than the fact that all criminal defendants are entitled to a full range of legal rights and constitutional protections.

A comprehensive view of the formal criminal process would normally include:

1. *Initial Contact*. The initial contact stage involves an act or incident that makes a person the subject of interest to the agencies of justice. In most instances, initial contact is a result of a police action: while they are on patrol, police officers observe a person acting suspiciously and conclude the suspect is under the influence of drugs; police officers are contacted by a victim who reports a robbery, and they respond by going to the scene of the crime; an informer tells police about some ongoing criminal activity in order to receive favorable treatment. In some instances, the initial contact is a result of the police department's responding to the request of the mayor or other political figures to control an ongoing social problem, such as gambling, prostitution, or teenage loitering.

2. *Investigation*. The purpose of the investigatory stage of the justice process is to gather enough evidence to identify, arrest, and bring the offender to trial. An investigation can take but a few minutes, as in the case where a police officer sees a crime in progress and is able to apprehend the suspect within minutes. Or it can take many months and involve hundreds of police officers, as was the case in the Atlanta child killings, which resulted in the apprehension, trial, and conviction of Wayne Williams.

3. *Arrest*. An arrest occurs when the police take a person in custody and the suspect believes that he or she has lost his or her liberty. An arrest is considered legal when all the following conditions exist: (a) the police officer believes there is sufficient evidence, referred to as **probable cause,** that a crime is being or has been committed and the suspect is the person who committed it; (b) the officer deprives the individual of freedom; and (c) the suspect believes that he or she is now in the custody of the police. The police officer is not required to use the word *arrest* or any similar term to initiate an arrest, nor does the officer have to bring the suspect to the police station. To make an arrest in a misdemeanor, the officer must have witnessed the crime personally, known as the **in-presence requirement,** while a felony arrest can be made based upon the statement of a witness or victim.

4. *Custody*. The moment after an arrest is made, the detained suspect is considered in police custody. At this juncture (commonly called *booking*), the police may wish to search the suspect for weapons or contraband, interrogate him or her in order to gain more information, find out if the person had any accomplices, or even encourage the suspect to confess to the crime. The police may wish to enter the suspect's home, car, or office to look for further evidence. Similarly, the police may want to bring witnesses to view the suspect in a **lineup** or in a one-to-one confrontation. And during custody, the police will take personal information from the suspect, such as name, address, fingerprints, and photo. Because these procedures are so crucial and can have a great bearing at a later trial, the U.S. Supreme Court has granted suspects in police custody protection from the unconstitutional abuse of police power, such as illegal searches and intimidating interrogations.

5. *Charging*. If sufficient evidence exists to charge a person with a crime, the case will be turned over to the prosecutor's office for additional processing. If the case involves a misdemeanor, the prosecutor will file a charges document generally called a complaint before the court that will try the case. If the case involves a felony, the prosecutor must decide whether to bring the case forward, depending on the procedures used in the jurisdiction and the nature of the crime, to either a grand jury or preliminary hearing (see below). In either event, the decision to charge the suspect with a specific criminal act involves many factors, including evidence sufficiency, crime seriousness, case pressure, and political issues. Prosecutors may decide to take no further action in a case, referred to as a "nolle prosqui."

6. *Preliminary hearing/grand jury*. Since a person faces great financial and personal costs when he or she is forced to stand trial for a felony, the U.S. Constitution mandates that the government must first prove that there is probable cause that the accused committed the crime he or she is charged with and that a trial is warranted under the circumstances. In about half the states and the federal system, this decision is rendered by a group of citizens brought together to form a grand jury. The grand jury considers the case in a closed hearing in which o

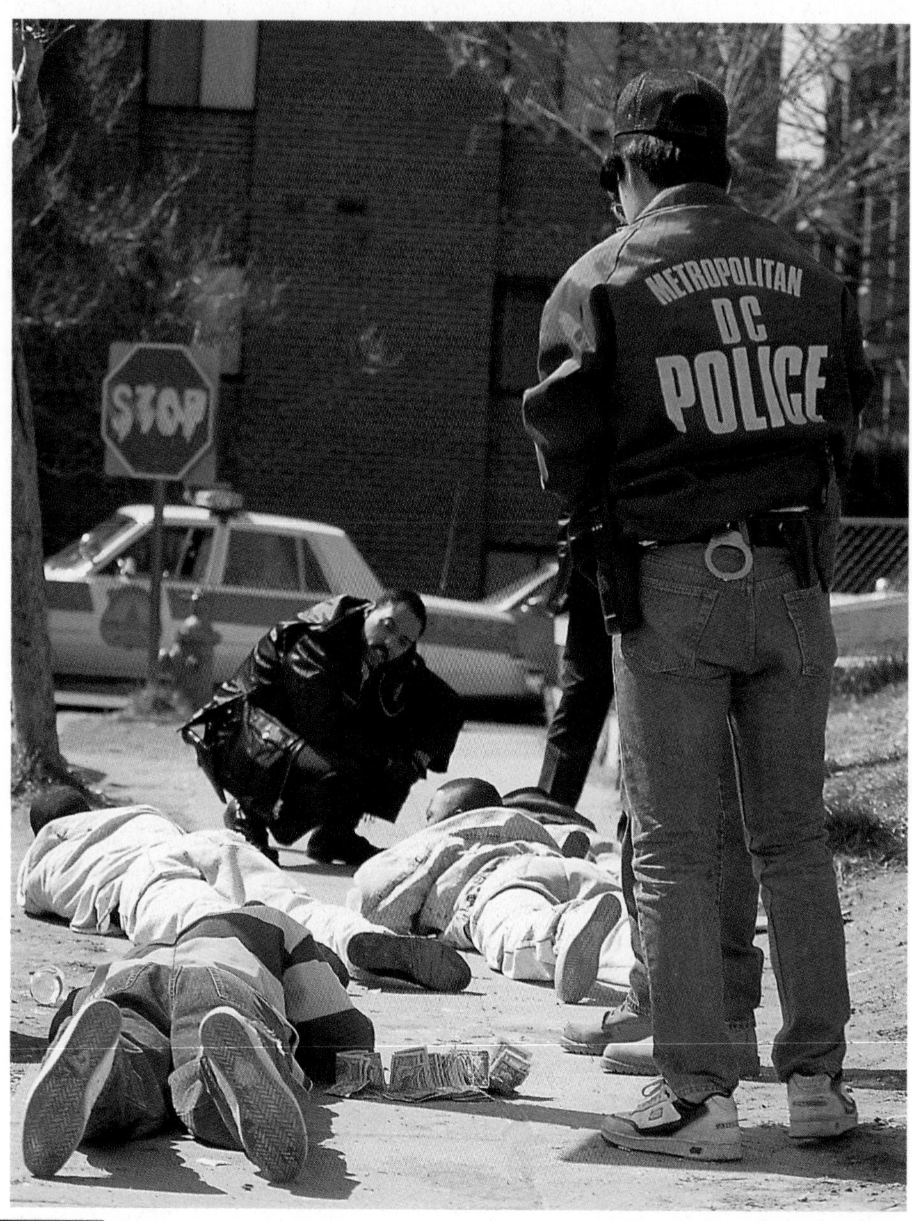

A detained suspect is considered in police custody the moment after an arrest is made.

the prosecutor presents evidence. If the evidence is sufficient, the jury will issue a **bill of indictment,** which specifies that the accused must stand trial for a specific crime. In the remaining states, the grand jury has been replaced with a preliminary hearing. In these jurisdictions, a charging document called an **information** is filed before a lower trial court, which then conducts an open hearing on the merits of the case. This procedure is sometimes referred to as a probable cause hearing. The defendant and his or her attorney may appear at this hearing and dispute the prosecutor's charges. If the prosecutor's evidence is accepted as factual and sufficient, the suspect will be called to stand trial for the crime.

7. *Arraignment.* Before the trial begins, the defendant will be **arraigned** or brought before the court that will hear the case. At the arraignment, the formal charges will be read, the defendant will be informed of his or her constitutional rights (for example, the right to be represented by legal counsel), an initial plea may be entered in the case (not guilty or guilty), a trial date set, and bail issues considered.

8. *Bail/Detention.* Bail is a money bond, the amount of which is set by judicial authority. The purpose of bail is to insure the return of a criminal defendant for trial while allowing the person pretrial freedom to prepare his or her defense. Defendants who do not show up for trial forfeit their bail. Those people who cannot afford to put up bail or who cannot borrow sufficient funds for it will remain in state custody prior to trial. In most instances, this means an extended stay in a county jail or house of correction. Most jurisdictions allow defendants awaiting trial to be released on their own recognizance (promise to the court), without bail, if they are stable members of the community and have committed nonviolent crimes.

9. *Plea Bargaining.* Soon after an arraignment, if not before, defense counsel will meet with the prosecution to see if the case can be brought to a conclusion without a trial. In some instances, this can involve filing the case while the defendant participates in a community-based treatment program for substance abuse or psychiatric care, for example. Most commonly, the defense and prosecution will discuss a possible guilty plea in exchange for reducing or dropping some of the charges or agreeing to a request for a more lenient sentence. It is generally accepted that almost 90 percent of all cases end in a plea bargain, rather than a criminal trial.

10. *Adjudication.* If an agreement cannot be reached or if the prosecution does not wish to arrange a negotiated settlement of the case, a full-scale inquiry into the facts of the case will commence. The criminal trial is held before a judge or jury who will decide whether the evidence against the defendant is *sufficient beyond a reasonable doubt*. The defendant may be found guilty or not guilty as charged. Sometimes in a jury trial, a decision cannot be reached, resulting in a deadlocked or hung jury and leaving the case unresolved and open for a possible retrial.

11. *Disposition.* If after a criminal trial the accused has been found guilty as charged, he or she will be returned to court for sentencing. Possible dispositions may include a fine, probation, a period of incarceration in a penal institution, or some combination of the above. In cases involving first-degree murder, more than thirty states and the federal government allow the death penalty.

Dispositions are usually made after the probation department conducts a presentence investigation that evaluates the defendant and determines his or her potential for successful rehabilitation if given a period of community supervision or whether he or she needs secure confinement. Sentencing is a key decision point in the criminal justice system because in many jurisdictions, judicial discretion can result in people receiving vastly different sentences though they have committed the same crime.

12. *Postconviction Remedies.* After conviction and if the defendant believes he or she was not treated fairly by the justice system, he or she may **appeal** the conviction before an appellate court. An appeals court reviews the procedures used during the processing of the case. It considers such questions as whether evidence was used properly, whether the judge conducted the trial in an approved fashion, whether the jury was representative, and whether the attorneys in the case acted appropriately. If the court rules that the appeal has merit, it can hold that the defendant be given a new trial or, in some instances, order his or her outright release. Outright release can be ordered when the state prosecuted the case in violation of the double jeopardy clause of the U.S. Constitution or when it violated the defendant's right to a speedy trial.

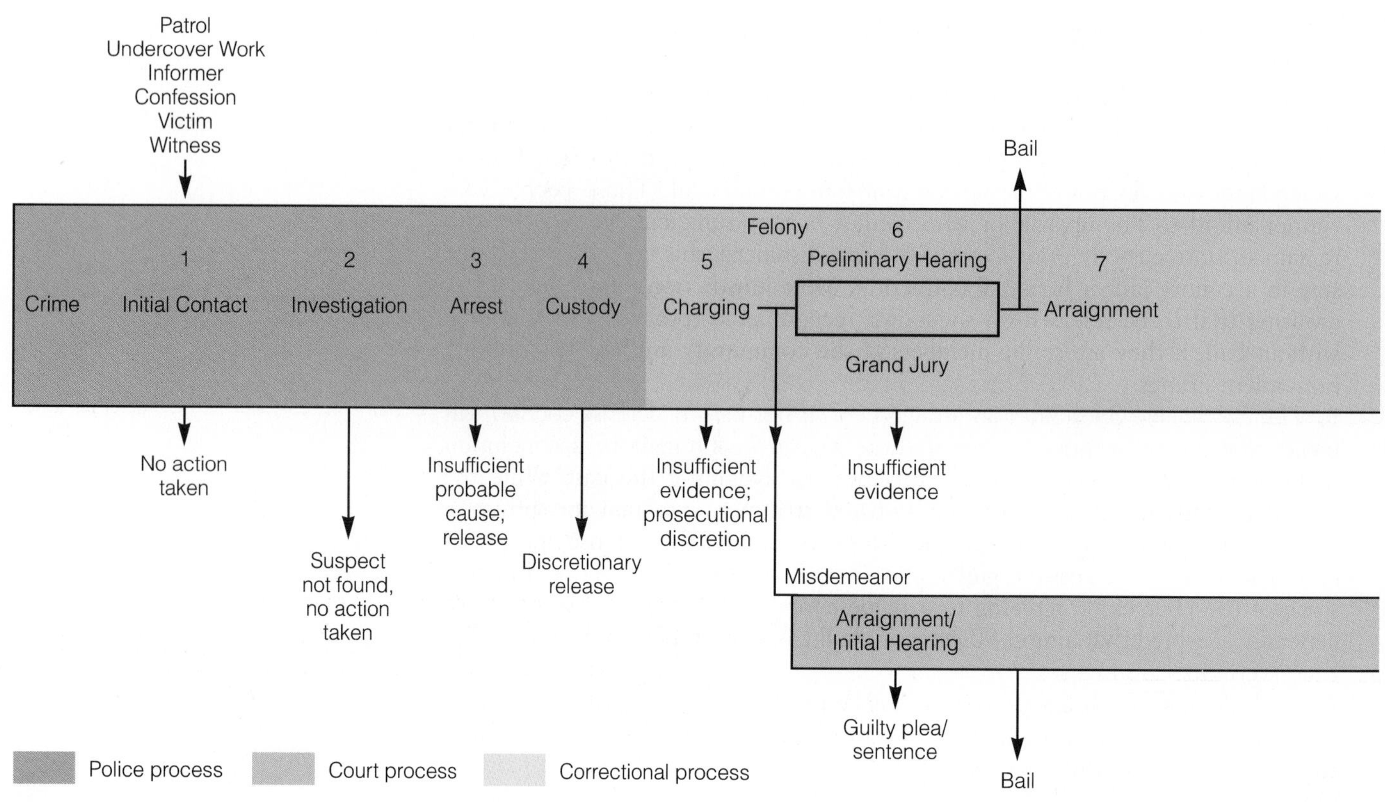

FIGURE 1.4
The Critical Stages in the Justice Process

13. *Correctional Treatment.* After sentencing, the offender is placed within the jurisdiction of state or federal correctional authorities. He or she may serve a probationary term, be placed in a community correctional facility, serve a term in a county jail, or be housed in a prison. During this stage of the criminal justice process, the offender may be asked to participate in rehabilitation programs designed to help him or her make a successful readjustment to society. He or she may be forced to radically adjust his or her personality and life-style.
14. *Release.* Upon completion of his or her sentence and period of correction, the offender will be free to return to society. Release may be earned by serving the maximum sentence given by the court or through an early-release mechanism, such as parole or pardon. Most inmates do not serve the full term of their sentence. Offenders sentenced to community supervision simply finish their term and resume their lives in the community.
15. *Postrelease.* After termination of correctional treatment, the offender will have to make a successful return to the community. This adjustment is usually aided by corrections department staff members who attempt to counsel the offender through the period of reentry into society. The offender may be asked to spend some time in a community correctional center, which acts as a bridge between a secure treatment facility and absolute freedom. Offenders may find that their conviction has cost them some personal privileges, such as the right to hold certain kinds of employment. These may be returned by court order once the offenders have proven their trustworthiness and willingness to adjust to society's rules.

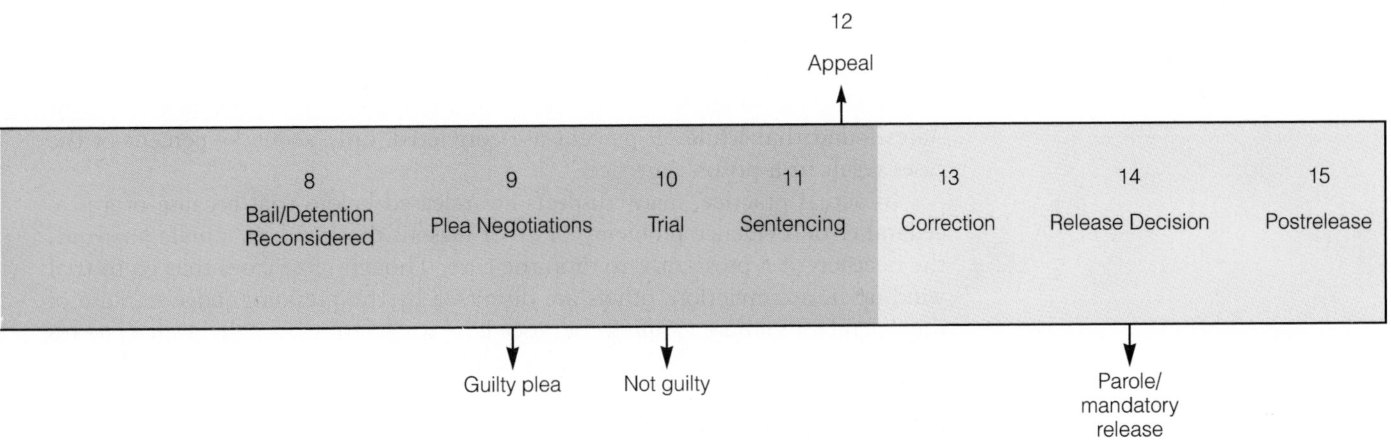

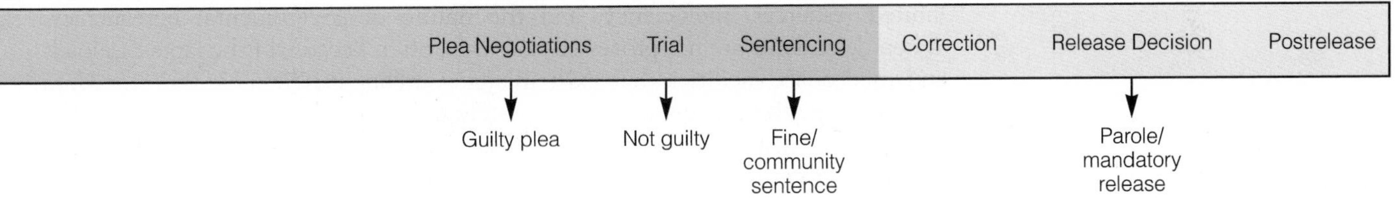

Criminal Justice Assembly Line

> The image that comes to mind is an assembly line conveyor belt down which moves an endless stream of cases, never stopping, carrying them to workers who stand at fixed stations and who perform on each case as it comes by the same small but essential operation that brings it one step closer to being a finished product, or to exchange the metaphor for the reality, a closed file. The criminal process is seen as a screening process in which each successive stage—pre-arrest investigation, arrest, post-arrest investigation, preparation for trial, trial or entry of plea, conviction, disposition—involves a series of routinized operations whose success is gauged primarily by their tendency to pass the case along to a successful conclusion.[51]

So Herbert Packer describes the criminal justice process. According to this view, each of the fifteen stages described above is actually a decision point through which cases flow (see Figure 1.4). For example, at the investigatory stage, police must decide whether to pursue the case or terminate involvement because there is insufficient evidence to identify a suspect, the case is considered trivial, the victim decides not to press charges, and so on. Or at the bail stage, a decision must be made whether to set so high a bail that the defendant remains in custody, set a reasonable bail, or release the defendant on his or her own recognizance without requiring any bail at all. Each of these decisions can have a critical effect on the defendant, the justice system, and society. If an error is made, an innocent person may suffer or a dangerous individual may be released to continue to prey upon society.

Figure 1.5 illustrates the approximate number of offenders removed from the criminal justice system at each stage of the process. As the figure shows, relatively few arrestees are bound over for trial, convicted, and eventually sentenced to prison. One recent study of more than half a million felony arrests made in eight states found that while 59 percent are convicted, only about 10 percent of the cases result in a prison sentence.[52]

In actual practice, many suspects are released before trial because of a procedural error, evidence problems, or other reasons that result in a ***nolle prosequi,*** the decision of a prosecutor to drop the case. Though most cases that go to trial wind up in a conviction, others are dismissed by the presiding judge because of the defendant's failure to appear or procedural irregularities. So, the justice process can be viewed as a funnel that holds a lot of cases at its mouth and relatively few at its end.

Theoretically, nearly every part of the process requires that individual cases be disposed of as quickly as possible. However, the criminal justice process is slower and more tedious than desired because of congestion, inadequate facilities, limited resources, inefficiency, and the nature of governmental bureaucracy. When defendants are not processed smoothly, often because of the large caseloads and inadequate facilities that exist in many urban jurisdictions, the procedure breaks down, the process within the system fails, and the ultimate goal of a fair and efficient justice system cannot be achieved. Table 1.1 represents the interrelationship of the component agencies of the criminal justice system and the criminal justice process.

The Informal Justice System

The traditional model of the criminal justice system outlined above depicts the legal process as a series of decision points through which cases flow. Each stage of the system, beginning with investigation and arrest and ending after a sentence has been served, is defined by time-honored administrative procedures and controlled by the rule of law. The public's perception of the system, fueled by the media, is that it is composed of daredevil, crime-fighting police officers who never ask for overtime or sick leave, crusading district attorneys who stop at nothing to send the mob boss up the river, wily defense attorneys who neither ask clients for upfront cash nor cut office visits to play golf, no-nonsense judges who are never inept political appointees, and tough wardens who rule the yard with an iron hand. Though this "ideal" model of justice still merits concern and attention, it would be overly simplistic to assume that the system works this way for every case. While there is little question that a few cases receive a full measure of rights and procedures, many are settled in an informal pattern of cooperation between the major actors in the justice process. For example, police may be willing to make a deal with a suspect in order to gain his or her cooperation, and the prosecutor bargains with the defense attorney to gain a plea of guilty as charged in return for a promise of leniency. Law enforcement agents and court officers are allowed tremendous discretion in their decision to make an arrest, bring formal charges, handle a case informally, substitute charges, and so on. Crowded courts operate in a spirit of getting the matter settled quickly and cleanly, rather than engage in long, drawn-out criminal proceedings with an uncertain outcome.

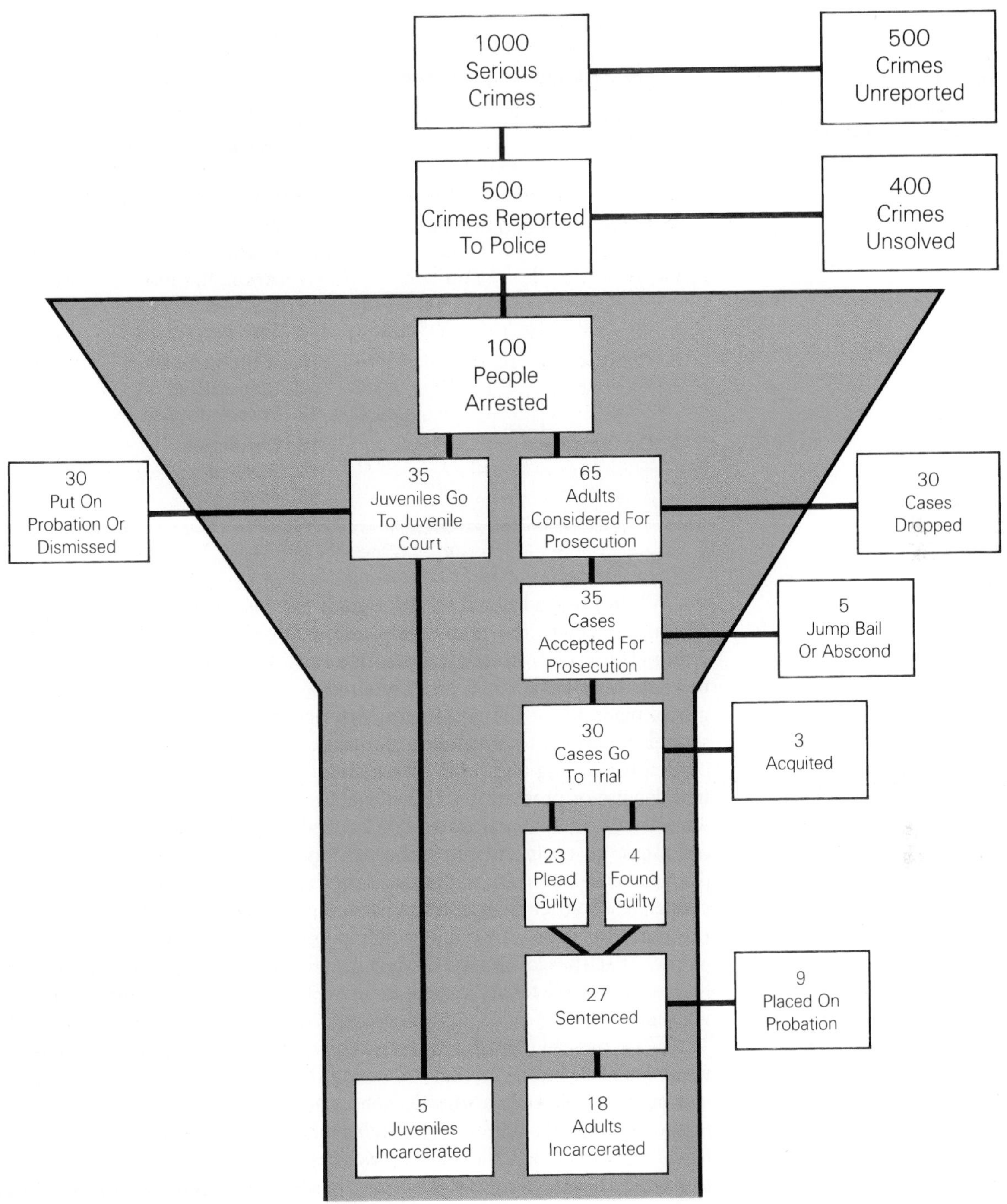

FIGURE 1.5

The Criminal Justice Funnel

SOURCE: Edward Lisefski and Donald Manson, *Tracking Offenders, 1984* (Washington, D.C.: Bureau of Justice Statistics, 1988); Patrick Langan, *Felony Sentences in State Courts, 1986* (Washington, D.C.: Bureau of Justice Statistics, 1989).

TABLE 1.1
The Interrelationship of the Criminal Justice System and the Criminal Justice Process

The System: Agencies of Crime Control	The Process
1. Police	1. Contact 2. Investigation 3. Arrest 4. Custody
2. Prosecution and defense	5. Complaint/charging 6. Grand jury/preliminary hearing 7. Arraignment 8. Bail/detention 9. Plea bargaining
3. Court	10. Adjudication 11. Disposition 12. Postconviction remedies
4. Corrections	13. Correction 14. Release 15. Postrelease

While the traditional model regards the justice process as an adversary proceeding in which the prosecution and defense are combatants, the majority of criminal cases are actually cooperative ventures in which all parties get together to work out a deal; this is often referred to as the **courtroom work group.**[53] This group, made up of the prosecutor, defense attorney, judge, and other court personnel, functions to streamline the process of justice through the extensive use of plea bargaining and other alternatives. Rather than looking to provide a spirited defense or prosecution, these legal agents, who have often attended the same schools and know each other and worked together for many years, try to work out a case to their advantage through an informal legal process that sometimes disregards the interests of the defendant and the public. In most criminal cases, cooperation rather than conflict between prosecution and defense appears to be the norm. It is only in a few widely publicized criminal cases involving rape or murder that the adversarial process is called into play. Consequently, upward of 80 percent of all felony cases and over 90 percent of misdemeanors are settled without trial.

What has developed is a system in which criminal court experiences can be viewed as a training ground for young defense attorneys looking for seasoning and practice, a means for newly established lawyers to receive government compensation for cases taken to get their practice going, or an arena in which established firms can place their new associates for experience before they are assigned to paying clients. Similarly, successful prosecutors can look forward to a political career or a highly paid partnership in a private firm. To further their career aspirations, prosecutors must develop and maintain a winning track record in criminal cases. No district attorney wants to become a Hamilton Burger, the fictional prosecutor who loses every case to the legendary Perry Mason. While the courtroom work group limits the constitutional rights of defendants, it may be essential for keeping our overburdened justice system afloat. Moreover, while informal justice exists, it is not absolutely certain that it is inherently unfair to both the victim and the offender. The research evidence shows that the defen-

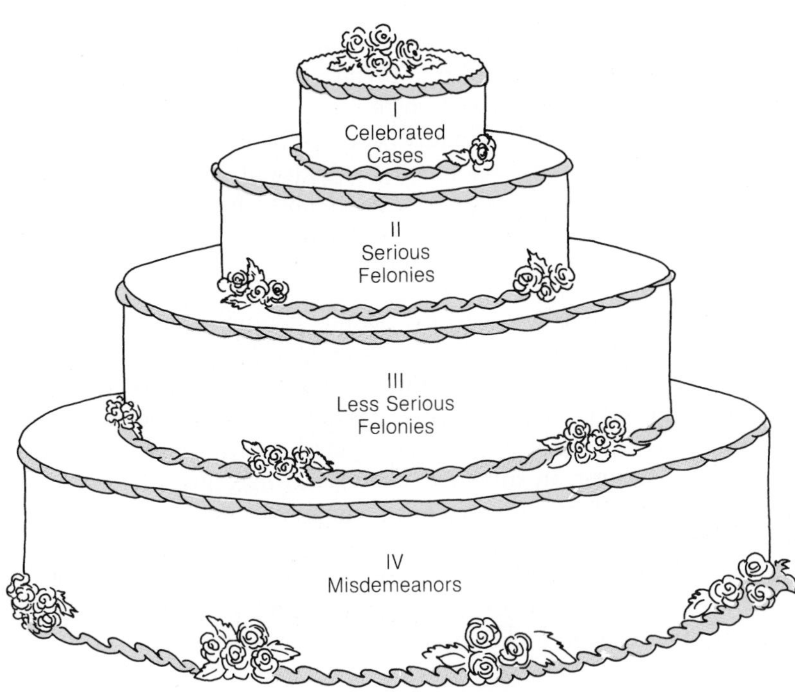

FIGURE 1.6
The Criminal Justice "Wedding Cake"

SOURCE: Based on Samuel Walker, *Sense and Nonsense about Crime* (Monterey, Calif.: Brooks/Cole, 1985).

dants who benefit the most from informal court procedures commit the least serious crimes, while the more chronic offender gains relatively little.[54]

The "Wedding Cake" Model of Justice

Samuel Walker, a justice historian and scholar of some renown, has come up with a rather dramatic way of describing this informal justice process: he compares it to a four-layer cake, as depicted in Figure 1.6.[55]

Level I. The first layer of Walker's model is made up of the celebrated cases involving the wealthy and famous, such as heavyweight boxing champion, Mike Tyson, socialite William Kennedy Smith, and financier Michael Milken, or the not so powerful who victimize a famous person—for example, John Hinckley, Jr., who shot President Ronald Reagan, or Sirhan Sirhan, who assassinated Senator Robert Kennedy.

Other cases fall into the first layer because they are widely reported in the media and become the subject of a TV miniseries. When New Hampshire teacher Pamela Smart plotted with her teenage lover William Flynn to kill her husband Greg, media coverage made it a first-layer case. The media usually focuses on hideous or unusual cases, such as Jeffrey Dahmer's killing of fifteen men in Milwaukee.

Also included within Level I are relatively unknown cases that become celebrated when they serve as vehicles for important Supreme Court decisions. *Miranda v. Arizona* and *Gideon v. Wainwright* reached legal prominence when they defined the defendant's right to legal counsel at arrest and trial.

Cases in the first layer of the criminal justice wedding cake usually receive the full array of criminal justice procedures, including competent defense attorneys, expert witnesses, jury trials, and elaborate appeals. Prosecutors are more than willing to bring these cases to trial because the media attention helps them launch political careers—but only when they win, of course. Consider the criticism leveled against Palm Beach County Assistant District Attorney Moira Lasch after William Kennedy Smith was found not guilty of rape. Because the public hears so much about these cases, it believes them to be a norm, but in reality, they are quite rare.

Level II. In the second layer are the serious felonies—rapes, robberies, and burglaries—which have become all too routine in U.S. society. They are in the second layer because they are serious crimes committed by experienced offenders. Burglaries are included if the amount stolen is quite high and the techniques used indicate the suspect is a real pro. Violent crimes, such as rape and assault, are vicious incidents against an innocent victim and may involve a weapon and extreme violence. Robberies involve large amounts of money and suspects who brandish handguns or other weapons and are considered career criminals. Police, prosecutors, and judges all agree that these are serious cases, worthy of the full attention of the justice system. Offenders in such Level II cases receive a full jury trial and, if convicted, can look forward to a prison sentence.

Level III. Though they can also be felonies, crimes that fall in the third layer of the wedding cake are either less serious offenses, committed by young or first-time offenders and/or involving people who knew each other or were otherwise related: an inebriated teenager commits a burglary and nets fifty dollars; the rape victim had gone on a few dates with her assailant before he attacked her; the robbery that involved members of rival gang and no weapons; the assault was the result of a personal dispute and where there is some question of who hit who first. Agents of the criminal justice system relegate these cases to the third level because they see them as less important and deserving of attention. Level III crimes may be dealt with by an outright dismissal, a plea bargain, reduction in charges, and, most typically, a probationary sentence or intermediate sanction, such as victim restitution.

Level IV. The fourth layer of the cake is made up of the millions of misdemeanors, such as disorderly conduct, shoplifting, public drunkeness, and minor assault. These are handled by the lower criminal courts in assembly-line fashion. Few defendants insist on exercising their constitutional rights because the delay would cost them valuable time and money. Since the typical penalty is a small fine, everyone wants to get the case over with. Malcolm Feeley's study of the lower court in New Haven, Connecticut, shows that in a sense, the experience of going to court is the real punishment in a misdemeanor case. Few (4.9 percent) of the cases involved any jail time.[56]

The informal justice system model depicts the justice system in political terms. Cases that are "important" because they involve famous people or generate media interest go to the top of the pile. In contrast, cases in which the poor victimize one another get little formal interest from the justice system. The typical criminal case is handled as if it were a civil complaint or lawsuit: a settlement agreeable to all parties involved—defendant, victim, defense attorney, prosecutor, and police—seems the best course of action.

The Justice System: A Final Word

The "wedding cake" model of informal justice is an intriguing alternative to the traditional criminal justice flow chart. Criminal justice officials do handle individual cases quite differently. Yet there is a high degree of consistency with which particular types or classes of cases are dealt in every legal jurisdiction. Police and prosecutors in Los Angeles and Boston, New York and San Antonio will each handle the murder of a prominent citizen in a similar fashion. They will also deal with the death of an unemployed street person killed in a brawl in a likewise manner. Yet, in each jurisdiction, the two cases will be handled very differently from one another. The bigwig's killer will receive a full-blown jury trial (with details on the six o'clock news); the drifter's killer will get a quick plea bargain. The model is useful because it helps us realize that all too often, public opinion about criminal justice is formed on the basis of what happened in a celebrated case that is actually quite atypical.

In sum, the justice system is large, complex, and multifaceted. It offers an intriguing challenge for those who desire to work within its structure and many career opportunities for motivated individuals who seek to understand and improve its operations.

Criminal Justice as a Career

The criminal justice system provides numerous career opportunities. The preceding sections identified some of the different roles in the justice process. Some who choose to go into the field are motivated by the desire to help people and get into social service work. Others are more interested in law enforcement and policing. Another choice is teaching and research, while others want to supplement their criminal justice education with legal studies in order to fill the role of defense counsel, prosecutor, or magistrate. Of course, some enterprising people are able to fill a number of these different endeavors some time during their criminal justice career: a police officer earns a doctorate and goes into teaching; a probation officer goes to law school and becomes a prosecutor; a professor is appointed head of a state corrections department, and so on. Let us now examine some of the specialties within the field of criminal justice to get an idea of what some of the career alternatives are.

Law Enforcement

Over a half million people are employed in policing and law enforcement in the United States. The following are but a few areas in which a person's criminal justice career can involve in the enforcement of the criminal law.

Municipal Police Officer. The majority of people in law enforcement work for city police departments. The work of the patrol officer, traffic cop, and detective is familiar to any one who watches TV or goes to a movie (though the accuracy of the portrayal by those entertainment vehicles is highly suspect). Beyond these familiar roles, however, police work also includes a great many administrative and service jobs, such as officer training, communications, records management, purchasing, and so on. A student interested in a police career but not necessarily excited by the idea of roaming the streets chasing after bad guys will find that police work has a great deal of other opportunities to offer.

State and County Law Enforcement. In addition to city police agencies, state and county governments also provide career opportunities in law enforcement. The state police and county sheriff's department do much the same work as city police agencies—traffic, patrol, and investigation—depending on their area of jurisdiction. These agencies commonly take on a greater law enforcement role in more rural areas and provide ancillary services, such as running the local jail or controlling traffic, in urban centers.

Federal Law Enforcement. The federal government also employs thousands of law enforcement personnel in such agencies as the Federal Bureau of Investigation, the Drug Enforcement Agency, the Secret Service, and so on. These agencies are often considered the elite of the law enforcement profession, and standards for entry are quite high. The duties of these federal agencies include upholding federal laws controlling counterfeiting, terrorism, espionage, bank robbery, and importation and distribution of controlled substances, among others.

Private Security. The field of private security also offers many career opportunities. Some positions are in large security companies, such as Pinkerton's or Wackenhut. Others are in company security forces, such as those maintained by large retail chains, manufacturing companies, and railroads. Public institutions such as hospitals, airports, and port facilities also have security teams.

These are but a few of the many careers in law enforcement. Table 1.2 provides a more complete list of opportunities.

Correctional Service Work

A significant number of people who work in the field of criminal justice become involved in its social service side. There are many opportunities to provide direct service to people both before they actually get involved with the law and after they come to the attention of criminal justice agencies.

Probation Officer. Probation officers supervise offenders who have been placed under community supervision by the criminal court. Their duties include counseling clients to help them to adjust to society. This may be done through family counseling, individual counseling, and group sessions. Probation officers are trained to use the resources of the community to help their clients. Their work involves them in the personal, family, and work problems of their clients.

Correctional Counselor. While some may view correctional work as a matter of guarding incarcerated inmates, that narrow perspective is far from accurate. Correctional treatment staff engage in such tasks as vocational and educational training, counseling, recreational work, and so on. Almost every correctional institution has a social service staff that helps inmates adjust to the institution and prepare for successful reentry into the outside world.

Community Correctional Counselor. There are thousands of community-based correctional facilities around the country. These house nonviolent criminals serving out their prison sentence and inmates transferred from high-security institutions near the completion of their prison term; separate facilities are main-

TABLE 1.2
Careers in Law Enforcement

arson investigator	investigator
attaché	jailer
ballistics expert	juvenile specialist
booking officer	K-9 handler
Border Patrol officer	narcotics agent
chaplain	operations specialist
chief of police	patrol officer
chief of staff	personnel specialist
commander of field operations	photographer
commissioner	pilot
communications officer	police attorney/legal advisor
community safety coordinator	police psychologist
community service officer	police/school liaison officer
conservation officer	police surgeon
crime lab technician	polygraph operator
crime prevention specialist	professor
customs officer	psychiatric advisor
data processing specialist	public relations officer
deputy	public safety director
deputy chief	radio communications
detective	records management director
detention officer	scientist
director of research and development	security specialist
director of scientific services	secret service agent
director of standards and training	serology specialist
document specialist	sheriff
emergency management coordinator	street crimes specialist
evidence technician	superintendent of police
FBI special agent	SWAT team member
fingerprint expert	traffic officer
firearms instructor	training director
forensic scientist	treasury agent
gaming enforcement agent	trooper
gang investigator	undercover operative
inspector	undersheriff
instructor	U.S. marshal
intelligence officer	water patrol
	witness protection agent

SOURCE: Harr & Hess, *Seeking Employment in Law Enforcement, Private Security, and Related Fields.* West Publishing Company © 1992. pp. 16–17.

tained for juvenile offenders. These settings also provide ample opportunity for direct service work, since the overwhelming majority of programs emphasize the value of rehabilitation and treatment. Community-based corrections provide the setting for some of the most innovative treatment techniques used in the criminal justice system.

Parole and After Care. Parole and after-care workers supervise offenders upon their release from correctional treatment. This involves helping them find jobs, achieve their educational objectives, sort out their family problems, and so on. Parole officers employ various counseling techniques to help clients clarify their goals and find ways of surmounting obstacles so that they can make a successful readjustment to the community.

Law and the Courts

The criminal justice system provides many opportunities for people interested in working in the legal system and the courts. Of course, in most instances, these careers require postgraduate education, such as law school or a course in court management.

Prosecutor. Prosecutors represent the state in criminal matters. They bring charges against offenders, engage in plea bargaining, conduct trials, and help determine sentences. Prosecutors work at the local, county, state, and federal levels of government. For example, an assistant U.S. attorney general would prosecute violations of federal law in one of the ninety-one U.S. district courts.

Defense Counsel. All criminal defendants are entitled to legal counsel. Therefore, agencies such as the public defender's office have been created to provide free legal services to indigent offenders. In addition, private attorneys often take on criminal cases without compensation as a gesture of community service or are assigned cases by the court for modest compensation (referred to as a ***pro bono*** case). Defense attorneys help clients gather evidence to support their innocence, represent them at pretrial, trial, and sentencing hearings, and serve as their advocate if an appeal is filed upon conviction.

Judge. Judges carry out many different functions during the trial stage of justice. They help in jury selection, oversee the admission of evidence, and control the flow of the trial. Most important, they are entrusted with the duty to ensure that the trial is conducted within the boundaries of legal fairness. While many criminal defense attorneys and prosecutors aspire to become judges, few are actually chosen for this honor.

Court Manager. Most court jurisdictions maintain an office of court administration. These individuals help in case management and ensure that the court's resources are used in the most efficient manner. Court administrators usually are required to receive advance education at programs that specialize in court management, such as the ones at the University of Southern California and American University in Washington, D.C.

Research, Administration, and Teaching

In addition to work within the agencies of justice themselves, a career in criminal justice that involves teaching, research or administration is also possible.

Private-Sector Research. A number of private-sector institutes and research firms, such as the Rand Corporation in Santa Monica, California, Abt Associates in Cambridge, Massachusetts, and the Battelle Institute in Seattle, employ research scientists who conduct criminal justice-related research. In addition, a number of private nonprofit organizations are devoted to the study of criminal justice issues, including the Police Executive Research Forum, the Police Foundation, and International Association of Chiefs of Police, each located in the Washington, D.C., area, and the National Council on Crime and Delinquency in San Francisco and the VERA Foundation in New York.

Many universities also maintain research centers that for many years have conducted ongoing efforts in criminal justice, often with funding from the government and private foundations. For example, the Institute for Social Research at the University of Michigan has conducted an annual survey of teenage substance abuse; the Hindelang Research Center at the State University of New York at Albany produces the *Sourcebook of Criminal Justice Statistics*, an invaluable research tool; the National Neighborhood Foot Patrol Center at Michigan State University conducts research on community policing; and the Criminal Justice Research Center at the University of Massachusetts-Lowell is involved in measuring the effectiveness of probation supervision.

Most people who work for these research centers hold advanced degrees in criminal justice or other applied social sciences. Some of the projects carried out by these centers, such as the study of career criminals conductd by Rand Corporation scientists and the Police Fondation's study of the deterrent effect of police patrol, have had a profound effect on policy-making within the criminal justice system.

Public-Sector Research. Most large local, state, and federal government agencies contain research arms that oversee the evaluation of ongoing criminal justice programs and plan for the development of innovative efforts designed to create positive change in the system. For example, most state corrections departments have planning and research units that monitor the flow of inmates in and out of the prison system and help evaluate the effectiveness of prison programs, such as work furloughs. On a local level, larger police departments commonly employ civilian research coordinators who analyze police data in order to improve the effectiveness and efficiency of police services.

The most significant contribution to criminal justice research made by the public sector is probably that of the federal government's Bureau of Justice Statistics and National Institute of Justice, which are the research arms of the U.S. Justice Department. In recent years, these agencies have supported some of the most impressive and important of all research on criminal justice issues, such as sentencing, plea bargaining, and victimization.

System Administration. It is also common for states and the federal government to maintain central criminal justice planning offices that are responsible for setting and implementing criminal justice policy or for distributing funds for its implementation. For example, the NIJ sets priorities for criminal justice research and policy on an annual basis and then distributes funds to local and state applicants who are willing to set up and evaluate demonstration projects. In 1989, for example, the NIJ targeted the following areas: apprehension, prosecution, and adjudication of criminal offenders; public safety and security; punishment and control of offenders; victims of crime; white-collar and organized crime; criminal careers; drugs and alcohol and crime; forensic science; offender classification; and violent criminal behavior.[57]

A number of states also have criminal justice administrative agencies that set policy agendas and coordinate state efforts to improve the quality of the system.

College Teaching. There are more than six-hundred criminal justice education programs in the United States. These include specialized criminal justice programs, programs where criminal justice is combined with another department, such as sociology or political science, and programs that offer a concentration in criminal justice as part of another major.

Criminal justice educators have a career track similar to most other teaching specialties. Regardless of the level they teach at—associate, baccalaureate, or graduate—their course will reflect the core subject matter of criminal justice, including courses on policing, the courts, and the correctional system.

Financial Reward in Criminal Justice

Many people believe that a criminal justice career is limited financially because it involves working for local, state, or federal governments. However, a great many careers within the criminal justice system involve substantial salary and financial benefits. A number of careers, such as federal law enforcement agent, local prosecutor, and state and federal court personnel, offer salaries that are competitive with other fields. For example, police officers in some cities in Massachusetts start at about thirty thousand dollars a year. If they receive an undergraduate degree, they earn an extra 20 percent on their base pay; a master's or law degree increases their starting pay by 25 percent. Overtime and special detail pay can add to this sum. It is not uncommon for uniformed police officers to double their salaries with extra work details (in Boston, the highest paid patrolman earned $118,472 in a single year); in 1991, 400 Boston police officers made over $70,000.[58]

SUMMARY

The term *criminal justice* became prominent around 1967, when the President's Commission on Law Enforcement and Administration of Justice began a nationwide study of the nation's crime problem. Since then, a field of study has emerged that uses knowledge from various disciplines in an attempt to understand what causes people to commit crimes and how to deal with the crime problem. Criminal justice, then, consists of the study of crime and of the agencies concerned with its prevention and control.

Criminal justice is both a system and a process. As a system, it ideally functions as a cooperative effort among the primary agencies—police, courts, and corrections. The process, on the other hand, consists of the actual steps the offender takes from the initial investigation through trial, sentencing, and appeal.

In many instances, the criminal justice system works informally in order to expedite the disposal of cases. Criminal acts that are very serious or notorious may receive the full complement of criminal justice processes, from arrest to trial. However, less serious cases are often settled when a bargain is reached between the prosecution and the defense.

Many careers are open to people interested in working within the criminal justice system. Among the options are police work, social service, research, administration, and teaching.

QUESTIONS

1. Which criminal behavior patterns pose the greatest threat to the public? Should the justice system devote greater resources to combating these crimes? If so, which crime patterns should be deemphasized?
2. Describe the differences between the formal and informal justice systems. Is it fair to treat some offenders informally?
3. What are the layers of the criminal justice "wedding cake"? Give an example of a crime for each layer.
4. What are the advantages and drawbacks to the various careers in criminal justice?

NOTES

1. Scott Rothschild, "Gunman Slays 22 in Texas," *Boston Globe* 17 October 1991, p. 1.

2. The Gallup Report, June 1989. Cited in Kathleen Maguire and Timothy Flanagan, *Sourcebook of Criminal Justice Statistics, 1990* (Washington, D.C.: U.S. Government Printing Office, 1991), p. 154.

3. The Harris Poll, 16 December 1990, cited in Kathleen Maguire and Timothy Flanagan, *Sourcebook of Criminal Justice Statistics, 1990* (Washington, D.C.: U.S. Government Printing Office, 1991), p. 158.

4. Charles Patrick Ewing, *When Children Kill* (Lexington, Mass.: Lexington Books, 1990), p. 22.

5. National Opinion Research Center data reported in Katherine Jamieson and Timothy Flanagan, *Sourcebook of Criminal Justice Statistics 1986* (Washington, D.C.: U.S. Government Printing Office, 1987), pp. 76, 109.

6. G. David Curry and Irving Spergel, "Gang Homicide, Delinquency, and Community," *Criminology* 26 (1988): 382; John Hagedorn, *People and Folks: Gangs, Crime and the Underclass in a Rustbelt City* (Chicago: Lake View Press, 1988); C. Ronald Huff, "Youth Gangs and Public Policy," *Crime and Delinquency* 35 (1989): 524–37; Jeffery Fagan, "The Social Organization of Drug Use and Drug Dealing Among Urban Gangs," *Criminology* 27 (1989): 633–67; Carl Taylor, *Dangerous Society* (East Lansing: Michigan State University Press, 1990).

7. James A. Fox and Jack Levin, *Mass Murder*, 2d ed. (New York: Plenum Press, 1991).

8. Ibid.

9. Study Findings, *National Incidence and Prevalence of Child Abuse and Neglect* (Washington, D.C.: U.S. Department of Health and Human Services, 1988).

10. Diana Russell, "The Incidence and Prevalence of Intrafamilial and Extrafamilial Sexual Abuse of Female Children," *Child Abuse and Neglect* 7 (1983): 133–46.

11. Richard Gelles and Murray Straus, *Intimate Violence* (New York: Simon and Schuster, 1988), p. 27.

12. Peggy Reeves Sanday, *Fraternity Gang Rape: Sex, Brotherhood, and Privilege on Campus* (New York: New York University Press, 1990).

13. Mark Starr, "The Writing on the Wall," *Newsweek*, 26 November 1990, p. 64.

14. Susan Estrich, *Real Rape* (Cambridge: Harvard University Press, 1987), pp. 72–79.

15. Janet Gornick, Martha Burt, and Karen Pittman, "Structure and Activities of Rape Crises Centers in the Early 1980's," *Crime and Delinquency* 31 (1985): 247–68.

16. Special Issue, "Drugs—The American Family in Crisis," *Juvenile and Family Court* 39 (1988): 45–46.

17. Associated Press, "Alcohol Deaths Stopped Declining," *Boston Globe*, 27 January 1991, p. 8.

18. George Speckart and M. Douglas Anglin, "Narcotics Use and Crime: An Overview of Recent Research Advances," *Contemporary Drug Problems* 13 (1986): 741–69; M. Douglas Anglin and George Speckart, "Narcotics Use and Crime: A Multisample, Multimethod Analysis," *Criminology* 26 (1988): 197–235.

19. Eric Wish, *Drug Use Forecasting, Drugs and Crime Annual Report, 1990* (Washington, D.C.: National Institute of Justice, 1991).

20. Ibid., p. 5.

21. Kitty Calavita and Henry Pontell, "Heads I Win, Tails You Lose: Deregulation, Crime, and Crisis in the Savings and Loan Industry," *Crime and Delinquency* 36 (1990): 309–41. Rich Thomas, "Sit Down Taxpayers," *Newsweek*, 4 June 1990, p. 60; L. Gordon Crovitz, "Milken's Tragedy: Oh How the Mighty Fall before RICO," *Wall Street Journal*, 2 May 1990, p. A17.

22. Tim Metz and Michael Miller, "Boesky's Rise and Fall Illustrate a Compulsion to Profit by Getting Inside Track on Market," *Wall Street Journal*, 17 November 1986, p. A28; Wade Lambert, "FDIC Receives Cooperation of Milken Aide," *Wall Street Journal*, 25 April 1991, p. A3.

23. Steven Waldman, "The HUD Ripoff," *Newsweek*, 7 August 1989, pp. 16–22, quote at p. 16.

24. John Braithwaite, "Toward a Theory of Organizational Crime." Paper presented at the annual meeting of the American Society of Criminology, Montreal, November 1987.

25. Travis Hirschi and Michael Gotffredson, "Causes of White Collar Crime," *Criminology* 25 (1987): 969–74.

26. See, generally, Jay Albanese, *Organized Crime in America*, 2d ed. (Cincinnati: Anderson Publishing, 1989), p. 68.

27. Alan Block, *East Side/West Side* (New Brunswick, N.J.: Transaction Books, 1983), pp. VII, 10–11.

28. Selwyn Raab, "A Battered and Ailing Mafia Is Losing Its Grip on America," *New York Times*, 22 October 1990, p. 1.

29. This section leans heavily on Ted Robert Gurr, "Historical Trends in Violent Crime: A Critical Review of the Evidence," in Michael Tonry and Norval Morris, eds., *Crime and Justice: An Annual Review of Research*, vol. 3 (Chicago: University of Chicago Press, 1981); Richard Maxwell Brown, "Historical Patterns of American Violence," in Hugh Davis Graham and Ted Robert Gurr, eds., *Violence in America: Historical and Comparative Perspectives* (Beverly Hills, Calif.: Sage Publications, 1979).

30. Cesare Beccaria, *On Crimes and Punishments* (1764, reprint ed., Indianapolis: Bobbs Merrill, 1963).

31. Samuel Walker, *Popular Justice* (New York: Oxford University Press, 1980).

32. Ibid.

33. Ibid.

34. President's Commission on Law Enforcement and the Administration of Justice, *Challenge of Crime in a Free Society* (Washington, D.C.: U.S. Government Printing Office, 1967).

35. See Public Law 90-351, Title I—Omnibus Crime Control Safe Streets Act of 1968, 90th Congress, 19 June 1968.

36. American Bar Association, *Project on Standards for Criminal Justice* (New York: Institute of Judicial Administration, 1968–1973); National Advisory Commission on Criminal Justice) Standards and Goals, *A National Strategy to Reduce Crime* (Washington, D.C.: U.S. Government Printing Office, 1973).

37. Frank Zarb, "Police Liability for Creating the Need to Use Deadly Force in Self-Defense," *Michigan Law Review* 86 (1988): 1982–2009.

38. See, for example, Stephen Schoenthaler and Walter Doraz, "Types of Offenses Which Can Be Reduced in an Institutional Setting Using Nutritional Intervention," *International Journal of Biosocial Research* 4 (1983): 74–84.

39. *Marbury v. Madison*, 1 Cranch 137 (1803).

40. Sue Lindgren, *Justice Expenditures and Employment, 1988* (Washington, D.C.: Bureau of Justice Statistics, 1990).

41. Federal Bureau of Investigation, *Crime in the United States, 1990* (Washington, D.C.: U.S. Government Printing Office, 1991).

42. Ibid., p. 240.

43. Louis Jankowski, *Probation and Parole, 1990* (Washington, D.C.: Bureau of Justice Statistics, 1991).

44. Daniel Skoler, "Antidote for the Non-System: State Criminal Justice

Superagencies," *State Government* 46 (1976): 1–23.

45. From an address by former Chief Justice Warren Burger, U.S. Supreme Court, as reported in *Criminal Law Reporter* (1972): 305.

46. President's Commission on Law Enforcement and the Administration of Justice, *Challenge of Crime*, p. 125.

47. *Powell v. Alabama*, 287 U.S. 45, 53 S.Ct. 55, 77 L.Ed. 158 (1932); *Gideon v. Wainwright*, 372 U.S. 335, 83 S.Ct. 792, 9 L.Ed. 2d 799 (1963); *Argersinger v. Hamlin*, 407 U.S. 25, 92 S.Ct. 2006, 32 L.Ed. 2d 530 (1972).

48. Jankowski, *Probation and Parole, 1990*, p. 5.

49. See Robyn Cohen, *Prisoners in 1990* (Washington, D.C.: Bureau of Justice Statistics, 1991).

50. For an analysis of this issue, see William Wilbanks, *The Myth of a Racist Criminal Justice System* (Monterey, Calif.: Brooks/Cole, 1987); Stephen Klein, Joan Petersilia, and Susan Turner, "Race and Imprisonment Decisions in California," *Science* 247 (1990): 812-16; Alfred Blumstein, "On the Racial Disproportionality of the United States Prison Population," *Journal of Criminal Law and Criminology* 73 (1982): 1259-81; Darnell Hawkins, "Race, Crime Type and Imprisonment," *Justice Quarterly* 3 (1986): 251–69.

51. Herbert L. Packer, *The Limits of the Criminal Sanction* (Stanford, Calif.: Stanford University Press, 1975), p. 21.

52. Jacob Perez, *Tracking Offenders, 1988* (Washington, D.C.: Bureau of Justice Statistics, 1991), p. 2.

53. James Eisenstein and Herbert Jacob, *Felony Justice* (Boston: Little Brown, 1977); Peter Nardulli, *The Courtroom Elite* (Cambridge, Mass.: Ballinger, 1978); Paul Wice, *Chaos in the Courthouse* (New York: Praeger, 1985); Marcia Lipetz, *Routine Justice: Processing Cases in Women's Court* (New Brunswick, N.J.: Transaction Books, 1983).

54. Douglas Smith, "The Plea Bargaining Controversy," *Journal of Criminal Law and Criminology* 77 (1986): 949–67.

55. Samuel Walker, *Sense and Nonsense about Crime*, (Belmont, Calif.: Wadsworth Publishers, 1985).

56. Malcolm Feeley, *The Process Is the Punishment* (New York: Russell Sage Foundation, 1979).

57. National Institute of Justice, *Research Program Plan, Fiscal Year 1989* (Washington, D.C.: National Institute of Justice, 1988).

58. Brian Mooney, "Salaries of 7 Boston Officers Topped $100,000," *Boston Globe*, 2 February 1989, p. 21.

The Nature of Crime and Victimization

CHAPTER 2

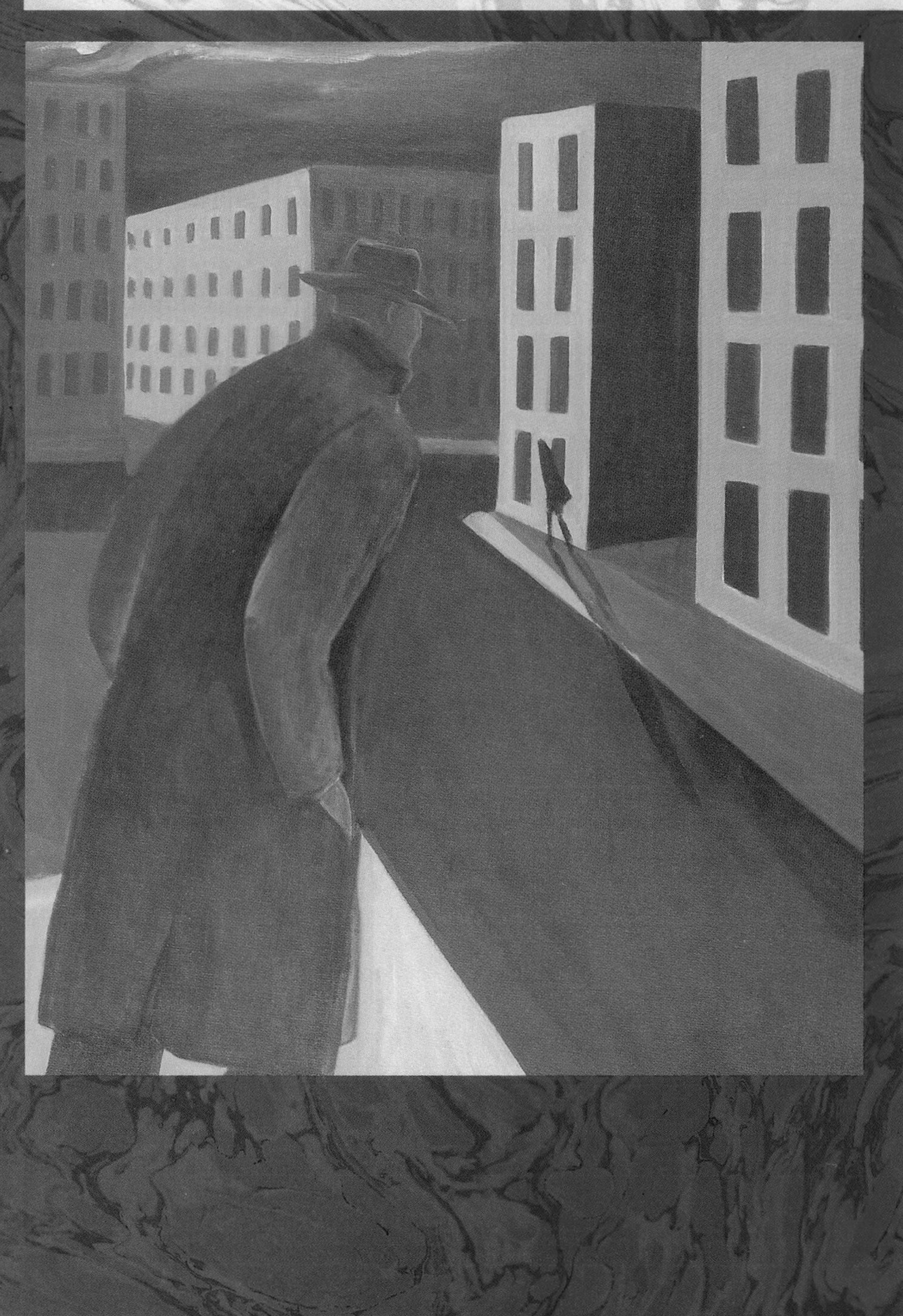

KEY TERMS

crime
criminal law
social control
interactionist view
moral entrepreneurs
conflict view
probability samples
official crime statistics
cohort research
longitudinal cohort study
participant observation
life history
index crimes
relative deprivation
self-report surveys
routine activities

Crime is an all too familiar and disturbing aspect of life in the United States. Surveys indicate that most people fear crime and are suspicious of the criminal justice system's ability to reduce its incidence. A majority of Americans tell public opinion surveyors that the crime rate in their neighborhood has been increasing.[1] About 56 percent of people who responded to a recent Hearst Corporation national survey reported they were fearful of violent crime in the 1990s.[2]

Public fear should come as no surprise, considering the daily barrage of newspaper stories, magazine articles, television series, and films that have crime as their principal topic or theme. It is probably because of the salience of crime to U.S. life, its impact on life-styles and behavior, and the widespread belief that something should be done to reduce the crime rate that programs in criminal justice have become so popular on the nation's college campuses.

If the criminal justice system is to become an effective instrument to reduce or control criminal behavior, administrators and policymakers must have up-to-date and accurate information about the nature and extent of crime. The policies and procedures of the justice system cannot exist in an informational vacuum. Unless accurate information about crime exists, we could never be sure whether a particular policy, process, or procedure has the effect its creators envisioned. For example, a state may enact a new law requiring that anyone who uses a firearm to commit a crime serve a mandatory prison term. The new statute is aimed directly at reducing the incidence of violent crimes, such as murder, armed robbery, and assault. The effectiveness of this statutory change cannot be demonstrated without hard evidence that the use of firearms actually declined after the law was instituted and, concomitantly, that the use of knives or other weapons did not increase. Without being able to measure crime accurately, it would be impossible to either understand its cause or plan its elimination.

This chapter discusses some of the basic questions in the study of crime and justice: How is crime defined? How is crime measured? How much crime is there, and what are its trends and patterns? How many people become victims of crime, and under what circumstances does victimization take place?

The Concept of Crime

The study of criminal justice is bound up in the concept of crime. To most people, the term **crime** invokes such familiar images as a bank robbery, an auto theft, or an assault. But legal scholars have long wrestled with the problem of defining crime so that it can be more easily studied. Currently, there are three distinct views on the subject.

Consensus View

According to the consensus view, crimes are behaviors that (1) are essentially harmful to a majority of citizens living in society and (2) have been controlled or prohibited by the existing **criminal law.** The term *consensus view* means that most people agree that the behaviors prohibited by the criminal law are generally harmful to the well-being of society. The consensus position is that the criminal law is a set of rules that express the norms, goals, and values of a majority of society. Consequently, the criminal law has a **social control** function—restraining those who would take advantage of others' weakness for their own personal gain and thereby endanger the social framework. While differences in behavior can be tolerated within a properly functioning social system, behaviors that are considered inherently destructive and dangerous are outlawed to maintain the social fabric and ensure the peaceful functioning of society.

Interactionist View

Those embracing the **interactionist view** agree that the criminal law defines crime, but they challenge the belief that the law represents the will and opinion of a majority of citizens. Instead, the interactionist view holds that the criminal law is influenced by people who hold social power and use it to mold the law to reflect their way of thinking. For example, various groups have tried to influence laws regulating the possession of handguns, the use of drugs and alcohol, and the availability of abortions. These **moral entrepreneurs** use their economic, social, and political influence to impose their definition of right and wrong on the rest of the population.[3]

According to this view, the criminal law is a flexible instrument that may change according to the whim of powerful individuals and groups who use it to reflect their views of right and wrong. A good example of this viewpoint can be found in the passage of law banning the sale and possession of marijuana. Al-

Public perception of crime is shaped by sensational news stories. Here Richard Ramirez, the Los Angeles Night Stalker, a serial killer, is held in custody. Cases such as the Night Stalker give the public the impression that crime is out of control.

though legal in this country until 1937, marijuana was criminalized as a result of the efforts of Harry Anslinger, head of the Federal Bureau of Narcotics. Through a series of graphic magazine articles and lurid newspaper stories, Anslinger personally led the national lobbying campaign that led to Congress passing the Marijuana Tax Act, which banned the drug. Today, though millions still use marijuana, it has remained illegal in most jurisdictions.[4]

Conflict View

The **conflict view** of crime maintains that the true purpose of the criminal law is to protect the power of the upper classes at the expense of the poor. The conflict approach depicts society as a collection of diverse groups—owners, workers, professionals, minority groups—who are in conflict with one another over a number of issues. Groups able to assert their political and economic power use the law and the criminal justice system to advance their own causes. Criminal laws, therefore, are viewed as acts created to protect the haves from the have-nots.[5]

The conflict position differs from the interactionist view because it has a distinctly political, rather than moral, orientation. It views the capitalist economic system, with its emphasis on money, power, and position, as a major controlling factor in the definition of crime. Crime is *created* by ruling authorities. The ability to confer criminal status is a privilege enjoyed by the propertied classes and suffered by the nonprivileged. The law is a function of political power that is held as a weapon over the heads of those unable or unwilling to enjoy or possess its resources.

Crime and Law

The three competing views of crime have significantly influenced research and policy-making in the field of criminal justice. How a person defines or views the concept of crime affects his or her positions on its prevention and control.

Despite the obviously wide theoretical gulf separating these views of crime and criminality, they do share some common ground. All three link crime to the existing legal code, agree that the law is constantly changing and evolving, conclude that social forces mold the definition of crimes, and view the criminal justice system as responsible for carrying out the criminal law's social control function. Since these concepts of crime overlap, elements of each view can be used to create an integrated definition:

> Crime is a violation of social rules of conduct, interpreted and expressed by a written criminal code, created by people holding social and political power. Its content may be influenced by prevailing public sentiments, historically developed moral beliefs, and the need to protect public safety. Individuals who violate these rules may be subject to sanctions administered by state authority, which include social stigma and loss of status, freedom, and, on occasion, their life.

How Crime Is Measured

Criminal justice scholars use a variety of techniques to study crime and its consequences. Some of the major sources of crime data will be discussed in this section.

Survey Data

Survey data is comprised of information obtained from interviews and questionnaires focusing on people's behaviors, attitudes, beliefs, and abilities. Most survey data comes from **probability samples** in which a limited number of subjects are randomly selected from a larger population. If the sample is carefully drawn, every individual in the population has an equal chance of being selected for the study. For example, a sample of ten thousand high school seniors is selected at random and asked about the frequency of their use of alcohol and drugs. Their answers would represent the behavior of millions of high school seniors in the United States.

Surveys can be conducted in a number of different ways. Some involve mailed or personally distributed questionnaires that participants are asked to complete and return. Sometimes surveyors interview subjects about their attitudes and behavior; occasionally both questionnaires and interviews are used. Subjects can also be selected randomly from the telephone book and interviewed over the telephone.

Criminological surveys provide a valuable source of information on particular crime problems, such as drug use, which are rarely reported to police and may therefore go undetected. Two important surveys of this type are the annual high school drug use survey conducted by researchers at the Univerity of Michigan's Institute for Social Research and the *Household Survey on Drug Abuse* conducted by the National Institute on Drug Abuse (NIDA), a branch of the U.S. Department of Health and Human Services.[6]

Surveys are also an invaluable source of information on the nature and extent of criminal victimization. The *National Crime Victimization Survey (NCVS)* conducted by the U.S. Department of Justice uses a large, carefully drawn sample of citizens to estimate the total number of criminal incidents that occur each year; it is one of the most important sources of crime data.[7]

Record Data

A significant proportion of criminal justice data involves the compilation and evaluation of official records. The records may be acquired from a variety of sources, including schools, courts, police departments, social service centers, and correctional agencies.

Records can be used for a number of purposes. Prisoners' files can be analyzed in an effort to determine what types of inmates adjust to prison and what types tend to be disciplinary problems or suicidal. Parole department records are evaluated to determine the characteristics of inmates who successfully adjust to living in society and of those who fail. Educational records are important indicators of intelligence, academic achievement, school behavior, and other information that can be related to delinquent behavior patterns. However, the most important source of crime data is those records compiled by police departments and annually collected and analyzed by the Federal Bureau of Investigation (FBI); these are referred to as the **official crime statistics.**

One important use of record data in criminal justice is in the conduct of **cohort research.** This involves the observation of a group of people who share a like characteristic over time. In order to conduct a **longitudinal cohort study,** researchers might select a cohort of subjects, for example, all boys born in Omaha, Nebraska, in 1982, and then follow their behavior patterns for a twenty-year

period. The research data might include their school, police, medical, and family records. Areas of interest might be the association of early childhood trauma and later criminality or the effect of dropping out of school on the likelihood of arrest. Because it is extremely difficult, expensive, and time-consuming to follow a cohort over time and since most of the sample do not become serious criminals, another approach is to take an intact group of known offenders and look back into their early life experiences; this format is known as a retrospective longitudinal study.

Other Sources of Crime Data

A variety of other sources of crime information exists in addition to surveys and record data. The systematic observation, recording, and deciphering of types of behavior within a sample or population is a common method of criminal justice data collection. Some observation studies are conducted in the field, where the researcher observes subjects in their normal environments; other observations take place in a contrived, artificial setting or a laboratory. Still another type of observation study is called **participant observation.** In this type of research, the criminologist joins the group being studied and behaves as a member of the group. It is believed that participation enables the scientist to better understand the motives subjects may have for their behavior and attitudes. Participation also enables the researcher to develop a frame of reference similar to that of the subjects and to better understand how the subjects interact with the rest of the world. Classic participant observation studies have been conducted by William F. Whyte on the lives of lower-class youth *(Street Corner Society)* and Laud Humphreys on homosexual behavior in public places *(Tearoom Trade)*.[8]

Observation is a time-consuming way to conduct research and occasionally contains some ethical risks, such as when the subjects engage in deviant behavior during the data-gathering stage of the research and the observer is faced with betraying their trust or letting a criminal act go unreported. Participant observation studies, however, do allow the researcher to gain insights into behavior that might never be available otherwise. In addition, since observation studies depend more on actual behavior than on surveyed opinions, the researcher can be fairly sure of the validity of the information because it will be more difficult for subjects to give false impressions or responses. It is difficult, if not impossible, to standardize the conditions or replicate the results of observation studies; thus, they usually stand as unique and valuable contributions of concerned scientists and scholars.

Another technique of criminal justice data collection is the **life history.** This method uses personal accounts of individuals who have had experience in crime, deviance, and other related areas. Diaries or autobiographies can be used; sometimes an account is given to an interested second party to record "as told to." Examples of this approach are contained in two important works by Carl Klockars and Darrell Steffensmeier on the lives of two criminal fences (people who buy and sell stolen merchandise).[9]

Life histories provide insights into the human condition that other, less personal research methods cannot hope to duplicate. They are sometimes moving, often revealing individual testimonies of the feelings, beliefs, values, and attitudes of convicts, delinquents, and criminals. Of course, life histories do not represent the average criminal. Most life histories are provided by talented, artistic individuals who eventually successfully readjust to society. Nonetheless, their stories often illustrate the conditions they had to overcome and the strengths they had to call on in order to reenter society.

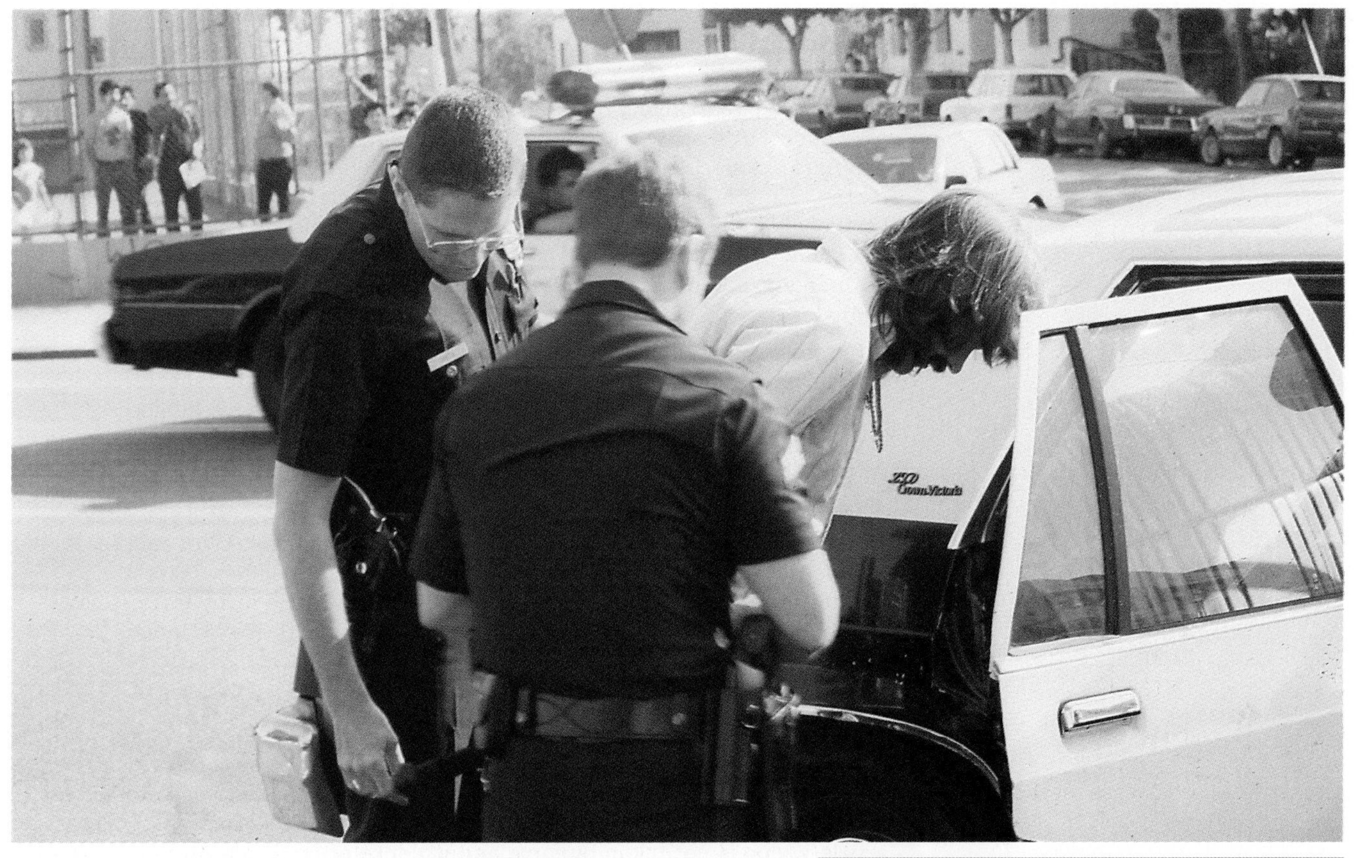

UCR part arrest data can be used to identify personal characteristics of criminal offenders.

Each of the research methods above helps criminal justice experts understand the nature and extent of criminal behavior in the United States. Usually three separate measures are used: official data, self-report data, and victim data. Each of these sources can be used independently, but taken together, they provide a detailed picture of the crime problem. While the data provided by these three sources of crime data diverge in many key areas, they have enough similarities to draw some conclusions about crime in the United States. Each method is discussed in detail below.

Official Crime Data

The national crime rate is usually equated with the amount and trends in crime contained in the aggregate criminal incidence data collected by the FBI from police departments around the United States.

Prepared by the FBI, the *Uniform Crime Reports (UCR)* are the best known and most widely cited source of criminal statistics.[10] The FBI receives and compiles reports from over sixteen thousand police departments serving a majority of the population of the United States. Its major unit of analysis is the *index crimes:* murder and nonnegligent manslaughter, forcible rape, robbery, aggravated assault, burglary, larceny-theft, arson, and motor vehicle theft (see Table 2.1). The FBI tallies and annually publishes the number of reported offenses by city, county, standard metropolitan statistical area, and geographical division of the United States. In addition to these statistics, the UCR provides information on the number and characteristics of individuals who have been arrested and the number and location of assaults on police officers.

TABLE 2.1
FBI Index Crimes

The Part I offenses are:

Criminal homicide. a. Murder and nonnegligent manslaughter: the willful (nonnegligent) killing of one human being by another. Deaths caused by negligence, attempts to kill, assaults to kill, suicides, accidental deaths, and justifiable homicides are excluded. Justifiable homicides are limited to: (1) the killing of a felon by a law enforcement officer in the line of duty; and (2) the killing of a felon by a private citizen. b. Manslaughter by negligence: the killing of another person through gross negligence. Traffic fatalities are excluded. While manslaughter by negligence is a Part I crime, it is not included in the Crime Index.

Forcible rape. The carnal knowledge of a female forcibly and against her will. Included are rapes by force and attempts or assaults to rape. Statutory offenses (no force used—victim under age of consent) are excluded.

Robbery. The taking or attempting to take anything of value from the care, custody, or control of a person or persons by force or threat of force or violence and/or by putting the victim in fear.

Aggravated assault. An unlawful attack by one person upon another for the purpose of inflicting severe or aggravated bodily injury. This type of assault usually is accompanied by the use of a weapon or by means likely to produce death or great bodily harm. Simple assaults are excluded.

Burglary—breaking or entering. The unlawful entry of a structure to commit a felony or a theft. Attempted forcible entry is included.

Larceny—theft (except motor vehicle theft). The unlawful taking, carrying, leading, or riding away of property from the possession or constructive possession of another. Examples are thefts of bicycles or automobile accessories, shoplifting, pocket-picking, or the stealing of any property or article which is not taken by force and violence or by fraud. Attempted larcenies are included. Embezzlement, "con" games, forgery, worthless checks, etc., are excluded.

Motor vehicle theft. The theft or attempted theft of a motor vehicle. A motor vehicle is self-propelled and runs on the surface and not on rails. Specifically excluded from this category are motorboats, construction equipment, airplanes, and farming equipment.

Arson. Any willful or malicious burning or attempt to burn, with or without intent to defraud, a dwelling, house, public building, motor vehicle or aircraft, personal property of another, etc.

SOURCE: Federal Bureau of Investigation, *Crime in the United States, 1990* (Washington, D.C.: U.S. Government Printing Office, 1991), p. 327.

In the following sections, we will review the methods the FBI uses to prepare the UCR, discuss some recent trends in crime statistics, and review criticism of the UCR.

How Is the UCR Compiled?

On a monthly basis, law enforcement agencies tabulate the number of index offenses.[11] A count of these crimes, which are also known as Part I offenses, is taken from records of all complaints of crime received by law enforcement agencies from victims, officers who discovered the infractions, and other sources. Whenever complaints of crime are determined through investigation to be unfounded or false, they are eliminated from the actual count. The number of "actual offenses known" is reported to the FBI, whether or not anyone is arrested for the crime, the stolen property is recovered, or prosecution is undertaken. In addition, each month, law enforcement agencies report the total number of these crimes "cleared." Crimes are cleared in one of two ways: (1) when at least one person is arrested, charged, and turned over to the court for prosecution; or (2) when some element beyond police control precludes the physical arrest of an offender (for example, the suspect dies). Data on the number of clearances involving only the arrest of offenders under the age of eighteen, the value of property stolen and recovered in connection with Part I offenses, and detailed information pertaining to criminal homicide are also reported.

Arrest data, which include the age, sex, and race of persons arrested, are reported monthly for both Part I and Part II offenses, by crime category. Part II offenses include all crimes other than traffic violations and those classified as Part I (for example, drug offenses, liquor law violations, sex offenses, juvenile offenses such as running away, and weapons offenses).

Data on law enforcement officers assaulted or killed are collected on a monthly basis. The number of full-time sworn officers and other personnel is reported as of October 31 of each calendar year.

The UCR employs three methods to express crime data. First, the number of crimes reported to the police and the number of arrests made are expressed as raw figures (for example, 24,000 murders occurred in 1991). Second, percent changes in the amount of crime between years is computed (for example, murder increased 7 percent between 1990 and 1991). Third, the crime rate per 100,000 people is computed. That is, when the UCR indicates that the murder rate was 9.5 in 1991, it means that about 9 people in every 100,000 fell victim to murder between January 1 and December 31 of 1991. The equation used is:

$$\frac{\text{Number of reported crimes}}{\text{Total U.S. population}} \times 100{,}000 = \text{Rate per } 100{,}000$$

Official Crime Trends

Crime is not new to this century.[12] Studies have indicated that a gradual increase in the crime rate, especially in violent crime, occurred from 1830 to 1860. Following the Civil War, this rate increased significantly for about fifteen years. Then, from 1880 up to the time of the First World War, with the possible exception of the years immediately preceding and following the war, the number of reported crimes decreased. After a period of readjustment, the crime rate steadily declined until the Depression (about 1930), whereupon another general increase or crime wave was recorded. Crime rates increased gradually following the 1930s until the 1960s, when the growth rate became much greater. The homicide rate, which had actually declined from the 1930s to the 1960s, also began a period of sharp increase that continued through the 1970s. In 1981, the number of index crimes peaked at about 13.4 million and then began a consistent decline to 1984, when 11.1 million crimes were recorded by police. Unfortunately, beginning in 1985, the crime rate once again began an upward trend, so that by 1991, about 14.6 million crimes were reported to police.

While there has not been a major new crime wave, Figure 2.1 indicates that since 1986, both the number of offenses known to the police and the rate of crime per 100,000 citizens have increased, up about 10 percent in number and 6 percent in rate.[13] While this increase is not as dramatic as those recorded in the

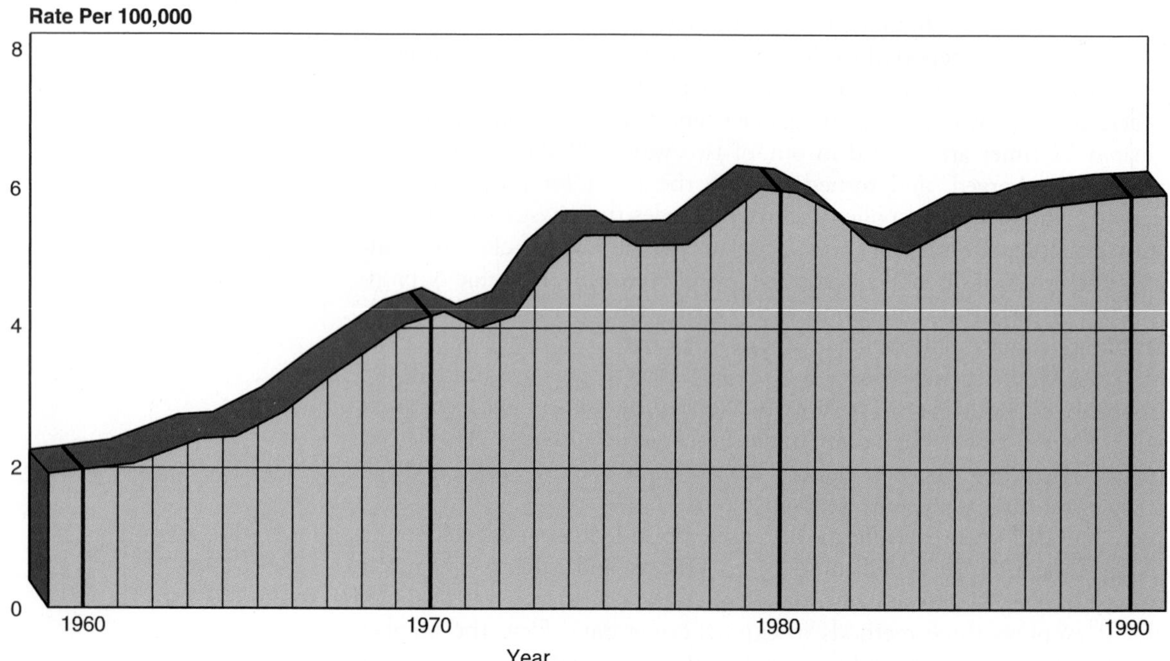

FIGURE 2.1
Crime Trends Rates 1960–1991

1960s and '70s, it indicates that crime is resistant to prevention and control efforts. After two decades of governmental efforts to deter, prevent, and otherwise eliminate crime, there are indications that neither an effective crime control policy has been found nor criminal behavior ceased being a major social problem.

Violent Crime Trends

The violent crimes reported by the FBI include murder, rape, assault, and robbery. In 1991, some 1.9 million violent crimes were reported to police, a rate of 753 per 100,000. According to the UCR, violence in the United States has increased dramatically in the past ten years. The number of reported violent acts increased 34 percent between 1981 and 1991, while the violence rate increased 25 percent (see Figure 2.2); the rate of rapes (more than 15 percent) and assaults (more than 47 percent) increased dramatically: Police received 82,500 reports of rape in 1981 and 106,000 in 1991; assaults jumped from 664,000 in 1980 to 1.08 million in 1991. Particularly troubling has been the steady increase in the number of murders. The murder statistics are generally regarded as the most accurate aspect of the UCR. Figure 2.3 illustrates homicide rate trends since 1900. Note how the rate peaked around 1930, then fell, rose dramatically around 1960, and peaked once again in 1991, when the number of murders topped twenty-four thousand for the first time in the nation's history.

Property Crime Trends

The property crimes reported in the UCR include robbery, larceny, motor vehicle theft, and arson. In 1991, 12.7 million property crimes were reported, a rate of about 5,000 per 100,000 population.

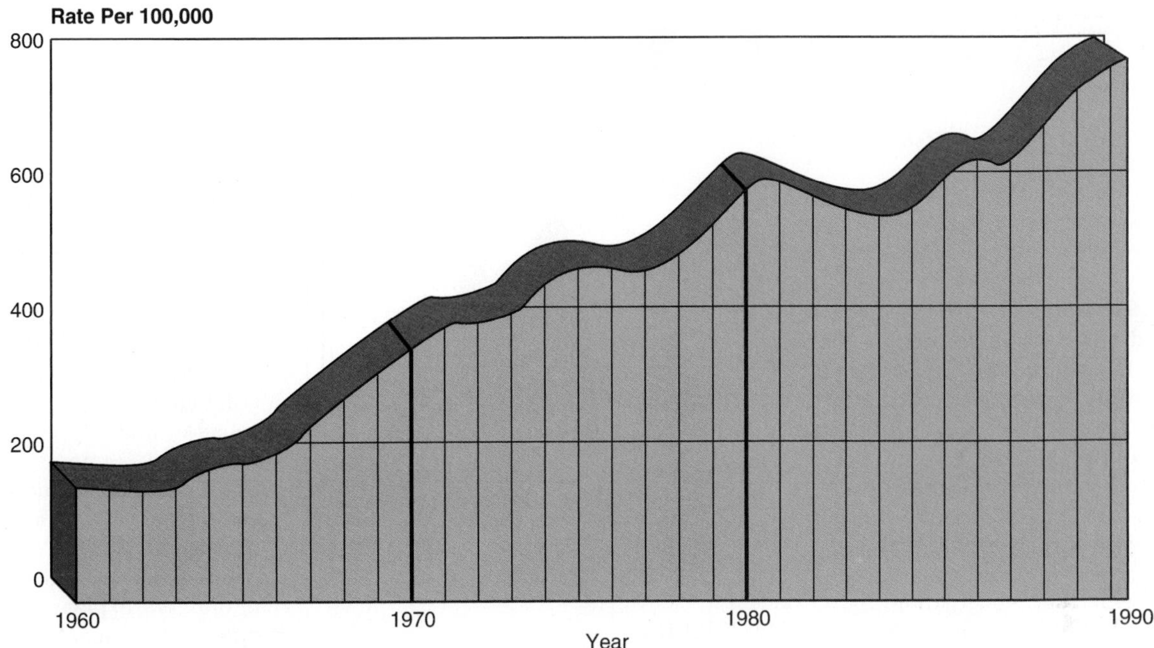

FIGURE 2.2
Violence Trends Rates 1960–1991

Unlike violent crime, property crime has remained relatively stable during the past decade. Since 1981, the number of property crimes increased about 5 percent (compared to the 34 percent increase in violent crime), while the property crime *rate* actually *declined* 3 percent (compared to the violent crime rate increase of 25 percent). Of the property crimes, only motor vehicle theft showed appreciable gains during the past decade, increasing more than 50 percent in number (to 1.7 million from 1.08 million) and 39 percent in rate per 100,000. In contrast, the number of burglaries declined 18 percent (from 3.7 million to 3.1 million) and 25 percent in rate.

While property crime rates have generally stabilized or declined, millions of offenses are still committed each year, far more than in other industrialized nations. A comparison of crime rates in the United States and other nations is made in Analyzing Criminal Justice Issues: International Crime Trends.

Arrest Trends

The FBI also records the number of people arrested each year for both index and nonindex crimes. In 1990, 14,195,000 arrests were recorded, including 2.9 million for index crimes; this represents a rate of 5,805 per 100,000, a slight increase over the preceding year. This data does not necessarily mean that more than 5,800 Americans in every 100,000 are arrested each year, because an individual may have multiple arrests during a calendar year.

In the past five years, the number of arrests has increased 19 percent, and during the past ten years, the annual number of arrests has risen almost 31 percent. During the 1981-to-1990 period, index crime arrests rose 20 percent, violent crime arrests went up 45%, and property crime arrests increased 13 percent.

ANALYZING CRIMINAL JUSTICE ISSUES

International Crime Trends

How do crime rates in the United States compare with those in other nations? According to the Senate Judiciary Committee on Violence, the United States is "the most violent and self-destructive nation on earth." The committee reports that the United States led the world with its murder, rape, and robbery rates, noting that the U.S. murder rate is four times as great as Italy's, nine times England's, and twice that of war-torn Northern Ireland. The robbery rate in the United States was 47 times higher than that in Ireland and over 100 times greater than that in Greece! If the United States had the same murder rate as England's, it would have experienced 2,500 homicides in 1990, instead of 23,500.

Violence against women is a particularly serious problem. The rape rate in the United States is eight times higher than France's, fifteen times higher than England's, twenty times that of Portugal, twenty-three times Italy's, twenty-six times greater than that of Japan, and forty-six times higher than that in Greece.

Nowhere is the disparity in crime rate more dramatic than between the United States and its economic rival Japan. Our murder rate is 11 times Japan's and the robbery rate is 150 times greater; if the United States had Japan's robbery rate, 4,500 robberies would have occurred in 1990, instead of the actual number of 630,000! Not only is the Japanese crime rate significantly lower than that of the United States, but it has gone down at a significant pace since 1950, while the U.S. rate has spiraled up.

How can these differences be explained? Certainly culture may play an important role in determining these crime rate differences. Individualism and self-gratification are emphasized in the United States, and success is defined in terms of possessing material goods and commodities. Americans are willing to risk interpersonal confrontations in order to achieve an upperclass lifestyle, increasing the likelihood of violence. Other cultural dynamics operating in the United States but not in Japan include: a large underclass; urban areas in which the poorest and wealthiest citizens reside in close proximity; racism and discrimination; the failure of the educational system; troubled families; and easy access to handguns.

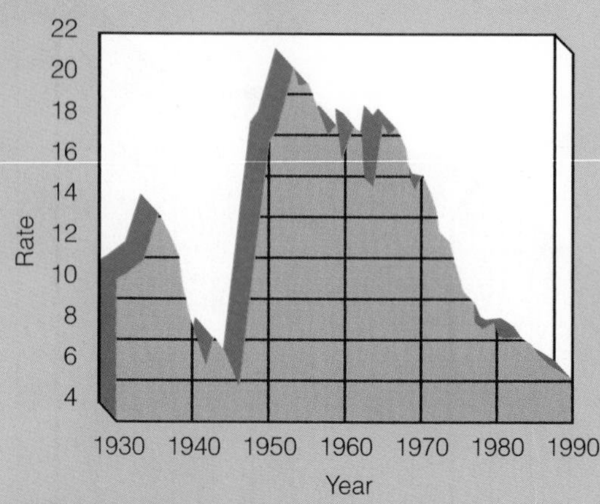

FIGURE A
Felony Rates per 100,000 in Japan from 1926 to 1987

In contrast, the Japanese maintain a strict code of personal honor. They have extraordinary patience, a cooperative approach to decision making, extreme respect for seniority and age, and a greater concern for society than for the individual. The Japanese subordinate personal feelings for the good of the group and avoid interpersonal confrontations at all costs. Nowhere is obedience and respect more important than in that shown toward family members and friends. Children owe parents total respect; younger siblings must obey older brothers and sisters; friends show reverence toward older acquaintances; and all show respect for the emperor. Bowing, a familiar Japanese custom, symbolizes this respect. Japanese are deterred from criminal behavior not because of moral principles of right and wrong but to avoid embarrassment to self, family, or acquaintances.

There may be other, more pragmatic, explanations for the relatively low Japanese crime rate, including the lack of an underclass, strict gun control laws, public cooperation with the police, a centralized criminal justice system, and the lack of racism and racial conflict. In any case, it is clear that U.S. society is much more crime-prone than that of Japan.

Critical Thinking Skills

1. Assume that U.S. society is more violent than other industrialized nations. What policies can be developed to bring the crime rate down? Is it feasible to tackle the social sources of crime by making families more cohesive, ending poverty, or reducing drug use? Regardless of why crime rates are so high, might it not be possible to reduce them through aggressive law enforcement policies and the incapacitation of known criminals?

SOURCE: Committee on the Judiciary of the United States Senate, *Fighting Crime in America: An Agenda for the 1990's* (Washington, D.C.: 12 March 1991); Michael Vaughn and Nobuho Tomita, "A Longitudinal Analysis of Japanese Crime from 1926–1987: The Pre-War, War and Post-War Eras," *International Journal of Comparative and Applied Criminal Justice* 14 (1990): 145–60.

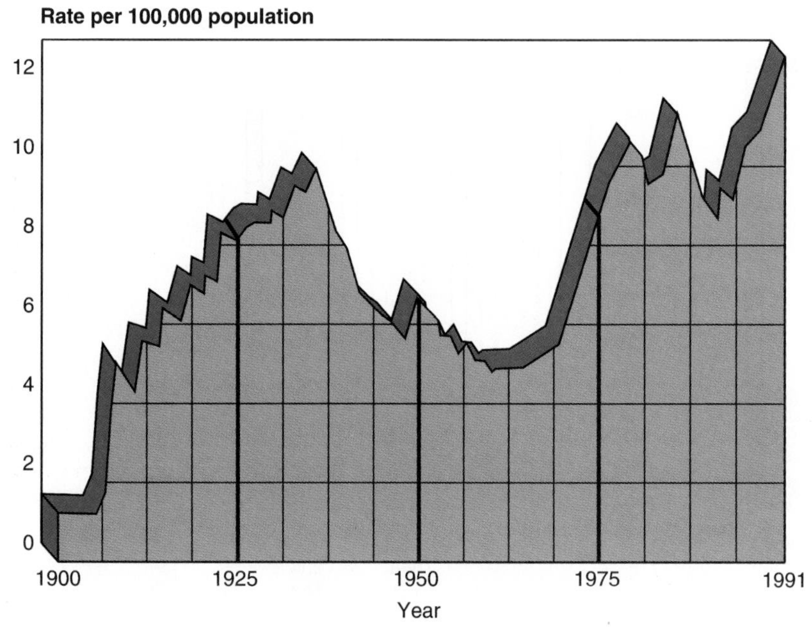

Rate per 100,000 population

12
10
8
6
4
2
0

1900 1925 1950 1975 1991
Year

FIGURE 2.3
Homicide Rate Trends, 1900–1991

SOURCE: Bureau of Justice Statistics, *Violent Crime in the United States* (Washington, D.C.: Bureau of Justice Statistics, 1991; updated, 1992).

One reason for the decade-long increase in the arrest rate has been the crackdown on crime involving alcohol and drugs. During the decade, drunk driving arrests increased 15 percent, liquor law violation arrests jumped 42 percent, and drug abuse arrests rose more than 70 percent. There were also significant increases in the number of arrests for other crime patterns, including assault, rape, and motor vehicle theft; the catchall "all other offenses" category jumped more than 75 percent.

Solving Crime

How successful are police agencies in solving reported crimes? To provide an answer, the FBI tallies crimes cleared by arrest (reported crimes in which at least one person is arrested and turned over for prosecution). The UCR indicates that police typically clear slightly more than 20 percent of all reported crimes, a rate that has remained stable over time.

As Figure 2.4 shows, police are able to "solve" (that is, arrest someone for) about three times as many violent crimes as property crimes (45 percent versus 18 percent). Victims of violent crime are usually able to describe or identify their assailant, most often because the perpetrator of a violent crime is likely to be a friend, acquaintance, or relative of the victim. Police departments generally devote more resources to solving violent crimes than property offenses.

UCR data consistently show that police are able to "solve" only one in five reported crimes. The inability of law enforcement agencies to improve arrest ratios has been one of the factors persuading police administrators to rethink the role of police as crime fighters and reorient their departments toward community service and neighborhood problem solving.[14]

In the following sections, some of the specific patterns identified in the UCR will be examined more closely.

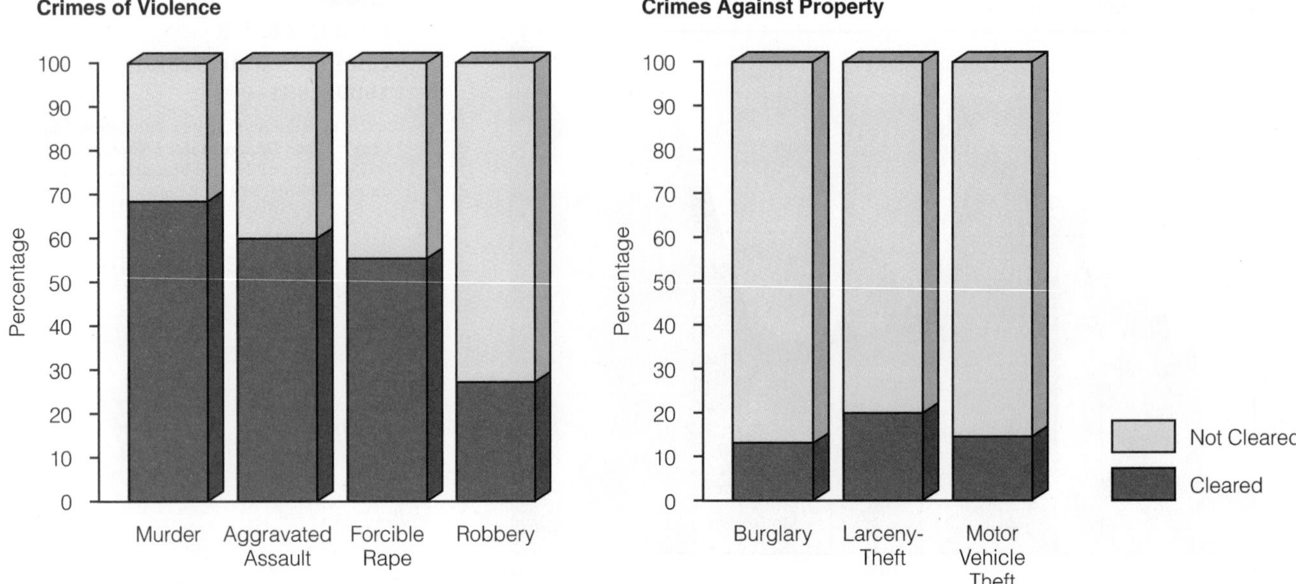

FIGURE 2.4
Percent of Crimes Cleared by Arrest

SOURCE: Federal Bureau of Investigation, *Crime in the United States, 1990* (Washington, D.C.: U.S. Government Printing Office, 1991), p. 164.

Patterns of Crime

Part I and Part II (arrest) data can both be used to tell us a lot about the patterns of crime in our nation.[15] Some of the most important patterns are discussed below.

Ecological and Seasonal Differences

A distinct relationship exists between crime rates and urbanization. Areas with rural and suburban populations are more likely to have much lower crime rates than large urban areas. This finding, consistent over many years, suggests that the crime problem is linked to the social forces operating in the nation's largest cities—overcrowding, poverty, social inequality, narcotics use, and racial conflict. This pattern is illustrated by the fact that approximately 25 percent of all homicides occur in just seven cities: New York, Los Angeles, Chicago, Detroit, Houston, Philadelphia, and Washington, D.C.

UCR data also show that crime rates are highest in the summer months, most likely because people spend so much time outdoors and are less likely to secure their homes, and schools are closed and young people have greater opportunity for criminal activity.

Crime rates are also related to the region of the country. The West and South usually have significantly higher rates than the Midwest and New England (see Figure 2.5).

Gender and Crime

UCR arrest data consistently show that males have a much higher crime rate than females. The overall arrest ratio is about 4 to 1 and approaches 8 to 1 for violent crimes.

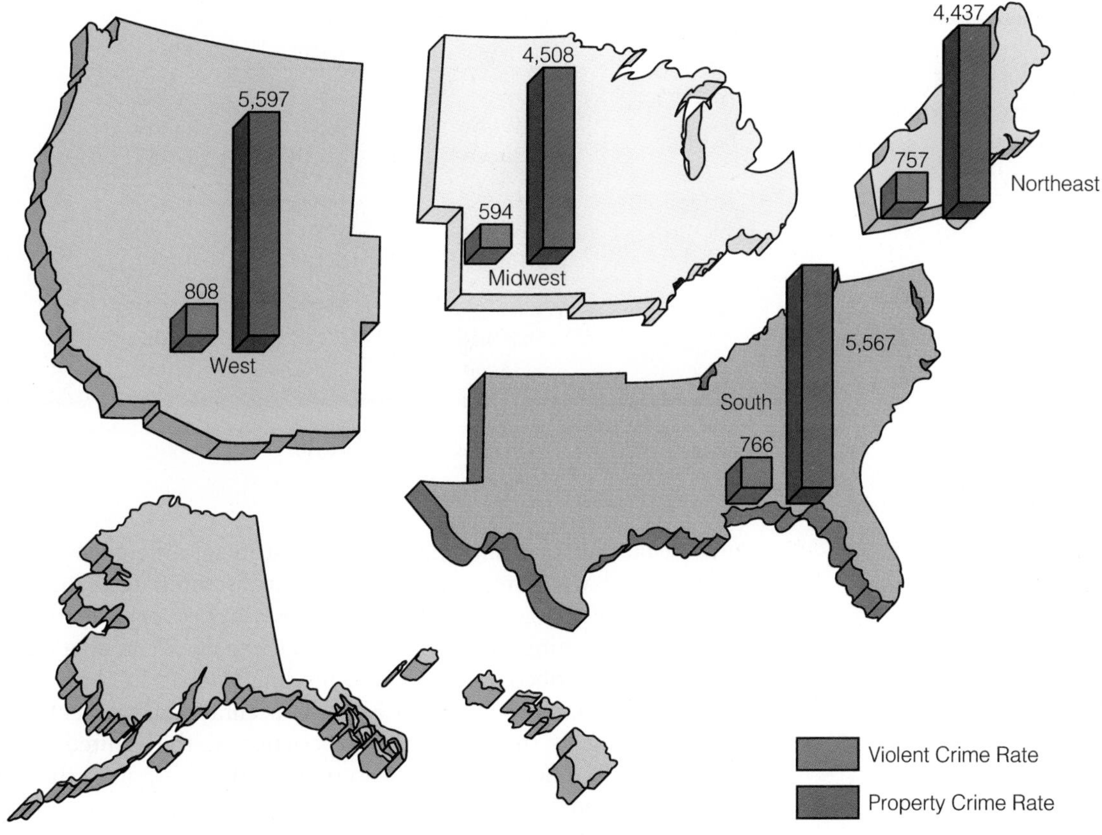

FIGURE 2.5
Regional Violent and Property Crime Rates (per 100,000 inhabitants)
SOURCE: Federal Bureau of Investigation, *Crime in the United States, 1990* (Washington, D.C.: U.S. Government Printing Office, 1989), p. 49.

In the past decade, the female serious crime rate has risen at a faster rate than that of males (more than 48 percent versus more than 27 percent). Some experts attribute this to the emergence of a "new female criminal" whose criminal activity mirrors the changing role of women in modern society.[16] Others disagree and find that female emancipation has had relatively little influence on criminality. It is possible that women are being arrested more often today not due to changes in their crime rate but because police are more willing to arrest and formally process female offenders, a result of the feminist movement's call for equal treatment for men and women.[17]

Race and Crime

UCR arrest statistics also reveal distinct racial patterns in the crime rate. Overall, about 29 percent of all people arrested are black, 69 percent are white, and the remainder are split between Native Americans and Alaskans, Asians, and Pacific Islanders.

African-Americans are arrested for murder, rape, and robbery at a rate higher than their relative representation in the population; an absolute majority of people arrested for murder and robbery are black. These data have proven to be

TABLE 2.2
Probability of Murder Victimization in the Remainder of One's Lifetime

Age	Race	Male	Female	Both Sexes
At birth	White	1/205	1/496	1/289
	Nonwhite	1/33	1/138	1/55
	All Races	1/114	1/348	1/171
At age 20	White	1/232	1/589	1/332
	Nonwhite	1/38	1/159	1/63
	All Races	1/131	1/413	1/199
At age 40	White	1/525	1/1,102	1/714
	Nonwhite	1/101	1/357	1/164
	All Races	1/342	1/868	1/494

SOURCE: Federal Bureau of Investigation, *Population-At-Risk Rates and Selected Crime Indicators 1990* (Washington, D.C.: U.S. Government Printing Office, 1991). NP.

controversial. Some criminologists argue that racial differences in the crime rate are caused by law enforcement practices that discriminate against blacks. Daniel Georges-Abeyie charges that police routinely employ "petit apartheid" policies of searching, questioning, and detaining all black males in an area if a violent criminal has been described as looking or sounding black.[18] In contrast, other experts view the official crime statistics as being an accurate reflection of the black crime rate. Their view is that the black experience in the United States, one that involves racism, differential opportunity, powerlessness, and other social disabilities, has resulted in a higher black crime rate as an expression of anger and frustration.[19]

Not only are African-Americans at risk for drug use and crime, they also have a significantly greater chance of being the target of violence. As the data in Table 2.2 show, nonwhites at birth are more than five times as likely to become murder victims as whites. These data indicate why the crime problem is of special significance for the black community.

Social Class and Crime

Researchers have used UCR data in conjunction with census data to determine whether crime is associated with poverty, unemployment, and lower class status.[20] Official data seem to indicate that crime rates are highest in deprived, inner-city slum areas and that the level of poverty in an area can predict its crime rate.[21]

A number of different explanations exist for the association between social class and official crime rates. One view is that the social forces in a high-risk, socially disorganized neighborhood—poverty, dilapidated housing, poor schools, broken families, drugs, and street gangs—significantly increase the likelihood that residents will engage in criminality.[22] Rodney Stark argues that as the social system in decayed urban areas breaks down and the rule of law becomes a distant threat, slum neighborhoods attract criminals and deviants who find the decayed environment suitable for their law-violating behavior. The moral vacuum of the slum acts as a magnet for deviants and undesirables who help conditions grow steadily worse.[23]

Another view is that crime rates are high in deteriorated areas where the disadvantaged and the affluent live side by side. In these neighborhoods, social

TABLE 2.3
Percent Distribution of Total U.S. Population and Persons Arrested for All Offenses, by Age Group, 1989

Age Group	U.S. Resident Population	Persons Arrested
Age 12 and younger	19.1%	1.7%
13 to 15	4.0	6.3
16 to 18	4.3	12.4
19 to 21	4.5	13.6
22 to 24	4.6	11.9
25 to 29	8.7	18.4
30 to 34	8.9	14.1
35 to 39	7.9	9.0
40 to 44	6.8	5.3
45 to 49	5.4	3.0
50 to 54	4.6	1.7
55 to 59	4.3	1.1
60 to 64	4.4	0.7
Age 65 and older	12.5	0.7

SOURCE: Kathleen Maguire and Timothy Flanagan, Sourcebook of Criminal Justice Statistics, 1990 (Washington, D.C.: U.S. Government Printing Office, 1991), p. 414.

differences are magnified, and less affluent residents perceive a feeling of **relative deprivation.** This perception of social inequality results in a higher crime rate.[24]

Though the class-crime relationship has been the subject of almost constant research, the true association between these variables is far from determined. While many research efforts do show a strong class-crime relationship, they are matched by others that indicate a weak or nonexistent relationship; that is, members of the lower class may be no more crime-prone than the middle class or wealthy.[25] The high official crime rates in lower-class neighborhoods may be a function of law enforcement policy and lower-class bias, rather than actual criminality.

One reason for the uncertainty about the class-crime relationship is the difficulty of measuring what is meant by the term *lower class*. Some studies define the lower class as welfare recipients; others consider lower-class status as having a below-average income or being chronically unemployed. The lack of consensus in defining this important research variable has helped obscure what may be the true relationship between social class and crime.[26]

Age and Crime

UCR arrest data consistently show that a significant relationship between age and crime: Young people between the ages of fifteen and twenty-five are responsible for an overwhelming number of all arrests; in contrast, people aged sixty and over are relatively crime-free. This relationship is clearly viewed in Table 2.3 and Figure 2.6, which compare age and arrest data. The peak age for property crime is about sixteen, and for violence, it is eighteen. In 1990, about 45 percent of all arrests involved people aged twenty-four and under, while 16 percent involved youths under eighteen. In contrast, people over forty-five accounted for only about 7.5 percent of all arrests.

How can the age-crime relationship be explained? One factor involves lifestyle; many young people are part of a youth culture that favors risk taking, short-

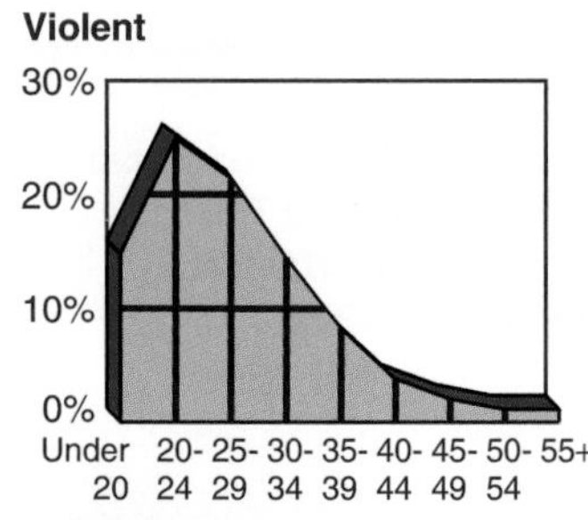

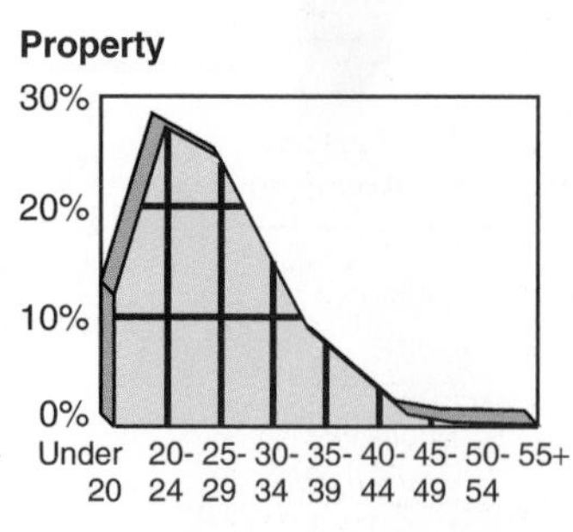

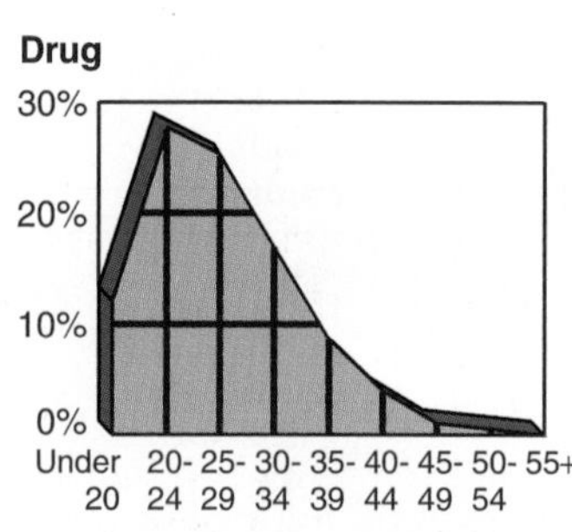

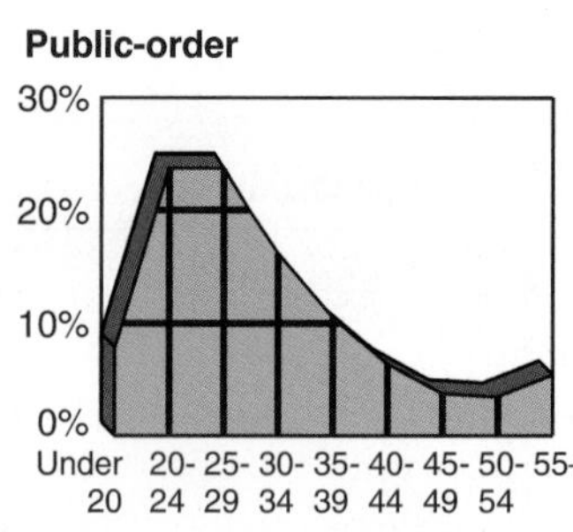

FIGURE 2.6

Percentage of Felony Arrests by Age People in their twenties have the largest percentage of felony arrests for all crimes. As age increases, arrests decrease.

SOURCE: Bureau of Justice Statistics, *Update* (Washington, D.C.: Bureau of Justice Statistics, Oct. 1991), p. 8.

run hedonism, and other forms of behavior that may involve them in law violation. Youths have limited financial resources and may resort to theft and drug dealing for income. The high-risk life-style of most youths ends as they mature and become involved in forming a family and a career.[27] Some adolescents may desist from crime when they begin to understand that the chances of winning friends, happiness, and wealth via crime is limited. A more simple explanation is biological: young people have the energy, strength, and physical skill needed to commit crime, all of which erode with age.[28]

Despite such overwhelming evidence, the true relationship between age and crime has proven to be one of enduring controversy. Some experts hold that all people commit less crime as they age. That is, regardless of race, gender, class, or any other personal characteristic, younger people commit more crime than older ones.[29] Even high-risk offenders and drug addicts eventually slow down. They may continue to commit crime in their maturity, but the *frequency* of their law violations is lower than in their youth.[30]

Not all crime experts agree with this view. Some argue that while it is true that most offenders reduce their criminal activity as they age, there is a group of offenders who enter into a life of crime early in their adolescence and maintain a high rate of criminal violations throughout their lifespan.[31] Chronic offenders are immune to both the ravages of age and the punishments of the justice system. More important, this small group may be responsible for a significant portion of all serious criminal behavior.[32]

Analysis of the Uniform Crime Reports

There is no question that the FBI and many of its contributing law enforcement agencies have made a serious attempt to measure the incidence and amount of crime and delinquency in the United States. Nonetheless, a great deal of criticism has been directed at the actual validity of the national crime statistics and official statistics in general. Methodological problems have compelled some experts to advocate total abandonment of the use of official crime statistics in criminal justice research.

Two issues most disturb critics: (1) the failure or refusal of many citizens to report criminal acts to police and (2) the problems caused by variations in law enforcement practices. Because each of these issues is important, they will be discussed separately below.

Reporting Influences

U.S. citizens are believed to report less than half of all criminal acts to police. The reasons for this are varied. Many individuals in lower-class areas neglect to carry property insurance and therefore believe it is useless to report theft-related offenses to police since "nothing can be done." In other cases, victims may fail to notify police because they fear reprisals from friends or family members of the offenders.

Victimization surveys indicate that the probability of crime reporting varies by the type of offense.[33] Rape victims do not report the crime if they believe it is a "private matter" or if they fear reprisals. Assaults also go unreported if victims feel they are a private matter. For the most part, people do not report such crimes as robbery, burglary, and larceny if they believe "nothing could be done" and the victimization is "not important enough" to interest the police.

Administrative Influences

The way police departments record and report criminal activity also affects the validity of UCR statistics. The manner in which police interpret the definitions of index crimes may affect reporting practices. For example, one study found that police in Boston report only completed rapes to the FBI, while those in Los Angeles reported completed rapes, attempted rapes, and sexual assaults. Such reporting practices helped account for the fact that the rape rate in Los Angeles is far higher than that in Boston.[34] A more recent study by Lawrence Sherman and Barry Glick for the Police Foundation found that local police departments make systematic errors in UCR reporting.[35] All 196 departments surveyed counted an arrest only after a formal booking procedure, although the UCR requires arrests to be counted if the suspect is released without a formal charge. Similarly, 29 percent did not include citations and 57 percent did not include summonses, though the UCR requires it. An audit of arrests found an error rate of about 10 percent in every Part I offense category. Similarly, Patrick Jackson found that the FBI's newest crime category, arson, may be seriously underreported because many fire departments do not report suspicious fires to the UCR and those that do exclude many fires that are probably set by arsonists.[36].

Of a more serious nature are the allegations that police officials may deliberately alter reported crimes to put their departments in a more favorable light with the public. Some critics have suggested that police administrators interested in lowering the crime rate and improving their departments' image may falsify crime reporting by deliberately undervaluing the cost of stolen goods so that an index larceny is relegated to a nonreportable offense category.[37]

At the same time, increased police efficiency and professionalism may actually help increase crime rates. As more sophisticated computer-aided technology is developed for police work and as the education and training of police employees increase, so too might their ability to record and report crimes, producing higher crime rates.

Rethinking the UCR

Methodological issues continue to cloud the validity of the UCR. Among the problems most often mentioned are:

1. No federal crimes are reported.
2. Reports are voluntary and vary in accuracy and completeness.

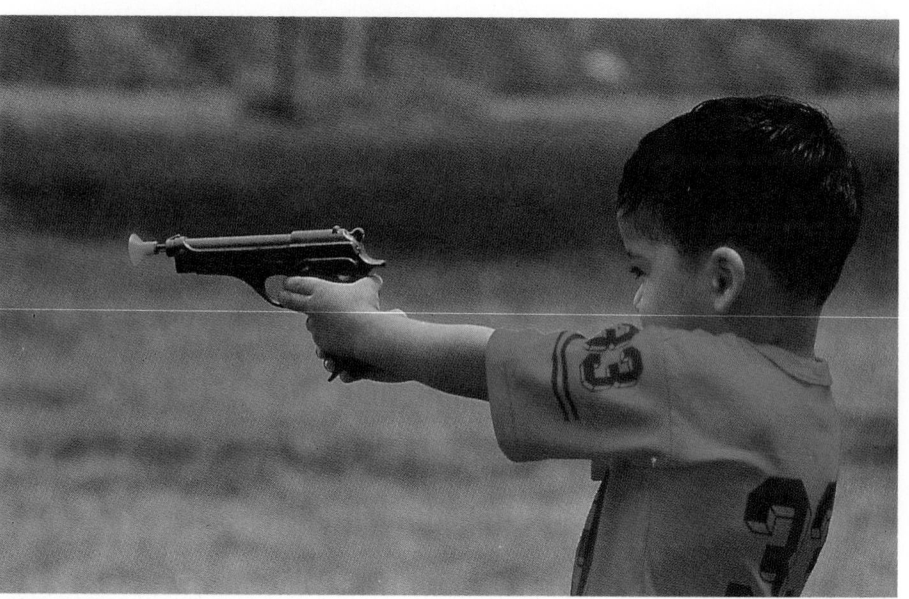

UCR data indicate that adolescents and teens have significantly higher crime rates than the elderly.

3. Not all police departments submit reports.
4. The FBI uses estimates in its total crime projections.
5. If multiple crimes are committed by an offender, only the most serious is recorded. Thus, if a narcotics addict rapes, robs, and murders a victim, only the murder is recorded as a crime.
6. For some crimes, each act is listed as a single offense. Thus, if a man robs six people in a bar, the act is listed as one robbery; but if he assaults them, it is listed as six assaults.
7. Uncompleted acts are lumped together with completed ones.
8. Important differences exist between the FBI's definition of a crime and those used in a number of states. Some crime categories, such as rape, may contain acts that in some states might be interpreted as molestation or assault, while burglary can include illegal trespass or breaking and entering.[38]

Because of these and other problems, justice experts often question the validity of the UCR as a source for criminal justice research. However, a number of important research efforts indicate that the UCR may be more accurate than previously believed.[39] In a significant analysis of the existing evidence on the subject, Walter Gove, Michael Hughes, and Michael Geerken found indications that the UCR is a valid indicator of serious crime.[40] While it is true that many crimes are not reported to the police, Gove and his colleagues found the nonreported crimes to be generally less serious ones that may not even satisfy the legal requirements of criminality. They found evidence that both citizens and police are in general agreement about what a serious crime entails: it involves bodily injury; it involves a significant amount of lost property; it is committed by a stranger; it involves breaking and entering. When the criminal act meets one or more of these criteria, it has a good chance of being reported to the FBI.

Even if the number of reported crimes is less than the total number of crimes committed, the overall reliability of the UCR makes it a valuable source of crime data. Because measurement errors are most likely constant over time, the UCR's ability to identify trends and patterns in the crime rate is probably more accurate than its ability to count the exact number of crimes committed annually. Because crime is counted in a consistent fashion, if the UCR says crime increased 10 percent between 1986 and 1990, we might not be sure how many crimes were committed in these years, but we would be confident that *more* crimes were committed in 1990 than in 1986 and the increase was about 10 percent.

Revising the UCR

To help improve the quality of UCR statistics, the FBI is revising its form and content to provide more detailed information on individual criminal incidents.

It is planned that instead of submitting statements of reported crimes and summary statements of resulting arrests, local police agencies would provide at least a brief account of each incident within the existing Part I crime categories. Police agencies will provide detailed reports on twenty-three crime patterns, including incident, victim, and offender information. Crime categories in which expanded information will be provided include such new areas as blackmail and bribery. These additional data will allow a national database on the nature of crime, victims, and criminals to be developed. More stringent auditing techniques will be imposed to ensure the accuracy and completeness of the material being submitted by the police.[41]

When implemented, the new UCR program may bring about greater uniformity in cross-jurisdictional reporting and improve the accuracy of official crime data. While three jurisdictions are already participating in the revised program, full national data is not available at the time of this writing.

Self-Report Data

While the UCR is the most significant method of measuring crime rates and trends, questions about its overall validity have persisted. In addition, the UCR does not measure important criminal behaviors, such as drug use, nor does it tell us much about individual criminals. Consequently, another method of collecting crime data called **self-report surveys** has been developed. Self-report surveys ask respondents to tell about their criminal and deviant activities. Typically, they are distributed to large groups of people in order to guarantee the anonymity of respondents. Self-report surveys have often been used in schools to measure the delinquent activity of youths, but they may also be used with adults, such as prison inmates, to measure their criminal behaviors.

A typical self-report instrument will provide a list of criminal acts and ask the subjects to tell how often in the past year (or their lifetime) they participated in each act. Sometimes in a single study, self-report surveys will be distributed to thousands of people chosen randomly in various sites around the United States.

Self-report studies have two main advantages: (1) they measure the so-called "dark figures" of crime—such acts as drug use, gambling, and alcohol abuse, which often are not reported in official data sources and victimization surveys, and (2) they can be used to collect personal information from offenders, such as intelligence level, attitudes, values, and family relationships, which is unavailable from other crime data sources.

What do self-report studies tell us? Overall, they reinforce the fact that crime is much more common than the UCR indicates.[42] Adolescents report significant and widespread involvement in delinquent activity and drug abuse. Self-report studies indicate that youth crime is spread throughout society; lower-, middle-, and upper-class kids all use drugs, engage in theft, and damage property.[43] When

TABLE 2.4
Self-Reported Delinquent Acts—High School Class of 1991

Delinquent Act	Percent Who Committed Act				
	Never	Once	Twice	Three or Four Times	Five Times
Serious Fight	82	10	4	2	2
Gang or Group Fight	80	11	5	2	2
Hurt Someone Badly	87	8	2	1	1
Used a Weapon	97	2	0.6	0.3	0.9
Stealing Less $50	68	14	8	4	6
Stealing More $50	90	5	2	2	2
Shoplifting	69	12	7	5	7
Car Theft	93	3	1	0.6	1
Joyriding	93	3	1	1	1
Breaking & Entering	76	11	7	3	4
Arson	98	1	0.4	0.1	0.5
Damaged School Prop.	87	7	3	1	2
Damaged Work Prop.	93	3	1	0.8	1

N = 2569

SOURCE: Jerald Bachman, Lloyd Johnston and Patrick O'Malley, *Monitoring the Future, 1991* (Ann Arbor, Michigan: Institute For Social Research, 1992).

truancy, alcohol consumption, petty theft, and recreational drug use are included in self-report scales, almost everyone tested is found to have violated some law. Furthermore, self-report surveys dispute the notion that criminals and delinquents specialize in one type of crime or another; offenders seem to engage in a "mixed bag" of crime and deviance.[44]

It has been estimated that almost 90 percent of all youths commit delinquent and criminal acts. It is not unusual for self-report surveys to find combined substance abuse, theft, violence, and damage rates of more than 50 percent among suburban, rural, and urban high school youths. What is surprising is the consistency of these findings in samples taken from southern, eastern, midwestern, and western states.

When the results of recent self-report surveys are compared with various studies conducted over a twenty-year period, a uniform pattern emerges. The use of drugs and alcohol increased markedly in the 1970s and then leveled off in the 1980s and declined in the 1990s; the rates of theft, violence, and damage-related crimes seem more stable. Although a self-reported crime wave has not occurred, neither has there been any visible reduction in self-reported criminality.[45]

One of the most important sources of self-report data is the annual national survey of over twenty-five hundred high school seniors conducted by the Institute for Social Research (ISR) at the University of Michigan.[46] Some data from a recent ISR survey is included in Table 2.4. This data shows that young people commit a great deal of crime: about one third of high school seniors reported stealing something in the last twelve months, 10 percent stole something worth more than fifty dollars, 32 percent admitted shoplifting, and 26 percent engaged in breaking and entering. High school kids also engaged in violent acts: 19 percent got into fights, and 13 percent said they injured someone badly. ISR surveys conducted during the past decade indicate that the extent of self-reported delinquency has been quite stable over time. The fact that at least one third of all U.S. high school students engaged in theft and at least 19 percent committed a violent act during the past year shows that criminal activity is widespread and not restricted to a few "bad apples."

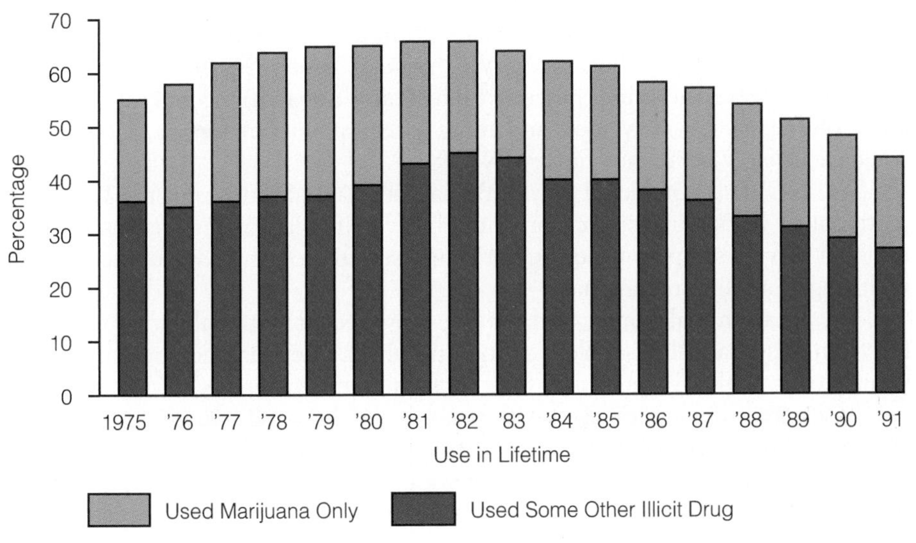

FIGURE 2.7
Trends in Lifetime Prevalence of an Illicit Drug Use Index, All High School Seniors

SOURCE: Lloyd Johnston, Patrick O'Malley, and Jerald Bachman, *Drug Use Among American High School Seniors, College Students, and Young Adults, 1975–1990* (Washington, D.C.: U.S. Department of Health and Human Services, 1991; updated 1992), p. 58.

Self-Reported Drug Use

Probably the most important use of self-report surveys has been efforts to monitor adolescent drug abuse. The most comprehensive research is being carried out by the University of Michigan's Institute for Social Research. ISR researchers have conducted a survey of about seventeen thousand high school seniors each year since 1975.[47]

ISR data indicate that since 1980, U.S. students have significantly decreased the extent and frequency of their drug use. As Figure 2.7 shows, far fewer kids today have tried drugs than in 1980. Reductions were observed in the use of the most common drug types, including cocaine, marijuana, and stimulants (such as amphetamines). Similar trends were recorded in annual and monthly drug usage. What is especially encouraging is that the use of both cocaine and its potent derivative crack has declined in the two most recent surveys (1990–1991).

While these data show that drug use in the general population may be declining, there is still a disturbing pattern of teenage substance abuse. About 44 percent of U.S. high school seniors have tried drugs in their life; about 30 percent have used them in the past year and 16 percent in the past month. About 88 percent have used alcohol, with 54 percent in the past month. About 63 percent of high school seniors have smoked cigarettes, with 28 percent in the last month. The fact that so many high school seniors drink, smoke, and take drugs on a regular basis indicates continued efforts are required in the fight against substance abuse.

The ISR's research on drug use illustrates how self-report surveys can be used to collect important information that is otherwise unobtainable and that may diverge sharply from the impression that is promoted in the media and accepted by the general public.

Victimization Data: The NCVS

On the receiving end of crime are its victims. For many years, victims and victimization were not considered important topics for criminal justice study. Victims were viewed as the passive receptors of a criminal's anger, greed, or frustration; they were simply in the wrong place at the wrong time. In the late 1960s, a number of pioneering studies found that victims actually could tell us a lot about the crime problem and that, contrary to popular belief, the victim's role is an important one in the crime process.[48] This early research encouraged development of the most widely used and most extensive victim survey to date, the *National Crime Victimization Survey* (NCVS).[49]

The NCVS is conducted by the Bureau of Justice Statistics of the U.S. Department of Justice in cooperation with the U.S. Bureau of the Census. In this national survey, samples of housing units are selected on the basis of a complex, multistage sampling technique.

The total annual sample size for the most recent national survey is about forty-nine thousand households, containing about one hundred thousand individuals over twelve years of age. The total sample is composed of six independently selected subsamples, each with about eight thousand households with sixteen thousand individuals. Each subsample is interviewed twice a year about victimizations suffered in the preceding six months. For example, sixteen thousand individuals are interviewed in January. In the following month—and in each of the four succeeding months—an independent probability sample of the same sample size is interviewed. In July, the housing units originally interviewed in January are revisited, and interviews are repeated; likewise, the original February sample units are revisited in August, the March units in September, and so on. Each time they are interviewed, respondents are asked about victimizations suffered during the six months preceding the month of interview. The crimes they are asked about include personal and household larcenies, burglary, motor vehicle theft, assault, robbery, and rape.

The data reported represent estimates of crimes occurring in the United States, based on weighted sample data. It is possible to make these estimates because a probability sample of respondents was surveyed. The interview completion rate in the national sample is about 95 percent or more of those selected to be interviewed in any given period; hence, population estimates are relatively unbiased.

General Victimization Patterns

How many people report being the victims of crime? According to the most recent NCVS data, some 35 million personal crimes occur annually. As Figure 2.8 shows, there was a steady increase in the total number of victimizations between 1973 and 1981, when over 41 million crimes were recorded. Since then, reported victimization has been declining slowly. Between 1981 and 1990, the number of victimizations actually fell by 17 percent (compared to an increase in the UCR during this period)[50]. However, as Figure 2.9 shows, the number of *violent* victimizations increased. Both the UCR and the NCVS report that the United States is becoming more violent.

The number of crimes reported in the NCVS is considerably larger than that reported by the FBI. For example, while the NCVS estimated that 200,000 rapes occurred in 1990, the UCR reported a little more than 100,000 cases. Similarly, while the UCR recorded about 1.05 million aggravated assaults in 1990, the NCVS estimated that about 1.7 million actually occurred. The reason for such discrepancies is that fewer than half the violent crimes, less than one-third the personal theft crimes (such as pocket picking), and less than half the household thefts are reported to police. If the NCVS findings are valid, the official statistics significantly underestimate the crime problem since many crimes are not reported to the police.

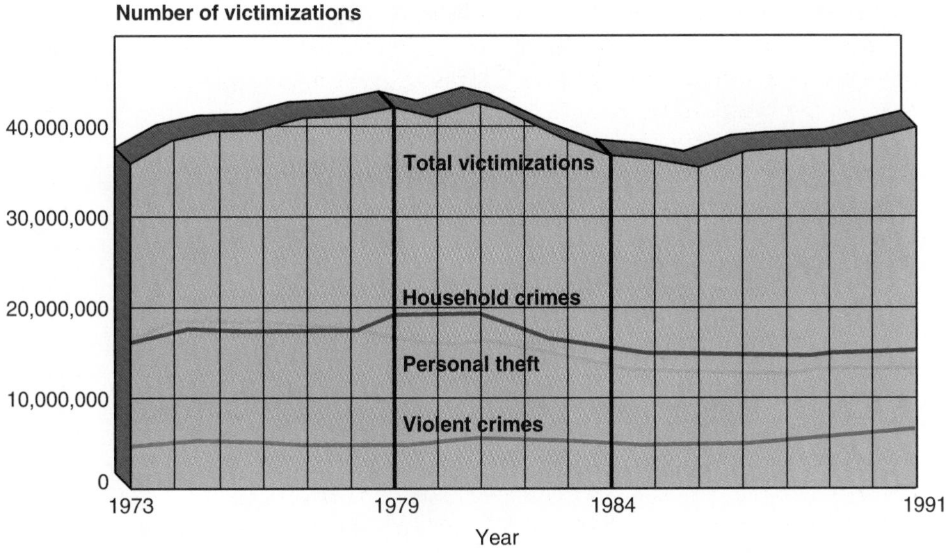

Number of victimizations

40,000,000
30,000,000
20,000,000
10,000,000
0

Total victimizations
Household crimes
Personal theft
Violent crimes

1973 1979 1984 1991

Year

FIGURE 2.8
Victimization Trends, 1973–1991

Victim Characteristics

The NCVS provides information on the background characteristics of the victims of crime. Men are about twice as likely as women to be victims of robbery and assault. Women, as might be expected, are far more likely to be rape victims.

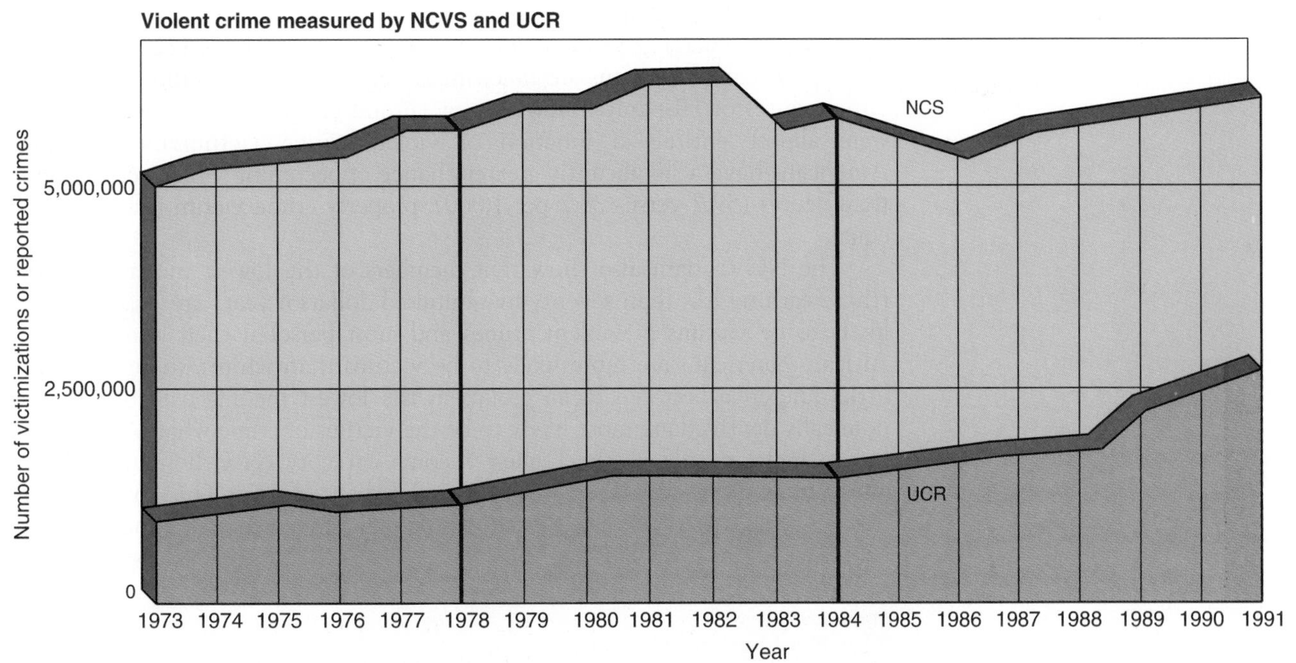

FIGURE 2.9
Violent Crime Trends, 1973–1991

Note: NCS measures the violent crimes of rape, robbery, and aggravated and simple assault. UCR measures the violent crimes of murder and nonnegligent manslaughter, forcible rape, robbery, and aggravated assault.

SOURCE: Bureau of Justice Statistics, *Violent Crime in the United States*, Washington, D.C.: Bureau of Justice Statistics, 1991, p. 4.

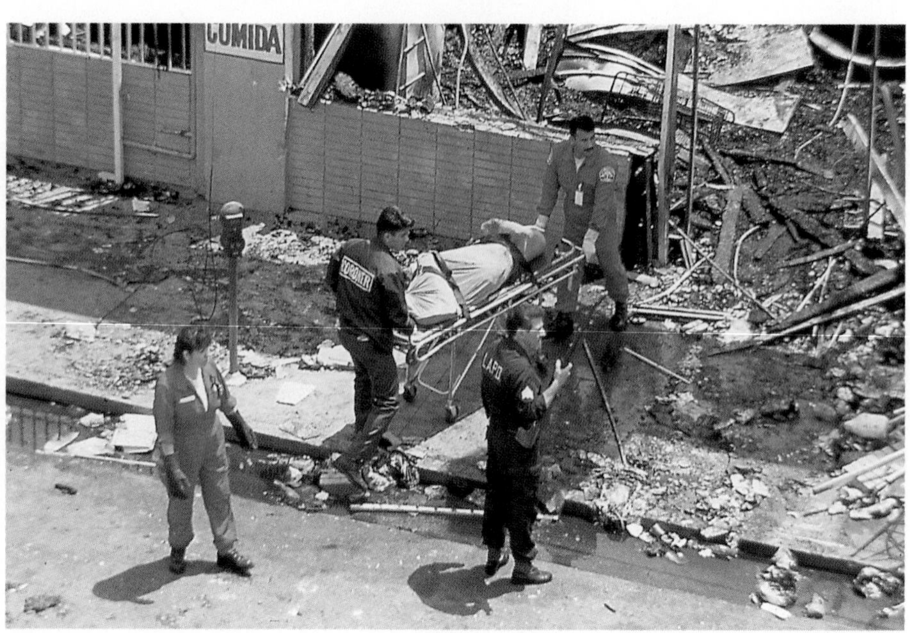

The National Crime Victimization Survey indicates that more than 35 million crimes occur annually.

However, while the rape rate for women is about ten times that of men, it is estimated that about seventy-five hundred men are rape victims each year. Women are also much more likely to be the victims of personal larcenies with contact, due to the inclusion of purse snatching in that category.

Racial characteristics also influence a person's chances of becoming a crime victim. African-Americans are much more likely to become crime victims than either whites or Hispanics. However, racial and ethnic victimization differences were almost entirely a function of violent crime victimizations. African-Americans have a significantly greater chance of becoming violent crime victims than whites (39.7 versus 28.2 per 1,000); property crime victim rates are almost equal.

The NCVS data also show that members of the lowest income categories (those earning less than seventy-five-hundred dollars a year) are by far the most likely to be victims of violent crimes and most personal theft crimes. Though African-Americans are more likely to be victims than whites, there is relatively little difference between racial groups in the lowest income category: the economically deprived are more likely to be the victims of crime whatever their race. Interestingly, people in the highest income category (fifty-thousand dollars or more annually) are the most likely victims of theft offenses. This finding suggests that criminals may calculate which targets offer the greatest chance of reward before deciding to commit a crime.

The Ecology of Victimization

The NCVS data parallel the crime patterns found in the UCR. Most victimizations occur in large urban areas; rural and suburban victim rates are far lower. Most incidents occur during the evening hours (6 P.M. to 6 A.M.). Generally, more serious crimes take place after 6 P.M.; less serious, before 6 P.M. For example, aggravated assaults occur at night, while simple assaults are more likely to take place during the daytime.

The most likely site for a victimization, especially a violent crime such as rape, robbery, and aggravated assault, is an open, public area, such as a street, a park, or a field. Sadly, one of the most dangerous public places is a public school building. A recent federal survey found that 9 percent of all U.S. youth ages twelve to nineteen (approximately 2 million kids) were crime victims while on school grounds over a six-month period.[51] The best way to avoid victimization is to stay home at night with the doors and windows locked.

An overwhelming number of victimizations involved a single person. Most victims report that their assailant was not armed. In the robberies and assaults involving injury, however, a majority of the assailants were reported armed. The use of guns and of knives was about equal, and there did not seem to be a pattern of a particular weapon being used for a particular crime.

The Victim and Their Criminal

The NCVS data can tell us something about the characteristics of people who commit crime. Of course, this information is available only on criminals who actually came in contact with the victim through such crimes as rape, assault, or robbery.

Most offenders and victims did not know one another; about 65 percent of all violent crimes are committed by strangers, and that number has remained stable for the past ten years. However, women seem much more likely than men to be victimized by acquaintances. In fact, a majority of female assault victims know their assailants.

A majority of the victims reported that the crime was committed by a single offender over the age of twenty. About one quarter of the victims indicated that their assailant was a young person twelve to twenty years of age. This may reflect the criminal activities of youth gangs and groups in the United States.

Whites were the offenders in a majority of single-offender rapes and assaults, but a majority of robberies were carried out by blacks; this pattern held true for crimes involving multiple offenders.

The NCVS has recently begun to ask victims if their assailants were under the influence of drugs or alcohol. Victims reported that substance use was involved in 36 percent of the violent crime incidents, including 46 percent of the rapes.[52]

The Likelihood of Victimization

The NCVS data also tell us that about 20 million U.S. households experience some form of criminal activity each year. Americans have a significant chance of becoming a victim sometime during their lifetime. The probability of the average twelve year old becoming the victim of violent crime sometime during his or her lifespan is over 80 percent; 25 percent of all U.S. citizens will experience violence three or more times. Even more startling is the fact that 99 percent of the U.S. population will experience personal theft and 87 percent will be theft victims three or more times.[53]

The NCVS data suggest that the risk of becoming a crime victim over one's lifetime is a function of personal characteristics and life-style. Victimization risk

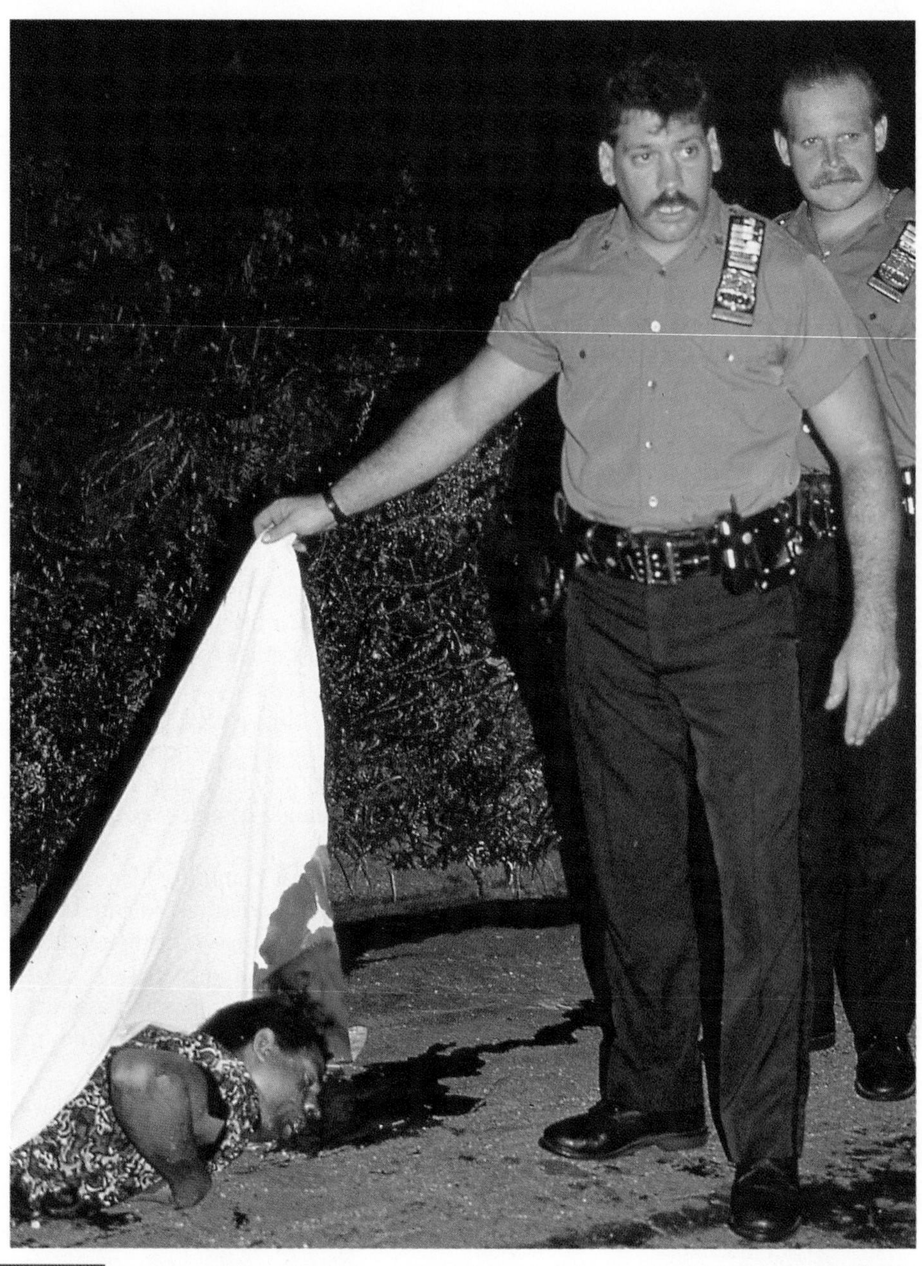

Over 80 percent of all adolescents age twelve and under will experience a violent attack sometime during their life.

can be increased by being in public places in urban areas late at night. Victimization can be reduced by moving to a suburb and avoiding public places in the evening.

The NCVS seems to be indicating that the likelihood of a crime occurring is dependent on victim behavior. This discovery has led to the development of a life-style approach to understanding victimization risk.[54] This view holds that victimization risk is related to the **routine activities** of human behavior. Crime occurs because victims place themselves in jeopardy. The crime rate is a function of victim behavior: if households filled with expensive goods are left unguarded, the crime rate will increase; crime rates will decline if households are defended like forts by well-armed guards and their contents have little value.

Critique of the NCVS

Like the UCR, the NCVS and all other victim surveys suffer from some methodological problems, so their findings must be interpreted with caution. Among the problems are:

1. Overreporting due to victims' misinterpretation of events. For example, a lost wallet is reported as stolen, or an open door is viewed as a burglary attempt.
2. Underreporting due to embarrassment in reporting crime to interviewers, fear of getting into trouble, or simply forgetting an incident.
3. Inability to record the personal criminal activity of those interviewed, such as drug use or gambling.
4. Failure to directly ask subjects about rape victimization; this topic is covered under the question "Did anyone try to attack you in some other way?" (other than the incidents included in the survey). This omission may invalidate the rape data.[55]

To relieve these problems, a committee of experts has been assembled to help redesign the NCVS instrument.

Are the Data Sources Compatible?

Are the various sources of criminal statistics compatible? Each has its own strengths and weaknesses. The UCR is carefully tallied and contains data on the number of murders and people arrested that the other sources lack; yet, it omits the many crimes that victims choose not to report to the police. The NCVS contains important information on the personal characteristics of victims and unreported crimes, but the data consist of population estimates made from relatively limited samples (about 100,000) so that even narrow fluctuations in the reporting rates of some crimes can have a major impact on findings; the NCVS is also subject to inaccurate reporting by victims. Self-report surveys can provide important information on the personal characteristics of offenders, unavailable from any other source. Yet, at their core, self-report surveys rely on the honesty of criminal offenders, a population not normally known for accuracy and integrity.

Despite these differences, a number of prominent criminologists have found that the various sources of crime data are more compatible than was first believed. For example, while the absolute numbers of crimes recorded by the NCVS and the UCR do not coincide, the crime patterns, changes, and fluctuations they record are often quite similar.[56] All three sources are in general agreement about the personal characteristics of serious criminals, where and when crime occurs, and general crime patterns.

Despite similarities, comparing the data sources can sometimes result in confusing and contradictory findings. Because each source of crime data uses a different method to obtain results, differences inevitably will occur between them. These differences must be carefully considered when interpreting the data on the nature of and trends in crime.

Explaining Crime Trends

While the findings of the crime data sources diverge in some areas, the patterns and trends they measure in the crime rate may be quite similar. Both the NCVS and the UCR now indicate that the number of violent crimes has increased since 1986. The NCVS shows that more than 6 million violent acts occur each year;

the UCR records over 1.8 million. In addition, the UCR has found a significant increase in the murder rate, a crime not included in the NCVS. So while general crime patterns seem stable, violent crimes remain unacceptably high and increasing.

How can we account for the recent patterns in the crime rate? This question has a number of possible answers. When crime rates skyrocketed between 1965 and 1980, the blame was placed on such targets as a large, alienated teenage population who did nothing but disobey their parents and listen to rock and roll, urban decay, racial disharmony, the rise of a drug culture, and the erosion of middle-class values. To some critics, it was not surprising that the postwar baby-boom generation brought up under the permissive rules of Dr. Spock, weaned on violent TV shows and Elvis Presley, and later influenced by urban riots and the war in Vietnam would turn to an increasing amount of crime and violence.[57]

When crime rates fell in the mid-1980s, experts believed that the drop was a result of a decline in the U.S. birthrate, which produced a smaller number of people in the most crime-prone age bracket, eighteen to twenty-five years old.[58] Young people maintain the highest overall crime rate, and with the "greying" of society, some experts believed that the crime rate had concomitantly declined.

Another popular explanation was that the "get tough" crime control policy that held sway during the Reagan administration helped deter criminal behavior. As prison and jail populations soared and judges put a greater percentage of convicted criminals behind bars, some believed that it stood to reason the crime rate would go down. It was also claimed that the "law and order" philosophy met with a great deal of public approval and that an increase in police-community cooperation helped stem the crime rate. Finally, the improved economy and low unemployment rate in the mid-1980s may have helped to control crime rates.

A number of explanations have been offered for the recent fluctuations in the crime rate. The most influential factors are discussed below.

Younger Criminals

One reason for fluctuations in the violence rate may be a change in the age structure of criminality. While the number of teens has not risen sharply, there are indications that kids are being arrested for violent acts earlier in their adolescence. As Table 2.5 shows, the violent crime arrest rate for teens has increased significantly since 1970. These data indicate either that police are now more

TABLE 2.5
Violent Crime Arrest Rates

Number of Arrests per 100,000 Population by Age							
Age	1965	1970	1975	1980	1985	1988	1989
12 or less	10	15	18	14	15	15	18
13–14	138	206	249	261	251	283	338
15	244	364	482	504	446	506	602
16	304	459	616	638	568	612	750
17	304	518	662	739	661	693	826
18	338	570	712	746	660	751	865

SOURCE: Uniform Crime Reporting Program, *Age-Specific Arrest Rates and Race-Specific Arrest Rates for Selected Crimes, 1965–1988* (Washington, D.C.: U.S. Government Printing Office 1990; updated 1991).

willing to arrest young people than they were twenty years ago or that adolescents are actually more violent today than in the past. Data from successive research studies conducted in Philadelphia show that adolescents are beginning their violent careers earlier today and engage in violence more frequently than their older brothers and sisters.[59]

Economic Problems

While an association between crime and the state of the economy would seem inherently logical, empirical evidence measuring this relationship has generally been inconclusive. There have been periods of relative national affluence, such as the 1960s, when *both* the economy and the crime rate increased significantly.[60]

A number of factors may help neutralize the crime-producing influence of a poor economy. Most criminals are chronically unemployed, so an economic slowdown may have little effect on their already desperate economic condition. It is also unlikely that otherwise law-abiding citizens will turn to crime because they have been temporarily laid off from their jobs. Few offenders actually begin their law-violating careers in middle age; most serious criminals are "early beginners."[61]

People also accumulate fewer valuables during periods of economic hardship, and they are likely to guard their hard-won possessions more closely. Unemployed parents are able to keep closer tabs on their teenage children, who normally maintain a high offense rate.

This pattern may now be changing. Some experts argue that the recent erosion of urban manufacturing jobs, tight local government budgets, and the economic downturn have placed an overwhelming financial burden on the urban poor.[62] The level of poverty and unemployment among youths in the nation's largest cities is shockingly high.[63] Kids who in the past might have hoped for a job at the local plant may now find it closed and the jobs transferred overseas. Getting shut out of the job market has encouraged disadvantaged youth to join criminal gangs in ever greater numbers.[64] An economic downturn has also widened the gulf between the nation's most impoverished and affluent citizens.[65] A number of studies have shown that the crime rate is extremely high when people who live in close proximity to one another in urban areas are at the opposite ends of the economic spectrum.[66]

Drug Abuse

While the overall rate of drug use has declined dramatically in recent years, the continuing abuse of cocaine and crack in inner-city areas may accentuate the crime problem.[67] A number of research efforts have shown that a single drug user commits an enormous amount of crime annually.[68] A significant number of all arrested criminals test positively for drugs.[69] The presence of even a relatively few hard-core drug users in the population may result in a significant increase in the crime rate.[70]

The Failure of Crime-Control Strategies

Throughout the 1980s and into the 1990s, the federal government and most state jurisdictions have advocated strict crime-control policies. Though court dockets have become filled and prisons overcrowded, the official crime rate has not dropped significantly and the number of victimizations has stabilized since 1985.

Little evidence exists that these "get tough" policies alone can reduce the level of criminal activity.[71]

Punishment-oriented strategies are ineffective for a number of reasons. Most convicted offenders repeat their criminal acts after they are released from correctional confinement. Programs designed to "get tough" on crime may have backfired because they create an expanding pool of ex-offenders who have little chance to succeed in conventional society. And, while get-tough policies may incapacitate known offenders, they do little to change the social, economic, and personal conditions that produce crime.

Statistical Validity

Change or movement in the crime rate may be more a matter of law enforcement reporting practices than actual fluctuations in criminal behavior. The UCR is dependent on accurate crime reporting and uniformity in the way crimes are defined and tallied. A reduction in the crime rate may reflect the desire of the nation's police departments to show they are on top of the crime problem: they can record a burglary as a breaking and entering and avoid counting it as an index crime; the value of a larceny can be underestimated so that the crime is not counted. In contrast, crime rate increases may reflect confidence in the police and the willingness of victims to report criminal events. Therefore, it is possible that changes in the overall crime rate may reflect the way citizens report crime to the police and the way police departments record the results, rather than any actual change in the amount or rate of crime.

SUMMARY

Crime has become a familiar and disturbing fact of life in the United States. When we speak about crime, we refer to a violation of existing societal rules of behavior that are expressed in the criminal code created by those holding political power. Individuals who violate these rules are subject to state sanctions.

Today, we get our information on crime from a number of sources. One of the most important of these is the uniform crime report compiled by the FBI. This national survey of serious criminal acts reported to local police departments indicates that about 14.5 million index crimes (murder, rape, burglary, robbery, assault, larceny-theft, and motor vehicle theft) occurred in 1990. This figure represents a steady increase in the crime rate beginning in the mid-1980s.

Critics have questioned the validity of the UCR. They point out that many people fail to report crime to police because of fear, apathy, or lack of respect for law enforcement. In addition, questions have been raised about the accuracy of police records and reporting practices.

To remedy this situation, the federal government has sponsored a massive victim survey designed to uncover the true amount of annual crime. The National Crime Victimization Survey, or NCVS, reveals that about 34 million serious personal crimes are committed every year and that the great majority are not reported to police. A third form of information is self-report surveys, which ask offenders themselves to tell about their criminal behaviors.

The various sources of criminal statistics tell us a lot about the nature and patterns of crime. The crime rate decline of the early 1980s has been reversed. Rate increases have been attributed to the influence of drugs, the economy, the age structure, social decay, and other factors.

Many crime victims do not report criminal incidents to the police because they believe that nothing can be done or that they should not get involved. However, recent evidence indicates that the crimes not reported to the police are less serious than reported crimes. Consequently, the crime patterns found in the UCR and the NCVS may be more similar than some critics believe.

There are distinct patterns to crime. It occurs more often in large cities during the summer and at night. Some geographic areas (the South and the Far West) have higher crime rates than others (the Midwest and New England).

Arrest and victim data indicate that males, minorities, the poor, and the young have relatively high rates of criminality. Victims of crime have many of the same demographic characteristics as criminals. They tend to be poor, young, male, and members of a minority group. However, households that experience crime tend to have a higher relative income than those that avoid victimization.

For the most part, criminals tend to victimize people who share their personal characteristics. For example, crime is intraracial. People can increase the risk of victimization by choosing a life-style that includes acts associated with high degrees of victimization, such as frequenting public places at night.

The police cannot do much about crime. About 20 percent of all reported crimes are solved by police. Since only half of all crimes are reported to police, this means that the success rate is only 10 percent. However, there is a positive relationship between crime seriousness and the probability of a successful clearance. That is, murders and rapes are much more often solved than car thefts or larcenies.

QUESTIONS

1. Why are crime rates higher in the summer than during other seasons?
2. Why would some police departments report more serious crimes than actually took place?
3. Would you answer a self-report survey honestly? Do you think such data is valid?
4. What factors account for the fact that adolescents are becoming increasingly violent?

NOTES

1. The Harris Survey, cited in Timothy Flanagan and Katherine Jamieson, *Sourcebook of Criminal Justice Statistics, 1987* (Washington, D.C.: U.S. Government Printing Office, 1988), p. 123.

2. Frank Bennack, *The American Public's Hopes and Fears for the Decade of the 1990's* (New York: Hearst Corporation, 1989), cited in Kathleen Maguire and Timothy Flanagan, *Sourcebook of Criminal Justice Statistics, 1990* (Washington, D.C.: U.S. Government Printing Office, 1991), p. 181.

3. Howard Becker, *Outsiders*, 2d ed. (New York: Macmillan, 1972).

4. Alfred Lindesmith, *The Addict and the Law* (New York: Vintage, 1965), chap. 1.

5. For a general discussion of Marxist thought, see Michael Lynch and W. Byron Groves, *A Primer in Radical Criminology*, 2d ed. (New York: Harrow and Heston, 1990), pp. 6–26.

6. *The Household Survey on Drug Abuse, 1990* (Washington, D.C.: U.S. Department of Health and Human Services, 1990).

7. Lisa Bastian and Marshall DeBerry, Jr., *Criminal Victimization, 1990* (Washington, D.C.: Bureau of Justice Statistics, 1991).

8. William F. Whyte, *Street Corner Society: The Social Structure of an Italian Slum* (Chicago: University of Chicago Press, 1955); Laud Humphreys, *Tearoom Trade: Impersonal Sex in Public Places*, rev. ed. (Chicago: Aldine Publishing, 1975).

9. Carl Klockars, *The Professional Fence* (New York: Free Press, 1976); Darrell Steffensmeier, *The Fence: In the Shadow of Two Worlds* (Totowa, N.J.: Rowman and Littlefield, 1986).

10. At the time of this writing, the latest volume of the UCR was the Federal Bureau of Investigation's *Crime in the United States, 1990* (Washington, D.C.: U.S. Government Printing Office, 1991). Wherever possible, statistics in this volume will be supplemented by estimates based on data from the 1991 crime survey, made public in *Crime in the United States, 1991, Preliminary Annual Report*.

11. Adapted from Federal Bureau of Investigation, *Crime in the United States, 1990*, pp. 2–3.

12. Clarence Schrag, *Crime and Justice: American Style* (Washington, D.C.: U.S. Government Printing Office, 1971), p. 17.

13. Federal Bureau of Investigation, *Crime in the United States, 1990*, p. 43.

14. Malcolm Sparrow, Mark Moore, and David Kennedy, *Beyond 911: A New Era for Policing* (New York: Basic Books, 1990).

15. The findings in this section are based on 1990 UCR statistics.

16. Freda Adler, *Sisters in Crime* (New York: McGraw Hill, 1975); Rita James Simon, *The Contemporary Woman and Crime* (Washington, D.C.: U.S. Government Printing Office, 1975).

17. Joseph Weis, "Liberation and Crime: The Invention of the New Female Criminal," *Crime and Social Justice* 1 (1976):17–27; Steven Box and Chris Hale, "Liberation/Emancipation, Economic Marginalization or Less Chivalry," *Criminology* 22 (1984):473–78.

18. Daniel Georges-Abeyie, "Race, Ethnicity, and the Spatial Dynamic: Toward a Realistic Study of Black Crime, Crime Victimization, and the Criminal Justice Processing of Blacks," *Social Justice* 16 (1989):35–54.

19. See, for example, James Comer, "Black Violence and Public Policy," in *American Violence and Public Policy*, ed. Lynn Curtis (New Haven: Yale University Press, 1985).

20. Emilie Andersen Allan and Darrell Steffensmeier, "Youth, Underemployment and Property Crime: Differential Effects of Job Availability and Job Quality on Juvenile and Young Adult Arrest Rates," *American Sociological Review* 54 (1989):107–23.

21. For a general view, see James Byrne and Robert Sampson, *The Social Ecology of Crime* (New York: Springer-Verlag, 1985).

22. Douglas Smith and G. Roger Jarjoura, "Social Structure and Criminal Victimization," *Journal of Research in Crime and Delinquency* 25 (1988):27–52; Janet Heitgerd and Robert Bursik, Jr., "Extracommunity Dynamics and the Ecology of Delinquency," *American Journal of Sociology* 92 (1987):775–87; Ora Simcha-Fagan and Joseph Schwartz, "Neighborhood and Delinquency: An Assessment of Contextual Effects," *Criminology* 24 (1986):667–703.

23. Rodney Stark, "Deviant Places: A Theory of the Ecology of Crime," *Criminology* 25 (1987):893–910.

24. Judith Blau and Peter Blau, "The Cost of Inequality: Metropolitan Structure and Violent Crime," *American Sociological Review* 47 (1982):114–29.

25. Charles Tittle and Robert Meier, "Specifying the SES/Delinquency Relationship," *Criminology* 28 (1990):271–95.

26. Colin Loftin and Robert Nash Parker, "An Errors-in-Variable Model of the Effect of Poverty on Urban Homicide Rates," *Criminology* 23 (1985):269–87.

27. Herman Schwendinger and Julia Schwendinger, "The Paradigmatic Crisis in Delinquency Theory," *Crime and Social Justice* 18 (1982):70–78.

28. Michael Gottfredson and Travis Hirschi, "The True Value of Lambda Would Appear to Be Zero: An Essay on Career Criminals, Criminal Careers, Selective Incapacitation, Cohort Studies and Related Topics," *Criminology* 24 (1986):213–34; further support for their position can be found in Lawrence Cohen and Kenneth Land, "Age Structure and Crime," *American Sociological Review* 52 (1987):170–83.

29. Travis Hirschi and Michael Gottfredson, "Age and the Explanation of Crime," *American Journal of Sociology* 89 (1983):552–84.

30. Gottfredson and Hirschi, "The True Value of Lambda Would Appear to Be Zero."

31. Alfred Blumstein, Jacqueline Cohen, and David Farrington, "Criminal Career Research: Its Value for Criminology," *Criminology* 26 (1988):1–35.

32. Arnold Barnett, Alfred Blumstein, and David Farrington, "Probabilistic Models of Youthful Criminal Careers," *Criminology* 25 (1987):83–107; David Greenberg, "Age, Crime, and Social Explanation," *American Journal of Sociology* 91 (1985):1–21.

33. NCVS data come from Timothy Flanagan and Katherine Jamieson, *Sourcebook of Criminal Justice Statistics, 1987* (Washington, D.C.: U.S. Government Printing Office, 1988), pp. 131–76.

34. Duncan Chappell et al., "Forcible Rape: A Comparative Study of Offenses Known to the Police in Boston and Los Angeles," in *Studies in Sociology of Sex*, ed. James Henslin (New York: Appleton-Century-Crofts, 1971), pp. 169–93.

35. Lawrence Sherman and Barry Glick, "The Quality of Arrest Statistics," *Police Foundation Reports* 2 (1984):1–8.

36. Patrick Jackson, "Assessing the Validity of Official Data on Arson," *Criminology* 6 (1988):181–95.

37. David Seidman and Michael Couzens, "Getting the Crime Rate Down: Political Pressure and Crime Reporting," *Law and Society Review* 8 (1974):457.

38. Leonard Savitz, "Official Statistics," in *Contemporary Criminology*, ed. L. Savitz and N. Johnston (New York: John Wiley & Sons, 1982), pp. 3–15.

39. Michael Hindelang, Travis Hirschi, and Joseph Weis, *Measuring Delinquency* (Beverly Hills, Calif.: Sage Publications, 1981).

40. Walter Gove, Michael Hughes, and Michael Geerken, "Are Uniform Crime Reports a Valid Indicator of the Index Crimes? An Affirmative Answer with Minor Qualifications," *Criminology* 23 (1985):451–501.

41. U.S. Department of Justice, *The Redesigned UCR Program* (Washington, D.C.: U.S. Department of Justice, n.d.).

42. For example, the following studies have noted the great discrepancy between official statistics and self-report studies: Maynard Erickson and LaMar Empey, "Court Records, Undetected Delinquency and Decision-making," *Journal of Criminal Law, Criminology, and Police Science* 54 (1963):456–69; Martin Gold, "Undetected Delinquent Behavior," *Journal of Research in Crime and Delinquency* 3 (1966):27–46; James Short and F. Ivan Nye, "Extent of Unrecorded Delinquency, Tentative Conclusions," *Journal of Criminal Law, Criminology, and Police Science* 49 (1958):296–302; David Farrington, "Self-Reports of Deviant Behavior: Predictive and Stable?" *Journal of Criminal Law and Criminology* 64 (1973):99–110.

43. Charles Tittle, Wayne Villemez, and Douglas Smith, "The Myth of Social Class and Criminality: An Empirical Assessment of the Empirical Evidence," *American Sociological Review* 43 (1978):643–46.

44. D. Wayne Osgood, Lloyd Johnston, Patrick O'Malley, and Jerald Bachman, "The Generality of Deviance in Late Adolescence and Early Adulthood," *American Sociological Review* 53 (1988):81–93.

45. D. Wayne Osgood, Patrick O'Malley, Jerald Bachman, and Lloyd Johnston, "Time Trends and Age Trends in Arrests and Self-Reported Illegal Behavior," *Criminology* 27 (1989):389–417.

46. Jerald Bachman, Lloyd Johnston, and Patrick O'Malley, *Monitoring the Future, 1990* (Ann Arbor: Institute for Social Research, 1991).

47. Lloyd Johnston, Patrick O'Malley, and Jerald Bachman, *Drug Use Among American High School Students, College Students, and Young Adults, 1975–1990* (Washington, D.C.: U.S. Department of Health and Human Services, 1991; updated with press release, 27 January 1992).

48. Philip Ennis, *Criminal Victimization in the United States*, Field Survey 2 (Washington, D.C.: President's Commission on Law Enforcement and Criminal Justice, 1967).

49. Data in these sections come from Lisa Bastian and Marshall DeBerry, Jr., *Criminal Victimization, 1990* (Washington, D.C.: Bureau of Justice Statistics, 1991).

50. Ibid.

51. Lisa Bastian and Bruce Taylor, *School Crime* (Washington, D.C.: Bureau of Justice Statistics, 1991), p. 1.

52. Catherine Whitaker, *The Redesigned National Crime Survey: Selected New Data* (Washington, D.C.: Bureau of Justice Statistics, 1989).

53. *Households Touched by Crime, 1987* (Washington, D.C.: Bureau of Justice Statistics, 1988).

54. Lawrence Cohen and Marcus Felson, "Social Change and Crime Rate Trends: A Routine Activities Approach," *American Sociological Review* 44 (1979):588–608; L. Cohen, James Kleugel, and Kenneth Land, "Social Inequality and Predatory Criminal Victimization: An Exposition and Test of a Formal Theory," *American Sociological Review* 46 (1981):505–24; Steven Messner and Kenneth Tardiff, "The Social Ecology of Urban Homicide: An Application of the 'Routine Activities' Approach," *Criminology* 23 (1985):241–67.

55. Helen Eigenberg, "The National Crime Survey and Rape: The Case of the Missing Question," *Justice Quarterly* 7 (1990):655–71.

56. Alfred Blumstein, Jacqueline Cohen, and Richard Rosenfeld, "Trend and Deviation in Crime Rates: A Comparison of UCR and NCS Data for Burglary and Robbery," *Criminology* 29 (1991):237–63.

57. James Gilbert, *A Cycle of Outrage, America's Reaction to the Juvenile Delinquent in the 1950's* (New York: Oxford University Press, 1986).

58. Michael Gottfredson and Travis Hirschi, "Science, Public Policy and the Career Paradigm," *Criminology* 26 (1988):37–57.

59. Marvin Wolfgang, "Delinquency in Two Birth Cohorts," in *Perspective Studies of Crime and Delinquency*, ed. Katherine Teilmann Van Dusen and Sarnoff Mednick (Boston: Kluwer-Nijhoff, 1983), pp. 7–17.

60. Theodore Chiricos, "Rates of Crime and Unemployment: An Analysis of Aggregate Research Evidence," *Social Problems* 34 (1987):187–212.

61. Jennifer White, Terrie Moffitt, Felton Earls, Lee Robins, and Phil Silva, "How Early Can We Tell? Predictors of Childhood Conduct Disorder and Adolescent Delinquency," *Criminology* 28 (1990):507–33.

62. E. Britt Patterson, "Poverty, Income Inequality, and Community Crime Rates," *Criminology* 29 (1991):755–76.

63. Daniel Lichter, "Racial Differences in Underemployment in American

Cities," *American Journal of Sociology* 93 (1988):771–92.

64. John Hagedorn, "Gangs, Neighborhoods and Public Policy," *Social Problems* 38 (1991):529–41.

65. Judith Blau and Peter Blau, "The Cost of Inequality: Metropolitan Structure and Violent Crime," *American Sociological Review* 147 (1982):114–29; Richard Block, "Community Environment and Violent Crime," *Criminology* 17 (1979):46–57; Robert Sampson, "Structural Sources of Variation in Race-Age-Specific Rates of Offending Across Major U.S. Cities," *Criminology* 23 (1985):647–73.

66. Robert Sampson and John Wooldredge, "Linking the Micro- and Macro-Level Dimensions of Lifestyle-Routine Activity and Opportunity Models of Predatory Victimization," *Journal of Quantitative Criminology* 3 (1987):371–93; Blau and Blau, "The Cost of Inequality."

67. Marcia Chaiken and Bruce Johnson, *Characteristics of Different Types of Drug-Involved Offenders* (Washington, D.C.: National Institute of Justice, 1988).

68. James Inciardi,"Heroin Use and Street Crime," *Crime and Delinquency* 25 (1979):335–46.

69. Eric Wish, *Drug Use Forecasting, 1990* (Washington, D.C.: National Institute of Justice, 1991).

70. Chaiken and Johnson, *Characteristics of Different Types of Drug-Involved Offenders*, pp. 5–7; see also M. Douglas Anglin, Elizabeth Piper Deschenes, and George Speckart, "The Effect of Legal Supervision on Narcotic Addiction and Criminal Behavior" (Paper presented at the Annual American Society of Criminology meeting, Montreal, November 1987).

71. Raymond Paternoster, "Examining Three-Wave Deterrence Models: A Question of Temporal Order and Specification," *Journal of Criminal Law and Criminology* 79 (1988):135–79; see also Lonn Lanza-Kaduce, "Perceptual Deterrence and Drinking and Driving Among College Students," *Criminology* 26 (1988):321–41; Raymond Paternoster, "The Deterrent Effect of the Perceived Certainty and Severity of Punishment," *Justice Quarterly* 4 (1987):173–217.

Similarly, a plan to reduce prison riots by eliminating the sugar intake of inmates is feasible only if research shows a link between diet and violence.

In addition to understanding the nature and cause of criminal behavior, it is also important for criminal justice policymakers to study and understand the role of victims in the crime process. Such knowledge is essential for developing strategies to reduce the probability of predatory crime while providing information that people can use to decrease their likelihood of becoming a target of predatory criminals.

This chapter will explore these fundamental questions: Why do people commit crime? Is crime a social, psychological, physical, or economic phenomenon? Is it a matter of free will or a reaction to uncontrollable external forces? Do people become victims because they are in the wrong place at the wrong time, or do crime victims control their own destiny?

Criminal Justice and Criminology

Because criminal justice professionals must understand the nature and causes of crime and victimization, many carefully evaluate the research and writing in the field of **criminology.** While criminal justice refers to the processes and policies of the justice system, criminology involves analyzing the nature and extent of criminal behavior. Criminologists attempt to derive explanations based on observable facts, or **theories,** which explain the onset of criminality. They also examine the nature of specific crime patterns, such as rape, murder, or burglary. Criminology also contains the subdisciplines of **victimology** (the study of the victim's role in the crime process), sociology of law (the study of the social foundation of legal rules and precedents), criminal statistics (the development of valid and reliable indicators of criminal behaviors), and **penology** (correctional treatment).

Criminology and criminal justice overlap a great deal. Criminologists must be aware of how the agencies of justice operate and how they influence criminal behavior. Similarly, criminal justice experts cannot begin to design programs of crime control or correction without some understanding of the nature of crime itself. Criminology courses are commonly taught in criminal justice programs, and criminology courses often include discussions of the criminal justice system. In fact, many criminologists belong to the *Academy of Criminal Justice Sciences*, the national criminal justice organization, and many criminal justice scholars belong to the *American Society of Criminology*, the national criminology organization.

Theories of Crime Causation: Why They Do It

Criminologists have attempted to create valid and accurate theories of crime causation and victimization. Social scientists define theory as:

- A general statement or set of statements that explain many different facts by reference to underlying principles and relationships.[2]
- A statement that organizes a set of concepts in a meaningful way by explaining the relationship among the concepts.[3]

Accordingly, criminologists have sought to collect many different facts about crime and use them to discover the underlying principles and relationships that control crime rates. By developing scientifically testable statements, or **hypotheses,** about crime and by organizing and explaining them in a meaningful way, they hope to identify the root causes of crime and victimization.

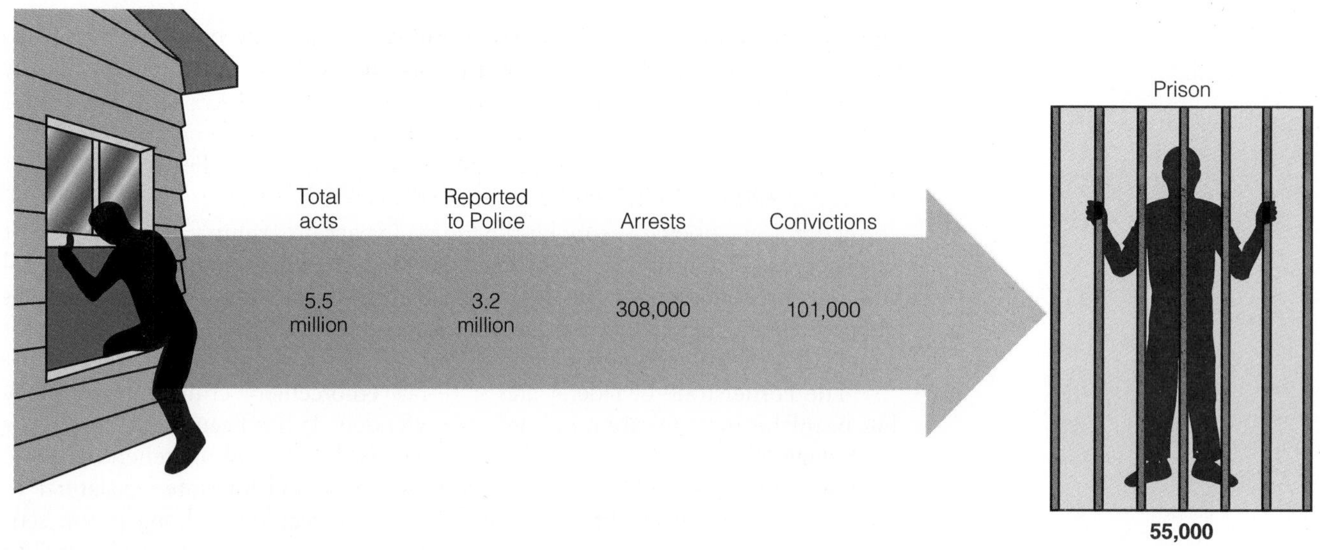

FIGURE 3.1
Burglary: The Chance of Punishment

SOURCE: Patrick Langan and John Davison, *Felony Sentences in State Courts,* 1988 (Washington, D.C.: Bureau of Justice Statistics, 1990).

Make 'Em Afraid II: Specific Deterrence

Even if the threat of punishment cannot deter would-be criminals, actual punishment at the hands of the justice system should be sufficient to convince arrested offenders never to repeat their criminal acts. If punishment is severe enough, a convicted criminal would never dare repeat his or her offense. What rational person would? This view is referred to as **special or specific deterrence.** Prior to the twentieth century, special deterrence became a motive for the extreme tortures and physical punishments commonly used on convicted criminals. By breaking the convicts physically, legal authorities hoped to control their spirit and behavior.[26]

While our more enlightened society no longer uses such "cruel and unusual punishments," we do employ long prison sentences in dangerous and forbidding prisons as a substitute. Yet such measures do not seem to deliver the promise of crime control inherent in the special deterrence concept. A majority of inmates repeat their criminal acts soon after returning to society, and most inmates had previously served time.[27]

Why have these punishments failed as a specific deterrent? Our current system of justice appears inconsistent and arbitrary, creating a sense of injustice in the inmate population. Most defendants plea-bargain for a reduced sentence, including probation for felony offenses; those sent to prison rarely serve their entire sentence before being granted parole or some other early release.[28] Rather than producing a specific deterrent effect, the correctional process enhances criminal involvement by reducing both the certainty and severity of punishment.

Specific deterrence also assumes a rational criminal, someone who learns from experience. It is possible that many offenders have impulsive personalities that may inhibit their ability to learn from experience. A majority of criminal offenders have life-styles marked by heavy substance abuse, lack of formal educa-

tion, and disturbed home lives, which inhibit conventional behavior. The pains of imprisonment and the stigma of a prison record do little to help an already troubled person readjust to society.

Choice Theory and Criminal Justice Policy

In recent years, choice theory has had great impact on criminal justice policy. It has been used to justify the "get tough" law-and-order approach to crime control that was predominant in the 1980s and continues into the 1990s. If criminals choose crime, then it follows that increasing the level of criminal punishment should deter crime and lower crime rates.

The cornerstone of federal and state law enforcement crime control policy has been the **incapacitation** of hard-core offenders. It has been common for law enforcement agencies to establish task forces to locate and apprehend chronic offenders, for prosecutors to target career criminals, and for state legislatures to enact laws providing lengthy prison sentences for recidivists. Long prison sentences are believed to be the best way to keep repeaters "out of circulation," to convince prospective offenders that crime does not pay, and to teach those who decide to commit crimes a lesson not soon forgotten. And, obviously, incapacitated criminals are in no position to choose crime.

While an incapacitation policy seems inherently logical, little evidence actually exists that putting large numbers of convicted criminals in prison can lower the crime rate.[29] A case in point: while crime rates increased between 1985 and 1991, judges were putting record numbers of convicted offenders behind bars. During this period, the prison population expanded by two hundred thousand. How can this puzzling phenomenon be explained? One reason may be that the economic benefits of crime may actually increase as more criminals are incarcerated.[30] As more experienced criminals are incapacitated, newcomers are free to take advantage of wide-open criminal opportunities.[31] If crime is indeed rational, newcomers should be able to sense the opportunities presented by the absence of large numbers of competitors from the street. For example, when large numbers of organized crime figures were imprisoned, weakening mob control over drug trafficking, local ethnic gangs and groups filled the gap in the narcotics trade.

The high recidivism (repeat offense) rate of convicted offenders also limits the effectiveness of incapacitation strategies. Surveys of young parolees aged seventeen to twenty-two found that 69 percent were rearrested within six years of their release from prison, 53 percent were convicted for a new offense, and 49 percent were returned to prison.[32] A prison experience probably does little to stifle and much to encourage criminality. Though chronic offenders cannot commit crime against society outside while they are incarcerated, the frequency and intensity of their criminality may be amplified by their experience.

Because They're Different: Biological Theories

As the nineteenth century came to a close, some criminologists began to suggest that crime was caused not so much by human choice but by inherited and uncontrollable biological and psychological traits: intelligence, body build, personality, diet. The newly developed **scientific method** was applied to the study of social relations, including criminal behavior.

The origins of scientific criminology is usually traced to the research of Cesare Lombroso (1835–1909). Lombroso was an Italian army physician fascinated by

human anatomy who became interested in finding out what motivated criminals to commit crimes. He physically examined hundreds of prison inmates and other criminals in order to discover any similarities between them. On the basis of his research, Lombroso proposed that criminals manifest **atavistic** or **degenerate anomalies;** in other words, the active criminal is a physical and biological throwback to early stages of human evolution who adjusts poorly to modern society and is thrust into criminal activities. Careful physical measurement of hundreds of convicted criminals led Lombroso to catalog attributes that denoted criminality: an asymmetric face or excessive jaw, eye defects, large eyes, a receding forehead, prominent cheekbones, long arms, a twisted nose, and swollen lips.[33]

With Lombroso's work as their focal point, a number of other early criminologists continued to search for a biological basis for crime. Raffaele Garofalo (1852–1934) found that criminals lacked compassion for others, a condition he believed was brought about by organic problems and inherited instincts.[34] Enrico Ferri (1856–1929) attempted to identify the biological, social, and organic factors associated with crime and delinquency.[35] Later, Ernest Hooton argued that criminals suffered from biological and social inferiority.[36] Richard Dugdale, Henry Goddard, and Arthur Estabrook each conducted research on the family trees of criminal offenders and attempted to show that crime proneness was an inherited characteristic passed down from one generation to the next.[37]

Biological Theory Today

In mid-twentieth century, sociology supplanted biology as the primary focus of crime theory. However, with the publication of Edward O. Wilson's book *Sociobiology: The New Synthesis* in 1975, interest was renewed in linking biological explanations to human social behavior.[38] Sociobiology differs from earlier theories of behavior because it focuses on an evolutionary explanation of human behavior. It assumes that social behavior has evolved as part of a genetic adaptation and that biological and genetic conditions affect perception and the learning of social behavior.

The popularity of sociobiology spurred a number of criminologists to look once again at the biological underpinnings of crime. At their core, biological theories assume that variation in human physical traits can explain behavior.[39] Rather than being born equal and influenced by social and environmental conditions, each person maintains a unique biochemical, neurological, and genetic makeup. But biocriminologists hold that no one factor absolutely controls behavior and that the interaction of physical and environmental factors influences behavior choices. If biological preconditions that promote antisocial acts could be treated or compensated for, then environmental factors would have less of an impact on crime.

Today, biocriminologists are attempting to link physical traits with tendencies toward violence, aggression, and other antisocial behavior. Their work, which is still in the early stages of development, can be divided into three broad areas of focus: biochemical factors, neurological problems, and genetic influence.

You Are What You Eat: Biochemical Factors

One major area of modern biocriminology involves identifying the influence of biochemical factors on criminal behavior. Some research efforts have linked vitamin and mineral deficiencies, improper diet, environmental contaminants, and

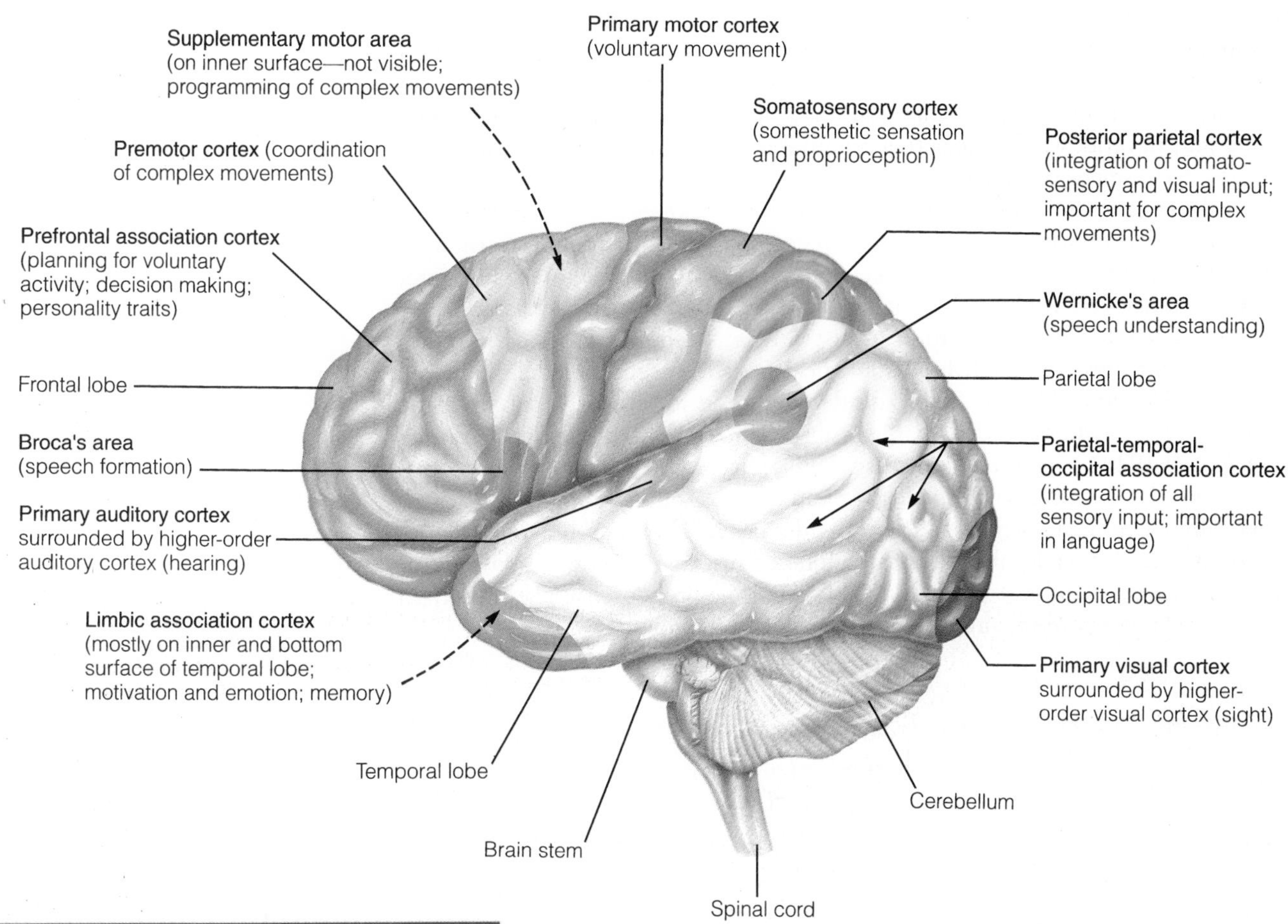

Some biocriminologists believe that brain structure controls behavior. People with an abnormal cerebral structure may be crime prone.

allergies to antisocial behavior.[40] Research focusing on the behavior of jailed inmates has shown that subjects who maintain high levels of sugar and caffeine in their diet were more likely to engage in antisocial behavior than control-group subjects who had diets low in those substances.[41] A number of research efforts have concluded that hypoglycemia, a lack of blood sugar, may contribute to outbursts of antisocial behavior and violence.[42] Similarly, allergic reactions to such common foods as milk, chocolate, and corn have been associated with hyperactivity and aggression in children.[43] Recent research by Paul Cromwell and his associates found that violent offenders test positively for abnormal quantities of trace minerals, such as copper, zinc, and chromium.[44] Louis Gottschalk and his associates found high traces of manganese in violent offenders.[45]

In sum, biochemical studies suggest that criminal offenders have abnormal levels of organic or inorganic substances that influence their behavior and in some way make them prone to antisocial behavior.

The Abnormal Brain: Neurological Problems

Another area of interest to biocriminologists is the relationship of brain activity to behavior. Biocriminologists have used the electroencephalogram (EEG) to record the electrical impulses given off by the brain. Preliminary studies indicate that while 5 to 15 percent of nonlaw-violating youths have abnormal EEG ratings,

50 to 60 percent of those with behavior disorders display abnormal recordings.[46] Studies of problem children have found that almost half have abnormal EEG ratings; studies using adult subjects have found that abnormal EEG patterns are associated with hostile, nonconforming, and impulsive behavior.[47] Tests of convicted murderers show that a disproportionate number manifest abnormal EEG ratings.[48]

People with an abnormal cerebral structure referred to as *minimal brain dysfunction* (MBD) may experience periods of explosive rage.[49] Brain dysfunction is sometimes manifested as an attention deficit disorder (ADD), another suspected cause of antisocial behavior. About 3 percent of all U.S. children, most often boys, are believed to suffer from this disorder, and it is the most common reason children are referred to mental health clinics. The condition usually results in poor school performance, bullying, stubbornness, and a lack of response to discipline. While the origin of ADD is still unknown, suspected causes include neurological damage, prenatal stress, and even food additives and chemical allergies. Research by Terrie Moffitt and Phil Silva seems to suggest that youths who suffer both ADD and MBD and who also grow up in a dysfunctional family are the most vulnerable to chronic delinquency that continues into their adulthood.[50]

The Bad Seed: Genetic Factors

Although the earliest biological studies of crime tried and failed to discover a genetic basis for criminality, modern biocriminologists are still concerned with the role heredity plays in producing crime-prone people. Interest in this area was spurred in the late 1960s by the case of Richard Speck, the convicted killer of eight nurses in Chicago, who was believed to have an abnormal chromosome structure, a condition known as the **47XYY syndrome.** Follow-up research produced little evidence that 47XYY males were any more dangerous than those with the normal 46XY configuration. Later, it was revealed that Speck, who died in 1991, did not actually have the 47XYY chromosome.[51]

More recent research efforts have focused on the behavior of twins. If inherited traits are related to criminality, it should be expected that twins would be more similar in their antisocial activities than other sibling pairs. Since most twins are brought up together, however, determining whether behavior similarities are a function of environmental influences or genetics is difficult. To overcome this problem, biocriminologists usually compare identical monozygotic (MZ) twins with fraternal or dizygotic (DZ) twins of the same sex. Since MZ twins are genetically identical, their behavior would be expected to be more similar than that of DZ twins. Preliminary studies have shown that there is indeed a greater similarity between the criminal behavior of MZ twin pairs than of DZ pairs. For example, Karl Christiansen studied the criminal behavior patterns of 3,586 male twin pairs and found a 52 percent similarity between MZ twins and only a 22 percent similarity between DZ twins.[52] A more recent evaluation of twin behavior by David Rowe and D. Wayne Osgood found that genetic makeup is a better predictor of criminality than either social or environmental variables.[53]

Another approach has been to evaluate the behavior of adopted children. If an adopted child's behavior patterns run parallel to his or her biological parents, it would be strong evidence to support a genetic basis for crime. Preliminary studies conducted in Europe have indicated that the criminality of the biological father is a strong predictor of a child's antisocial behavior.[54] The probability that a youth will engage in crime is significantly enhanced when *both* biological and adoptive parents exhibit criminal tendencies.

It's in Their Heads: Psychological Theories

The view that criminals may be suffering from psychological abnormality or stress has also had a long history. One of the earliest advocates of psychological theory, British psychologist Henry Maudsley (1835–1918), believed that criminals were *morally insane* and that moral insanity was an inherited quality; his theoretical statements implied that criminals are "born and not made."[55] According to Maudsley, crime was a way for the criminal to express or alleviate the pathological urges inherited from mentally or morally deficient ancestors.[56]

Today, psychological views of crime can be divided into four significant areas, described below.

The Disturbed Mind: Psychoanalytic Theory

Psychoanalysis, the creation of Viennese doctor Sigmund Freud (1856–1939), still holds a dominant position in psychological thought.[57] Freud saw the human personality as divided into three areas that make up the unconscious part of the mind. The *id* is the primitive aspect of personality present at birth; it demands instant gratification (known as the **pleasure principle**). The *ego* develops when the infant learns that its wishes cannot always be gratified and that it must cope with the practical and conventional standards of society; the ego operates on the **reality principle.** The *superego* incorporates the moral standards and values of parents and others; it forms our conscience. Freud also postulated the existence of two basic instinctual human drives present at birth, sex and aggression, which are normally repressed into unconsciousness and channeled into productive modes of behavior—career motivation, artistic endeavors, and so on.

According to the psychoanalytic view, some people encounter problems during their early development that cause an imbalance in their personality. **Neurotics** are people who are extremely anxious and fear that repressed, unacceptable impulses may break through and control their behavior. **Psychotics** are people

Psychopaths have a disturbed personality structure which makes them act in an anti-social and aggressive fashion. Some may join bizarre groups and engage in violent rituals.

whose primitive id functions actually control their personality. One type of psychosis is *schizophrenia*, a condition marked by incoherent thought processes, a lack of insight, hallucinations, feelings of persecution, and so on.

Psychoanalysts believe that law violators may have suffered damage to their egos or superegos early in their development that renders them powerless to control their impulses and urges. They may suffer delusions and feel persecuted, worthless, and alienated.[58] David Berkowitz, known as the "Son of Sam," John Hinckley, Jr., who attempted to assassinate President Ronald Reagan, and Milwaukee cannibal Jeffrey Dahmer are examples of people suffering from severe character disorders. However, even nonviolent criminals may be motivated by a lack of insight and control caused by personality disorders.[59] As a result, they seek immediate gratification of their needs without considering right and wrong or the needs of others.

While a link between mental instability and criminality seems logical (and a popular topic in horror films), little empirical evidence actually exists that mentally ill people are any more criminal than the mentally sound. Studies focusing on the criminal activity of the mentally ill have failed to establish a clear link between crime and psychiatrically diagnosed problems.[60] Mentally disordered inmates may actually pose less risk to society upon their release than the typical inmate.[61]

Learning to Commit Crime: Behavioral Theory

A second branch of psychological theory views behavior as learned through interactions with others. Simply put, behavior that is rewarded becomes habitual; behavior that is punished becomes extinguished. One branch of behavior theory that is of particular relevance to criminology is called **social learning theory.** According to social learning theorists, people act aggressively because, as children, they modeled their behavior after the violent acts of adults.[62] Later in life, antisocial behavior patterns are reinforced by peers and other acquaintances.[63]

Social learning theorists conclude that the antisocial behavior of potentially violent people can be triggered by a number of different influences: verbal taunts and threats; the experience of direct pain; and perceptions of relative social disability, such as poverty and racial discrimination. Those who have learned violence and have seen it rewarded are more likely to react violently under these stimuli than those who have not.

One area of particular interest to social learning theorists is whether the media can influence violence. Studies have shown that youths exposed to aggressive, antisocial behavior on television and in movies are likely to copy that violent behavior. Laboratory studies generally conclude that violence on television can lead to aggressive behavior by children and teenagers who watch such programs.[64] Whether the evidence obtained in controlled laboratory studies can be applied to the "real world" is still debatable. A number of studies have found little evidence of a link between the number of violent acts shown each week on TV and actual crime rates.[65] Considering that the average child watches more than twenty hours of TV a week, more research is needed on this crucial issue.

Developing Criminal Ideas: Cognitive Theory

Cognitive psychologists are concerned with the way people perceive and mentally represent the world in which they live. Some focus on how people process and store information, viewing the operation of human intellect as similar to the way computers analyze available information; this is referred to as **information processing.** Aggressive people may actually base their behavior on faulty information. They perceive other people to be more aggressive than they actually are; consequently, they are more likely to be vigilant, on edge, or suspicious. When they attack victims, they may believe they are actually defending themselves, even though they are simply misreading the situation.[66] The college student who rapes his date may have a cognitive problem rendering him incapable of distinguishing between behavior cues; he misidentifies rejection as a come-on or "playing hard to get."

Another area of cognitive psychology is referred to as **moral development theory.** According to this approach, people go through a series of stages beginning early in childhood and continuing through their adult years.[67] Each stage is marked by a different view of right and wrong. For example, a child may do what is right simply to avoid punishment and censure. Later in life, the same person will develop a sensitivity to others' needs and do what is right to avoid hurting others. On reaching a higher level of maturity, the same person may behave in accordance with his or her perception of universal principles of justice, equality, and fairness.

According to developmental psychologists, criminals may lack the ability to make moral judgments. Criminals report that their outlooks are characterized by self-interest and impaired moral development; they are unlikely to consider the rights of others, nor are they concerned with maintaining the rules of society.[68]

They Must Be Monsters: The Psychopath

Some psychologists view criminal behavior as a function of a disturbed personality structure. Personality can be defined as the reasonably stable patterns of behavior, including thoughts and emotions, that distinguish one person from another.[69] Individual personality reflects characteristic ways of adapting to life's demands and problems. The way we behave is a function of how our personality enables us to interpret life events and make appropriate behavioral choices.

Psychologists have explored the link between personality and crime. Evidence exists that aggressive youth have unstable personality structures often marked by hyperactivity, impulsiveness, and instability. One area of particular interest to criminology is the identification of the **psychopathic** (sometimes referred to as the **antisocial** or **sociopathic**) personality. Psychopaths are believed to be dangerous, aggressive, antisocial individuals who act in a callous manner. They neither learn from their mistakes nor are deterred by punishments.[70] Although they may appear charming and have at least average intelligence, psychopaths lack emotional depth, are incapable of caring for others, and maintain an abnormally low level of anxiety. They are likely to be persistent alcohol and drug abusers.[71] The concept of the psychopathic personality is important for criminology, because it has been estimated that somewhere between 10 and 30 percent of all prison inmates can be classified as psychopaths or sociopaths or as having similar character disorders.[72] Psychopathy has also been linked to the phenomenon of serial murder.[73]

Though psychologists are still not certain of its cause, a number of factors are believed to contribute to the development of a psychopathic personality. They include having a psychopathic parent, parental rejection and a lack of love during childhood, and inconsistent discipline. The early relationship between mother and child is also quite significant. Children who lack the opportunity to form an attachment to a mother figure in the first three years of life, who suffer sudden separation from the mother figure, or who see changes in the mother figure are most likely to develop psychopathic personalities.[74]

Some psychologists suspect that psychopathy is a function of physical abnormality, especially the activity of the autonomic nervous system (ANS). The ANS mediates the body's activities associated with emotions, such as heartbeat, blood pressure, muscle tension, and respiration. Studies measuring the physical makeup of clinically diagnosed psychopaths indicate that such persons react differently to pain and have lower arousal levels to noise and environmental stimuli than control subjects do. It has been found that clinically defined psychopaths who have had their levels of arousal increased through injections of the hormone adrenaline begin to respond as normal subjects do. It is possible that psychopaths are thrill seekers who engage in high-risk antisocial activities to raise their general neurological arousal level to a more optimal rate.[75] Another view is that the psychopathic personality is imprinted at birth and is relatively unaffected by socialization.[76]

Biological and Psychological Theory and Justice Policy

Biological and psychological explanations of some crimes—specifically irrational, violent, and antisocial criminal acts—have recently received increased attention. Critics have challenged their validity because the research methods used are often inadequate: samples are drawn from inmate populations, which are not representative of the general society; comparisons between experimental and control groups are often inadequate; key concepts such as psychopathy and aggression are inconsistently measured; and the interactive effect of environmental and physical conditions is not adequately controlled.[77]

Some well-publicized attempts have been made to use biological and psychological approaches in the treatment of criminal offenders. For example, a number of prisons and jails have instituted programs to change the diet of inmates to reduce levels of antisocial behavior.[78] In another well-known program, the state of Texas provides plastic surgery for inmates who suffer from physical deformities that are believed to contribute to their antisocial behavior. About 150 prisoners are treated each year to correct physical conditions that may have led them to retaliate against society.[79]

Judges almost always order that offenders who seem to be manifesting personality problems be psychologically evaluated by local social service agencies that may or may not be part of the criminal justice system. The evaluation can come right after arrest or during the trial or sentencing stages. Almost all people sent to prison are evaluated at classification centers in order to assess their personality and determine the psychological treatment that will become a routine part of their correctional rehabilitation.

The fact that criminal justice agencies spend time and money on treating offenders for psychological problems and assessing their diet and other biological needs shows that policymakers seem willing to accept that personal traits can be a contributing cause of criminality. One reason for this acceptance has been the discovery of the "chronic offender." Research indicates that a few hard-core criminals are responsible for a significant amount of all criminal behavior and seem immune to the deterrent effect of punishment. It seems logical that criminal offenders suffering from physical or mental impairment would be well represented within the cohort of chronic offenders. This issue is discussed in more depth in Analyzing Criminal Justice Issues: The Chronic Offender.

The Chronic Offender

One of the most dramatic recent developments in the study of crime and delinquency has been the "discovery" of the **chronic offender.** Researchers increasingly recognize that a relatively few offenders commit a significant percentage of all serious crimes in the community and that such offenders who are juveniles grow up to become chronic adult criminals who contribute significantly to the total adult crime rate.

Chronic offenders can be distinguished from conventional criminals. The latter category contains law violators who may commit and be apprehended for a single instance of criminal behavior, usually of relatively minor seriousness—shoplifting, simple assault, petty larceny, and so on. The chronic offender is one who has serious and persistent brushes with the law, who is building a career in crime, and whose behavior may be excessively violent and destructive.

The concept of the chronic career offender is most closely associated with the research efforts of **Marvin Wolfgang** and his associates at the University of Pennsylvania. In 1972, Wolfgang, Robert Figlio, and Thorsten Sellin published a landmark study, *Delinquency in a Birth Cohort,* that has had a profound influence on the very concept of the criminal offender. Wolfgang, Figlio, and Sellin used official records to follow the criminal careers of a **cohort** of 9,945 boys born in Philadelphia, Pennsylvania, in 1945, until they reached eighteen years of age in 1963.

About two-thirds of the cohort (6,470) never had contact with police authorities, while the remaining 3,475 had at least one contact with the police during their minority; they were responsible for a total of 10,214 arrests.

The cohort data indicated that 54 percent (1,862) of the offenders were **persisters** (repeat offenders) and 46 percent (1,613) were **desisters** (one-time offenders). The persisters could be further divided into **nonchronic recidivists** and **chronic recidivists.** The former consisted of 1,235 youths who had been arrested more than once but less than five times, while the latter was a group of 627 boys arrested *five times or more.* About 18 percent of all arrestees and 6 percent of the total sample of 9,945 were considered chronic offenders (hence, their designation as "the chronic 6 percent").

Chronic offenders were responsible for *5,305 arrests, 51.9 percent of the total.* Even more striking was the involvement of chronic offenders in serious criminal acts. Of the entire sample, they committed 71 percent of the homicides, 73 percent of the rapes, 82 percent of the robberies, and 69 percent of the aggravated assaults. Arrest and punishment did little to deter the chronic offender. In fact, punishment was inversely related to chronicity—the stricter the sanctions they received, the more likely they were to engage in repeated criminal behavior.

Wolfgang and his associates later followed a 10 percent sample of the original cohort (974 subjects) through their adulthood to age thirty. They found that those classified as chronic juvenile offenders in the original birth cohort had an 80 percent chance of becoming adult offenders and a 50 percent chance of being arrested four or more times as adults. The former chronic delinquents were involved in 74 percent of all arrests and 82 percent of all serious crimes, such as homicide, rape, and robbery.

Wolfgang and his colleagues conducted a second birth cohort study, this time with a group of 27,160 boys and girls born in Philadelphia in 1958, and again found the presence of a chronic offender. Subsequent cohort studies by Lyle Shannon, Donna Hamparian, D. J. West, and David Farrington have substantiated the Wolfgang findings.

The Cause of Chronic Offending

The existence of a chronic offender presents a dilemma for those who believe that the criminal offender can be successfully treated with some combination of educational, vocational, and psychological counseling and support. If in fact only a small group of offenders are responsible for almost all serious crimes, it follows that there must be some personal characteristic that sets chronic offenders apart from *both* noncriminals and nonchronic offenders. Environmental and socialization factors alone cannot explain why one young offender desists from crime, while another, living in the same area and experiencing similar environmental conditions, becomes a chronic offender who escalates the frequency and seriousness of his or her criminal activity.

A number of criminologists have suggested that chronic offending is caused by some individual trait, genetic condition, or physical characteristic. These preconditions may exist before birth or, as suggested by Elizabeth Kandel and Sarnoff Mednick, may be a function of birth complications, factors that for all practical purposes are uncontrollable. Some preliminary research efforts indicate that such factors as limited intelligence (as measured by IQ tests) and impulsive personality predict chronic offending. Terrie Moffitt and his associates found that chronic offenders manifested an abnormal amount of *minor physical anomalies,* observable physical malformations that result from disturbance in fetal development. However, the association of physical traits and chronic offending is very preliminary and needs further research and analysis.

Controlling Chronic Offenders

The chronic offender has become a central focus of criminal justice system policy at all levels. At the front end of the system, law enforcement agencies have developed regional task forces in which various agencies cooperate in identifying, tracking, and arresting career offenders. This task has been aided by local and state prosecutors who devote resources to the adjudication of persistent offenders.

Even more important has been the effect of the chronic offender on sentencing policy. Around the country, legal jurisdictions have developed sentencing policies designed to incapacitate repeat violent offenders for long periods of time. Among the programs spurred by the chronic offender concept is the use of mandatory prison sentences for repeat violent offenders. Keeping chronic criminals out of circulation seems to be the best approach to crime control. This strategy, referred to as **selective incapacitation,** requires that prison sentences escalate for multiple offenders and for those whose personal background characteristics indicate they are a real risk to continue a "life of crime."

To some experts, punishing people because they are believed to be chronic offenders is wrong because it is based on predicting what people will do in the future, not on what their current crime involves. It has also resulted in expanding the scope of the criminal justice system; the prison system now holds more than eight hundred thousand people.

Despite such reservations, as long as the violence rate remains high and fear of crime pervades the U.S. psyche, the justice system likely will continue to focus on the problem of chronic offenders and devote increasing resources to control their activities.

Critical Thinking Skills

1. The record number of inmates currently in prison and jail reflects the justice system's efforts to curb career offenders and the "lock 'em up and throw away the key" philosophy. This solution is troubling to civil libertarians since it involves possible errors in the prediction of a person's future behavior. Might not some people be unfairly punished because their background characteristics mistakenly indicate they are chronic offenders? Conversely, might not some serious offenders be overlooked because they have a more conventional background? No prediction method is totally accurate, and error can involve a significant infringement on a person's civil rights. Should people be punished because their past deeds indicate a risk of future criminality? Or should criminal punishment be based on the current criminal act?

SOURCES: Elizabeth Kandel and Sarnoff Mednick, "Perinatal Complications Predict Violent Offending," *Criminology* 29 (1991): 519–29; Marvin Wolfgang, Robert Figlio, and Thorsten Sellin, *Delinquency in a Birth Cohort* (Chicago: University of Chicago Press, 1972); Marvin Wolfgang, "Delinquency in Two Birth Cohorts," in *Perspective Studies of Crime and Delinquency,* ed. Katherine Teilmann Van Dusen and Sarnoff Mednick (Boston: Kluwer-Nijhoff, 1983), pp. 7–17; Lyle Shannon, *Changing Patterns of Delinquency and Crime* (Boulder, Colo.: Westview Press, 1991); D. J. West and David P. Farrington, *The Delinquent Way of Life* (London: Hienemann, 1977); Terrie Moffitt, Sarnoff Mednick and William Gabrielli, "Predicting Careers of Criminal Violence: Descriptive Data and Predispositional Factors," in *Current Approaches to the Prediction of Violence,* ed. D. A. Brizer and M. Crowner (Washington, D.C.: American Psychiatric Press, 1989), pp. 125–37; Donna Hamparian, Richard Schuster, Simon Dinitz, and John Conrad, *The Violent Few* (Lexington, Mass.: Lexington Books, 1978); Franklyn Dunford and Delbert Elliott, "Identifying Career Offenders Using Self-Reported Data," *Journal of Research in Crime and Delinquency* 21 (1984):57–86.

Is Crime a Social Phenomenon?

Sociological Theories

It seems plausible that an individual act of violence is motivated by some mental or physical abnormality; mass murderers and serial rapists are usually described as "demented" or "psychotic." It is, however, unlikely that crime patterns and trends can be explained by biological or psychological factors alone. Official, self-report, and victim data all indicate social patterns in the crime rate. Some regions are more crime-prone than others. There are distinct differences between the crime rate across states, cities, and neighborhoods. Crime rates, however, are probably not higher in New York than West Virginia because New Yorkers are more likely to suffer personality defects or eat more sugar. There is also an economic bias in the crime rate: prisons are filled with the poor and hopeless, not the rich and famous. Because crime patterns have a decidedly social orientation, sociological explanations of crime have predominated in criminology.

Sociological criminology is usually traced to the pioneering work of sociologist Emile Durkheim (1858–1917). Durkheim viewed crime as a social phenomenon.[80] In his formulation of the *theory of anomie* and his analysis of the division of labor, Durkheim concluded that crime is an essential part of society and a function of its internal conflict. As he used the term, **anomie** means the absence or weakness of rules and social norms in any person or group; the lack of these rules or norms may lead an individual to lose the ability to distinguish between right and wrong.

As the field of sociological criminology emerged in the twentieth century, greater emphasis was placed on environmental conditions, while the relationship between crime and physical and/or mental traits was neglected. Equating the cause of criminal behavior with social factors, such as poverty and unemployment, was instrumental for the development of treatment-oriented crime prevention techniques. If criminals are in fact made and not born—if they are forged in the crucible of societal action—then it logically follows that crime can be eradicated by the elimination of the social elements responsible for crime. The focus of crime prevention shifted from punishing criminals to treatment and rehabilitation.

We now turn to some of the most important criminological theories that have a sociological base.

Because They're Poor: Social Structure Theory

According to the social structure theory, the United States is a **stratified society.** Social strata are created by the unequal distribution of wealth, power, and prestige. Social classes are segments of the population whose members have relatively similar attitudes, values, and norms, and an identifiable life-style. In U.S. society, people can be identified as belonging to the upper, middle, or lower class, with a broad range of economic variation in each group.

The contrast between the life-styles of the wealthiest members of the upper class and the poorest segment of the lower class is striking. While the wealthiest 3 percent of U.S. families holds more than 28 percent of the nation's wealth, the poorest 20 percent have only 5 percent.[81] The gap between the richest and the poorest Americans seems to be growing wider; the number of families living in poverty doubled in the past decade. About 20 million high school dropouts face dead-end jobs, unemployment, and social failure. Because of their meager economic resources, lower-class citizens are often forced to live in slum areas marked

The crushing burden of urban poverty results in the development of a culture of poverty, marked by cynicism, helplessness, and distrust.

by substandard housing, inadequate health care, poor educational opportunities, underemployment, and despair. Many families are fatherless and husbandless, headed by a female who is the sole breadwinner and who is often forced to go on welfare.

The problems of lower-class culture are particularly acute for racial and ethnic minorities. African-Americans have an income level significantly lower than that of whites and an unemployment rate almost twice as high. They now face the deterioration of the manufacturing economy in the urban United States. Hundreds of thousands of jobs have been lost, further weakening the economic future of young black men and women. On top of this, research indicates an increase in negative racial stereotyping among potential employers.[82]

Young black males and females also suffer crime victimization rates that are far higher than those of whites. African-American men and women have a significantly greater chance of becoming a murder victim than white men and women, and this risk continues throughout their lifespan.

Poverty and Crime

The crushing burden of urban poverty results in the development of a **culture of poverty.**[83] This subculture is marked by apathy, cynicism, helplessness, and distrust. The culture is passed from one generation to another so that slum dwellers become part of a permanent underclass, "the truly disadvantaged."[84]

Considering the social disability suffered by lower-class slum dwellers, it is not surprising that they turn to crime as a means of support and survival. According to the social structure approach, a significant majority of people who commit violent crimes and serious theft offenses live in the lower-class culture, and a majority of all serious crimes occur in inner-city areas. The social forces operating in lower-class, inner-city areas produce high crime rates. What are these forces and how do they produce crime?

The Disorganized Neighborhood

Pioneering research on the ecology of the city by University of Chicago sociologists Clifford R. Shaw and Henry D. McKay found that the **disorganized neighborhood** in the inner city was a breeding ground of juvenile gangs and adult criminality.[85] Crime is a product of neighborhoods that are both deteriorating physically and maintaining conflicting values and social systems. Disorganized neighborhoods are undergoing the disintegration of their existing culture and services, the diffusion of cultural standards, and successive changes from purely residential to a mixture of commercial, industrial, transient, and residential populations. In these areas, the major sources of informal social control—family, school, neighborhood, civil service—are broken and ineffective.

The patterns found by Shaw and McKay are still relevant today. Urban slum areas are believed to be crime-prone because their most important social institutions cannot function properly. These neighborhoods are unable to realize the common values of their residents or solve commonly experienced problems.[86] Disorganized neighborhoods experience high population density, large numbers of single-parent households, unrelated people living together, and a lack of employment opportunities.[87] Their residents perceive significant levels of fear, alienation, and social dissatisfaction. These high-crime areas typically have rapid population turnover and lack the ability to socially integrate their residents.[88] Constant population turnover makes it difficult for these communities to understand or assimilate their newest members; hence, they acquire the reputation of being a "changing neighborhood."

The social, economic, and physical conditions that develop in disorganized neighborhoods have been associated with escalating crime rates. Areas that experience a high rate of housing abandonment, neighborhood decline, increased population density, and urban growth have also been found to have increasing crime rates.[89] All too often, these areas are racially segregated, illustrating the "subtle and pervasive racism that continues to divide the U.S. population into two separate and unequal societies."[90] The fact that a significant portion of African-Americans are forced to live in these conditions can help explain the distinct racial patterns in the official crime rate.

Developing Deviant Values

Living in deteriorated inner-city neighborhoods, forced to endure substandard housing and schools, and cut off from conventional society, lower-class slum dwellers are faced with a constant assault on their self-image and sense of worth. While the media bombards them with images glorifying a materialistic life-style, they cannot purchase fine clothes, a luxury automobile, or their own home. How, then, can they adjust to the reality of being shut out from the social and economic mainstream while being forced to live in a disorganized neighborhood?

One method of adjusting is to create an independent value system. While middle-class values favor education, hard work, sexual abstinence, honesty, and sobriety, lower-class values in slum areas applaud goals that are realistically obtainable in a disorganized society: being cool, promiscuous, intemperant, and fearless. Lower-class values extol scorning authority, living for today, seeking excitement, and scoffing at formal education. In a famous paper, sociologist Walter Miller identified the unique **focal concerns** present in lower-class areas: a need for excitement, street smarts, fate, independence, toughness, and trouble. Ghetto youth cherish these focal concerns and abhor middle-class values and behavior.[91]

These lower-class values are incorporated into an active code of behavior: the desire for excitement results in children born out of wedlock to teenage parents; toughness develops into violent gang membership; admiration of street smarts leads to a high drop out rate; trouble ends up in drug abuse and rebellion. Deviant values pit lower-class kids against teachers, police officers, welfare workers, merchants, and employers.

Deviant values are entrenched in the urban slum. They are both admired and passed down from one generation to the next in a process referred to as **cultural transmission.** Each generation of slum dwellers then provides a ready supply of recruits for the teenage gangs and groups that rule the streets.

In sum, the burden of poverty and urban decay in lower-class areas is thought to produce a unique set of values that conflict with conventional rules and laws. Obedience to these deviant values forces slum youths to disobey the rules of conventional society. The result is high rates of drug abuse, violence, and criminality.

Deviant Subcultures

The ultimate outcome of social disorganization and cultural deviance is the development of an independent lower-class **subculture.** Subcultures are small reference groups that provide members with a unique set of values, beliefs, and traditions distinct from conventional society. Within the subculture, lower-class youth can achieve success unobtainable within the larger culture, while gaining a sense of identity and achievement.

One type of lower-class subculture involves its members in behavior that is marginally deviant. Members of the **corner boy** subculture are truants who gather in neighborhood hangouts to gamble or commit petty crimes. The corner boy eventually ages out of crime and ekes out a marginal existence in the neighborhood.

Members of the **criminal subculture** adopt a set of norms and principles in direct opposition to middle-class society. They engage in **short-run hedonism,** living for today by taking drugs, drinking, and engaging in unsafe sex. Members of the criminal subculture resist efforts by family members and other authority figures to control their behavior and instead join autonomous peer groups and gangs.[92]

Lower-class youth who are unable to learn criminal skills from older, more experienced offenders form a **subculture of violence** whose members engage in senseless and destructive antisocial acts. Still others may become self-destructive dropouts and substance abusers and partake in the **retreatist subculture.**[93] All or some of these deviant subcultures may co-exist in lower-class areas.

Strain

Another by-product of life in lower-class slum areas is the frustration and anger people experience because they lack the ability to achieve legitimate social and financial success. This is referred to as **strain.** In lower-class slum areas, strain or *status frustration* occurs because legitimate avenues for success are all but closed. With no acceptable means for obtaining success openly, people may either use deviant methods for obtaining their goals, such as theft or violence, or reject socially acceptable goals and seek others that are more easily satisfied, such as being a gang leader. When people cannot hope to fulfill their ambitions and dreams because they come from a poor background, they then turn to crime and violence.

The concept of strain can be traced to the pioneering work of famed sociologist Robert Merton. Merton recognized that members of the lower-class undergo anomie, or normlessness, when the means they have for achieving culturally defined goals are insufficient.[94] As a result of anomie, people will begin to seek alternative solutions to their problems. While middle-class college students hope to achieve success by attending school, getting a good job, and saving their wages, lower-class slum youth, lacking the same educational and vocational opportunities, will steal, sell drugs, or extort money. Merton referred to this method of adaptation as *innovation*—using innovative but illegal behaviors to achieve success when legitimate means are closed off. Other youth, faced with the same dilemma, might reject conventional goals and choose to live as drug users, alcoholics, and wanderers; Merton referred to this as retreatism. Still others might join revolutionary political groups and work to change the system to one of their liking; this, according to Merton, is rebellion. In either event, strain leads to criminality because those who do not feel part of society break the law to either join it, change it, or retreat from the psychic pain caused by its rejection.

Relative Deprivation

One recent variation of the strain concept is called *relative deprivation*. According to relative deprivation, the burdens of economic hardship might go unnoticed if all people shared an equivalent economic status. After all, crime rates are lower in countries that are far less affluent than the United States. Economic status only becomes a central concern when people compare themselves with others. When haves and have-nots live in close proximity to one another, comparative economic disadvantage produces first a sense of social injustice and then anger and frustration.[95] Income inequality is magnified when professional families move into lower-class areas and renovate existing property, a process referred to as **gentrification.**[96] It is no wonder that making a few thousand dollars a week selling crack seems more attractive to slum kids than earning $3.50 an hour at the local fast-food restaurant.[97]

Gang Culture

An important part of social structure theories is the development of youth gangs and groups in disorganized ghettos. The gang gives the disadvantaged youth an opportunity to relieve strain and obtain money and respect. It provides a substitute for conventional opportunities and institutions.

Gangs are most active today in the nation's largest cities, especially Philadelphia, New York, Detroit, Los Angeles, and Chicago.[98] Authorities in California claim that there are six hundred gangs in operation containing approximately seventy thousand members in Los Angeles County alone. Many of the Los Angeles gangs are loosely incorporated into two huge gangs, the Bloods and the Crips, which control a significant portion of the drug trade. In Chicago, police estimates indicate 135 gangs with over 14,000 members. Even smaller cities, such as Cleveland and Columbus, Ohio; San Diego, California; and Milwaukee, Wisconsin, which had not experienced serious gang problems, have seen the emergence or importation of gangs.[99]

Social Structure and Social Policy

Social structure theory has had a prominent role in criminology and an important influence on criminal justice policy-making for most of the twentieth century. The belief that the lower-class slum is the breeding ground of serious crime has prompted the development of community action programs designed to give members of the lower-class opportunities to succeed legitimately. The Chicago Area Project developed by Clifford Shaw was the forerunner of numerous attempts to marshal the resources of the community to improve the lives of its citizens. More recent efforts include the Job Corps, Head Start, and various community action projects around the country.

Of course, efforts to reduce crime rates by revitalizing the community are extremely difficult because the problems of decayed, transitional neighborhoods are so overwhelming that any individual effort is dwarfed by the social problems ingrained in these areas. In addition, government budget deficits in the 1990s have severely curtailed the funds available for serious community development projects. Consequently, crime-control efforts have shifted from the community level to focusing on the individual offender.

Socialized to Crime: Social Process Theories

Not all criminologists agree that the root cause of crime can be found solely within the culture of poverty.[100] After all, self-report studies indicate that many middle- and upper-class youths take drugs and commit serious criminal acts. As adults, they commit white-collar and corporate crimes. Conversely, the majority of people living in the worst slum areas hold conventional values and forgo criminal activity. These patterns indicate that forces must be operating in all strata of society that influence individual involvement in criminal activity.

If crime is spread throughout the social structure, then it follows that the factors that cause crime should be found within all social and economic groups. People commit crime as a result of the experiences they have while they are being **socialized** by the various organizations, institutions, and processes of society. People are most strongly influenced toward criminal behavior by poor family relationships, destructive peer-group relations, educational failure, and labeling by agents of the justice system. Although lower-class citizens have the added burdens of poverty, strain, and blocked opportunities, even middle-class or upper-class citizens may turn to crime if their socialization is poor or destructive.

Social process theorists point to research efforts linking family problems to crime as evidence that socialization, not social structure, is the key to understanding the onset of criminality. The quality of family life is considered to be a significant determining factor in adolescent development.[101] Among the most important research efforts are those that show that inconsistent discipline, poor supervision and discipline, and a lack of warm parent-child relationships are closely related to a child's deviant behavior.[102] Positive parental relationships can insulate children from criminogenic influences in the environment.[103] It has also been suggested that child abuse is related both to delinquency and to the perpetuation of abusive behavior. In other words, abused children grow up to become child abusers themselves.[104]

Educational experience has also been found to have a significant impact on behavioral choices. Schools contribute to fostering criminality when they set problem youths apart by creating a track system that labels some as college-bound and others as academic underachievers. Studies show that chronic delinquents do poorly in school, lack educational motivation, and are frequently held back.[105] Research indicates that high school dropouts are more likely to become involved in crime than those who complete their education.[106]

In a similar vein, studies of prison inmates show that their relationships with the institutions of society are less than adequate. Most inmates grew up in a single-parent household, had relatives who served time in prison, were single or divorced with dependent children, had a dropout rate three times the national average, and were educational underachievers.[107]

In sum, significant evidence exists that the direction and quality of interpersonal interactions and relationships throughout the lifespan influence behavior. However, there is disagreement over the direction this influence takes. Some crime experts maintain that all people are "born innocent" but some are exposed to and learn criminal techniques and attitudes from peers and family members. Another view is that all people have the potential to engage in antisocial behavior, but most are controlled by the bonds they form with society. Still another view is that crime is a by-product of social *stigma* and the formation of a deviant identity. Each of these three branches of social process theory are described below.

Students of Crime: Learning Theories

Most of us can remember a time in our youth when a parent or some other adult warned us to stay away from one of our peers because he or she was a bad influence. Our wise elders feared that we would pick up bad habits from associating with "tough characters." Presumably, they were afraid that we would learn rough language and how to smoke, drink, and steal and, while we were at it, all about sex.

This common-sense approach to the cause of crime has not been lost on criminologists. Those who advocate **learning theories** hold that people enter into a life of crime when, as adolescents, they are taught the attitudes, values, and behaviors that support a criminal career. They may learn the techniques of crime from a variety of intimates, including parents and family members. Learning theorists believe that gang members and drug users have close and intimate relationships with other law-violating youth.[108]

The most well-known example of the learning perspective is Edwin Sutherland's **differential association theory.**[109] Sutherland, considered by many to be the preeminent American criminologist, believed that the attitudes and behaviors that cause crime are learned in close and intimate relationships with significant others. People learn to commit crime in the same fashion they learn any other behavior. For example, kids learn to ride a bike by observing more experienced riders, practicing riding techniques, and hearing how much fun it is to ride. In the same fashion, adolescents learn from more experienced drug users how to buy drugs, how to use them properly, and how to behave when they are high. Adolescents who are exposed to an excess of attitudes ("definitions") in support of deviant behavior will eventually view those behaviors as attractive, appropriate, and suitable. Because of the importance of the differential association view, its major premises are defined in Table 3.1.

Sutherland's theory has greatly influenced U.S. criminology. His learning theory can account for the disproportionate amount of crime in lower-class areas yet can also explain middle- and upper-class crime. After all, even middle-class kids can be exposed to a variety of pro-crime definitions from deviant, drug-abusing parents and friends.

TABLE 3.1
Principles of Differential Association Theory

1. Criminal behavior is learned. In this respect, crime is similar to all other forms of social behavior. Crime is neither inherited, nor is it invented by unsophisticated persons.
2. Criminal behavior is learned as a result of the communication that occurs in social interaction, and this communication is most effective in primary groups that are characterized by intimacy, consensus, and shared understandings. Impersonal communications, in general, are less effective.
3. When criminal behavior is learned, the learning includes both the techniques that are necessary to commit the crime and the motives, rationalizations, and social definitions that enable an individual to utilize criminal skills. In some situations (societies, neighborhoods, families, groups, and so on), an individual is surrounded by people who almost invariably define the laws as rules to be observed, while in other situations, the individual encounters many persons whose definitions are favorable to law violations. Although the relative numbers of people who endorse criminal and noncriminal definitions may vary in time, place, and other circumstances, it seems almost inevitable that there will be some conflict over the efficacy and the morality of legal codes, especially in pluralistic societies.
4. More specifically, criminal behavior is learned when the definitions favoring law violations an individual encounters exceed those that support conformity. This is the basic principle of differential association. It refers to the counteracting influences of both criminal and noncriminal contacts, and it maintains that the probability of criminal behavior varies directly with the number of criminal definitions. Hence, the generic formula for criminal behavior may be written as follows:

$$\text{Probability of crime} = \frac{\text{Definitions favorable to violations}}{\text{Definitions opposed to violations}}$$

5. Differential association with criminal and noncriminal behavior patterns may vary in frequency, duration, priority, and intensity. Frequency refers to the number of contacts during a given interval of time. Duration indicates the length of time during which a pattern of contacts is maintained. Priority designates an individual's age at the time of establishing contact with distinctive behavior patterns or developing certain modes of response. Intensity is not precisely defined but deals with such things as the prestige of the carriers of social norms or the affective attachments that may be generated among individuals involved in certain contact patterns.

Other Learning Theories

The learning theory model has a number of variations. Ronald Akers reformulated differential association theory using concepts developed by behavioral psychologists, such as B. F. Skinner. His **differential reinforcement theory** holds that deviant behavior is a function of conditioning and that positive reinforcements (rewards) will encourage behaviors while negative reinforcements (punishments) will help extinguish them.[110] Criminal behavior is initiated and persists when it is rewarded and is extinguished or avoided when it is punished. According to Akers, people learn to evaluate their own behavior through interaction with significant others and groups in their lives. The more individuals learn to define their behavior, even deviant acts, as good or at least as justified, rather than as undesirable, the more likely they are to choose deviance and crime.

Sociologist David Matza and his associate Gresham Sykes argue that youths become involved in criminality when they *learn* to throw off the moral constraints of society.[111] To do this, they must adopt as a personal code a series of justifications for crime that allows them to **drift** between illegal and conventional behavior. The most widely used **techniques of neutralization** include blaming the victim ("they had it coming"), denying responsibility ("they made me do it"),

FIGURE 3.2
Techniques of Neutralization

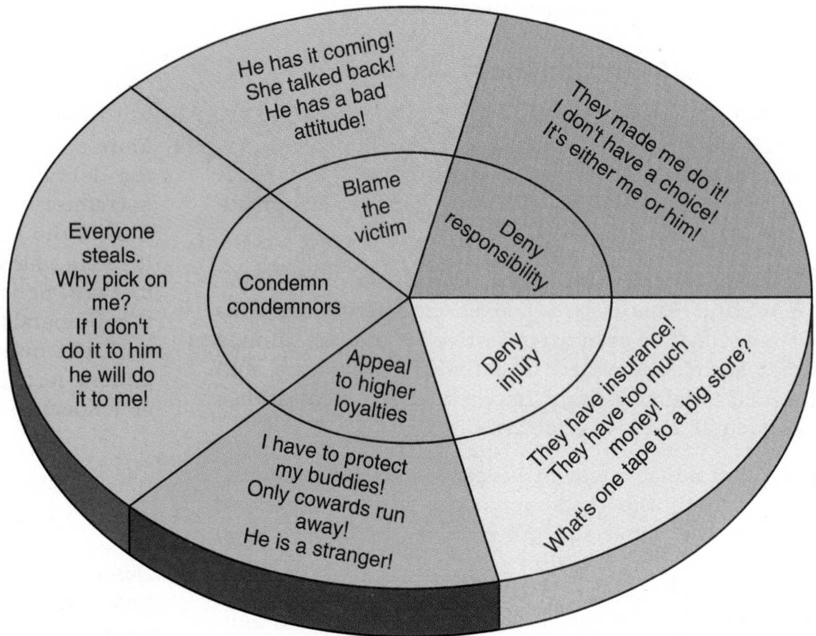

denying injury ("they have insurance") condemning the condemnors ("why pick on me, cops and judges take bribes"), and appealing to higher loyalties ("I had to protect my buddies") (see Figure 3.2). Sykes and Matza suggest that by learning these justifications, youths can free themselves from the constraints of social norms and participate in criminal behavior. Later, as adults, neutralizations allow them to evade taxes, take drugs, and drink and drive: after all, everyone is doing it, and it does not really hurt anyone.

While neutralization theory seems to have merit, it is difficult to determine whether criminals neutralize moral constraints *before* they engage in crime or simply rationalize their behavior *after* they have violated the law. That is, it is still uncertain whether neutralizations are a *cause* or an *effect* of criminality.[112]

They're Out of Control: Control Theories

When we were in high school, most of us knew a few kids who seemed detached and alienated from almost everything and everyone. They did not care about school, they had poor relationships at home, and, though they may have belonged to a tough crowd, their relationships with their peers were superficial and often violent. Very often these same kids got into trouble at school, had run-ins with the police, and were involved in drugs and antisocial behaviors.

These observations form the nucleus of **control theory.** This approach to understanding crime holds that all people may have the inclination to violate the law but most are held in check by their relationships to conventional institutions and individuals, such as the family, school, and their peer group. For some people, when these relationships are strained or broken, they are then freed to engage in deviant acts that otherwise would be avoided. Crime occurs when the influence of official and informal sources of social control is weakened or absent.

The most influential advocate of control theory is sociologist Travis Hirschi. Hirschi suggests that people have bonds to society that are formed from a number of different elements:

1. Attachment—caring for and valuing relationships with others, including parents, friends, teachers, and so on. A person with a strong sense of attachment will seek out the advice of teachers, associate with friends, and maintain strong ties with family members; these activities are believed to shield a person from criminal temptations.
2. Commitment—time, energy, and effort expended in the pursuit of conventional lines of action. Commitments may embrace such activities as spending time in school or working to save money for the future. The more commitment one has, the less risk one has of engaging in criminal activity.
3. Involvement—participation in conventional activities, such as school, recreation, church, family, or hobbies. The youth who is always active will not have time for delinquent acts.
4. Belief—adhering to commonly held moral values, such as sharing, sensitivity to others, obeying the law, and refraining from hurting others.

According to Hirschi, people whose bond to society is secure are unlikely to engage in criminal misconduct because they have a strong stake in society (see Figure 3.3). Those who find their social bond weakened are much more likely to succumb to the temptations of criminal activity. After all, crime does have rewards, such as excitement, action, material goods, and pleasures. While Hirschi does not give a definitive reason for what causes a person's social bond to weaken, the process likely has two main sources: disrupted home life and poor school ability (leading to subsequent school failure and dislike of school).

Control theory as articulated by Hirschi has become one of the preeminent social theories of crime. Ongoing research efforts have attempted to adapt its assumptions to different crime patterns and to determine whether control variables explain criminality among different groups and cultures.[113] While some variations exist, the findings tend to support Hirschi's control hypothesis.[114]

Self-Control Theory

In an important new work, *A General Theory of Crime*, Travis Hirschi, writing with Michael Gottfredson, has redefined his original version of social control theory.[115]

In this work, Gottfredson and Hirschi integrate the concept of social control with rational choice. They find that the concepts of "crime" and "criminal" are independent from one another. Crimes, such as car theft, are illegal deeds that people engage in when they perceive such acts to be advantageous. For example, burglaries are typically committed by young males looking for cash, liquor, and entertainment equipment; the crime provides easy, short-term gratification.

In contrast, criminals are people who maintain a status that maximizes the possibility that they will engage in crimes. People with criminal tendencies do not constantly commit crimes; their days are filled with noncriminal behaviors, such as going to school, parties, concerts, and church. But given the *opportunity*, people with criminal tendencies will have a much higher probability of committing crimes than noncriminals.

What, then, causes people to become excessively crime-prone? For Gottfredson and Hirschi, the explanation for individual differences in the tendency to commit criminal acts can be found in a person's level of **self-control.** People with limited self-control tend to be impulsive, insensitive, physical (rather than mental), risk-taking, short-sighted, and nonverbal. They have a "here and now" orientation and refuse to work for distant goals; they lack diligence, tenacity, and

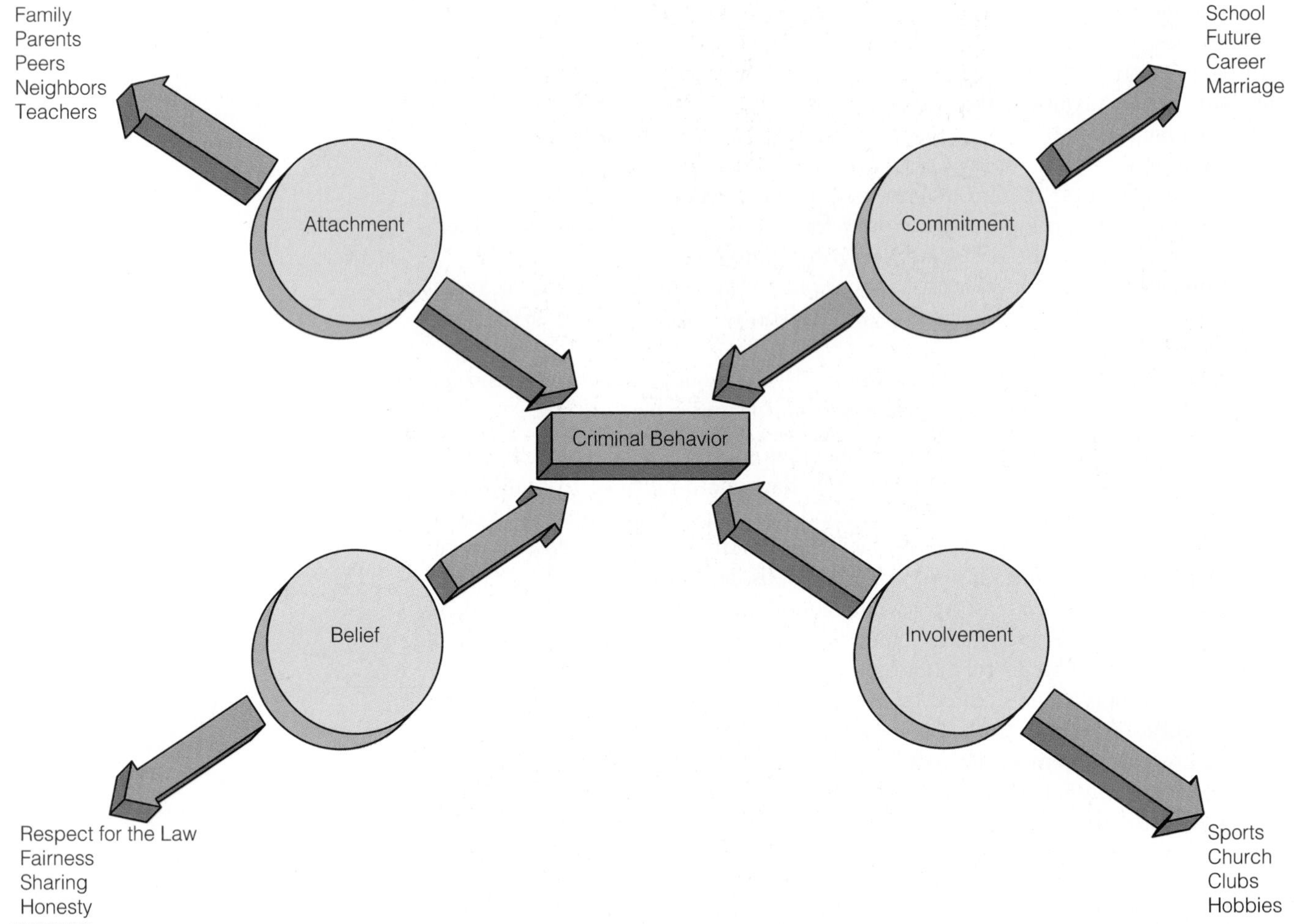

FIGURE 3.3
Elements of The Social Bond

persistence in a course of action. People lacking self-control tend to be adventuresome, active, physical, and self-centered. As they mature, they have unstable marriages, jobs, and friendships. Criminal acts are attractive to them because they provide easy and immediate gratification, or as Gottfredson and Hirschi put it, "money without work, sex without courtship, revenge without court delays."

Why do people lack self-control? The root cause of poor self-control can be traced to inadequate child-rearing practices. Parents who refuse or are unable to monitor a child's behavior, recognize deviant behavior when it occurs, and punish that behavior will produce children who lack self-control. Kids who are not attached to their parents, who are poorly supervised, and whose parents are criminal or deviant themselves are the most likely to develop poor self-control.

Gottfredson and Hirschi's general theory provides answers to many of the questions left unanswered by the original control model. By separating the concepts of criminality and crime, Gottfredson and Hirschi help explain why some people lacking in self-control remain virtuous: they lack criminal opportunity. In contrast, given the proper incentive, people who have a strong bond to social institutions may on occasion engage in law-violating behavior. The "good kid" who has a strong school record and positive parental relationships gets involved in drugs to impress his friends; the corporate executive with a spotless record gets caught up in business fraud because she expects to make millions in profits.

Gottfredson and Hirschi's self-control view is an important concept that requires further empirical testing and verification.

The Outsider: Labeling Theory

The **labeling** approach views society as creating criminals when social control agencies define people as "troublemakers" and stigmatize them with a permanent deviant label.

According to the labeling approach, people who commit undetected antisocial acts are called "secret deviants" or "primary deviants." Their illegal act has little influence or impact on their life-style or behavior. However, if another person commits the same act and his or her behavior is discovered by social control agents, the labeling process may be initiated. That person may be given a deviant label, such as "mentally ill" or "criminal." The deviant label transforms him or her into an **outsider,** shunned by the rest of society.

In time, the stigmatized person may believe that the deviant label is valid and assume it as a personal identity. For example, the student put in special education classes begins to view herself as "stupid" or "backward," the mental patient accepts society's view of him as "crazy," and the convicted criminal considers himself as "dangerous" or "wicked."

Accompanying the deviant label are a variety of degrading social and physical restraints—handcuffs, trials, incarceration, bars, cells, and a criminal record—which leave an everlasting impression on the accused. These sanctions are designed to humiliate and are applied in what labeling experts call **degradation ceremonies** in which the target is made to feel unworthy and despised.

Labels and sanctions work to define the whole person, meaning that a label evokes stereotypes that are used to forecast other aspects of the labeled person's character. A person labeled "mentally ill" is assumed to be dangerous, evil, cruel, or untrustworthy, even though he or she has exhibited none of these characteristics.

Faced with such condemnation, negatively labeled people may begin to adopt their new degraded identity. They may find no alternative but to seek others who are similarly stigmatized and form a deviant subculture. Supported by a deviant peer group that sports similar labels, they enter into a deviant or criminal career. Rather than deterring crime, labeling begins a **deviance amplification** process.

If apprehended and subjected to even more severe negative labels, the offender may be transformed into a "real" deviant—one whose view of self is in direct opposition to conventional society. The deviant label may become a more comfortable and personally acceptable social status than any other. The individual whose original crime may have been a relatively harmless act is transformed by social action into a career deviant, a process referred to as **secondary deviance.** The entire labeling process is illustrated in Figure 3.4.

Despite its widespread initial acceptance, labeling theory has received quite a bit of scholarly criticism. It has been attacked on the grounds that criminals are viewed as passive actors in crime, which is actually controlled by agents of the justice system.[116] However, there are indications that negative labels may impact heavily on some youth, helping them become chronic offenders; it is logical that repeat arrest, conviction, and punishment simply drive the point home that "you're bad, everyone knows it, so why even try to change?"[117]

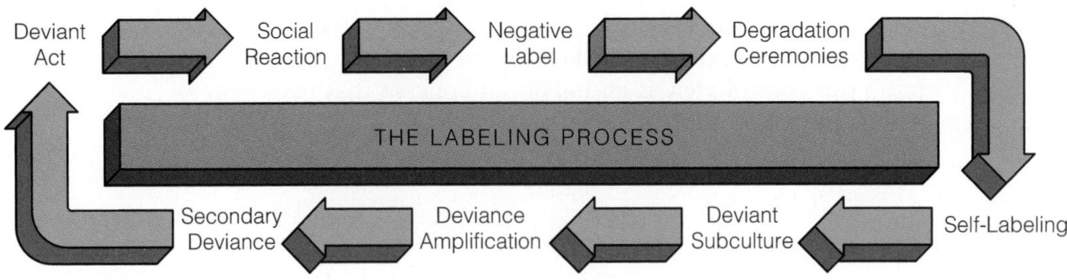

FIGURE 3.4
The Labeling Process

Policy Implications of Social Process Theory

Social process theories have significantly influenced criminal justice policy-making. For example, programs have been designed to present alternative values and life-styles to youths who have bought into a delinquent way of life. These programs often use group process and counseling to attack the criminal-behavior orientations of their clients and help them learn conventional values and beliefs.

Control theories have been the foundation of numerous community-based programs designed to strengthen a young person's bond to society. These involve family development and counseling programs and school-based prevention programs. In addition, various state youth and adult correctional authorities maintain inmate treatment programs that stress career development, work and educational furloughs, and self-help groups, all designed to help reestablish social bonds.

Labeling theory principles have been used to design programs that limit an offender's interface with the criminal justice system. The idea behind these programs is that any sort of official contact can only help promote the stigma that locks a young offender into a life of crime. Among the most prominent policy efforts based on the labeling approach are efforts to divert first offenders away from the normal justice process and into treatment programs, to order offenders to pay victim restitution, rather than enter into the justice process, and to deinstitutionalize noncriminal youth in the juvenile justice system (that is, remove runaways, truants, and incorrigible youth from secure lockups that also contain criminal youth).

Conflict Theory

Conflict theory views the economic and political forces operating in society as the fundamental causes of criminality. The criminal law and criminal justice system are viewed as vehicles for controlling the poor members of society. The criminal justice system is believed to help the powerful and rich impose their particular morality and standards of good behavior on the entire society, while it protects their property and physical safety from the have-nots, even though the cost may be the legal rights of the lower class. Those in power control the content and direction of the law and legal system. Crimes are defined in a way that meets with the needs of the ruling classes. The theft of property worth five dollars by a poor person can be punished much more severely than the misappropriation of millions by a large corporation. Those in the middle class are drawn into this pattern of control because they are led to believe they, too, have a stake in maintaining the status quo and should support the views of the upper-class owners of production.[118]

Conflict theory has a number of subdivisions. One approach—known as conflict criminology—views crime as a product of the class conflict that can exist in any society.[119] The second subbranch—called critical, radical, or Marxist criminology—focuses on the crime-producing forces contained within the capitalist system. Both branches agree that the law and justice systems are mechanisms with which those in power control the have-not members of society.

Conflict theorists devote their research efforts to exposing discrimination and class bias in the application of laws and justice. They trace the history of criminal sanctions to show how those sanctions have corresponded to the needs of the wealthy. They attempt to show how police, courts, and correctional agencies have served as tools of the powerful members of society. They work for praxis—the bringing about through writings, discussion, or social action a transformation of the current arrangements and relationships in society.

Critical criminology is now undergoing significant evolution, and a number of new perspectives have been suggested. **Left realists** are attempting to reconcile critical views with the social realities of crime and its impact on the lower class. Left realists recognize that predatory crimes are not "revolutionary" acts and that crime is an overwhelming problem for the poor. Regardless of its origins, according to left realists, crime must be dealt with by the police and courts.[120] **Radical feminists** have tried to explain how capitalism places particular stress on women and to explicate the role of male dominance in female criminality.[121] **Constitutive criminology** attempts to connect the concept of crime with the social forces and human agents that are responsible for its construction.[122] **Peacemaking criminology** views crime as just another form of violence among others, such as war and genocide. Peacemakers call for universal social justice as a means of eliminating antisocial acts.[123]

Policy Implications of Conflict Theory

Conflict theorists have identified inequities in the criminal justice system. The call for social justice has helped focus attention on the plight of the poor, women, and minority groups when they confront the agencies of the justice system. Programs that have been developed as a result include free legal services for indigent offenders, police civilian review boards, laws protecting battered women, and shelters for victims of domestic abuse.

Attempts have been made to increase fairness in the justice system. Sentencing laws have been structured to eliminate bias and discrimination. Enforcement of laws prohibiting white-collar crimes, such as price-fixing and stock fraud, has expanded. And though these acts are rarely punished in proportion to their seriousness, some widely publicized attempts have been made to punish upper-class tax cheats and inside traders.

Theories of Female Criminality

Most existing criminological theories are directed toward the explanation of male criminality.[124] The role of women in crime is usually treated as a unique and independent topic.

Early criminologists traditionally devoted little time or effort to studying female criminality, probably because the female crime rate was significantly lower than the male crime rate, the types of crime women committed were considered

Conflict theory views crime as a function of the class conflict which can occur in any society.

nonserious, and criminologists were generally males who had little interest in the problems of women.

At first, the female criminal was regarded as an oddity. Pioneer criminologists such as Cesare Lombroso made note of the physiobiological differences between men and women and suggested that those differences were responsible for women's passive, law-abiding nature.[125] Women were believed to be less "primitive" than men and thus less likely to be violent or offensive. The rare woman who did commit criminal acts was viewed as being more masculine in personality and demeanor than her law-abiding sisters (the "masculinity hypothesis"). Explanations of feminine crime were often based on the widely held belief that women engaged in crimes that were amoral or sexual in nature, rather than violent or motivated by profit.[126]

In the 1950s and 1960s, it was popular to portray the female criminal as emotionally disturbed.[127] Role conflict was produced by the lack of emotional support and understanding from family, friends, and society. The troubled female offender suffered from a low self-image and depression, resulting in criminal behavior or sexual promiscuity.

The "New" Female Offender

Criminologists began to reconsider the female criminal in the 1970s because gender differences in the arrest and incarceration rates seemed to be narrowing: women were committing more crime and going to prison at a faster rate than ever before. A sociopolitical view of female criminality was developed that linked expanded female participation in the crime rate to the changes brought about by the feminist movement. As a result of economic emancipation, the same social forces that affected male criminality were now having a similar effect on female criminality.[128] Feminist scholars noted that UCR data trends indicated a remarkable increase in the number of women arrested for white-collar crimes, such as embezzlement, larceny, and forgery, and a stabilization in the rate of moral and sexual offenses.[129] Rita Simon, a noted expert on gender differences in the crime rate, stated that emerging economic and legal rights, such as simplified divorce and legalized abortion, and a new sense of group identification via the women's movement meant that women would be less likely to be "victimized, dependent, and oppressed" by the men in their lives.[130] As a consequence, the liberated woman may be less likely to engage in violent acts born of frustration and despair and more likely to become involved in business-related crimes.[131]

Much debate continues over whether the economic opportunities that have come out of the women's liberation movement actually influenced female crime trends. Some authorities have argued that gender differences in the crime rate have not changed and that any increases in the female rate can be attributed to changes in the way agents of the justice system treat women; police may be more likely to arrest women than ever before and courts more likely to convict them. Those who dispute the analysis of feminists talk about the "invention" of the new female criminal.[132]

Feminist Views

Feminist criminologists have continued the search for the cause of female criminality. Scholars such as Meda Chesney-Lind find that a great deal of female criminality can be linked to sexual and physical abuse and male oppression. She argues:

> Young women, a large number of whom are on the run from homes characterized by sexual abuse and parental neglect, are forced by the very statutes designed to protect them into the lives of escaped convicts. Unable to enroll in school or take a job to support themselves because they fear detection, young female runaways are forced into the streets. Here they engage in panhandling, petty theft, and occasional prostitution in order to survive. Young women in conflict with their parents (often for very legitimate reasons) may actually be forced by present laws into petty criminal activity, prostitution and drug use.[133]

Chesney-Lind's research jibes with other efforts showing that female offenders grew up in dysfunctional homes lacking in adequate love, protection, and nurturing.[134] Other research efforts have shown that alcohol and substance abuse problems play a major role in determining the female criminal's behavior choices.[135]

Radical feminists view the cause of female crime as originating with the onset of male supremacy **(patriarchy),** the subsequent subordination of women, male aggression, and efforts of men to control females sexually.[136] They focus on the social forces that shape women's lives and experiences in order to explain female criminality. For example, they attempt to show how the sexual victimization of girls is a function of male socialization because so many young males learn to be aggressive and exploitive of women. Exploited at home, female victims try to cope by running away and engaging in premarital sex and substance abuse. The double standard means that female adolescents still have a much narrower range of acceptable behavior than male adolescents. Any sign of misbehavior is viewed as a substantial challenge to authority that requires immediate control. Feminist scholars view the female criminal as a victim of gender inequality.

Theories of Victimization

For many years, criminological theory focused on the actions of the criminal offender; the role of the victim was virtually ignored. Then a number of scholars found that the victim was not a passive target in crime but someone whose behavior can influence his or her own fate. Hans Von Hentig portrayed the crime victim as someone who "shapes and molds the criminal."[137] The criminal might have been a predator, but the victim may have helped the criminal by becoming a willing prey. Stephen Schafer continued this approach by focusing on the victim's responsibility in the "genesis of crime."[138] Schafer accused some victims of provoking or encouraging criminal behavior, a concept now referred to as **victim precipitation.**

These early works helped focus attention on the role of the victim in the crime problem and led to further research efforts that have sharpened the image of the crime victim.

Victim Precipitation

Victim precipitation refers to the fact that victims may have actually initiated the confrontation that led to their injury or death. The victim may have provoked or threatened the attacker, used "fighting words," or even attacked first.

The concept of victim precipitation was popularized by Marvin Wolfgang's 1958 study of criminal homicide. Wolfgang found that crime victims were often intimately involved in their demise and as many as 25 percent of all homicides could be classified as victim precipitated.[139] Wolfgang's concept was extended to the crime of rape by Menachim Amir, who suggested female victims often contributed to their attacks through a relationship with the rapist.[140]

The concept of victim precipitation implies that in some but not all crimes, the victim provoked or instigated the crime: the crime could not have taken place unless the victim actually cooperated with the criminal. Nowhere is this position more often abused than in the crime of rape, where juries have continued to return not-guilty verdicts if the victim's actions could in any way be construed as consenting to the crime.[141] As law professor Susan Estrich claims in her book *Real Rape*:

> . . . the force standard continues to protect, as "seduction," conduct which should be considered criminal. It ensures broad male freedom to "seduce" women who feel themselves to be powerless, vulnerable, and afraid. It effectively guarantees men freedom to intimidate women and exploit their weakness and passivity, so long as they don't "fight" with them. And it makes clear that the responsibility should be placed squarely on the women.[142]

Life-style Theories

The cause of victimization has also been linked to life-style and activity. NCVS data shows that most victimizations occur in public places, in urban areas, during the evening. Victimization is rare among married people who stay home at night in their rural home and avoid public places. People who engage in high-risk behaviors, such as consuming large amounts of alcohol or spending weekend nights away from home, put themselves at risk of being crime targets.[143]

Victimization data shows that the people most likely to become crime victims share many personal characteristics and traits, including gender, race, age, class, and environment, with those who are most likely to be arrested for criminal offenses. One reason is that both groups live in close physical proximity to one another and criminals tend to select victims who share similar backgrounds and circumstances. The **proximity hypothesis** is based on the fact that both victims and criminals live in the same environment and engage in similar routine activities. People who live in high-crime areas, spend time in public places, go out late at night, and so on are the ones most likely to interact with lawbreakers who have similar life-styles. In other words, crime is an inevitable consequence of having potential victims and criminals sharing a similar life-style.

The important point is that crime is not a random event unaffected by the actions of victims. People can avoid victimization by limiting their exposure to high-risk life-styles. Crime and victimization then are codependent: the probability of a crime occurring is dependent on the activities of the victim. Crime rates may continue to be high because people who seek the enjoyments of urban life are willing to overlook or ignore the potential of becoming crime victims.[144]

Routine Activities

The **routine activities** approach holds that the incidence of criminal activity and victimization is related to the nature of normal, everyday patterns of human behavior. According to originators Lawrence Cohen and Marcus Felson and their associates, predatory crime rates can be explained by three factors: the supply of motivated offenders (such as large numbers of unemployed teenagers); suitable targets (goods that have value and can be easily transported, such as VCRs); and the absence of effective guardians for protection (such as police and security forces or home security devices).[145]

The routine activities view of victimization suggests that people's daily activities may put them at risk of being the target of criminal behavior. If people leave unguarded valuables in their home, they increase the likelihood of becoming burglary victims; if they walk at night in public places, they increase the risk of becoming the target of violence.[146]

According to this approach, the likelihood of victimization is a function of both the behavior of potential victims as well as criminal motivation. For example, if family income increases because of the number of women employed in the workforce and because of this, the average family is able to afford more luxury goods, such as TVs and VCRs, we might expect a comparable increase in the crime rate because the number of "suitable targets" has expanded while the number of "capable guardians" left to protect the home has been reduced.[147] In contrast, crime rates may go down during times of high unemployment simply because there is less to steal and more people at home to guard their possessions. The routine activities approach seems a promising way of understanding crime and victimization patterns and predicting the probability of victim risk.

The Equivalent Group Hypothesis

The UCR and NCVS indicate that criminals and victims share many similar traits. Poor, young, unmarried, males predominate in both groups. One reason why victims and criminals share similar characteristics is that they are not in reality separate groups. Research shows that crime victims report significant amounts of criminal behavior themselves. For example, Joan McDermott found that the young victims of school crime were likely to strike back at other students to regain lost possessions or recover their self-respect.[148] In another study, Simon

TABLE 3.2
Concepts and Theories of Criminology: A Review

Theory	Major Premise
Choice	People commit crime when they perceive that the benefits of law violation outweigh the threat and pain of punishment:
Biosocial	
Biochemical	Crime, especially violence, is a function of diet,vitamin intake, hormonal imbalance, or food allergies.
Neurological	Criminals and delinquents often suffer brain impairment, as measured by the EEG. Attention deficit disorder and minimum brain dysfunction are related to antisocial behavior.
Genetic	Delinquent traits and predispositions are inherited. The criminality of parents can predict the delinquency of children.
Psychological	
Psychoanalytic	The development of the unconscious personality early in childhood influences behavior for the rest of a person's life. Criminals have weak egos and damaged personalities.
Behavioral	People commit crime when they model their behavior after others they see being rewarded for the same acts. Behavior is enforced by rewards and extinguished by punishment.
Cognitive	Individual reasoning processes influence behavior. Reasoning is influenced by the way people perceive their environment and by their moral and intellectual development.
Social Structure	
Social disorganization	The conflicts and problems of urban social life and communities control the crime rate.
Shaw and McKay's ecological theory	Crime is a product of transitional neighborhoods that manifest social disorganization and value conflict.
Strain theory	People who adopt the goals of society but lack the means to attain them seek alternatives, such as crime.
Relative deprivation	Crime occurs when the wealthy and poor live in close proximity to one another.
Cultural deviance theory	Citizens who obey the street rules of lower-class life (focal concerns) find themselves in conflict with the dominant culture.

Singer employed data from the Philadelphia cohort and found that the victims of violent assault were those most likely to become offenders themselves.[149] And a number of studies show that youths who are the victims of child abuse are quite likely to later victimize their own children and families.[150] Gary Jensen and David Brownfield conclude:

> . . . for personal victimizations, those most likely to be the victims of crime are those who have been most involved in crime; and the similarity of victims and offenders reflects that association.[151]

TABLE 3.2
Continued

Theory	Major Premise
Social Process	
Learning Theories	
Differential association theory	People learn to commit crime from exposure to antisocial definitions.
Differential reinforcement theory	Criminal behavior depends on the person's experiences with rewards for conventional behaviors and punishments for deviant ones. Being rewarded for deviance leads to crime.
Neutralization theory	Youths learn ways of neutralizing moral restraints and periodically drift in and out of criminal behavior patterns.
Control Theories	
Social control theory	A person's bond to society prevents him or her from violating social rules. If the bond weakens, the person is free to commit crime.
Self-control theory	Crime and criminality are separate concepts. People choose to commit crime when they lack self-control. People lacking self-control will seize criminal opportunities.
Labeling theory	People enter into law-violating careers when they are labeled for their acts and organize their personalities around the labels.
Conflict	
Conflict theory	People commit crime when the law, controlled by the rich and powerful, defines their behavior as illegal. The immoral actions of the powerful go unpunished.
Integrated	
	Youths who grow up in lower-class cultures are more likely to have weakened bonds to society and suffer other socialization problems.
Routine activities theory	Crime is a function of the availability of the victim, the presence of an offender, and the absence of an effective guardian.
Wilson and Herrnstein's human nature theory	People choose to commit crime when they are biologically and psychologically impaired.

Consequently, it may be foolish to separate criminals and victims into separate categories; the conditions that create criminality may be present in all people at some time in their lives.

The true nature of the victim-criminal association is far from certain. Some victims may commit criminal acts out of a sense of rage and frustration; some may have learned antisocial behavior as a consequence of their own experiences, as in the case of abused children; others may engage in law-violating behaviors as a means of revenge, self-defense, or social control. The relationship is a complex one. Certainly not all victims become criminals, nor have all criminals been victims. Some recent research by Jeffrey Fagan and his associates shows that while a relationship between victimization and criminality exists, the social processes that produce both events are not identical.[152] Further research is needed to fully understand this important interrelationship.

The Future of Crime Theory

Two recent trends in criminological theory will probably continue to influence the field in years to come. The first is the availability of powerful computer programs that enable researchers to use large data sets with many variables in very complex calculations. The second is the recognition of the fact that serious predatory crime is not spread evenly throughout the social structure: deviant individuals and deviant places do exist.[153] The concept of a career criminal who is a persistent offender living in an ecologically deteriorated neighborhood is now a familiar concept in criminology.[154]

These developments have caused criminologists to expand their horizons and produce integrated theoretical models that combine personal, social, physical, and economic concepts and borrow elements from all the various branches of social, biological, psychological, and choice theories.[155]

Integrated theoretical models that combine social as well as psychological and biological variables likely will become more prominent. The integration movement was popularized in James Q. Wilson and Richard Herrnstein's controversial 1985 book, *Crime and Human Nature*.[156] Wilson and Herrnstein argue that biological and psychological factors, such as body build, intelligence, and personality disorders, interact with social variables, such as family, economic, and educational problems, to produce crime. They maintain that people with physical abnormalities will be the ones most likely to succumb to the crime-producing influences in the environment.

The integration of social and physical factors has been embraced by such highly respected social scientists as Travis Hirschi and Michael Gottfredson, who now suggest that criminals are impulsive people who commit less crime as they age. If, as they maintain, getting older, weaker, and more tired requires that even impulsive people desist from crime, then it follows that such physical factors as youthful strength, vigor, energy, and pep promote criminality.[157]

Integrated theories have been praised as important reference points for organizing research findings and stimulating research strategies. Theory integration should continue to influence all branches of crime theory in the foreseeable future.

SUMMARY

This chapter has reviewed some of the most important theoretical models in criminology. Clearly, there is more than one approach to understanding the cause of crime and its consequences. Debate continues over whether crime is a social, economic, psychological, biological, or personal problem; whether it is a matter of free choice or the product of uncontrollable social and personal forces; and whether it can be controlled by the fear of punishment or the application of rehabilitative treatment. Consequently, a number of different and diverse schools of criminological theory exist, some focusing on the individual, while others view social factors as the most important element in producing crime.

Recent conceptualizations have tried to incorporate a number of different views into a complex theory of crime causation. For example, James Q. Wilson and Richard Herrnstein have proposed a theory of criminality that holds that crime is a matter of personal choice (classical approach) influenced by a person's physical traits (biological theory) and family life (social process theory). In other efforts, sociologists have attempted to combine elements of social learning, social structure, and social process theory.

The various theories of crime causation have had an important influence on criminal justice policy. Each has been used to formulate criminal justice policy and can be linked to one of the various perspectives in criminal justice.

QUESTIONS

1. What factors are present in a disorganized urban area that produce high crime rates?
2. What is meant by the term *cultural transmission?* Have you been a member of a social group whose culture is transmitted to newcomers?
3. It seems logical that biological and psychological factors might explain why some people commit crime. Why would these factors fail to explain crime patterns and trends?
4. Are criminals impulsive? How could impulsivity be used to explain white-collar and organized crime?
5. If crime is a routine activity, what steps should you take to avoid becoming a crime victim?

NOTES

1. Herbert Koppel, *Lifetime Likelihood of Victimization* (Washington, D.C.: Bureau of Justice Statistics, 1987).

2. Reece McGee, *Sociology*, 2d ed. (New York: Holt, Rinehart & Winston, 1980), p. 540.

3. Ian Robertson, *Sociology*, 2d ed. (New York: Worth, 1981), p. 16.

4. Cesare Beccaria, *On Crimes and Punishments*, 6th ed., trans. Henry Paolucci (Indianapolis: Bobbs-Merrill Co., 1977); Jeremy Bentham, *A Fragment on Government and an Introduction to the Principles of Morals and Legislation*, ed. Wilfred Harrison (Oxford, England: Basic Blackwell, 1967).

5. Beccaria, *On Crimes and Punishments*, p. 99.

6. Lawrence Cohen and Richard Machalek, "A General Theory of Expropriative Crime: An Evolutionary Ecological Approach," *American Journal of Sociology* 94 (1988):465–501.

7. See also Philip Cook, "The Demand and Supply of Criminal Opportunities," in *Crime and Justice*, vol. 7, ed. Michael Tonry and Norval Morris (Chicago: University of Chicago Press, 1986), pp.1–28; Ronald Clarke and Derek Cornish, "Modeling Offender's Decisions: A Framework for Research and Policy," in *Crime and Justice*, vol. 6, ed. Michael Tonry and Norval Morris (Chicago: University of Chicago Press, 1985), pp. 147–87; Morgan Reynolds, *Crime by Choice: An Economic Analysis* (Dallas: Fisher Institute, 1985).

8. Julia MacDonald and Robert Gifford, "Territorial Cues and Defensible Space Theory: The Burglar's Point of View," *Journal of Environmental Psychology* 9 (1989):193–205; Paul Cromwell, James Olson, and D'Aunn Wester Avary, *Breaking and Entering, An Ethnographic Analysis of Burglary* (Newbury Park, Calif.: Sage Publications 1991), pp. 48–51.

9. Paul Cromwell, Alan Marks, James Olson, and D'Aunn Avary, "Group Effects on Decision-Making by Burglars," *Psychological Reports* 69 (1991):579–88.

10. Ineke Haen Marshall and Julie Horney, "Motives for Crime and Self-Image among a Sample of Convicted Felons" (Paper presented at the annual meeting of the American Society of Criminology, San Francisco, November 1991).

11. James Wright and Peter Rossi, *Armed and Considered Dangerous: A Survey of Felons and Their Firearms* (New York: Aldine, 1986).

12. Jennifer Browdy, "Interview with Ann Rule," *Law Enforcement News*, 21 May 1984, p. 12.

13. James Q. Wilson, *Thinking About Crime* (New York: Basic Books, 1975); Ernest Van den Haag, *Punishing Criminals* (New York: Basic Books, 1975).

14. Herbert Packer, *The Limits of the Criminal Sanction* (Stanford, Calif.: Stanford University Press, 1968).

15. Ernest Van den Haag, "Could Successful Rehabilitation Reduce the Crime Rate?" *Journal of Criminal Law and Criminology* 73 (1985):1022–35.

16. Robert Bursik, Harold Grasmick, and Mitchell Chamlin, "The Effect of Longitudinal Arrest Patterns on the Development of Robbery Trends at the Neighborhood Level," *Criminology* 28 (1990):431–50.

17. See, generally, Hugo Bedeau, *The Death Penalty in America* 3d. ed. (New York: Oxford University Press, 1982).

18. For a recent view, see Ruth Peterson and William Bailey, "Felony Murder and Capital Punishment: An Examination of the Deterrence Question," *Criminology* 29 (1991):367–96.

19. Steven Klepper and Daniel Dagin, "Tax Compliance and Perceptions of the Risks of Detection and Criminal Prosecution," *Law and Society Review* 23 (1989):209–40.

20. Raymond Paternoster, "Decisions to Participate in and Desist from Four Types of Common Delinquency: Deterrence and the Rational Choice Perspective," *Law and Society Review* 23 (1989):7–29; Paternoster, "Examining Three-Wave Deterrence Models: A Question of Temporal Order and Specification," *Journal of Criminal Law and Criminology* 79 (1988):135–63.

21. Harold Grasmick and Robert Bursik, "Conscience, Significant Others and Rational Choice: Extending the Deterrence Model," *Law and Society Review* 24 (1990):837–61; Charles Tittle, *Sanctions and Social Deviance* (New York: Praeger, 1980).

22. Federal Bureau of Investigation, *Crime in the United States, 1990* (Washington, D.C.: U.S. Government Printing Office, 1991).

23. Ibid.

24. Patrick Langan and John Dawson, *Felony Sentences in State Courts, 1988* (Washington, D.C.: Bureau of Justice Statistics, 1990), p. 3.

25. Eric Wish, *Drug Use Forecasting, 1990* (Washington, D.C.: National Institute of Justice, 1991); U.S. Department of Justice, *Crime and Alcohol* (Washington, D.C.: U.S. Government Printing Office, 1983).

26. Michel Foucault, *Discipline and Punishment* (New York: Random House, 1978).

27. Allen Beck and Bernard Shipley, *Recidivism of Young Parolees* (Washington, D.C.: Bureau of Justice Statistics, 1987).

28. Joan Petersilia, Susan Turner, James Kahan, and Joyce Peterson, *Granting Felons Probation: Public Risks and Alternatives* (Santa Monica, Calif.: Rand Corporation, 1985).

29. See, generally, Alfred Blumstein, Jacqueline Cohen, and Daniel Nagen, *Deterrence and Incapacitation: Estimating The Effects of Legal Sanctions on Crime Rates* (Washington, D.C: National Academy of Science, 1978).

30. Gary Becker, "Crime and Punishment: An Economic Approach," *Journal of Political Economy* 76 (1968):174–82.

31. Charles Silberman, *Criminal Violence, Criminal Justice* (New York: Vintage Books, 1980), pp. 245–62.

32. Beck and Shipley, *Recidivism of Young Parolees.*

33. See, generally, Cesare Lombroso, *Crime, Its Causes and Remedies* (Montclair, N.J.: Patterson Smith, 1968).

34. Raffaele Garofalo, *Criminology*, trans. Robert Miller (Boston: Little, Brown & Co., 1914).

35. Enrico Ferri, *Criminal Sociology* (New York: D. Appleton & Co., 1909).

36. Ernest Hooton, *The American Criminal* (Cambridge: Harvard University Press, 1939).

37. Henry Goddard, *The Kallikak Family: A Study in the Heredity of Feeble Mindedness* (New York: Macmillan, 1927); Richard Dugdale, *The Jukes, A Study in Crime, Pauperism, Disease, and Heredity* (New York: G. P. Putnam, 1910); Arthur Estabrook, *The Jukes in 1915* (Washington, D.C.: Carriage Institute of Washington, 1916).

38. Edward O. Wilson, *Sociobiology: The New Synthesis* (Cambridge: Harvard University Press, 1975).

39. Daniel Nagin and David Farrington, "The Stability of Criminal Potential from Childhood to Adulthood" (Paper presented at the annual meeting of the American Society of Criminology, San Francisco, November 1991).

40. Leonard Hippchen, "Some Possible Biochemical Aspects of Criminal Behavior," *Journal of Behavioral Ecology* 2 (1981):1–6.

41. B. D'Asaro, C. Grossback, and C. Nigro, "Polyamine Levels in Jail Inmates," *Journal of Orthomolecular Psychiatry* 4 (1975):149–52.

42. J. A. Yaryura-Tobias and F. Neziroglu, "Violent Behavior, Brain Dysrhythmia and Glucose Dysfunction, a New Syndrome," *Journal of Orthopsychiatry* 4 (1975):182–88.

43. Ray Wunderlich, "Neuroallergy as a Contributing Factor to Social Misfits: Diagnosis and Treatment," in *Ecologic-Biochemical Approaches to Treatment of Delinquents and Criminals*, ed. Leonard Hippchen (New York: Van Nostrand Reinhold, 1978), pp. 229–53.

44. Paul Cromwell, Ben Abadies, Jay Stephens, and Marilee Kyler, "Hair Mineral Analysis: Biochemical Imbalances and Violent Criminal Behavior," *Psychological Reports* 64 (1989):259–66.

45. Louis Gottschalk, Tessio Rebello, Monte Buchsbaum, Howard Tucker, and Everett Hodges, "Abnormalities in Hair Trace Elements as Indicators of Aberrant Behavior," *Comprehensive Psychiatry* 32 (1991):229–37.

46. D. Williams, "Neural Factors Related to Habitual Aggression—Consideration of Differences Between Habitual Aggressives and Others Who Have Committed Crimes of Violence," *Brain* 92 (1969):503–20.

47. R. S. Aind and T. Yamamoto, "Behavior Disorders of Childhood," *Electroencephalography and Clinical Neurophysiology* 21 (1966):148–56.

48. Z. A. Zayed, S. A. Lewis, and R. P. Britain, "An Encephalographic and Psychiatric Study of 32 Insane Murderers," *British Journal of Psychiatry* 115 (1969):1115–24.

49. R. R. Monroe, *Brain Dysfunction in Aggressive Criminals* (Lexington, Mass.: D.C. Heath, 1978); L. T. Yeudall, *Childhood Experiences as Causes of Criminal Behavior* (Senate of Canada, issue no. 1, Thirteenth Parliament, Ottawa, Canada, 1977).

50. Terrie Moffitt and Phil Silva, "Self-Reported Delinquency, Neuropsychological Deficit, and History of Attention Deficit Disorder," *Journal of Abnormal Child Psychology* 16 (1988):553–69.

51. T. R. Sarbin and L. E. Miller, "Demonism Revisited: The XYY Chromosome Anomaly," *Issues in Criminology* 5 (1970):195–207.

52. See S. A. Mednick and Karl O. Christiansen, eds. *Biosocial Bases of Criminal Behavior* (New York: Gardner Press, 1977).

53. David Rowe and D. Wayne Osgood, "Heredity and Sociological Theories of Delinquency: A Reconsideration," *American Sociological Review* 49 (1984):526–40.

54. B. Hutchings and S. A. Mednick, "Criminality in Adoptees and Their Adoptive and Biological Parents: A Pilot Study," in S. A. Mednick and Karl O. Christiansen, eds. *Biosocial Bases of Criminal Behavior* (New York: Gardner Press, 1977).

55. See Peter Scott, "Henry Maudsley," in *Pioneers in Criminology*, ed. Hermann Mannheim (Montclair, N.J.: Patterson Smith, 1970), p. 212.

56. Traditionally, the law has recognized that some offenders are mentally ill and should therefore be excused from criminal responsibility. However, *insanity* is a legal, not psychological, term and will therefore be discussed in Chapter 4, where we review the criminal law.

57. For an analysis of Freud, see Spencer Rathus, *Psychology* (New York: Holt, Rinehart & Winston, 1990), pp. 412–20.

58. August Aichorn, *Wayward Youth* (New York: Viking, 1965).

59. Seymour Halleck, *Psychiatry and the Dilemmas of Crime* (New York: Harper & Row, 1967), pp. 99–115.

60. John Monahan and Henry Steadman, *Crime and Mental Disorder* (National Institute of Justice Research brief, Washington, D.C., September 1984); David Tennenbaum, "Research Studies of Personality and Criminality," *Journal of Criminal Justice* 5 (1977):1–19.

61. Carmen Cirincione, Henry Steadman, Pamela Clark Robbins, and John Monahan, "Mental Illness as a Factor in Criminality: A Study of Prisoners and Mental Patients" (Paper presented at the annual meeting of the American Society of Criminology, San Francisco, November 1991).

62. This discussion is based on three works by Albert Bandura: *Aggression: A Social Learning Analysis* (Englewood Cliffs, N.J.: Prentice-Hall, 1973); *Social Learning Theory* (Englewood Cliffs, N.J.: Prentice-Hall, 1977); "The Social Learning Perspective: Mechanisms of Aggression," in *The Psychology of Crime and Criminal Justice*, ed. H. Toch (New York: Holt, Rinehart and Winston, 1979), pp. 198–326.

63. Mark Warr and Mark Stafford, "The Influence of Delinquent Peers: What They Think or What They Do?" *Criminology* 29 (1991):851–66.

64. Department of Health and Human Services, *Television and Behavior* (Washington, D.C.: U.S. Government Printing Office, 1982).

65. Richard Kania, "T.V. Crime and Real Crime: Questioning the Link" (Paper presented at the annual meeting of the American Society of Criminology, Chicago, November 1988).

66. J. E. Lockman, "Self and Peer Perception and Attributional Biases of Aggressive and Nonaggressive Boys in Dyadic Interactions," *Journal of Consulting and Clinical Psychology* 55 (1987):404–10.

67. See, generally, Jean Piaget, *The Moral Judgement of the Child* (London: Kegan Paul, 1932).

68. Lawrence Kohlberg et al., *The Just Community Approach in Corrections: A Manual* (Niantic, Conn.: Connecticut Department of Corrections, 1973).

69. Walter Mischel, *Introduction to Personality*, 4th ed. (New York: Holt, Rinehart and Winston, 1986), p. 1.

70. See, generally, Albert Rabin, "The Antisocial Personality—Psychopathy and Sociopathy," in *The Psychology of Crime and Criminal Justice*, ed. H. Toch (New York: Holt, Rinehart and Winston, 1979), pp. 236–51.

71. Steven Smith and Joseph Newman, "Alcohol and Drug Abuse-Dependence Disorders in Psychopathic and Nonpsychopathic Criminal Offenders," *Journal of Abnormal Psychology* 99 (1990):430–39.

72. Ibid.

73. Jack Levin and James Alan Fox, *Mass Murder* (New York: Plenum Books, 1985).

74. Spencer Rathus and Jeffrey Nevid, *Abnormal Psychology* (Englewood Cliffs, N.J.: Prentice-Hall, 1991), pp. 310–16.

75. Ibid.

76. Samuel Yochelson and Stanton Samenow, *The Criminal Personality* (New York: Jason Aronson, 1977).

77. For a thorough discussion, see Diana Fishbein, "Biological Perspectives in Criminology," *Criminology* 28 (1990):27–72.

78. Paul Boccomini, Bill Strum, and Alexander Schauss, "Sub-Clinical Thiamine Deficiency and Behavior Disorders: Case History," *Journal of Behavioral Ecology* 2 (1981):5–6.

79. Associated Press, "Prison Surgeons Reshape Faces, Futures," *Omaha World Herald*, 13 January 1986, p. 25.

80. Emile Durkheim, *The Division of Labor in Society* (New York: Free Press, 1964); and *Rules of the Sociological Method*, trans. S. A. Solvay and J. H. Mueller, ed. G. Catlin (New York: Free Press, 1966).

81. William T. Grand Foundation, *The Forgotten Half* (Cambridge, Mass., 1988).

82. William Julius Wilson, "Poverty, Joblessness, and Family Structure in the Inner City: A Comparative Perspective" (Paper presented at the annual meeting of the American Society of Criminology, San Francisco, November 1991).

83. Oscar Lewis, "The Culture of Poverty," *Scientific American* 215 (1966):19–25.

84. William Julius Wilson, *The Truly Disadvantaged* (Chicago: University of Chicago Press, 1987).

85. Clifford R. Shaw and Henry D. McKay, *Juvenile Delinquency and Urban Areas*, rev. ed. (Chicago: University of Chicago Press, 1972).

86. Robert Bursik, "Social Disorganization and Theories of Crime and Delinquency: Problems and Prospects," *Criminology* 26 (1988):519–51, at 521.

87. Robert Sampson, "Structural Sources of Variation in Race-Age-Specific Rates of Offending Across Major U.S. Cities," *Criminology* 23 (1985):647–73; Janet Heitgerd and Robert Bursik, Jr., "Extracommunity Dynamics and the Ecology of Delinquency," *American Journal of Sociology* 92 (1987):775–87; Ora Simcha-Fagan and Joseph Schwartz, "Neighborhood and Delinquency: An Assessment of Contextual Effects," *Criminology* 24 (1986): 667–703.

88. E. Britt Patterson, "Poverty, Income Inequality, and Community Crime Rates," *Criminology* 29 (1991):755–76.

89. Leon Pettiway, "Urban Spatial Structure and Incidence of Arson: Differences Between Ghetto and Nonghetto Environments," *Justice Quarterly* 5 (1988):113–29.

90. Roland Chilton, "Twenty Years of Homicide and Robbery in Chicago: The Impact of the City's Changing Racial and Age Composition," *Journal of Quantitative Criminology* 3 (1987):195–213.

91. Walter Miller, "Lower Class Culture as a Generating Milieu of Gang Delinquency," *Journal of Social Issues* 14 (1958):5–19; see also Thorsten Sellin, *Culture Conflict and Crime*, Bulletin no. 41 (New York: Social Science Research Council, 1938).

92. Richard Cloward and Lloyd Ohlin, *Delinquency and Opportunity* (Glencoe, Ill.: Free Press, 1960).

93. Ronald Simons and Phyllis Gray, "Perceived Blocked Opportunity as an Explanation of Delinquency among Lower-Class Black Males: A Research Note," *Journal of Research in Crime and Delinquency* 26 (1989):90–101.

94. Robert Merton, "Social Structure and Anomie," in Robert Merton, ed. *Social Theory and Social Structure* (Glencoe, Ill.: Free Press, 1975).

95. Richard Rosenfeld, "Urban Crime Rates: Effects of Inequality, Welfare Dependency, Region and Race," in James Byrne and Robert Sampson, *The Social Ecology of Crime* (New York: Springer-Verlag, 1985), pp. 116–30; Leo Carroll and Pamela Irving Jackson, "Inequality, Opportunity, and Crime Rates in Central Cities," *Criminology* 21 (1983):178–94.

96. Ralph Taylor and Jeanette Covington, "Neighborhood Changes in Ecology and Violence," *Criminology* 26 (1988):533–89.

97. Judith Blau and Peter Blau, "The Cost of Inequality: Metropolitan Structure and Violent Crime," *American Sociological Review* 147 (1982):114–29; Richard Block, "Community Environment and Violent Crime," *Criminology* 17 (1979):46–57.

98. See, for example, G. David Curry and Irving Spergel, "Gang Homicide, Delinquency, and Community," *Criminology* 26(1988):382; John Hagedorn, *People and Folks: Gangs, Crime and the Underclass in a Rustbelt City* (Chicago: Lake View Press, 1988); C. Ronald Huff, "Youth Gangs and Public Policy," *Crime and Delinquency* 35 (1989):524–37; Carl Taylor, *Dangerous Society* (East Lansing: Michigan State University Press, 1990); Joan Moore, "Isolation and Stigmatization in the Development of an Underclass: The Case of Chicago Gangs in East Los Angeles," *Social Problems* 33 (1985):1–12.

99. Jeffrey Fagan, "The Social Organization of Drug Use and Drug Dealing Among Urban Gangs," *Criminology* 27 (1989):633–67.

100. Charles Tittle, Wayne Villemez, and Douglas Smith, "The Myth of Social Class and Criminality: An Empirical Assessment of the Evidence," *American Sociological Review* 43 (1978):643–56.

101. Rolf Loeber and Magda Stouthamer-Loeber, "Family Factors as Correlates and Predictors of Juvenile Conduct Problems and Delinquency," in *Crime and Justice*, vol. 7, eds. Michael Tonry and Norval Morris (Chicago: University of Chicago Press, 1986), pp. 29–151.

102. John Laub and Robert Sampson, "Unraveling Families and Delinquency: A Reanalysis of the Gluecks' Data," *Criminology* 26 (1988):355–80.

103. Joan McCord, "Family Relationships, Juvenile Delinquency, and Adult Criminality," *Criminology* 29 (1991):397–419.

104. Lawrence Rosen, "Family and Delinquency: Structure or Function?" *Criminology* 23 (1985):553–73.

105. Lyle Shannon, *Assessing the Relationship of Adult Criminal Careers to Juvenile Careers: A Summary* (Washington, D.C.: U.S. Government Printing Office, 1982); D. J. West and David P. Farrington, *The Delinquent Way of Life* (London: Heineman, 1977); Marvin Wolfgang, Robert Figlio, and Thorsten Sellin, *Delinquency in a Birth Cohort* (Chicago: University of Chicago Press, 1972).

106. Terence Thornberry, Melanie Moore, and R. L. Christenson, "The Effect of Dropping Out of High School on Subsequent Criminal Behavior," *Criminology* 23 (1985):3–18.

107. Christopher Innes, *Profile of State Prison Inmates* (Washington, D.C.: Bureau of Justice Statistics, 1988); Louis Jankowski, *Correctional Populations in the United States, 1988* (Washington, D.C.: Bureau of Justice Statistics, 1991).

108. Denise Kandel and Mark Davies, "Friendship Networks, Intimacy, and Illicit Drug Use in Young Adulthood: A Comparison of Two Competing Theories," *Criminology* 29 (1991):441–67.

109. Edwin Sutherland and Donald Cressey, *Criminology* (Philadelphia: J. B. Lippincott, 1970), pp. 71–91.

110. Ronald Akers, *Deviant Behavior: A Social Learning Approach* (Belmont, Calif.: Wadsworth, 1977).

111. David Matza, *Delinquency and Drift* (New York: John Wiley & Sons, 1964); Gresham Sykes and David Matza, "Techniques of Neutralization: A Theory of Delinquency," *American Sociological Review* 22 (1957):664–70; M. William Minor, "The Neutralization of Criminal Offense," *Criminology* 18 (1980):103–20; Robert Regoli and Eric Poole, "The Commitments of Delinquents to Their Misdeeds: A Reexamination," *Journal of Criminal Justice* 6 (1978):261–69.

112. For a discussion of the time ordering of neutralizations, see John

Hamlin, "The Misplaced Role of Rational Choice in Neutralization Theory," *Criminology* 26 (1988):425–38.

113. Jill Leslie Rosenbaum and James Lasley, "School, Community Context, and Delinquency: Rethinking the Gender Gap," *Justice Quarterly* 7 (1990):493–513.

114. See, for example, Randy La Grange and Helen Raskin White, "Age Differences in Delinquency: A Test of Theory," *Criminology* 23 (1985):19–45; Marvin Krohn and James Massey, "Social Control and Delinquent Behavior: An Examination of the Elements of the Social Bond," *Sociological Quarterly* 21 (1980):529–44.

115. Michael Gottfredson and Travis Hirschi, *A General Theory of Crime* (Stanford, Calif.: Stanford University Press, 1990).

116. Clarence Schrag, *Crime and Justice: American Style* (Washington, D.C.: U.S. Government Printing Office, 1971), pp. 89–91. A summary of Schrag's work is in William Pelfrey, *The Evolution of Criminology* (Cincinnati: Anderson Publishing, 1980), pp. 47–48.

117. Charles Tittle, "Two Empirical Regularities (Maybe) in Search of an Explanation: Commentary on the Age/Crime Debate," *Criminology* 26 (1988):75–85.

118. W. Byron Groves and Robert Sampson, "Critical Theory and Criminology," *Social Problems* 33 (1986):58–80.

119. Gresham Sykes, "The Rise of Critical Criminology," *Journal of Criminal Law and Criminology* 65 (June 1974):206; see also Ian Taylor et al., *The New Criminology—For a Social Theory of Deviance* (New York: Harper & Row, 1973).

120. See, generally, Jock Young, *Realist Criminology* (London: Sage, 1989).

121. Kathleen Daly and Meda Chesney-Lind, "Feminism and Criminology," *Justice Quarterly* 5 (1988):438–97.

122. Stuart Henry and Dragan Milovanovic, "Constitutive Criminology: the Maturation of Critical Theory," *Criminology* 29 (1991):293–315.

123. Harold Pepinsky, "Violence as Unresponsiveness: Toward a New Conception of Crime," *Justice Quarterly* 5 (1988):539–87.

124. Meda Chesney-Lind, "Girls' Crime and Woman's Place: Toward a Feminist Model of Female Delinquency," *Crime and Delinquency* 35 (1989):5–29.

125. Cesare Lombroso and William Ferrero, *The Female Offender* (New York: D. Appleton & Co., 1899).

126. Otto Pollak, *The Criminality of Women* (New York: A. S. Barnes & Co., 1950).

127. Gisela Konopka, *The Adolescent Girl in Conflict* (Englewood Cliffs, N.J.: Prentice-Hall, 1966).

128. Rachelle Canter, "Sex Differences in Self-Reported Delinquency," *Criminology* 20 (1982):373–94.

129. Roy Austin, "Women's Liberation and Increase in Minor, Major, and Occupational Offenses," *Criminology* 20 (1982):407–30.

130. Rita James Simon, "Women and Crime Revisited," *Social Science Quarterly* 56 (March 1976):658.

131. Fred Adler, *Sisters in Crime: The Rise of the Female Criminal* (New York: McGraw-Hill, 1975), p. 95.

132. Joseph Weis, "Liberation and Crime: The Invention of the New Female Criminal," *Crime and Social Justice* 1 (1976):17–27.

133. Meda Chesney-Lind, "Girl's Crime and a Woman's Place," p. 24.

134. Jill Leslie Rosenbaum, "Family Dysfunction and Female Delinquency," *Crime and Delinquency* 35 (1989): 31–44.

135. Brenda Miller, William Downs, and Dawn Gondoli, "Delinquency, Childhood Violence, and the Development of Alcoholism in Women," *Crime and Delinquency* 35 (1989):94–108.

136. For a general review of this issue, see Sally Simpson, "Feminist Theory, Crime and Justice," *Criminology* 27 (1989):605–32; Daly and Chesney-Lind, "Feminism and Criminology"; James Messerschmidt, *Capitalism, Patriarchy and Crime* (Totowa, N.J.: Rowman and Littlefield, 1986).

137. Hans Von Hentig, *The Criminal and His Victim: Studies in the Sociobiology of Crime* (New Haven: Yale University Press, 1948), p. 384.

138. Stephen Schafer, *The Victim and His Criminal* (New York: Random House, 1968), p. 152.

139. Marvin Wolfgang, *Patterns of Criminal Homicide* (Philadelphia: University of Pennsylvania Press, 1958).

140. Menachem Amir, *Patterns in Forcible Rape* (Chicago: University of Chicago Press, 1971).

141. Susan Estrich, *Real Rape* (Cambridge: Harvard University Press, 1987).

142. Ibid., p. 69.

143. James Lasley and Jill Leslie Rosenbaum, "Routine Activities and Multiple Personal Victimization," *Sociology and Social Research* 73 (1988):47–48.

144. Joseph Perry and M. D. Pugh, "Fear of Crime and City Nightlife" (Paper presented at the annual meeting of the American Society of Criminology, San Francisco, November 1991).

145. Lawrence Cohen and Marcus Felson, "Social Change and Crime Rate Trends: A Routine Activities Approach," *American Sociological Review* 44(1979):588–608; Lawrence Cohen, Marcus Felson, and Kenneth Land, "Property Crime Rates in the United States: A Macrodynamic Analysis, 1947–1977, with Ex-Ante Forecasts for the Mid-1980's," *American Journal of Sociology* 86 (1980):90–118; for a review, see James LeBeau and Thomas Castellano, "The Routine Activities Approach: An Inventory and Critique," (Center for the Studies of Crime, Delinquency and Corrections, Southern Illinois University, Carbondale, Ill., unpublished, 1987).

146. Steven Messner and Kenneth Tardiff, "The Social Ecology of Urban Homicide: An Application of the 'Routine Activities' Approach," *Criminology* 23 (1985):241–67; Philip Cook, "The Demand and Supply of Criminal Opportunities," in *Crime and Justice*, vol. 7, ed. Michael Tonry and Norval Morris (Chicago: University of Chicago Press, 1986), pp. 1–28; Ronald Clarke and Derek Cornish, "Modeling Offender's Decisions: A Framework for Research and Policy," in *Crime and Justice*, vol. 6, ed. Michael Tonry and Norval Morris (Chicago: University of Chicago Press, 1985), pp. 147–87.

147. Cohen, Felson, and Land, "Property Crime Rates in the United States: A Macrodynamic Analysis, 1947–1977."

148. Joan McDermott, "Crime in the School and in the Community: Offenders, Victims and Fearful Youth," *Crime and Delinquency* 29 (1983):270–83.

149. Simon Singer, "Homogeneous Victim-Offender Populations: A Review and Some Research Implications," *Journal of Criminal Law and Criminology* 72 (1981):779–99.

150. Ross Vasta, "Physical Child Abuse: A Dual Component Analysis," *Developmental Review* 2 (1982):128–35.

151. Gary Jensen and David Brownfield, "Gender, Lifestyles and Victimization: Beyond Routine Activities," *Violence and Victims* (1986):85–101.

152. Jeffrey Fagan, Elizabeth Piper, and Yu-Teh Cheng, "Contributions of Victimization to Delinquency in Inner Cities," *The Journal of Criminal Law and Criminology* 78 (1987):586–613.

153. Lawrence Sherman, Patrick Gartin, and Michael Buerger, "Hot Spots of Predatory Crime: Routine Activities and the Criminology of Place," *Criminology* 27 (1989):27–56.

154. Rodney Stark, "Deviant Places: A Theory of the Ecology of Crime," *Criminology* 25 (1987):893–911.

155. Delbert Elliott, David Huizinga, and Suzanne Ageton, *Explaining Delinquency and Drug Use* (Beverly Hills, Calif.: Sage Publications, 1985).

156. James Q. Wilson and Richard Herrnstein, *Crime and Human Nature* (New York: Simon and Schuster, 1985).

157. Michael Gottfredson and Travis Hirschi, "The True Value of Lambda Would Appear to Be Zero: An Essay on Career Criminals, Criminal Careers, Selective Incapacitation, Cohort Studies and Related Topics," *Criminology* 24 (1986):213–34.

CHAPTER 4

Criminal Law: Substance and Procedure

The law: it has honoured us, may we honour it.
I would invoke those who fill seats of justice,... that they execute the wholesome and necessary severity of the law.
DANIEL WEBSTER

OUTLINE

KEY TERMS

substantive criminal law
criminal procedure
procedural law
civil law
common law
Carriers case
law of precedent
stare decisis
torts
intent
folkways
mores
ex post facto laws
bills of attainder
substantive due process
procedural due process
mala in se
mala prohibitum
felony
misdemeanor
corpus delicti
actus reus
mens rea
criminal negligence
general or specific intent
transferred intent
strict liability
insanity
M'Naghten rule
irresistible impulse test
Durham rule
substantial capacity test
self-defense
entrapment
double jeopardy
RICO
Model Penal Code
preventive detention
separation of powers
Bill of Rights
exclusionary rule
self-incrimination
due process of law
incorporation theory
theory of selective incorporation
fundamental fairness

At the heart of the criminal justice system stands the rule of law. The criminal law defines crimes, dictates punishments, and controls the procedures used to process criminal offenders through the justice system.

This chapter focuses on the basic principles of the **substantive criminal law**, which regulates conduct in our society. In addition, constitutional **criminal procedure,** the law that governs judicial process, will be discussed to show how the rules of procedure, laid out in the U.S. Constitution and interpreted over time by the Supreme Court, control the operations of the justice system.

The substantive criminal law defines crime in U.S. society. Each state government, and the federal government as well, has its own criminal code, developed over many generations and incorporating moral beliefs, social values, political and economic matters, and other societal concerns. The criminal law is a living document, constantly evolving to keep pace with society and its needs.

The rules designed to implement the substantive law are known as **procedural law**. It is concerned with the criminal process—the legal steps through which an offender passes—commencing with the initial criminal investigation and concluding with release of the offender. Some elements of the law of criminal procedure are the rules of evidence, the law of arrest, the law of search and seizure, questions of appeal, and the right to counsel. Many of the rights that have been extended to offenders over the past two decades lie within procedural law.

A working knowledge of the law is critical for the criminal justice practitioner. In our modern society, the rule of law governs almost all phases of human enterprise, including commerce, family life, property transfer, and the regulation of interpersonal conflict. It contains elements that control personal relationships between individuals and public relationships between individuals and the government. The former is known as **civil law**, while the latter is criminal law, and both concepts are distinguished below.

Since the law defines crime, punishment, and procedure, which are the basic concerns of the criminal justice system, it is essential for students to know something of the nature, purpose, and content of the substantive and procedural criminal law.

Historical Development of the Criminal Law

The roots of the criminal codes used in the United States can be traced back to such early legal charters as the Babylonian Code of Hammurabi (2000 B.C.), the Mosiac Code of the Israelites (1200 B.C.), and the Roman Twelve Tables. During the sixth century, under the leadership of the Byzantine emperor Justinian, the first great codification of law in the western world was prepared. Justinian's *Corpus Juris Civilis*, or body of civil law, summarized the system of Roman law that had gradually developed for over a thousand years. Rules and regulations to ensure the safety of the state and the individual were organized into a code and served as the basis for future civil and criminal legal classifications. Centuries later, the French emperor Napoleon I created the French civil code, using Justinian's code as a model. France and the other countries that have modeled their legal systems on French and Roman law have what are known as civil law systems. Thus, the concept of law and crime has evolved over thousands of years.[1]

Before the Norman Conquest in 1066, the legal system among the early Anglo-Saxons was very decentralized. The law often varied from county to county, and there was very little written law, except for those covering crimes. Crimes were viewed prior to the year 1000 as personal wrongs, and compensation was often paid to the victim. Major violations of custom and law were violent acts, thefts, and disloyalty to the lord. For certain actions, such as treason, the penalty was often death. For other crimes, such as theft, compensation could be paid to the victim. Thus, to some degree, the early criminal law sought to produce an equitable solution to both private and public disputes.[2]

The Common Law

A more immediate source for much U.S. law is the English system of jurisprudence that developed after the Norman Conquest (1066). Prior to the ratification of the U.S. Constitution in 1788 and the development of the first state legal codes, formal law in the original colonies was adopted from existing English law, which is known today as the **common law**. Common law first came into being during the reign of King Henry II (1154–1189) when royal judges were appointed to travel to specific jurisdictions to hold court and represent the crown. Known as circuit judges, they followed a specific route (circuit) and heard cases that previously had been under the jurisdiction of local courts.[3] The royal judges began to replace local custom with a national law that was followed in courts throughout the country; thus, the law was "common" to the entire nation. The common law developed when English judges actually created many crimes by ruling that certain actions were subject to state control and sanction. The most serious offenses, such as murder, rape, treason, arson, and burglary, which had been viewed largely as personal wrongs (torts for which the victim received monetary compensation from the offender), were redefined by the judges as offenses against the state, or crimes.

The English common law evolved constantly to fit specific incidents that the judges encountered. In fact, legal scholars have identified specific cases in which judges created new crimes, some of which exist today. For example, in the **Carriers case** (1473), an English court ruled that a merchant who had been hired to

The English common law forms the basis of the substantive criminal law in the United States.

transport merchandise was guilty of larceny (theft) if he kept the goods for his own purposes.[4] Prior to the Carriers case, the common law had not recognized a crime when people kept something that was voluntarily placed in their possession, even if the rightful owner had only given them temporary custody of the merchandise. Breaking with legal tradition, the court recognized that the commercial system could not be maintained unless the law of theft were changed. Thus, larcenies defined by separate and unique criminal laws, such as embezzlement, extortion, and false pretenses, came into existence.

Another example of the historical basis for common law (case law) can be traced to what is known as "incomplete crime." A failed attempt to commit an illegal act was not a crime at common law. The modern doctrine that criminal attempt can be punished under law can be traced directly back to 1784 and the case law of *Rex v. Scofield.* In that case, Scofield was charged with having put a lit candle and combustible material in a house he was renting with the intention of burning it down; however, the house did not burn. He defended himself by arguing that an attempt to commit a misdemeanor was not actually a misdemeanor. In rejecting this argument, the court stated: "The intent may make an act, innocent in itself, criminal; nor is the completion of an act, criminal in itself, necessary to constitute criminality."[5] After *Scofield,* attempt became a common law crime, and today, all U.S. jurisdictions have enacted some form of criminal attempt law (inchoate crimes).

Over time, such common law decisions made by judges in England produced a body of rules and legal principles about crime and punishment that formed the basis of our early American legal system.

Prior to the American Revolution, this common law was the law of the land in the colonies. The original colonists abided by the various common law rulings and adopted them to fit their needs, making extensive changes in them when necessary. After the War of Independence, most state legislatures incorporated the common law into standardized legal codes. Over the years, some of the original common law crimes have changed considerably due to revisions. For example, the common law crime of rape originally applied only to female victims. This has been replaced in a number of jurisdictions by general sexual assault statutes that condemn sexual attacks against any person, male or female. Similarly, statutory offenses such as those banning the sale and possession of narcotics or outlawing the pirating of videotapes have been passed to control human behavior unknown at the time the common law was formulated.

Today, criminal behavior is defined primarily by statute. With few exceptions, crimes are removed, added, or modified by the legislature of a particular jurisdiction. In addition, many states have both a substantive criminal code and a code of criminal procedure that separates the definitions of crimes and the penalties from the various procedures used to process the defendant through the justice system.

The Principle of *Stare Decisis*

One of the principal components of the common law was its recognition of the **law of precedent**. Once a decision had been made by a court, that judicial decision was generally binding on other courts in subsequent cases. This principle is based on judge-made, or case, law created by judicial decisions. For example, if a homeowner who killed an unarmed intruder was found not guilty of murder on the ground that he had a right to defend his property, that rule would be applied in subsequent cases involving the same set of facts. In other words, a decision on the issue of self-defense in that case would be followed in that jurisdiction by the same court or a lesser court in future cases presenting the same legal problem. Since the common law represented decisions handed down by judges, as distinguished from law that is determined by statutes, it was essential that the rule of precedent be followed. This legal principle, known as ***stare decisis***, originated in England and is still used as the basis for deciding future legal cases.[6] *Stare decisis* is firmly rooted in our U.S. system of jurisprudence and serves to furnish the courts with a clear guide for the adjudication of similar issues.

The courts are generally bound by the principle of *stare decisis* to follow criminal law as it has been judicially determined in prior cases in the justice system. This principle is also used in interpreting evidence given in trials and in determining trial outcomes. The advantage of this legal doctrine is that it promotes stability and certainty in the process of making legal decisions. Predictability and uniformity in judicial decision making result from such a policy. However, where sufficient reason exists for varying from precedent, the court need not follow previous case decisions. For example, in the case of *Gideon v. Wainwright*, the U.S. Supreme Court ruled that a defendant in a felony case had the legal right to an attorney, although previous courts had decided such a right existed only in capital cases.[7] In other words, when a principle of law established by precedent is no longer appropriate because of changing economic, political, and social conditions, courts can redefine legal traditions and overrule precedent.[8] Because of this flexibility, the principle of *stare decisis* remains firmly embedded in our legal system.

Criminal Law and Civil Law

In modern U.S. society, law can be divided into two broad categories: criminal law and civil law. All law other than criminal law is known as civil law; it includes tort law (personal wrongs and damages), property law (the law governing the transfer and ownership of property), and contract law (the law of personal agreements).

The differences between criminal law and civil law are very significant because, in our legal system, criminal proceedings are completely separate from civil actions.

The major objective of the criminal law is to protect the public against harm by preventing criminal offenses. The primary concern of the civil law—in the area of private wrongs or **torts**, for example—is that the injured party be compensated for any harm done. The aggrieved person usually initiates proceedings to recover monetary damages. In contrast, when a crime is committed, the state initiates the legal process and imposes a punishment in the form of a criminal sanction. Furthermore, in criminal law, the emphasis is on the **intent** of the individual committing the crime; a civil proceeding gives primary attention to affixing the blame each party deserves for producing the damage or conflict.

Despite these major differences, criminal and civil law share certain features. Both areas of the law seek to control people's behavior by preventing them from acting in an undesirable manner, and both impose sanctions on those who commit violations of the law. The payment of damages to the victim in a tort case, for example, serves some of the same purposes as the payment of a fine in a criminal case. The criminal law sentences offenders to prison, while the civil law also imposes confinement on such individuals as the mentally ill, alcoholics, and the mentally defective. In addition, many actions, such as assault and battery, various forms of larceny, and negligence, are the basis for criminal as well as civil actions. Table 4.1 summarizes the similarities and differences between the criminal law and tort law.

In summary, the criminal law usually applies in an action taken by the local, state, or federal government against an individual who has been accused of committing a crime. The civil law comes into play when an individual or group seeks monetary recompense for harmful actions committed by another individual or group.

TABLE 4.1
A Comparison of Criminal and Tort Law

Similarities

Both criminal and tort law seek to control behavior.
Both laws impose sanctions.
Similar areas of legal action exist; for example, personal assault and control of white-collar offenses, such as environmental pollution.

Differences

Criminal Law	Tort Law
Crime is a public offense.	Tort is a civil or private wrong.
The sanction associated with criminal law is incarceration or death.	The sanction associated with a tort is monetary damages.
The right of enforcement belongs to the state.	The individual brings the action.
The government ordinarily does not appeal.	Both parties can appeal.
Fines go to the state.	The individual receives damages as compensation for harm done.

Purposes of the Criminal Law

Today, the criminal law serves a number of different purposes, five of the most important of which are discussed here. Underlying these broad purposes is the desire to prevent and control unacceptable behavior and protect the interests of society and its citizens.

Identification of Public Wrongs

One major purpose of the substantive criminal law is the identification of conduct that society deems unjustifiable. Such conduct inflicts or threatens to harm individuals or the public interest.[9] Conversely, acts that are not identified by the criminal law as crimes are protected from state sanction. In some instances, the law seeks an outright ban on acts such as murder, rape, and arson. In other situations, the law seeks to create boundaries of acceptable behavior. For example, consider the fifty-five-mile-per-hour speed limit, twenty-one-year-old drinking age, government lotteries in jurisdictions that prohibit other types of gambling, or the judicial age limitation over jurisdiction for juvenile delinquency.

Exertion of Social Control

The criminal law allows the state to control and sanction those people who commit crime. This distinguishes crimes from the unwritten rules of conventional society: ordinary customs and conventions referred to as **folkways** and universally followed behavior norms and morals known as **mores**. Where crime brings the offender into confrontation with the state and its authorities, infringement of unwritten rules is subject only to social disapproval and individual expressions of scorn. In other words, control of the criminal law is given to those in political power; violations of mores may only be informally punished.

Deterrence of Antisocial Behavior

Society must give fair warning of the nature of forbidden conduct and describe the sanctions associated with the outlawed behaviors. The well-publicized punishments connected to criminal law violations serve to deter potential criminals from carrying out their illegal plans and schemes. It is believed that if punishments of adequate severity are swiftly given and if criminals believe they are likely to be caught, the threat of the criminal law should be sufficient to deter crime.

Regulation of Punishments

The criminal law spells out the punishments given to law violators. In so doing, it safeguards offenders against excessive, disproportionate, or arbitrary punishments. In an ideal world, offenders who have similar criminal backgrounds and who commit similar crimes would receive identical sanctions. Of course, this does not always work in practice, but the criminal law attempts to regulate punishment or at least keep penalties within an acceptable range. In creating punishments, the framers of the criminal law should take into account such issues as public opinion about the crime's social harm, the ability of the justice system to carry out sanctions, and the latest scientific views on the prevention of crime and treatment of offenders. For example, society would be appalled if shoplifters were punished as severely as rapists or if traffic offenders were regularly sentenced to prison. (See Analyzing Criminal Justice Issues on the disproportionality in punishing the drunk driver.)

Today, the most common punishments are monetary fines, community supervision or probation, incarceration in prison, and, in rare instances, capital punishment.

Maintenance of the Social Order

An underlying principle of all legal systems is to support and maintain the boundaries of the social system they serve. In medieval England, the law protected the feudal system by defining an orderly system of property transfer and ownership. Similarly, the legal systems in communist or socialist countries are designed to curtail profiteering and private ownership of production. The U.S. free enterprise system is maintained by the power of the criminal law to protect the marketplace and allow commerce to exist. For example, if it were not for the various laws of theft—larceny, burglary, robbery—businesspeople would be prevented from accumulating large sums of money that they do not have in their direct possession. The banking system could not exist, nor could credit be extended. Thus, the criminal law is tailored to fit the social and economic system it serves.

Sources of the Criminal Law

The five major sources of the criminal law are (1) common law, (2) statutes, (3) case decisions, (4) administrative rules and regulations, and (5) constitutional laws.[10]

Common Law and Statutes

The common law crimes adopted into state codes form one major source of the substantive criminal law today. At common law, crimes had a general meaning, and everyone basically understood the definition of such actions as murder, larceny, and rape. Today, statutes, enacted by state and federal legislative bodies, have built on these common law meanings and often contain more detailed and specific definitions of the crimes. Statutes are thus a way in which the criminal law is created, modified, or expunged. They reflect existing social conditions and deal with issues of morality, such as gambling and sexual activity, as well as traditional common law crimes, such as murder, burglary, and arson.

Case Decisions

Case law and judicial decision making also change and influence laws. For example, a statute may define murder as the "unlawful killing of one human being by another with malice." Court decisions might help explain the meaning of the term *malice* or clarify whether *human being* includes a fetus. A judge may rule that a statute is vague or deals with an act no longer of interest to the public or is an unfair exercise of state control over an individual. Conversely, some judges may interpret the law so that behaviors that were previously acceptable become outlawed. For example, judges in a particular jurisdiction might find all people who sell magazines depicting nude men and women guilty of the crime of selling obscene material, whereas in the past, obscenity was interpreted much more nar-

ANALYZING CRIMINAL JUSTICE ISSUES

Punishing the Drunk Driver in Foreign Countries

Although penalties for driving under the influence are becoming increasingly severe in the United States, most jurisdictions still only require a fine, temporary suspension of the driver's license, and/or rehabilitation for drunk driving.

Such sentences are no match for those handed out in other countries.

- In Australia, the names of drunk drivers are sent to the local newspaper and published under the heading, "He's/She's drunk and in jail."
- In Bulgaria, a second conviction means execution.
- In El Salvador, a first conviction of driving while under the influence results in death by firing squad.
- In Malaysia, the driver is jailed and, if married, the spouse is jailed as well.
- In Turkey, drunk drivers are taken twenty miles from town and forced to walk back.
- And in Russia, the driver's license is revoked for life.

Critical Thinking Skills

This tells us that many other nations have concluded that drunk driving is so serious that harsh penalties are required. By imposing less severe sentences, the United States places itself in the position of being lenient on traffic offenders.

1. Does the fact that the United States is generally "easy" on drunk drivers mean that prison sentences are negligible as a deterrent? Does it make more sense to impose mandatory sentences for driving under the influence to ensure a deterrent effect?

2. Should traffic offenses be part of the criminal justice system? Research shows that alcoholism is a disease. Would this fact justify a massive effort to decriminalize such actions? If a drunk driver is suffering from alcoholism, does he or she have the intent to commit a crime?

3. Drunk drivers account for twenty-five to thirty thousand deaths each year in the United States, in addition to enormous personal injury and property damage. As a result, many states have passed "roadblock" laws under which police can stop traffic and inspect drivers for signs of intoxication. Is this a reasonable thing to do? At this point in your reading, can you identify any possible constitutional problems with sobriety checkpoints?

SOURCE: *National District Attorneys Association Bulletin* 10 (September/October 1991):9.

rowly. Or, some courts might consider drunken driving a petty crime, while others might interpret the driving-under-the-influence statute more severely.

Administrative Rule Making

Administrative agencies with rule-making authority also develop measures to control conduct in our society.[11] Some agencies regulate taxation, health, environment, and other public functions; others control drugs, illegal gambling, or pornographic material. The listing of prohibited drugs by various state health boards, for example, is an important administrative control function. Parole boards are administrative agencies that implement the thousands of parole regulations that govern the conduct of criminal offenders after their release from prison. Such rules are called administrative rules with criminal sanctions, and agency decisions about these rules have the force and authority of law.

Constitutional Law and Its Limits

Regardless of its source, all criminal law in the United States must conform to the rules and dictates of the U.S. Constitution.[12] In other words, any criminal law that conflicts with the various provisions and articles of the Constitution will eventually be challenged in the appellate courts and stricken from the legal code by judicial order (or modified to adhere to constitutional principles). As Chief Justice John Marshall's opinion in *Marbury v. Madison* indicated, "If the courts are to regard the constitution and the constitution is superior to any ordinary act of the legislature, the constitution and not such ordinary act must govern the case to which they apply." [13]

Among the general limitations set by the Constitution are those that forbid the government to pass ***ex post facto* laws.** Such laws create crimes (or penalties) that can be enforced retroactively (though civil penalties, such as those set in tax laws, can be retroactive). The Constitution also forbids **bills of attainder,** legislative acts that inflict punishment without a judicial trial. In addition, criminal laws have been interpreted as violating constitutional principles if they are too vague, or overbroad, to give clear meaning of their intent. For example, a law forbidding adults to engage in "immoral behavior" could not be enforced because it does not use clear and precise language or give adequate notice as to which conduct is forbidden.[14] The Constitution also forbids laws that make a person's status a crime. For example, addiction to narcotics cannot be made a crime, though laws can forbid the sale, possession, and manufacture of dangerous drugs.

In general, the Constitution has been interpreted to forbid any criminal law that violates a person's right to be treated fairly and equally; this principle is referred to as **substantive due process**. Usually, this means that before a new law can be created, the state must show that there is a compelling need to protect public safety or morals. However, a law that unfairly penalizes a particular group of people would be considered unconstitutional. Therefore, laws requiring drivers to buckle their seat belts to protect their physical well-being are considered a reasonable exercise in public safety; in contrast, a law requiring all people to attend church every Sunday to protect their moral well-being would be considered an infringement of the personal freedom guaranteed by the first Amendment. In the 1992 case of *R.A.V. v. St. Paul,* for example, the U.S. Supreme Court ruled that a St. Paul, Minnesota "hate crime" statute which defined cross-burning as a crime violated the defendants' First Amendment guarantee of free speech.

By the same token, constitutional provisions can be used to strike down administrative or judicial rules and regulations that do not meet the requirements of **procedural due process**. This means that the Constitution guarantees fairness and justice in such proceedings. The hearing must be fair; defendants must have the opportunity to defend themselves; the hearing must be held before an impartial tribunal, and so on. In this and subsequent chapters, the due process guarantees of criminal procedure will be discussed in detail.

Crimes and Classifications

The decision of how a crime should be classified rests with the individual jurisdiction. Each state has developed its own body of criminal law and consequently determines its own penalties for the different crimes. Thus, the criminal law of a given state defines and grades offenses, sets levels of punishment, and classifies crimes into different categories. Over the years, crimes have been generally grouped into the following classifications: (1) felonies, misdemeanors, and violations; and (2) other statutory classifications, such as juvenile delinquency, sex offender categories, and multiple- or first-offender classifications.

The Concepts of *Mala in Se* and *Mala Prohibitum*

In the early twentieth century, such terms as *mala in se* and *mala prohibitum* were also used to describe categories of crime.[15] ***Mala in se*** crimes were basically those that appeared inherently wrong or evil by their nature. Crimes involving gross immorality or depravity—such as murder, armed robbery, kidnapping, and rape—are all essentially evil and were considered to be *mala in se* offenses. Common law crimes were generally considered to be *mala in se* because the common law concerned itself with actions wrong in themselves and not with crimes forbidden by statutory law.

Mala prohibitum offenses were those that were sanctioned because they were prohibited by statute; that is, they had been defined as crimes by the penal code. The question of immorality does not exist in mala prohibitum crimes because these crimes are created by legislative enactment for the well-being of society. Such crimes included speeding, driving under the influence of alcohol, going through a red light, being disorderly or vagrant, and other similar breaches of the public peace. Over the years, many states have expanded *mala prohibitum* crimes through legislative enactment.

This historic distinction between *mala in se* and *mala prohibitum* offenses has been a useful reference for legislative substantive law revisions, particularly when they involve issues of criminal intent and liability. For instance, with regard to such crimes as manslaughter and battery, one whose conduct causes an unintentional death may be guilty of manslaughter (*mala in se*), but if his conduct is *mala prohibitum*, then the crime may only be a battery. In other words, the defendant would only be liable if death was the foreseeable consequence of the criminal act.[16] Practically speaking, however, such distinctions have little bearing on the classification of crimes today.

Crimes can also be grouped according to the harm done. Who and what is the legislature trying to protect from injury is the basic question with regard to this kind of classification. Some crimes, such as murder, manslaughter, rape, assault, and robbery, are classified offenses against a person. Other crimes, such as arson, burglary, and larceny, are classified as offenses against property to protect the home and the interest in personal property. Offenses against authority in the administration of justice include many public welfare crimes and serious offenses, such as perjury and treason. Crimes are categorized in this fashion in almost every state penal code. Such a classification helps the legislature locate particular crimes within the penal code and develop comparable sentences for the various offenses.

Felonies and Misdemeanors

The most common classification in the United States is the division between felonies and misdemeanors.[17] This distinction is based primarily on the degree of seriousness of the crime.

Distinguishing between a **felony** and a **misdemeanor** is sometimes difficult. Simply put, a felony is a serious offense and a misdemeanor a less serious one.

Black's Law Dictionary defines the two terms as follows:

> A felony is a crime of a graver or more atrocious nature than those designated as misdemeanors. Generally it is an offense punishable by death or imprisonment in a penitentiary. A misdemeanor is lower than a felony and is generally punishable by fine or imprisonment otherwise than in a penitentiary.[18]

Each jurisdiction in the United States determines by statute what types of conduct constitute felonies or misdemeanors. The most common definition for a felony is that it is a crime punishable in the statute by death or imprisonment in a state prison. In Massachusetts, for example, any crime that a statute punishes by imprisonment in the state prison system is considered a felony, and all other crimes are misdemeanors.[19] Another way of determining what category an offense falls into is by providing in the statute that a felony is any crime punishable by imprisonment for more than one year. In the former method, the place of imprisonment is critical; in the latter, the length of the prison sentence distinguishes a felony from a misdemeanor.

In the United States today, felonies include serious crimes against the person, such as criminal homicide, robbery, and rape, or crimes against property, such as burglary and larceny. Misdemeanors include petit (or petty) larceny, assault and battery, and the unlawful possession of marijuana. The least serious, or petty, offenses, often involving criminal traffic violations, are called infractions.

The felony-misdemeanor classification has a direct effect on the offender charged with the crime. A person convicted of a felony may be barred from certain fields of employment or from entering some professional fields of study, such as law or medicine. A felony offender's status as an alien in the United States might also be affected, or the offender might be denied the right to hold public office, vote, or serve on a jury.[20] These and other civil liabilities exist only when a person is convicted of a felony offense, not a misdemeanor.

Whether the offender is charged with a felony or a misdemeanor also makes a difference at the time of arrest. Normally, the law of arrest requires that if the crime is a misdemeanor and has not been committed in the presence of a police officer, the officer cannot make an arrest. This is known as the in-presence requirement. However, the police officer does not have the legal authority to arrest a suspect for a misdemeanor at a subsequent time by the use of a validly obtained arrest warrant. In contrast, an arrest for a felony may be made regardless of whether the crime was committed in the officer's presence, as long as the officer has reasonable grounds to believe that the person has committed the felony.

Another important effect of this classification is that a court's jurisdiction often depends on whether a crime is considered a felony or a misdemeanor. A person charged with a felony must be tried by a court that has jurisdiction over the type of offense. Similarly, some states prosecute felonies only on indictment. This means that a person accused of a felony ordinarily has a legal right to a preliminary hearing and presentment of the charges by indictment of a grand jury or information.

In addition to serious felony crimes and less serious offenses labeled misdemeanors, some jurisdictions also have a third category of least serious offenses called violations. These violations, ordinarily of town, city, or county ordinances, are regulatory offenses that may not require *mens rea* (criminal intent). Examples include health and sanitary violations, unlawful assembly, public disturbances, and traffic violations.

Behavioral Classifications

In addition to the felony-misdemeanor classifications, crimes may be classified according to the characteristics of the offender. All states, for example, have juvenile delinquency statutes that classify children under a certain age as juvenile delinquents if they commit acts that would constitute crimes if committed by adults. Some statutes have special statutory classifications for sex offenders, multiple offenders, youthful offenders, and first offenders. Generally, no special statutory classification exists for white-collar crimes, which usually involve nonviolent conduct, such as embezzlement, fraud, and income tax violation.

The Legal Definition of a Crime

There is no single universally accepted legal definition of a crime. Because the determination of what constitutes a crime rests with the individual jurisdiction, the federal government and each of the states have their own body of criminal law. Most general legal definitions of a crime are basically similar in nature, however. A crime can be defined as follows:

> A crime is (1) a legal wrong (2) prohibited by the criminal law (3) prosecuted by the state (4) in a formal court proceeding (5) in which a criminal sanction or sentence may be imposed.

As determined by most legal systems, crime can result from the commission of an act in violation of the law or from the omission of a required legal act. For example, a crime can be an intentional act of striking another person or of stealing someone else's property. A crime can also involve the failure of a person to act, such as the failure to file an income tax return, a parent's failure to care for a child, the failure to report a crime, or the failure to report an automobile accident.

The legal definition of a crime involves the elements of the criminal acts that must be proven in a court of law if the defendant is to be found guilty. For the most part, common criminal acts have both mental and physical elements, both of which must be present if the act is to be considered a legal crime. The following definition of the crime of burglary in the nighttime, as stated in the Massachusetts General Laws, is an example of the mental and physical elements of the substantive criminal law:

> Whoever breaks and enters a dwelling house in the nighttime, with intent to commit a felony, or whoever, after having entered with such intent, breaks such dwelling house in the nighttime, any person being lawfully therein, and the offender being armed with a dangerous weapon at the time of such breaking or entry, or so arming himself in such house or making an actual assault on a person lawfully therein, (commits the crime of burglary).[21]

The elements of the crime are:

1. Nighttime
2. Breaking and entering, or breaking or entering
3. A dwelling house
4. Being armed, or arming the self after entering, or committing an actual assault on a person lawfully therein
5. Intent to commit a felony

Notice how certain basic elements are required in order for an act to be considered a crime. For the crime of burglary, the state must prove that the defendant actually entered a home by force and was not invited in, that the defendant carried an identifiable weapon, that the crime occurred after sundown, and that the act was intentional. These elements form what is known as the ***corpus delicti***, or "body of the crime." The term *corpus delicti* is often misunderstood. Some people, for instance, wrongly believe that it refers to the body of the deceased in a homicide. *Corpus delicti* describes all the elements that together constitute a crime; it includes (1) the *actus reus*, (2) the *mens rea*, and (3) the combination of *actus reus* and *mens rea*.

Actus Reus

The term ***actus reus,*** which translates as "guilty act," refers to the forbidden act itself. The criminal law uses it to describe the physical crime and/or the commission of the criminal act (or omission of the lawful act). In *Criminal Law*, Wayne LaFave and Austin Scott state:

> Bad thought alone cannot constitute a crime, there must be an act, or an omission to act where there is a legal duty to act. Thus, the criminal law crimes are defined in terms of act or omission to act and statutory crimes are unconstitutional unless so defined. A bodily movement, to qualify as an act forming the basis of criminal liability, must be voluntary.[22]

The physical act in violation of the criminal statute is usually clearly defined within each offense. For example, in the crime of manslaughter, the unlawful killing of a human being is the physical act prohibited by a statute; in burglary, it is the actual breaking and entering into a dwelling house or other structure for the purpose of committing a felony.

Regarding an omission to act, many jurisdictions hold a person accountable if a legal duty exists and the offender avoids it. In most instances, the duty to act is based on a defined relationship such as parent-child or on a contractual duty such as lifeguard-swimmer. The law, for example, recognizes that a parent has a legal duty to protect a child. When a parent refuses to obtain medical attention for the child and the child dies, the parent's actions constitute an omission to act, and that omission is a crime.

Finally, the *actus reus* must be a measurable act; thought alone is not a crime. However, planning, conspiring, and soliciting for criminal purposes are considered an *actus reus,* even if the actual crime is never carried out or completed.

Mens Rea

The second element basic to the commission of any crime is the establishment of the ***mens rea,*** translated as "guilty mind." *Mens rea* is the element of the crime that deals with the defendant's intent to commit a criminal act and also includes such states of mind as concealing criminal knowledge (scienter), recklessness, negligence, and criminal purpose.[23] A person ordinarily cannot be convicted of a crime unless it is proven that he or she intentionally, knowingly, or willingly committed the criminal act.

The following case illustrates the absence of *mens rea.* A student at a university took home some books, believing them to be her own, and subsequently found that the books belonged to her classmate. When she realized that the books did not belong to her, she returned them to their proper owner. The student could not be prosecuted for theft because she did not intend to steal the books in the first place; she did not knowingly take the books and therefore lacked sufficient knowledge that her act was unlawful.

Another case that illustrates a lack of criminal intent, though harm occurs, is that in which a pedestrian is accidentally killed in an automobile accident. At the time of the accident, the driver is operating the motor vehicle legally and with appropriate care, but the victim steps out in front of the car and is struck and killed. The driver cannot be convicted of manslaughter unless evidence can be found that some intent or gross criminal negligence existed at the time of the accident. This situation would be considered in a completely different legal light if it could be proved that the driver actually intended to hit the pedestrian or had been driving the car in a willful and reckless manner, indicating criminal negligence.

Ordinary negligence is any conduct that falls below the normal standard established by law for the protection of others against unreasonable risk. **Criminal negligence,** on the other hand, exists where actions show a significant degree of carelessness that results in a culpable disregard for the safety of others. Thus, in order for an individual to be found guilty of committing most crimes, it must be proved that he or she committed the physical act itself and that he or she intended to do so with full awareness of the consequences of the act.

Other variations on the concept of criminal intent exist. Different degrees of intent are used to determine the mental state necessary for an individual to commit a particular crime. Where a criminal homicide occurs, it may be necessary to prove that a mental state of premeditation and malice existed in the accused before a judgment of first-degree murder can be reached; for a judgment of second-degree murder, it may be necessary to prove malice; and for a judgment of third-degree murder, it may be necessary to prove guilty knowledge or criminal negligence.

Mens rea conditions also differ among the types of crime when considering whether a **general or specific intent** to commit the crime exists. For most crimes, a general intent on the part of the accused to act purposefully or to accomplish a criminal result must be proved. A specific intent requires that the actor intended to accomplish a specific purpose as an element of the crime. Burglary, for example, involves more than the general intent of breaking and entering into a dwelling house; it usually also involves the specific intent of committing a felony, such as stealing money or jewels. Many other crimes such as robbery, larceny, assault with intent to kill, false pretense, and even kidnapping may require a specific intent.

Relationship of *Mens Rea* and *Actus Reus*

The third element needed to prove the *corpus delicti* of a crime is the relationship of the act to the criminal intent or result. The law requires that the offender's conduct must be the approximate cause of any injury resulting from the criminal act. If, for example, a man chases a victim into the street intending to assault him and the victim is struck and killed by a car, the accused could be convicted of murder if the court felt that his actions made him responsible for the victim's death. If, however, a victim dies from a completely unrelated illness after being assaulted, the court must determine whether the death was a probable consequence of the defendant's illegal conduct or whether it would have resulted even if the assault had not occurred.

In addition, to prove a crime, the state must show that the external physical act and the internal mental state were in some way connected to one another. For example, if a man breaks into another person's house to escape a violent storm and while in the home notices some jewels and steals them, he cannot be found guilty of the crime of burglary since he did not intend to commit a crime at the time he broke into the house. Nevertheless, he could be convicted of larceny and criminal trespass, since he had the necessary intent at the time he committed these crimes. However, evil intent and the act it produces do not

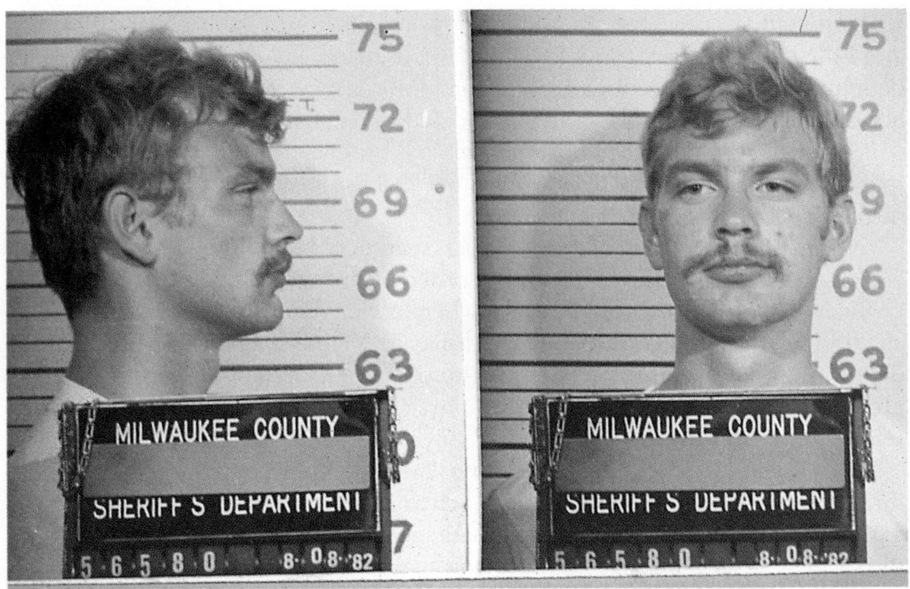

Though bizarre criminals such as Milwaukee Cannibal Jeffrey Dahmer may appear mentally ill, a jury found that he was legally sane. Dahmer was given a life sentence to prison.

necessarily have to take place at the same time. If a terrorist plants a bomb in an airport, but it does not go off until three weeks later, that would still be considered murder—assuming people are killed.

Criminal liability, as previously explained, cannot be imposed for simply having had bad thoughts about the victim at a previous time. Thus, a concurrence of act and intent—*actus reus* and *mens rea*—must be present if a crime is to occur. However, cases do exist where one person intends criminal action against another but harms a third party instead; for example, the accused intends to shoot one person but misses and shoots another. In this instance, the law transfers the original criminal intent to the innocent bystander. Under the legal doctrine of **transferred intent,** the accused would be considered criminally responsible for transferring wrongful intent to the other person.

Strict Liability

Existence of a criminal intent and a wrongful act must both be proved before an individual can be found guilty of committing a crime. However, certain statutory offenses exist in which *mens rea* is not essential. These offenses fall within a category known as public welfare, or **strict liability,** crimes. A person can be held responsible for such a violation independent of the existence of intent to commit the offense. Strict liability criminal statutes generally include narcotics control laws, traffic laws, health and safety regulations, sanitation laws, and other regulatory statutes. For example, a driver could not defend himself against a speeding ticket by claiming that he was unaware of how fast he was going and did not intend to speed, nor could a bartender claim that a juvenile to whom she sold liquor looked quite a bit older. No state of mind is generally required where a strict liability statute is violated.[24]

The general purpose of such laws is to protect the public and to provide the prosecution with an opportunity to convict offenders of crimes that would ordinarily be difficult to prove in court. Over the years, most legal commentators have been critical of strict liability offenses because it seems unfair to punish a person without referring to that person's state of mind when committing the crime.[25] However, these statutes still remain part of the legal codes in many jurisdictions.

Table 4.2 presents some categories of major substantive crimes common to all jurisdictions. The basic elements of each crime are contained within its definition.

Criminal Responsibility

The idea of criminal responsibility is also essential to any discussion of criminal law. The law recognizes that certain conditions of a person's mental state might excuse him or her from acts that otherwise would be considered criminal. These factors have been used in legal defenses to negate the intent required for the commission of a crime. For example, a person who kills another while insane may argue in court that he or she was not responsible for criminal conduct. Similarly, a child who violates the law may not be treated as an adult offender. Three major types of criminal defense are detailed in this section: insanity, intoxication, and age.

Insanity

Criminal **insanity** is a legal defense involving the use of rules and standards to determine if a person's state of mental balance negates criminal responsibility. Insanity is a legal concept and not one coined by the mental health field. Consequently, there are no standard symptoms of insanity or any specific behaviors that determine its existence. Instead, each legal jurisdiction defines insanity as it sees fit and then, at trial, attempts to determine whether the defendant meets the standards set forth in the state's criminal code. Usually, people who claim they are insane are examined by psychologists and psychiatrists who will then testify at trial on the defendant's mental condition. This procedure is often unsatisfactory because members of the mental health profession will disagree sharply on their diagnosis, and their conflicting opinions only serve to confuse the judge and the jury.

Stages of Insanity. If a person is declared insane at the time he or she committed a criminal act, a judgment of *not guilty by reason of insanity* is entered. The person is then held in an institution for the criminally insane until found to be sane and eligible for release. Defendants may also be incompetent to stand trial because of their mental condition. In this instance, they would be held in a mental institution until ready to stand trial. If after a reasonable period of time they are still unable to stand trial, the state might move to have them committed to an institution under civil commitment procedures.

On rare occasions, a person who was insane or temporarily insane at the time of committing a crime is treated successfully before coming to trial. Under those circumstances, the state would have no choice but to find the person not guilty and release him or her into the community, since psychiatric care is no longer needed.

Legal Definition of Insanity. Over the years, the legal system has struggled to define the rules relating to the use of insanity as a defense in a criminal trial. The different tests for criminal responsibility involving insanity followed by

TABLE 4.2
Common Law Crimes

Crimes Against the Person	Examples
First degree murder. Unlawful killing of another human being with malice aforethought and with premeditation and deliberation.	A woman buys some poison and pours it into a cup of coffee her husband is drinking, intending to kill him. The motive—to get the insurance benefits of the victim.
Second-degree murder. Unlawful killing of another human being with malice aforethought but without premeditation and deliberation.	A man intending to greatly harm his friend after a disagreement in a bar hits his friend in the head with a baseball bat, and the victim dies as a result of the injury. Hitting someone hard with a bat is known to cause serious injury. Because the act was committed in spite of this fact, it is second-degree murder.
Voluntary manslaughter. Intentional killing committed under extenuating circumstances that mitigate the killing, such as killing in the heat of passion after being provoked.	A husband coming home early from work finds his wife in bed with another man. The husband goes into a rage and shoots and kills both lovers with a gun he keeps by his bedside.
Involuntary manslaughter. Unintentional killing, without malice, that is neither excused nor justified, such as homicide resulting from criminal negligence.	After becoming drunk, a woman drives a car at high speed down a crowded street and kills a pedestrian.
Battery. Unlawful touching of another with intent to cause injury.	A man seeing a stranger sitting in his favorite seat in the cafeteria goes up to that person and pushes him out of the seat.
Assault. Intentional placing of another in fear of receiving an immediate battery.	A student aims an unloaded gun at her professor who believes the gun is loaded. She says she is going to shoot.
Rape. Unlawful sexual intercourse with a female without her consent.	After a party, a man offers to drive a young female acquaintance home. He takes her to a wooded area and, despite her protests, forces her to have sexual relations with him.
Statutory rape. Sexual intercourse with a female who is under the age of consent.	A boy, aged 18, and his girlfriend, aged 15, have sexual relations. Though the victim voluntarily participates, her age makes her incapable of legally consenting to have sexual relations.
Robbery. Wrongful taking and carrying away of personal property from a person by violence or intimidation.	A man armed with a loaded gun approaches another man on a deserted street and demands his wallet.

TABLE 4.2
Continued

Inchoate (Incomplete) Offenses	Examples
Attempt. An intentional act for the purpose of committing a crime that is more than mere preparation or planning of the crime. The crime is not completed, however.	A person intending to kill another places a bomb in the second person's car so that it will detonate when the ignition key is used. The bomb is discovered before the car is started. Attempted murder has been committed.
Conspiracy. Voluntary agreement between two or more persons to achieve an unlawful object or to achieve a lawful object using means forbidden by law.	A drug company sells larger-than-normal quantities of drugs to a doctor, knowing that the doctor is distributing the drugs illegally. The drug company is guilty of conspiracy.
Solicitation. Efforts by one person to encourage another person to commit or attempt to commit a crime by means of advising, enticing, inciting, ordering, or otherwise.	A person offers another a hundred dollars to set fire to a third person's house. The person requesting that the fire be set is guilty of solicitation, whether the fire is set or not.

Crimes Against Property	Examples
Burglary. Breaking and entering of a dwelling house of another in the nighttime with the intent to commit a felony.	Intending to steal some jewelry and silver, a young man breaks a window and enters another's house at 10 P.M.
Arson. Intentional burning of a dwelling house of another.	A secretary, angry that her boss did not give her a raise, goes to her boss's house and sets fire to it.
Larceny. Taking and carrying away the personal property of another with the intent to steal the property.	While a woman is shopping, she sees a diamond ring displayed at the jewelry counter. When no one is looking, the woman takes the ring and walks out of the store.
Embezzlement. Fraudulent appropriation of another's property by one already in lawful possession.	A bank teller receives a cash deposit from a customer and places it in the cash drawer with other deposits. A few minutes later, he takes the deposit out of the cash drawer and keeps it by placing it in his pocket.
Receiving stolen goods. Receiving of stolen property with the knowledge that the property is stolen and with the intent to deprive the owner of the property.	A "fence" accepts some television sets from a thief with the intention of selling them, knowing that the sets have been stolen.

United States courts are (1) the M'*Naghten rule*; (2) the *irresistible impulse test*; (3) the *Durham rule*; and (4) the *substantial capacity test*.

The **M'Naghten rule,** or the right-wrong test, is based on the decision in the M'*Naghten* case.[26] In 1843, Daniel M'Naghten shot and killed Edward Drummond, believing Drummond to be Sir Robert Peel, the British prime minister. M'Naghten was prosecuted for murder. At his trial, he claimed that he was not criminally responsible for his actions because he suffered from delusions at the time of the killing. M'Naghten was found not guilty by reason of insanity. Because of the importance of the case and the unpopularity of the decision, the House of Lords reviewed the decision and asked the court to define the law with respect to crimes committed by persons suffering from insane delusions. The court's answer became known as the M'Naghten rule and has subsequently become the primary test for criminal responsibility in the United States. The M'Naghten rule can be stated as follows:

> A defendant may be excused from criminal responsibility if at the time of the committing of the act the party accused was labouring under such a defect of reason, from a disease of the mind, as not to know the nature and quality of the act he was doing, or if he did know it, that he did not know that he was doing what was wrong.

Thus, according to the M'Naghten rule, a person is basically insane if he or she is unable to distinguish between right and wrong as a result of some mental disability.

Over the years, the courts have become critical of the M'Naghten rule. Many insane individuals are able to distinguish between right and wrong. Also, clear determinations by the courts of such terms as *disease of the mind, know*, and *the nature and quality of the act* have never been made. As a result, many jurisdictions that follow the M'Naghten rule have supplemented it with the **irresistible impulse test.** This rule excuses from criminal responsibility a person whose mental disease makes it impossible to control personal conduct. The criminal may be able to distinguish between right and wrong but may be unable to exercise self-control because of a disabling mental condition. Approximately twenty states use a combined M'Naghten rule-irresistible impulse test.

Another rule for determining criminal insanity is the **Durham rule.** Originally created in New Hampshire in 1871, the Durham rule was reviewed and subsequently adopted by the Court of Appeals for the District of Columbia in 1954, in the case of *Durham v. United States*.[27] In that opinion, Judge David Bazelon rejected the M'Naghten formula and stated that an accused is not criminally responsible if the unlawful act was the product of mental disease or defect. This rule, also known as the *products test*, is based on the contention that insanity represents many personality factors, all of which may not be present in every case. It leaves the question of deciding whether a defendant is insane in the hands of jurors.

The Durham rule has been viewed with considerable skepticism, primarily because the problem of defining *mental disease or defect* and *product* does not give the jury a reliable standard by which to make its judgment. Consequently, it has been dropped in the jurisdictions that experimented with it and is used in only New Hampshire today. Nevertheless, the Durham rule was probably the most important factor in stimulating rethinking of the entire insanity issue, and it revolutionized the law of insanity in the United States. It opened up the insanity defense to the urban poor, desegregated mental hospitals, and helped bring legal psychiatric services to the needy.

Another test for criminal insanity, which has become increasingly popular with many courts, is the **substantial capacity test.** In summary, as presented in Section 4.01 of the American Law Institute's Model Penal Code, this test states:

> A person is not responsible for criminal conduct if at the time of such conduct as a result of mental disease or defect he lacks substantial capacity whether to appreciate his criminality (wrongfulness) of his conduct or to conform his conduct to the requirements of law.[28]

This rule is basically a broader restatement of the M'Naghten rule-irresistible impulse test. It rejects the Durham rule because of its lack of standards and its inability to define the term *product*. The most significant feature of this test is that it requires only a lack of "substantial capacity," rather than complete impairment of the defendant's ability to know and understand the difference between right and wrong. Twenty-four states use the substantial capacity test as defined by the American Law Institute.[29]

For a summary of various rules for determining criminal insanity, see Table 4.3. In reality, only a small number of offenders actually use the insanity defense

TABLE 4.3
Various Insanity Defense Standards

Test	Legal Standard Because of Mental Illness	Final Burden of Proof	Who Bears Burden of Proof
M'Naghten	"didn't know what he was doing or didn't know it was wrong"	Varies from proof by a balance of probabilities on the defense to proof beyond a reasonble doubt on the prosecutor	
Irresistible Impulse	"could not control his conduct"		
Durham	"the criminal act was caused by his mental illness	Beyond reasonable doubt	Prosecutor
Substantial Capacity	"lacks substantial capacity to appreciate the wrongfulness of his conduct or to control it"	Beyond reasonable doubt	Prosecutor
Present Federal Law	"lacks capacity to appreciate the wrongfulness of his conduct"	Clear and convincing evidence	Defense

SOURCE: National Institute of Justice, *Crime Study Guide: Insanity Defense* by Norval Morris (Washington, D.C.: U.S. Department of Justice, 1986), p. 3.

because many cases involving insane offenders are processed through civil commitment proceedings.

Debate Over the Insanity Defense. The insanity defense has been controversial for many years. It has been criticized on the grounds that it (1) spurs crime, (2) releases criminal offenders, (3) requires extensive use of expert testimony, and (4) commits more criminals to mental institutions than to prisons.[30] In addition, according to Norval Morris, a University of Chicago law professor, defendants end up with a double stigma—namely, that they are "bad and mad" when they are found not guilty by reason of insanity.[31]

In the early 1980s, the case of John Hinckley, Jr. heightened the debate over the insanity plea.[32] Hinckley was charged with the attempted murder of President Ronald Reagan in 1981. At his criminal trial, expert testimony was offered to show that Hinckley suffered from a serious form of schizophrenia that grew worse with age. This caused Hinckley to be criminally insane. He was unable to appreciate his actions or control himself because he had a serious disease of the mind. The government, on the other hand, was required to show that Hinckley was sane beyond a reasonable doubt and responsible for his behavior at the time of the crime. After the trial, the general public, legal commentators, and experts in the criminal justice system were shocked at the jury decision that Hinckley was not guilty by reason of insanity.

Consequently, many prosecutors, judges, and even mental health experts feel that changes are needed in the insanity plea. Two law scholars, Charles Nesson of the Harvard Law School and Norval Morris of the University of Chicago Law School, suggest that the Hinckley verdict points up the need for a new verdict of *guilty but insane*.[33] Under this procedure, if a person uses the insanity defense but a judge or jury finds the evidence insufficient to find for legal insanity, a verdict of guilty but mentally ill can be reached. This indicates the defendant is suffering from an emotional disorder severe enough to influence behavior but insufficient to render him or her insane. Consequently, after such a finding, the court can impose any sentence it could have used on the crime charge. The convicted defendant is sent to prison, where the correctional authorities are required to provide therapeutic treatment. If the mental illness is cured, the offender is returned to the regular prison population to serve out the remainder of the sentence. Approximately twelve states provide for a verdict of guilty but mentally ill.[34]

Another approach is to ban from court all evidence of mental illness, as was recently done in Montana, Idaho, and Utah (Idaho does allow psychiatric evidence on the issue of intent to commit crime).[35] Some commentators suggest more moderate changes, such as eliminating pleas involving "diminished capacity," where defendants lack the ability to premeditate the crime, and limiting the role of expert witnesses at trial.

Lastly, the federal government and Indiana have adopted a new test of criminal responsibility known as the appreciation test. It resembles the M'Naghten test by relying on cognitive incapacity and differs from the substantial capacity test in that the defendant is not required to show lack of control regarding behavior. It also shifts the burden of proof to the defense.

Although such backlash against the insanity plea is intended to close supposed legal loopholes allowing dangerous criminals to go free, the public's fear may be misplaced. It is generally agreed that an infinitesimal number of criminal cases use the insanity defense. Moreover, evidence shows that relatively few insanity defense pleas are successful. Even Jeffrey Dahmer, who confessed in 1992 to killing fifteen persons in Wisconsin, was held criminally liable for his acts, which included necrophilia (sexual attraction to corpses) and cannibalism. He received fifteen consecutive life sentences without parole. If the insanity defense is successful, the offender must be placed in a secure psychiatric hospital. The state prison and the secure hospital are the two alternative ways of handling such criminal deviants.[36]

Despite efforts to ban its use, the insanity plea is probably here to stay. Most crimes require *mens rea*, and unless we are willing to forego that standard of law, we will be forced to find not guilty those people whose mental state makes it impossible for them to rationally control their behavior.

Intoxication

As a general legal rule, intoxication, which may include drunkenness or being under the influence of drugs, is not considered a defense. In the highly publicized 1989 criminal homicide child abuse case of Joel Steinberg in New York City, the court rejected the defense of drug use when it was shown that such behavior was voluntary on the defendant's part. However, a defendant who becomes involuntarily intoxicated under duress or by mistake may be excused for crimes committed. Voluntary intoxication may also lessen the degree of a crime—for example, a judgment may be decreased from first- to second-degree murder because the defendant may use intoxication to prove the lack of critical element of *mens rea*, or mental intent. Thus, the effect of intoxication upon criminal liability depends upon whether the defendant uses the alcohol or drugs voluntarily. For example, a defendant who enters a bar for a few drinks, becomes intoxicated, and strikes someone can be convicted of assault and battery. On the other hand, if the defendant ordered a nonalcoholic drink that was spiked by someone else, the defendant may have a legitimate legal defense.

Given the frequency of crime-related offenses with drugs and alcohol, the impact of intoxication on criminal liability is a frequent issue in the criminal justice system. The connection between drug use, alcoholism, and violent street crime has been well documented. Although those in law enforcement and the judiciary tend to emphasize the use of the penal process in dealing with problems of chronic alcoholism and drug use, others in corrections and crime prevention favor approaches that depend more on behavioral theories and the social sciences. For example, in the case of *Robinson v. California*, the U.S. Supreme Court struck down a California statute making addiction to narcotics a crime on the ground that it violated the defendant's rights under the Eighth and Fourteenth Amendments to the U.S. Constitution.[37] On the other hand, the landmark decision in *Powell v. Texas*, which is highlighted in the Law in Review on page 148 placed severe limitations on the behavioral science approach in *Robinson* when it rejected the defense of chronic alcoholism of a defendant charged with the crime of public drunkenness.[38]

Age

The law holds that a child is not criminally responsible for actions committed at an age that precludes a full realization of the gravity of certain types of behavior. Under common law, there is generally a conclusive presumption of incapacity for a child under age seven; a reliable presumption for a child between the ages of seven and fourteen; and no presumption for a child over the age of fourteen. This

LAW IN REVIEW

Powell v. Texas (1968)

The decision in *Powell v. Texas* placed significant constitutional limitations on the ruling in *Robinson v. California,* which had held unconstitutional a ninety-day sentence for the crime of being addicted to the use of narcotics. In *Powell,* the U.S. Supreme Court rejected the defense of chronic alcoholism, claiming that persons inflicted with the disease cannot use their disease as a defense to a criminal charge.

Facts

In December 1966, the defendant in *Powell* was arrested and charged with being found in a state of intoxication in a public place in violation of the Texas Penal Code, which reads as follows: "Whoever shall get drunk or being found in a state of intoxication in any public place shall be fined not exceeding $100."

The defendant was tried in the Austin, Texas Corporation Court, found guilty, and fined twenty dollars. A *de novo* trial was subsequently held where the defense attorney argued that the defendant was afflicted with the disease of chronic alcoholism and that his public drunkenness was not of his own volition and that to punish him criminally would be cruel and unusual punishment in violation of the Eighth and Fourteenth Amendments to the U.S. Constitution. The trial judge ruled that chronic alcoholism was not a defense to the charge of public drunkenness and found the defendant guilty as charged. The case was subsequently appealed to the U.S. Supreme Court.

Testimony given during the trial of the defendant indicated that he was a chronic alcoholic who was unable to control his intoxication and had an uncontrollable compulsion to drink. Psychiatric testimony was also admitted to indicate that the defendant had no willpower to resist the excessive consumption of alcohol. Based on such expert testimony, the trial court agreed (1) that chronic alcoholism was a disease; (2) that a chronic alcoholic does not appear in public by his own volition but under a compulsion symptomatic of the disease of chronic alcoholism; and (3) that Leroy Powell was in fact a chronic alcoholic afflicted with such disease.

But, in light of the uncertain medical knowledge at this time, it appears that chronic alcoholics do not necessarily suffer from an irresistible compulsion to drink and to get drunk in public, nor are they utterly unable to control their actions.

Decision

The Supreme Court was asked to decide whether alcoholism was a condition of such an involuntary nature that to punish an individual for public intoxication would be cruel and unusual punishment under the Eighth and Fourteenth Amendments to the U.S. Constitution. Prior to this case, the Court had ruled in *Robinson v. California* that a state

generally means that a child under seven years old who commits a crime will not be held criminally responsible for these actions and that a child between seven and fourteen may be held responsible. These common law rules have been changed by statute in most jurisdictions. Today, the maximum age of criminal responsibility for children ranges from fourteen to seventeen, while the minimum age may be set by statute at seven or under fourteen.[39] In addition, every jurisdiction has established a juvenile court system to deal with juvenile offenders and children in need of court and societal supervision. Thus, the mandate of the juvenile justice system is to provide for the care and protection of children under a given age established by state statute. In certain situations, a juvenile court may transfer a more serious chronic youthful offender to the adult criminal court. The juvenile court system is discussed in Chapter 19.

Criminal Defense: Justification and Excuse

Criminal defenses may also be based on the concept of justification or excuse. In other words, certain defenses allow for the commission of a crime to be justified or excused on grounds of fairness and public policy. In these instances, defendants normally acknowledge that they committed the act but claim that they cannot

statute making it a crime to be addicted to the use of narcotics was unconstitutional. On its face, however, according to the Court, the *Powell* case did not fall within that same meaning, since the defendant was convicted not of being a chronic alcoholic but of being in public while drunk on a particular occasion. According to the Court, this is a far cry from convicting someone for being an addict, being mentally ill, or being a leper. Although *Robinson* forbade punishing a person for being afflicted with any disease or predisposition, Powell was a chronic alcoholic who was prosecuted for being drunk in a public place, not for being an alcoholic per se. According to the majority, if Leroy Powell could not be convicted of public intoxication, it was difficult to see how a state could convict an individual for murder, if that individual while exhibiting normal behavior suffers from a compulsion to kill, which is an exceedingly strong but not overpowering influence.

Therefore, the Supreme Court concluded that Powell was not convicted for being a chronic alcoholic but for being drunk in public. His actions did not fall within the ruling of *Robinson,* which held that conviction for being a drug addict alone is cruel and unusual punishment. In *Powell,* the conviction protected public safety and health and was constitutionally permissible.

Significance of the Case

Although the decision in *Robinson v. California* supported the position that a chronic alcoholic with a compulsion to consume alcohol should not be punished for drinking per se, the defendant in *Powell* was convicted for the crime of being drunk in a public place. Even though the defendant showed that he was compelled to drink, medical evidence and testimony does not indicate whether alcohol is physically addicting or psychologically habit-forming. Given the state of the record and current medical knowledge, the public has an interest in controlling behavior and actions that result from public intoxication that violates criminal laws. Consequently, a conviction for public drunkenness must be sustained even where the defendant is a chronic alcoholic whose alcoholism resulted in his being intoxicated in public, the crime for which he was arrested. The decision in *Powell* makes clear, however, that punishment for a status is particularly obnoxious and in many instances is cruel and unusual because it involves punishment for a mere propensity and desire to commit a crime, and the mental element, or *mens rea,* is not part of the criminal activity. Chronic alcoholism, even defined as a disease, however, is not a defense to being found intoxicated in a public place if such behavior violates a legitimate public intoxication statute.

be prosecuted because they were justified in doing so. The following major types of criminal defenses involving justification or excuse are explained in this section: (1) consent, (2) self-defense, (3) entrapment, (4) double jeopardy, and (5) mistake, compulsion, and necessity.

Consent

As a general rule, the victim's consent to a crime does not justify or excuse the defendant who commits the action. The type of crime involved generally determines the validity of consent as an appropriate legal defense. Such crimes as common law rape and larceny require lack of consent on the part of the victim. In other words, a rape does not occur if the victim consents to sexual relations. In the same way, a larceny cannot occur if the owner voluntarily consents to the taking of the property. Consequently, in such crimes, consent is an essential element of the crime, and it is a valid defense where it can be proven or shown that it existed at the time the crime was committed. In statutory rape, however, consent is not an element of the crime and is considered irrelevant, because the state presumes that young people are not capable of providing consent.

Consent is also not an appropriate defense in cases involving assault and battery, mayhem, or homicide or in any crime where serious harm can come to a person. In addition, regardless of whether both parties consent to a fight, if there is a likelihood of serious bodily injury, mutual consent is not a valid defense.

Self-Defense

In certain instances, the defendant who admits to the acts that constitute a crime may claim to be not guilty because of an affirmative **self-defense.** To establish the necessary elements to constitute self-defense, the defendant must have acted under a reasonable belief that he or she was in danger of death or great harm and had no means of escape from the assailant.

As a general legal rule, however, a person defending himself or herself may use only such force as is reasonably necessary to prevent personal harm. A person who is assaulted by another with no weapon is ordinarily not justified in hitting the assailant with a baseball bat. A person verbally threatened by another is not justified in striking the other party. If a woman hits a larger man, generally speaking, the man would not be justified in striking the woman and causing her physical harm. In other words, to exercise the self-defense privilege, the danger to the defendant must be immediate. In addition, the defendant is obligated to look for alternative means of avoiding the danger, such as escape or retreat or looking for assistance from others.[40]

The 1984 case of Bernhard Goetz, the celebrated "subway shooter," is a much publicized example of legal self-defense versus unlawful vigilantism in an urban setting.[41] Goetz, a thirty-seven-year-old businessman, shot four black teenagers on a New York City subway train after being asked for five dollars. Three of the teens were carrying sharpened screwdrivers and had prior arrest records; they had allegedly threatened Goetz. New York state law allows a victim to shoot in self-defense only if there is reasonable belief that the assailant will use deadly force and if the victim cannot escape.

After a much publicized refusal by a first grand jury to indict Goetz for attempted murder, Goetz was subsequently indicted, tried, and acquitted in 1987 of attempted murder and assault but convicted of illegal possession of an unlicensed concealed handgun. Goetz claimed he shot the four youths in self-defense because he feared he was about to be robbed. This bitter and controversial case finally came to an end in January 1989, when Goetz was given a one-year jail sentence for the illegal handgun charge. According to the prosecution, Goetz had taken the law into his own hands. Goetz maintained that society needs to be protected from criminals.

The elements that constitute self-defense are also applicable to the defense of another and to the defense of one's property. The right to defend another is based on the responsibility of a citizen to use force to exercise a citizen arrest and to defend members of a family group. The right to defend one's property is dependent on the exercise of reasonable force to retain property or to remove a trespasser. Most jurisdictions use the "reasonableness" test determined by the facts of the action to decide what constitutes an appropriate defense of property. In some other jurisdictions, force has been accepted as a reasonable way to prevent a burglary. Generally speaking, however, force is ordinarily an acceptable means of protecting property only when it is used as a last resort when the police are unavailable or when reasonable requests to control trespass or unlawful action have been ignored.[42] The use of deadly force is not considered reasonable when only the protection of property is involved. This is based on society's belief that human life is more important than property.

Entrapment

The term **entrapment** refers to an affirmative defense in the criminal law that excuses a defendant from criminal liability when law enforcement agents use traps, decoys, and deception to induce criminal action. It is generally legitimate for law enforcement officers to set traps for criminals by getting information about crimes from informers, undercover agents, and codefendants. Police officers are allowed to use ordinary opportunities for defendants to commit crime and to create these opportunities without excessive inducement and solicitation to commit and involve a defendant in a crime. However, when the police instigate the crime, implant criminal ideas, and coerce individuals into bringing about a crime, defendants have the defense of entrapment available to them. Entrapment is not a constitutional defense but has been created by court decision and statute in most jurisdictions.

The degree of government involvement in a criminal act leading to the entrapment defense has been defined in a number of U.S. Supreme Court decisions beginning in 1932. The majority view of what constitutes entrapment can be seen in the 1932 case of *Sorrells v. United States*.[43] During Prohibition, a federal officer passed himself off as a tourist while gaining the defendant's confidence. The federal agent eventually enticed the defendant to buy illegal liquor for him. The defendant was then arrested and prosecuted for violating the National Prohibition Act. The Supreme Court held that the officer used improper inducements that amounted to entrapment. In deciding this case, the Court settled on the "subjective" view of entrapment, which means that the predisposition of the defendant to commit the offense is the determining factor in entrapment. Following the *Sorrells* case, the Supreme Court stated in *Sherman v. United States* that the function of law enforcement is to prevent crime and to apprehend criminals, not to implant a criminal design, which originates with the officials of the government, in the mind of an innocent person.[44]

In 1973, the U.S. Supreme Court ruled on the entrapment case of *United States v. Russell*.[45] In this case, an agent of the Federal Bureau of Narcotics offered to supply defendants with the ingredients necessary to manufacture the drug "speed." The defendants showed the agent the laboratory where the speed was produced. The agent eventually obtained a search warrant and arrested the defendants for the unlawful manufacture, sale, and delivery of drugs. Defendant Russell raised the defense of entrapment in his criminal trial. The Court ruled that the participation of the narcotics agent was not entrapment in this case and rejected the "objective" test of entrapment, which looks solely to the police conduct to determine if a law-abiding citizen has been persuaded to commit crime.

In a 1976 case, *Hampton v. United States*, the Court ruled that the defendant's predisposition rendered the entrapment defense unavailable to him even when a federal informant had provided the heroin that the defendant was charged with selling.[46] According to Justice William Rehnquist, "[T]he police conduct in *Hampton* no more deprived the defendant of any right secured to him by the U.S. Constitution than did the police conduct in *Russell* deprive Russell of any rights."[47]

Consequently, the major legal rule today considers entrapment primarily in light of the defendant's predisposition to commit a crime. A defendant with a criminal record would have a tougher time using this defense successfully than one who had never been in trouble before. An example is the case of automobile manufacturer John DeLorean, who was acquitted of selling cocaine, even though the jury was shown videotapes of DeLorean freely engaging in the sale of the drug. The jury felt that a well-respected businessman would never have gotten involved in such a crime without government entrapment.

Over the last decade, the defense of entrapment has resulted in a great deal of litigation concerning undercover police work and criminal liability. Sting and scam operations are often employed to obtain evidence on burglars, drug manufacturers, and corrupt public officials. The Abscam operation, for example, in which FBI agents paid bribes to government officials, resulted in the conviction of several congressmen. And Operation Greylord uncovered attorneys, judges, and other court personnel "on the take" in the Chicago court system.[48] "Government activity in the criminal enterprise," a phrase used in the decision in *United States v. Russell,* has become an increasingly commonplace tool in the justice system.[49]

Double Jeopardy

By virtue of the Fifth Amendment, "no person shall be subject for the same offense to be twice put in jeopardy of life or limb."[50] The objective of this constitutional protection is to prohibit the reprosecution of a defendant for the same offense by the same jurisdiction. Thus, a person who has been tried for armed robbery in the state of Massachusetts by a judge or jury may not be tried again in that state for the same incident.

A review of the **double jeopardy** question involves a number of issues: (1) Does prosecution for the same or similar offenses by the state and federal governments constitute double jeopardy? (2) When does double jeopardy attach in a criminal prosecution? (3) What effect does the double jeopardy clause have on sentencing provisions?

The issue of federal versus state prosecutions arises from the existence of offenses that are crimes against the state as well as against the federal government. The U.S. Supreme Court has held, in the case of *Bartkus v. Illinois* (1959) and in numerous other cases, that both state and federal prosecutions against a defendant for the same crime are not in violation of the Fifth Amendment.[51] The Court reasoned that every citizen is a citizen of the United States and of a state. Consequently, either or both jurisdictions can try to punish an offender.

On the other hand, a state can try an accused only once. The state has the responsibility either to convict the defendant legally or to acquit the defendant on all charges. The Fifth Amendment prohibits a second prosecution, unless there has been an appeal by the defendant. The state may obtain a second trial in cases involving a mistrial, a hung jury, or some other trial defect.

With regard to when double jeopardy attaches, the general rule is that the Fifth Amendment applies when a criminal trial begins before a judge or jury. In the case of *Benton v. Maryland* (1969), the U.S. Supreme Court held the double jeopardy provisions of the Fifth Amendment applicable to the states.[52] The accused has the right to be tried until a final determination of the case is made. Jeopardy may exist when a jury is selected and sworn or even when a defendant is indicted for a crime. However, in the case of *Illinois v. Somerville* (1973), the double jeopardy clause did not bar the retrial of a defendant where a mistrial was caused because of a fatal defect in the government's indictment.[53] Also, a dismissal that occurs prior to jeopardy attaching does not prohibit a second prosecution under the Fifth Amendment. In other words, double jeopardy normally does not apply until after a criminal trial has started; thus, early pretrial dismissals do not bar further prosecutions.

In terms of the sentence itself, the double jeopardy clause does not restrict the court's decision with regard to the length of the sentence imposed on a defendant in a second trial. However, the court is required to sentence fairly in accordance with due process of law. Vindictiveness or harshness against a defendant for being successful in overturning the first conviction is not appropriate grounds for imposing a sentence in the second trial. Thus, although the double jeopardy clause does not prevent or restrict harsh sentences on retrial, the case of *North Carolina v. Pearce* (1969) makes clear that sentences on retrial must be realistic and in accordance with fair principles of law and procedure.[54]

Pearce was convicted of assault with intent to commit rape in North Carolina. He was given a sentence of twelve to fifteen years in prison. After a reversal of his conviction, Pearce was retried, convicted, and sentenced to a longer sentence than originally imposed. The Court made clear that, although the double jeopardy clause is not an absolute bar to a more severe sentence, vindictiveness against a defendant can play no part in the new sentence.[55]

Mistake, Compulsion, and Necessity

Mistake or ignorance of the law is generally no defense to a crime. According to the great legal scholar William Blackstone, "Ignorance of the law, which everyone is bound to know, excuses no man."[56] Consequently, a defendant cannot present a legitimate defense by saying he or she was unaware of a criminal law, had misinterpreted the law, or believed the law to be unconstitutional.

On the other hand, mistakes of fact, such as taking someone else's coat that is similar to your own, may be a valid defense. If the jury or judge as trier of fact determines that criminal intent was absent, such an honest mistake may remove the defendant's criminal responsibility.

Compulsion or coercion may also be a criminal defense under certain conditions. In these cases, the defendant is forced into committing a crime. For this defense to be upheld, a defendant must show that the actions were the only means of preventing death or serious harm to self or others. For example, a bank employee might be excused from taking bank funds if she can prove that her family was being threatened and that consequently she was acting under duress. But there is widespread general agreement that duress is no defense to an intentional killing.

Closely connected to the defense of compulsion is that of necessity. According to the Model Penal Code, "necessity may be an acceptable defense, provided the harm to be avoided is greater than the offense charged."[57] In other words, the defense of necessity is justified when the crime was committed because other circumstances could not be avoided. For example, a husband steals a car to bring his pregnant wife to the hospital for an emergency delivery, or a hunter shoots an animal of an endangered species that was about to attack her. The defense has been found inapplicable, however, where defendants sought to shut down nuclear power plants or abortion clinics or to destroy missile components under the belief that the action was necessary to save lives or prevent a nuclear war. Even those who use a controlled substance such as marijuana for medicinal purposes often cannot claim vindication based on medical necessity, although some courts have viewed this as a legitimate defense.[58]

In addition, the courts have grappled with such controversial defenses as euthanasia (or mercy killing), civil disobedience, and the "cultural" (taking into account the beliefs, customs, and traits of racial and ethnic groups) defense.[59]

In sum, affirmative defenses—consent, self-defense, entrapment, and double jeopardy—refer primarily to situations where the defendants admit that they committed the act but claim that they should not be punished. Such is the case when a person exercises proper self-defense, when the police deliberately entice a defendant to commit a crime, or when someone is tried twice for the same offense.

Substantive Criminal Law Reform

In recent years, many states and the federal government have been examining and revising their substantive and procedural criminal codes. An ongoing effort has been made to update legal codes so that they provide an accurate reflection of public opinion, social change, technological innovation, and other important social issues.

What was a crime thirty years ago—such as performing an abortion—may no longer be a crime today. In this instance, clouds of protest continue to surround the issue as pro- and antiabortion groups argue the merits of such decisions by the government. Conversely, what was unregulated behavior in the past, such as using children to pose for adult sex publications, may be outlawed because of public concern and outrage.[60]

One aspect of criminal law reform involves weeding out laws that seem archaic in light of what is now known about human behavior. For example, alcoholism is now considered a disease that should be treated, not an offense that should be punished. Many experts believe that offenses like drunkenness, disorderly conduct, vagrancy, gambling, and minor sexual violations are essentially social problems and should not be dealt with by the criminal justice system.

The RICO Statute

Other criminal law revisions reflect increasing awareness about problems that confront U.S. society. As mentioned previously, a number of states have eliminated traditional rape laws and replaced them with sexually neutral assault statutes that recognize that men as well as women can be the victims of rape. Most jurisdictions have adopted laws that require people in certain occupations, such as teachers and doctors, to report suspected cases of child abuse to the proper authorities. In an effort to control organized crime, Congress passed the Racketeer Influenced and Corrupt Organization Act (RICO). This law prevents people from acquiring or maintaining an interest in an ongoing enterprise, such as a union or legitimate business, with funds derived from illegal enterprises and racketeering activities.[61]

RICO did not create new categories of crime, but it did create new categories of offenses in racketeering activity, which it defined as involvement in two or more acts prohibited by twenty-four existing federal statutes and eight state statutes. The offenses listed in RICO include such state-defined crimes as murder, kidnapping, gambling, arson, robbery, bribery, extortion, and narcotic violations and such federally defined crimes as bribery, counterfeiting, transmission of gambling information, prostitution, and mail fraud.

RICO is designed to limit "patterns" of organized criminal activity by defining racketeering as an act intended to:

The RICO statutes were devised as a weapon against organized crime. John Gotti, the "Dapper Don," smiles for the cameras before being sentenced to a long prison term.

- Derive income from racketeering or the unlawful collection of debts and to use or invest such income.
- Acquire through racketeering an interest in or control over any enterprise engaged in interstate or foreign commerce.
- Conduct business enterprises through a pattern of racketeering.
- Conspire to use racketeering as a means of generating income, collecting loans, or conducting business.

An individual convicted under RICO is subject to twenty years in prison and a twenty-five-thousand-dollar fine. Additionally, the accused must forfeit to the U.S. government any interest in a business in violation of RICO. These penalties are much more potent than simple conviction and imprisonment. In addition, there is a separate civil provision of the law that permits private parties to sue for racketeering and obtain treble damages.

Using RICO, the U.S. attorneys for New York, Boston, and Chicago have attacked the leadership of major organized crime families and obtained convictions of high-ranking mafiosi during the late 1980s and early 1990s. In 1986 and 1987, in a trail-blazing case, the U.S. attorney for New York used RICO and language in the Securities and Exchange Act of 1934 to prosecute and convict Ivan Boesky and others for insider trading crimes.[62] Boesky agreed to pay a $100 million penalty for trading on inside stock information supplied by others and was subsequently sentenced to three years in prison. RICO indictments have also helped prosecutors plea bargain criminal cases involving the investment banking firm of Drexel Burnham Lambert Inc. and junk-bond kingpin Michael Milken, as well as the government-influenced Wedtech Corporation scandal, the Charles Keating savings and loan scandal and the Bank of Commerce and Credit International (BCCI) criminal forfeiture of 1991. Although slow to respond to such criminal violations over the years, the federal government now maintains that insider trading violations will receive full attention in the future. With such activities as junk bond underwriting, mergers and acquisitions, and venture capital investing, the number of people exposed to confidential information has increased

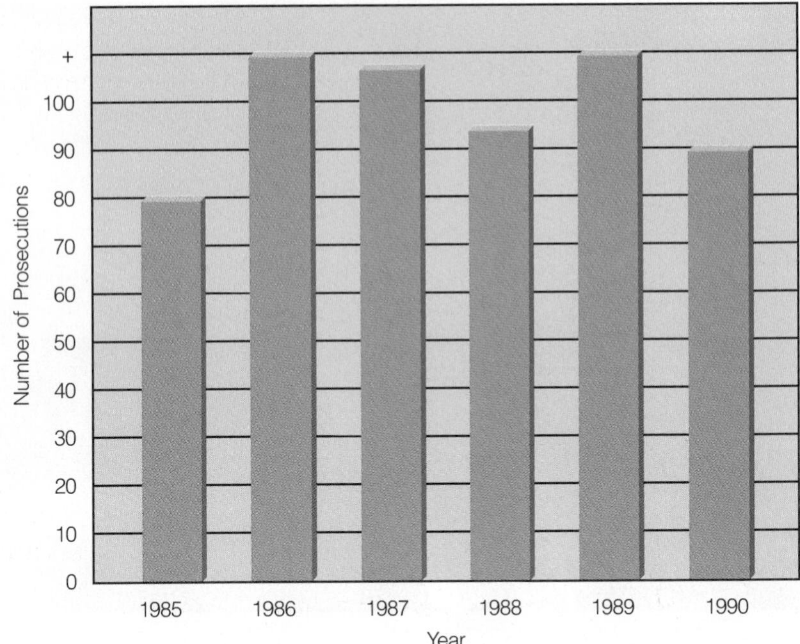

FIGURE 4.1
RICO Prosecutions, 1980–1990
SOURCE: U.S. Department of Justice, Office of the Attorney General, Office of the Attorney General, 1991.

enormously. In addition, the number of people able to reap huge potential profits illegally has resulted in a proliferation of insider trading abuses. Although it may seem astonishing that for decades the stock market remained unscathed by criminal prosecutions, the government's ability to use RICO and other such statutes has further increased the number of prosecutions in the area of white-collar crime (see Figure 4.1).

The federal courts are currently divided over RICO's "pattern of activity requirement."[63] The constitutionality of this twenty-year-old statute has suddenly been thrown into question because of RICO's ambiguous and vague language. Convictions obtained by the aggressive U.S. attorney in Manhattan, Rudolph Giuliani, have been overturned on procedural grounds. And some courts claim that the "pattern requirement" lacks sufficient definition such that ordinary people cannot understand what conduct is prohibited. Ultimately, it will be the U.S. Supreme Court that will determine RICO's fate.[64]

Model Penal Code

There have been a number of ongoing efforts to help states make changes in their criminal laws. Beginning in 1952, the American Law Institute, a private organization of lawyers, judges, and judicial experts, began a movement to draft a model penal code. Its purpose was to encourage states to revise their penal statutes and eliminate vague, inconsistent, and redundant laws. The project was completed in 1962. Known as the Proposed Official Draft, it is a modernized version of what the criminal law ought to be and deals with both specific crimes and the general principles of the criminal law.[65]

Today, the **Model Penal Code** of the American Law Institute continues to be a comprehensive model of the substantive criminal law and serves as a guide for the elimination of outdated federal and state laws. Comprehensive revisions of criminal legislation have been undertaken in over thirty states since the establishment of the Model Penal Code.

In virtually all jurisdictions, some aspect of the common law has been replaced by the statutory language of the Model Penal Code. An example of how the common law and the Model Penal Code view two different crimes—rape and arson—can be seen in Table 4.4. At common law, rape is unlawful "sexual intercourse with a female without her consent," while arson is "the malicious burning of the dwelling of another." Both definitions are expanded and more precise under the Model Penal Code.

Federal Crime Legislation

One of the most significant criminal law revisions in the last decade was the 1984 Federal Crime Bill.[66] This legislation reforms a code that has been criticized for

TABLE 4.4
Model Penal Code

Model Penal Code—Arson	Model Penal Code—Rape
Section 220.1. Arson and Related Offenses. (1) Arson. A person is guilty of arson, a felony of the second degree, if he starts a fire or causes an explosion with the purpose of: (a) destroying a building or occupied structure of another; or (b) destroying or damaging any property, whether his own or another's, to collect insurance for such loss. It shall be an affirmative defense to prosecution under this paragraph that the actor's conduct did not recklessly endanger any building or occupied structure of another or place any other person in danger of death or bodily injury.	**Section 213.1. Rape and Related Offenses.** (1) Rape. A male who has sexual intercourse with a female not his wife is guilty of rape if: (a) he compels her to submit by force or by threat of imminent death, serious bodily injury, extreme pain or kidnapping, to be inflicted on anyone; or (b) he has substantially impaired her power to appraise or control her conduct by administering or employing without her knowledge drugs, intoxicants or other means for the purpose of preventing resistance; or (c) the female is unconscious; or (d) the female is less than 10 years old. Rape is a felony of the second degree unless (i) in the course thereof the actor inflicts serious bodily injury upon anyone, or (ii) the vitim was not a voluntary social companion of the actor upon the occasion of the crime and had not previously permitted him sexual liberties, in which cases the offense is a felony of the first degree.

SOURCE: *Model Penal Code, Official Draft* (copyright 1962 by the American Law Institute). Reprinted with permission of the American Law Institute.

its complexity and inconsistency. Among the most important changes is the treatment of the insanity defense. In the past, federal prosecutors had the burden of proving that a defendant was sane. Now the burden of proof for insanity has shifted to the defendant. In addition, the new federal code eliminated parole and required that criminal punishments be imposed more fairly and evenhandedly. Another important provision allowed judges to detain offenders in jail prior to their trials if they were considered a danger to the community and themselves. **Preventive detention** was a significant change in the nation's bail system. Despite these changes, in comparison with the revisions that have taken place in many states, the federal criminal law has not been extensively overhauled.

In addition, amid much national concern about drugs, the Congress passed the Omnibus Drug Bill of 1988.[67] Earmarking over $2 billion for antidrug activities, the law called for increased drug education and treatment programs and broader federal drug interdiction efforts. Some of its major provisions included: (1) the establishment of an office of national drug control policy, headed by a so-called drug czar, to coordinate a national drug policy; (2) increased funding for school drug abuse and mental health programs; (3) more funding for drug abuse education throughout the country; (4) increased efforts to deal with international narcotic problems; and (5) stricter criminal sanctions, including the use of the death penalty for major drug traffickers who intentionally kill someone as part of their drug-related transactions. Although opponents of the death penalty say its imposition has no deterrent value, even in controlling drugs, proponents argue that it reflects a determination on the part of our society to be tough on major drug suppliers. This legislation is the basis for U.S. drug enforcement policy today.

Under the Bush administration, the 101st Congress passed the Crime Control Act of 1990. This recent legislation was probably more significant for what was left out than what was enacted. Among the measures deleted from the legislation were increasing the number of crimes for which the death penalty could be imposed, enacting reforms to the federal habeas corpus process, creating a good-faith exception to the Fourth Amendment exclusionary rule, and barring the sale or production of semiautomatic weapons.

On the other hand, some significant changes were part of the 1990 legislation. These include: improvements in public defender services; the implementation of "shock incarceration" programs in federal and state correctional systems; reforms for the investigation of child abuse cases; efforts to aid crime victims through the Victims Rights and Restitution Act of 1990; authorization for a study of mandatory sentencing by the U.S. Sentencing Commission; provisions dealing with drugs; and the development of new offenses and penalties relating to the savings and loan scandals.[68]

Efforts to pass an anticrime package in 1991 failed when the Congress and President Bush could not agree on substantially the same unresolved issues detailed in 1990, namely gun control, the death penalty, and the use of evidence seized in good faith without warrants. These issues will continue to be the basis for criminal justice debate during the 1990s.[69]

Constitutional Criminal Procedure

Whereas substantive criminal law primarily defines crimes, the law of criminal procedure consists of the rules and procedures that govern the pretrial processing of criminal suspects and the conduct of criminal trials. As codified in the modern Federal Rules of Criminal Procedure, such rules provide for the "just and fair determination of all criminal proceedings." The principles that govern criminal procedure flow from the relationship between the individual and the state and include: (1) a belief in the presumption of innocence; (2) the right to a defense against criminal charges; and (3) the requirement that the government should act in a lawful manner. In general, these policies are mandated by the provisions of state constitutions. A sound understanding of criminal procedure requires an awareness of constitutional law.

The U.S. Constitution

The U.S. Constitution has played and continues to play a critical role in the development of the criminal law used in the criminal justice system. The forerunner of the Constitution was the Articles of Confederation, adopted by the Continental Congress in 1781. The Articles were found to be generally inadequate as the foundation for effective government because they did not create a proper balance of power between the states and the central government. As a result, in 1787, the Congress of the Confederation adopted a resolution calling for a convention of delegates from the original states. Meeting in Philadelphia, the delegates' express purpose was to revise the Articles of Confederation. The work of that convention culminated in the drafting of the Constitution; it was ratified by the states in 1788 and put into effect in 1789.

In its original form, the Constitution consisted of a preamble and seven articles. The Constitution divided the powers of government into three independent but equal parts: the executive, the legislative, and the judicial branches. The purpose of the **separation of powers** was to ensure that no single branch of the government could usurp power for itself and institute a dictatorship. The measures and procedures initiated by the Framers of the Constitution have developed over time into our present form of government.

How does the Constitution, with its formal set of rights and privileges, affect the operations of the criminal justice system? One way is to guarantee that no one branch of government can in and of itself determine the fate of those accused of crimes. The workings of the criminal justice process illustrate this principle. A police officer, who represents the executive branch of government, makes an arrest on the basis of laws passed by the legislative branch, and the accused is subsequently tried by the judiciary. In this way, citizens are protected from the arbitrary abuse of power by any single element of the law.

The Bill of Rights—Two Hundred Years Old

In addition to providing protection by ensuring a separation of powers within the government, the Constitution also controls the operations of the criminal justice system. It does this by guaranteeing individual freedoms in the ten amendments added to it on December 15, 1791, which are collectively known as the Bill of Rights.[70]

The **Bill of Rights** was added to the Constitution to prevent any future government from usurping the personal freedoms of citizens. In its original form, the Constitution contained few specific guarantees of individual rights. The Founders, aware of the past abuses perpetrated by the British government, wanted to ensure that the rights of citizens of the United States would be safe in the future. The Bill of Rights was adopted only to protect individual liberties from being abused by the national government, however, and did not apply to the actions of state or local officials. This oversight resulted in abuses that have been rectified only with great difficulty and even today remain the subject of court action.

Police officers may seize some personal information and effects, such as fingerprints, without a warrant and still use such evidence in court.

Over the last four decades, the U.S. Supreme Court's interpretation of the Constitution has served as the basis for the creation of legal rights of the accused. The principles that govern criminal procedure are required by the U.S. Constitution and Bill of Rights. Of primary concern are the Fourth, Fifth, Sixth, and Eighth Amendments, which limit and control the manner in which the federal government operates the justice system. In addition, the due process clause of the Fourteenth Amendment has helped define the nature and limits of governmental action against the accused on a state level. Because these key amendments furnish the basis for our system of criminal procedure, they are examined carefully.

The Fourth Amendment. The Fourth Amendment to the U.S. Constitution provides some of the major limits on police behavior. It states:

> The right of the people to be secure in their persons, houses, papers, and effects, against unreasonable searches and seizures, shall not be violated, and no warrants shall issue, but upon probable cause, supported by oath or affirmation, and particularly describing the place to be searched, and the persons or things to be seized.

The Framers of the Constitution were greatly concerned about the power of the central government to interfere in personal matters. After all, the Constitution's authors had just engineered a revolution against a government they viewed as tyrannical and opposed to individual freedom. In addition, the predominant philosophical movement of the time, known today as the Enlightenment, stressed limitations on the state's power to interfere with the rights of its citizens. Such issues as liberty and privacy were of central concern when the Bill of Rights was formulated. Considering these goals, it is not surprising that the Fourth Amendment is designed to protect citizens from unnecessary intrusions by the government into their private affairs. The Fourth Amendment is especially important for the criminal justice system because it means that police officers cannot indiscriminately use their authority to investigate a possible crime or arrest a suspect unless either or both actions are justified by the law and the facts of the case. Stopping, questioning, or searching an individual without legal justification represents a serious violation of the Fourth Amendment right to personal privacy.

The right to privacy is not unlimited, however, because it must be properly balanced against the need for public protection. The police can search for and seize evidence under certain circumstances with a properly authorized *search warrant*, issued when a magistrate has been presented with sufficient evidence to convince him or her that a crime has been committed and that the place to be searched contains seizable evidence. The police can also perform a search without a warrant under special circumstances, such as when they have legally arrested a person and wish to search him or her for weapons or contraband.

Because the police are constantly involved in street encounters with suspects, Fourth Amendment issues are always before the courts. For example, a person accused of a crime who believes that an illegal search was conducted can have an attorney file a motion before the court to suppress any evidence obtained during that search. Federal courts have formulated the rule that any evidence seized by authorities in violation of the Fourth Amendment cannot be used against suspects in a court of law; this is known as the **exclusionary rule**. A large body of complex legal decisions, known as the law of *search and seizure*, deals with the rights protected by the Fourth Amendment. These issues will be discussed in detail in Chapter 9.

In addition, the U.S. Supreme Court has extended Fourth Amendment privacy protections to such diverse areas as wiretapping and issues involving criminal abortion statutes. In 1973, the constitutionally derived right to privacy was made explicit by the Supreme Court in *Roe v. Wade*, where the Court declared unconstitutional a Texas statute that made it a crime to procure an abortion.[71] In this case, the Court held that a person's body is private and that the government therefore cannot make laws to control it.

The Fifth Amendment Limiting the admissibility of confessions that have been obtained unfairly is another method of controlling police behavior. The right against self-incrimination is frequently asserted by a defendant in an effort to exclude confessions or admissions that might be vital to the government's case. In such instances, the meaning of the Fifth Amendment to the U.S. Constitution is critical. The amendment states:

> No person shall be held to answer for a capital, or otherwise infamous crime, unless on a presentment or indictment of a grand jury, except in cases arising in the land or naval forces, or in the militia, when in actual service in time of war or public danger; nor shall any person be subject for the same offense to be twice put in jeopardy of life or limb; nor shall be compelled in any criminal case to be a witness against himself, nor be deprived of life, liberty, or property, without due process of law, nor shall private property be taken for public use, without just compensation.

It was a common practice in Europe to subject people awaiting trial to horrible tortures designed to elicit confessions and implicate co-conspirators. Often a trial became superfluous when suspects had already been broken on the rack or had their arms and shoulders dislocated on the strappado. To prevent such practices from continuing in the United States, the Framers of the Constitution added the rights contained in the Fifth Amendment.

One of the primary purposes of the Fifth Amendment is to prevent torture and coercion of suspects by providing that no person shall be compelled to be a

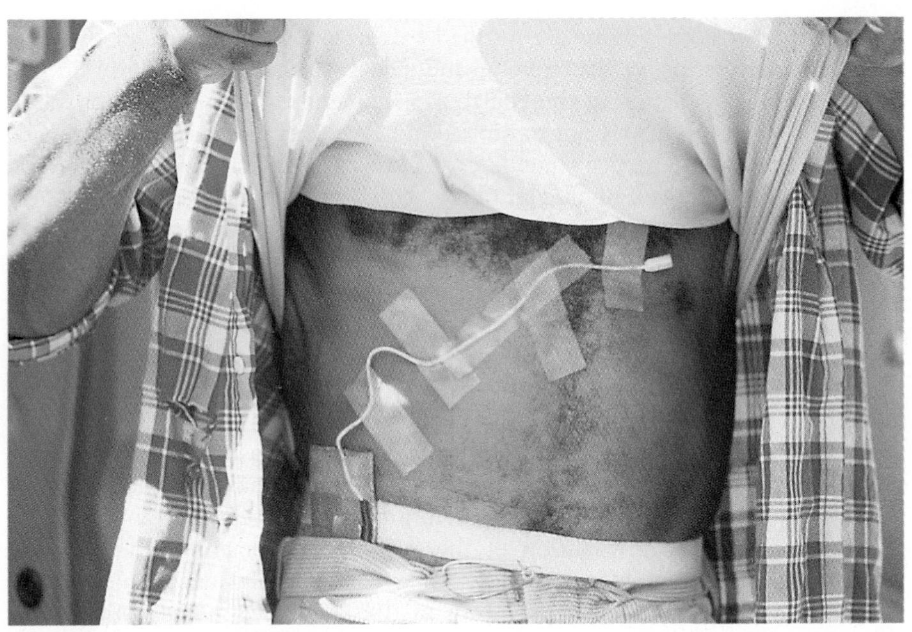

The Fourth Amendment restrictions on searching and seizing evidence apply to speech. Here an undercover agent is being wired to record a conversation.

witness against himself or herself. This protection has two separate parts: First, the witness has the right not to answer questions that would tend to be self-incriminating. A witness can claim the Fifth Amendment right against **self-incrimination** in a congressional investigation, grand jury proceeding, or criminal trial. This privilege normally extends to all kinds of proceedings, including those of a civil as well as a criminal nature. Second, under the Fifth Amendment, the defendant has the right not to take the stand in a criminal trial. If the defendant decides not to testify, the prosecution cannot comment on the silence or infer in any way that failure to testify is evidence of guilt.

The Fifth Amendment has had a tremendous impact on the U.S. criminal justice system. In 1966, in the landmark case of *Miranda v. Arizona,* the U.S. Supreme Court held that a person accused of a crime has the right to refuse to answer questions when placed in police custody.[72] As a result of the *Miranda* case, which is discussed in Chapter 9, the Supreme Court developed a set of rules with which the police must comply when questioning a suspect prior to trial.

The Fifth Amendment right against self-incrimination does not stand alone but is often combined with the Fourth Amendment protections against unreasonable searches and seizures. For example, when the police investigate a crime and make an arrest, or when they question a suspect to obtain a confession or admission, they may use information obtained from the defendant to locate incriminating evidence. An illegal interrogation can result in an improper search for evidence; an illegal search can trigger an arrest and subsequent interrogation. Thus, in each step of the criminal justice process, the police must respect the rights accorded to every individual under the law. Since constitutional violations against both amendments are often present in the same case, the amendments represent a dual constitutional protection against governmental intrusions.

In addition to the prohibition against forcing people to incriminate themselves, the Fifth Amendment forbids the government from trying people more than one time on the same charge—double jeopardy. The amendment also establishes the concept of **due process of law**, or the right of people to be treated fairly and openly when they are confronted by state authority.

The Sixth Amendment. The Sixth Amendment States:

> In all criminal prosecutions, the accused shall enjoy the right to a speedy and public trial, by an impartial jury of the state and district wherein the crime shall have been committed, which district shall have been previously ascertained by law, and to be informed of the nature and cause of the accusation; to be confronted with the witnesses against him; to have compulsory process for obtaining witnesses in his favor, and to have the assistance of counsel for his defense.

One of the goals of the Framers of the Constitution was to ensure that criminal defendants received a fair trial. Their concern stemmed from the abuses to human rights that had occurred in England and other European nations. For example, in the seventeenth century, an English court known as the Star Chamber tried persons charged with political crimes in secret and passed judgment upon them with little regard to fairness or due process of law. To protect U.S. citizens from such practices, the Sixth Amendment set out rights guaranteed to all people facing criminal charges.

The Sixth Amendment guarantees the defendant the right to a speedy and public trial by an impartial jury, the right to be informed of the nature of the charges, and the right to confront any prosecution witnesses. This amendment has had a profound effect on the treatment of persons accused of crimes and has been the basis for numerous significant Supreme Court decisions that have increased the rights of criminal defendants. Regarding the right to a speedy trial, the Sixth Amendment demands that a defendant be brought to trial within a reasonable time following accusation without undue delay by the prosecution. The Sixth Amendment has also been interpreted to mean that a defendant must be given a trial by a jury of his or her peers in all criminal cases where imprisonment for more than six months may be authorized. The right to a trial by an impartial jury means that the jury must be free from any prejudice, bias, or preconceived notions of the defendant's guilt. The right to a public trial protects the accused from being tried secretly or in a closed trial.

Many Supreme Court decisions regarding the Sixth Amendment have also concerned the individual's right to counsel. The right of a defendant to be represented by an attorney has been extended to numerous stages of the criminal justice process, including pretrial custody, identification and lineup procedures, preliminary hearing, submission of a guilty plea, trial, sentencing, and postconviction appeal. The major legal decisions and statutes involving the right to jury trial, counsel, self-representation (the right to represent oneself), and speedy and public trial are examined in Chapter 13.

The Eighth Amendment. According to the Eighth Amendment,

> Excessive bail shall not be required, nor excessive fines imposed, nor cruel and unusual punishments inflicted.

Bail is a money bond put up by the accused in order to attain freedom between arrest and trial. Bail is meant to ensure a trial appearance, since the bail money is forfeited if the defendant misses the trial date.

The Eighth Amendment does not guarantee a constitutional right to bail but rather prohibits the exactment of excessive bail. Nevertheless, since many state statutes place no precise limit on the amount of bail a judge may impose, many defendants who cannot make bail are often placed in detention while awaiting trial. It has become apparent over the years that the bail system is discriminatory in that a defendant who is financially well-off is more likely to be released on bail than one who is poor. In addition, placing a person in jail results in serious financial burdens on local and state governments—and, in turn, on taxpayers—which must pay for the cost of confinement. These factors have given rise to bail reform programs that depend on the defendant's personal promise to appear in court for trial (recognizance), rather than on the financial ability to meet bail (see Chapter 12). Despite reforms that have enabled many deserving but indigent offenders to go free, another trend has been to deny people bail on the grounds that they are a danger to themselves or others in the community. Although the Supreme Court has not dealt with the issue with respect to adults, the Court has ruled that the preventive detention of minors is permitted to promote public safety.[73]

The Eighth Amendment restriction on excessive bail may also be interpreted to mean that the sole purpose of bail is to ensure that the defendant returns for trial; bail may not be used as a form of punishment, nor may it be used to coerce or threaten a defendant.

Another goal of the Framers was to curtail the use of torture and excessive physical punishment. In the early history of Europe, convicted criminals were often subjected to bizarre and cruel methods of execution, including burning, being slowly crushed with heavy objects, and even being pulled apart by horses. Consequently, the prohibition against cruel and unusual punishment was added to the Eighth Amendment. This prohibition has affected the imposition of the death penalty and other criminal dispositions and has become a guarantee that serves to protect the accused and convicted offenders from actions regarded as unacceptable by a civilized society. Many prison reforms—such as those moderating prison discipline, isolation, and segregation and allowing prisoners to express grievances—have resulted from litigation based on the prohibition against cruel and unusual punishment. Nevertheless, the Supreme Court has not outlawed the use of physical punishment per se, since it has upheld the use of *capital punishment* and the use of physical discipline in schools. It has, however, banned the use of force in a discriminatory or excessive fashion.

The State Criminal Justice System under the Constitution

Fourteenth Amendment

The Fourteenth Amendment has been the vehicle most often used to apply the protection of the Bill of Rights to the states. The Fourteenth Amendment states:

> All persons born or naturalized in the United States, and subject to the jurisdiction thereof, are citizens of the United States and of the state wherein they reside. No state shall make or enforce any law which shall abridge the privileges or immunities of citizens of the United States; nor shall any state deprive any person of life, liberty, or property, without due process of the law; nor deny to any person within its jurisdiction the equal protection of the laws.

As we have seen, the first ten amendments came into being in 1791. As the years passed and the new republic grew, however, it became apparent that in spite of the Bill of Rights, many oppressive conditions remained. Slavery existed in many states, while some men were forced into military service and others worked for the state without pay. The states confiscated land and property and frequently denied rights guaranteed by the Bill of Rights to individuals and their families.

At the conclusion of the Civil War, the Thirteenth Amendment (abolishing slavery) was added to the Constitution. Because other substantial infringements of individual rights continued to exist, the Fourteenth Amendment was adopted in 1868. The most important aspect of this amendment is the clause that says no state shall "deprive any person of life, liberty, or property, without due process of law." This meant that the same general constitutional restrictions previously applicable to the federal government were to be imposed on the states. It is essential to keep the following constitutional principles in mind while examining the Fourteenth Amendment:

1. The first ten amendments, ordinarily referred to as the Bill of Rights, originally applied only to the federal government. They were designed to protect citizens against injustices inflicted by federal authorities. The Bill of Rights restricts the actions of the federal government and does not apply to the states.
2. The Fourteenth Amendment's *due process* clause applies to state governments. It has been used to provide individuals in all states with the basic liberties guaranteed by the Bill of Rights.
3. The U.S. Supreme Court has expanded the rights of defendants in the criminal justice system by interpreting the due process clause to mean that the states must be held to standards similar to those applicable to the federal government by the Bill of Rights.

Application of the Bill of Rights to the States

From its inception until about the middle of the twentieth century, the Bill of Rights had little bearing on the state criminal justice process. Individuals charged with federal crimes were guaranteed rights under the Fourth, Fifth, and Sixth Amendments, but defendants charged with criminal acts in state cases were denied similar treatment. The fact that the Bill of Rights was originally designed to govern the relationship between the individual and the federal government was pointed out by Chief Justice John Marshall in the case of *Barron v. Baltimore* in 1833.[74] In *Barron*, Justice Marshall rejected the claim that the Fifth Amendment was applicable to the states and held that the Constitution was binding only on the federal government. The question of whether the Bill of Rights was applicable to the states was further explored by the U.S. Supreme Court in 1884 in the case of *Hurtado v. California*.[75] This case raised the question of whether the due process clause of the Fourteenth Amendment contains the liberties expressed in the Bill of Rights. The Court held that the provisions of the Bill of Rights were not binding on the states through the Fourteenth Amendment.

Theories of Incorporation

Gradually, however, through a long series of decisions, the Supreme Court has held that the guarantees of the First, Fourth, Fifth, Sixth, and Eighth Amendments apply to the states as well as to the federal government. The movement to make the Bill of Rights applicable to the states has gained impetus during the latter half of the twentieth century. It is based on a number of legal theories that describe the relationship of the Bill of Rights to the Fourteenth Amendment. The first theory, known as the **incorporation theory,** states that all the provisions of the Bill of Rights are incorporated into the Fourteenth Amendment's due process clause. Thus, such fundamental rights as freedom from unreasonable

search and seizure, the right to jury trial, and the right to counsel are all considered binding on the states through the Fourteenth Amendment. The idea of total incorporation has never received majority support in any Supreme Court decision, however, nor has it been accepted in any substantial way by legal scholars or historians. Those supporting total incorporation argue that an individual is a citizen of both the federal government and a state government and should receive similar protections from each, while those arguing against this position suggest that the states should be allowed to develop their own criminal procedures.

The most widely recognized theory of constitutional responsibility is the **theory of selective incorporation,** which states that the Bill of Rights does apply to the states through the due process clause of the Fourteenth Amendment but only on a case-by-case basis. Advocates of this theory believe that some of the provisions of the Bill of Rights may be binding on the states—such as the right to a jury trial or the right to be free from self-incrimination—but that these should apply only after a careful consideration of the facts, or merits, of each case.

One way of determining which federal rights must be incorporated into the states' criminal justice systems was set forth in the decision in *Palko v. Connecticut* in 1937.[76] That case questioned whether the defendant's second trial for a state crime constituted double jeopardy and violated the due process clause of the Fourteenth Amendment. The U.S. Supreme Court decided that the defendant's due process rights were not violated because the Fourteenth Amendment applied to the states only those aspects of the Bill of Rights "which are the very essence of a scheme of ordered liberty."[77] Double jeopardy was not considered "fundamental" or "so rooted in the traditions and conscience of our people" that it should apply to the states as well as to the federal government.

From the Supreme Court decisions such as *Palko* evolved a new legal theory called **fundamental fairness.** If the Supreme Court decided that a particular guarantee in the Bill of Rights was "fundamental" to and "implicit" in the U.S. system of justice, it would hold that right applicable to the states. This became the method by which states could be held to the same standards of criminal due process as the federal government.

Using the formula derived from the *Palko* case, the incorporation of the provisions of the Bill of Rights into the Fourteenth Amendment moved forward slowly on a case-by-case basis, accelerating in 1953 when Earl Warren became chief justice of the Supreme Court. Under his leadership, the due process movement reached its peak. The Court decided numerous landmark cases focusing on the rights of the accused and brought about a revolution in the area of constitutional criminal procedure. The Warren Court granted many new rights to those accused of crimes and went so far as to impose specific guidelines on the policies of police, courts, and correctional services that ensured that due process of law would be maintained.

Today, the Fourteenth Amendment's due process clause has been interpreted by the U.S. Supreme Court to mean that an accused in a state criminal case is entitled to the same protections available under the federal Bill of Rights. Some of the major Supreme Court decisions making the Bill of Rights applicable to the states have been *Mapp v. Ohio* (1961),[78] which guaranteed the right of an individual to be free from unreasonable searches and seizures and to exclude the illegally seized evidence from criminal trials; *Malloy v. Hogan* (1964),[79] which guaranteed the right of an individual to be free from forced self-incrimination; *Gideon v. Wainwright* (1963),[80] which guaranteed the right to counsel; and *Klopfer v. North Carolina* (1967),[81] which overturned *Palko v. Connecticut* and guaranteed the right to be free from double jeopardy. These are some of the pertinent de-

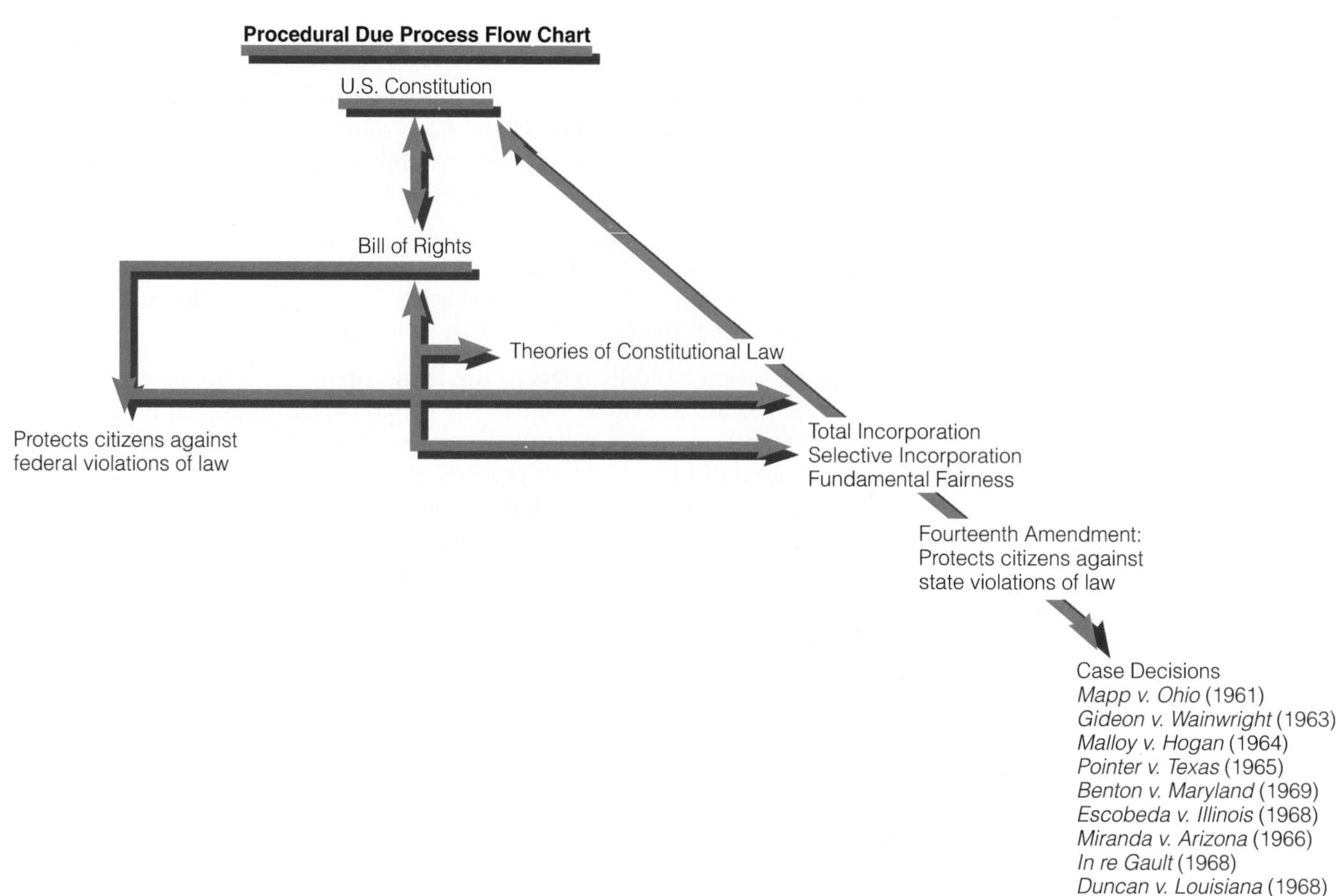

FIGURE 4.2
Relationship of the Bill of Rights and the Fourteenth Amendment to the Constitutional Rights of the Accused

cisions that grant similar rights to an accused person on both state and federal levels. A diagram of the relationship between the Bill of Rights and the Fourteenth Amendment is presented in Figure 4.2.

Procedural Due Process of Law

The concept of due process has been used as a basis for incorporating the Bill of Rights into the Fourteenth Amendment. Due process has also been used to evaluate the constitutionality of legal statutes and to set standards and guidelines for fair procedures in the criminal justice system.

Due process has often been divided into its substantive and procedural areas. The substantive aspects of due process are generally used to determine whether a statute is a fair, reasonable, and appropriate use of the legal power of the legislature. The concept of substantive due process was used extensively in the 1930s and 1940s to invalidate minimum wage standards, price-fixing, and employment restriction statutes. Today, substantive due process is used relatively sparingly; it is employed occasionally, however, to hold that a criminal statute—

such as an act prohibiting disorderly conduct, imposing capital punishment, or banning pornography—is unconstitutional because it is arbitrary or unreasonable.

Much more important today are the procedural aspects of due process of law. In seeking to define the meaning of the term, most legal experts believe that it refers to the essential elements of fairness under law.[82] *Black's Law Dictionary* presents an elaborate and complex definition of due process:

> Due process of law in each particular case means such an exercise of the powers of government as the settled maxims of law permit and sanction, and under such safeguards for the protection of individual rights as those maxims prescribe for the class of cases to which the one in question belongs.[83]

This definition basically refers to the legal system's need for rules and regulations that protect individual rights. The actual objectives of due process help define the term even more explicitly. Due process seeks to ensure that no person will be deprived of life, liberty, or property without notice of charges, assistance from legal counsel, a hearing, and an opportunity to confront those making the accusations. Basically, due process is intended to guarantee that fundamental fairness exists in each individual case. This doctrine of fairness as expressed in due process of law is guaranteed under both the Fifth and Fourteenth Amendments.[84] Abstract definitions are only one aspect of due process. Much more significant are the procedures that give meaning to due process in the everyday practices of the criminal justice system. In this regard, due process provides numerous procedural safeguards for the offender, including the following:

1. Notices of charges
2. A formal hearing
3. The right to counsel or some other representation
4. The opportunity to respond to charges
5. The opportunity to confront and cross-examine witnesses and accusers
6. The privilege to be free from self-incrimination
7. The opportunity to present one's own witnesses
8. A decision made on the basis of substantial evidence and facts produced at the hearing
9. A written statement of the reasons for the decision
10. An appellate review procedure

The Nature of Due Process—Its Real Meaning

Exactly what constitutes due process in a specific case depends on the facts of the case, the federal and state constitutional and statutory provisions, previous court decisions, and the ideas and principles that society considers important at a given time and in a given place.[85] Justice Felix Frankfurter emphasized this point in *Rochin v. California* (1952):

> Due process of law requires an evaluation based on a disinterested inquiry pursued in the spirit of science on a balanced order of facts, exactly and clearly stated, on the detached consideration of conflicting claims . . . on a judgment not ad hoc and episodic but duly mindful of reconciling the needs both of continuity and of change in a progressive society.[86]

Both the elements and the definition of due process seem to be flexible and constantly changing. For example, at one time, the concept of due process did not require a formal hearing for parole revocation, but it does today. Prior to

1968, juvenile offenders did not have the right to an attorney at their adjudication; counsel is now required in the juvenile court system. Prior to 1972, defendants were often unable to receive a speedy trial because of court delays. Today, state and federal laws safeguard the defendant's right to a speedy trial. In the 1970s and 1980s, the secrecy of the grand jury proceeding was a matter of much controversy. Recent reforms provide new due process protections that open the proceeding to outside review. Thus, the interpretations of due process of law are not fixed but rather reflect what society deems fair and just at a particular time and place. The degree of loss suffered by the individual (victim or offender) balanced against the state's interests also determines which and how many due process requirements are ordinarily applied. When a person's freedom is at stake in the criminal justice system, he or she is usually granted all applicable due process rights; in other cases, due process may be circumscribed.

Due process has been increasingly applied to protect individual rights when the government seeks to deprive a person of life, liberty, or property. The trend toward a wider use of procedural safeguards to prevent abuses of power has spread to many fields, including criminal justice, public welfare, mental health, juvenile delinquency, and public education. More than ever before, due process of law based on the Fifth and Fourteenth Amendments is used to challenge various types of arbitrary actions, such as the termination of aid by welfare officials or the imposition of punishment on prison inmates. Consistent judicial intervention has made these and other fields more responsive to reform through the application of constitutional rights.

Future Directions in Criminal Law and Procedure

Despite present problems with the criminal justice system, much progress has been made in the field of criminal law and constitutional procedure over the past twenty-five years. The future direction of the criminal law in the United States remains unclear. Yet there seems to be less tolerance for government corruption, more public interest in fixed sentences and capital punishment, and more conservative decision making by our judicial bodies. Attention probably will be paid to the substantive nature of criminal law in the future, particularly where it is important in the preservation of U.S. society. Special prosecutors, for example, using criminal statutes involving conspiracy, perjury, and fraud were able to uncover the illegal operations in the Nixon administration of the 1970s and to examine the Reagan administration's activities in the Iran-Contra affair in the 1980s. In the Bush administration of the 1990s, efforts have been made to prosecute such diverse crimes as those in the scandal involving the savings and loan associations and the alleged international drug scheme of deposed dictator, General Manuel Noriega of Panama. The criminal law system has demonstrated amazing resilience in its ability to prosecute public officials and private citizens whose behavior has damaged the very government they work so hard to promote.

Both an expansion and a contraction of the criminal law itself can also be anticipated. Areas of expansion probably will include a greater emphasis on controlling career criminals. Laws making it easier for states to punish serious juvenile offenders and incarcerate them in secure adult institutions will probably be passed. More attention will be given to white-collar crimes, as well as to drug-related crimes and terrorism. Corporations are almost certainly going to be held accountable for their illegal acts, especially those that result in physical as well as economic harm. Stock market and computer activities will receive close scrutiny by

law enforcement agencies. In addition, there are likely to be greater efforts to sever the link between organized crime and legitimate businesses, similar to the efforts being made to stop banks from laundering illegal cash.

Lastly, the legal system will also be faced with difficult challenges involving the AIDS (acquired immune deficiency syndrome) disease. Currently, there are some criminal laws that specifically attempt to control the activities of prisoners, prostitutes, drug users, and criminal defendants who may be spreading the AIDS virus, including mandatory drug-testing programs.[87] AIDS testing for all inmates, for instance, is viewed by correctional authorities as a special preventive measure to protect others from contracting the disease.

Other offenses, such as those involving the use of some controlled drugs (most likely, marijuana), and petty criminal offenses may be reduced in importance or removed entirely from the criminal law system. To make criminal sentencing fairer and more certain for the justice system, the public, and the offender, a system of judicially fixed sentences—and possibly the elimination of parole in some jurisdictions—will continue to become more commonplace.

Regardless of what changes occur in the future, the criminal law system will continue to be faced with four fundamental problems: (1) defining and classifying antisocial behavior; (2) establishing appropriate criminal sanctions or punishments; (3) applying the proper degree of criminal responsibility; and (4) determining what departures from due process of law safeguards may require the reversal of a conviction.

The Supreme Court Turns to the Right

More than any other factor, the role of the Supreme Court will dominate the future direction of criminal law and procedure in the United States. The Supreme Court has been the setting for some of the important recent events in the administration of criminal justice. For example, the Court took a decidedly liberal turn in granting individual rights for the accused during the Earl Warren era of the 1960s. In the 1970s and 1980s, Nixon's conservatives—Justices Warren Burger and William Rehnquist—curbed the growth of criminal procedure rights. With the replacement of liberal Justice William Brennan by conservative David Souter of New Hampshire in 1990, the court continued to hand down legally conservative opinions favoring state law enforcement over criminal defendants. This conservative trend was apparent in the 1990–91 term of the Court. The justices made it easier for police with no warrants to search buses for drugs or to open and examine suitcases found in car trunks.[88] The Court also allowed prosecutors to use coerced confessions as evidence against defendants and even authorized the jailing of individuals for up to forty-eight hours without a hearing.[89] In addition, the Court's decision to permit the use of evidence about a victim's character and the impact on the victim's family at the sentencing phase of death penalty cases overturned an earlier ban against the use of such information.[90] These decisions, which are discussed in more detail in Chapter 9, illustrate the conservative trend in the Supreme Court. This trend should become more pronounced with the controversial appointment of conservative U.S. Court of Appeals Judge Clarence Thomas to the high court in 1991, replacing retiring liberal Justice Thurgood Marshall.[91] The Court is now positioned to change or reverse the 1960s expansion of rights of the accused and become a "law and order" court of the 1990s. Figure 4.3 identifies how the individual justices on the U.S. Supreme Court might view actual cases on criminal justice issues in the twenty-first century.

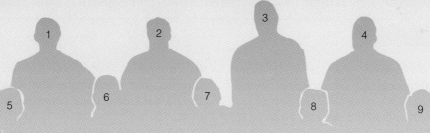

1 David H. Souter
Age: 52 1990*
In conservative camp on criminal procedure

2 Antonin Scalia
Age: 56 1986
A constitutional scholar

3 Anthony M. Kennedy
Age: 55 1988
Often upholds states' position on criminal procedure

4 Clarence Thomas
Age: 44 1991
Conservative Republican ?

5 John Paul Stevens
Age: 72 1975
Middle of the road on rights of the underdog

6 Byron R. White
Age: 75 1962
To the right on criminal justice issues

7 William H. Rehnquist
Age: 67 1972
Leader of conservative crime and justice revolution

8 Harry A. Blackmun
Age: 83 1970
His votes are mixed on criminal procedure

9 Sandra Day O'Connor
Age: 62 1981
Generally votes to limit criminal's rights

*Year appointed to Supreme Court

FIGURE 4.3
The Law and Order Court of the Twenty-first Century?

SUMMARY

The criminal justice system is basically a legal system. Its foundation is the criminal law, which is concerned with people's conduct. The purpose of criminal law is to regulate behavior and maintain order in society. What constitutes a crime is defined primarily by the state and federal legislatures and reviewed by the courts.

What is considered criminal conduct changes from one period to another. Social norms, values, and community beliefs play major roles in determining what conduct is antisocial. Crimes are generally classified as felonies or misdemeanors, depending on their seriousness. Since a crime is a public wrong against the state, the criminal law imposes sanctions in the form of fines, probation, or imprisonment on a guilty defendant.

Under the criminal law, all adults are presumed to be aware of the consequences of their actions, but the law does not hold an individual blameworthy unless that person is capable of intending to commit the crime of which he or she is accused. Such factors as insanity, a mental defect, or age mitigate a person's criminal responsibility.

States periodically revise and update the substantive criminal law and the procedural laws in their penal codes; the latter deals with the rules for processing the offender from arrest through trial, sentencing, and release. An accused must be provided with the guarantees of due process under the Fifth and Fourteenth Amendments to the U.S. Constitution.

The U.S. Supreme Court has held that the due process clause protects citizens against two basic types of state intrusion. One involves substantive due process that "shocks the conscience" of society.[92] The second deals with the implementation of fair and just procedures—often referred to as procedural due process. Both principles hold the government responsible where an individual's liberty is at stake.

The relationship of the Bill of Rights to the Fourteenth Amendment of 1868 remains a source of great controversy in the justice system. Drug trafficking and RICO laws impinge on Fourth Amendment protections; the meaning of cruel and unusual punishment under the Eighth Amendment conflicts with the death penalty; and equal rights under the law is often threatened by arbitrary procedures. These kinds of issues require constant vigilance by the Supreme Court.

QUESTIONS

1. What are the specific aims and purposes of the criminal law? To what extent does the criminal law control behavior?
2. What kinds of activities should be labeled criminal in contemporary society? Why?
3. What is a criminal act? What is a criminal state of mind? When are individuals liable for their actions?
4. Discuss the various kinds of crime classifications. To what extent or degree are they distinguishable?
5. In recent years, numerous states have revised their penal codes. What are some of the major categories of substantive crimes you think should be revised?
6. Entrapment is a defense when the defendant was entrapped into committing the crime. To what extent should law enforcement personnel induce the commission of an offense?
7. What legal principles can be used to justify self-defense? Considering that the law seeks to prevent crime, not promote it, are such principles sound?
8. What are the minimum standards of procedure required in the criminal justice system?
9. Discuss the relationship between the U.S. Constitution and the Bill of Rights. What particular provisions does the incorporation theory involve?

NOTES

1. Some of the historical criminal law concepts are a synthesis of those contained in Fred Inbua, James Thompson, and James Zagel, *Criminal Law and Its Administration* (Mineola, NY: Foundation Press, 1974); Jerome Hall, *General Principles of Criminal Law* (Charlottesville, Va.: Michie, 1961); Richard Singer and Martin Gardner, *Crimes and Punishment: Cases Materials and Readings in Criminal Law* (New York: Matthew Bender, 1989).

2. See, generally, Sanford Kadish and Monrad Paulsen, *Criminal Law and Its Processes* (Boston: Little, Brown, 1975); also, J. Dressler, *Understanding Criminal Law* (New York: Matthew Bender, 1987).

3. See T. F. Pluckett, *A Concise History of the Common Law* (Boston: Little, Brown, 1956); also, E. Allan Farnworth, *An Introduction to the Legal System of the United States* (New York: Oceana Publications, 1963).

4. *Carriers Case Yearbook*, 13 Edward IV 9.pL.5 (1473).
5. *Rex v. Scofield*, Caldwell, 397 (1784), 400.
6. 372 U.S. 335, 83 S.Ct. 792, 9 L.Ed.2d 799 (1963).
7. Ibid.
8. T. Maltz, "The Nature of Precedent," *North Carolina Law Review* 66 (1988):367–93.
9. *Robinson v. California*, 370 U.S. 660, 82 S.Ct. 1417, 8 L.Ed.2d 758 (1962); see also American Law Institute, *Model Penal Code, Proposed Official Draft* (Philadelphia: American Law Institute, 1962), Sec. C.
10. See, generally, Wayne R. LaFave and Austin W. Scott, *Criminal Law* (St. Paul: West Publishing Horn Book Series, 1986).
11. E. Gellhorn, *Administrative Law and Process* (St. Paul: West Publishing Nutshell Series, 1981).
12. See John Weaver, *Warren—The Man, the Court, the Era* (Boston: Little, Brown, 1967); see also, "We the People," *Time*, 6 July 1987, p. 6.
13. *Marbury v. Madison*, 5 U.S. (1 Cranch) 137, 2 L.Ed. 60 (1803).
14. Thomas Gardner, *Criminal Law* (St. Paul: West Publishing, 1985), pp. 15–18.
15. See *State v. Horton*, 139 N.C. 588, 51 S.E. 945 (1905).
16. See Wayne R. LaFave and Austin W. Scott, *Criminal Law*, 2d ed. (St. Paul: West Publishing Horn Book Series, 1988), p. 34.
17. See American Law Institute, *Model Penal Code*, Sec. 104.
18. Henry Black, *Black's Law Dictionary*, rev. 5th ed. (St. Paul: West Publishing, 1979), pp. 744, 1150.
19. Mass. Gen. Laws, Chap. 274, Sec. 1.
20. Sheldon Krantz, *Law of Corrections and Prisoners' Rights, Cases and Materials*, 3d ed. (St. Paul: West Publishing, 1986), p. 702; Barbara Knight and Stephen Early, Jr., *Prisoners' Rights in America* (Chicago: Nelson-Hall, 1986), chapter 1; see also Fred Cohen, "The Law of Prisoners' Rights—An Overview," *Criminal Law Bulletin* 24 (188):321–49.
21. See Mass. Gen. Laws Ann. Chapter 266, Sec. 14.
22. LaFave and Scott, *Criminal Law*, p. 177; see, generally, Frank Miller, Robert Dawson, George Dix, and Raymond Parnas, *Cases and Materials on Criminal Justice Administration*, 3d ed. (New York: Foundation Press, 1988).
23. See American Law Institute, *Model Penal Code*, Sec. 2.02; see also *United States v. Bailey*, 444 U.S. 394, 100 S.Ct. 624, 62 L.Ed.2d 575 (1980).
24. See *United States v. Balint*, 258 U.S. 250, 42 S.Ct. 301, 66 L.Ed. 604 (1922); see also *Morissette v. United States*, 342 U.S. 246, 72 S.Ct. 240, 96 L.Ed. 288 (1952).
25. See Henry Hart, "The Aims of the Criminal Law," *Law and Contemporary Problems* 23 (1956):402.
26. 8 English Reporter 718 (1943).
27. 94 U.S. App. D.C. 228, 214 F.2d 862 (1954).
28. American Law Institute, *Model Penal Code*, Sec. 4.01.
29. See Bureau of Justice Statistics, *Report to the Nation on Crime and Justice*, 2d ed. (Washington, D.C.: Bureau of Justice Statistics, 1988), p. 87.
30. "The Insanity Defense: Should It Be Abolished?" *Newsweek*, 24 May 1982, pp. 56–70; "Hinckley Bombshell—End of Insanity Plea?" *U.S. News and World Report*, 5 July 1982, pp. 12–14.
31. See, generally, Norval Morris, *Madness and the Criminal Law* (Chicago: University of Chicago Press, 1982), chapter 2; see also Rita Simon and David Aaronson, *The Insanity Defense: A Critical Assessment of Law and Policy in the Post-Hinckley Era* (New York: Praeger, 1988), p. 45.
32. Joseph di Genova and Victoria Toensing, "Bringing Sanity to the Insanity Defense," *American Bar Association Journal* 69 (1983):467.
33. "Hinckley Decision Points Up Need for New Verdict," *New York Times*, 1 July 1982; "It's a Mad, Mad Verdict," *New Republic*, 12 July 1983, pp. 13–19; "Straight Talk about the Insanity Defense," *The Nation*, 24 July 1982, pp. 70–72.
34. Bureau of Justice Statistics, *Report to the Nation on Crime and Justice*, p. 87; see also John Klofas and Janette Yandrasits, "Guilty But Mentally Ill and the Jury Trial: A Case Study," *Criminal Law Bulletin* 24 (1989):424.
35. "The Insanity Defense: Should It Be Abolished," pp. 56–60. For excellent references on crime and insanity, see Katherine Ellison and Robert Buckhout, *Psychology and Criminal Justice: Common Grounds* (New York: Harper & Row, 1982); Willard Gaylin, *The Killing of Bonnie Garland: A Question of Justice* (New York: Simon & Schuster, 1982); Abraham Goldstein, *The Insanity Defense* (Westport, Conn.: Greenwood Press, 1980); William Winslade and Judith Wilson, *The Insanity Plea* (New York: Scribner, 1983).
36. Comprehensive Crime Control Act of 1984. Title 18; see also B. McGraw et al., "The Guilty But Mentally Ill Plea and Verdict: Current State of the Knowledge," *Villanova Law Review* (1985):30; Pedro Portes, Dennis Wagner, and Eleanor Lore, "How Just Is the Guilty But Mentally Ill Verdict? An Exploration into Personality and Intellectual Factors," *Journal of Criminal Justice* 19 (1991):471–479; Richard Moran, "His Insanity Plea Can't Free Dahmer," *Boston Globe*, 9 February 1992, p. 60.
37. 370 U.S. 660, 82 S.Ct. 1417, 8 L.Ed.2d 758 (1962).
38. 392 U.S. 514, 88 S.Ct. 2145, 20 L.Ed.2d 1254 (1968).
39. Samuel M. Davis, *Rights of Juveniles: The Juvenile Justice System* (New York: Boardman, 1974); chapter 2; Larry Siegel and Joseph Senna, *Juvenile Delinquency: Theory, Practice and Law* (St. Paul: West Publishing, 1988).
40. See Thomas Gardner and Victor Manian, *Criminal Law—Principles, Cases, and Readings* (St. Paul: West Publishing, 1975), p. 144.
41. *People v. Goetz*, 68 N.Y.2d 96, 497 N.E.2d 41, 506 N.Y.S.2d 18 (1986); see also "New York Court Upholds Goetz Gun Conviction," *Boston Globe*, 23 November 1988, p. 5.
42. See the interesting case of *Katko v. Briney*, 183 N.W.2d 657 (Iowa 1971), which deals with the question of whether an owner may protect personal property in an unoccupied farmhouse against trespassers by a spring gun capable of inflicting death.
43. 287 U.S. 435, 53 S.Ct. 210, 77 L.Ed. 413 (1932).
44. 356 U.S. 369, 78 S.Ct. 819, 2 L.Ed.2d 848 (1958).
45. 411 U.S. 423, 93 S.Ct. 1637, 36 L.Ed.2d 366 (1973).
46. 425 U.S. 484, 96 S.Ct. 1646, 48 L.Ed.2d 113 (1976).
47. Ibid., at 489, 96 S.Ct. at 1649.
48. Thomas Gardner, *Criminal Law Principles and Cases*, 3d ed. (St. Paul: West Publishing, 1985), p. 133; see also James Tuohy and Rob Warden, *Greylord: Justice Chicago Style* (New York: Putnam Press, 1989).
49. 411 U.S. 423, 93 S.Ct. 1637, 36 L.Ed.2d 366 (1973).
50. See U.S. Constitution, Fifth Amendment.
51. 359 U.S. 121, 72 S.Ct. 676, 3 L.Ed.2d 684 (1959).
52. 395 U.S. 784, 89 S.Ct. 2056, 23 L.Ed.2d 707 (1969).
53. 410 U.S. 458, 93 S.Ct. 1066, 35 L.Ed.2d 425 (1973).
54. 395 U.S. 711, 89 S.Ct. 2072, 23 L.Ed.2d 656 (1969).
55. Ibid., at 721, 89 S.Ct. at 2078.
56. William Blackstone, *Commentaries on the Law of England*, vol. 1, ed. Thomas Cooley (Chicago: Callaghan, 1899), pp. 4, 26. Blackstone was an English barrister who lectured on the English common law at Oxford University in 1753.
57. American Law Institute, *Model Penal Code*, Sec. 2.04.
58. *Commonwealth v. Berrigan*, 509 Pa. 118, 501 A.2d 226 (1985); see also *State v. Tate*, 102 N.J. 64, 505 A.2d 941 (1986).
59. See Associated Press, "Michigan Senate Acts to Outlaw Aiding Suicides," *Boston Globe*, 20 March 1991, p. 22; also see Note, *Harvard Law Review* 99 (1986):1293, which gives several examples of whether a defendant's cultural background has bearing on criminal responsibility.
60. In *New York v. Ferber*, 458 U.S. 747, 102 S.Ct. 3348, 73 L.Ed.2d 1113 (1982), the Supreme Court upheld state laws that ban the use of children in sexually explicit publications even if they are not legally obscene.
61. 18 U.S.C. §§ 1961–1968 (1970). Enterprise includes both legitimate and illegitimate associations.
62. See John Brooks, *The Takeover Game* (New York: E.P. Dutton, 1987), p. 319; also James Stewart, *Den of Thieves* (New York: Simon & Schuster,

1991). This book is a complete analysis of the insider trading scandal.
63. David W. Fassett, "Mother of Mercy, Is This the End of RICO?" *American Bar Association Journal on Criminal Justice*, 6 (1991):12.
64. See, generally, "Reforming RICO: If, Why and How—A Symposium," *Vanderbilt Law Review* 43 (1990). This issue presents nine articles with varied perspectives on the use and possible reform of the RICO Act.
65. Three additional and more current sources include the updated Model Penal Code and commentaries of American Law Institute, 1985; the "Working Papers" of National Commission on Reform of the Federal Criminal Law (1970); and Jeremy Miller, "An Outline for a Model Penal Code II," *The Prosecutor Journal of National District Attorneys Association* 25 (1991):21.
66. Comprehensive Crime Control Act of 1984, Title 18, U.S.C.; also Albert P. Melone, "The Politics of Criminal Code Revision," *Capital U.S. Review* 15 (1986):191.
67. Omnibus Drug Law, H5210, *Congressional Quarterly*, 29 October 1988, p. 3145.
68. Tom Smith, "Legislative and Legal Developments in Criminal Justice," *Journal on Criminal Justice* 5 (1991):36–37.
69. See "U.S. House Ok's $1.1 Billion Anti-Crime Package—Will It Pass?" *Boston Globe*, 23 October 1991:23.
70. For a real-world application and impact of the Bill of Rights on criminal justice in particular, see Ellen Alderman and Caroline Kennedy, *In Our Defense—The Bill of Rights in Action* (New York: William Morrow, 1991).
71. 410 U.S. 113, 93 S.Ct. 705, 35 L.Ed.2d 147 (1973).
72. 384 U.S. 436, 86 S.Ct. 1602, 16 L.Ed.2d 694 (1966).
73. *Schall v. Martin*, 467 U.S. 253, 104 S.Ct. 2403, 81 L.Ed.2d 207 (1984).
74. 32 U.S. (7 Peters) 243, 8 L.Ed. 672 (1833).
75. 110 U.S. 516, 4 S.Ct. 111, 28 L.Ed. 232 (1884).
76. 302 U.S. 319, 58 S.Ct. 149, 82 L.Ed. 288 (1937).
77. Ibid., at 325, 58 S.Ct. at 152.
78. 367 U.S. 643, 81 S.Ct. 1684, 6 L.Ed.2d 1081 (1961).
79. 378 U.S. 1, 84 S.Ct. 1489, 12 L.Ed.2d 653 (1964).
80. 372 U.S. 335, 83 S.Ct. 792, 9 L.Ed.2d 799 (1963).
81. 386 U.S. 213, 87 S.Ct. 988, 18 L.Ed.2d 1 (1967).
82. See Essay, *Time*, 26 February 1973, p. 95; also for a tribute to the Bill of Rights and due process, see James MacGregor Burns and Steward Burns, *The Pursuit of Rights in America* (New York: Knopf, 1991).
83. Black, *Black's Law Dictionary*, p. 449.
84. See, generally, Joseph J. Senna, "Changes in Due Process of Law," *Social Work* 19 (1974):319; see also the interesting student rights case *Goss v. Lopez*, 419 U.S. 565, 95 S.Ct. 729, 42 L.Ed.2d 725 (1975).
85. 342 U.S. 165, 72 S.Ct. 205, 95 L.Ed. 183 (1952).
86. Ibid., at 172, 72 S.Ct. at 209.
87. See Alan Dershowitz, *Taking Liberties—A Decade of Hard Cases, Bad Laws, and Bum Raps* (Chicago: Contemporary Books, 1988) p. 148; see also Theodore Hammett, *AIDS in Correctional Facilities—Issues and Options* (Washington, D.C.: U.S. Department of Justice, 1986); The Administrative Office of the United States Courts, *Demonstration Program of Mandatory Drug Testing of Criminal Defendants* (Washington, D.C.: Office of U.S. Courts, March 29, 1991).
88. *Florida v. Bostick*, 49 Criminal Law Reporter 2270 (1991):2270; *California v. Acevedo* 49 Criminal Law Reporter 2210 (1991).
89. *Arizona v. Fulminante*, 48 Criminal Law Reporter 2107 (1991); *Riverside v. McLaughlin*, 49 Criminal Law Reporter 2104 (1991).
90. *Payne v. Tennessee*, ____ U.S. ____, 111 S.Ct. 2597, 115 L.Ed.2d 720 (1991).
91. For more detailed information on the controversial appointment of Clarence Thomas to the U.S. Supreme Court, see *Time*, 21 October 1991; *U.S. News & World Report*, 21 October 1991; also T. Rosenthal, "Marshall Retires from High Court: Blow to Liberals," *New York Times*, 28 June 1991, p. 1.
92. See *Rochin v. California*, 342 U.S. 165, 72 S.Ct. 205, 95 L.Ed. 183 (1952).

Confronting Crime

CHAPTER 5

OUTLINE

KEY TERMS

crime control
rehabilitation
due process model
nonintervention
decriminalization
victimless crimes
deinstitutionalization
pretrial diversion
widening the net
determinate sentencing
conflict
white-collar crimes
source control
DARE
methadone
legalization
social control

Now that some understanding of the agencies and processes of justice, the nature and cause of crime, and the functions of the criminal law has been developed, it is time to focus attention directly on the criminal justice system and its efforts to confront and control crime in the United States.

Though it has been more than twenty-five years since the field of criminal justice began to be the subject of both serious academic study and attempts at unified policy formation, significant debate continues over the general direction the system should take, how the problem of crime control should be approached, and the most effective method of dealing with known criminal offenders. After decades of effort in research and policy analysis, it is clear that criminal justice is far from a unified field. Practitioners, academics, and commentators alike have expressed irreconcilable differences concerning its goals, purpose, and direction. This lack of consensus is particularly vexing when the multitude of problems facing the justice system is considered. The agencies of justice must attempt to eradicate such seemingly diverse social problems as substance abuse, gang violence, and environmental contamination, while at the same time respecting individual liberties and civil rights. It is also assumed that the agencies of the justice system can efficiently carry out a multiplicity of diverse tasks and that their representatives possess a wide range of knowledge on law, psychology, and social welfare.

This chapter will review the major perspectives on justice and some of the critical issues facing the field. First, the focus is on the different perspectives of justice: what are the goals and objectives of the criminal justice system? Then the chapter turns to a discussion of how the system is confronting some of the major forms of crime in the United States: how can drug abuse, violence, white-collar crime, and chronic offending be controlled or eliminated? The chapter then addresses the risks of social control: what are the unforeseen costs of crime control?

Perspectives on Justice

Considering the complexity of criminal justice, it should not be surprising that no single view of the concept dominates the field. Those who work within the profession or study its processes often hold competing views on how the justice system works and how it should operate in the future. In fact, people who hold opposing views sometimes share the same job responsibilities or duties, resulting in intraagency conflict. In academic departments, opposing views on the nature of justice can heat up faculty politics.

What are the dominant views of the criminal justice system today? What is the role of the justice system, and how should it approach its tasks? The different perspectives on criminal justice are discussed below.

Crime Control Perspective

Advocates of the **crime control** perspective believe that the proper role of the justice system is to prevent crime through the judicious use of criminal sanctions. If the justice system operated in an effective manner, potential criminals would be deterred from committing law violations, while those who did commit crime would be apprehended, tried, and punished. The justice system would be capable of meting out sufficient punishment to convince the offender that "crime does not pay."

According to the crime control perspective, the focus of justice should be on the victim of crime, not the criminal. The ultimate goal of the criminal justice system is to protect innocent people from the ravages of crime. This objective can be achieved through more effective police protection, tough sentences (including liberal use of the death penalty), and the construction of prisons designed to safely incapacitate hardened criminals.

Crime control enthusiasts believe in swift and sure justice. They do not want legal technicalities to help the guilty go free and tie the hands of justice. They lobby for the abolition of legal restrictions that control a police officer's ability to search for evidence and interrogate suspects with a free hand. They are angry at judges who let obviously guilty people go free because a law enforcement officer made an unintentional procedural error. They argue for the abolition of the exclusionary rule and the *Miranda* decision and applaud when the Supreme Court hands down rulings that increase police power. Overzealous, publicity-seeking defense lawyers who specialize in freeing notorious killers and rapists on legal technicalities or the insanity defense are the subject of unrestrained scorn.

Advocates of the crime control perspective also are skeptical of the criminal justice system's ability to rehabilitate offenders. Most treatment programs are ineffective because the justice system is simply not equipped to treat people who have a long history of antisocial behavior. From both a moral and a practical standpoint, the role of criminal justice should be the control of antisocial people. If not to the justice system, then to whom can the average citizen turn for protection from society's criminal elements?

Crime Control in Action. The crime control perspective was one of the first views of criminal justice and is still a dominant force today. Its roots can be traced to the eighteenth century, when philosophers such as Cesare Beccaria and Jeremy Bentham argued that punishment should be designed to deter crime without resorting to sadism and brutality. It fell out of favor in the mid-twentieth century, when a more liberal view of criminal justice, favoring offender treatment and rehabilitation, dominated. However, during the conservative resurgence in the 1970s and 1980s, the crime control perspective emerged once again as an important factor in justice policy. Its ascendency was marked by conservative appointments to the Supreme Court and other federal courts, the toughening of

Advocates of the crime control perspective believe that police officers should be professional and efficient crime fighters.

federal and state sentencing codes, and the resumption of the use of capital punishment.

Today, the crime control perspective still exerts a powerful influence on criminal justice policy. A great deal of recent state and federal legislation has created "law and order" oriented programs, such as mandatory prison sentences for those convicted of violent crimes. The Supreme Court has generally eased restrictions on police operations. Even views of the cause of crime and the nature of criminality have become more conservative. It is common today to see books and journal articles that indicate that criminal tendencies are inherited and that criminals are "wicked" people who should be set aside from society. The crime control perspective seems a logical approach for those people concerned with law and order and the control of street crime.

Nowhere can the influence of the crime control perspective be more clearly seen than in the adoption of capital punishment by a majority of states and the federal government. To a crime control advocate, the use of the death penalty is morally justified because the state has a duty to protect the lives of its citizens. Capital punishment also is a reflection of the public will, since most U.S. citizens favor the death penalty for convicted murderers. Crime control advocates also favor the death penalty because they are concerned about research that shows that convicted killers who are sent to prison often serve a small percentage of their sentence in confinement and that people on death row have prior convictions for murder.[1]

Rehabilitation Perspective

If the crime control perspective views the justice system in terms of protecting the public and controlling criminal elements, then those who advocate the **rehabilitation** perspective may be said to see the justice system as a means of caring for and treating people who cannot manage themselves. They view crime as an expression of frustration and anger created by social inequality. Crime can be controlled by giving people the means to improve their life-style through conventional endeavors.

The rehabilitation concept assumes that people are at the mercy of social, economic, and interpersonal conditions and interactions. Criminals themselves are the victims of racism, poverty, strain, blocked opportunities, alienation, family disruption, and other social problems. They live in socially disorganized neighborhoods that are incapable of providing proper education, health care, or civil services. Society must help them in order to compensate for their social problems.

Crime can be controlled by helping people find legitimate ways of obtaining wealth, power, and prestige and coping with their life situations. Methods to achieve these goals include job training, family counseling, educational services, and crisis intervention. It is far less expensive and more efficient and humane to treat potential young offenders and help them become established in the community than to wait until they violate the law and then punish them with a prison sentence and lock them into a life of crime.

In contrast to the crime control perspective, the rehabilitation perspective places its emphasis on the criminal offender. It disputes the crime control perspective's emphasis on punishment and control. Even if every criminal were apprehended and incarcerated, destructive social conditions would create a new generation of law violators in the nation's ghettos and poverty areas. Society has a choice: pay now, by funding treatment and educational programs, or pay later, when disenfranchised youth enter costly correctional facilities.

A rehabilitation advocate rejects the concept of capital punishment because of its inherent brutality and futility. Its use signifies that society has given up on offenders and precludes any hope they can be turned into law-abiding citizens. Advocates of the death penalty feed the public with images of maniacal killers who must be executed to protect innocent children; in truth, the typical person sentenced to death is a young man who kills someone during an armed robbery. The mass murderer is actually rarely sentenced to death. Has society not progressed beyond the cruel punishments used in ancient civilizations?

Rehabilitation in Action. The rehabilitation view was extremely influential in the 1960s and early 1970s, when the government's ability to devise programs to counteract crime was viewed with optimism. The Kennedy and Johnson administrations invited well-known liberal academics and social policy experts to Washington to help shape government programs. The federal government lent support to direct service programs at the grass-roots level. Large-scale anticrime and delinquency prevention programs were implemented that emphasized community development, job training, educational enrichment, and political organizing. In addition, a multitude of programs was created at every level of government to offer social services to known offenders who desired to "go straight." Among the most well-known were the *detached street worker* program, in which social workers were matched and worked closely with street gangs.[2] Other programs, among the most notable being Mobilization for Youth on New York City's lower east side and Boston's Mid-City Project, attempted to revitalize entire city neighborhoods with a variety of work and education programs.[3]

In the 1980s, the rehabilitation view fell into disfavor with many members of the general public and the professional community. Despite costly government interventions, treatment efforts apparently failed to reduce the crime rate. A series of research studies found that most programs designed to rehabilitate known offenders did not really work as well as expected.[4] The failure of rehabilitation

ANALYZING CRIMINAL JUSTICE ISSUES

Confronting Crime Again

In 1985, Elliott Currie published a well-received book, *Confronting Crime,* in which he set out a liberal agenda for reducing the crime problem. Currie's book helped clarify the goals of the rehabilitation perspective and provided a blueprint for change in the justice system.

Currie argued that prevailing efforts to reduce the crime rate, most of which rested on conservative social control policies, were highly confused and ineffectual. The crime rate could be reduced if efforts focused instead on young offenders before they actually became enmeshed in the justice system. The crime problem can be traced directly to social inequality, great extremes of poverty and hopelessness, ineffective national policies to deal with un- and underemployment, the destruction of community and family ties due to social mobility, and the pressure placed on the family by our technical society. As a result, the justice system must ease social problems and reduce tensions within the most important institutions of human socialization. This effort might include more formal police responses to domestic violence disputes and the strengthening of community ties through using foot patrols and hiring teens to be auxiliary police officers. According to Currie's vision, the justice system must combine control efforts with more effective rehabilitation policies. For example, intensive probation and restitution should be used as alternatives to incarceration. Every effort should be made to expand intensive rehabilitation services for youthful offenders at the local community level. Aid must be provided to the victims of family violence. Neighborhood dispute resolution teams and community-based family support programs, especially those that respect cultural diversity, can be directed at improving family services, helping teenaged parents, and providing educational enrichment for youths.

Currie's prescription for a lower crime rate based on social engineering was scoffed at by conservative thinkers. And throughout the 1980s, the conservative crime control model of criminal justice dominated. In more recent writings, Currie argues that just as conservatives proclaimed the death of liberalism in the early 1980s, the conservative movement may run out of steam in the 1990s. After a decade of toughened criminal penalties, the threat of capital punishment, and the tripling of the prison population, the crime rate remains unacceptably high and the nation's cities are wracked by drug abuse and gang violence. If the failure to reduce the crime rate ended the dominance of liberal policies, might the continu-

programs to receive unqualified support eroded confidence in the ability of the justice system to improve the lives of known criminals and offer alternatives to potential offenders. The cost of funding effective rehabilitation efforts, coupled with the public's fear of violent crime, helped erode the dominance of the rehabilitation philosophy in the criminal justice system.

The justice system has by no means terminated its efforts to treat offenders, however. While some research evaluations question the effectiveness of rehabilitation, others show that many programs do produce desired effects.[5] Numerous treatment programs continue to exist in the various criminal justice agencies around the United States. Most long-term correctional facilities maintain counseling programs, educational efforts, and job training courses. Probation departments operate a full range of community-based programs for offenders who are not in need of secure confinement. Agencies of the juvenile justice system generally remain committed to a rehabilitation orientation. While it is wrong to say that everything works, it may be premature to say that nothing works.[6] As Analyzing Criminal Justice Issues: Confronting Crime Again suggests, the rehabilitation perspective may have a resurgence.

Due Process Perspective

In his classic work *The Limits of the Criminal Sanction*, Herbert Packer contrasted the crime control perspective with a view that he referred to as the **due process**

ing urban crisis have the same effect on conservative approaches?

In his more recent writings, Currie confirms his view that crime can be controlled by "human-ecological" means. This includes: (1) an emphasis on high-quality early education, such as the Head Start program; (2) expanded health and mental health services for high-risk children and adults, including pre- and postnatal care; and (3) greater commitment to family support programs. While these short-term objectives can have an immediate influence, they are not sufficient to bring about a society in which crime is a historical curiosity. To reach this end, Currie suggests that the social and economic inequality that wracks the United States must be ended. Disadvantaged Americans must be offered the opportunity to engage in labor that brings adequate reward and compensation. Work must be geared to the realities of family life to relieve the pressure on that battered institution. Greater attention must also be paid to local communities so that they can give the proper support to families and provide a helping network to those in need.

Critical Thinking Skills

1. According to Currie, crime rates could be slashed if income inequality were reduced and the underemployed given better work opportunities. Is the socioeconomic class system in the United States so rigid that the lower class is actually prevented from entering mainstream society? Are there not existing programs in almost every community that already provide educational opportunities for the "deserving poor"? And considering the success of the free market system, would increased government control and regulation of the marketplace threaten our economic structure?

2. Currie finds that the family is key to reducing crime rates. Is it not naive to suppose that family relations can be improved by outside social action? Divorce, family conflict, spouse abuse, and child abuse have long been recognized as major social problems and, despite many efforts, have resisted change. If the quality of family life cannot be changed, are crime control efforts inherently futile?

3. Suppose for a moment that research shows that for every 10 percent increase in the prison population, the crime rate is reduced 5 percent. Would this finding justify a massive effort to build and fill prisons with the hope of eradicating crime?

SOURCE: Elliott Currie, *Confronting Crime: An American Challenge* (New York: Pantheon, 1985); idem, "Confronting Crime: Looking toward the Twenty-Fifth Century," *Justice Quarterly* 6 (1989):6–25.

model.[7] According to Packer, due process combines elements of the liberals' concern for the individual with the concept of legal fairness guaranteed by the U.S. Constitution.

Advocates of the due process perspective argue that the greatest concern of the justice system should be providing fair and equitable treatment to those accused of crime. This means providing impartial hearings, competent legal counsel, equitable treatment, and reasonable sanctions. It follows that the use of discretion within the justice system should be strictly monitored to ensure that no one suffers from racial, religious, or ethnic discrimination.

Those who advocate the due process orientation are quick to point out that the justice system remains an adversary process that pits the forces of an all-powerful state against those of a solitary individual accused of a crime. If concern for justice and fairness did not exist, the defendant who lacked resources could easily be overwhelmed. They point to miscarriages of justice, such as the Gary Dotson case, as examples of what could happen if we slacken in our vigilance. Dotson was imprisoned for rape only to be released years later when his accuser recanted her testimony. Since such mistakes can happen, even the most apparently guilty offender deserves all the protection the justice system can offer.

Due Process in Action. In the 1960s, the Supreme Court under the leadership of Chief Justice Earl Warren began a slow process of expanding the due process rights of offenders. Criminal defendants were granted the right to an attorney at almost all stages of the justice process; the exclusionary rule was applied to the states; for the first time, juvenile offenders were eligible for due process rights; and efforts were made to grant prison inmates fundamental legal entitlements. Since 1980, this due process revolution has waned. A more conservative Supreme Court, filled with Reagan and Bush appointees, has handed down decisions expanding the police officer's ability to search for and seize evidence and to question suspects and curtailing the rights of juveniles and inmates.

Evidence is growing that the desire to protect the public and control crime now overshadows concern for the civil rights of criminal defendants. While the most important legal rights won by criminal defendants in the 1960s and 1970s remain untouched (for example, the right to have a fair and impartial jury of one's peers), there is little urgency today to increase the scope of their civil rights. Considering the Court's present makeup, this conservative trend probably will not soon end. As the more liberal justices on the Supreme Court have retired and been replaced with conservatives, it is more likely that due process considerations will be placed farther back on the burners of justice.

Nonintervention Perspective

The fourth approach to criminal justice is known as the **nonintervention** perspective. Those who espouse this model of justice hold that justice agencies should limit their involvement with criminal defendants when at all possible. Regardless of whether intervention is designed to punish or treat people, its ultimate effect is often harmful. Whatever their goals or design, programs that involve people with a social control agency, such as the police, a mental health department, the correctional system, or a criminal court, will have long-term negative effects. Once involved with such an agency, criminal defendants may be watched, people might consider them dangerous and untrustworthy, and they can develop a lasting record that has negative connotations. Eventually, they may even come to believe what their official record suggests; they may view themselves as bad, evil, outcasts, troublemakers, or crazy. Noninterventionists are concerned about the effect of stigma and were influenced by labeling theory.

The noninterventionist philosophy was highly influential throughout the 1970s, when distrust of government cast doubt on any effort that bore the stamp of "big brother." The doctrine of nonintervention called for limiting government's ability to take control of the lives of people, especially minors, who ran afoul of the law. Calls went out for the **decriminalization** (reduction of penalties) and/or legalization of nonserious **victimless crimes,** such as the possession of small amounts of marijuana, public drunkenness, and vagrancy. Noninterventionists demanded the removal of nonviolent offenders from the nation's correctional system, a policy referred to as **deinstitutionalization.** First offenders who committed minor crimes were to be removed from the formal trial process and placed in informal, community-based treatment programs, a process referred to as **pretrial diversion.** Each of these initiatives was designed to help people avoid the stigma associated with contact with the criminal justice system.

Nonintervention in Action. Efforts to place a barrier between the defendant and the criminal justice system have cooled. Little evidence has been developed that shows that efforts to restrict intervention work any better than programs based on crime control or rehabilitation. *Beyond Probation*, an important study by Charles Murray and Louis Cox, found that the deterrent effect of punitive programs may actually reduce recidivism far more effectively than innovative, community-based efforts founded on the principles of deinstitutionalization.[8] Evidence exists that the impact of punishment can be a crime deterrent, while the stigma of formal criminal justice processing has relatively little influence on behavior.[9]

There has also been suspicion that efforts designed to avoid intervention actually work to enmesh those accused of crime more firmly in the grasp of the agencies of justice, a process called **widening the net.** This refers to the phenomenon in which such programs actually create more contact with the justice system; in some cases, one type of deviant label is substituted for another. Some treatment-oriented diversion programs actually increase intervention because they require clients to participate in long-term counseling programs, rather than simply pay a fine or be placed on probation; clients are considered "emotionally unstable," rather than "criminal."

Despite such criticism, the nonintervention philosophy still flourishes. Pretrial, trial, and posttrial programs developed to reduce intervention are quite active today. Efforts continue to be made to keep as many young offenders as possible out of secure detention facilities by making bail readily more available and out of prisons and jails through the use of alternative sanctions, such as house arrest and electronic monitoring.[10]

Despite such efforts, conservative sentiments toward crime control have caused the prison admission rate to steadily increase. Even the number of incarcerated juvenile offenders, the most important target of nonintervention strategies, has increased over the past decade. So while efforts still exist to remove the nonserious offender from the justice system, a more strenuous effort has been made to exert social control over serious offenders.

The conflict perspective holds that the justice system serves as an instrument of social control, which prevents the socially deprived from exercising their civil rights.

Justice Perspective

The justice perspective combines both liberal and conservative views of justice. On the conservative side, it stresses that the purpose of the justice system is to control crime and punish those who violate the law. On the liberal side, it stresses fairness, equality, and strict control of discretion.

The justice perspective holds that rehabilitating criminals through correctional treatment efforts is futile. Correctional institutions are places of punishment and confinement and therefore cannot serve as treatment centers. Any effort to individualize treatment and distinguish between criminal offenders will create a sense of unfairness that can interfere with readjustment to society. If two people commit the same crime but receive different sentences due to treatment considerations, the injustice will increase frustration and anger among the inmate population.

The criminal justice system must increase fairness by reducing discretion and unequal treatment. Law violators should be evaluated on the basis of their current behavior, and not on how their treatment will influence others. The justice model holds that the deterrent effects of a criminal sentence should not be considered because it is unfair to punish someone solely to prevent others from committing crimes. Nor should criminals be incapacitated because they are believed to be dangerous; it is unfair to incarcerate people based on often misguided predictions of their future behavior. The core principle of the justice model is that the treatment of criminal offenders must be based solely on present behavior: punishment must be equitably administered and based on "just desert."

Justice in Action. The justice model plays an extremely influential role in the criminal justice system today. One effort has been the creation of **determinate sentencing** models that authorize similar sentences for every offender convicted of a particular crime. Just desert-based sentences make use of guidelines to control judicial authority in sentencing. The federal criminal code mandates that judges use sentencing guidelines to control their decision making and reduce discretion. The justice perspective influence has also caused some states to abolish parole (early release from prison) in an effort to ensure that each inmate serves the full sentence he or she received at trial. In sum, efforts are being made to take the discretion out of the justice system and reduce the disparity with which people are treated.

Conflict Perspective

The **conflict** view holds that the justice system is a state-supported institution designed to control the have-not members of society and keep power in the hands of the affluent. The justice system is required because society is dominated by inter- and intragroup conflict. The criminal process serves as an instrument of control, preventing the socially deprived from exercising their civil rights and allowing members of the privileged classes to accumulate an unequal distribution of the nation's wealth. Police are used to interfere with strikes and union activities. Law enforcement agencies infiltrate and compromise dissident political groups. The courts have one standard for the poor and another for the wealthy. Only the affluent can afford private attorneys, pay investigators and expert witnesses, and employ the legal tools needed to win acquittal. And in the rare instance when a member of the upper class is found guilty of serious crime, he or she is either granted probation or allowed to serve time in a low-security, "country club" facility, rather than in a dangerous state institution. The lenient treatment given white-collar criminals in the nation's courts can be contrasted with the harsh punishments meted out to lower-class property offenders. Conflict scholars have tried to promote change in the system of justice by pointing up such problems as discrimination and inequality in the way the law is enforced.

Conflict in Action. There is little question that policymakers are more sensitive today than ever to issues that are of considerable importance to conflict thinkers: the misuse of power; discrimination by government officials; unfair application of the law; and the disadvantages suffered by the poor. This heightened sensitivity has been translated into efforts to correct some major abuses: indigent defendants are now entitled to free legal counsel; police officers are strictly scrutinized when they use their weapons; and the government has pledged to prosecute businesspeople who commit corporate or **white-collar crimes.** In our post-Watergate, post-Iran-Contra society, where suspicion of the government is common, some major conflict propositions seem to be receiving increasingly greater public interest. Incidents such as the Rodney King case fuel speculation that the justice system is inherently unfair and biased.

Perspectives in Perspective

The influence of each perspective can be seen in the justice system today (see Figure 5.1). During the past decade, the crime control and justice models have dominated. Laws have been toughened and the rights of the accused curtailed, the prison population has grown, and the death penalty has been employed against convicted murderers. In the mid-1980s, when the crime rate was dropping, these policies seemed to be effective. They may be questioned now that crime rates have once again begun to rise.

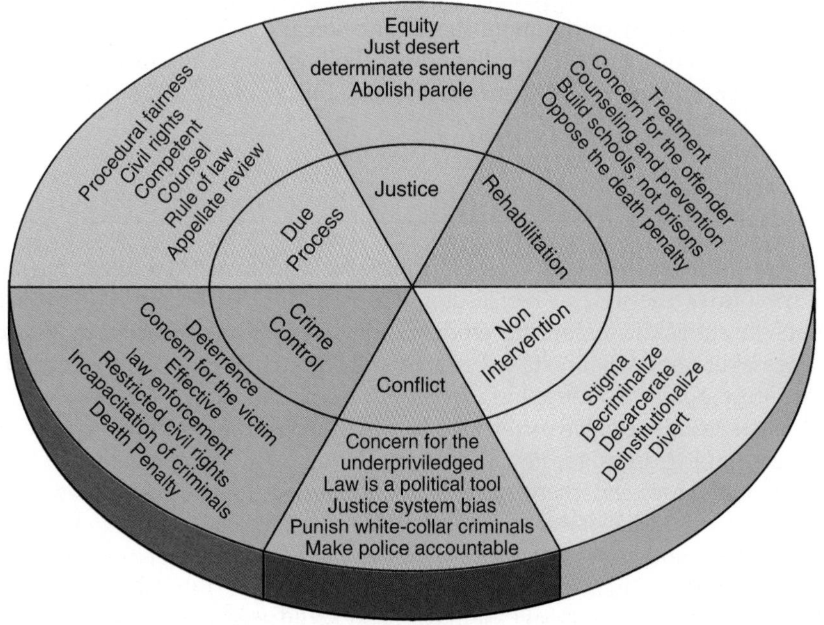

FIGURE 5.1
Perspectives on Justice: Key Concerns and Concepts

While the general public still favors punitive policies, efforts to rehabilitate offenders, to provide them with elements of due process, and to give them the least intrusive treatment possible are still made. Police, courts, and correctional agencies supply a wide range of treatment and rehabilitation programs to offenders in all stages of the criminal justice system. Whenever possible, those accused of crime are treated informally in nonrestrictive, community-based programs, and the effects of stigma are guarded against. While the legal rights of offenders are being closely scrutinized by the courts, the basic constitutional rights of the accused remain inviolate. Guardians of due process have made sure that defendants are allowed the maximum protection possible under the law. For example, criminal defendants have been awarded the right to competent legal counsel at trial; merely having a lawyer to defend them is not considered sufficient legal protection.[11]

In sum, understanding the justice system today requires analyzing a variety of occupational roles, institutional processes, legal rules, and administrative doctrines. Each of the predominant views of criminal justice provides a vantage point for understanding and interpreting these rather complex issues. No single view is the right or correct one. Each individual must choose the perspective that best fits his or her own ideas and judgment—or they can all be discarded and the individual's own view substituted.

Confronting Crime

Considering the multiplicity of perspectives and goals in the criminal justice system, it should come as no surprise that there are many unresolved issues that present an important challenge to scholars and practitioners alike. Debate continues over the direction of criminal justice policy and the role the system should play in controlling the behavior of criminals, victims, and the general public. How far should the justice system go in confronting crime? What should be sacrificed when the legal rights of individuals interfere with effective crime control? What is the most efficient approach to controlling the crime patterns of greatest concern to the U.S. public. The sections below examine the efforts being made to control a few of the more significant illegal forms of behavior including drug abuse, violence and white-collar crimes. Following this discussion is an analysis of how current efforts to control crime may interfere with personal rights and liberties.

Controlling the Drug Trade

For both political and social reasons, a massive and concerted effort has been made to control the flow of illegal drugs into the United States. The most important reason is the mounting evidence of a significant association between substance abuse and criminality. Research indicates that about 75 percent of all arrestees test positively for some drug use.[12] It is still uncertain whether drug abuse causes criminal behavior, since most users began committing crime before they began taking drugs and few users report committing crimes solely to obtain drug money.[13] However, there seems to be evidence that both drugs and crime are part of a deviant life-style, characterized by substance abuse, criminality, illegal sexual activity, and other antisocial behaviors.[14] Adolescent drug users show a disturbing trend to engaging in sex for profit to finance their drug habits. Sex with multiple partners and drug use have been intimately linked to the spread of the HIV virus and AIDS.[15]

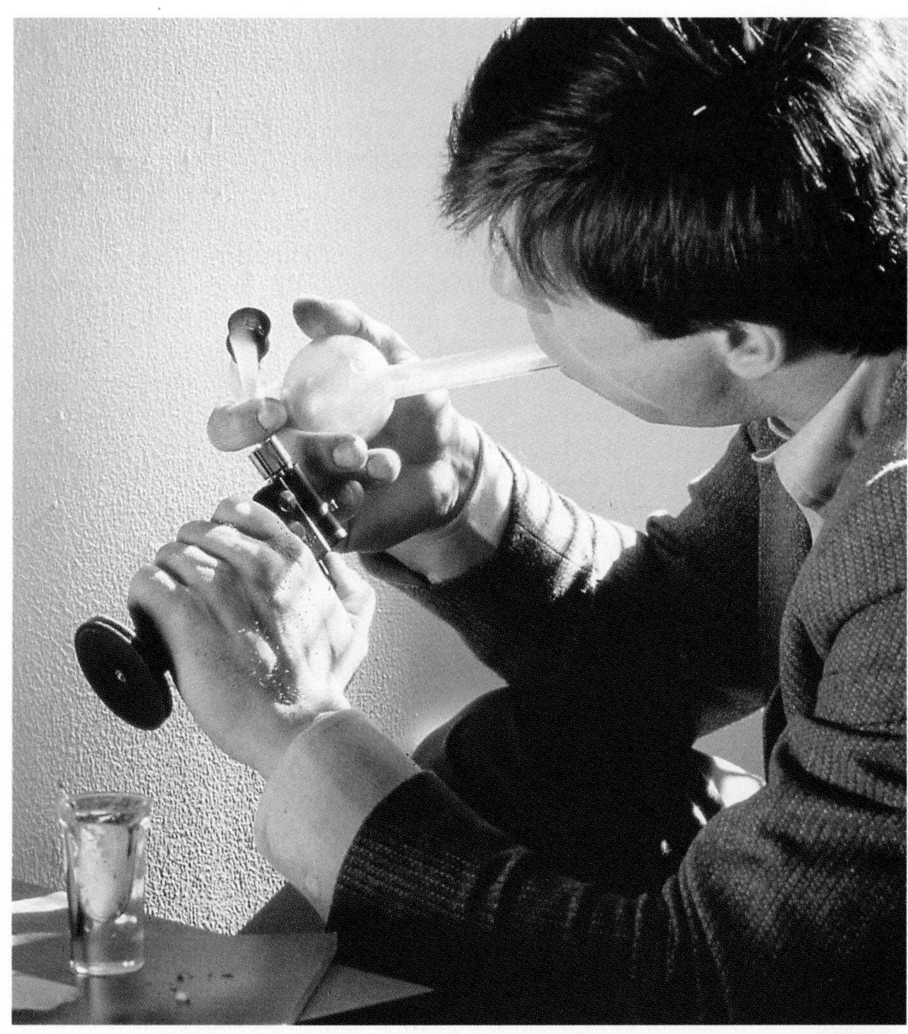

There is evidence that both drugs and crime are part of a deviant lifestyle.

One reason it has proven so difficult to control drug sales is the enormous profits involved: five hundred kilos of coca leaves worth four thousand dollars to a grower yields about eight kilos of street cocaine valued at half a million dollars. A drug dealer who can move a hundred pounds of coke into the United States can make $1.5 million in one shipment. An estimated one thousand tons of cocaine are produced in Latin America each year, and law enforcement officials are able to seize about one third. Government crackdowns simply serve to drive up the price of drugs and encourage more illegal entrepreneurs to enter the market. Today, youth gangs have become a prime source of cocaine and crack sales in urban areas, and the Hell's Angels motorcycle club is thought to be a primary distributor of amphetamines.

Agencies of the criminal justice system have used a number of strategies to reduce drug trafficking and the use of drugs. Some have relied on a strict crime control orientation, while others feature rehabilitation strategies.

Source Control

One approach to drug control is to deter the sale and importation of drugs through the systematic apprehension of large-volume drug dealers, coupled with the enforcement of strict drug laws that carry heavy penalties. This approach is designed to punish known drug dealers and users and deter those who are considering entering the drug trade.

A major effort has been made to cut off supplies of drugs by destroying crops and arresting members of drug cartels in drug-producing countries; this approach is known as **source control.** The federal government's Drug Enforcement Administration has been in the vanguard of encouraging exporting nations to step up efforts to destroy drug crops and prosecute dealers. More than five hundred U.S. soldiers are stationed in Central and South America to help train local narcotics forces and aid their intelligence gathering.[16] Three South American nations, Peru, Bolivia, and Colombia have agreed with the United States to coordinate control efforts. In 1989, the United States invaded Panama with twenty thousand troops to stop its leader, General Manuel Noriega, from assisting drug traffickers.

Translating words into deeds is a formidable task. Drug lords are willing and able to fight back through intimidation, violence, and corruption. The Cali and Medellin drug cartels in Colombia do not hesitate to use violence and assassination to protect their interests. Drug trafficking to the United States increased even after government crackdowns in Colombia put some leaders of the Medellin cartel on the run or in prison.

Adding to control problems is the fact that the drug trade is an important source of foreign revenue for the exporting countries, and destroying the drug trade undermines their economy. For example, about 60 percent of the raw coca leaves used to make cocaine for the United States is grown in Peru. The drug trade supports 250,000 Peruvians and brings in over $3 billion annually. Bolivia, which supplies 30 percent of the raw cocaine for the U.S. market, supports 350,000 people with profits from the drug trade; coca is its single leading export. About 20 percent of Colombia's overseas exports are made by drug cartels that refine the coca leaves into cocaine, which is then shipped to the United States.[17] It would take billions in annual U.S. economic aid to convince farmers in these countries to give up cultivating drugs. And even if the government of one nation would be willing to cooperate in vigorous drug suppression efforts, suppliers in other nations, eager to cash in on the seller's market, would be encouraged to turn more acreage over to coca, poppy, or marijuana production.

Interdiction Strategies

Another crime control approach to the drug problem has been to interdict drug supplies as they enter the country. Border patrols and military personnel using sophisticated hardware have been involved in massive interdiction efforts; many impressive multimillion-dollar seizures have been made. Yet the United States' borders are so vast and unprotected that meaningful interdiction is quite difficult. To aid law enforcement agencies, the U.S. military has become involved in stemming the flow of drugs across the border. The cost of staffing listening posts and patrolling borders is growing rapidly. In 1989, the military's antidrug budget was $439 million; by 1992, it reached $1.2 billion. In 1989, U.S. military aircraft flew fifty-four hundred hours of drug missions over the Atlantic Ocean; by 1991, they flew more than thirty-seven thousand hours.[18]

Border control may be an inherently limited drug control strategy. Even if all importation were eliminated, home-grown marijuana and lab-made drugs, such as LSD and PCP, could become drugs of choice. Even now, their easy availability and relatively low cost are increasing their popularity.

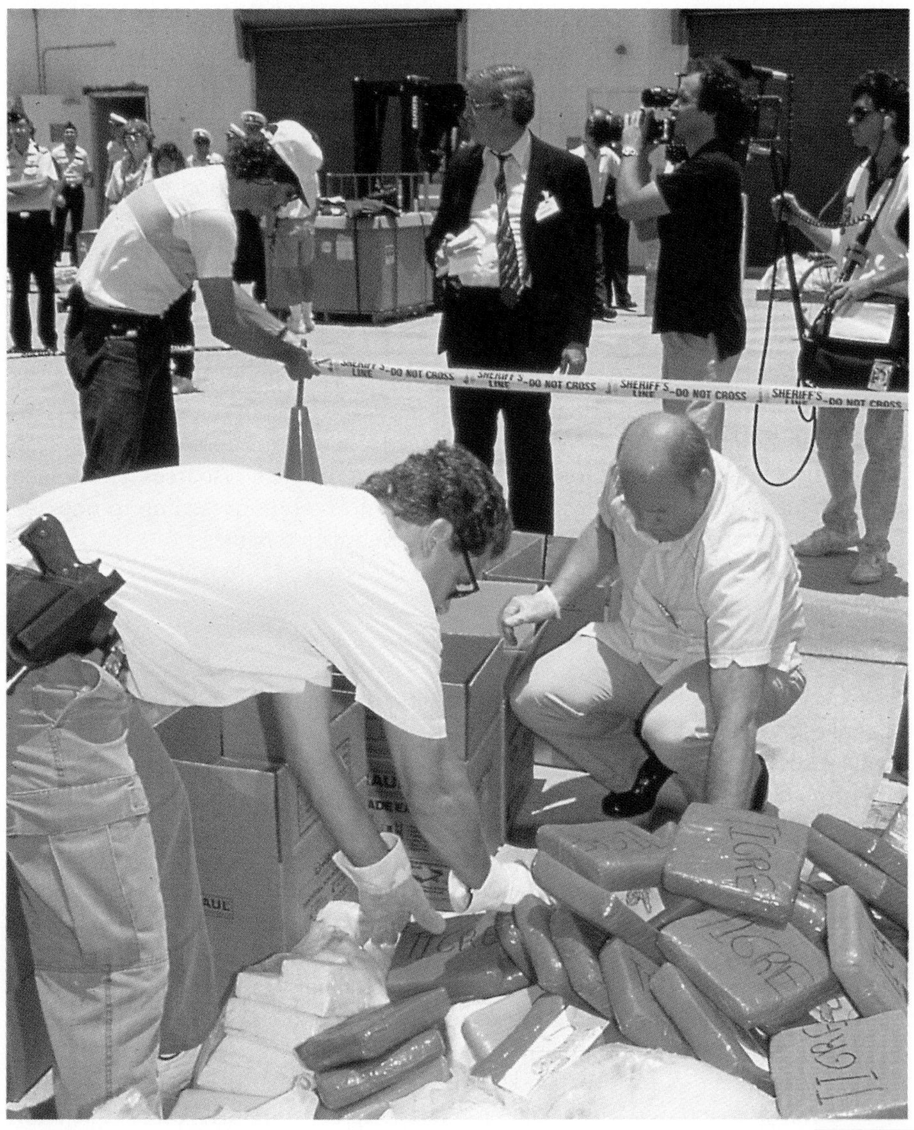

No matter how frequently drugs are seized by police officers, the enormous profits in drug trafficking encourages importation of controlled substances.

Law Enforcement Strategies

Local, state, and federal law enforcement agents have also been engaged in an active fight against drugs. One approach is to direct efforts at large-scale drug rings. Federal and local narcotics agencies routinely announce the seizure of large quantities of drugs. For example, on December 3, 1991, Drug Enforcement and Customs officials discovered twelve tons of cocaine hidden in two thousand hollowed-out fence posts in a warehouse in Miami. While breaking the large-scale international drug ring responsible for importing this cocaine was considered an important achievement, the success was tempered by the fact that in the previous two-year period, the warehouse had shipped sixty-two thousand fence posts.[19]

Even if efforts directed at large-scale dealers were always effective, little evidence exists that law enforcement efforts alone could end drug distribution. A largely successful effort by the FBI to smash traditional organized crime families has helped decentralize drug dealing. Filling the void has been Asian, Latin

American, and Jamaican groups, motorcycle clubs, and local gangs, such as Los Angeles's Crips and Bloods.[20] Ironically, it has proven easier for federal agents to infiltrate and prosecute traditional organized crime groups than to take on drug-dealing gangs.

Police can also target, intimidate, and arrest street-level dealers and users in an effort to make drug use so much of a hassle that consumption is cut back and the crime rate reduced. Among the approaches tried are "reverse stings," in which undercover agents pose as dealers in order to arrest users who approach them for a buy. Police have attacked fortified crack houses with heavy equipment in order to breach their defenses. They have used federal racketeering laws to seize the assets of known dealers. Special task forces of local and state police have used undercover operations and drug sweeps to discourage both dealers and users.[21]

While some street-level enforcement efforts have been successful, others are considered failures. Drug sweeps have clogged courts and correctional facilities with petty offenders while proving a costly drain on police resources. A displacement effect is also suspected: stepped-up efforts to curb drug dealing in one area or city simply encourage dealers to seek out friendlier territory.[22]

Punishment Strategies

Another crime control approach is intensifying criminal punishments for drug dealing. If the benefits of drug dealing can be offset by the pains of punishment and imprisonment, then the "rational" drug trafficker will look for a new line of employment.

A number of initiatives have been undertaken to make the prosecution and punishment of drug offenders a top priority. The Federal Anti-Drug Abuse Act of 1988 provides minimum mandatory prison sentences for serious drug crimes, with especially punitive sentences for anyone caught distributing drugs within one thousand feet of a school playground, youth center, or other areas where minors congregate.[23] The federal government has made the arrest and conviction of drug traffickers a top priority, increasing the number of drug-related convictions in federal courts by more than 130 percent since 1980.

State prosecutors have expanded their investigations into drug importation and distribution and created special prosecutors to expedite drug cases. The effort may be working in some jurisdictions. One study of court processing in New York found that cases involving crack had a higher probability of pretrial detention, felony indictment, and incarceration sentences than other criminal cases.[24] Some states, such as New Jersey and Pennsylvania, report sharp increases in the number of convictions for drug-related cases.[25] Once convicted, drug dealers are subject to very long sentences. Research by the federal government shows that the average sentence for drug offenders sent to federal prison is now about six years.[26]

Punishment strategies can have their downside. Defense attorneys consider delay tactics as sound legal maneuvering in drug-related cases. Courts are so backlogged that prosecutors are anxious to plea-bargain. The consequence is that less than half of the people convicted on drug charges are sent to prison.[27] Despite the uniformly "get tough" rhetoric of politicians, many narcotics dealers are treated leniently. Even so, many of the inmates who are jamming the prisons were involved in drug-related crimes. To relieve overcrowded conditions, many drug offenders sent to prison do not serve their entire sentence. The average prison stay is slightly more than one year. In fact, of all criminal types, drug offenders spend the least amount of their sentence behind bars.[28]

Prevention Strategies

Advocates of the rehabilitation model have suggested strategies aimed at reducing the desire to use drugs and increasing incentives for users to eliminate substance abuse. One approach relies on drug prevention—convincing nonusers to not start using drugs. This effort relies heavily on educational programs that teach kids to say no to drugs. One of the most familiar is the "McGruff, the Crime Dog" advertisements sponsored by the federal government's National Citizen's Crime Prevention Campaign. This friendly symbol, which is familiar to 99 percent of all children between the ages of six and twelve, has been used extensively in the media to warn kids about the dangers of drug use and crime. A multimedia drug prevention kit containing antidrug materials and videos has been distributed to almost every school district in the nation. A McGruff drug prevention curriculum featuring a McGruff puppet and accompanying audio cassette has been distributed to over 75,000 elementary classroom teachers, and more than 1.5 million McGruff antidrug comic books have been given away to students. Students in the program appear to have learned and improved their antidrug attitudes, teachers like the program, and parents endorse the content and the need for the program.[29]

Another familiar program is Drug Abuse Resistance Education, or **DARE.** This is an elementary school course designed to give students the skills for resisting peer pressure to experiment with tobacco, drugs, and alcohol. It is unique because it employs uniformed police officers to carry the antidrug message to the students before they enter junior high school. The program focuses on five major areas:

1. Providing accurate information about tobacco, alcohol, and drugs;
2. Teaching students techniques to resist peer pressure;
3. Teaching students respect for the law and law enforcers;
4. Giving students alternatives to drug use; and
5. Building the self-esteem of students.

DARE is based on the concept that young students need specific analytical and social skills to resist peer pressure and say no to drugs. Instructors work with children to raise their self-esteem, provide them with decision-making tools, and help them identify positive alternatives to substance use. So far, police in more than eight hundred jurisdictions have received DARE training and given the program to more than 3 million students.[30]

Despite the fact that a "just say no" strategy almost seems like wishful thinking, indirect evidence shows that prevention programs may be having a positive effect on the general population. Drug use among high school students has declined significantly in the past decade, and a majority of students now hold attitudes that disparage drug abuse.[31] While it is still unknown whether drug awareness programs can reach the hard-core user, the data suggests that drug use can be curtailed or restricted in the general population by making information readily available to adolescents.[32]

Treatment Strategies

The rehabilitation model suggests that it is possible to treat known users, get them clean of drugs and alcohol, and help them to reenter conventional society.

A number of drug offender treatment strategies have been implemented. One approach rests on the assumption that users have low self-esteem and holds that treatment efforts must focus on building a sense of self. In this approach, users participate in outdoor activities and wilderness training in order to create self-reliance and a sense of accomplishment.[33]

More intensive efforts use group therapy approaches relying on group leaders who once were substance abusers. Group sessions try to give users the skills and support that can help them reject the social pressure to use drugs. These programs are based on the Alcoholics Anonymous approach that says that users must find within themselves the strength to stay clean and that peer support from those who understand the users' experiences can help them achieve a drug-free life.

Residential programs have been established for the more heavily involved users, and a large network of drug treatment centers has been developed. Some are detoxification units that use medical procedures to wean patients from the more addicting drugs to others, such as methadone, the use of which can be more easily regulated. **Methadone,** a drug similar to heroin, is given to addicts at clinics under controlled conditions. Methadone programs have been undermined because some users sell their methadone on the black market, while others supplement their dosages with illegally obtained heroin.

Other therapeutic communities attempt to deal with the psychological causes of drug use. Hypnosis, aversion therapy (getting users to associate drugs with unpleasant sensations, such as nausea), counseling, biofeedback, and other techniques are often used.

Despite their good intentions, little evidence exists that these treatment programs can efficiently end substance abuse. A stay can help stigmatize residents as "addicts," even though they never used hard drugs; while in treatment, they may be introduced to hard-core users with whom they may associate upon release. Users often do not enter these programs voluntarily and have little motivation to change.[34] Even those who could be helped soon learn that there are simply more users who need treatment than there are beds in treatment facilities. Many programs are restricted to users whose health insurance will pay for short-term residential care; when the insurance coverage ends, the patients are often released before their treatment program is completed. Simply put, if treatment strategies are to be successful, far more programs and funding are needed.

Legalization

Despite the massive effort to control drug usage through both crime control and rehabilitation strategies, the fight has not been successful. Getting people out of the drug trade is difficult because drug trafficking involves enormous profits and dealers and users both lack meaningful economic alternatives. Controlling drugs by convincing known users to quit is equally hard; few treatment efforts have proven successful.

Considering these problems, some commentators, relying on a noninterventionist strategy, have called for the **legalization** of drugs. If drugs were legalized, the argument goes, distribution could be controlled by the government. Price and the distribution method could be regulated, reducing addict's cash requirements. Crime rates would be cut because drug users would no longer need the same cash flow to support their habit. Drug-related deaths would decrease since government control would reduce the sharing of needles and thus the spread of AIDS. Legalization would also destroy the drug-importing cartels and gangs. Since drugs would be bought and sold openly, the government would reap a windfall from both taxes on the sale of drugs and on the income of drug dealers, which now is untaxed as part of the hidden economy. Drug distribution would be regulated,

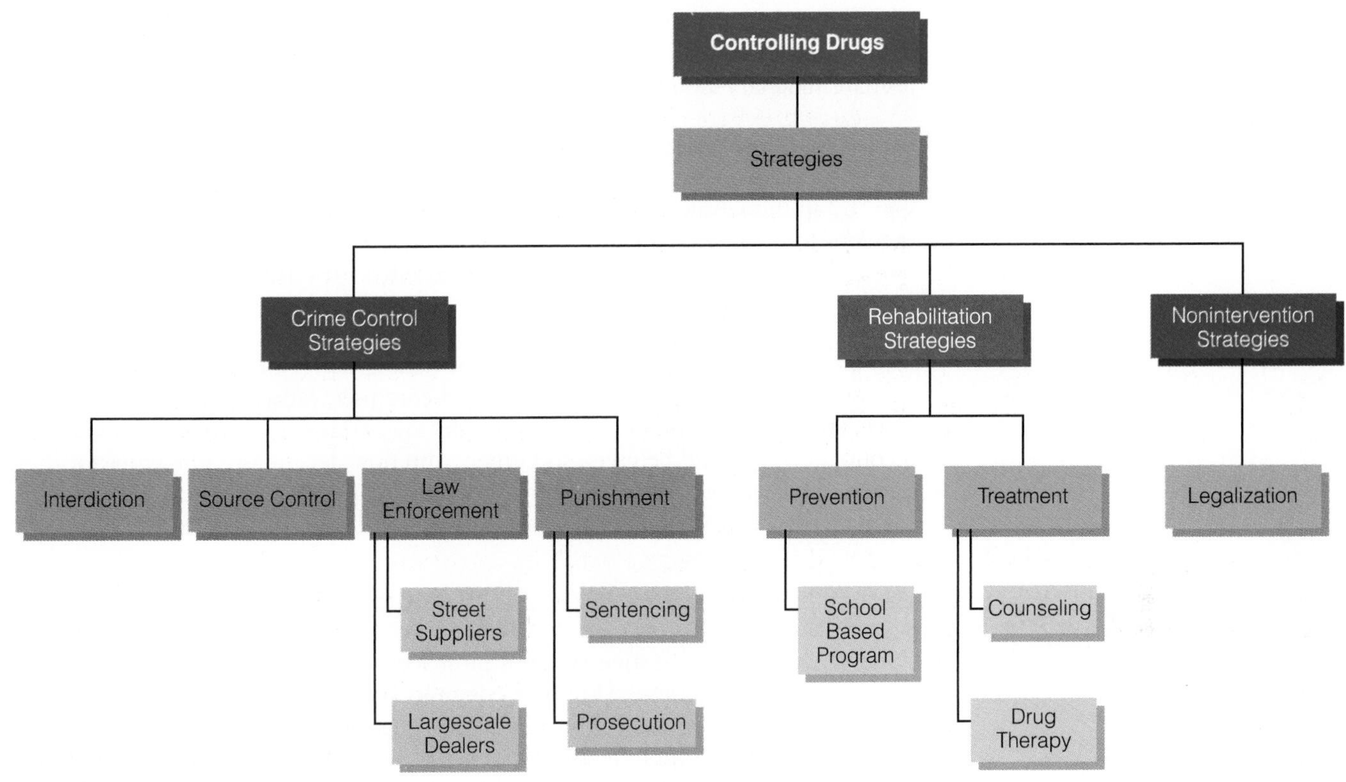

FIGURE 5.2
Strategies for Controlling Drugs

keeping narcotics out of the hands of adolescents. Those who favor legalization point to the Netherlands as a country that has legalized drugs and remains relatively crime-free.[35]

While this approach might reduce the association between drug use and crime in the short-run, it may also have grave social consequences. In the long-term, drug use might increase, creating an overflow of nonproductive drug-dependent people who must be cared for by the rest of society. The problems of alcoholism should serve as a warning of what can happen when controlled substances are made readily available. The number of drug-dependent babies could begin to match or exceed the number who are delivered with fetal alcohol syndrome.[36] Drunk driving fatalities, which today number about twenty-five thousand per year, could be matched by deaths caused by driving under the influence of pot or crack. And while distribution would be regulated, adolescents likely would have the same opportunity to obtain potent drugs as they now have with beer and liquor.

Are Drug Control Strategies Working?

Are any of these drug control strategies working? (See Figure 5.2.) It depends on whom you ask. National surveys sponsored by the federal government indicate that drug use today is far lower than in the past (see Chapter 2). This dramatic evidence is used as an indicator that the war on drugs is being won with a combination of interdiction, source control, and strict law enforcement.

Critics question whether the war on drugs is really successful. Some are troubled by the fact that so many criminal offenders are involved with drugs; more than half of all arrestees test positively for drugs. It is also disturbing that so many young people are still experimenting with addicting drugs. A 1992 report by the Senate Judiciary Committee notes:

- 1.1 million Americans used crack cocaine for the first time in 1991—up 40 percent in one year
- 1.2 million Americans became heroin users for the first time in 1991—up 75 percent from the year before
- 1.4 million Americans began using LSD in 1991—the sixth straight year use of this drug increased.[37]

The Senate committee believes that if drug use is to be controlled, greater efforts must be devoted to target the hard-core user, rather than the recreational user. Pressure must also be placed on producing nations to reduce drug production; economic aid should be given to farmers who now depend on drug crops for their living. These efforts, coupled with increased treatment and education programs, may be the key to reducing the use of drugs in the United States.

Controlling Violence

One of the criminal justice system's most formidable tasks is to control the incidence of violent crime. The most common strategy relies on the crime control model: deter violent crime through fear of legal punishments. Most legal jurisdictions emphasize apprehending violent criminals, bringing them to trial, and giving them long prison sentences. In some places, the death penalty has been enacted as a deterrent to violent crimes.

The effort to control violent crimes through deterrence strategies alone has not met with success. One reason for this failure is the nature of violent crime itself. Many violent episodes are the result of emotion-laden, interpersonal conflicts that are quite difficult to deter. As you may recall, most murderers knew their victims; the target of violence is commonly a family member, sweetheart, or friend. Many violent criminals were under the influence of drugs or alcohol at the time they committed their crime. Some have a disturbed personality or are psychopathic, which by definition makes them immune to the threat of punishment. Crime control strategies cannot do much to deter this kind of violence.

What alternatives have been suggested, then, to reduce violence? Certainly one approach is to reduce the root causes of crime—poverty, social inequality, racism, family conflict, and drug abuse. Yet to be effective, such measures must be carried out on a scale that has seemed unachievable.

A more realistic approach has been to encourage community cooperation with police, improve police effectiveness, discourage plea bargaining, and increase prison sentences for the chronic violent offender. Controlling violence through legal action has had the unfortunate side effect of creating an overcrowded prison system whose size is increasing at a far faster pace than the crime rate. Research studies give little support to such policies because former inmates have a significant chance of returning to prison.

The physical environment has also been the focus of violence-control efforts.[39] People are installing private security systems and other control mechanisms in their homes and businesses.[39] There are indications that the environment can be altered to reduce the threat of violence. For example, neighborhood watch programs have been hailed for their crime-reducing potential.[40]

The most often debated violence control program is efforts to restrict or ban the sale and possession of the major instruments of violence: handguns.

Banning Handguns and Assault Rifles

The use of handguns in political crimes, such as the Robert Kennedy assassination and the shooting of President Ronald Reagan and his press secretary James Brady, has spurred advocacy for controls on the sale of handguns and a ban on cheap "Saturday night specials." Ongoing gang and street violence has spurred calls for laws limiting gun availability. UCR data tell us that about half of all murders and a third of all robberies involve a firearm, including many crimes on school grounds (see Figure 5.3). Handguns are the cause of death for two-thirds of all police killed in the line of duty. The presence of firearms in the home has been found to significantly increase the risk of suicide among adolescents, regardless of how carefully the guns are secured or stored.[41] It seems logical, then, that a ban on the sale and ownership of handguns might help reduce the violence rate.

Controlling guns is a formidable job. About 1.4 million handguns are manufactured each year in the United States.[42] About one third of these are cheaply made Saturday night specials. Guns such as the Raven Arms MP-25, Davis In-

- Weapons are a big problem in schools.
- One fourth of all major urban schools use metal detectors.
- Some school districts practice "fire drills"–teaching students and staff what to do if gunshots are heard.
- During the 1991–1992 school year, New York City schools had more than fifty shooting incidents.
- An estimated 5 percent of all students carry weapons to school.
- The NCVS estimates more than 3 million crimes occur on school grounds each year—one every six seconds.

FIGURE 5.3
Guns in the Schools

SOURCE: Lisa Bastian and Bruce Taylor, School Crime: A National Crime Victimization Survey Report (Washington, D.C.: Bureau of Justice Statistics, 1991); Ronald Stephens, G. Ellis Butterfield, Ronald Garrison, Bernard James, *Weapons in Schools,* National School Safety Center, Pepperdine University, Malibu, Cal. 1991.

dustries Davis .38, and Jennings/Bryco Arms J-22 semiautomatic can be made for about fifteen dollars each because zinc alloy is injected into molds in their manufacture; expensive guns, such as Smith and Wessons or Rugers, use precision-crafted stainless steel. A Colt .45 takes about three hours to make; a Raven is assembled in three minutes. These mass-produced weapons are favored by young street toughs because they are easily concealed and can be bought for as little as fifty dollars on the street; about thirty thousand are made and sold each month. Since 1990, the federal Bureau of Alcohol, Tobacco, and Firearms has been able to trace twenty-four thousand guns used in violent felonies; of these 41 percent were made by Davis, Raven, and Jennings/Bryco. These companies are now expanding into the manufacture of more powerful 9 mm automatics.[43]

The growth in the number of firearms in the United States has not been limited to handguns: more than one hundred thousand semiautomatic assault rifles, such as the UZI and the AK-47, are imported each year. The Bureau of Alcohol, Tobacco, and Firearms estimates that Americans possess two to three million automatic weapons. In 1989, the U.S. government moved to reduce the use of guns for both criminal and self-protection purposes by banning the importation and sale of forty-three types of assault rifles, a ban voluntarily followed by U.S. manufacturers. These weapons have been used in some highly publicized shootouts and are particularly disturbing to police officials.

Why Do People Own Guns?

Despite its logic, banning handguns and automatic weapons has proven to be difficult. Gun advocacy groups, led by the National Rifle Association, argue that the right to bear arms is guaranteed by the Second Amendment to the U.S. Constitution and that an armed citizenry is a free one.

Gun advocacy is supported by the fact that many gun owners purchase weapons to protect themselves from armed intruders and criminals. Research indicates that people who carry guns are often motivated by self-protection and not violence-prone personalities.[44] Eduard Ziegenhagen and Dolores Brosnan's survey of New York City subway riders found that passengers are likely to carry self-protective devices such as handguns if they believe that local crime is on the increase, that they themselves are likely to become crime victims, and that they are unlikely to be helped if they are attacked; many had prior experience as victims.[45] Laura Moriarty and E. Duane Davis surveyed North Carolina residents and found that most gun owners bought handguns for self-protection; gun owners rarely, if ever, used their weapons or had accidents. Many handgun owners reported getting their guns as gifts; most gun owners said their family almost always had a gun in the house.[46] Store owners in Los Angeles reported that gun purchases increased significantly after the 1992 rioting.

Gun advocates believe that fear of crime is a legitimate reason to bear arms and that people have a right to protect themselves and their family from armed intruders. They point to such studies as the one conducted by Gary Kleck, who found that each year between fifteen hundred and twenty-eight hundred predatory criminals are killed by gun-wielding crime victims and that between eighty-seven hundred and sixteen thousand are wounded.[47] And as William Calathes notes, while a ban on assault rifles is politically appealing, relatively few crimes involve these weapons.[48]

Gun advocates also challenge the role of handguns in crime. While FBI data show handguns are used in a great many violent crimes, the NCVS indicates that

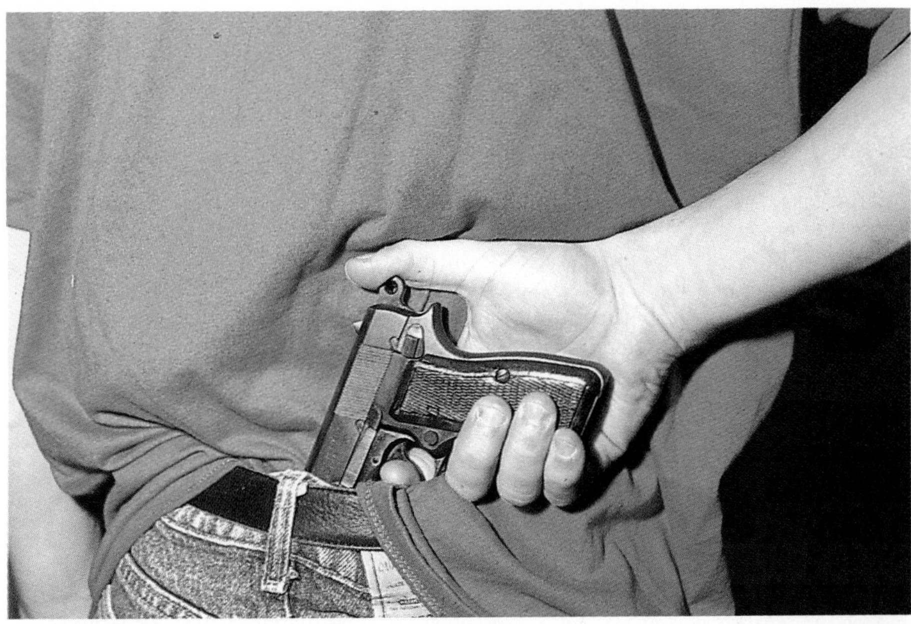

Many gun owners carry weapons to protect themselves from armed intruders and criminals.

guns are used in only 10 percent of all violent acts (about 27 percent of those in which the assailant was armed with a weapon).[49] These facts are all too often ignored or misrepresented by the media, which has an "antigun" bias.[50]

Rather than legal controls, gun advocates call for strict punishment being meted out to anyone who uses a handgun during the commission of a crime.

Does Gun Control Work?

Efforts to control gun ownership have many different sources. Each state and many local jurisdictions have laws banning or restricting sales or possession of guns. Other laws regulate dealers who sell guns. For example, the Federal Gun Control Act prohibits dealers from selling guns to minors, ex-felons, and known drug users.[51] A number of states and the federal government have passed legislation banning or restricting assault rifles. Some laws, such as California's, allows those who owned such weapons prior to the ban to register and keep them, while New Jersey's requires all owners to sell, destroy, or register such weapons as legitimate target-shooting rifles.[52] Regulations may not work because authorities lack the resources to enforce rules and monitor dealers. Guns can be purchased from unregulated private parties at gun shows, bought on the black market, or stolen.

Can laws penalizing the use of handguns to commit crime make a difference in the violent crime rate?[53] Some jurisdictions have set mandatory sentences for any crime involving a handgun. A well-known example is Michigan's Felony Firearm Statute, which requires that persons convicted of a crime in which a handgun was used receive an additional two years tacked on to their sentence. Analysis of the statute's effectiveness found that the Michigan law had (1) little effect on the sentence given to convicted offenders and (2) little effect on violent crime in Detroit.[54]

Massachusetts passed the Bartley-Fox Law in 1975, which provides a mandatory one-year prison term for possession of a handgun (outside the home) with-

ANALYZING CRIMNAL JUSTICE ISSUES

Can Gun Control Backfire?

While gun control advocates believe that strict gun laws can help reduce the violence rate, opponents charge that restricting gun ownership can backfire, taking guns out of the hands of crime victims who need them for self-protection and leaving the criminal offender's access to guns undisturbed. Which position is correct?

Evidence exists that many gun owners do in fact buy handguns for self-protection and that gun ownership is highest among people who have already been the victims of crime, who perceive police protection as being inadequate, who believe the crime rate is increasing in their neighborhood, and who believe they are likely candidates for additional victimization. Fear of crime has also prompted citizens to take courses in firearms training; there is some evidence that these measures are associated with lower crime rates. Self-protection efforts are supported by research conducted by James Wright and Peter Rossi, who found that convicted criminals will avoid potential victims who they believe are carrying guns.

Though many gun owners purchase weapons with the intent of preventing crime, the evidence that gun ownership can reduce crime rates is inconclusive. A recent review of gun ownership and gun control programs conducted by David McDowall, Alan Lizotte, and Brian Wiersma found little evidence that gun availability reduces crime rates. Jurisdictions that toughened their standards on gun ownership did not experience increases in violent crimes. The authors conclude that there is "no solid empirical support" for the hypothesis that firearm ownership can deter crime.

How successful are people who use weapons to fight back against crime on an individual level? Gary Kleck's research suggests that victims who fight back in crimes such as rape are better off than those who remain passive and unresponsive. Fighting back significantly reduces the chances of a crime being completed.

While Kleck's findings can be used to support the claim that victims who fight back frustrate their attackers, evidence also exists that those victims who use force also increase the likelihood that they will be physically harmed during the criminal attack. A recent analysis of rape victimization data by Polly Marchbanks and her associates found that fighting back does decrease the odds of a rape being completed but at the same time increases a victim's chances of physical injury. Marchbanks speculates that while resistance may draw the attention of bystanders and make the rape physically difficult to complete, it may also cause an offender to escalate his use of violence and further endanger the rape victim.

Even if armed victims are actually safer, their self-defense measures do not make crime go away. Gary Green's research on firearms training programs found that gun ownership for self-protection may displace crime to unarmed victims. In

out a permit. A detailed analysis of violent crime in Boston in the years after the law's passage found that the use of handguns in robberies and murders did decline substantially (35 percent in robberies and 55 percent in murders in a two-year period). However, these optimistic results must be tempered by two facts: rates for similar crimes dropped significantly in comparable cities that did not have gun control laws and the use of other weapons, such as knives, increased.[55]

More persuasive findings have been derived from an evaluation of the District of Columbia's Firearms Control Regulations Act of 1976. This act restricts possession of firearms to persons who already owned and reregistered guns at the time the law was passed.[56] After the initial reregistration, handguns could not be registered and therefore became illegal (it is still possible to buy shotguns and rifles). The law also requires that registered gun owners keep firearms unloaded and disassembled or locked up, except when they are being used for lawful recreational purposes. A longitudinal study by Colin Loftin and his associates compared homicide and suicide trends in the District of Columbia with the trends in surrounding areas of Virginia and Maryland.[57] They found that while gun-related homicides and suicides remained rather stable in surrounding areas, they significantly declined in the District of Columbia after the gun control law went into effect. Especially significant was the fact that the nongun homicide and suicide rate remained stable in the District, a finding that confirms that the reduction in

addition, Green found that firearms ownership brings with it many other social problems, including accidental deaths and guns stolen in burglaries being used in other crimes. According to Green, the benefits of violent self-protection are often offset by its drawbacks.

So while there is evidence that armed citizens can effectively protect themselves, it is also true that fighting back can endanger victims and displace, rather than control, crime. In sum, the evidence seems to indicate that gun ownership can backfire.

Critical Thinking Skills

1. Research indicates that gun-toting citizens stand a good chance of frustrating criminal attempts. There is evidence, though, that fighting back is related to physical injuries sustained during criminal attempts. What are some of the other risks associated with gun ownership? On balance, do the benefits of gun possession outweigh the drawbacks?

2. If you were in charge of gun policy in the United States, what steps would you take to restrict or expand the ability to own a firearm? Would you ease gun ownership rules because the Constitution's provision on the "right to bear arms" empowers citizens to be armed as they wish? Considering the failure of police to control crime, are people entitled to own guns for self-protection? Or would you ban the possession of all handguns in order to deny criminals and the mentally unstable easy access to guns? Or would a legal ban on handguns leave criminals armed and noncriminals defenseless?

SOURCES: David McDowall, Alan Lizotte, and Brian Wiersema, "General Deterrence through Civilian Gun Ownership: An Evaluation of the Quasi-Experimental Evidence," *Criminology* 29 (1991):541-59, at 556; James Wright and Peter Rossi, *Armed and Considered Dangerous: A Survey of Felons and Their Firearms* (New York: Aldine, 1986); Gary Kleck, "Crime Control through the Private Use of Armed Force," *Social Problems* 35 (1988):1-21; idem, "Rape and Resistance," *Social Problems* 7 (1990): 149-62; Robert Young, David McDowall, and Colin Loftin, "Collective Security and Ownership of Firearms for Protection," *Criminology* 25 (1987):47–62; Gary Green, "Citizen Gun Ownership and Criminal Deterrence: Theory, Research and Policy," *Criminology* 25 (1987):63–81; Douglas Smith and Craig Uchida, "The Social Organization of Self-Help: A Study of Defensive Weapon Ownership," *American Sociological Review* 53 (1988):94–102; Gary Kleck and David Bordua, "The Factual Foundation for Certain Key Assumptions of Gun Control," *Law and Policy Quarterly* 5 (1983):271–98; Alan Lizotte, "Determinants of Completing Rape and Assault," *Journal of Quantitative Criminology* 2 (1986):203–17; Polly Marchbanks, Kung-Jong Lui, and James Mercy, "Risk of Injury from Resisting Rape," *American Journal of Epidemiology* 132 (1990):540-49.

handgun violence was not part of a general decline in the crime rate. The Loftin research is one of the strongest statements in support of the effectiveness of handgun control laws.

Gun Control Problems

Controlling guns through legislation alone may be difficult to achieve.[58] There are so many guns in the United States today—a conservative estimate is 50 million illegal handguns—that banning their sale would have a relatively small effect for years to come.[59] And if guns are made more valuable by banning their manufacture or sale, illegal importation of guns might increase, as it has for another controlled product, narcotics.

Increasing penalties for gun-related crimes may also be a limited approach because judges are usually reluctant to alter their sentencing policies to accommodate legislators. Regulating dealers is difficult and encourages private sales and bartering. Little evidence exists that if criminals were prevented from easily purchasing cheap, low-caliber Saturday night specials, they would terminate their criminal careers. They might instead turn to using larger-caliber weapons with deadlier effects.[60]

In part because of these conflicting and often inconclusive data, the debate over gun control will not go away. Some combination of control and penalty may prove useful. But it is important to determine whether gun control efforts can actually backfire.

Controlling White-Collar Crime

Until recently, the justice system seemed to pay scant attention to business-related *white-collar crimes*. Then in the late 1980s, several highly publicized criminal incidents took place that severely damaged the national economy and produced widespread economic misery. First, the insider stock trading and junk bond scandals involving Ivan Boesky and Michael Milken rocked Wall Street and shook public confidence in the nation's financial institutions. Then it was revealed that officials at the federal government's Department of Housing and Urban Development (HUD) had used their influence to fraudulently divert billions in public money to politically connected contractors. In the nation's most costly business fraud, officials in some of the country's largest savings and loan (S&L) banks fraudulently converted deposits to their own pockets and those of their partners; the S&L crisis will cost taxpayers over billions.[61] The S&L scandal was followed by the bankruptcy of the Bank of Credit and Commerce; fraud in this case will cost additional billions.

The effect of these large-scale frauds helped undermine the national economy and played no small role in causing an economic recession.

Punishing White-Collar Criminals

In the past, white-collar criminals rarely suffered criminal prosecution and, when convicted, received relatively light sentences. Unlike lower-class street crimes, most white-collar law violations were treated as civil infractions and punished economically with fines. Though white-collar criminals may have caused millions of dollars of losses and endangered human life, judges tended to view them as misguided businesspeople and not as dangerous criminals. Public humiliation of these criminals, some of whom were "pillars of the community," was deemed punishment enough; criminal prosecution and a prison sentence seemed unnecessarily cruel.[62]

In the wake of the HUD, Wall Street, and S&L scandals, the government has begun to take a more hardline "crime control" stance with white-collar criminals. This move was prompted by the belief that fear of criminal punishment can have a more powerful deterrent effect on white-collar crime than fear of civil fines.[63] On the federal level, detection of white-collar crime is primarily in the hands of administrative departments and agencies, such as the General Accounting Office and the Federal Communication Commission. Any evidence of criminal activity is then sent to the Department of Justice or the FBI for investigation. Some federal agencies, such as the Securities and Exchange Commission and the Postal Service, have their own investigative arms.

If criminal prosecution is called for, the case will be handled by attorneys from the Criminal, Tax, Antitrust, and Civil Rights Divisions of the Justice Department. If insufficient evidence is available to warrant a criminal prosecution, the case will be handled civilly or administratively by some other federal agency or brought before a federal court. For example, the Federal Trade Commission can issue a cease-and-desist order in antitrust or merchandising fraud cases, or a federal judge can fine a company found in violation of the Clean Air Act.

On the state and local levels, enforcement of white-collar laws is often disorganized and inefficient. Confusion may exist over the jurisdiction of the state attorney general and local prosecutors. The technical expertise of the federal government is often lacking on the state level. Local prosecutors do not consider white-collar crimes particularly serious problems when compared to common law violence and theft cases. They seem willing to prosecute a case only if the offense causes substantial harm and federal agencies fail to take action.[64] Aiding the investigation of white-collar offenses is a movement toward protecting employees who blow the whistle on their firm's violations. Five states—Michigan, Connecticut, Maine, California, and New York—have passed laws protecting workers from being fired if they testify about violations.[65] Without such help, the hands of justice are often tied.

Surveys conducted by the federal government show that the justice system is now taking white-collar crime more seriously.[66] One review of enforcement practices in nine states found that (1) white-collar crimes account for about 6 percent of all arrest dispositions, (2) 88 percent of all those arrested for white-collar crimes were prosecuted, and (3) 74 percent subsequently were convicted in criminal court. The survey also showed that while 60 percent of all white-collar criminals convicted in state court were incarcerated (a number comparable to the incarceration rate of most other offenders), relatively few white-collar offenders (18 percent) received a prison term of more than a year.

A second survey followed white-collar cases prosecuted by the U.S. government between 1980 and 1985. Consistent with the government's "get tough" policy on white-collar crime, convictions rose 18 percent between 1980 and 1985, and the conviction rate for white-collar offenders (85 percent) was higher than that for all other federal crimes (78 percent). However, as was found in state courts, federal white-collar criminals received more lenient sentences than other offenders. For example, of those white-collar offenders sentenced to prison (about 40 percent of all those convicted), the average period of incarceration was twenty-nine months, while all other federal offenders (54 percent of whom were incarcerated) averaged fifty months. Of equal importance is the finding that almost all white-collar cases included in the two surveys involved individual common law crimes—forgery, fraud, embezzlement, and counterfeiting—and relatively few corporate or regulatory crimes.

The Scope of Social Control

While the agencies of justice are charged with using all appropriate means to control drugs, violence, and white-collar and other crimes, they are also expected to be considerate of the civil rights and privacy of both the general public and criminal suspects. Those who champion the due process perspective are constantly wary of intrusions by the justice system, made in the name of "efficient crime control," into the personal life of "suspects" who maintain a life-style or political beliefs that are perceived as threatening. Similarly, there are questions about the scope of **social control.** What behaviors should society control with a firm hand and which should remain beyond the grasp of the law? For example, is the distribution of sexually oriented material a public menace or a protected incidence of free speech? Should sexual relations between consenting adults be subject to government regulation? Should marijuana be legalized? Should abortions be outlawed? While efforts have been made to increase society's control over some behaviors that are considered a danger to the general public, in other instances, efforts by noninterventionists have limited the power of the justice system to regulate human interaction.

A number of recent efforts stand out to illustrate the extension of social control by the justice system. For example, the federal government's most recent drug control legislation significantly extends the government's ability to control drug importers and distributors through the use of mandatory prison sentences.[67] A number of states have passed legislation toughening penalties for drunk drivers to curb the flood of alcohol-related highway fatalities. The federal government has attempted to crack down on the distribution of pornography by significantly increasing the number of its obscenity prosecutions.[68] In synch with the federal effort, local prosecutors brought highly publicized obscenity charges against the curators of the Cincinnati's Contemporary Art Center for mounting an exhibit of homoerotic photographs by Robert Mapplethorpe and prosecutors in Florida filed charges against the rap group 2 Live Crew for producing an allegedly obscene record album.[69] Though neither case resulted in a conviction, they illustrate efforts to control behavior considered by some to be private and nonthreatening.

Reducing Social Control

While the scope of social control has increased in some areas of the law, many experts in criminal justice, law, and the social sciences have suggested that certain offenses should be removed from the criminal statutes. These include public drunkenness, pornography, vagrancy, gambling, the use of marijuana, prostitution, and sexual acts between consenting adults in private. The reduction or elimination of legal penalties for such acts is referred to as **decriminalization.**[70] Advocates of the decriminalization approach suggest that the criminal law is overextended when it invokes criminal sanctions in regard to social and moral problems; they believe that the primary purpose of criminal law should be to control serious crimes affecting persons and property. As a result, it is argued that these "victimless" crimes, as they are often called, should be the responsibility not of the criminal justice system but of mental health or other social service-type agencies.

Decriminalization efforts aim to make the criminal law reflective of current social values and attitudes while at the same time allowing the overburdened criminal justice system to concentrate on more serious criminal offenses. The decriminalization process has been aided by legal change. For example, the movement to decriminalize the behavior of chronic alcoholics was originally influenced by two federal court decisions, *Easter v. District of Columbia*[71] and *Driver v. Hinnant*,[72] which declared that a chronic alcoholic could not be found guilty of the crime of public intoxication. In 1968, the U.S. Supreme Court decision of *Powell v. Texas* recognized the criminal justice system's inability to provide rehabilitation for the alcoholic and in so doing removed alcoholics from the control of the justice system.[73]

The move to decriminalize victimless crimes received a setback in 1986, when in the case of *Bowers v. Hardwick*, the Supreme Court upheld a Georgia statute that holds sexual relations between consenting adults of the same sex to be a crime (sod-omy). The majority found that homosexuality has long been condemned in Western society and that it is therefore within the state's interest to limit homosexual activity.[74]

The *Bowers* case represents a major setback for civil liberties groups that had hoped the Court would decriminalize homosexual behavior in the same manner

it had dealt with other sexual matters, such as the use of contraceptives and abortion. However, sexually related behavior has always presented a dilemma for lawmakers, even when there is little conclusive evidence that it is harmful to society. For example, all states continue to ban obscene magazines and films, even though sexually related material has not been clearly linked to crime or violence.[75]

The Privacy Issue

The scope of social control has become a critical issue because government agents now have so many new tools, including computerized databases, aerial surveillance cameras, DNA testing, and highly sensitive listening devices, at their disposal. Civil libertarians and advocates of due process are troubled that the government can use this new technology to monitor suspected and convicted criminals. How far should the government go in an effort to control crime? Are we in danger of becoming dominated by an all-seeing, all-knowing "big brother"?

The new surveillance techniques operate on a number of different levels. Computers are used in extensive data retrieval systems to cross-reference people and activities. Information available in national and local databases includes credit ratings, bank accounts, stock transfers, medical information, and outstanding loans.

Computer networks also contain criminal justice system information. The most extensive network is the National Crime Information Center, operated by the Justice Department, which contains an extensive collection of arrest records, allowing local police departments to instantly determine whether a suspect has a record.

Technology has also been improved in the area of visual and audio surveillance. The FBI has made national headlines filming and taping drug deals and organized crime activities. Hundreds of high-tech devices make listening and watching more extensive and virtually self-sufficient. For example, audio listening devices now use lasers that permit eavesdropping without having to enter a home or secure a warrant. Airborne cameras can monitor human movement from thirty-thousand feet and help spot fields of marijuana and other illegal drugs.

Electronic equipment is also used to monitor offenders in the community. Instead of a prison or jail sentence, convicted offenders are placed under house arrest and kept under surveillance by a central computer. A government agency, most typically the probation department, keeps track of offenders by requiring them to wear a nonremovable ankle or neck device that signals a computer if they move from their home without permission.

The Danger of Overcontrol

The dangers represented by the new electronic surveillance is the subject of an important book by sociologist Gary Marx.[76] He lists the following characteristics of these surveillance techniques that set them apart from traditional methods of social control:

1. The new surveillance transcends distance, darkness, and physical barriers.
2. It transcends time; its records can be stored, retrieved, combined, analyzed, and communicated.
3. It has low visibility or is invisible.
4. It is often involuntary.

5. Prevention of future crimes is a major concern.
6. It is capital, rather than labor, intensive.
7. It involves decentralized self-policing.
8. It triggers a shift from targeting a specific suspect to categorical suspicion of everyone.
9. It is more intensive.
10. It is more extensive.[77]

According to Marx, the use of electronic eavesdropping and other modern surveillance methods has changed the relationship between police and the public. New techniques have overcome the physical limitations that existed when surveillance was a function of human labor. Today's electronic devices never rest, are virtually undetectable, and can store information forever. People now may be required to aid in their own monitoring by wearing devices that keep them under scrutiny; electronic devices can follow suspects everywhere, gather extensive information on them, and include thousands in the information net. As Marx puts it:

> Between the camera, tape recorder, the identity card, the metal detector, the tax form, and the computer, everyone becomes a reasonable target.[78]

Marx warns that the dangers of the new surveillance can include a redefinition of the concept of invasion of privacy in which almost any personal information is open to scrutiny, "fishing expeditions" in which the government can do a general check on a citizen without a court order, and the chance that machine error will destroy the lives of innocent people. He cautions us:

> The first task of a society that would have liberty and privacy is to guard against the misuse of physical coercion on the part of the state and private parties. The second task is to guard against "softer" forms of secret and manipulative control. Because these are often subtle, indirect, invisible, diffuse, deceptive, and shrouded in benign justifications, this is clearly the more difficult task.[79]

SUMMARY

The role of criminal justice can be interpreted in many ways. People who study the field or work within its agencies bring their own ideas and feelings to bear when they try to decide on the right course of action to take or recommend. There are a number of different perspectives on criminal justice today. The crime control perspective is oriented toward deterring criminal behavior and incapacitating serious criminal offenders. In contrast, the rehabilitation model views the justice system as a treatment agency focused on helping offenders. Counseling programs are stressed over punishment and deterrence strategies. Those who hold the due process perspective see the justice system as a legal process. Their concern is that every defendant receive the full share of legal rights granted under law.

In addition to these views, the nonintervention model is concerned about stigma and helping defendants avoid the net of justice; advocates call for the least intrusive methods possible. Those who advocate the justice model are concerned with making the system equitable. The arrest, sentencing, and correctional process should be structured so that every person is treated equally. Finally, the conflict view focuses on exposing the political and economic forces that shape justice policy and promote bias and discrimination.

The justice system is now confronting some major crime problems. One important area is the so-called war on drugs. A number of strategies have been attempted, including some based on crime control strategies, such as source control and interdiction at the border. Some ef-

forts are based on the rehabilitation model; for example, treatment and education programs. One approach that may be tried is a noninterventionist strategy of legalizing drugs. So far, the war on drugs has had mixed results: drug use is down in the general population, but hard-core users still commit a lot of crime.

Another concern is violent crime. One method is to control handguns. Efforts to regulate guns by law or punishment strategies have not worked because there are so many guns, they can be bought on the black market, and many people feel the general public has the right to own guns for self-protection. Efforts are also being made to crack down on white-collar crime.

While the justice system is confronting crime, a danger exists that these efforts will intrude on privacy. New methods of surveillance and data collection make the privacy issue critical.

QUESTIONS

1. What are the basic elements of each model or perspective on justice? Which best represents your own point of view?

2. How would each perspective on criminal justice consider the use of the death penalty as a sanction for first-degree murder?

3. What are the primary strategies being used to fight the war on drugs? Why are they failing to control hard-core drug use? Which strategy is the most effective?

4. Should possession of all handguns be banned? What about assault rifles? Before you answer, remember how successful efforts to ban narcotics have been.

NOTES

1. Lawrence Greenfeld, *Capital Punishment, 1990* (Washington, D.C.: Bureau of Justice Statistics, 1991).

2. Malcolm Klein, *Street Gangs and Street Workers* (Englewood Cliffs, N.J.: Prentice-Hall, 1971); New York City Youth Board, *Reaching the Fighting Gang* (New York: New York City Youth Board, 1960).

3. Walter Miller, "The Impact of a 'Total Community' Delinquency Control Project," *Social Problems* 10 (1962):168–91.

4. See, for example, Robert Martinson, "What Works?—Questions and Answers about Prison Reform," *Public Interest* 35 (1974):22–54; Charles Murray and Louis Cox, *Beyond Probation* (Beverly Hills, Calif.: Sage Publications, 1979); for further analysis, see John Whitehead and Steven Lab, "A Meta-Analysis of Juvenile Correctional Treatment," *Journal of Research in Crime and Delinquency* 26 (1989):223–36.

5. D. A. Andrews, Ivan Zinger, Robert Hoge, James Bonta, Paul Gendreau, and Francis Cullen, "Does Correctional Treatment Work? A Clinically Relevant and Psychologically Informed Meta-Analysis," *Criminology* 28 (1990):369–404.

6. Paul Gendreau and Robert Ross, "Revivification of Rehabilitation: Evidence from the 1980's," *Justice Quarterly* 4 (1987):349–407; see also Carol Garrett, "Effects of Residential Treatment on Adjudicated Delinquents: A Meta-Analysis," *Journal of Research in Crime and Delinquency* 22 (1985):287–308.

7. Herbert Packer, *The Limits of the Criminal Sanction* (Stanford, Calif.: Stanford University Press, 1968), p. 175.

8. Charles Murray and Louis Cox, *Beyond Probation: Juvenile Corrections and the Chronic Offender* (Beverly Hills, Calif.: Sage Publications, 1979).

9. Douglas Smith and Patrick Gartin, "Specifying Specific Deterrence: The Influence of Arrest on Future Criminal Activity," *American Sociological Review* 54 (1989):94–105.

10. Joan Petersilia, *Expanding Options for Criminal Sentencing* (Santa Monica: Rand Corporation, 1987).

11. *Strickland v. Washington*, 466 U.S. 668, 104 S.Ct. 2052, 80 L.Ed.2d 674 (1984).

12. Eric Wish, *Drug Use Forecasting, 1990* (Washington, D.C.: National Institute of Justice, 1991).

13. David Altschuler and Paul Brounstein, "Patterns of Drug Use, Drug Trafficking, and Other Delinquency Among Inner-City Adolescent Males in Washington, D.C.," *Criminology* 29 (1991):589–621.

14. George Speckart and M. Douglas Anglin, "Narcotics Use and Crime: An Overview of Recent Research Advances," *Contemporary Drug Problems* 13 (1986):741–69; Charles Faupel and Carl Klockars, "Drugs-Crime Connections: Elaborations from the Life Histories of Hard-core Heroin Addicts," *Social Problems* 34 (1987):54–68.

15. James Inciardi, Anne Pottieger, Mary Ann Forney, Dale Chitwood, and Duane McBride, "Prostitution, IV Drug Use, and Sex-for-Crack Exchanges Among Serious Delinquents: Risks for HIV Infection," *Criminology* 29 (1991):221–35.

16. Charles Lane, "The Newest War," *Newsweek*, 6 January 1992, p. 18.

17. Brook Larmer, "A Booming Grass-Roots Business," *Newsweek*, 6 January 1992, p. 23; Drug Enforcement Administration, *National Drug Control Strategy* (Washington, D.C.: U.S. Government Printing Office, 1989).

18. Lane, "The Newest War."

19. "Cocaine hidden in concrete seized," *Boston Globe*, 3 December 1991, p. 3.

20. Rick Graves and Ed Allen, *Narcotics and Black Gangs* (Los Angeles: Los Angeles County Sheriff's Department, n.d.); Scott Armstrong, "Los Angeles Gangs Go National," *Christian Science Monitor*, 19 July 1988, p. 3; Walter Shapiro, "Going after the Hell's Angels," *Newsweek*, 13 May 1985, p. 41.

21. David Hayeslip, "Local-Level Drug Enforcement: New Strategies," *NIJ*

Reports, March/April 1989.
22. Mark Moore, *Drug Trafficking* (Washington, D.C.: National Institute of Justice, 1988).
23. Anti-Drug Abuse Act of 1988, Public Law 100-6901 21 U.S.C. § 1501; Subtitle A-Death Penalty, Sec. 001, Amending the Controlled Substances Abuse Act, 21 USC 848.
24. Steven Belenko, Jeffrey Fagan, and Ko-Lin Chin, "Criminal Justice Responses to Crack," *Journal of Research in Crime and Delinquency* 28 (1991):55–74.
25. Bureau of Justice Assistance, *FY 1988 Report on Drug Control* (Washington, D.C.: Bureau of Justice Assistance, 1989) p. 103.
26. Carol Kaplan, *Sentencing and Time Served* (Washington, D.C.: Bureau of Justice Statistics, 1987).
27. Patrick Langan and John Dawson, *Felony Sentences in State Courts, 1988* (Washington, D.C.: Bureau of Justice Statistics, 1990), p. 3.
28. Herbert Koppel, *Time Served in Prison and on Parole* (Washington, D.C.: Bureau of Justice Statistics, 1988).
29. *FY 1988 Report on Drug Control*, p. 50.
30. Ibid.
31. Lloyd Johnston, Jerald Bachman, and Patrick O'Malley, "Annual Survey of Drug Abuse, 1990," University of Michigan News Release, January 24, 1991.
32. For an analysis of this issue, see Cheryl Tieman, William Tolone, and Lisa Zuelke, "Drug Education and Drug Use Decline: An Assessment of Trends from 1976–1984" (Paper presented at the annual meeting of the American Society of Criminology, San Francisco, November 1991).
33. See, generally, Peter Greenwood and Franklin Zimring, *One More Chance* (Santa Monica, Calif.: Rand Corporation, 1985).
34. Eli Ginzberg, Howard Berliner, and Miriam Ostrow, *Young People at Risk, Is Prevention Possible?* (Boulder, Colo.: Westview Press, 1988), p. 99.
35. See, generally, Ralph Weisheit, *Drugs, Crime and the Criminal Justice System* (Cincinnati: Anderson, 1990).
36. James Inciardi and Duane McBride, "Legalizing Drugs: A Gormless, Naive Idea," *The Criminologist* 15 (1990):1–4.
37. Majority Staff, The Senate Judiciary Committee, *Fighting Drug Abuse: Tough Decisions for Our National Strategy* (Washington, D.C.: U.S. Senate, 1992).
38. Charles Murray, "The Physical Environment and Community Control of Crime," in *Crime and Public Policy*, ed. James Q. Wilson (San Francisco: ICS Press, 1983), pp. 107–25.
39. Oscar Newman, *Defensible Space: Crime Prevention through Urban Design* (New York: MacMillan, 1972).
40. Peter Finn, *Block Watches Help Crime Victims in Philadelphia* (Washington, D.C.: National Institute of Justice, 1986).
41. David Brent, Joshua Perper, Christopher Allman, Grace Moritz, Mary Wartella, and Janice Zelenak, "The Presence and Accessibility of Firearms in the Home and Adolescent Suicides," *Journal of the American Medical Association* 266 (1991):2989–95.
42. Estimates supplied by the Bureau of Alcohol, Tobacco, and Firearms, 1992.
43. Alix Freedman, "A Single Family Makes Many of Cheap Pistols That Saturate Cities," *Wall Street Journal*, 28 February 1992, pp. A1, 6–7.
44. John Whitehead and Robert Langworthy, "Gun Ownership and Willingness to Shoot: A Clarification of Current Controversies," *Justice Quarterly* 6 (1989):262–82.
45. Eduard Ziegenhagen and Dolores Brosnan, "Citizen Recourse to Self-Protection: Structural, Attitudinal, and Experiential Factors," *Criminal Justice Policy Review* 4 (1990):91–104.
46. Laura Moriarty and E. Duane Davis, "Firearms, Self-Protection and Crime Prevention: A Citizen Survey," *Journal of Security Administration* (in press, 1992).
47. Gary Kleck, "Crime Control Through the Private Use of Armed Force," *Social Force* 35 (1988):1–21.
48. William Calathes, "The New Jersey Assault Firearms Act" (Paper presented at the annual meeting of the American Society of Criminology, San Francisco, November 1991).
49. Michael Rand, *Handgun Crime Victims* (Washington, D.C.: Bureau of Justice Statistics, 1990), p. 1.
50. Paul Blackman, "The Bigotry of the Anti-Gun Press: A Year in the Lies of the *Washington Post*" (Paper presented at the annual meeting of the American Society of Criminology, San Francisco, November 1991).
51. Franklin Zimring, "Firearms and Federal Law: The Gun Control Act of 1968," *Journal of Legal Studies* 4 (1975):133–98.
52. Calathes, "The New Jersey Assault Firearms Act," p. 2.
53. David Lester, *Gun Control* (Springfield, Ill.: Charles Thomas, 1984).
54. Colin Loftin, Milton Heumann, and David McDowall, "Mandatory Sentencing and Firearms Violence: Evaluating an Alternative to Gun Control," *Law and Society Review* 17 (1983):287–319.
55. Glenn Pierce and William Bowers, "The Bartley-Fox Gun Law's Short-Term Impact on Crime," *The Annals* 455 (1981): 120–37; Samuel Walker, *Sense and Nonsense about Crime* (Monterey, Calif.: Brooks/Cole, 1985), pp. 70–71.
56. Adopted from Colin Loftin, David McDowall, Brian Wiersema, and Talbert Cottey, "Effects of Restrictive Licensing of Handguns on Homicide and Suicide in the District of Columbia," *New England Journal of Medicine* 325 (1991):1615–20.
57. Ibid.
58. See, generally, James Wright, Peter Rossi, and Kathleen Daly, *Under the Fun: Weapons, Crime and Violence in America* (New York: Aldine, 1983).
59. Walker, *Sense and Nonsense about Crime*, p. 152.
60. James Wright, "Second Thoughts about Gun Control," *The Public Interest* 91 (1988):23–39.
61. See Kitty Calavita and Henry Pontell, "Heads I Win, Tails You Lose: Deregulation, Crime and Crisis in the Savings and Loan Industry," *Crime and Delinquency* 36 (1990):309–11.
62. Stanton Wheeler, David Weisburd, Elin Waring, and Nancy Bode, "White-Collar Crimes and Criminals," *American Criminal Law Review* 25 (1988):331–57.
63. Steven Klepper and Daniel Nagin, "The Deterrent Effect of Perceived Certainty and Severity of Punishment Revisited," *Criminology* 27 (1989):721–46.
64. Michael Benson, Francis Cullen, and William Maakestad, "Local Prosecutors and Corporate Crime," *Crime and Delinquency* 36 (1990):356–72.
65. Alan Otten, "States Begin to Protect Employees Who Blow Whistle on Their Firms," *Wall Street Journal*, 31 December 1984, p. 11.
66. Donald Manson, *Tracking Offenders: White-Collar Crime* (Washington, D.C.: Bureau of Justice Statistics, 1986); Kenneth Carlson and Jan Chaiken, *White Collar Crime* (Washington, D.C.: Bureau of Justice Statistics, 1987).
67. Anti-Drug Abuse Act of 1988.
68. Bob Cohn, "The Trials of Adam & Eve," *Newsweek*, 7 January 1991, p. 48.
69. Richard Lacayo, "The Rap Against a Rap Group," *Time*, 25 June 1990, p. 18.
70. See Norval Morris and Gordon Hawkins, *The Honest Politician's Guide to Crime Control* (Chicago: University of Chicago Press, 1970).
71. 361 F.2d 50 (D.C. Cir. 1966).
72. 356 F.2d 761 (4th Cir. 1966).
73. 392 U.S. 514, 88 S.Ct. 2145, 20 L.Ed.2d 1254 (1968).
74. 478 U.S. 186, 106 S.Ct. 2841, 92 L.Ed.2d 140 (1986), rehearing denied 478 U.S. 1039, 107 S.Ct. 29, 92 L.Ed.2d 779 (1986).
75. *The Report of the Commission on Obscenity and Pornography* (Washington, D.C.: U.S. Government Printing Office, 1970); *Attorney General's*

Commission Report on Pornography, Final Report (Washington, D.C.: U.S. Government Printing Office, 1986), pp. 837–902; Berl Kutchinsky, "The Effect of Easy Availability of Pornography on the Incidence of Sex Crimes," *Journal of Social Issues* 29 (1973):95–112; Michael Goldstein, "Exposure to Erotic Stimuli and Sexual Deviance," *Journal of Social Issues* 29 (1973):197–219; John Court, "Sex and Violence: A Ripple Effect," in *Pornography and Aggression*, ed. Neal Malamuth and Edward Donnerstein, (Orlando,. Fla.: Academic Press, 1984); see Edward Donnerstein, Daniel Linz, and Steven Penrod, *The Question of Pornography* (New York: Free Press, 1987).

76. Gary Marx, *Undercover, Police Surveillance in America* (Berkeley: University of California Press, 1988).

77. Ibid., pp. 217–19.

78. Ibid., p. 219.

79. Ibid., p. 233.

PART TWO

THE POLICE AND LAW ENFORCEMENT

CHAPTER 6

Police in Society: History and Organization

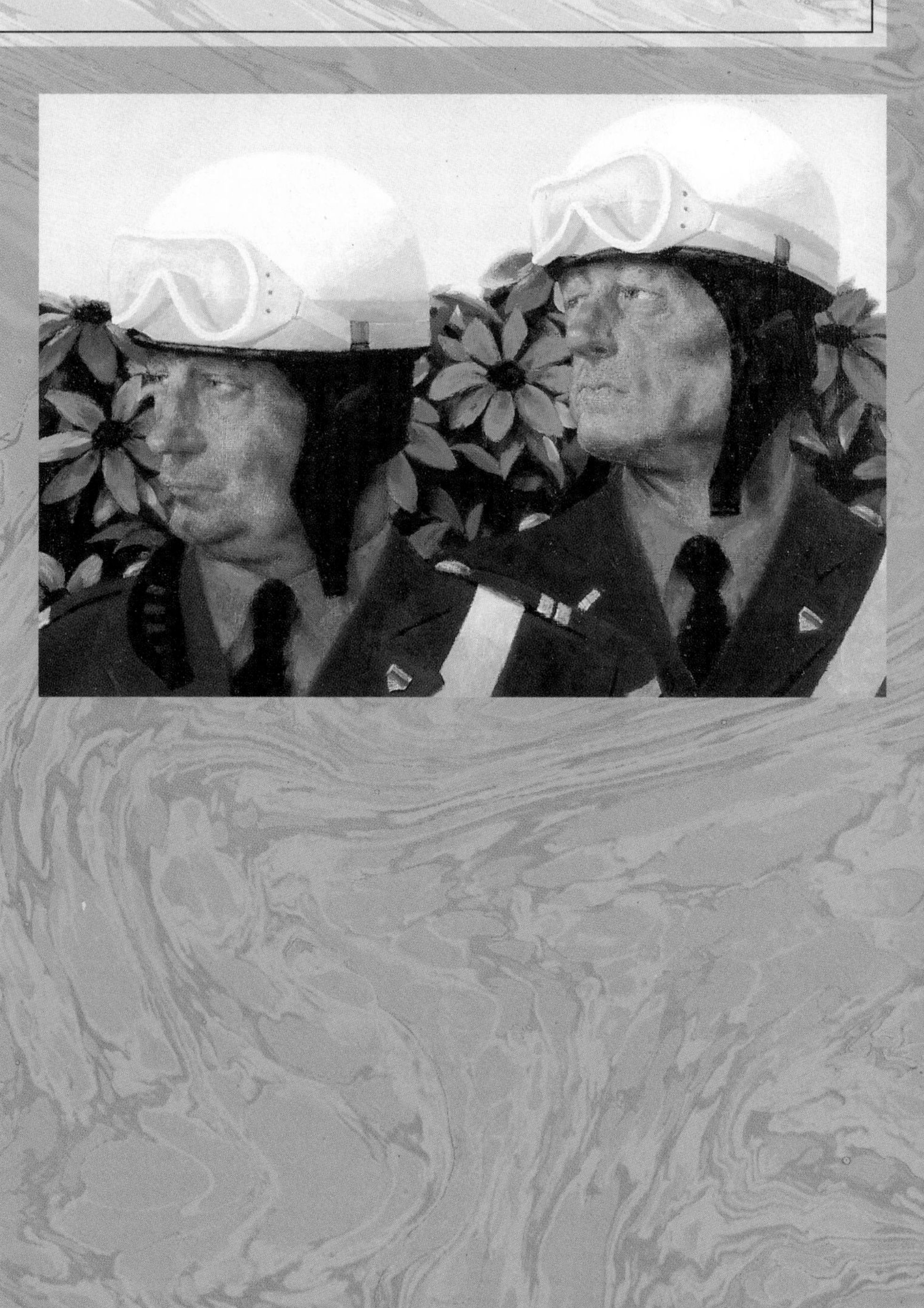

OUTLINE

KEY TERMS

pledge system
tithings
hue and cry
constable
hundred
shires
shire reeve
watch system
justice of the peace
Sir Robert Peel
vigilantes
Wickersham Commission
International Association of Chiefs of Police (IACP)
August Vollmer
O. W. Wilson
sheriff
state police
U.S. Department of Justice
Federal Bureau of Investigation (FBI)
Drug Enforcement Administration (DEA)
DNA profiling
teleconferencing
Hallcrest Report
proprietary security
contractual services
moonlighting

On March 3, 1991, Rodney King, an African-American motorist, was chased by members of the California Highway Patrol after failing to heed their order to pull over for speeding. After he was finally stopped, patrol officers radioed for backup help. Members of the Los Angeles Police Department arrived and took control of the situation. When King resisted being handcuffed and flailed his arms, the police officers began a long and bloody beating, including kicks and baton blows to the head. An area resident videotaped the beating, and the video was broadcast by the national media. Los Angeles Police Chief Daryl Gates, under fire from community groups, was encouraged to announce his retirement date. Four white officers were charged and tried for assault.[1] A Gallup Poll conducted shortly after the King beating found that confidence in the police had declined significantly: the number of citizens saying they had a great deal of respect for police in their area had deteriorated 60 percent from a high of 77 percent in 1965; in 1965, 9 percent of Americans polled believed police in their area were brutal, and by 1991, that number had reached 35 percent.[2] When a jury found the four officers "not guilty," rioting broke out which caused hundreds of millions of dollars in damage and cost more than fifty lives.

The King case has become a symbol of the problems facing police departments in the United States. Law enforcement and police agencies and their sworn personnel—police officers, sheriffs, state troopers, and federal agents—are the most numerous and visible elements of the criminal justice system. Citizens who may never knowingly interact with judges, prosecutors, wardens, or prison guards are keenly aware when they are in the presence of law enforcement officers. To the average citizen, the police officer is the active symbol of justice in the United States.[3] The general public has greater concerns about the quality of police work and the caliber of police behavior than about any other aspect of the criminal justice system. When police pursue their job too vigorously, citizens are quick to cry out against a "police state" atmosphere. If police fail to control crime effectively, the same citizens will decry the "fear stalking the city" and call for increased police protection. When scandal rocks a police department, the very essence of justice comes under attack: If the keepers are imperfect, how can we blame the kept? The general public's "damned if you do, damned if you don't" attitude frustrates police officers, and job stress is a major issue for them. Overall, less than half of the general public is confident that the police can protect them from harm and/or believes that police officers are highly ethical and honest.[4]

While these results are discouraging, interest in careers in police work continues to expand. Metropolitan police departments are swamped with applications by job seekers who value an exciting, well-paid job that also holds the opportunity to provide valuable community service. So while police agencies are still trying to define their role and effectively marshal their resources, they continue to be held in high esteem by the public they serve.

In this and the following three chapters, we will evaluate the history, role, organizational issues, and procedures of police agents and agencies and discuss the legal rules that control police behavior.

The History of Police

The origin of U.S. police agencies, like that of the criminal law, can be traced back to early English society.[5] Before the Norman Conquest, there was no regular English police force. Every person living in the villages scattered throughout the countryside was responsible for aiding neighbors and protecting the settlement from thieves and marauders. This was known as the **pledge system.** People were grouped in collectives of ten families, called **tithings,** and entrusted with policing their own minor problems. When trouble occurred, the citizen was expected to make a **hue and cry.** Ten tithings were grouped into a **hundred,** whose affairs were supervised by a **constable** appointed by the local nobleman. The constable, who might be considered the first real police officer, dealt with more serious breaches of the law.[6]

Shires, which resembled the counties of today, were controlled by the **shire reeve** appointed by the crown or local landowner to supervise the territory and ensure that order would be kept. The shire reeve, a forerunner of today's sheriff, soon began to pursue and apprehend law violators as part of his duties.

In the thirteenth century, during the reign of King Edward I, the **watch system** was created to help protect property in England's larger cities and towns. Watchmen patrolled at night and helped protect against robberies, fires, and disturbances. They reported to the area constable, who became the primary metropolitan law enforcement agent. In larger cities, such as London, the watchmen were organized within church parishes and were usually members of the parish they protected.

In 1326, the office of **justice of the peace** was created to assist the shire reeve in controlling the county. Eventually, these justices took on judicial functions in addition to their primary role as peacekeeper. The local constable became the operational assistant to the justice of the peace, supervising the night watchmen, investigating offenses, serving summonses, executing warrants, and securing prisoners. This system helped delineate the relationship between police and the judiciary that has continued for five hundred years.

At first, the position of constable was an honorary one given to a respected person in the village or parish for a one-year period. Often these men were wealthy merchants who had little time for their duties. They commonly employed paid and unpaid assistants to help them fulfill their obligations, thereby creating another element of a paid police force. By the seventeenth century, the justice of the peace, the constable, his assistants, and the night watchmen formed the nucleus of the local metropolitan justice system. (The sheriff's duties lay outside the cities and towns.)

The police-community tension in the 1990s has sparked riots and conflict. Thirty-five percent of the general public today consider the local police "brutal."

Eighteenth-Century Developments

By the end of the eighteenth century, the Industrial Revolution lured thousands from the English countryside to work in the factory towns. The swelling population of urban poor, whose minuscule wages could hardly sustain them, heightened the need for police protection. Henry Fielding, the famed author of *Tom Jones*, organized the Bow Street Runners of London, one of the first local police agencies, to investigate crimes and attempt to bring offenders to justice.

This disorganized system of public protection was inadequate to stem the growing tide of urban crime and violence. In response to public pressure, the government passed statutes creating new police offices in London. These offices employed three justices of the peace who were each authorized to employ six paid constables. Law enforcement began to be more centralized and professional, but many parishes still maintained their own foot patrols, horse patrols, and private investigators.

In 1829, **Sir Robert Peel,** England's home secretary, guided through Parliament an "Act for Improving the Police in and near the Metropolis." The Metropolitan Police Act established the first organized police force in London. Composed of over one thousand men, the London police force was structured along military lines; its members would be known ever after as bobbies, after their creator. They wore a distinctive uniform and were led by two magistrates, who were later given the title of commissioner. However, the ultimate responsibility for the police fell to the home secretary and consequently the Parliament.

The early bobbies suffered many of the same problems that have befallen their heirs. Many were corrupt, they were unsuccessful at stopping crime, and they were influenced by the wealthy. Owners of houses of ill repute who in the past had guaranteed their undisturbed operations by bribing watchmen, now turned their attention to the bobbies. Metropolitan police administrators fought constantly to terminate cowardly, corrupt, and alcoholic officers, dismissing in the beginning about one third of the bobbies each year.

Anglo-Saxon constables on duty in the 11th century.

Despite its recognized shortcomings, the London experiment proved a vast improvement over what had come before. It was considered so successful that the metropolitan police soon began providing law enforcement assistance to outlying areas that requested it. Another act of Parliament allowed justices of the peace to establish local police forces, and by 1856, every borough and county in England was required to form its own police force.

The American Colonial Experience

Law enforcement in colonial America paralleled the British model. In the colonies, the county sheriff became the most important law enforcement agent. In addition to keeping the peace and fighting crime, sheriffs collected taxes, supervised elections, and handled a great deal of other legal business.

The colonial sheriff did not patrol or seek out crime. Instead, he reacted to citizens' complaints and investigated crimes that had occurred. His salary was related to his effectiveness and paid on a fee system. Sheriffs received a fixed amount for every arrest made. Unfortunately, their tax-collecting chores were more lucrative than fighting crime, so law enforcement was not one of their primary concerns.

In the cities, law enforcement was the province of the town marshal, who was aided, often unwillingly, by a variety of constables, night watchmen, police justices, and city council members. However, local governments had little power of administration, and enforcement of the criminal law was largely an individual or community responsibility.

In rural areas in the South, "slave patrols" charged with recapturing escaped slaves were an early if odious form of law enforcement.[7] In the western territories, individual initiative was encouraged by the practice of offering rewards for the capture of felons. If trouble arose, the town "vigilance committee" might form a posse to chase offenders. These **vigilantes** were called upon to eradicate social problems, such as theft of livestock, through force or intimidation; the San Francisco Vigilance Committee actively pursued criminals in the mid-nineteenth century.

As cities grew, it became exceedingly difficult for local leaders to organize ad hoc citizen vigilante groups. Moreover, the early nineteenth century was an era of widespread urban unrest and mob violence. Local leaders began to realize that a more structured police function was needed to control demonstrators and keep the peace.

Early Police Agencies

The modern police department was born out of urban mob violence that wracked the nation's cities in the nineteenth century. Boston created the first formal U.S. police department in 1838. New York formed its police department in 1844; Philadelphia, in 1854. The new police departments replaced the night-watch system and relegated constables and sheriffs to serving court orders and running jails.

At first, the urban police departments inherited the functions of the institutions they replaced. For example, Boston police were charged with maintaining public health until 1853, and in New York, the police were responsible for street sweeping until 1881.

Politics dominated the departments and determined the recruitment of new officers and promotion of supervisors. An individual with the right connections could be hired despite a lack of qualifications. "In addition to the pervasive brutality and corruption," writes one justice historian, Samuel Walker, "the police did little to effectively prevent crime or provide public services. . . . Officers were primarily tools of local politicians; they were not impartial and professional public servants."[8]

In the late nineteenth century, police work was highly desirable, because it paid more than most other blue-collar jobs. By 1880, the average factory worker earned $450 a year, while large cities paid police $900 annually. For immigrant groups, having enough political clout to be appointed to the police department was an important step up the social ladder.[9] However, job security was uncertain, because it depended on the local political machine's staying in power.

Police work itself was primitive. There were few of even the simplest technological innovations common today, such as call boxes or centralized record keeping. Most officers patrolled on foot, without backup or the ability to call for help. Officers commonly were taunted by local toughs and responded with force and brutality. The long-standing conflict between police and the public was born in the difficulty that untrained, unprofessional officers had in patrolling the streets of nineteenth-century United States and in breaking up and controlling labor disputes. Police were not crime fighters as we know them today. Their major role was maintaining order, and their power was almost unchecked. As historian Dennis Rousey found in his study of police in nineteenth-century New Orleans, the average officer had little training, no education in the law, and a minimum of supervision, yet the police became virtual judges of law and fact with the ability to exercise unlimited discretion.[10]

At mid-nineteenth century, the detective bureau was set up as part of the Boston police. Until then, "thief-taking" had been the province of amateur bounty hunters, who hired themselves out to victims for a price. When professional police departments replaced bounty hunters, the close working relationships that developed between police detectives and their underworld informants produced many scandals and consequently high personnel turnover.

Police during the nineteenth century were generally incompetent, corrupt, and disliked by the people they served. The police role was only minimally directed at law enforcement. Its primary function was serving as the enforcement arm of the reigning political power, protecting private property, and keeping control of the ever-rising numbers of foreign immigrants.

Uniformed police in New York City, 1856.

Twentieth-Century Reform

Police agencies evolved slowly through the latter half of the nineteenth century and into the twentieth century. Uniforms were introduced in 1853 in New York. The first technological breakthroughs in police operations came in the area of communications. The linking of precincts to central headquarters by telegraph began in the 1850s. In 1867, the first telegraph police boxes were installed; an officer could turn a key in a box, and his location and number would automatically register at headquarters. Additional technological advances were made in the area of transportation. The Detroit police department outfitted some of its patrol officers with bicycles in 1897. By 1913, the motorcycle was being employed by departments in the eastern part of the nation. The first police car was used in Akron, Ohio, in 1910, and the police wagon became popular in Cincinnati in 1912.[11] Nonpolice functions, such as care of the streets, began to be abandoned after the Civil War.

Despite any impetus toward improvement, big-city police were neither respected by the public, successful in their role as crime stoppers, nor involved in progressive activities. The control of police departments by local politicians impeded effective law enforcement and fostered an atmosphere of graft and corruption.

In an effort to control police corruption, civic leaders in a number of jurisdictions created police administrative boards to reduce local officials' control over the police. These tribunals were responsible for appointing police administrators and controlling police affairs. In many instances, these measures failed, because the private citizens appointed to the review boards lacked expertise in the intricacies of police work.

Another reform movement was the takeover of some big-city police agencies by state legislators. Although police budgets were paid through local taxes, control of police was usurped by rural politicians in the state capitals. New York City temporarily lost control of its police force in 1857. It was not until the first decades of the twentieth century that cities regained control of their police forces.

The Boston police strike of 1919 heightened interest in police reform. The strike came about basically because police officers were dissatisfied with their status in society. Other professions were unionizing and increasing their standards of living, but police salaries lagged behind. The Boston police officers' organization, the Boston Social Club, voted to become a union affiliated with the American Federation of Labor. The officers struck on September 9, 1919. Rioting and looting broke out, resulting in Governor Calvin Coolidge's mobilization of the state militia to take over the city. Public support turned against the police, and the strike was broken. Eventually all the striking officers were fired and replaced by new recruits. The Boston police strike ended police unionism for decades and solidified power in the hands of reactionary, autocratic police administrators.

In the aftermath of the strike, various local, state, and federal crime commissions began to investigate the extent of crime and the ability of the justice system to deal with it effectively. The **Wickersham Commission** was created by President Herbert Hoover to study the criminal justice system on a national scale. In its 1931 report, the commission found that the average police supervisor's term of office was too short and that his responsibility to political officials made his position insecure. The commission also said that there was a lack of effective, efficient, and honest patrolmen. It found that no intensive effort was being made to educate prospective recruits, to train and discipline officers, or to terminate those who were incompetent. The Wickersham Commission concluded that, with few exceptions, police forces in cities with populations above three hundred thousand had neither adequate communications systems nor the equipment necessary to enforce the law effectively. Policing, according to the commission, was made much more difficult by the excessively rapid growth of U.S. cities in the previous half-century and by the tendency of ethnic groups to retain their languages and customs in large cities. Finally, the commission said too many duties were cast on each officer.[12] The Missouri Crime Commission reported that in a typical U.S. city, the police were expected to be familiar with and enforce thirty thousand federal, state, and local statutes and ordinances.[13] However, with the onset of the Depression, justice reform became a less important issue than economic revival, and for many years, little changed in the nature of policing.

The Emergence of Professionalism

Around the turn of the century, a number of nationally recognized leaders called for measures to help improve and professionalize the police. In 1893, a professional society, the **International Association of Chiefs of Police (IACP),** was formed. Under the direction of its first president (District of Columbia Chief of Police Richard Sylvester), the IACP became the leading voice for police reform during the first two decades of the twentieth century. The IACP called for creating a civil service police force and for removing political influence and control. It also advocated centralized organizational structure and record keeping to curb the power of politically aligned precinct captains. Still another professional reform the IACP fostered was the creation of specialized units, such as delinquency control squads.

The most famous police reformer of the time was **August Vollmer.** While serving as police chief of Berkeley, California, Vollmer instituted university training for young officers. He also helped develop the School of Criminology at the

University of California at Berkeley, which became the model for justice-related programs around the United States. Vollmer's disciples included **O. W. Wilson,** who pioneered the use of advanced training for officers when he took over and reformed the Wichita, Kansas, police department in 1928. Wilson was also instrumental in applying modern management and administrative techniques to policing. His text, *Police Administration*, became the single most influential work on the subject. Wilson eventually took over as dean of the School of Criminology at Berkeley and ended his career in Chicago, where he had gone in 1960 at the request of Mayor Richard J. Daley to take over and reform that city's police department.

From 1920 to 1960, police departments for the most part stayed out of the public eye. Most departments used the "watchman" style of policing, which stressed keeping "a lid on things," rather than aggressive police work. The quality of police work often depended on the ethnic and racial composition of the community; more affluent areas received better services.

During this period, police professionalism was equated with an incorruptible, tough, highly trained, rule-oriented department organized along militaristic lines. The most respected department was that in Los Angeles, led by a no-nonsense chief, William Parker. It is not merely coincidence that one of the most popular police television shows of the period, "Dragnet," stressed the high motivation, competence, and integrity of Los Angeles police officers. The Los Angeles style emphasized police as incorruptible crime fighters who would not question the authority of Parker's central command. Later, the Los Angeles police would be severely criticized for allegedly treating minority citizens brutally.

Policing: 1960 to 1990

Police work has experienced turmoil, crisis, and reexamination in the thirty-year period from 1960 to 1990. The dramatic changes during this period had several causes. Throughout the 1960s, the Supreme Court handed down a number of decisions designed to control police operations and procedures. Police officers were now required to obey strict legal guidelines when questioning suspects, conducting searches and wiretapping, and so on. As the civil rights of suspects were significantly expanded, police complained they were being "handcuffed by the courts."

Also during the 1960s, civil unrest produced a growing tension between police and the public. African-Americans, who were battling for increased rights and freedoms in the civil rights movement, found themselves confronting police lines. When riots broke out in New York, Detroit, Los Angeles, and other cities between 1964 and 1968, the spark that ignited conflict often involved the police. And when students across the nation began marching in anti-Vietnam War demonstrations, it was the local police departments who were called on to keep order. An entire generation of minorities and college students came to openly resent local police, who were viewed as the most enduring symbol of the oppressive status quo. Police forces were ill-equipped and poorly trained to deal with these social problems; it is not surprising that the 1960s were marked by a number of bloody confrontations between the police and the public.

Confounding these problems was a rapidly growing crime rate. The number of violent and property crimes increased rapidly during the 1960s. Drug addiction and abuse grew to be national concerns, common in all social classes. Urban police departments were unable to control the crime rate, and police officers resented the demands placed on them by dissatisfied citizens.

Law enforcement officers must be able to handle the problems of a variety of special needs populations.

The 1970s witnessed many structural changes in police agencies themselves. The end of the war in Vietnam significantly reduced tensions between students and police. However, the relationship between police and minorities was still rocky. Pamela Irving Jackson has documented how early in the 1970s, public expenditures on police grew in urban areas where the minority population was increasing.[14] Local fears and distrust, combined with conservative federal policies, encouraged the growth of police departments to control what was perceived as an emerging minority "threat."

As the decade wore on, police departments began to reexamine their relations with the minority community. Public service officers, sensitivity training, and community advisory boards became standard features in most large police departments. Special police services for juveniles, rape victims, crime prevention, and community relations were created.

Increased federal government support for criminal justice greatly influenced police operations. During the 1970s, the Law Enforcement Assistance Administration (LEAA) devoted a significant portion of its funds to police agencies. Although a number of police departments used this money to purchase little-used hardware, such as antiriot gear, most of it went to supporting innovative research on police work and advanced training for police officers. Perhaps most significant, LEAA's Law Enforcement Education Program helped thousands of officers further their college education. Hundreds of criminal justice programs were developed on college campuses around the country, providing a pool of highly educated police recruits. LEAA funds were also used to import or transfer technology originally developed in other fields into law enforcement. Technological innovations involving computers transformed the way police kept records, investigated crimes, and communicated with one another. State training academies improved the way police learn to deal with such issues as job stress, community conflict, and interpersonal relations.

The 1970s also saw more women and minorities recruited to police work. Affirmative action programs helped, albeit slowly, alter the ethnic, racial, and gender composition of U.S. policing.

As the 1980s began, the police role seemed to be changing significantly. A number of experts acknowledged that the police were not simply crime fighters and called for police to develop a greater awareness of community issues, which resulted in the emergence of the community policing concept.[15]

Police unions, which began to grow in the late 1960s, continued to have a great impact on departmental administration in the 1980s. Unions fought for and won increased salaries and benefits for their members; starting salaries of thirty thousand dollars are not uncommon in metropolitan police agencies. In many instances, unions eroded the power of the police chief to make unquestioned policy and personnel decisions. During the 1980s chiefs of police commonly consulted with union leaders before making major decisions concerning departmental operations.

While police operations improved markedly in the 1980s, police departments were also beset by problems that impeded their effectiveness. State and local budgets were cut back during the Reagan administration, while federal support for innovative police programs was severely curtailed with the demise of the LEAA.

In the 1980s, police-community relations continued to be a major problem. Riots in Miami in 1980, 1982, and 1989 sparked by police-citizen conflicts, the destruction of the MOVE headquarters by Philadelphia police in 1985 in which eleven people were killed, and revelations that the New York City police used a fifty thousand-volt electric stun gun to obtain confessions from minority males exemplified the continual conflict between police and minority groups.[16] Incidents such as these triggered public outcry and skepticism about the police role, especially in inner-city neighborhoods. Toward the end of the decade, several police experts decreed that the nation's police forces should be evaluated, not on their crime-fighting ability, but on their courteousness, deportment, and helpfulness. Interest renewed in reviving an earlier style of police work featuring foot patrols and increased citizen contact.

Law Enforcement Today

There are approximately 17,000 law enforcement agencies in the United States, including:

- 3,093 sheriff's departments
- 12,288 municipal police agencies
- 1,531 special police forces (those with limited jurisdictions, such as parks, transit systems, airports, colleges, and schools)
- 49 state police (all states except Hawaii)
- 50 federal law enforcement agencies[17]

In total, these agencies employ more than eight hundred thousand people, including six hundred thousand sworn officers and about two hundred thousand civilians. The following sections review the operations and functions of these agencies in greater detail.

Metropolitan Police

City police comprise the majority of the nation's authorized law enforcement personnel.[18] Metropolitan police departments range in size from the New York City Police Department with its approximately twenty-five thousand sworn officers and eight thousand civilian employees, to police departments in Murdo,

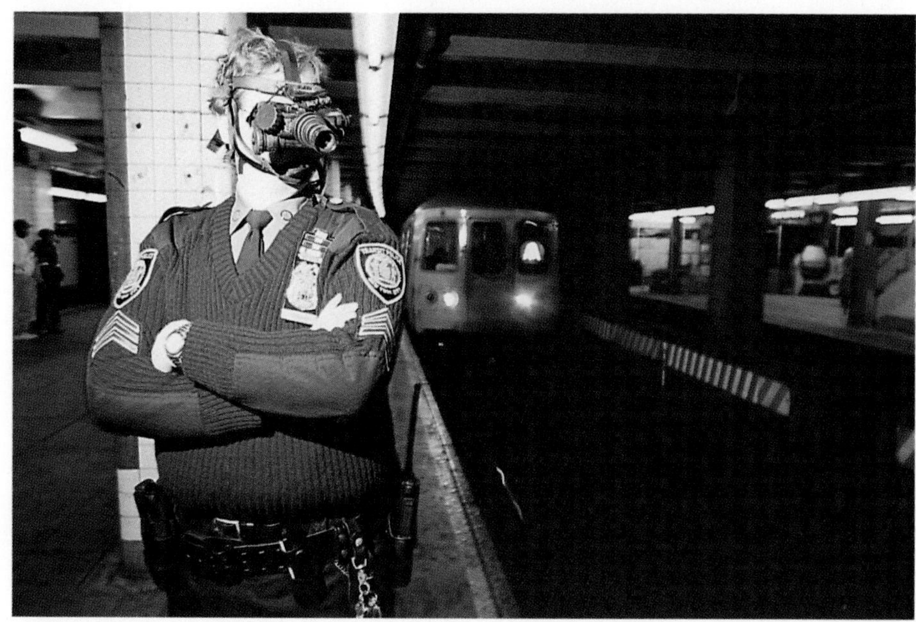

In addition to metropolitan police departments, there are more than 1,500 special police agencies which have jurisdiction over parks, transit systems, and similar public areas. Here a New York City Transit Authority police officer models military style night vision goggles which enable him to apprehend vandals and law violators in dark subway tunnels.

South Dakota, and Schoharie, New York, which have a single officer. While most TV police shows feature the trials of big-city police officers, the overwhelming number of departments actually have fewer than fifty officers and serve a population of under twenty-five thousand. As Figure 6.1 shows, thirty-eight departments have a thousand or more officers, while about a thousand have a single employee; the modal department has between ten to twenty-four officers.

As Table 6.1 shows, the cost of maintaining these police forces is high. The average police officer costs taxpayers about fifty-five thousand dollars per year including salary, benefits, and other costs; this amounts to an annual cost of over one hundred dollars for every resident in the jurisdiction. Residents in larger jurisdictions who want and receive greater police protection pay more than 40 per cent more each year for police services than those living in small towns.

Regardless of its size, most individual metropolitan police departments perform a standard set of functions and tasks and provide similar services to the community. These include traffic enforcement, accident investigation, patrol and peacekeeping, property and violent crime investigation, death investigation, narcotics and vice enforcement, and radio communications. Less universal but certainly not uncommon are a profusion of other services, including fingerprint processing, search and rescue, emergency medical care, court security, civil defense, civil process service, fire services, jail operation, training academy operation, crime laboratories and ballistic testing, tourist information, crowd control at public events, and license and permit issuance. The police role is currently expanding, so procedures must be developed to aid special-needs populations, including AIDS-infected suspects, the homeless, and victims of domestic and child abuse.[19]

These are only a few examples of the multiplicity of roles and duties assumed today in some of the larger urban police agencies around that nation. Smaller agencies can have trouble effectively carrying out these tasks; the hundreds of small police agencies in each state often provide duplicative services. Whether unifying smaller police agencies into "super agencies" would improve services is often debated among police experts. Smaller municipal agencies can provide im-

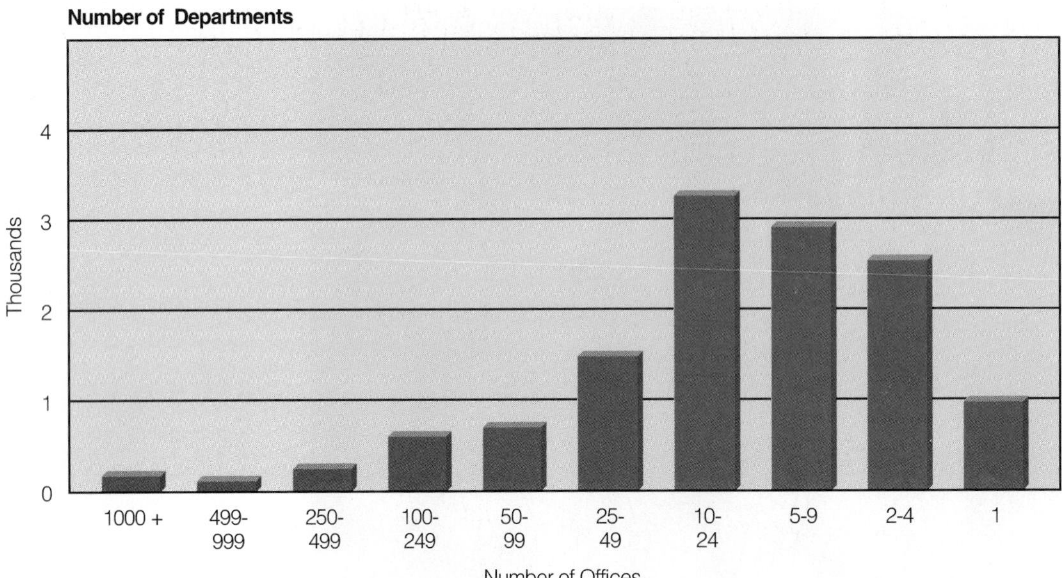

FIGURE 6.1
Number and Size of Police Agencies

SOURCE: Brian Reaves, *State and Local Police Departments, 1990* (Washington, D.C.: Bureau of Justice Statistics, 1992), p. 2.

portant specialized services that might have to be relinquished if they were combined and incorporated into larger departments.

County Law Enforcement

Most of the nation's county police departments, with their two hundred thousand employees, are independent agencies whose senior officer, the **sheriff,** is usually an elected political official (in all states except Rhode Island and Hawaii). The county sheriff's role has evolved from that of the early English shire reeve, whose primary duty was to assist the royal judges in trying prisoners and enforcing sentences. From the time of the westward expansion in the United States until municipal departments were developed, the sheriff was often the sole legal authority over vast territories.

The duties of a county sheriff's department vary according to the size and degree of development of its county. The standard tasks of a typical sheriff's department are serving civil process (summons and court orders), providing court security, operating the county jail, and investigating crimes. Less commonly, sheriff's departments may serve as coroners, tax collectors, overseers of highways and bridges, custodians of the county treasury, and providers of fire, animal control, and emergency medical services; in years past, sheriff's offices also conducted executions. Typically, a sheriff's department's law enforcement functions today are restricted to unincorporated areas within a county, unless a city or town police department requests its help.

Some sheriff's departments are exclusively law enforcement-oriented; some carry out court-related duties only; some are involved solely in correctional and judicial matters and not in law enforcement; a majority are full-service programs that carry out judicial, correctional, and law enforcement activities. As a rule, agencies serving large population areas (over 1 million) are devoted to maintain-

TABLE 6.1
Operating Expenditures of Local Police Departments, by Size of Population Served, 1990

Population Served	Operating Expenditures, Fiscal Year 1990			
	Per Department	Per Sworn Officer	Per Employee	Per Resident
All sizes	$1,675,000	$54,900	$42,300	$108
1,000,000 or more	$334,542,000	$62,600	$48,300	$144
500,000–999,999	79,567,000	63,400	48,400	114
250,000–499,999	46,500,000	62,600	46,800	128
100,000–249,999	16,268,000	59,600	44,000	108
50,000–99,999	6,528,000	54,400	40,600	95
25,000–49,999	3,225,000	55,200	42,100	93
10,000–24,999	1,513,000	51,600	40,400	96
2,500–9,999	442,000	39,800	31,800	85
Under 2,500	115,000	31,500	27,400	95

Note: Figures are for fiscal year ending June 30, 1990, or the most recent fiscal year completed prior to that date. Figures do not include capital expenditures, such as equipment purchases or construction costs. Computation of per officer and per employee average includes both full-time and part-time employees, with a weight of 0.5 assigned to part-time employees.

SOURCE: Brian Reaves, *State and Local Police Departments, 1990* (Washington, D.C.: Bureau of Justice Statistics, 1992), p. 3.

ing county correctional facilities, while those in smaller population areas are focused on law enforcement.

In the past, sheriff's salaries were almost always based on the fees they received for the performance of official acts. They received fees for every summons, warrant, subpoena, writ, or other process they served; they were also compensated for summoning juries or locking prisoners in cells. Today, almost all sheriffs are salaried in order to avoid conflict of interest.

State Police

Unlike municipal police departments, state police were legislatively created to deal with the growing incidence of crime in nonurban areas, a consequence of the increase in population mobility and the advent of personalized mass transportation in the form of the automobile. County sheriffs—elected officials with occasionally corrupt or questionable motives—had proven to be ineffective in dealing with the wide-ranging criminal activities that developed during the latter half of the nineteenth century. In addition, most local police agencies were unable to effectively protect against highly mobile lawbreakers who randomly struck at cities and towns throughout a state. In response to citizens' demands for effective and efficient law enforcement, state governors began to develop plans for police agencies that would be responsible to the state, instead of being tied to local politics and corruption.

The Texas Rangers, created in 1835, was one of the first state police agencies formed. Essentially a military outfit that patrolled the Mexican border, it was followed by the Massachusetts state constables in 1865 and the Arizona Rangers in 1901. Pennsylvania formed the first truly modern state police in 1905.[20]

Today, about twenty-three **state police** agencies have the same general police powers as municipal police and are territorially limited in their exercise of law enforcement regulations only by the state's boundaries. In some jurisdictions, state police are also given special police powers. New York, Pennsylvania, and West Virginia employ their state police as fire, fish, and game wardens. In Michigan,

TABLE 6.2
Functions Performed by State Police Departments, 1990

Function	Percent of Departments
Accident investigation	100
Traffic enforcement	100
Patrol and first response	96
Communications and dispatch	76
Narcotics/vice enforcement	69
Training academy operation	69
Fingerprint processing	59
Death investigation	55
Property crime investigation	51
Violent crime* investigation	51
Ballistics testing	45
Laboratory testing of substances	45
Search and rescue operations	45
Emergency medical services	27
Lockup facility operation	12
Civil defense	12
Court security	4
Fire services	4
Serving civil process	4
Animal control	0
Jail operation	0

*Rape, robbery, or serious assault

SOURCE: Brian Reaves, *State and Local Police Departments, 1990* (Washington, D.C.: Bureau of Justice Statistics, 1992), p. 10.

state police may be required to execute civil process in actions to which the state is a party, while in Connecticut and Pennsylvania, they conduct driver's licensing road tests. The remaining state police agencies are primarily responsible for highway patrol and traffic law enforcement. Some state police, such as those in California, direct most of their attention to the enforcement of traffic laws.

Most state police organizations are restricted by legislation from becoming involved in the enforcement of certain areas of the law. In Connecticut, Pennsylvania, New York, and New Hampshire, for example, state police are prohibited from entering incorporated areas to suppress riots or civil disorders, except when directed by the governor or by a mayor with the governor's approval. In some states, such as Massachusetts and Colorado, state police are prohibited from becoming involved in strikes or other labor disputes, unless violence erupts.

As Table 6.2 indicates, the nation's seventy-seven thousand state police employees (fifty-two thousand officers and twenty-five thousand civilians) are not only involved in law enforcement and highway safety but also carry out a variety of functions, including maintaining a training academy and providing emergency medical services. State police crime laboratories aid local departments in investigating crime scenes and analyzing evidence. State police also provide special services and technical expertise in such areas as bomb-site analysis and homocide investigation. Other state police departments, such as California's, are involved in highly sophisticated traffic and highway safety programs, including the use of helicopters for patrol and rescue, the testing of safety devices for cars, and the conducting of postmortem examinations to determine the causes of fatal accidents.

Federal Law Enforcement Agencies

The federal government has a number of law enforcement agencies designed to protect the rights and privileges of U.S. citizens; no single agency has unlimited jurisdiction, and each has been created to enforce specific laws and cope with particular situations. Federal police agencies have no particular rank order or hierarchy of command or responsibility, and each reports to a specific department or bureau. The most important of these include the following.

The Justice Department

The **U.S. Department of Justice** is the legal arm of the U.S. government. Headed by the attorney general, it is empowered to (1) enforce all federal laws, (2) represent the United States when it is party to court action, and (3) conduct independent investigations through its law enforcement services. The branches and responsibilities of the Department of Justice are outlined below.

Legal Divisions. The Department of Justice maintains several separate divisions that are responsible for enforcing federal laws and protecting U.S. citizens. The *Civil Rights Division* proceeds legally against violations of federal civil rights laws that protect citizens from discrimination on the basis of their race, creed, ethnic background, age, or sex. Areas of greatest concern include discrimination in education (e.g., school busing), housing, and employment, including affirmative action cases. The *Tax Division* brings legal actions against tax violators. The *Criminal Division* prosecutes violations of the Federal Criminal Code. Its responsibility includes enforcing statutes relating to bank robbery (since bank deposits are federally insured), kidnapping, mail fraud, interstate transportation of stolen vehicles, and narcotics and drug trafficking.

The Justice Department also maintains administrative control over a number of independent investigative and enforcement branches, described below.

The Federal Bureau of Investigation

The Justice Department first became involved in law enforcement in 1910, when the attorney general hired investigators to enforce the Mann Act (forbidding the transportation of women between states for immoral purposes). These investigators were formalized in 1908 into a distinct branch of the government, the Bureau of Investigation; the agency was later reorganized into the **Federal Bureau of Investigation (FBI),** under the direction of J. Edgar Hoover (1924–1972).

Today's FBI is not a police agency but an investigative agency with jurisdiction over all matters in which the United States is, or may be, an interested party. It limits its jurisdiction, however, to federal laws, including all federal statutes not specifically assigned to other agencies. Areas covered by these laws include espionage, sabotage, treason, civil rights violations, murder and assault of federal officers, mail fraud, robbery and burglary of federally insured banks, kidnapping, and interstate transportation of stolen vehicles and property.

The FBI has been the most glamorous and widely publicized law enforcement agency. In the 1920s and 1930s, its agents pursued such gangsters as John Dillinger, "Mad Dog" Coll, Bonnie and Clyde Barrow, "Machine Gun" Kelly, and "Pretty Boy" Floyd. During World War II, they hunted Nazi agents and prevented any major sabotage on U.S. military bases. After the war, they conducted a cru-

sade against Soviet intelligence agents and investigated organized-crime figures. They have been instrumental in cracking tough criminal cases, which has brought the FBI enormous public respect.

After J. Edgar Hoover's death, the agency was subjected to public criticism concerning its alleged harassment of civil rights leader Martin Luther King, Jr., its use of questionable investigation practices with subversives and antiwar activists, and its failure to investigate white-collar and organized criminals.[21] In the post-Watergate era, however, the FBI, under the leadership of William H. Webster and its current director, William Sessions, has attempted to steer a new course. Greater executive control has been exercised over domestic intelligence operations, and enforcement has been concentrated on white-collar and organized-crime violations and the control of terrorist groups. There have been a few recent trouble spots, including the five-year probe of the Committee in Solidarity with the People of El Salvador (CISPES), a group opposed to the Reagan administration's Latin American policies in the 1980s. The FBI was accused of illegally investigating CISPES and helping the Salvadoran National Guard identify its opponents in that country.[22] Nonetheless, the FBI seems to have restored its image of incorruptible, efficient law enforcement.

The FBI offers a number of important services to local law enforcement agencies. Its identification division, established in 1924, collects and maintains a vast fingerprint file that can be used by local police agencies. Its sophisticated crime laboratory, established in 1932, aids local police in testing and identifying evidence, such as hairs, fibers, blood, tire tracks, and drugs. The uniform crime reports are another service of the FBI. The UCR is an annual compilation of crimes reported to local police agencies, arrests, police killed or wounded in action, and other information. Finally, the FBI's National Crime Information Center is a computerized network linked to local police departments that provides ready information on stolen vehicles, wanted persons, stolen guns, and so on. Today, the FBI is one of the few federal agencies slated to expand. It employs about 21,500 people, a number that should increase by almost 1,000 in the next few years. Similarly, the agency will be spending millions on artificial intelligence models that combine investigation techniques with computer systems in order to develop leads in criminal cases.[23]

The FBI mission has been evolving to keep pace with world events. With the end of the Cold War and the reduction of East-West tensions, the FBI's counterintelligence mission has diminished. In some offices, agents have been reassigned to antigang efforts. Agency officials believe that the surveillance and information-gathering techniques that worked against East German spies will help in breaking up gangs and controlling drugs.[24]

Drug Enforcement Administration

Government interest in drug trafficking can be traced back to 1914, when the Harrison Act established federal jurisdiction over the supply and use of narcotics. A number of drug enforcement units, including the Bureau of Narcotics and Dangerous Drugs, were charged with enforcing drug laws. In 1973, however, these agencies were combined to form the **Drug Enforcement Administration (DEA).**

Agents of the DEA assist local and state authorities in investigating illegal drug use and carrying out independent surveillance and enforcement activities to control the importation of narcotics. For example, DEA agents work with foreign governments in cooperative efforts aimed at destroying opium and marijuana crops at their source, hard-to-find fields tucked away in the interiors of Latin

America, Asia, Europe, and Africa. Undercover DEA agents infiltrate drug rings and simulate buying narcotics to arrest drug dealers.

The DEA maintains regional laboratories that are essential to testing seized drugs so that accurate records and measures can be presented at the trials of drug offenders. The DEA also has an Office of Intelligence, which coordinates information and enforcement activities with local, state, and foreign governments. Recently, the DEA has been instructed to share some of its duties with the FBI, and the two agencies now have similar administrative controls.

Other Justice Department Agencies

Other federal law enforcement agencies under the direction of the Justice Department include the U.S. Marshals, the Immigration and Naturalization Service, and the Organized Crime and Racketeering Unit. The U.S. Marshals are court officers who help implement federal court rulings, transport prisoners, and enforce court orders. The Immigration and Naturalization Service is responsible for the administration of immigration laws governing the exclusion and deportation of illegal aliens and the naturalization of aliens lawfully present in the United States. This service also maintains border patrols to prevent illegal aliens from entering the United States. The Organized Crime and Racketeering Unit, under the direction of the U.S. attorney general, coordinates federal efforts to curtail organized crime primarily through the use of federal racketeering laws.

Treasury Department

The U.S. Treasury Department maintains the following enforcement branches:

The Bureau of Alcohol, Tobacco, and Firearms. The Bureau of Alcohol, Tobacco, and Firearms helps control sales of untaxed liquor and cigarettes and, through the Gun Control Act of 1968 and the Organized Crime Control Act of 1970, has jurisdiction over the illegal sales, importation, and criminal misuses of firearms and explosives.

The Internal Revenue Service. The Internal Revenue Service (IRS), established in 1862, enforces violations of income, excise, stamp, and other tax laws. Its Intelligence Division actively pursues gamblers, narcotics dealers, and other violators who do not report their illegal financial gains as taxable income. For example, the career of Al Capone, the famous 1920s gangster, was brought to an end by the efforts of IRS agents.

The Customs Service. The Customs Service guards points of entry into the United States and prevents smuggling of contraband into (or out of) the country. It ensures that taxes and tariffs are paid on imported goods and helps control the flow of narcotics into the country.

The Secret Service. The Secret Service was originally charged with enforcing laws against counterfeiting. Today, it is also accountable for the protection of the president and the vice-president and their families, presidential candidates, and former presidents. The Secret Service maintains the White House Police Force, which is responsible for protecting the executive mansion, and the Treasury Guard, which protects the mint.

Law Enforcement in the Year 2000

What changes can we expect in U.S. police agencies by the year 2000? What are the trends in policing? Where is police work heading?

One view is that police departments will be reshaping their role, deemphasizing crime fighting and stressing community organization and revitalization.[25] Around the country, citizens are demanding that police departments reconsider their image as disinterested outsiders. Community leaders are asking that, instead of riding around anonymously in patrol cars, police officers become actively involved in neighborhood affairs. Already functioning programs that do this include neighborhood-based ministations and foot patrols. Departments are also increasing their use of civilian employees, thereby freeing sworn officers for law enforcement tasks.

Police departments are evolving because leaders recognize that traditional models have not been effective: the streets are still not safe; the fear of crime is not declining; respect for the justice system has not been increasing. In the future, the police role may shift farther away from a legalistic style that isolates officers from the public to a service orientation that holds officers accountable to the community and encourages them to learn from the people they serve. This means that the police must actively create a sense of community where none has existed and recruit neighborhood cooperation for crime control and prevention activities.

Another change that police agencies will continue to emphasize is the decentralization of command through the creation of specialized units, substations, and direct response teams. While decentralization does not automatically ensure greater citizen cooperation, it is believed to increase sensitivity to citizen needs, create special knowledge of and commitment to the area served, and foster heightened community trust in the police.

Another innovation that will probably mushroom in the future is the employment of civilians for tasks that are now carried out by sworn officers. As police salaries and benefits increase, civilian employees will become an economic necessity. In addition, employing citizens from the community can help police departments become sensitive to the cultural environment that they serve.[26]

Police departments will become increasingly more proactive and focus their attention on solving particular community problems. These problems will include domestic abuse, drug dealing, and drunk driving, because police administrators believe that arrests for these crimes may help reduce recidivism and because vocal community groups demand action against violators.

The demographic structure of policing will also evolve. The numbers of minority and female police officers should continue to grow. In the past, white males followed their fathers into a police career. A new generation of minority kids will now be able to follow their mothers into police work.

As the private security industry mushrooms (see below), police departments may become more sensitive to their role in law enforcement. Patrol and investigation work may be coordinated with private security managers, many of whom began on the local force and employ local police.

One of the biggest problems police will face is shrinking municipal budgets and taxpayer revolts. Being forced to do more with less, police may shift from being labor-intensive, with the stress on random patrols to deter crime, to a more focused approach. This change will be enabled, in part, through relying on technology to improve effectiveness, to shorten response time, and to allow fewer police officers to accomplish more tasks efficiently. Police administrators must also be aware of the potential hazards of placing too much emphasis on constantly increasing performance.

An Era of Technological Change

Another trend will be relying on technology to improve the effectiveness of police resources. Budget realities demand that police leaders make the most effective use of their forces, and technology seems to be an important method of increasing productivity at a relative low cost.

The introduction of technology has already been explosive. In 1964, for example, only one city, St. Louis, had a police computer system; by 1968, ten states and fifty cities had state-level criminal justice information systems; today, almost every city of more than fifty thousand has some sort of computer support services.[27] Table 6.3 illustrates some of the services that have been computerized as of 1992.

One of the most important computer-aided tasks is the identification of criminal suspects. Computers now link neighboring agencies so that they can share information on cases, suspects, and warrants. One such system is the Police Information Network, which electronically links the ninety-three independent law enforcement agencies in the San Francisco area to enable them to share information. On a broader jurisdictional level, the FBI implemented the National Crime Information Center in 1967. This system provides rapid collection and retrieval of data about persons wanted for crimes anywhere in the fifty states.

TABLE 6.3
Computerized Functions in Police Departments, 1992

Percentage of Departments Using Computers for:	
Record keeping	45
Criminal investigations	30
Crime analysis	25
Budgeting	23
Dispatching	20
Fleet management	14
Personnel allocation	13
Jail management	3

SOURCE: Brian Reaves, *State and Local Police Departments, 1990* (Washington, D.C.: Bureau of Justice Statistics, 1992), p. 9.

Identifying Suspects. Computers are also being used to expedite the analysis of evidence. Los Angeles police can instantly cross-reference computer databases (e.g., compare the files on suspects who own brown Chevrolets with those who have facial scars).[28]

Some police departments are using computerized imaging systems to replace mug books. Photos are stored in computer memory and easily retrieved for viewing. New York City has an automated mug-shot file called the Computer-Assisted Terminal Criminal Hunt (CATCH). A witness who can remember a few details (e.g., a gold tooth or a scar on the cheek) or the way a crime was committed

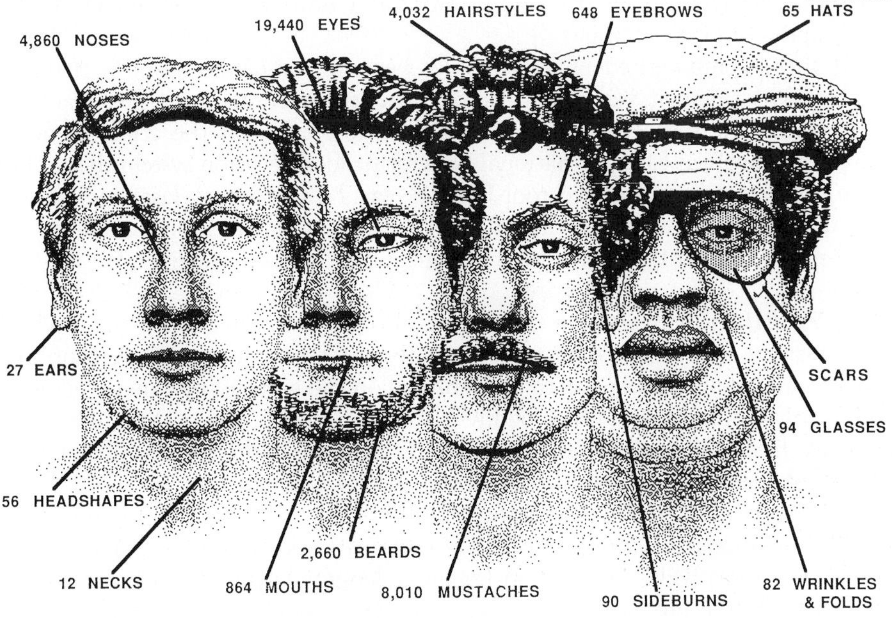

Computer generated composites can be used to help a witness create a precise sketch of criminal suspects. The Compusketch program developed by the Visatex Corporation of Campbell, California, contains thousands of facial features and details.

will be shown pictures of only those known suspects who have such characteristics, saving countless hours of looking through old-fashioned mug-shot books. CATCH can also check for fingerprints on file and match them to prints found at the scene of the crime. Several software companies have developed identification programs that help witnesses create a composite of the perpetrator. A vast library of photographed facial features can be stored in computer files and accessed on a terminal screen. Witnesses can scan through thousands of noses, eyes, and lips until they find those that match the suspect's. Eyeglasses, mustaches, and beards can be added; skin tones can be altered. When the composite is created, an attached camera makes a hard copy for distribution.[29]

Computer systems now used in the booking process, can also help in the suspect identification process. During the booking procedure, a visual image of the suspect is stored in a computer's memory along with other relevant information. Police can then easily create a "photo lineup" by calling up color photos on the computer monitor of all suspects having a particular characteristic described by a witness.

New techniques are constantly being developed. Soon, through the use of genetic algorithms (mathematical models), a computerized composite image of a suspect's face will be constructed from relatively little information.[30] Digitation of photographs will enable the reconstruction of blurred images. Videotapes of bank robbers or blurred photos of license plates, even bite marks, can be digitized using highly advanced mathematical models.

Fingerprint Analysis. The use of computerized fingerprint systems is growing around the United States. Using mathematical models, automated fingerprint identification systems (AFIS) can classify fingerprints and identify up to 250 characteristics (minutiae) of the print.[31] These automated systems use high-speed silicon chips to plot each point of minutiae and count the number of ridge lines between that point and its four nearest neighbors, which substantially improves its speed and accuracy over earlier systems. Some police departments, such as the District of Columbia's, report that computerized print systems are allowing them to make over one hundred identifications a month from fingerprints taken at a crime scene. AFIS files have been regionalized. For example, the Western Identification Network serves Alaska, California, Idaho, Nevada, Oregon, Utah, Washington, and Wyoming.[32]

If these computerized fingerprint files become standardized and a national database is formed, it would be possible to check records in all fifty states to determine if the suspect's fingerprints match those taken at the crime scene of previously unsolved cases. A national fingerprint identification system should become an even more effective tool by the year 2000, because laser technology should vastly improve fingerprint analysis. Investigators will soon be able to recover prints that in the past were too damaged to be used as evidence.

DNA Profiling. Advanced technology is also spurring new forensic methods of identification and analysis. The most prominent technique is **DNA profiling.** This technique allows suspects to be identified on the basis of the genetic material found in hair, blood, and other bodily tissues and fluids. When DNA is used as evidence in a rape trial, DNA segments are taken from the victim, the suspect, and blood and semen found on the victim. A DNA match indicates a 4 billion-to-one chance that the suspect is the offender.

Two methods of DNA matching are currently used. The most popular technique, known as RFLP (restriction fragment length polymorphism), uses radioactive material to produce a DNA image on an X ray film. The second method,

Computerized fingerprint identification systems will help investigators make rapid identification of criminal suspects. This program was created by Printrak International Inc. of Anaheim, CA.

PCR (polymerase chain reaction), amplifies DNA samples through molecular photocopying.[33]

In the future, genetic samples may be taken from every infant at birth and each child's unique patterns kept on computer files for instant identification.[34] DNA fingerprinting is now commonly used as evidence in criminal trials.[35] The use of DNA evidence to gain convictions has also been upheld on appeal.[36] Though some scientists have questioned the accuracy of DNA testing and dispute the infallability of a DNA match, the use of genetic evidence in criminal trials is likely to continue. (Some states have halted the use of DNA evidence pending further testing.)

Leading the way in the development of the most advanced forensic techniques is the Forensic Science Research and Training Center operated by the FBI in Washington, D.C., and Quantico, Virginia; the lab provides information and services to over three hundred crime labs throughout the United States.[37] The National Institute of Justice is also sponsoring research to identify a wider variety of DNA segments for testing and is involved in developing a PCR-based DNA profiling examination, using fluorescent detection, that will reduce the time required for DNA profiling.

Administration and Communication. Computers will certainly be used in training officers, both in terms of learning, performance evaluation, and field testing.[38] Departments are already using computer simulations to train officers in the use of deadly force.[39]

Some programs appear to be highly successful. For example, the St. Petersburg, Florida, police department has equipped all of its officers with portable computers, which has significantly cut down the time needed to write and duplicate reports.[40] Police can now use terminals to draw accident diagrams, communicate with the city traffic engineers, and merge their incident reports into other databases.

In addition to computer-driven information systems, future police technology will involve more efficient communications systems. Some departments are using

TABLE 6.4
Computerized Record Keeping in Police Departments

Records and Percentage of Departments Maintaining Them on Computers	
Arrests	39
Calls for service	34
Traffic citations	34
Stolen Property	32
Warrants	31
Criminal histories	30
UCR data	30
Inventory	21
Evidence	20
Payroll personnel	18
License registration	15
Summons	15

SOURCE: Brian Reaves, *State and Local Police Departments, 1990* (Washington, D.C.: Bureau of Justice Statistics, 1992), p. 9.

cellular phones in their cars to facilitate communications with victims and witnesses.[41] Departments that cover wide geographical areas and maintain independent precincts and substations are experimenting with **teleconferencing** systems that provide both audio and video linkages. Police agencies may use advanced communications gear to track stolen vehicles. Car owners will be able to buy transmitters that give off a signal to a satellite or other listening device, which can then be monitored and tracked by the specially equipped patrol cars; the system is now being tested.[42] Finally, some departments are linking advanced communications systems with computers. The Vancouver, British Columbia, police are already using a highly effective mobile digital communications system that allows patrol officers to personally access remote law enforcement data files without having to go through dispatch personnel at central headquarters.[43]

The Threat of Technology

By the year 2000, police departments will be relying more heavily on the new technologies for investigation efficiency. The use of improved computer-based record keeping and long-range electronic surveillance devices may pit modernized police agencies against civil libertarians who fear the power police have to intrude into the private lives of citizens.[44] Table 6.4 shows the percentage of departments that already use computers to keep records.

Justice experts Mark Moore and George Kelling question the wisdom of administrators who emphasize the technological aspects of police productivity at the expense of public service.[45] They state:

> The enormous investment in telephone, radios, and cars that now allow the police to respond to crime calls in under five minutes (often with more than one car) has bought little crime control, no greater sense of security, and has prevented the police from taking order maintenance and service functions seriously.[46]

Moore and Kelling believe that a truly productive police department is more concerned with public well-being and security than with a futile effort to control crime. David Farmer suggests that this effort is essentially cooperative: police agencies must be able to work with other public agencies in identifying the optimum levels of law, order, and justice to achieve social order.[47]

In the future, as now, police will be asked to do more with less, so they will need to be aware of potential breakdowns and stress levels. When they crack and use excessive force, the potential for civil suits increases. Despite efforts to promote positive change within departments, the most important source of police innovation and action may be external: the threat of major damage claims when they act too precipitously or when they fail to act precipitously enough.

Private Policing and Security

Since police forces alone can have only a limited influence on controlling crime and protecting victims, alternative methods of policing have been developed. In the next decade, private security forces should significantly affect law enforcement.

The emergence of the private security industry has been dramatic, increasing at a much greater pace than public policing.[48] In fact, as Figure 6.2 shows, it is now estimated that more money is spent on private protection than on state-sponsored law enforcement agencies; by the year 2000, over $100 billion will be

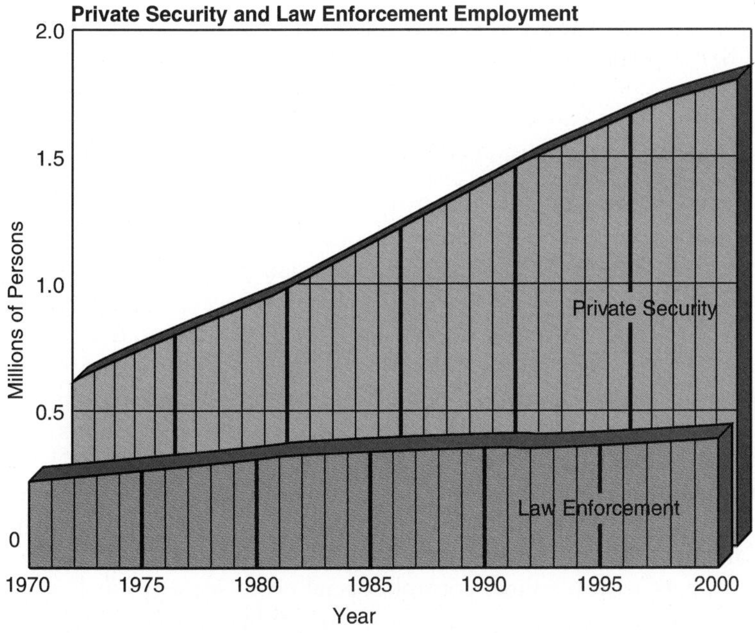

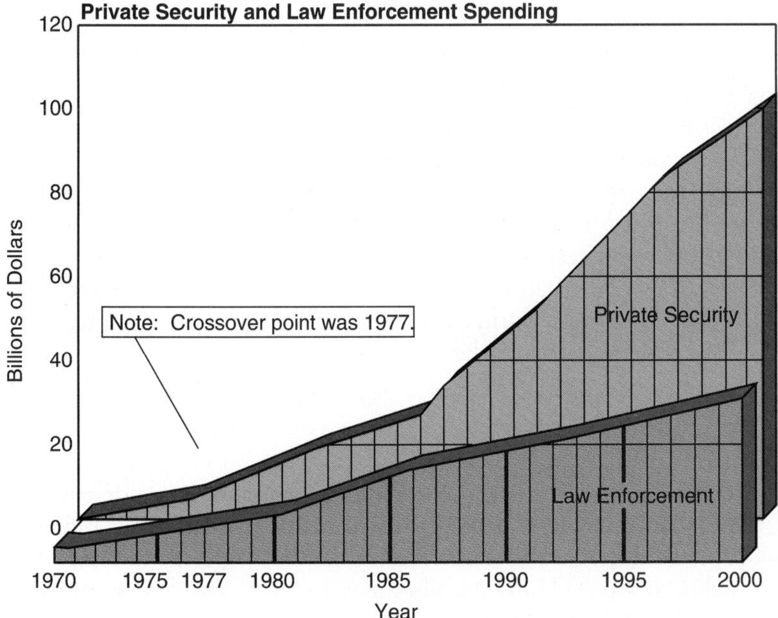

FIGURE 6.2
Private Security Employment and Spending

SOURCE: William Cunningham, John Strauchs, and Clifford Van Meter, *Private Security: Patterns and Trends* (Washington, D.C.: National Institute of Justice, 1991), p. 3.

spent on private security.[49] Today, more than 1.5 million people work in private security—far more than the total number of sworn police officers.

Much of what is known about the national trends in private policing comes from the **Hallcrest Report,** a government-financed survey of the industry, which found that the use of private security falls into two major areas.[50] **Proprietary security** is undertaken by an organization's own employees and includes both plainclothes and uniformed agents directed by the organization's head of security. The second type of private security is **contractual services,** such as guards, investigators, and armored cars, which are provided by private companies, such as Wackenhut and Pinkerton's. Also included within the category of contractual security is the wide variety of security products, such as safes, electronic access-control devices, and closed-circuit television.

Public-Private Cooperation

Private security forces take on responsibilities that are also within the domain of local police agencies. These include responding to burglar alarms, investigating misdemeanors, enforcing parking restrictions, and providing court security. Despite this overlap, there was customarily little contact or cooperation between private and public policing agents. In the 1980s, the International Association of Chiefs of Police, the National Sheriff's Association, and the American Society for Industrial Security began joint meetings to improve relations between the public and private sectors. In 1986, the Joint Council on Law Enforcement and Private Security Associations was formed.

One reason public-private cooperation is essential is the rise of a movement to privatize services that have been within the jurisdiction of public police agencies. Candidates for privatization include public building security, parking enforcement, park patrol, animal control, special event security (such as rock concerts), funeral escorts, prisoner escorts, and public housing security. About eighteen states already have privatized some police functions. In some small towns, private police may even replace the town police force. Reminderville, Ohio, experimented with an all-private police force and found that it produced great savings without any drop in service.

One area that may be ideal for privatization is responding to private security systems. The number of private security systems has grown rapidly, along with a corresponding increase in the number of false alarms. In some jurisdictions, 30 percent of all calls for police service are false alarms. This problem will intensify because the number of residences with alarm systems should double by the year 2000 (about 20 percent of all homes). One approach has been to fine or charge homeowners for repeat false alarm calls. Private firms may be contracted to handle alarm calls and screen out false alarms before notifying police.

Moonlighting

At one time, the image of the private security guard was that of being undertrained, undereducated, and underpaid. Research by William Walsh indicates that the background and personal characteristics of private police are actually quite similar to public police.[51] However, most states still do not require private companies to provide employees with stringent training in the use of firearms or other police techniques, nor are there any national standards to ensure quality.

Because of the important role played by private security, the lack of training in certain key areas, and the need for increased public protection, police officers are commonly hired by private agencies for part-time work, referred to as **moonlighting** or "details."[52] There is no single method for administering the private employment of public police. In some instances, individual officers make their own arrangements with employers; in others, the police union handles detail work, or the department itself regulates work contracts. These methods are described in Table 6.5. Though about 20 percent of police departments prohibit moonlighting, an estimated 150,000 police officers moonlight as private security agents.

Moonlighting has benefits and drawbacks. It puts law enforcement officers on the street and at "hot spots," such as sporting events, without cost to the public.

TABLE 6.5
Three Management Models for the Private Employment of Police

Officer contract model
- Each officer finds own secondary employment.
- Officer independently contracts conditions of work, hours, pay.
- Officer than applies for permission to accept off-duty job.
- Department grants permission, provided job meets minimum standards.
- Employer pays officer in cash (work is called "cash detail"). Departments in Atlanta, Charlotte, Cincinnati, Minneapolis, and Omaha generally follow this model, differing on what work is permitted. Arlington County permits uniformed employment only by permission of the police chief and only at activities funded or sponsored by the county, state, or U.S. government. In Peoria, most secondary employment is independently contracted, but the department itself contracts for civic center jobs and permits officers and department heads to broker work. In Cincinnati, work for private parties is independently contracted, but the department contracts for city, county, or state agencies.

Union brokerage model
- Union, guild, or association finds paid details.
- Union assigns officers who have volunteered.
- Union sets assignment conditions for paid details.
- Union bargains with the department over status, pay, and conditions of paid details.
- Most off-duty employment of Seattle police is coordinated by the Seattle Police Officers' Guild, although the officers act as independent contractors. For privately sponsored special events at the Seattle Center complex, off-duty officers are employed by the center's security officer and paid through an outside accounting firm.

Department contract model
- Police agency contracts with employers.
- Agency assigns officers and pays them from reimbursements by employers.
- Agency assigns an off-duty employment coordinator to receive employer requests, issue work permits, and assign officers to paid details.
- Agency negotiates with union or guild on pay and job conditions. Boston, Colorado Springs, New Haven, and St. Petersburg fit this model. Metro-Dade contracts for police-related work (including, unlike most departments, work for private security firms) but lets officers contract for nonpolice jobs, each of which requires a permit.

Moonlighters are better trained and carry more authority than other security personnel. Moonlighting, however, raises questions of liability and conflict of interest. For example, if an off-duty police officer uses a firearm while working a security detail, is the local police department responsible if a lawsuit results from the officer's actions? Is there a conflict of interest if police serve private rather than municipal purposes? Should the public pay sick leave if an officer is injured while working privately? What happens if a police officer is permanently injured while working a security detail and forced to retire? Should police officers be allowed to wear municipal uniforms while working private details? Can they use police radios, vehicles, and other equipment? Despite these questions and potential problems, the private employment of public police continues to grow.

The Future of Private Security

The Hallcrest Report estimates that by the year 2000, there will be 750,000 contract guards and 410,000 proprietary security forces. The technology that supports the field will grow rapidly, with more sophisticated alarm systems, access control, and closed-circuit television.

The expanded role of private security is not without its perils. Many law enforcement executives are critical of the quality of private security and believe it has little value as a crime control mechanism. One complaint heard by the

ANALYZING CRIMINAL JUSTICE ISSUES

Private Justice

The Hallcrest Report highlights an area of the justice process that generates relatively little empirical research. While police discretion and style has long been the focus of criminal justice research, decision making by private security forces has not received the same degree of attention.

To fill this knowledge gap, Melissa Davis, Richard Lundman, and Ramiro Martinez, Jr., recently investigated the loss prevention unit in a branch store of a large national retail chain. They uncovered a private justice system that works parallel to but independent of the public justice system. Private security officers have many law enforcement powers also granted to municipal police officers. They may arrest suspects, conduct a search of their person, seize evidence, and file criminal charges in court. They are actually given more legal leeway than local police because state courts have ruled that as "private persons," they are not bound by *Mapp vs. Ohio* and other civil liberties cases. Security agents are therefore given a free hand to detain suspects, interrogate them, and conduct more intrusive searches with less cause than local police have. In addition, a "merchant's privilege statute" immunizes store police from criminal or civil liability charges stemming from false arrest, a privilege local police must certainly envy.

Private police decision making seems to be influenced by state law allowing stores to recover civil damages from shoplifters. In the twenty-eight states that have implemented this type of legislation, shoplifters may be required to compensate store owners for the value of the goods they attempted to steal, for costs incurred because of their illegal acts, and for punitive damages. Store detectives used the civil damages route to defray the costs of their operation. The researchers found that the availability of civil damages had important effects on decision making. Store police "skim" the more affluent shoplifters for civil recovery and "ship" the poor to the public criminal justice system.

The Davis, Lundman, and Martinez research has important consequences for the criminal justice system. It implies that decisions made by private police agents can have a considerable impact on the number and type of cases processed in the criminal courts. Shoplifting cases make up a considerable portion of the criminal cases reported to the FBI. Therefore, the actions of private police help create the illusion of a class-crime relationship. If security forces permit the affluent to pay civil damages while passing the needy on to police agencies, then official crime data will be spuriously weighted by the exclusion of middle-class criminals. This research highlights the need for further research on the nature of private police activities and their impact on the crime rate.

Critical Thinking Skills

1. Is it fair to have a hidden justice system that places a higher value on a person's ability to pay than on the seriousness of his or her actions? Does this undermine Fourteenth Amendment guarantees of equal protection and due process? Should these apply to private companies?

2. Taking this concept a bit farther, if private firms have the right to decide to arrest or release suspects, might they not also conduct their own quasi-trials and then exact penalties? The case would be turned over to public authorities if the "convicted" offender refuses to obey the judgment. Private courts could reduce case pressure in the public court system. Could such a system of private justice actually work?

SOURCE: Melissa Davis, Richard Lundman, and Ramiro Martinez, Jr., "Private Corporate Justice: Store Police, Shoplifters, and Civil Recovery," *Social Problems* 38 (1991):395–408.

Hallcrest researchers was the lack of training and standards in the profession. Still another source of contention between private security and local police agencies is the increasing number of police calls that are a function of private security measures.

The Hallcrest report recommends a number of strategies to improve the quality of private security: upgrade employee quality; create statewide regulatory bodies and statutes for controlling security firms; require mandatory training; increase police knowledge of private security; expand the interaction between police and private security providers, such as sharing information; and transfer some police functions, such as burglar alarm checking, to the private sector. The report rec-

A Pinkerton investigator conducts a surveillance assignment.

ommends that the industry create its own standards similar to those adopted by the British Security Industry Association to professionalize the trade. Analyzing Criminal Justice Issues: Private Justice discusses the relationship between public and private policing.

SUMMARY

Present-day police departments have evolved out of early European and colonial American crime-control forces. Today, most police agencies operate in a militaristic fashion; policy generally emanates from the top of the hierarchy, and it is difficult for both police officers and the public to understand or identify the source of orders and directives. Most police officers therefore use a great deal of discretion when making on-the-job decisions.

Many different types of organizations are involved in law enforcement activities on the local, state, and federal levels of government. The most visible law enforcement agencies are local police departments, which carry out patrol, investigative, and traffic functions, as well as many support activities. Police departments have also been concerned with developing proper techniques for training their leaders, recruiting new officers, promoting deserving veterans, and developing technical expertise.

By the year 2000, police departments will begin to rely on advanced computer-based technology to identify suspects and collate evidence. Automated fingerprint systems and computerized identification systems will become widespread. There is danger that technology may make police overly intrusive and interfere with civil liberties.

In addition to public law enforcement agencies, a large variety of private policing enterprises have developed. These include a multibillion dollar private security industry and the private employment of public police.

QUESTIONS

1. List the problems faced by police departments today that were also present during the early days of policing.
2. Distinguish between the duties of the state police, sheriff's, and local police departments.
3. Why has the private security industry blossomed? What factors will influence the role of private policing during the coming decade?
4. What are some of the technological advances that should help the police solve more crimes? What are the dangers of these advances?
5. Discuss the trends that will influence policing during the coming decade. What other social factors may affect police?

NOTES

1. Associated Press, "California officer describes beating of motorist," *Boston Globe*, 7 March 1992, p. 4.

2. Gallup Poll results cited in Kathleen Maguire and Timothy Flanagan, *Sourcebook of Criminal Justice Statistics, 1990* (Washington, D.C.: U.S. Government Printing Office, 1991), p. 167.

3. Edward Zamble and Phyllis Annesley, "Some Determinants of Public Attitudes Toward the Police," *Journal of Police Science and Administration* 15 (1987):285–91.

4. Ibid., p. 289.

5. This section relies heavily on such sources as Malcolm Sparrow, Mark Moore, and David Kennedy, *Beyond 911, A New Era for Policing* (New York: Basic Books, 1990); Daniel Devlin, *Police Procedure, Administration, and Organization* (London: Butterworth, 1966); Robert Fogelson, *Big City Police* (Cambridge: Harvard University Press, 1977); Roger Lane, *Policing the City, Boston 1822–1885* (Cambridge: Harvard University Press, 1967); Roger Lane, "Urban Police and Crime in Nineteenth-Century America," in *Crime and Justice*, vol. 2, ed. Norval Morris and Michael Tonry (Chicago: University of Chicago Press, 1980), pp. 1–45; J. J. Tobias, *Crime and Industrial Society in the Nineteenth Century* (New York: Schocken Books, 1967); Samuel Walker, *A Critical History of Police Reform: The Emergence of Professionalism* (Lexington, Mass.: Lexington Books, 1977); Samuel Walker, *Popular Justice* (New York: Oxford University Press, 1980); President's Commission on Law Enforcement and the Administration of Justice, *Task Force Report: The Police* (Washington, D.C.: U.S. Government Printing Office, 1967), pp. 1–9.

6. Devlin, *Police Procedure, Administration, and Organization*, p. 3.

7. Phillip Reichel, "Southern Slave Patrols as a Transitional Type," *American Journal of Police* 7 (1988):51–78.

8. Walker, *Popular Justice*, p. 61.

9. Ibid., p. 8.

10. Dennis Rousey, "Cops and Guns: Police Use of Deadly Force in Nineteenth-Century New Orleans," *American Journal of Legal History* 28 (1984):41–66.

11. Law Enforcement Assistance Administration, *Two Hundred Years of American Criminal Justice* (Washington, D.C.: U.S. Government Printing Office, 1976).

12. National Commission on Law Observance and Enforcement, *Report on the Police* (Washington, D.C.: U.S. Government Printing Office, 1931), pp. 5–7.

13. Preston William Slossom, *A History of American Life*, vol. 12 of *The Great Crusade and After, 1914–1929*, ed. Arthur M. Schlesinger and Dixon Ryan Fox (New York: Macmillan, 1931), p. 102.

14. Pamela Irving Jackson, *Minority Group Threat, Crime, and Policing* (New York: Praeger, 1989).

15. James Q. Wilson and George Kelling, "Broken Windows," *Atlantic Monthly* 249 (March 1982):29–38.

16. Frank Tippett, "It Looks Just Like a War Zone," *Time*, 27 May 1985, pp. 16–22; "San Francisco, New York Police Troubled by Series of Scandals," *Criminal Justice Newsletter* 16 (1985):2–4; Karen Polk, "New York police: Caught in the middle and losing faith," *Boston Globe*, 28 December 1988, p. 3.

17. Bureau of Justice Statistics, *Report to the Nation on Crime and Justice* (Washington, D.C.: Bureau of Justice Statistics, 1988), p. 63.

18. This section relies heavily on data from Brian Reaves, *State and Local Police Departments, 1990* (Washington, D.C.: Bureau of Justice Statistics, 1992); see also Federal Bureau of Investigation, *Crime in the United States, 1990* (Washington, D.C.: U.S. Government Printing Office, 1991).

19. See, for example, Susan Martin and Edwin Hamilton, "Police Handling of Child Abuse Cases: Policies, Procedures and Issues," *American Journal of Police* 9 (1990):1–16.

20. Bruce Smith, *Police Systems in the United States* (New York: Harper & Row, 1960), p. 72.

21. Tony Poveda, "The FBI and Domestic Intelligence: Technocratic or Public Relations Triumph?" *Crime and Delinquency* 28 (1982):194–210.

22. Ross Gelbspan, "FBI misled Congress on its Latin inquiry," *Boston Globe*, 2 January 1989, p. 5.

23. "New Budget Builds Up FBI, DEA, Prisons, Marshals; Cuts Grants," *Criminal Justice Newsletter*, 18 February 1986, p. 1.

24. Kathleen Grubb, "Cold War to gang war," *Boston Globe*, 22 January 1992, p. 1.

25. This section leans heavily on Jerome Skolnick and David Bayley, *The New Blue Line* (New York: Free Press, 1986), pp. 210–30.

26. See Stephen Matrofski, "The Prospects of Change in Police Patrol: A Decade in Review," *American Journal of Police* 9 (1990):1–69.

27. Mark Birchler, "Computers in a Small Police Agency," *FBI Law Enforcement Bulletin*, January 1989, pp. 7–9.

28. Kristen Olson, "LAPD's Newest Investigative Tool," *The Police Chief* 55 (1988):30.

29. See Judith Blair Schmitt, "Computerized ID Systems," *The Police Chief* 59 (1992):33–45.

30. Richard Rau, "Forensic Science and Criminal Justice Technology: High-Tech Tools for the 90's," *National Institute of Justice Reports*, 224 (June 1991):6–10.

31. William Stover, "Automated Fingerprint Identification—Regional Application of Technology," *FBI Law Enforcement Bulletin* 53 (1984):1–4.

32. Schmitt, "Computerized ID Systems," p. 35.

33. Rau, "Forensic Science and Criminal Justice Technology."

34. Matt Rodriguez, "The Acquisition of High Technology Systems by

Law Enforcement," *FBI Law Enforcement Bulletin* 57 (1988):10–15.
35. "California Attorney General Endorses DNA Fingerprinting," *Criminal Justice Newsletter*, 1 March 1989, p. 1.
36. *State v. Ford*, 301 S.C. 485, 392 S.E.2d 781 (1990).
37. Colleen Wade, "Forensic Science Information Resource System," *FBI Law Enforcement Bulletin* 57 (1988):14–15.
38. Paul Smith, "Inservice Training for Law Enforcement Personnel," *FBI Law Enforcement Bulletin* 57 (1988):20–21.
39. John LeDoux and Henry McCaslin, "Computer-Based Training for the Law Enforcement Community," *FBI Law Enforcement Bulletin* 57 (1988):8–10.
40. Brewer Stone, "The High-Tech Beat in St. Pete," *Police Chief* 55 (1988):23–28.
41. Ibid., p. 24.
42. Mark Thompson, "Police Seeking Radio Channel for Stolen Auto Tracking System," *Criminal Justice Newsletter*, 15 March 1989, p. 1.
43. James McRae and James McDavid, "Computer-Based Technology in Police Work: A Benefit-Cost Analysis of a Mobile Digital Communications System," *Journal of Criminal Justice* 16 (1988):47–55.
44. Office of Technology Assessment, *Criminal Justice: New Technologies and the Constitution* (Washington, D.C.: U.S. Government Printing Office, 1988).
45. Mark Moore and George Kelling, "To Serve and Protect: Learning from Police History," *The Public Interest* 70 (1983):49–65.
46. Ibid., p. 62.
47. David Farmer, *Crime Control: The Use and Misuse of Police Resources* (New York: Plenum, 1984).
48. Material in this section leans heavily on two sources: William Cunningham, John Strauchs, and Clifford Van Meter, *The Hallcrest Report I: Private Security and Police in America* (Stoneham, Mass.: Butterworth-Heineman, 1985); idem, *The Hallcrest Report II: Private Security Trends, 1970–2000* (Stoneham, Mass.: Butterworth-Heineman, 1990). Both reports are summarized in William Cunningham and Todd Taylor, *The Growing Role of Private Security* (Washington, D.C.: National Institute of Justice, 1984) and William Cunningham, John Strauchs, and Clifford Van Meter, *Private Security: Patterns and Trends* (Washington, D.C.: National Institute of Justice, 1991).
49. National Institute of Justice, *Research Program Plan, Fiscal Year 1989* (Washington, D.C.: National Institute of Justice, 1990), p. 3.
50. William Cunningham and Todd Taylor, *The Growing Role of Private Security* (Washington, D.C.: U.S. Government Printing Office, 1984).
51. William Walsh, "Private/Public Police Stereotypes: A Different Perspective," *Security Journal* 1 (1989):21–27.
52. Albert Reiss, *Private Employment of Public Police* (Washington, D.C.: National Institute of Justice, 1988).

CHAPTER 7

The Police: Organization, Role, and Function

OUTLINE

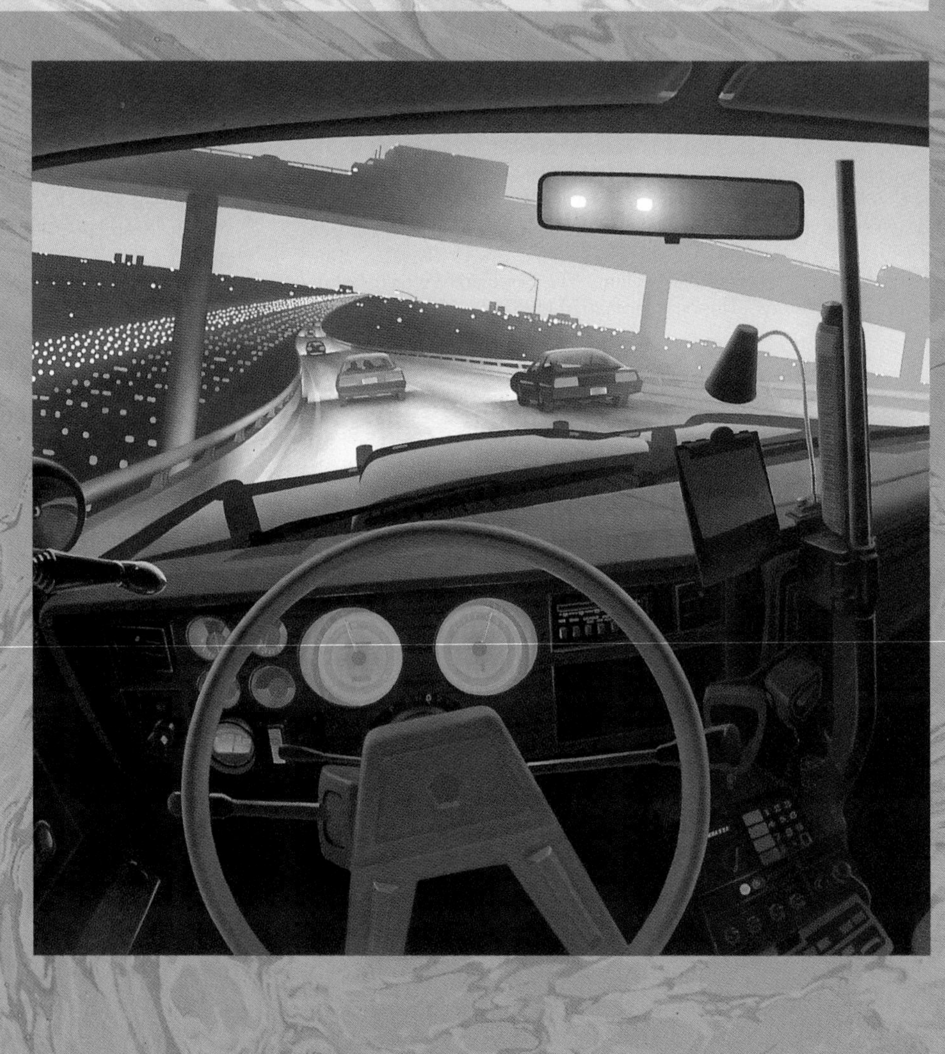

KEY TERMS

detective bureau
time-in-rank system
special-needs populations
order maintenance or peacekeeping
Kansas City study
vice squad
detection
sting operations
proactive
reactive
police-community relations (PCR)
team policing
"broken windows"
foot patrol
neighborhood policing
problem-oriented policing
hot spots of crime
roll call training
participatory management
police productivity

Most municipal police departments in the United States are independent agencies, located within the executive branch of government, operating without specific administrative control from any higher governmental authority. On occasion, police agencies will cooperate and participate in mutually beneficial enterprises, such as sharing information on known criminals, or they may help federal agencies investigate interstate criminal cases. Aside from such cooperative efforts, police departments tend to be functionally independent organizations with unique sets of rules, policies, procedures, norms, budgets, and so on. The unique structure of police agencies greatly influences their function and effectiveness.

This chapter describes the organization of police departments and their various operating branches: patrol, investigation, service, and administration. It discusses the realities and ambiguities of the police role and how the concept of the police mission has been radically changing. The chapter concludes with a brief overview of some of the most important administrative issues confronting U.S. law enforcement agencies.

Police Organization

Most police agencies are still organized in a militaristic, hierarchical manner, as illustrated in Figure 7.1. Within this organizational model, each element of the department normally has its own chain of command. For example, in a large municipal department, the **detective bureau** might have a captain as the director of a particular division (e.g., homicide), while a lieutenant oversees individual cases and acts as liaison with other police agencies, and sergeants and inspectors carry out the actual field work. Smaller departments may have a captain as head of all detectives, while lieutenants supervise individual subsystems (e.g., robbery or homicide). At the head of the organization is the chief, who sets policy and has general administrative control over all of the department's various operating branches. Most departments also follow a military-like system in promoting personnel within the ranks; at an appropriate time, a promotion test may be given and, based on his or her scores and other recommendations, an officer may be advanced in rank. This organizational style frustrates some police officers from furthering their education, since a college or advanced degree may have little direct impact on their promotion potential or responsibilities. Furthermore, some otherwise competent police officers are unable to increase their rank due to their inability to take tests well.

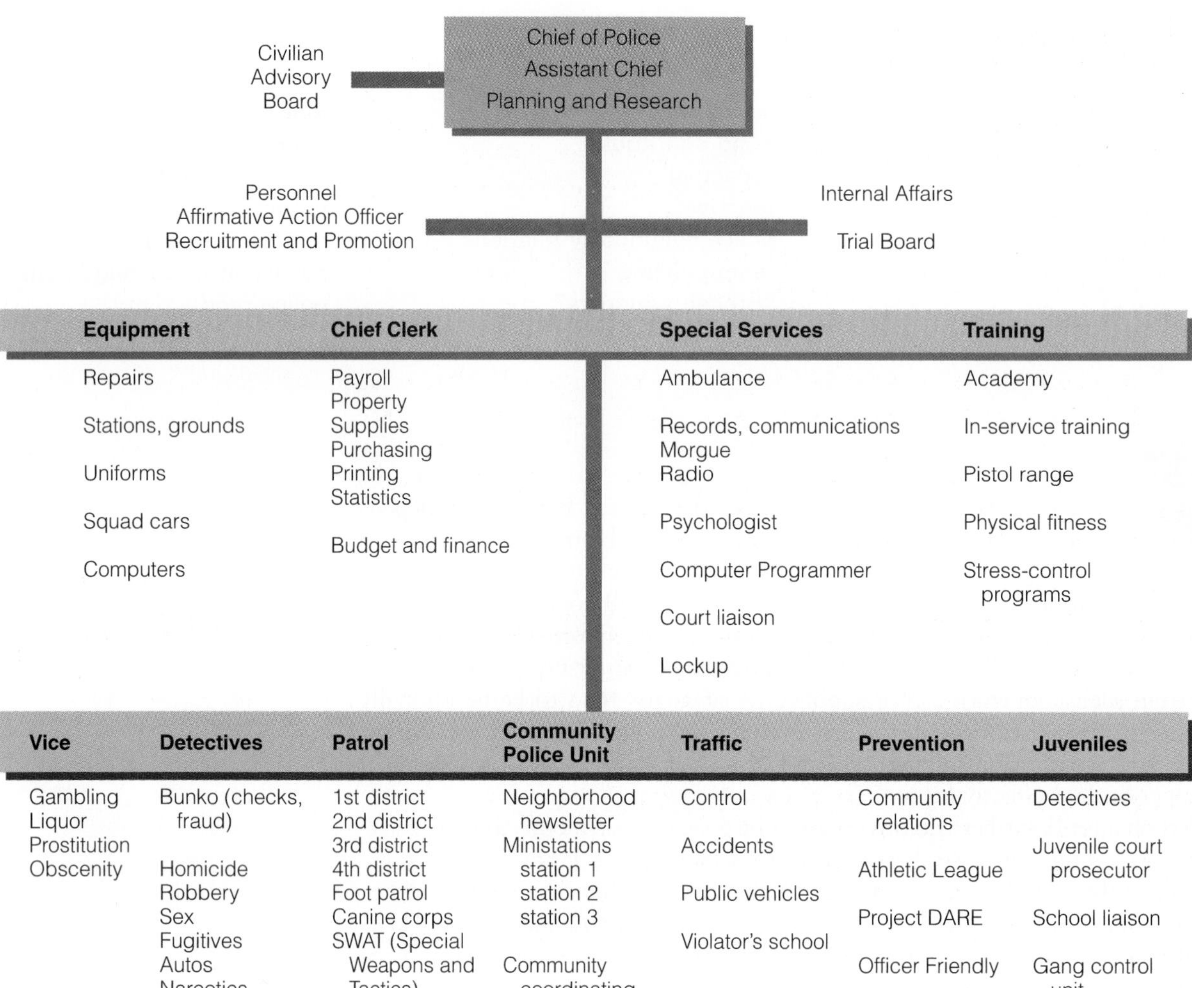

FIGURE 7.1
Organization of a Metropolitan Police Department

The typical police department's organizational structure has several other problems. First, the overlapping assignments between the top administrators (chief and assistant or deputy chief) make it difficult for citizens to determine who is actually responsible for the department's policies and operations. Second, the large number of operating divisions and the lack of any clear relationship among them almost guarantees that the decision-making practices of one branch will be unknown to another; two divisions may unknowingly compete with each other over jurisdiction on a particular case. Even where cooperation is assured, the absence of a close working relationship among the various divisions of a department often causes inefficiency in the allocation and use of resources.[1]

The Time-in-Rank System

Most police departments employ a **time-in-rank system** for determining promotion eligibility. This means that before moving up the administrative ladder, an officer must spend a certain amount of time in the next lowest rank; a sergeant cannot become a captain without serving an appropriate amount of time as a lieutenant. While this system is designed to promote fairness and limit favoritism, it also restricts administrative flexibility. Unlike the private sector, where talented people can be pushed ahead in the best interests of the company, the time-in-rank system prohibits rapid advancement. A police agency would probably not be able to hire a computer systems expert with a Ph.D. and give her a command position in charge of its data analysis section. The department would be forced to hire the expert as a civilian employee under the command of a ranking senior officer who may not be as technically proficient.

Under this rank system, a title can rarely be taken away or changed once it is earned. Police administrators become frustrated when qualified junior officers cannot be promoted or reassigned to appropriate positions because they lack time in rank or because less qualified officers have more seniority. Inability to advance through the ranks convinces numerous educated and ambitious officers to seek private employment. Conversely, the rank system means that talented people cannot transfer to other departments or sell their services to the highest bidder. Time in rank ensures the stability—for better or worse—of police agencies.

The Police Role

In countless books, movies, and TV shows, the public has been presented with a view of policing that romanticizes police officers as fearless crime fighters who think little of their own safety as they engage in daily shootouts with Uzi-toting drug runners, psychopathic serial killers, and organized-crime hit men. Occasionally, but not often, fictional patrol officers and detectives seem aware of departmental rules, legal decisions, citizen groups, civil suits, or physical danger. They are rarely faced with the economic necessity of moonlighting as security guards, caring about an annual pay raise, or griping when someone less deserving gets promoted ahead of them for political reasons.

How close is this portrayal of a selfless crime fighter to "real life"? Not very, according to most research efforts. Police officers are asked to deal with hundreds of incidents each year. For example, the Los Angeles Police Department's force of eighty-two hundred officers receives about 5 million calls for assistance each year; Houston's four thousand receive 2.4 million service calls annually.[2] This translates into fourteen thousand calls each day in Los Angeles and almost seven thousand in Houston. The Police Foundation's study of police in the nation's six largest cities found that in a given year, each police car in New York City is dispatched to an average of 2,900 service calls; in Philadelphia, each car goes to 2,566 calls.[3]

How many of these are directly related to enforcing laws? Most research efforts show that a police officer's crime-fighting efforts are only a small part of his or her overall activities. Studies of police work indicate that a significant portion of an officer's time is spent handling minor disturbances, service calls, and administrative duties. Studies conducted over the past two decades have found that social-service and administrative tasks consume more than half a police officer's time and account for more than half of his or her calls.[4] In contrast, crime-related calls fall in a range, depending on the department, of between 5 and 20 percent of a police officer's total activity.[5]

Law Enforcement Activity

These results are not surprising when UCR arrest data are considered: Each year, about six hundred thousand local, county, and state police officers make about

FIGURE 7.2
Annual Violent Crime and Property Crime Arrests Per Sworn Officer in the Nation's Six Largest Departments

SOURCE: Anthony Pate and Edwin Hamilton, *The Big Six, Policing America's Largest Cities* (Washington, D.C.: Police Foundation, 1990), pp. 129–30.

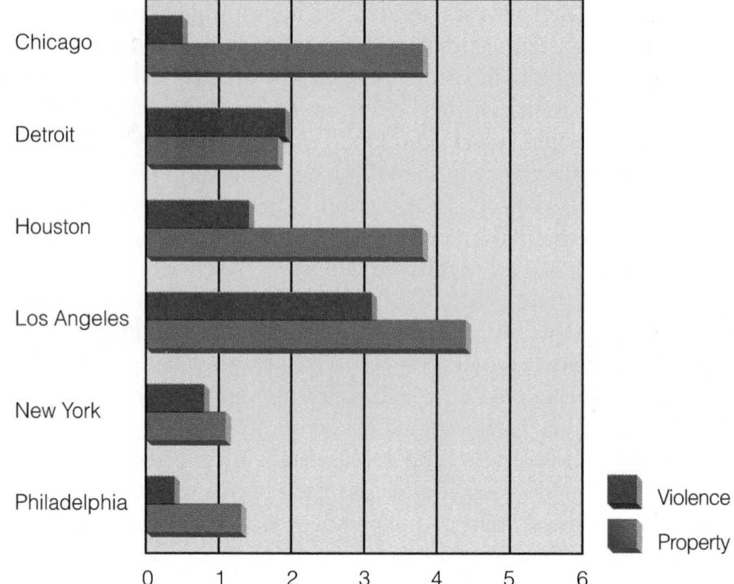

14 million arrests, or about twenty-three each.[6] Of these, about 3 million are for serious index crimes (Part I), or about five yearly per officer. Given an even distribution of arrests, it is evident that the average police officer is making two arrests per month and less than one felony arrest every two months. If the geographic distribution of crime is considered, urban police should make significantly more arrests than suburban or rural officers. Yet, a Police Foundation study indicates that police in the largest cities make between three and seven property and violent crime arrests per sworn officer each year (see Figure 7.2). These figures should be interpreted with caution, because not all police officers are engaged in activities that allow them to make arrests, such as patrol or detective work. As Figure 7.3 shows, between 17 and 32 percent of the sworn officers in the nation's largest police departments are in such units as communications, antiterrorism, administration, and personnel. Even if the number of arrests per officer were adjusted by 30 percent, it would still only amount to between five and nine arrests per year. So while police handle thousands of calls each year they may make only five or six criminal arrests.

The evidence, then, shows that the police role involves a preponderance of noncrime-related activities and is similar in both large and small departments. Although officers in large urban departments may be called on to handle more felony cases than those in small towns, they, too, like it or not, will probably find that the bulk of their daily activities are not crime-related. In the future, police officers will probably spend even more of their time learning to deal with the social problems exploding across the United States, ranging from women battered in domestic disputes to runaway children.[7] More attention will also be paid to **special-needs populations:** substance abusers; the homeless; the mentally ill; and runaways.[8] Unlike their fictional counterparts who arrest ten people per hour (and shoot about five), most police officers rarely spend their days directly fighting crime. The activities of most police departments are illustrated in Figure 7.1. As this figure shows, large metropolitan police departments carry out a wide variety of tasks and maintain a number of highly specialized roles. The most important of these, the patrol and investigation functions, are described below.

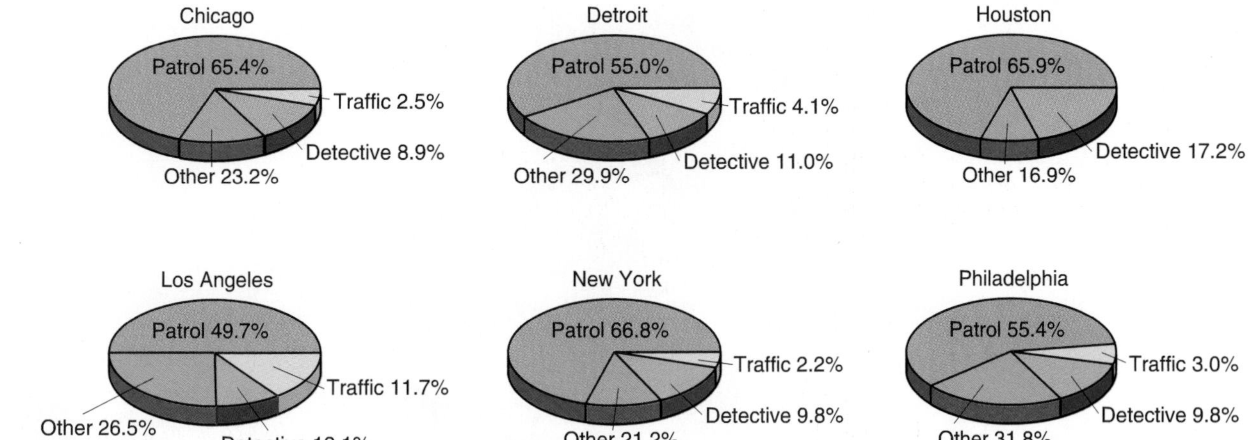

FIGURE 7.3
Sworn Police Personnel by Unit in the Nation's Six Largest Departments

SOURCE: Adapted from Anthony Pate and Edwin Hamilton, *The Big Six, Policing America's Largest Cities* (Washington, D.C.: Police Foundation, 1990), p. 60.

Patrol Function

Regardless of the style of policing employed, patrol officers are the backbone of the police department, usually accounting for about 60 percent of a department's personnel. Patrol officers are the most highly visible components of the entire criminal justice system. They are charged with supervising specific areas of their jurisdiction, called *beats*, whether on foot, in a patrol car, or by motorcycle, horse, helicopter, or even boat.[9] Each beat or patrol area is covered twenty-four hours a day by different shifts. The major purpose of patrol is to (1) deter crime by maintaining a visible police presence, (2) maintain public order (peacekeeping) within the patrol area, (3) enable the police department to respond quickly to law violations or other emergencies, (4) identify and apprehend law violators, (5) aid individuals and care for those who cannot help themselves, (6) facilitate the movement of traffic and people, and (7) create a feeling of security in the community.[10]

Patrol officers' responsibilities are immense; they may suddenly be faced with an angry mob, an armed felon, or a suicidal teenager and be forced to make split-second decisions on what action to take. At the same time, they must be sensitive to the needs of citizens who are often of diverse racial and ethnic backgrounds.

Patrol Activities

For many years, the major role of police patrol was considered law enforcement, but research conducted in the 1960s and 1970s showed that very little of a patrol officer's time was spent on crime-fighting duties. For example, Albert Reiss found that the typical tour of duty does not involve a single arrest.[11] Egon Bittner concluded that patrol officers average about one arrest per month and only three arrests for index crimes per year.[12] While arrests alone cannot be equated with law enforcement duties, they do give an indication of the activities of patrol officers. Most experts today agree that the great bulk of police patrol efforts is devoted to what has been described as **order maintenance or peacekeeping.**[13]

Police today are called upon to handle many different roles. Here a police officer conducts a crime prevention program in a grammar school class.

Order maintenance functions fall on the border between criminal and noncriminal behavior. The patrol officer's discretion often determines whether a noisy neighborhood dispute involves the crime of disturbing the peace or whether it can be controlled with street-corner diplomacy and the combatants sent on their way. Similarly, teenagers milling around in the shopping center parking lot can be brought in and turned over to the juvenile authorities or handled in a less formal and often more efficient manner.

James Q. Wilson's pioneering work *Varieties of Police Behavior* was one of the first to view the major role of police as "handling the situation." Wilson believed that police encounter many troubling incidents that need some sort of "fixing up." [14] Enforcing the law might be one tool a patrol officer uses; threat, coercion, sympathy, understanding, and apathy might be others. Most important is "keeping things under control so that there are no complaints that he is doing nothing or that he is doing too much." [15] This early research by Wilson led him to regard the real police role as community problem solvers.

Police officers, then, actually practice a policy of selective enforcement, concentrating on some crimes but handling the majority in an informal, noncriminal manner. A police officer is supposed to know when to take action and when not to, whom to arrest and who can be dealt with by issuing a warning or some other informal action. If a mistake is made, the officer can come under fire from his or her peers and superiors, as well as the general public. Consequently, the patrol officer's job is extremely demanding and often unrewarding and unappreciated. It is not surprising that the attitudes of police officers toward the public have been characterized by ambivalence, cynicism, and tension.[16]

Does Patrol Work?

For many years, preventive police patrol has been considered one of the greatest deterrents of criminal behavior. The visible presence of patrol cars on the street and the rapid deployment of police officers to the scene of a crime were viewed as particularly effective law enforcement techniques. However, research efforts have questioned the basic assumptions of patrol. The most widely heralded attempt at measuring patrol effectiveness was undertaken in Kansas City, Missouri, under sponsorship of the Police Foundation.[17]

To evaluate the effectiveness of patrol, fifteen separate police districts were divided into three groups; one group retained normal police patrol; the second ("proactive") set of districts were supplied with two to three times the normal amount of patrol forces; and the third ("reactive") group had its preventive patrol entirely eliminated and police officers responded only when summoned by citizens to the scene of a particular crime.

Data from the **Kansas City study** indicated that these variations in patrol techniques had little effect on the crime patterns in the fifteen districts. The presence or absence of patrol did not seem to affect residential or business burglaries, motor vehicle thefts, larcenies involving auto accessories, robberies, vandalism, or other criminal behavior.[18] Moreover, variations in police patrol techniques appeared to have little effect on citizens' attitudes toward the police, their satisfaction with police, or their fear of future criminal behavior.[19]

Proactive Patrol

The Kansas City project, though subject to criticism because of its research design, greatly influenced the way police experts viewed the effectiveness of patrol. Its rather lukewarm findings set the stage for community and problem-oriented policing models, which stress social service over crime deterrence (see later in this chapter).

While the mere presence of police may not be sufficient to deter crime, the manner in which they approach their task may make a difference. In an important paper, James Q. Wilson and Barbara Boland found that police departments that use a proactive, aggressive law enforcement style may help reduce crime rates. Jurisdictions that encourage patrol officers to stop motor vehicles to issue citations and to aggressively arrest and detain suspicious persons also experience lower crime rates than jurisdictions that do not follow such proactive policies.[20] In a more recent analysis of police activities in 171 U.S. cities, Robert Sampson and Jacqueline Cohen found that departments that more actively enforced disorderly conduct and traffic laws also experienced lower robbery rates.[21]

Pinpointing why proactive policing works so effectively is difficult. It may have a direct deterrent effect: aggressive policing increases community perception that police arrest a lot of criminals and that most violators get caught. Its effect may be indirect: aggressive police arrest more suspects and their subsequent conviction gets them off the street; fewer criminals produce lower crime rates.

Before a general policy of vigorous police work can be adopted, the downside of aggressive tactics must be considered. Proactive police strategies breed resentment in minority areas where citizens believe they are targets of police suspicion and reaction.[22] Evidence exists that such aggressive police tactics as stopping and frisking and rousting teenagers who congregate on street corners are the seeds from which racial conflict grows.[23] Despite such reservations, many large police jurisdictions have insisted that patrol officers become more aggressive and concentrate on investigating and deterring crimes.

In sum, while the Kansas City study questioned the value of police patrol as a crime deterrent, later research efforts raise the possibility that it may be a more effective, albeit socially costly, crime suppression mechanism than earlier thought.

Research indicates that aggressive patrol tactics may reduce crime rates.

Making Arrests

If the Kansas City study found that the mere presence of police patrol officers cannot reduce crime rates, what is the effect of formal police contact, such as an arrest? A number of experts have expressed doubt that formal police action can have any general deterrent effect, or, if it does, that it would be anything but short-lived and temporary.[24] However, research studies do show that contact with the police may cause some offenders to forgo repeat criminal behavior; formal police action, such as arrest, may have a specific deterrent function. In one study using data acquired in Scandinavia, Perry Shapiro and Harold Votey found that an arrest for drunk driving can actually reduce the probability of offender recidivism. An arrest apparently increases people's belief that they will be rearrested if they drink and drive and also heightens their perception of the unpleasantness associated with an arrest.[25] Similarly, Douglas Smith and Patrick Gartin's research shows that getting arrested reduces the likelihood that first time offenders will continue their criminal activity; repeaters also seem to reduce offending rates after an arrest.[26] Some evidence also exists that an increase in the arrest rate can help reduce an area's overall crime rate.[27]

Even if formal action does deter crime, police chiefs may find it difficult to convince patrol officers to make more arrests. Despite a departmental policy requiring officers to be more active, police officers may be reluctant to change their style and tactics.[28] Research efforts indicate that departmental directives to make more arrests may have relatively little effect on police behavior.[29] So influencing actual police activities in the field may prove a difficult task.

Controlling Domestic Violence

One of the most significant tests of the deterrent effect of police arrest was conducted in Minneapolis, Minnesota, by the research team of Lawrence Sherman and Bernard Berk.[30]

Sherman and Berk focused on the effect of arrest on domestic violence cases. These cases are particularly vexing for police administrators because they typically involve repeat incidents and situations to which it is difficult for the officer on the scene to respond effectively.

To test the most appropriate response, Sherman and Berk had police officers randomly assign treatments to the domestic assault cases they encountered on their beat. One approach was to give some sort of advice and mediation; another was to send the assailant from the home for a period of eight hours; and the third was to arrest the assailant.

The data indicated that when police took formal action (arrest), the chance of recidivism was substantially less than when they took less punitive measures, such as warning offenders or ordering them out of the house for a cooling-off period. A six-month follow-up found that only 10 percent of those who were arrested repeated their violent behavior, while 19 percent of those advised and 24 percent of those sent away repeated their offenses.

To supplement the official police data, Sherman and Berk also interviewed 205 of the victims. The victims also reported that an arrest had the greatest benefit in controlling domestic assaults. While 19 percent of the women whose men were arrested reported their mates had assaulted them, 37 percent of those whose mates were advised and 33 percent of those whose mates were sent away reported further assaults. If, in addition to arresting the assailant, the police also took the time to listen to the victim, the reported assault rate declined to 9 percent. These results were only for nonlethal misdemeanor assault cases and did not include life-threatening situations. In sum, Sherman and Berk found that a formal arrest was the most effective means of controlling domestic violence, regardless of what happened to the offender in court.[31]

The Minneapolis experiment has deeply affected police operations. The data suggested that actual contact with police and their use of formal actions may have a special deterrent effect on future crime. Not surprisingly, Atlanta, Chicago, Dallas, Denver, Detroit, New York, Miami, San Francisco, and Seattle, among other large cities, have adopted policies encouraging arrests in domestic violence cases.

Though the findings of the Minneapolis experiment received quick acceptance, government-funded research replicating the experimental design in other locales, including Omaha, Nebraska, and Charlotte, North Carolina, has so far failed to duplicate them; in these locales, formal arrest was not a greater deterrent to domestic abuse than warning or advising the assailant.[32] There are also indications that police officers in Minneapolis failed to assign cases randomly, which altered the experimental findings.[33]

Nevertheless, there are indications that police actions can in fact deter domestic abuse. More recent research by Lawrence Sherman and his associates in Milwaukee found that the specific deterrent effect of arrest may be a much more complex phenomenon than previously thought. Among the factors that influence deterrence are the personal characteristics and background of suspects and the amount of time they spend in detention after arrest.[34] A short-term arrest (custody lasting about three hours) has a different impact, and may actually be more effective, than an arrest followed by a longer period of detention (about twelve hours). Sherman and his associates found that a significant deterrent effect may be produced by a short-term arrest that then decays over time. Measurements taken one year after the initial experiment, however, also indicate that while initially a deterrent, short-term arrests may in the long-run escalate the frequency of repeat domestic violence.[35]

In a similar fashion, Franklyn Dunford reevaluated domestic abuse cases in Omaha in which the offender was *not* on the scene when officers arrived. Offender-absent cases in which probable cause to arrest existed were randomly assigned to warrant and nonwarrant groups. In the former, the police automatically had a warrant issued, while in the latter, they advised the victims of their right to apply for a warrant through the prosecutor's office. Dunford found that the automatic issuance of a warrant had a significant short- and long-term deterrent effect on domestic violence.[36]

Explaining why the initial deterrent effect of arrest decays over time is difficult. It is possible that offenders who suffer arrest are initially fearful of punishment but eventually replace fear with anger and violent intent toward their mate when their case does not result in severe punishment. Another possibility is that the true recidivism rate is hidden from researchers. Victims of domestic abuse, realizing that an initial call to the police produced an arrest but not much else, may be reluctant to make subsequent calls for service or even discuss their predicament with evaluators.[37] Arrests also do little to redress the underlying cause of domestic abuse. Michael Steinman has found that formal police action coupled with coordinated treatment efforts may significantly impact domestic abuse recidivism rates.[38]

While much research is being conducted, more is needed to determine the true nature of this complex phenomenon.

Does Increasing Resources Help?

One reason patrol activity may be less effective than desired is the lack of adequate resources. Does adding more police help bring the crime rate down? Craig Uchida and Robert Goldberg compared police expenditures in eighty-eight U.S. cities between 1938 and 1982 and found that cities with the highest crime rates also spent the most on police services; adding police officers had little effect on the crime rate.[39] Other research efforts have found that the actual number of law enforcement officers in a jurisdiction has little effect on area crimes.[40]

Adding resources may not bring the crime rate down, but it may improve the overall effectiveness of the justice system. A recent Rand Corporation study looked at reasons for case attrition between arrest and trial. As you may recall from Chapter 1, up to half of all criminal cases are dropped by prosecutors before trial. The Rand team found that communities with relatively high crime rates that devoted fewer resources to police had high case attrition rates.[41] It is possible that overworked police in high-crime areas may be processing cases with little hope of prosecution in order to give the public the message that they are trying "to do something." Adding resources, in this instance, could possibly improve the quality of police arrests.

Investigation Function

Since the first independent detective bureau was established by the London Metropolitan Police in 1841,[42] criminal investigators have been romantic figures vividly portrayed in novels, movies, including *Beverly Hills Cop,* the *Dirty Harry* series, and television shows such as "Columbo," "Hill Street Blues" and "Law and Order." The fictional police detective is usually depicted as a loner, willing to break departmental rules, perhaps even violate the law, in order to capture the suspect. The average fictional detective views departmental policies and U.S. Supreme Court decisions as unfortunate roadblocks to police efficiency. Civil rights are either ignored or actively scorned.[43]

Although every police department probably has a few "hell-bent for leather" detectives who take matters into their own hands at the expense of citizens' rights, the modern criminal investigator is most likely an experienced civil servant, trained in investigatory techniques, knowledgeable about legal rules of evidence and procedure, and at least somewhat cautious about the legal and administrative consequences of his or her actions.[44] Though detectives are often handicapped by limited time, money, and resources, they are certainly aware of how their actions will one day be interpreted in a court of law. Police investigators are sometimes accused of being more concerned with the most recent court cases regarding search and seizure and custody interrogation than they are with engaging in shootouts with suspected felons.

Detectives are probably the elite of the police force: they are usually paid more than patrol officers, engage in interesting tasks, wear civilian clothes, and are subject to a less stringent departmental control than patrol officers.[45]

Detectives investigate the causes of crime and attempt to identify the individuals or groups responsible for committing particular offenses. They may enter a case after patrol officers made the initial contact, such as when a patrol car interrupts a crime in progress and the offenders flee before they can be apprehended. They can investigate a case entirely on their own, sometimes by following up on leads provided by informants.

Detective divisions are typically organized into sections or bureaus, such as homicide, robbery, or rape. Some jurisdictions maintain morals or vice squads, which are usually staffed by plainclothes officers and/or detectives specializing in victimless crimes, such as prostitution or gambling. In this latter capacity, **vice squad** officers may set themselves up as customers for illicit activities in order to make arrests. For example, undercover detectives may frequent public men's rooms and make advances toward entering men; those who respond are arrested for homosexual soliciting. In other instances, female police officers may pose as prostitutes. These covert police activities have often been criticized as violating the personal rights of citizens, and their appropriateness and fairness have been questioned.

James Q. Wilson described the function of investigation as containing four separate types of action:

> In the first [case], a suspect has been apprehended, or a subject placed under control and there is adequate information about the person's behavior.
>
> In the second case, there is reliable information that a crime has been committed, but the suspect has not been identified, or if identified, not apprehended. . . . This is the classic problem of **detection:** to discover reliable information that will permit the identification and arrest of a perpetrator.
>
> In the third case, a suspect or subject may be known or even under continuous observation or control, but there is no reliable or adequate information about this person's past behavior, present connections, or future intentions. . . . This case is to be distinguished from the preceding one by noting that the investigators are not reacting to the fact that a crime has been committed but are hoping to discover a crime that can implicate a targeted individual or his confederates.
>
> The final case involves the absence of both an identified subject and adequate information. Nonetheless, there are reasons, ranging from a hunch to the tips of untested informants to the implications of other investigative reports, that "something may be up" or something bears watching.[46]

Within the framework described above, the detective branch maintains discretion over the amount and intensity of effort put into each case.

Effectiveness of Investigation

Serious criticism has been leveled at the nation's detective forces for being bogged down in paperwork and relatively inefficient in clearing cases. In 1975, a study conducted by the Rand Corporation of 153 detective bureaus found that a great deal of a detective's time was spent in nonproductive work and that investigative expertise did little to solve cases; the Rand researchers estimated that half of all detectives could be replaced without negatively influencing crime-clearance rates.[47] The Rand survey's findings were duplicated in a study of detective work by Mark Willman and John Snortum, who found in an analysis of 5,336 cases reported to a suburban police department that the majority of cases were solved when the perpetrator was identified at the scene of the crime and that scientific detective work was rarely called for; the researchers did conclude that detectives do make a valuable contribution to police work because their skilled interrogation and case-processing techniques are essential to eventual criminal conviction.[48]

The effectiveness of detectives is also questioned by data gathered by the Police Executive Research Forum (PERF), which disclosed that if a crime is reported while in progress, the police have about a 33 percent chance of making an arrest; the arrest probability declines to about 10 percent if the crime is reported one minute later and to 5 percent if more than fifteen minutes have elapsed before the crime is reported. Also, as time elapses between the crime and the arrest, the chances of a conviction are reduced, probably because the ability to recover evidence is lost. Put another way, once a crime has been completed and the investigation is put in the hands of detectives, the chances of identifying and arresting the perpetrator diminish rapidly.[49]

Improving Investigation Effectiveness

A number of efforts have been made to revamp and improve investigation procedures. One practice has been to give patrol officers greater responsibility to conduct preliminary investigations at the scene of the crime. In addition, the old-fashioned precinct detective has been replaced by specialized units, such as homicide or burglary squads, that operate over larger areas and can bring specific expertise to bear. Technological advances in DNA and fingerprint identification have also aided investigation effectiveness.

Another approach is suggested by data gathered by researchers at the Police Executive Research Forum on 3,360 burglary and 320 robbery cases committed in DeKalb County, Georgia; St. Petersburg, Florida; and Wichita, Kansas. The data included a wide range of information on the crime, the investigation, and the outcome of the investigation. The research contained a number of key findings:

- Unsolved Cases: Almost 50 percent of the burglary cases were screened out before assignment to a detective for a follow-up investigation. Of those assigned, 75 percent were dropped after the first day of the follow-up investigation. While all robbery cases were assigned to detectives, 75 percent of them were also dropped after one day of investigation.
- Length of Investigation: The vast majority of cases were investigated for no more than four hours stretching over a three-day period. An average of eleven

Sophisticated computer identification systems help witnesses identify suspects from a few facial features. Such technological advances should improve the quality of investigation.

days elapsed between the initial report of a crime and the suspension of the investigation.

- Sources of Information: Early in an investigation, the focus is on the victim; as the investigation is pursued, emphasis is shifted to the suspect. The most critical information for determining case outcome is the name and description of the suspect and related crime information. Victims are most often the source of information; unfortunately, witnesses, informants, and members of the police department are consulted far less often. However, when these sources are tapped, they are likely to produce useful information.
- Effectiveness: Preliminary investigations by patrol officers and follow-ups by detectives are equally important for solving crimes. Even in situations where the preliminary investigation by patrol officers did not develop information on the suspect, detectives were able to make an identification in about 14 percent of the cases and make an arrest in 8 percent.[50]

Unlike earlier studies, the PERF research found that detectives do make a meaningful contribution to the solution of criminal cases. To improve investigatory effectiveness, PERF recommends that greater emphasis be placed on collecting physical evidence at the scene of the crime, identifying witnesses, checking departmental records, and using informants. The probability of successfully settling a case is improved if patrol officers carefully gather evidence at the scene of a crime and effectively communicate it to detectives working the case. Moreover, police managers should pay more attention to screening cases, monitoring case flow and activity, and creating productivity measures to make sure individual detectives and detective units are meeting their goals. Also recommended is the use of targeted investigations that direct attention at a few individuals, such as career criminals, who are known to have engaged in the behavior under investigation.

ANALYZING CRIMINAL JUSTICE ISSUES

Undercover Work

One police investigation technique that has widespread notoriety is undercover work. According to sociologist Gary Marx, undercover work can take a number of forms. A lone agent can infiltrate a criminal group or organization in order to gather information on future criminal activity. For example, a DEA agent may go undercover in order to gather intelligence on drug smugglers. Undercover officers can also pose as victims in order to capture predatory criminals who have been conducting street robberies and muggings.

Another approach to undercover work, commonly referred to as **sting operations,** involves organized groups of detectives who deceive criminals into openly committing illegal acts or conspiring to engage in criminal activity. Numerous sting operations have been aimed at capturing professional thieves and seizing stolen merchandise. Undercover detectives pose as fences, set up ongoing fencing operations, and encourage thieves interested in selling stolen merchandise. Transactions are videotaped to provide prosecutors with strong cases. Sting operations have netted millions of dollars in recovered property and resulted in the arrests of many criminals. While these results seem impressive, Robert Langworthy's sophisticated analysis of sting operations in Birmingham, Alabama, failed to show that they are an effective crime deterrent (though they do meet with public approval and improve community relations).

While undercover work can be vital to police operations, it is not without its drawbacks. By its very nature, it involves deceit by police agents that often comes close to being entrapment. Sting operations may encourage criminals to commit new crimes because they have a new source for fencing stolen goods. Innocent people may hurt their reputations by buying merchandise from a sting operation when they had no idea the items had been stolen.

In 1992 the Supreme Court recognized the dangers of over-zealous sting operations in the case of *Jacobson v. U.S.* Jacobson's name was on a list of subscribers to pornographic material because he had legally ordered sexually explicit magazines. After obtaining the list, two Federal government agencies sent mail to him through a fictitious organization which promoted sexual freedom and claimed to be against censorship. After two-and-one-half years of mailings, Jacobson was sent a letter that described censorship as nonsense. When he responded he received a catalog from which he ordered a magazine depicting young boys engaged in sexual activities. He was arrested for and convicted on charges that he violated the Child Protection Act of 1984 which made the receipt through the mails of sexually explicit depictions of children illegal.

In its ruling the Court held that the Government's two-and-one-half year campaign to interest Jacobson in pornography amounted to illegal entrapment against a person who was not originally disposed to commit a criminal act. The fact that Jacobson had previously ordered child pornography merely showed that he was inclined toward certain acts within a broad range of behavior, but was not sufficient to indicate specific criminal tendencies. By their long term campaign, government investigators had pressured him to obtain and read illegal material in order to fight censorship and maintain individual rights. The *Jacobson* case is important because it mandates that sting operations cannot entrap otherwise law-abiding citizens to commit crimes they might not have perpetrated had not law enforcement agents applied pressure or even interested them in criminal behavior.

Undercover work also endangers the police agent. Police officers may

Changing Concepts of Policing

Many police officers feel unappreciated by the public they serve, which may be due to the underlying conflicts inherent in the police role. Police may want to be **proactive** crime fighters who initiate actions against law violators; yet most remain **reactive,** responding when a citizen calls for service. The desire for direct action is often blunted because police are expected to perform many civic duties that in earlier times were the responsibility of every citizen: keeping the peace; performing emergency medical care; dealing with family problems; helping during civil emergencies. While most of us agree that a neighborhood brawl must be stopped, that shelter must be found for the homeless, and that the inebriate taken

be forced to engage in illegal or immoral behavior to maintain their cover. They also face significant physical danger in playing the role of a criminal and dealing with mobsters, terrorists, and drug dealers. In far too many cases, undercover officers are mistaken for real criminals and injured by other law enforcement officers or private citizens trying to stop a crime. Arrest situations involving undercover officers may also provoke violence when suspects do not realize they are in the presence of police and therefore violently resist arrest.

Undercover officers also experience psychological problems. Being away from home, keeping late hours, and always worrying that their identity will be uncovered all create enormous stress. Officers have experienced postundercover stress resulting in trouble at work and, in many instances, ruined marriages and botched prosecutions. Some have even turned to crime themselves.

The FBI is taking this problem quite seriously and now monitors undercover work very closely. Veteran agents interview former undercover agents four to six months after they have left the field to monitor for such stress-related trouble. The bureau also has retained a team of psychologists to deal with the problem.

Examples of undercover officers who succumbed to the stress of their work are legion. FBI agent Dan Mitrione got so caught up in his undercover drug dealing that he took $850,000 in drug profits for himself. Robert Delaney, a New Jersey state police officer, got so involved in his role as "Robert Alan Covert," a fence, that he could not shake his underground identity. His private life suffered as he reverted to the life-style of the mobster that he had successfully adopted for two years. And Patrick Livingstone, who participated in the pornography business for nearly three years under the alias "Pat Salamone," continued to visit his old bars, bookmakers, and criminal associates after the investigation he conducted was over. He maintained a bank account and a driver's license in his alias's name and was happy to be known as Pat Salamone. When he was arrested for shoplifting, defense attorneys working for the pornographers he helped identify used his tainted character to get some charges against their clients dismissed.

Despite its glamour, undercover work has many drawbacks. Sting operations have been criticized for encouraging people to commit crime. By putting the government in the fencing business, such operations blur the line between law enforcement and criminal activity. Undercover work also places serious and potentially fatal stress on detectives. Nonetheless, the FBI reports that as many as six hundred agents are on a waiting list to be placed undercover.

Critical Thinking Skills

1. Undercover work involves police officers on the fringe of criminal activity. Even if sting operations result in arrests, do their social costs outweigh the law enforcement benefits? Would a sting operation encourage local people to get involved in crimes they might have avoided because they now have a convenient place to fence stolen goods? Might not the presence of an undercover agent encourage crime because a new, enthusiastic criminal agent is on the scene?

SOURCES: *Jacobson v. United States,* 60 WSLW 4307 (1992); Robert Langworthy, "Do Stings Control Crime? An Evaluation of a Police Fencing Operation," *Justice Quarterly* 6 (1989):27–45; Gary Marx, *Undercover, Police Surveillance in America* (Berkeley, Calif.: University of California Press, 1988); Anthony DeStefano, "Undercover Jobs Carry Big Psychological Risk after the Assignment," *Wall Street Journal,* 4 November 1985, p. 1.

safely home, few of us want to personally jump into the fray; we would rather call the cops. The police officer has become a "social handyman" called in to fix up problems that the average citizen wishes would simply go away. As sociologist Egon Bittner argues, police work has, from its earliest origins, been a "tainted occupation":

> The taint that attaches to police work refers to the fact that policemen are viewed as the fire it takes to fight fire, that in the natural course of their duties they inflict harm, albeit deserved, and that their very existence attests that the nobler aspirations of mankind do not contain the means necessary to insure survival.[51]

Note how Bittner identifies the inherent role conflict faced by the modern police officer. The public needs the police to perform those duties that the average citizen finds distasteful or dangerous, for example, breaking up a domestic quarrel. At the same time, the public resents the power the police have to use force, to arrest people, and to deny people their vices. Put another way, the average citizen wants the police to crack down on undesirable members of society while excluding his or her own behavior from legal scrutiny.

Because of these natural role conflicts, the relationship between the police and the public has been the subject of a great deal of concern. As you may recall, the respect Americans have for police effectiveness, courtesy, honesty, and conduct seems to be dwindling. Citizens may be less likely to go to police for help, to report crimes, to step forward as witnesses, or to cooperate with and aid police. Victim surveys indicate that many citizens have so little faith in the police that they will not report even serious crimes, such as rape or burglary. In some communities, citizen self-help groups have sprung up to supplement police protection.[52] In return, police officers often feel ambivalent and uncertain about the public they are sworn to protect.

Because of this ambivalence and role conflict, more communities are adapting new models of policing that reflect the changing role of the police. Some administrators now recognize that police officers are better equipped to be civic problem solvers than effective crime fighters. Rather than ignore, deny, or fight this reality, police departments are being reorganized to maximize their strengths and minimize their weaknesses. What has emerged is the community policing movement, a new concept of policing designed to bridge the gulf between police agencies and the communities they serve.

Community Policing

A quiet revolution is reshaping American policing.[53]

Police agencies have been trying to gain the cooperation and respect of the community they serve for more than thirty years. At first, efforts at improving the relationships between police departments and the public involved programs with the general title of **police-community relations (PCR).** These initial PCR programs were developed at the station house and departmental levels and designed to make citizens more aware of police activities, alert them to methods of self-protection, and improve general attitudes toward policing. In the socially turbulent 1960s, many larger departments instituted specialized PCR units, while others pursued improving relations through specialized programs, such as neighborhood watch groups, which instructed citizens in home security measures and enlisted their assistance in watching neighbor's homes. Operation ID, first implemented in Monterey Park, California, in 1963, had police officers passing out engraving tools with which citizens could mark their valuables for easy identification if they were stolen and tags to be placed on the front of a home alerting potential thieves that the valuables inside had been marked. Other early PCR programs were crime prevention clinics, citizen's police alert programs, and similar efforts to help citizens identify suspicious characters in their neighborhoods.

To some observers, these efforts could be classified as noble failures. PCR programs were criticized for their "Band-Aid" approach to overwhelming social problems; little evidence existed that they either improved police effectiveness or raised citizen evaluation of police departments. Coupled with the less than overwhelming success of local police agencies in bringing the crime rate down, the inability to attract citizen cooperation troubled many police leaders. Many of these programs remain in operation, though fiscal belt-tightening in the 1990s threatens their existence.[54]

Team Policing. One important effort in the 1970s to change the police role was the development of **team policing** models, which took aim at the on-going conflict between community residents and police departments.

The teams were semiautonomous units that had jurisdiction over particular neighborhoods. Each team was responsible for distributing police services in the community and coordinating activities with neighborhood groups. Team officers appeared at local group meetings and offered advice on crime prevention. Decision making was decentralized so that teams could easily respond to neighborhood problems. Some teams employed proactive policing techniques, identifying community problems and designing strategies to eliminate them.

Team policing models eventually were discontinued. Evaluations failed to show they effectively cut the crime rate or reduced the fear of crime. Officers assigned to teams developed morale problems because they felt they were being overlooked for promotions and honors. Team policing was also opposed by conservative police managers who considered decentralized decision making a threat to their traditional authority. Some teams were led by officers holding the rank of lieutenant or sergeant, and granting decision-making power to the lower ranks irritated autocratic police managers.[55]

"Broken Windows." The second wave of efforts to reacquaint police departments with the community they serve began a decade ago. In a critical 1982 paper, two justice policy experts, George Kelling and James Q. Wilson, articulated a new approach to improving police relations in the community that has come to be known as the **"broken windows"** model.[56] Kelling and Wilson made three points:

1. Neighborhood disorder creates fear. Urban areas filled with street people, youth gangs, prostitutes, and the mentally disturbed are the ones most likely to maintain a high degree of crime.
2. Neighborhoods give out crime-promoting signals. A neighborhood filled with deteriorated housing, unrepaired broken windows, and untended disorderly behavior gives out crime-promoting signals. Honest citizens live in fear in these areas, and predatory criminals are attracted to them.
3. Police need citizens' cooperation. If police are to reduce fear and successfully combat crime in these urban areas, they must have the cooperation, support, and assistance of the citizens.

According to Kelling and Wilson, community relations and crime control effectiveness cannot be the province of a few specialized units housed within a traditional police department. Instead, they argue, the core police role must be altered if community involvement is to be won and maintained. To accomplish this goal, urban police departments should return to an earlier style of policing in which officers on the beat had intimate contact with the people they served.

Police departments must totally alter their crime control strategy. Modern police departments generally rely on motorized patrol to cover wide areas, to maintain a visible police presence, and to ensure rapid response time. While effective and economical, the patrol car removes officers from the mainstream of the community, alienating people who might otherwise be potential sources of information and help to the police.

According to the community policing concept, broken windows give out crime promoting signals.

According to the "broken windows" approach, police administrators would be well served by deploying their forces where they can encourage public confidence, strengthen feelings of safety, and elicit cooperation from citizens. Community preservation, public safety, and order maintenance—not crime fighting—should become the primary focus of patrol. Put another way, just as physicians and dentists practice preventive medicine and dentistry, police should help maintain an intact community structure, rather than simply fight crime.

Community Policing in Action

The community policing concept was implemented through a number of innovative demonstration projects.[57] Among the most publicized were experiments in **foot patrol,** which took officers out of cars and into walking beats in the neighborhood. Foot patrol efforts were aimed at forming a bond with community residents by acquainting them with the individual officers who patroled their neighborhood, letting them know that police were caring and available. The first foot patrol experiments were conducted in cities in Michigan and New Jersey. An evaluation of foot patrol conducted by the Police Foundation focused on efforts in twenty-seven New Jersey cities, with special emphasis on Newark and Elizabeth.[58] Evaluations indicated that while foot patrol efforts did not bring the crime rate down, residents in areas where foot patrol was added perceived greater safety and were less afraid of crime. Though foot patrol did not deter crime per se, it helped citizens improve their attitudes toward the police.

Similar results came out of the well-documented Flint, Michigan, foot patrol experiment.[59] This carefully monitored study evaluated the effects of community policing in fourteen areas of Flint that included about 20 percent of the city's population. The Flint experiment yielded data indicating that foot patrol, as a supplement to motor patrol, can increase both citizen cooperation and police officer job satisfaction, while at the same time reducing calls for service and the need for assistance. Since the advent of these programs, hundreds of communities have adopted innovative forms of nonmotorized patrol (including bicycle patrols) that show early signs of success.[60]

soon as possible. As a result, police provide superficial relief; they do not solve problems, they attempt to cope with tough situations.[71]

In contrast, the core of problem-oriented policing is a proactive orientation. As spelled out by Herman Goldstein, problem-oriented police strategies require police agencies to identify particular long-term community problems—street level drug dealers, prostitution rings, gang hangouts—and develop strategies to eliminate them.[72] As in community policing, being problem solvers requires that police departments rely on local residents and private resources. This means that police managers must learn how to develop community resources, design cost-efficient and effective solutions to problems, and become advocates as well as agents of reform.[73]

Problem-oriented policing models are supported by pioneering research efforts that showed that a great deal of urban crime is concentrated in a few "hot spots." [74] Lawrence Sherman, Patrick Gartin, and Michael Buerger found that a significant portion of all police calls in Minneapolis emanated from a relatively few locations: bars, malls, the bus depot, hotels, certain apartment buildings.[75] By implication, concentrating police resources on these **hot spots of crime** could appreciably reduce crime.[76]

While the new community police models are essentially problem-oriented, problem-oriented strategies can be developed within traditional police organizations.[77] One of the first evaluations of this approach conducted by police in Newport News, Virginia, found that it was effective in reducing theft from cars, problems associated with prostitution, and household burglaries.[78] In Madison, Wisconsin, police focused on people who were disrupting shoppers in a downtown mall. Discovering that many of these people were already involved in counseling programs, police worked with mental health authorities to tighten client supervision, and mall security improved.[79]

A more elaborate model was Operation Pressure Point, a massive police initiative in which an additional 240 officers were dispatched to a high-drug use area on the lower east side of New York. The program combined aggressive law enforcement tactics, including the arrest and detention of all suspects and undercover surveillance work. Enforcement strategies were combined with community organization programs designed to strengthen neighborhood structure and increase resident support for police operations. An impressive review of Operation Pressure Point by Lynn Zimmer found that it successfully reduced drug trafficking in the area while reviving community spirit.[80] But, as Zimmer warns, the success of street-level problem-solving efforts must be interpreted with caution. It is possible that the criminals will be displaced to other, "safer" areas of the city and will return shortly after the program is called a success and the additional police forces pulled from the area.[81]

In Baltimore County, Maryland, a problem-oriented unit was formed which operated on the individual and neighborhood level. The Citizen-Oriented Police Enforcement (COPE) teams developed their own plan of action to reduce fear caused by violent crime. In one instance, an elderly woman was seriously beaten. Though she could identify her assailants, fear drove her to move from the community, rather than seek justice. COPE officers conducted a community meeting and found that the culprits were a band of teenage burglars who had invaded the area through a hole in a fence. The COPE team responded to the environmental problem by fixing the fence and installing lights to discourage congregating teenagers. They convinced the woman to testify, even providing a van to transport neighborhood supporters to and from the trial. The result: the victim moved back, reported crime was reduced, and respect for police increased.[82]

As the name suggests, problem-oriented policing programs focus on area problems that in the long run can produce crime. For example, as described in Chapter 5, police are attacking the problem of adolescent drug abuse by actively participating in drug education programs such as DARE. Problem-oriented programs cannot be evaluated on the basis of how many criminals were apprehended or crimes solved by a rapid police response but only on the basis of reduced community fear, marshalled community resources, and long-term change.

Problems of Community Policing

The core concepts of police work are changing as administrators recognize its limitations and realities in modern society. The oft-repeated charge that police catch relatively few criminals and have little deterrent effect has had a tremendous influence on police policy. On the one hand, many departments are experimenting with programs designed to bring police officers into closer contact with the community to increase citizen cooperation in the fight against crime. Major cities such as New York have made implementing community policing models a priority.

On the other hand, community policing is not without its critics. Jack Greene, for example, has argued that the most significant problem in designing community policing strategies is accurately defining *community*. Greene finds that in most community policing projects, the concept of community is defined in terms of administrative areas that are convenient for police administrators and correspond to existing patrol areas. Police departments rarely identify a *community* in terms of an ecological area defined by common norms, shared values, and interpersonal bonds.[83] According to Greene, correcting this oversight is vital to the future success of community policing. After all, the main focus of community policing is to activate the community norms that make neighborhoods more crime-resistant. To do so requires a greater identification with ecological areas: if community policing projects cross the boundaries of many different neighborhoods, any hope of learning and accessing community norms, strengths, and standards will be lost. Research by Roger Dunham and Geoffrey Alpert shows that residents of different neighborhoods have distinct views of the police role and that no single approach to community policing can possibly be correct for all areas.[84]

In addition to the need to understand and identify actual community areas, police departments must also establish the exact role of community police agents. How should they integrate their activities with those of regular patrol forces? For example, should foot patrols have primary responsibility for policing in an area, or should they coordinate their activities with officers assigned to patrol cars? Should community police officers be solely problem identifiers and neighborhood organizers, or should they also be expected to be law enforcement agents who get to the crime scene rapidly and later do investigative work? Can community police teams and regular patrols work together, or must a department abandon traditional police roles and become purely community policing-oriented?

Community policing activists also assume that citizens actually *want* increased police presence in their neighborhoods. This assumption ignores the fact that the same citizens who fear crime may also fear the police.[85] A victim callback program of the Houston police department, originally designed to provide aid and support for victims, was found to have a generally negative effect on some minority groups (Asians and Hispanics) whose members may have been suspicious of the police department's intentions.[86] A similar program in Detroit also met with suspicion and generated disappointing results.[87]

On the other side, police officers have learned to distrust the general public. Police have often been described as being isolated from and suspicious of the people they serve.[88] Since the community policing model calls for a revision of the police role from law enforcer to community organizer, police training must now be revised to reflect this new mandate. Mid-level managers must be recruited and trained who are receptive to and can implement community-change strategies.[89] If community policing is to be adopted on a wide scale, a whole new type of police officer must be recruited and trained in a whole new way.

Support Functions

As the model of a typical police department in Figure 7.1 indicates, not all members of a police department engage in what the general public regards as "real police work"—patrol, detection, and traffic control. Even in departments that are embracing community- and problem-oriented policing, a large part of police resources is actually devoted to support and administrative functions. While there are too many tasks to mention all in detail, the most important include the following:

Personnel. Many police departments maintain their own personnel service, which carries out such functions as recruiting new police officers, creating exams to determine the most qualified applicants, and handling promotions and transfers. Later in this chapter, we will discuss in more detail the specific problems and issues associated with the complex task of creating adequate entrance exams.

Internal Affairs. Larger police departments often maintain an internal affairs branch, which is charged with policing the police. Internal affairs officers process citizen complaints of police corruption, investigate what may be the unnecessary use of force by police officers, and even probe police participation in actual criminal activity, such as burglaries or narcotics violations. In addition, internal affairs divisions may assist police management personnel when disciplinary action is brought against individual officers.

Internal affairs is a controversial function since investigators are feared and distrusted by fellow police officers. Nonetheless, rigorous self-scrutiny is the only way police departments can earn the respect of citizens.

Budget and Finance. Most police departments are responsible for the administration and control of their own budgets. This task includes administering payroll, purchasing equipment and services, planning budgets for future expenditures, and auditing departmental financial records.

In smaller police departments, police chiefs and other officers in charge of budgetary considerations often lack the requisite skills to manage finances accurately and effectively. Recently, police managers seeking to maximize the growth and efficiency of their departments have turned to a planning-programming budgeting system (PPBS) to improve their financial operations. This new method requires police administrators to identify goals and objectives by systematically allotting available funding to them.[90] The use of PPBS and similar modern management techniques may significantly improve police operations during the coming decade.

Records and Communication. Police departments maintain separate units that are charged with maintaining and disseminating information on wanted offenders, stolen merchandise, traffic violators, and so on. Modern data management systems enable police to use their records in a highly sophisticated fashion. For example, officers in a patrol car who spot a suspicious-looking vehicle can instantly receive a computer-based rundown on whether it has been stolen, or if property is recovered during an arrest, police using this sort of system can determine who reported the loss of the merchandise and arrange for its return.

Another important function of police communication is the effective and efficient dispatching of patrol cars. Again, modern computer technologies have been used to make the most of available resources. For example, most large cities now use the computer-assisted 911 emergency number.[91]

Training. In many departments, training is continuous throughout an officer's career. Training usually begins at a police academy, which may be run exclusively for larger departments or be part of a regional training center servicing smaller and varied governmental units. About 92 percent of all police departments require preservice training, including almost all departments in larger cities (population over one hundred thousand). The average officer receives about 543 hours of preservice training, including 402 in the classroom and 141 in the field. Police in large cities receive over one thousand hours of instruction divided almost evenly between classroom and field instruction.[92] Among the topics usually covered are law and civil rights, firearms handling, emergency medical care, and restraint techniques. One recent survey found that the typical state police officer spends about twenty weeks and municipal officers, eighteen weeks in a training academy.[93]

After assuming their police duties, new recruits are assigned to field-training officers who break them in on the job. However, training does not stop here. On-the-job training is a continuous process in the modern police department and includes such areas as weapons skills, first aid, crowd control, and community relations. Some departments use **roll call training,** in which superior officers or outside experts address police officers at the beginning of the workday. Other departments allow police officers time off to attend annual training sessions to sharpen their skills and learn new policing techniques.

The amount and nature of police training vary widely. Most training programs stress the nuts-and-bolts technical aspects of police work, such as weapons handling, criminal law, and patrol procedures. Some departments have included community relations, sensitivity training, emergency medical training, and minimizing the use of deadly force in their curriculum.

Community Relations. Police departments provide emergency aid to the ill, counsel youngsters, speak to school and community agencies on safety and drug abuse, and provide countless other services designed to improve citizen-police interactions.

Crime Prevention. Larger police departments maintain specialized units that help citizens to protect themselves from criminal activity. For example, they advise citizens on effective home security techniques or conduct Project ID campaigns—engraving valuables with an identifying number so that they can be returned if recovered after a burglary.

Laboratory. Police agencies maintain (or have access to) forensic laboratories that enable them to identify substances to be used as evidence and classify fingerprints.

Planning and Research. Planning and research functions include designing programs to increase police efficiency and strategies to test program effectiveness. Police planners monitor recent technological developments and institute programs to adapt them to police services.

Property. Police handle evidence such as weapons and narcotics seized during investigations; hold recovered stolen property; maintain prisoners' personal effects, lost property, and abandoned or towed motor vehicles.

Detention. Police stations maintain detention facilities for the temporary custody of suspects after their arrest.

Issues in Police Administration and Management

For the past twenty-five years, a major effort has been made to professionalize U.S. police forces. The growth of administrative and management skills has improved the quality of policing and paved the way for reform in management and administration. Orlando Wilson's classic text, *Police Administration*, served as an early source for police administrators attempting to improve their department's management.[94] Wilson stressed the need for a rational organizational framework that encouraged the free flow of communication, a clear chain of command, and a strict set of controls on officers' conduct backed up by written guidelines. Wilson's efforts have been furthered by such groups interested in promoting efficient police administration, such as the International Association of Chiefs of Police, the Police Executive Research Forum, and the Police Foundation.

Civil-service rules govern criteria for hiring, promotion, discipline, and appeals. Civil service has helped remove much of the politics from policing. Although some departments, usually smaller ones, are still run by an authoritarian chief who uses personal power to control all departmental policies and actions, most larger departments use more sophisticated management techniques.

Modern police chiefs rely on the advice of ranking officers who have authority over specific areas of the department. Some chiefs have experimented with advisory boards made up of police officers of all ranks who consult with them on policy and procedural problems. An effort has been made to democratize many police departments and take note of the needs and ideas of even the lowest-ranking patrol officers, and police unions have had a hand in changing management's operational procedures. But the impetus for change has also come from management studies, which stress the utility of teamwork and group decision making. Experts and reformers such as John Angell have consistently called for the end of the military model of policing.[95] However, while many police approve of the idea of **participatory management,** most report that they see little of it in action; police managers have not yet fully embraced democracy.[96]

While an entire text could be devoted to the subject of police personnel administration and the management of a modern department, this section will focus on only a few of the more important issues in this area.

Recruitment and Selection

In recent years, a number of political and social factors have resulted in better and more effective police recruitment. The depressed labor market and the scarcity of good jobs have made the security of a police career seem particularly inviting; the end of the military draft has increased the pool of eligible candidates; and the growing numbers of criminal justice programs in colleges have attracted a pool of educated young people seeking law enforcement careers. Equally important has been the development of a competitive salary structure in larger communities, which, with the addition of educational pay incentives, has provided patrol officers with annual starting salaries in the neighborhood of 30,000 dollars in larger cities. Surveys indicate that candidates are attracted to the variety, pay, and public service aspects of a police career.[97]

Most police departments have specific criteria and means for selecting police candidates: written tests; oral interviews; psychological appraisals; physical fitness, height, weight, and strength requirements; background investigations; biographical data; and medical exams.[98] More than half of all police departments employ polygraphs (lie detectors) to screen applicants.[99] Almost all departments will disqualify a candidate who has an adult or juvenile felony conviction, but only about half disqualify people with misdemeanor convictions.

Entrance Exams. Most metropolitan police departments place heavy emphasis on written examinations administered by themselves or by the state civil service commission. These range from published aptitude tests measuring reading and verbal comprehension, such as the Cattell Intelligence Test and the Culture Fair Intelligence Test, to locally created tests made up of items that reflect the department's operating manual.

Minority groups have charged that police entrance exams are discriminatory and culturally biased. When model tests have been created in which culturally relevant terms have been substituted for standard items, African-Americans improved their scores by as much as 30 percent. Those questioning the validity of written police tests also point to studies that show the tests do not actually predict effective police performance in the field. To find a middle ground in the testing controversy, some departments have created job-related examinations that measure a candidate's ability to take quick and reasonable action in stress situations. A sample question from this type of test might read:

> While on patrol, you find a panicked group of people standing at the shore of a frozen lake, staring helplessly at a youth, fifteen feet offshore, who has fallen through the ice. You would:
>
> A. Dash across the ice to rescue the boy.
> B. Radio headquarters for help and wait by the lake.
> C. Try to form a "human chain" to attempt rescue.
> D. Proceed with patrol since this is not a criminal matter.

The candidate is then asked to rank the answers according to their correctness. The right answers in this type of test are determined by analyzing the responses of experienced, qualified police officers. Even job-related tests have been successfully challenged in the courts on the grounds that using only the "best" officers to test the items is unfair and nonrepresentative of the general police department.

About 60 percent of all police departments employ both individual or group simulation models. The former tests provide candidates with materials familiar to police agencies (police blotters, logs, memorandums, etc.) and ask them to make decisions. Group simulation allows candidates to interact with one another in a problem-solving situation. For example, candidates may be asked to role-play a conflict situation that has little to do with police work to see if they have general problem-solving and leadership skills; one test included the question, "I want you to imagine you are a lifeguard and an individual is running on the pool deck in violation of the rules. How would you stop him?" Verbal skills, interpersonal relations, sensitivity, and other qualities can all be assessed using this method.

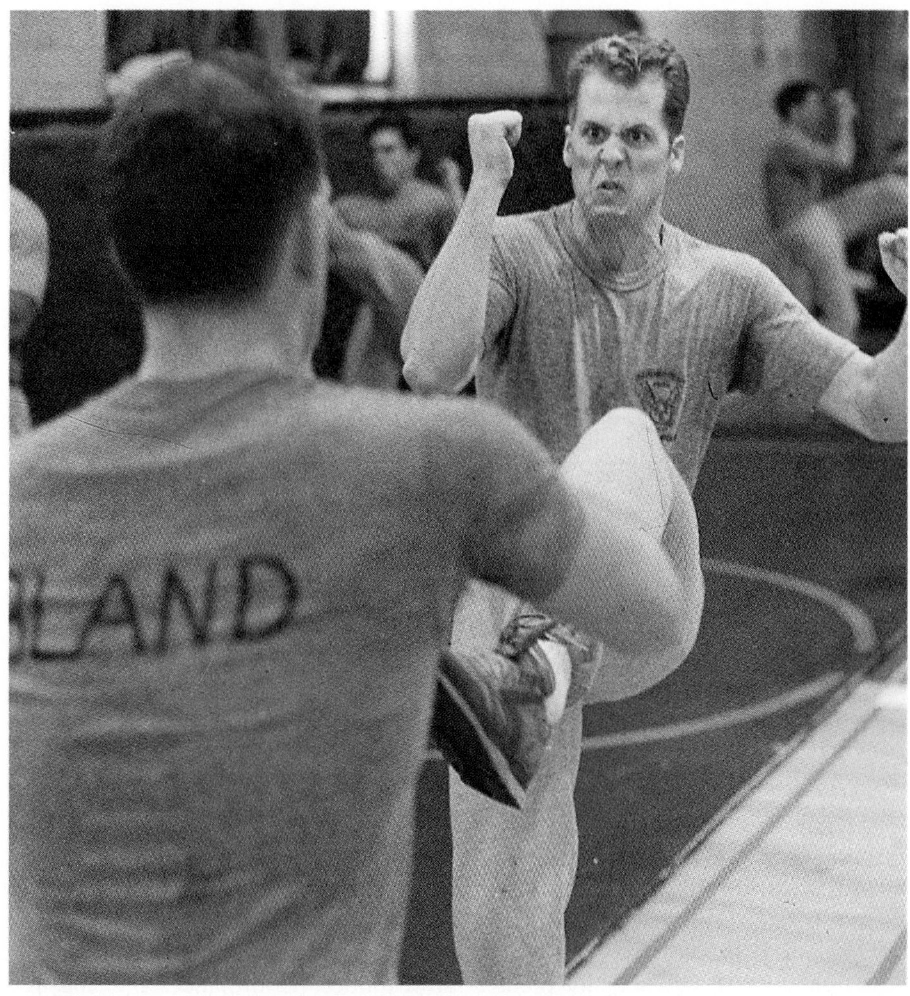

Physical agility and strength are hotly debated issues of police selection criteria.

Despite years of effort, no existing police exam has proven to be a 100 percent reliable predictor of successful field performance. Some experts have suggested that the practice of ranking applicants according to their scores on entrance exams be abolished in favor of selecting candidates on the basis of nonwritten, objective measures. For example, candidates might be asked to demonstrate their ability to remember faces and license plate numbers. Selection could also depend heavily on demonstrated past performance in school or prior work experience.[100]

Physical Requirements. Police departments have universally placed height, weight, and physical ability restrictions on their recruits. The traditional method of testing required candidates to perform a minimal number of push-ups, sit-ups, and running and jumping exercises. Court reviews suggesting these requirements discriminated against women and some minority groups have prompted departments to rely more often on body proportion and agility than on absolute minimum requirements. Another trend has been the development of job-related tests. Physical agility tests are based on the typical activities of local police officers; for example, how far they actually run in a critical incident, how many stairs they have to climb each day, and how many hours they spend on their feet. Strength tests are geared to how much the typical arrestee weighs and the amount of resistance he or she usually gives officers.[101]

Personality Testing. In recent years, there has been a shift from relying on physical requirements and cognitive ability to an increased use of intelligence and personality test measures. More than half of all larger police departments now use such sophisticated screening devices as the Wechsler Adult Intelligence Scale-Revised to measure intelligence and the California Test of Personality, the Minnesota Multiphasic Personality Inventory, and the Inwald Personality Inventory, among others, to evaluate personality structure.[102]

Research findings on the ability of psychological tests to predict police performance are inconclusive. Some studies indicate that these tests taken independently or in conjunction with clinical interviews are valid predictors of future police performance.[103] Others find little relationship between scores on psychological profiles and subsequent performance.[104] Still other evaluations have found that psychological tests are valid, though somewhat limited predictors of future job performance; their predictive value tends to diminish over time.[105] A review of the literature by Elizabeth Burbeck and Adrian Furnham found significant methodological problems in the administration of psychological tests and that most have little success in contrasting between good and bad police officers. Psychological tests may have some value for screening out candidates with mental problems but less for selecting recruits who will become skilled police officers.[106] Some critics have called for the development of guidelines to ensure that psychological profiles are used fairly and equitably.[107] Another approach is to abandon standard psychological screening devices and develop job-related or -oriented tests and rely more on intensive investigation of recruits' prior behavior patterns.[108]

Predicting Good Performance. The real purpose of selection criteria is to choose police recruits who will eventually become effective and efficient officers. A number of efforts have been made to determine empirically whether current selection criteria can actually predict future police performance.[109] Some evidence exists that recruits who do well on written civil service tests subsequently excel in arrest activity, investigative skills, evidence gathering, and crime scene management and receive superior supervisory ratings and career advancement.[110] Other factors that predict above-average performance are oral interviews, prior work experience, numerical ability, intelligence, age, and education. Unsatisfactory performances have been related to deficient educational levels, prior work problems, and poor performance during probationary periods. Other important findings: shorter officers were more likely to become assault victims; single and highly educated officers were more likely to resign (probably because they have greater career mobility); and factors that predict superior police performance do not vary by race or gender.[111]

The debate over selection criteria continues to rage. Should emphasis be placed on cognitive ability? Strength? Intelligence? As the police role shifts toward community policing and problem solving, selection criteria must also change. Police may need to be smarter and more competent than ever before.[112] Keep in mind, however, that when a professor applies for a job in a university, an attorney in a law firm, or an engineer in an aerospace company, no written test is given nor are there any in existence that hope to measure teaching, law, or engineering competence. Decisions are based on past performance and current competence; should police recruits also be chosen this way?

Improving Police Productivity

Government spending cutbacks forced by inflation and legislative tax-cutting measures have prompted belt-tightening in many areas of public service. Police departments have not been spared the budgetary pinch caused by decreased government spending. To combat the probable damage that would result from police service cutbacks, police administrators have sought to increase the productivity of their line, support, and administrative staff.

As used today, the term **police productivity** refers to the amount of actual order, maintenance, crime control, and other law enforcement activities provided by individual police officers and concomitantly by police departments as a whole. By improving police productivity, a department could keep the peace, deter crime, apprehend criminals, and provide useful public services without necessarily increasing its costs. This goal is accomplished by having each police officer operate with greater efficiency, thus using fewer resources to achieve greater effectiveness.

Confounding the situation and heightening its importance has been the dramatic increase in the cost of maintaining police personnel, including such items as salaries, fringe benefits, and retirement plans. The modern police department depends on expensive electronic gear, communications systems, computers, weapons, and transportation, and the cost of basic supplies from gasoline to paper is constantly increasing. It has been estimated that the cost of running U.S. police departments has increased to almost $14 billion annually.[113]

Despite the emphasis on increasing police effectiveness, serious questions have been raised about how the police accomplish their assigned tasks. As previously mentioned, in the Rand Corporation study of police detective services, the productivity of investigators was strongly assailed.[114] This nationwide study found that police investigators give only limited attention to about half the serious cases reported to them. Even cases in which the suspect was caught immediately required more time for paperwork and administrative tasks than was devoted to identifying the criminal. The study also found that a patrol officer's gathering of information at the site of the crime was more important to the crime's solution than the subsequent efforts of the detective force.

Patrol forces have also been concerned about their productivity. One basic complaint has been that the average patrol officer spends relatively little time on what is considered real police work. More often than not, highly skilled police officers can be found writing reports, waiting in court corridors, getting involved in domestic disputes, and handling what are generally characterized as "miscellaneous noncriminal matters."

Productivity Measures. How have police administrators responded to the challenge of improving police productivity? Applying modern technology to information, communication, and record-keeping systems has helped police improve their ability to respond to calls in a more effective fashion. For example, the 911 emergency code has been used in cities to improve police response time.

Another productivity improvement measure has been to simply ask individual police officers to shoulder a greater workload. Many jurisdictions have decreased the number of officers in patrol cars from two to one, saving approximately one hundred thousand dollars per beat annually (since three shifts are assigned to each patrol area). Research indicates that officers in one-person cars are as safe and productive as officers in two-person cars.[115]

Consolidation. Another move to increase police efficiency has come in the area of consolidating police services. This means combining small departments (usually with under ten employees) in adjoining areas into a superagency that services the previously fragmented jurisdictions. Consolidation has the benefit of creating departments large enough to use expanded services, such as crime labs, training centers, communications centers, and emergency units, that are not cost-effective in smaller departments. This procedure is controversial, since it demands that existing lines of political and administrative authority be drastically changed. Nonetheless, consolidation of departments or special services (such as a regional computer center) has been attempted in California (the Los Angeles Sheriff's Department), Massachusetts, New York, and Illinois.[116]

Some of the popular police department consolidation and productivity improvement techniques are:[117]

1. *Informal arrangements*—unwritten cooperative agreements between localities to perform a task collectively that would be mutually beneficial (e.g., monitoring neighboring radio frequencies so that needed backup can be provided). For example, the Metro Task Force program implemented in New Jersey in 1981 committed state troopers to help local police officers in urban areas for limited times and assignments.[118]

2. *Sharing*—the provision or reception of services that aid in the execution of a law enforcement function (e.g., the sharing of a communications system by several local agencies).

3. *Pooling*—the combination of resources by two or more agencies to perform a specified function under a predetermined, often formalized arrangement with direct involvement by all parties (e.g., the use of a city-county law enforcement building or training academy or the establishment of a crime task force, such as those used in St. Louis, Kansas City, Topeka, Tuscaloosa, and Des Moines). In Phoenix, the police department has a shared relationship with the Phoenix South Community Mental Health Center called the Family Stress Team. Two-person teams conduct on-site crisis intervention and attempt to stabilize family disputes in order to prevent repeated requests for police services. An evaluation indicates that the project has been a major labor-saving device.[119]

4. *Contracting*—a limited and voluntary approach in which one government enters into a formal binding agreement to provide all or certain specified law enforcement services (e.g., communications, patrol service) to another government for an established fee. Many communities that contract for full law enforcement service do so at the time they incorporate to avoid the costs of establishing their own police capability. For example, six small towns in Florida (Pembroke Park, Lauderdale Lakes, Tamarac, Dania, and Deerfield Beach) contract with the Broward County Sheriff's Department to provide law enforcement for their communities; contracting saved each town millions of dollars.[120]

5. *Police service districts*—areas, usually within an individual county, where a special level of service is provided and financed through a special tax or assessment. In California, residents of an unincorporated portion of a county may petition to form such a district to provide more intensive patrol coverage than is available through existing systems. Such service may be provided by a sheriff, another police department, or a private person or agency. This system is used in Contra Costa and San Mateo counties in California and Suffolk and Nassau counties in New York.

6. *Civilian employees*—a practice of using civilians in administrative support or even in some line activities. Civilians' duties have included operating communications gear; performing clerical work, planning, and research; and staffing traffic control (e.g., meter monitors). Using civilian employees can be a considerable savings to taxpayers, since their salaries are considerably lower than those of regular police officers. In addition, they allow trained, experienced officers to spend more time on direct crime control and enforcement activities. It is not surprising that the FBI estimates that today almost 20 percent of police employees are civilians.[121]

7. *Multiple tasks*—police officers are trained to carry out other functions of municipal government. For example, in a number of smaller departments, the roles of fire fighters and police officers have been merged into a job called a public safety officer. The idea is to increase the number of people trained in both areas to have the potential for putting more cops at the scene of a crime or more fire fighters at a blaze than was possible when the two tasks were separated. The system provides greater coverage at far less cost. While employees initially resisted the multiple-task system, it seems to have become established as a labor- and cost-saving device.[122]

8. *Use of technology*—computers are not the only technology that can improve productivity. For example, Raymond Surette has described the use of video patrol to increase police surveillance of downtown shopping districts without increasing personnel costs. This project entailed the use of one hundred video housings on traffic light poles that actually contained only twenty-one television cameras operated around the clock by volunteers. An ongoing evaluation found the program helped reduce crime in the area while increasing citizen feeling of security.[123]

9. *Special assignments*—officers are trained for special assignments that are required only occasionally. For example, the Special Enforcement Team in Lakewood, Colorado, is trained in a variety of police tasks, such as radar operation, surveillance, traffic investigation, and criminal investigations but specializes in tactical operations, such as crowd control and security. Use of the team where needed helps save thousands of dollars that normally would be required for overtime pay.[124]

10. *Budget supplementation*—the seeking of innovative sources of income to supplement a police department's limited budget. For example, Chicago police instituted a private fund drive that raised over $1.5 million to purchase protective clothing, and other departments have created private foundations to raise funds to support police-related activities. In New York City, $1.3 million was raised in one year for scholarships, health care, and training. Other schemes involve raising funds from the sale of property seized in crime-related activity, such as drug smuggling. The Fort Lauderdale, Florida, police raised $5.5 million in three years by selling forfeited goods. Additional budget supplementing activities include conducting fund-raising events, using traffic fines for police services, and enacting special taxes that go directly for police services.[125]

SUMMARY

Today's police departments operate in a military-like fashion; policy generally emanates from the top of the hierarchy, and both police officers and the public have difficulty understanding or identifying the source of orders and directives. Most police officers, therefore, use a great deal of discretion when making on-the-job decisions.

The most common law enforcement agencies are local police departments, which carry out patrol and investigative functions, as well as many different support activities. Many questions have been raised about the effectiveness of police work, and some research efforts seem to indicate that police are not effective crime fight-

ficking," *American Journal of Police* 9 (1990):43–65.

81. Ibid., pp. 64–65.

82. Cited in Malcolm Sparrow, Mark Moore, and David Kennedy, *Beyond 911, A New Era for Policing* (New York: Basic Books, 1990), p. 69.

83. Jack R. Greene, "The Effects of Community Policing on American Law Enforcement: A Look at the Evidence" (Paper presented at the International Congress on Criminology, Hamburg, Germany, September 1988), p. 19.

84. Roger Dunham and Geoffrey Alpert, "Neighborhood Differences in Attitudes Toward Policing: Evidence for a Mixed-Strategy Model of Policing in a Multi-Ethnic Setting," *Journal of Criminal Law and Criminology* 79 (1988):504–22.

85. Jack Greene and Ralph Taylor, "Community-Based Policing and Foot Patrol: Issues of Theory and Evaluation," in *Community Policing, Rhetoric or Reality*, ed. Jack Greene and Stephen Mastrofski (New York: Praeger, 1988).

86. Wesley Skogan and Mary Ann Wycoff, "Some Unexpected Effects of a Police Service for Victims," *Crime and Delinquency* 33 (1987):490–501.

87. Dennis Rosenbaum, "Coping with Victimization: The Effects of Police Intervention on Victim's Psychological Readjustment," *Crime and Delinquency* 33 (1987):502–19.

88. See, for example, Gary Cordner, "Fear of Crime and the Police: An Evaluation of a Fear-Reduction Strategy," *Journal of Police Science and Administration* 14 (1986):223–28.

89. Riechers and Roberg, "Community Policing: A Critical Review of Underlying Assumptions," pp. 112–13.

90. For a more complete description of these functions, see Robert Sheehan and Gary Cordner, *Introduction to Police Administration*, 2d ed. (Reading, Mass.: Addison-Wesley, 1986).

91. See, for example, Richard Larson, *Urban Police Patrol Analysis* (Cambridge: MIT Press, 1972).

92. Brian Reaves, *State and Local Police Departments, 1990* (Washington, D.C.: Bureau of Justice Statistics, 1992), p. 6.

93. Philip Ash, Karen Slora, and Cynthia Britton, "Police Agency Officer Selection Practices," *Journal of Police Science and Administration* 17 (1990):258–69.

94. Orlando W. Wilson, *Police Administration*, 2d ed. (New York: McGraw-Hill, 1963).

95. John Angell, "Toward an Alternative to the Classic Police Organizational Arrangements: A Democratic Model," *Criminology* 9 (1971):185–206.

96. Jeffrey Witte, Lawrence Travis, and Robert Langworthy, "Participatory Management in Law Enforcement: Police Officer, Supervisor, and Administrator Perceptions," *American Journal of Police* 9 (1990):1–23.

97. Harold Slater and Martin Reiser, "A Comparative Study of Factors Influencing Police Recruitment," *Journal of Police Science and Administration* 16 (1990):168–76.

98. This section leans heavily on Alan Benner, "Psychological Screening of Police Applicants," in *Critical Issues in Policing*, ed. Roger Dunham and Geoffrey Alpert (Prospect Heights, Ill.: Waveland Press, 1989), pp. 72–87; Elizabeth Burbeck and Adrian Furnham, "Police Officer Selection: A Critical Review of the Literature," *Journal of Police Science and Administration* 3 (1985):58–69; George Hargrave and Deirdre Hiatt, "Law Enforcement Selection with the Interview, MMPI, and CPI: A Study of Reliability and Validity," *Journal of Police Science and Administration* 15 (1987):110–14; Jack Aylward, "Psychological Testing and Police Selection," *Journal of Police Science and Administration* 13 (1985):201–10.

99. Ash, Slora, and Britton, "Police Agency Officer Selection Practices," p. 265.

100. T. Kenneth Moran, "Pathways Toward a Nondiscriminatory Recruitment Policy," *Journal of Police Science and Administration* 16 (1988):274–87.

101. Ken Peak, Douglas Farenholtz, and George Coxey, "Physical Abilities Testing of Police Officers: A Flexible, Job-Related Approach," *The Police Chief* 59 (1992):51–56.

102. George Pugh, "The California Psychological Inventory and Police Selection," *Journal of Police Science and Administration* 3 (1985):172–77; Charles Bartel, "Psychological Characteristics of Small Town Police Officers," *Journal of Police Science and Administration* 10 (1982):58–63.

103. Joyce McQuilkin, Vickey Russell, Alan Frost, and Wayne Faust, "Psychological Test Validity for Selecting Law Enforcement Officers," *Journal of Police Science and Administration* 17 (1990):289–94; Hargrave and Hiatt, "Law Enforcement Selection with the Interview, MMPI, and CPI."

104. Benjamin Wright, William Doerner, and John Speir, "Pre-employment Psychological Testing as a Predictor of Police Performance During an FTO Program," *American Journal of Police* 9 (1990):65–79.

105. Benner, "Psychological Screening of Police Applicants"; Hargrave and Hiatt, "Law Enforcement Selection with the Interview, MMPI and CPI."

106. Burbeck and Furnham, "Police Officer Selection: A Critical Review of the Literature," p. 66–68.

107. Robin Inwald, "Administrative Legal and Ethical Practices in the Psychological Testing of Law Enforcement Officers," *Journal of Criminal Justice* 13 (1985):367–72.

108. William Dwyer, Erich Prien, and J. L. Bernard, "Psychological Screening of Law Enforcement Officers: A Case for Job-Relatedness," *Journal of Police Science and Administration* 17 (1990):176–82.

109. Allan Roe and Norma Roe, *Police Selection: A Technical Summary of Validity Studies* (Provo, Utah: Diagnostic Specialists, 1982).

110. Bernard Cohen and Jan Chaiken, *Investigators Who Perform Well* (Washington, D.C.: National Institute of Justice, 1987), pp. 16–20.

111. Ibid., p. 20.

112. Dennis Jay Kenney and Stewart Watson, "Intelligence and the Selection of Police Recruits," *American Journal of Police* 9 (1990):39–61.

113. Bureau of Justice Statistics *Report to the Nation on Crime and Justice* (Washington, D.C.: U.S. Government Printing Office, 1988), p. 36.

114. Greenwood and Petersilia, *Summary and Policy Implications;* Peter Greenwood et al., *Observations and Analysis*, vol. 3 of *The Criminal Investigation Process* (Santa Monica, Calif.: Rand Corporation, 1975).

115. George Kelling, *What Works—Research and the Police*.

116. Thomas McAninch and Jeff Sanders, "Police Attitudes Toward Consolidation in Bloomington/Normal, Illinois: A Case Study," *Journal of Police Science and Administration* 16 (1988):95–105.

117. Adapted from Terry Koepsell and Charles Gerard, *Small Police Agency Consolidation: Suggested Approaches* (Washington, D.C.: U.S. Government Printing Office, 1979).

118. James Garofalo and Dave Hanson, *The Metro Task Force: A Program of Intergovernmental Cooperation in Law Enforcement* (Washington, D.C.: National Institute of Justice, 1984).

119. Thomas Jahn and Maryann Conrad, "The Family Stress Team Approach in Curbing Domestic Violence," *Police Chief* 52 (1985):66–67.

120. Nick Navarro, "Six Broward County Cities Turn to the Green and Gold," *Police Chief* 59 (1992):60.

121. Federal Bureau of Investigation, *Crime in the United States, 1987* (Washington, D.C.: U.S. Government Printing Office, 1988), p. 236.

122. For a detailed review of this issue, see John Crank, "Patterns of Consolidation Among Public Safety Departments, 1978–1988," *Journal of Police Science and Administration* 17 (1990):277–88.

123. Raymond Surette, "Video Street Patrol: Media Technology and Street Crime," *Police Science and Administration* 13 (1985):78–85.

124. Kenneth Perry, "Tactical Units Reduce Overtime Costs," *Police Chief* 52 (1985):57–58.

125. Lindsey Stellwagen and Kimberly Wylie, *Strategies for Supplementing the Police Budget* (Washington, D.C.: National Institute of Justice, 1985).

Issues in Policing

CHAPTER 8

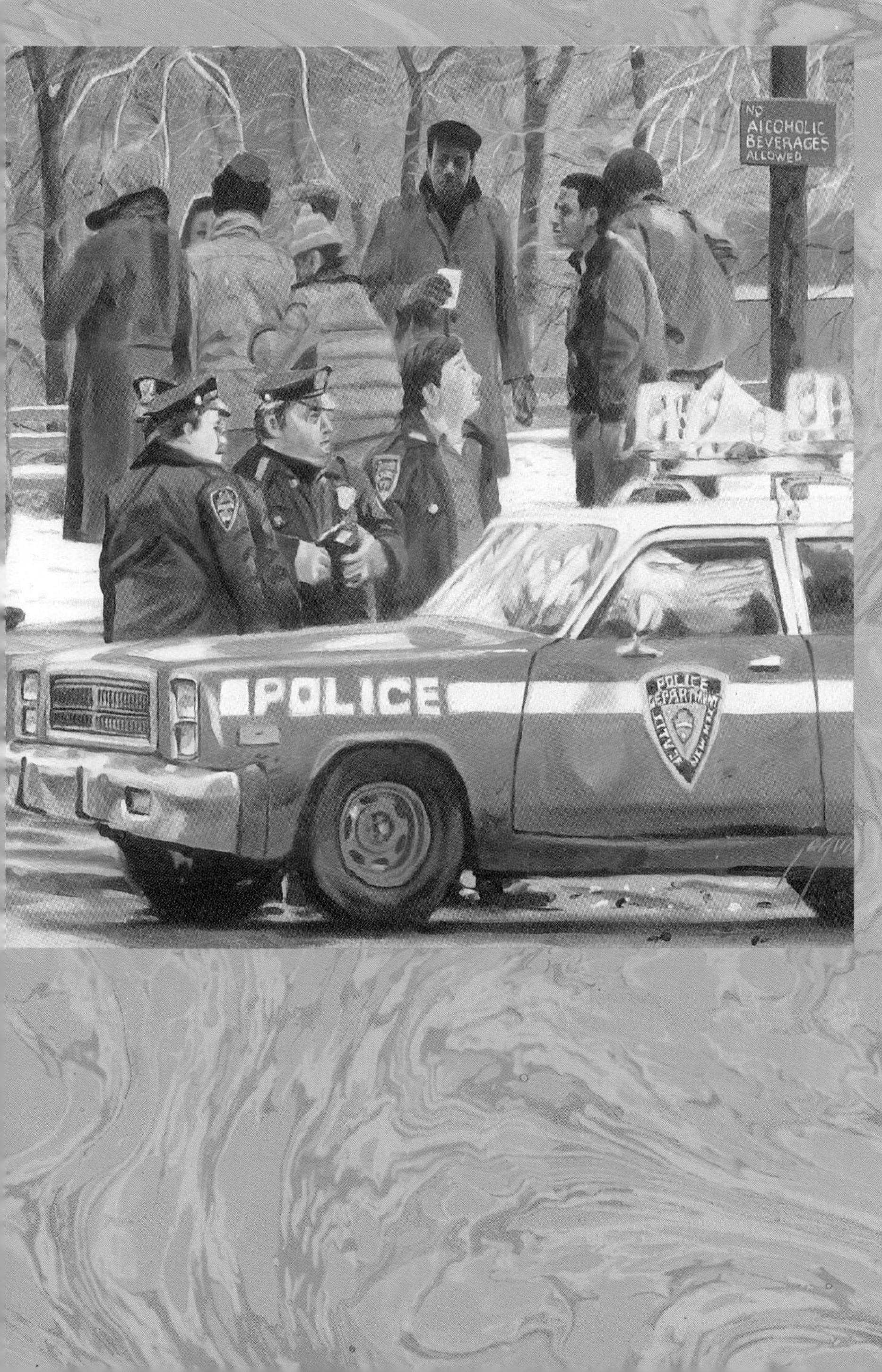

OUTLINE

KEY TERMS

blue curtain
cynical
authoritarian
field training officer
style
crime fighter
social agent
law enforcer
watchman
discretion
demeanor
Sherman Report
"double marginality"
"defeminization"
police brutality
Christopher Commission
deliberate indifference
deadly force
Knapp Commission
meat eaters
grass eaters
accountability system

For the past three decades, a great deal of public interest has focused on the function of police. The U.S. public seems genuinely concerned today about the quality and effectiveness of local police. Most citizens seem to approve of their local police, yet only 14 percent say that they have a great deal of confidence that police can protect them from harm.[1] It is not, therefore, surprising that citizens are arming themselves in record numbers, depending on private security forces, and organizing self-help groups to reduce their fear of crime.

The general public is not the only group concerned about police attitudes and behavior. Police administrators and other law enforcement experts have focused their attention on issues that may influence the effectiveness and efficiency of police performance in the field. Some of their concerns are outgrowths of the development of policing as a profession: Does an independent police culture exist, and what are its characteristics? Do police officers develop a unique "working personality," and if so, does it influence their job performance? Are there police officer "styles" that make some police officers too aggressive while others are inert and passive? Is policing too stressful an occupation?

Another area of concern involves the social composition of police departments: Who should be recruited as police officers? Are minorities and women being attracted to police work, and what have been their experiences on the force? Should police officers have a college education?

Important questions are also being raised about the problems police departments face interfacing with the society they are entrusted with supervising: Are police officers too forceful and brutal, and do they discriminate in their use of deadly force? Are police officers corrupt, and how can police deviance be controlled?

The Police Profession

All professions contain unique characteristics that distinguish them from other occupations and institutions. Policing is no exception. Police experts have long sought to understand the unique nature of the police experience and determine how the challenges of police work shape the field and its employees. In this section, some of the factors that make policing unique are discussed in detail.

Culture

Police experts have found that the experience of becoming a police officer and the nature of the job itself cause most officers to band together in a police subculture, characterized by clannishness, secrecy, and insulation from others in society (the so-called **blue curtain**). Police officers tend to socialize together and believe that their occupation cuts them off from relationships with civilians. Joining the police subculture means always having to stick up for fellow officers against outsiders, maintaining a tough, macho exterior personality, and distrusting the motives and behavior of outsiders.[2]

In their review of modern policing, *Beyond 911, A New Era for Policing,* Malcom Sparrow, Mark Moore, and David Kennedy identify six core beliefs at the heart of the police culture today:

1. We are the only real crime fighters. The public wants the police officer to fight crime; other agencies, both public and private, only play at crime fighting.
2. No one else understands the real nature of police work. Lawyers, academics, politicians, and the public in general have little concept of what it means to be a police officer.
3. Loyalty to colleagues counts above everything else. Police officers have to stick together because everyone is out to get the police and make the job more difficult.
4. It is impossible to win the war against crime without bending the rules. Courts have awarded criminal defendants too many civil rights.
5. Members of the public are basically unsupportive and unreasonably demanding. People are quick to criticize police unless they need one themselves.
6. Patrol work is the pits. Detective work is glamorous and exciting.[3]

These cultural beliefs make police reluctant to accept new ideas and embrace innovative concepts, such as community policing.

The forces that support a police culture generally are believed to develop out of on-the-job experiences. Most officers, both male and female, originally join police forces because they want to help people, to fight crime, and to have an interesting, exciting, prestigious career with a high degree of job security.[4] Recruits often find the social reality of police work does not mesh with their original career goals. They are unprepared for the emotional turmoil and conflict that accompany police work today. Membership in the police culture helps recruits adjust to the rigors of police work and provides the emotional support needed for survival.

In his well-respected work, *Working the Street,* Michael K. Brown argues that a police culture is created to meet the recurring anxiety and emotional stress that are part of police work.[5] The culture encourages decisiveness in the face of uncertainty and the ability to make split-second judgments that may later be subject to extreme criticism. Brown finds that the police culture is grounded on three principles: honor, loyalty, and individualism. Honor is given and received for risk-taking behavior, such as facing an armed assailant, which a civilian could never fully understand or appreciate. To be honored, the officer must be loyal to his or her partner and peers. Loyalty demands secrecy and the maintenance of the belief that the most important obligation a police officer has is to back up and support fellow officers. At the same time, the police culture idealizes the individualistic officer who is autonomous and aggressive and can take charge of any situation. Brown finds that individualism is compatible with loyalty, since police officers will need the backup and support of their partners when they take action that does not go along with accepted police procedures. Research by Stan Shernock does in fact show that police who view their role as "crime fighters" are most likely to value solidarity and depend on the support and camaraderie of their fellow officers.[6]

In sum, the police culture has developed in response to the insulated, dangerous life-style of police officers. As Egon Bittner plainly states, "Policing is a

Police experts find that police officers band together in a subculture referred to as the "blue curtain."

dangerous occupation and the availability of unquestioned support and loyalty is not something officers could readily do without."[7]

Personality

Some experts believe that police officers develop a unique set of personality traits that distinguish them from the average citizen. The typical police personality has been described as dogmatic, authoritarian, suspicious, racist, hostile, insecure, conservative, and **cynical.**[8] Cynicism has been found on all levels of policing, including among chiefs of police, and throughout all stages of a police career.[9] Maintenance of these negative values and attitudes is believed to cause police officers to be secretive and isolated from the rest of society, producing what William Westly calls the "blue curtain."[10]

In a similar vein, Jerome Skolnick says the policeman's "working personality" is shaped by constant exposure to danger and the need to use force and authority to reduce and control threatening situations.[11] Police feel suspicious of the public they serve and defensive about the actions of their fellow officers.

There are two opposing viewpoints on the cause of this phenomenon. One position holds that police departments attract recruits who are by nature cynical, **authoritarian,** secretive, and so on. Other experts maintain that socialization and experience on the police force itself cause these character traits to develop in police officers. Since research has found evidence supportive of both viewpoints, no one position dominates on the issue of how the police personality develops, or even if one actually exists.

A number of research studies have attempted to describe the development of the police personality. One of the most influential early efforts was conducted by social psychologist Milton Rokeach with police officers in Lansing, Michigan. When Rokeach and his associates compared police officers' personality traits with those of a national sample of private citizens, they found some significant differences: police officers seemed more oriented toward self-control and obedience than the average citizen, and they were more interested in personal goals, such as "an exciting life," and less interested in social goals, such as "a world at peace."[12] When comparing the values of veteran officers with those of recruits, Rokeach and his associates found evidence that police officers' on-the-job experience did not significantly influence their personalities and that most police officers probably had a unique value orientation and personality when they first embarked on their police career.

Developing the Police Personality

There is probably more evidence that a police personality is developed through the process of doing police work. In his study of one urban police department, John Van Maanen found that the typical police recruit is a sincere individual motivated to join the force for the salary and job security and out of a belief that the job will be interesting and flexible, in addition to a desire to enter an occupation that can be of benefit to society.[13] Van Maanen argues that the police personality is developed through the experience of becoming an officer. At the police academy, highly idealistic recruits are first taught to have a strong sense of camaraderie with fellow recruits. They begin to admire the exploits of the experienced officers who serve as their instructors. From them, police trainees learn when to play it by the book and when to ignore departmental rules and rely on personal discretion.

When rookies are finally assigned street duty, their **field training officer** teaches them the ins and outs of police work, helping them through the rite of passage of becoming a "real cop." The department's folklore, tales, myths, and legends are communicated to rookies. Soon, they begin to understand the rules of police work. Van Maanen suggests that "the adjustment of a newcomer in police departments is one which follows the line of least resistance."[14] By becoming similar to their peers in sentiments and behavior, rookies avoid censure by their department, their supervisor, and, most important, their colleagues. Thus, young officers adapt their personality to that of the "ideal cop."

George Kirkham, a professor who became a police officer, has described how the explosive and violent situations he faced as a police officer changed his own personality:

> As someone who had always regarded policemen as a "paranoid" lot, I discovered in the daily round of violence which became part of my life that chronic suspiciousness is something that a good cop cultivates in the interest of going home to his family each evening.[15]

Egon Bittner concludes that an esprit de corps develops in police work as a function of the dangerous and unpleasant tasks police officers are required to do. Solidarity and a "one for all, and all for one" attitude are two of the most cherished aspects of the police occupation.[16]

The Cynicism Factor

In what is probably the most well-known study of police personality, *Behind the Shield,* Arthur Niederhoffer examined the assumption that most police officers develop into cynics as a function of their daily duties.[17] William Westly had earlier maintained that being constantly faced with keeping people in line and believing that most people are out to break the law or harm a police officer caused officers to learn to distrust the citizens they protect.[18] Niederhoffer tested Westly's assumption by distributing a survey measuring attitudes and values to 220 New York City police officers. Among his most important findings were that police cynicism did increase with length of service, that patrol officers with college educations become quite cynical if they are denied promotion, and that military-like police academy training caused new recruits to quickly become cynical about themselves. For example, Niederhoffer found that nearly 80 percent of first-day recruits believed that the police department was an "efficient, smoothly operating organization"; two months later, less than a third professed that belief. Similarly, half the new recruits believed that a police superior was "very interested in the welfare of his subordinates"; two months later, that number declined to 13 percent.[19]

The development and maintenance of negative attitudes and values by police officers may have an extremely detrimental effect on their job performance. In a review of police literature, Robert Regoli and Eric Poole found evidence that a police officer's feelings of cyncism intensify the need to maintain respect and increase the desire to exert authority over others.[20] Unfortunately, as police escalate their use of authority, citizens learn to distrust and fear them. These feelings of hostility and anger in turn create feelings of potential danger among police officers, resulting in "police paranoia." [21] Regoli and Poole also find that by maintaining negative attitudes, police tend to be very conservative and resistant to change, factors that interfere with the efficiency of police work.[22]

While cynicism may hurt the relationship between police and the public, it might actually help the police officer's career within the department. Richard Anson and his associates found in a longitudinal study of police officers in Georgia that those exhibiting the most cynical attitudes were the most likely to get high ratings from supervisors. They conclude:

> . . . cynicism is a valued quality of the personality of the police officer and is positively evaluated by important individuals in police organizations.[23]

Is There a Police Personality?

Since the first research measuring police personality was published, numerous efforts have been made to determine whether the typical police recruit does indeed possess a unique personality that sets him or her apart from the average citizen. The results have been a mixed bag.[24] While some research concludes that police values are different from those of the general adult population, other efforts reach an opposing conclusion; some have found that police officers are actually more psychologically healthy than the normative population, less depressed and anxious and more social and assertive.[25] Recent research on police personality found that police officers highly value such personality traits as warmth, flexibility, and emotion; these traits are far removed from rigidity and cynicism.[26]

There may be within-group differences in the distribution of a police personality. George Reming compared "supercops," who were in the upper tenth of arrest activity, with average performers. The supercops were significantly more aggressive, vigilant, rebellious, energized, frank, extroverted, sociable, jealous, possessive and headstrong than the average officer. Interestingly, Reming found that the so-called supercops had personalities indistinguishable from a sample of habitual criminals, while the so-called average officers and members of the general public exhibited similar personality traits.[27]

Style

Policing involves a multitude of diverse tasks, including peacekeeping, criminal investigation, traffic control, and providing emergency medical service. Part of the socialization as a police officer is developing a working attitude, or **style,** through which he or she approaches policing. For example, some police officers may view their job as a well-paid civil service position that stresses careful compliance with written departmental rules and procedures. Other officers may see themselves as part of the "thin blue line" that protects the public from wrongdoers. They will use any means to get the culprit, even if it involves such cheating as planting evidence on an obviously guilty person who so far has escaped arrest. Should the police bend the rules in order to protect the public? Carl Klockars has referred to this dilemma as the "Dirty Harry problem," after the popular Clint Eastwood movie character who routinely (and successfully) violates all known standards of police work.[28]

Several studies have attempted to define and classify police styles into behavioral clusters. These classifications, called typologies, attempt to categorize law enforcement agents by groups, each of which has a unique approach to police work. The purpose of such classifications is to demonstrate that the police are not a cohesive, homogeneous group, as many believe, but rather are individuals with differing approaches to their work. Police administrators and others who wish to modify or improve police performance should be aware of the nature and extent of these stylistic undercurrents.[29] Do all officers within their jurisdiction operate with similar, unique, or conflicting styles? Is one style more effective than another? Does the existence of numerous styles within a single jurisdiction detract from good police work?

An examination of the literature suggests that the following four styles of police work seem to fit the current behavior patterns of most police agents: the Crime Fighter, the Social Agent, the Law Enforcer, and the Watchman. These four types are discussed in detail below.

The Crime Fighter

To the **Crime Fighter,** the most important police work consists of investigating serious crimes and prosecuting criminals. This type of police officer believes that murder, rape, and other major personal crimes should be the primary concerns of police agencies. Property crimes are considered less significant, while such matters as misdemeanors, traffic control, and social service functions would be better handled by other agencies of government. This type of police officer believes that the ability to investigate criminal behavior that poses a serious threat to life and safety, combined with the power to arrest criminals, separates a police department from other municipal agencies. To dilute these functions with minor social-service and nonenforcement duties is seen as harmful to police efforts to create a secure society.

Crime Fighters are primarily interested in dealing with hard crimes; on patrol, their senses are attuned to assaults, rapes, burglaries, and the like, and situations are interpreted by the degree of their relationship to these crimes. Some occurrences considered by others as appropriate occasions for police intervention (such as minor traffic violations or requests for enforcement in nonemergency situations) may be ignored or brushed off by Crime Fighters on the grounds that they are relatively unimportant and undeserving of their attention and time.

A number of police experts have recognized the existence of the Crime Fighter type. William Muir labels them "enforcers"—supercops who lack sym-

Crime fighters concentrate on arresting suspects for serious felony offenses.

pathy for the common citizen.[30] Michael Brown calls them "old-style crime fighters," who use force and violence to maintain control of the streets.[31]

The Social Agent

Strongly opposed to the Crime Fighter is the sort of police officer described as the **Social Agent.** Defenders of this type of officer note that police departments are merely part of a larger organization of several government agencies and feel that officers are responsible for a wide range of duties other than crime fighting. They argue that police could better spend their time trying to do well those things that have to be done, rather than conceiving of worlds where most police contacts are crime-related. Proponents of the Social Agent approach argue that establishing new governmental agencies or modifying existing ones to perform the duties relinquished by the Crime Fighter would create an exorbitant drain on municipal resources.

The Social Agent believes that police should be involved in a wide range of activities without regard for their connection to law enforcement. The Social Agent does not believe enforcement to be the essence of policing and may point out that the world *police* is commonly used in contexts that have at best only a tenuous relation to law enforcement (e.g., in such phrases as "the state's police powers" and "police the parade grounds"). The Social Agent who is well versed in the history of police in the United States will note, for example, that the Boston Police Department was developed in the early nineteenth century as much in response to a health and sanitary crisis as to criminal apprehension needs.

Rather than viewing themselves as criminal catchers, Social Agents consider themselves problem solvers. They are troubleshooters who patch the holes that appear where the social fabric wears thin.

The Law Enforcer

Like the Crime Fighter, the **Law Enforcer** tends to emphasize the detection and apprehension aspects of police work. Unlike the Crime Fighter, this police officer does not distinguish between major and minor crimes. Although a Law Enforcer may prefer working on serious crimes—they are more intriguing and rewarding in terms of achievement, prestige, and status—he or she sees the police role as one of enforcing all statutes and ordinances. According to this officer's view, duty is clearly set out in law, and the Law Enforcer stresses playing it by the book. Since the police are specifically charged with apprehending all types of lawbreakers, they are viewed in this typology as generalized law enforcement agents. They do not perceive themselves as lawmakers or as judges of whether existing laws are fair; quite simply, legislators legislate, courts judge, and police officers perform the functions of detecting violations, identifying culprits, and taking the lawbreakers before a court. The law enforcer is devoted to the profession of police work and is the most likely officer to aspire to command rank.

The Watchman

James Q. Wilson's study of interdepartmental differences in police orientations provides the fourth major typology.[32] In Wilson's analysis, three general departmental styles were observed and related to different demographic characteristics of U.S. cities. One of the styles Wilson noted, the Service Type, was similar to the Social Agent, while a second, the Legalist, seemed to resemble parts of the Crime Fighter and the Law Enforcer. A third orientation, which Wilson called the **Watchman** style, was characterized by an emphasis on the maintenance of public order as the police goal, rather than on law enforcement or general service. Police in Watchman-type departments choose to ignore many infractions and requests for service unless they believe that the social or political order is jeopardized:

> Juveniles are "expected" to misbehave, and thus infractions among this group—unless they are serious or committed by a "wise guy"—are best ignored or treated informally. . . . Motorists . . . will often be left alone if their driving does not endanger or annoy others. . . . Vice and gambling are . . . problems only when the currently accepted standards of public order are violated. . . . Private disputes—assaults among friends or family—are treated informally or ignored unless the circumstances . . . require an arrest. . . . The police are watchmanlike not simply in emphasizing order over law enforcement but also in judging the seriousness of infractions less by what the law says about them than by their immediate and personal consequences. . . . In all cases, circumstances of person and condition are taken seriously into account.[33]

The watchman is the most passive officer, concerned with retirement benefits rather than crime rates.

The Watchman type of police officer appears similar to Muir's concept of the "avoider" and to one of the groups Brown labels as the "service style."[34]

Figure 8.1 illustrates each police style.

Do Police Styles Exist?

As you may recall, the police role involves a great deal of time spent in noncrime service-related activities, ranging from providing emergency medical care to directing traffic. Although officers who admire one style of policing may emphasize one area of law enforcement over another, their daily activities likely will require them to engage in police duties they consider trivial or unimportant. While some pure types exist, an officer probably cannot specialize in one area of policing while ignoring the others.

FIGURE 8.1
Police Styles

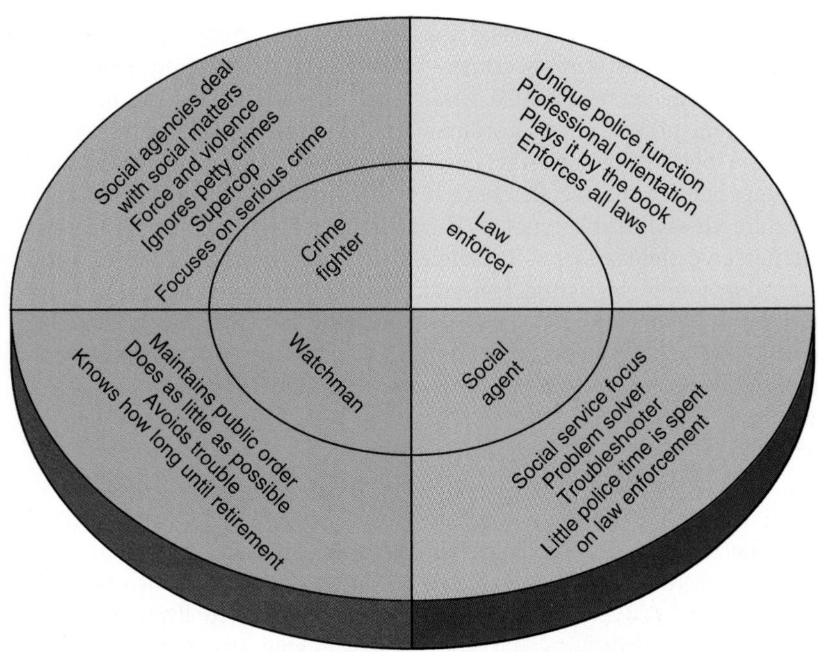

Support for this position comes from two studies. One, by Ellen Hochstedler, found that police officers in Dallas could not easily be categorized into one of the popular police styles cited above.[35] Similarly, Kathryn Golden has shown that students studying for careers in law enforcement are well aware that the police role stresses such diverse activities as crisis intervention and general service activities, and they do not join the force expecting to be the next "Dirty Harry." [36] Though further research is needed to clarify this issue, it is possible that today's police officer is more of a generalist than ever before and that future police recruits understand that they will be required to engage in a great variety of police tasks.

Discretion

No aspect of the police profession is more important than the great individual responsibility given to each field officer. Police have the ability to deprive people of their liberty, to arrest them and take them away in handcuffs, and even to use deadly force to subdue them. A critical aspect of this professional responsibility is the personal **discretion** each officer has in carrying out his or her daily activities. Discretion can involve the selective enforcement of the law, for example, when a vice squad plainclothes officer decides not to take action against a tavern that is serving drinks after hours. Patrol officers use discretion when they decide to arrest one suspect for disorderly conduct but escort another one to her home.

Most scholars have concluded that few police officers do not use a high degree of personal discretion in carrying out daily tasks. Jerome Skolnick termed the exercise of police discretion a prime example of "low visibility decision-making" in criminal justice.[37] This statement suggests that, unlike members of almost every other criminal justice agency, police are neither regulated in their daily procedures by administrative scrutiny nor subject to judicial review (except when their behavior clearly violates an offender's constitutional rights). As a result, the exercise of discretion by police may sometimes deteriorate into discrimination, violence, and other abusive practices. The following sections describe the factors that influence police discretion and review suggestions for its control.

Environment and Discretion

The degree of discretion an officer will exercise is at least partially defined by the living and working environment.[38] Police officers may work or dwell within a community culture that either tolerates eccentricities and personal freedoms or expects extremely conservative, professional, no-nonsense behavior on the part of its civil servants. The police officer who lives in the community he or she serves is probably strongly influenced by and shares a large part of the community's beliefs and values and is likely to be sensitive to and respect the wishes of neighbors, friends, and relatives. Conflict may arise, however, when the police officer commutes to an assigned area of jurisdiction, as is often the case in the urban inner-city precincts. The officer who holds personal values in opposition to those of the community can exercise discretion in such a way as to conflict with the community and result in ineffective law enforcement.

Dennis Powell has found that a community's racial makeup may influence police discretion.[39] After studying five adjacent police jurisdictions, Powell found that police in a predominantly black urban community demonstrated the highest use of discretion and punitive behavior toward whites, compared to blacks. Conversely, police in predominantly white areas were significantly more punitive to black offenders than whites. Douglas Smith and Jody Klein found that the socioeconomic status of the neighborhood greatly influenced a police officer's use of discretion in domestic abuse cases. Police were much more likely to use formal arrest procedures in lower-class than in middle- and upper-class neighborhoods. Smith and Klein also found that income level influenced whether police officers would be willing to take citizen's complaints seriously.[40]

A final environmental factor affecting the police officer's performance is his or her perception of community alternatives to police intervention. A police officer may exercise discretion to arrest an individual in a particular circumstance if it seems that nothing else can be done, even if the officer does not believe that an arrest is the best possible example of good police work. In an environment that has a proliferation of social agencies—detoxification units, drug control centers, and child-care services, for example—a police officer will obviously have more alternatives to choose from in deciding whether to make the arrest. In fact, referring cases to these alternative agencies saves the officer both time and effort—records do not have to be made out and court appearances can be avoided. Thus, social agencies provide for greater latitude in police decision making.

Departmental Influences

The policies, practices, and customs of the local police department provide another influence on discretion. These conditions vary from department to department and strongly depend on the judgment of the chief and others in the organizational hierarchy. For example, departments can issue directives that have as their goal the influence of police conduct. Patrol officers may be asked to issue more tickets and make more arrests or to refrain from arresting under certain circumstances. Occasionally, a directive will instruct officers to be particularly alert for certain types of violations or to make some sort of interagency referral when specific events occur. For example, the department may order patrol officers to crack down on street panhandlers or to take formal action in domestic violence cases. These factors affect the decisions of the police officer who has to produce appropriate performance statistics by the end of the month or be prepared to offer justification for following a course of action other than that officially prescribed.

The ratio of supervisory personnel to subordinates may also influence discretion: departments with a high proportion of sergeants to patrol officers may experience fewer officer-initiated actions than one in which more eyes are observing the action in the streets. The size of the department may also determine the level of officer discretion. In larger departments, looser control by supervisors seems to encourage a level of discretion unknown in smaller, more tightly run police agencies.

Police discretion is also subject to peer pressure.[41] Police officers suffer a degree of social isolation, because the job involves strange working conditions and hours, including being on twenty-four-hour call, and their authority and responsibility to enforce the law cause embarrassment during social encounters. At the same time, officers must handle irregular and emotionally demanding encounters involving the most personal and private aspects of people's lives. As a result, police officers turn to their peers both for on-the-job advice and for off-the-job companionship, essentially forming a subculture to provide a source of status, prestige, and reward.

The peer group affects how police officers exercise discretion on two distinct levels. In an obvious, direct manner, other police officers dictate acceptable responses to street-level problems by displaying or withholding approval in office discussions. The officer who takes the job seriously and desires the respect and friendship of others will take their advice, abide by their norms, and seek out the most experienced and most influential patrol officers on the force and follow their behavior models.

Situational Influences

The situational factors attached to a particular crime provide another extremely important influence on police actions and behavior. Regardless of departmental or community influences, the officer's immediate interaction with a criminal act, offender, citizen, or victim will weigh heavily on the use of discretionary powers.

While it is difficult to catalog every situational factor influencing police discretion, a few stand out as having major significance. Studies have found that police officers rely heavily on **demeanor** (the attitude and appearance of the offender) in making decisions. Some early research efforts all reached that conclusion. These studies found that if the offender was surly, talked back, or otherwise challenged the officer's authority, formal action was more likely to be taken.[42]

Another set of situational influences on police discretion concerns the manner in which a crime or situation is encountered. If, for example, a police officer stumbles on an altercation or break-in, the discretionary response may be quite different from a situation in which the officer is summoned by police radio. If an act has received official police recognition, such as the dispatch of a patrol car, police action must be taken or an explanation made as to why it was not. Or if a matter is brought to an officer's attention by a citizen observer, the officer can ignore the request and risk a complaint or take discretionary action. When an officer chooses to become involved in a situation, without benefit of a summons or complaint, maximum discretion can be used. Even in this circumstance, however, the presence of a crowd or witnesses may influence the officer's decision making.

And, of course, the officer who acts alone is also affected by personal matters—physical condition, mental state, police style, and whether there are other duties to perform.

Extralegal Factors

One often-debated issue is whether police take race, class, and gender into account when making arrest decisions. The question is whether police discretion works against the young, males, the poor, and minority-group members and favors the wealthy, the politically connected, and majority-group members. Research has uncovered evidence supporting both sides of this argument.[43] For example, Dale Dannefer and Russell Schutt found that racial bias was often present in the patrol officer's decision to process youths to juvenile court.[44] Christy Visher found that police were more likely to arrest women whose attitude and actions deviated from the stereotype of proper female behavior.[45] Visher found that older, white female suspects were less likely to be arrested than younger, black, or hostile women. A study of twenty-four police departments by Douglas Smith and Christy Visher found that race (and demeanor) do in fact play an important role in police discretion. Surprisingly, Smith and Visher also found that males and females were equally likely to be arrested and formally processed for law violations.[46]

The belief that police are more likely to use formal sanctions against minority citizens has not been consistently supported by research. A number of studies have produced data indicating that racial bias does not influence the decision to arrest and process a suspect.[47] However, racial influences on police decision making are often quite subtle and hard to detect. For example, there are some indications that the victim's race, and not the criminal's, is the key to racial bias: police officers are more likely to take formal action when the victim of crime is white than when the victim is a minority-group member.[48]. Cecil Willis and Richard Wells found that police are more likely to report child abuse cases involving white families than those involving black families.[49] The inference Willis and Wells draw from their data is that either (a) police officers view a case involving a white victim as more deserving of official attention and action than one involving a black child or (b) the officers hold negative stereotypes of black family life, including the perception that violence is normal. This data suggests that any study of police discretion must take into account both victim and offender characteristics if it is to be truly valid.

All police officers do not operate in an unfair and unjust manner, nor can all police departments be accused of operating with a racial bias. Evidence exists that the influence of race on police discretion varies from jurisdiction to jurisdiction and may be a function of the professionalism of the individual department.[50] Similarly, there is evidence that gender bias has decreased.[51]

Police discretion is one of the most often-debated issues in criminal justice (see Figure 8.2). On its face, the unequal enforcement of the law smacks of unfairness and violates the Constitution's doctrines of due process and equal protection. Yet were some discretion not exercised, police would be forced to function as automatons merely following the book. Administrators have sought to control discretion so that its exercise may be both beneficial to citizens and nondiscriminatory.

Today, no clear answer to the management of police discretion exists. Advocates of specialized units, policy statements, legal mandates, and other approaches can only assume that the officer in the field will comply with the intent and spirit of the administrator's desire. Little knowledge is currently available

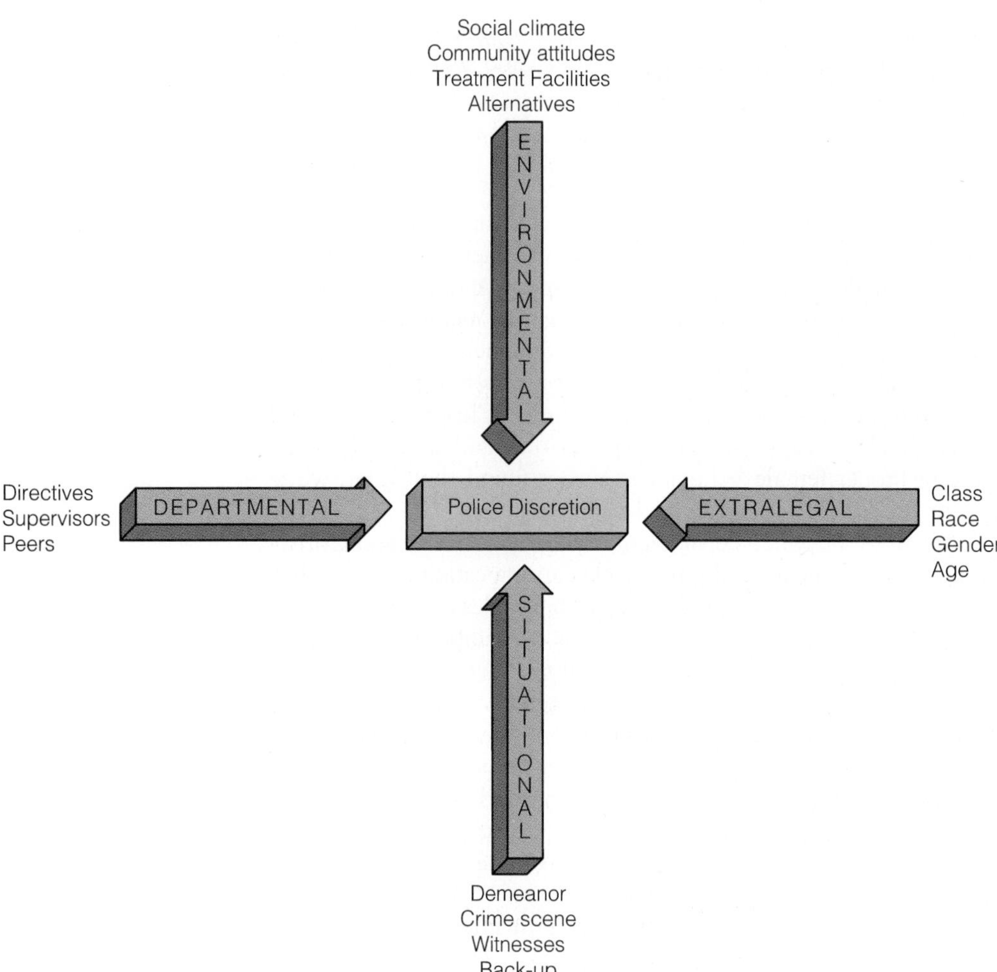

FIGURE 8.2
Influences on Police Discretion

concerning the specific influence any particular legal or administrative measure will have on police discretion, whether it will affect all officers equally, or why some officers will be affected one way and others will respond in an opposite fashion. Michael Brown argues that discretion is an important and necessary part of policing and should only be tampered with carefully. "We should be less concerned with worrying about how much discretion patrolmen have and searching for ways to eliminate it," he argues, "than with trying to enlarge their qualities of judgment and making them responsive to the people they serve." [52]

Who Are the Police?

The composition of the nation's police forces is changing. Traditionally, police agencies were comprised of white males with a high school education who viewed policing as a secure position that brought them the respect of their family and friends and a step up the social ladder. It was not uncommon to see police families in which one member of each new generation would enter the force. This picture has been changing and will continue to change. As criminal justice programs turn out thousands of graduates every year, an increasing number of police officers have received at least some college education. In addition, affirmative action programs have helped slowly change the racial and gender composition of police departments to reflect community makeup. The following sections explore these changes in detail.

Police Education

In recent years, many police experts have argued that police recruits should have a college education. This development is not unexpected, considering that higher education for police officers has been recommended by national commissions on policing since 1931.[53] Though the great majority of U.S. police departments do not require a college education of their recruits, the trend for police officers to seek post-high-school training has been spurred by the development of law enforcement and criminal justice academic programs and the availability of federal and state tuition aid.

What are the benefits of higher education for police officers? Better communication with the public, especially minority and ethnic groups, is believed to be one. Educated officers write better and more clearly and are more likely to be promoted. Police administrators believe that education enables officers to perform more effectively, generate fewer citizen complaints, show more initiative in performing police tasks, and generally act more professionally. In addition, educated officers are less likely to have disciplinary problems and are viewed as better decision makers.[54] As Bruce Berg points out, education is essential for officers who would one day become training academy instructors.[55]

Considering its advantages, what is the status of higher education in policing today? A recent Bureau of Justice Statistics survey of U.S. police departments found that few require higher education for entry-level jobs. As Figure 8.3 shows, about 2 percent of local police forces require some college-level courses and 4 percent require a two-year degree; about 8 percent of state police departments require a two-year college degree.[56]

David Carter and Allen Sapp conducted a 1988 survey on behalf of the Police Executive Research Forum of all state and local police agencies serving populations of more than fifty thousand.[57] Of the 699 agencies that responded to the survey, 62 percent had at least one formal policy in support of officers pursuing higher education and 58 percent required course work to be job-related. While the scope of job-related education included a variety of subjects, about half (49 percent) of the surveyed departments expressed a preference for criminal justice majors, most often because of their enhanced knowledge of the entire criminal justice system and issues in policing. Another promising trend: while they did not require college credits for promotion, 82 percent recognized that college education is an important element in promotion decisions.

In some respects, the findings of the Carter and Sapp survey can be considered disappointing. Only 14 percent of the departments had a formal college requirement for employment, and 75 percent had no policy or practice requiring college education for promotion. In addition, most (75 percent) of the departments that supported in-service higher education did not require the course work to be part of a degree program.

Does Higher Education Matter?

Despite the growth of educational opportunities for police, the issue of higher education for police officers is not a simple one. A number of factors have

FIGURE 8.3
Education Requirements of Police and Sheriffs

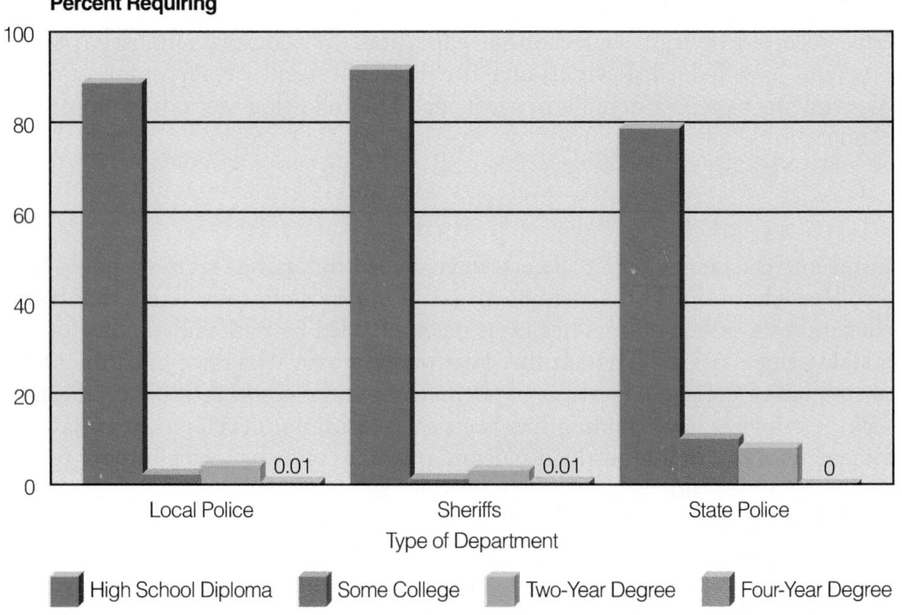

impeded police departments from requiring aspiring officers to attain college credits. The most often-cited reason is that many potential candidates, especially those from minority communities, will be dissuaded from police work if a college degree is required. In addition, a college-educated police force would be more costly to recruit and, assuming they would want higher salaries than a less-educated force, more costly to maintain.

Still another factor is the lack of clear-cut evidence that college-educated police perform better than less-educated officers. For example, one recent survey by Robert Worden found that education had relatively little influence on police officer attitudes or behavior.[58] The diversity of the police role, the need for split-second decision making, and the often boring and mundane tasks police are required to do are all considered reasons formal education for police officers may be a waste of time.[59]

In addition, there is no agreement on which education model is the most effective for training the modern police officer. For example, liberal arts may be too general, criminal justice too focused, and law enforcement too technical to be of use to the street cop. This important issue has been addressed by the report of the National Advisory Commission on Higher Education for Police Officers (commonly called the **Sherman Report**).[60] The Sherman Report examined the findings of a national study of existing college curricula and educational delivery systems for police education in the United States and recommended that prospective police officers should receive a liberal education and that criminal justice courses and course material should emphasize ethical considerations and moral values in law enforcement, not the nuts and bolts of police procedures.

While the jury is still out on the value of police education, a number of research efforts indicate that a college education does influence police performance beneficially. Studies have shown that college-educated police officers generate fewer citizen complaints and have better behavioral and performance characteristics than their less-educated peers.[61] Higher education has been associated with fewer on-the-job injuries, injuries by assault and battery, disciplinary actions from accidents, and physical-force allegations and less use of sick leave. Other research has shown that higher education promotes higher aspirations and greater acceptance of minorities; decreases dogmatism, authoritarianism, rigidity, and conservatism; lessens disciplinary problems, citizen complaints, and discretionary arrests; and increases promotions, the perception of danger, and the ability to tolerate job-related excitement.[62] While the Worden research found few benefits of police education, it did note that superiors find educated officers to be more reliable employees and better report writers and citizens found them to be exceptional in the use of good judgment and problem solving.[63]

While it is generally recognized that education benefits law enforcement officers, public finances and the ability to recruit college-educated candidates will probably determine whether police departments will increase their educational requirements. The difficulty of finding appropriate college-educated recruits has caused some cities to ignore educational requirements. On the other hand, some cities, such as San Diego, San Jose, and Sacramento, Calif., and Tulsa, Oklahoma, and state police agencies, such as in New York and Minnesota, have recently adopted measures requiring at least two years of college education for prospective recruits.[64]

The Changing Composition of Police

For the past two decades, U.S. police departments have made a concerted effort to attract female and minority police officers. The reasons for this effort are varied. Viewed in its most positive light, police departments recruit minority citizens to field a more balanced force that truly represents the community it serves. A heterogeneous police force can be instrumental in gaining the public's confidence by helping to dispel the view that police departments are generally bigoted or biased organizations. Futhermore, minority police officers possess special qualities that can serve to improve police performance. For example, Spanish-speaking officers are essential in Hispanic neighborhoods, while Asian officers are essential for undercover or surveillance work with Asian gangs and drug importers. As Figure 8.4 indicates, however, white males continue to predominate in U.S. police departments.

Minority Police Officers

The earliest known date of when an African-American was hired as a police officer was 1861, in Washington, D.C.; Chicago hired its first black officer in 1872.[65] By 1890, an estimated two thousand minority police officers were employed in the United States. At first, black officers suffered a great deal of discrimination. Their work assignments were restricted, as were their chances for promotion. Minority officers were often assigned solely to the patrol of black neighborhoods, and in some cities, they were required to call a white officer to make an arrest. White officers held highly prejudicial attitudes, and as late as the 1950s, some refused to ride with blacks in patrol cars.[66]

The experience of black police officers has not been an easy one. In his well-known book, *Black in Blue,* Nicholas Alex points out that blacks suffer **double marginality**."[67] On the one hand, black officers must deal with the expectation that they will give members of their own race a break. On the other hand, they often experience overt racism from their police colleagues. Alex found that black officers' adaptation to these pressures ranged from denying that black suspects should be treated differently from whites to treating black offenders more harshly than white offenders to prove their lack of bias. Alex offered several reasons for

FIGURE 8.4

Gender, Race, and Ethnic Background of Full-Time Police Officers

SOURCE: Brian Reaves, *State and Local Police Departments, 1990* (Washington, D.C.: Bureau of Justice Statistics, 1992), p. 5.

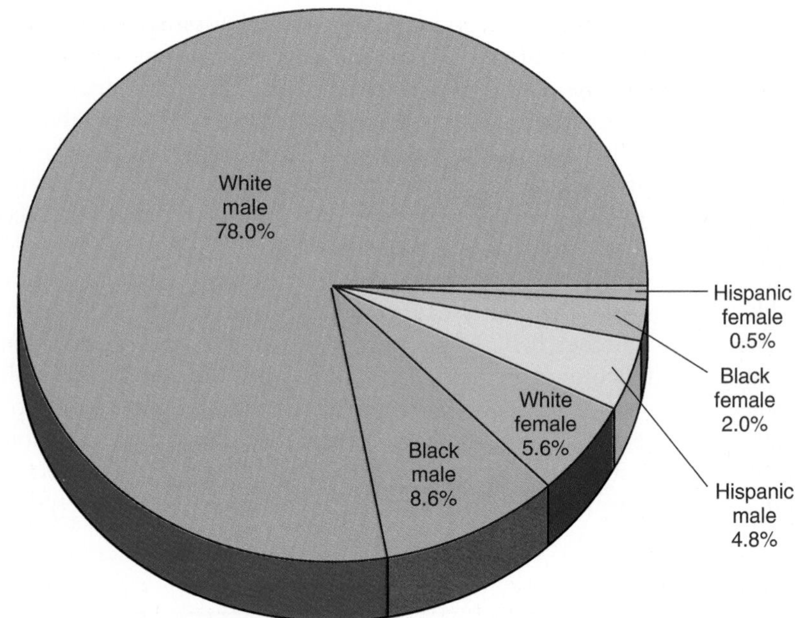

some black police officers being tougher on black offenders: they desire acceptance from their white colleagues; they are particularly sensitive to any disrespect given them by black teenagers; they view themselves as protectors of the black community.

These attitudes may be changing, however. In a more recent book, *New York Cops Talk Back,* Alex claims to have found a more aggressive and self-assured black police officer, one who is less willing to accept any discriminatory practices by the police department.[68] Similarly, Eva Buzawa found that black officers in Michigan generally were satisfied with their profession and believed they had good chances for advancement.[69] And in a study conducted in the aftermath of the Miami riots in the early 1980s, Bruce Berg and his associates found that black police officers were actually far less detached and alienated from the local community than white or Hispanic police officers.[70] Thus, it appears that black officers are overcoming the problems of *double marginality*.

This is not to say that the black police officer's problems are over. For example, some police officials believe that black officers have trouble relating to the community because they often identify with their white peers, who have limited understanding of cultural differences. As one high-ranking police official put it, "Many black police officers in this area are insensitive to the people in the community because they don't understand the black community problems any better than nonblack police officers."[71]

Another significant problem is the difficulty black officers have in attaining command positions. Despite the growing number of minorities in supervisory positions, the percentage of minority officers of senior rank actually lags behind their total representation on police forces. Consequently, minority police organizations have filed lawsuits over the promotion practices of some of the nation's largest police departments, including those in Chicago, Omaha, and Miami. Courts have ordered that minorities and women be promoted so that the racial and gender composition of the department's supervisory staff reflects the number of minorities and women in the department. However, it should be noted that there are now black chiefs in some of the nation's largest cities. For example, Lee Brown was appointed as chief in Houston in 1982 and has since been named

New York City police chief upon the retirement of Benjamin Ward, another African-American; Willie Williams was named to replace Daryl Gates in Los Angeles in the wake of the Rodney King case.[72]

Legal Issues. Despite these positive changes, minority police officers have been victims of intentional and sometimes unintentional departmental discrimination. For example, some departments, in an effort to provide representative coverage to minority areas of the city, assign all their black, Hispanic, or Asian officers to a single patrol area or beat. In one Florida city, an inner-city patrol zone was staffed entirely by black officers, and all the department's black officers were assigned to this one zone.[73] The U.S. Fifth Circuit Court of Appeals labeled this practice discriminatory and ordered it stopped. Nonetheless, this practice is not unusual, and minority police officers have resorted to lawsuits to seek relief from what they consider to be discriminatory or demeaning activity.[74]

A series of legal actions brought by minority representatives have resulted in local, state, and federal courts ordering police departments either to create hiring quotas to increase minority representation or to rewrite entrance exams and requirements in order to increase minority hiring. Court-ordered hiring was deemed necessary because as late as 1940, less than 1 percent of all police officers were minorities, and by 1950, the numbers had increased to only 2 percent.[75]

Numerous hiring plans have been implemented under court supervision. For example, the Virginia state police signed a consent decree in federal court in which they agreed to recruitment levels of at least 30 percent black and 25 percent female applicants.[76] Until the agreement was reached, only 4 percent of their force of 1,345 officers was black and 2 percent, female.

Sometimes the drive to recruit and promote minority officers forces police and city officials to reevaluate the results of normal testing procedures. This occurred in 1985 in New York City, when the annual promotion exam was challenged on the basis that it discriminated against black and Hispanic officers. As a result, the city decided to promote 1,041 officers of all races who passed the test and the 200 highest-scoring black and Hispanic candidates among the 2,355 who had failed.[77]

In 1987, in the case of *United States v. Paradise*, the Supreme Court upheld racial quotas as a means of reversing the effects of past discrimination. Ordering the Alabama Department of Public Safety to promote an equal number of black and white highway patrol officers, the Court said, "Discrimination at the entry level necessarily precluded blacks from competing and resulted in a departmental hierarchy dominated exclusively by nonminorities." The Alabama state patrol had no minority majors, captains, lieutenants, or sergeants, and only four of sixty-six corporals were black. The Court justified its ruling on the grounds that only qualified people would be promoted, the restriction was temporary, and it did not require layoffs of white officers.[78]

Court-ordered hiring has sometimes generated resentment among white officers who view affirmative action hiring and promotion programs as a threat to their job security. In Chicago, white officers intervened on the side of the city when a black police officer organization filed suit to change promotion criteria.[79] The Detroit Police Officers' Association filed suit to prevent the police department from setting up a quota plan for hiring black police sergeants. The court upheld the white officers' claim and struck down the promotional scheme. The court stated:

> Inevitably race quotas do not accomplish the result of equal employment opportunity. The polarization of races that quotas exhibit creates a divided police

department—instead of unifying and strengthening it, the quota underscores differences and sows seeds of internal hatred.[80]

Considering this conflict, it was not surprising when some Boston police officers were accused of misrepresenting their racial identity in order to take advantage of departmental affirmative action programs. Though the Boston police claimed its investigation of the situation found no white officers had misrepresented their race, the fire department uncovered five fire fighters whose claimed minority status was successfully challenged.[81]

In the 1990s, many cities around the country are either under court order to hire and promote more minority police officers or have voluntarily complied with minority hiring plans. While it has often proven difficult to achieve an effective prescription for racial equality, some jurisdictions have achieved impressive results. Michael Charles has described how a citizen advisory committee was able to solve promotional discrimination in the Fort Wayne, Indiana, police in just a few weeks of effort. Representation by all concerned groups, an open atmosphere, and political support resulted in a plan that was fair and acceptable.[82]

Minorities will continue to increase their presence on police forces, especially if the recruitment mechanisms ordered by courts are followed. At the same time, police administrators will be challenged to provide the most effective law enforcement possible while at the same time easing morale problems presented by court ordered police hiring, promotion, and administration.

Female Police Officers

The first women were admitted to police departments in 1910. For more than half a century, they endured separate criteria for selection, given menial tasks, and denied the opportunity for advancement.[83] Some relief was gained with the passage of the Civil Rights Act of 1964 and its subsequent amendments. Courts have consistently supported the addition of women to police forces by striking down entrance requirements that eliminated almost all female candidates but could not be proven to predict job performance (such as height and upper-body strength).[84] Nonetheless, the role of women in police work is still restricted by social and administrative barriers that have been difficult to remove. Today, about 7 percent of all sworn officers are women. Women continue to be underrepresented in the senior administrative ranks, and many believe they are assigned duties that underutilize their skills and training.[85] Eric Poole and Mark Pogrebin found that after three years on the job, few policewomen aspire to rise in police organizations. By then, most recognize that few women get promoted, and they lack successful female role models on which to shape their career aspirations.[86]

Gender bias is certainly not supported by existing research that indicates that female officers are highly successful police officers.[87] In an important study of recruits in the Metropolitan Police Department of Washington, D.C., conducted by the Police Foundation, policewomen were found to exhibit extremely satisfactory work performances.[88] Compared to male officers, women were found to respond to similar types of calls, and the arrests they made were as likely to result in conviction. Women were more likely than their male colleagues to receive support from the community and were less likely to be charged with improper conduct. One study by Robert Homant and Daniel Kennedy found that policewomen could be more understanding and sympathetic of the victims of domestic abuse and were more likely than male officers to refer them to shelters.[89]

Traditionally, female officers received somewhat lower supervisory ratings than males and made fewer felony and misdemeanor arrests.[90] Female police of-

ficers have also been described as having lower evaluations of their own competency than male officers and more fears regarding the consequences of women being promoted to the superior officer level.[91] However, more recent analysis of the issue suggests that these differences have diminished. A study of the behavior of 2,293 officers in Texas and Oklahoma by James David found that the arrest rates of male and female officers were almost identical.[92] In a study of policewomen's performance conducted in New York City, the results prove equally favorable to female patrol officers. Based on 3,625 hours of observation of patrol, including 2,400 police-civilian encounters, the study found that female officers were perceived by civilians as being more competent, pleasant, and respectful, and their performance seemed to create a better civilian regard for police. The study also found that female officers performed better when serving with other women. Females paired with male colleagues seemed to be intimidated by their partners and were less likely to be assertive and self-sufficient.[93]

Sean Grennan's important study of patrol teams in New York City examined an enduring myth about policewomen: because they are less capable of subduing a suspect physically, they will be more likely to use their firearms. Grennan found exactly the opposite: policewomen are less likely to use a firearm in violent confrontations than their male partners, are more emotionally stable, are less likely to seriously injure a citizen, and are no more likely to suffer injuries than their male partners.[94] These generally positive results are similar to findings developed in other studies conducted in major U.S. cities.[95]

Gender Conflicts

Despite the overwhelming evidence supporting their performance, policewomen have not always been fully accepted by their male peers or the general public. Male officers complain that policewomen lack the emotional and physical strength to perform well in situations involving violence.[96] Some officers' wives resent their husbands having a female partner because they consider the policewoman a sexual threat and inadequate support in a violent encounter.[97] If evidence of gender equality could be proven beyond a doubt, it would be a blow to some male officers who have long been schooled in a macho police culture that is disrespectful of women; they could no longer regard police work as the "manly" profession they entered.[98]

The general public may believe that policewomen are well suited for some tasks, such as "settling family disputes" or "dealing with a rape victim," but are inadequate for action-oriented activities, such as "stopping a fistfight."[99] Female officers face the additional problem that a great majority of the people they must control are male. Sometimes this can be an advantage, for example, when a normally belligerent male suspect surrenders peacefully, rationalizing that he does not want to fight with or hurt a woman.[100]

Those female officers who try to catch on to the unwritten police subculture are often written off as "bad police material."[101] Women who prove themselves tough enough to gain respect as police officers are then labeled as "lesbians" or "bitches" in order to neutralize their threat to male dominance, a process referred to as **defeminization.**[102] Male officers also generally assume that female officers who adopt an aggressive style of policing will be quicker to use deadly force than their male counterparts (an assumption disputed by the Grennan research).

These perceptions of female officers are often based on gender stereotypes and consequently incorrect. In a careful review of the literature, Michael Charles found that women can train themselves to achieve a level of strength and fitness

well within the normal demands of the police profession.[103] Nonetheless, female officers are often caught in the classic catch-22 dilemma: if they are physically weak, male partners view them as a risk in street confrontations; if they are actually more powerful and aggressive than their male partners, they are regarded as an affront to the policeman's manhood.

Given the sometimes hostile reception they get from their male peers and the general public, policewomen have been forced to perform their jobs under extreme pressure.[104] This condition is bound to affect their performance. Sociologist Susan Martin describes the roles female police officers adopt as a consequence of this pressure as falling somewhere on a continuum between two idealized professional identities, the *police*woman and police*woman*. The *police*woman gains her peers' acceptance by trying to adhere closely to the norms of behavior governing police in general and exhibits a strong law enforcement orientation.[105] She tries to be more loyal, professional, hardworking, and tough than women are generally expected to be. *Police*women are not afraid to engage in physical action or take punishment. Martin quotes one *police*woman:

> You have to fight the way the people fight out here. . . . You fight to win. . . . You have to be physical. Hit, kick, do what you can . . . and the person who doesn't do that should be disciplined. Often, it's the women, and they are said not to know any better. But they've been trained; they *do* know better. Generally, the women aren't aggressive enough, but once you've been punched a couple of times, you learn to get the punch in first.[106]

On the other end of the spectrum are police*women*, who behave in a "traditionally feminine manner." They make few arrests, rarely attempt to engage in hazardous physical activity, and emphasize "being a lady." Police*women* feel comfortable in the role of being of secondary importance in a police agency. Martin's interviews with thirty-two female officers reveal that seven could be classified as typical police*women* and eight as *police*women, with the remaining falling in between.

The Future of Women in Policing

What does the future hold for female police officers? One of the main concerns is the number of female officers in supervisory positions. So far, women, especially black female officers, have been woefully underrepresented in the police command hierarchy. A number of lawsuits have been filed to reverse this situation. For example, a consent decree required that one-third of all promotions in the Miami police department be given to women (and minorities).[107] However, change in this area continues to be slow. Male officers may find it difficult to take orders from female supervisors; some female officers may not seek promotion because they fear rejection from their male colleagues.[108]

Another area of concern is the development of an effective maternity policy. Most departments do not yet have policies that identify when pregnant officers are unfit for patrol or other duties and whether they should be reassigned to lighter duties and what these should entail. If the number of women on police forces continues to grow, maternity issues are bound to become an important staffing issue for police administrators.[109]

Despite these problems, the future of women in policing grows continually brighter.[110] As Eric Poole and Mark Pogrebin point out, female officers want to remain in policing because it pays a good salary, offers job security, and is considered a challenging and exciting occupation.[111] These factors should continue to bring women to policing for years to come.

Problems of Policing

Law enforcement is not an easy job. Role ambiguity, social isolation, and the threat of danger present in "working the street" are the police officer's constant companions. What effects do these strains have on police? This section discusses three of the most significant problems: stress, violence, and corruption.

Stress

The complexity of their role, the need to exercise prudent discretion, the threat of using violence and having violence used against them, and isolation from the rest of society all take a toll on law enforcement officers. It is not surprising, then, that police experience tremendous stress, a factor that leads to alcoholism, divorce, depression, and even suicide. Even civilian employees, such as dispatchers, have been found to exhibit elevated stress levels.[112]

A number of factors have been associated with police stress.[113] The pressure of being on duty twenty-four hours a day leads to stress and emotional detachment from both work and public needs. Police stress has been related to internal conflict with administrative policies that deny officers support and a meaningful role in decision making. In addition, police suffer stress in their personal lives when they bring the job home or when their work hours are shifted, causing family disruptions.[114] Other stressors include poor training, substandard equipment, inadequate pay, lack of opportunity, job dissatisfaction, role conflict, exposure to brutality, and fears about competence, success, and safety.[115] Some officers believe that their superiors care little about their welfare. For example, Harvey McMurray studied officers in two jurisdictions who were physically assaulted while on the job and found they perceived inadequate support from supervisors. Among the comments McMurray heard were "Seems like everyone abandons you. You're criticized more about what mistakes you made or your involvement. Any help you get seems like just a formality" and the "Department doesn't give a damn about the officers"; such perceptions must certainly create stress.[116]

Police psychologists have divided these stressors into four distinct categories:

1. External stressors, such as verbal abuse from the public, justice system inefficiency, and liberal court decisions that favor the criminal.
2. Organizational stressors, such as low pay, excessive paperwork, arbitrary rules, and limited opportunity for advancement.
3. Duty stressors, such as rotating shifts, work overload, boredom, fear, and danger.
4. Individual stressors, such as discrimination, marital difficulties, and personality problems.[117]

The effects of stress can be shocking. Police work has been related to both physical and psychological ailments. Police have a significantly high rate of premature death caused by such diseases as coronary heart disease and diabetes. They also experience a disproportionate number of divorces and other marital problems. Research indicates that police officers in some departments, but not all, have higher suicide rates than the general public.[118]

How can stress be combated? Research efforts have shown that the more support police officers get at the workplace, the lower their feelings of stress and anxiety.[119] Consequently, departments have attempted to fight job-related stress by training officers to cope with its effects. Today, stress training includes infor-

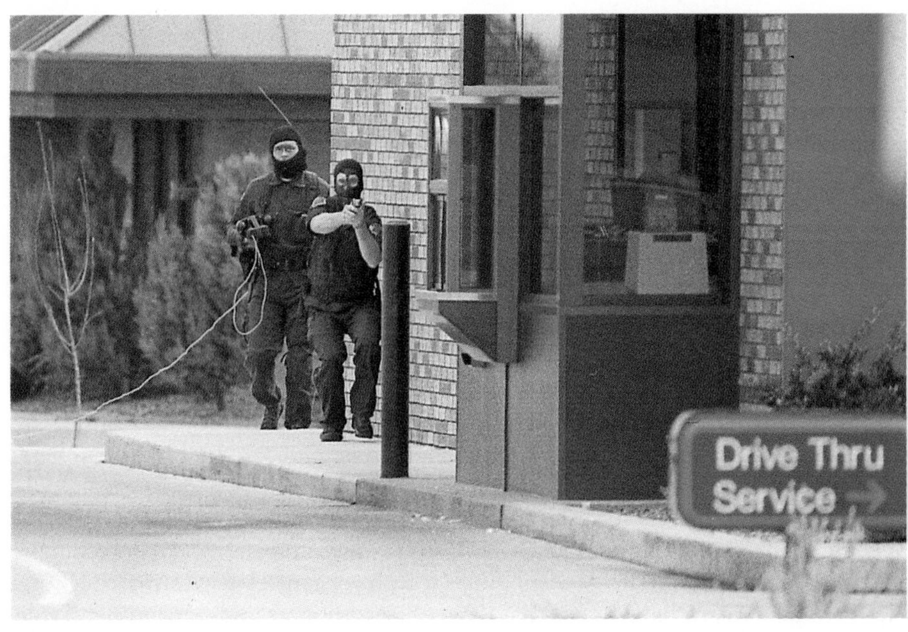

Though police make relatively few felony arrests each year, the threat of violent encounters helps to produce stress. Here a SWAT team approaches a hostage scene in Oklahoma City. After storming the restaurant, they found two gunmen dead from bullet wounds.

mation on diet, biofeedback, relaxation and meditation, and exercise. Some programs have included family members because if they have more knowledge about the difficulties of police work, they may be better able to help the officer cope. Still other efforts promote "total wellness programming," which enhances the physical and emotional well-being of officers by emphasizing preventive physical and psychological measures.[120]

Stress is a critically important aspect of police work. Further research is needed to create valid methods of identifying police officers under considerable stress and devising effective stress-reduction programs.[121]

Violence and the Police

Since their creation, U.S. police departments have wrestled with the charge that they are brutal, physically violent organizations. Early police officers resorted to violence and intimidation to gain the respect that was not freely given by citizens. In the 1920s, the Wickersham Commission detailed numerous instances of police brutality, including the use of the third degree to extract confession.

Police violence first became a major topic for discussion in the 1940s, when rioting provoked serious police backlash. Retired Supreme Court Justice Thurgood Marshall, when he was chief counsel of the National Association for the Advancement of Colored People's Legal Defense Fund, referred to the Detroit police as a "gestapo" after a 1943 race riot left thirty-four people dead.[122] Twenty-five years later, excessive police force was again an issue when television cameras captured police violence against protestors at the Democratic National Convention in Chicago.

Today, **police brutality** continues to be a concern, especially when police use excessive violence against members of the minority community. The nation looked on in disgust when a videotape was aired on network newscasts showing members of the Los Angeles Police Department beating, kicking, and using electric stun guns on Rodney King. Earlier, Los Angeles police stopped using a re-

straining choke hold that cuts off circulation of blood to the brain after minority citizens complained that it caused permanent damage and may have killed as many as seventeen people. Use of excessive force is not restricted to Los Angeles. The use of force against minority citizens was the spark that set off three riots in Miami in the 1980s. The last disturbance, which occurred in January 1989, was set off by the shooting of an unarmed black motorcyclist by a Hispanic police officer; eleven citizens were wounded and thirteen buildings burned to the ground.[123]

The question of police use of force has two main aspects: (1) Are average police officers generally brutal, violent, and disrespectful to the citizens with whom they come in daily contact? (2) Are the police overzealous and discriminatory in their use of **deadly force** when apprehending suspected felons? Let us examine each of these issues separately.

Police Brutality

Police brutality usually involves such actions as the use of abusive language, unnecessary use of force or coercion, threats, prodding with nightsticks, stopping and searching people in order to harass them, and so on. Charges of generalized police brutality were common between the 1940s and 1960s. Surveys undertaken by the President's Commission on Law Enforcement and the Administration of Justice and other national commissions found that many citizens believed that police discriminated against minorities when they used excessive force in handling suspects, displayed disrespect to innocent bystanders, and so on.[124] However, by 1967, the President's Commission on Law Enforcement and the Administration of Justice concluded that the police use of physical brutality had somewhat abated:

> The Commission believes that physical abuse is not as serious a problem as it was in the past. The few statistics which do exist suggest small numbers of cases involving excessive use of force. Although the relatively small number of reported complaints cannot be considered an accurate measure of the total problem, most persons, including civil rights leaders, believe that verbal abuse and harassment, not excessive use of force, is the major police-community relations problem today.[125]

While charges of police brutality continue to be made in many jurisdictions, the evidence suggests that actual instances of physical abuse of citizens by police officers are less frequent than commonly imagined. In a classic study, Albert Reiss employed thirty-six college students to observe police-citizen interactions in high-crime areas in Washington, D.C., Chicago, and Boston.[126] Reiss found that while verbal abuse of citizens was quite common, the excessive use of physical force was relatively rare. In only 44 cases out of the 5,360 observations made by Reiss's researchers did police seem to employ excessive or unreasonable force. There appeared to be little difference in the way police treated blacks and whites; when force was used, it was against more selective groups—those who showed disrespect or disregard for police authority once they were arrested.

Some experts believe that police officers have reduced their violent interactions with citizens of all races.[127] John Dugan and Daniel Breda studied citizen complaints against police officers in the state of Washington and found that only 4 percent could be substantiated or sustained; most complaints were for "verbal conduct" and not physical brutality.[128] David Bayley and James Garofalo observed 350 eight-hour tours of duty in three precincts in New York City. They discovered

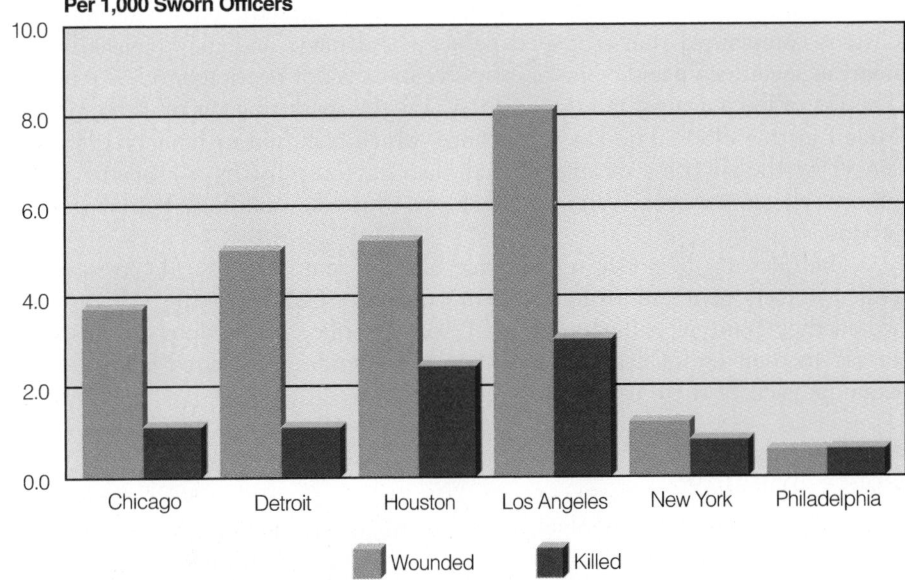

FIGURE 8.5
Civilians Wounded and Killed by Police

SOURCE: Anthony Pate and Edwin Hamilton, *The Big Six, Policing America's Largest Cities* (Washington, D.C.: Police Foundation, 1990), p. 138.

that even in a large urban area such as New York, incidents of police violence are relatively rare. Of the 467 potentially violent incidents they encountered, only 78 resulted in some type of actual conflict. In only forty-two encounters was force used by police against citizens or citizens against police officers. The force used by police consisted almost exclusively of grabbing and restraining; firearms were never used.[129]

Is Brutality Reemerging?

Despite such reassuring research findings, widely publicized incidents of police brutality have continued to plague departments around the country. Some of these incidents have been captured on film and later viewed by the public. One such incident occurred in January 1989, when Don Jackson, a black police officer from a neighboring town, rode through the streets of Long Beach, California. Jackson, who wanted evidence of the Long Beach Police Department's harassment of minorities, was secretly accompanied by an NBC camera crew. In less than three minutes after he entered Long Beach, his car was pulled over, he was verbally abused by a police officer, and his head was pushed through a plate glass window and then pounded on the trunk of a police car.

The Rodney King and Don Jackson cases focused attention on an alleged increase in urban police brutality.[130] In Los Angeles, the **Christopher Commission,** set up to review police operations in the wake of the King beating, found that Los Angeles police wound and kill more citizens (per one thousand officers) than police in any other big-city department. As Figure 8.5 shows, Los Angeles police are about eight times more likely to shoot and wound citizens than police in New York City.[131] The Los Angeles Police Department's Special Investigations Section, a nineteen man surveillance team, was accused of being a death squad assigned to kill career criminals.[132] In 1990, the team shot and killed three men who were sitting in a car after they had robbed a McDonald's. Prosecutors in the King case charged that the Los Angeles department has honed itself into an elite paramilitary force that depends on high-tech weapons ranging from motorized battering rams to French-built helicopters.[133]

The beating of Rodney King by Los Angeles police focused attention on police brutality. Here King awaits the outcome of the trial in which the officers who clubbed and kicked him were found not guilty.

Curbing Brutality

Since incidents of brutality undermine efforts to build a bridge between police and the public, police departments around the United States have instituted specialized training programs to reduce them. Departments in cities such as New York and Boston are now implementing or considering implementing neighborhood and community policing models to improve relations with the public. In addition, detailed rules of engagement that limit the use of force are now common in major cities. However, the creation of departmental rules limiting behavior is often haphazard and, as Samuel Walker points out, usually a reaction to a crisis situation (for example, a citizen is seriously injured), rather than part of a systematic effort to improve police-citizen interactions.[134]

What may be the greatest single factor that can control the use of police brutality is the threat of civil judgments against individual officers who use excessive force, police chiefs who ignore or condone violent behavior, and the cities and towns in which they are employed. This issue is discussed further in Analyzing Criminal Justice Issues: Suing the Police.

Deadly Force

In 1986, the citizens of New York City were shocked to hear that a police officer shot and killed a sixty-six-year-old woman with a shotgun as she was being evicted from her apartment. Was this a most extreme instance of police brutality? Later, the facts of the case revealed a more complex situation: the woman was mentally unstable; she weighed over 275 pounds; she had attacked the police with a ten-inch-long knife while they had tried their best to restrain her with protective shields; and the woman was shot twice to stop her charging at the officers. Were the officers justified in using deadly force? A New York court indicted the officers for involuntary manslaughter, but they were later exonerated.[135]

ANALYZING CRIMINAL JUSTICE ISSUES

Suing the Police

A major inducement for police departments to control violence is the growing number of civil lawsuits being filed and won against individual officers and agencies. For example, in December 1988, Boston paid half a million dollars to the parents of a teenager shot to death by an officer, despite the fact the youth was involved in a high-speed chase with a stolen car. On December 1, 1988, a federal jury ordered Los Angeles Police Chief Daryl Gates to pay $170,000 in punitive damages to a family injured when police roughed them up while conducting a search. This was the largest judgment ever imposed on a police chief and possibly the first case in which a chief was held responsible for the behavior of his officers, even though the chief was not at the scene, did not know about the incident, and had not explicitly condoned the behavior.

People can sue the police for the use of excessive force if they can show that the force used was unreasonable, considering all the circumstances known to the officer at the time he or she acted. A suit can also be brought if the police fail to act in a matter, for example, when despite a (court) restraining order, they fail to arrest a husband who is battering his wife.

Civil suits became common after the Supreme Court ruled in 1978 (*Monell v. Department of Social Services*) that local agencies could be held liable under the federal Civil Rights Act (42 U.S.C. 1983) for actions of their employees. Before *Monell,* attorneys were reluctant to file civil actions against police officers because even if the case could be won, there was often no way to collect damages from individuals who in most instances were without attachable financial resources. After *Monell,* police agencies, with their "deep pockets," could be held liable if in some way the officer's behavior could be attributed to an official policy or behavior. Liability increases if the policy or behavior is sanctioned by a high-ranking official, such as the chief.

A victim can seek redress against the department and the municipality it serves if he or she can show that the incident stemmed from a practice that, although not necessarily an official policy, was so widespread that it had become a "custom" that fairly represented official policy. To make the department liable under this standard, the victim might show that the actions that led to his or her injury were practices accepted by supervisors, that many police officers frequently engaged in these practices, that the police department failed to investigate or discipline officers involved in similar incidents, and that the department knew about such practices and did little to prohibit them. For example, a municipality could be held liable under the Civil Rights Act if police officers made it a custom to use excessive force in making arrests, police officials ignored the problem despite many complaints and incidents, brutality complaints were rarely investigated, and neither rules to limit force nor special training programs to aid police in making arrests were created.

Training

One area of particular concern has been the failure of police departments to properly train officers. Mu-

As commonly used, the term **deadly force** refers to the actions of a police officer who shoots and kills a suspect who is either fleeing from arrest, assaulting a victim, or attacking the officer.[136] The justification for the use of deadly force can be traced to English common law, in which almost every criminal offense was a felony and bore the death penalty. The use of deadly force in the course of arresting a felon was considered expedient, saving the state the burden of trial.[137]

Today, no other issue facing the police is more critical than the use of deadly force. Police violence can be the spark that ignites racial unrest and community uprisings, as was the case of the Miami riot of January 1989, which began when an unarmed black man was killed by an Hispanic police officer.[138]

How Frequently Is Deadly Force Used?

To determine the frequency of police shootings, researchers generally rely on data provided by the FBI (supplementary homicide reports) and the National Center for Health Statistics ("death by legal intervention of the police") and information

nicipalities have been held liable if an officer uses excessive force and that officer has not been trained in the use of force or the training was forgotten, obsolete, and inadequate. The Supreme Court in *Canton v. Harris* ruled that to be liable for their failure to train, police departments must be "deliberately indifferent" to the needs of people injured by the untrained officers. Some commentators believe that *Harris* had made suing police more difficult because of the need to prove **deliberate indifference,** and not mere negligence or misconduct. Though it is difficult to define *deliberate indifference,* it would most likely include situations where the need for training was so obvious that its absence seems a clear-cut violation of Constitutional rights; for example, where police are not given any firearms training after they leave the police academy, even though the department has switched its standard weapon from the .38-caliber revolver to the 9mm automatic. Deliberate indifference might also involve failure to train officers in dealing with a particular crime problem, such as domestic abuse, even though police officials should recognize it as a significant area of concern.

The threat to police departments posed by civil litigation is significant. Not only are they liable for large dollar awards to victims, but they must also pay hefty legal fees. It is not uncommon for a plaintiff in a civil rights case to be awarded a nominal amount of damages, with ten times that amount going to his or her attorney in legal fees.

The threat of large civil penalties may prove the most effective deterrent yet to the police use of excessive force. It will certainly cause police departments to carefully consider whom they hire, how they train, when they investigate, and what action they take against officers who are brutal or negligent.

Critical Thinking Skills

Policing is a dangerous, stressful job. Is it fair to hold officers and towns liable for the occasional use of excessive force? Many offenders are disrespectful to officers and provoke violent responses. Even Rodney King, who was brutally beaten by police, resisted being handcuffed and flailed his arms around, rather than meekly consenting to arrest. Would the threat of civil suits prevent officers from taking the necessary steps to subdue dangerous criminals? People want police to make neighborhoods safe, even if it means putting their lives at risk. Research by Forrest Scogin and Stanley Brodsky found that many officers have a real fear of lawsuits and maintain an "us versus them" mentality. Will these concerns undermine police-community relations at a time when they are seen as critical to effective policing? Should officers be immune from punishment if they use too much force in this dangerous undertaking?

SOURCE: Rolando del Carmen and Victor Kappeler, "Municipalities and Police Agencies as Defendants: Liability for Official Policy," *American Journal of Police* 10 (1991):1–17; Barbara Roberts, "Legal Issues in Use-of-Force Claims," *The Police Chief* 59 (1992):16–29; Forrest Scogin and Stanley Brodsky, "Fear of Litigation among Law Enforcement Officers," *American Journal of Police* 10 (1991): 41–45; *Graham v. Connor,* 490 U.S. 386 (1989); *Monell v. Department of Social Services,* 436 U.S. 658 (1978); *Canton v. Harris,* 109 S.Ct. 1197 (1989).

volunteered by local police departments. These data indicate that on average about 250 citizens are killed by the police each year. While these sources provide some indication of patterns and trends, no systematic effort has been made to gather accurate national data on police shootings, and the existing data is at best problematic and suspected of error.[139] This lack of reliable data is particularly vexing, considering the seriousness of the problem.

In one of the most often-cited surveys of police use of force, Kenneth Matulia surveyed 57 of the nation's largest cities and found that approximately 260 citizens are killed by police each year, a rate of 2.41 per 1,000 officers and 0.62 per 100,000 citizen population.[140] Matulia also found indications that the average number of citizens killed by police is steadily decreasing, probably due to both legal and administrative efforts to control police use of force.[141] For example, he estimates that in 1975, 360 people were killed by police, while by 1983, that number had declined to 229.

Though these data are encouraging, some researchers believe that the actual number of police shootings is far greater and may be hidden or masked by a number of sources. For example, coroners may be intentionally (or accidentally) underreporting police homicides by almost half.[142] In an impressive review of the evidence, James Fyfe estimates that one thousand citizens are killed by police each year. Though Fyfe recognizes that no accurate measure of fatalities exists, he reaches this figure by applying the data recorded in the nation's largest jurisdictions to the population as a whole.[143]

Factors Related to Police Shootings

Is police use of deadly force a random occurrence, or are there social, legal, and environmental factors associated with its use? The following patterns have been related to police shootings.

Variation by Jurisdiction. Research indicates that cities differ markedly in percentage of police shootings. For example, while police in Portland, Oregon, annually shoot 0.81 civilians per 1,000 population, New York City police shoot 1.4, Oakland, California, police shoot 5.2, and Jacksonville, Florida, police shoot 7.1.[144] Scholars are still uncertain about the reasons for these differences. Police practices, population characteristics, social trends, and so on may be responsible.

Exposure to Violence. Most police shootings involve suspects who are armed and who either attack the officer or are engaged in violent crimes. Richard Kania and Wade Mackey found that fatal police shootings were closely related to reported violent crime rates and criminal homicide rates.[145]

Police Workload. A correspondence exists between police violence and the number of police on the street, the number of calls for service, the number and nature of police dispatches, the number of arrests made in a given jurisdiction, and police exposure to stressful situations.[146]

Firearms Availability. Cities that experience a large number of crimes committed with firearms are also likely to have high police violence rates. In a study of forty-eight cities, Lawrence Sherman and Robert Langworthy found a strong association between police use of force and "gun density" (the proportion of suicides and murders committed with a gun).[147]

Social Variables. Research suggests that many individuals shot by police are transients or nonresidents caught at or near the scenes of robberies or burglaries of commercial establishments.[148] David Jacobs and David Britt found the greatest number of police shootings in states where there were great disparities in economic opportunity.[149]

Administrative Policies. The philosophy, policies, and practices of individual police chiefs and departments significantly influence the police use of deadly force.[150] Departments that stress restrictive policies on the use of force generally have lower shooting rates than those that favor tough law enforcement and encourage officers to shoot when necessary. Poorly written or ambivalent policies encourage shootings because they allow the officer at the scene to decide when deadly force is warranted, often under conditions of undue stress and tension.

Race and Police Shootings

No other issue is as important to the study of the police use of deadly force than that of racial discrimination. A number of critics have claimed that police are more likely to shoot and kill minority offenders than they are whites. In a famous statement, Paul Takagi charged that police have "one trigger finger for whites and another for blacks."[151] Takagi's complaint is supported by a number of research studies showing that a disproportionate number of police killings involve minority citizens—almost 80 percent in some of the cities surveyed.[152]

Do these findings alone indicate that police discriminate in the use of deadly force? Some pioneering research by James Fyfe helps provide an answer to this question. In his study of New York City shootings over a five-year period, Fyfe found that police officers are most likely to shoot suspects who are armed and with whom they become involved in violent confrontations. Once such factors as being armed with a weapon, being involved in a violent crime, and attacking an officer were considered, the racial differences in the police use of force ceased to be significant. In fact, Fyfe found that black officers were almost twice as likely as white officers to have shot citizens. Fyfe attributes this finding to the fact that (1) black officers work and live in high-crime, high-violence areas where shootings are more common and (2) black officers hold proportionately more line positions and fewer administrative posts than white officers, which would place them more often on the street and less often behind a desk.[153]

Shootings of Police

Although police officers are often taken to task for being too violent, the public sometimes forgets that police are all too often injured and killed by armed assailants. This situation has not been improved by the fact that professional criminals and drug dealers are armed with automatic weapons, such as UZI machine guns, while police officers carry .38-caliber revolvers. The danger in this disparity made national headlines when two FBI agents were killed and five seriously wounded when they intercepted two well-armed robbers on April 23, 1986, in Miami; the two slain officers were the twenty-eighth and twenty-ninth agents killed in the FBI's seventy-eight-year history.[154] As Barbara Raffel Price of John Jay University puts it:

> It would be foolish not to recognize that the violence associated with the drug business puts the police and citizens in greater jeopardy and that it makes the job of policing almost impossible.[155]

Every year, between fifty and one hundred law enforcement and public safety officers are feloniously killed in the line of duty (sixty-five in 1990); about two thirds of these are shooting victims.[156] The most common incident that results in the death of an officer is an arrest situation, followed by a disturbance call and the aftermath of an investigation of suspicious persons and circumstances. In addition, about seventy officers are killed each year in job-related incidents, such as traffic accidents.

What are the factors that predict the shooting of police officers? The majority of incidents were initiated by the officers themselves, as opposed to an unexpected attack by a hidden assailant; black officers had a greater risk of getting killed than white officers and by black assailants. Police officers faced the greatest danger when they were attempting to arrest an armed assailant. Contrary to popular myth, Konstantin did not find that police were at greatest risk while dealing with domestic disputes.[157] Ecological patterns may also be present when a police officer becomes the victim of violent crime. Southern cities, with high violence and gun-ownership rates, experience the highest numbers of police officer fatalities.[158] Some of the incidents that resulted in the death of a police officer are described in detail in Table 8.1.

TABLE 8.1
Line of Duty Deaths: Missouri and Ohio

Missouri

While attempting to execute a Federal search warrant in St. Louis County, a 13-year veteran FBI Special Agent was shot and killed. On January 19, 1990 at approximately 7 p.m., the St. Louis FBI SWAT team assembled to effect entry and search of a residence for weapons and drugs. Announcing their presence and forcibly entering through the front door, the 47-year-old agent was one of a four-man clearing room team. After assuring the first room was clear, the victim agent proceeded to a second room where he observed an armed male. The agent and the suspect fired almost simultaneously. Although wearing protective armor, the agent was fatally struck in the forehead with a round from a .38-caliber Taurus revolver. Other members of the team returned fire, killing the 45-year-old assailant. Two other agents were wounded in the gun battle; both have recovered from their wounds.

A 23-year-old St. Louis Metropolitan Police Department officer was shot and killed on June 12. At approximately 9:20 p.m., the off-duty officer, with less than 2 years' experience, drove to a laundromat, exited his vehicle, and was walking to its rear when accosted by a male who attempted to rob him. When the officer pulled his weapon in an attempt to arrest the robber, shots were exchanged, and the officer was fatally struck in the head with a round from a Smith & Wesson .38-caliber revolver. A 20-year-old male, shot three times and critically injured, was arrested and charged with first-degree murder and armed robbery.

Ohio

On the evening of April 17, [1990], a Washington County Sheriff's Office deputy was shot and killed during an attempted arrest. The Noble County Sheriff had gone to a Macksburg residence to serve a warrant for attempted murder and felonious assault. Upon arriving at the residence, the sheriff was fired upon while sitting in his vehicle. Shots went through the left front glass of his vehicle, with bullet fragments and glass striking him in the left shoulder and exiting through the rear glass. In response to the sheriff's call for assistance, officers from the Washington and Monroe County Sheriffs' Offices responded. Arriving at the scene, the officers checked several buildings on the property and located the man named on the warrant barricaded on the second floor of a barn-type garage. After the perimeter was secured, the victim deputy positioned himself below the man behind an embankment. At approximately 11:15 p.m., one shot was fired from within the barn, striking the deputy in the face. The 30-year-old male victim, with over 3 years' law enforcement experience, died instantly from the shot fired from a Remington, model 700, .243-caliber bolt-action rifle with a mounted scope. It is believed the assailant fired through a space in the siding on the barn. The man remained barricaded in the barn and a gun battle ensued. Over 200 rounds were expended by law enforcement officers and numerous attempts to negotiate with the 29-year-old male failed. Tear gas failed to bring the suspect out. Subsequently, the barn was set on fire and the assailant perished in the fire. The Noble County Sheriff has since recovered.

SOURCE: Federal Bureau of Investigation, *Law Enforcement Officers Killed and Assaulted, 1990* (Washington, D.C.: U.S. Government Printing Office, 1991), pp. 30–32.

Research also shows that off-duty police and plainclothes officers are very likely to be shot. One reason is that off-duty officers, who are usually armed, are expected to take appropriate action yet suffer tactical disadvantages, such as a lack of communication and backup.[159] Plainclothes officers are often mistaken for perpetrators or unwanted interveners.

Can the shooting of police be prevented? Annesley Schmidt believes that wearing protective equipment can significantly reduce police fatalities. She cites the wearing of Kevlar body armor, which is believed to have saved the lives of six hundred officers and reduced fatalities from gunshots by almost 30 percent.[160]

Controlling Deadly Force

Since the police use of deadly force is such a serious problem, ongoing efforts have been made to control its use.

One of the most difficult problems influencing its control was the continued use of the fleeing felon rule in a number of states. However, in 1985, the Supreme Court outlawed the indiscriminate use of deadly force with its decision in the case of *Tennessee v. Garner;* because of the importance of this case for the criminal justice system, it is set out in Law in Review. With *Garner*, the Supreme Court effectively put an end to any local police policy that allowed officers to shoot unarmed or otherwise nondangerous offenders if they resisted arrest or attempted to flee from police custody. However, the Court did not ban the use of deadly force or otherwise control police shooting policy. Consequently, in *Graham v. Connor*, the Supreme Court created a reasonableness standard for the use of force: force is excessive when, considering all the circumstances known to the officer at the time he or she acted, the force used was unreasonable.[161] For example, a police officer is approached in a threatening manner by someone wielding a knife. The assailant fails to stop when warned and is killed by the officer. The officer would not be held liable if it turns out that the shooting victim was deaf and could not hear the officer's command and the officer at the time of the incident had no way of knowing the person's condition.

Individual state jurisdictions still control police shooting policy. Some states have adopted statutory policies that restrict the police use of violence. Others have upgraded training in the use of force. The Federal Law Enforcement Training Center has developed the FLETC use of force model, illustrated in Figure 8.6, to teach officers the proper method to escalate force in response to the threat they face. As the figure shows, resistance ranges from compliant and cooperative to assaultive with the threat of serious bodily harm or death. Officers are taught via lecture, demonstration, computer-based instruction, and training scenario to assess the suspect's behavior and apply an appropriate and corresponding amount of force.[162]

Another method of controlling police shootings is through internal review and policy-making by police administrative review boards. For example, New York's Firearm Discharge Review Board was established over ten years ago to investigate and adjudicate all police firearm discharges. Among the dispositions available to the board are:

1. The discharge was in accordance with law and department policy.
2. The discharge was justifiable, but the officer should be given additional training in the use of firearms or in the law and department policy.
3. The shooting was justifiable under law but violated department policy and warrants department disciplinary action.

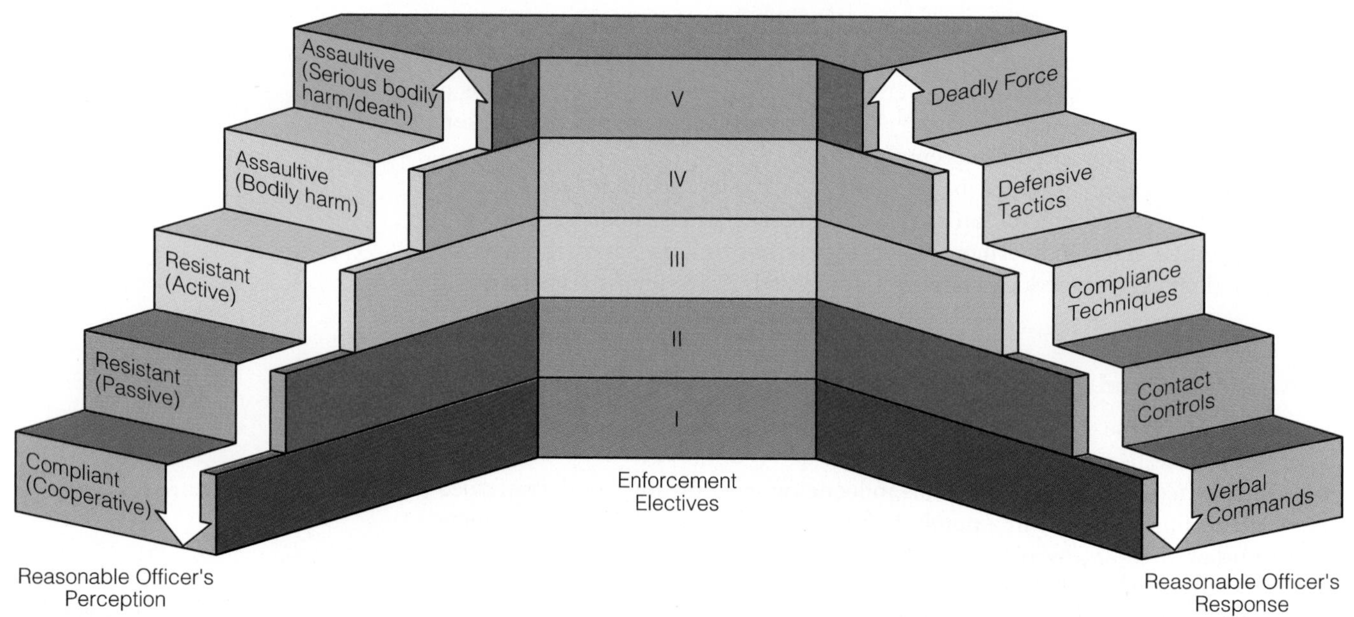

FIGURE 8.6
Federal Law Enforcement Training Center's Use of Force Model
SOURCE: Dr. Franklin Graves and Professor Gregory Connor, The Federal Law Enforcement Training Center, Glynco, Georgia.

4. The shooting was in apparent violation of law and should be referred to the appropriate prosecutor if criminal charges have not already been filed.
5. The officer involved should be transferred (or offered the opportunity to transfer) to a less sensitive assignment.
6. The officer involved should receive testing or alcoholism counseling.[163]

The review board approach is controversial because it can mean that the department recommends that one of its own officers be turned over for criminal prosecution, an outcome with which some legal scholars disagree.[164] In an analysis of the effect of the firearm review board (and the development of a restrictive shooting policy based on the Model Penal Code), James Fyfe found that "fleeing felon" shootings, warning shots, and opponent and officer deaths decreased significantly.[165]

Because of the positive results of instituting administrative reform, an increasing number of police departments are turning to administrative guidelines and policy reform, such as those formulated by the Commission for Accreditation for Law Enforcement Agencies, as a means of reducing civilian complaints about violence and the legal judgments and increases in liability insurance payments that soon follow.[166]

Corruption

From their creation, U.S. police departments have wrestled with the problem of controlling illegal and unprofessional behavior by their officers. Writing of early nineteenth-century police departments, historian Samuel Walker has stated:

> Corruption pervaded the American police. In fact, one could almost say that corruption was their main business. The police systematically ignored laws related to drinking, gambling, and prostitution in return for regular payoffs; they entered into relationships with professional criminals, especially pickpockets, tolerating

LAW IN REVIEW

Tennessee v. Garner (1985)

This case establishes the rule of law on the police use of deadly force to prevent the escape of a suspected felon.

Facts

On October 3, 1974, at about 10:45 P.M., two Memphis police officers were dispatched to answer a prowler call. Upon arriving, they encountered a neighbor who told them she had heard someone breaking into the house next door. While one of the officers radioed for help, the other went behind the house. The pursuing officer saw someone run across the backyard. The fleeing suspect stopped at a chain-link fence at the end of the yard. When the officer shone his flashlight at the suspect, he saw what appeared to him to be a seventeen- or eighteen-year-old youth who may have been about five feet seven inches tall. The officer called out, "Police! Halt!" The suspect, however, began to climb the fence. Convinced that the suspect would get away, the police officer shot him; the bullet struck the suspect in the back of the head, and he later died on an operating table.

The dead suspect turned out to be Edward Garner, an eighth grader who was 15 years old and weighed between 100 and 110 pounds. At trial, the officer admitted that he knew Garner was unarmed and trying to flee from his pursuit. However, he felt justified in using deadly force because the much younger suspect had a good chance of evading his pursuit and Tennessee law allowed him to use his weapon under those circumstances. The Tennessee statute read in part, "If after notice of the intention to arrest the defendant, he either flees or forcibly resists, the officer may use all the necessary means to effect the arrest" (section 40-7-108 [1982]).

Decision

The U.S. Supreme Court ruled that the use of deadly force against apparently unarmed and nondangerous fleeing felons is an illegal seizure of their person under the Fourth Amendment. Deadly force may not be used unless it is necessary to prevent the escape and the officer has probable cause to believe that the suspect poses a significant threat of death or serious injury to the officer or others. The majority opinion stated, "The use of deadly force to prevent the escape of all felony suspects, whatever the circumstances, is constitutionally unreasonable. It is not better that all felony suspects die than they escape. Where the suspect poses no immediate threat to the officer and no threat to others, the harm resulting from failing to apprehend them does not justify the use of deadly force to do so. It is no doubt unfortunate when a suspect who is in sight escapes, but the fact that the police arrive a little late or are a little slower afoot does not always justify killing the suspect. A police officer may not seize an unarmed, nondangerous suspect by shooting him dead."

Significance of the Case

In deciding *Garner,* the Supreme Court recognized the changes that have occurred in the justice system since the common law fleeing felon doctrine was formulated. No longer are all felonies punished by death, nor are law enforcers limited to personal-contact weapons, such as a club. If the fleeing felon rule remained a police policy, future tragedies like the shooting of Edward Garner would surely occur. The fact that if this nonviolent adolescent had been caught, he would probably have served a probation sentence was not lost on the Court.

Garner, however, was not a unanimous decision. Three justices argued that police should be able to use whatever force is necessary to capture criminals who commit serious crimes, such as burglary. The dissenters espoused a public safety doctrine—the rights of the criminal are less important than the right of honest citizens to be adequately protected by police. Despite such disagreement, *Garner* should end use of the fleeing felon rule in the United States.

illicit activity in return for goods or information; they actively supported a system of electoral fraud; and they sold promotions to higher rank within the department.[167]

Since the early nineteenth century, scandals involving police abuse of power have occurred in many urban cities, and elaborate methods have been devised to control or eliminate the problem. Though most police officers are probably not corrupt, the few that are dishonest bring discredit to the entire profession.

Police deviance can include a number of different activities. In a general sense, it involves misuse of authority by police officers in a manner designed to produce personal gain for themselves or others.[168] However, debate continues over whether a desire for personal gain is an essential part of corruption. Some experts argue that police misconduct also involves such issues as the unnecessary use of force, unreasonable searches, or an immoral personal life and that these should be considered as serious as corruption devoted to economic gain. However, the broadening of misconduct categories can have unforeseen consequences. While most police departments have regulations governing police officer misconduct (conduct unbecoming an officer), their application can lead to lawsuits, especially when the proscribed conduct involves the officer's personal life. For example, some departments prohibit police officers from engaging in off-duty homosexual conduct or ban cohabitation by unmarried officers. The courts have been divided on whether police officers have the same rights of privacy as other citizens.[169]

Varieties of Police Corruption

When we think about corrupt police officers, the image that usually comes to mind is of the greedy cop taking a bribe from a drug dealer, being on the payroll of the racketeer, or shaking down a motorist who should be getting a ticket. But corruption is actually much more complex and takes on many different forms, ranging from abuse of power to outright criminality. For example, a Boston police officer was convicted of larceny after receiving eighty-eight thousand dollars in salary while he was on a fully paid job-related medical leave and working as a safety and security officer at a local high school.[170]

Scholars have attempted to create typologies categorizing the forms that the abuse of police powers can take. For example, when investigating corruption among police officers in New York, the **Knapp Commission** classified abusers into two categories: "**meat eaters**" and "**grass eaters**."[171] Meat eaters aggressively misuse police power for personal gain by demanding bribes, threatening legal action, or cooperating with criminals. Across the country, police officers have been accused, indicted, and convicted of shaking down club owners and other business people.[172] In contrast, grass eaters accept payoffs when their everyday duties place them in a position to be solicited by the public. For example, police officers have been investigated for taking bribes to look the other way while neighborhood bookmakers ply their trade.[173] The Knapp Commission concluded that the vast majority of police officers on the take are grass eaters, although the few meat eaters who are caught capture all the headlines.

Other police experts have attempted to create models to better understand police corruption. Michael Johnston divides police corruption into four major categories:[174]

1. *Internal corruption*—takes place among police officers themselves, involving both the bending of departmental rules and the outright performance of illegal acts. For example, in Chicago, police officers conspired to sell relatively new police cars to other officers at cut-rate prices, forcing the department to purchase new cars unnecessarily. In Boston, a major scandal hit the police department when a police captain was indicted in an exam tampering and selling scheme. Numerous officers bought promotion exams from the captain, while others had him lower the scores of rivals who were competing for the same job.[175]

2. *Selective enforcement or nonenforcement*—occurs when police abuse or exploit their discretion. If an officer frees a drug dealer in return for valuable information, that would be considered a legitimate use of discretion; if the police officer did it for money, that would be an abuse of police power.

3. *Active criminality*—involves participation by police in serious criminal behavior. Police may use their positions of trust and power to commit the very crimes they are entrusted with controlling. For example, a police burglary ring in Denver was so large it prompted one commentator to coin the phrase "burglars in blue." During the past twenty years, police burglary rings have been uncovered in Chicago, Reno, Nashville, Cleveland, and Burlington, Vermont, among other cities.[176] Another disturbing trend has been police use of drugs. Peter Kraska and Victor Kappeler found that more than 20 percent of the officers in a local police department used marijuana and dangerous nonprescription drugs while on active duty.[177]

4. *Bribery and extortion*—refers to practices in which law enforcement roles are exploited specifically to raise money. Bribery is initiated by the citizen, extortion is initiated by the officer. Bribery or extortion can be a one-shot transaction, as when a traffic violator offers a police officer twenty dollars to forget about issuing a summons and the bribe is accepted. Or the relationship can be an ongoing one, in which the officer solicits (or is offered) regular payoffs to ignore criminal activities, such as gambling or narcotics dealing. This is known as being *on the pad.* When Ellwyn Stoddard interviewed a former police officer who had been indicted on charges of robbery and grand larceny, he uncovered additional categories of "blue-coat crime":[178]

5. *Mooching*—receiving free gifts of coffee, cigarettes, meals, and so on, in exchange for possible future acts of favoritism.

6. *Chiseling*—demanding admission to entertainment events or price discounts.

7. *Shopping*—taking small items such as cigarettes from a store whose door was accidentally left unlocked after business hours.

8. *Shakedown*—appropriating expensive items from a crime scene and blaming the loss on the criminal.

9. *Favoritism*—giving immunity to friends or relatives from traffic or other violations.

Lawrence Sherman suggests that police departments themselves can be categorized on the basis of the level and type of corruption existing within them.[179] He identifies three different types:

Type I: Rotten apples and rotten pockets. This type of police department has a few corrupt officers who use their position for personal gain. When these corrupt officers band together, they form a *rotten pocket*. Robert Daley described the activities of such a group in his book *Prince of the City*. Agents of New York City's Special Investigations Unit kept money they confiscated during narcotics raids and used illegal drugs to pay off informers. Rotten pockets help institutionalize corruption because their members expect newcomers to conform to their illegal practices and to a code of secrecy. For example, *Prince of the City* tells the story of New York Detective Frank Leuci, whose testimony against his partners before investigating committees made him an outcast in the police department.

Type II: Pervasive unorganized corruption. According to Sherman, a Type II department contains a majority of personnel who are corrupt but have little relationship to one another. Though many officers are involved in taking bribes and extortion, they are not cooperating with one another for personal gain.

Type III: Pervasive organized corruption. This describes a department in which almost all members are involved in systematic and organized corruption. The Knapp Commission found this type of relationship in New York City's vice divisions, where payoffs and bribes were an organized and accepted way of police life.

The Causes and Control of Corruption

No single explanation satisfactorily accounts for the various forms the abuse of power takes. One view puts the blame on the type of person who becomes a police officer. This position holds that policing tends to attract lower-class individuals who do not have the financial means to maintain a coveted middle-class life-style. As they develop the cynical, authoritarian police personality, accepting graft seems an all-too-easy method of achieving financial security.[180]

A second view is that the wide discretion police enjoy, coupled with the low visibility they maintain with the public and their own supervisors, makes them likely candidates for corruption. In addition, the "code of secrecy" maintained by the police subculture helps insulate corrupt officers from the law. Similarly, police managers, most of whom have risen through the ranks, are reluctant to investigate corruption or punish wrongdoers. Thus, corruption may also be viewed as a function of police institutions and practices.[181]

A third position holds that corruption is a function of society's ambivalence toward many forms of vice-related criminal behavior that police officers are sworn to control. As Samuel Walker states:

> Unenforceable laws governing moral standards promote corruption because they create large groups with an interest in subverting law enforcement. Interest groups include both consumers and suppliers. The consumers—people who gamble, or wish to drink after the legal closing hour, or patronize a prostitute—do not want to be deprived of their chosen form of recreation. Even though the consumers may not actively corrupt police officers (by offering bribes, for example), their existence creates a climate that tolerates active corruption by others.[182]

Since vice cannot be controlled and the public apparently wants it to continue, the police officer may have little resistance to inducements for monetary gain offered by law violators. A good example of this problem can be found in Dade County, Florida. In 1985 alone, eleven police officers there were arrested on drug-related charges. Two were charged with making off with 150 pounds of cocaine valued at $2 million from a raided boat. Another four officers were indicted on murder charges when they hijacked a boatload of cocaine and caused the drug runners to jump into the sea and drown.[183]

How can police corruption be controlled? One approach is to strengthen the internal administrative review process within police departments. A strong and well-supported internal affairs division has been linked to lowered corruption rates.[184] Another approach, instituted by then New York Commissioner Patrick Murphy in the wake of the Knapp Commission, is the **accountability system.** This holds that supervisors at each level are directly accountable for the illegal behaviors of the officers under them. Consequently, a commander can be forced to resign or be demoted if one of his or her command is found guilty of corruption.[185]

Close scrutiny by a department can lower officer morale and create the suspicion that the officers' own supervisors distrust them. Another similar approach is to create outside review boards or special prosecutors, such as the Christopher Commission, to investigate reported incidents of corruption. However, outside investigators and/or special prosecutors are often limited by their lack of intimate knowledge of day-to-day police operations. As a result, they depend on the testimony of a few officers who are willing to cooperate, either to save themselves from prosecution or because they have a compelling moral commitment. Outside evaluators also face the problem of the "blue curtain," which is quickly drawn closed when police officers feel their department is under scrutiny.

Another approach to controlling police corruption is through court review of police behavior. In the past decade, courts have tended to remove restrictions limiting litigation against the police. While it is difficult to analyze the precise effects of legal action on police behavior, the resulting higher insurance rates caused by large settlements and increased media coverage have almost certainly caused police administrators to take the matter quite seriously.[186]

It is also possible that corruption can be controlled by intensive training and education programs begun when a police officer first enters a training academy. Thomas Barker has shown that police recruits believe that a certain degree of corruption is present in every department.[187] Therefore, recruits should be made aware of the enticements to police deviance and the steps that can be taken to control it.

A more realistic solution to police corruption, albeit a difficult one, might be to change the social context of policing. Police operations must be made more visible and the public must be given freer access to controlling police operations. All too often the public finds out about police problems only when a scandal hits the newspaper. Some of the vice-related crimes the police now deal with might be decriminalized or referred to other agencies. Although decriminalization of vice cannot in itself end the problem, it could lower the pressure placed on individual police officers and help eliminate their moral dilemmas.

SUMMARY

Police departments today are faced with many critical problems in their development and relationship with the public.

Police are believed to be insulated from the rest of society. Some experts hold that police officers have distinct personality characteristics marked by authoritarianism and cynicism. It is also alleged that police maintain a separate culture with distinct rules and loyalties. A police personality also influences their working style. Four distinct police styles have been identified, and each influences police decision making. The complexity and danger of the police role produce an enormous amount of stress that harms police effectiveness.

Social concerns also affect police operations. Today, many police officers are seeking higher education. The jury is still out on whether educated police officers are actually more effective. Women and minorities are now being recruited into the police in increasing numbers. Research indicates that, with few exceptions, they perform equally well or even better than other officers. The percentage of minorities on police forces reflects their representation in the general population, but the number of female officers still lags behind. Of greater importance is increasing the number of women and minorities in supervisory positions.

Police departments have also been concerned about limiting police stress and improving police-community relations. One critical concern is the police use of deadly force. Research indicates that antishooting policies can limit deaths resulting from police action. Another effort has been to identify and eliminate police corruption, which still mars the reputation of police forces.

QUESTIONS

1. Should male and female officers have exactly the same duties in a police department?
2. Do you think that working the street will eventually produce a cynical personality and distrust for civilians?
3. How would education help police officers? Can it actually hinder them?

4. Do you think that police work is any more stressful than other professions?
5. Should a police officer who accepts a free meal from a restaurant owner be dismissed from the force?
6. A police officer orders an unarmed person running away from a burglary to stop; the suspect keeps running and is shot and killed by the officer. Has the officer committed murder?
7. Would you like to live in a society that abolished police discretion and used a full enforcement policy?

NOTES

1. Kathleen Maguire and Timothy Flanagan, *Sourcebook of Criminal Justice Statistics, 1990* (Washington, D.C.: Bureau of Justice Statistics, 1991), p. 159.
2. See, for example, Richard Harris, *The Police Academy: An Inside View* (New York: John Wiley & Sons, 1973); John Van Maanen, "Observations on the Making of a Policeman," in *Order Under Law*, ed. R. Culbertson and M. Tezak (Prospect Heights, Ill.: Waveland Press, 1981), pp. 111–26; Jonathan Rubenstein, *City Police* (New York: Ballantine Books, 1973); John Broderick, *Police in a Time of Change* (Morristown, N.J.: General Learning Press, 1977).
3. Malcolm Sparrow, Mark Moore, and David Kennedy, *Beyond 911, A New Era for Policing* (New York: Basic Books, 1990), p. 51.
4. M. Steven Meagher and Nancy Yentes, "Choosing a Career in Policing: A Comparison of Male and Female Perceptions," *Journal of Police Science and Administration* 16 (1986):320–27.
5. Michael K. Brown, *Working the Street* (New York: Russel Sage Foundation, 1981), p. 82.
6. Stan Shernock, "An Empirical Examination of the Relationship Between Police Solidarity and Community Orientation," *Journal of Police Science and Administration* 18 (1988):182–98.
7. Egon Bittner, *The Functions of Police in Modern Society* (Cambridge, Mass: Oelgeschlager, Gunn & Hain, 1980), p. 63.
8. Richard Lundman, *Police and Policing* (New York: Holt, Rinehart & Winston, 1980); see also, Jerome Skolnick, *Justice Without Trial* (New York: John Wiley & Sons, 1966).
9. Robert Regoli, Robert Culbertson, John Crank, and James Powell, "Career Stage and Cynicism Among Police Chiefs," *Justice Quarterly* 7 (1990):592–614.
10. William Westly, *Violence and the Police: A Sociological Study of Law, Custom, and Morality* (Cambridge: MIT Press, 1970).
11. Skolnick, *Justice Without Trial*, pp. 42–68.
12. Milton Rokeach, Martin Miller, and John Snyder, "The Value Gap Between Police and Policed," *Journal of Social Issues* 27 (1971):155–71.
13. Van Maanen, "Observations on the Making of a Policeman," p. 50.
14. Ibid, p. 66.
15. George Kirkham, "A Professor's Street Lessons," in *Order Under Law*, ed. R. Culbertson and M. Tezak (Prospect Heights, Ill.: Waveland Press, 1981), p. 81.
16. Bittner, *Functions of Police in Modern Society*, p. 63.
17. Arthur Niederhoffer, *Behind the Shield: The Police in Urban Society* (Garden City, N.Y.: Doubleday, 1967).
18. Westly, *Violence and the Police;* idem, "Violence and the Police," *American Journal of Sociology* 49 (1953):34–41.
19. Niederhoffer, *Behind the Shield*, pp. 216–20.
20. Robert Regoli and Eric Poole, "Measurement of Police Cynicism: A Factor Scaling Approach," *Journal of Criminal Justice* 7 (1979):37–52.
21. Ibid., p. 43.
22. Ibid., p. 44.
23. Richard Anson, J. Dale Mann, and Dale Sherman, "Niederhoffer's Cynicism Scale: Reliability and Beyond," *Journal of Criminal Justice* 14 (1986):295–307.
24. Bruce Carpenter and Susan Raza, "Personality Characteristics of Police Applicants: Comparisons Across Subgroups and with Other Populations," *Journal of Police Science and Administration* 15 (1987):10–17.
25. Larry Tifft, "The 'Cop Personality' Reconsidered," *Journal of Police Science and Administration* 2 (1974):268; David Bayley and Harold Mendelsohn, *Minorities and the Police* (New York: Free Press, 1969); Robert Balch, "The Police Personality: Fact or Fiction?" *Journal of Criminal Law, Criminology, and Police Science* 63 (1972):117.
26. Lowell Storms, Nolan Penn, and James Tenzell, "Policemen's Perception of Real and Ideal Policemen," *Journal of Police Science and Administration* 17 (1990):40–43.
27. George Reming, "Personality Characteristics of Supercops and Habitual Criminals," *Journal of Police Science and Administration* 16 (1988):163–67.
28. Cark Klockars, "The Dirty Harry Problem," *Annals* 452 (1980):33–47.
29. Jack Kuykendall and Roy Roberg, "Police Manager's Perceptions of Employee Types: A Conceptual Model," *Journal of Criminal Justice* 16 (1988):131–35.
30. William Muir, *Police: Streetcorner Politicians* (Chicago: University of Chicago Press, 1977).
31. Brown, *Working the Street*, pp. 234–35.
32. James Q. Wilson, *Varieties of Police Behavior* (Cambridge: Harvard University Press, 1968), chapter 7.
33. Ibid., p. 141.
34. Muir, *Police: Streetcorner Politicians;* Brown, *Working the Street*.
35. Ellen Hochstedler, "Testing Types, A Review and Test of Police Types," *Journal of Criminal Justice* 9 (1981):451–66.
36. Kathryn Golden, "The Police Role: Perceptions and Preferences," *Journal of Police Science and Administration* 10 (1982):108–11.
37. Skolnick, *Justice Without Trial*.
38. Gregory Howard Williams, *The Law and Politics of Police Discretion* (Westport, Conn.: Greenwood Press, 1984).
39. Dennis Powell, "Race, Rank, and Police Discretion," *Journal of Police Science and Administration* 9 (1981):383–89.
40. Douglas Smith and Jody Klein, "Police Control of Interpersonal Disputes," *Social Problems* 31 (1984):468–81.
41. Westly, *Violence and the Police*.
42. Nathan Goldman, *The Differential Selection of Juvenile Offenders for Court Appearance* (New York: National Council on Crime and Delinquency, 1963).
43. Powell, "Race, Rank, and Police Discretion."
44. Dale Dannefer and Russell Schutt, "Race and Juvenile Justice Processing in Court and Police Agencies," *American Journal of Sociology* 87 (1982):1113–32.
45. Christy Visher, "Arrest Decisions and Notions of Chivalry," *Criminology* 21 (1983):5–28.
46. Douglas Smith and Christy Visher, "Street-Level Justice: Situational Determinants of Police Arrest Decisions," *Social Problems* 29 (1981):267–77.
47. See, generally, William Wilbanks, *The Myth of a Racist Criminal Jus-*

tice System (Monterey, Calif.: Brooks/Cole, 1987); see also Douglas Smith and Jody Klein, "Police Control of Interpersonal Disputes," *Social Problems* 31 (1984):368–481.

48. Douglas Smith, Christy Visher, and Laura Davidson, "Equity and Discretionary Justice: The Influence of Race on Police Arrest Decisions," *Journal of Criminal Law and Criminology* 75 (1984):234–49.

49. Cecil Willis and Richard Ward, "The Police and Child Abuse: An Analysis of Police Decisions to Report Illegal Behavior," *Criminology* 26 (1988):695–716.

50. See, for example, Wilson, *Varieties of Police Behavior;* see James Fyfe, "Blind Justice? Police Shootings in Memphis" (Paper presented at the Annual Meeting of the Academy of Criminal Justice Sciences, Philadelphia, March 1981).

51. Marvin Krohn, James Curry, and Shirley Nelson-Kilger, "Is Chivalry Dead? An Analysis of Changes in Police Dispositions of Males and Females," *Criminology* 21 (1983):417–37.

52. Brown, *Working the Street*, p. 290.

53. See Larry Hoover, *Police Educational Characteristics and Curricula* (Washington, D.C.: U.S. Government Printing Office, 1975).

54. David Carter and Allen Sapp, *The State of Police Education: Critical Findings* (Washington, D.C.: Police Executive Research Forum, 1988), p. 6.

55. Bruce Berg, "Who Should Teach Police: A Typology and Assessment of Police Academy Instructors," *American Journal of Police* 9 (1990):79–100.

56. Brian Reaves, *State and Local Police Departments, 1990* (Washington, D.C.: Bureau of Justice Statistics, 1992).

57. Carter and Sapp, *The State of Police Education: Critical Findings*.

58. Robert Worden, "A Badge and a Baccalaurate: Policies, Hypotheses, and Further Evidence, *Justice Quarterly* 7 (1990):565–92.

59. See Lawrence Sherman and Warren Bennis, "Higher Education for Police Officers: The Central Issues," *Police Chief* 44 (1977):32.

60. Lawrence Sherman et al., *The Quality of Police Education* (San Francisco: Jossey-Bass, 1978).

61. See, for example, B.E. Sanderson, "Police Officers: The Relationship of a College Education to Job Performance," *Police Chief* 44 (1977):62.

62. Lee Bowker, "A Theory of Educational Needs of Law Enforcement Officers," *Journal of Contemporary Criminal Justice* 1 (1980):17–24.

63. Worden, "Badge and a Baccalaurate," pp. 587–89.

64. David Carter, Allen Sapp, and Darrel Stephens, "Higher Education as a Bona Fide Occupational Qualification (BFOQ) for Police: A Blueprint," *American Journal of Police* 7 (1988):1–29.

65. Jack Kuykendall and David Burns, "The Black Police Officer: An Historical Perspective," *Journal of Contemporary Criminal Justice* 1 (1980):4–13.

66. Ibid.

67. Nicholas Alex, *Black in Blue: A Study of the Negro Policeman* (New York: Appleton-Century-Crofts, 1969).

68. Nicholas Alex, *New York Cops Talk Back* (New York: John Wiley & Sons, 1976).

69. Eva Buzawa, "The Role of Race in Predicting Job Attitudes of Patrol Officers," *Journal of Criminal Justice* 9 (1981):63–78.

70. Bruce Berg, Edmond True, and Marc Gertz, "Police, Riots, and Alienation," *Journal of Police Science and Administration* 12 (1984):186–90.

71. Daniel Georges-Abeyie, "Black Police Officers: An Interview with Alfred W. Dean, Director of Public Safety, Harrisburg, Pennsylvania," in *The Criminal Justice System and Blacks*, ed. D. Georges-Abeyie (Beverly Hills, Calif.: Sage Publications, 1984).

72. "Profiles of Black Police Chiefs of Selected Cities," *Blacks in Criminal Justice* Spring/Summer (1985):18–24.

73. *Baker v. City of St. Petersburg*, 400 F.2d 294 (5th Cir. 1968).

74. See, for example, *Allen v. City of Mobile*, 331 F.Supp. 1134 (1971), *affirmed* 466 F.2d 122 (5th Cir. 1972).

75. Kuykendall and Burns, "The Black Police Officer."

76. "Two Cities Take Different Paths in College Education for Recruits," *Police* 6 (January 1983):35.

77. "The Police Exam That Flunked," *New York Times*, News of the Week in Review, 24 November 1985, p. 20.

78. *United States v. Paradise*, 480 U.S. 149, 107 S.Ct. 1053, 94 L.Ed.2d 203 (1987).

79. See *Afro American Patrolmen's League v. Duck*, 366 F.Supp. 1095 (N.D. Ohio 1973); 503 F.2d 294 (6th Cir. 1974); 538 F.2d 328 (6th Cir. 1976).

80. *Detroit Police Officers Association v. Young*, 446 F.Supp. 979 (E.D. Mich. 1978).

81. Steven Marantz, "City review turns up no racial fraud by police, some question finding," *Boston Globe*, 19 October 1988, p. 21.

82. Michael Charles, "Resolving Discrimination in the Promotion of Fort Wayne Police Officers," *American Journal of Police* 10 (1991):67–87.

83. Susan Martin, "Female Officers on the Move? A Status Report on Women in Policing," in *Critical Issues in Policing*, ed. Dunham and Alpert (Grove Park, Ill.: Waveland Press, 1988), pp. 312–31 at 312.

84. *Le Bouef v. Ramsey*, 26 FEP Cases 884 (9/16/80).

85. Carole Garrison, Nancy Grant, and Kenneth McCormick, "Utilization of Police Women," *Police Chief* 55 (1988):32–33.

86. Eric Poole and Mark Pogrebin, "Factors Affecting the Decision to Remain in Policing: A Study of Women Officers," *Journal of Police Science and Administration* 16 (1988):49–55 at 54.

87. Merry Morash and Jack Greene, "Evaluating Women on Patrol: A Critique of Contemporary Wisdom," *Evaluation Review* 10 (1986):230–55.

88. Peter Bloch and Deborah Anderson, *Policewomen on Patrol: Final Report* (Washington, D.C.: Police Foundation, 1974).

89. Robert Homant and Daniel Kennedy, "Police Perceptions of Spouse Abuse: A Comparison of Male and Female Officers," *Journal of Criminal Justice* 13 (1985):49–64.

90. Bloch and Anderson, *Policewomen on Patrol*, pp. 1–7.

91. Judie Gaffin Wexler and Vicki Quinn, "Considerations in the Training and Development of Women Sergeants," *Journal of Police Science and Administration* 13 (1985):98–105.

92. James David, "Perspectives of Policewomen in Texas and Oklahoma," *Journal of Police Science and Administration* 12 (1984):395–403.

93. Joyce Sichel et al., *Women on Patrol: A Pilot Study of Police Performances in New York City* (Washington, D.C.: National Criminal Justice Reference Service, 1978).

94. Sean Grennan, "Findings on the Role of Officer Gender in Violent Encounters with Citizens," *Journal of Police Science and Administration* 15 (1988):78–85.

95. See, for example, Jack Molden, "Female Police Officers: Training Implications," *Law and Order* 33 (1985):62–63.

96. Joseph Balkin, "Why Policemen Don't Like Policewomen," *Journal of Police Science and Administration* 16 (1988):29–38.

97. Anthony Bouza, "Women in Policing," *FBI Law Enforcement Bulletin* 44 (1975):2–7.

98. Balkin, "Why Policemen Don't Like Policewomen," p. 36.

99. Kenneth Kerber, Steven Andes, and Michelle Mittler, "Citizen Attitudes Regarding the Competence of Female Police Officers," *Journal of Police Science and Administration* 5 (1977):337–46.

100. Martin, "Female Officers on the Move?" p. 322.

101. Adriane Kinnane, *Policing* (Chicago: Nelson-Hall, 1979), p. 58.

102. Bruce Berg and Kimberly Budnick, "Defeminization of Women in Law Enforcement: A New Twist in the Traditional Police Personality," *Journal of Police Science and Administration* 14 (1986):314–19.

103. Michael Charles, "Women in Policing: The Physical Aspects," *Journal of Police Science and Administration* 10 (1982):194–205.

104. Daniel Bell, "Policewomen: Myths and Reality," *Journal of Police*

Science and Administration 10 (1982):112–20.
105. Susan Martin, "*Police*women and Police*women*: Occupational Role Dilemmas and Choices of Female Officers," *Journal of Police Science and Administration* 7 (1979):314.
106. Ibid., pp. 317–318; see also idem, *Breaking and Entering* (Berkeley: University of California Press, 1980).
107. Roi Dianne Townsey, "Black Women in American Policing: An Advancement Display," *Journal of Criminal Justice* 10 (1982):455–68.
108. J. G. Wexler and V. Quinn, "Considerations in the Training and Development of Women Sergeants."
109. Martin, "Female Officers on the Move?" pp. 325–26.
110. Ibid.
111. Poole and Pogrebin, "Factors Affecting the Decision to Remain in Policing: A Study of Women Officers," pp. 54–55.
112. Roy Roberg, David Hayhurst and Harry Allen, "Job Burnout in Law Enforcement Dispatchers: A Comparative Analysis," *Journal of Criminal Justice* 16 (1988):385–94.
113. For an impressive review, see Richard Farmer, "Clinical and Managerial Implication of Stress Research on the Police," *Journal of Police Science and Administration* 17 (1990):205–17.
114. Francis Cullen, Terrence Lemming, Bruce Link, and John Wozniak, "The Impact of Social Supports on Police Stress," *Criminology* 23 (1985):503–22.
115. Farmer, "Clinical and Managerial Implications of Stress Research on the Police"; Nancy Norvell, Dale Belles, and Holly Hills, "Perceived Stress Levels and Physical Symptoms in Supervisory Law Enforcement Personnel," *Journal of Police Science and Administration* 16 (1988):75–79.
116. Harvey McMurray, "Attitudes of Assaulted Police Officers and Their Policy Implications," *Journal of Police Science and Administration* 17 (1990):44–48.
117. John Blackmore, "Police Stress," in *Policing Society*, ed. Clinton Terry (New York: John Wiley & Sons, 1985), p. 395.
118. Rose Lee Josephson and Martin Reiser, "Officer Suicide in the Los Angeles Police Department: A Twelve-Year Follow-Up," *Journal of Police Science and Administration* 17 (1990):227–30.
119. Ibid.
120. Farmer, "Clinical and Managerial Implications of Stress Research on the Police," p. 215.
121. Vivian Lord, Denis Gray, and Samuel Pond, "The Police Stress Inventory: Does It Measure Stress?" *Journal of Criminal Justice* 19 (1991):139–49.
122. Samuel Walker, *Popular Justice* (New York: Oxford University Press, 1980), p. 197.
123. George Hackett, "All of Us Are in Trouble," *Newsweek*, 30 January 1989, p. 41; Pamela Reynolds, "Legacy of hostility pervades Overton," *Boston Globe*, 19 January 1989, p. 1.
124. See, for example, President's Commission on Law Enforcement and Administration of Justice, *Task Force Report: The Police* (Washington, D.C.: U.S. Government Printing Office, 1967), pp. 181–82; National Advisory Commission on Civil Disorders, *Police and the Community* (Washington, D.C.: U.S. Government Printing Office, 1968), pp. 158–59.
125. President's Commission on Law Enforcement and the Administration of Justice, *Task Force Report: The Police*, pp. 181–82.
126. Albert Reiss, *The Police and the Public* (New Haven: Yale University Press, 1972).
127. Lawrence Sherman, "Causes of Police Behavior, The Current State of Quantitative Research," *Journal of Research in Crime and Delinquency* 17 (1980):80–81.
128. John Dugan and Daniel Breda, "Complaints About Police Officers: A Comparison Among Types and Agencies," *Journal of Criminal Justice* 19 (1991):165–71.
129. David Bayley and James Garofalo, "The Management of Violence by Police Patrol Officers," *Criminology* 27 (1989):1–27.
130. Bill Girdner, "Charges of racism by Calif. police is latest in long line," *Boston Globe*, 19 January 1989, p. 3.
131. Anthony Pate and Edwin Hamilton, *The Big Six, Policing America's Largest Cities* (Washington, D.C.: Police Foundation, 1990), p. 138.
132. Michael Meyer, "LAPD: A Force Unto Itself," *Newsweek*, 16 March 1992, p. 37.
133. Ibid.
134. Samuel Walker, "The Rule Revolution: Reflections on the Transformation of American Criminal Justice, 1950–1988," Working Papers, Series 3, Institute for Legal Studies, University of Wisconsin Law School, Madison, December 1988.
135. *People v. Sullivan*, 116 A.D.2d 101, 500 N.Y.S.2d 644 (1986).
136. Lawrence Sherman and Robert Langworthy, "Measuring Homicide by Police Officers," *Journal of Criminal Law and Criminology* 4 (1979): 546–60.
137. Ibid.
138. "Killing of a Black by Police Again Triggers Riots in Miami," *Criminal Justice Newsletter*, 1 February 1989) p. 3.
139. James Fyfe, "Police Use of Deadly Force: Research and Reform," *Justice Quarterly* 5 (1988):165–205.
140. Kenneth Matulia, *A Balance of Forces*, 2d ed. (Gaithersburg, Md.: International Association of Chiefs of Police, 1985).
141. William Geller, "Deadly Force: What We Know," *Journal of Police Science and Administration* 10 (1982):151–77.
142. Sherman and Langworthy, "Measuring Homicide by Police Officers."
143. Fyfe, "Police Use of Deadly Force: Research and Reform."
144. Ibid., pp. 178–79.
145. Sherman and Langworthy, "Measuring Homicide by Police Officers"; Richard Kania and Wade Mackey, "Police Violence as a Function of Community Characteristics," *Criminology* 15 (1977):27–48.
146. Ibid.
147. Sherman and Langworthy, "Measuring Homicide by Police Officers."
148. Ibid.
149. David Jacobs and David Britt, "Inequality and Police Use of Deadly Force: An Empirical Assessment of a Conflict Hypothesis," *Social Problems* 26 (1979):403–12.
150. Fyfe, "Police Use of Deadly Force: Research and Reform," p. 181.
151. Paul Takagi, "A Garrison State in a 'Democratic' Society," *Crime and Social Justice* 5 (1974):34–43.
152. Mark Blumberg, "Race and Police Shootings: An Analysis in Two Cities," *Contemporary Issues in Law Enforcement*, ed. James Fyfe (Beverly Hills,Calif.: Sage Publications, 1981), pp. 152–66; Catherine Milton et al., *Police Use of Deadly Force* (Washington, D.C.: Police Foundation, 1977).
153. James Fyfe, "Shots Fired," Ph.D. diss., State University of New York, Albany, 1978.
154. Jacob Lamar, "A Twisted Trail of Blood," *Time*, 28 April 1986, p. 38.
155. Quoted in Karen Polk, "New York police: Caught in the middle and losing faith," *Boston Globe*, 28 December 1988, p. 3.
156. Federal Bureau of Investigation, *Law Enforcement Officers Killed and Assaulted, 1990* (Washington, D.C.: U.S. Government Printing Office, 1991); Annesley Schmidt, "Deaths in the Line of Duty," *NIJ Reports 1989* 4 (1985):6–8.
157. David Konstantin, "Law Enforcement Officers Feloniously Killed in the Line of Duty: An Exploratory Study," *Justice Quarterly* 1 (1984):29–45.
158. David Lester, "The Murder of Police Officers in American Cities," *Criminal Justice and Behavior* 11 (1984):101–13.
159. "Number of Officers Killed Declined in '81," *Justice Assistance News* 6 (August 1982):13; see also Geller, "Officer Restraint in the Use of Deadly Force," pp. 166–67.
160. Schmidt, "Deaths in the Line of Duty," p. 8.

161. *Graham v. Connor*, 490 U.S. 386, 109 S.Ct. 1865, 104 L.Ed.2d 443 (1989).
162. Franklin Graves and Gregory Connor, "The FLETC Use-of-Force Model," *Police Chief* 59 (1992):56–58.
163. See James Fyfe, "Administrative Interventions on Police Shooting Discretion: An Empirical Examination," *Journal of Criminal Justice* 7 (1979):313–25.
164. Frank Zarb, "Police Liability for Creating the Need to Use Deadly Force in Self-Defense," *Michigan Law Review* 86 (1988):1982–2009.
165. Ibid.; for an opposing finding, see William Waegel, "The Use of Lethal Force by Police: The Effect of Statutory Change," *Crime and Delinquency* 30 (1984):121–40.
166. For information, contact Commission for Accreditation for Law Enforcement Agencies, 4242B Chain Bridge Road, Fairfax, Virginia 22030.
167. Walker, *Popular Justice*, p. 64.
168. Herman Goldstein, *Police Corruption* (Washington, D.C.: Police Foundation, 1975), p. 3.
169. Michael Woronoff, "Public Employees or Private Citizens: The Off-Duty Sexual Activities of Police Officers and the Constitutional Right of Privacy," *University of Michigan Journal of Law Reform* 18 (1984):195–219.
170. John Kennedy, "Officer found guilty of collecting sick pay while on second job," *Boston Globe*, 26 February 1987, p. 61.
171. *Knapp Commission Report on Police Corruption* (New York: George Braziller, 1973), pp. 1–34.
172. Elizabeth Neuffer, "Seven additional detectives linked to extortion scheme," *Boston Globe*, 25 October 1988, p. 60.
173. Kevin Cullen, "US probe eyes bookie protection," *Boston Globe*, 25 October 1988.
174. Michael Johnston, *Political Corruption and Public Policy in America* (Monterey, Calif.: Brooks/Cole, 1982), p. 75.
175. William Doherty, "Ex-sergeant says he aided bid to sell exam," *Boston Globe*, 26 February 1987, p. 61.
176. Anthony Simpson, *The Literature of Police Corruption*, vol. 1 (New York: John Jay Press, 1977), p. 53.
177. Peter Kraska and Victor Kappeler, "Police On-Duty Drug Use: A Theoretical and Descriptive Examination," *American Journal of Police* 7 (1988):1–28.
178. Ellwyn Stoddard, "Blue Coat Crime," in *Thinking About Police*, ed. Carl Klockars (New York: McGraw-Hill, 1983), pp. 338–49.
179. Lawrence Sherman, *Police Corruption: A Sociological Perspective* (Garden City, N.Y.: Doubleday, 1974).
180. Johnston, *Political Corruption and Public Policy in America*, p. 82.
181. Sherman, *Police Corruption*, pp. 40–41.
182. Samuel Walker, *Police in Society* (New York: McGraw-Hill, 1983), p. 181.
183. "Slice of Vice," *Time*, 6 January 1986, p. 72.
184. Sherman, *Police Corruption*, p. 194.
185. Barbara Gelb, *Tarnished Brass: The Decade After Serpico* (New York: Putnam and Sons, 1983).
186. Candace McCoy, "Lawsuits Against Police: What Impact Do They Have?" *Criminal Law Bulletin* 20 (1984):49–56.
187. Thomas Barker, "Rookie Police Officers' Perceptions of Police Occupational Deviance," *Police Studies* 6 (1983):30–38.

CHAPTER 9

Police and the Rule of Law

OUTLINE

KEY TERMS

exclusionary rule
search and seizure
Fourth Amendment
search warrant
unreasonableness
probable cause
particularity
hearsay evidence
searches incident to a lawful arrest
field interrogations
California v. Hodari
threshold inquiry
stop and frisk
Terry v. Ohio
detain
Michigan v. Chesternut
Florida v. Jimeno
California v. Acevedo
Colorado v. Bertine
consent
Florida v. Bostick
bus sweep
drug courier profiles
plain view
open fields
curtilage
arrest
Miranda v. Arizona
Escobedo v. Illinois
Minnick v. Mississippi
inevitable discovery rule
public safety doctrine
Arizona v. Fulminante
Patterson v. Illinois
Mapp v. Ohio
good faith exception
Illinois v. Krull
Arizona v. Youngblood
California v. Greenwood

The police are charged with both preventing crime before it occurs and identifying and arresting criminals who have already broken the law. To carry out these tasks, police officers want a free hand to search for evidence, to seize contraband such as guns and drugs, to interrogate suspects, and to have witnesses and victims identify suspects. They know their investigation must be thorough. For trial, they will need to provide the prosecutor with sufficient evidence to prove guilt "beyond a reasonable doubt." Therefore, soon after the crime is committed, they must make every effort to gather physical evidence, obtain confessions, and take witness statements that will be adequate to prove the case in court. Police officers also realize that evidence the prosecutor is counting on to prove the case, such as the testimony of a witness or co-conspirator, may evaporate before the trial begins. Then the case outcome may depend on some piece of physical evidence or a suspect's statement taken early during the investigation.

The need for police officers to gather conclusive evidence can conflict with the constitutional rights of citizens. For example, although police want a free hand to search homes and cars for evidence, the Fourth Amendment restricts police activities by requiring that they obtain a warrant before conducting a search. When police wish to vigorously interrogate a suspect, they are bound to honor the Fifth Amendment's prohibition against forcing people to incriminate themselves.

Over the years, the confrontation between police and the criminal suspect has been moderated by the courts. Most important, the U.S. Supreme Court has used its power of case review and constitutional interpretation to set limits on police operations. At one time, the Court did little to curb police, leaving their authority unchecked. In the 1960s, the Warren Court moved vigorously to restrict police activities, going so far as to "punish" police by excluding from trial any evidence obtained in violation of the suspect's constitutional rights (the so-called **exclusionary rule**). Some critics charged that Court decisions "handcuffed" the police while giving criminal suspects a free hand to continue their law-violating activities; the rising crime rate in the 1960s and 1970s was blamed on the Warren Court's "submissiveness." Since then, under the leadership of the Court by Chief

There has been tension between the police, who desire a free hand to investigate crimes and interrogate suspects, and the courts, which seek to uphold civil liberties and to protect the rights of the accused.

Justices Warren Burger and William Rehnquist, the balance seems to be shifting: criminal suspects have received fewer protections, and police officers find it easier to obtain search warrants, interrogate suspects, and conduct lineups. Getting tough with criminals also seems to be the trend of the early 1990s (see Chapter 4).

In sum, police are controlled in their investigatory activities by the rule of law. At some junctures in the nation's history, the Court has sided with the police, while at others, it has put the civil liberties of criminal suspects first. This chapter reviews these issues and shows how the changes in Court rulings have influenced police operations and investigations.

Identification of Criminal Behavior

Once a crime has been committed and the purpose of the investigation has been determined, the police may use various means to collect the evidence needed for criminal prosecution. With each crime, police must decide how best to investigate it. Should surveillance techniques be employed to secure information? Is there reasonable suspicion to justify stopping and frisking a suspect? Has the investigation shifted from a general inquiry and begun to focus on a particular suspect so that the police can start a legally appropriate interrogation? Depending on the circumstances, one investigative technique may be more appropriate than another.

The American Bar Association's *Standards Relating to the Urban Police Function* identifies many of the investigative methods police use in situations involving both criminal and noncriminal activity:[1]

1. Engaging in surveillance (keeping a situation under observation—overtly or covertly—with the objective of acquiring additional information or evidence, with the objective of discouraging certain forms of activity).

2. Frisking and searching of persons and searching of vehicles and premises (in connection with an arrest or, independent of an arrest, as a means of protecting the officer, acquiring evidence of a crime, acquiring information generally, or simply making the presence of the police known).

3. Confiscating illegal objects (drugs, guns, gambling devices, paraphernalia, or money—either in connection with an arrest or simply as a means of removing such items from use and circulation).

4. Trading immunity from enforcement for information or cooperation (in allowing a narcotics user, a petty gambler, or a prostitute to continue to operate despite evidence of a violation of the law in exchange for their providing information leading to the identity and prosecution of those engaged in more serious forms of behavior).

5. Detaining persons temporarily (the use of arrest and subsequent detention for purposes other than prosecution, such as further investigation, safekeeping, or simply harassment).[2]

Criminal detection, apprehension, and arrest are the primary investigative functions performed by law enforcement officers. Proper police investigations involve collecting facts and information that will lead to the identification, arrest, and conviction of the criminal. Many police operations are informational—such as referring an alcoholic to a hospital or resolving a family dispute—and based on agency policy or police discretion. In contrast, the primary techniques of investigation—such as stopping and questioning people or interrogating a suspect—are controlled by statute and constitutional case law and are subject to review by the courts.

Police and the Courts

The U.S. Supreme Court has taken an active role in considering the legality of police operations. The Court has reviewed numerous appeals charging that police violated a suspect's rights during the investigation, arrest, and custody stages of the justice process. Of primary concern has been police conduct in obtaining and serving search and arrest warrants and in conducting postarrest interrogations and lineups. In some instances, the Court has expanded police power, for example, by increasing the occasions when police can search without a warrant. In other cases, the Court has restricted police operations, for example, by ruling that every criminal suspect has a right to an attorney when being interrogated by police. Changes in the law often reflect such factors as the justices' legal philosophy, their emphasis on the ability of police to control crime, their views on public safety, and their commitment to the civil liberties of criminal defendants. The issues and cases discussed in the following sections reflect the endless ebb and flow of judicial decision making and its impact on the law enforcement process.

Search and Seizure

Evidence collected by the police is governed by the **search and seizure** requirements of the **Fourth Amendment** of the U.S. Constitution.[3] The Fourth Amendment protects the defendant against unreasonable searches and seizures resulting from unlawful activities. Although there are exceptions, the general rule regarding the application of the Fourth Amendment is that any search or seizure undertaken without a validly obtained **search warrant** is unlawful. Furthermore, the amendment provides that no warrant shall be issued unless there is probable cause to believe that an offense has been or is being committed. A police officer concerned with investigating a crime can undertake a proper search and seizure if a valid search warrant has been obtained from the court or if the officer is functioning under one of the many exceptions to the search warrant requirement.

A search warrant is an order from a court authorizing and directing the police to search a designated place for property stated in the order and to bring that property to court. The order must be based on the sworn testimony of the police officer that the facts on which the request for the search warrant is made are trustworthy.

Search Warrant Requirements

Three critical concepts in the Fourth Amendment are directly related to the search warrant: **unreasonableness, probable cause,** and **particularity.**

"Unreasonableness" in searches and seizures generally refers to whether an officer has exceeded the scope of police authority. Most unreasonable actions are those in which the police officer did not have sufficient information to justify the search. In discussing "probable cause," the Fourth Amendment provides clearly that no warrants shall be issued unless probable cause is supported by oath or affirmation; in other words, a search warrant can be obtained only if the request for it is supported by facts that convince the court that a crime has been or is being committed.

"Particularity" generally refers to the search warrant itself; the Fourth Amendment requires that a search warrant specify the place to be searched and the reasons for searching it. When the police request a search warrant, the warrant must identify the premises and the personal property to be seized, and it must be signed under oath by the officer requesting it. The essential facts and information justifying the need for the search warrant are set out in an affidavit requesting the warrant. The requirement of particularity was addressed in the 1987 U.S. Supreme Court case of *Maryland v. Garrison*.[4] On the basis of information received from an informant, the police obtained a search warrant for the third-floor premises of a building, believing only one apartment existed there; upon arriving, they found that the third floor actually contained two apartments. They proceeded to search the entire floor and seized incriminating evidence that was later used to convict Garrison. Garrison challenged the search of the entire third floor, claiming that the warrant was imprecise in its description of the premises. The Supreme Court concluded that the factual mistake did not invalidate the warrant, even though a complete understanding of the building's floor plan was missing. In other words, when it comes to the essence of *particularity* regarding the place to be searched, the validity of the warrant must be judged on the basis of the information available to the police and disclosed to the issuing magistrate.

In practice, law enforcement officers do not often rely on a search warrant to enter a home or search a person, but in certain kinds of cases—such as investigations of organized crime, gambling, drug, and pornography cases—search warrants are particularly useful. Police also request warrants during investigations of other offenses when they are reasonably sure that the evidence sought cannot be removed from the premises, destroyed, or damaged by the suspect. The police are generally reluctant to seek a warrant, however, because of the stringent evidentiary standards courts require for obtaining one and the availability of search-and-seizure alternatives.

Use of Informers

The U.S. Supreme Court has played an active role in interpreting the legal requirements of a search warrant. One of the major issues considered by the Court has been the reliability of the evidence contained in the affidavit. In many instances, the evidence used by the police in requesting a search warrant originates with a police informer, rather than with the police officer. Such information is normally referred to as **hearsay evidence.**

The Supreme Court has determined that such evidence must be corroborated to serve as a basis for probable cause and thereby justify the issuance of a warrant. In the case of *Spinelli v. United States* (1969), the Supreme Court held that statements by an informer that he or she had personal knowledge of the facts about the crime and had supplied prior truthful information were sufficient corroboration.[5] In an earlier case, *Aguilar v. Texas* (1964), the Court articulated a two-part test for issuing a warrant on the word of an informant: (1) the police had to show why they believed the informant and (2) how the informant acquired personal knowledge of the crime had to be explained.[6] Later, in *Illinois v. Gates* (1983), the Court eased the process of obtaining search warrants by developing a new test.[7] The "two-pronged test" of *Spinelli* and *Aguilar* was replaced with a "totality of the circumstances" test to determine probable cause for issuing a search warrant. This means that to obtain a warrant, the police must prove to a judge that, considering the "totality of the circumstances," an informant has relevant and factual knowledge that a fair probability exists that evidence of a crime will be found in a certain place. Some states have rejected the standard of the "totality of the circumstances." For example, in *Commonwealth v. Upton* (1985), a Massachusetts court held that the standard set out in *Gates* was "unacceptably shapeless and permissive" and lacking in precision. It used the old *Spinelli-Aguilar* doctrine in deciding that a police officer's use of an anonymous telephone tip to obtain a warrant was improper.[8]

In sum, to obtain a search warrant, the following procedural requirements must be met: (1) the police officer must request the warrant from the court; (2) the officer must submit an affidavit establishing the proper grounds for the warrant; and (3) the affidavit must state the place to be searched and the property to be seized. Whether the affidavit contains sufficient information to justify issuing the warrant is what determines the validity of the warrant once it is issued.

Warrantless Searches

There are some significant exceptions to the search warrant requirement of the Fourth Amendment. Two critical exceptions are: (1) **searches incident to a lawful arrest** and (2) **field interrogations.** Other specialized warrantless searches include automobile searches, consent searches, and drug courier profiles. These exceptions, as well as the doctrine of plain view and the law of electric surveillance, are discussed below.

Searches Incident to a Lawful Arrest

Traditionally, a search without a search warrant is permissible if it is made incident to a lawful arrest. For example, if shortly after the armed robbery of a grocery store, officers arrest a suspect with a briefcase hiding in the basement, a search of the suspect's person and of the briefcase would be a proper search incident to a lawful arrest and without a warrant. The legality of this type of search depends almost entirely on the lawfulness of the arrest. The arrest will be upheld if the police officer observed the crime being committed or had probable cause to believe that the suspect committed the offense. If the arrest is found to have been invalid, then any warrantless search made incident to the arrest would be considered illegal, and the evidence obtained from the search would be excluded from trial.

The police officer who searches a suspect incident to a lawful arrest must generally observe two rules. First, it is important that the officer search the suspect at the time of or immediately following the arrest. Second, the police may search only the suspect and the area within the suspect's immediate control; that is, when a police officer searches a person incident to a lawful arrest, such a search may not legally go beyond the area where the person can reach for a weapon or destroy any evidence. The U.S. Supreme Court dealt with the problem of the permissible scope of a search incident to a lawful arrest in the case of *Chimel v. California*, which is summarized in the Law in Review on page 325.[9]

According to the *Chimel* doctrine, the police can search a suspect without a warrant after a lawful arrest in order to protect themselves from danger and to secure evidence. This rule can be interpreted loosely so that the search can be conducted even though the threat of danger is not really imminent. For example, in 1981 in *New York v. Belton*, the Court upheld the search of a defendant's jacket pursuant to an arrest for a traffic violation.[10] Belton and three other men had been stopped on a highway for speeding. The police officer discovered that none of the four occupants owned the vehicle. He also smelled marijuana and noticed an envelope marked "Supergold," which he associated with marijuana, on the floor of the car. The officer ordered the men out of the car and stationed them some distance from the vehicle. He then searched the men and the passenger compartment of the car, where Belton's black leather jacket was on the back seat. The officer searched the jacket and found cocaine. The Court concluded that the search of the jacket was a search incident to a lawful arrest and that the jacket was within the area of immediate control within the meaning of *Chimel*, even though the defendants were not close to the jacket at the time of the search.

One of the problems with the exception for the search incident to a lawful arrest is defining what is a "lawful arrest." In common law, an arrest ordinarily occurs if a person believes he or she cannot leave the scene and the police officer conveys this to the subject. In the recent case of ***California v. Hodari*** (1991), the subject, Hodari, fled when police approached and, before being apprehended, threw down a rock of crack cocaine.[11] The question in the case was whether or not Hodari, after fleeing from police, was under their control and therefore "seized" at the time he dropped the drugs.[12] The Supreme Court ruled that the crack was admissible evidence because it had been abandoned by the suspect and was not obtained by an illegal search and seizure.

The dissenting judges argued that the chase by police adequately conveyed the message that Hodari was not free to leave and that he therefore had been legally "seized."

The majority, however, felt it was unnecessary to apply the concept of a common law arrest to this police situation. The *Hodari* case stands for the proposition that a person is not seized under the Fourth Amendment until he or she has either been subjected to physical force or has submitted to the assertion of governmental control.[13]

LAW IN REVIEW

Chimel v. California (1969)

This case illustrates how the U.S. Supreme Court changed its legal position with regard to the scope of a search incident to a lawful arrest.

Facts

On the afternoon of September 13, 1965, three police officers arrived at the Santa Ana, California, home of Ted Chimel with a warrant authorizing his arrest for the burglary of a coin shop. The officers knocked on the door, identified themselves to Chimel's wife, and asked if they could come inside. She admitted the officers into the house, where they waited ten or fifteen minutes until Chimel returned home from work. When he entered the house, one of the officers handed him the arrest warrant and asked for permission to look around. Chimel objected but was advised that the officers could conduct a search on the basis of the lawful arrest. No search warrant had been issued.

Accompanied by Chimel's wife, the officers then looked through the entire three-bedroom house. The officers told Chimel's wife to open drawers in the master bedroom and sewing room and "to physically move contents of the drawers from side to side so that [they] might view any items that would have come from [the] burglary." After completing the search, the officers seized numerous items, including some coins. The entire search took between forty-five minutes and an hour.

At the defendant's subsequent state trial on two charges of burglary, the coins taken from his house were admitted into evidence against him over his objection that they had been unconstitutionally seized. He was convicted, and the judgment was affirmed by the California Supreme Court.

Decision

The U.S. Supreme Court decided that the search of Chimel's home went far beyond any area where he might conceivably have obtained a weapon or destroyed any evidence and that no constitutional basis existed for extending the search to all areas of the house. The court concluded that the scope of the search was unreasonable under the Fourth Amendment as applied through the Fourteenth Amendment, and Chimel's conviction was overturned.

Significance of the Case

The *Chimel* case changed the policy with regard to the scope of a search made by an officer incident to a lawful arrest. In the past, a police officer was permitted to search all areas under the control of the defendant. The Court's ruling in the *Chimel* case allows the officer to search only the defendant and the immediate physical surroundings under the defendant's control, generally interpreted as an arm's length distance around the defendant. No longer can a police officer who arrests a person in that person's home search the entire house without a valid search warrant.

Field Interrogation: Stop and Frisk

Another important exception to the rule requiring a search warrant is the **threshold inquiry,** or the **stop-and-frisk** procedure. Police examination of a suspect on the street does not always occur during or after arrest; officers frequently stop persons who appear to be behaving in a suspicious manner or about whom complaints are being made. Ordinarily, police are not required to have sufficient evidence for an arrest in order to stop a person for brief questioning. If the only way in which the police could stop a person was by making an arrest, they would be prevented from investigating many potentially criminal situations. For this reason, the courts have given the police the authority to stop a person, ask questions, and search the person in a limited way, such as frisking for a concealed weapon. The courts have concluded that it is unreasonable to expect a police officer to decide immediately whether to arrest a suspect. With a limited power to stop and frisk, the police officer is able to investigate suspicious persons and situations without having to meet the probable cause standard for arrest. If the police officer did not have this authority, many innocent individuals would probably be arrested.

The threshold inquiry, or the stop-and-frisk procedure, applies to an important point of contact between the police officer and the citizen—the street encounter. Stopping a suspect allows for brief questioning of the person, while frisking affords the officer an opportunity to avoid the possibility of attack. For instance, a police officer patrolling a high-crime area observes two young men loitering outside a liquor store after dark. The two men confer several times and stop to talk to a third person who pulls up alongside the curb in an automobile. From this observation, the officer may conclude that the men are casing the store for a possible burglary. He can then stop the suspects and ask them for some identification and an explanation of their conduct. If, after questioning the suspects, the officer has further reason to believe that they are planning to engage in criminal activity and that they are a threat to his safety, the officer can conduct a proper frisk, or a carefully limited search of the suspects' outer clothing.

In the case of ***Terry v. Ohio*** (1968), the Supreme Court upheld the right of the police to conduct brief threshold inquiries of suspicious persons when they have reason to believe that such persons may be armed and dangerous to the police or others.[14] The Court's intention was to allow the officer, who interacts with members of the community many times each day, to conduct proper investigations where necessary, while at the same time keeping invasions of personal rights to a minimum and protecting the officer from harm.[15]

The field interrogation process is based primarily on the ability of the police officer to determine whether suspicious conduct exists that gives the officer reason to believe a crime is about to be committed. Some jurisdictions have enacted legislation authorizing the stop-and-frisk procedure, thereby codifying the standard established in *Terry v. Ohio*. Courts have ruled that frisking must be limited to instances in which the police officer determines that his or her safety or that of others is at stake. The stop-and-frisk exception cannot be used to harass citizens or conduct exploratory searches.

The Supreme Court has continued to treat the *Terry v. Ohio* ruling as an exception to the general rule requiring probable cause for arrest. In 1979, the Court's decision in *Dunaway v. New York* limited the scope of *Terry v. Ohio* to stop-and-frisk actions.[16] In this case, the police obtained information from an informant that implicated Dunaway in a murder and robbery. He was taken into custody but not arrested. Dunaway then implicated himself during a police interrogation. The Court raised the question of the legality of the custodial questioning on less than probable cause for a full arrest. It concluded that such police action violated the defendant's Fourth and Fourteenth Amendment rights.

Field Detention

Despite the restrictions of *Dunaway*, the police have been given the right to **detain** suspects with less than probable cause. In *Michigan v. Summers* (1981), the Supreme Court held that initial detention of the defendant did not violate his constitutional right to be free from unreasonable search of his person.[17] As the police officers were about to execute a warrant to search a house, they encountered the defendant descending the steps. They requested his assistance to gain entry and detained him while searching the premises. After finding narcotics in the basement, the police searched the defendant and found heroin in his coat pocket. The Court said that because it was lawful to require the suspect to reenter the house until evidence establishing probable cause was found, his subsequent arrest and search did not violate any stop-and-frisk provisions of the Fourth Amendment.

In a different contextual situation, and applying a more traditional approach to field detention and seizure, was the Supreme Court's decision in ***Michigan v. Chesternut*** (1988).[18] While on a routine patrol, the police observed a car pull up to a curb and an individual exit and approach the defendant, Chesternut. When Chesternut saw the police cruiser, he ran off and was observed to pull several packets from his pocket and discard them. The police examined the discarded packets and concluded that they contained cocaine. Chesternut was arrested, and a search revealed that he possessed other drugs, including heroin. The Court rejected both the position that any pursuit is a seizure and the argument that no seizure can occur until the officer apprehends the person. Instead, the Court said that in view of all the circumstances, a reasonable person would not have felt free to leave the scene and therefore Chesternut's detention was neither a seizure nor a violation of the Fourth Amendment.

Automobile Searches

The U.S. Supreme Court has also established that certain situations justify the warrantless search of an automobile on a public street or highway. For example, evidence can be seized from an automobile when a suspect is taken into custody subject to a lawful arrest. In *Carroll v. United States*, which was decided in 1925, the Supreme Court ruled that distinctions should be made between searches of automobiles, persons, and homes. The Court also concluded that a warrantless search of an automobile is valid if the police have probable cause to believe that the car contains evidence they are seeking.[19]

The legality of searching automobiles without a warrant has always been a trouble spot for police and the courts. Should the search be limited to the interior of the car, or can the police search the trunk? What about a suitcase in the trunk? What about the glove compartment? Does a traffic citation give the police the right to search an automobile? These questions have produced significant litigation over the years. To clear up the matter, the Supreme Court decided the landmark case of *United States v. Ross* in 1982.[20]

In *Ross*, the Court held that if probable cause exists to believe that an automobile contains criminal evidence, a warrantless search by the police is permissible, including a search of closed containers in the vehicle (see the Law in Review on page 329 for a detailed discussion).

Almost a decade later, in 1991, conservative opinions were also handed down in additional auto search cases. In ***Florida v. Jimeno,*** a police officer asked Jimeno, a motorist who had been stopped for a traffic violation, for permission to search his car for drugs. Jimeno gave the officer permission, and during the subsequent search, the officer opened a paper bag that contained cocaine. The issue was whether the consent to search the auto extended to the closed bag. The Court ruled that by giving permission to search the car, Jimeno had also consented to the search of all closed containers within the car and therefore the cocaine could be used as evidence.[21] In ***California v. Acevedo,*** the Court ruled that police had the right to open the trunk of a car and search a closed container without a warrant if they believed that the container held drugs, even if they had no reason to search the rest of the car.[22] In this case, the police had probable cause to believe that a brown bag that the defendant placed in the trunk contained marijuana but no probable cause to believe drugs were otherwise in the car. Justice Harry Blackmun said there is no distinction regarding privacy between the *Ross* situation, which resulted from an informant's tip, and this case.[23] The decisions in these two cases permit the warrantless search of closed containers or suitcases in cars. Ironically, police officers would not be allowed to search these containers if they were being held by the drivers as they walked down the street!

Other unique cases in this area include *California v. Carney* (1985) and ***Colorado v. Bertine*** (1987). In the *Carney* case, the Court held that a mobile home is to be treated as an automobile and does not enjoy the same protection from a police search as a stationary home.[24] And in *Bertine*, the Court addressed the validity of an inventory inspection of the contents of containers found in a van. Police departments conduct inventory searches to make an accurate tally of an arrestee's possessions so that they may be returned upon his or her release. If police discover contraband while making an inventory search, it can be used as evidence in court. In the present case, police arrested Bertine for driving under the influence of alcohol and impounded the van he was driving. During their examination of the van, the police found canisters of cash and drugs. On appeal, the Supreme Court said that a warrant was not required and, in so doing, further strengthened the *Ross* holding.[25]

In sum, the most important requirement for a warrantless search of an automobile is that it must be based on the legal standard of probable cause that a crime related to the automobile has been or is being committed. Police who undertake the search of a vehicle must have reason to believe that it contains evidence pertaining to the crime.

Roadblock Searches. Police departments often wish to set up roadblocks to check driver's licenses or the condition of drivers. Is such a stop an illegal search and seizure? In *Delaware v. Prouse* in 1979, the Supreme Court forbade the practice of random stops in the absence of any reasonable suspicion that some traffic or motor vehicle law has been violated.[26] Unless there is at least reasonable belief that a motorist is unlicensed, that an automobile is not registered, or that the occupant is subject to seizure for violation of the law, stopping and detaining a driver to check his or her license violates the Fourth Amendment.

One important purpose of the *Prouse* decision was to eliminate the individual police officer's use of discretion to stop cars. However, what has developed from this case is tacit approval for police roadblocks that are set up to stop cars in some systematic fashion. As long as the police can demonstrate that the checkpoints are conducted in a uniform manner and that the operating procedures have been determined by someone other than the officer at the scene, roadblocks can be used to uncover violators of even minor traffic regulations.

Roadblocks have recently become popular for combatting drunk driving. Courts have ruled that police can stop a predetermined number of cars at a checkpoint and can request each motorist to produce his or her license, registration, and insurance card. While doing so, they can check for outward signs of intoxication. Nevertheless, some state jurisdictions find that such behavior intrudes on citizens' privacy. Stopping an automobile without suspicion is ordinarily unreasonable under the Fourth Amendment. There must be reason to believe the motorist is unlicensed, the vehicle is not registered, or the vehicle or the occupant is in violation of some law.

Consent Searches

Police officers may also undertake warrantless searches when the person in control of the area or object voluntarily consents to the search. Those who **consent** to a search essentially waive their constitutional rights under the Fourth Amendment.

LAW IN REVIEW

United States v. Ross (1982)

Facts

Acting on information from an informant that a described individual was selling narcotics kept in the trunk of a certain car parked at a specified location, District of Columbia police officers immediately drove to the location, found the car there, and a short while later stopped the car and arrested the driver, who matched the informant's description. One of the officers opened the car's trunk, found a closed brown paper bag, and, after opening the bag, discovered glassine bags containing white powder (later determined to be heroin). The officer then drove the car to headquarters, where another warrantless search of the trunk revealed a zippered leather pouch containing cash. The defendant was subsequently convicted of possession of heroin with intent to distribute, the heroin and currency found in the searches having been introduced in evidence after a pretrial motion to suppress the evidence had been denied. The court of appeals reversed the decision, holding that while the officers had probable cause to stop and search the car, including the trunk, without a warrant, they should not have opened either the paper bag or the leather pouch found in the trunk without first obtaining a warrant.

Decision

The U.S. Supreme Court reversed the lower-court ruling, stating, "Police officers who have legitimately stopped an automobile and who have probable cause to believe that contraband is concealed somewhere within it may conduct a warrantless search of the vehicle as thoroughly as a magistrate could authorize by warrant." Furthermore, the rationale justifying the automobile exception does not apply so as to permit a warrantless search of any movable container that is believed to be carrying an illicit substance and that is found in a public place, even when the container is placed in a vehicle not otherwise believed to be carrying contraband. However, where police officers have probable cause to search an entire vehicle, they may conduct a warrantless search of every part of the vehicle and its contents, including all containers and packages, that may conceal the object of the search. The scope of the search is not defined by the nature of the container in which the contraband is secreted. Rather, it is defined by the object of the search and the places in which there is probable cause to believe that it may be found. For example, probable cause to believe that undocumented aliens are being transported in a van will not justify a warrantless search of a suitcase.

Significance of the Case

The U.S. Supreme Court has attempted to clarify the law of warrantless searches of automobiles by applying the singular concept of probable cause to the search of the vehicle and any material, including closed containers, found in the vehicle. The Court emphasized that police officers who have legitimately stopped an automobile and who have probable cause to believe that contraband is concealed somewhere within it may conduct a warrantless search of the vehicle as thoroughly as a magistrate could authorize by warrant. Also, the automobile exception to the Fourth Amendment's warrant requirement established in *Carroll v. United States,* 267 U.S. 132, 45 S.Ct. 280, 69 L.Ed. 543 (1925), applies to searches of vehicles that are supported by probable cause to believe that the vehicle contains contraband. In this kind of case, a search is not unreasonable if based on objective facts that would justify the issuance of a warrant, even though a warrant has not actually been obtained.

This decision should result in some order in the area of legal decision making on warrantless automobile searches, but at a loss of privacy to the individual.

Ordinarily, courts are reluctant to accept such waivers and require the state to prove that the consent was voluntarily given. In addition, the consent must be given intelligently, and in some jurisdictions, consent searches are valid only after the suspect is informed of the option to refuse consent.

The major legal issue in most consent searches is whether the police can prove that consent was given voluntarily. For example, in the case of *Bumper v. North Carolina* (1968), police officers searched the home of an elderly woman

In Florida v. Bostick, *the Supreme Court upheld the right of police agents to board a bus and question suspects.*

after informing her that they possessed a search warrant.[27] At the trial, the prosecutor informed the court that the search was valid because the woman had given her consent. When the government was unable to produce the warrant, the court decided that the search was invalid because the woman's consent was not given voluntarily. On appeal, the U.S. Supreme Court upheld the lower court's finding that the consent had been illegally obtained by the false claim of the police that they had a search warrant.

In most consent searches, however, voluntariness is a question of fact to be determined from all the circumstances of the case. In *Schneckloth v. Bustamonte*, for example, where the defendant actually helped the police by opening the trunk and glove compartment of the car, the Court said this demonstrated that the consent was voluntarily given.[28] Furthermore, the police are usually under no obligation to inform a suspect of the right to refuse consent. Failure to tell a suspect of this right does not make the search illegal, but it may be a factor used by courts to decide if the suspect gave consent voluntarily. In terms of the obligation of police to inform a suspect of this right, the right of refusal is not equivalent to other constitutional safeguards. Under the *Miranda* decision, for instance, where the Supreme Court held that a defendant has a right to counsel and a right to be free from self-incrimination, the defendant must be informed of these rights before being able to waive them.

The Bus Sweep

Today, consent searches have additional significance because of their use in drug control programs. On June 20, 1991, the U.S. Supreme Court, in ***Florida v. Bostick,*** upheld the police drug interdiction technique of boarding buses and, without suspicion of illegal activity, questioning passengers, asking for identification, and requesting permission to search luggage.[29] Known as the **"bus sweep,"** police in the *Bostick* case boarded a bus bound from Miami to Atlanta during a stopover in Fort Lauderdale. Without suspicion, the officers picked out the defendant and asked to inspect his ticket and identification. After identifying themselves as narcotics officers looking for illegal drugs, they asked to inspect the defendant's luggage. Although there was some uncertainty about whether the defendant consented to the search in which contraband was found and whether he was informed of this right to refuse to consent to the search, the defendant was convicted.

The Supreme Court was faced with deciding whether consent was freely given or the nature of the bus sweep search negated the defendant's consent. Justice Sandra Day O'Connor, writing for the majority, said that police may approach individuals without any suspicion and that asking questions and requesting to search luggage does not constitute a "seizure" in every instance.[30] In other words, drug enforcement officers, after obtaining consent, may search luggage on a crowded bus without meeting the Fourth Amendment requirements for a search warrant or probable cause.

This case raises fundamental questions about the legality of new techniques used to discourage drug trafficking. Law enforcement officials are concerned about intercepting large amounts of drugs and sums of money. Bus sweeps are one answer to the drug menace. But is the Supreme Court also compromising individual Fourth Amendment rights when it considers these encounters between police and citizens to be consensual in nature?

Drug Courier Profiles

Another controversial method of police investigation that can conflict with the law of search and seizure is the use of **drug courier profiles** to spot potential drug violators at transportation centers, such as airports.

The profiles are based on physical and psychological descriptions of past offenders. They contain such characteristics as: using a number of different airlines, taking a circuitous route, not picking up baggage, being the last one off the plane (in order to look out for agents), and appearing very nervous. A person displaying such traits may come under the suspicion of narcotics agents but may not have openly broken any law or provided probable cause sufficient for a search of his or her clothing or carryon baggage. However, the courts have ruled under the *Terry* doctrine that agents can approach a suspect, ask for identification, and ask him or her to submit to a search.

In *United States v. Mendenhall* (1980), the Supreme Court upheld the search of a woman detained at an airport after she was identified by a drug courier profile as a suspicious person who might be carrying narcotics.[31] The defendant was not able to explain why she was using a different name on her airline tickets. She subsequently agreed to a voluntary search, which revealed she was in possession of illegal drugs. Since the search of the defendant was not preceded by an impermissible seizure of her person, the Court concluded that the search was legal. As long as the defendant had consented to her search freely and voluntarily, the stop-and-frisk procedure did not violate the law.

In 1983, however, in *Florida v. Royer,* the Court limited the ability of the police to search suspects who fit drug courier profiles.[32] Royer fit the description of a drug courier: he carried heavy luggage, he was young, and he was casually dressed. In addition, Royer had paid for his ticket in cash and had written only a name and destination—not an address and phone number—on his luggage ID tags. The police approached him, requested his driver's license and airline ticket, and then asked him to accompany them to an interrogation room. There, Royer was asked to open his luggage, and he voluntarily produced a key. The suitcases contained marijuana. The Court ruled that Royer's detention was a seizure because when his ticket and license were taken, the police actually prevented him from leaving voluntarily. Furthermore, the long detention (fifteen minutes) in the interrogation room was greater than that permitted by the *Terry* doctrine (since Royer was not under arrest).

The Doctrine of Plain View

One final instance in which police can search for and seize evidence without benefit of a warrant is if it is in **plain view.** For example, if a police officer is conducting an investigation and notices while questioning some individuals that one has drugs in her pocket, the officer could seize the evidence and arrest the suspect. Or if the police are conducting a search under a warrant enabling them to look for narcotics in a person's home and they come upon a gun, the police could seize the gun, even though it is not mentioned in the warrant. The 1986 case of *New York v. Class* illustrates the plainsight doctrine.[33] A police officer stopped a car for a traffic violation. Wishing to check the vehicle identification number (VIN) on the dashboard, he reached into the car to clear away material that was obstructing his view. While clearing the dash, he noticed a gun under the seat—"in plain view." The U.S. Supreme Court upheld the seizure of the gun as evidence because the police officer had the right to check the VIN; therefore, the sighting of the gun was legal.

The doctrine of plain view was applied and further developed in *Arizona v. Hicks* in 1987.[34] Here, the Court held that moving a stereo component in plain view a few inches to record the serial number constituted a search under the Fourth Amendment. When a check with police headquarters revealed the item had been stolen, the equipment was seized and offered for evidence at Hick's trial. The Court held that a plain-view search and seizure could only be justified by probable cause, and not reasonable suspicion, and suppressed the evidence against the defendant. In this case, the Court decided to take a firm stance on protecting Fourth Amendment rights. The *Hicks* decision is uncharacteristic in an era when most decisions have tended to expand the exceptions to the search warrant requirement.

The Concept of Curtilage. An issue long associated with plain view is whether police can search **open fields,** which are fenced in but are otherwise open to view. In *Oliver v. United States* (1984), the U.S. Supreme Court distinguished between the privacy granted persons in their own home or its adjacent grounds **(curtilage)** and a field. The Court ruled that police can use airplane surveillance to spot marijuana fields and then send in squads to seize the crops, or they can peer into fields from cars for the same purpose.[35]

In *California v. Ciraola* (1986), the Court expanded the police ability to spy on criminal offenders. In this case, the police received a tip that marijuana was growing in the defendant's backyard.[36] The yard was surrounded by fences, one of which was ten feet high. The officers flew over the yard in a private plane at an altitude of one thousand feet to ascertain that it contained marijuana plants. On the basis of this information, a search warrant was obtained and executed, and using the evidence, Ciraola was convicted on drug charges. On appeal, the Supreme Court found that the defendant's privacy had not been violated.

This holding was expanded in 1989 in *Florida v. Riley*, when the Court ruled that police do not need a search warrant to conduct even low-altitude helicopter searches of private property.[37] The Court allowed Florida prosecutors to use evidence obtained by a police helicopter that flew four hundred feet over a greenhouse in which defendants were growing marijuana plants. The Court said the search was constitutionally permissible because the flight was within airspace legally available to helicopters under federal regulations.

These cases illustrate how the concepts of curtilage and open fields have added significance in defining the scope of the Fourth Amendment in terms of the doctrine of plain view.

Electronic Surveillance

The use of wiretapping to intercept conversations between parties has significantly affected police investigative procedures. Electronic devices allow people to listen to and record the private conversations of other people over telephones, through walls and windows, and even over long-distance phone lines. Using these devices, police are able to intercept communications secretly and obtain information related to criminal activity.

The earliest and most widely used form of electronic surveillance is wiretapping. With approval from the court and a search warrant, law enforcement officers place listening devices on telephones to overhear oral communications of suspects. Such devices are also often placed in homes and automobiles. The evidence collected is admissible and used in the defendant's trial.

More sophisticated devices have come into use in recent years. A pen register, for instance, is a mechanical device that records the numbers dialed on a telephone. "Trap and tracer" devices ascertain the number from which calls are placed to a particular telephone. Law enforcement agencies also obtain criminal evidence through electronic communication devices, such as electronic mail, video surveillance, and computer data transmissions.

The Law of Electronic Surveillance

Electronic eavesdropping by law enforcement personnel, however, represents an invasion of an individual's right to privacy unless a court gives prior permission to intercept conversations in this manner. Police can obtain criminal evidence by eavesdropping only if such activities are controlled under rigid guidelines established under the Fourth Amendment, and they must normally request a court order based on probable cause before using electronic eavesdropping equipment.

Many citizens believe that electronic eavesdropping through hidden microphones, radio transmitters, and telephone taps and bugs represents a grave threat to personal privacy.[38] Although the use of such devices is controversial, the police are generally convinced of their value in investigating criminal activity. Others, however, believe that these techniques are often used beyond their lawful intent to monitor political figures, harass suspects, or investigate cases involving questionable issues of national security.

In response to concerns about invasions of privacy, the U.S. Supreme Court has increasingly limited the use of electronic eavesdropping in the criminal justice system. *Katz v. United States* (1967) is an example of a case in which the government failed to meet the requirements necessary to justify electronic surveillance.[39] (See the Law in Review on page 335.) The *Katz* doctrine is usually interpreted to mean that the government must obtain a court order if it wishes to listen into conversations in which the parties have a reasonable expectation of privacy, such as in their own homes or on the telephone; public utterances or actions are fair game. *Katz* concluded that electronic eavesdropping is a search, even though there is no actual trespass. Therefore, it is unreasonable and a warrant is needed.

The concept of privacy is still unclear in many instances. For example, in *United States v. Knotts* (1983), the Court upheld the right of police agencies to attach a battery-operated radio transmitter to chemicals related to illegal drug manufacture to aid their surveillance. The Court noted that "nothing in the Fourth Amendment prohibited the police from augmenting the sensory faculties bestowed upon them at birth with such enhancement as science and technology afforded them in this case." [40] In *United States v. Karo* (1984), the Court ruled that although the government can use tracking devices, it cannot monitor them without a court order once they are taken into a home.[41]

The Supreme Court also has held that if the police conduct warrantless electronic surveillance of conversations, as long as one of the parties consented to the monitoring, the warrantless search does not violate the Fourth Amendment.[42] Law enforcement personnel often rely on this exception when they "wire" or bug an informant or undercover agent. It is generally referred to as the "consensual monitoring theory."

Federal Controls

As a result of the controversy surrounding the use of electronic eavesdropping over the last twenty years, Congress has passed legislation to control the interception of oral communications. The Omnibus Crime Control Act (Title III) of 1968 initially prohibited lawful interceptions except by warrant or with consent.[44] It established procedures for judicial approval to be obtained based on "probable cause" and upon application of the attorney general or a designate. Statutory provisions also provide for the suppression of evidence when recordings are obtained in violation of the law.

The federal electronic surveillance law was modified by the Electronic Communications Privacy Act of 1986.[45] In light of technological changes, Title III of the new act was expanded to include not only all forms of wire and oral communications but also virtually all types of nonaural electronic communication. The law added new offenses to the previous list of crimes for which electronic surveillance could be used and liberalized court procedures for permitting such surveillance and issuing court orders. In addition to this important legislation, the American Bar Association has created standards on the use of electronic surveillance in the criminal system.[46] These guidelines are helpful to jurisdictions planning changes in their electronic surveillance law.

In general, the basic principle of the law of electronic surveillance is that wiretapping and other devices that violate privacy are contrary to the Fourth Amendment. As a result of technological advances, such devices probably pose a greater threat to personal privacy than physical searches. The U.S. Supreme Court has permitted only narrow exceptions, such as court-ordered warrants and consensual monitoring.[47]

Arrest

The arrest power of the police involves taking a person into custody in accordance with lawful authority and holding that person to answer for a violation of the criminal law. For all practical purposes, the authority of the police to arrest a

LAW IN REVIEW

Katz v. United States (1967)

This case deals with government intrusion by electronic eavesdropping and establishes the important principle that the Fourth Amendment protects people and not places and that searches without prior judicial approval are unlawful, with some exceptions.

Facts

Katz was convicted of transmitting wagering information by telephone in violation of a federal statute. At his trial, the government was permitted to introduce evidence of Katz's end of the telephone conversations, which had been overheard by FBI agents who had attached an electronic listening and recording device to monitor the outgoing calls. Katz appealed, claiming that the actions of the FBI violated his search and seizure rights under the Fourth Amendment.

Decision

Justice Potter Stewart of the U.S. Supreme Court, speaking for the majority, reversed the conviction, holding that the interception and recordings of Katz's telephone conversations represented unreasonable searches and seizures of the conversations in violation of the Fourth Amendment. Stewart said, "The government agents here ignored 'the procedure of antecedent justification . . . that is central to the Fourth Amendment,' a procedure that we hold to be a constitutional precondition of the kind of electronic surveillance involved in this case. Because surveillance here failed to meet the condition, and because it led to the petitioner's conviction, the judgment must be reversed."

Significance of the Case

In *Katz,* the U.S. Supreme Court declared that the Fourth Amendment was not to apply solely to protected places involving privacy but that such protections also relate to the privacy of individuals. Thus, the Court abandoned the definition of a search based on property and concluded that a search results whenever police violate a person's privacy.

People in telephone booths, offices, apartments, rooms, and taxicabs, the Court stated, should be able to rely on the safeguards of the Fourth Amendment. The right of privacy protects the person anywhere and is not restricted to certain physical places.

suspect is the basis for crime control; without such authority, the police would be powerless to implement the criminal law.

The arrest power is used primarily by law enforcement officers. Generally, law enforcement personnel are employed by public police agencies, derive their authority from statutory laws, and take an oath to uphold the laws of their jurisdiction. Most police officers have complete law enforcement responsibility and unrestricted powers of arrest in their jurisdictions; they carry firearms, and they give evidence in criminal trials. In the United States, private citizens also have the right to make an arrest, generally when a crime is committed in their presence. For the most part, though, private citizens rarely exercise their power of arrest, except when they apprehend offenders who have committed crimes against them.

An **arrest,** the first formal police procedure in the criminal justice process, occurs when a police officer takes a person into custody or deprives a person of freedom for having allegedly committed a criminal offense. Since the police stop unlimited numbers of people each day for a variety of reasons, the time when an arrest actually occurs may be hard to pinpoint. Some persons are stopped for short periods of questioning, others are informally detained and released, and still others are formally placed under arrest. An actual arrest occurs when the following conditions exist: (1) the police officer believes that sufficient legal evidence exists that a crime is being or has been committed and intends to restrain the suspect; (2) the police officer deprives the individual of freedom; and (3) the suspect believes that he or she is in the custody of the police officer and cannot voluntarily leave. The police officer is not required to use the term *arrest* or some similar word in order to initiate arrest, nor does the officer first have to bring the suspect to the station house. For all practical purposes, a person who has been deprived of liberty is under arrest.

Arrests can be initiated with or without an arrest warrant and must be based on probable cause. The arrest warrant, an order issued by the court, determines that an arrest should be made and directs the police to bring the named person before the court. An arrest warrant must be based on probable cause that the person to be arrested has committed or is attempting to commit a crime. The police will ordinarily go before a judge and obtain a warrant where no danger exists that the suspect will leave the area, where a long-term investigation of organized crime is underway, or where a probable cause exists to arrest the suspect.

Most arrests are made without a warrant. The decision to arrest is often made by the police officer during contact with the suspect. An arrest may be made without a warrant only in the following circumstances:

1. Where the arresting officer is able to establish probable cause that a crime has been committed and that the defendant is the person who committed it.
2. Where the law of a given jurisdiction allows for arrest without a warrant.

In the case of a felony, most jurisdictions provide that a police officer may arrest a suspect without a warrant where probable cause exists, even though the officer was not present when the offense was committed. In the case of a misdemeanor, probable cause and the officer's presence at the time of the offense are required. When there is some question as to the legality of an arrest, it usually involves whether the police officer has probable cause or a reasonable belief based on reliable evidence that the suspect has committed a crime. The issue is reviewed by the judge when the suspect is brought before the court for a hearing.

Postarrest Time Frame

As a general rule, if the police make an arrest without a warrant, the person arrested must ordinarily be brought before a magistrate promptly for a probable cause hearing.

The U.S. Supreme Court dealt with the meaning of *promptness* in the 1991 case of *Riverside County v. McLaughlin*.[48] The Court said that the police may detain an individual arrested without a warrant for up to forty-eight hours without a court hearing on whether the arrest was justified. This decision takes into account the state's interest in taking suspects into custody and the individual's concern about prolonged custody affecting employment and family relations. Some justices believed that a probable cause hearing should be held immediately after the suspect is booked. Others felt, however, that some police processing delays are inevitable and that a probable cause determination on arrest within forty-eight hours seemed reasonable. While great concern surrounds the rights of individuals at the postarrest stage, prompt judicial determination should allow for proper administrative processing, without resulting in a violation of the Fourth Amendment. Many states use more stringent standards, such as a twenty-four- or thirty-six-hour time frame to bring suspects to a probable cause hearing.

Custodial Interrogation

A suspect who comes into police custody at the time of arrest—on the street, in a police car, or in the police station—must be warned of the right under the Fifth Amendment to be free from self-incrimination before police conduct any

After an arrest, police must inform suspects of their Miranda *rights if they wish to use the suspects' statements and admissions in a court of law. Here police in South Central Los Angeles question youths suspected of possessing a handgun.*

questioning. In the landmark case of ***Miranda v. Arizona*** (1966), the Supreme Court held that the police must give the *Miranda* warning to a person in custody before questioning begins.[49] Suspects in custody must be told that they have the following rights:

1. They have the right to remain silent.
2. If they decide to make a statement, the statement can and will be used against them in a court of law.
3. They have the right to have an attorney present at the time of the interrogation, or they will have an opportunity to consult with an attorney.
4. If they cannot afford an attorney, one will be appointed for them by the state.

Most suspects choose to remain silent, and since oral as well as written statements are admissible in court, police officers often do not elicit any statements without making certain a defense attorney is present. If an accused decides to answer any questions, he or she may also stop at any time and refuse to answer further questions. A suspect's constitutional rights under *Miranda* can be given up (waived), however. Consequently, a suspect should give careful consideration before abrogating any custodial rights under the *Miranda* warning.

Over twenty-five years have passed since this warning was established by the Warren Court. During this time, U.S. appellate courts have heard literally thousands of cases involving alleged violations of the *Miranda* rights, custodial interrogation, right to counsel, and statements made to persons other than the police, among others. Some experts believe felons have been freed because *Miranda* is the heart of our privilege to be free from self-incrimination. What follows is a detailed analysis of this often litigated and hotly contested legal issue.

Historical Perspective on *Miranda*

Prior to the *Miranda* safeguards, confessions could be obtained from a suspect who had not consulted with an attorney. An early ruling in *Brown v. Mississippi* (1936) held that statements obtained by physical coercion were inadmissible evidence, but it also limited the use of counsel to aid the accused at this early stage of the criminal process.[50] Not until 1964 in ***Escobedo v. Illinois*** was the groundwork laid for the landmark *Miranda* decision.[51] In *Escobedo,* the Supreme Court finally recognized the critical relationship between the Fifth Amendment privilege against self-incrimination and the Sixth Amendment right to counsel. Danny Escobedo was a convicted murderer who maintained that the police interrogation forced him to make incriminating statements that were regarded as a voluntary confession. In *Escobedo,* the Court recognized that he had been denied the assistance of counsel, which was critical during police interrogation. With this decision, the Court made clear its concern that the accused should be permitted certain due process rights during interrogation.

Two years later came the *Miranda* decision, which has had an historic impact on police interrogation practices at the arrest stage of the criminal justice process. Prior to *Miranda,* the police often obtained confessions through questioning methods that violated the constitutional privilege against self-incrimination. The Supreme Court declared in *Miranda* that the police have a duty to inform defendants of their rights. Certain specific procedures (that is, the *Miranda* warning) must be followed, or any statements by a defendant will be excluded from evidence. The purpose of the warning is to implement the basic Fifth Amendment right to be free from self-incrimination.

As a result, the interrogation process is protected by the Fifth Amendment, and if the accused is not given the *Miranda* warning, any evidence obtained during interrogation is not admissible to prove the state's case. It is important to note, however, that the *Miranda* decision does not deny the police the opportunity to ask a suspect general questions as a witness at the scene of an unsolved crime, as long as the person is not in custody and the questioning is of an investigative and nonaccusatory nature. In addition, a suspect can still offer a voluntary confession after the *Miranda* warning has been issued. The *Miranda* decision is summarized in the Law in Review on page 342.

After the *Miranda* decision, many people became concerned that the Supreme Court under Chief Justice Earl Warren had gone too far in providing procedural protections to the defendant. Some nationally prominent persons expressed opinions that made it seem as if the Supreme Court were emptying the prisons of criminals, and law enforcement officers throughout the nation generally have been disturbed by the *Miranda* decision, believing that it seriously hampers their efforts to obtain confessions and other self-incriminating statements from defendants. Research indicates, however, that the decision has had little or no effect on the number of confessions obtained by the police and that it has not affected the rate of convictions.[52] Since *Miranda,* little empirical evidence has been produced showing that the decision has had a detrimental impact on law enforcement efforts. Instead, it has become apparent that the police formerly relied too heavily on confessions to prove a defendant's guilt. Other forms of evidence, such as witness statements, physical evidence, and expert testimony, have proved more than adequate to win the prosecution's case. Blaming *Miranda* for increased crime rates is apparently not correct.[53] The real reasons crime may be out of control lie in the drug problem and an overwhelmed justice system, not the enforcement of constitutional rights.

The Legacy of *Miranda*

Despite its apparent clarity, the *Miranda* decision has given rise to a series of litigations. One of the central issues has been the need to define the specific instances in which the *Miranda* warning must be given. Questions here involve,

for example, ascertaining what custodial interrogation is, who the interrogator is, and whether damaging statements result from a specific interrogation. Other problems generally focused on whether the *Miranda* warning was properly given. Was the warning adequate? Did the defendant waive his or her rights? Was the defendant capable of understanding the meaning of the warning? Did statements made after the initial interrogation require the repetition of the *Miranda* warning? Can persons be questioned without an attorney present after they ask for counsel (or have counsel appointed)?

This latter question was raised in *Brewer v. Williams* (1977), otherwise known as the "Christian burial case."[54] In this case, Robert Williams was being transported by the police. Williams's attorney had warned the police not to question him about the killing of a young girl. On the trip, the officers asked Williams to tell where her body was buried so that she could get a "Christian burial." Williams remorsefully complied, leading the police to the woods where he had left the victim's body. The body and his statements were later used against him at trial. Williams was convicted of the sex slaying of the ten-year-old girl and sentenced to life in prison. Though shocked by the gravity of the case, the Supreme Court overturned his conviction on the grounds that the police questioning was improper given the fact that his counsel was not present, that the officers had used psychological coercion, and that they had been warned not to interrogate the suspect without his attorney present. The case of ***Minnick v. Mississippi*** (1991) reinforced the important proposition that once an accused person has invoked the *Miranda* right to request an attorney, the police cannot resume interrogation without legal counsel being present.[55] *Minnick* sought to suppress information given to the police after a second interrogation without counsel. The Court agreed and said that reinterrogation requires the presence of counsel unless the conversation is initiated by the accused. This rule often prevents the police from badgering or harassing suspects and avoids placing the burden on the government of determining when consultation with counsel is actually required.

Not all decisions have upheld a strict interpretation of *Miranda*. For example, in *Harris v. New York* (1971), the Court agreed that evidence obtained in violation of the *Miranda* warning could be used by the government to impeach a defendant's testimony during trial.[56] In *Michigan v. Tucker* (1974), the Court allowed the testimony of a witness whose identity was revealed by the suspect, even though a violation of the *Miranda* rule occurred.[57] And in the case of *Michigan v. Mosely* (1975), the Court upheld the renewed questioning of a suspect who had already been given the *Miranda* warning and had refused to answer any questions.[58]

Other cases stand out as illustrations of the erosion of the protections granted by *Miranda*. *Nix v. Williams* (1984) was the rehearing of the *Brewer v. Williams* case (see above).[59] At Williams's second trial, the court ruled that the body of the young girl located by Williams was admissible as evidence since it would probably have been found anyway by search parties. Although the interrogation of Williams in the patrol car was ruled illegal, the girl's body did not fall under the exclusionary rule because it would have eventually been found in the same condition; this is known as the **inevitable discovery rule.** In the second case, *New York v. Quarles* (1984), the police arrested a man who fit the description of an armed rapist.[60] After frisking the suspect, Quarles, and finding an empty holster, the police asked where his gun was. Quarles nodded in the direction of some empty cartons and responded, "The gun is over there." Although the lower courts disallowed the use of the gun as evidence at trial on the grounds that Quarles had not been given his *Miranda* warning, the Supreme Court allowed its use on

the grounds that the police had the right to protect public safety by immediately asking Quarles to produce the gun (known as the **public safety doctrine**). If the gun had not been quickly found, the Court reasoned, it could have been picked up and discharged accidentally by a passerby.

In *Moran v. Burbine* (1986), a confession by a murder suspect was allowed to be used against him, even though the police failed to let him know that his sister had obtained an attorney for him and had assured the attorney that they would not question the suspect until the following day.[61] The Court ruled that the police do not have to tell suspects that someone else has hired a lawyer for them, nor do they have to be honest with the lawyer; they simply must make sure that suspects know they have the right to remain silent.

With regard to the important problem of coerced confessions, the Supreme Court issued a Fifth Amendment decision that upset liberals in 1991. The case, ***Arizona v. Fulminante,*** involved a murder confession by a prisoner to a fellow inmate who was a police informant.[62] The Court ruled that even if a confession is found to be "coerced," that fact will not automatically cause a mistrial if it can be shown, beyond a reasonable doubt, that the error did not determine the outcome of the trial. Despite the fact that a confession often has a tremendous impact on a jury, it is now possible for a judge to allow a trial to continue to a decision even though the jury has been exposed to an improperly obtained confession. However, it remains to be seen when and under what circumstances a coerced confession will be allowed in court proceedings and how *coercion* and *harmless error* will be defined. In *Fulminante*, the Court concluded that the introduction of the coerced confession was not harmless because of its likely impact on the verdict and ordered a new trial. Nonetheless, this case leaves the door open to admit confessions into evidence that violate the voluntariness standard.[63]

The impact of *Miranda* has also been felt in cases where the defendant raises the issue of the proper application of the Sixth Amendment right to counsel to interrogation proceedings. For instance, in the recent important case of ***Patterson v. Illinois*** (1988), the Court reviewed whether the interrogation of the accused after indictment violated the Sixth Amendment right to counsel.[64] The defendant was charged with a street gang murder after he had been given his *Miranda* warning and volunteered to answer questions put to him by police. After the indictment, while being transferred to jail, the defendant gave a lengthy statement to police about his involvement in the murder, among other things. This statement followed another *Miranda* warning and waiver, which the defendant initiated and signed for the police officer. The defendant claimed that questioning him about the murder without counsel present violated the Sixth Amendment and that he had not validly waived his right to have an attorney present during the interview. The Supreme Court decided, however, that the *Miranda* warning given the defendant (1) had made him aware of his right to have counsel present at the time of interrogation and (2) had made him aware of the consequences of his waiver. In other words, as long as the waiver was given "knowingly and intelligently," the confession obtained in the postindictment questioning was admissible.

The rulings in these cases indicate that the Supreme Court has somewhat weakened the *Miranda* ruling in recent years. The Court has held that statements made to police can be used in a court, even though they seem to have been made at the expense of the defendant's right to remain silent and to be represented by counsel. Overall, it seems that the Burger-Rehnquist court of the 1970s, 1980s, and early 1990s has chipped away at the Warren Court's original decision. Never-

theless, *Miranda* remains an historic and often symbolic decision whose progeny continue to affect the philosophical thrust of U.S. criminal jurisprudence.

Table 9.1 summarizes some of the most significant Fourth and Fifth Amendment Supreme Court decisions that have an impact on law enforcement practices and individual rights.

The Pretrial Identification Process

After the accused is arrested, he or she is ordinarily brought to the police station, where the police list the possible criminal charges. At the same time, they obtain other information, such as a description of the offender and the circumstances of the offense, for booking purposes. The booking process is a police administrative procedure in which generally the date and time of the arrest are recorded; arrangements are made for bail, detention, or removal to court; and any other information needed for identification is obtained. The defendant may be fingerprinted, photographed, and required to participate in a **lineup.** In a lineup, a suspect is placed in a group for the purpose of being viewed and identified by a witness. In accordance with the U.S. Supreme Court decisions in *United States v. Wade* (1967)[65] and *Kirby v. Illinois* (1972),[66] the accused has the right to have counsel present at this postindictment lineup or identification procedure.

In the *Wade* case, the Supreme Court held that a defendant has a right to counsel if the lineup takes place after the suspect has been formally charged with a crime. This decision was based on the Court's belief that the postindictment lineup procedure is a critical stage of the criminal justice process. In contrast, the suspect does not have a comparable right to counsel at a pretrial lineup where a complaint or indictment has not been issued. When the right to counsel is violated, the evidence of any pretrial identification must be excluded from the trial.

Suggestive Lineups

One of the most difficult legal issues in this area is determining if the identification procedure is "suggestive" and consequently in violation of the due process clause of the Fifth and Fourteenth Amendments. In *Simmons v. United States* (1968), the Supreme Court said, "The primary evil to be avoided is a very substantial likelihood of irreparable misidentification."[67] In its decision in *Neil v. Biggers* (1972), the Court established the following general criteria to judge the suggestiveness of a pretrial identification procedure: (1) the opportunity of the witness to view the criminal at the time of the crime; (2) the degree of attention by the witness and the accuracy of the prior description by the witness; (3) the level of certainty demonstrated by the witness; and (4) the length of time between the crime and the confrontation.[68]

The offense in the *Biggers* case was a rape. In regard to the witness's opportunity to view the suspect at the time of the crime, the victim spent a considerable period of time with her assailant, up to a half an hour. She was with him under adequate artificial light in her house and under a full moon outdoors, and at least twice, once in the house and later in the woods, she faced him directly and intimately. She was no casual observer but rather the victim of one of the most personally humiliating of all crimes. Her description to the police, which included the assailant's approximate age, height, weight, complexion, skin texture, build, and voice was thorough. She had no doubt that he was the person who raped her. Rarely are there witnesses to a rape other than the victim, who often has

LAW IN REVIEW

Miranda v. Arizona (1966)

Miranda v. Arizona is a landmark decision that climaxed a long line of self-incrimination cases in which the police used unlawful methods to obtain confessions from suspects accused of committing a crime.

Facts

Ernesto Miranda, a twenty-five-year-old mentally retarded man, was arrested in Phoenix, Arizona, and charged with kidnapping and rape. Miranda was taken from his home to a police station, where he was identified by a complaining witness. He was then interrogated and, after about two hours, signed a written confession. Miranda was subsequently convicted and sentenced to twenty to thirty years in prison. His conviction was affirmed by the Arizona Supreme Court, and he appealed to the U.S. Supreme Court, claiming that he had not been warned that any statement he made would be used against him and that he had not been advised of any right to have counsel present at his interrogation.

The *Miranda* case was one of four cases heard simultaneously by the U.S. Supreme Court, which dealt with the legality of confessions obtained by the police from a suspect in custody. In *Vignera v. New York* (1966), the defendant was arrested in connection with a robbery and taken to two different detective headquarters, where he was interrogated and subsequently confessed after eight hours in custody. In *Westover v. United States* (1966), the suspect was arrested by the Kansas City police, placed in a lineup, and booked on a felony charge. He was interrogated by the police during the evening and in the morning and by the FBI in the afternoon, when he signed two confessions. In *California v. Stewart,* the defendant was arrested at his home for being involved in a robbery. He was taken to a police station and placed in a cell, where over a period of five days he was interrogated nine times. The U.S. Supreme Court in *Miranda* described the common characteristics of these four cases:

In each, the defendant was questioned by the police in a room in which he was cut off from the outside world. In none of these cases was the defendant given a full and effective warning of his rights at the outset of the interrogation process. In all the cases, the questioning elicited oral admissions, and in three of them, signed statements as well which were admitted at their trials. They all thus share salient features—incommunicado interrogation of individuals in a police-dominated atmosphere, resulting in self-incriminating statements without full warnings of constitutional rights.

Decision

The major constitutional issue in *Miranda,* as in the other three cases, was the admissibility of statements obtained from a defendant questioned while in custody or while otherwise deprived of his freedom. The Fifth Amendment provides that no person shall be compelled to be a witness against himself. This means that a defendant cannot be required to testify at his

limited opportunity for observation. The victim, a practical nurse by profession, had an unusual opportunity to observe and identify her assailant. She testified at the habeas corpus hearing that there was something about his face "I don't think I could ever forget."

Seven months lapsed between the rape and the confrontation. This would be a serious negative factor in most cases, but the testimony was undisputed that the victim had made no previous identification at any of the showups, lineups, or photographic showings. Her record for reliability was thus a good one, as she had previously resisted whatever suggestiveness inheres in a lineup. Weighing all these factors, the Court found no substantial likelihood of misidentification and upheld the defendant's conviction. This is the approach the Court takes in analyzing the issue of suggestiveness in a lineup identification procedure.

The Exclusionary Rule

No review of the legal aspects of policing would be complete without a discussion of the exclusionary rule, the principal means used to restrain police conduct. As previously mentioned, the Fourth Amendment guarantees individuals the right to be secure in their persons, homes, papers, and effects against unreasonable searches and seizures. The exclusionary rule provides that all evidence obtained

trial and that a suspect who is questioned before trial cannot be subjected to any physical or psychological pressure to confess.

In the opinion of Chief Justice Earl Warren in the *Miranda* case, "the third degree method was still 'sufficiently widespread to be the object of concern.' " Of greater concern, he believed, was the increased use of sophisticated psychological pressures on suspects during interrogation. Thus, in a 5 to 4 decision, Miranda's conviction was overturned, and the Court established specific procedural guidelines for police to follow before eliciting statements from persons in police custody.

The Court's own summary of its decision is:

> Our holding will be spelled out with some specificity in the pages which follow but briefly it is this: the prosecution may not use statements, whether exculpatory or inculpatory, stemming from custodial interrogation of the defendant unless it demonstrates the use of procedural safeguards effective to secure the privilege against self-incrimination. By custodial interrogation, we mean questioning initiated by law enforcement officers after a person has been taken into custody or otherwise deprived of his freedom of action in any significant way. As for the procedural safeguards to be employed, unless fully effective means are devised to inform accused persons of their right of silence and to assure a continuous opportunity to exercise it, the following measures are required. Prior to any questioning the person must be warned that he has a right to remain silent, that any statement he does make may be used as evidence against him, and that he has a right to the presence of an attorney, either retained or appointed. The defendant may waive effectuation of these rights, provided the waiver is made voluntarily, knowingly and intelligently. If, however, he indicates in any manner and at any stage of the process that he wishes to consult with an attorney before speaking there can be no questioning. Likewise, if the individual is alone and indicates in any manner that he does not wish to be interrogated, the police may not question him. The mere fact that he may have answered some questions or volunteered some statements on his own does not deprive him of the right to refrain from answering any further inquiries until he has consulted with an attorney and thereafter consents to be questioned.

Significance of the Case

The *Miranda* decision established that the Fifth Amendment privilege against self-incrimination requires that a criminal suspect in custody or in any other manner deprived of freedom must be informed of his or her rights. If the suspect is not warned, then any evidence given is not admissible by the government to prove its case.

by illegal searches and seizures is inadmissible in criminal trials. Similarly, it excluded the use of illegal confessions under Fifth Amendment prohibitions.

For many years, evidence obtained by unreasonable searches and seizures that should consequently have been considered illegal was admitted by state and federal governments in criminal trials. The only criteria for admissibility was whether the evidence was incriminating and whether it would assist the judge or jury in ascertaining the innocence or guilt of the defendant. How the evidence was obtained was unimportant; its admissibility was determined by its relevance to the criminal case.

In 1914, however, the rules on the admissibility of evidence underwent a change of direction when the Supreme Court decided the case of *Weeks v. United States*.[69] The defendant, Freemont Weeks, was accused by federal law enforcement authorities of using the mails for illegal purposes. After his arrest, the home in which Weeks was staying was searched without a valid search warrant. Evidence in the form of letters and other materials was found in his room and admitted at the trial. Weeks was then convicted of the federal offense based on incriminating evidence. On appeal, the Supreme Court held that evidence obtained by unreasonable search and seizure must be excluded in a federal criminal trial. The Court stated:

TABLE 9.1

Notable Case Doctrines and Exceptions to the Fourth Amendment (Search and Seizure) and Fifth Amendment (Self-incrimination) Clauses

Fourth Amendment Doctrine	Case Decision	Holding
Expectation of Privacy	*Katz v. United States* 1968	Electronic eavesdropping is a search.
Plain View	*Arizona v. Hicks* 1967	Fourth Amendment may not apply when the object is in plain view.
Open Fields	*Oliver v. United States* 1984	To what extent can police search a field and curtilage?
Exigent or Emergency		Exception to the warrant requirement is allowed.
Warrant Requirements	**Case Decision**	**Holding**
Particularity	*Maryland v. Garrison* 1987	Particularity is a critical aspect of the warrant to be evaluated by the court.
Probable Cause	*Illinois v. Gates* 1983	Probable cause to issue a warrant is based on a "totality of circumstances."
Exceptions to the Warrant Requirement	**Case Decision**	**Holding**
Federal Requirement of Exclusionary Rule	*Weeks v. United States* 1914	U.S. Supreme Court applied the exclusionary rule to federal prosecutions.
State Application	*Mapp v. Ohio* 1961	U.S. Supreme Court applied the exclusionary rule to state prosecutions.
Automobile Search	*United States v. Ross* 1982	Warrantless search of an auto is permissible when it is based on probable cause.
Inventory Search	*Colorado v. Bertine* 1987	Inventory search of a vehicle is constitutional.
Search Incident to Arrest	*Chimel v. California* 1969	Permissible scope for a search is the area "within the arrestee's immediate control."

If letters and private documents can thus be seized and held and used in evidence against a citizen accused of an offense, the protection of the Fourth Amendment declaring his right to be secure against such searches and seizures is of no value, and, so far as those thus placed are concerned, might as well be stricken from the Constitution. The efforts of the courts and their officials to bring the guilty to punishment, praiseworthy as they are, are not to be aided by the sacrifice of those great principles established by years of endeavor and suffering which have resulted in their embodiment in the fundamental law of the land.[70]

TABLE 9.1
Continued

Fourth Amendment Doctrine	Case Decision	Holding
Stop and Frisk	*Terry v. Ohio* 1967	Police are authorized to stop and frisk suspicious persons.
Road Block Stop	*Delaware v. Prouse* 1979	Random stops require reasonable suspicion.
Consent	*Schneckloth v. Bustamonte* 1973	Consent to search must be voluntarily given.
Bus Sweep	*Florida v. Bostick* 1991	Police, after obtaining consent, may conduct a search of luggage without a search warrant or probable cause.
Exceptions to the Exclusionary Rule	**Case Decisions**	**Holding**
Good Faith	*United States v. Leon* 1984	When police rely on "good faith" in a warrant, the evidence seized is admissible even if the warrant is subsequently deemed defective.
Inevitable Discovery Rule	*Nix v. Williams* 1984	Illegal evidence is admissible if it is discovered independent of the illegality.
Fifth Amendment Doctrine	**Case Decisions**	**Holding**
Self-Incrimination	*Miranda v. Arizona* 1966	Defendant must be given the *Miranda* warning before questioning begins.
Definition of Interrogation and Waiver	*Brewer v. Williams* 1977	Absence of counsel is grounds for reversal.
Confessions (Harmless Error)	*Arizona v. Fulminante* 1991	Coerced confessions can sometimes be used as evidence.
Consultation with Counsel	*Minnick v. Mississippi* 1990	Once the accused has invoked *Miranda,* police cannot resume questioning without a lawyer present.

Thus, for the first time, the Court held that the Fourth Amendment barred the use in a federal prosecution of evidence obtained through illegal search and seizure. With this ruling, the Court established the exclusionary rule. The rule was based not on legislation but on judicial decision making.

Over the years, subsequent federal and state court decisions have gradually applied the exclusionary rule to state court systems. These decisions have not always been consistent, however. For instance, in 1949, the states received notice that the Supreme Court was considering making the *Weeks* doctrine binding on the state courts in the case of *Wolf v. Colorado*.[71] Wolf was charged in a Colorado state court with conspiring to perform abortions. Evidence in the form of patients' names was secured by a sheriff from a physician's office without a valid search warrant. The patients were subsequently questioned, and the evidence was used at Wolf's trial. The case was appealed, and the Supreme Court was asked to decide the question "Does a conviction by a state for a state offense deny the defendant due process of law because evidence admitted at the trial was obtained under circumstances which would have rendered it inadmissible in a federal trial?" [72] In a 6-to-3-decision, the Court decided that the evidence was admissible and not in violation of the Fourteenth Amendment. The Court recognized that the Fourth Amendment forbade the admissibility of illegally seized evidence but did not see fit to impose federal standards of criminal procedure on the states. One important fact the court considered in reaching its decision in *Wolf* was that only sixteen states were in agreement with the exclusionary rule, while thirty-one had rejected it by 1949.

However, many states changed their positions, and by 1961, approximately half had adopted the exclusionary rule. In that same year, the Supreme Court, despite past decisions, reversed itself and made the exclusionary rule applicable to state courts in the landmark decision of ***Mapp v. Ohio*** (1961).[73] Because of the importance of the *Mapp* case, it is discussed in the Law in Review on page 347.

Current Status and Controversy

The U.S. Supreme Court, with its conservative bent of recent years, has been diminishing the scope of the exclusionary rule. In *Illinois v. Gates* (1983), the Court made it easier for police to search a suspect's home by allowing an anonymous letter to be used as evidence in support of a warrant.[74] In another critical case, *United States v. Leon* (1984), the Court ruled that evidence seized by police relying on a warrant issued by a detached and neutral magistrate can be used in a court proceeding, even if the judge who issued the warrant may have relied on less than sufficient evidence.[75] In this case, the Court articulated a **good faith exception** to the exclusionary rule: evidence obtained with less than an adequate search warrant may be admissible in court if the police officers acted in good faith in obtaining court approval for their search. However, deliberately misleading a judge or using a warrant that the police know is unreasonably deficient would be grounds to invoke the exclusionary rule. A 1988 empirical study of the effects of *United States v. Leon* on police warrant practices found virtually no impact on the judicial suppression of evidence.[76] Although prosecutors initially applauded the decision and defense lawyers feared that the police would be inclined to secure warrants from sympathetic judges, both groups agree that *Leon* has had little practical effect on the processing of criminal cases. Further, most experts believe that no important data exist to prove that the exclusionary rule has had a direct impact on police behavior.

The Supreme Court appears to have expanded the good faith exception to the exclusionary rule in its decision in ***Illinois v. Krull*** (1987).[77] A Chicago police officer engaged in a warrantless search of a junkyard, relying on a state statute allowing such inspections. The Court held that the evidence the officer found was admissible, even though the statute allowing the search was subsequently found to be unconstitutional. In this case, the Court felt the police officer could not be responsible for an illegal search when the legislature had passed the law and the officer relied in good faith on that law.

LAW IN REVIEW

Mapp v. Ohio (1961)

In this historic case, the U.S. Supreme Court held that all law enforcement agents, federal and state, are affected by the exclusionary rule, which bars the admission of illegally obtained evidence in a criminal trial.

Facts

On May 23, 1957, three police officers arrived at Dolree Mapp's residence pursuant to information that "a person [was] hiding out in the home, who was wanted for questioning in connection with a recent bombing and that there was a large amount of police paraphernalia being hidden in the home." Mapp and her daughter by a former marriage lived on the top floor of the two-family dwelling. Upon their arrival at the house, the officers knocked on the door and demanded entrance, but Mapp, after telephoning her attorney, refused to admit them without a search warrant.

The officers again sought entrance three hours later when four or more additional officers arrived on the scene. When Mapp did not immediately come to the door, the police forcibly opened one of the doors to the house and gained admittance. Meanwhile, Mapp's attorney arrived, but the officers would not permit him to see Mapp or to enter the house. Mapp was halfway down the stairs from the upper floor to the front door when the officers broke into the hall. She demanded to see the search warrant. A paper, claimed to be a search warrant, was held up by one of the officers. She grabbed the "warrant" and placed it in her bosom. A struggle ensued in which the officers recovered the piece of paper and handcuffed Mapp because she had ostensibly been belligerent.

Mapp was then forcibly taken upstairs to her bedroom, where the officers searched a dresser, a chest of drawers, a closet, and some suitcases. They also looked into a photo album and through personal papers belonging to her. The search spread to the rest of the second floor, including the child's bedroom, the living room, the kitchen, and the dinette. In the course of the search, the police officers found pornographic literature. Mapp was arrested and subsequently convicted in an Ohio court of possessing obscene materials.

Decision

The question in the *Mapp* case was whether the evidence was seized in violation of the search and seizure provisions of the Fourth Amendment and therefore inadmissible in the state trial, which resulted in an obscenity conviction. The Supreme Court of Ohio found the conviction valid. However, the U.S. Supreme Court overturned it, stating that the Fourth Amendment's prohibition against unreasonable searches and seizures, enforceable against the states through the due process clause, had been violated by the police. Justice Tom Clark, delivering the majority opinion of the Court, made clear the importance of this constitutional right in the administration of criminal justice when he stated:

> There are those who say, as did Justice [then Judge] Cardozo, that under our constitutional exclusionary doctrine "[t]he criminal is to go free because the constable has blundered." In some cases this will undoubtedly be the result. But . . . there is another consideration—the imperative of judicial integrity. . . . The criminal goes free, if he must, but it is the law that sets him free. Nothing can destroy a government more quickly than its failure to observe its own laws, or worse its disregard of the charter of its own existence.

Significance of the Case

In previous decisions, the U.S. Supreme Court had refused to exclude evidence in state court proceedings based on Fourth Amendment violations of search and seizure. The *Mapp* case overruled such decisions, including that of *Wolf v. Colorado,* and held that evidence gathered in violation of the Fourth Amendment would be inadmissible in a state prosecution. For the first time, the Court imposed federal constitutional standards on state law enforcement personnel. In addition, the Court reemphasized the point that a relationship exists between the Fourth and Fifth Amendments, which forms the constitutional basis for the exclusionary rule.

The Court has also ruled that evidence discovered in violation of the exclusionary rule can be used at trial if it would have been found within a short time by independent means. This is known as the "inevitable discovery rule." Thus, if police seize evidence in violation of the exclusionary rule, it may still be used at trial if a judge rules that it would most likely have been found anyway (for example, it was in an open field and people were already looking for it).[78]

Finally, the Supreme Court continued this conservative trend by ruling in a 1988 case ***(Arizona v. Youngblood)*** that a criminal defendant's rights are not violated when police lose or destroy evidence that might prove the person's innocence, unless the police acted maliciously.[79] In *Youngblood,* the Court ruled that police failure to preserve important evidence properly simply because of incompetence or mistake is not sufficient reason to reserve a conviction. According to conservative Chief Justice William Rehnquist, "unless a defendant can show bad faith on the part of the police, failure to preserve potentially useful evidence does not constitute a denial of due process of law."

In these and other cases, the Court seems to be making it easier for the police to conduct searches of criminal suspects and their possessions and then use the seized evidence in court proceedings. The Court has indicated that as a general rule, the protection afforded the individual by the Fourth Amendment may take a back seat to concerns about public safety if criminal actions pose a clear threat to society.[80]

The Future of the Exclusionary Rule

The exclusionary rule has long been a controversial subject in the administration of criminal justice. It was originally conceived to control illegitimate police practices, and that remains its primary purpose today. It is justified on the basis that it deters illegal searches and seizures. Yet most experts believe that no impartial data exist to prove that the rule has a direct impact on police behavior. This is by far the most significant criticism of the rule. By excluding evidence, the rule has a more direct effect on the criminal trial than on the police officer on the street. Furthermore, the rule is powerless when the police have no interest in prosecuting the accused or in obtaining a conviction. In addition, it does not control the wholesale harassment of individuals by law enforcement officials bent on disregarding constitutional rights.

The most popular criticism of the exclusionary rule, however, is that it allows guilty defendants to go free. Because courts frequently decide in many types of cases (particularly those involving victimless offenses, such as gambling and drug use) that certain evidence should be excluded, the rule is believed to result in excessive court delays and to negatively affect plea-bargaining negotiations.[81] However, the rule appears to result in relatively few case dismissals.

Because the exclusionary rule may not deter illegal police action and because its use may result in some offenders escaping conviction, proposals for modifying the rule have been suggested. The American Law Institute's *Model Code of Pre-Arraignment Procedure* limits the use of the exclusionary rule to substantial violations by law enforcement officials. This means that evidence should be suppressed only if the court finds that the constitutional violations are substantial. The code does not precisely define the term *substantial,* but it enumerates six criteria for determining substantial violations:

1. [The] extent of deviation from lawful conduct
2. [The] extent to which [the] violation was willful
3. [The] extent to which privacy was invaded
4. [The] extent to which exclusion will tend to prevent violations of this Code
5. [W]hether, but for the violation, the things seized would have been discovered
6. [The] extent to which the violation prejudiced the moving party's ability to support his motion, or to defend himself in the proceedings in which the things seized are sought to be offered in evidence against him.[82]

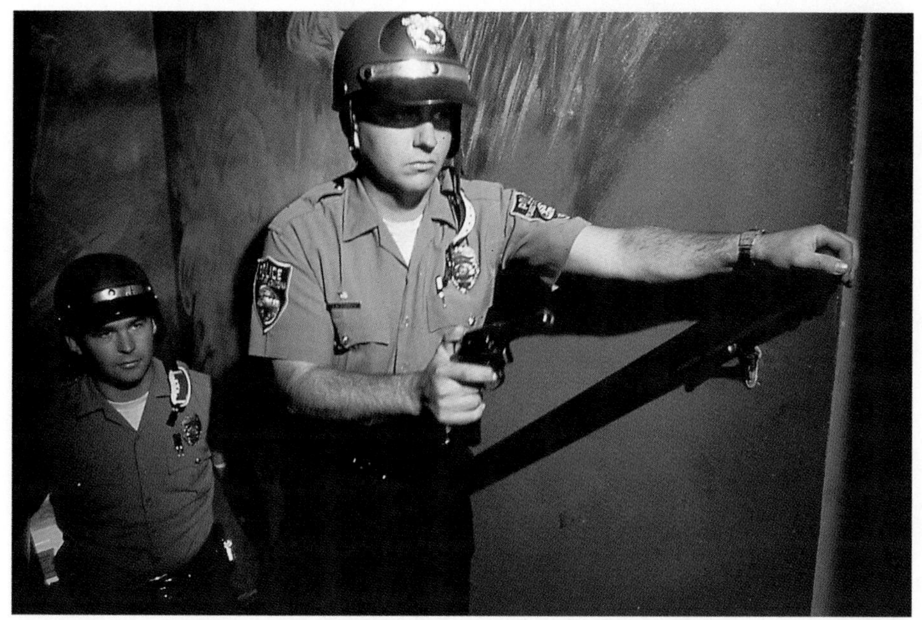

In recent years the Supreme Court has relaxed restrictions on the police officer's ability to search for and seize evidence.

Although the code is only a proposed model, its modification of the exclusionary rule would seem to offer some relief from the problem of having to free criminals due to minor Fourth Amendment violations by police officials. On the other hand, modification of the rule could lead police to become sloppy in their application of constitutional rights and cause them to care more about developing excuses for their actions, such as "we acted in good faith" or "the evidence would have been discovered anyway," than about individuals' rights.[83]

Another approach has been to legislate the exclusionary rule out of existence. Voters in California attempted to do this when they passed Proposition 8 in the early 1980s. The proposition stated: "That relevant evidence should not be excluded in any criminal proceeding." In 1988, the U.S. Supreme Court considered this issue in the case of ***California v. Greenwood.***[84] Concerned that the defendant Greenwood might be involved in selling drugs, the police collected Greenwood's trash bags from the curb of his home, searched them without a warrant, and found items indicating the defendant used drugs. A subsequent search of Greenwood's home with a warrant disclosed additional drugs. The California Supreme Court held that the police officers' conduct was an impermissible and illegal search. The U.S. Supreme Court, however, took cognizance of the 1982 amendment to the California State Constitution that provided that evidence was not to be excluded in criminal trials on this basis. Greenwood argued that since state law prohibited the police from examining the trash, this gave him a right of privacy protected by the Fourth Amendment. But the Supreme Court rejected Greenwood's argument, holding that the state could establish the scope of its exclusionary rule and weigh the benefits of controlling police misconduct against the price of excluding reliable evidence. The *Greenwood* case certainly suggests that the exclusionary rule could be modified so long as it pertains to police parameters established by the U.S. Supreme Court.

Other suggested approaches to dealing with violations of the exclusionary rule include (1) criminal prosecution of police officers who violate constitutional rights; (2) internal police control; (3) civil lawsuits against state or municipal

ANALYZING CRIMINAL JUSTICE ISSUES

The Exclusionary Rule in Australia

In 1914, the U.S. Supreme Court created the exclusionary rule in the case of *Weeks v. United States.* Known as the bane of police and prosecutors, it was mandated in state courts in 1961 by *Mapp v. Ohio.* Its major purpose then and now is to deter police misconduct. Mandatory exclusion of illegally seized evidence to achieve this goal, with certain exceptions defined by the court, is the rule in the United States.

Australia's legal system on the other hand—based on the British common law like that of the United States—holds that illegally seized evidence is admissible and that the "voluntariness" test regarding confessions is the only area for mandatory evidentiary exclusion. Adhering to the British rule, the Australians allow the admission of almost any evidence regardless of how it was obtained. This approach is based to some degree on the fact that Australia does not have a Bill of Rights and its rules are established by parliaments and state courts, while U.S. rules of criminal procedure have a constitutional foundation.

Consequently, Australia uses a discretionary or balanced approach to evidentiary exclusion. Evidence is ordinarily excluded if the cost to society of imposing the rule is less than the benefit of enforcing it. Discretionary exclusion revolves around three possible grounds: (1) prejudice, (2) unfairness, and (3) police misconduct. In other words, a trial judge can exclude a confession if it has low prohibitive value but great prejudicial effect; the judge must balance the desirability of convicting the offender against approving unlawful police conduct. In some respects, this discretionary exclusionary rule has not worked well because judges have shown little interest in deterring police misconduct through evidentiary exclusion. As a result, the Australian states, such as South Wales and Victoria, have moved toward a statutory approach to regulating police behavior. Even national legislation may be approved since the rules of procedure are partly statutory already.

This discretionary approach to the exclusionary rule is also used in West Germany and most other European nations.

Critical Thinking Skills

According to law enforcement and judicial experts, crime rates could be reduced if the exclusionary rule in the United States were eliminated and the prosecutor given a greater chance to obtain a conviction. On the other hand, some social scientists believe the rule plays only a minor role in the total disposition of criminal cases. However, the primary purpose of the exclusionary rule is to deter unconstitutional police behavior. This goal must be balanced against the probability that a dangerous defendant may go free. How would you decide the following issues?

1. Should rules of criminal procedure be developed by statute, instead of case law?
2. Should the United States consider a national code of criminal procedure that safeguards constitutional rights while protecting the law-abiding citizen?
3. Instead of adopting the Australian or British model of discretion, should we abandon the exclusionary rule for certain crimes, such as murder or kidnapping?

SOURCES: Craig M. Bradley, "Criminal Procedure in the "Land of Oz": Lessons for America," *The Journal of Criminal Law and Criminology* 81 (1990): 99–134; also Marvin Zalman and Larry Siegel, *Criminal Procedures—Constitution and Society* (St. Paul: West Publishing, 1991) p. 393.

police officers; and (4) federal lawsuits against the government under the Federal Tort Claims Act. An individual using any of these alternatives, however, would be faced with such obstacles as the cost of bringing a lawsuit, proving damages, and dealing with a bureaucratic law enforcement system.

In the end, of all the civilized countries in the world, only the United States applies an exclusionary rule to illegal searches and seizures of material evidence.[85] (See Analyzing Criminal Justice Issues: The Exclusionary Rule in Australia.) Whether the Supreme Court or legislative bodies adopt any more significant changes to the rule will depend largely on efforts by police to discipline themselves. It will also depend on a tough civil tort remedy that allows lawsuits and claims for damages against offending police officers.

The fate of the exclusionary rule will remain difficult to predict. Although it is a simple rule of evidence, it involves complex issues of fairness, justice, and crime control.[86]

SUMMARY

Law enforcement officers use many different investigatory techniques to detect and apprehend criminal offenders. These include searches, electronic eavesdropping, interrogation, the use of informants, surveillance, and witness identification procedures. Over the past three decades, in particular through U.S. Supreme Court decisions, serious constitutional limitations have been placed on the pretrial process. Under interpretations of the Fourth Amendment, for example, police are required to use warrants to conduct searches except in some clearly defined situations. The exceptions to the search warrant rule include searches of automobiles used in a crime, stop and frisks, searches incident to an arrest, searches of material in plain view, and some instances of electronic eavesdropping.

Police interrogation procedures have also been reviewed extensively. Through the *Miranda* rule, the Supreme Court established an affirmative procedure as a requirement for all custodial interrogations. Many issues concerning *Miranda* continue to be litigated. Lineups and other suspect identification practices have also been subject to court review. The degree to which a defendant's rights should be protected at the pretrial stage while maintaining the government's interest in crime control remains a source of constant debate in the criminal justice system.

The exclusionary rule continues to be one of the most controversial issues in the criminal justice system. Even though the courts have curtailed its application in recent years, it still generally prohibits the admission of evidence that violates the defendant's constitutional rights. The exclusionary rule is an example of a federal rule made binding on the states.

QUESTIONS

1. Should obviously guilty persons go free because police originally arrested them with less than probable cause?
2. Should illegally seized evidence be excluded from trial, even though it is conclusive proof of a person's criminal acts?
3. Should police be personally liable if they violate a person's constitutional rights? How might this influence their investigations?
4. Should a person be put in a lineup without the benefit of counsel?
5. Have criminals been given too many rights? Should courts be more concerned with the rights of victims or the rights of offenders?
6. Does the exclusionary rule effectively deter police misconduct?
7. Can a search and seizure be "reasonable" if it is not authorized by a warrant?

NOTES

1. See, generally, American Bar Association, *Standards Relating to the Urban Police Function* (New York: Institute of Judicial Administration, 1973); see also Herman Goldstein, *Policing a Free Society* (Cambridge, Mass.: Ballinger, 1977).
2. American Bar Association, *Standards Relating to the Urban Police Function*, pp. 91–93. Reprinted with the permission of the American Bar Association, which authored these standards and holds the copyright.
3. See Wayne R. LaFave, *Arrest: The Decision to Take a Suspect into Custody* (Boston: Little, Brown & Co., 1965); Lawrence P. Tiffany, Donald McIntyre, and Daniel Rotenberg, *Detection of Crime: Stopping and Questioning, Search and Seizure* (Boston: Little, Brown & Co., 1967); Wayne R. LaFave, *Search and Seizure: A Treatise on the Fourth Amendment* (St. Paul: West Publishing, 1978).
4. 480 U.S. 79, 107 S.Ct. 1013, 94 L.Ed.2d 72 (1987).
5. 393 U.S. 410, 89 S.Ct. 584, 21 L.Ed.2d 637 (1969).
6. 378 U.S. 108, 84 S.Ct. 1509, 12 L.Ed.2d 723 (1964).
7. 462 U.S. 213, 103 S.Ct. 2317, 76 L.Ed.2d 527 (1983).
8. 394 Mass. 363, 476 N.E.2d 548 (1985).

9. 395 U.S. 752, 89 S.Ct. 2034, 23 L.Ed.2d 685 (1969).
10. 453 U.S. 454, 101 S.Ct. 2860, 69 L.Ed.2d 768 (1981).
11. ___ U.S. ___, 111 S.Ct. 1547, 113 L.Ed.2d 690 (1991).
12. Ibid., at ___, 111 S.Ct. at 1547.
13. Ibid., at ___, 111 S.Ct. at 1549.
14. 392 U.S. 1, 88 S.Ct. 1868, 20 L.Ed.2d 889 (1968).
15. Ibid., at 20–27, 88 S.Ct. at 1879–1883.
16. 442 U.S. 200, 99 S.Ct. 2248, 60 L.Ed.2d 824 (1979).
17. 452 U.S. 692, 101 S.Ct. 2587, 69 L.Ed.2d 340 (1981).
18. 486 U.S. 567, 108 S.Ct. 1975, 100 L.Ed.2d 565 (1988).
19. 267 U.S. 132, 45 S.Ct. 280, 69 L.Ed. 543 (1925).
20. 456 U.S. 798, 102 S.Ct. 2157, 72 L.Ed.2d 572 (1982); see also Barry Latzer, "Searching Cars and Their Contents: *U.S. v. Ross*," *Criminal Law Bulletin* 6 (1982):220; Joseph Grano, "Rethinking the Fourth Amendment Warrant Requirements," *Criminal Law Review* 19 (1982):603.
21. ___ U.S. ___, 111 S.Ct. 1801, 114 L.Ed.2d 297 (1991).
22. *California v. Acevedo*, ___U.S. ___, 111 S.Ct. 1982, 114 L.Ed.2d 619 (1991).
23. Ibid., at ___, 111 S.Ct. at 1982.
24. 471 U.S. 386, 105 S.Ct. 2066, 85 L.Ed.2d 406 (1985).
25. 479 U.S. 367, 107 S.Ct. 738, 93 L.Ed.2d 739 (1987).
26. 440 U.S. 648, 99 S.Ct. 1391, 59 L.Ed.2d 660 (1979); see also Lance Rogers, "The Drunk-Driving Roadblock: Random Seizure or Minimal Intrusion?" *Criminal Law Bulletin* 21 (1985):197–217.
27. 391 U.S. 543, 88 S.Ct. 1788, 20 L.Ed.2d 797 (1968).
28. 412 U.S. 218, 93 S.Ct. 2041, 36 L.Ed.2d 854 (1973).
29. *Florida v. Bostick*, ___ U.S. ___, 111 S.Ct. 2382, 115 L.Ed.2d 389 (1991).
30. Joseph Cronin, "Working the Buses: Leave the Searching to Us," *Suffolk University Law School Journal* 22 (1991):31–37.
31. 446 U.S. 544, 100 S.Ct. 1870, 64 L.Ed.2d 497 (1980).
32. 460 U.S. 491, 103 S.Ct. 1319, 75 L.Ed.2d 229 (1983).
33. 475 U.S. 106, 106 S.Ct. 960, 89 L.Ed.2d 81 (1986).
34. 480 U.S. 321, 107 S.Ct. 1149, 94 L.Ed.2d 347 (1987); see also Note, "Fourth Amendment Requires Probable Cause for Search and Seizure under Plain View Doctrine," *Journal of Criminal Law and Criminology* 78 (1988):763.
35. 466 U.S. 170, 104 S.Ct. 1735, 80 L.Ed.2d 214 (1984).
36. 476 U.S. 207, 106 S.Ct. 1809, 90 L.Ed.2d 210 (1986).
37. 488 U.S. 445, 109 S.Ct. 693, 102 L.Ed.2d 835 (1989).
38. Gary T. Marx, *Undercover: Police Surveillance in America* (Berkeley: University of California Press, 1988).
39. 389 U.S. 347, 88 S.Ct. 507, 19 L.Ed.2d 576 (1967).
40. 460 U.S. 276, 103 S.Ct. 1081, 75 L.Ed.2d 55 (1983).
41. 468 U.S. 705, 104 S.Ct. 3296, 82 L.Ed.2d 530 (1984).
42. See *United States v. White*, 401 U.S. 745, 91 S.Ct. 1122, 28 L.Ed.2d 453 (1971).
43. 400 Mass. 61 (1987).
44. Omnibus Crime Control Act, Title III, 90th Congress 1968; 18 U.S.C. §§ 2511–2520.
45. Electronic Communications and Privacy Act of 1986, Public Law No. 99–508, Title 18 U.S.C. § 2510.
46. American Bar Association, *Standards Relating to Electronic Surveillance*, 2d ed. (New York: Institute of Judicial Administration, 1980).
47. See Michael Goldsmith, "The Supreme Court and Title III: Rewriting the Law of Electronic Surveillance," *Journal of Criminal Law and Criminology* 74 (1983):76–85.
48. ___ U.S. ___, 111 S.Ct. 1661, 114 L.Ed.2d 49 (1991).
49. 384 U.S. 436, 86 S.Ct. 1602, 16 L.Ed.2d 694 (1966).
50. 297 U.S. 278, 56 S.Ct. 461, 80 L.Ed. 682 (1936).
51. 378 U.S. 478, 84 S.Ct. 1758, 12 L.Ed.2d 977 (1964).
52. Michael Wald et al., "Interrogations in New Haven: The Impact of Miranda," *Yale Law Journal* 76 (1967):1519.
53. "Don't Blame Miranda," *Washington Post*, 2 December 1988, p. A26.
54. 430 U.S. 387, 97 S.Ct. 1232, 51 L.Ed.2d 424 (1977).
55. ___ U.S. ___, 111 S.Ct. 486, 112 L.Ed.2d 489 (1990).
56. 401 U.S. 222, 91 S.Ct. 643, 28 L.Ed.2d 1 (1971).
57. 417 U.S. 433, 94 S.Ct. 2357, 41 L.Ed.2d 182 (1974).
58. 423 U.S. 96, 46 S.Ct. 321, 46 L.Ed.2d 313 (1975).
59. 467 U.S. 431, 104 S.Ct. 2051, 81 L.Ed.2d 377 (1984).
60. 467 U.S. 649, 104 S.Ct. 2626, 81 L.Ed.2d 550 (1984).
61. 475 U.S. 412, 106 S.Ct. 1135, 89 L.Ed.2d 410 (1986); see also Walter Lippman, "*Miranda v. Arizona*—Twenty Years Later," *Criminal Justice Journal* 9 (1987):241; Stephen J. Scholhofer, "Reconsidering Miranda," *University of Chicago Law Review* 54 (1987):435–61.
62. ___ U.S. ___, 111 S.Ct. 1246, 113 L.Ed.2d 302 (1991).
63. Marvin Zalman, "Reflections on *Arizona v. Fulminante*—Harmless Error, Coerced Confessions and Precedent" (draft paper, November 1991).
64. 487 U.S. 285, 108 S.Ct. 2389, 101 L.Ed.2d 261 (1988).
65. 388 U.S. 218, 87 S.Ct. 1926, 18 L.Ed.2d 1149 (1967).
66. 406 U.S. 682, 92 S.Ct. 1877, 32 L.Ed.2d 411 (1972).
67. 390 U.S. 377, 88 S.Ct. 967, 19 L.Ed.2d 1247 (1968).
68. 409 U.S. 188, 93 S.Ct. 375, 34 L.Ed.2d 401 (1972).
69. 232 U.S. 383, 34 S.Ct. 341, 58 L.Ed. 652 (1914).
70. Ibid., at 393, 34 S.Ct. at 344.
71. 338 U.S. 25, 69 S.Ct. 1359, 93 L.Ed. 1782 (1949).
72. Ibid., at 25, 26, 69 S.Ct. at 1360.
73. 367 U.S. 643, 81 S.Ct. 1684, 6 L.Ed.2d 1081 (1961).
74. 462 U.S. 213, 103 S.Ct. 2317, 76 L.Ed.2d 527 (1983).
75. 468 U.S. 897, 104 S.Ct. 3405, 82 L.Ed.2d 677 (1984).
76. Craig V. Chida et al., *The Effects of U.S. v. Leon on Police Search Warrant Practices*, (Washington, D.C.: U.S. Government Printing Office, 1988).
77. 480 U.S. 340, 107 S.Ct. 1160, 94 L.Ed.2d 364 (1987).
78. *Nix v. Williams*, 467 U.S. 431, 104 S.Ct. 2501, 81 L.Ed.2d 377 (1984).
79. 488 U.S. 51, 109 S.Ct. 333, 102 L.Ed.2d 281 (1988).
80. *New Jersey v. T.L.O.*, 469 U.S. 325, 105 S.Ct. 733, 83 L.Ed.2d 720 (1985).
81. See, generally, Arnold Enker, "Prospectives on Plea Bargaining" in President's Commission on Law Enforcement and the Administration of Justice, *Task Force Report: The Courts* (Washington, D.C.: U.S. Government Printing Office, 1967), pp. 109–19.
82. American Law Institute, *A Model Code of Pre-Arraignment Procedure* (Washington, D.C.: American Law Institute, 1975), Articles 290 and 290.2(4).
83. See, generally, James Fyfe, "In Search of the 'Bad Faith' Search," *Criminal Law Bulletin* 18 (1982):260–64.
84. 486 U.S. 35, 108 S.Ct. 1625, 100 L.Ed.2d 30 (1988).
85. See "The Exclusionary Rule," *American Bar Association Journal* 19 (February 1983):3; "Rule Prohibiting Illegal Evidence Faces Limitation," *Wall Street Journal*, 30 November 1982.
86. See Bradford Wilson, *Exclusionary Rule* (Washington, D.C.: U.S. Government Printing Office, 1986); see also Jana Nestlerode, "Distinguishing the Exclusionary Rule Exceptions," *Journal of National Association of District Attorneys* 24 (1991):29–35.

PART THREE

COURTS AND ADJUDICATION

CHAPTER 10

Courts and the Judiciary

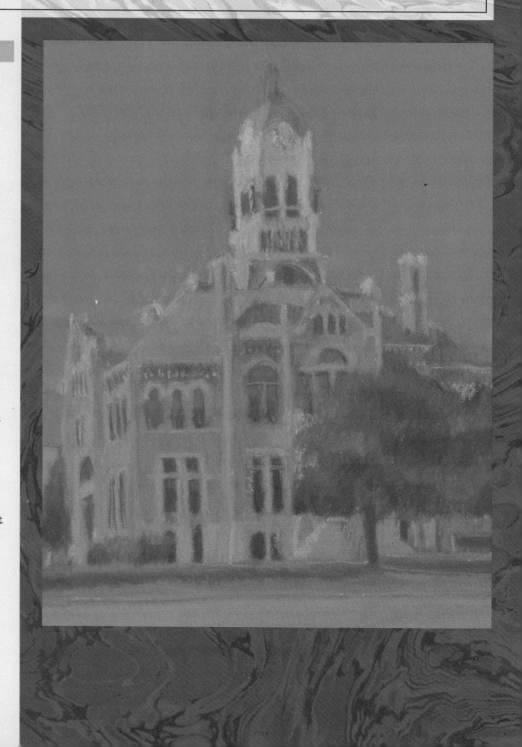

OUTLINE

KEY TERMS

defendants
assembly-line justice
courts of limited jurisdiction
lower courts
courts of general jurisdiction
felony courts
appellate courts
court of last resort
intermediate appellate courts
U.S. District Courts
U.S. Circuit Courts
U.S. Supreme Court
writ of certiorari
landmark decision
judge
charges the jury
jury trial
sentencing
Missouri Plan

The criminal court is the setting in which many of the most important decisions in the criminal justice system are made: bail, trial, plea negotiations, and sentencing all involve court-made decisions. Within the confines of the court, those accused of crime (**defendants**) call on the tools of the legal system to provide them with a fair and just hearing, with the burden of proof resting on the state; crime victims ask the government to provide them with justice for the wrongs done them and the injuries they have suffered; agents of the criminal justice system attempt to find solutions that benefit the victim, the defendant, and society in general. The court process is designed to provide an open and impartial forum for deciding the truth of the matter and reaching a solution which, though punitive, is fairly arrived at and satisfies the rule of law.

Regardless of the parties or issues involved, the presence of these parties in a courtroom should guarantee them that a hearing will be held and conducted under fair, equitable, and regulated rules of procedure, that the outcome of the hearing will be clear, and that the hearing will take place in an atmosphere of legal competence and objectivity. If either party, the defendant or the prosecutor, feels that these ground rules have been violated, he or she may take the case to a higher court, where the procedures of the original trial will be examined. If, on reexamination, it is found that criminal procedure has been violated, the appellate court may deem the findings of the original trial improper and either order a new hearing or hold that some other measure must be carried out—for example, the court may dismiss the charge outright.

As you already know, in today's crowded court system, such abstract goals are often impossible to achieve. In reality, the U.S. court system is often the scene of accommodation and "working things out," rather than an arena for a vigorous criminal defense. Plea negotiations and other nonjudicial alternatives, such as diversion, are far more common than the formal trial process.

In this and the following four chapters, the structure and function of the court system will be closely examined. Here, we set out the structure of the U.S. court system and its guiding hand, the judge. The following chapters cover the prosecutor and the defense attorney, the pretrial process, the trial, and finally, sentencing and punishment.

Criminal Court Process

The court is a complex social agency with many independent but interrelated subsystems, each of which has a role in the court's operation: police, prosecutor, defense attorney, judge, and probation department. It is also the scene of many

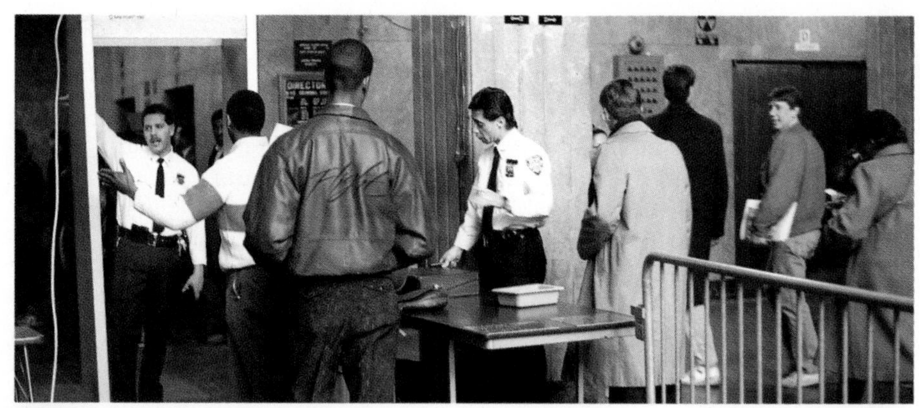

The nation's criminal courts are dangerous, overcrowded, and congested. In cities such as New York, visitors to criminal courts are required to undergo weapon screenings before entering.

important elements of criminal justice decision-making: bail, detention, charging, jury selection, trial, and sentencing. As you may recall, there are two ways to view the criminal court process. In the traditional model, the court is seen as a setting for an adversarial procedure that pits the defendant against the state, the defense counsel against the prosecutor. Procedures are fair and formalized, controlled by the laws of criminal procedure and the rule of evidence.

In the second model, the court is viewed as a system that encourages settling matters in the simplest, quickest, and most efficient manner possible. Rather than being adversaries, prosecutors and defense attorneys form a "work group" with the judge and other court personnel that tries to handle the situation with as little fuss as possible. This usually involves dropping the case if the defendant agrees to make restitution or enter a treatment or diversion program, plea bargaining, or some other "quick fix." In Malcom Feeley's study of a lower court in Connecticut, not one defendant in 1,640 cases analyzed insisted on having a jury trial, and only half made use of legal counsel. Because cases dragged on endlessly, people were encouraged to plea-bargain. And the haphazard nature of justice produced a situation in which the defendant's prior criminal record and the seriousness of the current charge had little influence on case outcome. Felons with prior records fared as well as first-time misdemeanants.[1]

The U.S. court system has evolved over the years into an intricately balanced legal process that has recently come under siege because of the sheer numbers of cases it must consider and the ways in which it is forced to handle such overcrowding. Overloaded court dockets have given rise to charges of **assembly-line justice,** in which a majority of defendants are induced to plead guilty, jury trials are rare, and the speedy trial is highly desired but unattainable.

Overcrowding causes the poor to languish in detention while the wealthier go free on bail. The possibility increases that an innocent person may be frightened into pleading guilty and, conversely, a guilty person released because a trial has been delayed too long.[2] Whether providing more judges or new or enlarged courts will solve the problem of overcrowding remains to be seen. Meanwhile, diversion programs, decriminalization of certain offenses, and bail reform provide other avenues of possible relief. More efficient court management and administration is also seen as a step that might ease the congestion of the courts. These issues are extremely important if defendants are going to view their experience as a fair one in which they were able to present their side of the case and influence its outcome. Ironically, there is evidence that the informal justice system, which is often deplored by experts, may provide criminal suspects a greater degree of satisfaction than the more formal criminal trial.[3]

To house this rather complex process, each state maintains its own state court organization and structure. Usually three (or more) separate court systems exist within each state jurisdiction. These are described below.

Courts of Limited Jurisdiction

There are approximately thirteen thousand **courts of limited jurisdiction** in the United States. Most (87 percent) are organized along town, municipal, and county lines of government; about seven hundred are controlled by state governments.[4]

Courts of limited jurisdiction (sometimes called municipal courts, or **lower courts**) are restricted in the types of cases they may hear. Usually, they will handle misdemeanor criminal infractions, violations of municipal ordinances, traffic violations, and civil suits where the damages involve less than a certain amount of money (usually ten thousand dollars). These courts also conduct preliminary hearings for felony criminal cases.

The lower criminal courts are restricted in the criminal penalties they can impose. Most can levy a fine of one thousand dollars or less and incarcerate a person for twelve months or less in the local jail.

Included within the category of courts of limited jurisdictions are special courts, such as juvenile and family courts and probate (divorce, estate issues, and custody) courts. Some states separate limited courts into those that handle civil cases only and those which settle criminal cases.

Process and Punishment in Lower Courts

The nation's lower courts are the ones most often accused of providing assembly-line justice. Since the matters they decide involve minor personal confrontations and conflicts—family disputes, divorces, landlord-tenant conflicts, barroom brawls—the rule of the day is "handling the situation" and resolving the dispute. Social commentator Charles Silberman describes his experience in such a criminal court:

> My first visit to a criminal court, in fact, reminded me of nothing quite so much as a long evening spent in the emergency room of a large city hospital, trying to get medical care for an elderly relative who had been knocked down by an automobile. In the courtroom, defendants, witnesses, and complainants, along with their families, sat in hard-backed chairs, waiting with the same air of resignation that patients and their families had displayed in the hospital emergency room; waiting sometimes seems to be a principal occupation of the poor.[5]

In his well-received book, *The Process Is the Punishment,* Malcolm Feeley describes the lower courts as a "world apart . . . their facilities are terrible. Courtrooms are crowded, chambers are dingy, and libraries are virtually nonexistent. Even the newer courtrooms age quickly, worn down by hard use and constant abuse."[6] According to Feeley, lower courts are basically informal institutions in which all parties work together to settle the situation in an equitable fashion. In this respect, the criminal process is similar to the civil justice system. According to Feeley, the "process is the punishment in lower courts." By this, he means that nothing much happens by way of formal punishment in the lower courts. Just having to go to hearings, retain counsel, miss work, and so on is the real punishment for offenders. So many cases are settled by plea bargains because defendants are trying to avoid the pains of the court process, not the pains of imprisonment.

Defendants are aided in this by the court personnel, who practice accommodative rather than adversarial justice.

Courts of General Jurisdiction

Approximately 3,235 **courts of general jurisdiction,** or **felony courts,** exist in the United States and process about 1.5 million cases each year.[7] Courts of general jurisdiction handle the more serious felony cases (e.g., murder, rape, robbery), while courts of limited jurisdiction handle misdemeanors (e.g., simple assault, shoplifting, bad checks). About 90 percent of the general courts are state-administered, and the remainder are controlled by counties or municipalities. The overwhelming majority (95 percent) of general courts hear both serious civil and criminal matters (felonies).

About three-fourths of the courts of general jurisdiction also are responsible for reviewing cases on appeal from courts of limited jurisdiction. In some cases, they will base their decision on a review of the transcript of the case, while in others, they can actually grant a new trial; this latter procedure is known as the trial *de novo* process.

Appellate Courts

If defendants believe that the procedures used in their case were in violation of their constitutional rights, they may appeal the outcome of their case. For example, defendants can file an appeal if they believe that the law they were tried under violates constitutional standards (e.g., it was too vague) or if the procedures used in the case contravened principles of due process and equal protection or were in direct opposition to a constitutional guarantee (e.g., the defendants were denied the right to have competent legal representation). Appellate courts do not try cases; they review the procedures of the case in order to determine whether an error was made by judicial authorities. Judicial error can include admitting into evidence illegally seized material, improperly charging a jury, allowing a prosecutor to ask witnesses improper questions, and so on. The appellate court can either order a new trial, allow the defendant to go free, or uphold the original verdict.

State criminal appeals are heard in one of the approximately ninety-four **appellate courts** in the fifty states and the District of Columbia. Each state has at least one **court of last resort,** usually called a state supreme court, which reviews issues of law and fact appealed from the trial courts; two states, Texas and Oklahoma, have two high courts, one for civil appeals and the other for criminal cases. In addition, thirty-six states have established **intermediate appellate courts** to review decisions by trial courts and administrative agencies before they reach the supreme court stage. Five states, including New York, Pennsylvania, and Indiana, have established more than one type of intermediate appellate court. In Hawaii, Idaho, Iowa, Oklahoma, and South Carolina, intermediate courts do not have original jurisdiction over appeals but are assigned cases when the supreme court's caseload overflows.

Appellate Overflow?

Many people believe that criminal appeals clog the nation's court system because so many convicted criminals try to "beat the rap" on a technicality. Actually,

A defendant listens as he is given a sentence to probation in a New York narcotics court.

criminal appeals represent a small percentage of the total number of cases processed by the nation's appellate courts. For example, only about 17 percent of the appeals in federal courts are criminal matters, and the number of criminal appeals has been relatively stable (about five thousand per year).[8]

State courts have witnessed an increase in the number of appellate cases of about 9 percent a year; in the meantime, the number of judges has increased at one sixth that rate.[9] Courts in some states, such as New York and Florida, process about nine thousand appeals each year.[10] The resulting imbalance has led to the increased use of intermediate courts to screen cases.

Though criminal cases do in fact make up only a small percentage of appellate cases, they are still of concern to the judiciary. Steps have been taken to make appealing more difficult. For example, the Supreme Court has tried to limit access to federal courts by prisoners being held in state prisons who have complaints arising out of the conditions of their captivity. Prisoner complaints more than doubled in the 1970s.

The State Court Structure

Figure 10.1 illustrates the interrelationship of appellate and trial courts in a model state court structure. Of course, each state's court organization varies from this standard pattern. Each state has a tiered court organization (lower, upper, and appellate courts), but states vary somewhat in the way they have delegated responsibility to a particular court system, as shown by the court organizations of Texas and New York in Figures 10.2 and 10.3. Note the complexity of their structures in comparison to the "typical" model court structure. For example, Texas separates its highest appellate divisions into civil and criminal courts. The Texas Supreme Court hears civil, administrative, and juvenile cases, while an independent Court of Criminal Appeals has the final say on criminal matters. New York's unique structure features two separate intermediate appellate courts with different geographic jurisdiction and an independent family court that han-

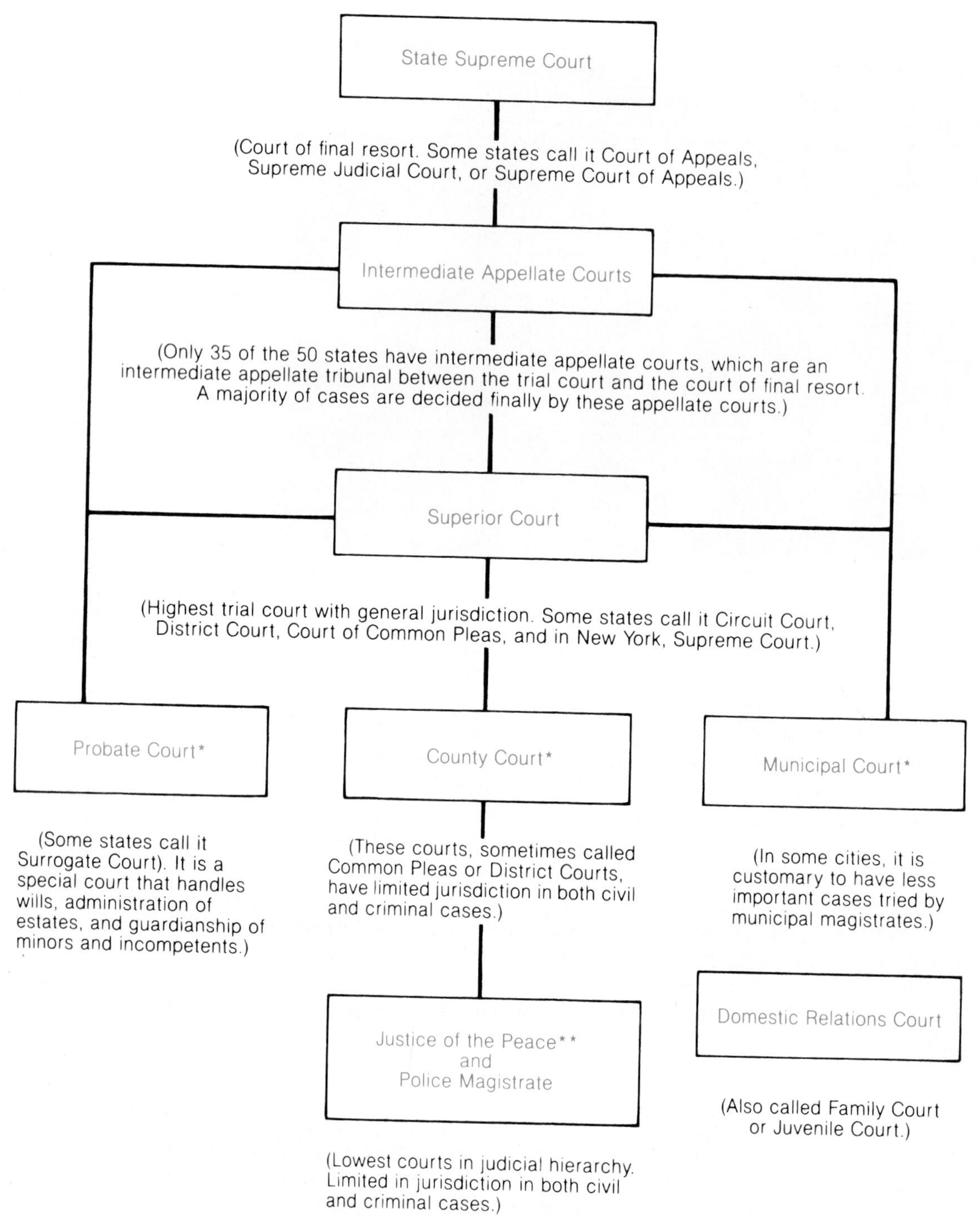

FIGURE 10.1

State Judicial System

*Courts of special jurisdiction, such as probate, family, or juvenile courts, and the so-called inferior courts, such as common pleas or municipal courts, may be separate courts or part of the trial court of general jurisdiction.

**Justices of the peace do not exist in all states. Where they do exist, their jurisdictions vary greatly from state to state.

SOURCE: American Bar Association, *Law and the Courts* (Chicago: American Bar Association, 1974), p. 20. Updated information provided by West Publishing Company, St. Paul, Minnesota.

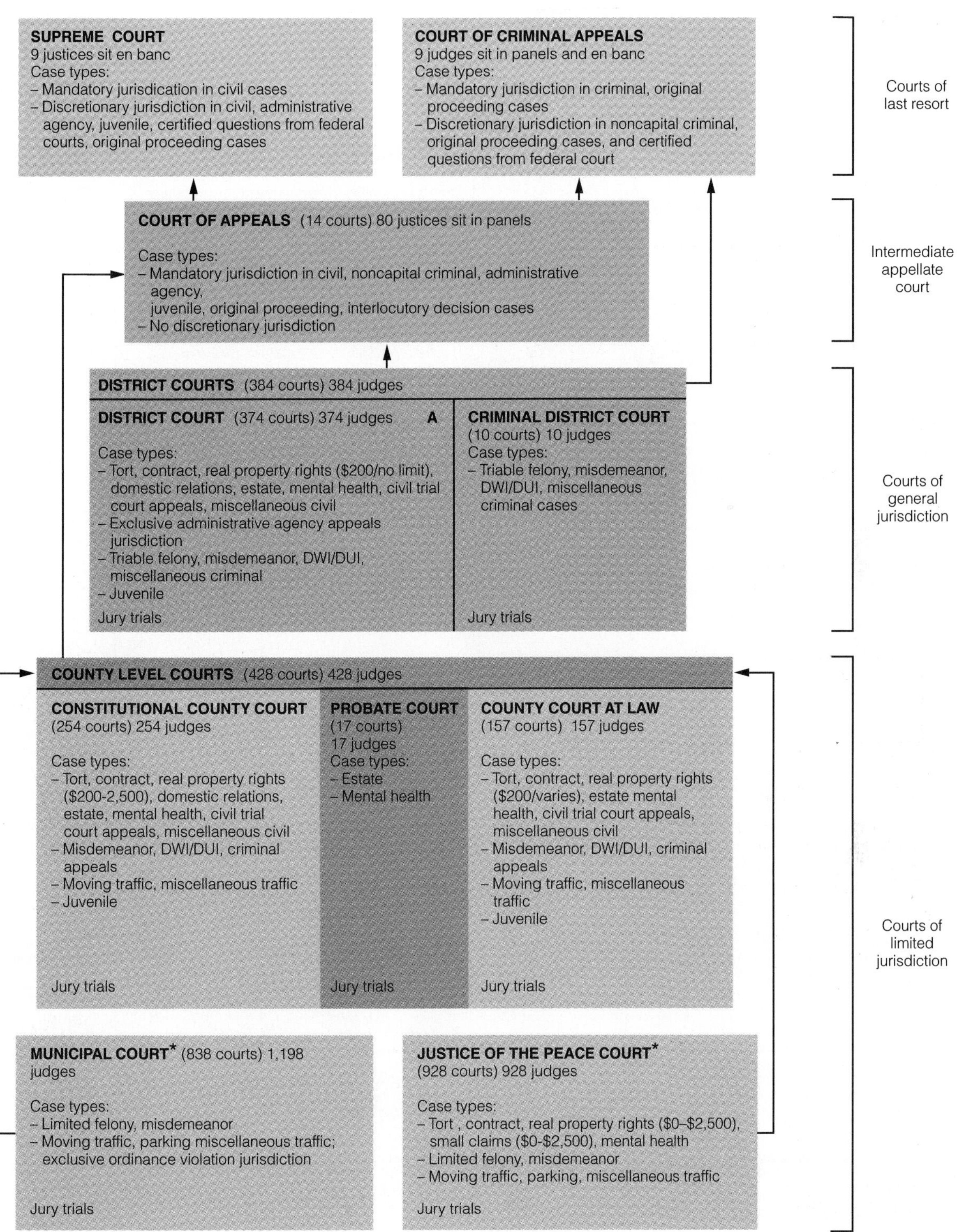

FIGURE 10.2

Texas Court Structure, 1990

*Some municipal and justice of the peace courts may appeal to the district court.

SOURCE: Court Statistics Project, *State Court Caseload Statistics: Annual Report 1990* (Williamsburg,Va.: National Center for State Courts in cooperation with the Conference of State Court Administrators, 1992).

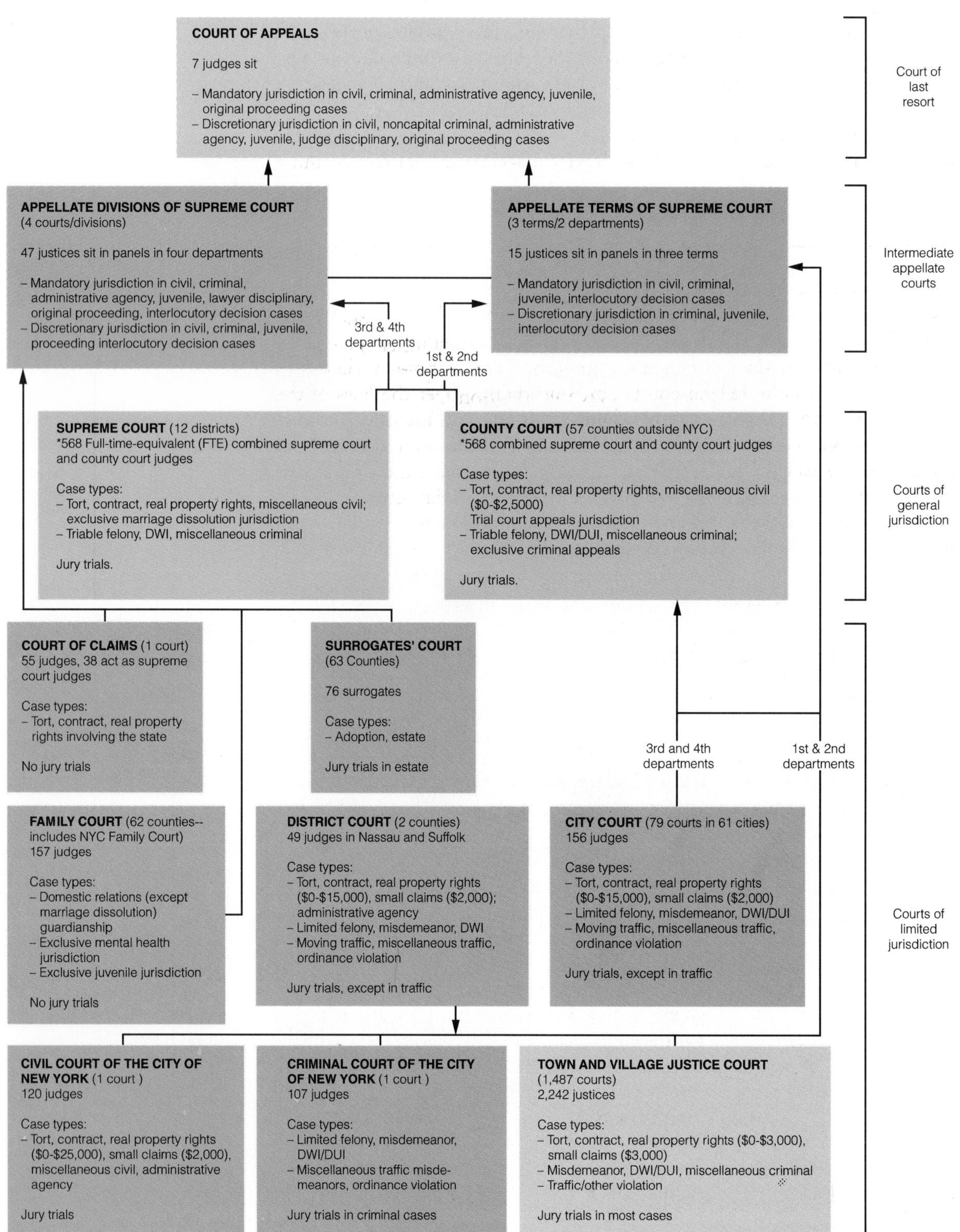

FIGURE 10.3

New York Court Structure, 1990

*Includes acting supreme court justices assigned administratively.

SOURCE: Court Statistics Project, *State Court Caseload Statistics: Annual Report 1990* (Williamsburg, Va.: National Center for State Courts in cooperation with the Conference of State Court Administrators, 1992).

dles both domestic relations (such as guardianship and custody), neglect and abuse, and juvenile delinquency. New York also maintains a surrogate court that handles adoptions and settles disagreements over estate transfers; the court of claims handles civil matters in which the state is a party. In contrast to New York, which has ten independent courts, six states (Idaho, Illinois, Iowa, Massachusetts, Minnesota, and South Dakota) have unified their trial courts into a single system.

The Federal Courts

The legal basis for the federal court system is contained in Article 3, section 1, of the U.S. Constitution, which provides that "the judicial power of the United States shall be vested in one Supreme Court, and in such inferior courts as Congress may from time to time ordain and establish." The important clauses in Article 3 indicate that the federal courts have jurisdiction over the laws of the United States and treaties and cases involving admiralty and maritime jurisdiction, as well as over controversies between two or more states and citizens of different states.[11] This complex language generally means that state courts have jurisdiction over all legal matters, *unless* they involve a violation of a federal criminal statute or a civil suit between citizens of different states or between a citizen and an agency of the federal government.

Within this authority, the federal government has established a three-tiered hierarchy of court jurisdiction that, in order of ascendancy, consists of the (1) U.S. District Courts, (2) U.S. Courts of Appeals (circuit courts), and (3) the U.S. Supreme Court (see Figure 10.4).

District Courts

U.S. District Courts are the trial courts of the federal system. They have jurisdiction over cases involving violations of federal laws, including civil rights abuses; interstate transportation of stolen vehicles; and kidnappings. They may also hear cases on questions involving citizenship and the rights of aliens. The jurisdiction of the U.S. District Court will occasionally overlap that of state courts. For example, citizens who reside in separate states and are involved in litigation of an amount in excess of ten thousand dollars may choose to have their cases heard in either of the states or the federal court. Finally, federal district courts hear cases in which one state sues a resident (or firm) in another state, where one state sues another, or where the federal government is a party in a suit.

Federal district courts were organized by Congress in the Judicial Act of 1789, and today, ninety-four independent courts are in operation. Originally, each state was allowed one court; as the population grew, however, so did the need for courts. Now each state has from one to four district courts, and the District of Columbia has one for itself.

In most cases, a single judge presides over trials; a defendant may request that a jury also be present. In complex civil matters, a three-judge panel may be convened.

Federal Appeals Court

Approximately thirty-five thousand appeals from the district courts are heard each year in the twelve federal courts of appeals, sometimes referred to as **U.S. circuit**

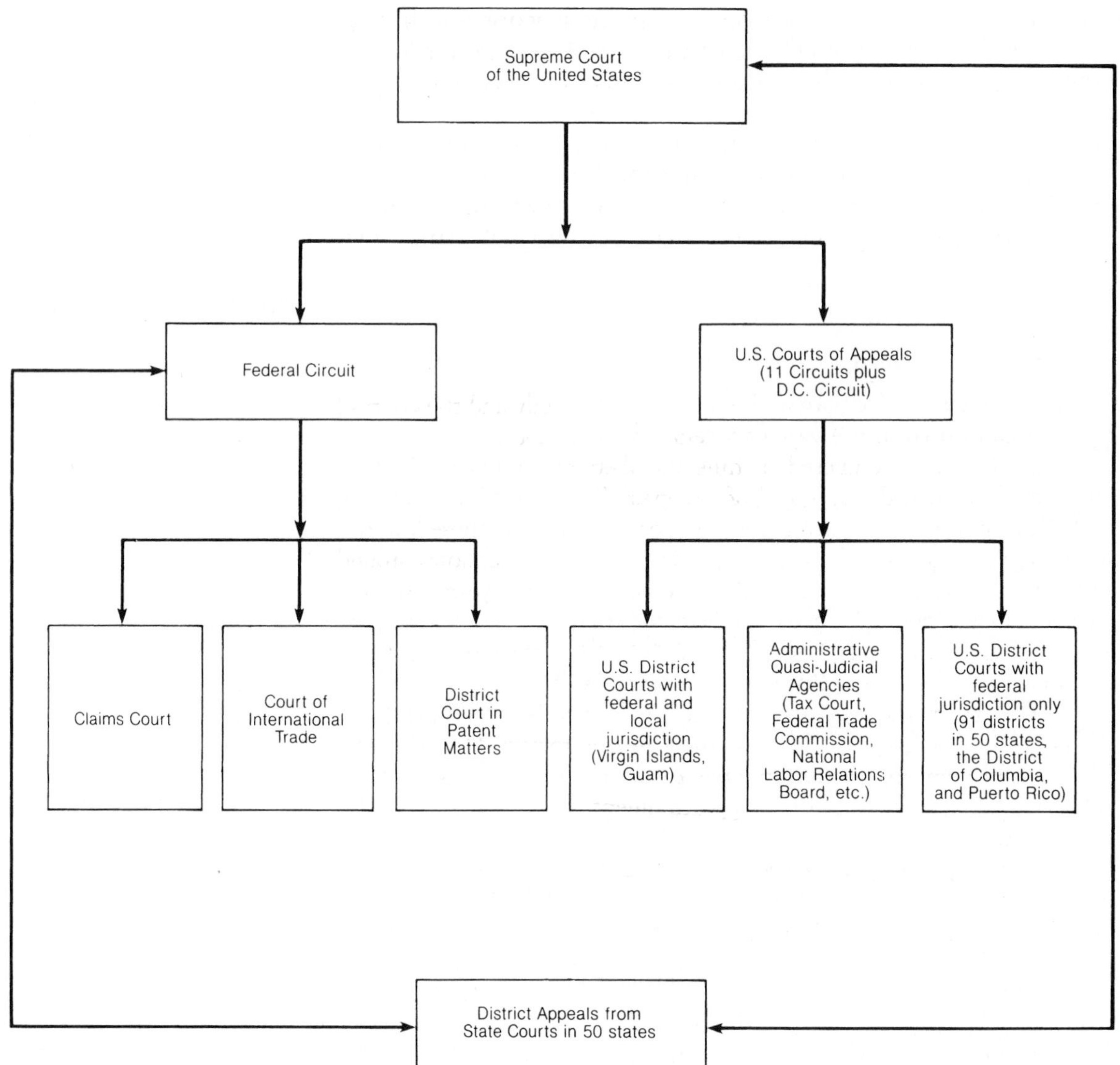

FIGURE 10.4
Federal Judicial System

SOURCE: American Bar Association, *Law and the Courts* (Chicago: American Bar Association, 1974), p. 21. Updated information provided by the Federal Courts Improvement Act of 1982 and West Publishing Company, St. Paul, Minnesota.

courts. This name is derived from the historical practice of having judges ride the circuit and regularly hear cases in the judicial seats of their various jurisdictions. Today, appellate judges are not required to travel (though some may sit in more than one court), and each federal appellate court jurisdiction contains a number of associate justices who share the caseload. Circuit court offices are usually located in major cities, such as San Francisco and New York, and cases must be brought to these locations by attorneys in order to be heard.

The circuit court is empowered to review federal and state appellate court cases on substantive and procedural issues involving rights guaranteed by the Constitution. Circuit courts do not actually retry cases, nor do they determine whether the facts brought out during trial support conviction or dismissal. Instead, they analyze judicial interpretations of the law, such as the charge (or instructions) to the jury, and reflect on the constitutional issues involved in each case they hear.

Federal appellate courts also enforce orders of federal administrative agencies, such as the Food and Drug Administration and the Securities and Exchange Commission. Federal decisions in these matters are final, except when reviewed by the U.S. Supreme Court. Any dissatisfied litigant in a federal district court has the right to appeal the case to a circuit court.

The U.S. Supreme Court

The **U.S. Supreme Court** is the nation's highest appellate body and the court of last resort for all cases tried in the various federal and state courts.

The Supreme Court is composed of nine members appointed for lifetime terms by the president with the approval of Congress. The Court has discretion over most of the cases it will consider and may choose to hear only those it deems important, appropriate, and worthy of its attention. The Court chooses around three hundred of the five thousand cases that are appealed each year; only half of these receive full opinions. Evidence exists that the Supreme Court has decided to reduce the number of cases it hears by one third. In 1991, the Court rendered 109 full opinions, the lowest total since the 1970–71 term.[12]

When the Court decides to hear a case, it grants a **writ of certiorari,** requesting a transcript of the proceedings of the case for review. However, the Supreme Court must grant jurisdiction in a few instances, such as decisions from a three-judge federal district court on reapportionment or cases involving the Voting Rights Act.

When the U.S. Supreme Court rules on a case, usually by majority decision (at least five votes), its rule becomes a precedent that must be honored by all lower courts. For example, if the Court grants a particular litigant the right to counsel at a police lineup, then all similarly situated clients must be given the same right. This type of ruling is usually referred to as a **landmark decision.** The use of precedent in the legal system gives the Supreme Court power to influence and mold the everyday operating procedures of the police, trial courts, and corrections agencies. In the past, this influence was not nearly as pronounced as it was during the tenure of Chief Justices Earl Warren and Warren Burger, who greatly amplified and extended the power of the Court to influence criminal justice policies. Under Chief Justice William Rehnquist, the Court has continued to influence criminal justice matters, ranging from the investigation of crimes to the execution of criminals. The personal legal philosophy of the justices and their orientation toward the civil and personal rights of victims and criminals significantly affect the daily operations of the justice system.

How a Case Gets to the Supreme Court

No court in this nation is as unique as its highest court. First of all, it is the only court established by constitutional mandate, rather than federal legislation. Second, it decides basic social and political issues of grave consequence and importance to the nation. Third, the Court's nine justices shape the future meaning of the U.S. Constitution. Their decisions identify the rights and liberties of citizens throughout the United States.

When our nation was first established, the U.S. Supreme Court did not review state court decisions involving issues of federal law. Even though Congress had given the Supreme Court jurisdiction to review state decisions, much resistance and controversy surrounded the relationship between the states and the federal government. However, in a famous decision called *Martin v. Hunter's Lessee* (1816), the Supreme Court reaffirmed the legitimacy of the Court's jurisdiction over state court decisions when such courts handled issues of federal or constitutional law.[13] This decision allowed the Supreme Court to actively review actions by states and their courts and reinforced the Court's power to make the supreme law of the land. Since that time, a defendant who indicates that governmental action—whether state or federal—violates a constitutional law is in a position to have the Supreme Court review such action.

To carry out its responsibilities, the Court had to develop a method of dealing with a large volume of cases coming from the state and federal courts for final review. In the early years of its history, the Court sought to review every case brought before it. Since the middle of the twentieth century, however, the court has used a technical device known as a writ of certiorari to decide what cases it should hear. *Certiorari* is a Latin term that means "to bring the record of a case from a lower court up to a higher court for immediate review." When applied, it means that an accused in a criminal case is requesting the U.S. Supreme Court to hear the case. More than 90 percent of the cases heard in the Supreme Court are brought by petition for a writ of certiorari. Under this procedure, the Court's justices have discretion to select cases that they will review for a decision. Of the thousands of cases filed before the Court every year, only 100–150 receive a full opinion. Four of the nine justices sitting on the U.S. Supreme Court must vote to hear a case brought by a writ of certiorari for review. Generally, these votes are cast in a secret meeting attended only by the justices.

After the Supreme Court decides to hear a case, written and oral arguments are reviewed by the Court. The written materials are referred to as legal briefs, and oral arguments are normally presented to the justices at the Court in Washington, D.C.

After the material is reviewed and the oral arguments heard, the justices normally meet in what is known as a "case conference." At this case conference, they discuss the case and vote to reach a decision. The cases voted on by the Court generally come from the judicial systems of the various states, or from the U.S. courts of appeals, and represent the entire spectrum of law.

Supreme Court Decision Making

In reading a decision, the Supreme Court reevaluates and reinterprets state statutes, the U.S. Constitution, and previous case decisions. Based on a review of the case, the Court either affirms or reverses the decision of the lower court. When the justices reach a decision, the chief justice of the Court assigns someone of the majority group to write the opinion. Another justice normally writes a dissent or minority opinion. In the final analysis, the justices join with either the majority opinion or the dissenting opinion. When the case is finished, it is submitted to the public and becomes the law of the land. The decision represents the legal precedents that add to the existing body of law on a given subject, change it, and guide its future development.

In the area of criminal justice, the decisions of the U.S. Supreme Court have had the broadest impact on the reform of the system. The Court's action is the final step in settling constitutional criminal disputes throughout the nation. By discretionary review through a petition for certiorari, the U.S. Supreme Court

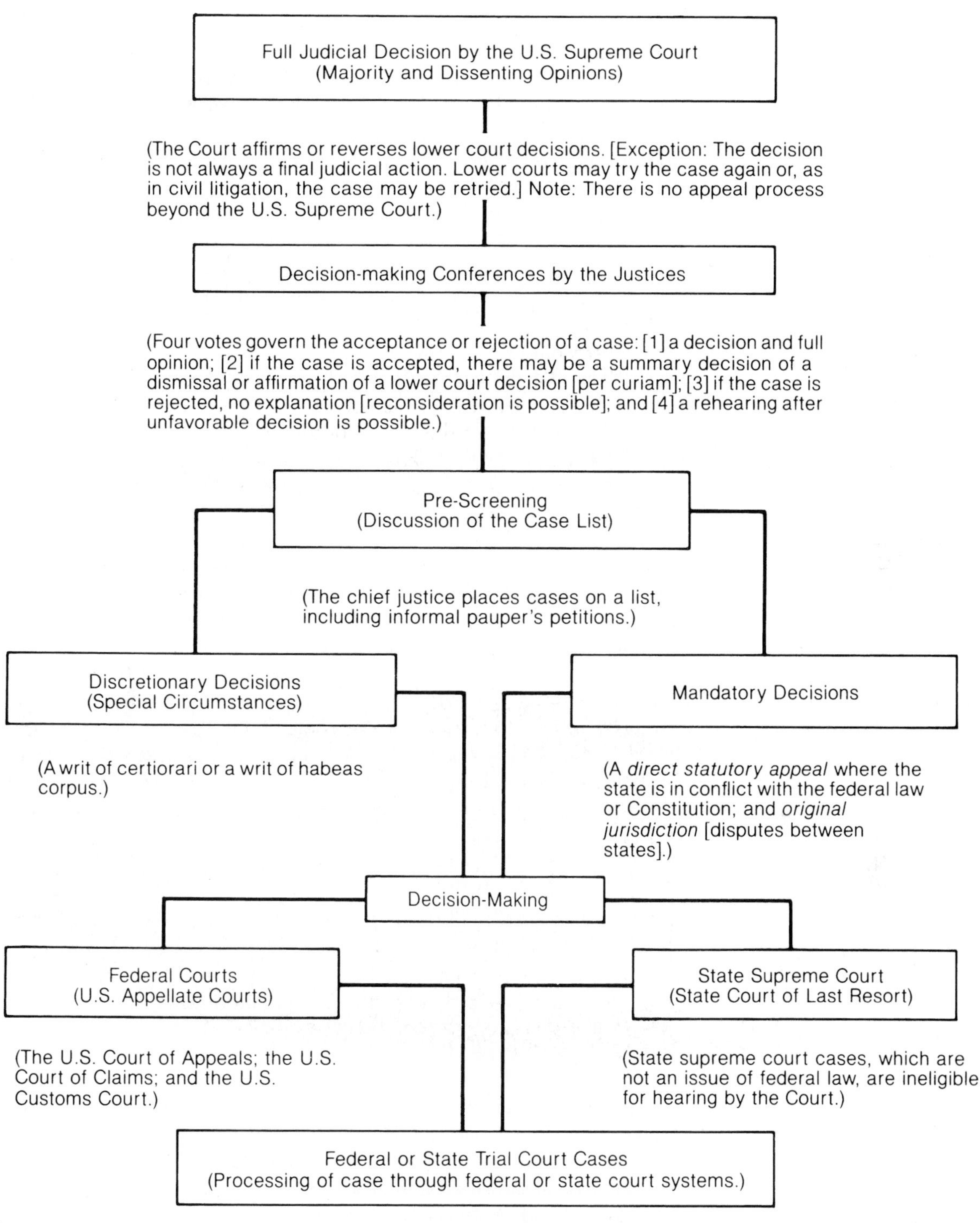
Full Judicial Decision by the U.S. Supreme Court
(Majority and Dissenting Opinions)
(The Court affirms or reverses lower court decisions. [Exception: The decision is not always a final judicial action. Lower courts may try the case again or, as in civil litigation, the case may be retried.] Note: There is no appeal process beyond the U.S. Supreme Court.)
Decision-making Conferences by the Justices
(Four votes govern the acceptance or rejection of a case: [1] a decision and full opinion; [2] if the case is accepted, there may be a summary decision of a dismissal or affirmation of a lower court decision [per curiam]; [3] if the case is rejected, no explanation [reconsideration is possible]; and [4] a rehearing after unfavorable decision is possible.)
Pre-Screening
(Discussion of the Case List)
(The chief justice places cases on a list, including informal pauper's petitions.)
Discretionary Decisions
(Special Circumstances)
Mandatory Decisions
(A writ of certiorari or a writ of habeas corpus.)
(A *direct statutory appeal* where the state is in conflict with the federal law or Constitution; and *original jurisdiction* [disputes between states].)
Decision-Making
Federal Courts
(U.S. Appellate Courts)
State Supreme Court
(State Court of Last Resort)
(The U.S. Court of Appeals; the U.S. Court of Claims; and the U.S. Customs Court.)
(State supreme court cases, which are not an issue of federal law, are ineligible for hearing by the Court.)
Federal or State Trial Court Cases
(Processing of case through federal or state court systems.)

FIGURE 10.5
Tracing the Course of a Case to the U.S. Supreme Court

requires state courts to accept its interpretation of the federal Constitution. In doing so, the Court has changed the day-by-day operations of the criminal justice system. Figure 10.5 describes the steps required to appeal a case to the Supreme Court.

Court Caseloads

The nation's courts handle over 100 million civil, criminal, and traffic cases each year, resulting in backlogs, delays, and what is sometimes called "assembly-line justice."[14] Of these cases, approximately 13 million were criminal matters. In addition, the federal district courts hear approximately forty-five thousand criminal and two hundred thousand civil cases a year.[15]

While these figures seem overwhelming, they are even more disturbing due to the sharp increase in both civil and criminal litigation in the past few years. For example, in 1980, federal district courts disposed of twenty-nine thousand criminal cases; by 1990, the number had increased to forty-two thousand. In 1980, about nineteen thousand appeals were heard in federal circuit courts; by 1990, the number had grown to almost thirty-five thousand.[16] In state courts, the number of felony case filings increased from 690,000 in 1984 to more than 1 million by 1990, an increase of almost 50 percent in six years.

The significant increases in both criminal and civil litigation have forced state and local governments to allocate ever greater resources to the courts. Court services, including the judiciary, prosecution, legal services such as public defenders, and other court-related matters (juries, stenographers, clerks, bailiffs, maintenance), today run over $13 billion per year.[17] Despite such resource allocation, there is no guarantee that services will significantly improve.[18] Budget cuts and cost-reduction measures have resulted in layoffs and cutbacks in a number of state court systems. Conditions have become so extreme in New York that the Chief Judge Sol Wachtler took the unusual step of filing a lawsuit against Governor Mario Cuomo charging that the state has failed to fulfill its constitutional obligation to adequately fund the court system—despite a court budget of about $900 million.[19] Conditions are particularly acute in courts serving minorities. A commission set up to study the problem found that some New York City courts are infested with rats and roaches and are so crowded that defendants have no privacy to meet with their attorneys.[20]

Reducing Court Congestion

What causes court caseloads to overflow? In a survey of judges and trial court administrators, two factors that stood out were the excessive number of continuances demanded by attorneys and the increasing number of pretrial motions on evidence and procedural issues.[21] As the law becomes more complex and involves such issues as computer crimes, the need for a more involved court process has escalated. Ironically, efforts being made to reform the criminal law may also be helping to overload the courts. For example, the increase of mandatory prison sentences for some crimes may reduce the use of plea bargaining and increase the number of jury trials because defendants fear that a conviction will lead to an incarceration sentence and thus must be avoided at all costs. Second, the recent explosion in civil litigation has added to the backlog because most courts handle both criminal and civil matters.

If relief is to be found, it will probably be in the form of better administrative and management techniques that improve the use of existing resources. For example, it may be possible for legal jurisdictions to create policies mandating speedy trials in order to reduce trial delay. An analysis of the Federal Speedy Trial Act of 1974 and Rule 50(b) of the *Federal Rules of Criminal Procedure*, policy initiatives designed to facilitate federal case processing, shows that these initiatives actually produced a significant reduction in the processing time of federal criminal cases.[22]

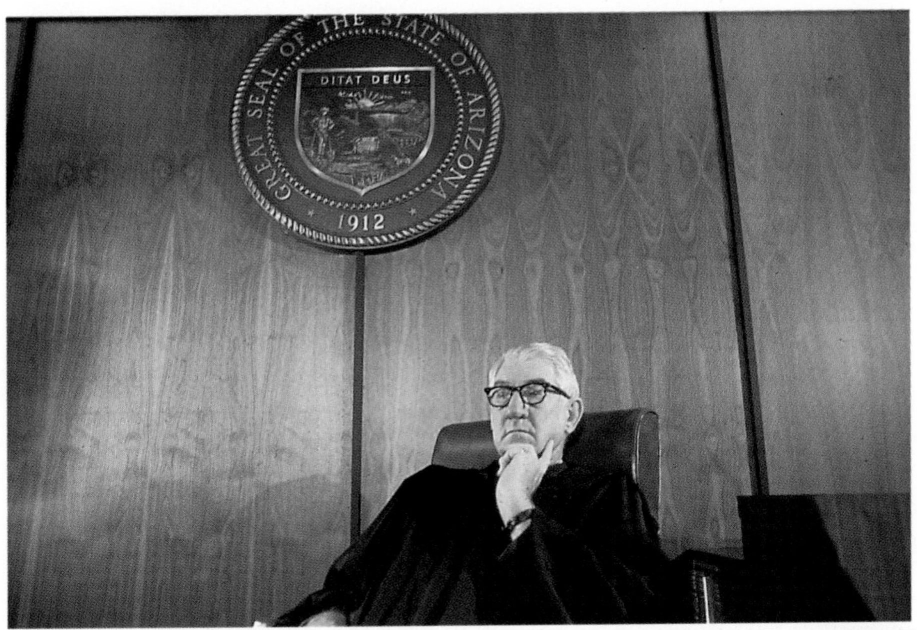

Individuals entrusted with the awesome powers of judgeship should ideally be chosen from the highest levels of the legal profession.

Another possible method of creating a more efficient court system is to unify existing state courts into a single administrative structure employing modern management principles. Massachusetts, Illinois, Iowa, Minnesota, South Dakota, and Idaho have implemented unified court systems. In contrast, fourteen states have complex court systems in which several courts have overlapping jurisdiction with other courts (see the discussion of court unification at the end of this chapter).

Regardless of its source, some immediate relief must be provided: about 39 percent of all judges reported recently that workloads were so heavy that they needed stress management training to reduce job-related tension.[23] One reason for such stress has been repeated threats against judges; security officers detected 137,000 weapons in courthouses during 1990 alone.[24]

The Judiciary

The **judge** is the senior officer in a court of criminal law. His or her duties are quite varied and are actually far more extensive than might be expected. During trials, the judge rules on the appropriateness of conduct, settles questions of evidence and procedure, and guides the questioning of witnesses. In a jury trial, the judge must instruct jurors on which evidence is proper to examine and which should be ignored. The judge also formally **charges the jury** by instructing its members on what points of law and evidence they must consider in order to reach a decision of either guilty or innocent. When a **jury trial** is waived, the judge must decide whether to hold for the complainant or the defendant. Finally, if a defendant is found guilty, the judge must decide on the sentence (in some cases, this is legislatively determined); this includes choosing the type of sentence, its length, and in the case of probation, the conditions under which it may be revoked.

Beyond these stated duties, the trial judge has extensive control and influence over the other agencies of the court: probation, the court clerk, the police, and the district attorney's office. Probation and the clerk may be under the judge's explicit control. In some courts, the operations, philosophy, and procedures of these agencies are within the magistrate's administrative domain. In others, for example, where a state agency controls the probation department, the attitudes of the county or district court judge greatly influence the way a probation department is run and how its decisions are made. Judges often consult with probation staff on treatment decisions, and many judges are interested in providing the most innovative and up-to-date care possible.[25]

Police and prosecutors are also directly influenced by the judge, whose sentencing discretion affects the arrest and charging processes. For example, if a judge usually chooses minimal sentences—such as a fine for a particular offense—the police may be reluctant to arrest offenders for that crime, knowing that doing so will basically be a waste of their time. Similarly, if a judge is known to have a liberal attitude toward police discretion, then the local department may be more inclined to engage in practices that border on entrapment or to pursue cases through easily obtained wiretaps. However, a magistrate oriented toward strict use of due process guarantees would stifle such activities by dismissing all cases involving apparent police abuses of personal freedoms. The district attorney's office may also be sensitive to judicial attitudes. The district attorney might forgo indictments in cases that the presiding magistrate expressly considers trivial or quasi-criminal and in which the judge has been known to take only token action in, such as the prosecution of pornographers.

Finally, the judge considers requests by police and prosecutors for leniency (or severity) in **sentencing.** The judge's reaction to these requests is important if the police and the district attorney are to honor the bargains they may have made with defendants in order to secure information, cooperation, or guilty pleas. For example, when police tell informers that they will try to convince the judge to go easy on them in order to secure required information, they will often discuss the terms of the promised leniency with representatives of the court. If a judge ignores police demands, then the department's bargaining power is severely diminished and communication within the criminal justice system is impaired.

There is always concern that the judges will discriminate against defendants on the basis of their gender, race, or class. While this issue is of great social concern, most research efforts have failed to find consistent bias in judicial decision making. For example, analyzing case processing in Los Angeles, Huey-Tsyh Chen found that judges tend to dismiss cases that they consider weak and less serious. During the sentencing stage, judges were more likely to consider offense seriousness, the defendants' cooperation with the judicial process, their potential for rehabilitation, and their potential danger to the community; social and demographic factors, such as gender and race, were less important than critics have believed.[26]

Judicial Qualifications

The qualifications for appointment to one of the existing twenty-six thousand judgeships vary from state to state and court to court. Most typically, the potential judge must be a resident of the state, licensed to practice law, a member of the state bar association, and at least twenty-five and less than seventy years of age.[27] However, a significant degree of diversity in the basic qualifications exists, depending on the level of court jurisdiction. While almost every state requires judges to have a law degree if they are to serve on appellate courts or courts of general jurisdiction, it is not uncommon for municipal or town court judges to lack a legal background, even though they maintain the power to incarcerate criminal defendants. Surprising as it may seem, about 43 percent of lower-court judges are not trained attorneys. For example, of 1,176 municipal judges in Texas, 706 were not legally trained; and of the 2,050 town and village judges in New York, 1,585 were not attorneys. Yet, as Figures 10.2 and 10.3 indicate, municipal courts in Texas and town and village courts in New York routinely handle criminal matters.[28] In contrast, fourteen states, including California, Florida, Nebraska, and New Jersey, make possession of a law degree or being "learned in the law" a requirement for all judicial appointments.[29]

Judicial Selection

Many different methods are used to select judges, depending on the level of court jurisdiction.[30] In some jurisdictions, the governor simply appoints judges. In others, the governor's recommendations must be confirmed by either (1) the state senate, (2) the governor's council, (3) a special confirmation committee, (4) an executive council elected by the state assembly, or (5) an elected review board. Some states employ a judicial nominating commission that submits names to the governor for approval.

Another form of judicial selection is popular election. In some jurisdictions, judges run as members of the Republican, Democratic, or other parties, while in others, they run without party affiliation. Thirteen states have partisan elections for selecting judges in courts of general jurisdiction, seventeen states have nonpartisan elections, and in the remainder, upper trial-court judges are appointed by the governor or the legislature.

Sixteen states have adopted some form of what is known as the **Missouri Plan** to select appellate court judges, and six states also use it to select trial court judges. This plan consists of three parts: (1) a judicial nominating commission to nominate candidates for the bench, (2) an elected official (usually from the executive branch) to make appointments from the list submitted by the commission, and (3) subsequent nonpartisan and noncompetitive elections in which incumbent judges run on their records and voters can choose either their retention or dismissal.[31]

Some states use a variety of methods for selecting judges. For example, in New York, appellate court judges are appointed by the governor from a group of candidates selected by a judicial nominating commission with the consent of the state Senate; partisan elections are held to select general jurisdiction, limited jurisdiction, and family court judges; and the mayor appoints criminal court and family court judges in New York City.

Problems of Judicial Selection

The quality of the judiciary is a concern. Although merit plans, screening committees, and popular elections are designed to ensure a competent judiciary, it has often been charged that many judicial appointments are made to pay off political debts or to reward cronies and loyal friends. Also not uncommon are charges that those desiring to be nominated for judgeships are required to make significant political contributions.

Another problem is the limited requirements for judicial appointments. As you may recall, a majority of the states still do not require lower-court judges to be attorneys, to be members of the bar, or to have any legal experience at all.

A great deal of concern has been raised about the qualification of judges. In most states, people appointed to the bench have had little or no training in how to be a judge. Others may have held administrative posts and may not have appeared before a court in years.

A number of agencies have been created to improve the quality of the judiciary. The National Conference of State Court Judges and the National College of Juvenile Justice both operate judicial training seminars and publish manuals and guides on state-of-the-art judicial technologies. Their ongoing efforts are designed to improve the quality of the nation's judges.

Judicial Alternatives

Increased judicial caseloads have prompted the use of alternatives to the traditional judge. For example, to expedite matters in civil cases, it has become common for both parties to agree to hire a retired judge and abide by his or her decision. Jurisdictions have set up dispute resolution systems for settling minor complaints informally upon the agreement of both parties. An estimated seven hundred dispute resolution programs are now handling domestic conflicts, landlord/tenant cases, misdemeanors, consumer/merchant disputes, and so on.[32]

Other jurisdictions have created new quasi-judicial officers, such as referees or magistrates, to relieve the traditional judge of time-consuming responsibilities. The Magistrate Act of 1968 created a new type of judicial officer in the federal district court system who handles pretrial duties.[33] Federal magistrates also handle civil trials if both parties agree to the arrangement.[34]

Other jurisdictions use part-time judges. Many of these are attorneys who carry out their duties *pro bono*—for no or limited compensation. These "judicial adjuncts" assist the courts on a temporary basis while maintaining an active law practice.[35] The use of alternative court mechanisms should continue to grow as court congestion increases.

Court Administration

Former Chief Justice Warren Burger has stated, "The days are . . . past when a chief judge, with the help of a secretary and the clerk of the court, can manage the increasingly complex tasks required of them to keep courts functioning effectively. We must be constantly alert to new ideas, new methods, new ways of looking at the judiciary." [36]

The need for efficient management techniques in an ever-expanding criminal court system has led to the recognition of improved court administration as a way to relieve court congestion. Management goals include improving organization and scheduling of cases, devising methods to allocate court resources efficiently, administering fines and monies due the court, preparing budgets, and overseeing personnel.

The federal courts have led the way in creating and organizing court administration. In 1939, Congress passed the Administrative Office Act, which established the Administrative Office of the United States Courts. Its director was charged with gathering statistics on the work of the federal courts and preparing the judicial budget for approval by the Conference of Senior Circuit Judges. One clause of the act created a judicial council with general supervisory responsibilities for the district and circuit courts.

Unlike the federal government, the states have experienced a slow and uneven growth in the development and application of court management principles.

The first state to establish an administrative office was North Dakota in 1927. Today, all states employ some form of central administration.

The federal government has encouraged the development of state court management through funding assistance. In addition, the federal judiciary has provided the philosophical impetus for better and more effective court management. A court system is an extremely complex organization that is far more difficult to manage than the typical business enterprise or government agency because:

1. Its key people are accustomed to working as individuals and do not take kindly to regimentation.
2. A very high value is placed on judicial independence, and this severely limits the pressures that can be brought to bear to produce desired administrative results.
3. Many persons involved in the judicial process—attorneys, jurors, witnesses, litigants—are not employed by the judiciary.
4. Participants in the judicial process often have conflicting goals.[37]

Another obstacle facing court administration is the generally low profile of the courts themselves. Except in times of unusual stress, judicial performance is hidden from public view, and mismanagement is rarely noted by taxpayers. Despite increased efforts to manage courts efficiently, successes have been few and far between. For example, a survey of the nation's state and local courts revealed that many have fragmented and overlapping jurisdictions, lack sufficiently trained personnel, and have no consistent procedures for handling various types of proceedings. The study concluded:

> Each court in each county in each state is different. Each has its own set of challenges. These are closely tied to the experience and temperament of the judge, the size and quality of the bar, the people who live in the area and the kind of justice they demand.[38]

Despite the multitude of problems in reforming court management, some progress is being made. By order of its state supreme court, effective February 1, 1973, Florida became the first state to implement most of the American Bar Association standards by formal court rule. Under the state constitution, the Florida Supreme Court exercised the power to prescribe rules of practice and procedures for all courts in the state. By 1974, Florida had adopted some 85 percent of the principles in the standards that needed statutory implementation.

Today, centralized court administrative services perform numerous functions with the help of sophisticated computers that free the judiciary to fulfill their roles as arbiters of justice. Table 10.1 lists some of the varied duties of centralized court administration.

Technology and Court Management

Computers are becoming an important aid in the administration and management of courts. Rapid retrieval and organization of data can be used for such functions as

1. Maintaining case histories and statistical reporting
2. Monitoring and scheduling of cases
3. Preparing documents
4. Indexing cases
5. Issuing summonses
6. Notifying witnesses, attorneys, and others of required appearances

TABLE 10.1
Activities of State Court Central Administration

Activities and Services

Management activities
- Appears before legislative committees dealing with court-related legislation
- Obtains sponsors for legislation relating to work
- Represents judiciary before agencies of the executive branch
- Recommends to court of last resort the creation or dissolution of judgeships
- Recommends to court of last resort the assignment of judges
- Nominates trial court administrators for selection by trial courts

Information systems activities
- Responsible for records management systems
- Responsible for managing data processing
- Responsible for forms design
- Responsible for managing information systems
- Establishes records for automated administrative systems
- Responsible for budgeting financial requirements of state information system
- Responsible for statewide inventory control of facilities and equipment

Court support services
- Provides secretarial services to boards and committees
- Researches court organization and function
- Supplies reports and documents to the legislature as required
- Provides technical assistance to court jurisdiction
- Manages physical facilities for courts
- Supervises probation services
- Supervises court reporter services
- Responsible for managing indigent defense
- Assists court in exercise of its rule-making function

Finance and budget activities
- Prepares budget for submission to the court of last resort
- Conducts audit of judicial expenditures
- Requires accounting and budget report from the courts
- Approves requisitions for capital equipment and construction
- Determines compensation for nonjudicial court personnel

Personnel services
- Establishes qualifications for nonjudicial court personnel

Education and training activities
- Responsible for judicial training programs and seminars
- Responsible for nonjudicial training programs and seminars
- Responsible for managing state law libraries

Public information and liaison activities
- Disseminates information on court operations to the media and the public
- Disseminates information on court decisions to the media and the public

Planning and research activities
- Responsible for court planning and grant management
- Collects, analyzes, and publishes court caseload statistics
- Requires caseload reports from the courts
- Collects statistics on expenditures of state funds

SOURCE: Bureau of Justice Statistics, *State Court Organization, 1980* (Washington, D.C.: U.S. Government Printing Office, 1982), p. 96.

7. Selecting and notifying jurors
8. Preparing and administering budgets and payrolls[39]

The federal government has encouraged the states to experiment with computerized information systems. Federal funds were used to begin fifty-state consortium for the purpose of establishing a standardized crime-reporting system called SEARCH (Systems for the Electronic Analysis and Retrieval of Criminal Histories).

Computer technology is also being applied in the courts in such areas as videotaped testimonies, new court reporting devices, information systems, and data-processing systems to handle such functions as court docketing and jury management. In 1968, only ten states had state-level automated information systems; today, all states employ such systems for a mix of tasks and duties. A recent survey of Georgia courts found that 84 percent used computers for three or more court administration applications.[40]

Another modern technology being used for court administration is the facsimile machine (fax). In Minnesota, fax machines allow the courts to relay criminal arrest or search warrants, juvenile warrants, and temporary restraining orders instantly to police officers. The Minnesota Supreme Court even allows fax documents to be filed as permanent court documents.[41]

Court jurisdictions are also cooperating with police departments in the installation of communications gear that allows defendants to be arraigned via closed-circuit TV while they are in police custody. Closed-circuit TV has been used for judicial conferences and scheduling meetings. Courts in Kentucky, Michigan, North Carolina, and Washington are using voice-activated cameras to record all testimony during trials; these are the sole means of keeping trial records. Four videos are made: one each for the prosecution and the defense and two for the court records.[42]

The American Bar Association standards have classified the uses of computerized information retrieval into the following three categories:[43]

1. Judicial and administrative decision making
   a. Rules on motions
   b. Assigning cases for trial
2. Information handling
   a. Making entries into official records
   b. Sending out notices
   c. Computerizing financial accounts
3. Monitoring and planning in court administration
   a. Analyzing case flow
   b. Preparing budgets
   c. Projecting future needs

The standards stress that many essential procedures and vital decisions in a court system are determined outside the direct supervision of the judges.

The computer cannot replace the judge, but it can be used as an ally to help speed the trial process by identifying backlogs and bottlenecks that can be eradicated by applying intelligent managerial techniques. Just as an industrialist must know the type and quantity of goods on hand in a warehouse, so an administrative judge must have available information concerning those entering the judge's domain, what happened to them once they were in it, and how they have fared since judgment has been rendered.

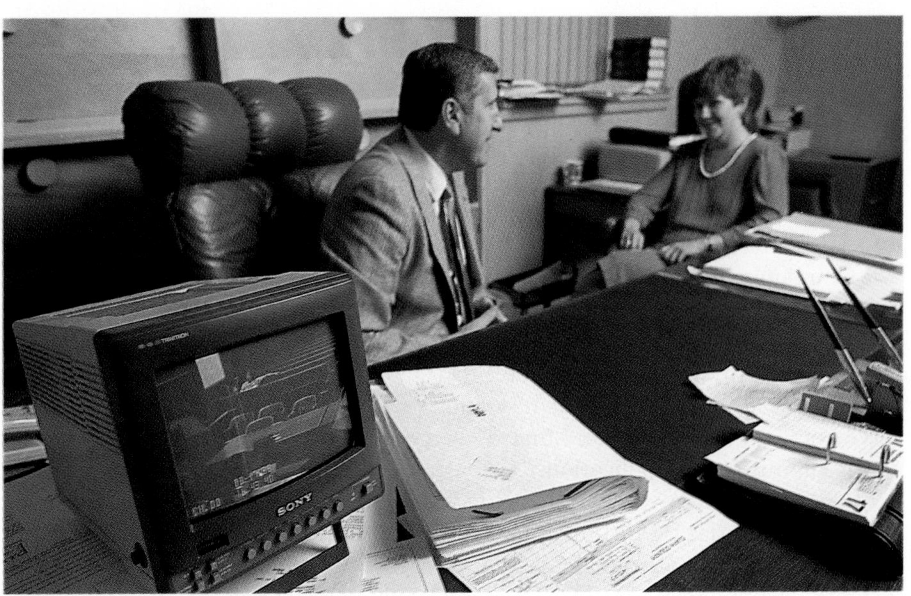

A closed-circuit monitor on a judges desk is part of the technological changes in court administration and management.

Court Unification Models

One method being used to improve court efficiency is to unify trial courts into a single administrative entity. A number of states, such as Massachusetts and Minnesota, have already done this, while other states are considering it.[44] Right now, courts are organized in one of four models, some that have unified all court processes into a single jurisdiction and others that maintain complex court structures (such as Texas and New York) with several jurisdictions and overlapping responsibilities (see Figure 10.6). These models are briefly described below:

- The constellation model is a loose association of courts that form a unified system in only the most general terms. The various trial courts operate with local rules and procedures. The formal line of authority among the courts is a function of their cooperation in legal processes such as appeals.
- The confederation model of a court system is characterized by a relatively consolidated trial court structure and a centralized state authority that exercises limited power over the courts. While the state has guidelines for running the courts, local authorities maintain great discretion either because of inaction by the court administration or because they have a legal right to exercise autonomy.
- The federation model involves a very complex trial court structure with local units bound together at the state level by a strong, central authority. For example, Colorado and New Jersey have several trial courts that operate independently at the local level but are supervised by a strong state administrative office.
- The union model is a tightly integrated approach characterized by a fully consolidated, highly centralized system of courts with a single, coherent source of authority. No court or subunit has independent powers or discretion in matters

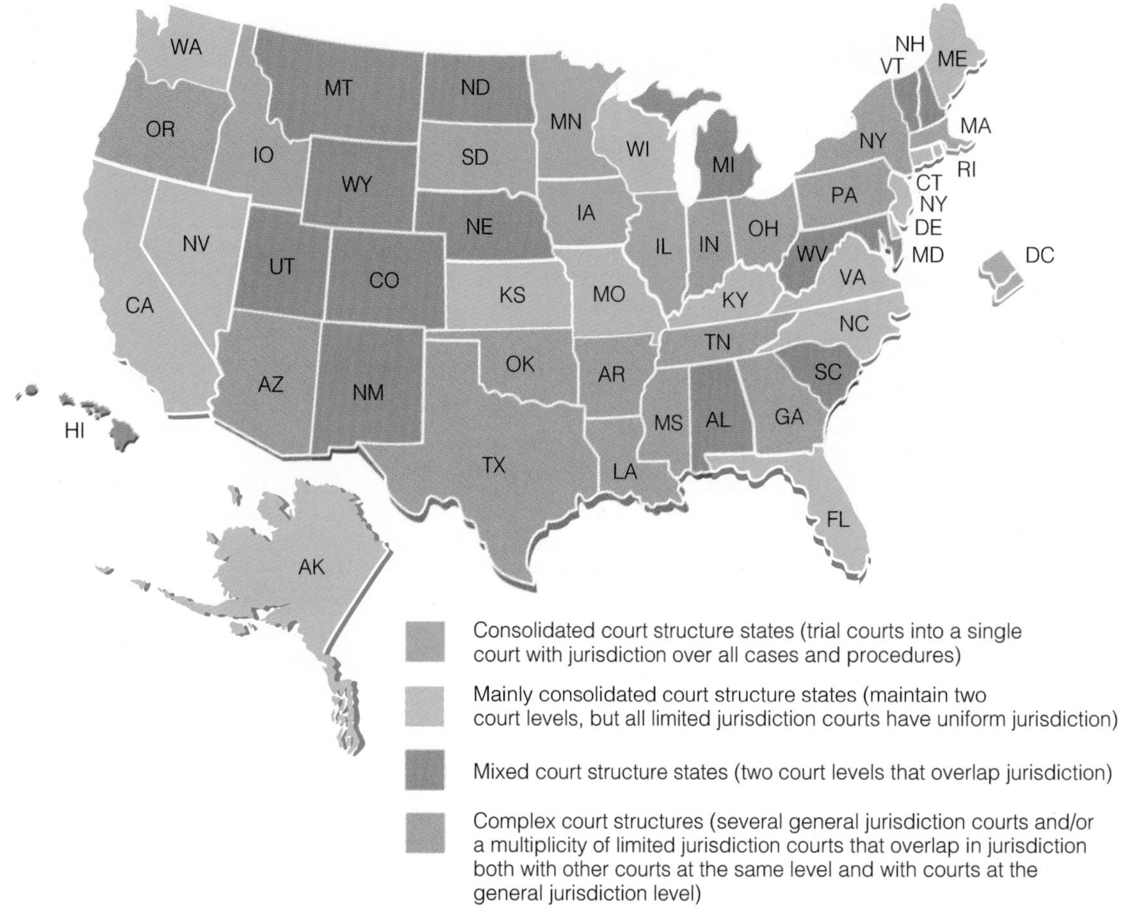

FIGURE 10.6
Trial Court Structure Maps, 1990

SOURCE: Court Statistics Project, *State Court Caseload Statistics, Annual Report, 1990* (Williamsburg, Va.: National Center for State Courts in Cooperation with the Conference of State Court Administrators, 1992).

of basic policy. For example, Connecticut's court system has been assembled by numerous legislative amendments into a single statewide trial court system. The Office of Chief Administrator has supervisory authority over all areas of judicial administration and policy. The result is a highly centralized and consolidated formal structure.

A federally sponsored research study in five states found that these various models of court organization had little influence on court performance. Courts with loose organizations functioned about as well as those that used the highly structured union model. Nonetheless, the researchers found that consolidation allows court administrators to allocate resources where needed, especially in time of crisis.[45]

The concept of a unified court system and a supreme court was introduced into postwar Japan by that nation's constitution, which U.S. authorities helped develop. This system is described in Analyzing Criminal Justice Issues: The Japanese Court System.

ANALYZING CRIMINAL JUSTICE ISSUES

The Japanese Court System

The Japanese court system is organized in a tier style somewhat similar to that of the United States. There are 570 summary courts that deal with cases in which the penalty is a fine or short detention, such as those involving gambling, larceny, embezzlement, and fencing offenses. The fifty family courts have jurisdiction over all juvenile cases and cases involving adults who have violated laws protecting the rights of children. Fifty district courts have jurisdiction over all other criminal cases except insurrection, which is handled by judges in one of the eight appellate or high courts; at the top of the system is a supreme court.

Unlike in the United States, Japan's system has no jury trials; instead, trials are held before professional jurists. Most cases are handled by a single judge (*tandoku jiken*). When the crime is serious, such as robbery or a homicide, a mandatory collegiate court (*hotei gogi jiken*) consisting of three judges handles the case. A three-judge discretionary collegiate court can also be called to handle lesser charges that are extremely complex or technical (*saitei gogi jiken*). However, as in the United States, most cases are handled informally and end in summary judgments. In fact, in most cases, upon a prosecutor's petition and agreement from the defendant, all hearings are waived and a judge makes a determination of guilt and imposes a penalty without anyone ever appearing in court. This practice allows the accused to avoid a court appearance but retain the right to appeal. About 70 percent of all cases are handled by summary judgments; less than 10 percent of all cases are seriously contested, and about 3 percent end in acquittal.

The Supreme Court of Japan

On May 3, 1947, the constitution of Japan became effective and radically altered Japan's judicial system. Before 1868, Japan had been governed by a feudal system ruled by the *Tokugawa* shogunate and a powerless emperor. The shogunate administered a legal system based on the codification of customary laws that emphasized social status. Confucianism was the official ideology and provided moral ideals. The laws of Japan were actually a means of enforcing the government's authority and sustaining the prevailing social order with a strict behavioral code. In 1868, the emperor was returned to power and the shogunate was abolished. The new system that resulted included a strong executive, a weak legislature, and a developing judiciary. There were no checks and balances or separation of powers. The emperor had sovereign power. Japan made major changes in its legal system around 1900 that followed the European models. Judgeships were career positions in Japan and required that candidates for them pass a national examination.

SUMMARY

The U.S. court system is a complex social institution. There is no set pattern of court organization, and court structure varies considerably between the various state jurisdictions.

Courts are organized on the federal, state, county, and local levels of government. States commonly maintain felony and misdemeanant cases separately, as well as operate independent trial and appellate courts. This structure is repeated on the federal level of jurisdiction. However, federal appellate courts also rule on state cases, and the U.S. Supreme Court is the court of last resort for all cases decided in the United States.

Directly supervising our nation's courts is the judiciary. Judges have a variety of backgrounds, skills, and qualifications. Their functions vary according to the courts in which they sit; some rule at the trial level, others handle appellate cases. Judges also serve as decision makers in administering probation departments and in working with district attorneys and police. Some judges are appointed by the state's chief executive, the governor, while others are elected to office by popular vote.

A recent trend has been the creation of administrative bodies to oversee court operations. Within this operational sphere are court administrators, who have used sophisticated computer operations to ease the flow of cases and improve court efficiency.

The 1947 constitution provided for separation of powers among distinct branches of government and granted judicial power to the supreme court and inferior courts. This marked the beginning of judicial independence and supremacy for the judiciary. The supreme court of Japan, as is the Supreme Court of the United States, is the court of ultimate instance.

The supreme court of Japan is located in Tokyo. The cabinet appoints fifteen judges to the court, and the emperor appoints one judge as chief justice on the recommendation of the cabinet. The appointments are subject to later approval by the voters. This electoral review is conducted at the first general election and every ten years thereafter. This process was intended to assure democratic control over the supreme court's appointments. However, due to the long-standing dominance of the ruling Liberal Democratic Party, no justice has been removed using the review process, and the court has not involved itself in partisan politics. Popular review is essentially a symbolic gesture of the ultimate sovereignty of the people.

At least ten of the judges on the supreme court must have served as judges on a lower court for twenty years or more. Five justices need not have any experience as judges, lawyers, or law professors. They must demonstrate great insight and knowledge of the law. Five justices are generally selected from lower courts and five from the practicing bar. The other five may be former law professors, government bureaucrats, or public prosecutors. Regional balance is given much consideration. The majority of the lawyers appointed to the supreme court have been presidents of the Tokyo and Osaka bar associations. Interestingly, many lawyers decline to accept the appointment because it means financial sacrifice. The average age for justices at appointment is sixty-two, and they usually serve until the mandatory retirement age of seventy. Justices are appointed with the expectation they will serve for less than ten years.

Critical Thinking Skills

1. There is far less crime in Japan than in the United States. Yet, despite lower caseload pressures in Japan, most criminal charges are handled informally. Though both systems stress adversarial justice, both rely heavily on informal procedures. Does this suggest that deal making is an inherent part of justice and that efforts to curb or eradicate it are doomed to failure?

SOURCES: Nobuyoshi Araki, "The Flow of Criminal Cases in the Japanese Criminal Justice System," *Crime and Delinquency* 31 (1985):601–29; P. R. Luney, Jr., "Judiciary: Its Organization and Status in the Parliamentary System," *Law and Contemporary Problems* 53 (1990): 135–62.

QUESTIONS

1. What qualities should a judge have? Should the judgeship be a lifetime appointment, or should judges be reviewed periodically?
2. Do the pomp and formality of a courtroom impede justice by setting it apart from the common person?
3. What is meant when we say that the Supreme Court is "the court of last resort"?
4. Should all judges be lawyers? When can people with no legal training be of benefit to the court system?
5. What are the benefits and drawbacks of holding judicial elections?

NOTES

1. Malcolm Feeley, *The Process Is the Punishment* (New York: Russell Sage Foundation, 1979), pp. 9–11.
2. Thomas Henderson, *The Significance of Judicial Structure: The Effect of Unification on Trial Court Operations* (Washington, D.C.: National Institute of Justice, 1984).
3. Johnathan Casper, Tom Tyler, and Bonnie Fisher, "Procedural Justice

in Felony Cases," *Law and Society Review* 22 (1988):497–505.

4. This section relies heavily on Conference of State Court Administrators and National Center for State Courts, *State Court Caseload Statistics, Annual Report, 1990* (Williamsburg, Va.: National Center for State Courts, 1992). Herein cited as *State Court Statistics*.

5. Charles Silberman, *Criminal Violence/Criminal Justice* (New York: Vintage Books, 1980), p. 347.

6. Feeley, *The Process Is the Punishment*, p. 3.

7. Patrick Langan, *State Felony Courts and Felony Laws* (Washington, D.C.: Bureau of Justice Statistics, 1987).

8. Timothy Flanagan and Katherine Jamieson, *Sourcebook of Criminal Justice Statistics*, (Washington, D.C.: U.S. Government Printing Office, 1988), p. 450.

9. Bureau of Justice Statistics, *Report to the Nation on Crime and Justice* (Washington, D.C.: U.S. Government Printing Office, 1988), p. 88.

10. Ibid.

11. *U.S. Constitution*, Art. 3, secs.1 and 2.

12. Linda Greenhouse, "Lightening Scales of Justice: High Court Trims Its Docket," *New York Times*, 7 March 1992, p. 1.

13. 1 Wharton 304, 4 L.Ed. 97 (1816).

14. *State Court Statistics*, updated.

15. Administrative Office of the United States Courts, *Annual Report of the Director, 1990* (Washington, D.C.: Administrative Office of the United States Courts, 1991).

16. Kathleen Maguire and Timothy Flanagan, *Sourcebook of Criminal Justice Statistics, 1990* (Washington, D.C.: U.S. Government Printing Office, 1991), pp. 529.

17. Sue Lindgren, *Justice Expenditures and Employment, 1988* (Washington, D.C.: Bureau of Justice Statistics, 1990).

18. H. Jacobs with D. Swank, J. Beecher, and M. Rich, "Keeping Pace: Court Resources and Crime in Ten U.S. Cities," *Judicature* 66 (1982):73–83.

19. "New York Chief Judge Sues Cuomo and Legislature over Budget," *Criminal Justice Newsletter* 22 (1991):1.

20. "Panel Says New York Courts Are 'Infested with Racism'," *Criminal Justice Newsletter*, 17 June 1991, p. 1.

21. "Too Many Continuances #1 Factor in Court Delays, Survey Finds," *Criminal Justice Newsletter*, 15 November 1988, p. 7.

22. Joel Garner, "Delay Reduction in the Federal Courts: Rule 50(B) and the Federal Speedy Trial Act of 1974," *Journal of Quantitative Criminology* 3 (1987):229–50.

23. "Too Many Continuances #1 Factor in Court Delays, Survey Finds," *Criminal Justice Newsletter*.

24. "Federal Judges Seeking Authority to Carry Firearms," *Criminal Justice Newsletter* 21 (1990):3.

25. Robert Sigler, Joan Crowley, and Ida Johnson, "Judicial and Prosecutorial Endorsement of Innovative Techniques in the Trial of Domestic Abuse Cases," *Journal of Criminal Justice* 18 (1990):443–53.

26. Huey-Tsyh Chen, "Dropping in and Dropping out: Judicial Decisionmaking in the Disposition of Felony Arrests," *Journal of Criminal Justice* 19 (1991):1–17.

27. *State Court Statistics*.

28. Ibid., pp. 204–07.

29. Ibid., p. 10.

30. *State Court Statistics*, pp. 5–10.

31. Sari Escovitz with Fred Kurland and Nan Gold, *Judicial Selection and Tenure* (Chicago: American Judicature Society, 1974), pp. 3–16.

32. "State Adoption of Alternative Dispute Resolution," *State Court Journal* 12 (1988):11–15.

33. Pub. L. 90-578, Tit. I sec. 101, 82 Stat. 1113 (1968); amended. Pub.L. 94-577, sec. 1, Stat. 2729 (1976); Pub.L. 96-82 sec. 2, 93 Stat. 643 (1979).

34. See, generally, Carroll Seron, "The Professional Project of Parajudges: The Case of U.S. Magistrates," *Law and Society Review* 22 (1988):557–75.

35. Alex Aikman, "Volunteer Lawyer-Judges Bolster Court Resources," *NIJ Reports*, January 1986, pp. 2–6.

36. Warren Burger, "Rx for Justice: Modernize the Courts," *Nation's Business*, September 1974, p. 62.

37. Cited in National Advisory Commission on Criminal Justice Standards and Goals, *Courts* (Washington, D.C.: U.S. Government Printing Office, 1973), p. 171.

38. Edward McConnell, in *Justice in the States*.

39. National Center for State Courts, *Report on Trends in the State Courts* (Williamsburg, Va.: National Center for State Courts, 1988).

40. Ibid.

41. Ibid.

42. Ibid.

43. See, generally, American Bar Association, *Standards Relating to Court Organization* (New York: Institute for Judicial Administration, 1973).

44. Malcolm Feeley, *Court Reform on Trial* (New York: Basic Books, 1983).

45. Ibid.

The Prosecution and the Defense

CHAPTER 11

OUTLINE

KEY TERMS

prosecutor
district attorney
U.S. attorney
attorney general
Town of Newton v. Rumery
United States v. Goodwin
Burns v. Reed
defense attorney
public defender
adversarial process
indigent
Sixth Amendment
Gideon v. Wainwright
Argersinger v. Hamlin
recoupment
ad hoc assigned counsel system
coordinated assigned counsel system
contract system
plea bargaining
Burger v. Kemp
Taylor v. Illinois
surprise witness rule
reasonable competence standard
Strickland v. Washington

After a criminal defendant has been processed by police agencies and relevant evidence has been gathered in the case, the focus of justice shifts from the law enforcement to the criminal court system. In the preceding chapter, we discussed the organization of the court system and the manner in which the criminal court, as a complex social agency, deals with different types of cases. Issues involving court administration, judicial selection, and court reform were analyzed.

This chapter explores the role of the prosecutor and the defense attorney in the criminal process. The prosecutor, to a great extent, is the person who single-handedly controls the "charging" decision. To charge or not, and for what offense, is the prosecutor's great discretionary authority. The defense attorney acts in a different capacity. Although defendants have a right to defend themselves, most are represented by a lawyer who is knowledgeable about the criminal law. The criminal lawyer has a legal obligation to make every effort to provide a competent and adequate defense.

Although the formal criminal trial is an important aspect of our justice system, it is actually used in a small minority of cases. Most criminal cases are decided rather informally through negotiations and other actions by the attorneys in the case: the prosecutor who represents the state and the defense counsel who represents the accused. Questions about the critical roles of the prosecutor and the defense attorney, whether they are acting formally in a trial or informally through negotiated settlements, pervade the system.

The Prosecutor

Depending on the level of government and the jurisdiction in which he or she functions, the **prosecutor** may be known as a **district attorney,** a county attorney, a state's attorney, or a **U.S. attorney.** Whatever the title, the prosecutor is ordinarily a member of the practicing bar who has been appointed or elected to be a public prosecutor.

Although the prosecutor participates with the judge and defense attorney in the adversary process, the prosecutor is responsible for bringing the state's case against the accused. The prosecutor focuses the power of the state on those who disobey the law by charging them with a crime, releasing them from prosecution, or eventually bringing them to trial.

Although the prosecutor's primary duty is to enforce the criminal law, his or her fundamental obligation as an attorney is to seek justice as well as to convict

Depending on the level of government they serve, the prosecutor may be known as a district attorney, county attorney, state's attorney or U.S. attorney.

those who are guilty. For example, if the prosecutor discovers facts suggesting that the accused is innocent, he or she must bring this information to the attention of the court. The American Bar Association's Code of Professional Responsibility, Canon 7-103, deals with the ethical duties of the attorney as a public prosecutor:

> Dr 7-103 Performing the Duty of Public Prosecutor or Other Government Lawyer
> A. A public prosecutor or other government lawyer shall not institute or cause to be instituted criminal charges when he knows or it is obvious that the charges are not supported by probable cause.
> B. A public prosecutor or other government lawyer in criminal litigation shall make timely disclosure to counsel for the defendant, or to the defendant, if he has no counsel, of the existence of evidence, known to the prosecutor or other government lawyer, that tends to negate the guilt of the accused, mitigate the degree of the offense, or reduce the punishment.[1]

The senior prosecutor must make policy decisions on the exercise of prosecutorial enforcement powers in a wide range of cases in criminal law, consumer protection, housing, and other areas. In so doing, the prosecutor determines and ultimately shapes the manner in which justice is exercised in society.[2]

Many individual prosecutors are often caught between being compelled by their supervisors to do everything possible to obtain a guilty verdict and acting as a concerned public official to ensure that justice is done. Sometimes this conflict can lead to prosecutorial misconduct. According to some legal authorities, unethical prosecutorial behavior is often motivated by the desire to obtain a conviction and by the fact that prosecutorial misbehavior is rarely punished by the courts.[3] Some prosecutors may conceal evidence or misrepresent it or influence juries by impugning the character of opposing witnesses. Even where a court may instruct a jury to ignore certain evidence, a prosecutor may attempt to sway the jury or the judge by simply mentioning the tainted evidence. Since appellate courts generally uphold convictions where such misconduct is not considered serious (the harmless error doctrine), prosecutors are not penalized for their misbehavior, nor are they personally liable for their conduct. Overzealous, excessive, and even cruel prosecutors, motivated by political gain or notoriety, produce wrongful convictions, thereby abusing their office and the public trust.[4] According to legal expert Stanley Fisher, prosecutorial excesses appear when the government (1) always seeks the highest charges; (2) interprets the criminal law expansively; (3) wins as many convictions as possible; and (4) obtains the most severe penalties.[5]

Politics and Prosecutors

The prosecutor is either elected or appointed and is, consequently, a political figure in the criminal justice system. The prosecutor normally has a party affiliation, a constituency of voters and supporters, and a need to respond to community pressures and interest groups. In this regard, the American Bar Association's *Standards Relating to the Prosecution Function and Defense Function* states:

> The political process has played a significant part in the shaping of the role of the American prosecutor. Experience as a prosecutor is a familiar stepping stone to higher political office. The "DA" has long been glamorized in fiction, films, radio, television, and other media. Many of our political leaders had their first exposure to public notice and political life in this office. A substantial number of executive and legislative officials as well as judges have served as prosecuting attorneys at some point in their careers. The political involvement of a prosecutor varies. In most jurisdictions he is required to run with a party designation. In some places prosecutors are elected on a nonpartisan basis. The powers of a prosecutor are formidable and he is an important personage in his community. If he is not truly independent and professional, his powers can be misused for political or other improper purposes. Perhaps even more than other American public officials, the prosecutor's activity is in large part open to public gaze—as it should be—and spotlighted by the press. The importance of his function is such that his least mistake is likely to be magnified, as are many of his successful exploits.[6]

The political nature of the prosecutor's office can heavily influence decision making. When deciding if, when, and how to handle a case, the prosecutor cannot forget that he or she may be up for election soon and have to answer to an electorate who will scrutinize his or her actions. For example, in a murder trial involving a highly charged issue, such as child killing, the prosecutor's decision to ask for the death penalty may hinge on his or her perception of the public's will. The role of politics in the prosecutor's office is discussed in great detail in Analyzing Criminal Justice Issues: The Role of Politics and Partisanship in Law Enforcement on page 386.

The Duties of the Prosecutor

The prosecutor is also the chief law enforcement officer of a particular jurisdiction. His or her participation spans the entire gamut of the justice system, from the time search and arrest warrants are issued or a grand jury empaneled to the final sentencing decision and appeal. General duties of a prosecutor include (1) enforcing the law, (2) representing the government, (3) maintaining proper standards of conduct as an attorney and court officer, (4) developing programs and legislation for law and criminal justice reform, and (5) being a public spokesperson for the field of law. Of these, representing the government while presenting the state's case to the court is the prosecutor's most frequent task. In this regard, the prosecutor does many of the following:

1. Investigates possible violations of the law
2. Cooperates with police in investigating a crime
3. Determines what the charge will be
4. Interviews witnesses in criminal cases
5. Reviews applications for arrest and search warrants
6. Subpoenas witnesses
7. Represents the government in pretrial hearings and in motion procedures
8. Enters into plea-bargaining negotiations
9. Tries criminal cases
10. Recommends sentences to courts upon convictions
11. Represents the government in appeals

Many jurisdictions have also established special prosecution programs aimed at seeking indictments and convictions of those committing major felonies, violent offenses, rapes, and white-collar crimes. In a recent national survey of prosecutorial practices, Michael Benson found an apparent increase in the local prosecution of corporate offenders.[7] According to Benson, the federal government historically played the dominant role in controlling white-collar crime. But there appears to be an increased willingness to prosecute corporate misconduct on a local level if an offense causes substantial harm. The National District Attorneys Association has responded to the concerns of prosecutors faced with the need to enforce complex environmental laws by creating the National Environmental Crime Prosecution Center. This center, modeled after the National Center for Prosecution of Child Abuse, lends assistance to district attorneys who are prosecuting environmental crimes.

In addition, a form of priority prosecutions commonly known as the career criminal prosecution program is very popular in many jurisdictions. Such programs involve identifying dangerous offenders who commit a higher rate of crime so that prosecutors could target them for swift prosecution (see Figure 11.1).[8]

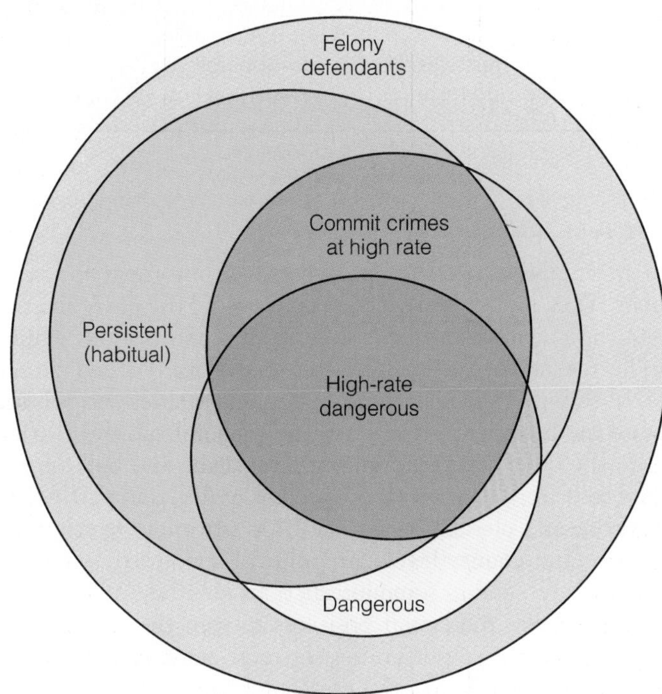

FIGURE 11.1
Priority Prosecution Candidates for Career Criminal Prosecution

Felony defendants include three groups that could fit the term "career criminal" in its broadest sense: persistent offenders, high-rate offenders, and dangerous offenders. Defendants who are dangerous and also commit crimes at a high rate are the subject of this report.

SOURCE: Marcia and Jan Chaiken, *Priority Prosecution of High-Rate Dangerous Offenders* (Washington, D.C.: National Institute of Justice, 1991), pp. 1–8.

ANALYZING CRIMINAL JUSTICE ISSUES

The Role of Politics and Partisanship in Law Enforcement

[The following article describes the relationship between politics and criminal prosecution.]

Politics, properly understood, is the essence of democracy. It is the way a free and vigorous people seek to determine and then change public policy. Federal law enforcement is, in this sense, political. As we have recently observed, criminal justice issues such as drug enforcement are often important to citizens, and presidential candidates regularly address them in their campaigns.

When a president is elected, he is entitled to be served by an attorney general and others, including the 94 U.S. attorneys, who share his law enforcement priorities and—where the law is uncertain—who share the interpretation of the law the president prefers. It is natural that a president who believes in his law enforcement program and will be held accountable for it at the next election will likely seek members of his own party to implement that program.

Once appointed, however, an attorney general or U.S. attorney must recognize that politics is limited to the development of policies. There can be no political favoritism or partisan bias in the enforcement of those policies. In law enforcement there simply can be no friends or enemies. The law must treat important and anonymous interests alike. To achieve this, neutral standards and procedures for initiating investigations and authorizing prosecutions must be established and then applied without fear or favor.

A corollary of this is that an attorney general or U.S. attorney should be a person who has earned a reputation as trustworthy and professional, rather than partisan, because often he cannot properly explain what his office is doing, or why it has failed to act. For example, a prosecutor usually has a responsibility not to confirm or deny the existence of an investigation. This is a matter of fairness to the subjects of investigations and of self-interest to the government, because public disclosure of the details of an investigation may facilitate its frustration. Similarly, a prosecutor can rarely properly explain why an indictment was not sought in a matter known to have been investigated.

Thus, it is essential that the public trust the integrity and ability of an attorney general or U.S. attorney. Immediately after Watergate, it was widely recognized that it would be inappropriate to continue the tradition of appointing [as] attorney general someone such as the president's campaign manager—be he Robert Kennedy or John Mitchell—because it would be difficult for the person to cease making partisan decisions and virtually impossible for the public to believe he had done so. Although this lesson of Watergate has not always been faithfully followed, the deviations may, perhaps, remind us of its continuing validity.

It should also be recognized, however, that neither an attorney general nor a U.S. attorney is solely responsible for federal law enforcement. Rather, he or she is the cap-

Types of Prosecutors

In the federal system, prosecutors are known as U.S. attorneys and are appointed by the president. They are responsible for representing the government in federal district courts. The chief prosecutor is usually an administrator, while assistants normally handle the actual preparation and trial work. Federal prosecutors are professional civil service employees with reasonable salaries and job security.

On the state and county levels, the **attorney general** and the district attorney, respectively, are the chief prosecutorial officers. Again, the bulk of the criminal prosecution and staff work is performed by scores of full- and part-time attorneys, police investigators, and clerical personnel. Most attorneys who work for prosecutors on the state and county levels are political appointees who earn low salaries, handle many cases, and in some jurisdictions maintain private law practices. Many young lawyers take these staff positions to gain the trial experience that will qualify them for better opportunities. In most state, county, and municipal jurisdictions, however, the office of the prosecutor can be described as having the highest standards of professional skill, personal integrity, and working conditions.

tain—but not necessarily the star—of a team of prosecutors, usually attracted by the highest tradition of public service, who tend to endure from administration to administration. They work with dedicated professionals in the federal investigative agencies. As Edward Levi said when President Ford appointed him attorney general in the aftermath of Watergate, the nation has been fortunate because the Department of Justice has historically been staffed by people who understand that "if we are to have a government of laws and not men, then it particularly takes dedicated men and women to accomplish this through their zeal and determination, and also their concern for fairness and impartiality."

Indeed, this may be an appropriate time to recall an exemplar of that tradition. Emory Buckner was an assistant U.S. attorney in New York when Felix Frankfurter served as Henry Stimson's deputy in that office. Buckner went on to become the U.S. attorney in New York and also a special prosecutor of public corruption. When Buckner died in 1941, Frankfurter described Buckner's "uncompromising conception of the functions and standards of a prosecutor."

"He was," Frankfurter said, "an instinctive ethical nature, but one whose comic spirit precluded the taint of self-righteousness and the dullness of moralizing. . . . Buckner displayed uncommon energy and skill in the successful prosecution of subtle and complicated crimes, against powerful opposition."

"But what is much more important is that . . . Buckner realized that he who wields the instruments of criminal justice wields the most terrible instruments of government. In order to assure their just and compassionate use, a prosecutor must have an almost priest-like attitude toward his duties. Buckner practiced this attitude without deviation."

Critical Thinking Skills

1. In the United States, federal prosecutors are appointed, while state prosecutors are often elected. Both approaches are ingrained in our political traditions. The overwhelming number of jurisdictions, however, elect prosecutors on a local level. Is one system superior to the other? Can you point to any program where a nonelective office is more effective? Which system promotes a greater degree of accountability? Loyalty? Which encourages more career prosecutors?

2. According to the author, Judge Wolf, it is essential that the public trust the integrity and ability of an attorney general, a U.S. attorney, or a district attorney. In light of Watergate and the Iran-Contra affair do you share the same vision?

SOURCE: Mark Wolf, "U.S. Federal Court Judge," *Boston Globe,* 3 February 1989. p. 37.

In urban jurisdictions, the structure of the district attorney's office is often specialized, with separate divisions for felonies, misdemeanors, and trial and appeal assignments. In rural offices, chief prosecutors will handle many of the criminal cases themselves. Where assistant prosecutors are employed, they often work part-time, have limited professional opportunities, and depend on the political patronage of chief prosecutors for their positions.

The personnel practices, organizational structures, and political atmospheres of many prosecutor's offices often restrict the effectiveness of individual prosecutors in investigating and prosecuting criminal offenses. For many years, prosecutors have been criticized for bargaining justice away, for using their positions as a stepping stone to higher political office, and often for failing to investigate or simply dismissing criminal cases. Lately, however, the prosecutor's public image has improved. Violations of federal laws, such as white-collar crime, drug peddling, and corruption, are being more aggressively investigated by the ninety-four U.S. attorneys and the nearly two thousand assistant U.S. attorneys. The National Drug Prosecution Center of the National District Attorneys Association, for instance, is assisting state and federal prosecutors in enforcing complex drug laws.

At every level of government, the prosecutor represents the government in trying criminal cases.

Aggressive federal prosecutors in New York have made extraordinary progress in the war against insider trading and security fraud on Wall Street using informants, wiretaps, and federal racketeering law. Through RICO (Racketeer Influenced and Corrupt Organization Law, detailed in Chapter 4), the government has successfully obtained convictions of important Mafia gangsters.[9] Prosecutors in Boston were credited with the recent dramatic and hard-won conviction of Gennaro (Jerry) Angiulo and the collapse of his Mafia family.[10] From 1987 to 1990, many major organized crime figures were indicted, convicted, and sentenced to long prison terms.[11]

State crimes ranging from murder to larceny are prosecuted in state courts by district attorneys who are stepping up their efforts against career criminals, shortening the time it takes to bring serious cases to trial, and addressing the long-neglected problems of victims and witnesses. With such actions, the prosecutor will continue to be one of the most powerful and visible professionals in the justice system.

The Law Enforcement Role of Prosecutors

One of the most important of the prosecutor's many functions involves the relationship between the prosecutor and the police officer. The prosecutor has broad discretion in decisions to charge the suspect with a crime and is generally the chief law enforcement official of the jurisdiction. When it comes to processing everyday offenses and minor fines, the prosecutor often relies on law enforcement officers to provide and initiate the formal complaint. With more serious offenses, such as felonies, the prosecutor is involved in the criminal investigation. Some offices of the district attorney carry out special investigations of organized crime, corruption of public officials, and corporate and white-collar crime, as well as vice and drug offenses. Much of the investigative work in such offices is handled by police personnel.

Police and prosecutorial relationships vary from one jurisdiction to another and often depend on whether the police agency is supplying the charge or the district attorney is investigating the matter. In either case, the prosecutor is required to maintain regular contact with the police department to develop the criminal prosecution properly. Some of the areas where the police officer and the prosecutor work together include:

1. *The police investigation report*. This report is one of the most important documents in the prosecutor's case file. It is basically a statement by the police of the details of the crime, including all the evidence needed to support each element of the offense. It is a critical first step in developing the government's case against a suspect.
2. *Providing legal advice*. Often the prosecutor advises the police officer about the legal issues in a given case. The prosecutor may also assist the officer by limiting unnecessary court appearances, informing the officer of the disposition of the case, and preparing the officer for pretrial appearances. While the prosecutor should advise the police on the legal aspects of criminal investigations, he or she also needs to be particularly careful about prosecutorial immunity from civil liability in light of the *Burns v. Reed* case outlined on page 397.
3. *Training police personnel*. In many jurisdictions, prosecutors help train police officers in securing warrants, making legal arrests, interrogating persons in custody, and conducting legal lineups. Some police departments have police legal advisers who work with the prosecutor in training new and experienced police personnel in legal matters.[12]

Police-Prosecutor Conflicts. Although the police and the prosecutor work together in many ways, in others they function with minimal cooperation and even distrust because of their different roles. The police and the prosecutor often compete with each other in seeking credit for the successful arrest, prosecution, and conviction of a particular defendant. In some cases, the prosecutor is insensitive to the problem of unnecessary court appearances by police officers. And in some jurisdictions, the police and the prosecutor may be outright antagonistic toward each other if there is little or no exchange of information about a particular case. Futhermore, the police may be unwilling to understand the prosecutor's decision not to charge a suspect with a crime after they have put much work into an investigation. The police may not agree with alternative procedures developed by the prosecutor and would prefer to press for full enforcement in the charging decision. In some cases, the prosecutor may not handle the witnesses or informants properly, which may place the police officer in an embarrassing position. On the other hand, the prosecutor may believe that the police have legally bungled an investigation and mishandled evidence. Such problems between prosecutors and police officers vary in degree from one jurisdiction to another.

At the same time, the prosecutor, as the chief law enforcement official of a jurisdiction, ordinarily depends on police and other investigative agencies for information on criminal violations. A large part of the prosecutor's work comes from complaints made by citizens or arrests made directly by police agencies. Consequently, the prosecutor needs the cooperation of the police in processing the case. Even when the prosecutor initiates investigations of suspected criminal acts, the investigations are generally conducted by police personnel. Most prosecutors willingly cooperate with law enforcement personnel so they have the most impact possible on the investigation and a higher probability of successfully prosecuting their cases.

Prosecutorial Discretion

One might expect that after the police arrest and bring a suspect to court, the entire criminal court process would be mobilized. This is often not the case, however. For a variety of reasons, a substantial percentage of defendants are never brought to trial. The prosecutor decides whether to bring a case to trial or to dismiss it outright. Even if the prosecutor decides to pursue a case, the charges may later be dropped if conditions are not favorable for a conviction in a process called *nolle prosequi*.

Even in felony cases, the prosecutor ordinarily exercises much discretion in deciding whether to charge the accused with a crime.[13] After a police investigation, the prosecutor may be asked to review the sufficiency of the evidence to determine if a criminal complaint should be filed. In some jurisdictions, this may involve presenting the evidence at a preliminary hearing. In other cases, the prosecutor may decide to seek a criminal complaint through the grand jury or other information procedure. These procedures, representing the formal methods of charging the accused with a felony offense, are discussed in Chapter 12.

There is little question that prosecutors exercise a great deal of discretion in even the most serious cases. Figure 11.2 illustrates the flow of felony cases through three jurisdictions in the United States: Golden, Colorado; Manhattan, New York; and Salt Lake City, Utah. Barbara Boland collected the data for a study of the differences in how prosecutors handle felony arrests.[14] Note that although procedures were different in the three districts, prosecutors used their discretion to dismiss a high percentage of the cases before trial. Also note that when cases were forwarded for trial, very few defendants were actually acquitted, indicating that the prosecutorial discretion was exercised to screen out the weakest cases. In addition, of those cases accepted for prosecution, a high percentage ended with the defendant pleading guilty. All the evidence here points to the conclusion that prosecutorial discretion is used to reduce potential trial cases to a minimum.

The reasons some cases are rejected or dismissed are reviewed in the Analyzing Criminal Justice Issues on page 393.

The prosecutor may also play a limited role in exercising discretion in minor offenses. This may consist of simply consulting with the police after their investigation results in a complaint being filed against the accused. In such instances, the decision to charge a person with a crime may be left primarily to the discretion of the law enforcement agency. The prosecutor may decide to enter this type of case after an arrest has been made and a complaint has been filed with the court and subsequently determine whether to adjust the matter or proceed to trial. In some minor crimes, the prosecutor may not even appear until the trial stage of the process (or not at all); the police officer sometimes handles the entire case, including its prosecution.

Extent of Discretion

The power to institute formal charges against the defendant is the key to the prosecutorial function. The ability to initiate or discontinue charges against a defendant represents the control and power the prosecutor has over an individual's liberty. The prosecutor has broad discretion in the exercise of his or her duties. The prosecutor is primarily responsible for instituting criminal proceedings against the defendant; this discretionary decision is subject to few limitations and often puts the prosecutor in the position of making difficult decisions without appropriate policies and guidelines. Over fifty years ago, Newman Baker commented on the problems of prosecutorial decision making:

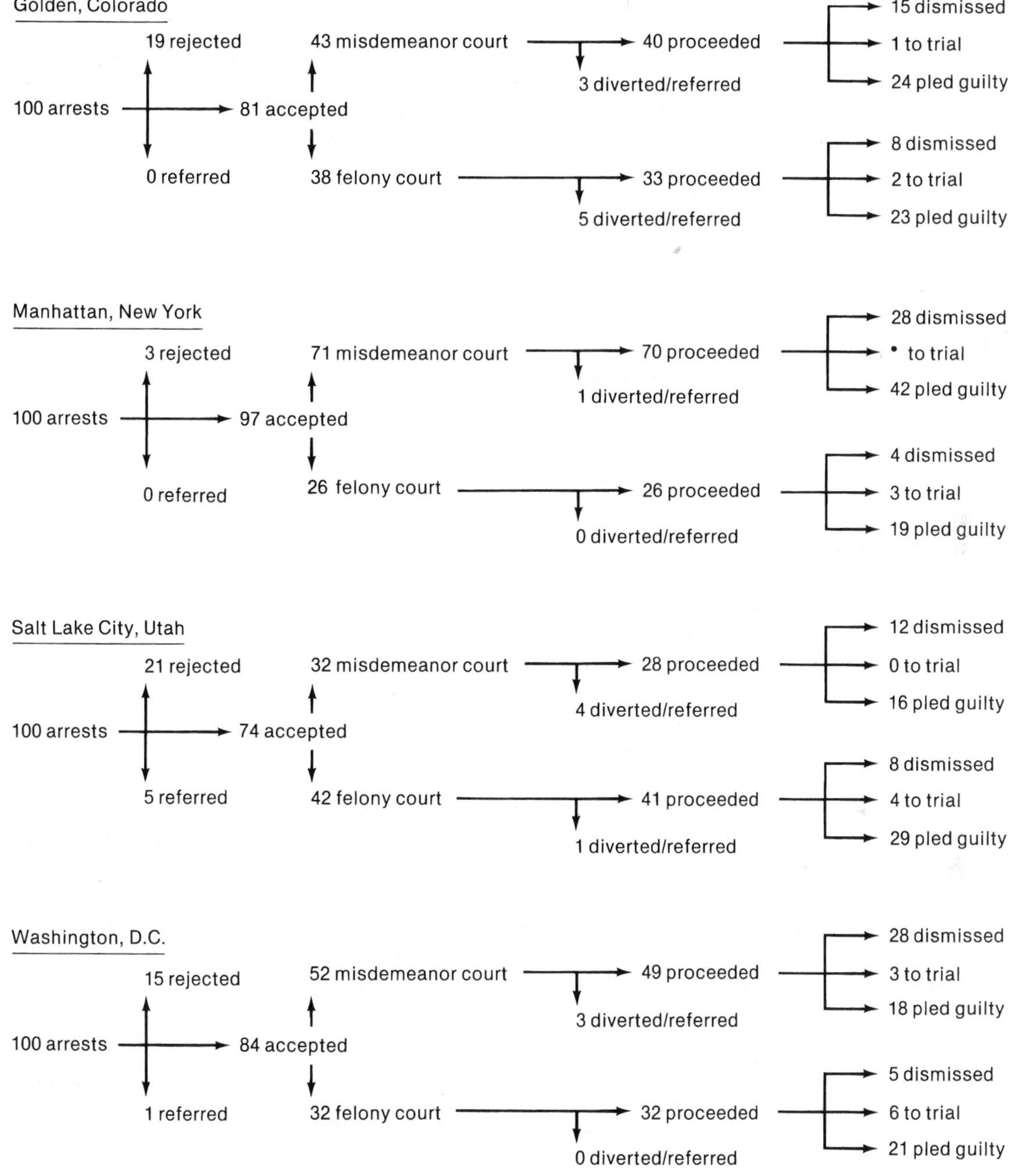

FIGURE 11.2

Differences in How Prosecutors Handle Felony Cases Can Be Seen in Three Jurisdictions

SOURCE: Bureau of Justice Statistics, *Report to the Nation on Crime and Justice,* 2d ed. (Washington, D.C.: U.S. Government Printing Office, 1988), p. 71; adapted from Barbara Boland, INSLAW, Inc., *The Prosecution of Felony Arrests* (Washington, D.C.: U.S. Government Printing Office, 1983).

"To prosecute or not to prosecute?" is a question which comes to the mind of this official scores of times each day. A law has been contravened and the statute says he is bound to commence proceedings. His legal duty is clear. But what will be the result? Will it be a waste of time? Will it be expensive to the state? Will it be unfair to the defendant (the prosecutor applying his own ideas of justice)? Will it serve any good purpose to society in general? Will it have good publicity value? Will it cause a political squabble? Will it prevent the prosecutor from carrying the offender's home precinct when he, the prosecutor, runs for Congress after his term as prosecutor? Was the law violated a foolish piece of legislation? If the offender is a friend, is it the square thing to do to reward friendship by initiating criminal proceedings? These and many similar considerations are bound to come to the mind of the man responsible for setting the wheels of criminal justice in motion.[15]

Once involved in a case, the prosecutor must also determine the formal charge. Deciding whether or not to charge a person with a crime is often not easy—nor is determining the appropriate charge. Should a seventeen-year-old boy be charged with burglary or handled as a juvenile offender in the juvenile court? Would it be more appropriate to reduce a drug charge from sale of marijuana to mere possession? What if the offense could be considered mayhem, battery, or simple assault? What then are the factors that influence prosecutorial decision making?

System Factors. In determining what course of action to take, the prosecutor has a significant effect on the criminal justice system. Initiating formal charges against all defendants arrested by the police would clog the courts with numerous petty crimes and cases in which little chance of conviction exists. The prosecutor would waste time on minor cases that could have been better spent on the investigation and prosecution of more serious crimes. Effective screening by prosecutors can eliminate many cases from the judicial system in which convictions cannot reasonably be obtained or that may be inappropriate for criminal action, such as petty thefts, minor crimes by first offenders, and criminal acts involving offenders in need of special services (for example, emotionally disturbed or mentally retarded offenders). The prosecutor can then concentrate on bringing to trial offenders who commit serious personal and property crimes, such as homicide, burglary, rape, and robbery.[16]

Case Factors. Since they are ultimately responsible for deciding whether to prosecute, prosecutors must be aware of the wide variety of circumstances that affect their decisions. Frank Miller has identified a list of factors that affect discretion and the charging decision. Some of these include (1) the attitude of the victim, (2) the cost of prosecution to the criminal justice system, (3) the avoidance of undue harm to the suspect, (4) the availability of alternative procedures, (5) the use of civil sanctions, and (6) the willingness of the suspect to cooperate with law enforcement authorities.[17]

Recent evidence indicates that the relationship between the victim and the criminal may greatly influence whether a prosecutor wishes to pursue a case. Barbara Boland found that conviction rates were much lower in cases involving friends (30 percent) or relatives (19 percent) than they were in cases involving strangers (48 percent).[18] Prosecutors who are aware of the drop-off in conviction probability in friend-relative cases may be reluctant to pursue them unless they involve serious offenses.

Disposition Alternatives. While determining which cases should be eliminated from the criminal process or brought to trial, the prosecutor has the opportunity to select more appropriate alternative actions. There are many situations in which the prosecutor must decide if noncriminal alternatives are more appropriate. For example, offenders may be alcoholics or narcotics addicts; they

ANALYZING CRIMINAL JUSTICE ISSUES

What Are the Most Common Reasons for Rejection or Dismissal of a Criminal Case?

Many criminal cases are rejected or dismissed because of:

- *Insufficient evidence* that results from a failure to find sufficient physical evidence that links the defendant to the offense.
- *Witness problems* that arise, for example, when a witness fails to appear, gives unclear or inconsistent statements, is reluctant to testify, or is unsure of the identity of the offender or where a prior relationship may exist between the victim/witness and the offender.
- *The interests of justice,* wherein the prosecutor decides not to prosecute certain types of offenses, particularly those that violate the letter but not the spirit of the law (for example, offenses involving insignificant amounts of property damage).
- *Due process problems* that involve violations of the constitutional requirements for seizing evidence and for questioning the accused.
- *A plea on another case,* for example, when the accused is charged in several cases and the prosecutor agrees to drop one or more of the cases in exchange for a plea of guilty on another case.
- *Pretrial diversion,* in which the prosecutor and the court agree to drop charges when the accused successfully meets the conditions for diversion, such as completion of a treatment program.
- *Referral for other prosecution,* such as when there are other offenses, perhaps of a more serious nature, in a different jurisdiction, or deferral to federal prosecution.

Critical Thinking Skills

A study of prosecutorial practices in a number of jurisdictions in the United States shows that evidence problems are the most common reasons prosecutors reject cases. Many other cases are dropped because defendants plead guilty to lesser crimes.

U.S. prosecutors have great discretionary power to decide not to prosecute—and are often immune from review by other officials and the courts. Contrast this discretionary power with the role of the prosecutor in West Germany. According to Kenneth Davis, "The most important distinction between the German system and the American system is that the German prosecutor is without discretionary power to withhold prosecution." When there are doubts about whether to prosecute, the system of prosecution in West Germany requires judicial review. What system is preferable? How can the U.S. prosecutorial system control unchecked discretion? Since the U.S. prosecutor is a representative of the public, shouldn't society impose standards that compel prosecution in certain cases? Wouldn't mandatory laws and policies limit discretion and curb any favoritism or partisan bias?

SOURCES: Bureau of Justice Statistics, *Report to the Nation on Crime and Justice,* 2d ed. (Washington, D.C.: U.S. Government Printing Office, 1988); John Kaplan, Jerome Skolnick, and Malcolm Feeley, *Criminal Justice—Introductory Cases,* 5th ed. (Westbury, N.Y.: Foundation Press, 1991), p. 310.

may be mentally ill; they may have been led to crime by their family situation or by their inability to get a job. If they are not helped, they may well return to crime. In many cases, only minimal intrusions on defendants' liberty seem necessary. Often it will be enough simply to refer offenders to the appropriate agency in the community and hope that they will take advantage of the help offered. The prosecutor might, for example, be willing to drop charges if a man goes to an employment agency and makes a bona fide effort to get a job, seeks help from a social service agency, or resumes his education. The prosecutor retains legal power to file a charge until the period of limitations has expired, but as a practical matter, unless the offense is repeated, reviewing the initial charge would be unusual.[19]

Today, particularly in those jurisdictions where alternative programs exist, prosecutors are identifying and diverting offenders to community agencies in cases where the full criminal process does not appear necessary. This may occur in certain juvenile cases, with alcoholic and drug offenders, and in nonsupport paternity, prostitution, and gambling offenses. The American Bar Association recommends the use of social service programs as appropriate alternatives to prosecution.[20]

Dealing with the accused in a noncriminal fashion is what has come to be known as pretrial diversion. In this process, the prosecutor postpones or eliminates criminal prosecution in exchange for the alleged offender's participation in a rehabilitation program.[21] In recent years, the reduced cost and general utility of such programs have made them an important factor in prosecutorial discretion and a major part of the criminal justice system. A more detailed discussion of pretrial diversion is found in Chapter 12.

The Role of Prosecutorial Discretion

Regardless of its source, the proper exercise of prosecutorial discretion can improve the criminal justice process. For example, its use can prevent unnecessarily rigid implementation of the criminal law. Discretion allows the prosecutor to consider alternative decisions and humanize the operation of the criminal justice system. If prosecutors had little or no discretion, they would be forced to prosecute all cases brought to their attention. Judge Charles Breitel has stated, "If every policeman, every prosecutor, every court, and every post sentence agency performed his or its responsibility in strict accordance with rules of law, precisely and narrowly laid down, the criminal law would be ordered but intolerable."[22]

On the other hand, too much discretion can lead to abuses that result in the abandonment of law. One of the nation's most eminent legal scholars, Roscoe Pound, has defined discretion as

> an authority conferred by law to act in certain conditions or situations in accordance with an official's or an official agency's considered judgment and conscience. It is an idea of morals, belonging to the twilight between law and morals.[23]

In terms of prosecutorial practices, this definition of discretion implies the need to select and choose among alternative decisions—to remove cases from the criminal process, to modify criminal charges, or to prosecute to the fullest intent of legal authority. Because there is no easy way to make these decisions, it has been recommended that the prosecutor establish standards for evaluating whether criminal proceedings should be brought against an accused.

Judicial Restraints

The prosecutor's charging discretion has been considered by the U.S. Supreme Court. For example, in ***Town of Newton v. Rumery*** (1987), a defendant entered into an agreement with a prosecutor under which the criminal charges against him would be dropped in exchange for his agreeing not to file a civil suit against the town police. The defendant later filed the suit anyway, maintaining that the original agreement was coercive and interfered with his right to legal process. He lost the case when the trial court ruled that his earlier agreement not to file suit against the town was binding. On appeal, the Supreme Court found for the town. It upheld the legality of the prosecutor's actions because the idea for the bargain had originated with the defense and therefore was not inherently coercive. *Rumery* illustrates that prosecutors maintain significant discretion to work out bargains and deals as long as they do not deprive defendants of their legal rights.[24]

The courts have also reviewed such prosecutorial behavior issues as (1) disciplining a prosecutor for making disruptive statements in court; (2) the failure of a prosecutor to adhere to sentence recommendations pursuant to a plea bargain; (3) disqualifying a prosecutor who represented a criminal defendant presently under indictment; and (4) removing a prosecutor for making public statements harmful to the office of the district attorney not constitutionally protected under the First Amendment.

Prosecutors need to exercise control and discretion. In accordance with the national prosecution standards of the National District Attorneys Association, the broad discretion given to the prosecutor necessitates that the greatest effort be made to use this power fairly.[25] When decisions are not based on accurate and pertinent evidence and on fair procedures, the prosecutor can expect court intervention and judicial review.

Prosecutorial Vindictiveness. Courts have been more concerned about prosecutors who use their discretion in a vindictive manner to punish defendants who exercise their legal rights. For example, in *North Carolina v. Pearce* (1969), the U.S. Supreme Court held that a judge in a retrial cannot impose a sentence more severe than that originally imposed. In other words, a prosecutor cannot seek a stricter sentence for a defendant who succeeds in getting his or her first conviction set aside.[26] In *Blackledge v. Perry* (1974), the Court dealt with the issue of vindictiveness on the part of the prosecutor and found that imposing a penalty on a defendant for having successfully pursued a statutory right of appeal is a violation of due process of law.[27] But in *Bordenkircher v. Hayes* (1978), the Court allowed the prosecutor to carry out threats of increased charges made during plea negotiations when the defendant refused to plead guilty to the original charge.[28] This case is highlighted in Chapter 12.

In 1982, the Supreme Court dealt with prosecutorial discretion in ***United States v. Goodwin.*** In *Goodwin*, the Court held that no realistic likelihood of vindictiveness exists where the prosecutor increases charges after the plea negotiations fail and the defendant asserts his or her right to a trial by jury.[29] The defendant, Goodwin, was stopped for speeding. After Goodwin stepped out of his car, the officer noticed a clear plastic bag under the car's armrest and instructed Goodwin to return to the car. Goodwin placed the car in gear and accelerated, knocking the officer aside. A complaint was filed, charging Goodwin with various misdemeanor offenses. When Goodwin chose to plead guilty, the U.S. attorney's office obtained an indictment that, unlike the original charges, included a felony charge of assaulting an officer. The defendant was convicted, and he appealed on the basis that the case presented a genuine effort at retaliation by the prosecutor. Although the federal circuit court set aside the conviction, the Supreme Court held that the increased charges did not present a likelihood of vindictiveness on the prosecutor's part. First, the Court reasoned that in preparing a case, the prosecutor may uncover additional relevant information, thus justifying the increased charges. Second, the Court felt there was a greater likelihood that posttrial actions are more vindictively motivated than pretrial changes in criminal charges. The prosecutor is often faced with the issue of vindictiveness when he or she files increased charges after a guilty plea is withdrawn. If the additional charges are the result of a reevaluation of evidence and there is no indication of malice on the part of the prosecutor, then no vindictiveness can be found.

These decisions provide the framework of the "prosecutorial vindictiveness" doctrine: Due process of law may be violated if the prosecutor retaliates against a defendant and there is proof of actual vindictiveness. The prosecutor's legitimate exercise of discretion must be balanced against the defendant's legal rights.

Government Immunity—Suing the Prosecutor

The prosecutor is an attorney, public servant, and officer of the court. As such, he or she generally enjoys civil immunity when pursuing a criminal prosecution. This means that a prosecutor is not liable to a criminal defendant in a civil suit. Traditionally, prosecutors have benefited from the so-called "absolute immunity" rule, which provided them with virtually complete immunity in the performance of their duties. Occasional conflicts have arisen over the scope of the immunity. Some states, for instance, have designated prosecutorial immunity only for those actions connected with the prosecutor's role in judicial proceedings. The question has often been raised about whether statutory protection included all administrative, investigative, and judicial functions. As we have already discussed, the prosecutor's duties are extensive and span the entire spectrum of the judicial system. Whether immunity is absolute or qualified is critical because it may affect how the prosecutor performs these duties. At the same time, there is the issue of what civil redress is available against a prosecutor whose wrongful, malicious, or even dishonest action deprives a defendant of his or her freedom.

The U.S. Supreme Court pronounced the most significant opinion affecting prosecutor's civil immunity in the case of ***Burns v. Reed*** in 1991.[30] In *Burns*, the Court held that a prosecutor had absolute immunity from damages under the Civil Rights Act (42 U.S.C. § 1983) while participating in a probable cause hearing but no immunity for giving legal advice to the police. Leaving prosecutors with a qualified or limited immunity was justified, according to the Court, because such a standard protects prosecutors by permitting lawsuits to be resolved by a summary judgement. Under *Burns*, if a prosecutor is now sued as a civil defendant based on his or her giving legal advice to the police, the prosecutor will have to demonstrate that no reason exists in order to preclude summary judgment (a device used to seek a prompt disposition) against him or her. Because of the importance of this decision in the performance of the prosecutor's duties, it is outlined in the Law in Review on page 397.

The Defense Attorney

The **defense attorney** is the counterpart of the prosecuting attorney in the criminal process. The accused has a constitutional right to counsel, and when the defendant cannot afford an attorney, the state must provide one. The accused may obtain counsel from the private bar if he or she can afford to do so; if the defendant is indigent, private counsel or a **public defender** may be assigned by the court. (See the discussion on the defense of the indigent later in this chapter.)

For many years, much of the legal community looked down on the criminal defense attorney and the practice of criminal law. This attitude stemmed from the kinds of legal work a defense attorney was forced to do—working with shady characters, negotiating for the release of known thugs and hoods, and often overzealously defending alleged criminals in the criminal trial. Lawyers have been reluctant to specialize in criminal law because they receive comparatively low pay and often provide services without any compensation. In addition, law schools in the past seldom offered more than one or two courses in the criminal law and trial practices.

In recent years, however, with the advent of constitutional requirements regarding the assistance of counsel, interest has grown in criminal law. Almost all law schools today have clinical programs that employ students as voluntary defense attorneys. They also offer courses in trial tactics, brief writing, and appellate

LAW IN REVIEW

Burns v. Reed (1991)

The decision in *Burns v. Reed* placed important constitutional limitations on the absolute immunity rule affecting prosecutors' civil liability. In *Burns,* the U.S. Supreme Court said that prosecutors are not completely immune from liability for civil damages when providing legal advice to the police.

Facts

In September 1982, an unknown person entered the home of Cathy Burns, knocked her unconscious, and seriously shot her two small children. The assailant scrawled a message on a bathroom mirror that read, "I took what you loved most." After some investigation, the police considered Cathy Burns to be a suspect and theorized that she suffered from a multiple personality disorder. One of the officers suggested that Burns be hypnotized in an effort to identify her other personalities. Uncertain if hypnosis was an appropriate legal investigative device, the police officers requested and received permission from the prosecuting attorney to proceed. As a result of the hypnosis, the officers concluded that Burns had a multiple personality disorder and most likely had committed the shooting. The prosecutor advised the police officers that they had probable cause to proceed against Burns and subsequently questioned the officers at a hearing regarding an application for a search warrant.

Burns was charged with attempted murder and confined to a state psychiatric hospital, where medical experts concluded that she did not suffer from a multiple personality disorder. After the case was dismissed, Burns brought suit under the Civil Rights Act seeking damages against the police officers and prosecutor. At the trial level, the court granted a directed verdict in favor of the prosecutor, and the U.S. Court of Appeals affirmed.

In 1990, the Supreme Court decided to consider whether the prosecutor was absolutely immune while participating in the hearing for the warrant as well as for giving legal advice to the police.

Decision

The Supreme Court affirmed the lower court ruling regarding absolute immunity for actions connected with the prosecutor's role in judicial proceedings, but it concluded that there was no precedent for extending such immunity to the prosecutorial duty of giving legal advice to the police. The Court regarded the prosecutor's role as legal adviser to the police as separate from that carried out in the formal stages of the criminal justice process. Prior to this case, prosecutors generally enjoyed absolute immunity from civil rights actions brought under 42 U.S.C. Sec. 1983 when acting within the scope of their duties in initiating and pursuing a criminal prosecution. But the law was often unclear with respect to prosecutorial functions viewed as "administrative or investigative" in nature. Therefore, the Supreme Court concluded that prosecutors would be entitled to qualified immunity for giving legal advice to the police. Even though there was some risk of litigation in giving advice, the Court felt that the function was concerned primarily with actions closely related to the judicial process. Absolute immunity, according to the Supreme Court, should be reserved for prosecutorial duties in judicial proceedings so that the judicial process itself is kept free from any harassment and intimidation associated with litigation.

Significance of the Case

The *Burns* decision did not extend absolute immunity to actions of a prosecuting attorney outside the scope of his or her duties in the process of criminal prosecution. If sued over advise they give to police, prosecutors will not be able to have the suit dismissed on grounds of absolute immunity. As a civil defendant, they will be required to deal with the litigation and demonstrate that no liability exists.

Prosecutors will now face greater risk in their role as advisers to police officers. While performing this role, prosecutors will have to use extreme caution and deliberation to avoid the risk of suit by a defendant. At a minimum, they must be current on the law, as well as have a clear understanding of the facts of each case developed by the police officer. The mere fact that they do not have absolute immunity will probably have a chilling effect on their relationship with the police. Routine prosecutorial duties handled in a perfunctory manner may well result in an increase in civil litigation against both prosecutors and police officers.

procedures. In addition, legal organizations such as the American Bar Association, the National Legal Aid and Defenders Association, and the National Association of Criminal Defense Lawyers have assisted in recruiting able lawyers to do criminal defense work. As the American Bar Association has noted, "An almost indispensable condition to fundamental improvement of American criminal justice is the active and knowledgeable support of the bar as a whole."[31]

The Role of the Criminal Defense Attorney

The defense counsel is an attorney as well as an officer of the court. As an attorney, the defense counsel is obligated to uphold the integrity of the legal profession and to observe the requirements of the Code of Professional Responsibility in the defense of a client. According to the code, the duties of the lawyer to the adversary system of justice are as follows:

> Our legal system provides for the adjudication of disputes governed by the rules of substantive, evidentiary, and procedural law. An adversary presentation counters the natural human tendency to judge too swiftly in terms of the familiar that which is not yet fully known; the advocate, by his zealous preparation of facts and law, enables the tribunal to come to the hearing with an open and neutral mind and to render impartial judgments. The duty of a lawyer to his client and his duty to the legal system are the same: To represent his client zealously within the boundaries of the law.[32]

The defense counsel performs many functions while representing the accused in the criminal process. These include but are not limited to:

1. investigating the incident;
2. interviewing the client, police, and other witnesses;
3. discussing the matter with the prosecutor;
4. representing the defendant at the various pretrial procedures, such as arrest, interrogation, lineup, and arraignment;
5. entering into plea negotiations;
6. preparing the case for trial, including developing tactics and strategy;
7. filing and arguing legal motions with the court;
8. representing the defendant at trial;
9. providing assistance at sentencing; and
10. determining the appropriate basis for appeal.

These are some of the major duties of any defense attorney, whether privately employed by the accused, appointed by the court, or serving as a public defender.

Because of the way the U.S. system of justice operates today, criminal defense attorneys face many role conflicts. They are viewed as the prime movers in what is essentially an **adversarial process:** The prosecution and the defense engage in conflict over the facts of the case at hand, with the prosecutor arguing the case for the state and the defense counsel using all the means at his or her disposal to aid the client.

However, as members of the legal profession, defense counsels must be aware of their role as officers of the court. As an attorney, the defense counsel is obligated to uphold the integrity of the legal profession and to rely on constitutional ideals of fair play and professional ethics (discussed below) to provide adequate representation for a client.

Ethical Issues

As an officer of the court, along with the judge, prosecutors, and other trial participants, the defense attorney seeks to uncover the basic facts and elements of the criminal act. In this dual capacity of being both a defensive advocate and an officer of the court, the attorney is often confronted with conflicting obligations to his or her client and profession. Monroe Freedman identifies three of the most difficult problems involving the professional responsibility of the criminal defense lawyer:

1. Is it proper to cross-examine for the purpose of discrediting the reliability or credibility of an adverse witness whom you know to be telling the truth?
2. Is it proper to put a witness on the stand when you know he will commit perjury?
3. Is it proper to give your client legal advice when you have reason to believe that the knowledge you give him will tempt him to commit perjury?[33]

There are other, equally important issues with respect to a lawyer's ethical responsibilities. Suppose, for example, a client confides that he is planning to commit a crime. What are the defense attorney's ethical responsibilities in this case? Obviously, the lawyer would have to counsel the client to obey the law; if the lawyer assisted the client in engaging in illegal behavior, the lawyer would be subject to charges of unprofessional conduct and even criminal liability. In another area, suppose the defense attorney is aware that the police made a procedural error and that the guilty client could be let off on a technicality. What are the attorney's ethical responsibilities in this case? The criminal lawyer needs to be aware of these troublesome situations in order to properly balance the duties of being an attorney with those of being an officer of the court.

Since the defense attorney and the prosecutor have different roles, their ethical dilemmas may also vary. The defense attorney must maintain confidentiality and advise his or her client of the constitutional requirements of counsel, the privilege against self-incrimination, and the right to trial. On the other hand, the prosecutor represents the public and is not required to abide by such restrictions in the same way. In some cases, the defense counsel may even be justified in withholding evidence by keeping the defendant from testifying at the trial. In addition, while prosecutors are prohibited from expressing a personal opinion as to the defendant's guilt on summation of a case, defense attorneys are not altogether barred from expressing their belief about a client's innocence.

As a practical matter, therefore, ethical rules may differ because the state is bringing the action against the defendant and must prove the case beyond a reasonable doubt. This is also why a defendant who is found guilty can appeal, while a prosecutor must live with an acquittal, and why defense attorneys generally have more latitude in performing their duties on behalf of their clients, although neither side should encourage unethical practices.[34] Examine the ethical violations in the following two situations:

1. Legal Ethics in the Movies. In the Martin Scorsese thriller, *Cape Fear*, Sam Bowden, a lawyer played by Nick Nolte, is threatened and intimidated by Max Cady (Robert DeNiro), an ex-con released from prison after serving fourteen years for sexual battery. It seems that Cady blamed Bowden for his imprisonment because as Cady's public defender, Bowden did not reveal a report on the rape victim's sexual history, which might have gotten Cady off. Bowden apparently looked down on Cady and was critical of his background and criminal history. The movie depicts the horror to which Bowden and his family are subjected by Cady.

A defense attorney is obligated to provide the best legal representation for his or her client. Because Bowden let his prejudices interfere with his legal defense, he excluded important evidence that might have exonerated his client.

Bowden's action constituted a serious breach of his professional ethics as a defense attorney.

2. Legal Ethics in Real Life. In 1989, the nation was shocked by the fatal shooting of Carol Stuart as she and her husband Charles were leaving a childbirth class in Boston. Charles, who also was shot, told police that a black man had attacked them in a robbery. Later, however, Charles's brother, Matthew, confessed through his attorney to police that he and a friend had helped his brother dispose of the murder weapon and the woman's purse; Matthew and his friend apparently were unwitting accomplices in the plot to kill Carol Stuart. After prosecutors announced that Charles Stuart was the prime suspect in the slaying, he committed suicide. Matthew Stuart and his attorney believed that Matthew and his friend were protected from any criminal charges by prosecutorial immunity; however, because they apparently made statements to prosecutors without written immunity, they could possibly be brought to trial.

Are there any ethical issues in this case? Did Matthew Stuart's attorney bungle his client's defense and that of his friend by not getting written immunity for them? On the other hand, did the prosecutors renege on a deal? Developing evidence on possible violations of legal ethics by the defense and prosecution in such complex legal investigations may be as impossible as trying to pin down what actually happened in the Stuart murder case.

The Right to Counsel

Over the past decade, the rules and procedures of criminal justice administration have become extremely complex. Bringing a case to court involves a detailed investigation of a crime, knowledge of court procedures, the use of rules of evidence, and skills in criminal advocacy. Both the state and the defense must have this specialized expertise, particularly when an individual's freedom is at stake. Consequently, the right to the assistance of counsel in the criminal justice system is essential if the defendant is to have a fair chance of presenting a case in the adversary process.

One of the most critical issues in the criminal justice system has been whether an **indigent** defendant has the right to counsel. Can the accused who is poor and cannot afford an attorney have a fair trial without the assistance of counsel? Is counsel required at preliminary hearings? Should the convicted indigent offender be given counsel at state expense in appeals of the case? Questions such as these have arisen constantly in recent years. The federal court system has long provided counsel to the indigent defendant on the basis of the **Sixth Amendment** to the U.S. Constitution, unless he or she waived this right.[35] This constitutional mandate clearly applies to the federal courts, but its application to state criminal proceedings has been less certain.

In the landmark case of ***Gideon v. Wainwright*** in 1963, the U.S. Supreme Court took the first major step on the issue of right to counsel by holding that state courts must provide counsel to indigent defendants in felony prosecutions.[36] Almost ten years later, in the case of ***Argersinger v. Hamlin*** in 1972, the Court extended the obligation to provide counsel to all criminal cases where the penalty includes imprisonment—regardless of whether the offense is a felony or misdemeanor.[37] These two major decisions relate to the Sixth Amendment right to counsel as it applies to the presentation of a defense at the trial stages of the criminal justice system.[38]

F. Lee Bailey, shown here at a news conference, is one of the handful of nationally famous criminal defense lawyers.

In numerous Supreme Court decisions since *Gideon v. Wainwright*, the states have been required to provide counsel for indigent defendants at virtually all other stages of the criminal process, beginning with arrest and concluding with the defendant's release from the system.

Today, the Sixth Amendment right to counsel and the Fourth Amendment guarantee of due process of law have been judicially interpreted together to provide the defendant with counsel by the state in all types of criminal proceedings. The right to counsel attaches at the earliest stages of the justice system, usually when a criminal suspect is interrogated while in the custody of the police: *Miranda v. Arizona* (see Chapter 9) held that any statements made by the accused when in custody are inadmissible at trial unless the accused is informed of the right to counsel and to have an attorney appointed by the state if indigent.[39]

In addition to guaranteeing the right of counsel at the earliest stages of the justice system, as well as at trials, the Supreme Court has moved to extend the right to counsel to postconviction and other collateral proceedings, such as probation and parole revocation and appeal. When, for example, the court intends to revoke a defendant's probation and impose a sentence, the probationer has a right to counsel at the deferred sentence hearing.[40] Where the state provides for an appellate review of the criminal conviction, the defendant is entitled to the assistance of counsel for this initial appeal.[41] The defendant does not have the right to counsel for an appellate review beyond the original appeal or for a discretionary review to the U.S. Supreme Court. The Supreme Court has also required the states to provide counsel in other proceedings that involve the loss of personal liberty, such as juvenile delinquency hearings[42] and mental health commitments.[43]

Areas still remain in the criminal justice system where the courts have not required assistance of counsel for the accused. These include (1) preindictment lineups; (2) booking procedures, including the taking of fingerprints and other forms of identification; (3) grand jury investigations; (4) appeals beyond the first review; (5) disciplinary proceedings in correctional institutions; and (6) postre-

TABLE 11.1
Major U.S. Supreme Court Cases Granting Right to Counsel throughout the Pretrial, Trial, and Posttrial Stages of Criminal Justice Process

Case	Stage and Ruling
Escobedo v. Illinois, 378 U.S. 478 (1964)	The defendant has the right to counsel during the course of any police interrogation.
Miranda v. Arizona, 384 U.S. 436 (1966)	Procedural safeguards, including the right to counsel, must be followed at custodial interrogation to secure the privilege against self-incrimination.
Brewer v. Williams, 430 U.S. 387 (1977) (see also *Massiah v. United States,* 377 U.S. 201 [1964])	Once adversary proceedings have begun against the defendant, he or she has a right to the assistance of counsel.
Hamilton v. Alabama, 368 U.S. 52 (1961)	The arraignment is a critical stage in the criminal process, so that denial of the right to counsel is a violation of due process of law.
Coleman v. Alabama, 399 U.S. 1 (1970)	The preliminary hearing is a critical stage in a criminal prosecution requiring the state to provide the indigent defendant with counsel.
Moore v. Illinois, 434 U.S. 220 (1977)	An in-court identification at a preliminary hearing after a criminal complaint has been initiated requires counsel to protect the defendant's interests.
United States v. Wade, 388 U.S. 218 (1967)	A defendant in a pretrial postindictment lineup for identification purposes has the right to assistance of counsel.
Moore v. Michigan, 355 U.S. 155 (1957)	The defendant has the right to counsel when submitting a guilty plea to the court.
Powell v. Alabama, 287 U.S. 45 (1932)	Defendants have the right to counsel at their trial in a state capital case.
Gideon v. Wainwright, 372 U.S. 335 (1963)	An indigent defendant charged in a state court with a noncapital felony has the right to the assistance of free counsel at trial under the due process clause of the Fourteenth Amendment.
Argersinger v. Hamlin, 407 U.S. 25 (1972)	A defendant has the right to counsel at trial whenever he or she may be imprisoned for any offense, even for one day, whether classified as a misdemeanor or felony.

TABLE 11.1
Continued

Case	Stage and Ruling
Scott v. Illinois, 440 U.S. 367 (1979)	A criminal defendant charged with a statutory offense for which imprisonment on conviction is authorized but not imposed does not have the right to appointed counsel.
In re Gault, 387 U.S. 1 (1967)	Procedural due process, including the right to counsel, applies to juvenile delinquency adjudication that may lead to a child's commitment to a state institution.
Faretta v. California, 422 U.S. 806 (1975)	A defendant in a state criminal trial has a constitutional right to proceed without counsel when he or she voluntarily and intelligently elects to do so.
Townsend v. Burke, 334 U.S. 736 (1948)	A convicted offender has a right to counsel at the time of sentencing.
Douglas v. California, 372 U.S. 353 (1963)	An indigent defendant granted a first appeal from a criminal conviction has the right to be represented by counsel on appeal.
Mempa v. Rhay, 389 U.S. 128 (1967)	A convicted offender has the right to assistance of counsel at probation revocation hearings where the sentence has been deferred.
Gagnon v. Scarpelli, 411 U.S. 778 (1973)	Probationers and parolees have a constitutionally limited right to counsel on a case-by-case basis at revocation hearings.

lease revocation hearings. Nevertheless, the general rule of thumb is that no person can be deprived of freedom or lose a "liberty interest" without representation by counsel.

The right to counsel can also be spelled out in particular federal or state statutes. For example, beyond abiding by present constitutional requirements, a state may provide counsel by statute at all stages of juvenile proceedings, in dealing with inmate prison infractions or pretrial release hearings, or when considering temporary confinement of drug or sex offenders for psychiatric examination.

Today, the scope of representation for the indigent defendant is believed to cover virtually all areas of the criminal process and most certainly those critical points at which a person's liberty is at stake. Table 11.1 summarizes the major U.S. Court decisions granting defendants counsel throughout the criminal justice system.

The Private Bar

Today, the lawyer whose practice involves a substantial proportion of criminal cases is often considered a specialist in the field. Since most lawyers are not prepared in law school for criminal work, their skill often results from their experience in the trial courts. Lawyers such as F. Lee Bailey, Alan Dershowitz, Melvin Belli, William Kunstler, James St. Clair, Gerry Spence, and Roy Black of William Kennedy Smith fame are the elite of the private criminal bar; they are nationally known criminal defense attorneys who often represent defendants for large fees in celebrated and widely publicized cases. Attorneys like these are relatively few in number and do not regularly defend the ordinary criminal defendant. Bruce Cutler of New York, for instance, is noted for his career defense work of Mafia chiefs, Joseph Bunanno in the 1970s and John Gotti in 1990s. Brendan Sullivan offers top-flight legal representation to political figures charged with crimes, such as Oliver North.

In addition to this limited group of well-known criminal lawyers, some lawyers and law firms serve as house counsel for such professional criminals as narcotics dealers, gamblers, prostitutes, and even big-time burglars. These lawyers, however, constitute a very small percentage of the private criminal bar.

A large number of criminal defendants are represented by lawyers who often accept many cases for small fees. These lawyers may belong to small law firms or work alone, but a sizable portion of their practice involves representing those accused of crime. Other private practitioners occasionally take on criminal matters as part of their general practice. Criminal lawyers often work on the fringe of the legal business, and they receive little respect from the professional respect of their colleagues or the community as a whole. As one prominent authority put it:

> All but the most eminent criminal lawyers are bound to spend much of their working lives in overcrowded, physically unpleasant courts, dealing with people who have committed questionable acts, and attempting to put the best possible construction on those acts. It is not the sort of working environment that most people choose. Finally, the professional status of the criminal lawyer tends to be low. To some extent the criminal lawyer is identified unjustifiably in the public eye with the client he represents. Indeed some criminal lawyers are in fact house counsel for criminal groups engaged in gambling, prostitution, and narcotics. The reprehensible conduct of the few sometimes leads the public to see honest, competent practitioners as "mouthpieces" also. Furthermore, in nearly every large city a private defense bar of low legal and dubious ethical quality can be found. Few in number, these lawyers typically carry large caseloads and in many cities dominate the practice in routine cases. They frequent courthouse corridors, bondsmen's offices, and police stations for clients, and rely not on legal knowledge but on their capacity to manipulate the system. Their low repute often accurately reflects the quality of the services they render. This public image of the criminal lawyer is a serious obstacle to the attraction of able young lawyers, and reputable and seasoned practitioners as well, to the criminal law.[44]

Another problem associated with the private practice of criminal law is the fact that the fee system can create a conflict of interest. Since private attorneys are usually paid in advance and do not expect additional funds if their client is convicted and since many are aware of the guilt of their client before the trial begins, they earn the greatest profit if they get the case settled as quickly as possible. This usually means bargaining with the prosecutor, rather than going to trial. Even if attorneys win the case at trial, they may lose personally since the time expended will not be compensated by more than the gratitude of their client. And, of course, many criminal defendants cannot afford even a modest legal fee and therefore cannot avail themselves of the services of a private attorney. For these reasons, an elaborate, publicly funded legal system has developed.

Legal Services for the Indigent

To satisfy the constitutional requirements that indigent defendants be provided with the assistance of counsel at various stages of the criminal process, the federal government and the states have had to evaluate and expand criminal defense services. Prior to the Supreme Court's mandate in *Gideon v. Wainwright*, public defendant services were provided mainly by local private attorneys appointed and paid for by the court, called assigned counsels, or by limited public defendant programs. In 1961, for example, public defender services existed in only 3 percent of the countries in the United States, serving only about a quarter of the country's population.[45] The general lack of defense services for indigents traditionally stemmed from these causes, among others: (1) until fairly recently, the laws of most jurisdictions did not require the assistance of counsel for felony offenders and others; (2) only a few attorneys were interested in criminal law practice; (3) the organized legal bar was generally indifferent to the need for criminal defense assistance; (4) the caseloads of lawyers working in public defender agencies were staggering; and (5) financial resources for courts and defense programs were limited.

However, beginning with the *Gideon* case in 1963 and continuing through the *Argersinger* decision in 1972, the criminal justice system has been forced to increase public defender services. Today, about three thousand state and local agencies are providing indigent legal services in the United States.

Types of Indigent Defender Systems

Providing legal services for the indigent offender is a huge undertaking. Over 4.4 million offenders are given free legal services. And, although most states have a formal set of rules to signify who is an indigent and 75 percent require indigents to repay the state for at least part of their legal services (known as **recoupment**), indigent legal services in 1988 still cost over $1 billion annually. This is an increase of over 65 percent from the $600 million spent to provide legal representation to the poor in 1982.

Programs providing assistance of counsel to indigent defendants can be divided into three major categories: public defender systems, assigned counsel systems, and contract systems. In addition, other approaches to the delivery of legal services include the use of mixed systems, such as representation by both the public defender and the private bar, law school clinical programs, and prepaid legal services. Of the three major approaches, assigned counsel systems dominate defender programs, with about 60 percent of U.S. courts using this method. Thirty-four percent use public defenders, and 6 percent employ contract attorneys (see Figure 11.3).[46] Although many jurisdictions have a combination of these programs, public defender programs seem to be on the increase.

Public Defenders. Approximately eleven hundred public defender offices are located in about 37 percent of the counties in the United States.[47] However, since public defender services are housed in forty-three of the fifty largest counties,

FIGURE 11.3
Indigent Criminal Defense Systems in the United States

SOURCE: Carla Gaskins. *Criminal Defense for the Poor—1986* (Washington, D.C.: Bureau of Justice Statistics, September 1988).

State defense systems, by type
In majority of counties, 1986

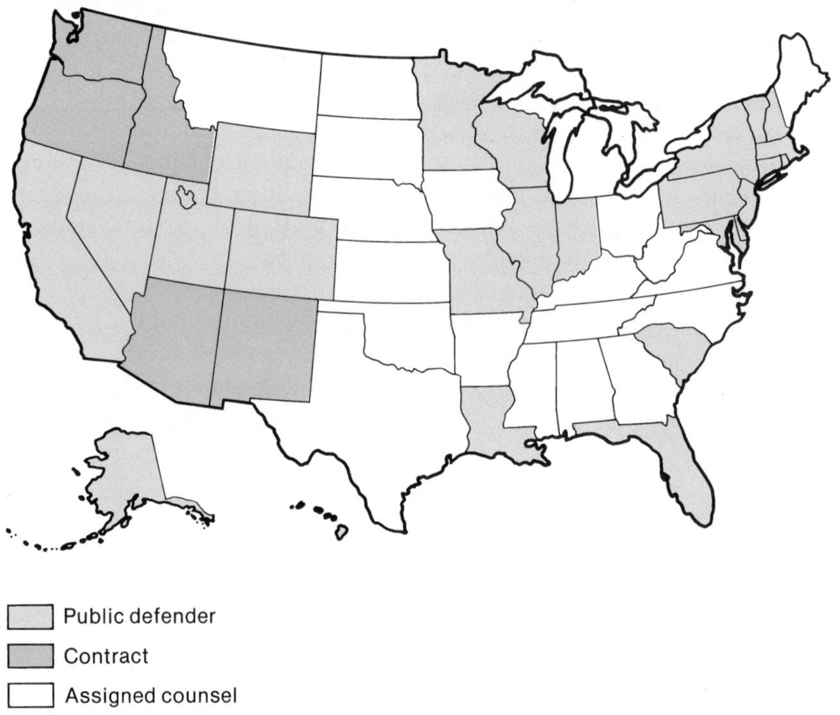

they serve a majority (68 percent) of the population; all but two states (Maine and North Dakota) have some form of public defender services.

The first public defender program in the United States opened in 1913 in Los Angeles. Over the years, primarily as a result of efforts by judicial leaders and bar groups, the public defender program became the model for the delivery of legal services to indigent defendants in criminal cases throughout the country.

Most public defender offices can be thought of as law firms whose only clients are criminal offenders. However, there is a major division in the administration of public defender services. Sixteen states, including Connecticut, Colorado, and Wyoming, have a statewide public defender's office headed by a chief public defender who administers the operation. In some of these states, the chief defender establishes offices in all counties around the state, while in others, the chief defender relies on part-time private attorneys to provide indigent legal services in rural counties. Statewide public defenders are organized as either part of the judicial branch, as part of the executive branch, as an independent state agency, or even as a private, nonprofit organization.

In the remaining thirty-two states, the public defender's office is organized on the county level of government, and each office is autonomous. For example, in Florida, elected public defenders operate separately in each of the twenty judicial circuits in the state. In Pennsylvania, a local public defender is legislatively mandated in each of the state's sixty-seven counties. In Illinois, each county with a population over thirty thousand has a legislatively mandated public defender's office.

Major changes have recently occurred in indigent services in such states as Massachusetts, Minnesota, and New Hampshire, where state-funded public defender programs are made available to all counties in each state. In South Carolina, each county is represented by an independent public defender program.[48] Oklahoma created a state indigent defense system in 1990, highlighted by the establishment of a statewide board administered by an executive director, an updated delivery system, services at the trial and appellate levels, and access to post-conviction relief [appeals] for all poor people accused of crimes. The Oklahoma program is funded by a surcharge on every fee assessed in adult and juvenile criminal cases.[49]

Assigned Counsel System. In contrast to the public defender system, the assigned counsel system involves the use of private attorneys appointed by the court to represent indigent defendants. The private attorney is selected from a list of attorneys established by the court and is reimbursed by the state for any legal services rendered to the client. Today, about 60 percent of all counties, containing 27 percent of the U.S. population, use an assigned counsel system. Assigned counsels are usually used in rural areas, which do not have sufficient criminal caseloads to justify a full-time public defender staff. Only two states, Maine and North Dakota, use predominantly assigned counsel in all jurisdictions.

There are two main types of assigned counsel systems. In the first, which makes up about 75 percent of all assigned counsel systems, the presiding judge appoints attorneys on a case-by-case basis; this is referred to as an **ad hoc assigned counsel system.** In a **coordinated assigned counsel system,** an administrator oversees the appointment of counsel and sets up guidelines for the adminsitration of indigent legal services. The fees awarded assigned counsels can vary widely, ranging from a low of $10 per hour in South Carolina for handling a misdemeanor out of court to a high of $104 per hour for a serious felony handled in court in California. Some jurisdictions may establish a maximum allowance per case of $750 for a misdemeanor and $1,500 for a felony. Average rates seem to be between forty and eighty dollars per hour, depending on the nature of the case. Proposals for higher rates are pending. One court has already concluded that caps on legal fees for appointed counsel are an unconstitutional infringement on the services of an attorney.[50] Restructuring the attorney fee system is undoubtedly needed to maintain fair standards for the payment of such legal services.

The assigned counsel system, unless organized properly, suffers from such problems as unequal assignments, inadequate legal fees, and the lack of supportive or supervisory services. Other disadvantages are the frequent use of inexperienced attorneys and the tendency to use the guilty plea too quickly. Some judicial experts believe the assigned counsel system is still no more than an ad hoc approach that presents serious questions about the quality of representation. However, the assigned counsel system is simple to operate.[51] It also offers the private bar an important role in providing indigent legal services, since most public defender systems cannot represent all needy criminal defendants. Thus, the appointed counsel system gives attorneys the opportunity to do criminal defense work.

Contract System. The **contract system** is a relative newcomer to providing legal services to the indigent; it is being used in 11 percent (330) of the counties around the United States. In this system, a block grant is given to a lawyer or law firm to handle indigent defense cases. In some instances, the attorney is given a set amount of money and is required to handle all cases assigned. In other jurisdictions, contract lawyers agree to provide legal representation for a set number of cases at a fixed fee. A third system involves representation at an estimated cost per case until the dollar amount of the contract is reached. At that point, the contract may be renegotiated, but the lawyers are not obligated to take new cases. The contract program payment method has recently come under attack by state courts claiming that assigning indigent defense services to the lowest bidder violates the Fifth and Sixth Amendments of the U.S. Constitution.[52]

The contract system is used quite often in counties that also have public defenders. Such counties may need independent counsel when a conflict of interests arises or when there is a constant overflow of cases. It is also used in sparsely populated states that cannot justify the structure and costs of full-time public defender programs. Pauline Houlden and Steven Balkin recently found that contract attorneys were at least as effective as assigned counsel and were most cost-effective.[53] The per-case cost in any jurisdiction for indigent defense services is determined largely by the type of program offered. In most public defender programs, funds are obtained through annual appropriations; assigned counsel costs relate to legal charges for appointed counsel, and contract programs negotiate a fee for the entire service. No research currently available indicates which method is the most effective way to represent the indigent on a cost-per-case basis. However, Lawrence Spears reports that North Dakota adopted the contract model in 1990 with much success. Advantages include the provision of comprehensive legal services, controlled costs, and improved coordination in counsel programs.[54]

Mixed Systems. A mixed system uses both public defenders and private attorneys in an attempt to draw on the strengths of both. In this approach, the public defender system operates simultaneously with the assigned counsel system or contract system to offer total coverage to the indigent defendant. This need occurs when the caseload increases beyond the capacity of the public defender's office. In addition, many counties (34 percent) supply independent counsel to all co-defendants in a single case to prevent a conflict of interest. In most others, separate counsel will be provided if a co-defendant requests it or if the judge or public defender perceives a conflict of interest. Since all lawyers in a public defender's office are considered to be working for the same firm, outside counsel is required if co-defendants are in conflict with one another. It is estimated that 60 percent of all counties having public defenders also have a program to assign counsel in overflow and conflict-of-interest cases; the cost of this program amounts to 12 percent of the total budget for indigent defense. Public defender services supplemented by contract programs and an assigned counsel system often provide the best model to uphold the Sixth Amendment right to counsel for indigent defendants.

Other methods of providing counsel to the indigent include the use of law school students and prepaid legal service programs (similar to comprehensive medical insurance). Most jurisdictions have a student practice rule of procedure; third-year law school students in clinical programs provide supervised counsel to defendants in nonserious offenses. In *Argersinger v. Hamlin*, Supreme Court Justice William Brennan suggested that law students are an important resource in fulfilling constitutional defense requirements.[55]

In the future, government-prepaid legal service programs may offer criminal defense services, as well as legal aid in civil matters, to the indigent. Federal or state governments may even legislate support for the development of prepaid defense services for persons unable to afford their own attorneys.

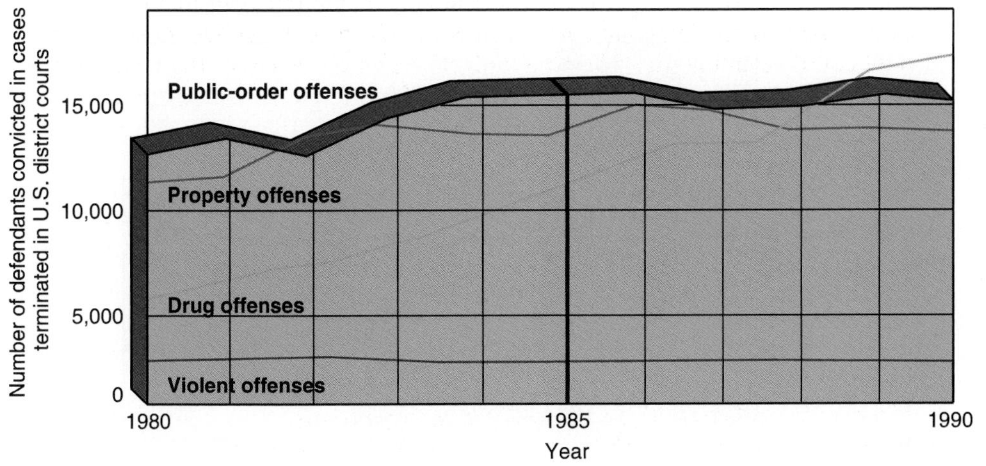

FIGURE 11.4
Number of Federal Offenders Convicted of Drug Offenses, 1980 to 1990 Convictions for federal drug offenses increased 213 percent from 1980 to 1990.

- The number of defendants convicted of federal drug offenses rose from 5,135 in 1980 to 16,077 in 1990.
- About a third of all federal offenders were convicted of drug offenses in 1990.
- Almost half of all federal offenders sentenced to prison in 1990 were convicted of drug offenses.

SOURCE: Bureau of Justice Statistics, *National Update, Federal Criminal Case Processing 1980–1991*, 1 (January 1992).

Costs of Defending the Poor

Over the past decade, the justice system has been faced with extreme pressure to provide counsel for all indigent criminal defendants. Inadequate funding has made implementation of this Sixth Amendment right an impossible task. The chief reasons for underfunded defender programs are: (1) caseload problems; (2) lack of available attorneys; and (3) legislative restraints. Increasing numbers of drug cases, mandatory sentencing, and even overcharging have put tremendous stress on defender services. The number of federal offenders convicted of drug offenses, for instance, has more than doubled from 1980 to 1990 (see Figure 11.4).[56] The system is also overloaded with appeals by indigent defendants convicted at the trial level whose representation involves filing complex briefs and making oral arguments. Such postconviction actions often consume a great deal of time and result in additional backlog problems. Death penalty litigation is another area where legal resources for the poor are strained.

In some jurisdictions, attorneys are just not available to provide defense work. Burnout due to heavy caseloads, low salaries, and poor working conditions are generally the major causes for the limited supply of attorneys interested in representing the indigent defendant. Some attorneys even refuse to accept appointments in criminal cases because the fees are too low.

Lack of government funding is the most significant problem today. While the entire justice system is often underfunded, the prosecutor-defense system is usually in the worse shape. Ordinarily, providing funding for indigent criminal defendants is not the most politically popular thing to do. Edward Monahan, in a recent survey of defender services, illustrates the reality of this situation.[57] In Kentucky, for instance, criminal defense programs receive 0.1 percent of the state budget and 2 percent of the funding for criminal justice agencies. In Alabama, where about $7 million was spent on indigent defense in 1990, it was estimated that over $14 million was really needed. An examination of the Ohio criminal justice system indicates that it overwhelmingly favors corrections versus defense

FIGURE 11.5
Funding for Public Defender Services

SOURCE: Edward C. Monahan, "Who Is Trying to Kill the Sixth Amendment?" *American Bar Association Journal on Criminal Justice* 26:6 (1991):24–28. Reprinted with permission.

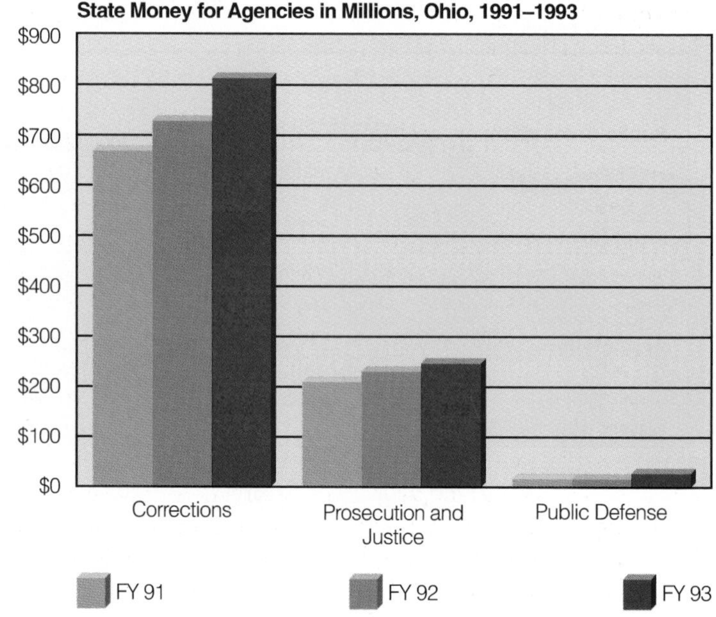

and prosecution services (see Figure 11.5). As a result, demands placed on the system by constitutional requirements are not being completely satisfied.

Obviously, the Sixth Amendment means little without counsel. The constitutional mandate that calls for legal representation requires adequate funding for these services. The National Center for State Courts, the National Legal Aid and Defenders Association, the American Bar Association, and many other legal and citizen groups indicate that the public defender system is losing the battle for funding to the enormous increase in drug cases.[58]

Current funding for defender programs is ordinarily the responsibility of state and local government. As a result of an amendment to the Crime Control Act of 1990, however, federal funds are also available through the Drug Control Act of 1988.[59] According to most experts on defense funding, jurisdictions whose legislatures have been relatively generous in funding such programs in the past have continued to do so, while underfunded programs have become more seriously hampered.

Indigent defense services are a critical component of the justice system. If there is growing disparity in the resources allocated to police, courts, and correctional agencies, then very few cases will go to trial, and most will have to be settled by informal processing, such as plea bargaining or diversion.

The Defense Lawyer as a Professional Advocate

The problems of the criminal bar are numerous. Private attorneys are accused of sacrificing their clients' interests for the pursuit of profit. Many have a bad reputation in the legal community because of their unsavory clientele and reputation as "shysters" who hang out in court hoping for referrals. Attorneys who specialize in criminal work base their reputation on their power and influence. A good reputation is based on the ability to get obviously guilty offenders off on legal technicalities, to arrange the best deal for clients who cannot hope to evade punishment, and to protect criminals whose illegal activities are shocking to many citizens. Consequently, the private criminal attorney is not often held in high esteem by his or her colleagues.

Public defenders are in the unenviable position of being paid by the government, yet acting in the role of the government's adversary. They may be considered at the bottom of the legal profession's hierarchy because they represent clients without social prestige for limited wages.[60] Public defenders are often young attorneys who are seeking trial practice before they go on to high-paying jobs in established law firms. Today, the top-rated firms pay partners around half a million dollars per year, and some New York firms start associates at a salary of sixty-five thousand dollars, far outstripping any income state-compensated attorneys can hope for. In addition, public defenders are forced to work under bureaucratic conditions, which can lead to routine processing of cases. Their large caseloads prevent them from establishing more than a perfunctory relationship with their clients. To keep their caseload under control, they may push for the quickest and easiest solution to a case—plea bargaining.

Assigned counsel and contract attorneys may also be young lawyers just starting out and hoping to build their practice by taking on indigent cases. Since their livelihood depends on getting referrals from the court, public defender, or other governmental body, they risk the problem of conflict of interest. If they pursue too rigorous a defense or handle cases in a way not approved by the presiding judge or other authorities, they might risk being removed from the assigned counsel lists. And, though the fees of an assigned counsel are not as high as those paid the private bar, billings at fifty dollars per hour can mount up significantly in a long felony trial. In a recent Nebraska murder case, the assigned counsels billed a total of $145,000.[61]

Very often, large firms will contribute the services of their newest members for legal aid to indigents, referred to as *pro bono* work. Although such efforts may be made in good spirit, they mean that inexperienced lawyers are handling legal cases in which a person's life may be at stake.

What has emerged is a system in which **plea bargaining** predominates because little time and insufficient recourses are available to give criminal defendants a full-scale defense. Moreover, because prosecutors are under pressure to win their cases, they are often more willing to work out a deal than pursue a case to trial. After all, half a loaf is better than none. Defense attorneys, too, often find it easier to encourage their clients to plead guilty and secure a reduced sentence or probation, rather than seek an acquittal and risk a long prison term.

The Adversary System Reconsidered

These conflicts have helped erode the formal justice process. As you may recall, the formal justice system is based on the adversary system: prosecutors and defense attorneys meet in the arena of the courtroom to do battle over the merits of the case. Through the give and take of the trial process, the truth of the matter becomes known. Guilty defendants are punished and the innocent go free. Yet the U.S. legal system seldom works that way. Because of the pressures faced by defense attorneys and prosecutors, more frequently today the prosecution and defense work together in a spirit of cooperation to get the case over with, rather than to "fight it out," wasting each other's time and risking an outright loss. In the process of this working relationship, the personnel in the courtroom—judge, prosecutor, defense attorney—form working groups that leave the defendant on the outside. Criminal defendants may find that everyone they encounter in the

Attorney competence is a critical issue in the justice system. Here Roy Black addresses perspective jurors in the William Kennedy Smith rape trial. Black's spirited defense helped gain Smith's acquittal.

courtroom seems to be saying "plead guilty," "take the deal," "let's get it over with."

The informal justice system revolves around the common interest of its members to move the case along and settle matters. In today's criminal justice system, defense attorneys share a common history, goals, values, and beliefs with their colleagues in the prosecution. They are alienated by class and social background from the clients they defend. Considering the reality of who commits crime, who are its victims, and who defends, prosecutes, and tries the case, it should not be surprising that the adversary system has suffered.

The Competence of Defense Lawyers

The presence of competent and effective counsel has long been a basic principle of the adversary system. With the Sixth Amendment's guarantee of counsel for virtually all defendants, the performance of today's attorneys has come into question.

Inadequacy of counsel may occur in a variety of instances. The attorney may refuse to meet regularly with his or her client, fail to cross-examine key government witnesses, or fail to investigate the case properly. A defendant's plea of guilty may be based on poor advice, where the attorney may misjudge the admissibility of evidence. When co-defendants have separate counsel, conflicts of interest between the defense attorneys may arise. On an appellate level, the lawyer may decline to file a brief, instead relying on a brief submitted for one of the co-appellants. Such problems as these are being raised with increasing frequency.

The U.S. Supreme Court dealt with the issue of conflict of interest between defense lawyers in ***Burger v. Kemp*** (1987).[62] Two defendants charged with murder were represented by law partners. Each defendant was tried separately, but the attorneys conferred and assisted each other in the trial process. One defendant, who was found guilty and sentenced to death, claimed ineffective legal representation because he believed his attorney failed to present mitigating circumstances to show that he was less culpable than the co-defendant. But the Supreme Court said this view was unfounded because the defendant claiming the conflict of interest actually perpetrated the crime. The Court also said it is not per se a violation of constitutional guarantees of effective assistance of counsel when a single attorney represents two defendants or when two partners supplement one another in the trial defense.

Even a legally competent attorney sometimes makes mistakes that can prejudice a case against his or her client. For example, in ***Taylor v. Illinois*** (1988), a defense lawyer sprung a surprise witness against the prosecution. The judge ruled the witness out of order (invoking the **surprise witness rule**), thereby depriving the defendant of valuable testimony and evidence.[63] The Supreme Court affirmed the conviction despite the defense attorney's error in judgment because the judge had correctly ruled that surprising the prosecutor was not legally defensible.

The key issue is the level of competence that should be required of defense counsel in criminal cases. This question concerns appointed counsel, as well as counsel chosen by the accused. Some appellate court decisions have overturned lower court convictions when it was judged that the performance of counsel had reduced the trial to a farce or a mockery. Other appellate courts have held that there was ineffective counsel where gross incompetence had the effect of eliminating the basis for a substantial defense.

In recent years, the courts have adopted a **reasonable competence standard,** but differences exist on the formulation and application of this standard. For example, is it necessary for defense counsel to answer on appeal every nonfrivolous issue requested by his or her convicted client? What if counsel does not provide the court with all the information at the sentencing stage and the defendant feels counsel's performance is inadequate? Whether any of these instances is an appropriate situation for stating that counsel is incompetent requires court review. In other words, while there may be general agreement regarding the use of the reasonable competence standard, a defendant must demonstrate that counsel has substantially departed from the standard governing his or her performance. In addition, it may also be necessary to prove prejudice to the defendant.

Defining Attorney Competence

The concept of attorney competence was defined by the U.S. Supreme Court in the case of ***Strickland v. Washington*** in 1984.[64] Strickland had been arrested for committing a string of extremely serious crimes, including murder, torture, and kidnapping. Against his lawyer's advice, Strickland pleaded guilty and threw himself on the mercy of the trial judge at a capital sentencing hearing. He also ignored his attorney's recommendation that he exercise his right to have an advisory jury at his sentencing hearing.

In preparing for the hearing, the lawyer spoke with Strickland's wife and mother but did not otherwise seek character witnesses. Nor was a psychiatric examination requested since, in the attorney's opinion, Strickland did not have psychological problems. The attorney also did not ask for a presentence investigation because he felt such a report would contain information damaging to his client.

Though the presiding judge had a reputation for leniency in cases where the defendant confessed, he sentenced Strickland to death. Strickland appealed on the grounds that his attorney had rendered ineffective counsel, citing his failure to seek psychiatric testimony and present character witnesses.

The case eventually went to the Supreme Court, which upheld Strickland's sentence. The justices found that a defendant's claim of attorney incompetence must have two components. First, the defendant must show that the counsel's performance was deficient and that such serious errors were made as to eliminate the presence of counsel guaranteed by the Sixth Amendment. Second, the defendant must also show that the deficient performance prejudiced the case to an extent that the defendant was deprived of a fair trial (that is, a trial with reliable results). In the case at hand, the Court found insufficient evidence that the attorney had acted beyond the boundaries of professional competence. Though the strategy he had adopted might not have been the best one possible, it certainly was not unreasonable, considering minimum standards of professional competence.

The Court recognized the defense attorney's traditional role as an advocate of the defendant's cause, which includes such duties as consulting on important decisions, keeping the client informed of important developments, bringing knowledge and skill to the trial proceeding, and making the trial a reliable adversary proceeding. Yet the Court found that a mechanical set of rules that define competency would be unworkable.

Developing a workable standard, however, is solving only half the problems. According to Judge Irving Kaufman of the U.S. Court of Appeals, an influential spokesman on judicial issues, competency of counsel at all stages of the criminal process, particularly at trial, is an elusive concept, and remedies must be adopted to reduce the claims of inadequate representation.[65]

Postconviction review by the appellate courts is one approach, but this has limitations because the appellate judge cannot get a full picture of trial counsel's performance from the record. Counsel's knowledge of the law, ability to handle legal issues, and capacity to conduct effective examination of witnesses cannot be personally observed by the appellate judge. What is needed, according to Judge Kaufman, is more penetrating supervision by the trial judge, a reduction in caseloads, and a review of traditional methods of legal education in criminal law, so that advocacy skills and trial techniques can be developed.[66] Through such efforts, competent counsel in prosecutorial and defense work will help the adversary system arrive at the truth and produce fairer trials.[67]

Relations between Prosecutor and Defense Attorney

In the final analysis, the competency of the prosecutor and the defense attorney depends on their willingness to work together in the interest of the client, the criminal justice system, and the rest of society. Serious adversarial conflicts have arisen between both in recent years. The prosecutor, for instance, should exercise discretion in seeking to subpoena other lawyers to testify about any relationship with their clients. Although not all communication between a lawyer and his or her client is privileged, confidential information entrusted to a lawyer is ordinarily not available for prosecutorial investigation. Often, however, overzealous prosecutors try to use their subpoena power against lawyers whose clients are involved in drug or organized crime cases in order to obtain as much evidence as possible. As a result, prosecutors interested in confidential information about defendants have subpoenaed lawyers to testify against them. Court approval should be needed before a lawyer is forced to give information about a client. Otherwise, the defendant is really not receiving his or her right to effective legal counsel under the Sixth Amendment. In addition, prosecutors should refrain from using their grand jury subpoena power to obtain information from private investigators employed by the defense attorney. Judicial remedies for violations of these rules often include suppression of subpoenaed evidence and even dismissal of a criminal indictment.

By the same token, some criminal lawyers ignore situations where a client informs them of his or her intention to commit perjury. The purpose of the defense attorney's investigation is to learn the truth from the client. The defense attorney also has a professional responsibility to persuade the defendant not to commit perjury, which is a crime.

While it is the duty of the prosecutor to seek justice, and not merely to obtain a conviction, this goal also applies to the criminal defense attorney. As legal scholar David G. Bress so aptly stated twenty-five years ago, "A defense attorney does not promote the attainment of justice when he secures his client's freedom through illegal and improper means."[68] This warning is equally accurate today.

SUMMARY

The judge, the prosecutor, and the defense attorney are the major officers of justice in the judicial system. The judge approves plea bargains, tries cases, and determines the sentence given the offender. The prosecutor, who is the people's attorney, has discretion to decide the criminal charge and disposition. The prosecutor's daily decisions significantly impact police and court operations.

The role of the defense attorney in the criminal justice system has grown dramatically during the past thirty years. Today, providing defense services to the indigent criminal defendant is an everyday practice. Under landmark decisions of the U.S. Supreme Court, particularly *Gideon v. Wainwright* and *Argersinger v. Hamlin*, all defendants who may be imprisoned for any offense must be afforded counsel at trials. Methods of providing counsel include systems for assigned counsel, where an attorney is selected by the court to represent the accused, and public defender programs, where public employees provide legal services. Lawyers doing criminal defense work have discovered an increasing need for their services, not only at trial, but also at the pre- and postjudicial stages of the criminal justice system. Consequently, the issue of their competency has become an important one for judicial authorities. The prosecutor and the defense attorney are the principle adversaries in the courtroom because they represent the public and the accused. How they fulfill their respective roles and responsibilities all too often reflects society's fundamental ability to control crime and the public's perception of the justice system.

QUESTIONS

1. Should attorneys disclose information given them by their clients concerning participation in an earlier unsolved crime?
2. Should defense attorneys cooperate with a prosecutor if it means that their clients will go to jail?
3. Should a prosecutor have absolute discretion over which cases to proceed on and which to drop?
4. Should clients be made aware of an attorney's track record in court?
5. Does the assigned counsel system present an inherent conflict of interest since attorneys are hired and paid by the institution they are to oppose?
6. Which kind of cases do you think are most likely to be handled informally?
7. Do you believe prosecutors have a great deal of discretion? Why?

NOTES

1. American Bar Association, *Code of Professional Responsibility* (Chicago: American Bar Association, 1970), p. 87; John Jay Douglas, *Ethical Issues in Prosecution* (Houston: University of Houston Law Center, National College of District Attorneys, 1988); National District Attorneys Association, *National Prosecution Standards*, 2d ed. (Alexandria, Va.: National District Attorneys Association, 1991).

2. *Berger v. United States*, 295 U.S. 78, 88, 55 S.Ct. 629, 633, 79 L.Ed. 1314 (1935).

3. See Bennett Gershman, "Why Prosecutors Misbehave," *Criminal Law Bulletin* 22 (1986):131–43.

4. American Bar Association, *Model Rules of Professional Conduct* (Chicago: American Bar Association, 1981), Rule 3.8; see also Stanley Fisher, "In Search of the Virtuous Prosecutor: A Conceptual Framework," *American Journal of Criminal Law* 15 (1988):197.

5. Stanley Fisher, "Zealousness and Overzealousness: Making Sense of the Prosecutor's Duty to Seek Justice," *Prosecutor* 22 (1989):9; see also Bruce Green, "The Ethical Prosecutor and the Adversary System," *Criminal Law Bulletin* 24 (1988):126–45.

6. American Bar Association, *Standards Relating to the Prosecution Function and Defense Function* (New York: Institute of Judicial Administration, 1971), pp. 18–19. Reprinted with the permission of the American Bar Association, which authored these standards and holds the copyright.

7. Michael Benson, Francis Cullan, and William Maakestad, "Local Prosecutors and Corporate Crime," *Crime and Delinquency* 36 (July 1990):356–72.

8. "NDAA Establishes Environmental Center," *National District Attorneys Association Bulletin* 10 (October 1991):1; Marcia Chaiken and Jan Chaiken, *Priority Prosecutors of High-Rate Dangerous Offenders* (Washington, D.C.: National Institute of Justice, 1991).

9. "Litigator's Legacy," *Wall Street Journal*, 11 January 1989, p. 1; Selwyn Raab, "A Battered and Ailing Mafia Is Losing Its Grip on America," *New York Times*, 22 October 1990, p. 1.

10. See, generally, Gerard O'Neill and Dick Lehr, *The Underboss—The Rise and Fall of a Mafia Family* (New York: St. Martin's Press, 1989).

11. Kevin Cullen, "Gotti v. U.S.—Round 4 Could Be His Last," *Boston Globe*, 20 January 1992, p. 1.

12. National Advisory Commission on Criminal Justice Standards and Goals, *Courts* (Washington, D.C.: U.S. Government Printing Office, 1973), p. 439.

13. Kenneth C. Davis, *Discretionary Justice* (Baton Rouge: Louisiana State University Press, 1969), p. 180; see also James B. Stewart, *The Prosecutor* (New York: Simon and Schuster, 1987).

14. Barbara Boland, *The Prosecution of Felony Arrests* (Washington, D.C.: U.S. Government Printing Office, 1983).

15. Newman Baker, "The Prosecutor—Initiation of Prosecution," *Journal of Criminal Law, Criminology, and Police Science* 23 (1933):770–71; see also Joan Jacoby, *The American Prosecutor: A Search for Identity* (Lexington, Mass.: Lexington Books, 1980).

16. See, generally, W. Jay Merrill, Marie N. Malks, and Mark Sendrow, *Case Screening and Selected Case Processing in Prosecutor's Offices* (Washington, D.C.: National Institute of Law Enforcement and Criminal Justice, March 1973).

17. Frank W. Miller, *Prosecution: The Decision to Charge a Suspect with a Crime* (Boston: Little, Brown & Co., 1970).

18. Boland, *Prosecution of Felony Arrests*.

19. President's Commission on Law Enforcement and the Administration of Justice, *Task Force Report: The Courts* (Washington, D.C.: U.S. Government Printing Office, 1967), pp. 8–9.

20. American Bar Association, *Standards Relating to the Prosecution Function and Defense Function*, Standard 3.8, p. 33.

21. See, generally, "Pretrial Diversion from the Criminal Process," *Yale Law Journal* 83 (1974):827.

22. Charles D. Breitel, "Controls in Criminal Law Enforcement," *University of Chicago Law Review* 27 (1960):427.

23. Roscoe Pound, "Discretion, Dispensation, and Mitigation: The Problem of the Individual Special Case," *New York University Law Review* 35 (1960):925; "Unleashing the Prosecutor's Discretion: *United States v. Goodwin*," *American Criminal Law Review* 20 (1983):507.

24. 480 U.S. 386, 107 S.Ct. 1187, 94 L.Ed.2d 405 (1987).

25. National District Attorneys Association, *National Prosecution Standards*.

26. 395 U.S. 711, 89 S.Ct. 2072, 23 L.Ed.2d 656 (1969).

27. 417 U.S. 21, 94 S.Ct. 2098, 40 L.Ed.2d 628 (1974).

28. 434 U.S. 357, 98 S.Ct. 663, 54 L.Ed.2d 604 (1978).

29. 457 U.S. 368, 102 S.Ct. 2485, 73 L.Ed.2d 74 (1982).

30. ___ U.S. ___, 111 S.Ct. 1934, 114 L.Ed.2d 547 (1991).

31. President's Commission on Law Enforcement and the Administration of Justice, *The Challenge of Crime in a Free Society* (Washington, D.C.: U.S. Government Printing Office, 1968), p. 150; American Bar Association, *Report of Standing Committee on Legal Aid and Indigent Defendants*, (Chicago: American Bar Association, 1991).

32. See American Bar Association, *Code of Professional Responsibility*, p. 81.

33. Monroe H. Freedman, "Professional Responsibility of the Criminal Defense Lawyer: The Three Hardest Questions," *Michigan Law Review* 64 (1966):1468.

34. Bennett Brummer, *Ethics Resource Guide for Public Defenders* (Chicago: American Bar Association February 1992).

35. The Sixth Amendment provides: "In all criminal prosecutions, the accused shall enjoy the right . . . to have the assistance of counsel for his defense."

36. 372 U.S. 335, 83 S.Ct. 792, 9 L.Ed.2d 799 (1963).

37. 407 U.S. 25, 92 S.Ct. 2006, 32 L.Ed.2d 530 (1972).

38. See Sheldon Krantz et al., *The Right to Counsel in Criminal Cases: The Mandate of Argersenger v. Hamlin* (Washington, D.C.: National Institute of Justice, March 1976).

39. 384 U.S. 436, 86 S.Ct. 1602, 16 L.Ed.2d 694 (1966).

40. *Mempa v. Rhay*, 389 U.S. 128, 88 S.Ct. 254, 19 L.Ed.2d 336 (1967).

41. *Douglas v. California*, 372 U.S. 353, 83 S.Ct. 814, 9 L.Ed.2d 811 (1963).

42. *In re Gault*, 387 U.S. 1, 875 S.Ct. 1428, 18 L.Ed.2d 527 (1967).

43. *Specht v. Patterson*, 386 U.S. 605, 87 S.Ct. 1209, 18 L.Ed.2d 326 (1967).

44. President's Commission on Law Enforcement and the Administration of Justice, *The Challenge of Crime in a Free Society*, p. 152.

45. See F. Brownell, *Legal Aid in the United States* (Chicago: National Legal Aid and Defender Association, 1961); for an interesting study of Cook County, Illinois, Office of Public Defenders, see Lisa McIntyre, *Public Defenders—Practice of Law in Shadows of Dispute* (Chicago: University of Chicago Press, 1987).

46. Carla Gaskins, *Criminal Defense for the Poor—1986* (Washington, D.C.: Bureau of Justice Statistics, September 1988), p. 2.

47. Ibid, pp. 1–8.

48. Ibid, p. 7.

49. John Arango, "Defense Services for the Poor," *American Bar Association Journal on Criminal Justice*, 6 (1991):48.

50. See the case of *State ex rel. Stephan v. Smith*, 242 Kan. 336, 747 P.2d 816 (1987).

51. Note, "Providing Counsel for the Indigent Accused: The Criminal Justice Act," *American Criminal Law Review* 12 (1975):794.

52. See *State v. Smith*, 140 Ariz. 355, 681 P.2d 1374 (1984).

53. Pauline Houlden and Steven Balkin, "Quality and Cost Comparisons of Private Bar Indigent Defense Systems: Contract vs. Ordered Assigned Counsel," *Journal of Criminal Law and Criminology* 76 (1985):176–200.

54. Lawrence Spears, "Contract Counsel: A Different Way to Defend the Poor—How It's Working in North Dakota," *American Bar Association Journal on Criminal Justice* 6 (1991):24–31.

55. 407 U.S. 25, 92 S.Ct. 2006, 32 L.Ed.2d 530 (1972).

56. Bureau of Justice Statistics, *National Update* (Washington, D.C.: Office of Justice Programs, January 1991), p. 5.

57. Edward Monahan, "Who Is Trying to Kill the Sixth Amendment?" *American Bar Association Journal on Criminal Justice* 6 (1991):24–28.
58. Timothy Murphy, "Indigent Defense and the War on Drugs—The Public Defender's Losing Battle," *American Bar Association Journal on Criminal Justice* 6 (1991):14–20.
59. See Drug Control Act of 1988, 42 U.S.C. §375(G)(10).
60. J. P. Heinz and E. O. Laumann, *Chicago Lawyers: The Social Structure of the Bar* (New York: Russell Sage Foundation, 1983).
61. "Judge, 8 Attorneys in Rulo Case Dispute Review of Fee Payment," *Omaha World Herald,* 19 May 19 1986.
62. 483 U.S. 776, 107 S.Ct. 3114, 97 L.Ed.2d 638 (1987).
63. 484 U.S. 400, 108 S.Ct. 646, 98 L.Ed.2d 798 (1988).
64. 466 U.S. 668, 104 S.Ct. 2052, 80 L.Ed.2d 674 (1984).
65. Irving Kaufman, "Attorney Incompetence: A Plea for Reform," *American Bar Association Journal* 69 (1983):308.
66. Ibid., at p. 311.
67. See *Culver v. Sullivan*, 446 U.S. 335, 100 S.Ct. 1708, 64 L.Ed.2d 333 (1980), where a state prisoner sought habeas corpus relief by showing that counsel represented a potential conflicting interest, but he did not prevail.
68. David G. Bress, "Professional Ethics in Criminal Trials," *Michigan Law Review* 64 (1966):1493; John Mitchell, "The Ethics of the Criminal Defense Attorney," *Stanford Law Review* 32 (1980):325.

CHAPTER 12

Pretrial Procedures

OUTLINE

KEY TERMS

pretrial procedures
booking
complaint
initial hearing
indictment
grand jury
preliminary hearing
probable cause hearing
nolo contendere
bail
bail bonding
deposit bail
release on recognizance (ROR)
Manhattan Bail Project
Bail Reform Act of 1966
Bail Reform Act of 1984
pretrial detention
pretrial detainees
presentment
subpoena
true bill
no bill
waiver
plea bargaining
Boykin v. Alabama
Santobello v. New York
diversion
continuance
widen the net

Between arrest and trial occurs a series of events that are critical links in the chain of justice. These include arraignments, grand jury investigations, bail hearings, plea bargaining negotiations, and predisposition treatment efforts. These **pretrial procedures** are critically important components of the justice process because the *great majority* of all criminal cases are resolved informally at this stage and never come before the courts. Although television and the media like to focus on the elaborate jury trial with its dramatic elements and impressive setting, formal criminal trials are relatively infrequent. The adversary system is not a myth, but the social reality of justice in the United States is that it is more often handled than fought over. Consequently, understanding the events that take place during the pretrial period is essential to grasp the reality of criminal justice policy.

Cases are settled during the pretrial stage in a number of ways. Prosecutors can use their discretion to drop cases before formal charges are filed because of insufficient evidence, office policy, witness conflicts, or similar problems. Even if charges are filed, the prosecutor can decide not to proceed against the defendant (*nolle prosequi*) because of a change in the circumstances of the case.

In addition, the prosecution and the defense almost always meet to try to arrange a nonjudicial settlement for the case. Plea bargaining, in which the defendant exchanges a guilty plea for some consideration such as a reduced sentence, is commonly used to terminate the formal processing of the case. The prosecution and/or the defense may believe, for example, that a trial is not in the best interests of the victim, the defendant, or society because the defendant is physically or emotionally incapable of understanding the charges or controlling his or her behavior. In this instance, the defendant may have a competency hearing before a judge and be placed in a secure treatment facility until ready to stand trial. Or the prosecutor may waive further action so that the defendant can be placed in a special treatment program, such as a detoxification unit at a local hospital.

Students must be aware of the pretrial stage of justice not only because so many cases are dealt with at this time but also because the procedures used are often insulated from external scrutiny. That is, deals are made and decisions are reached in secret, often with little regard for the public's will or the defendant's rights.

Procedures Following Arrest

After arrest, the accused is ordinarily taken to the police station, where the police list the possible criminal charges against him or her and obtain other information for **booking** purposes. This may include a description of the suspect and the circumstances of the offense. The suspect may then be fingerprinted, photographed, and required to participate in a lineup. During this stage, the police will compile additional information on the suspect that can have little to do with the charge for which he or she was arrested. For example, a person picked up in a break-in may admit to committing other burglaries, or witnesses brought in to view suspects may implicate them in additional crimes. All this information is then turned over to the prosecutor who has jurisdiction in the case for possible legal action.

Misdemeanor Procedures

Individuals arrested on a misdemeanor charge are ordinarily released from the police station on their own recognizance to answer the criminal charge before the court at a later date. They are usually detained by the police until it is decided whether a criminal complaint will be filed. The **complaint** is the formal written document identifying the criminal charge, the date and place where the crime occurred, and the circumstances of the arrest. The complaint is sworn to and signed under oath by the complainant, usually a police officer. The complaint will request that the defendant be present at an **initial hearing** held soon after the arrest was made; in some jurisdictions, this may be referred to by other names, such as "arraignment." The defendant may plead guilty at the initial hearing, and the case may be disposed of immediately. Defendants who plead not guilty to a minor offense are informed of the formal charge, provided with counsel if they are unable to afford a private attorney, and asked to plead guilty or not guilty as charged. A date in the near future is set for trial, and the defendants are generally released on bail or on their own recognizance to await trial.

Felony Procedures

Where a felony or more serious crime is involved, the U.S. Constitution requires an intermediate step before a person can be tried. This involves proving to an objective body that there is probable cause to believe that a crime has taken place and that the accused should be tried on the matter. This step of the formal charging process is ordinarily an **indictment** from a **grand jury** or an *information* issued by a lower court. An indictment is a written accusation charging a person with a crime that is drawn up by a prosecutor and submitted to a grand jury. The grand jury, after considering the evidence presented by the prosecutor, votes to endorse or deny the indictment. An information is a charging document drawn up by a prosecutor in jurisdictions that do not employ the grand jury system. The information is brought before a lower-court judge in a **preliminary hearing** (sometimes called a **probable cause hearing**). The purpose of this hearing is to require the prosecutor to present the case so that the judge can determine whether the defendant should be held to answer for the charge in a felony court.

After an indictment or information is filed, the accused is brought before the trial court for arraignment, during which the judge informs the defendant of the charge, ensures that the accused is properly represented by counsel, and determines whether he or she should be released on bail or some other form of release pending a hearing or trial.

The defendant who is arraigned on an indictment or information can ordinarily plead guilty, not guilty, or ***nolo contendere,*** which is equivalent to a guilty plea but cannot be used as evidence against the defendant in a civil case on the same matter. For example, a plea of *nolo contendere* in a rape case could not be used as an admission of guilt if the offender is later sued for damages by the victim.

Where a guilty plea is entered, the defendant admits to all the elements of the crime, and the court begins a review of the person's background for sentencing purposes. A plea of not guilty sets the stage for a trial on the merits or for negotiations, known as plea bargaining, between the prosecutor and the defense attorney.

Before discussing these issues, it is important to address the question of pretrial release and bail, which may arise at the police station, at the initial court appearance in a misdemeanor, or at the arraignment in most felony cases.

Pretrial Services

As we have described, many jurisdictions today are faced with significant increases in criminal cases, particularly those involving drugs. The police have responded with an unprecedented number of arrests, which has clogged an already overburdened jail system. Of these arrestees, the justice system must determine which can safely be released pending trial. Pretrial services help courts deal with this problem.

Often, there is some confusion about the meaning of "pretrial services." According to D. Alan Henry, director of the Pretrial Services Resources Center, pretrial services are those practices and programs that screen arrestees to provide the bail-setting magistrate concise summaries of the arrestees' personal background as it relates to bail.[1] This definition is distinguished from *diversion,* in which criminal prosecution is bypassed for alternative measures, such as treatment or counseling; diversion is discussed at the end of this chapter.

Pretrial service programs seek to:

1. Improve the release/detention decision process in criminal courts by providing complete, accurate, nonadversarial information to judicial officers;
2. Identify those for whom alternative forms of supervision may be more appropriate than incarceration; and
3. Monitor released pretrial arrestees to ensure they comply with the conditions of release imposed by the judicial officer for the benefit of public safety.[2]

Virtually all jurisdictions in the United States have pretrial release in one form or another. Court-administered programs comprise the greatest percentage of pretrial programs (38 percent), while probation-administered programs constitute the next largest segment (24 percent). The general criteria used to assess eligibility for release center around the defendant's community ties and prior criminal justice involvement. According to a 1991 report prepared by the National Association of Pretrial Services, over three-quarters of the programs in the United States have a wide variety of release options.[3] Many jurisdictions have conditional and supervised release and third-party custody release, in addition to release on a person's own recognizance.

In recent years, many states have also begun to rely on programs to detect illicit drug use by defendants. The aim is to provide a judge with an objective measure of a defendant's drug use for pretrial release determination and to serve as a tool for controlling possible misconduct during the pretrial release period. A recent demonstration program of mandatory drug testing of criminal defendants in eight federal judicial districts revealed that over 31 percent of the defendants who submitted to urinalysis provided positive samples.[4] Judges and magistrates generally believe that pretrial drug testing is a very valuable tool in implementing the statutory requirements of any pretrial release program. Any expansion of drug testing as part of the pretrial decision making, however, would obviously result in considerable additional cost for the criminal justice system.

Effective pretrial release programs benefit the justice system in many ways. Judicial officers are able to make more effective decisions about who may be released safely. The compliance of pretrial arrestees with their conditions of release can be monitored. In addition, pretrial programs can operate at different stages of the judicial process, thereby increasing the number of release options available to the courts. Table 12.1 shows an extensive list of such pretrial release mechanisms.

Bail

Bail is money or some other security provided to the court to ensure the appearance of the defendant at every subsequent stage of the criminal justice process. Its purpose is to obtain the release from custody of a person charged with a crime. Once the amount of bail is set by the court, the defendant is required to deposit all or a percentage of the entire amount in cash or security (or to pay a professional bonding agent to submit a bond). If the defendant is released on bail but fails to appear in court at the stipulated time, the bail deposit is forfeited. A defendant who fails to make bail is confined in jail until the court appearance.

The Legal Right to Bail

The Eighth Amendment to the U.S. Constitution does not guarantee a constitutional right to bail but rather prohibits "excessive bail." Since many state statutes place no precise limit on the amount of bail a judge may impose, many defendants who cannot make bail are placed in detention while awaiting trial. It has become apparent over the years that the bail system is discriminatory because defendants who are financially well-off are able to make bail, while indigent defendants languish in pretrial detention in the county jail. In addition, keeping a person in jail imposes serious financial burdens on local and state governments—and, in turn, taxpayers—who must pay for the cost of confinement. These factors have given rise to bail reform programs that depend on the defendant's personal promise to appear in court for trial (recognizance), rather than on financial ability to meet bail. While these reforms have enabled many deserving but indigent offenders to go free, another trend has been to deny people bail on the grounds that they are a danger to themselves or others in the community.

The Eighth Amendment restriction on excessive bail may also be interpreted to mean that the sole purpose of bail is to ensure that the defendant return for trial; bail may not be used as a form of punishment, nor may it be used to coerce or threaten a defendant. In most cases, a defendant has the right to be released on reasonable bail. Many jurisdictions also require a bail review hearing by a higher court in cases in which the initial judge set what might be considered excessive bail.

The U.S. Supreme Court's interpretation of the Eighth Amendment's provisions on bail was set out in the case of *Stack v. Boyle* (1951).[6] Here, the Supreme

TABLE 12.1
Pretrial Release Mechanisms

Stage	
Police	(1) **Field citation release**—An arresting officer releases the arrestee on a written promise to appear in court, at or near the actual time and location of the arrest. This procedure is commonly used for misdemeanor charges and is similar to issuing a traffic ticket.
Police	(2) **Station house citation release**—The determination of an arrestee's eligibility and suitability for release and the actual release of the arrestee are deferred until after he or she has been removed from the scene of an arrest and brought to the station house or police headquarters. Station house release allows the police officer or pretrial services officer to verify the information provided by the arrestee prior to the issuance of a citation and permits the release of an arrestee without booking.
Police/ Pretrial	(3) **Jail citation release**—The determination of an arrestee's eligibility and suitability for citation release and the actual release of the arrestee are deferred until after he or she has been delivered by the arresting department to a jail or other pretrial detention facility for screening, booking, and/or admission.
Pretrial/ Court	(4) **Direct release authority by pretrial program**—To streamline release processes and reduce the length of stay in detention, courts may authorize pretrial programs to release defendants without direct judicial involvement. Where court rule delegates such authority, the practice is generally limited to misdemeanor charges, but felony release authority has been granted in some jurisdictions.
Police/ Court	(5) **Bail schedule**—An arrestee can post bail at the station house or jail according to amounts specified in a bail schedule. The schedule is a list of all bailable charges and a corresponding dollar amount for each. Schedules may vary widely from jurisdiction to jurisdiction. An arrestee may effect release by posting the full amount of bail required or by engaging a bonding agent who will post the bail amount for a fee (usually 10 percent of the total bail).
Court	(6) **Judicial release**—Arrestees who have not been released either by the police or the jailer and who have not posted bail appear at the hearing before a judge, magistrate, or bail commissioner within a set period of time. In jurisdictions with pretrial release programs, program staff often interview arrestees detained at the jail prior to the first hearing, verify the background information, and present recommendations to the court at arraignment. At the arraignment hearing, the judicial officer can authorize a variety of nonfinancial and financial release options.[5]

Court found bail to be a traditional right to freedom before trial that permits unhampered preparation of a defense and prevents the criminal defendant from being punished prior to conviction. The Court held that bail is excessive when it exceeds an amount reasonably calculated to ensure that the defendant will return for trial. The Court indicated that bail should be in the amount that is generally set for similar offenses. Higher bail can be imposed when evidence supporting the increase is presented at a hearing at which the defendant's constitutional rights can be protected. Although *Stack* did not mandate an absolute right to bail, it did set guidelines for state courts to follow: if a crime is bailable, the amount set should not be frivolous, unusual, or beyond a person's ability to pay under similar circumstances.

Receiving Bail

Whether a defendant can be expected to appear at the next stage of the criminal proceeding is a key issue in determining bail. Bail cannot be used to punish an accused, nor can it be denied or revoked at the indulgence of the court. Many experts believe that money bail is one of the most unacceptable aspects of the criminal justice system: it is discriminatory because it works against the poor; it is costly because the government must pay to detain those offenders who are unable to make bail but would otherwise be in the community; it is unfair because a higher proportion of detainees receive longer sentences than people released on bail; and it is dehumanizing because innocent people who cannot make bail suffer in the nation's deteriorated jail system.

Another question is whether discrimination occurs in setting the amount of bail. Are minorities asked to pay larger amounts of bail, increasing the probability they will be detained in jail and receive longer prison sentences upon conviction?

A survey of bail practices in federal courts conducted by William Rhodes sheds some light on this issue.[7] The study found that, contrary to the fears of some critics, little actual relationship exists between the amount of bail and a person's race, age, economic status, and/or other other social variables. Instead, Rhodes found that the amount of bail requested by judges was more closely associated with the seriousness of the offense and the defendant's prior record, two factors that by most legal standards should legitimately influence the bail decision. Rhodes also found significant differences in bail practices within and between legal jurisdictions. This indicates that the probability of making bail is often a function of which judge hears the case and the jurisdiction in which the case is brought to justice. Rhodes's data are important because they show that extralegal factors such as race and social class do not play an important a role in determining bail amounts, as some critics have feared.

The Success of Bail

How successful are bail and pretrial release? The answer depends on your perspective. Mary Toborg evaluated bail procedures in eight urban jurisdictions (including Baltimore, Washington, D.C., Miami, Tucson, Louisville, and San Jose) and found that about 85 percent of all defendants received bail. Of these, about 15 percent did not return for trial because they absconded. An additional 15 percent were rearrested for another crime prior to their trial date. Thus, about 30 percent of those released on bail could be considered failures for one reason or another.[8]

A 1985 study found that about 10 percent of the defendants released by federal trial courts failed to honor their bail; the reasons included rearrest, failure to appear, or violation of the conditions of bail.[9] Those rearrested tended to (1) be on bail longer (nine months or more); (2) have a serious prior record; (3) abuse drugs; (4) have a poor work record; and (5) be disproportionately young, male, and minority-group members.

The differences between the state and federal studies may be attributed to the type of offenders who pass through their jurisdictions. The federal courts probably see more white-collar offenders and fewer violent offenders. Thus, although the state statistics are less than encouraging, the 10 percent failure rate recorded by the federal government indicates that pretrial release has been quite successful in some jurisdictions.

The most recent study of the National Pretrial Reporting Program found that about 24 percent of the released defendants failed to appear in court, while about 18 percent were rearrested for a felony while on pretrial release. These findings were drawn from a sample of felony cases in 1988 representing the seventy-five most populous counties in the United States involving 44,719 defendants, of which over two-thirds, or almost 30,000, were released prior to trial.[10] Some of the conclusions resulting from this important study are that: (1) significant numbers of defendants are given pretrial release; (2) the failure-to-appear rate varied according to the type of arrest charge and the type of release; and (3) defendants in different age groups and those with different criminal backgrounds were rearrested at different rates. The rates of rearrest and of failure to appear, which range from 18 to 24 percent, respectively, are similar to results of previous research in the area. The study presents new and convincing evidence that pretrial release continues to be a successful component in the criminal justice system, providing pivotal services at key stages of the criminal process. To improve success rates, further research is probably needed on the way pretrial personnel and judges handle bail decisions. One such approach to limit disparity and improve decision making is the use of bail guidelines, which is discussed later in this chapter.

Bail Bonding Today

One of the collateral developments of the bail system is the practice of **bail bonding.** For a fee, bonding agents lend money to people who cannot make bail on their own. Powerful ties often exist between bonding agents and the court, with the result that defendants are steered toward particular bonding agents. Charges of kickbacks and cooperation accompany such arrangements. Allegations of corruption associated with the bail-bonding system have long been made. Consequently, five states—Nebraska, Wisconsin, Kentucky, Oregon, and Illinois—have abolished bonding agents at the time of this writing. They have replaced them with bail systems in which the state itself acts as a bonding agency. Defendants put up 10 percent of the total bail but are responsible for paying the entire amount if they abscond, referred to as the "10 percent cash match," or **deposit bail,** system. Nevertheless, an estimated five thousand professional bail bonding agents operate in the United States today.[11] The potential for abuse inherent in the system has led many critics to suggest that in many instances, the traditional bail system is an unsatisfactory pretrial release procedure.[12]

A recent article by D. Alan Henry and Bruce Beaudin supports this recommendation and raises questions about the bail bond system itself. Should the decision of whether to release a defendant before trial be based primarily on money? And, second, should the decision as to release be the responsibility of a nonjudicial officer? On both counts, the authors find virtually all pretrial organizations calling for the elimination of such compensated sureties, particularly where bonding agents are involved.[13]

History of Bail Reform

Efforts have been made to reform and even eliminate money bail and reduce the importance of bonding agents. Until the early 1960s, the justice system relied primarily on money bonds as the principal form of pretrial release. Many states now allow defendants to be released on their own recognizance without any money bail. **Release on recognizance (ROR)** was pioneered by the Vera Institute of Justice in an experiment called the **Manhattan Bail Project,** which began in 1961 with the cooperation of the New York City criminal courts and local law students.[14] It came about because defendants with financial means were able to post bail to secure pretrial release, while indigent defendants remained in custody. This project found that if the court had sufficient background information about the defendant, it could make a reasonably good judgment as to whether the accused would return to court. When release decisions were based on such information as the nature of the offense, family ties, and employment record, most defendants returned to court when released on their own recognizance. The results of the Vera Institute's initial operation show that from October 16, 1961, through April 8, 1964, out of a total of 13,000 defendants, 3,000 fell into the excluded offense category, 10,000 were interviewed, 4,000 were recommended, and 2,195 were given ROR. Only fifteen of these failed to show up in court, a default rate of less than seven-tenths of 1 percent. The bail project's experience suggested that releasing a person on the basis of verified information more effectively guaranteed appearance in court than did money bail. Highly successful ROR projects were set up in major cities around the country, including Philadelphia and San Francisco.

By 1980, more than 120 formal programs were in operation, and today, they exist in almost every major jurisdiction.[15] These programs are organized as part of the court structure itself, as part of the probation department, or under some other public agency, such as the sheriff's department, the district attorney, or the county board of supervisors. In some jurisdictions, pretrial programs are administered by private nonprofit organizations on a voluntary or contractual basis.

The success of ROR programs resulted in further bail reforms that culminated with the enactment of the federal **Bail Reform Act of 1966,** the first change in federal bail laws since 1789.[16] This legislation sought to ensure that release would be granted in all noncapital cases where there was sufficient reason to believe that the defendant would return to court. The law clearly established the presumption of ROR that must be overcome before money bail is required, authorized 10 percent-deposit bail, introduced the concept of conditional release, and stressed the philosophy that release should be under the least restrictive method necessary to ensure court appearance.

During the 1970s and early 1980s, the pretrial movement was hampered by public pressure over pretrial increases in crime. As a result, the more recent federal legislation, the **Bail Reform Act of 1984,** mandated that no defendants shall be kept in pretrial detention simply because they cannot afford money bail, established the presumption for ROR in all cases in which a person is bailable, and formalized restrictive preventive detention provisions, which are explained later in this chapter.[17] The 1984 act required that community safety, as well as the risk of flight, be considered in the release detention decision. A number of innovative alternative bail programs are discussed in Table 12.2.

Critique of Bail Reform. Bail reform is considered one of the most successful programs in the recent history of the criminal justice system. Yet it is not without critics who suggest that emphasis should be put on controlling the behavior of serious criminals, rather than on making sure that nondangerous defendants are released prior to their trials. In addition, research conducted by John Goldkamp has uncovered evidence that race and other social variables may play an important role in the decision to grant ROR.[18] This is particularly troubling, since suspicion of social bias in granting bail was among the most important reasons for bail reform in the first place. Because of these considerations, recent efforts have concentrated on improving the standards for bail, rather than on easing its application.

One way to eliminate disparity in the delivery of bail is to set up guidelines for bail decision makers. This approach has been tried in Philadelphia and other cities under the guidance of researchers Michael Gottfredson and John Goldkamp.[19] Their approach is to provide judges with a tool that uniformly defines the criteria for bail decision making but is flexible enough to deal with individual differences. Gottfredson and Goldkamp created a two-dimensional grid that can be used to define an accused's bail risk. One dimension lists fifteen categories relating to the severity of the current offense, while the other dimension is a five-point scale associated with the suspect's personal characteristics, such as demeanor, probability of conviction, and probability he or she will interfere with witnesses. The resulting information can then be used to determine whether the defendant receives ROR or a particular amount of cash bail.

Evaluation of the use of guidelines in the Philadelphia court indicate that disparity among judges using the guidelines was significantly reduced. The guidelines did not change the number of people receiving ROR, cash bail, or detention. In addition, although equity was increased, failure-to-appear rates and pretrial arrest rates did not decline.

The Preventive Detention Controversy

Those who promote bail reform point to the Eighth Amendment of the Constitution as evidence that bail should be made available to almost all people accused of crime. The presumption of bail is challenged by those who believe that releasing dangerous criminals before trial poses a threat to public safety. They point to the evidence showing that many people released on bail commit new crimes while at large and often fail to appear for trial. One response to the alleged failure of the bail system to protect citizens is the adoption of preventive detention statutes. These require that certain dangerous defendants be confined prior to trial for their own protection and that of the community. Preventive detention is an important manifestation of the crime control perspective on justice, since it favors the use of incapacitation to control the future behavior of suspected criminals.

The most striking use of preventive detention can be found in the federal Bail Reform Act of 1984, which contrasts sharply with previous law.[20] Although the act does contain provisions for ROR, it also allows judges to order preventive detention if they determined "that no condition or combination of conditions will reasonably assure the appearance of the person as required and the safety of

TABLE 12.2
Innovative Bail Systems

NONFINANCIAL RELEASE

(1) **Release on recognizance**—The defendant is released on a promise to appear, without any requirement of money bond. This form of release is unconditional; that is, without imposition of special conditions, supervision, or specially provided services. The defendant must simply appear in court for all scheduled hearings.

(2) **Conditional release**—The defendant is released on a promise to fulfill some stated requirements that go beyond those associated with release on recognizance. Four types of conditions are placed on defendants, all of which share the common aims of increasing the defendant's likelihood of returning to court and/or maintaining community safety: (1) status quo conditions, such as requiring that the defendant maintain residence or employment status; (2) restrictive conditions, such as requiring that the defendant remain in the jurisdiction, stay away from the complainant, or maintain a curfew; (3) contact conditions, such as requiring that the defendant report by telephone or in person to the release program or a third party at various intervals; and (4) problem-oriented conditions, such as requiring that the defendant participate in drug or alcohol treatment programs.

FINANCIAL RELEASE

(3) **Unsecured bail**—The defendant is released with no immediate requirement of payment. However, if the defendant fails to appear, he or she is liable for the full amount.

(4) **Privately secured bail**—A private organization or individual posts the bail amount, which is returned when the defendant appears in court. In effect, the organization provides services akin to those of a professional bonding agent, but without cost to the defendant.

(5) **Property bail**—The defendant may post evidence of real property in lieu of money.

(6) **Deposit bail**—The defendant deposits a percentage of the bail amount, typically 10 percent, with the court. When the defendant appears in court, the deposit is returned, sometimes minus an administrative fee. If the defendant fails to appear, he or she is liable for the full amount of the bail.

(7) **Surety bail**—The defendant pays a percentage of the bond, usually 10 percent, to a bonding agent who posts the full bail. The fee paid to the bonding agent is not returned to the defendant if he or she appears in court. The bonding agent is liable for the full amount of the bond should the defendant fail to appear. Bonding agents often require posting of collateral to cover the full bail amount.

(8) **Cash bail**—The defendant pays the entire amount of bail set by the judge in order to secure release. The bail is returned to the defendant when he or she appears in court.

SOURCE: Adapted from Andy Hall, *Pretrial Release Program Options* (Washington, D.C.: National Institute of Justice, 1984), pp. 32–33.

any other person and the community. . . ." The decision to detain is evaluated at a hearing where the accused has the right to counsel, to testify, and to confront and cross-examine witnesses, and the government must present clear and convicting evidence of dangerousness. In addition, the act creates a presumption against release while the case is being appealed. This means that the judicial officer must find that there is clear and convincing evidence that the convicted offender is not dangerous and that the appeal is not frivolous. Finally, the act orders judges to detain bail violators for up to ten days after their arrest.[21]

In addition to the federal act, a number of state jurisdictions have incorporated elements of preventive detention into their bail systems. Table 12.3 lists the various restrictions now placed on the granting of bail. Although most of them do not constitute outright preventive detention, they serve to narrow the scope of bail eligibility.

The Effects of Preventive Detention

To better understand the effects of preventive detention, Stephen Kennedy and Kenneth Carlson compared the pretrial experiences of people released in 1983 before the 1984 federal Bail Reform Act went into effect with 1985 cases that were handled under the new law. Kennedy and Carlson found that although the Bail Reform Act's preventive detention provisions significantly affected federal pretrial release and detention practices, the number of defendants released before trial remained relatively stable (76 percent in 1983 and 71 percent in 1985). About 54 percent of all defendants received ROR in both 1983 and 1985.[22]

At the same time, the preventive detention statute did result in a number of changes. Although about 2 percent of all defendants were denied bail outright in 1983, by 1985, the number held without bail rose to 19 percent. The number of defendants making bail remained stable because a higher percentage of defendants in 1985 who were eligible for bail were able to put up the required funds. It is evident that before the Bail Reform Act took effect, judges detained the most dangerous defendants by requiring bail amounts they simply could not afford; after 1985, judges relied more on the Bail Reform Act's pretrial detention provisions.

Who received preventive detention? Most (40 percent) were charged with drug, immigration, and violent offenses. There was little relationship between social variables, such as race and economic status, and the probability of preventive detention.

In a 1987 study of four judicial districts by Thomas Scott involving over two thousand defendants, the findings revealed that: (1) more defendants were detained under the Bail Reform Act (31 percent compared to 26 percent) than under the prior statute; (2) fewer defendants were detained because of their inability to make surety or cash bail; (3) the rate of failure to appear was 2.1 percent under the old bail act, compared to 1.8 percent under the new act, while the percentage of defendants who were rearrested for committing new crimes was equally low under both statutes.[23]

The data seem to suggest that judges will use preventive detention, but that its actual effect on the total number of people detained before trial may be marginal. Those defendants who are now subject to preventive detention would in the past have been assigned high bail amounts designed to keep them incarcerated before trial. Rather than being a new "get tough" approach, preventive detention

TABLE 12.3
Legislative Provisions to Assure Community Safety

Type of Provision	States That Have Enacted the Provision
Exclusion of certain crimes from automatic bail eligibility	Colorado, District of Columbia, Florida, Georgia, Michigan, Nebraska, Wisconsin
Definition of the purpose of bail to ensure appearance and safety	Alaska, Arizona, California, Delaware, District of Columbia, Florida, Hawaii, Minnesota, South Carolina, South Dakota, Vermont, Virginia, Wisconsin
Inclusion of crime control factors in the release decision	Alabama, California, Florida, Georgia, Minnesota, South Dakota, Wisconsin
Inclusion of release conditions related to crime control	Alaska, Arkansas, Delaware, District of Columbia, Florida, Hawaii, Illinois, Minnesota, New Mexico, North Carolina, South Carolina, Vermont, Virginia, Washington, Wisconsin
Limitations on the right to bail for those previously convicted	Colorado, District of Columbia, Florida, Georgia, Hawaii, Michigan, New Mexico, Texas, Wisconsin
Revocation of pretrial release when there is evidence that the accused committed a new crime	Arkansas, Colorado, Illinois, Indiana, Massachusetts, Nevada, New York, Rhode Island, Virginia, Wisconsin
Limitations on the right to bail for crimes alleged to have been committed while on release	Colorado, District of Columbia, Florida, Maryland, Michigan, Nevada, Tennessee, Texas, Utah
Provisions for pretrial detention to ensure safety	Arizona, California, District of Columbia, Florida, Georgia, Hawaii, Michigan, Wisconsin

SOURCE: Bureau of Justice Statistics, *Report to the Nation on Crime and Justice,* 2d ed. (Washington, D.C.: U.S. Government Printing Office, 1988), p. 59.

continues the judiciary's long-standing practice of detaining defendants it views as dangerous and releasing those who meet its standards of behavior.

In addition, the statute assists those making pretrial decisions by giving specific criteria to use in defining dangerous defendants. Despite its potential drawbacks in terms of costs, jail overcrowding, loss of freedom, and legality, preventive detention probably will become more common in the years ahead.

The Legality of Preventive Detention

Preventive detention has been a source of concern for civil libertarians who believe it violates the due process clause of the U.S. Constitution since it means that a person will be held in custody before proven guilty. In two recent cases, the U.S. Supreme Court disagreed with this analysis. In *Schall v. Martin*, the

Court upheld the application of preventive detention statutes to juvenile defendants on the grounds that such detention is useful to protect the welfare of the minor and society as a whole.[24] In *United States v. Salerno*, the Court upheld the Bail Reform Act's provision on preventive detention.[25] According to Chief Justice William Rehnquist, the statute conforms to the principle that "[i]n our society liberty is the norm, and detention prior to trial or without trial is the carefully limited exception."[26] Because of the importance of this case, it is analyzed in the Law in Review on page 432.

Pretrial Detention

The criminal defendant who is not eligible for bail or ROR is subject to **pretrial detention** in the local county jail. The jail has long been a trouble spot for the criminal justice system. Conditions tend to be poor and rehabilitation nonexistent.

In terms of the number of persons affected per year, pretrial custody accounts for more incarceration in the United States than does imprisonment after sentencing.[27] In the late 1980s, on any given day in the United States, almost three hundred thousand people were held in more than thirty-five hundred local jails. Over the course of a year, many times that number pass through these jails. More than 50 percent of those held in local jails have been accused of crimes but not convicted. They are **pretrial detainees.** In the United States, people are detained at a rate twice that of neighboring Canada and three times that of Great Britain. Hundreds of jails are overcrowded, and many are under court orders to reduce their populations and improve conditions.

This national jail-crowding crisis has worsened over the years. Nationwide, local jails held about 210,000 persons on June 30, 1982, and 405,320 on June 29, 1990, an increase of 93 percent. There were nearly 20 million admissions and releases from local jails during the year ending June 29, 1990, compared to about 14 million just eight years earlier in the year ending June 30, 1982, an increase of 43 percent. The occupancy rate of jails rose from 85 percent in 1982 to 104 percent in 1990. Experts believe that five hundred new jail beds per week, or twenty-six thousand per year, will be needed just to keep up with the current rate of growth in the jail population.[28]

Jails are often considered the weakest link in the criminal justice process: they are frequently dangerous, harmful, decrepit, and filled by the poor and friendless. Costs of holding a person in jail range up to more than eighty-five dollars per day and thirty-thousand dollars per year.[29] In addition, detainees are often confined with those convicted of crimes and those who have been transferred from other institutions because of overcrowding. Many felons are transferred to jails from state prisons to ease crowding. It is possible to have in close quarters a convicted rapist, a father jailed for nonpayment of child support, and a person awaiting trial for a crime that he did not actually commit. Thus, jails contain a mix of inmates that can lead to violence, brutality, and suicide.

In light of these efforts, why does the jail crisis persist? The likelihood is that societal problems, such as drug use, the needs of the mentally ill, and cutbacks in federal and state social service funding, provide a partial answer.

The Consequences of Detention

What happens to people who do not get bail or who cannot afford to put up bail money? Traditionally, they find themselves getting a long prison sentence if they

LAW IN REVIEW

United States v. Salerno (1987)

In this case, the U.S. Supreme Court held that the use of preventive detention is constitutionally permissible.

Facts

On March 21, 1986, Anthony Salerno and co-defendant Vincent Cafaro were charged in a twenty-nine-count indictment alleging various racketeering violations, including gambling, wire fraud, extortion, and conspiracy to commit murder. At their arraignment, the government moved to have them detained on the grounds that no condition of release could assure community safety. At a detention hearing, the prosecution presented evidence that Salerno was the "boss" of the Genovese crime family and that Cafaro was a "captain." Wiretap evidence indicated that the two men had participated in criminal conspiracies including murder. The court heard testimony from two witnesses who had personally participated in the murder conspiracies. In rebuttal, Salerno provided character statements, presented evidence that he had a heart condition, and challenged the veracity of the government's witnesses. Cafaro claimed the wiretaps had merely recorded "tough talk." The trial court allowed the detention on the grounds that the defendants wanted to use their pretrial freedom to continue their "family" business and "when business as usual involves threats, beatings, and murder, the present danger such people pose to the community is self-evident."

On appeal, the U.S. Court of Appeals for the Second Circuit agreed with the defendants' claim that the government could not detain suspects simply because they were thought to represent a danger to the community. The circuit court found that the criminal law system holds people accountable for their past deeds, not their anticipated future actions. The government then reappealed the case to the Supreme Court.

Decision

The Supreme Court held that the preventive detention act had a legitimate and compelling regulatory purpose and did not violate the due process clause. Preventive detention was not designed to punish dangerous individuals but to find a solution for the social problem of people committing crimes while on bail; preventing danger to the community is a legitimate societal goal.

The Court also stated that society's need for protection can outweigh an individual's liberty interest: under some circumstances, individuals can be held without bail. The act provides that only the most serious criminals can be held and mandates careful procedures to ensure that the judgment of future dangerousness is made after careful deliberation. Finally, the Court found that the Eighth Amendment does not limit the setting (or denial) of bail simply to prohibit defendants' flight to avoid trial and held that considerations of dangerousness are a valid reason to deny pretrial release.

Significance of the Case

Salerno legitimizes the use of preventive detention as a crime control method. It permits the limitations on bail already in place in many state jurisdictions to continue. *Salerno* further illustrates the concern for community protection that has developed in the past decade. It is a good example of the recent efforts by the Court to give the justice system greater control over criminal defendants. At this time, it is still unclear how often judges will rely on preventive detention statutes that require a hearing on the facts or whether they will simply continue to set extremely high bail for defendants they wish to remain in pretrial custody.

are convicted at trial.[30] Data on cases processed through the federal court system indicate that detainees received significantly longer sentences than those who had been released on bail; for some crime categories, the detainees' sentences were double that of bailees.[31]

Although this evidence indicates that failure to receive bail is associated with longer prison sentences, the bail-conviction relationship is less clear. John Goldkamp's well-known study of bail in Philadelphia found no relationship between defendants' custody status before trial and the probability they would be convicted at trial. Goldkamp also found, however, that convicted offenders who did not receive bail were much more likely to receive prison terms than those who were not detained.[32]

How can these relationships be explained? It is possible that people who do not make bail are the more violent chronic offenders who, upon conviction, are punished more severely by sentencing judges. However, this explanation would not apply to individuals involved in white-collar crimes, such as fraud and forgery, for it is unlikely that detainees for those crimes are more dangerous than those receiving bail; research indicates, however, that even among those charged with white-collar crimes, detainees are punished far more severely than those who make bail.[33] It is also likely that judges are reluctant to give probation or even a relatively short prison sentence to people who have already been detained in jail. The justice system would look foolish if a person who has already spent a considerable period behind bars did not receive a prison sentence that at least matched the jail time.

It is also likely that judges' decision making is influenced by the pretrial behavior of bailees. People who make bail have a chance to demonstrate they can adjust to society and make use of community social services; detainees are not afforded this opportunity to prove themselves. While bailees can demonstrate that they have refrained from any further criminal activity, detainees are not given a chance to show their trustworthiness. Consequently, detainees may receive a greater period of secure confinement than bailees, who may be considered better risks.

In sum, the evidence suggests that, if convicted, people who do not receive bail are much more likely to be sent to prison and to do more time than people who avoid pretrial detention. More information on the issue of local jails is contained in Chapter 16.

The Indictment Process—The Grand Jury

The grand jury was an early development of the English common law. Under the Magna Charta (1215), no freeman could be seized and imprisoned unless he had been judged by his peers. To determine fairly who was eligible to be tried, a group of freemen from the district where the crime was committed would be brought together to examine the facts of the case and determine whether the charges had merit. Thus, the grand jury was created as a check against arbitrary prosecution by a judge who might be a puppet of the government.

The concept of the grand jury was brought to the American colonies by early settlers and later incorporated into the Fifth Amendment of the U.S. Constitution, which states that "no person shall be held to answer for a capital, or otherwise infamous crime, unless on presentment or indictment of a grand jury."

Today, the use of the grand jury is diminishing. In 1961, thirty-three states required grand jury indictments (eight for all prosecutions, twenty-two for all felonies, and three for offenses leading to capital punishment or prison). Currently, fourteen states require a grand jury indictment to begin all felony proceedings, and two others (Florida and Rhode Island) use it for capital cases.[34] About twenty-five states allow a grand jury to be called at the option of the prosecutor. The federal government employs both the grand jury and the preliminary hearing systems.

What is the role of the grand jury today? First, the grand jury has the power to act as an independent investigating body. In this capacity, it examines the possibility of criminal activity within its jurisdiction. These investigative efforts are directed toward general rather than individual criminal conduct. After an investigation is completed, a report called a **presentment** is issued. The present-

The bail decision is a critical stage of the justice process because pretrial detention can mean months awaiting trial in a county jail.

ment contains not only information concerning the findings of the grand jury but also usually a recommendation of indictment.

The grand jury's second and better known role is accusatory in nature. In this capacity, the grand jury acts as the community's conscience in determining whether the accusation of the state (the prosecution) justifies a trial. The grand jury relies on the testimony of witnesses called by the prosecution through its **subpoena** power. After examining the evidence and the testimony of witnesses, the grand jury decides whether probable cause exists for prosecution. If it does, an indictment, or **true bill,** is affirmed. If the grand jury fails to find probable cause, a **no bill** (meaning that the indictment is ignored) is passed. In some states, a prosecutor can present evidence to a different grand jury if a no bill is returned; in other states, this action is prohibited by statute.

A grand jury is ordinarily comprised of from sixteen to twenty-three individuals, depending on the requirements of the jurisdiction. This group theoretically represents a county. Selection of members varies from state to state, but for the most part, they are chosen at random (e.g., from voting lists). To qualify to serve on a grand jury, an individual must be at least eighteen years of age, a U.S. citizen, and a resident of the jurisdiction for one year or more and possess sufficient English-speaking skills for communication.

The grand jury usually meets at the request of the prosecution. Hearings are closed and secret. The prosecuting attorney presents the charges and calls witnesses who testify under oath to support the indictment. Usually, the accused individuals are not allowed to attend the hearing unless they are asked to testify by the prosecutor or grand jury.

The effectiveness and efficiency of the grand jury procedure have been questioned for a number of reasons. One usual complaint is that the grand jury is costly in terms of space, personnel, and money. The members must be selected, notified, sworn, housed, fed, and granted other considerations. More important, the grand jury has been criticized as being a "rubber stamp" for the prosecution.

The presentation of evidence is under prosecutorial control, and the grand jury merely assents to the actions of the prosecutor.[35]

Studies of grand jury effectiveness have noted that the grand jury indicts almost all cases presented to it and has a negligible effect—other than delay—on the criminal process. The general view is that the grand jury should be avoided except in cases where a community voice is needed in a troublesome or notorious case.[36]

It is generally agreed, however, that the investigative role of the grand jury is a valuable and necessary function that should not only be maintained but expanded. Because the grand jury is often controlled solely by the state prosecutor, however, some legal experts believe that the system should provide the defendant with more due process protection. The American Bar Association's Grand Jury Policy and Model Act suggests the following changes in state grand jury statutes: (1) witnesses should have their own attorneys when they give testimony; (2) prosecutors should be required to present evidence that might show that a suspect is innocent; (3) witnesses should be granted constitutional privileges against self-incrimination; and (4) grand jurors should be informed of all the elements of the crimes being presented against the suspect.[37] Such changes would permit the grand jury to perform its complex investigative tasks, while avoiding any serious abuses of its powers. A federally sponsored study of the implementation of these reforms in various sites across the country found that they are being complied with in varying degrees. The study concluded that each jurisdiction must determine the alternatives to the traditional grand jury that meet its particular needs.[38]

The Preliminary Hearing

The preliminary hearing is employed in about half the states as an alternative to the grand jury. Although the purpose of preliminary and grand jury hearings is the same—to establish whether probable cause is sufficient to merit a trial—the procedures differ significantly.

The preliminary hearing is conducted before a magistrate or inferior court judge and, unlike the grand jury hearing, is open to the public unless the defendant requests otherwise. Also present at the preliminary hearing are the prosecuting attorney, the defendant, and the defendant's counsel, if already retained. The prosecution presents its evidence and witnesses to the judge. The defendant or the defense counsel then has the right to cross-examine witnesses and to challenge the prosecutor's evidence.

After hearing the evidence, the judge decides whether there is sufficient probable cause to believe that the defendant committed the alleged crime. If the answer is in the affirmative, the defendant is bound over for trial, and the prosecuting attorney's information (same as an indictment) is filed with the superior court, usually within fifteen days. When the judge does not find sufficient probable cause, the charges are dismissed, and the defendant is released from custody.

A unique aspect of the preliminary hearing is the defendant's right to waive the proceeding. In most states, the prosecutor and the judge must agree to this **waiver.** A waiver has advantages and disadvantages for both the prosecutor and the defendant. In most situations, a prosecutor will agree to a waiver because it avoids revealing evidence to the defense before trial. However, if the state believes it is necessary to obtain a record of witness testimony because of the possibility that a witness or witnesses may be unavailable for the trial or unable to

The grand jury can investigate criminal activity and decide whether those accused of a crime should be tried on criminal charges.

remember the facts clearly, the prosecutor might override the waiver. In this situation, the record of the preliminary hearing can be used at the trial.

The defendant will most likely waive the preliminary hearing for one of three reasons: (1) he or she has already decided to plead guilty; (2) he or she wants to speed up the criminal process; or (3) he or she hopes to avoid the negative publicity that might result from the hearing. On the other hand, the preliminary hearing is of obvious advantage to the defendant who believes that it will result in a dismissal of the charges. In addition, the preliminary hearing gives the defense the opportunity to learn what evidence the prosecution has.

Arraignment

An arraignment takes place after an indictment or information is filed following a grand jury or preliminary hearing. At the arraignment, the judge informs the defendant of the charges against him or her and appoints counsel if it has not yet been retained. According to the Sixth Amendment of the U.S. Constitution, the accused has the right to be informed of the nature and cause of the accusation; thus, the judge at the arraignment must make sure that the defendant clearly understands the charges.

After the charges are read and explained, the defendant is asked to enter a plea. If a plea of not guilty or not guilty by reason of insanity is entered, a trial date is set. When the defendant pleads guilty or *nolo contendere*, a date for sentencing is arranged. The magistrate then either sets bail or releases the defendant on personal recognizance.

The Plea

Ordinarily, a defendant in a criminal trial will enter one of the following pleas:

Guilty. More than 90 percent of defendants appearing before the courts plead guilty prior to the trial stage. A guilty plea has several consequences:

> Such a plea functions not only as an admission of guilt but also as a surrender of the entire array of constitutional rights designed to protect a criminal defendant against unjustified conviction, including the right to remain silent, the right to confront witnesses against him, the right to a trial by jury, and the right to be proven guilty by proof beyond a reasonable doubt.[39]

As a result, a judge must take certain procedures when accepting a plea of guilty. First, the judge must clearly state to the defendant the constitutional guarantees automatically waived by this plea. Second, the judge must believe that the facts of the case establish a basis for the plea and that the plea is made voluntarily. Third, the defendant must be informed of the right to counsel during the pleading process. In many felony cases, the judge will insist on the presence of defense counsel. Finally, the judge must inform the defendant of the possible sentencing outcomes, including the maximum sentence that can be imposed.

After a guilty plea has been entered, a sentencing date is arranged. In a majority of states, a guilty plea may be withdrawn and replaced with a not guilty plea at any time prior to sentencing if good cause is shown.

Not Guilty. At the arraignment or prior to the trial, a not guilty plea is entered in two ways: (1) it is verbally stated by the defendant or the defense counsel, or (2) it is entered for the defendant by the court when the defendant stands mute before the bench.

Once a plea of not guilty is recorded, a trial date is set. In misdemeanor cases, trials take place in the lower court system, whereas felony cases are normally transferred to the superior court. At this time, a continuance or issuance of bail is once again considered.

Nolo contendere. The plea *nolo contendere*, which means "no contest," is essentially a plea of guilty. This plea has the same consequences as a guilty plea, with one exception: it may not be held against the defendant as proof in a subsequent civil matter because technically there has been no admission of guilty.

The *nolo contendere* plea is used where the defendant is also subject to a civil suit for damages (e.g., extortion of corporate funds). This plea is accepted in federal court cases and in about half the states. It may be entered only at the discretion of the judge and the prosecutor, however.

Plea Bargaining

One of the most common practices in the criminal justice system today, and a cornerstone of the "informal justice" system, is **plea bargaining.** More than 90 percent of criminal convictions are estimated to result from negotiated pleas of guilty. Even in serious felony cases, some jurisdictions will have about four bargains for every trial. Figure 12.1 shows the high percentage of cases resulting in a guilty plea in seven major cities. Although the rates range from 41 to 82 percent, the lower rates often reflect the use of all other prerelease options.

Plea bargaining has been defined concisely as the exchange of prosecutorial and judicial concessions for pleas of guilty.[40] Normally, a bargain can be made between the prosecutor and the defense attorney in four ways: (1) the initial charges may be reduced to those of a lesser offense, thus automatically reducing

FIGURE 12.1

Percentage of Cases Resulting in a Plea of Guilty in Seven Selected Jurisdictions

NOTE: Lower rates may reflect more reliance on such options as diversion, screening, dismissal, and trial.

SOURCE: Barbara Boland with Ronald Sones, INSLAW, Inc., *Prosecution of Felony Arrests, 1981* (Washington, D.C.: Bureau of Justice Statistics, 1986).

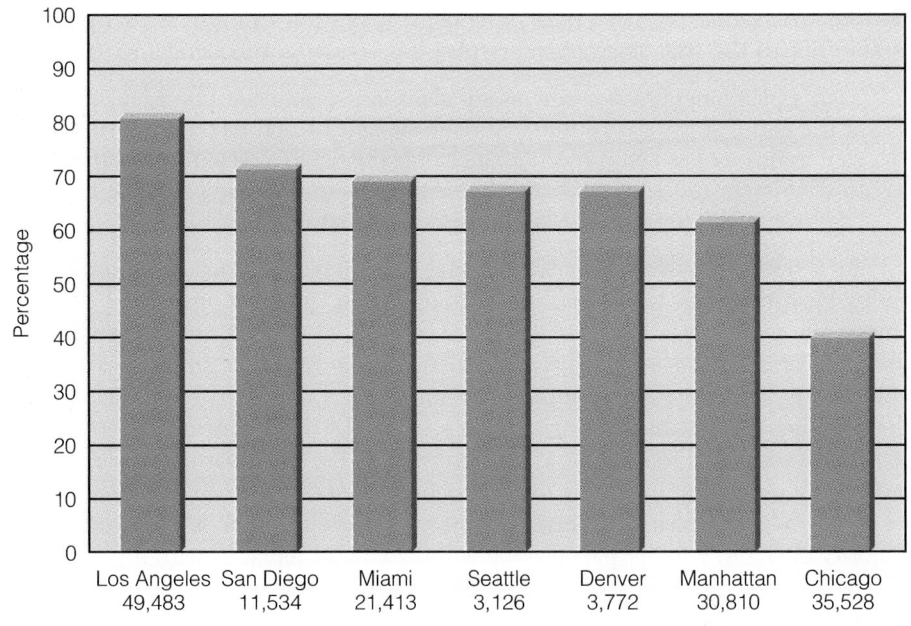

the sentence imposed; (2) in cases where many counts are charged, the prosecutor may reduce the number of counts; (3) the prosecutor may promise to recommend a lenient sentence, such as probation; and (4) when the charge imposed has a negative label attached (e.g., child molester), the prosecutor may alter the charge to a more "socially acceptable" one (e.g., assault) in exchange for a plea of guilty. In a jurisdiction where sentencing disparities exist between judges, the prosecutor may even agree to arrange for the defendant to appear before a lenient judge in exchange for a plea; this practice is known as "judge shopping."

Because of excessive criminal court caseloads and the personal and professional needs of the prosecution and the defense (to get the case over with in the shortest amount of time), plea bargaining has become an essential yet controversial part of the administration of justice. Proponents contend that plea bargaining actually benefits both the state and the defendant in the following ways: (1) the overall financial costs of the criminal prosecution are reduced; (2) the administrative efficiency of the courts is greatly improved; (3) the prosecution is able to devote more time to more serious cases; and (4) the defendant avoids possible detention and an extended trial and may receive a reduced sentence.[41] Those who favor plea bargaining believe it is appropriate to enter into plea discussions where the interests of the state in the effective administration of justice will be served.

Opponents of the plea-bargaining process believe that the negotiated plea should be eliminated. In 1973, the National Advisory Commission on Criminal Justice Standards and Goals stated:

> As soon as possible, but in no event later than 1978, regulations between prosecutors and defendants—either personally or through their attorneys—concerning concessions to be made in return for guilty pleas should be prohibited.[42]

This has never been accomplished.

Some argue that plea bargaining is objectionable because it encourages defendants to waive their constitutional right to trial. In addition, some experts suggest that sentences tend to be less severe when a defendant enters a guilty plea than in actual trials and that plea bargains result in even greater sentencing disparity. Particularly in the eyes of the general public, this allows the defendant to beat the system and further tarnishes the criminal process. Plea bargaining also raises the danger that an innocent person will be convicted of a crime if he or she is convinced that the lighter treatment from a guilty plea is preferable to the risk of conviction with a harsher sentence following a formal trial.

It is unlikely that plea negotiations will be eliminated or severely curtailed in the near future. Supporters of the total abolition of plea bargaining are in the minority. As a result of abuses, however, efforts are being made to improve plea-bargaining operations. Such reforms include: (1) the development of uniform plea practices, (2) the representation of counsel during plea negotiations, and (3) the establishment of time limits on plea negotiations.

Legal Issues in Plea Bargaining

The U.S. Supreme Court has reviewed the propriety of plea bargaining in several decisions, particularly in regard to the voluntariness of guilty pleas. Defendants are entitled to the effective assistance of counsel to protect them from pressure and influence. The Court ruled in *Hill v. Lockhart* (1985) that to prove ineffectiveness, the defendant must show a "reasonable probability that, but for counsel's errors, he would not have pleaded guilty and would have insisted on going to trial."[43]

In ***Boykin v. Alabama*** (1969), the court held that an affirmative action (such as a verbal statement) that the plea was made voluntarily must exist on the record before a trial judge may accept a guilty plea.[44] This is essential because a guilty plea basically constitutes a waiver of the defendant's Fifth Amendment privilege against self-incrimination and Sixth Amendment right to a jury trial. Subsequent to *Boykin*, the Court ruled in *Brady v. United States* (1970) that a guilty plea is not invalid merely because it is entered to avoid the possibility of the death penalty.[45]

When the question arose about whether a guilty plea may be accepted by a defendant maintaining his or her innocence, the Supreme Court, in *North Carolina v. Alford* (1970), said that such action was appropriate where a defendant was seeking a lesser sentence. In other words, a defendant could plead guilty without admitting guilt.[46]

In ***Santobello v. New York*** (1971), the Court held that the promise of the prosecutor must be kept and that the breaking of a plea-bargaining agreement by the prosecutor required a reversal for the defendant.[47] In *Ricketts v. Adamson* (1987), the Court ruled that defendants must also keep their side of a bargain in order to receive the promised offer of leniency. In this case, the defendant was charged with first-degree murder but was allowed to plead guilty to second-degree murder in exchange for testifying against his accomplices. The testimony was given, but the co-defendants' conviction was later reversed on appeal. Ricketts refused to testify a second time, and the prosecutor withdrew the offer of leniency. On appeal, the Supreme Court allowed the recharging and held that Ricketts had to suffer the consequences of his voluntary choice not to retestify.[48]

How far can prosecutors go to convince a defendant to plead guilty? The Supreme Court ruled in the 1978 case of *Bordenkircher v. Hayes* that a defendant's

TABLE 12.4
Notable U.S. Supreme Court Cases on the Regulation of Plea Bargaining

Case	Ruling
1. *Boykin v. Alabama* (1969)	The defendant must make an affirmative statement that the plea is voluntary before the judge can accept it.
2. *Brady v. United States* (1970)	Avoiding the possibility of the death penalty is not grounds to invalidate a guilty plea.
3. *North Carolina v. Alford* (1970)	Accepting a guilty plea from a defendant who maintains his or her innocence is valid.
4. *Santobello v. New York* (1971)	The promise of a prosecutor that rests on a guilty plea must be kept in a plea-bargaining agreement.
5. *Bordenkircher v. Hayes* (1978)	A defendant's constitutional rights are not violated when a prosecutor threatens to reindict the accused on more serious charges if he or she is not willing to plead guilty to the original offense.
6. *Hill v. Lockhart* (1985)	To prove ineffectiveness of defense counsel, the defendant needs to show a reasonable probability that, except for counsel's errors, the defendant would not have pleaded guilty.
7. *Ricketts v. Adamson* (1987)	The defendant is required to keep his or her side of the bargain in order to receive the promised offer of leniency since plea bargaining rests on an agreement between the parties.

due process rights are not violated when a prosecutor threatens to reindict the accused on more serious charges if he or she does not plead guilty to the original offense.[49]

From repeated actions by the Supreme Court, we realize that plea bargaining is a constitutionally accepted practice in the United States. Table 12.4 summarizes the major Supreme Court decisions regulating plea-bargaining practices.

Plea-Bargaining Decision Making

Because the plea-bargaining process is largely informal, lacking in guidelines, and discretionary in nature, some effort has been made to determine what kinds of information and how much is used by the prosecutor to make plea-bargaining decisions. A study conducted by Stephen Lagoy, Joseph Senna, and Larry Siegel found that certain information weighed heavily in the prosecutorial decision to accept a plea negotiation.[50] Such factors as the offense, the defendant's prior record and age, and the type, strength, and admissibility of evidence were considered important in the plea-bargaining decision. It was also discovered that the attitude of the complainant was an important factor in the decision-making process; for example, in victimless cases, such as heroin possession, the police attitude

Plea negotiations between prosecution and defense settle more than ninety percent of all criminal cases.

was most often considered, whereas in victim-related crimes, such as rape, the attitude of the victim was a primary concern. The study also revealed that prosecutors in low-population or rural jurisdictions not only employ more information while making their decisions but also seem more likely than their urban counterparts to accept bargains. It was suggested that "this finding tends to dispute the notion that plea bargaining is a response to overcrowding in large urban courts."[51] It appears that where caseload pressures are less, the acceptance of a plea bargain is actually more probable.

Similar conclusions were reached by William McDonald in a study of plea bargaining in six court jurisdictions. McDonald found that plea negotiations were not conducted in a haphazard manner, nor were they used by prosecutors to engage in frauds or other deceptive practices. For example, prosecutors did not overcharge suspects with the idea of forcing them to plea to a more reasonable charge.[52] Figure 12.2 identifies how decisions made by police, prosecutors, and defense attorneys play a critical role in disposing of criminal felony cases prior to trial. Taken from a study of one hundred typical cases, it shows that most cases are not brought to trial but were handled by guilty pleas, diversion, or dismissal.

The Nature of Plea Bargaining

A federal study of plea negotiations sheds some light on the plea-bargaining process. The study by Barbara Boland and Brian Forst looked at fourteen jurisdictions around the country and found a wide discrepancy in the use of pleas.[53] Although the overall average was one trial for every eleven plea bargains, the range was between one for every thirty-seven in Geneva, Illinois, and one for every four in Portland, Oregon. Interestingly, the high plea bargain jurisdictions were not exclusively high-crime areas where case pressure was a factor. Correspondingly, some of the jurisdictions that hold a large number of trials, such as Washington, D.C., St. Louis, and New Orleans, are big cities with high caseloads. Thus, case pressure does not seem to play as an important a role in plea negotiations as might have been thought. The study also found that jurisdictions that hold a great many trials tend to be more selective in the cases they process and are more likely to screen out weak cases before trial.

FIGURE 12.2
What Happens to Felony Arrests?

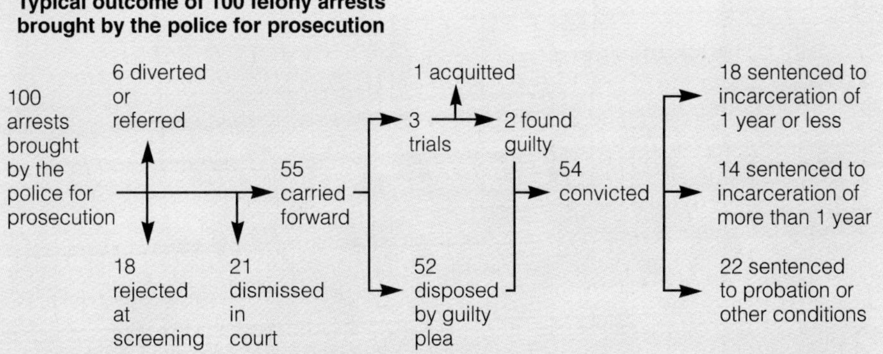

The data collected for this report indicate that for every 100 adult arrests for a felony, 54 will result in a conviction to either a felony or a misdemeanor. Of those 54—

- 52 will be guilty pleas, and
- 2 will be convictions at trial.

Of the 54 arrests resulting in conviction, 32 will lead to a sentence of incarceration—

- 18 will result in a sentence of 1 year or less, and
- 14 will result in a sentence of more than 1 year.

Of the 46 arrests that do not result in conviction—

- 6 will result in the defendants' being referred to diversion programs or to other courts for prosecution,
- 18 will be rejected for prosecution at screening, before court charges are filed,
- 21 will be dismissed in court, and
- 1 will result in an acquittal at trial.

SOURCE: Barbara Boland, Paul Mahanna, and Ronald Sones, *The Prosecution of Felony Arrests, 1988* (Washington, D.C.: Bureau of Justice Statistics, February 1992), p. 3.

One of the most important issues regarding the nature of plea bargaining is determining its effect on the outcome of a case. Many people believe that "coping a plea" lets a criminal "get away with murder." This charge is supported by research conducted by Mark Cuniff in twenty-eight large jurisdictions. As Table 12.7 shows, Cuniff found that people convicted after a plea bargain were much less likely to be sent to prison than those convicted after a jury trial. Interestingly, those convicted after a bench trial (before a judge alone) had the same probability of being sent to prison as defendants who plea-bargained.[54] Table 12.5 also indicates that those who plea-bargain receive lower average prison terms than those who go to trial, which supports the argument that plea bargaining helps the defendant avoid punishment.

Other research, however, indicates that plea bargains may not be that helpful to criminal defendants. Douglas Smith's study of 3,397 felony cases in six separate jurisdictions found that the probability of receiving an incarceration sentence was roughly equal for those who pleaded guilty and for those who actually went to trial.[55] Those defendants who seemed to benefit the most from plea bargaining committed the least serious offenses and had the best prior records.

Another project conducted by the federal government found that about 60 percent of the defendants pleaded guilty to the top charge filed against them.[56] A plea to the top charge did not necessarily mean the absence of negotiation or concession. The study found that bargaining often included judicial agreement to give a more lenient sentence than might be expected if the defendant went to trial. In other cases, the negotiation involved the dropping of other charges or pending cases. Sometimes the lesser charges involved acts that required add-ons to a sentence, such as possession of a handgun; dropping the lesser offense automatically shortened the defendant's prison term. People who pleaded guilty

TABLE 12.5
The Effect of Plea Bargaining on Prison Sentences and Prison Terms

Conviction Offense	Percentage of Prison Sentences by Type of Conviction					Average Prison Term by Type of Conviction			
	Jury Trial	Bench Trial	Trial, but Type Not Known	Guilty Plea	Total	Jury Trial	Bench Trial	Trial, but Type Not Known	Guilty Plea
Overall average	82%	42%	76%	43%	46%	194 months	98 months	133 months	13 months
Homicide	93	88	96	79	84	272	168	125	162
Rape	90	63	83	60	65	247	146	274	132
Robbery	89	50	82	66	67	210	113	142	89
Aggravated assault	73	37	50	39	42	139	115	100	66
Burglary	79	31	81	49	49	152	57	114	61
Larceny	54	29	50	32	32	152	42	46	43
Drug trafficking	69	36	68	26	27	121	34	96	51

SOURCE: Mark Cuniff, *Sentencing Outcomes in 28 Felony Courts, 1985* (Washington, D.C.: Bureau of Justice Statistics, 1987), pp. 26–28.

were also less likely to do their time in a state prison and more likely to be sent to a less restrictive correctional facility, such as a county jail. This conclusion is supported by McDonald's study of plea bargaining in six court jurisdictions. He found that in five of the six jurisdictions, people who did not plead guilty increased their chances of receiving a prison sentence and also received significantly longer prison terms.[57]

In sum, although punishment is a certainty when defendants decide to plead guilty, it is likely to be somewhat less severe than if they were found guilty after a trial. The plea-bargaining process reflects the "wedding cake" model of justice: pleas are a quick and efficient way of disposing of cases that fall into the bottom layers. Plea bargains also reduce the time the defendant is involved with the justice system: cases that go to trial take significantly longer than those that are bargained. So defendants, especially those placed in pretrial detention, have the extra burden of remaining with the justice system if they refuse to plea bargain, a burden few wish to bear.

The Role of the Prosecutor in Plea Bargaining

The prosecutor in the U.S. system of criminal justice has broad discretion in the exercise of his or her responsibilities. Such discretion includes deciding whether to initiate a criminal prosecution, determining the nature and number of the criminal charges, and choosing whether to plea-bargain a case and under what conditions. Plea bargaining is one of the major tools the prosecutor uses to control and influence the criminal justice system (the other two are the decision to initiate a charge and the ability to take the case to trial). Few states have placed limits on the discretion of prosecutors in plea-bargaining situations. Instead, in making a plea-bargaining decision, the prosecutor is generally free to weigh competing alternatives and factors, such as the seriousness of the crime, the attitude of the victim, the police report of the incident, and applicable sentencing provisions. Plea bargaining frequently occurs in cases where the government believes the evidence is weak, for example, where a key witness seems unreliable or unwilling to testify. Bargaining permits a compromise settlement in a weak case where the criminal trial outcome is in doubt.

On a case-by-case basis, the prosecutor determines the concessions to be offered in the plea bargain and seeks to dispose of each case quickly and efficiently. On the broader scale, however, the role of the chief prosecutor as an administrator also affects plea bargaining. While the assistant prosecutor evaluates and moves individual cases, the chief prosecutor must establish plea-bargaining guidelines for the entire office. In this regard, the prosecutor may be acting as an administrator.[58] In the Manhattan district attorney's office, for example, guidelines cover such aspects as avoiding overindictment and controlling nonprovable indictments, reducing felonies to misdemeanors, and bargaining with defendants.

Some jurisdictions have established guidelines to provide consistency in plea-bargaining cases. For instance, a given office may be required to define the kinds and types of cases and offenders that may be suitable for plea bargaining. In other jurisdictions, approval to plea bargain may be required. Other controls might include procedures for internally reviewing decisions by the chief prosecutor and the use of written memorandums to document the need and acceptability for a plea bargain in a given case. For example, in New Orleans, pleas are offered on a "take it or leave it" basis. In each case, a special prosecutor, whose job it is to screen cases, sets the bargaining terms. If the defense counsel cannot accept the agreement, there is no negotiation, and the case must go to trial. Only if complications arise in the case, such as witnesses changing their testimony, can negotiations be reopened.[59]

The prosecutor's role in plea bargaining is also important on a state- or systemwide basis because it involves exercising leadership in setting policy. The most extreme example of a chief prosecutor influencing the plea negotiation process has occurred where the prosecutor has attempted to eliminate plea bargaining. In Alaska, such efforts met with resistance from assistant prosecutors and others in the system, namely, judges and defense attorneys.[60] The more moderate approach by prosecutors in providing leadership in plea bargaining generally involves establishing guidelines for assistant prosecutors to follow in evaluating cases for plea bargaining. Thus, the prosecutor plays a role in setting plea-bargaining policy, as well as in using the technique on a case-by-case basis.

The Role of the Defense Counsel in Plea Bargaining

Both the U.S. Supreme Court and such organizations as the American Bar Association in its *Standards Relating to Pleas of Guilty* have established guidelines for the court receiving a guilty plea and for the defense counsel representing the accused in plea negotiations.[61] No court should accept a guilty plea unless the defendant has been properly advised by counsel and the court has determined that the plea is voluntary and has a factual basis; the court has the discretion to reject a plea if it is inappropriately offered. The defense counsel—a public defender or a private attorney—is required to play an advisory role in plea negotiations. The defendant's counsel is expected to be aware of the facts of the case and of the law and to advise the defendant of the alternatives available. The defense attorney is basically responsible for making certain that the accused understands the nature of the plea-bargaining process and the guilty plea. This means that the defense counsel should explain to the defendant that by pleading guilty, he or she is waiving certain rights that would be available on going to trial. In addition, the defense attorney has the duty to keep the defendant in-

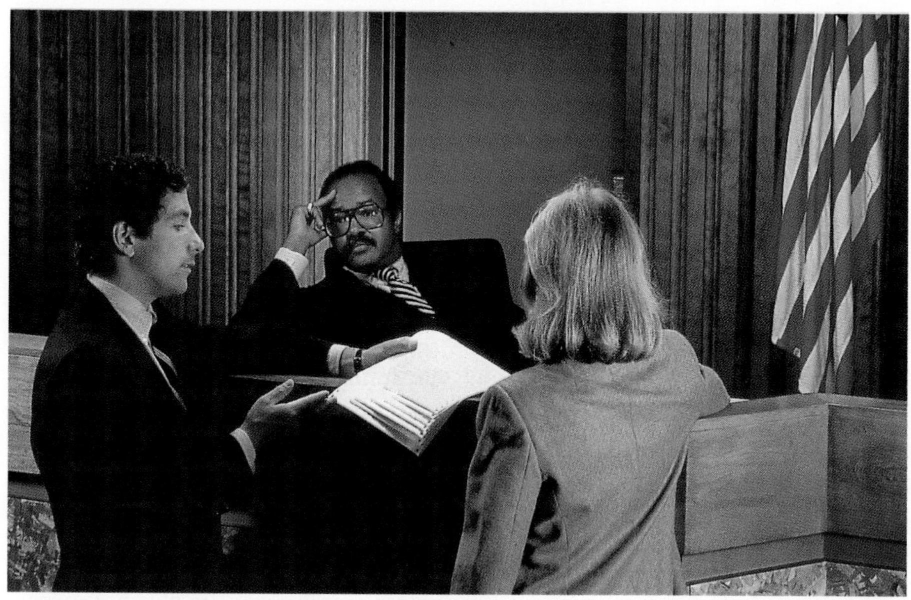

While experts disagree, it appears that judges play an active role in the plea negotiation process.

formed of developments and discussions with the prosecutor regarding plea bargaining. While doing so, the attorney for the accused cannot misrepresent evidence or mislead the client into making a detrimental agreement.

In reality, most plea negotiations occur in the chambers of the judge, in the prosecutor's office, or in the courthouse hallway. Under these conditions, it is often difficult to assess the actual roles played by the prosecutor and the defense attorney. Even so, it is fundamental that a defendant should not be required to plead guilty until advised by counsel and that a guilty plea should not be made unless it is done so with the consent of the accused.

The Judge's Role in Plea Bargaining

One of the most confusing problems in the plea-bargaining process has been the proper role of the judge. Should the judge act only in a supervisory capacity or actually enter into the negotiation process? The leading national legal organizations, such as the American Bar Association, are opposed to judicial participation in plea negotiations.[62] The American Bar Association sets out its position on the role of the judge in the plea-bargaining process as follows:

> Standard 3.3: Responsibilities of the Trial Judge:
>
> A. The trial judge should not participate in plea discussions.
>
> B. If a tentative plea agreement has been reached which contemplates entry of a plea of guilty in the expectation that other charges before that court will be dismissed, or that sentence concessions will be granted, upon request of the parties, the trial judge may permit the disclosure to him of the agreement and the reasons therefore in advance of the time for tender of the plea. He may then indicate to the prosecuting attorney and defense counsel whether he will concur in the proposed disposition, if the information in the pre-sentence report is consistent with the representations made to him. That the trial judge concurs but the final disposition does not include the charge or sentence concessions contemplated in the plea agreement, he shall state for the record what information in the pre-sentence report contributed to his decision not to grant these concessions.[63]

In addition, the *Federal Rules of Criminal Procedure* prohibit federal judges from participating in plea negotiations.[64] A few states disallow any form of judicial involvement in plea bargaining, but others permit the judge to participate.

The American Bar Association objects in general to the judge participating in plea negotiations because of his or her position as chief judicial officer. A judge should not be a party to arrangements for the determination of a sentence, whether as a result of a guilty plea or a finding of guilty based on proof. Furthermore, judicial participation in plea negotiations (1) creates the impression in the mind of the defendant that he or she could not receive a fair trial; (2) lessens the ability of the judge to make an objective determination of the voluntariness of the plea; (3) is inconsistent with the theory behind the use of presentence investigation reports; and (4) may induce an innocent defendant to plead guilty because he or she is afraid to reject the disposition desired by the judge.[65]

On the other hand, those who suggest that the judge should participate directly in plea bargaining argue that such an approach would make sentencing more uniform and ensure that the plea-bargaining process would be fairer and more efficient.

It appears that judges play an active role in the negotiation process in most jurisdictions in the United States. Where judges simply supervise plea bargaining, they oversee the taking of the guilty plea, determine a factual basis for the plea, inform the defendant of the sentencing consequences, and control the withdrawal of the plea. McDonald found that this type of judicial involvement can have a beneficial effect but that judges usually play an extremely neutral role and do not look into how a plea was arrived at nor examine the strength of the state's case.[66]

When judges participate more actively in plea bargaining, they may influence the kind and type of agreement that is reached, encourage prosecutors and defense attorneys to arrive at an agreement, expedite cases, and contribute to the efficient management of the court.

Plea-Bargaining Reform

Plea bargaining is so widespread that it is recognized as one of the major elements of the criminal justice system. Despite its prevalence, its merits are hotly debated. Those opposed to the widespread use of plea bargaining assert that it is coercive in its inducement of guilty pleas, that it encourages the unequal exercise of prosecutorial discretion, and that it complicates sentencing as well as the job of correctional authorities. Others argue that it is unconstitutional and that it results in cynicism and disrespect for the entire system.

On the other hand, its proponents contend that the practice ensures the flow of guilty pleas essential to administration efficiency. It allows the system the flexibility to individualize justice and inspires respect for the system because it is associated with certain and prompt punishment.[67]

In recent years, efforts have been made to convert plea bargaining into a more visible, understandable, and fair dispositional process. Many jurisdictions have developed safeguards and guidelines to prevent violations of due process and to ensure that innocent defendants do not plead guilty under coercion. Such safeguards include the following: (1) the judge questions the defendant about the facts of the guilty plea before accepting the plea; (2) the defense counsel is present and able to advise the defendant of his or her rights; (3) the prosecutor and the defense attorney openly discuss the plea; and (4) full and frank information about the defendant and the offenses is made available at this stage of the process. In addition, judicial supervision ensures that plea bargaining is conducted in a fair manner.

Another reform involves the development of specific guidelines by the office of the chief prosecutor[68] Some jurisdictions have also adopted prepleading investigations, which provide summaries of the case before a plea, rather than after the plea is given to the court. The prepleading report provides information to all participants in the negotiations. The pretrial settlement conference also improves the visibility and fairness of plea bargaining. The participants in such a conference include the judge, the victim, the defendant, and the police, as well as the prosecutor and the defense attorney. Generally, the parties assume that the defendant is guilty as charged and negotiate from there to settle the case. If a settlement is reached and approved by the judge, the defendant enters a plea in open court.

Banning Plea Negotiations. What would happen if plea bargaining were banned outright, as its critics advocate? Numerous jurisdictions throughout the United States have experimented with bans on plea bargaining. In 1975, Alaska eliminated the practice. Honolulu, Hawaii, also attempted to abolish plea bargaining. Other jurisdictions, including Iowa, Arizona, Delaware, and the District of Columbia, sought to limit the use of plea bargaining.[69] The U.S. Coast Guard banned plea bargaining in service-related crimes.[70] In theory, eliminating plea bargains means that prosecutors in these jurisdictions give no consideration or concessions to a defendant in exchange for a guilty plea.

In reality, however, in these and most jurisdictions, sentence-related concessions, charge-reduction concessions, and alternative methods for prosecution continue to be used in one fashion or another.[71] Where plea bargaining is limited or abolished, the number of trials may increase, the sentence severity may change, and more questions regarding the right to a speedy trial may arise. Discretion may also be shifted farther up the system. Instead of spending countless hours preparing for and conducting a trial, prosecutors may dismiss more cases outright or decide not to prosecute them after initial action has been taken.

These predictions have been supported by experience. An evaluation of the Alaska experiment in 1980 found that the ban on plea bargaining effectively increased sentence severity in minor cases that would ordinarily have been dealt with informally; at the same time, it had no effect on serious cases (robberies, murders, and rapes), probably because these were the cases that were going to trial before the ban was put into effect.[72]

In 1991, Alaska offered additional findings regarding its plea bargaining ban. They were: (1) tight screening of cases had resulted in an increase in the number of cases not accepted for prosecution; (2) routine sentence agreements between the prosecutor and defense attorneys had been virtually eliminated; (3) most defendants were being sentenced by a judge at an open hearing, and the responsibility for sentencing had shifted from the attorneys to the judge; (4) charge bargaining (which involves charge reduction and dismissals) had become more prevalent; (5) and sentences had increased in length, with a greater likelihood of incarceration for most offenses. According to the study, some of the changes could be attributed to criminal code revisions, but overall, the ban has significantly and positively reduced the number of cases traditionally processed by plea bargaining. Whether or not current methods of settlement, such as charge bargaining, clash with due process values remains to be seen.

California's attempt to reduce plea negotiations in drunk driving cases did not meet expectations: although some forms of plea bargaining were initially reduced, they soon rose back to their early levels; trial rates increased; rates of conviction at trial decreased; court congestion became a problem; and sentence disparity increased.[73]

Studies have also shown that a ban on plea bargaining will push discretion farther up the line. For example, when New York's narcotics control law banned plea bargaining in serious drug-related cases in 1973, it was hailed as a "get tough" measure that would certainly help control the drug trade. An evaluation conducted three years later found that the law's effect was somewhat less than expected.[74] The same percentage (11 percent) of people arrested for heroin sale or possession were incarcerated both before and after the law went into effect. One reason was that prosecutors began to process fewer cases, indicting 25 percent of arrested drug traffickers after the law went into effect, as opposed to about 40 percent before. Though the length of prison sentences increased, the drug trade was virtually unaffected. The law was amended three years later. These results suggest that, despite the attempts of policymakers to abolish plea bargaining, the system will not easily change its ways.

In view of the problems associated both with plea bargaining and with its reform, there appears to be no ideal system of adjudication and disposition in the criminal justice process. Current trends include the development of guidelines and safeguards, as well as the experimental banning of plea bargaining in some jurisdictions. Efforts are also being made to examine prosecutorial discretion and to make plea bargaining a more visible and structured process. Despite all the efforts to reform, control, or even ban plea bargaining, it remains one of the key elements of the informal justice process. (See Analyzing Criminal Justice Issues: Is Plea Bargaining Inevitable? on page 449.)

Pretrial Diversion

Another important feature in the early court process is the placing of offenders into noncriminal **diversion** programs prior to their formal trial or conviction. Pretrial diversion programs were first established in the late 1960s and early 1970s, when it became apparent that a viable alternative to the highly stigmatized criminal sentence was needed. In diversion programs, formal criminal proceedings against an accused are suspended while that person participates in a community treatment program under court supervision. Diversion helps the offender avoid the stigma of a criminal conviction and enables the justice system to reduce costs and alleviate prison overcrowding.

Many diversion programs exist throughout the United States. These programs vary in size and emphasis but generally pursue the same goal: to constructively bypass criminal prosecution by providing a reasonable alternative in the form of treatment, counseling, or employment programs.

The prosecutor often plays the central role in the diversion process. Decisions about nondispositional alternatives are based on (1) the nature of the crime, (2) special characteristics of the offender, (3) whether the defendant is a first-time offender, (4) whether the defendant will cooperate with a diversion program, (5) the impact of diversion on the community, and (6) consideration for the opinion of the victim.[75]

Diversion programs can take many forms. Some are separate, independent agencies that were originally set up with federal funds but are now being continued with county or state assistance. Others are organized as part of a police, prosecutor, or probation department's internal structure. Still others are a joint venture between the county government and a private, nonprofit organization that actually carries out the treatment process.

ANALYZING CRIMINAL JUSTICE ISSUES

Is Plea Bargaining Inevitable?

According to Chief Supreme Court Justice Warren Burger in *Santobello v. New York* over thirty years ago, "Plea Bargaining is an essential component of the administration of justice. Properly administered, it is to be encouraged . . . and leads to prompt and largely final disposition of most criminal cases."

A review of the history of plea bargaining reveals that it has not been particularly popular in the United States. Criticisms range from charges that it violates constitutional rights to complaints of a lack of uniform plea practices. Yet plea-bargaining has grown primarily as a result of the rise in the volume of crime and the legal procedures that have increased the length and complexity of criminal trials. All of the key players in the judicial process seem to promote it. The prosecution is concerned about granting concessions, the problem of overcharging, and reaching a plea agreement. The defense attorney often works on strategies that lead to a plea. The judge's role focuses on ensuring that the plea is voluntary and determining its influence on the sentence. From various U.S. Supreme Court decisions it appears that the plea bargain is constitutional. Affording the defendant a trial seems unnecessary, particularly if the prosecutor and the defense attorney intend to settle the case by negotiation.

Critical Thinking Skills

1. According to most knowledgeable judicial scholars, plea bargaining seems to be a viable and effective criminal justice procedure. It is believed to be one of the efficient methods of criminal case disposition. Yet it has poor stature in the eyes of the public. With this in mind, is it possible to argue that plea bargaining may be contained in the 1990s?

2. In recent years, efforts have been made to convert the practice of plea bargaining into a more visible, understandable, and fair dispositional process. Safeguards and guidelines have been developed to prevent due process violations and to ensure that innocent defendants do not plead guilty under duress. Can the system really be reformed by administrative means? Doesn't every defendant charged with a crime have a right to a genuine adversary proceeding?

3. Research shows that plea bargaining is the key to managing criminal caseloads. If plea bargaining were eliminated, wouldn't legislatures have to provide the courts with more resources and possibly build additional prisons?

SOURCE: The title is taken from Stephen Schulhofer, "Is Plea Bargaining Inevitable?" *Harvard Law Review* 97 (1984):125.

The Diversion Process

Many pretrial diversion programs have similar operating processes and procedures, yet each maintains its own unique characteristics.[76]

All diversion programs have admission criteria that control the selection of clients. Diversion priority is given to first-offender misdemeanors. The age, residency, and employment status of diversion candidates are also taken into consideration.

Diversion is considered after the arrest and arraignment of the individual but before the trial. The defendant chosen for a diversion program is released on a **continuance**—that is, the trial is postponed—if the relevant court personnel (judge, probation officer, assistant district attorney, arresting officer) and the program representative agree on the potential of the accused to succeed in the program. During this initial period, the program's staff assesses the potential client's suitability for the program. Acceptance may begin with a long continuance (the time limit varies from program to program) without entry of a plea and on the written waiver by the defendant of the right to a speedy trial.

Once the defendant is in the program, one of three things may occur:

1. The charges may be dismissed if the client successfully completes the program.

2. The continuance may be extended if program staff are unsure of the client's progress.
3. The client's participation in the program may be terminated because of his or her failure to comply with program guidelines and structures; in this case, the normal court process of trial and disposition takes place.

Some of the most important goals and purposes of the typical diversion program include:

1. To divert selected individuals from trial to fruitful training, employment, and counseling experiences;
2. To free up much needed resources for the court and legal system;
3. To help the court system become more aware of its rehabilitative role;
4. To help break a beginning pattern of crime and failure;
5. To sensitize employers to offenders' needs and to help alter restrictive hiring practices;
6. To create effective pretrial resources, where none exist;
7. To assist in reintegrating potential career offenders into the community; and
8. To help establish pretrial diversion as a permanent part of the state's criminal justice system.

Critique of Diversion

First viewed as a panacea that could reduce court congestion and help treat minor offenders, diversion programs have come under fire for their alleged failures. Some national evaluations have concluded that diversion programs are no more successful at avoiding stigma and reducing recidivism than traditional justice processing.[77] The most prominent criticism is that they help **widen the net** of the justice system. By this, critics mean that the people put in diversion programs are the ones most likely to have been dismissed after a brief hearing with a warning or small fine.[78] Those who would have ordinarily received a more serious sentence are not eligible for diversion anyway. Thus, rather than limiting interface with the system, the diversion programs actually increase it. Of course, not all justice experts agree with this charge, and some, such as Arnold Binder and Gilbert Geis, have championed diversion as a worthwhile exercise of the criminal justice system's rehabilitation responsibility.[79] As supporters such as Binder and Geis point out, though diversion may not be a cure-all for criminal behavior, it is an important effort that continues to be made in most jurisdictions across the United States.

While the diversion movement was originally supported by federal funds, most existing programs are now underwritten with local money. The financial limitations of the 1990s may well place many diversion programs in jeopardy due to local budget cuts. Nonetheless, the diversion alternative is an effective mechanism for dealing with certain types of offenders.

SUMMARY

Many important decisions about what happens to a defendant are made prior to trial. Hearings, such as before the grand jury and the preliminary hearing, are held to determine if probable cause exists to charge the accused with a crime. If so, the defendant is arraigned, enters a plea, is informed of his or her constitutional rights, particularly the right to the assistance of counsel, and is considered for pretrial diversion. The use of money bail and other alternatives, such as release on recognizance, allow most defendants to be free pending their trial. Bail provisions are beginning to be toughened, resulting in the preventive detention of people awaiting trial. Preventive detention has been implemented because many believe that significant numbers of criminals violate their bail and commit further crimes while on pretrial release.

The issue of discretion plays a major role at this stage of the criminal process. Since only a small percentage of criminal cases eventually go to trial, many defendants agree to plea bargains or are placed in diversion programs. Not enough judges, prosecutors, defense attorneys, and courts exist to try every defendant accused of a crime. As a result, subsystems such as plea bargaining and diversion are essential elements in the administration of the criminal justice system. Research indicates that most cases never go to trial but are bargained out of the system. Though plea bargaining has been criticized, efforts to control it have not met with success. Similarly, diversion programs have not been overly successful, yet they continue to be used throughout the United States.

QUESTIONS

1. Should criminal defendants be allowed to bargain for a reduced sentence in exchange for a guilty plea?
2. Should those accused of violent acts be subjected to preventive detention instead of bail, even though they have not been convicted of a crime?
3. What purpose does a grand jury or preliminary hearing serve in felony offenses?
4. Should a judge participate in plea bargaining? Is this a conflict of interest?
5. Do rehabilitation-oriented programs, such as pretrial diversion, create a whole new set of problems for people, such as net widening, or are they essentially beneficial?

NOTES

1. D. Alan Henry, "Pretrial Services: Today and Yesterday," *Federal Probation* (June 1991):54.
2. Bureau of Justice Assistance, *Pretrial Services Program*, (Washington, D.C.: U.S. Government Printing Office, 1990), p. 3.
3. Kristen Segebarth, *Pretrial Services and Practices in the 1990's* (Washington, D.C.: Pretrial Resource Center, March 1991), p. 3.
4. Director of Administrative Office of the United States Courts, *The Demonstration Program of Mandatory Drug Testing of Criminal Defendants* (Washington, D.C.: Bureau of Justice Assistance, March 29, 1991).
5. Andy Hall, *Pretrial Release Program Options* (Washington, D.C.: National Institute of Justice, 1984), pp. 30–31.
6. 342 U.S. 1, 72 S.Ct. 1, 96 L.Ed. 3 (1951).
7. William Rhodes, *Pretrial Release and Misconduct* (Washington, D.C.: Bureau of Justice Statistics, 1985).
8. Mary Toborg, *Pretrial Release: A National Evaluation of Practices and Outcomes* (Washington, D.C.: National Institute of Justice, 1982).
9. Rhodes, *Pretrial Release and Misconduct*.
10. Bureau of Justice Statistics, *Pretrial Release of Felony Defendants, 1988* (Washington, D.C.: U.S. Government Printing Office, February 1991), p. 1.
11. Hall, *Pretrial Release Program Options*.
12. President's Commission on Law Enforcement and the Administration of Justice, *Task Force Report: The Courts* (Washington, D.C.: U.S. Government Printing Office, 1967), p. 38.
13. D. Alan Henry and Bruce D. Beaudin, "Bail Bondsmen," *American Jails* 4 (1990):8–16.
14. Vera Institute of Justice, *1961–1971: Programs in Criminal Justice* (New York: Vera Institute of Justice, 1972).
15. Chris Eskridge, *Pretrial Release Programming* (New York: Clark Boardman, 1983), p. 27.
16. 4 Public Law 89–465, 18 U.S.C. § 3146 (1966).
17. 18 U.S.C. § 3142 (1984).
18. John Goldkamp, "Judicial Reform of Bail Practices: The Philadelphia Experiment," *Court Management Journal* 17 (1983):16–20.
19. John Goldkamp and Michael Gottfredson, *Judicial Decision Guidelines for Bail: The Philadelphia Experiment* (Washington, D.C.: National Institute of Justice, 1983).
20. 18 U.S.C. § 3142 (1984).
21. See, generally, Fred Cohen, "The New Federal Crime Control Act," *Criminal Law Bulletin* 21 (1985):330–37.
22. Stephen Kennedy and Kenneth Carlson, *Pretrial Release and Detention: The Bail Reform Act of 1984* (Washington, D.C.: Bureau of Justice Statistics, 1988).
23. Thomas Scott, "Pretrial Detention under Bail Reform Act of 1984," *American Criminal Law Review* 21 (1989):19.
24. 467 U.S. 253, 104 S.Ct. 2403, 81 L.Ed.2d 207 (1984).
25. 481 U.S. 739, 107 S.Ct. 2095, 95 L.Ed.2d 697 (1987).
26. Ibid, at 742, 107 S.Ct. at 2098.
27. Susan Kline, *Jail Inmates, 1987* (Washington, D.C.: Bureau of Justice Statistics, 1988).
28. "Jail Crowding," *Pretrial Reporter*, October-November, pp. 8–9.
29. National Coalition for Jail Reform, "Position Paper on Pre-trial Release," *Prisons Journal* 61 (1981):28–41; see also *Pretrial Reporter*, Pretrial Services Resource Center, Washington D.C., October 1991, p. 4.
30. Two excellent studies are Caleb Foote, "Compelling Appearance in Court: Administration of Bail in Philadelphia," *University of Pennsylvania Law Review* 102 (1956):1056, and idem, "A Study of Administration of Bail in New York City," *University of Pennsylvania Law Review* 106 (1960):693–730.
31. Rhodes, *Pretrial Release and Misconduct;* see also Foote, "A Study of Administration of Bail in New York."

32. John Goldkamp, *Two Classes of Accused* (Cambridge, Mass.: Ballinger, 1979).
33. Rhodes, *Pretrial Release and Misconduct*, p. 2.
34. Conference of State Court Administrators and National Center for State Courts, *State Court Organization, 1987* (Williamsburg, Va.: National Center for State Courts, 1988), p. 12.
35. National Advisory Commission on Criminal Justice Standards and Goals, *Task Force Report on Courts*, p. 74.
36. Ibid.
37. American Bar Association, *Grand Jury Policy and Model Act* (Chicago: American Bar Association, 1982).
38. Deborah Day Emerson, *Grand Jury Reform: A Review of Key Issues* (Washington, D.C.: National Institute of Justice, 1983).
39. National Advisory Commission on Criminal Justice Standards and Goals, *Task Force Report on Courts*, p. 42.
40. Alan Alschuler, "The Prosecutor's Role in Plea Bargaining," *University of Chicago Law Review* (1968):36 (1968):50–112.
41. For arguments favoring plea bargaining, see John Wheatley, "Plea Bargaining—A Case for Its Continuance," *Massachusetts Law Quarterly* 59 (1974):31.
42. National Advisory Commission on Criminal Justice Standards and Goals, *Task Force Report on Courts*, p. 46.
43. 474 U.S. 52, 106 S.Ct. 366, 88 L.Ed.2d 203 (1985).
44. 395 U.S. 238, 89 S.Ct. 1709, 23 L.Ed.2d 274 (1969).
45. 397 U.S. 742, 90 S.Ct. 1463, 25 L.Ed.2d 747 (1970).
46. 400 U.S. 25, 91 S.Ct. 160, 27 L.Ed.2d 162 (1970).
47. 404 U.S. 257, 92 S.Ct. 495, 30 L.Ed.2d 427 (1971).
48. 483 U.S. 1, 107 S.Ct. 2680, 97 L.Ed.2d 1 (1987).
49. 434 U.S. 357, 98 S.Ct. 663, 54 L.Ed.2d 604 (1978).
50. Stephen P. Lagoy, Joseph J. Senna, and Larry J. Siegel, "An Empirical Study on Information Usage for Prosecutorial Decision Making in Plea Negotiations," *American Criminal Law Review* 13 (1976):435–71.
51. Ibid., p. 462.
52. William McDonald, *Plea Bargaining: Critical Issues and Common Practices* (Washington, D.C.: U.S. Government Printing Office, 1985).
53. Barbara Boland and Brian Forst, *The Prevalence of Guilty Pleas* (Washington, D.C.: Bureau of Justice Statistics, 1984).
54. Mark Cuniff, *Sentencing Outcomes in 28 Felony Courts, 1985* (Washington, D.C.: Bureau of Justice Statistics, 1987), p. 25.
55. Douglas Smith, "The Plea Bargaining Controversy," *Journal of Criminal Law and Criminology* 77 (1986):949–67.
56. Boland and Forst, *The Prevalence of Guilty Pleas*.
57. McDonald, *Plea Bargaining: Critical Issues and Common Practices*, p. 97.
58. Alschuler, "The Prosecutor's Role in Plea Bargaining."
59. Boland and Forst, *The Prevalence of Guilty Pleas*, p. 3.
60. National Institute of Law Enforcement and Criminal Justice, *Plea Bargaining in the United States* (Washington, D.C.: Georgetown University, 1978), p. 8.
61. See American Bar Association, *Standards Relating to Pleas of Guilty* (New York: Institute of Judicial Administration, 1968); see also *North Carolina v. Alford*, 400 U.S. 25, 91 S.Ct. 160, 27 L.Ed.2d 162 (1970).
62. American Bar Association, *Standards Relating to Pleas of Guilty*, standard 3.3; National Advisory Commission on Criminal Justice Standards and Goals, *Task Force Report on Courts*, p. 42.
63. American Bar Association, *Standards Relating to Pleas of Guilty*, standards 3.3, p. 71.
64. *Federal Rules of Criminal Procedure*, rule 11.
65. American Bar Association, *Standards Relating to Pleas of Guilty*, p. 73; see also Alan Alschuler, "The Trial Judge's Role in Plea Bargaining," *Columbia Law Review* 76 (1976):1059.
66. McDonald, *Plea Bargaining: Critical Issues and Common Practices*, p. 27.
67. *Santobello v. New York*, 404 U.S. 257, 92 S.Ct. 495, 30 L.Ed.2d 427 (1971).
68. See Donald Purdy and Lawrence Jeffrey, "Plea Agreements under Federal Sentencing Guidelines," *Criminal Law Bulletin* 26 (1990):483–508.
69. National Institute of Law Enforcement and Criminal Justice, *Plea Bargaining in the United States*, pp. 37–40.
70. Jack Call, David England, and Susette Talarico, "Abolition of Plea Bargaining in the Coast Guard," *Journal of Criminal Justice* 11 (1983):351–58.
71. For a discussion of this issue, see Michael Tonry, "Plea Bargaining Bans and Rules," *Sentencing Reform Impacts* (Washington, D.C.: U.S. Government Printing Office, 1987).
72. Michael Rubenstein, Steven Clarke, and Theresa White, *Alaska Bans Plea Bargaining* (Washington, D.C.: U.S. Government Printing Office, 1980); see Theresa White Carns and John Kruse, *Alaska's Plea Bargaining Ban Re-evaluated* (Anchorage: Alaska Judicial Council, 1991).
73. Rodney Kingsworth and Michael Jungsten, "Driving under the Influence: The Impact of Legislative Reform on Court Sentencing Practices," *Crime and Delinquency* 34 (1988):3–28.
74. U.S. Department of Justice, *The Nation's Toughest Drug Law: Evaluating the New York Experience* (Washington, D.C.: U.S. Government Printing Office, 1978).
75. National District Attorneys Association, National Prosecution Standards, 2d ed. Alexandria, VA, NDAA, 1991, p. 130.
76. The information in this and the following section was adapted from the Court Resource Program, *A Program Manual Describing the Purpose, History, and Implementation of Pre-Trial Diversion in Boston* (Boston: Justice Resource Institute, 1974); see also Roberta Rovner-Pieczenik, *Pretrial Intervention Strategies: An Evaluation of Policy-Related Research and Policymaker Perceptions* (Chicago: American Bar Association, 1974).
77. Franklyn Dunford, D. Wayne Osgood, and Hart Weichselbaum, *National Evaluation of Diversion Programs* (Washington, D.C.: U.S. Government Printing Office, 1982).
78. Sharla Rausch and Charles Logan, "Diversion from Juvenile Court, Panacea or Pandora's Box?" in *Evaluating Juvenile Justice*, James Kleugel, ed. (Beverly Hills, Calif.: Sage Publications, 1983), pp. 19–30.
79. Arnold Binder and Gilbert Geis, "Ad Populum Argumentation in Criminology: Juvenile Diversion as Rhetoric," *Criminology* 30 (1984):309–88.

The Criminal Trial

CHAPTER 13

OUTLINE

KEY TERMS

adjudication
confrontation
six-person jury
Fourteenth Amendment
pro se
Speedy Trial Act
First Amendment
Court TV
adversary proceeding
venire
voir dire
challenges for cause
peremptory challenges
bench trials
direct examination
cross-examination
real evidence
directed verdict
rebuttal evidence
surrebuttal
charge
sequestration
verdict
hung jury
sentence
habeas corpus
in forma pauperis
reasonable doubt
preponderance of the evidence

The **adjudication** stage of the criminal justice process begins with a hearing that seeks to determine the truth of the facts of a case. This process is usually referred to as the criminal trial. As mentioned previously, the classic jury trial of a criminal case is an uncommon occurrence. The greatest proportion of individuals charged with crimes plead guilty. Others have their cases dismissed by the judge for a variety of reasons: the government may decide not to prosecute (*nolle prosequi*); the accused may be found emotionally disturbed and unable to stand trial; the court may be unwilling to attach the stigma of a criminal record to a particular defendant.

Still other defendants waive their constitutional right to a jury trial. In this situation, which occurs daily in the lower criminal courts, the judge may initiate a number of formal or informal dispositions, including dismissing the case, finding the defendant not guilty or guilty and imposing a sentence, or even continuing the case indefinitely. The decision the judge makes often depends on the seriousness of the offense, the background and previous record of the defendant, and the judgment of the court as to whether the case can be properly dealt with in the criminal process.

In a minor case in some jurisdictions, for example, the continuance is a frequently used disposition. In this instance, the court holds a case in abeyance without a finding of guilt in order to induce the accused to improve his or her behavior in the community; if the defendant's behavior does improve, the case is ordinarily closed within a specific amount of time.

Thus, the number of actual criminal jury trials is small in comparison to all the cases processed through the criminal justice system. Since upward of 90 percent of all defendants plead guilty and about 5 percent are dealt with by other methods, it appears that fewer than 5 percent ever reach the trial stage. Those cases that are actually tried before a jury often involve serious crimes. Such crimes require a formal inquiry into the facts to determine the guilt or innocence of the accused.

Even though proportionately few cases are actually tried by juries, the trial process remains a focal point in the criminal justice system. It symbolizes the U.S. system of jurisprudence, in which an accused person can choose to present a defense against the government's charges. The fact that the defendant has the option of going to trial significantly affects the operation of the criminal justice system. A federal government commission has stated:

Although most criminal prosecutions do not involve the adversary determination of guilt or innocence that occurs at the formal trial of a criminal case, the trial process remains a matter of vital importance to the criminal justice system. Whether or not a defendant chooses to invoke his right to trial, he has an interest in the trial process because in many cases it represents to him a legal option guaranteed by the Constitution of the United States. The opportunity to go to trial provides a valuable safeguard against abuse of informal processing and a basis for encouraging faith in the system.

Since informal disposition of a case often occurs only after the case proceeds along the formal route towards trial, procedures for formal processing at the earlier court stages may be used for a much greater number of cases than actually comes to trial. Because all other means of processing cases must be evaluated as alternatives to formal trial, the attractiveness of trial is a major consideration in both prosecution and defense willingness to process a case administratively.[1]

Legal Rights During Trial

Underlying every trial are constitutional principles, complex legal procedures, rules of court, and interpretations of statutes, all designed to ensure that the accused will receive a fair trial. This section discusses the most important constitutional rights of the accused at the trial stage of the criminal justice system and reviews the legal nature of the trial process. The major legal decisions and statutes involving the right to confront witnesses and the rights to jury trial, counsel, self-representation, and speedy and public trial are all examined.

The Right to Confront Witnesses

The Sixth Amendment states that "In all criminal prosecutions, the accused shall enjoy the right . . . to be confronted with the witnesses against him."[2] The **confrontation** clause is essential to a fair criminal trial because it restricts and controls the admissibility of hearsay evidence. In other words, second-hand evidence, which depends on a witness not available in court, is ordinarily limited in preference to the personal knowledge of a witness or victim of a crime. The Framers of the Constitution sought face-to-face accusations in which the defendant has a right to see and cross-examine all witnesses against him or her. The idea that it is always more difficult to tell lies about people to their face than behind their back illustrates the meaning of the confrontation clause. In other words, a witness in a criminal trial may have more difficulty repeating his or her testimony when facing the accused in a trial than in providing information to the police during an investigation. The accused has the right to confront the witnesses and challenge their assertions and perceptions: Did they really see what they believe? Are they biased? Can they be trusted? What about the veracity of their testimony? Generally speaking, the courts have been nearly unanimous in their belief that the right of confrontation and cross-examination is an essential requirement for a fair trial.[3]

This face-to-face presence has been reviewed recently by the Supreme Court in matters involving a child as a witness in criminal proceedings. In the case of *Coy v. Iowa* (1988), the Supreme Court limited the protection available to child sex abuse victims at the trial stage.[4] In *Coy*, two girls were allowed to be cross-examined behind a screen that separated them from the defendant. The Court ruled that the screen violated the defendant's right to confront witnesses and

Trials can be a terrifying experience for a child witness. The Supreme Court has allowed states to replace in-court testimony with cross examination via closed circuit television.

overturned his conviction. However, in her supporting opinion, Justice Sandra Day O'Connor made it clear that ruling out the protective screen did not bar the states from using videotapes or closed-circuit television. Although Justice O'Connor recognized that the Sixth Amendment right to confront witnesses was violated, she indicated that an exception to a literal interpretation of the confrontation clause may be appropriate.

In *Maryland v. Craig* (1990), the second case in this area, the Supreme Court carved out an exception to the Sixth Amendment confrontation clause by deciding that alleged child abuse victims could testify by closed-circuit television if face-to-face confrontation would cause them trauma.[5] In allowing the states to take testimony via closed-circuit television, the Supreme Court has found that circumstances exist in child sex abuse cases that override the defendant's right of confrontation.

As a result of these decisions, it appears that the confrontation clause does not guarantee criminal defendants the absolute right to a face-to-face meeting with witnesses at their trial. Instead, according to *Maryland v. Craig*, it reflects a preference for such a guarantee. *Craig* signals that the Court is willing to compromise a defendant's right to confront his or her accuser in order to achieve a social objective, the prosecution of a child abuser.

The Right to a Jury Trial

The defendant has the right to choose whether the trial will be before a judge or a jury. Although the Sixth Amendment to the U.S. Constitution guarantees to the defendant the right to a jury trial, the defendant can and often does waive this right. In fact, a substantial proportion of defendants, particularly those charged with misdemeanors, are tried before the court without a jury.

The major legal issue surrounding jury trial has been the question of whether all offenders, both misdemeanants and felons, have an absolute right to a jury trial. Because the U.S. Constitution is silent on this point, the U.S. Supreme

Court has ruled that all defendants in felony cases have this right. In *Duncan v. Louisiana* (1968), the Court held that the Sixth Amendment right to a jury trial is applicable to the states, as well as to the federal government, and that it can be interpreted to apply to all defendants accused of serious crimes.[6] The Court in *Duncan* based its holding on the premise

> that in the American States, as in the federal judicial system, a general grant of jury trial for serious offenses is a fundamental right, essential for preventing miscarriages of justice and for assuring that fair trials are provided for all defendants.[7]

The *Duncan* decision did not settle whether all defendants charged with crimes in state courts are constitutionally entitled to jury trials. It seemed to draw the line at only those charged with serious offenses, leaving the decision to grant jury trials to defendants in minor cases to the discretion of the individual states.

In 1970, in the case of *Baldwin v. New York*, the Supreme Court departed from the distinction of serious versus minor offenses and decided that a defendant has a constitutional right to a jury trial when facing a prison sentence of six months or more, regardless of whether the crime committed was a felony or a misdemeanor.[8] Where the possible sentence is six months or less, the accused is not entitled to a jury trial unless it is authorized by state statute.

The latest U.S. Supreme Court decision on jury trials occurred in 1989 in the case of *Blanton v. North Las Vegas*.[9] Here, the Court ruled unanimously that when a state defines the crime of drunk driving as a petty offense, the U.S. Constitution does not require that the defendant receive a jury trial. If, however, a state treats driving under the influence as a serious crime, a jury trial would be required. This decision upheld a Nevada law classifying drunk driving as a petty offense and similar procedures in at least five other jurisdictions in the United States.

Jury Size. Other important issues related to the defendant's rights in a criminal jury trial include the right to a jury consisting of twelve people or less and the right to a unanimous verdict.

The actual size of the jury has been a matter of great concern. Can a defendant be tried and convicted of a crime by a jury of fewer than twelve persons? Traditionally, twelve jurors have deliberated as the triers of fact in criminal cases involving misdemeanors or felonies. However, the U.S. Constitution does not specifically require a jury of twelve persons. As a result, in *Williams v. Florida* in 1970, the U.S. Supreme Court held that a **six-person jury** in a criminal trial does not deprive a defendant of the constitutional right to a jury trial.[10] The Court made clear that the twelve-person panel is not a necessary ingredient of a trial by jury and upheld a Florida statute permitting the use of a six-person jury in a robbery trial. The majority opinion in the *Williams* case traced the Court's rationale for its decision:

> We conclude, in short, as we began: the fact that a jury at common law was composed of precisely twelve is a historical accident, unnecessary to effect the purposes of the jury system and wholly without significance "except to mystics." [11]

Justice Byron White, writing further for the majority, said, "In short, while sometime in the 14th century the size of the jury came to be fixed generally at 12, that particular feature of the jury system appears to have been a historical accident, unrelated to the great purpose which gave rise to the jury in the first place." [12]

On the basis of this decision, many states are using six-person juries in misdemeanor cases, and some states, such as Florida, Louisiana, and Utah, even use them in felony cases (except in capital offenses). In the *Williams* decision, Justice White emphasized, "We have occasion to determine what minimum number can still constitute a jury, but do not doubt that six is above that minimum." [13] The six-person jury can play an important role in the criminal justice system because it promotes court efficiency and also helps implement the defendant's rights to a speedy trial. It should be noted, however, that the Supreme Court has ruled that a jury comprised of fewer than six people is unconstitutional[14] and that if a six-person jury is used in serious crimes, its verdict must be unanimous.[15]

In addition to the convention of twelve-person juries in criminal trials, tradition also had been that the jurors' decision must be unanimous. However, in the case of *Apodica v. Oregon* (1972), the Supreme Court held that the Sixth and Fourteenth Amendments do not prohibit criminal convictions by less than unanimous jury verdicts in noncapital cases.[16] In the *Apodica* case, the Court upheld an Oregon statute requiring only ten of twelve jurors to convict the defendant of assault with a deadly weapon, burglary, and grand larceny. It is not unusual to have such verdicts in civil matters, but much controversy remains regarding their place in the criminal process. Those in favor of less-than-unanimous verdicts argue, as the Court stated in *Apodica*, that unanimity does not materially contribute to the exercise of commonsense judgment. Some also believe that it would be easier for the prosecutor to obtain a guilty verdict if the law required only a substantial majority to convict the defendant. Today, the unanimous verdict remains the rule in most state jurisdictions and in the federal system.

The Right to Counsel at Trial

Mention has already been made in previous chapters of the defendant's right to counsel at numerous points in the criminal justice system. Through a series of leading U.S. Supreme Court decisions (*Powell v. Alabama* in 1932,[17] *Gideon v. Wainwright* in 1963,[18] and *Argersinger v. Hamlin* in 1972[19]), the right of a criminal defendant to have counsel in state trials has become a fundamental right in the U.S. criminal justice system. Today, state courts must provide counsel at trial to indigent defendants who face the possibility of incarceration.

It is interesting to note the historical development of the law regarding right to counsel, for it shows the gradual process of decision making in the Supreme Court, as well as reiterates the relationship between the Bill of Rights and the **Fourteenth Amendment.** The Bill of Rights protects citizens against federal encroachment, while the Fourteenth Amendment provides that no state shall deprive any person of life, liberty, or property without due process of law. A difficult constitutional question has been whether the Fourteenth Amendment incorporates the Bill of Rights and makes its provisions binding on individual states. In *Powell v. Alabama* (also known as the *Scottsboro Boys* case), for example, nine young black men were charged in an Alabama court with raping two young white women. They were tried and convicted without the benefits of counsel. The U.S. Supreme Court concluded that the presence of a defense attorney is so vital to a fair trial that the failure of the Alabama trial court to appoint counsel was a denial of due process of law under the Fourteenth Amendment. In this instance, due process meant the right to counsel for defendants accused of committing a capital offense. The *Powell* decision is discussed in detail in the Law in Review on page 459.

LAW IN REVIEW

Powell v. Alabama (1932)

Facts

The defendants, nine black youths, were charged with the crime of raping two white women. While they were riding on a freight train through Alabama with two white women and some white men, a fight broke out, and all the white male participants were thrown off the train. After the fight was reported, a sheriff's posse seized the defendants. All the black youths were taken to Scottsboro, Alabama, the county seat, where the two women claimed they were raped on the train. In an atmosphere of hostility in which the militia was called out to safeguard the prisoners, the "Scottsboro Boys" were indicted, arraigned, and held for trial. The pretrial proceedings began when a lawyer expressed an interest in assisting the court as counsel for the defense. Separate trials were held for groups of the defendants, and in spite of the evidence to the contrary, eight were convicted and sentenced to death. The record of the trial indicated that the exact ages of the youths were unknown, that all were illiterate, and that they had been arrested, charged, convicted, and sentenced in an atmosphere of public hostility under close surveillance by the militia. They were not allowed to contact family or friends, and the court failed to give them reasonable time and the opportunity to secure legal counsel to represent them. It was also alleged that the two women were known to be prostitutes.

Decision

The trial began six days after the indictment. The court did not ask the defendants whether they were able to obtain counsel but simply appointed "all members of the bar" as counsel for the limited purpose of representing the defendants at the initial arraignment. One attorney assisted at the trial and represented the defendants in only a perfunctory, haphazard, and *pro forma* manner. The defendants were convicted of rape, a capital offense, and appealed their conviction on the ground that they had not been accorded the right to counsel in a trial involving a capital offense. The Supreme Court of Alabama upheld the convictions of seven of the eight defendants, and the case was eventually appealed to the U.S. Supreme Court on the ground that the defendants had been denied their due process rights under the Fourteenth Amendment. In a limited and narrow opinion, the Court agreed that the defendants had been denied their rights to counsel because they were not afforded a reasonable time to secure counsel to defend themselves against very serious charges. Accordingly, the Court held that because it was a capital case, the defendants' Fourteenth Amendment rights to due process had been violated, and it reversed the judgments of the Alabama state courts.

Significance of the Case

The *Scottsboro Boys* case began in 1931, and appeals lasted until the 1940s. The case marked the beginning of a long line of cases that eventually would guarantee every criminal defendant in the criminal justice system the right to counsel. It also reveals the legal struggle and life-and-death ordeal of a group of black youths, falsely accused of raping two white women, who fought for almost a decade to secure their freedom.

Then, in the case of *Gideon v. Wainwright* almost thirty years later, the Supreme Court in a unanimous and historic decision stated that while the Sixth Amendment does not explicitly lay down a rule binding on the states, right to counsel is so fundamental and ethical to a fair trial that states are obligated to abide by it under the Fourteenth Amendment's due process clause. Thus, the Sixth Amendment requirement regarding the right to counsel in the federal court system is also binding on the states. The Law in Review on page 460 examines the *Gideon* case.

The *Gideon* decision made it clear that a person charged with a felony in a state court has an absolute constitutional right to counsel. But while some states applied the *Gideon* ruling to all criminal trials, others did not provide a defendant with an attorney in misdemeanor cases. Then, in 1972, in the momentous decision of *Argersinger v. Hamlin*, the Supreme Court held that no person can be imprisoned for any offense—whether classified as a petty offense, a misdemeanor,

LAW IN REVIEW

Gideon v. Wainwright (1963)

Facts

Clarence Gideon was charged in a Florida state court with having broken into and entered a poolroom with intent to commit a misdemeanor. This offense is a felony under Florida law. Appearing in court without funds and without a lawyer, the petitioner asked the court to appoint him counsel. The court replied that it could not appoint counsel because under Florida law the only time the court can appoint counsel for a defendant is when that person is charged with a capital offense.

Put to a trial before a jury, Gideon conducted his defense about as well as could be expected from a layperson. He made an opening statement to the jury, cross-examined the state's witnesses, presented witnesses in his own defense, declined to testify himself, and made a short argument emphasizing his innocence of the charge contained in the information filed in the case. The jury returned a verdict of guilty, and Gideon was sentenced to serve five years in the Florida state prison.

Gideon filed a habeas corpus petition in the Florida Supreme Court attacking his conviction and sentence on the ground that the trial court's refusal to appoint counsel for him denied him rights guaranteed by the Constitution and the Bill of Rights. Relief was denied.

Gideon then filed an *in forma pauperis* appeal to the U.S. Supreme Court, which granted certiorari and appointed counsel to represent him. The Supreme Court took on this case to review its earlier decision in *Betts v. Brady* (1942), which held that the refusal to appoint counsel is not so "offensive to the common and fundamental ideas of fairness" as to amount to a denial of due process.

The issues faced by the Supreme Court were simple but of gigantic importance: (1) Is an indigent defendant charged in a state court with a noncapital felony entitled to the assistance of a lawyer under the due process clause of the Fourteenth Amendment? (2) Should *Betts v. Brady* be overruled?

Decision

Justice Hugo Black delivered the opinion of the Court. "We accept *Betts v. Brady's* assumption, based as it was on our prior cases, that a provision of the Bill of Rights which is fundamental and essential to a fair trial is made obligatory upon the States by the Fourteenth Amendment. We think the Court in *Betts v. Brady* was wrong, however, in concluding that the Sixth Amendment's guarantee is not one of the fundamental rights. In our adversary system of criminal justice, any person brought into court, who is too poor to hire a lawyer, cannot be assured a fair trial unless counsel is provided for him. That government hires lawyers to prosecute and defendants who have the money to hire lawyers to defend, are the strongest indications of the widespread belief that lawyers in criminal court are necessities, not luxuries. The right of one charged with crime to counsel may not be deemed essential to fair trial in some countries, but it is in ours."

Significance of the Case

The U.S. Supreme Court unanimously overruled its earlier decision in *Betts v. Brady* and explicitly held that the right to counsel in criminal cases is fundamental and essential to a fair trial and as such applicable to the states by way of the Fourteenth Amendment. The *Gideon* decision thus guarantees the right to counsel in criminal cases in both federal and state proceedings. The refusal to appoint counsel for indigent defendants consequently violates the due process clause of the Fourteenth Amendment and the right to counsel of the Sixth Amendment.

or a felony—unless he or she is offered representation by counsel at trial. (See the Law in Review on page 462.) The decision extended this right to virtually all defendants in state criminal prosecutions. The timeline in Figure 13.1 indicates how it has taken almost two hundred years to establish what the U.S. Constitution stated in 1791, namely that "in all criminal prosecutions, the accused shall enjoy the right . . . to have the assistance of counsel for his defense." [20]

The Right to Self-Representation

Another important question regarding the right to counsel is whether criminal defendants are guaranteed the right to represent themselves, that is, to act as

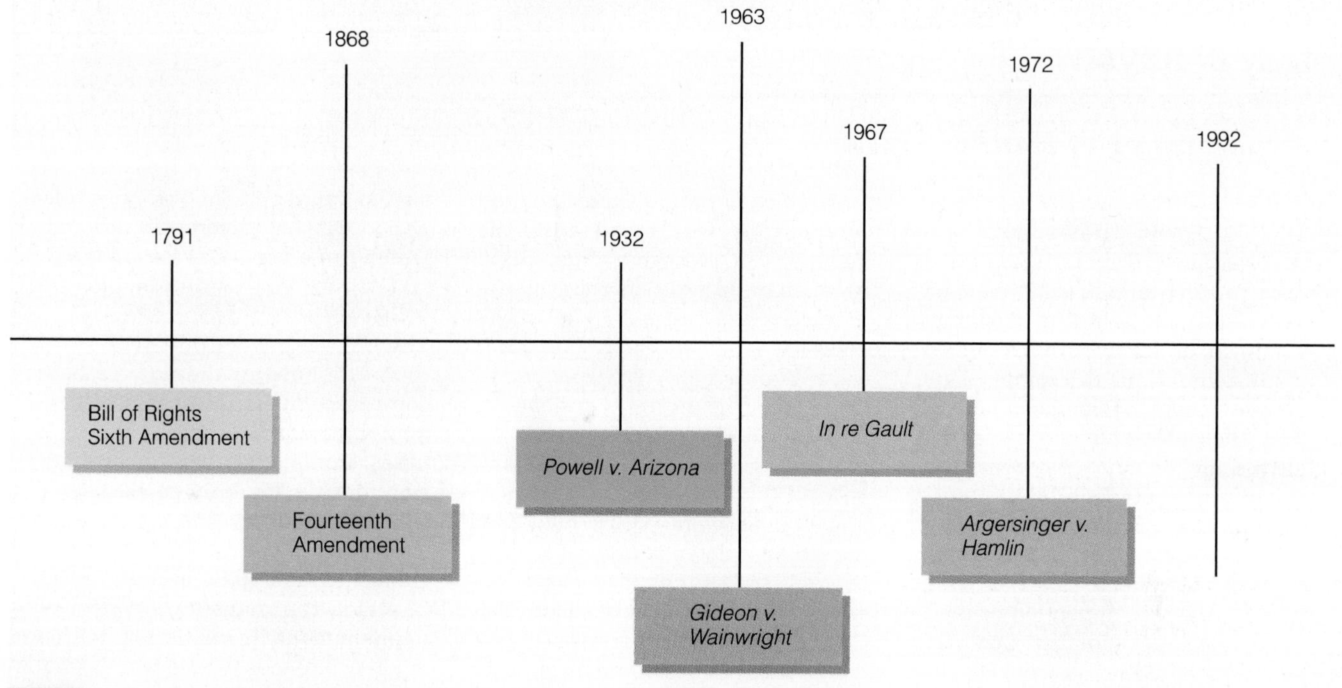

FIGURE 13.1
Timeline for Right to Counsel at Criminal Trials

SOURCE: The idea for this timeline was adapted from Edward Monahan, "Who is Trying to Kill the Sixth Amendment?" *American Bar Association Journal of Criminal Justice* 6 (1991):26, reprinted with permission.

their own lawyers. Prior to the U.S. Supreme Court decision in *Faretta v. California* in 1975,[21] defendants in most state courts and in the federal system claimed the right to proceed ***pro se,*** or for themselves, by reason of federal and state statutes and on state constitutional grounds. This permitted defendants to choose between hiring counsel or conducting their own defense. Whether a constitutional right to represent oneself in a criminal prosecution existed remained an open question until the *Faretta* decision.

The defendant, Anthony Faretta, was charged with grand theft in Los Angeles County. Before his trial, he requested that he be permitted to represent himself. The judge told Faretta that he believed this would be a mistake but accepted his waiver of counsel. The judge then held a hearing to inquire into Faretta's ability to conduct his own defense and subsequently ruled that Faretta had not made an intelligent and knowing waiver of his right to the assistance of counsel. As a result, the judge appointed a public defender to represent Faretta, who was brought to trial, found guilty, and sentenced to prison. He appealed, claiming that he had a constitutional right to self-representation.

Upon review, the U.S. Supreme Court recognized Faretta's *pro se* right on a constitutional basis, while making it conditional on a showing that the defendant could competently, knowingly, and intelligently waive his right to counsel. The Court's decision was based on the belief that the right of self-representation finds support in the structure of the Sixth Amendment, as well as in English and colonial jurisprudence from which the amendment emerged.[22] Thus, in forcing Faretta to accept counsel against his will, the California trial court deprived him of his constitutional right to conduct his own defense.

LAW IN REVIEW

Argersinger v. Hamlin (1972)

Facts

The indigent defendant was charged in a Florida state court with carrying a concealed weapon, an offense for which a maximum sentence of six months imprisonment, a fine of one thousand dollars, or both could be imposed. At his trial, the defendant was not represented by counsel. He was convicted and sentenced by the judge to ninety days in jail. The defendant brought a habeas corpus petition to the Florida Supreme Court, arguing that he was not appointed counsel as an indigent defendant and consequently could not present his defense to the charges against him. The defendant's claim was rejected by the Florida Supreme Court in a 4-to-3 vote, holding that the right to court-appointed counsel extended only to trials for nonpetty offenses punishable by more than six months' imprisonment.

The U.S. Supreme Court granted certiorari. It was faced with the question of whether the Sixth Amendment's right to counsel, applicable to the states by way of the Fourteenth Amendment (see *Gideon v. Wainwright* [1963]), extended to include the right to counsel in misdemeanors.

Decision

The U.S. Supreme Court held that the indigent defendant has a right to counsel in all criminal cases for which he or she could be jailed. The Court stated that because defendants charged with crimes punishable by imprisonment for less than six months may be tried without a jury, this does not mean that they may be tried without a lawyer. Assistance of counsel is often requisite to the very existence of a fair trial. In a misdemeanor case, the Court emphasized, the questions that can lead to imprisonment even for a brief period can be as complex as those leading to a sentence for a felony.

Significance of the Case

The U.S. Supreme Court was asked to decide how far the right to have court-appointed counsel for indigent defendants would extend. In other words, did the *Gideon* decision include the right to counsel in all criminal cases? The Court specifically held that this right to counsel should extend to all criminal cases in which the defendant could face imprisonment. It was not a matter of petty offenses versus felonies but a matter of whether imprisonment could be imposed for the crime charged.

It is important to recognize that the *Faretta* case dealt only with the constitutional right to self-representation. It did not provide guidelines for administering the right during the criminal process.[23]

Today, a defendant in a criminal trial is able to waive the right to the assistance of counsel. Generally, however, the courts have encouraged defendants to accept counsel so that criminal trials may proceed in an orderly and fair manner. Where defendants ask to be permitted to represent themselves and are found competent to do so, the court normally approves their requests. The defendants in these cases are almost always cautioned by the courts against self-representation. When *pro se* defendants' actions are disorderly and disruptive, the court can terminate their right to represent themselves.

Joint representation by counsel and defendant, in which the attorney would be retained on a standby basis, has been suggested as an alternative to the exclusive use of either representation by counsel or self-representation.[24] However, under current federal and state law, the defendant who has waived the right to counsel and is proceeding with the trial *pro se* is not entitled to standby counsel.

The Right to a Speedy Trial

The requirement of the right to counsel at trial in virtually all criminal cases often causes delays in the formal processing of defendants through the court system. Counsel usually seeks to safeguard the interests of the accused and in so doing may employ a variety of legal devices—pretrial motions, plea negotiations, trial procedures, and appeals—that require time and extend the decision-making period in a particular case. The involvement of counsel, along with inefficiencies in the court process—such as the frequent granting of continuances, poor scheduling procedures, and the abuse of time by court personnel—has made the problem of delay in criminal cases a serious and constitutional issue. As the American Bar Association's *Standards Relating to Speedy Trial* state, "Congestion in the trial courts of this country, particularly in urban centers, is currently one of the major problems of judicial administration."[25]

The Sixth Amendment guarantees a criminal defendant the right to a speedy trial in federal prosecutions. This right has been made applicable to the states by the decision in *Klopfer v. North Carolina* (1967).[26] In this case, the defendant Klopfer was charged with criminal trespass. His original trial ended in a mistrial, and he sought to determine if and when the government intended to retry him. The prosecutor asked the court to take a "*nolle prosequi* with leave," a legal device discharging the defendant but allowing the government to prosecute him in the future. The U.S. Supreme Court held that the effort by the government to postpone Klopfer's trial indefinitely without reason denied him the right to a speedy trial guaranteed by the Sixth and Fourteenth Amendments.

In *Klopfer*, the Supreme Court emphasized the importance of the speedy trial in the criminal process by stating that this right was "as fundamental as any of the rights secured by the Sixth Amendment."[27] Its primary purposes are

1. To improve the credibility of the trial by seeking to have witnesses available for testimony as early as possible;
2. To reduce the anxiety for the defendant in awaiting trial, as well as to avoid pretrial detention;
3. To avoid extensive pretrial publicity and questionable conduct of public officials that would influence the defendant's right to a fair trial; and
4. To avoid any delay that can affect the defendant's ability to defend himself or herself.

Definition of Speedy Trial. Because of court backlogs, the government has been forced to deal with the problem of how to meet the constitutional requirement of a speedy trial. In 1967, the President's Commission on Law Enforcement and the Administration of Justice suggested that nine months would be a reasonable period of time in which to litigate the typical criminal felony case through appeal. The process from arrest through trial would involve four months, with the decision of an appeals court, an additional five months.[28] Then in 1973, the National Advisory Commission on Criminal Justice Standards and Goals recommended that the period from the arrest of the defendant in a felony prosecution to the beginning of the trial generally should not be longer than sixty days and that the period from arrest to trial in a misdemeanor prosecution should be no more than thirty.[29]

Today, most states and the federal government have statutes fixing the period of time during which an accused must be brought to trial. These ensure that a person's trial cannot be unduly delayed and that the suspect cannot be held in custody indefinitely. Congress enacted the **Speedy Trial Act** of 1974 to guarantee the accused the right to a speedy trial by establishing the following time limits: (1) an information or indictment charging a person with a crime must be filed within thirty days of the time of arrest; (2) the arraignment must be held within ten days of the time of the information or indictment; and (3) the trial must be held within sixty days of the arraignment.[30] This means that the accused must be brought to trial in the federal system within one hundred days. Other special provisions of the Speedy Trial Act include the gradual phasing in of time standards, the use of fines against defense counsels for causing delays, and the allocation of funds with which to plan speedy trial programs in the federal judicial districts. The Speedy Trial Act was amended in 1979 to give further precision to the guarantee of a speedy trial and to encourage state jurisdictions to adopt similar procedures. Many state speedy trial statutes provide even shorter time limits when a defendant is detained in jail.

In a very important recent case involving the federal Speedy Trial Act, *United States v. Taylor* (1988), the Supreme Court considered the legality of a U.S. District Court's discretion to dismiss charges against a defendant who failed to appear for trial, rather than permit reprosecution.[31] The District Court found that the government had exhibited "lackadaisical" behavior and slow processing in returning the defendant for trial. According to the District Court, fifteen nonexcludable days in the speedy trial time clock had passed since the defendant's failure to appear for his trial and therefore, dismissal of the original indictment was mandated. But the Supreme Court found that the district court had ignored other relevant facts, such as the brevity of the delay, the lack of prejudice to the defendant, and the defendant's own illegal contribution to the delay. Thus, according to the Supreme Court, barring reprosecution as a remedy was an abuse of the District Court's discretion.

Fair Trial Versus Free Press

Every person charged with a crime also has a fundamental right to a fair trial. What does it mean to have a fair trial in the criminal justice system? A fair trial is one before an impartial judge and jury, in an environment of judicial restraint, orderliness, and fair decision making. Although it is not expressly stated in the U.S. Constitution, the right of the accused to a fair trial is guaranteed by the due process clauses of the Fifth and Fourteenth Amendments. This fair trial right may be violated in a number of ways. A hostile courtroom crowd, improper pressure on witnesses, or any behavior that produces prejudice toward the accused, among other things, can preclude a fair trial. When, for example, a defendant was required to go to trial in prison clothing, the U.S. Supreme Court found a violation of the due process clause of the Fourteenth Amendment.[32] Adverse pretrial publicity can also deny a defendant a fair trial. The release of premature evidence by the prosecutor, extensive and critical reporting by the news media, and vivid and uncalled for details in indictments can all prejudice a defendant's case.

Recently, one of the controversial issues involving the conduct of a trial has been the apparent conflict between the constitutional guarantees of fair trial and freedom of the press. When there is wide pretrial publicity, as in the Jean Harris murder case, the John Delorean case, the Atlanta child killings, and the Rodney King police-brutality case, whether an accused can have a fair trial as guaranteed by the Fifth, Sixth, and Fourteenth Amendments has been a matter of great concern. Think about the intense media coverage in the Pamela Smart murder case and the William Kennedy Smith rape trial.

The murder conviction of Dr. Sam Sheppard over twenty years ago was reversed by the U.S. Supreme Court because negative publicity generated by the government denied Sheppard a fair trial.[33] More recently, in one of the most highly publicized trials in U.S. history, Claus von Bulow was acquitted of the

The right of the press to cover criminal trials has become an increasingly controversial issue, involving questions of fairness and privacy.

attempted murder of his wife after two trials.[34] Both the prosecution and the defense used the media to reflect their side. Press conferences, leaked news stories, and daily television and radio coverage all contributed to a media sideshow. Even jury sequestration was not successful since many of the jurors had prior knowledge of the case. In the end, the media played a critical role in both the initial conviction and the subsequent acquittal on retrial of the defendant.

Judges involved in newsworthy criminal cases have attempted to place restraints on media coverage to preserve the defendant's right to a fair trial; at the same time, it is generally believed that the media has a constitutional right to provide news coverage. In the politically significant and highly publicized trial of Oliver North, U.S. District Court Judge Gerhard Gesell struggled with the fair trial/free press issue. North's lawyers argued that the defendant's constitutional right to a fair trial and complete defense required the disclosure of classified information. The U.S. Justice Department showed that national security concerns prevented certain material from being made public, however, and the court was forced to dismiss conspiracy and theft charges against North, although he was subsequently convicted on other criminal matters. In light of such problems, the U.S. Supreme Court approved an agreement designed to protect classified data so that North's trial in regard to the Iran-Contra affair could proceed.

Some critics of the media have even suggested that the media should be prohibited from reporting about ongoing criminal trials. Such an approach, however, would inhibit the role of the press in monitoring the criminal justice system and violate the constitutional right to a free press under the First Amendment. Public information about criminal trials, the judicial system, and other areas of government is an essential and indispensable characteristic of a free society. At the same time, trial by the media violates a defendant's right to a fair trial.

The Law of Fair Trial

The U.S. Supreme Court dealt with the fair trial/free press issue in the case of *Nebraska Press Association v. Stuart* (1976).[35] The Court ruled unconstitutional a

COURT TV is a cable network devoted to televising criminal cases. Here jurors in Palm Beach, Florida listen to testimony in the William Kennedy Smith rape trial. Though Smith was acquitted, the high profile case made him a familiar household name.

trial judge's order prohibiting the press from reporting the confessions implicating the defendant in the crime. The Court's decision was based primarily on the fact that "prior restraints on speech and publication are the most serious and least tolerable infringement on First Amendment rights."[36]

In *Gannett Co. v. DePasquale* (1979), the court was asked to decide if the public had an independent constitutional right of access to a pretrial judicial hearing, even though all the parties agreed to closure to guarantee a fair trial.[37] Justice Potter Stewart, writing for the Court, said that the trial court was correct in finding that the press had a right of access of constitutional dimensions but that this right was outweighed by the defendant's right to a fair trial.[38] In other words, the Court balanced competing social interests and found that denial of access by the public did not violate the First, Sixth, or Fourteenth Amendment rights of the defendant. The interest of justice requires that the defendant's case should not be jeopardized, and the desire for a fair trial far outweighed the public's right of access to a pretrial suppression hearing. The *Gannett* decision is not ordinarily cited as precedent to determine whether a right of access to trials is constitutionally guaranteed, since the Court believes that motion hearings are not trials.

The question of the **First Amendment** right of access to preliminary hearings was raised again in the case of *Press-Enterprise Co. v. Superior Court* (1986).[39] The defendant, charged with murder, agreed to have the preliminary hearing closed to the press and the public. But the Supreme Court said that closure is permissible under the First Amendment only if there is a substantial probability that the defendant's right to a fair trial would be prejudiced by publicity that closed proceedings would prevent. According to the Court, preliminary hearings have traditionally been open to the public and should remain so.

The Right to a Public Trial

The U.S. Supreme Court has also interpreted the First Amendment to mean that members of the press (and the public) have a right to attend trials. The most important case on this issue is *Richmond Newspapers, Inc. v. Virginia* (1980).[40] Here, the Supreme Court clearly established that criminal trials must remain public. Following the *Richmond Newspapers* case, the Supreme Court extended the right of the press to attend trials involving even highly sensitive, sexually related matters in which the victim was under eighteen years of age.[41] The right was further extended to the selection and question of potential jurors[42] and to the hearing on pretrial motions.[43]

Although the Court has ruled that criminal trials are open to the press, the right to a public trial is basically for the benefit of the accused.[44] The familiar language of the Sixth Amendment clearly states that "the accused shall enjoy the right to a speedy and public trial." Underlying this provision is the belief that a trial in the criminal justice system must be a public activity. The amendment is rooted in the principle that justice cannot survive behind walls of silence.[45] It was enacted because the Framers of the Constitution distrusted secret trials and arbitrary proceedings. In the 1948 case of *In re Oliver,* for instance, the Supreme Court held that the secrecy of a criminal contempt trial violated the right of the defendant to a public trial under the Fourteenth Amendment.[46] In *Oliver,* the Court recognized the constitutional guarantee of a public trial for the defendant in state and federal courts. Three decades later, the *Richmond Newspapers* decision clearly affirmed the right of the public and the press to attend criminal trials.

High-Profile Criminal Trials

Other fair trial/free press issues remain, however. Whether jury trials should be televised, for instance, is one of the most controversial questions in the criminal justice system today. The legal community was divided over the use of TV cameras in the courtroom for the highly publicized ten-day rape trial of William Kennedy Smith in 1991.[47] Smith's acquittal also raised the question of whether the media should protect the privacy rights of the rape victim (name and picture) from the public. In addition, the case proved to be a financial boom for **Court TV** (Courtroom Television Network), a private cable network devoted exclusively to televising trials.

In another case that received a great deal of media coverage, Mike Tyson, the former heavyweight boxing champion, was convicted in 1992 of raping a Miss Black America contestant who said he lured her to his hotel room and overpowered her. Because of the interest in the trial, closed-circuit TV was used to accommodate the more than one hundred news organizations that covered the trial.

Judges involved in such high-profile trials are not only faced with placing restraints on press coverage but also on television coverage. In the Tyson trial, the state of Indiana, which normally does not allow TV cameras in its courts, acquiesced in the use of closed-circuit TV. Florida, on the other hand, refused to allow television coverage of the Manuel Noriega drug trial, as did California in the Rodney King trial.

Today, many state courts permit such coverage, often at the judge's discretion, but the use of television cameras, video recorders, and still photography is banned in the federal court system.[48] In addition, Chief Supreme Court Justice William Rehnquist opposes televising Court proceedings. Yet, the truth is that televising criminal proceedings has significant advantages: judges would be better prepared; the public would be informed about important legal issues; and the proceedings would provide an educational function that would offset the simplistic views offered by such popular movies and television programs as "The People's Court," "Miller's Court," and "L.A. Law."

The extent to which judges, witnesses, and the accused would be influenced by the use of modern technology in the courtroom remains unknown, however, and is the major argument against adopting complete and total media coverage. In extreme cases, the judge might clear the courtroom where violence is threatened or where the rights of the accused and the state are at risk. Also, under the statutes of different jurisdictions, spectators and the press, for example, might be excluded from the trial of juvenile cases, certain sordid sex crimes, or national security offenses. Regardless of the kind of crime committed, a defendant is always permitted to have family, close associates, and legal counsel at his or her trial. In the final analysis, the Supreme Court has held, in *Chandler v. Florida* (1981), that, subject to certain safeguards, a state may allow electronic media coverage by television stations and still photography of public criminal proceedings over the objection of the defendant in a criminal trial.[49] Although the Supreme Court did not maintain in *Chandler* that the media had a constitutional right to televise trials, it left it up to state courts to decide whether they wished trials televised in their jurisdictions.

The controversy surrounding the televising of trials has prompted bar and media groups to develop standards in an attempt to find an acceptable middle ground between the First and Sixth Amendment rights concerning public trials. To be sure, the defendant has a constitutional right to a public trial, but it is equally imperative that the media exercise its First Amendment rights. And, above all, the court must seek to protect the rights of the accused to a fair trial by an unbiased jury. In the Analyzing Criminal Justice Issues on page 470, the issue of televising criminal trials is reviewed.

The Trial Process

The trial of a criminal case is a formal process conducted in a specific and orderly fashion in accordance with rules of criminal law, procedure, and evidence. Unlike what transpires in popular television programs involving lawyers—where witnesses are often asked leading and prejudicial questions and where judges go far beyond their supervisory role—the modern criminal trial is a complicated and often time-consuming technical affair. It is a structured **adversary proceeding** in which both the prosecution and defense follow specific procedures and argue the merits of their cases before the judge and jury. Each side seeks to present its case in the most favorable light. When possible, the prosecutor and the defense attorney will object to evidence they consider damaging to their positions. The prosecutor will use direct testimony, physical evidence, and a confession, if available, to convince the jury that the accused is guilty beyond a reasonable doubt. On the other hand, the defense attorney will rebut the government's case with his or her own evidence, make certain that the rights of the criminal defendant under the federal and state constitutions are considered during all phases of the trial, and determine whether an appeal is appropriate if the client is found guilty. The defense attorney will use his or her skill at cross-examination to discredit government witnesses: perhaps they have changed their statements from the time they gave them to the police; perhaps their memory is faulty; perhaps their background is unsavory, and so on. From the beginning of the process to its completion, the judge promotes an orderly and fair administration of the criminal trial.

Although each jurisdiction in the United States has its own trial procedures, all jurisdictions conduct criminal trials in a generally similar fashion. The basic

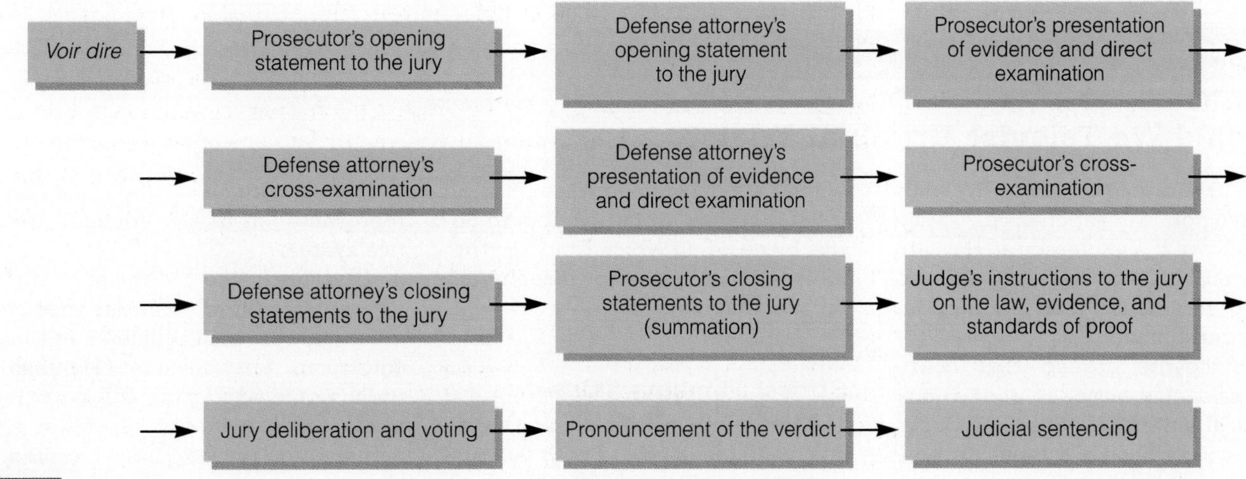

FIGURE 13.2
The Steps of a Jury Trial

SOURCE: Marvin Zalman and Larry Siegel, *Criminal Procedure: Constitution and Society* (St. Paul: West Publishing, 1991), p. 655.

steps of the criminal trial, which proceed in an established order, are described in this section and outlined in Figure 13.2.

Jury Selection

Jurors are selected randomly in both civil and criminal cases from tax assessment or voter registration lists within each court's jurisdiction.

Few states impose qualifications on those called for jury service. Over thirty states mandate a residency requirement.[50] There is also little uniformity in the amount of time served by jurors, with the term ranging from one day to months, depending on the nature of the trial. In addition, most jurisdictions also prohibit convicted felons from serving on juries, as well as others exempted by statute, such as public officials, medical doctors, and attorneys. The initial list of persons chosen, which is called **venire,** or jury array, provides the state with a group of potentially capable citizens able to serve on a jury. Many states, by rule of law, review the venire to eliminate unqualified persons and to exempt those who by reason of their professions are not allowed to be jurors. The actual jury selection process begins with those remaining on the list.

The court clerk, who handles the administrative affairs of the trial—including the processing of the complaint, evidence, and other documents—randomly selects enough names (sometimes from a box) to fill the required number of places on the jury. In most cases, the jury in a criminal trial consists of twelve persons, with two alternate jurors standing by to serve should one of the regular jurors be unable to complete the trial.

Once the prospective jurors are chosen, the process of ***voir dire*** is begun, in which all persons selected are questioned by both the prosecution and the defense to determine their appropriateness to sit on the jury. They are examined under oath by the government, the defense, and sometimes the judge about their backgrounds, occupations, residences, and possible knowledge or interest in the case. A juror who acknowledges any bias for or prejudice against the defendant—if the

ANALYZING CRIMINAL JUSTICE ISSUES

Should We Televise Criminal Trials?

In a 1992 article entitled "TV Trials Thrive on Sensationalism," Alan Dershowitz, a professor at Harvard Law School, encouraged the televising of trials but not for the purpose of entertainment.

Dershowitz argued that courtrooms should not be rented to commercial enterprises to sell products. The courts should establish a noncommercial television network whose role would be to educate. The goal of televising the courts and Congress is not to maximize the number of viewers, he said. It is to make our institutions of government accessible to those viewers who wish to watch.

According to Dershowitz, Court TV, a commercial enterprise that televised the rape trial of William Kennedy Smith, is not interested in the most educational trials but only those that sensationalize and titillate the public. Since there is so much crime in our society, Dershowitz believes, newspapers and TV should focus more on the day-to-day crime that threatens almost everyone and less on sensational crimes. A noncommercial court television network would be able to do this by deciding which trials are the most educational and meaningful for the general public.

Critical Thinking Skills

1. Most state courts allow television cameras in courts with various restrictions. Florida, for instance, has liberal rules regarding TV coverage. In light of Dershowitz's comments about television coverage of trials being worthwhile for educational purposes, do you consider the case of *Florida v. William Kennedy Smith* to be a landmark learning opportunity? Although the trial offered the public intimate details of a sexual encounter, didn't it also educate us about the serious crime of "date rape"?

2. Isn't it true that only certain trials, such as those involving the most heinous crimes (serial killer Jeffrey Dahmer) or celebrities (boxer Mike Tyson or Mafia chief John Gotti), are likely to be televised? Do such trials really provide the public with an accurate and fair representation of the criminal justice system?

3. Lawyers who represent the news media often point out cogent arguments for using cameras in the courtroom. They include: (1) public trials would encourage the participants to do a better job; (2) in a democratic society, the public should have access to all trials, even those of a scandalous nature; and (3) television coverage can contribute to educating the public about the justice system. On the other hand, some defense lawyers and judges believe that televised trials should be restricted because they are only a form of entertainment and suppress the search for the truth. Others question whether the public interest outweighs the defendant's ability to obtain a fair trial.

SOURCE: Adapted from Alan Dershowitz, "TV Trials Thrive on Sensationalism," *Boston Herald,* 10 February 1992, p. 23.

defendant is a friend or relative, for example, or if the juror has already formed an opinion about the case—is removed for "cause" and replaced with another. Thus, any prospective juror who declares he or she is unable to be impartial and render a verdict solely on the evidence to be presented at the trial may be removed by either the prosecution or the defense. Because normally no limit is placed on the number of **challenges for cause** that can be exercised, it often takes considerable time to select a jury for controversial and highly publicized criminal cases.

Jury selection in the famous 1989 Iran-Contra trial of Oliver North lasted for over three months, and hundreds of prospective jurors were examined. The *voir dire* process was made especially difficult because the trial judge insisted on disqualifying all jurors who had heard or read anything about the defendant's public testimony before congressional committees. According to some experts, this is an example of an extreme application of the impartiality requirement (no knowledge of the case), as opposed to simply determining that a jury lacks any prejudice toward the accused.[51]

In certain instances, the court may also want to ask prospective jurors "content" questions about how they became familiar with a particular case. In *Mu'Min v. Virginia* (1991), the trial judge did not allow questions from the defendant as to the content of the prospective jurors' acquired information in a highly publicized murder case.[52] While the jurors were asked whether they had read or heard about the case and formed an opinion based on outside information, content questions that would give legal depth to a finding of impartiality were not asked. In other words, should the judge have asked about the type and extent of pretrial information that would disqualify a juror? The Supreme Court said such content questions are not constitutionally compelled in a *voir dire* hearing, unless the failure to ask them would result in an unfair trial. Thus, the failure to ask such questions in those cases involving pretrial publicity is not ordinarily a violation of the defendant's Sixth Amendment right to an impartial jury.

Peremptory Challenges. In addition to challenges for cause, both the prosecution and the defense are allowed **peremptory challenges,** which enable the attorneys to excuse jurors for no particular reason or for undisclosed reasons. For example, a prosecutor might not want a bartender as a juror in a drunk driving case, believing that a person with that occupation would be sympathetic to the accused. Or the defense attorney might excuse a prospective male juror because the attorney prefers to have a predominantly female jury. The number of peremptory challenges permitted is limited by state statute and often varies by case and jurisdiction.

The peremptory challenge has been criticized by legal experts who question the fairness and propriety with which it has been employed.[53] The most significant criticism is that it has been used to exclude blacks from hearing cases in which the defendant is also black. In *Swain v. Alabama* (1964), the U.S. Supreme Court upheld the use of peremptory challenges in isolated cases to exclude jurors by reason of racial or other group affiliations.[54] This policy was extremely troublesome because it allowed what seemed to be legally condoned discrimination against minority-group members. Consequently, in 1986, the Court struck down the *Swain* doctrine in *Batson v. Kentucky*.[55] Because of the importance of this case, it is set out in the Law in Review on page 472. James Archer, in a recent analysis of the peremptory challenge since the *Batson* decision, suggested that this legal procedure can still be used fairly with improved systematic jury selection, appropriate judicial discretion, and the identification of *prima facie* constitutional violations in the jury process.[56] Other authors believe that if the *Batson* standard is to work and maximize legal protection under the law, its success depends primarily on the discretion of the trial judge.[57] Marvin Steinberg makes a case for eliminating peremptory challenges altogether to end racial discrimination in the jury systems.[58]

In sum, the *Batson* case held that the use of peremptory challenges against potential jurors by prosecutors in criminal cases violated the Constitution if they were based on race. Since that decision six years ago, the issue of race discrimination in the use of peremptory challenges has been raised by defendants in numerous cases. In 1991, in *Powers v. Ohio*, for instance, the Supreme Court was faced with deciding the legality of peremptory challenges involving jurors not of the same race as the defendant. The Court held that the racial identity of "*Batson*-excluded prospective jurors" and the defendant need not be the same. In other words, the Equal Protection Clause prohibits a prosecutor from using the peremptory challenge to exclude qualified and unbiased persons from a jury solely by reason of race. In so ruling, the Court rejected the government's contention

LAW IN REVIEW

Batson v. Kentucky (1986)

Facts

During the criminal trial of a black defendant in Kentucky, the prosecutor used his peremptory challenges to remove four blacks from the venire. Consequently, an all-white jury was selected. Although defense counsel protested that this deprived Batson, his client, of a fair jury representing a cross-section of the community, the trial judge denied the motion. Batson was ultimately convicted. The Kentucky Supreme Court relied on the *Swain* doctrine in upholding the case, arguing that the defense did not demonstrate systematic exclusion of black jurors in other cases.

Decision

The U.S. Supreme Court held that defendants have no right to a jury composed of members in whole or in part of their own race. However, the Fourteenth Amendment's Equal Protection Clause guarantees that the state will not exclude jury members on account of race or under the false assumption that members of the defendant's own race cannot render a fair verdict. This would also discriminate against the jury members and undermine public confidence in the jury system. Thus, the state is forbidden to preempt jurors solely on the basis of their race.

In addition, if defendants wish to show racism in the use of the peremptory challenge, they no longer must show a pattern of discrimination as the *Swain* doctrine indicated. Defendants may show purposeful racial discrimination in selection of the venire by relying solely on the facts of their own case. They must show that they are members of a particular race and that the prosecutor has exercised his or her peremptory challenges to remove members of that racial group from the jury. They may rely on the fact that such practices permit "those to discriminate who have a mind to discriminate." The burden is then on the prosecutor to come forward with a neutral explanation for challenging the jurors.

Finally, the Court argued that the peremptory challenge can still play an important role in the adversarial process. It can be used in most criminal cases as long as it is not employed in a racially biased manner.

Significance of the Case

Batson strikes down a legal procedure that was out of synch with modern ideas of justice and fairness. It prevents an element of racial discrimination from entering into the trial stage of justice, which is one of the cornerstones of American freedom. Yet it preserves, under controlled circumstances, the use of the peremptory challenge, which is an integral part of the jury selection process.

that the jurors be of the same race as the defendant. Similarly, in the 1991 case of *Georgia v. McCollum*, the Supreme Court said that criminal defendants may not seek to exclude potential jurors strictly on the basis of race. Race-based peremptory challenges to potential jurors in civil lawsuits have also been declared unconstitutional.

Impartial Juries. The Sixth Amendment provides for the right to a speedy trial by an impartial jury. This concept of an impartial jury has always been controversial. For one thing, research indicates that jury members often have little in common with their criminal "peers." Moreover, studies of jury deliberations indicate that the dynamics of decision making often involve pressure to get the case over with and convince recalcitrant jurors to join the majority. Nevertheless, jurors also appear to take cases seriously and reach decisions not too different from those made by legal professionals.[59] Judges, for instance, often agree with jury decisions. However, jurors often have problems understanding judicial instructions and legal rule-making in criminal trials.

The Supreme Court has sought to ensure compliance with this constitutional mandate of impartiality by decisions eliminating racial discrimination in jury selection. For instance, in *Ham v. South Carolina* in 1973, the Court held that the defense counsel of a black civil rights leader was entitled to question each juror on the issue of racial prejudice.[60] In *Taylor v. Louisiana* in 1975, the Court overturned the conviction of a man by an all-male jury because a Louisiana statute allowed women but not men to exempt themselves from jury duty.[61]

The issue of the racial composition of the jury is particularly acute in cases involving the death penalty. In 1986, the Court ruled in *Turner v. Murray* that a defendant accused of an interracial crime in which the death penalty is an option can insist that prospective jurors be informed of the victim's race and be questioned on the issue of their racial bias. A trial judge who refuses this line of questioning during *voir dire* risks having the death penalty vacated but not the reversal of the conviction.[62] These and other similar decisions have had the effect of providing safeguards against jury bias.

Jury selection can be made even more difficult in capital punishment cases where jurors are asked their views about the death penalty. In *Lockhart v. McCree* (1986), the Supreme Court decided that jurors who strongly oppose capital punishment may be disqualified from determining a defendant's guilt or innocence in capital cases.[63]

The *Lockhart* decision raises certain questions, however. Juries are not supposed to represent only one position or another. An impartial jury of one's peers is rooted in the idea that the defendant should be judged by a cross-section of members of the local community. Their views should not be disproportionate on any one issue. Consequently, a ruling such as *Lockhart* could theoretically result in higher conviction rates in murder cases.

Defendants often appeal their convictions on the ground of jury bias but are ordinarily unsuccessful with this approach. A recent federal appeals court decision held, however, that if a juror deliberately lies during the jury selection process, the defendant's conviction can be vacated.[64] What are the implications of this when jurors are asked their opinions of the death penalty in capital cases? Or about racial bias? And what are the implications where jurors fail to disclose personal relationships? The Supreme Court has not yet answered fully all of the important questions of impartiality in the role and qualifications of jurors in criminal cases.

Opening Statements

Once the jury has been selected and the criminal complaint has been read to the jurors by the court clerk, the prosecutor and the defense attorney may each make an opening statement about the case to the jury. The purpose of the prosecutor's statement is to introduce the judge and the jury to the particular criminal charges, to outline the facts, and to describe how the government will prove the defendant guilty beyond a reasonable doubt. The defense attorney reviews the case and indicates how the defense intends to show that the accused is innocent of the charge.

Usually, the defense attorney makes an opening statement after the government reads its case. In some jurisdictions, the court in its discretion can permit the defense to make opening remarks before any evidence is introduced. But, for the most part, present rules dictate that the prosecutor is entitled to offer an opening statement first.

The opening statement gives the jury a concise overview of the evidence that is to follow. In the opening statement, neither attorney is allowed to make

During the jury selection process, both the prosecution and the defense can challenge and dismiss jurors who may be biased or otherwise unsuitable.

prejudicial remarks or inflammatory statements or mention irrelevant facts. Both are free, however, to identify what they will eventually prove by way of evidence, which includes witnesses, physical evidence, and the use of expert testimony. The actual content of the statement is left to the discretion of the trial judge. As a general rule, the opening statements used in jury trials are important because they provide the finders of fact (the jury) with an initial summary of the case. They are infrequently used and less effective in **bench trials,** however, where juries are not employed. Most lower-court judges have handled hundreds of similar cases and do not need the benefit of an opening statement.

Presentation of the Prosecutor's Evidence

Following the opening statements, the government begins its case by presenting evidence to the court through its witnesses. Those called as witnesses—such as police officers, victims, or experts—provide testimony via **direct examination.** During direct examination, the prosecutor questions the witness to reveal the facts believed pertinent to the government case. Testimony involves what the witness actually saw, heard, or touched and does not include opinions. However, a witness's opinion can be given in certain situations, such as when describing the motion of a vehicle or indicating whether a defendant appeared to act intoxicated or insane. Witnesses may also qualify to give opinions because they are experts on a particular subject relevant to the case; for example, a psychiatrist may testify as to a defendant's mental capacity at the time of the crime.

After the prosecutor finishes questioning a witness, the defense cross-examines the same witness by asking questions in an attempt to clarify the defendant's role in the crime. The right to cross-examine witnesses is an essential part of a trial, and unless extremely unusual circumstances exist (such as a person's being hospitalized), witness statements will not be considered unless they are made in court and open for question. For example, in a recent case, *Lee v. Illinois* (1986), the U.S. Supreme Court ruled that a confession made to police by a co-defendant in a criminal trial cannot be used in court unless the person making the confession is available for **cross-examination.**[65] If desired, the prosecutor may seek a second direct examination after the defense attorney has completed cross-examination; this allows the prosecutor to ask additional questions about information brought out during cross-examination. Finally, the defense attorney may then question or cross-examine the witness once again. All witnesses for the trial are sworn in and questioned in the same basic manner.

Types of Evidence at a Criminal Trial

In addition to testimonial evidence given by police officers, citizens, and experts, the court also acts on **real,** or nonverbal, **evidence.**[66] Real evidence often consists of the exhibits taken into the jury room for review by the jury. A revolver that may have been in the defendant's control at the time of a murder, tools in the possession of a suspect charged with a burglary, and a bottle allegedly holding narcotics are all examples of real or physical evidence. Photographs, maps, diagrams, and crime scene displays are further types of real evidence. The criminal court judge will also review documentary evidence, such as writings, government reports, public records, and business or hospital records.

In general, the primary test for the admissibility of evidence in either a criminal or civil proceeding is its relevance.[67] In other words, the court must ask itself whether the gun, shirt, or photograph, for instance, has relevant evidentiary value in determining the issues in the case. Ordinarily, evidence that establishes an element of the crime is acceptable to the court. For example, in a prosecution for possession of drugs, evidence that shows the defendant to be a known drug user might be relevant. In a prosecution for bribery, monies received in the form of a cancelled check identified as the amount received would clearly be found relevant to the case.

Circumstantial, or indirect, evidence is also often used in trial proceedings. Such evidence is often inferred or indirectly used to prove a fact in question. On the issue of malice in a criminal murder trial, for instance, it would be appropriate to use circumstantial evidence to prove the defendant's state of mind. Such evidence has often been the controversial issue in many celebrated criminal cases. The Dr. George Parkman case, more than a century ago, attracted national attention when Parkman's colleague at Harvard University, Dr. Webster, was convicted of murder after Parkman disappeared.[68] Because there was no *corpus delecti*, Webster's conviction was based on circumstantial evidence.

And in the famous Sacco-Vanzetti trial in the 1920s, two men were tried and convicted of murder and finally executed seven years later, based on circumstantial evidence and possibly because they were Italian anarchists.[69] Circumstantial evidence bearing on or establishing the facts in a crime is ordinarily admissible, but evidence that is prejudicial, remote, or unrelated to the crime should be excluded by the court. In general, however, the admissibility of such evidence remains governed by the laws recognizing the constitutional rights of the accused, such as the right to be free from unreasonable search and seizure, the privilege against self-incrimination, and the right to counsel.

Motion for a Directed Verdict

Once the prosecution has provided all the government's evidence against a defendant, it will inform the court that it rests the people's case. The defense

During the Middle Ages, it was common to torture suspects to extract a confession. Modern trials rely on cross examination of witnesses.

attorney at this point may enter a motion for a **directed verdict.** This is a procedural device by means of which the defense attorney asks the judge to order the jury to return a verdict of not guilty. The judge must rule on the motion and will either sustain it or overrule it, depending on whether he or she believes that the prosecution proved all the elements of the alleged crime. In essence, the defense attorney argues in the directed verdict that the prosecutor's case against the defendant is insufficient to prove the defendant guilty beyond a reasonable doubt. If the motion is sustained, the trial is terminated. If it is rejected by the court, the case continues with the defense portion of the trial.

Basically, the defense usually makes a motion for a directed verdict so that a finding of guilt can later be appealed to a higher court. If the judge refuses to grant the motion, this decision can be the focus of an appeal charging that the judge did not use proper procedural care in making his or her decision. In some cases, the judge may reserve decision on the motion, submit the case to the jury, and consider a decision on the motion before a jury verdict or order a verdict of guilty.

Presentation of Evidence by the Defense Attorney

The defense attorney has the option of presenting many, some, or no witnesses on behalf of the defendant. In addition, the defense attorney must decide if the client should take the stand and testify in his or her own behalf. In a criminal trial, the defendant is protected by the Fifth Amendment right to be free from self-incrimination, which means that a person cannot be forced by the state to testify against himself or herself in a criminal trial. However, defendants who choose voluntarily to tell their side of the story can be subject to cross-examination by the prosecutor.

After the defense concludes its case, the government may then present **rebuttal evidence.** This normally involves bringing evidence forward that was not used when the prosecution initially presented its case. The defense may examine the rebuttal witnesses and introduce new witnesses in a process called a **surrebuttal.** After all the evidence has been presented to the court, the defense attorney may again submit a motion for a directed verdict. If the motion is denied, both the prosecution and the defense prepare to make closing arguments, and the case on the evidence is ready for consideration by the jury.

Closing Arguments

Closing arguments are used by the attorneys to review the facts and evidence of the case in a manner favorable to each of their positions. At this stage of the trial, both prosecution and the defense are permitted to draw reasonable inferences and to show how the facts prove or refute the defendant's guilt. Often both attorneys have a free hand in arguing about the facts, issues, and evidence, including the applicable law. They cannot comment on matters not in evidence, however, or on the defendant's failure to testify in a criminal case. Normally, the defense attorney will make a closing statement first, followed by the prosecutor. Either party can elect to forgo the right to make a final summation to the jury.

Instructions to the Jury

In a criminal trial, the judge will instruct, or **charge,** the jury members on the principles of law that ought to guide and control their decision on the defendant's innocence or guilt. Included in the charge will be information about the elements of the alleged offense, the type of evidence needed to prove each element, and the burden of proof required to obtain a guilty verdict. Although the judge commonly provides the instruction, he or she may ask the prosecutor and the defense attorney to submit instructions for consideration; the judge will then use discretion in determining whether to use any of their instructions. The instructions that cover the law applicable to the case are extremely important because they may serve as the basis for a subsequent appeal. Procedurally, in highly publicized and celebrated cases, the judge may have sequestered the jury to prevent it from having contact with the outside world. This process, called **sequestration,** is discretionary with the trial judge, and most courts believe "locking a jury up" is needed only in sensational cases.

The Verdict

Once the charge is given to the jury members, they retire to deliberate on a verdict. As previously mentioned, the **verdict** in a criminal case—regardless of whether the trial involves a six-person or a twelve-person jury—is usually required to be unanimous. A review of the case by the jury may take hours or even days. The jurors are always sequestered during their deliberations, and in certain lengthy and highly publicized cases, they are kept overnight in a hotel until the verdict is reached. In less sensational cases, the jurors may be allowed to go home, but they are cautioned not to discuss the case with anyone.

If a verdict cannot be reached, the trial may result in a **hung jury,** after which the prosecutor must bring the defendant to trial again if the prosecution desires a conviction. If found not guilty, the defendant is released from the criminal process. On the other hand, if the defendant is convicted, the judge will normally order a presentence investigation by the probation department before imposing a sentence. Prior to sentencing, the defense attorney will probably submit a motion for a new trial, alleging that legal errors occurred in the trial proceedings. The judge may deny the motion and impose a sentence immediately, a practice quite common in most misdemeanor offenses. In felony cases, however, the judge will set a date for sentencing, and the defendant will either be placed on bail or held in custody until that time. Mike Tyson, for example, after his conviction for rape, was set free on thirty thousand dollars bail to await sentencing a month after his conviction.

The Sentence

The imposition of the criminal **sentence** is normally the responsibility of the trial judge. In some jurisdictions, the jury may determine the sentence or make recommendations involving leniency for certain offenses. Often, the sentencing decision is based on information and recommendations given to the court by the probation department after a presentence investigation of the defendant. The sentence itself is determined by the statutory requirements for the particular crime as established by the legislature; in addition, the judge ordinarily has a great deal of discretion in reaching a sentencing decision. The different criminal sanctions available include fines, probation, imprisonment, and even commitment to a state hospital. The sentence may be a combination of all these. Sentencing is discussed in detail in the following chapter.

The Appeal

Defendants have as many as three possible avenues of appeal: the direct appeal, postconviction remedy, and federal court review.[70] Both the direct appeal and federal court review provide the convicted person with the opportunity to appeal to a higher state or federal court on the basis of an error that affected the conviction in the trial court. Extraordinary trial court errors, such as the denial of the right to counsel or the inability to provide a fair trial, are subject to the "plain error" rule of the federal courts.[71] "Harmless errors," such as the use of innocuous identification procedures or the denial of counsel at a noncritical stage of the proceeding, would not necessarily result in the overturning of a criminal conviction. A postconviction appeal, on the other hand, or what is often referred to as "collateral attack," takes the form of a legal petition, such as **habeas corpus,** and is the primary means by which state prisoners have their convictions or sentence reviewed in the federal court. A writ of habeas corpus (meaning "you take the body") seeks to determine the validity of a detention by asking the court to release the person or give legal reasons for the incarceration.

In most jurisdictions, direct criminal appeal to an appellate court is a matter of right. This means that the defendant has an automatic right to appeal a conviction based on errors that may have occurred during the trial proceedings. A substantial number of criminal appeals are the result of disputes over points of law, such as the introduction at the trial of illegal evidence detrimental to the defendant or statements made during the trial that were prejudicial to the defendant. Through objections made at the pretrial and trial stages of the criminal process, the defense counsel will reserve specific legal issues on the record as the basis for appeal. A copy of the transcript of these proceedings will serve as the basis on which the appellate court will review any errors that may have occurred during the lower court proceedings.

Because an appeal is an expensive, time-consuming, and technical process involving a review of the lower court record, the research and drafting of briefs, and the presentation of oral arguments to the appellate court, the defendant has been granted the right to counsel at this stage of the criminal process. In the case of *Douglas v. California* (1963), the Supreme Court held that an indigent defendant has a constitutional right to the assistance of counsel on a direct first appeal.[72] If the defendant appeals to a higher court, the defendant must have private counsel or apply for permission to proceed ***in forma pauperis,*** meaning that the defendant may be granted counsel at public expense if the court believes the appeal has merit.

The right of appeal normally does not extend to the prosecution in a criminal case. In the United States, according to the American Bar Association, considerable differences among the states and the federal government exist as to the appropriate scope of prosecution appeals.[73] At one extreme are states that grant no right of appeal to the prosecution in criminal cases. On the other hand, some jurisdictions permit the prosecution to appeal in those instances that involve the unconstitutionality of a statute or from pretrial orders that terminate the government's case. However, the prosecutor cannot bring the defendant to trial again on the same charge after an acquittal or a conviction; this would violate the defendant's right to be free from double jeopardy under the Fifth Amendment. As discussed in Chapter 4, the purpose of the double jeopardy guarantee is to protect the defendant from a second prosecution for the same offense.

After an appeal has been fully heard, the appeals court renders an opinion on the procedures used in the case. If an error of law is found—such as an improper introduction of evidence or an improper statement by the prosecutor that was prejudicial to the defendant—the appeals court may reverse the decision of the trial court and order a new trial. If the lower court's decision is upheld, the case is finished, unless the defendant seeks a discretionary appeal to a higher state or federal court.

Over the last decade, criminal appeals have increased significantly in almost every state and the federal courts. Criminal case appeals make up close to 50 percent of the state appellate caseload and over 35 percent of the total federal caseload, which includes prisoner petitions and ordinary criminal appeals.[74] Today, a substantial number of these appeals involve drug-related cases.

Although the steps in the criminal trial might seem totally mechanical and inflexible, informal procedures and subjective judgments affect how judicial decisions are made. Such questions as how the judge relates to the prosecutor and the defense attorney, how the jury feels toward the defendant, or whether certain witnesses are credible and competent all bring a human element to play in the trial process.

Evidentiary Standards

Proof beyond a **reasonable doubt** is the standard required to convict a defendant charged with a crime at the adjudicatory stage of the criminal process. This requirement dates back to early American history and over the years has become the accepted measure of persuasion needed by the prosecutor to convince the judge or jury of the defendant's guilt. Many twentieth-century U.S. Supreme Court decisions have reinforced this standard by making "beyond a reasonable doubt a due process and constitutional requirement."[75] In *Brinegar v. United States* (1948), for instance, the Supreme Court stated:

> Guilt in a criminal case must be proved beyond a reasonable doubt and by evidence confined to that which long experience in the common-law tradition, to some extent embodied in the Constitution, has crystallized into rules of evidence consistent with that standard. These rules are historically grounded rights of our system, developed to safeguard men from dubious and unjust convictions with resulting forfeitures of life, liberty, and property.[76]

And in the earlier case of *Davis v. United States* (1895), where a murder conviction was reversed because the judge had instructed the jury to convict when the evidence was equally balanced regarding the sanity of the accused, the Supreme Court held that the defendant is entitled to an acquittal where there is reasonable doubt of the capability in law of committing a crime.[83] The Court further stated, "No man should be deprived of his life under the forms of law unless the jurors who try him are able, upon their consciences, to say that the evidence before them . . . is sufficient to show beyond a reasonable doubt the existence of every fact necessary to constitute the crime charged."[78]

The reasonable doubt standard is an essential ingredient of the criminal justice process. It is the prime instrument for reducing the risk of convictions based on factual errors.[79] The underlying premise of this standard is that it is better to release a guilty person than to convict someone who is innocent. Since the defendant is presumed innocent until proven guilty, this standard forces the prosecution to overcome this presumption with the highest standard of proof. Unlike the civil law, where a mere **preponderance of the evidence** is the standard, the criminal process requires proof beyond a reasonable doubt for each element of the offense. As the Supreme Court pointed out in *In re Winship* (1970), where the reasonable doubt standard was applied to juvenile trials, "[i]f the standard of proof for a criminal trial were a preponderance of the evidence rather than proof

TABLE 13.1
Evidentiary Standards of Proof—Degrees of Certainty

Standard	Definition	Where Used
Absolute certainty	No possibility of error; 100 percent certainty	Not used in civil or criminal law
Beyond reasonable doubt; moral certainty	Conclusive and complete proof, while leaving any reasonable doubt as to the innocence or guilt of the defendant; allowing the defendant the benefit of any possibility of innocence	Criminal trial
Clear and convincing evidence	Prevailing and persuasive to the trier of fact	Civil commitments, insanity defense
Preponderance of evidence	Greater weight of evidence in terms of credibility; more convincing than an opposite point of view	Civil trial
Probable cause	U.S. constitutional standard for arrest and search warrants, requiring existence of facts sufficient to warrant that a crime has been committed	Arrest, preliminary hearing, motions
Sufficient evidence	Adequate evidence to reverse a trial court	Appellate review
Reasonable suspicion	Rational, reasonable belief that facts warrant investigation of a crime on less than probable cause	Police investigations
Less than probable cause	Mere suspicion; less than reasonable to conclude criminal activity exists	Prudent police investigation where safety of an officer or others is endangered

beyond a reasonable doubt, there would be a smaller risk of factual errors that result in freeing guilty persons, but a far greater risk of factual errors that result in convicting the innocent." [80] According to Oliver Wendell Holmes, one of the best known Supreme Court justices of the twentieth century, "We have to choose, and for my part I think it a less evil that some criminals should escape than that the government should play an ignoble part." [81] The various evidentiary standards of proof are analyzed and compared in Table 13.1.

SUMMARY

The number of cases disposed of by trials is relatively small in comparison to the total number that enter the criminal justice system. Nevertheless, the criminal trial provides the defendant with a very important option. Unlike other steps in the system, the U.S. criminal trial allows the accused to assert the right to a day in court. The defendant may choose between a trial before a judge alone or a trial by jury. In either case, the purpose of the trial is to adjudicate the facts, ascertain the truth, and determine the guilt or innocence of the accused.

Criminal trials represent the adversary system at work. The state uses its authority to seek a conviction, and the defendant is protected by constitutional rights, particularly those under the Fifth and Sixth Amendments. When they involve serious crimes, criminal trials are complex legal affairs. Each jurisdiction relies on rules and procedures that have developed over many years to resolve legal issues. As the U.S. Supreme Court has extended the rights of the accused, as described in this chapter, the procedures have undoubtedly contributed to the complexities and delays within the system. Some solutions have included smaller juries, more efficient control of police misconduct (see Chapter 7), and reducing time delays between arrest, indictment, and trial.

An established order of steps is followed throughout a criminal trial, beginning with the reading of the complaint, proceeding through the introduction of evidence, and concluding with closing arguments and a verdict. The criminal trial serves both a symbolic and a pragmatic function for defendants who require a forum of last resort to adjudicate their differences with the state.

QUESTIONS

1. Identify the steps involved in the criminal trial. Consider the pros and cons of a jury trial versus a bench trial.
2. What are the legal rights of the defendant in the trial process? Trace the historical development of the right to counsel at the trial stage of the criminal justice system.
3. Discuss the significance of the Supreme Court decisions in *Gideon v. Wainwright* and *Argersinger v. Hamlin*.
4. The burden of proof in a criminal trial to show that the defendant is guilty beyond a reasonable doubt is on the government in the adversary system of criminal justice. Explain the meaning of this statement in terms of other legal standards of proof.
5. If a seventeen-year-old youth is tried by a jury, should the jurors also be under twenty-one years of age to maintain fairness?
6. Devise a charge to the jury for a first-degree murder case.
7. What is the meaning of "prior restraint"?
8. What factors support televising criminal trials?

NOTES

1. National Advisory Commission on Criminal Justice Standards and Goals, *Courts* (Washington, D.C.: U.S. Government Printing Office, 1973), p. 66; see also Donald Newman, *Conviction: The Determination of Guilt or Innocence Without Trial* (Boston: Little, Brown & Co., 1966).
2. *United States Constitution*, Amend. VI.
3. *Pointer v. State of Texas*, 380 U.S. 400, 85 S.Ct. 1065, 13 L.Ed.2d 923 (1965).
4. 487 U.S. 1012, 108 S.Ct. 2798, 101 L.Ed.2d 857 (1988).
5. 497 U.S. 836, 110 S.Ct. 3157, 111 L.Ed.2d 666 (1990).
6. 391 U.S. 145, 88 S.Ct. 1444, 20 L.Ed.2d 491 (1968).
7. Ibid., at 157–158, 88 S.Ct. at 1451–1452.
8. 399 U.S. 66, 90 S.Ct. 1886, 26 L.Ed.2d 437 (1970).
9. 489 U.S. 538, 109 S.Ct. 1289, 103 L.Ed.2d 550 (1989).
10. 399 U.S. 78, 90 S.Ct. 1893, 26 L.Ed.2d 446 (1970).
11. Ibid., at 102–3, 90 S.Ct. at 1907.
12. Ibid., at 101, 90 S.Ct at 1906.
13. Ibid., at 102, 90 S.Ct. at 1907.
14. *Ballew v. Georgia*, 435 U.S. 223, 98 S.Ct. 1029, 55 L.Ed.2d 234 (1978).
15. *Burch v. Louisiana*, 441 U.S. 130, 99 S.Ct. 1623, 60 L.Ed.2d 96 (1979).
16. 406 U.S. 404, 92 S.Ct. 1628, 32 L.Ed.2d 184 (1972).
17. 287 U.S. 45, 53 S.Ct. 55, 77 L.Ed. 158 (1932).
18. 372 U.S. 335, 83 S.Ct. 792, 9 L.Ed.2d 799 (1963); see also Yale Kamisar, "*Gideon v. Wainwright, a Quarter Century Later*," *Pace Law Review* 10 (1990):343.
19. 407 U.S. 25, 92 S.Ct. 2006, 32 L.Ed.2d 530 (1972).
20. *United States Constitution*, Amend. VI.
21. 422 U.S. 806, 95 S.Ct. 2525, 45 L.Ed.2d 562 (1975).
22. Ibid.
23. Ibid., at 592.
24. See "Criminal Defendants at the Bar of Their Own Defense—*Faretta v. California*," *American Criminal Law Review* 60 (1975):335.
25. See American Bar Association, *Standards Relating to Speedy Trial* (New York: Institute of Judicial Administration, 1968), p. 1.
26. 386 U.S. 213, 87 S.Ct. 988, 18 L.Ed.2d 1 (1967).
27. Ibid., at 223, 87 S.Ct. at 993.
28. President's Commission on Law Enforcement and the Administration of Justice, *Task Force Report: The Courts* (Washington, D.C.: U.S. Government Printing Office, 1967), pp. 86–87; see also B. Mahoney et al., *Implementing Delay Reduction and Delay Prevention: Programs in Urban Trial Courts* (Williamsburg, Va.: National Center for State Courts, 1985).
29. National Advisory Commission on Criminal Justice Standards and Goals, *Courts*, pp. xx–xxi; see also Gregory S. Kennedy, "Speedy Trial," *Georgetown Law Journal* 75 (1987):953–64.
30. 18 U.S.C.A. § 3161 (Supp. 1975). For a good review of this legisla-

tion, see Marc I. Steinberg, "Right to Speedy Trial: The Constitutional Right and Its Applicability to the Speedy Trial Act of 1974," *Journal of Criminal Law and Criminology* 66 (1975):229.

31. 487 U.S. 326, 108 S.Ct. 2413, 101 L.Ed.2d 297 (1988).

32. *Estelle v. Williams,* 425 U.S. 501, 96 S.Ct. 1691, 48 L.Ed.2d 126 (1976).

33. *Sheppard v. Maxwell,* 384 U.S. 333, 86 S.Ct. 1507, 16 L.Ed.2d 600 (1966).

34. See *State v. von Bulow,* 475 A.2d 995 (R.I. 1984); see also Alan Dershowitz, *Reversal of Fortune: The von Bulow Affair* (New York: Random House, 1986).

35. 427 U.S. 539, 96 S.Ct. 2791, 49 L.Ed.2d 683 (1976).

36. Ibid., at 547, 96 S.Ct. at 2797.

37. 443 U.S. 368, 99 S.Ct. 2898, 61 L.Ed.2d 608 (1979).

38. Ibid., at 370, 99 S.Ct. at 2900.

39. 478 U.S. 1, 106 S.Ct. 2735, 92 L.Ed.2d 1 (1986).

40. 448 U.S. 555, 100 S.Ct. 2814, 65 L.Ed.2d 973 (1980).

41. *Globe Newspaper Co. v. Superior Court for County of Norfolk,* 457 U.S. 596, 102 S.Ct. 2613, 73 L.Ed.2d 248 (1982).

42. *Press-Enterprise Co. v. Superior Court,* 464 U.S. 501, 104 S.Ct. 819, 78 L.Ed.2d 629 (1984).

43. *Waller v. Georgia,* 467 U.S. 39, 104 S.Ct. 2210, 81 L.Ed.2d 31 (1984).

44. Nicholas A. Pellegrini, "Extension of Criminal Defendant's Right to Public Trial," *St. John's University Law Review* 611 (1987):277–89.

45. 333 U.S. 257, 68 S.Ct. 499, 92 L.Ed. 682 (1948).

46. 333 U.S. at 270, 68 S.Ct. at 506.

47. See "Smith Trial Offers Mixed Message about Date Rape," Editorial, *USA Today,* 12 December 1991, p. 10A.

48. T. Dyk and B. Donald, "Cameras in the Supreme Court," *American Bar Association Journal* (January 1989):34.

49. 449 U.S. 560, 101 S.Ct. 802, 66 L.Ed.2d 740 (1981).

50. Conference of State Court Administrators, *State Court Organization, 1987* (Williamsburg, Va.: National Center for State Courts, 1988), p. 10.

51. See Richard Moran and Peter D'Errico, "The Law—An Impartial Jury or an Ignorant One," *Boston Globe,* 12 February 1989, p. A18.

52. ____ U.S. ____, 111 S.Ct. 1899, 114 L.Ed.2d 493 (1991).

53. George Hayden, Joseph Senna, and Larry Siegel, "Prosecutorial Discretion in Peremptory Challenges: An Empirical Investigation of Information Use in the Massachusetts Jury Selection Process," *New England Law Review* 13 (1978):768.

54. 380 U.S. 202, 85 S.Ct. 824, 13 L.Ed.2d 759 (1964).

55. 476 U.S. 79, 106 S.Ct. 1712, 90 L.Ed.2d 69 (1986).

56. James Archer, "Exercising Peremptory Challenges after Batson," *Criminal Law Bulletin* 24 (1988):187–211.

57. Brian Sern and Mark Maney, "Racism, Peremptory Challenges and the Democratic Jury—The Jurisprudence of Delicate Balance," *Journal of Criminal Law and Criminology* 79 (1988):65.

58. Marvin Steinberg, "The Case for Eliminating Peremptory Challenges," *Criminal Law Bulletin* 27 (1991):216–29.

59. For a review of jury decision making, see John Baldwin and Michael McConville, "Criminal Juries," in *Crime and Justice,* vol. 2, ed. Norval Morris and Michael Tonry (Chicago: University of Chicago Press, 1980), pp. 269–320.

60. 409 U.S. 524, 93 S.Ct. 848, 35 L.Ed.2d 46 (1973).

61. 419 U.S. 522, 95 S.Ct. 692, 42 L.Ed.2d 690 (1975).

62. 476 U.S. 28, 106 S.Ct. 1683, 90 L.Ed.2d 27 (1986). See James Gobert, "In Search of an Impartial Jury," *Journal of Criminal Law and Criminology* 79 (1988):269; see also Martin Levin, "The Jury in a Criminal Case—Obstacles to Impartiality," *Criminal Law Bulletin* 24 (1988):321.

63. 476 U.S. 162, 106 S.Ct. 1758, 90 L.Ed.2d 137 (1986).

64. See *United States v. Klan,* 869 F.2d 149 (2d Cir. 1989).

65. 476 U.S. 530, 106 S.Ct. 2056, 90 L.Ed.2d 514 (1986).

66. See Charles McCormick, Frank Elliott and John Sutton, Jr., *Evidence—Cases and Materials* (St. Paul: West Publishing, 1981), chapter 1.

67. Ibid.

68. See the fascinating case study of the *State's Case v. Dr. Webster* in Helen Thomson, *Murder at Harvard* (Boston: Houghton-Mifflin, 1971).

69. See Francis Russell, *Sacco and Vanzetti—The Case Resolved* (New York: Harper & Row, 1986).

70. Bureau of Justice Statistics, *Report to the Nation on Crime and Justice,* 2d ed. (Washington, D.C.: U.S. Government Printing Office, 1988), p. 88.

71. *Chapman v. California,* 386 U.S. 18, 87 S.Ct. 824, 17 L.Ed.2d 705 (1967).

72. 372 U.S. 353, 83 S.Ct. 814, 9 L.Ed.2d 811 (1963).

73. American Bar Association, *Standards Relating to Criminal Appeals* (New York: Institute of Judicial Administration, 1970), p. 88.

74. Bureau of Justice Statistics, *Report to the Nation on Crime and Justice,* p. 88.

75. See *Brinegar v. United States,* 338 U.S. 160, 69 S.Ct. 1302, 93 L.Ed. 1879 (1949); *Speiser v. Randall,* 357 U.S. 513, 78 S.Ct. 1332, 2 L.Ed.2d 1460 (1958); *In re Winship,* 397 U.S. 358, 90 S.Ct. 1068, 25 L.Ed.2d 368 (1970).

76. 338 U.S. 160, 174, 69 S.Ct. 1302, 1310, 93 L.Ed. 1879 (1949).

77. 160 U.S. 469, 16 S.Ct. 353, 40 L.Ed. 499 (1895).

78. Ibid., at 493, 16 S.Ct. at 360.

79. See *In re Winship,* 397 U.S. 358, 90 S.Ct. 1068, 25 L.Ed.2d 368 (1970).

80. Ibid., at 371, 90 S.Ct. at 1076.

81. See *Olmstead v. United States,* 277 U.S. 438, 48 S.Ct. 564, 72 L.Ed. 944 (1928).

CHAPTER 14

Punishment and Sentencing

OUTLINE

History of Punishment
Public Work and Transportation
The Rise of the Prison
The Goals of Criminal Punishment
General Deterrence
Incapacitation
Specific Deterrence
Retribution/Desert
Rehabilitation
Restitution
Sentencing Strategies
The Indeterminate Sentence
The Determinate Sentence
Calls for a New Determinacy
Presumptive Sentencing
Structured Sentencing
Problems of Sentencing Guidelines
Mandatory Minimum Sentences
■ Analyzing Criminal Justice Issues: Federal Sentencing Guidelines
Habitual Criminal Statutes
Sentencing Practices
Extralegal Factors in Sentencing
Sentencing Reform
Capital Punishment
Arguments for the Death Penalty
Arguments against the Death Penalty
The Law of Capital Punishment
Limiting Capital Punishment
Death-Qualified Juries
Does the Death Penalty Deter Murder?
Capital Punishment Today

KEY TERMS

sanction
punishment
sentencing process
specific deterrence
wergild
wite
bot
poor laws
penitentiaries
incapacitation
recidivism
just desert
equity
legislatively fixed model
judicially fixed model
administrative model
concurrent sentence
consecutive sentence
Progressives
indeterminate sentence
indefinite sentence
determinate sentence
disparity
presumptive sentencing
descriptive guidelines
prescriptive guidelines
base penalty
brutalization effect
cruel and unusual punishment

After a defendant has been found guilty of a crime by a jury, a judge, or their own admission of guilt, the state has the right to impose a criminal **sanction** or **punishment.** In the modern criminal justice system, the procedure in which the nature and extent of punishment is decided is referred to as the **sentencing process.**

Historically, a full range of punishments was inflicted on criminal defendants, including physical torture, branding, whipping, and, for most felony offenses, death. At one time, the philosophy of punishment was to "torment the body for the sins of the soul."[1] People who violated the law were considered morally reprehensible and in need of strong discipline. If punishment was harsh enough, it was assumed, they would never repeat their mistakes, a concept referred to today as **specific deterrence.**

Punishment was also viewed as a spectacle that taught a moral lesson. The more gruesome and public the sentence, the greater the impact it would have on the local populace.[2] Harsh physical punishments would control any thoughts of rebellion and dissent against the central government and those who held political and economic control.

In modern U.S. society, four of the most important forms of criminal punishment are:

1. fines—monetary payments made to the court reflecting the costs to society of the criminal act.
2. community sentences—periods of supervision in the community during which the criminal is required to obey predetermined rules of behavior and may be asked to perform tasks, such as make restitution to the victim.
3. incarceration—a period of confinement in a state or federal prison, jail, or community-based treatment facility.
4. capital punishment—death in the electric chair or gas chamber or by lethal injection. While relatively uncommon, the death penalty has had a disproportionately significant impact on concepts of fairness and justice.

Punishing criminal offenders continues to be one of the most complex and controversial issues in the criminal justice system. Its complexity stems from the wide variety of sentences available and the discretion judges have in applying them. The proper sanction for a particular criminal defendant is often difficult to determine, and there is little coordination in judicial decision making. The controversy over punishment involves both its nature and extent: Are too many people being sent to prison? What is the impact of sentencing disparity? Is there discrimination in sentencing based on race, gender, or social class?[3] These are but a few of the most significant issues in the sentencing process.

This chapter first examines the history of punishment and then focuses on incarceration and capital punishment, the two most traditional and punitive forms of criminal sanctions used today. Chapter 15 reviews sentences that have been developed to reduce the strain on the overburdened correctional system; these sentences provide intermediate sanctions designed to control people whose behavior and personality makes an incarceration sentence unnecessary.

History of Punishment

The punishment and correction of criminals has changed considerably through the ages, reflecting custom, economic conditions, and religious and political ideals.[4]

In early Greece and Rome, the most common state-administered punishment was banishment or exile. Only slaves were commonly subjected to harsh physical punishment for their misdeeds. In the earliest period of Roman history, for example, the only crime for which capital punishment could be administered was *furtum manifestum*—a thief caught in the act was executed on the spot. More common were economic sanctions and fines, levied for such crimes as assault on a slave, arson, or housebreaking.

In both ancient Greece and Rome (prior to 400 B.C.), interpersonal violence, even that resulting in death, was viewed as a private matter. The laws of Greece and Rome (until quite late in its history) did not provide for punishment of a violent crime. Execution of an offender was considered the prerogative of the deceased's family.

During the Middle Ages (fifth to eleventh centuries A.D.), there was little law or governmental control. Offenses were settled by blood feuds carried out by the families of the injured parties. When possible, the Roman custom of settling disputes by fine or an exchange of property was adopted as a means of resolving interpersonal conflicts with a minimum of bloodshed.

After the eleventh century, during the feudal period, forfeiture of land and property was common punishment for persons who violated law and custom or who failed to fulfill their feudal obligations to their lord. The word *felony* actually comes from the twelfth century, when the term *felonia* referred to a breach of faith with one's feudal lord.

During this period, the main emphasis of criminal law and punishment was on maintaining public order.[5] If in the heat of passion or while intoxicated a person severely injured or killed his or her neighbor, freemen in the area would gather to pronounce a judgment and make the culprit do penance or pay compensation called **wergild.** Wergild contained two elements: the **wite,** which went to the local nobleman for disturbing the peace; and the **bot,** which was compensatin to the victims or their family. The purpose of the fine was to assauge the vengence of the injured party and ensure that the conflict would not develop into a blood feud and anarchy. The inability of the peasantry to pay a fine led to the use of corporal punishment, such as whipping or branding, as a substitute penalty.

The development of the common law in the eleventh through thirteenth centuries brought some standardization to penal practices. However, corrections remained an amalgam of fines and brutal physical punishments. By the fifteenth century, changing social conditions influenced the relationship between crime and punishment. First, the population of England and Europe began to increase after a century of decimation by constant warfare and plagues. At the same time, the developing commercial system caused large tracts of agricultural fields to be converted to grazing lands. Soon, unemployed peasants and landless noblemen were flocking to developing urban centers, such as London and Paris, or taking to the roads as highwaymen, beggars, or vagabonds.

The later Middle Ages also saw the rise of strong monarchs, such as Henry VIII and Elizabeth I of England, who were determined to keep a powerful grip on their realm. The administration of the "King's Peace" under the shire reeve and constable became stronger.

These developments led to the increased use of capital and corporal punishment to control the criminal poor. While the wealthy could buy their way out of punishment and into exile, the poor were executed and mutilated at ever-increasing rates. It is estimated that seventy-two thousand thieves were hanged during the reign of Henry VIII alone.[6] Execution, banishment, mutilation, branding, and flogging were used on a whole range of offenders, from murderers and robbers to vagrants and gypsies. Punishments became unmatched in their cruelty, featuring a gruesome variety of physical tortures. Also during this period, punishment became a public spectacle, presumably so that the sadistic sanctions would act as deterrents. But the variety and imagination of the tortures inflicted on even minor criminals before their death suggest that retribution, sadism, and spectacle were more important than any presumed deterrent effect.

Public Work and Transportation

By the end of the sixteenth century, the rise of the city and overseas colonization provided tremendous markets for manufactured goods. In England and France, population growth was checked by constant warfare and internal disturbances. Labor was scarce in many manufacturing areas of England, Germany, and Holland. The Thirty Years' War in Germany and the constant warfare among England, France, and Spain helped reduce the population.

Punishment of criminals changed to meet the demands created by these social conditions. Instead of being tortured or executed, many offenders were made to do hard labor for their crimes. **Poor laws,** developed at the end of the sixteenth century, required that the poor, vagrants, and vagabonds be put to work in public or private enterprise. Houses of correction were developed to make it convenient to assign petty law violators to work details. In London, a workhouse was developed at Brideswell in 1557, and its use became so popular that by 1576, Parliament ordered a "Brideswell" type workhouse be built in every county in England. Many convicted offenders were pressed into sea duty as galley slaves, a fate considered so loathsome that many convicts mutilated themselves rather than submit.

The constant shortage of labor in the European colonies also prompted authorities to transport convicts overseas. In England, the Vagrancy Act of 1597 legalized deportation for the first time. Similarly, an Order in Council of 1617 granted a reprieve and stay of execution to people convicted of robbery and other felonies who were strong enough to be employed overseas. Similar measures were employed in France and Italy to recruit galley slaves and workers.

Transporting convicts to the colonies became popular; it supplied labor, cost little, and was actually profitable for the government, since manufacturers and plantation owners paid for convicts' services. The Old Bailey Court in London supplied at least ten thousand convicts between 1717 and 1775.[7] Convicts would serve a period as workers and then become free again.

Transportation to the colonies waned as a method of punishment with the increase in colonial population, the further development of colonial lands, and the increasing importation of African slaves in the eighteenth century. The American Revolution ended transportation of felons to North America, although it continued in Australia and New Zealand. Between 1787 and 1875, when the practice was finally abandoned, over 135,000 felons were transported to Australia.

While transportation in lieu of a death sentence may at first glance seem advantageous, transported prisoners endured enormous hardships. Those who were sent to Australia suffered incredible physical abuse, including severe whippings and mutilation. Many of the British prison officials placed in charge of the Australian penal colonies could best be described as sociopaths or sadists. The popular book, *The Fatal Shore*, described in gory detail the almost inhuman treatment of both male and female prisoners transported to Australian penal colonies and the harsh discipline that often resulted in disfigurement or death. Female convicts suffered physical, sexual, and psychological abuse. Conditions were so brutal that some inmates mutilated themselves in order to get a hospital stay, while others volunteered to be killed by their fellow inmates so that their slayers would have a few good meals while awaiting execution.[8]

The Rise of the Prison

Between the American Revolution in 1776 and the first decades of the nineteenth century, the population of Europe and the United States increased rapidly. Transportation of convicts to North America was no longer an option. The increased use of machinery made industry capital- and not labor-intensive. As a result, there was less need for unskilled laborers in England, and many workers could not find suitable employment.

The gulf between poor workers and wealthy landowners and merchants widened. The crime rate rose significantly, prompting a return to physical punishment and increased use of the death penalty. During the later part of the eighteenth century, 350 types of crime in England were punishable by death.[9] While many people sentenced to death for trivial offenses were spared the gallows, the use of capital punishment was extremely common in England during the mid-eighteenth century.[10]

Prompted by the excessive use of physical and capital punishment, legal philosophers such as Jeremy Bentham and Cesare Beccaria argued that physical punishment should be replaced by periods of confinement and incapacitation. Jails and workhouses were commonly used to hold petty offenders, vagabonds, the homeless, and debtors. However, these institutions were not meant for hard-core criminals. One solution to imprisoning a growing criminal population was to keep prisoners in abandoned ships anchored in rivers and harbors throughout England. The degradation under which prisoners lived in these ships inspired John Howard, the sheriff of Bedfordshire, to write the *State of the Prisons* in 1777, which led Parliament to pass the Penitentiary Act in 1779 mandating the construction of secure and sanitary structures to house prisoners.

By 1820, long periods of incarceration in walled institutions called reformatories or **penitentiaries** began to replace physical punishment in England and the United States. These institutions were considered liberal reforms during a time when harsh physical punishment and/or incarceration in filthy holding facilities was the norm. The history of the prison will be explored more fully in Chapter 16.

Incarceration has remained the primary mode of punishment for serious offenses in the United States since it was introduced early in the nineteenth century. Ironically in our high-tech society, some of the institutions constructed soon after the Revolutionary War are still in use today. In recent times, prison as a method of punishment has been supplemented by a sentence to community supervision for less serious offenders, while the death penalty is reserved for those considered to be the most serious and dangerous criminals.

The Goals of Criminal Punishment

When we hear about a notorious criminal, such as Jeffery Dahmer or Ted Bundy, receiving a long prison sentence or the death penalty for a particularly heinous crime, each of us has a distinct reaction: some of us are gratified that a truly evil person "got just what he deserved"; many people feel safer because a dangerous person is now "where he can't harm any other innocent victims"; others hope the punishment serves as a warning to potential criminals that "everyone gets caught in the end"; some of us may actually feel sorry for the defendant—"she got a raw deal, she needs help not punishment"; still others hope that "when he gets out, he'll have learned his lesson"; and when an offender is forced to pay a large fine, we say, "What goes around comes around."

Each of these sentiments may be at work when criminal sentences are formulated. After all, sentences are devised and implemented by judges, many of whom are elected officials and share the general public's sentiments and fears. The objectives of criminal sentencing today can usually be grouped into six distinct areas: general deterrence, incapacitation, specific deterrence, retribution/desert, rehabilitation, and restitution.

General Deterrence

One consideration in sentencing is the impact of punishment on the community. By punishing an offender severely, the state can demonstrate its determination to control crime and deter potential offenders. Too lenient a sentence might encourage criminal conduct; too severe a sentence might reduce the system's ability to dispense fair and impartial justice and actually encourage criminality. For example, if the crime of rape was punished with death, rapists might be encouraged to kill their victims in order to dispose of the one person who could identify them; since they would already be facing the death penalty for rape, they have nothing more to lose. Maintaining a balance between fear and justice is an ongoing quest in the justice system.

Pursuing general deterrence reflects faith in the impact punishment can have on social behavior. Placing a student in jail for a month for a drunk driving conviction should convince his or her dorm mates not to drink and drive.[11] Sentencing for the purposes of general deterrence, then, has little to do with the offender's own behavior and more to do with how the rest of society perceives and reacts to the punishment.

Questions of justice and propriety arise when punishment is designed to serve as an example. It is fair to punish someone solely to frighten others? For example, executing a traitor may serve as a warning to those who might consider betraying their country to a foreign power. The death sentence in this case serves no other practical purpose beyond deterrence: the damage has already been done, and even if the spy were released, he or she presents no future danger to society (since the

One of the goals of sentencing is to punish offenders severely enough to convince them to never repeat their criminal offenses. A stay in a correctional boot camp is designed to deter young offenders.

offender would never again have access to any sensitive material). Is it fair to execute someone for no other reason than to influence and deter others? Is it just to "take a life to save a life"?

Sentencing for the purposes of deterrence may be a case of wishful thinking. Little clear-cut evidence exists that severe punishments actually influence criminal behavior trends.[12] The violence rate in the United States has increased at the same time judges are employing longer and more severe criminal punishments. More evidence exists that shame and social rejection are actually greater crime deterrents than the fear of legal sanctions.[13] For example, research conducted by Richard Hawkins and Kirk Williams indicates that potential spouse abusers are deterred when they fear personal humiliation and loss of social standing, not because they fear legal punishment and incarceration.[14]

Incapacitation

Sentencing judges consider whether the offender is a risk to society and requires a period of secure confinement. **Incapacitation** is justified because inmates will not be able to repeat their criminal acts while they are under state control. For some offenders, this means a period in a high-security state prison where behavior is strictly controlled. Fixing sentence length involves determining how long a particular offender needs to be incarcerated to ensure that society is protected.

Incapacitation strategies also depend on a form of prediction: offenders are confined to prevent additional criminality. This means punishing people not for what they have done but for what they may do in the future, something that is impossible to accurately predict.

Incapacitation strategies also seem of questionable utility because there appears to be little association between the number of criminals behind bars and the crime rate: though more convicted criminals are now in prison than ever before, the crime rate has not declined and the violence rate has steadily increased.[15] Yet the "get tough" sentencing approaches now in vogue have led to a U.S. jail and prison inmate population of more than 1 million people.[16] Because of overcrowding, some judges have sought alternatives to incapacitation, including house arrest monitored electronically by computers (see Chapter 15). In 1992, eager to reduce the prison population, one Texas judge approved a bizarre offer made by an accused child molester: the offender would be surgically castrated in return for criminal charges being dropped; public outcry (and the refusal of physicians to perform the operation) eventually led to the offer being withdrawn.[17]

Specific Deterrence

Specific deterrence refers to the ability of punishments to convince the convicted that **recidivism** would not be in their best interests. The theory is that suffering an extended prison stay or paying a large fine should inhibit future law violations.

Judges have had difficulty formulating sentences that are of sufficient length and severity to act as a specific deterrent, yet do not preclude or interfere with the offender's successful rehabilitation and return to society.[18] A few research efforts have found that punishment can have a significant specific deterrent effect on future criminality.[19] However, these are not conclusive, and punishment alone probably cannot convince offenders never to repeat their illegal acts.[20] After all, more than 70 percent of prison inmates have had prior convictions.

Retribution/Desert

Offenders are also punished because they deserve retribution for what they have done; "the punishment should fit the crime."[21] This approach is illustrated by the extremely large fines and assessments, some in excess of $100 million, handed down to investment bankers who profited from illegal stock market practices, such as insider trading. Since these criminals benefited by reaping millions in illicit profits, it seems fair that they should have to return their illegal gains—and then some—to society.

The **just desert** philosophy of punishment holds that criminal sentences should be proportional to the seriousness of an offender's criminal act.[22] Offenders are punished for what they have already done, not for what they may do in the future (incapacitation) or for what others may do unless they learn to fear punishment (deterrence).

Desert is based on **equity**; the criminals profited from their misdeeds, so now they must repay society to restore the social balance. Desert-based sentencing evaluates the weight of the criminal act, not the needs of the offender or the community. It demands that punishments be equally and fairly distributed to all people who commit similar illegal acts. Determining just punishments can be difficult because there is generally little consensus about the treatment of criminals, the seriousness of crimes, and the proper response to criminal acts.[23]

Rehabilitation

How can criminal offenders be effectively treated so that they can eventually readjust to society? Rehabilitation is required, because in a sense, society has failed the criminal offender, many of whom have grown up in disorganized neighborhoods and dysfunctional families.

In some cases, rehabilitation efforts can be implemented in the community through the probation department. Community supervision is used to teach commitment, conformity, and responsibility and to help people readjust to society.

Even serious criminals, including armed robbers and rapists, may be eligible for probationary sentences if they are not considered risks to society.[24]

If the gravity of the crime is great and the offender considered dangerous or unstable, rehabilitation takes place in a secure environment under the auspices of state correctional authorities. In this instance, the judge will remand the convicted offender to a secure treatment facility, such as a prison or jail, for correctional treatment.

The rehabilitation aspect of sentencing is also based on a prediction of the future needs of the offenders and not on the gravity of their current offense. For example, if a judge sentences a person convicted of a felony to a period of community supervision, the judge believes that the offender can be successfully treated and presents no further threat to society.

Recently, the rehabilitation aspect of sentencing has come under increased criticism from those advocating desert- or deterrence-based sentences, yet surveys indicate that the general public still supports treatment efforts.[25]

Restitution

In the early common law, wergild and fines represented the concept of restitution to both the victim and the state. Today, judges continue to require that offenders pay victims for their losses.

Restitution means that convicted criminals must pay back their victims for their loss, the justice system for the costs of processing their case, and society for any disruption they may have caused. In a so-called victimless crime, such as drug dealing, the social costs might include the expense of drug enforcement efforts, drug treatment centers, and care for infants born to drug-addicted mothers. To help defray these costs, convicted offenders might be required to pay a fine, forfeit the property they acquired through illegal gain, do community service work, make financial restitution to their victim, and reimburse the state for the costs of the criminal process.

The factors influencing sentencing are illustrated in Figure 14.1.

Sentencing Strategies

When a convicted offender is sentenced, the statutes of a jurisdiction provide the possible penalities that may be imposed by the court. Over the years, the states have adopted a variety of sentencing approaches usually defined by the legislature, which has power over the content of the criminal law. However, there is no single format for criminal sentencing, and most state codes can be categorized as falling into one of three groupings (or combine elements of all three): the legislative, judicial, and administrative models.[26]

In the **legislatively fixed model**, the state legislature determines the penalty for specific crimes, such as a minimum three-year prison term for a second drug offense, and all people convicted of that crime receive that sentence. Judicial and/or administrative discretion is severely reduced. Flexibility and discretion in the system is shifted to the law enforcement officers, who decide which cases to investigate, and the prosecutor's office, which determines the charge and arranges plea negotiations to lesser offenses.

In the **judicially fixed model**, the legislature sets a general range of prison sentences for a given crime, and the sentencing judge then determines a sentence

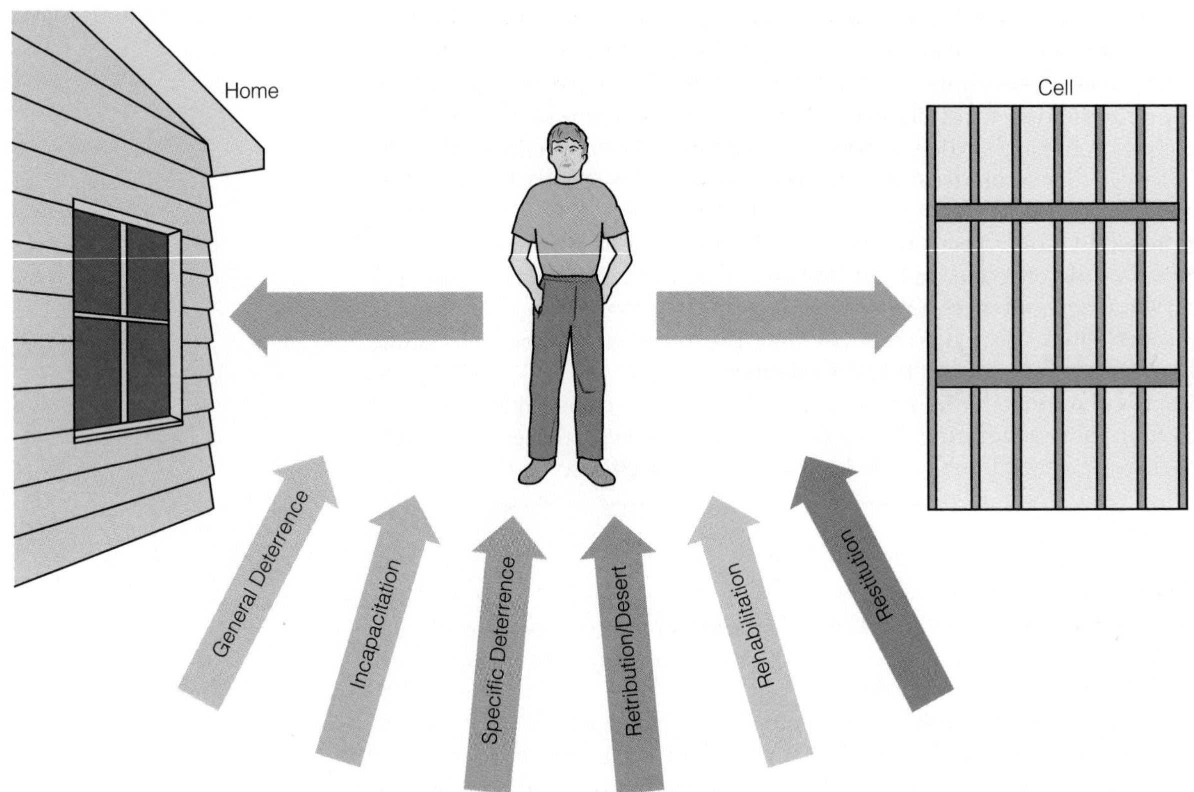

FIGURE 14.1
The Factors Influencing Sentencing Decisions

within that range. For example, the legislature creates a sentence of no less than one year but no more than ten years for a robbery, and the judge determines the sentence in each case somewhere between these ranges, for example, five years for a particular robber, seven for another. The sentence cannot be increased or reduced by any other state authority. Discretion is vested with the sentencing judge within the range authorized by the legislature.

In the **administrative model**, the legislature creates an extremely wide range of sentences for a particular crime, for example, from one to fifty years for robbery. The sentencing judge must—or may—impose this sentence. The actual duration of the sentence is controlled by an administrative agency that monitors the offenders while they serve their prison sentence. For example, a judge sentences a person for robbery to a prison term of not less than two years nor more than twenty-five; after serving twenty-two months, the offender is released on parole. In this model, control over criminal punishment is for all practical purposes in the hands of correctional administrative authorities, the parole board.

Regardless of which model is used, most sentencing schemes give the judge some discretion to impose a particular type of sentence. Based on his or her discretion, the judge can order a first time nonviolent offender to serve a relatively long prison sentence or sentence them to a term of probation only. When an offender is convicted on two or more charges, the judge also determines how these sentences are to be served. If the convicted offender is given a **concurrent sentence**, the sentence is completed after the longest term has been served. For example, if a defendant is convicted of rape and two counts each of assault and robbery and is sentenced to ten years for the rape, eight years on each of the robbery charges, and five on each of the assault charges, to run concurrently, the person would be released after ten years (the term of the single most serious offense). If, however, the sentences were imposed consecutively, the defendant would begin serving time for the second charge at the completion of the time for the first. If serving a **consecutive sentence**, the criminal in this example could serve thirty-six years, instead of ten. In most instances, sentences are served concurrently, and consecutive sentences are reserved for the most serious, chronic, unrepentant, and uncooperative defendants.

A variety of sentencing structures are used today. Some reflect reliance on judicial discretion, while others adhere to legislatively fixed or administrative models. In the sections below, the four most common types of sentencing models are discussed in some detail.

The Indeterminate Sentence

The first prison sentences used in the United States were for a fixed period of years that the offender was forced to serve before release. Harsh prison conditions and rules enforced by physical punishment left inmates with little incentive for rehabilitation or self-improvement.

By 1870, penal reformers in Australia (Alexander Maconochie) and Ireland (Sir Walter Crofton) had instituted plans in which inmates could earn early release by exhibiting a positive attitude and work habits (see Chapter 18). In that year, at a meeting of the National Congress on Penitentiary and Reformatory Discipline in Cincinnati, progressive prison reformers, such as Enoch Wines and Zebulon Brockway, called for inmates to be released from prison once they were reformed. **Progressives** were firmly convinced that government agencies, using scientific methods, could be the agents of social reform. They believed that prison sentences should be tailored to fit individual needs and that offenders should only be placed in confinement until they were rehabilitated. Brockway called for the development of **indeterminate sentences** that require that criminals serve a short minimum stay in prison during which they would be encouraged to work on self-improvement. Prison administrators would be empowered to release them back into the community via parole once they were reformed. Rather than the "punishment fitting the crime," reformers believed the "treatment should fit the offender."

Reform did not come at once. By 1900, five states had adopted the indeterminate sentencing model, however, with another thirty-two states following suit over the next twenty years.[27] The indeterminate sentence became the most widely used type of sentence in the United States. Some states went so far as developing true **indefinite sentences** with very brief minimums and very long maximums, allowing inmates to be released as soon as a parole board concluded they were rehabilitated.

The indeterminate sentence is still used in a majority of states. Under most sentencing models, convicted offenders who are not eligible for community supervision are given a short minimum sentence that must be served and a lengthy maximum sentence that is the outer boundary of the time that can possibly be served. For example, the legislature might set a sentence of a minimum of one year and a maximum of twenty years for burglary.

Under this scheme, the actual length of time served by the inmate is controlled by the corrections agency. The inmate can be paroled after serving the minimum sentence whenever the institution and parole personnel believe that he or she is ready to live in the community. The minimum (or maximum) might also be reduced by programs giving inmates time off for good behavior or for participating in counseling and vocational training programs. In many instances, sentencing reduction programs enable inmates to serve only a fraction of their minimum sentence.

The underlying purpose of the indeterminate sentencing approach is to individualize each sentence in the interests of rehabilitating the offender. This type of sentencing allows for flexibility not only in the type of sentence to be imposed but also in the length of time to be served.

A number of variations on the indeterminate sentence are possible. The most common is for the judge to set both the maximum and the minimum sentence within guidelines established by the legislature. For example: The minimum and maximum sentence for burglary is one to twenty years. Offender A gets one to twenty; offender B, four to ten; offender C, three to six. The maximum the judge uses cannot exceed twenty years; the minimum cannot be less than one. Another variation on this model is to have the judge set a maximum within an upper limit, with the minimum determined by the legislature. For example: All sentenced burglars do at least one year in prison but not more than twenty. Offender A receives one to ten; offender B, one to twenty; offender C, one to five.

Today, about forty states still use indeterminate sentencing. Most have statutes that specify minimum and maximum terms but allow the judge to fix the actual sentence within those limits. The typical minimum sentence is at least one year; a few state jurisdictions require at least a two-year minimum sentence for felons.[28]

The indeterminate sentence is the predominant form of sentence used in the criminal process. It is the heart of the rehabilitation model of justice, because offenders may be released after a relatively short prison stay if they convince correctional authorities that they can forgo a criminal career. Yet, because many policymakers believe that the rehabilitation of offenders has generally failed, alternative sentencing schemes are being given more consideration.

The Determinate Sentence

Determinate sentences were the first kind of sentences used in the United States. With these, judges could impose a sentence, based on their personal and professional judgments, that fell within limits set by statute. For example, a state criminal code could set the punishment for the crime of burglary at up to twenty years in prison. After evaluating each case, a judge could impose a sentence of five years on a first-time defendant, ten on a more experienced criminal, and the full twenty on a third who may have both been a repeater and carried a weapon to the crime scene. Unlike the indeterminate models in which release dates are controlled by correctional authorities, a **determinate sentence** is one in which the duration of the offender's prison stay is determined by the judiciary at the time the sentence is imposed.

When the original determinate sentencing statutes were replaced by indeterminate sentences and discretionary parole early in the twentieth century, judicial discretion remained quite broad. Both determinate and indeterminate sentences allowed judges to place one defendant on probation while sentencing another to a lengthy prison term for essentially the same crime. Such unbridled discretion left the door open to disparity and unfairness in the sentencing process. In addition, there was dramatic evidence that indeterminate sentences give correctional authorities quasi-judicial power, allowing them to decide when an inmate was to be returned to society. Correctional discretion could then be used to control the inmate population. The publication of *Soledad Brother* by George Jackson exposed efforts to deny parole to dissident or politically active inmates who campaigned for prison reform. Jackson served eleven years in the California correctional system after he was convicted on charges stemming from a seventy-dollar gas station robbery. Jackson's parole was continually denied because his political writings and activity indicated he had not yet been "rehabilitated." Jackson was convinced the authorities would never release him alive, and he was killed while trying to escape; his death was considered a political assassination by many of his supporters.[29]

Calls for a New Determinacy

In 1969, Kenneth Culp Davis published *Discretionary Justice*, followed in 1972 by Judge Marvin Frankel's landmark study *Law Without Order*.[30] These works exposed the **disparity** in sentencing and called for reform of the criminal law. Frankel stated, "The almost wholly unchecked and sweeping powers we give to judges in the fashioning of sentences are terrifying and intolerable for a society that professes devotion to the rule to law." [31]

Concern focused on the degree to which disparity existed in the sentencing process. Widely disparate sentences were often given to offenders who were convicted of similar offenses and who had identical criminal records. All too often discretion seemed to aid the wealthy and powerful and harm the poor, the vulnerable, and members of minority groups.[32] Those favoring the justice model (see Chapter 5), such as noted scholar Andrew von Hirsch, argued that if the justice system could neither reform criminals nor bring down the crime rate, then it should at least be able to "do justice" in a fair and equitable manner.[33] Those espousing a crime-control orientation, led by James Q. Wilson, called for sentencing reforms that would ensure that chronic criminal offenders would at least be incapacitated. "Wicked people exist," he concluded, adding: "Nothing avails except to set them apart from innocent people."[34] Conservative politicians wanted to control the rising crime rate by putting more offenders behind bars, while liberals were concerned about the uncertainty of indeterminate sentencing and inequities in the parole process.

In response to these concerns, a number of jurisdictions adopted alternatives to the indeterminate sentence aimed at controlling judicial discretion by calibrating sentences according to a defendant's criminal record and activities and abolishing discretionary parole release. These modern versions of determinate sentencing reflect an orientation toward desert, deterrence, and equality at the expense of treatment and rehabilitations.[35]

A variety of determinate sentencing structures are used today. The two most common approaches are presumptive sentences and guidelines, or structured sentences, which are discussed below in detail.

Presumptive Sentencing

For the past decade, advocates of the justice model of criminal justice and the just-desert philosophy have argued that sentencing decisions must be fair, equal, and based primarily on the seriousness of the current offense; deterring future criminality or rehabilitating offenders should be of secondary importance in the

Fighter Mike Tyson was sentenced under Indiana's presumptive sentencing model after his conviction on a rape charge.

sentencing decision.[36] It is often the case that similar offenses are committed in different ways, and each offender has unique characteristics. To attain this sentencing goal, a number of states, including Illinois, Indiana, and North Carolina, have instituted a form of determinancy referred to as **presumptive sentencing**.

In presumptive sentencing, the legislature sets an expected sentence range for a particular crime. Offenders convicted for this crime are expected to serve the sentence presumed by the legislature, unless mitigating or aggravating circumstances are found in the commission of the offense or the offender's personal background. Judges are then permitted to sentence below or above the prescribed sentence but must give the reasons, in writing, justifying such action. For example, the legislature might set a presumptive sentence of seven years for armed robbery in the first degree and allow judges to add or subtract three years, depending on aggravating or mitigating circumstances. The "average" robber sent to prison should expect a prison sentence of at least seven years. However, the sentencing judge can raise the sentence up to ten years in a particularly serious case or lower it to four where there are unusual mitigating circumstances. In this situation, the legislature retains the authority to exercise policy decisions, and the judge maintains some degree of sentencing discretion. Though discretionary parole is abolished, an inmate can reduce his sentence by earning time off for good behavior.

California's Determinate Sentencing Act of 1977 is an example of this approach. It allows judges to assign either a short, middle or long term for each offense. The middle term is required unless mitigating circumstances suggest the short term be used or aggravating circumstances require the longer term. Judges must specify and document why they deviated from the suggested middle term. A formal fact-finding hearing must be held if the long term is applied for such aggravating circumstances as a prior record or use of a handgun in the commission of the crime.[37]

Most presumptive sentencing jurisdictions carefully spell out the factors that enable judges to mitigate or extend suggested sentences. This approach has the advantage of retaining flexibility in sentencing while providing a substantial degree of certainty about the imposition of the sentence for the offender and the general public. It also seeks to eliminate the problem of widely disparate sentences for similar crimes imposed by judges with different sentencing philosophies.

Thus, the important objectives of presumptive sentencing are (1) to reduce sentencing disparity, (2) to limit judicial discretion without completely eliminating it, and (3) to impose a sentence that the offender is required to serve. Marvin Zalman points out that presumptive sentencing proposals have grown out of a climate of distrust of judicial and parole board discretion.[38] To restrict such discretion, legislatures are expanding their role in the sentencing process.

Structured Sentencing

Another approach to creating "rational sentences" has been the development of guidelines to control and structure the sentencing process. Guidelines are usually based on the seriousness of a crime and the background of an offender: the more serious the crime and the more extensive the offender's criminal background, the longer the prison term recommended by the guidelines. For example, guidelines might require that all people convicted of robbery who had no prior offense record and who did not use excessive force or violence be given an average of a five-year sentence; those who used force and had a prior record will have three years added on their sentence. Guidelines eliminate discretionary parole but also allow inmates to reduce their sentence by acquiring time off for good behavior.

In some states, including Delaware and Maryland, **descriptive guidelines**, were devised by analyzing how similar offenders were treated in the past; judges were then asked to voluntarily comply with suggested sentences. In contrast, **prescriptive guidelines,** used by such states as Michigan, Washington, Oregon, Pennsylvania, and Minnesota and by the federal government, are created by appointed sentencing commissions. The commission members determine what an "ideal" sentence would be for a particular crime and offender. Prescriptive guidelines are generally mandatory and generate a much higher rate of judicial compliance than voluntary guidelines.

Sentencing guidelines can be computed for a variety of offenses and offender types. Table 14.1 illustrates the guidelines used in Minnesota. Each case is evaluated on the basis of offense seriousness and the offender's prior record to determine where it fits in the guideline grid. Those that fall above the incarceration line give the judge the opportunity to choose probation or sentence the offender to up to twelve months in jail.[39] In more serious cases, judges may impose the guideline sentence but are granted discretion to increase or decrease the sentence based on mitigating or aggravating circumstances. The range of sentences in the Minnesota guideline grid has been altered over the years with some penalties being increased and others decreased. For example, in the original guidelines, an offender convicted of a first-level offense with a criminal history score of six was eligible for a probation sentence, while today, offenders falling in that category get nineteen months in prison. In 1989, the Minnesota legislature adopted get-tough policies, including mandatory minimum prison terms for certain drug crimes and life without parole for certain first-degree murderers. The legislation changed the mandate of the sentencing commission to develop sentences based on public safety as its primary goal without considering the conservation of correctional resources.[40]

Perhaps the most important attempt to create sentencing guidelines is the U.S. government's establishment of a sentencing commission to structure sentences. This commission's work is set out in Analyzing Criminal Justice Issues: Federal Sentencing Guidelines.

TABLE 14.1
Minnesota Guideline Grid, Presumptive Sentence Lengths in Months

Severity Levels of Conviction Offense		Criminal History Score						
		0	1	2	3	4	5	6 or more
Sale of a Simulated Controlled Substance	I	12*	12*	12*	13	15	17	19 *18–20*
Theft Related Crimes ($2,500 or less) Check Forgery ($200–$2500)	II	12*	12*	13	15	17	19	21 *20–22*
Theft Crimes ($2,500 or less)	III	12*	13	15	17	19 *18–20*	22 *21–23*	25 *24–26*
Nonresidential Burglary Theft Crimes (over $2,500)	IV	12*	15	18	21	25 *24–26*	32 *30–34*	41 *37–45*
Residential Burglary Simple Robbery	V	18	23	27	30 *29–31*	38 *36–40*	46 *43–49*	54 *50–58*
Criminal Sexual Conduct 2nd Degree (a) & (b)	VI	21	26	30	34 *33–35*	44 *42–46*	54 *50–58*	65 *60–70*
Aggravated Robbery	VII	48 *44–52*	58 *54–62*	68 *64–72*	78 *74–82*	88 *84–92*	98 *94–102*	108 *104–112*
Criminal Sexual Conduct, 1st Degree Assault, 1st Degree	VIII	86 *81–91*	98 *93–103*	110 *105–115*	122 *117–127*	134 *129–139*	146 *141–151*	158 *153–163*
Murder, 3rd Degree Murder, 2nd Degree (felony murder)	IX	150 *144–156*	165 *159–171*	180 *174–186*	195 *189–201*	210 *204–216*	225 *219–231*	240 *234–246*
Murder, 2nd Degree (with intent)	X	306 *299–313*	326 *319–333*	346 *339–353*	366 *359–373*	386 *379–393*	406 *399–413*	426 *419–433*

First-degree murder is excluded from the guidelines by law and continues to have a mandatory life sentence. See section II.E. Mandatory Sentences for policy regarding those sentences controlled by law.

*One year and one day.

Italicized numbers within the grid denote the range within which a judge may sentence without the sentence being deemed a departure.

Offenders with nonimprisonment felony sentences are subject to jail time according to law.

■ At the discretion of the judge, up to a year in jail and/or other nonjail sanctions can be imposed as conditions of probation.

■ Presumpive commitment to state imprisonment.

SOURCE: Minnesota Sentencing Guideline Commission, 1990.

Problems of Sentencing Guidelines

Guidelines will likely continue to be used now that the federal government has adopted structured sentencing and the U.S. Supreme Court has upheld its use.[41] A number of states, including Louisiana, Oregon, Tennessee, Vermont, and New Mexico, are considering adopting such guidelines.[42]

Despite the widespread acceptance of guidelines, some nagging problems remain. Analysis of Minnesota's guideline experiment found that judges closely followed the guideline's recommended sentences during the first year they were in effect (1980) but that sentences began to diverge after two years. Some racial disparity was indicated the first year after the guidelines were adapted, but it diminished over time. Most important, the incarceration rate for serious offenders increased 73 percent, while the rate for petty offenders decreased 72 percent.[43]

Some results were troubling. Research by Terance Miethe and Charles Moore found that the effects of race and economic status continued to influence sentencing.[44] For example, black offenders were more likely to be charged with weapons violations, so they were more likely to receive prison terms than white offenders.[45] Richard Frase found that the Minnesota guidelines did not eliminate gender bias and that regional differences can still be detected in sentencing outcomes.[46] However, there are also indications that the Minnesota guidelines produced positive change. Michael Tonry found that the Minnesota guidelines helped conserve state resources, were resistant to political pressures, and increased overall fairness in the sentencing system.[47] Similarly, the Frase research found that the Minnesota guidelines relieved correctional overcrowding while retaining judicial sentencing flexibility.[48]

Charges of racial disparity continue to plague guideline efforts. Joan Petersilia and Susan Turner's national evaluation of sentencing guidelines found many of the criteria used in determining sentence length resulted in racial differences in sentencing.[49] For example, some jurisdictions give enhanced sentences to prior juvenile convictions or for being on juvenile probation or parole at the time of an arrest. Guidelines could increase racial disparity in sentencing because black offenders are more likely than white offenders to have a prior record as a juvenile.

Research also indicates that judges deviate from the sentences suggested by their state's guidelines. David Griswold found that such factors as whether the case was settled by plea or trial, whether the offender was a probation violator, and the defendant's gender all influenced sentencing disparity in Florida, a state that uses guidelines.[50]

Some defense attorneys oppose the use of guidelines because they result in longer prison terms, prevent judges from considering mitigating circumstances, and reduce the use of probation. So, the debate over sentencing guidelines has not ended. As Chris Eskridge warns:

> . . . sentencing guidelines as implemented to date have not had the impacts anticipated by guideline proponents. There is some evidence, in fact, that sentencing guidelines may only be making the problem worse. In other words, the cure may be worse than the ailment. Presumptive sentencing guidelines, therefore, should not be adopted.[51]

Mandatory Minimum Sentences

Another effort to limit judicial discretion has been the development of the mandatory (minimum) sentences that require the incarceration of all offenders convicted of specific crimes. Most states now employ some form of mandatory sentencing. Some make offenders convicted of certain offenses, such as drug trafficking or handgun crimes, ineligible for probation; some exclude recidivists, while others bar certain offenders from being considered for parole.

Mandatory sentencing legislation may impose indeterminate minimum-maximum terms or a single determinate prison sentence. Mandatory prison sentences are most often provided for murder and multiple convictions for such crimes as rape, drug violations, and robbery. On the one hand, mandatory sen-

ANALYZING CRIMINAL JUSTICE ISSUES

Federal Sentencing Guidelines

One of the most important developments in the criminal justice system has been the adoption of sentencing guidelines by the federal judicial system. Consequently, when a defendant appears in federal court for sentencing, his or her fate will not be solely in the hands of the judge but will be determined by a very complex set of rules that have been set down by a seven-member U.S. Sentencing Guideline Commission, which also abolished the federal parole system.

The guidelines themselves are quite extensive and detailed. To determine the actual sentence, a magistrate must first determine the **base penalty** that a particular charge is given in the guidelines. Table A gives the base score and mitigation factors for robbery. Robbery has a base offense level of eighteen. The base level can be adjusted upward if the case was particularly serious or violent. For example, seven points could be added to the robbery base if a firearm was discharged during the crime and five points if the weapon was just in the offender's possession. Similarly, points can be added to a robbery if a large amount of money was taken; a victim was injured; a person was abducted or restrained in order to facilitate an escape; or the object of the robbery was to steal weapons or drugs. Upward adjustments can also be made if the defendant was a ringleader in the crime, obstructed justice, or used a professional skill or position of trust (such as doctor, lawyer, or politician) to commit crime. Offenders designated as "career criminals" by a court can likewise receive longer sentences.

Once the base score is computed, judges determine the sentence by consulting a sentencing table that converts scores into months to be served. Offense levels are set out in the vertical column, and the criminal history (ranging from one to six prior offenses) is displayed in a horizontal column, forming a grid that contains the various sentencing ranges (similar to the Minnesota guideline grid). By matching the applicable offense level and the criminal history, the judge can determine the sentence that applies to the particular offender.

Some gray areas remain in these guidelines. Some offenses, especially petty misdemeanors, are not covered; other offenses can overlap more than one category. It is also difficult to determine the exact sentence when there are multiple counts of a single offense, for example, importing narcotics on four different occasions. According to the guidelines, importing 40 kilograms of cocaine four times would be treated as if the offender imported 160 kilograms once; however, committing four burglaries would result in each offense being treated separately. If there are multiple counts of multiple offenses, the calculation becomes more complex.

Analysis of case processing indicates that judges sentence within range of the guidelines about 80 percent of the time, exceed guideline standards in about 2 percent of the cases because of aggravating circumstances, and give lower sentences due to mitigating circumstances in 7 percent of all cases. In another 7 percent of all cases, judges lower sentences because defendants are willing to provide substantial assistance in other criminal prosecutions. Research by Jim Beck and Elaine Wolf found that the substantial assistance clause gives prosecutors and judges a significant degree of discretion over charging and sentencing in federal courts.

While decreasing sentencing disparity, the guidelines will also have some dubious effects. The use of probation will probably diminish, and the size of the federal prison population will most likely increase. The prison time added by the guidelines will be compounded by other federal statutes increasing penalties for particular crimes, such as drug dealing (the Anti-Drug Abuse Act of 1986), and for career offenders with multiple convictions. The guidelines adjust for these sentencing provisions by giving base scores commensurate with the crime's seriousness; crimes that call for mandatory minimum sentences of at least ten years are assigned a base score of thirty-two. The amount of time served by offenders will almost double due to the impact of guidelines coupled with sentencing enhancement statutes. For example, robbers who served approximately forty-five months before the guidelines were implemented now serve seventy-five; drug offenders will see their sentences increase on average from twenty-three months to fifty-seven months. These sentencing enhancements will boost the federal prison population by up to sixty thousand inmates over preguideline estimates by the year 2002. So, while guidelines may enhance equity, they are not without their costs.

tencing generally limits the judge's discretionary power to impose any disposition but that authorized by the legislature; as a result, it destroys the idea of the individualized sentence, impeding rehabilitation efforts by the courts. On the other hand, mandatory sentencing provides equal treatment for all offenders who

TABLE A

Base Score and Mitigation Factors for Robbery

§ 2B3.1. *Robbery*

(a) Base Offense Level: 18

(b) Specific Offense Characteristics

(1) If the value of the property taken or destroyed exceeded $2,500, increase the offense level as follows:

	Loss	Increase in Level
(A)	$2,500 or less	no increase
(B)	$2,501–$10,000	add 1
(C)	$10,001–$50,000	add 2
(D)	$50,001–$250,000	add 3
(E)	$250,001–$1,000,000	add 4
(F)	$1,000,001–$5,000,000	add 5
(G)	more than $5,000,000	add 6

Treat the loss for a financial institution or post office as at least $5,000.

(2) (A) If a firearm was discharged increase by 7 levels; (B) if a firearm or a dangerous weapon was otherwise used, increase by 6 levels; (C) if a firearm or other dangerous weapon was brandished, displayed or possessed, increase by 5 levels.

(3) If any victim sustained bodily injury, increase the offense level according to the seriousness of the injury:

	Degree of Bodily Injury	Increase in Level
(A)	Bodily Injury	add 2
(B)	Serious Bodily Injury	add 4
(C)	Permanent or Life-Threatening Bodily Injury	add 6

Provided, however, that the cumulative adjustments from (2) and (3) shall not exceed 9 levels.

(4) (A) If any person was abducted to facilitate commission of the offense or to facilitate escape, increase by 4 levels; or (B) if any person was physically restrained to facilitate commission of the offense or to facilitate escape, increase by 2 levels.

(5) If obtaining a firearm, destructive device, or controlled substance was the object of the offense, increase by 1 level.

Critical Thinking Skills

Guidelines seem like an equitable way of dispensing justice. While many people believe that incarcerating thousands of offenders is essentially self-defeating, as long as incarceration is used, guidelines at least help create equity in the sentencing process. Are there problems with structured sentences beyond technical glitches? Is it fair to treat all criminals the same? For example, let's say that guidelines add ten years to a sentence because of a prior record of drug dealing. Offender A was sentenced to probation fifteen years ago, when he was caught selling marijuana to school mates when he was eighteen; offender B, age thirty-three, was sentenced to prison two years ago for selling cocaine to minors. Though both offenders have a prior record of drug dealing, are they really equivalent?

SOURCE: U.S. Sentencing Commission, *Mandatory Minimum Penalties in the Federal Criminal Justice System* (Washington, D.C.: U.S. Government Printing Office, 1991); Anti-Drug Abuse Act of 1986 (21 U.S.C. § 841 [1986], Pub.L. 99-570 [1986]); Jim Beck and Elaine Wolf, "Departures for Substantial Assistance under the Federal Sentencing Guidelines" (Paper presented at the annual meeting of the American Society of Criminology, San Francisco, November 1991); Sentencing Reform Act of 1984 (18 U.S.C. 3551 et seq.); *Federal Sentencing Guideline Manual* (St. Paul: West Publishing, 1987); Stefan Cassella, "A Step-by-Step Guide to the New Federal Sentencing Guidelines," *The Practical Lawyer* 34 (1988):13–23.

commit the same crime, regardless of age, gender, or other individual characteristics.

The most well-known mandatory sentencing laws include: New York's 1973 effort (since repealed) to control narcotics use and trafficking through prescribed

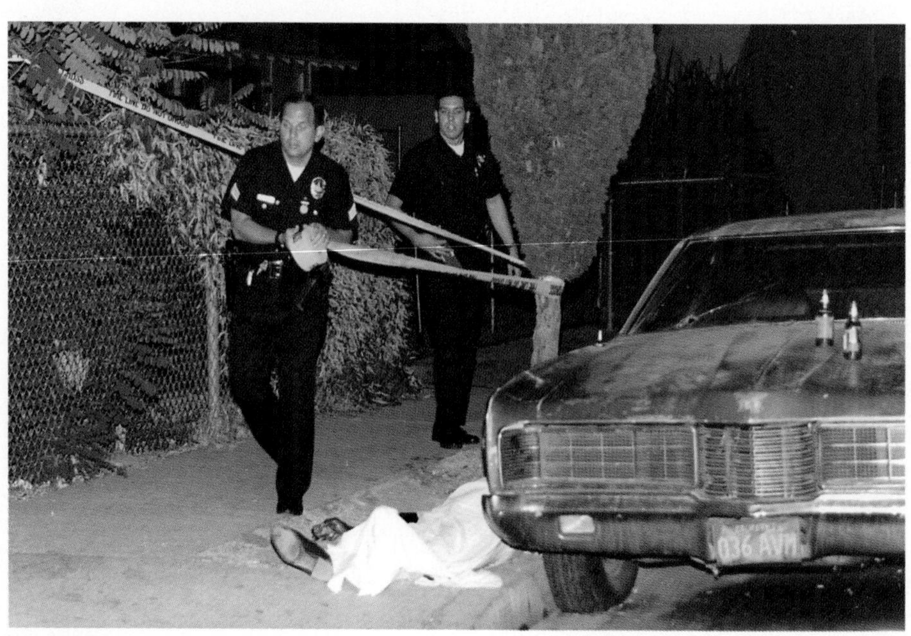

Fear of a growing predatory crime rate has prompted state legislators to institute mandatory minimum sentences for violent and drug related crimes.

mandatory sentences for narcotics offenses; the Massachusetts firearms control law, which gives offenders caught in possession of an unregistered handgun a mandatory one-year prison sentence that cannot be suspended by the court; the Michigan Felony Firearm Statute, which provides a two-year add-on sentence for possessing a handgun during the commission of a felony; and the federal drug control act of 1986 and 1988, which mandate long minimum sentences for drug trafficking and double these sentences if there has been a prior conviction.[52]

It is difficult to say if depriving the judiciary of discretion and placing all sentencing power in the hands of the legislature will have a deterrent effect on the commission of these offenses. Grouping all offenders who commit a particular crime into one category can result in hardships on defendants with particular personal characteristics. For example, the use of mandatory minimum sentences can lead to an increase in plea bargaining as offenders seek avenues to escape harsh sentences, and prosecutors use the threat of mandatory sentences to force guilty pleas to lesser offenses. A critique of mandatory sentencing by the Twentieth Century Fund found that it may lead to court delays, arbitrary judicial decision making, and increases in prosecutorial discretion and prison overcrowding.[53] Similarly, Michael Tonry makes these claims after reviewing the literature on mandatory sentencing:

1. Lawyers and judges will take steps to avoid application of laws they consider unduly harsh;
2. Dismissal rates typically increase at early stages of the criminal justice process after implementation of mandatory laws as practitioners attempt to shield some defendants from the laws' reach;
3. Defendants whose case is not dismissed or diverted make more vigorous efforts to avoid conviction and delay sentencing;
4. Defendants who are convicted of the target offense are often sentenced more severely than they would be in the absence of the mandatory law;
5. Because declines in conviction rates for those arrested tend to offset increases in imprisonment rates for those convicted, the overall probability that defendants will be incarcerated remains about the same after enactment of a mandatory sentencing law.[54]

A report by the National Council on Crime and Delinquency found that the use of mandatory sentences in Florida has led to overcrowding and chaos in the correctional system. Because of a combination of stiff mandatory penalties and an escalating "war on drugs," the prison system, which admitted ten thousand people in 1980, admitted forty-four thousand in 1989. Despite spending $750 million in the 1980s to build thousands of new cells, Florida did not experience a reduction in the crime rate and instead was forced to initiate the nation's most ambitious early release program to reduce overcrowding.[55]

So, while some of the desired effects of mandatory sentencing have been achieved (serious criminals do get longer sentences), they are counterbalanced by the efforts of justice system personnel to shield some offenders from the more punitive aspects of mandatory sentencing, by prison overcrowding, and by the resultant early release of offenders.

Habitual Criminal Statutes

Habitual criminal statutes mandate that people who have been convicted of and served time for multiple felony offenses receive either an enhanced punishment for the current crime or a mandatory life term without hope of parole.[56]

Enhanced punishment statues are designed to get tough with chronic and persistent offenders and keep them off the streets for an extended period of time. Civil libertarians fear that these statutes can be used in an indiscriminate fashion to punish petty offenders or pressure defendants to plea bargain or testify against others.[57]

The Supreme Court has limited the use of habitual criminal statutes. In *Rummel v. Estelle*, the Court mandated that defendants could be sentenced to life in prison for repeated petty crime (Rummel was convicted of obtaining $120 through false pretenses and had two prior convictions for petty crimes) as long as they retain some avenue of release, through parole, commutation, or other means.[58] In contrast in *Solem v. Helm*, the Court ruled that a life sentence without the chance of parole was inappropriate for a relatively minor crime (Helm had passed a bad check for one hundred dollars), even if the defendant had numerous prior convictions.[59] In *Helm*, the Court ruled that a sentence of imprisonment can be cruel and unusual if it is disproportionate to the crime committed.

The concern for offender rights may be waning. In *Harmelin v. Michigan*, a more conservative Court held that states could institute mandatory life sentences for convicted drug dealers.[60] Harmelin was arrested for being in the possession of 650 grams of cocaine and was sentenced to a mandatory term of life in prison without the possibility of parole. The Supreme Court (in a contested 5 to 4 vote) disagreed with his contention that the punishment was disproportionate to the severity of his crime and denied him a chance for individualized justice. The *Harmelin* decision guarantees that mandatory life sentences for chronic offenders, even those who have not committed overtly serious or life-threatening crimes, will be upheld by the courts.

Sentencing Practices

What kind of sentence can a criminal defendant expect if found guilty as charged? To answer this question, the federal government's Bureau of Justice Statistics has conducted a number of national surveys that track sentencing practices around

TABLE 14.2
Felony Sentences Imposed by State Courts, 1988

Most serious conviction offense	Total	Percent of felons sentenced to: Incarceration			Nonincarceration		
		Total	Prison	Jail	Total	Probation	Other
Total	100%	69%	44%	25%	31%	30%	1%
Murder[a]	100	95	91	4	5	5	(b)
Rape	100	87	69	18	13	13	(b)
Robbery	100	89	75	14	11	11	(b)
Aggravated assault	100	72	45	27	28	27	1
Burglary	100	75	54	21	25	25	(b)
Larceny[c]	100	65	39	26	35	34	1
Drug trafficking	100	71	41	30	29	28	1
Other felonies	100	62	35	27	38	37	1

Note: For persons receiving a combination of sentences, the sentence designation came from the most serious penalty imposed—prison being the most serious, followed by jail, then probation. "Prison" includes sentences to death. Sentence designation "other" includes unknown sentences (0.7 percent of cases).
[a]Includes nonnegligent manslaughter.
[b]Less than 0.5 percent.
[c]Includes motor vehicle theft.

SOURCE: Patrick Langan and John Dawson, *Felony Sentences in State Courts, 1988.* (Washington, D.C.: Bureau of Justice Statistics, 1990), p. 2, table 2.

the United States.[61] The major findings from one of these, National Judicial Reporting Program (NJRP) studies are presented in Tables 14.2 and 14.3.

This national survey makes an important contribution to the understanding of sentencing dynamics. First, as Table 14.2 indicates, people who commit the most serious crimes have the greatest likelihood of receiving an incarceration sentence. However, a surprising number of convicted felons receive a sentence of probation or community supervision only: 5 percent of convicted murderers, 12 percent of rapists, 26 percent of burglars, and 36 percent of those convicted on drug trafficking charges did not receive incarceration. These findings are not dissimilar from other federally sponsored sentencing surveys.[62]

The NJRP also tells us something about the average (mean) and middle range (median) sentence received for typical felony offenses (the mean is usually greater because it can be influenced by a few extreme cases). As the data in Table 14.3 indicate, the national average for a sentence to a state prison was nearly seven years; and the median term was four years. As might be expected, offenders committing the most serious crimes—rape, murder, and robbery—received the longest maximum sentences. About 24 percent of all those convicted on murder charges received a life sentence, and 2 percent got the death penalty.

These data show the surprising amount of flexibility and disparity built into the adjudicatory system. Not all criminals convicted of the most serious crimes actually go to prison or jail, and those who do can receive significantly different sentences. Why this disparity occurs is a very critical issue and the springboard for the call for reforming the sentencing process.

Extralegal Factors in Sentencing

One suspected cause of sentencing disparity is the consideration of race, gender, and economic factors when sentencing decisions are made. Considerations of such

TABLE 14.3
Average Length of Felony Sentences Imposed by State Courts, 1988

Most serious conviction offense	Average maximum sentence length (in months) for felons sentenced to:			
	Incarceration			
	Total	Prison	Jail	Probation
Average sentence	51	76	7	43
Murder[A]	226	239	16	62
Rape	146	183	10	64
Robbery	100	114	16	54
Aggravated assault	59	90	7	42
Burglary	56	74	9	49
Larceny[B]	33	50	7	40
Drug trafficking	41	66	7	43
Other felonies	34	55	6	42
Median sentence	24	48	5	36
Murder[A]	240	252	12	60
Rape	84	120	8	60
Robbery	60	84	12	60
Aggravated assault	24	54	6	36
Burglary	36	48	6	36
Larceny[B]	24	36	5	36
Drug trafficking	24	48	6	36
Other felonies	16	36	3	36

Note: The median sentence is the sentence length that marks the point below which and above which 50 percent of all sentence lengths fall. Averages exclude sentences to death or to life in prison. Sentence length data were available for 94 percent of incarceration sentences and 95 percent of probation sentences.

[A]Includes nonnegligent manslaughter.
[B]Includes motor vehicle theft.

SOURCE: Partick Langan and John Dawson, *Felony Sentences in State Courts, 1988.* (Washington, D.C.: Bureau of Justice Statistics, 1990), p. 3, table 3.

variables would be a direct violation of constitutional due process and equal protection, as well as of federal statutes, such as the Civil Rights Act. Do these extralegal factors actually play a role in criminal sentencing? Research so far has not provided any definitive answers.

Class. Evidence exists to support an association between social class and sentencing outcomes. Where economic status has been found to be related to sentence length, the relationship has been influenced by the inability of poor defendants to obtain quality legal representation and to make bail and their reluctance to plea-bargain.[63]

Gender. Women are less likely to receive incarceration sentences than men. Most research indicates that women receive more favorable outcomes the farther they go up the criminal justice system: they are more likely to receive preferential treatment from a judge at sentencing than they are from the police officer making the arrest or the prosecutor seeking the indictment.[64] Gender bias may be present because judges perceive women as better risks than male defendants. Recent research by Ellen Hochstedler Steury and Nancy Frank found that females were more likely than males to be granted lenient pretrial release and lower bail amounts; women were also more likely to spend less time in pretrial detention.[65] Bail release has generally been related to more attractive sentencing outcomes.

Age. Another extralegal factor that may play a role in sentencing is age. Recent research by Dean Champion found that judges are generally more lenient toward elderly defendants and more punitive toward younger ones.[66] While sentencing leniency may be a result of judges' perception that the elderly pose little risk to society, Champion views such practices as a violation of the civil rights of younger defendants.[67]

Race. Racial disparity in sentencing has been suspected because a disproportionate number of black inmates are in state prisons and on death row.[68] Recent analysis of sentencing practices in New York found that while African-Americans and Hispanics make up about 25 percent of the state's population, they account for 80 percent of its prison population and 67 percent of its jail population. While there were intercounty differences, the general pattern was for white defendants to receive fines, while minorities got jail and prison time.[69]

While such findings are disturbing, research on sentencing has failed to show a definitive pattern of racial discrimination. While some works do indicate that a defendant's race has a direct impact on sentencing outcomes, other efforts show that the influence of race on sentencing is less clear-cut than anticipated.[70]

Two studies are widely cited as indications that race has a direct or indirect influence on sentencing outcomes. Alfred Blumstein approached this issue by focusing on the racial disparity in the nation's prison system.[71] While almost half of all prison inmates are black, blacks account for only 12 percent of the total U.S. population. Blumstein concludes that most of this discrepancy can be explained by arrest rate differentials: blacks account for a percentage of the arrest rate that is similar to the percentage of black inmates in the prison population. However, the percentages are not identical: at least some (5 or 6 percent) of the racial difference in the prison population could not be explained by legal factors; racial disparity in the sentencing process then might help explain *at least part* of the overrepresentation of blacks in the prison system. Joan Petersilia's analysis of racial disparity also found that black defendants receive somewhat longer sentences than whites and actually serve more time in prison. Petersilia attributed these differences to legal factors correlated with race, such as the fact that white defendants more frequently plea bargain and people who plead guilty as charged are more likely to receive shorter sentences.[72]

One reason that the relationship between race and sentencing is so complex and difficult to establish is that the association may not be linear: while black defendants may be punished more severely in some areas for some crimes, they are treated more leniently in other jurisdictions for others.[73] As sociologist Darnell Hawkins explains:

> Certain crime types are considered less "appropriate" for blacks than for whites. Blacks who are charged with committing these offenses will be treated more severely than blacks who commit crimes that are considered more "appropriate." Included in the former category are various white collar offenses and crimes against political and social structures of authority. The latter groups of offenses would include various forms of victimless crimes associated with lower social status (e.g., prostitution, minor drug use, or drunkenness). This may also include various crimes against the person, especially those involving black victims.[74]

Racial bias may be obscured because it does not impact equally on all crimes and in all jurisdictions. Cassia Spohn and Jerry Cederblom found that race affects sentence length in less serious cases while having a less significant impact on cases considered more severe. They reason that when the crime is serious and the evidence is strong, judges rely more on relevant legal facts to make sentencing decisions. When cases are weak and crimes insignificant, judges are free to use more discretion and allow extralegal factors, such as the offender's race, to cloud their judgment.[75]

Another factor obscuring the impact of race on sentencing is that racial bias may be distributed unequally between and within legal jurisdictions: some judges operate in a racially biased manner, while others do not; some judges favor black defendants, while others give preferential treatment to white defendants.[76] This pattern would mask the true extent of racial bias in sentencing.

Racial bias has also been linked to the victim-offender relationship. For example, black defendants are sanctioned more severely if their victim is white than if their target is a fellow minority-group member.[77] Judges may base sentencing decisions on the race of the victim and not the race of the defendant.

While racial discrepancies exist, new sentencing laws may be helping to reduce disparity in some jurisdictions. For example, research shows that California's revised criminal sentencing code (which created presumptive sentences) has helped reduce racial disparity in sentencing.[78] Similarly, a national survey of sentencing practices conducted by the Bureau of Justice Statistics found that while white defendants are somewhat more likely to receive probation and other nonincarceration sentences than black defendants (34 percent versus 31 percent), there was little racial disparity in the *length* of prison sentences.[79]

In sum, while there is some evidence that judges let extralegal factors influence their sentencing decisions, it would be unfair to say that the court system practices systematic discrimination. Yet, race, class, gender, and age may be *associated* with factors that influence sentencing outcomes (such as making bail, plea bargaining, having dependent children, appearing "nondangerous"), thus creating the *appearance* of bias in the sentencing process. Outcomes that favor one group over another, regardless of their cause or implementation, cannot be tolerated in a democratic society.

Sentencing Reform

During the past two decades, almost every state and the federal government have been examining their penal codes in an effort to simplify the classification of offenses and create a more rational approach to sentencing. In some instances, sentencing reform has been motivated by a growing fear of violent crime and can be considered a response to the public's demand for law and order. Some critics view sentencing reform efforts with suspicion, charging that they were veiled efforts to control rebellious lower-class populations of young people and minority-group members.[80]

Both the states and the federal government have set up sentencing review commissions to revise and restructure their codes. Efforts to create mandatory, persumptive, and structured sentences have already been mentioned. In addition, national law reform groups have attempted to create model sentencing standards that can be accepted in full or in part by state jurisdictions. These model codes include the American Law Institute's *Model Penal Code;*[81] The Model Sentencing Act of the National Council on Crime;[82] and the American Bar Association's *Standards Relating to Sentencing Alternatives and Procedures*. These standards include recommendations regarding sentence authority, statutory structure, judicial discretion, an information base for sentencing, and the development of sentencing criteria. They have been used as guidelines to assist jurisdictions in amending their sentencing codes to conform more closely with the needs of a modern criminal justice system.

How have these reform efforts influenced the justice system? The answer can be observed in the manner of release of inmates from the nation's prisons. In 1977, about 72 percent of all inmates were released on parole granted at the discretion of correctional authorities and about 6 percent were subject to mandatory release after serving their sentence. Today, the percentage of parolees has declined to 40 percent, and the percentage of mandatory releasees has risen to about 30 percent.[83] This trend indicates that a dramatic change has occurred in the nation's sentencing policy. Control over the length of sentences has shifted in some large jurisdictions from the judicial and administrative to the legislative branches of government. More than half the states now employ at least some sentencing schemes, such as guideline-based or other forms of determinate sentencing or mandatory sentences, that are legislatively determined and insulated from judicial or administrative discretion.

Of course, such changes do not always work the way policy makers envisioned. Judges rebel against sentencing policies that handcuff their discretion and often ignore guideline suggestions or work around them. And change in the way sentences are handed down can move discretion farther up and farther down the system. For example, when California restricted plea bargaining for sentence reductions in felony cases, prosecutors began bringing the cases to the lower courts, where bargaining was permitted.[84]

Where reform has occurred, it has moved criminal sentencing toward a model that stresses an equitable but firm distribution of sentences. A greater proportion of people are going to prison than ever before, but the sentences they receive are less subject to large swings than in previous years. By taking the discretion out of sentencing, state and federal legislative bodies hope to reduce discretion and eliminate disparity.

Capital Punishment

The most severe sentence used in our nation is capital punishment, or execution. More than 14,500 confirmed executions have been carried out in America under civil authority, starting with the execution of Captain George Kendall in 1608.[85] Most of these executions were for murder and rape. However, federal, state, and military laws have conferred the death penalty for other crimes, including robbery, kidnapping, treason, (offenses against the federal government), espionage, and desertion from military service.

In recent years, the Supreme Court has limited the death penalty to first-degree murder, and only then when aggravating circumstances, such as murder for profit or murder using extreme cruelty, are present.[86] The federal government still has provisions for granting the death penalty for espionage by a member of the armed forces, treason, and killing during a criminal conspiracy, such as drug trafficking.[87] Some states continue to sentence criminals to death for crimes such as aircraft piracy, ransom kidnapping, and the aggravated rape of a child, but it remains to be seen whether the courts will allow criminals to be executed today for any crime less than aggravated first-degree murder.

Currently, about twenty-five hundred people are on death row. Of these, the majority are white (58 percent) males (98 percent) with an average age of thirty-four, who have completed the eleventh grade and are not married (70 percent).[88] One of the most controversial issues surrounding the death penalty is whether

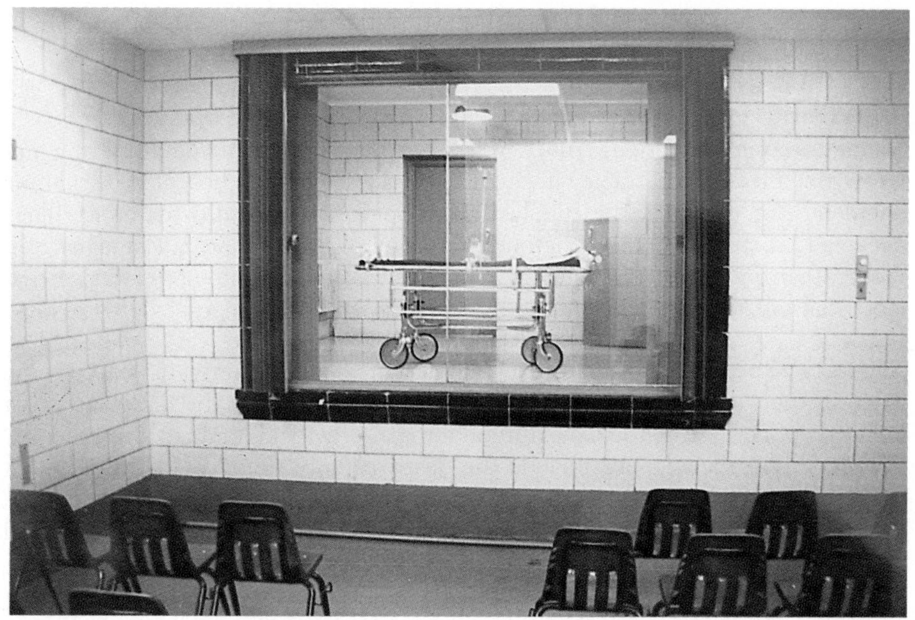

A gurney and observation room, part of the process used to execute inmates by lethal injection of fatal drugs.

black defendants are more likely to be sentenced to death than white defendants; today, about 41 percent of the inmates on death row are black, and about 2 percent are members of other minority groups.

No issue in the criminal justice system is more controversial or emotional than the implementation of the death penalty. Opponents and proponents have formulated a number of powerful arguments in support of their positions, and these will be reviewed in the following sections.

Arguments for the Death Penalty

The most common arguments for retaining the death penalty in the United States are examined below.

Incapacitation. Supporters argue that death is the "ultimate incapacitation" and the only one that can ensure that convicted killers can never be pardoned or paroled or escape. Most states that do not have capital punishment provide the sentence of "life in prison without the chance of parole." However, forty-eight states grant their chief executive the right to grant clemency and commute a life sentence, and may give "lifers" eligibility for various furlough and release programs.[89] As you may recall, the work furlough program in Massachusetts from which "lifer" Willie Horton escaped became one of the central issues in the 1988 presidential contest between Massachusetts Governor Michael Dukakis and Vice-President George Bush (despite the fact that the federal government also maintains an extensive furlough program).

Death penalty advocates believe that the potential for recidivism is a serious enough threat to require that murderers be denied further access to the public. Stephen Markman and Paul Cassell analyzed the records of 52,000 state prison inmates serving time for murder and found that 810 had previously been convicted of homicide and that these recidivists had killed 821 people following their first convictions.[90] About 9 percent of all inmates on death row today have had prior convictions for homicide.[91] If all these people had been executed after their first conviction, many innocent lives would have been saved.

Deterrent. Proponents of capital punishment argue that executions serve as a strong deterrent for serious crimes. While capital punishment could probably not deter the mentally unstable, it could have an effect on the cold, calculating murderer, for example, the hired killer or someone who kills for profit. They believe that studies, such as the one by Stephen Layson, that indicate that executions can produce a substantial decline in the murder rate are evidence that potential killers are swayed by the threat of capital punishment.[92]

Morally Correct. Advocates of capital punishment justify its use on the grounds that it is morally correct because it is mentioned in the Bible and other religious works. While the Constitution forbids "cruel and unusual punishments," this prohibition could not include the death penalty since capital punishment was widely used at the time the Constitution was drafted. The "original intent" of the Founding Fathers was to alow the states to use the death penalty; capital punishment may be cruel, but it is not unusual.

The death penalty has been accepted by criminal justice experts who consider themselves "humanists," concerned with the value and dignity of human beings. As David Friedrichs argues, there are a number of reasons capital punishment is not inconsistent with a progressive humanistic perspective.[93] Friedrichs maintains that a civilized society has no choice but to hold responsible those who commit horrendous crimes. The implementation of the death penalty provides the greatest justice for the victim and helps alleviate the psychic pain of the victim's family and friends. The death penalty makes a moral statement: there is behavior that is so unacceptable to a community of human beings that one who engages in such behavior forfeits his or her right to live.

Proportional. Putting dangerous criminals to death also conforms to the requirement that the punishment must be proportional to the seriousness of the crime. Since we currently use a system of escalating punishments, it follows that the most serious punishment should be employed to sanction the most serious crime. And before the brutality of the death penalty is considered, the cruelty with which the victim was treated should not be forgotten.

Reflects Public Opinion. Those who favor capital punishment charge that a majority of the public believes that criminals who kill innocent victims should forfeit their own life. Recent public opinion polls show that up to 80 percent of the public favors the death penalty, almost double the percentage of twenty years ago.[94] Public approval is based on the rational belief that the death penalty is an important instrument of social control, that it can deter crime, and that it is less costly than maintaining a murderer in prison for his or her entire life.[95]

Public opinion in favor of the death penalty was an important factor in the Supreme Court's decision to uphold the use of the death penalty in *Gregg v. Georgia:*

> Indeed, the decision that capital punishment may be the appropriate sanction in extreme cases is an expression of the community's belief that certain crimes are themselves so grievous an affront to humanity that the only adequate response may be the penalty of death.[96]

Unlikely Chance of Error. The many legal controls and appeals currently in use make it almost impossible for an innocent person to be executed or for the death penalty to be used in a racist or capricious manner. While some unfortunate mistakes may have been made in the past, death penalty proponents argue, the current system makes it virtually impossible to execute an innocent person. Federal courts closely scruitinize all death penalty cases and rule for the defendant in an estimated 60 to 70 percent of the appeals. Such judicial care should ensure that only those who are both truly guilty and deserving of death are executed.[97]

In sum, those who favor the death penalty find it to be traditional punishment for serious crimes, one that can help prevent criminality, is in keeping with the traditional moral values of fairness and equity, and is highly favored by the public.

Arguments against the Death Penalty

Arguments for the death penalty are matched by those that support it abolition:

Possibility of Error. Critics of the death penalty believe the death penalty has no place in a mature democratic society.[98] They have pointed to the finality of the act and the real possibility that innocent persons can be executed. Examples of people wrongfully convicted of murder abound. In March 1992, Clarence Chance and Benny Powell were released after spending seventeen and a half years in California prisons for a murder of a county sheriff that they did not commit.[99] Randall Adams spent many years on death row in Texas before being released in 1989 after the movie *The Thin Blue Line* drew attention to his case. Boxer Rubin "Hurricane" Carter spent twenty years in New Jersey prisons after being convicted of murdering three people in a tavern holdup. Singer Bob Dylan helped fight for Carter's release and wrote the song "The Hurricane" about his case; Carter was released in 1992 after new evidence revealed that the one person who could place him at the scene may have lied to avoid a burglary charge.

According to Michael Radelet and Hugo Bedeau, there have been about 350 wrongful murder convictions this century, of which 23 led to executions. They estimated about three death sentences are returned every two years in cases where the defendant has been falsely accused. More than half the errors stem from perjured testimony, false identifications, coerced confessions, and suppression of evidence. In addition to the 23 who were executed, 128 of the falsely convicted served more than six years in prison; 39 served more than sixteen years in confinement, and 8 died while serving their sentence.[100] It is their view that even though the system attempts to be especially cautious in capital cases, unacceptable mistakes can occur.[101]

Is the execution of even one innocent person too great a burden for our modern ("kinder and gentler") society to bear? This question must be answered carefully. As the number of people on death row increases, there will be renewed pressure on the justice system to process and review death penalty decisions. Inmates often file multiple appeals in order to delay their executions as long as possible. The Supreme Court has attempted to reduce the right of death row inmates to appeal their case by mandating in *McKlesky v. Zant* that multiple (habeas corpus) appeals by inmates are permissible only if the inmates can show why they did not raise the legal issues in their first appeal. This decision reduces the appeal process, which could result in the type of error that Bedeau and Radelet have warned about.[102]

Unfair Use of Discretion. Critics also frown upon the tremendous discretion used in seeking the death penalty and the arbitrary manner in which it is imposed.[103] Of the approximately 10,000 persons convicted each year on homicide charges, only 250 to 300 are sentenced to death, while 500 receive a sentence of probation or community supervision only![104] While it is true that many convicted murderers do not commit first-degree murder and therefore are ineligible for execution, it is also likely that many serious criminals who could have received the death penalty are not sentenced to death because of prosecutorial discretion. Some cooperate in prosecution or give testimony against others. It is fair to spare the life of a dangerous killer who cooperates with the prosecutor while executing another who does not?

The Most Serious Criminals Often Escape Punishment. A person who commits a particularly heinous crime and knows full well that he or she will receive the death penalty if convicted may be moved to plea-bargain to avoid capital punishment. In contrast, persons who protest their innocence and demand a trial will be the ones most likely to receive the death penalty. When serial killer Ted Bundy was executed in January 1989, he was actually one of the few notorious murderers to be put to death in modern times. Criminals who commit the most gruesome crimes often escape the death penalty because they may be the ones most motivated to plea-bargain.

Some vicious criminals who grievously injure victims during murder attempts are spared death because of a physician's skill. Some notable cases come to mind. Lawrence Singleton used an axe to cut off the arms of a woman he raped, yet he served only eight years in prison because the victim's life was saved by prompt medical care; "David," a boy severely burned in a murder attempt, lives in fear because his assailant, his father, Charles Rothenberg, was paroled from prison after serving a short sentence; the boys who attacked, beat, and raped the "Central Park Jogger" received relatively short prison sentences because their victim lived, despite losing most of her blood.[105] Though these horrific crimes received national attention and the intent to kill the victim was present, the death penalty could not be applied because of the availability of effective medical treatment. Research shows that areas that have superior medical resources actually have lower murder rates than less well-equipped areas; for example, ambulance response time can reduce the death rate by expeditiously transporting victims to an appropriate treatment center.[106] It makes little sense to punish someone for an impulsive murder, while sparing the life of those who intentionally maim and torture their victims, who happen by chance to live because of prompt medical care.

Misplaced Vengeance. While critics of the death penalty acknowledge that the use of the death penalty is approved by the general public, they maintain that prevailing attitudes reflect a primitive desire for revenge and not "just desert." Public acceptance of capital punishment has been compared to approval for human sacrifices practiced by the Aztecs in Mexico five hundred years ago.[107] The Supreme Court's justification of the death penalty on the basis that it reflects public opinion should be reassessed.[108]

No Deterrence. Those opposed to the death penalty also find little merit in the argument that capital punishment deters crime. They charge that insufficient evidence exists that the threat of a death sentence can convince potential murderers to forgo their criminal activity. Most murders involve people who knew each other, very often friends and family members. Since murderers are often under the influence of alcohol or drugs or are suffering severe psychological turmoil, no penalty will likely be a deterrent. Little current research concludes that the death penalty is an effective deterrent.[109]

William Bowers and Glenn Pierce have argued that far from being a deterrent, capital punishment actually produces more violence than it prevents; they label this the **brutalization effect.**[110] Executions actually increase murder rates because they raise the general violence level in society and because violence-prone people actually identify with the executioner, not with the target of the death penalty. Consequently, when someone gets in a conflict with them or challenges their authority, they execute them in the same manner the state executes people who violates its rules. The brutalization effect has been substantiated by other researchers, including William Bailey in his study of the effect of executions in Chicago.[111]

Hope of Rehabilitation. The death sentence also rules out any hope of offender rehabilitation. There is evidence that convicted killers actually make good parole risks. James Marquart and Jonathan Sorensen followed the careers of murderers originally sentenced to death but given a legal reprieve. Marquart and Sorensen found that while in prison, convicted murderers are actually model inmates and, once released, commit fewer crimes than other parolees. Their conclusion: executing convicted murderers would have little benefit for society.[112] Similarly, Gennaro Vito and his associates found that death-row inmates who had their sentences commuted because of changes in state capital punishment laws made surprisingly successful adjustments to society while on parole.[113]

Racial Bias. One of the most compelling arguments against the use of the death penalty is that it is employed in a racially discriminatory fashion. Since the death penalty was first instituted in the United States, a disproportionate number of minorities have been executed. Charges of racial bias are supported by the disproportionate numbers of blacks who have received the death sentence, are currently on death row, and who have been executed (53.5 percent of all executions). Racism was particularly blatant when the death penalty was employed in rape cases: 90 percent of those receiving death for rape in the South and 63 percent of those in the North and West were black.[114] Today, about 41 percent of the inmates on death row are black, a number disproportionate to the minority representation in the population.

At the same time, white criminals arrested for homicide actually have a slightly greater chance of getting the death penalty than blacks arrested for murder, and a majority of murderers executed since 1980 have also been white.[115] Does this mean that discrimination in the use of the death penalty has abated? Simply calculating the relative proportion of each racial group sentenced to death may not tell the whole story. A number of researchers have found that the death penalty is associated with the race of the *victim*; rather than the race of the *offender*.[116] In most instances, prosecutors are more likely to ask for the death penalty if the victim is white. The fact that most murders involving a white victim also involve a white attacker (86 percent) accounts for the higher death sentence rate for white murderers.[117] With few exceptions, the relatively infrequent interracial murder cases involving a black criminal and a white victim (14 percent) are the most likely to result in the death penalty.[118]

It is possible that prosecutors are more likely to ask for the death penalty when a black offender kills a white victim because they believe it will be easier to obtain a conviction or because they are under public pressure to take a "hard line" in such cases. Though prosecutors may not hold racist attitudes themselves, the fact remains that racial discrimination is still present in the capital sentencing process.[119]

Brutality. Abolitionists believe that executions are unnecessarily cruel and inhuman and come at a high moral and social cost on society.[120] Our society does not punish criminals by subjecting them to the same acts they themselves committed. Rapists are not sexually assaulted, and arsonists do not have their house burned down; why then should murderers be killed?

Robert Johnson has described the execution process as a form of torture in which the condemned are first tormented psychologically by being made to feel powerless and alone while on death row; suicide is a constant problem among those on death row.[121] The execution itself is a barbaric affair marked by the smell of burning flesh and stiffened bodies. The executioners themselves suffer from delayed stress reactions, including anxiety and a dehumanized personal identity.

Expense. Some people complain that they do not want to support "some killer in prison for thirty years." Abolitionists counter that legal appeals drive the cost of executions far higher than years in prison. If the money spent on the judicial process were invested, the interest would more than pay for the lifetime upkeep of death-row inmates. At least thirty states now have a sentence of life in prison without parole, and this can more than make up for an execution. Being locked up in a hellish prison without any chance of release (barring a rare executive reprieve) may be a worse punishment than a painless death by lethal injection. If vengeance is the goal, life without parole may eliminate the need for capital punishment.[122]

The Law of Capital Punishment

In recent years, the constitutionality of the death penalty has been a major concern to both the nation's courts and its concerned social scientists. In 1972, the Supreme Court in *Furman v. Georgia*[123] decided that the discretionary imposition of the death penalty was **cruel and unusual punishment** under the Eighth and Fourteenth Amendments of the Constitution. This case not only questioned whether capital punishment is a more effective deterrent than life imprisonment but also challenged the very existence of the death penalty on the grounds of its brutality and finality. The Court, however, did not rule out the use of capital punishment as a penalty; rather, it objected to the arbitrary and capricious manner in which it was imposed. After *Furman*, many states changed statutes that had allowed jury discretion in imposing the death penalty. In some states, this was accomplished by enacting statutory guidelines for jury decisions; in others, the death penalty was made mandatory for certain crimes only. Despite these changes in statutory law, no further executions were carried out while the Supreme Court pondered additional cases concerning the death penalty.

Then, in July 1976, the Supreme Court ruled on the constitutionality of five state death penalty statues. In the first case, *Gregg v. Georgia*,[124] the Court found valid the Georgia statute that held that a finding by the jury of at least one "aggravating circumstance" out of ten is required in pronouncing the death penalty in murder cases. In the *Gregg* case, for example, the jury imposed the death penalty after finding beyond a reasonable doubt two aggravating circumstances: (1) the offender was engaged in the commission of two other capital felonies, and (2) the offender committed the offense of murder for the purpose of receiving money and other financial gains (e.g., an automobile). In delivering the opinion of the court, Justice Potter Stewart stated:

> The basic concern of *Furman* centered on those defendants who were being condemned to death capriciously and arbitrarily. Under the procedures before

> the Court in that case, sentencing authorities were not directed to give attention to the nature or circumstance of the crime committed or to the character or record of the defendant. Left unguided, juries imposed the death sentence in a way that could only be called freakish. The new Georgia sentencing procedures, by contrast, focus the jury's attention on the particularized nature of the crime and the particularized characteristics of the individual defendant. While the jury is permitted to consider any aggravating or mitigating circumstances, it must find and identify at least one statutory aggravating factor before it may impose a penalty of death. In this way the jury's discretion is channeled. No longer can a jury wantonly and freakishly impose the death sentence; it is always circumscribed by the legislative guidelines. In addition, the review function of the Supreme Court of Georgia affords additional assurance that the concerns that prompted our decision in *Furman* are not present to any significant degree in the Georgia procedure applied here.
>
> For the reasons expressed in this opinion, we hold that the statutory system under which Gregg was sentenced to death does not violate the Constitution. Accordingly, the judgment of the Georgia Supreme Court is affirmed.[125]

The Court also upheld the constitutionality of a Texas statute on capital punishment in *Jurek v. Texas*[126] and of a Florida statute in *Proffitt v. Florida.*[127] The statutes of these states are similar to those of Georgia in that they limit sentencing discretion not only by specifying the crimes for which capital punishment can be handed down but also by stipulating criteria concerning the circumstances surrounding the crimes. For example, the Texas statute required that the death sentence could be imposed only if the jury in a proceeding following the verdict responded in the affirmative to two and sometimes three of the following questions:

1. Was the conduct of the defendant that caused the death of the deceased committed deliberately and with the reasonable expectation that the death of the deceased or another would result?
2. Was there a probability that the defendant would commit criminal acts of violence that would constitute a continuing threat to a society?
3. If raised by the evidence, was the conduct of the defendant in killing the deceased unreasonable in response to the provocation, if any, by the deceased?[128]

The Supreme Court, however, overruled the death penalty statutes of Louisiana in *Roberts v. Louisiana*[129] and North Carolina in *Woodson v. North Carolina.*[130] These two statutes provided for a mandatory death penalty in all first-degree murder cases. The rationale for the decision that the statutes were unconstitutional was expressed in *Woodson:*

> The history of mandatory death penalty statutes in the United States thus reveals that the practice of sentencing to death all persons convicted of a particular offense has been rejected as unduly harsh and unworkably rigid. . . . While the prevailing practice of individualizing sentencing determinations generally reflects simply enlightened policy rather than a constitutional imperative, we believe that in capital cases, the fundamental respect of humanity underlying the Eighth Amendment requires consideration of the character and record of the individual offender and the circumstances of the particular offense as a constitutionally indispensable part of the process of inflicting the penalty of death.[131]

The Supreme Court continued to deal with the death penalty and the "cruel and unusual punishment" question when it handed down decisions in the major cases of *Coker v. Georgia, Gardner v. Florida,* and *Lockett v. Ohio.* In *Coker,* the Court ruled unconstitutional a death penalty sentence in Georgia for the crime of rape but left unanswered the issue of imposing a death penalty to prevent and deter other types of crime.[132] The Court overruled the death sentence penalty in *Gardner* because information contained in the presentence report was not disclosed to the defense attorney.[133] And in *Lockett v. Ohio*, the Court declared that the imposition of a capital punishment sentence must be based on reason, not emotion. Limiting a judge's sentencing discretion to the narrow circumstances of the crime and the record of the offender makes it impossible to consider an indivdualized decision, which is essential in capital cases.[134] In other cases, the Supreme Court has upheld the right of a trial judge to disregard a jury's recommendation for leniency in a capital case and has ruled that it is not necessary for an appellate court to determine whether the sentence in a particular case was proportional to those given to others in that state, though most states hold proportionality hearings anyway.[135]

In probably the most important death penalty case of the past few years, *McLesky v. Kemp*, the Court upheld the conviction of a black defendant in Georgia despite social science evidence that black criminals who kill white victims have a significantly greater chance of receiving the death penalty than white offenders who kill black victims. The Court ruled that the evidence of racial patterns in capital sentencing was not persuasive absent a finding of racial bias in the immediate case.[136] Many observers believe that *McLesky* presented the last significant legal obstacle that death penalty advocates had to overcome and that, as a result, capital punishment will be a sentence in the United States for years to come (McLesky was executed in 1991).

Limiting Capital Punishment

While the Court has generally supported the death penalty, it has also placed some limitations on its use. Rulings have promoted procedural fairness in the capital sentencing process. For example, the Court has prohibited prosecutors from presenting damaging evidence about the defendant's background unless it is directly relevant to the case. In *Dawson v. Delaware* (1992), a prosecutor's mention of Dawson's membership in the Aryan Brotherhood prison gang was ruled irrelevant to his committing a murder after escaping from prison; membership in a gang is protected by the First Amendment's guarantee of the freedom of association.[137] It also overturned a judge's death penalty sentence in a case in which the prosecutor had discussed prison terms only. In *Lankford v. Idaho* (1991), the Court ruled that had the defense been given warning that capital punishment was being considered, it would have been able to prepare mitigating evidence, which it did not.[138]

The Court has also reinforced the idea that mental and physical conditions such as age, while not excusing criminal behavior, can be considered as mitigating factors in capital sentencing decisions.[139] In *Wilkins v. Missouri* and *Stanford v. Kentucky* the Court set a limit of sixteen years old on the age of defendants who could be sentenced to death.[140] (Seven inmates are currently on death row who committed their crime at age seventeen or younger.) These rulings effectively barred the use of capital punishment from underage minors who have been waived or transferred from the juvenile to the adult court system (see Chapter 19).

The Court also moved to make sure that the aggravating circumstances needed to qualify an offender for the death penalty be clearly stated and carefully considered. In *Clemons v. Mississippi*, the Court mandated that aggravating circumstances be defined precisely and that terms such as "especially heinous, atrocious and cruel" are so vague that they fail to adequately guide the sentencing judge's discretion.[141] And in *Stringer v. Black* (1992), the Court ruled that when sentencing judges are asked to weigh aggravating circumstances versus mitigating ones, the presence of illegal or vague factors (such as the murder being described as "heinous" or "especially cruel") makes the capital sentencing process unconstitutional.[142] And the Court ruled that appellate courts must carefully consider the presence of mitigating evidence when they review capital sentencing decisions.[143]

With these controls, the Court seems committed to maintaining the death penalty. It has reduced a defendant's ability to reappeal in a capital case by raising claims that were not included in the original legal motion.[144] It now allows victim impact statements to be made and gives prosecutors the right to include such statements in their closing argument describing how the victims will be missed by their family and friends.[145] These rulings, plus the failure to grant stays in numerous capital cases, underscore the Court's willingness to retain the death sentence.

Death-Qualified Juries

"Death-qualified" juries are ones in which any person opposed in concept to capital punishment has been removed during *voir dire*. Defense attorneys are opposed to death qualification because it bars citizens who oppose the death penalty and who may also be more liberal and less likely to convict defendants from serving on juries. Death qualification creates juries that are nonrepresentative of the 20 percent of the public that opposes capital punishment.

In *Witherspoon v. Illinois* (1968), the Supreme Court upheld the practice of excusing jurors who are opposed to the death penalty.[146] The Court has made it easier to convict people in death penalty cases by ruling that any juror can be excused if his or her views on capital punishment are deemed by a trial judge to "prevent or substantially impair the performance of their duties."[147] The Court has also ruled that jurors can be removed because of their opposition to the death penalty at the guilt phase of a trial, even though they would not have to consider the issue of capital punishment until a separate sentencing hearing. In *Lockhart v. McCree* (1986), the Court also ruled that removing anti-capital punishment jurors does not violate the Sixth Amendment's provision that juries represent a fair cross-section of the community, nor does it unfairly tip the scale toward juries who are prone to convict people in capital cases.[148] So, it appears that for the present, prosecutors will be able to excuse jurors who feel that the death penalty is wrong or immoral.

Does the Death Penalty Deter Murder?

Despite its inherent cruelty, capital punishment might be justified if it proved to be an effective crime deterrent which could save many innocent lives. Considerable empirical research has been carried out on the effectiveness of capital punishment as a deterrent. In particular, studies have tried to discover whether the death sentence serves as a more effective deterrent than life imprisonment for capital crimes such as homicide. Three methods have been used: immediate impact studies, which calculate the effect a well-publicized execution has on the short-term murder rate; time-series analysis, which compares long-term trends in murder and capital punishment rates; and contiguous-state analysis, which compares murder rates in states that have the death penalty with a similar state that has abolished capital punishment.

Impact Studies. One of the first noteworthy impact studies was conducted in Philadelphia in 1935 by Robert Dann.[149] He chose five highly publicized executions of convicted murderers in different years and determined the number of homicides in the sixty-day period before and after each execution. Each 120-day period had approximately the same number of homicides, as well as the same number of days on which homicides occurred. Dann's rationale was that if capital punishment does deter crime, this deterrent effect should cause a drop in the number of homicides in the days immediately following an execution. However, his study revealed that more homicides occurred during the sixty days following an execution than prior to it, suggesting that executions might actually serve to increase the incidence of homicide. Dann concluded that no deterrent effect was demonstrated.

One contemporary evaluation of executions in the United States (from 1950 to 1980) by Steven Stack concluded that capital punishment does indeed have an immediate impact and that sixteen well-publicized executions may have saved 480 lives.[150] While persuasive, Stack's methodology has been challenged.[151] Most recent studies have found that publicity about executions has little influence on murder rates.[152] In an important recent impact study, Ruth Peterson and William Bailey limited their focus to only those homicides that legally qualify for capital sentencing and again found that the influence of execution publicity on murder rates is insignificant.[153]

Contiguous State Analysis. One of the most noted capital punishment studies was conducted by Thorsten Sellin in 1959.[154] Contiguous states were grouped in threes wherever at least one in the group differed from the others in maximum penalties for homicide; in each set, at least one state did not provide the death penalty for the research period in question, while the other two did. Within these clusters of similar jurisdictions, the homicide rates in states with capital punishment were compared with the homicide rates in states without a mandatory death penalty. Since the homicide trends in all states studies were found to be similar, regardless of whether the death penalty was provided, Sellin concluded that capital punishment did not appear to have any influence on the reported rate of homicide. A recent update of the Sellin research by Richard Lempert was consistent in showing that there is no reason to believe that executions deter homicide.[155]

Another contiguous-state analysis was conducted in 1969 by Walter Reckless, who compared nine states in which the death penalty had been abolished with nine states in which it still applied.[156] Using data from the 1967 uniform crime reports, Reckless compared rates of murder, aggravated assault, and combined violent crimes. He found that five out of seven abolition states had lower crime rates than their contiguous death penalty states, while the remaining two states tied. He concluded that the death penalty is not an effective deterrent in such capital crimes.

Time-Series Studies. Time-series studies look at the long-term association between capital sentencing and murder. If capital punishment is a deterrent, then periods that have an upswing in executions should also experience a downturn in violent crime and murder.

A classic example of this form of research is Karl Schuessler's analysis of murder rates in eleven states from 1930 to 1949.[157] Schuessler found that homicide rates and execution risks (the number of executions for murder per one thousand homicides per year) move independently of each other. Extending this analysis to include the examination of European countries before and after the abolition of the death penalty, Schuessler found nothing in the data to suggest that homicide trends were influenced by the abolition of capital punishment.

More recent research by Dane Archer, Rosemary Gartner, and Marc Beittel comparing homicide rates in fourteen nations found evidence that homicide rates declined in more than half the countries studied after capital punishment was abolished, a direct contradiction to its supposed deterrent effect.[158]

Only a few studies have found that the long-term application of capital punishment may actually reduce the murder rate. The most often-cited was conducted in 1975 by Isaac Ehrlich of the University of Chicago.[159] Using highly advanced and complex statistical techniques, Ehrlich found a significant inverse relationship between murder and execution rates. Ehrlich reached the conclusion that homicides are quite often the product of interpersonal conflicts and that the perception of a high "execution risk" (the percentage of people executed after conviction for murder) can deter murder. As a result of his analysis, Ehrlich reached the controversial conclusion that each additional execution would save seven or eight people from becoming murder victims. This finding was supported by further analysis by Stephen Layson, who concluded that each execution can potentially save eighteen lives.[160]

The Ehrlich and Layson research has been widely cited by death penalty advocates as empirical evidence of the deterrent effect of capital punishment. Ehrlich's results were used in the solicitor general's brief in the case of *Gregg v. Georgia* as new proof of the effectiveness of the death penalty. However, subsequent analyses have questioned the methodology used in these studies and indicate that the deterrent effects they uncover are an artifact of the statistical techniques used in the research.[161] Subsequent time-series analyses have found little evidence that capital punishment can deter murder or other violent crimes.[162]

Why Doesn't The Death Penalty Deter Murder?

The general consensus among death penalty researchers today is that the threat of capital punishment has little effect on murder rates. While it is still unknown why capital punishment fails as a deterrent, the cause may lie in the nature of homicide itself: murder is often a crime of passion involving people who knew each other. Only 14 percent of all murder incidents recorded by the FBI in which the relationship between victim and offender could be determined involved strangers.[163] Many murders are committed by people under the influence of drugs and alcohol; more than 50 percent of all people arrested for murder test positively for drug use.[164] People involved in interpersonal conflict with friends, acquaintances, and family members and who may be under the influence of drugs and alcohol are not likely to be capable of considering the threat of the death penalty.

Murder rates have also been linked to the burdens of poverty and income inequality. Desperate adolescents caught up in the cycle of urban violence and who become members of criminal groups and gangs may find that their life situation gives them little choice except to engage in violent and deadly behavior; they have few chances to ponder the deterrent impact of the death penalty.

The failure of the "ultimate deterrent" to deter the "ultimate crime" has been used by critics to question the value of capital punishment. Nevertheless, many people still hold to the efficacy of the death penalty as a crime deterrent, and recent Supreme Court decisions seem to justify its use. Of course, even if the death penalty were no greater a deterrent than a life sentence, some people would still advocate its use on the grounds that it was the only way to permanently rid society of dangerous criminals who deserve to die.

Capital Punishment Today

When Utah executed Gary Gilmore, a convicted murderer, by firing squad on January 17, 1977, it was the first execution in the United States in over a decade; since then, there have been more than 160 executions and the number of people being executed is now about 40 per year.

Opinion polls show a majority of people believe that murderers ought to be given the death penalty and that public support for the death penalty has increased markedly in recent years. For example, in 1972, only 53 percent of those surveyed approved of the use of capital punishment, while today, the figure is about 80 percent; approval cuts across racial, religious, and economic lines.[165] At least thirty-six states and the federal government now allow capital punishment for murder and other serious crimes. New laws allowing the death penalty are seriously being considered in some of the other states . Executions are carried out by a variety of methods, including hanging, electrocution, gas, and the most recent and common method, death by an injection of lethal drugs.

Since the *Furman* decision, the number of persons sentenced to death each year by state courts has increased markedly. There have been numerous recent executions, including that of Warren McKlesky, whose two appeals resulted in important Supreme Court rulings. As a result of recent court decisions, the go-ahead by the U.S. Supreme Court, and the implementation of death penalty statutes, many other states where offenders are on death row may accelerate the imposition of death sentences in the near future. Capital punishment will continue to be a controversial issue in the U.S. justice system in the 1990s.

SUMMARY

Punishment and sentencing have gone through various phases throughout the history of Western civilization. Initially, punishment was characterized by retribution and the need to fix sentences for convicted offenders. Throughout the middle years of the twentieth century, individualized sentencing was widely accepted, and the concept of rehabilitation was used in sentencing and penal codes. During the 1960s, however, experts began to become disenchanted with rehabilitation and concepts related to treating the individual offender. There was less emphasis on treatment and more on the legal rights of offenders. Entering the 1980s, many states returned to the concept of punishment in terms of mandatory and fixed sentences.

Theorists suggest that the philosophy of sentencing has thus changed from a model of rehabilitation to a model of "retributive justice," where the focus is on the offense and a sentence likely to achieve equality of punishment and justice in the law.

The practice of sentencing can be traced back to ancient times, when retaliation and physical abuse were used to punish offenders. Sentencing in today's criminal justice system is based on deterrence, incapacitation, and rehabilitation. Traditional dispositions include fines, probation, and incarceration, with probation being the most common choice.

One of the most significant features of the sentencing process is its tripartite structure involving the legislature, the judge, and the correctional agency. Actions of each of these agencies affect the type of sentence, the length of sentence, and the conditions for release imposed on the offender.

While the courts today seek to fit the sentence to the individual and not to the crime, this philosophy often results in sentencing disparity. A number of states have developed determinate sentences that eliminate parole and attempt to restrict judicial discretion. Methods for making dispositions more uniform include appellate reviews of sentences and the use of sentencing guidelines, councils, and institutes.

The death penalty continues to be the most controversial sentence, with over half the states reinstituting capital punishment laws since the *Furman v. Georgia* decision of 1972. Though there is little evidence that the death penalty deters murder, supporters still view it as necessary in terms of incapacitation and retribution. Opponents point out that mistakes can be made, that capital sentences are apportioned in a racially biased manner, and that the practice is cruel and barbaric. Nonetheless, the courts have generally supported the legality of capital punishment, and it has been used more frequently in recent years.

QUESTIONS

1. Discuss the sentencing dispositons in your jurisdiction. What are the pros and cons of each?
2. Compare the different types of incarceration sentences. What are the similarities and differences? Why are many jurisdictions considering the passage of mandatory sentencing laws?
3. Discuss the issue of capital punishment. In your opinion, does it serve as a deterrent? What new rulings has the U.S. Supreme Court made on the legality of the death penalty?
4. Why does the problem of sentencing disparity exist? Do programs exist that can reduce disparate sentences? If so, what are they?
5. Should all people who commit the same crime receive the same sentence?
6. Should convicted criminals be released from prison when correctional authorities are convinced they are rehabilitated?

NOTES

1. Michel Foucault, *Discipline and Punishment* (New York: Vintage Books, 1978).

2. Graeme Newman, *The Punishment Response* (Philadelphia: J. B. Lippincott, 1978), p. 13.

3. Kathleen Daly, "Neither Conflict nor Labeling nor Paternalism Will Suffice: Intersections of Race, Ethnicity, Gender, and Family in Criminal Court Decisions," *Crime and Delinquency* 35: (1989) 136–68.

4. Among the most helpful sources for this section are Benedict Alper, *Prisons Inside-Out* (Cambridge, Mass.: Ballinger, 1974); Gustave de Beaumont and Alexis de Tocqueville, *On the Penitentiary System in the United States and Its Applications in France* (Carbondale: Southern Illinois University Press, 1964); Orlando Lewis, *The Development of American Prisons and Prisons Customs, 1776–1845* (Montclair, N.J.: Patterson-Smith, 1967); Leonard Orland, ed., *Justice, Punishment, and Treatment* (New York: Free Press, 1973); J. Goebel, *Felony and Misdemeanor* (Philadelphia: University of Pennsylvania Press, 1976); George Rusche and Otto Kircheimer, *Punishment and Social Structure* (New York: Russell & Russell, 1939); Samuel Walker, *Popular Justice* (New York: Oxford University Press, 1980); Newman, *The Punishment Response;* David Rothman, *Conscience and Convenience* (Boston: Little, Brown & Co., 1980).

5. Rusche and Kircheimer, *Punishment and Social Structure*, p. 9.

6. Ibid., p. 19.

7. George Ives, *A History of Penal Methods* (Montclair, N.J.: Patterson-Smith, 1970).

8. Robert Hughes, *The Fatal Shore* (New York; Knopf, 1986).

9. Leon Radzinowicz, *A History of English Criminal Law*, vol. 1 (London: Stevens, 1943), p. 5.

10. Newman, *The Punishment Response*, p. 139.

11. Lonn Lanza-Kaduce, "Perceptual Deterrence and Drinking and Driving among College Students," *Criminology* 26 (1988):321–41.

12. Ibid.

13. Charles Tittle, "Sanction Fear and the Maintenance of the Social Order," *Social Forces* 55 (1977):579–96.

14. Kirk Williams and Richard Hawkins, "The Meaning of Arrest for Wife Assault," *Criminology* 27 (1989):163–81; see also, Donald Dutton, *The Domestic Assault of Women: Psychological and Criminal Justice Perspectives* (Boston: Allyn and Bacon, 1988).

15. Bureau of Justice Statistics, *Report to the Nation on Crime and Justice*, 2d ed. (Washington, D.C.: U.S. Government Printing Office, 1988), p. 105.

16. "Inmate Population Predicted to Surpass 1 Million This Year," *Criminal Justice Newsletter*, 15 February 1989, p. 5.

17. Associated Press, "Judge Approves Castration Plea," *Boston Globe*, 7 March 1992, p. 5A.

18. Gerald Wheeler and Rodney Hissong, "Effects of Sanctions on Drunk Drivers: Beyond Incarceration," *Crime and Delinquency* 34 (1988):29–42.

19. Douglas Smith and Patrick Gartin, "Specifying Specific Deterrence: The Influence of Arrest in Future Criminal Activity," *American Sociological Review* 54 (1989):94–105.

20. Jeffrey Fagan, "Cessation of Family Violence: Deterrence and Dissuasion," in *Crime and Justice*, vol. 11, ed. Lloyd Ohlin and Michael Tonry (Chicago: University of Chicago Press, 1989), p. 100–51.

21. Alexis Durham, "The Justice Model in Historical Context: Early Law, the Emergence of Science, and the Rise of Incarceration," *Journal of Criminal Justice* 16 (1988):331–46.

22. Andrew von Hirsh, *Doing Justice: The Choice of Punishments* (New York: Hill and Wang, 1976).

23. Alexis Durham, "Crime Seriousness and Punitive Severity: An Assessment of Social Attitudes," *Justice Quarterly* 5 (1988):131–53.

24. Joan Petersilia, Susan Turner, James Kahan, and Joyce Peterson, *Granting Felons Probation: Public Risks and Alternatives* (Santa Monica, Calif.: Rand Corp., 1986).

25. Francis Cullen, John Cullen, and John Wozniak, "Is Rehabilitation Dead? The Myth of the Punitive Public," *Journal of Criminal Justice* 16 (1988):303–16.

26. Adapted from Alan Dershowitz, *Fair and Certain Punishment: Report of the Twentieth Century Task Force on Criminal Sentencing* (New York: Twentieth Century Fund, 1976).

27. David Rothman, *Incarceration and Its Alternatives in 20th Century America* (Washington, D.C.: U.S. Government Printing Office, 1979).

28. Patrick Langan, *State Felony Courts and Felony Laws* (Washington, D.C.: Bureau of Justice Statistics, 1987), p. 6.

29. George Jackson, *Soledad Brother* (New York: Bantam Books, 1970).

30. Kenneth Culp Davis, *Discretionary Justice, A Preliminary Inquiry* (Baton Rouge: Louisiana State University Press, 1969); Marvin Frankel, *Criminal Sentences: Law Without Order* (New York: Hill and Wang, 1972).

31. See Frankel, *Criminal Sentences: Law Without Order* p. 5.

32. American Friends Service Committee, *Struggle for Justice: A Report on Crime and Punishment in America* (New York: Hill and Wang, 1971).

33. Andrew von Hirsch, *Doing Justice: The Choice of Punishments* (New York: Hill and Wang, 1976).

34. James Q. Wilson, *Thinking About Crime* (New York: Random House, 1975), p. 236.

35. Kay Knapp, "Structured Sentencing: Building on Experience," *Judicature* 72 (1988):47–52.

36. Andrew von Hirsch, *Past or Future Crimes* (New Brunswick, N.J.: Rutgers University Press, 1985).

37. Determinate Sentencing Act, 1977, Cal. Penal Code 1170 (a)(1).

38. Marvin Zalman, "The Rise and Fall of the Indeterminate Sentence," *Wayne Law Review* 24 (1978):857–88 at 877.

39. John Kramer, Robin Lubitz, and Cynthia Kempinen, "Sentencing Guidelines: A Quantitative Comparison of Sentencing Policies in Minnesota, Pennsylvania, and Washington," *Justice Quarterly* 6 (1989):565–87.

40. Richard Frase, "Implementing Commission-Based Sentencing Guidelines: The Lessons of the First Ten Years in Minnesota" (Paper presented at the annual meeting of the American Society of Criminology, San Francisco, November 1991,) p. 5.

41. *Mistretta v. United States*, 44 Cr.L. 3061 (January 15, 1989).

42. Kay Knapp, "Structures Sentencing: Building on Experience," p. 52.

43. Minnesota Sentencing Guidelines Commission, *The Impact of the Minnesota Sentencing Guidelines: Three-Year Evaluation* (St. Paul, Minnesota Sentencing Guidelines Commission, 1984), p. 162.

44. Terance Miethe and Charles Moore, "Socioeconmic Disparities under Determinate Sentencing Systems: A Comparison of Preguideline and Postguideline Practices in Minnesota," *Criminology* 23 (1985):337–63.

45. Ibid.

46. Frase, "Implementing Commission-Based Sentencing Guidelines."

47. Michael Tonry, "The Politics and Process of Sentencing Commissions," *Crime and Delinquency* 37 (1991):307–29.

48. Frase, "Implementing Commission-Based Sentencing Guidelines," p. 23.

49. Joan Petersilia and Susan Turner, *Guideline-Based Justice: The Implications for Racial Minorities* (Santa Monica, Calif.: Rand Corp., 1985).

50. David Griswold, "Deviation from Sentencing Guidelines: The Issue of Unwarranted Disparity," *Journal of Criminal Justice* 16 (1988):317–29.

51. Chris Eskridge, "Sentencing Guidelines: To Be or Not to Be," *Federal Probation* 50 (1986):70–76.

52. Timothy Bynum, "Prosecutorial Discretion and the Implementation of a Legislative Mandate," in *Implementing Criminal Justice Policies*, ed. Merry Morash (Beverly Hills, Calif.: Sage Publications, 1982); Massachusetts General Laws, chap. 269, 10, chap. 649, acts of 1974.

53. Dershowitz, *Fair and Certain Punishment*.

54. Michael Tonry, *Sentencing Reform Impacts* (Washington, D.C.: U.S. Government Printing Office, 1987), pp. 26–27.

55. James Austin, *The Consequences of Escalating the Use of Imprisonment: The Case Study of Florida* (San Francisco: National Council on Crime and Delinquency 1991).

56. Derral Cheatwood, "The Life-Without-Parole Sanction: Its Current Status and a Research Agenda," *Crime and Delinquency* 34 (1988):43–59.

57. Paul Woodard, *Statutes Requiring the Use of Criminal History Record Information* (Washington, D.C.: Bureau of Justice Statistics, 1991).

58. 445 U.S. 263, 100 S.Ct. 1133, 63 L.Ed.2d 382 (1980).

59. 463 U.S. 277, 103 S.Ct. 3001, 77 L.Ed.2d 637 (1983).

60. ___ U.S. ___, 111 S.Ct. 2680, 115 L.Ed.2d 836 (1991).

61. Patrick Langan, *Felony Sentences in State Courts, 1988* (Washington, D.C.: Bureau of Justice Statistics, 1990).

62. Edward Lisefski and Donald Manson, *Tracking Offenders, 1984* (Washington, D.C.: Bureau of Justice Statistics, 1988).

63. For a general look at the factors that affect sentencing, see Susan Welch, Cassia Spohn, and John Gruhl, "Convicting and Sentencing Differences among Black, Hispanic, and White Males in Six Localities," *Justice Quarterly* 2 (1985):67–80.

64. See, generally, Janet Johnston, Thomas Kennedy, and I. Gayle Shuman, "Gender Differences in the Sentencing of Felony Offenders," *Federal Probation* 87 (1987):49–56; Cassia Spohn and Susan Welch, "The Effect of Prior Record in Sentencing Research: An Examination of the Assumption That Any Measure Is Adequate," *Justice Quarterly* 4 (1987):286–302; David Willison, "The Effects of Counsel on the Severity of Criminal Sentences: A Statistical Assessment," *Justice System Journal* 9 (1984):87–101.

65. Ellen Hochstedler Steury and Nancy Frank, "Gender Bias and Pretrial Release: More Pieces of the Puzzle, *Journal of Criminal Justice* 18 (1990):417–32.

66. Dean Champion, "Elderly Felons and Sentencing Severity: Interregional Variations in Leniency and Sentencing Trends," *Criminal Justice Review* 12 (1987):7–15.

67. Ibid., p. 13.

68. Alfred Blumstein, "On the Racial Disproportionality of the United States Prison Population," *Journal of Criminal Law and Criminology* 73 (1982):1259–81.

69. "Racial Disparities Cited in New York's Justice System," *Criminal Justice Newsletter 22 (10 October 1991):6.*

70. Gary Kleck, "Racial Discrimination in Criminal Sentencing: A Critical Evaluation of the Evidence with Additional Evidence on the Death Penalty," *American Sociological Review* 46 (1981):783–805.

71. Blumstein, "On the Racial Disproportionality of the United States Prison Population."

72. Joan Petersilia, *Racial Disparities in the Criminal Justice System* (Santa Monica, Calif.: Rand Corp., 1983).

73. Darnell Hawkins, "Race, Crime Type and Imprisonment," *Justice Quarterly* 3 (1986):251–69; James Unnever and Larry Hembroff, "The Prediction of Racial/Ethnic Sentencing Disparities: An Expectation States Approach." *Journal of Research in Crime and Delinquency* 25 (1988):53–82.

74. Ibid., p. 267.

75. Cassia Spohn and Jerry Cederblom, "Race and Disparities in Sentencing: A Test of the Liberation Hypothesis," *Justice Quarterly* 8 (1991):305–27.

76. George Bridges, Robert Crutchfield, and Edith Simpson, "Crime, Social Structure and Criminal Punishment: White and Nonwhite Rates of Imprisonment," *Social Problems* 34 (1987):345–61; Terance Miethe and Charles Moore, "Racial Differences in Criminal Processing: The Consequences of Model Selection on Conclusions about Differential Treatment," *Sociological Quarterly* 27 (1987):217–37.

77. See, generally, Martha Myers, "Offended Parties and Official Reactions: Victims and the Sentencing of Criminal Defendants," *Sociological Quarterly* 20 (1979):529–40.

78. Stephen Klein, Joan Petersilia, and Susan Turner, "Race and Imprisonment Decisions in California," *Science* 247 (1990):812–17.

79. Patrick Langan and John Dawson, *Profile of Felons Convicted in State Courts, 1986* (Washington, D.C.: Bureau of Justice Statistics, 1990), p. 4.

80. Chistopher Link and Neal Shover, "The Origins of Sentencing Reforms," *Justice Quarterly* 3 (1986):329–41.

81. American Law Institute, *Model Penal Code*, Proposed Official Draft, 1962.

82. National Council on Crime and Delinquency, *Model Sentencing Act*, 1963 and 1972.

83. Louis Jankowski, *Probation and Parole, 1990* (Washington, D.C.: Bureau of Justice Statistics, 1991), p. 5.

84. Scott Paltrow, "New Anti-Crime Law in California Is Helping Some Accused Felons," *Wall Street Journal*, 26 November 1982.

85. Victoria Schneider and John Ortiz Smykla, "A Summary Analysis of Executions in the United States, 1608–1987: The Espy File," in *The Death Penalty in America,:Current Research*, ed. Robert Bohm (Cincinnati: Anderson Publishing, 1991), pp. 1–19.

86. *Coker v Georgia*, 433 U.S. 584, 97 S.Ct. 2861, 53 L.Ed.2d 982 (1977).

87. Espionage (10 U.S.C. § 906[a]); treason, (18 U.S.C. § 2381).

88. Lawrence Greenfield, *Capital Punishment, 1990* Washington, D.C.: Bureau of Justice Statistics, 1991), p. 7.

89. Cheatwood, "The Life-Without-Parole Sanction: Its Current Status and a Research Agenda," p. 49.

90. Stephen Markman and Paul Cassell, "Protecting the Innocent: A Response to the Bedeau-Radelet Study," *Stanford Law Review* 41 (1988):121–70, at 153.

91. Greenfield, *Capital Punishment, 1990*, p. 9.

92. Stephen Layson, "United States Time-Series Homicide Regressions with Adaptive Expectations," *Bulletin of the New York Academy of Medicine* 62 (1986):589–619.

93. David Friedrichs, "Comment—Humanism and the Death Penalty: An Alternative Perspective," *Justice Quarterly* 6 (1989):197–209.

94. James Fox, Michael Radelet, and Julie Bonsteel, "Death Penalty Opinion in the Post-*Furman* Years," *New York University Review of Law and Social Change* 18 (1990):499–528.

95. For an analysis of the formation of public opinion on the death penalty, see Kimberly Cook, "Public Support for the Death Penalty: A Cultural Analysis" (Paper presented at the annual meeting of the American Society of Criminology, San Francisco, November 1991).

96. 428 U.S. 153, 96 S.Ct. 2909, 49 L.Ed.2d 859 (1976).

97. Julian Wright, "Life Without Parole: The View From Death Row," *Criminal Law Bulletin* 27: (1991):334–57.

98. See, generally, Hugo Bedeau, *Death Is Different: Studies in the Morality, Law, and Politics of Capital Punishment* (Boston: Northeastern University Press, 1987); Keith Otterbein, *The Ultimate Coercive Sanction* (New Haven: HRAF Press, 1986).

99. "Capital Punishment's Injustice," *Boston Globe*, 30 March 1992, p. 10.

100. Michael Radelet and Hugo Bedeau, "Miscarriages of Justice in Potentially Capital Cases," *Stanford Law Review* 40 (1987):21–181.

101. For a response that questions the Bedeau and Radelet research, see Stephen Markman and Paul Cassell, "Protecting the Innocent: A Response to the Bedeau-Radelet Study," *Stanford Law Review* 41 (1988):121–70; for their response, see Hugo Adam Bedeau and Michael Radelet, "The Myth of Infallibility: A Reply to Markman and Cassell," *Stanford Law Review* 42 (1989):161–70.

102. *McKlesky v. Zant*, 49 Crim.L.Rep. 2031 (1991).

103. Barry Nakell and Kenneth Hardy, *The Arbitrariness of the Death Penalty* (Philadelphia: Temple University Press, 1987).

104. Patrick Langan and John Dawson, *Felony Sentences in State Courts, 1988* (Washington, D.C.: Bureau of Justice Statistics, 1990), p. 2.

105. "A Victim's Progress," *Newsweek*, 12 June 1989, p. 5.

106. William Doerner, "The Impact of Medical Resources on Criminally Induced Lethality: A Further Examination," *Criminology* 26 (1988):171–77.

107. Elizabeth Purdom and J. Anthony Paredes, "Capital Punishment and Human Sacrifice," *Facing the Death Penalty: Essays on Cruel and Unusual Punishment*, ed. Michael Radelet (Philadelphia: Temple University Press, 1989), pp. 152–53.

108. James Finckenauer, "Public Support for the Death Penalty: Retribution as Just Deserts or Retribution as Revenge?" *Justice Quarterly* 5 (1988):81–100.

109. See, generally, Bohm, ed., *The Death Penalty in America*.

110. William Bowers and Glenn Pierce, "Deterrence or Brutalization: What Is the Effect of Executions?" *Crime and Delinquency* 26 (1980):453–84.

111. William Bailey, "Disaggregation in Deterrence and Death Penalty Research: The Case of Murder in Chicago," *Journal of Criminal Law and Criminology* 74 (1986):827–59.

112. James Marquart and Jonathan Sorensen, "Institutional and Postrelease Behavior of *Furman*-Commuted Inmates in Texas," *Criminology* 26 (1988):677–93.

113. Gennaro Vito, Pat Koester, and Deborah Wilson, "Return of the Dead: An Update on the Status of *Furman*-Commuted Death Row Inmates," in *The Death Penalty in America: Current Research*, ed. Robert Bohm (Cincinnati: Anderson Publishing, 1991), pp. 89–100; Gennaro Vito, Deborah Wilson, and Edward Latessa, "Comparison of the Dead: Attributes and Outcomes of *Furman*-Commuted Death Row Inmates in Kentucky and Ohio," *The Death Penalty in America: Current Research*, ed. Robert Bohm (Cinncinnati: Anderson Publishing, 1991), pp. 101–12.

114. Schneider and Smykla, "A Summary Analysis of Executions in the United States, 1608–1987: The Espy File," p. 12.

115. Lawrence Greenfield and David Hinners, *Capital Punishment, 1984* (Washington, D.C.: Bureau of Justice Statistics, 1985).

116. Gennaro Vito and Thomas Keil, "Capital Sentencing in Kentucky: An Analysis of the Factors Influencing Decision Making in the Post-*Gregg* Period," *Journal of Criminal Law and Criminology* 79 (1988):493–503; David Baldus, C. Pulaski, and G. Woodworth, "Comparative Review of Death Sentences: An Empirical Study of the Georgia Experience," *Journal of Criminal Law and Criminology* 74 (1983):661–85; Raymond Paternoster, "Race of the Victim and Location of Crime: The Decision to Seek the Death Penalty in South Carolina," *Journal of Criminal Law and Criminology* 74 (1983):754–85.

117. Federal Bureau of Investigation, *Crime in the United States, 1990* (Washington, D.C.: U.S. Government Printing Office, 1989), p. 11.

118. Paternoster found that prosecutors in North Carolina did not use the death penalty on the basis of race; Raymond Paternoster, "Prosecutorial Discretion and Capital Sentencing in North and South Carolina, in *The Death Penalty in America: Current Research*, ed. Robert Bohm (Cincinnati: Anderson Publishing, 1991), pp. 39–52.

119. Vito and Keil, "Capital Sentencing in Kentucky," pp. 502–3.

120. Robert Bohm, "Humanism and the Death Penalty, with Special Emphasis on the Post-*Furman* Experience," *Justice Quarterly* 6 (1989):173–93.

121. Robert Johnson, *Death Work: A Study of the Modern Execution Process* (Belmont, Calif.: Brooks/Cole, 1990).

122. See, generally, Wright, "Life Without Parole: The View from Death Row."

123. 408 U.S. 238, 92 S.Ct. 2726, 33 L.Ed.2d 346 (1972).

124. 428 U.S. 153, 96 S.Ct. 2909, 49 L.Ed.2d 859 (1976).

125. Ibid., at 205–207, 96 S.Ct. at 2940–2941.

126. 428 U.S. 262, 96 S.Ct. 2950, 49 L.Ed.2d 929 (1976).

127. 428 U.S. 242, 96 S.Ct. 2960, 49 L.Ed.2d 913 (1976).

128. *Jurek*, 428 U.S. at 269, 96 S.Ct. at 2955.

129. 428 U.S. 325, 96 S.Ct. 3001, 49 L.Ed.2d 974 (1976).

130. 428 U.S. 280, 96 S.Ct. 2978, 49 L.Ed.2d 944 (1976).

131. Ibid., at 294, 304, 96 S.Ct. at 2986, 2991.

132. 438 U.S. 584, 97 S.Ct. 2861, 53 L.Ed.2d 982 (1977).

133. 430 U.S. 349, 97 S.Ct. 1197, 51 L.Ed.2d 393 (1977).

134. 438 U.S. 801, 98 S.Ct. 2981, 57 L.Ed.2d 973 (1978).

135. *Spaziano v. Florida*, 468 U.S. 447, 104 S.Ct. 3154, 82 L.Ed.2d 340 (1984); *Pulley v. Harris*, 465 U.S. 37, 104 S.Ct. 871, 79 L.Ed.2d 29 (1984).

136. *McLesky v. Kemp*, 478 U.S. 1019, 106 S.Ct. 3331, 92 L.Ed.2d 737 (1986).

137. *Dawson v. Delaware*, ___ U.S. ___, 112 S.Ct. 1093, 117 L.Ed.2d 309 (1992).

138. *Lankford v. Idaho*, 49 Cr.L. 2160 (1991).

139. *Eddings v. Oklahoma*, 455 U.S. 104, 102 S.Ct. 869, 71 L.Ed.2d 1 (1982).

140. 492 U.S. 361, 109 S.Ct. 2969, 106 L.Ed.2d 306 (1989).

141. 494 U.S. 738, 110 S.Ct. 1441, 108 L.Ed.2d 725 (1990).

142. *Stringer v. Black*, ___ U.S. ___, 112 S.Ct. 1130, 117 L.Ed.2d 367 (1992).

143. *Parker v. Dugger*, 48 Cr.L. 2084 (1991).

144. McKlesky *v. Zant*, 49 Cr.L. 2031 (1991).

145. *Payne v. Tennessee*, ___ U.S. ___, 111 S.Ct. 2597, 115 L.Ed.2d 720 (1991).

146. 391 U.S. 510, 88 S.Ct. 1770, 20 L.Ed.2d 776 (1968).

147. *Wainwright v. Witt*, 469 U.S. 412, 105 S.Ct. 844, 83 L.Ed.2d 841 (1985).

148. *Lockhart v.* McCree, 476 U.S. 162, 106 S.Ct. 1758, 90 L.Ed.2d 137 (1986).

149. Robert H. Dann, "The Deterrent Effect of Capital Punishment," *Friends Social Service Series* 29 (1935):1.

150. Steven Stack, "Publicized Executions and Homicide, 1950–1980," *American Sociological Review* 52 (1987):532–40.

151. William Bailey and Ruth Peterson, "Murder and Capital Punishment: A Monthly Time-Series Analysis of Execution Publicity," *American Sociological Review* 54 (1989):722–43.

152. David Phillips, "The Deterrent Effect of Capital Punishment," *American Journal of Sociology* 86 (1980):139–48; Sam McFarland, "Is Capital Punishment a Short-Term Deterrent to Homicide? A Study of the Effects of Four Recent American Executions," *Journal of Criminal Law and Criminology* 74 (1984):1014–32.

153. Ruth Peterson and William Bailey, "Felony Murder and Capital Punishment: An Examination of the Deterrence Questions," *Criminology* 29 (1991):367–96.

154. Thorsten Sellin, "Effect of Repeal and Reintroduction of the Death Penalty on Homicide Rates," in *The Death Penalty*, ed. Thorsten Sellin (Philadelphia: American Law Institute, 1959).

155. Richard Lempert, "The Effect of Executions on Homicides: A New Look in an Old Light," *Crime and Delinquency* 29 (1983):88–115.

156. Walter C. Reckless, "Use of the Death Penalty," *Crime and Delinquency* 15 (1969):43.

157. Karl F. Schuessler, "The Deterrent Influence of the Death Penalty," *Annals* 284 (1952):54.

158. Dane Archer, Rosemary Gartner, and Marc Beittel, "Homicide and the Death Penalty: A Cross-National Test of a Deterrence Hypothesis," *Journal of Criminal Law and Criminology* 74 (1983):991–1014.

159. Isaac Ehrlich, "The Deterrent Effect of Capital Punishment: A Question of Life or Death," *American Economic Review* 65 (1975):397.

160. Layson, "United States Time-Series Homicide Regressions with Adaptive Expectations."

161. William J. Bowers and Glenn L. Pierce, "The Illusion of Deterrence in Isaac Ehrlich's Research on Capital Punishment," *Yale Law Journal* 85 (1975):187–208.

162. For a review, see William Bailey, "The General Prevention Effect of Capital Punishment for Non-Capital Felonies," in *The Death Penalty in America: Current Research*, ed. Robert Bohm (Cincinnati: Anderson Publishing, 1991), pp. 21–38.

163. Federal Bureau of Investigation, *Crime in the United States*, 1990, p. 13.

164. National Institute of Justice, *Drug Use Forecasting, 1989* (Washington, D.C.: National Institute of Justice, 1990).

165. Hans Zeisel and Alec Gallup, "Death Penalty Sentiment in the United States," *Journal of Quantitative Criminology* 5 (1989):285–96.

PART FOUR

CORRECTIONS

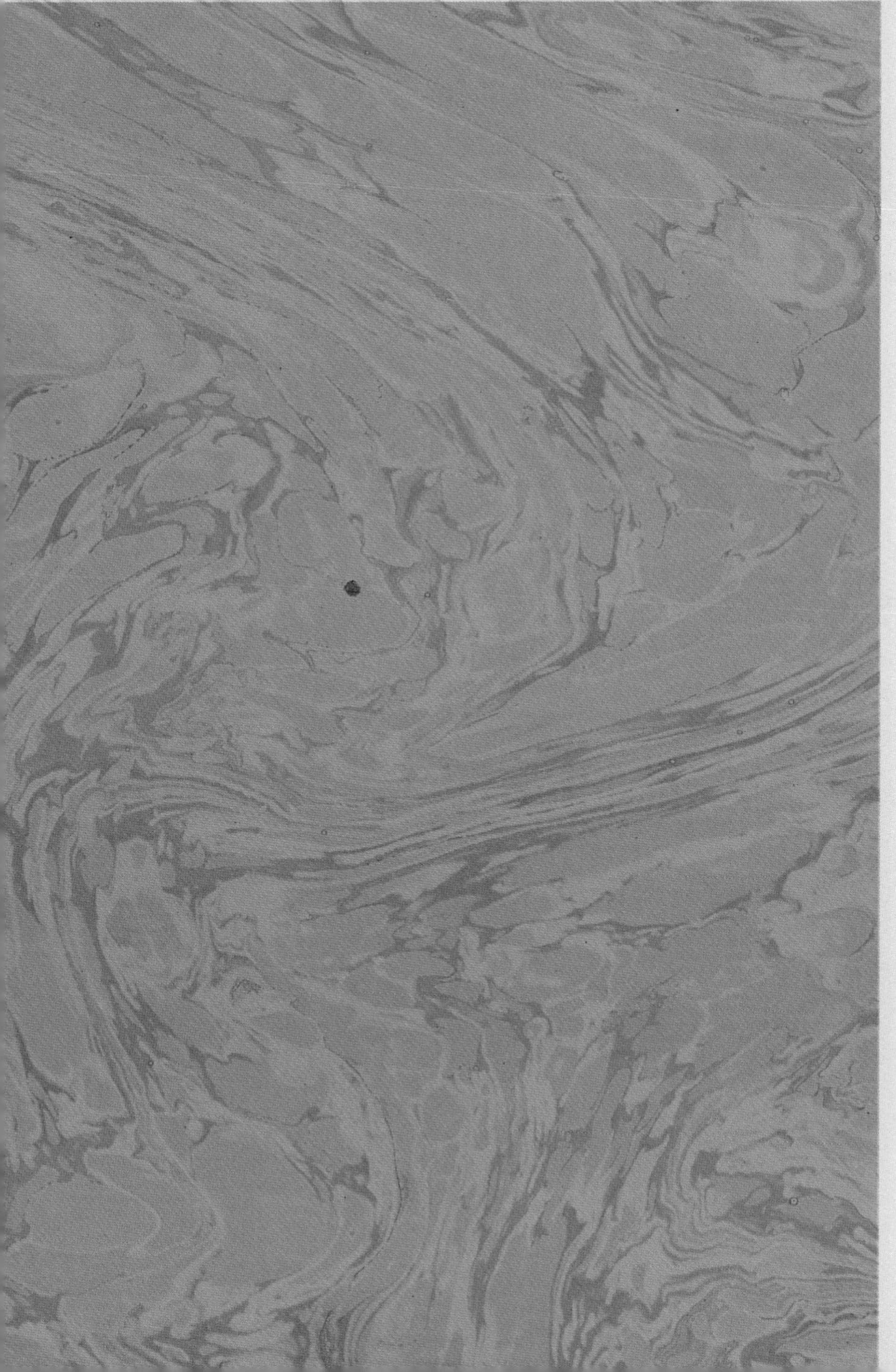

CHAPTER 15

Probation and Intermediate Sanctions

OUTLINE

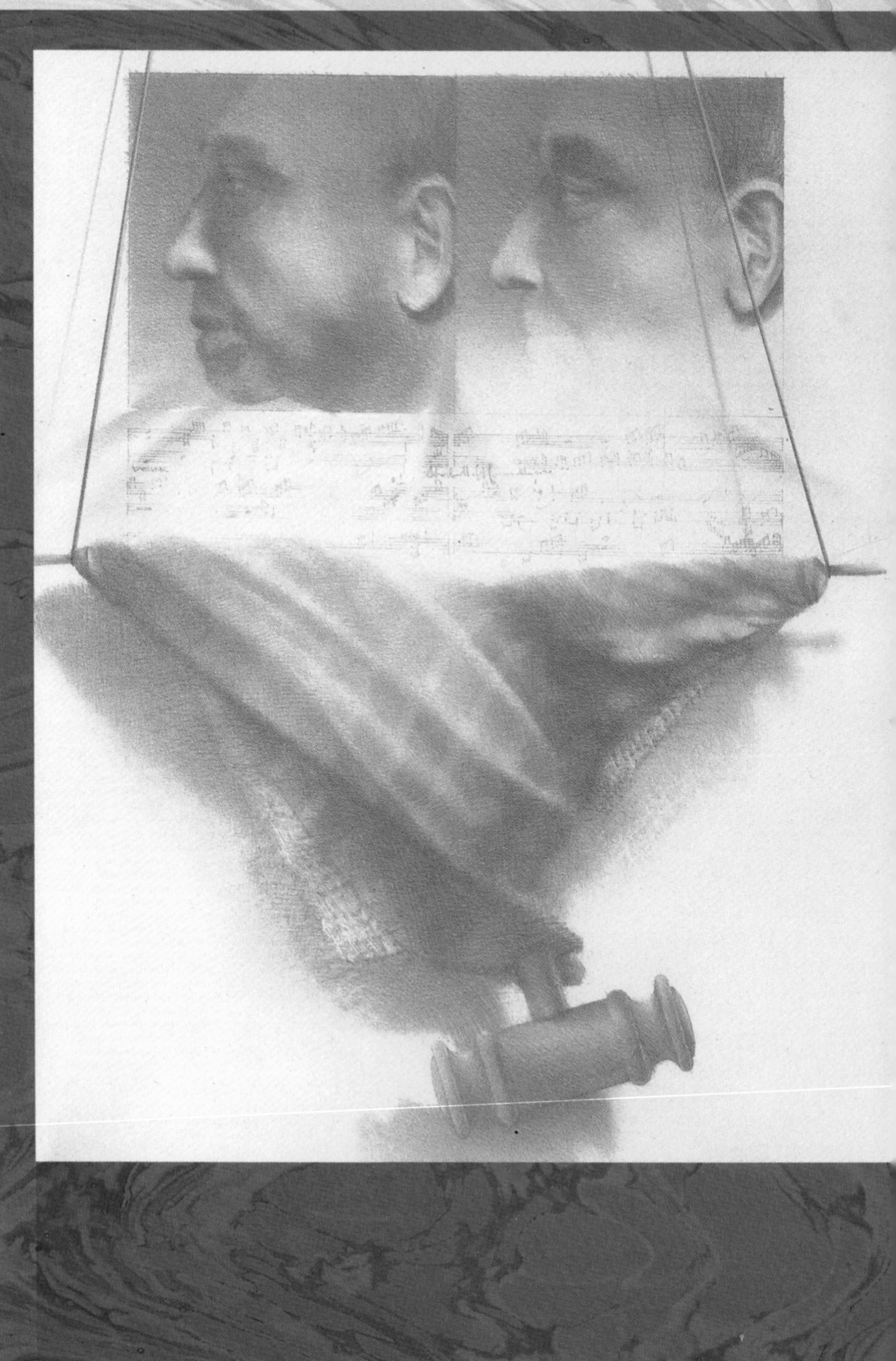

KEY TERMS

probation
judicial reprieve
recognizance
sureties
John Augustus
revoked
suspended sentence
Model Penal Code
chief probation officer
presentence investigation
intake
diagnosis
risk classification
day fees
alternative sanctions
intermediate sanctions
pretrial diversion
fines
day fines
forfeiture
zero tolerance
monetary restitution
community-service restitution
split sentencing
shock probation
intensive probation supervision
diversion
control
reintegration
house arrest
surveillance officers
electronic monitoring
reintegrate
day reporting centers

Though many people would like to see dangerous offenders "do hard time," incarcerating every convicted criminal is both expensive and unworkable. The prison system is already overcrowded and dangerous. New prison construction is a costly option for cash-strapped states. Little evidence exists that a prison stay can effectively rehabilitate many inmates; almost 70 percent of parolees are rearrested within six years of their release.[1] The perceived failure of traditional correctional models has prompted criminal justice policymakers to create alternatives to incarceration that are both effective and economical. The most traditional and common alternative sanction, probation, involves maintaining an offender in the community under a set of behavioral rules created and administered by judicial authority. Considering the potential benefits and cost effectiveness of a probation sentence, it is not surprising that the number of probationers is at an all-time high—about 2.7 million.[2]

The need to create effective and efficient methods of controlling offenders in the community has also prompted correctional policymakers to develop and amplify the use of new forms of community-based intermediate sanctions: fines, forfeiture, restitution, shock probation/split sentencing, house arrest, electronic monitoring, inensive probation supervision, and residential community corrections. These are designed to provide greater control over an offender and increase the level of sanction without resorting to a prison sentence.

Both traditional probation and the newer intermediate sanctions have the potential to become reasonable answers to many of the economic and social problems faced by correctional administrators: they are less costly than jail or prison sentences; they help the offender maintain family and community ties; they can be structured to maximize security and maintain public safety; and they can be scaled in severity to correspond to the seriousness of the crime. Because of their importance and utility, no area of the criminal justice system is undergoing more change and greater expansion than probation and intermediate sanctions.

This chapter reviews these criminal sanctions. It begins with a brief history of probation and covers probation as an organization, sentence, and correctional practice. Then attention is focused on such intermediate sanctions as intensive supervision, house arrest, and electronic monitoring.

History of Probation

The roots of **probation,** the practice of maintaining convicted criminal offenders in the community under supervision of court authority, can be traced back to the traditions of the English common law. During the Middle Ages, judges wishing to spare deserving offenders from the pains of the then commonly used punishments of torture, mutilation, and death used their power to grant clemency and stays of execution. The common law practice of **judicial reprieve** allowed judges to suspend punishment so that convicted offenders could seek a pardon, gather new evidence, or demonstrate that they had reformed their behavior. Similarly, the practice of **recognizance** enabled convicted offenders to remain free if they agreed to enter into a debt obligation with the state. The debt would have to be paid only if the offender was caught engaging in further criminal behavior. Sometimes **sureties** were required. Sureties were people who made themselves responsible for the behavior of the offender after the offender was released.

Early U.S. courts continued the practice of indefinitely suspending sentences of offenders who seemed deserving of a second chance, but it was **John Augustus** of Boston who is usually credited with originating the modern probation concept. Although a private citizen, in 1841, Augustus began to supervise offenders released to his custody by a Boston judge. Over an eighteen-year period, Augustus supervised close to two thousand probationers and helped them get jobs and establish themselves in the community. Augustus had an amazingly high success rate, and few of his charges became involved in crime again.

In 1878, Augustus's work inspired the Massachusetts Legislature to pass a law authorizing appointment of a paid probation officer for the city of Boston. In 1880, probation was extended to other jurisdictions in Massachusetts, and by 1898, the probation movement had spread to the superior (felony) courts.[3] The Massachusetts experience was copied by Missouri (1887), Vermont (1898), and soon after by most other states. In 1925, the federal government established a probation system for the U.S. district courts. While some critics, such as historian David Rothman, view these early efforts as ineffectual and merely widening society's control over the poor, the probation concept soon became the most widely used correctional mechanism in the United States.[4]

The Concept of Probation

Probation is a criminal sentence mandating that a convicted offender be placed and maintained in the community under the supervision of a duly authorized agent of the court. Once on probation, the offender is subject to certain rules and conditions that must be followed in order for that person to remain in the community. The probation sentence is managed by a probation department that supervises offenders' behavior and treatment and carries out other tasks for the court. Although the term has many meanings, *probation* usually indicates a non-punitive form of sentencing for convicted criminal offenders and delinquent youth, emphasizing maintenance in the community and treatment without institutionalization or other forms of punishment.[5]

The philosophy of probation is that the average offender is not actually a dangerous criminal or a menace to society. Advocates of probation suggest that when offenders are institutionalized instead of being granted community release, the prison community becomes their new reference point, they are forced to interact with hardened criminals, and the "ex-con" label prohibits them from making successful adjustments to society. Probation provides offenders with the opportunity to prove themselves, gives them a second chance, and allows them to be closely supervised by trained personnel who can help them reestablish proper forms of behavior in the community.

In practice, probation usually involves suspension of the offender's sentence in return for the promise of good behavior in the community under the supervision of the probation department. As practiced in all fifty states and by the federal government, probation implies a contract between the court and the offender in which the former promises to hold a prison term in abeyance while the latter promises to adhere to a set of rules or conditions mandated by the court. If the rules are violated, and especially if the probationer commits another criminal offense, probation may be **revoked;** this means that the contract is terminated and the original sentence enforced. If an offender on probation commits a second offense that is more serious than the first, he or she may also be indicted, tried, and sentenced on that second offense. However, probation may be revoked simply because the rules and conditions of probation have not been met; it is not necessary for an offender to commit another crime.

Each probationary sentence is for a fixed period of time, depending on the seriousness of the offense and the statutory law of the jurisdiction. Probation is considered served when offenders fulfill the conditions set by the court for that period of time; they can then live without state supervision.

Awarding Probation

Probationary sentences may be granted by state and federal district courts and state superior (felony) courts.

In some states, juries may recommend probation as part of their sentencing power, or they may make recommendations to judges that the judges will usually follow if the case meets certain legally regulated criteria (e.g., if it falls within a certain class of offenses as determined by statute). While juries can recommend probation, judges have the final say in the matter and may grant probation at their discretion. In nonjury trials, probation is granted solely by judicial mandate.

In most jurisdictions, all juvenile offenders are eligible for probation, as are most adults. Some state statutes prohibit probation for certain types of adult offenders, usually those who have engaged in repeated and serious violent crimes, such as murder or rape, or those who commit crimes for which mandatory prison sentences have been legislated.

The most common manner in which a probationary sentence is imposed is for the judge to formulate a prison sentence and then suspend it if the offender agrees to obey the rules of probation while living in the community (a **suspended sentence).** About 50 percent of all probationary sentences are imposed in this manner.[6] The term of a probationary sentence may extend to the limit of the suspended prison term, or the court may set a time limit that reflects the sentencing period. For misdemeanors, probation usually extends for the entire period of the jail sentence, while felonies are more likely to warrant probationary periods that are actually shorter than their prison sentences would have been.

Probation may also be granted to an offender whose sentence is deferred pending successful completion of his or her probationary period (about 6 percent of all cases).[7] This step is usually taken to encourage the defendant to pursue a specific rehabilitation program, for example, treatment for alcohol abuse. If the program is successfully completed, further legal action is usually not taken. Probation can also be a sole sentence (42 percent) with no prison sentence imposed or contemplated, but if the rules are violated, the probationer can be brought in for resentencing.

The Extent of Probation

There are approximately 1,920 adult probation agencies in the United States. Most (56 percent) are associated with a state-level agency, while the remainder are organized at the county or municipal level of government. About thirty states combine probation and parole supervision into a single agency.

The 2.7 million adults under probation supervision (as of 1991) amounted to 63 percent of all adults under some form of correctional supervision. Probation has remained the sentence of choice in U.S. courts, and the number of those on probation has increased 36 percent since 1985.

Probation is used more frequently in some states than others. In thirty-one states, led by Georgia (2.8 percent of all adults), more than 1 percent of the adult residents were on probation; six states had more than 2 percent of their populations on probation. Overall, about 1.4 of every hundred adults were on probation at the start of 1991.

The extensive use of probation is probably a reflection of its low cost and its importance to the efficient operation of the justice system; it is used today in about 52 percent of felony cases.[8] Without probation, the correctional system would be rapidly overcrowded and undoubtedly in serious financial distress. However, research by Mark Cuniff, Dale Sechrest, and Robert Cushman, indicates that there has been relatively little change in the judicial use of probationary sentences. Cuniff and his associates find that expansion of the probation population is a product of the increase in the number of people coming into felony court. The one notable exception is drug trafficking cases: the chances of someone receiving a probation sentence after conviction for drug trafficking declined significantly between 1983 and 1990, from 70 percent to 55 percent.

Eligibility for Probation

Several criteria are involved in granting probation. On one level, the statutes of many states determine the factors that a judge should take into account when deciding whether to grant probation. Some states limit the use of probation in serious felony cases and for specific crimes whose penalties are controlled by mandatory sentencing laws. However, the granting of probation to serious felons is not unknown.

Many states have attempted to control judicial discretion by creating guidelines for granting probation. The American Law Institute's **Model Penal Code** standard for probation eligibility is representative of the factors considered before a person is eligible for probation.[9] The code's provisions are listed in Table 15.1.

While these guidelines are often followed by judges, probation decision making is quite varied: an individual offender granted probation in one jurisdiction might not be if tried in another. In addition to being provided for by statutory mandate, probation is often granted by a discretionary decision based on the beliefs and attitudes of the presiding judge and the probation staff.

A significant issue involving eligibility for probation is community supervision of convicted felons. Many people believe that probation is given to minor or first offenders who are deserving of "a break." This is not actually the case. Many serious criminal offenders are given probation sentences. One study of

TABLE 15.1
Suggested Criteria for Granting Probation

1. The court shall deal with a person who has been convicted of a crime without imposing sentence of imprisonment unless, having regard to the nature and circumstances of the crime and the history, character and condition of the defendant, it is of the opinion that his imprisonment is necessary for protection of the public because:
   a. there is undue risk that during the period of a suspended sentence or probation the defendant will commit another crime; or
   b. the defendant is in need of correctional treatment that can be provided most effectively by his commitment to an institution; or
   c. a lesser sentence will depreciate the seriousness of the defendant's crime.
2. The following grounds, while not controlling the direction of the court, shall be accorded weight in favor of withholding sentence of imprisonment:
   a. the defendant's criminal conduct neither caused nor threatened serious harm;
   b. the defendant did not contemplate that his criminal conduct would cause or threaten serious harm;
   c. the defendant acted under a strong provocation;
   d. there were substantial grounds tending to excuse or justify the defendant's criminal conduct, though failing to establish a defense;
   e. the victim of the defendant's criminal conduct induced or facilitated its commission;
   f. the defendant has compensated or will compensate the victim of his criminal conduct for the damage or injury that he sustained;
   g. the defendant has no history of prior delinquency or criminal activity or has led a law-abiding life for a substantial period of time before the commission of the present crime;
   h. the defendant's criminal conduct was the result of circumstances unlikely to recur;
   i. the character and attitudes of the defendant indicate that he is unlikely to commit another crime;
   j. the defendant is particularly likely to respond affirmatively to probationary treatment;
   k. the imprisonment of the defendant would entail excessive hardship to himself or his dependents.
3. When a person has been convicted of a crime and is not sentenced to imprisonment, the court shall place him on probation if he is in need of the supervision, guidance, assistance or direction that the probation service can provide.

SOURCE: American Law Institute, *Model Penal Code* § 7.01. Copyright 1962 by the American Law Institute. Reprinted with the permission of the American Law Institute.

sentencing procedures in twenty-eight large jurisdictions found that about 25 percent of all convicted felons are granted probation, including people convicted on homicide (8 percent), rape (16 percent), robbery (13 percent) and burglary (25 percent) charges.[10] While originally conceived as a way to provide a second chance for young offenders, probation today is also a means of reducing the population pressures on an overcrowded and underfunded correctional system.

Conditions of Probation

A probation sentence is usually viewed as an act of mercy on the part of court and is reflective of the rehabilitative aspects of the criminal justice system. Yet there are two distinct sides to the probationary contract drawn up between the offender and the court. One side involves the treatment and rehabilitation of the offender through regular meetings with trained probation staff or other treatment personnel; the other side reflects the supervision and enforcement aspects of probation. Probation as practiced today often saddles the probationer with rules and conditions that may impede achieving the stated treatment goals of the probation department by emphasizing the punitive aspects of criminal justice.

When probation is fixed as a sentence, the court sets down certain rules as conditions for qualifying for community treatment. In many jurisdictions, statutory law mandates that certain conditions be applied in every probation case; the sentencing judge usually has broad discretion to add to or lessen these standard conditions on a case-by-case basis. A presiding judge may not, of course, impose capricious or cruel conditions, such as requiring an offender to make restitution out of proportion to the seriousness of his or her criminal act. In one case, a federal court rejected a probation order requiring that the offender do sixty-two hundred hours of volunteer time over a three-year period (an amount equivalent to a full-time job).[11] The court used the following test to determine whether probation rules are reasonable:

> First we consider the purposes for which the judge imposed the conditions. If the purposes are permissible, the second step is to determine whether the conditions are reasonably related to the purposes. In conducting the latter inquiry the court examines the impact which the conditions have on the probationer's rights. If the impact is substantially greater than is necessary to carry out the purposes, the conditons are impermissible.[12]

In addition to standard conditions, judges may legally impose on a probationer restrictions tailored both to fit his or her individual needs and to protect society from additional harm.[13] The most common of these special conditions include residential placement, alcohol- or drug-abuse treatment and testing, mental health counseling, house arrest, and community service (the latter two conditions are discussed below); almost half of all probationers are given one or more special conditions.[14]

Some special conditions are tailored to the particular needs of the probationer. A judge may limit the interpersonal relationships a probationer may have if they are potential threats to society; for example, a child molester can be forbidden to associate with minor children.[15] In *United States v. Cothran*, for example, the Eleventh U.S. Court of Appeals upheld a judge's decision to order a probationer banished from the county in which he lived on the grounds that he was a popular figure among drug-using adolescents to whom he sold cocaine; barring him from his residence also gave him an opportunity for a fresh start.[16]

Probationers can be ordered to abstain from using alcohol and illegal drugs and to take chemical tests at the request of their probation officer to determine if they have recently used controlled substances.[17] Some courts have permitted probation officers to demand drug tests even though such testing was not part of the original conditions of probation.[18] Probationers can be required to cooperate with legal authorities; for instance, they may be required to testify against others in grand jury hearings.[19] Similarly, probation rules can require periodic reporting of personal practices; for example, tax violators can be required to submit their tax returns.[20] A common procedure today is to require probationers to make restitution to the victims of their crimes (restitution will be discussed later in this chapter). However, an Illinois appeals court ruled that requiring a probationer to make a public apology in the local newspaper for driving drunk was too punitive and a more drastic rule than those authorized by the state's probation laws.[21]

Courts have upheld probation conditions as long as they are reasonably related to the purposes of probation. Probation conditions may even infringe on some constitutional rights, as long as they are not capricious or cruel.[22] Probationers have a right to challenge rules imposed at the time of sentencing or others imposed later by the court (for example, if the original rules are violated). Some courts have ruled that probationers may bring legal challenges to rules even before they have been charged with their violation.[23]

Administration of Probation Services

Probation services are organized in a variety of different ways, depending on the state and the jurisdiction in which they are located. Some states have a statewide probation service, but each court jurisdiction actually controls the local departments. Other states maintain a strong statewide authority with centralized control and administration. Thirty states combine probation and parole services in a single unit; some combine juvenile and adult probation departments, while others maintain these departments separately.

The typical probation department is situated in a single court district, such as a juvenile, superior, district, or municipal court. The relationship between the department and court personnel (especially the judge) is extremely close.

In the typical department, the **chief probation officer** (CPO) sets policy, supervises hiring, determines training needs, and may personally discuss with or recommend sentencing to the judge. In state-controlled departments, some of the CPO's duties are mandated by the central office; training guidelines, for example, may be determined at the state level. If, on the other hand, the department is locally controlled, the CPO is invested with great discretion in the management of the department.

Most large probation departments also have one or more assistant chiefs. Sometimes, in departments of moderate size, each of these middle managers will be responsible for a particular aspect of probation services: one assistant chief will oversee training; another will supervise treatment and counseling services; another will act as a liaison with police or other agencies. In smaller departments, the CPO and the executive officers may also maintain a caseload or investigate cases for the court. For example, the chief may handle a few of the most difficult cases personally and concentrate on these. In larger municipal departments, however, the probation chief is a purely administrative figure.

The line staff, or the probation officers (POs), may be in direct and personal contact with the entire supervisory staff, or they may be independent from the chief and answer mainly to the assistant chiefs. Line staff perform the following major functions: (1) they supervise or monitor cases assigned to them to ensure that the rules of probation are followed; (2) they attempt to rehabilitate their cases through specialized treatment techniques; (3) they investigate the lives of convicted offenders to enable the court to make intelligent sentencing decisions; (4) they occasionally collect fines due the court or oversee the collection of delinquent payments, such as child support; and (5) they interview complainants and defendants to determine whether criminal action should be taken, whether cases can be decided informally, or whether diversion should be advocated, and so on. This last procedure, called *intake*, is common in juvenile probation.

In some major cities, the probation department is quite complex, controlling detention facilities, treatment programs, research, and evaluation staffs. In such a setting, the CPO's role is similar to that of a director of a multiservice public facility. This CPO rarely comes into direct contact with clients, and his or her behavior, attitudes, and values are quite different from those of the rural CPO who maintains a full caseload.

Duties of Probation Officers

Staff officers in probation departments are usually charged with four primary tasks: investigation, intake, diagnosis, and treatment supervision.

The number of people on probation is growing because the crime rate has resisted prevention and deterrence efforts.

In the investigative stage, the probation officer (PO) conducts an inquiry within the community in an effort to discover the factors related to the criminality of the offender. As was discussed in Chapter 14, the **presentence investigation** is conducted primarily to gain information for judicial sentences, but in the event the offender is placed on probation, the investigation becomes a useful testimony on which to base treatment and supervision.

Intake is a process by which probation officers interview cases that have been summoned to the court for initial appearances. Intake is most commonly used with juvenile offenders but may also be employed in adult misdemeanant cases. During juvenile court intake, the petitioner (i.e., the juvenile) and the complainant (i.e., the private citizen or the police officer) may work with the probation officer to determine an equitable resolution of the case. The PO may settle the case without further court action, recommend restitution or other compensation, initiate actions that result in a court hearing, or recommend unofficial or informal probation.

Diagnosis is the analysis of the probationer's personality and the subsequent development of a personality profile that may be helpful in treating the offender. Diagnosis involves evaluating the probationer based on information from an initial interview (intake) or the presentence investigation for the purpose of planning a proper treatment program. The diagnosis should not merely reflect the desire or purpose of labeling the offender neurotic or psychopathic, for example, but should "codify all that has been learned about the individual, organized in such a way as to privide a means for the establishment of future treatment goals."[24]

Treatment Supervision

Based on a knowledge of psychology, social work, or counseling and the diagnosis of the offender, the probation officer plans a treatment program that will, it is hoped, allow the probationer to fulfill the probation contract and make a reasonable adjustment to the community.

In years past, the probation staff had primary responsibility for supervision and treatment. Probation officers today rarely have "hands-on" treatment responsibility and instead employ the resources of the community to carry out this function. Attitudes toward treatment also seem to be changing. Probation officers seem less interested today in treating clients than in controlling their behavior.[25] Some experts have called for totally eliminating the personal involvement of probation officers in supervising treatment.[26] However, with the increasing number of narcotics abusers in probation caseloads and the lack of effective community-based programs to deal with substance abuse problems, probation officers have been forced to rely on their own skills to provide treatment services. A recent survey of 231 probation departments found that more than half continue to provide hands-on counseling and behavior modification techniques with drug abusers.[27]

The treatment function is a product of both the investigative and diagnostic aspects of probation. It is based on the PO's perceptions of the probationer, including family problems, peer relationships, and employment background. Treatment may also involve the use of community resources. For example, a probation officer who discovers that a client has a drinking problem may find a detoxification center willing to accept the client, while a chronically underemployed offender may be given job counseling or training and a person undergoing severe psychological stress may be placed in a therapeutic treatment program.[28] Or in the case of juvenile delinquency, a probation officer may work with teachers and other school officials to help a young offender stay in school. Of course, most cases do not (or cannot) receive such individualized treatment.

Failure to adequately supervise probationers and determine whether they are obeying the rules of probation can result in the officer and the department being held legally liable for civil damages. For example, a probationer with a history of child molestation attacks a child while working as a school custodian. The probationer's case supervisor could be held legally responsible if he or she had failed to check on the probationer's employment activities.[29]

The proper diagnostic, treatment, and investigative skills needed for effective probation work are difficult to find in a single individual. Probation officers often have social work backgrounds, and a master's degree may be a prerequisite for advancement in large departments. Today, most jurisdictions require officers to have a background in the social sciences and to hold at least a bachelor's degree.

Presentence Investigations

Another important task of probation officers is the investigation and evaluation of defendants coming before the court for sentencing. The court uses presentence investigation reports in deciding whether to grant probation, incarcerate, or use other forms of treatment.

The style and content of presentence investigations may vary among jurisdictions and also among individual probation officers within the same jurisdiction. Some departments require voluminous reports covering every aspect of the defendant's life; other departments, which may be rule-oriented, require that officers stick to the basic facts, such as the defendant's age, race, sex, and previous offense record. Each department also has its own standards for presentence investigations.

At the conclusion of most presentence investigations, a recommendation is made to the presiding judge that reflects the department's sentencing posture on the case at hand. This is a crucial aspect of the report because the probation department's recommendation is followed in many but not all cases. Probation officers make critical decisions when recommending sentences to a judge, and a number of environmental and situational factors are thought to influence their decisions.

One obvious influence on presentence recommendations is the working environment of the department and the court. Close working relationships between the probation department's staff and the chief and between the chief and the trial judge will greatly influence the decision making of junior officers. Dissonance within a department, either among staff members or between staff and administration, may lead to the department having less influence on the kinds of recommendations POs make. In larger departments, where the chief may be functionally separated from the staff and where close personal supervision is rare, guidance in decision making may come from middle managers (assistant chiefs) or more experienced staff.

The personal and individual characteristics of offenders and the clients' relationship to probation officers are also believed to significantly affect the probation officer's recommendations. Among the factors that have been found to influence probation decision making are the probationer's attitude, family data, prior arrest record, gravity of the present offense, interview impression, educational achievement, psychological profile, interests and activities, and involvement in religious activities. Of course, the crime and the offender's prior record play important roles in this decision making.

Presentence investigations are extremely important since the recommendations developed out of them are closely followed by the sentencing judge. Thus, the probation officer exercises discretion similar to that used by a judge in making sentencing decisions.[30] Federal courts have prohibited defendants from suing probation officers who have made errors in their presentence investigations on the grounds that liability "would seriously erode the officers' independent fact finding function and would as a result impair the sentencing judge's ability to carry out his judicial duties."[31]

Risk Classification

One presupervision task related to both the PO's investigation and management functions is **risk classification.** This involves classifying cases chosen for probation on the basis of the clients' particular needs and then assigning the cases to a level and type of probation based on these needs and the risks the clients present to the community. For example, some clients may receive frequent (intensive) supervision, while others are assigned to minimum probation officer monitoring.

While a number of different risk assessments are used, most employ such measures as the offender's age, employment status, drug abuse history, prior felony convictions, and number of address changes in the year prior to sentencing (see Table 15.2).[32]

Does classification make a dramatic difference in the success of probation? Peter Kratcoski evaluated existing programs and found that while classification did not have a substantial impact on reducing recidivism, it may be a useful tool in case management and treatment delivery.[33] The classification of offenders aids the most important goal of supervision: reducing the risk the probationer presents to the community. In addition, classification schemes are in synch with desert-based sentencing models: The most serious cases get the most intensive supervision.[34]

TABLE 15.2
Risk Prediction Scale

Automatic Component: Automatically places an individual in low-activity supervision if two conditions are satisfied.

A. Offender has a twelfth-grade education or better; and
B. The individual has a history free of opiate usage

If the two conditions are not met, the remaining items are scored.

C. Twenty-eight years of age or older at time of offense (7 points) If not, score as 0.
D. Arrest-free period of five or more consecutive years (4 points) If not, score as 0.
E. Few prior arrests (none, one, or two = 10 points) If not, score as 0.
F. History free of opiate usage (9 points) If not, score as 0.
G. At least four months of steady employment immediately prior to arraignment for present offense (3 points) If not, score as 0.

Risk Score	Supervisor Level	Minimum Personal Contacts	Maximum Personal Contacts	Collateral Contacts
Automatic Assignment or 20–33	Low activity	1 per quarter	1 per quarter	Unlimited
0–19	High activity	1 per month	No maximum	Unlimited

SOURCE: Adopted from the Classification and Supervision Planning System, Probation Division, Administrative Office, U.S. Courts, January 1981.

How Successful Is Probation?

Probation is the most commonly used alternative sentence for a number of reasons: it is humane; it helps offenders maintain community and family ties; it is cost effective. While the prison cost per inmate is over twenty thousand dollars per year, the cost of probation runs about two thousand dollars per year (though some programs in California have been found to cost up to six thousand dollars per client annually).[35] While unquestionably inexpensive, is probation successful? If most probation orders fail, the costs of repeated criminality would certainly outweigh the cost savings of a probation sentence.

The evidence documenting the success of probation is mixed. A 1988 federal survey of probation practices in thirty-seven states found that about 81 percent of all people who complete their probation orders could be classified as "successful." Of the 19 percent classified as "failures," about 11 percent are incarceratd for a new offense while the remaining 8 percent either absconded, were discharged to another jurisdiction, or were released because a warrant had been issued against them.[36]

While the typical client completes probation successfully, the most serious offenders may be the ones most likely to commit new crimes. Since felons are commonly granted probation today, this issue is an important one. Tracking the outcome of felony probation was the goal of Joan Petersilia and her colleagues at the Rand Corporation when they traced 1,672 men convicted of felonies and granted probation in Los Angeles and Alameda counties in California.[37] They found that of that total, 1,087 (65 percent) were rearrested; of those rearrested, 853 (51 percent) were convicted; and of those convicted, 568 (34 percent) were sentenced to jail or prison! Of the probationers who had new charges filed against them, 75 percent were charged with burglary, theft, robbery, and other predatory crimes; 18 percent were convicted of serious, violent crimes.

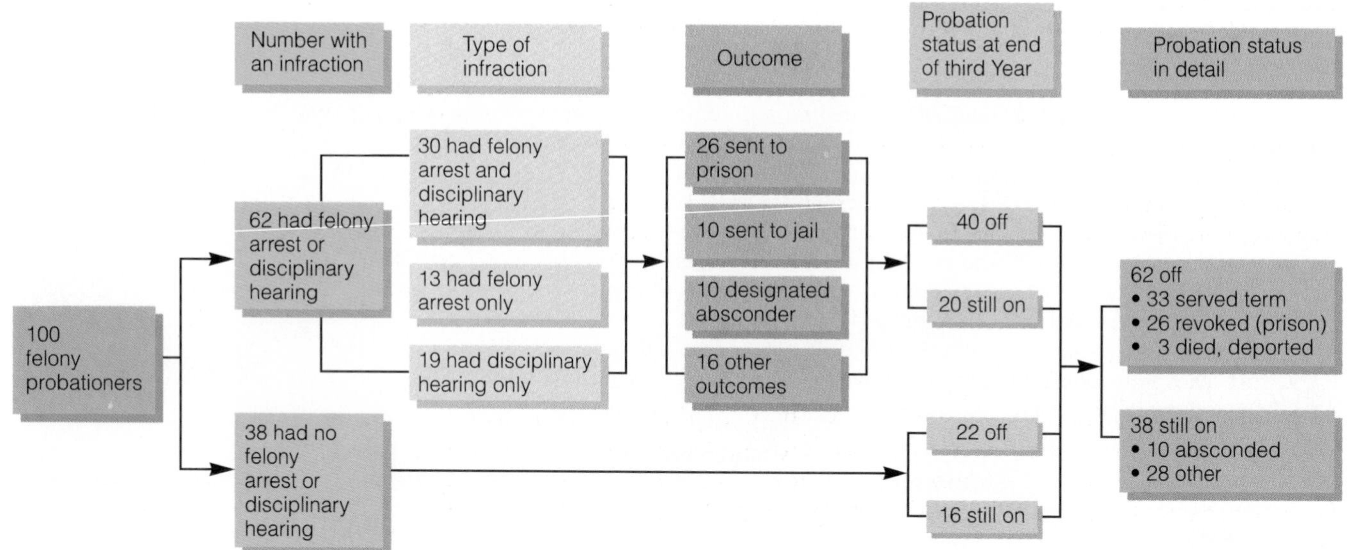

FIGURE 15.1
Probation Outcomes of One Hundred Felons

SOURCE: Patrick Langan and Mark Cuniff, *Recidivism of Felons on Probation,* 1986–1989 (Washington, D.C.: Bureau of Justice Statistics, 1992).

The Rand researchers found that probation is by far the most common sentencing alternative to prison, used in about 60 to 80 percent of all criminal convictions. What is disturbing, however, is that the crimes and criminal records of about 25 percent of all probationers are indistinguishable from those offenders who go to prison.

Another, more recent seventeen-state analysis of felony probation by Patrick Langan and Mark Cuniff also found that community supervision could only be considered a qualified success.[38] About 62 percent of the probationers in their sample of seventy-nine thousand either had a disciplinary hearing for violating a condition of probation or were arrested for another serious criminal offense within three years of their release. Within three years, 46 percent of the probationers had been sent to prison or jail or had absconded from the jurisdiction. This pattern is illustrated in Figure 15.1. Though murderers and rapists were the least likely of all probationers to lapse into criminal behavior, they were the most likely to commit new murders and rapes while on probation. Langan and Cuniff found that probationers who were frequent drug abusers were arrested at a far higher rate (55 percent) than nonabusers (36 percent); drug treatment and testing efforts did not seem to lower recidivism rates. In another analysis, Cuniff and his associates found that the chances of rearrest were associated with risk classification scores: probationers considered the greatest risk were also the ones most likely to be arrested while on probation.[39]

While the recidivism rate of probationers seems high, it is still somewhat lower than the recidivism rate of prison inmates.[40] To improve probation effectiveness, Petersilia and her colleagues suggest that probation be supplemented with more stringent rules, such as curfews, and closer supervision. Even though such measures can dramatically increase the cost of probation, they would still be far less expensive than the cost of incarceration.

While these results indicate the need for improvement, the low cost of probation and its relative effectiveness make it the sentence of choice in almost half of all felony cases, including 6 percent of murder cases, 20 percent of rapes, and 54 percent of felony drug cases.

Legal Rights of Probationers

A number of important legal issues surround probation, one set involving the civil rights of probationers and another involving the rights of probationers during the revocation process.

Civil Rights

The Supreme Court has ruled that probationers have a unique status and therefore are entitled to fewer constitutional protections than other citizens. One area of law involves the Fifth Amendment right of freedom from self-incrimination. The Court dealt with this issue in the case of *Minnesota v. Murphy* (1984).[41] In this case, Murphy was ordered to seek psychological counseling. During his therapy session, he admitted to his counselor that he had engaged in a rape and murder. Murphy's counselor reported this admission to Murphy's probation officer. Though Murphy had earlier been suspected of these crimes, the evidence was insufficient to try him on those charges; his conviction had been on a lesser offense. The probation officer confronted Murphy about the rape and murder, and Murphy admitted that he had committed them. The probation officer brought the information to the police who now had sufficient evidence to bring the case to the prosecutor.

Murphy contested his subsequent conviction on rape and murder on the grounds that the information he gave the probation officer was an in-custody interrogation, and therefore he should have been given the *Miranda* warning. However the Supreme Court disagreed and held that the interrogation was noncustodial and that a probation officer has every right to turn information over to the police. That a probation officer can require a probationer to show up for an interview does not constitute a police arrest; therefore, the self-incrimination protections do not apply.

This case holds that the probation officer-client relationship does not hold a right of confidentiality, as do doctor-patient or attorney-client relationships. Furthermore, the *Murphy* decision held that a probation officer could even use trickery or psychological pressure to get information and turn it over to police.

A second area of law involving probationers is search and seizure. In *Griffin v. Wisconsin*, the Supreme Court held that a probationer's home may be searched without a warrant on the grounds that probation departments "have in mind the welfare of the probationer" and must "respond quickly to evidence of misconduct." The usual legal standards were deemed inapplicable to probation because to do so "would reduce the deterrent effect of the supervisory arrangement" and "the probation agency must be able to act based upon a lesser degree of certainty than the Fourth Amendment would otherwise require in order to intervene before a probationer does damage to himself or society."[42]

Revocation Rights

During the course of a probationary term, a violation of the rules or terms of probation or the commitment of a new crime can result in probation being revoked, at which time the offender may be placed in an institution. Revocation is often not an easy decision, since it conflicts with the treatment philosophy of most probation departments.

When revocation is chosen, the offender is notified, and a formal hearing is scheduled. If the charges against the probationer are upheld, the offender can then be placed in an institution to serve the remainder of the sentence. Most departments will not revoke probation unless the offender commits another crime or seriously violates the rules of probation.

Because placing a person on probation implies that probation will continue unless the probationer commits some major violation, the defendant has been given certain procedural due process rights at this stage of the criminal process. In three significant decisions, the U.S. Supreme Court provided procedural safeguards to apply at proceedings to revoke probation (and parole).

In *Mempa v. Rhay*, in 1967, the Court unanimously held that a probationer was constitutionally entitled to counsel in a revocation-of-probation proceeding where the imposition of sentence had been suspended.[43] Prior to the *Mempa* case, it was traditionally held that a probationer was not entitled to be represented or assisted by counsel at a proceeding to revoke probation.

The *Mempa* case resulted in a variety of judicial interpretations. Most lower-court rulings treated *Mempa* as a sentencing case, limiting its application to probation revocation proceedings involving deferred sentencing, and did not apply it to cases where the probationer was sentenced at the time of the trial. Other courts, however, extended *Mempa* to mean that every probation revocation required counsel because the probation revocation hearing itself was a critical stage needing total due process protection. Thus, some jurisdictions provided counsel to indigent offenders at probation revocation hearings, while others did not.

Then, in 1972, the Supreme Court, in the case of *Morrissey v. Brewer*, handed down an important decision detailing the procedures required for parole revocation.[44] Because the revocations of probation and parole were similar in nature, the standards in the *Morrissey* case affected the probation process as well. In *Morrissey*, the Court required an informal inquiry to determine if there was probable cause to believe the arrested parolee had violated the conditions of parole, as well as a formal revocation hearing with minimum due process requirements. However, in *Morrissey*, the Court did not deal with the issue of right to counsel. Chief Justice Warren Burger stated, "We do not reach or decide the question whether the parolee is entitled to the assistance of retained counsel or to appointed counsel if he is indigent." The *Morrissey* case is discussed further in Chapter 18.

The question of the right to counsel in revocation proceedings did come up again in the 1973 case of *Gagnon v. Scarpelli*.[45] In that decision, which involved a probationer, the Supreme Court held that both probationers and parolees have a constitutionally limited right to counsel in revocation proceedings.

The *Gagnon* case can be viewed as a step forward in the application of constitutional safeguards to the correctional process. It provides some control over the unlimited discretion exercised in the past by probation and parole personnel in revocation proceedings. In practice, almost all states today provide counsel to indigent defendants at probation revocation hearings, while fewer states provide counsel at parole proceedings.

With the development of innovative probation programs, courts have had to review the legality of changing probation rules and their effect on revocation. For example, courts have, in general, upheld the demand that restitution be made to the victim of crime.[46] Since restitution is designed to punish and reform the offender, rather than simply repay the victim, the probationer can be made legally responsible for paying restitution. Similarly, courts have ruled that a probationer could be required to receive psychological counseling unless it forced him or her to undergo drug therapy or to be placed in seclusion.[47]

Future of Probation

Probation will likely continue to be the most popular alternative sentence used by U.S. courts, and if anything, its use as a community-based correction will continue to grow in the 1990s.[48] Part of its appeal stems from its flexibility, which allows it to be coupled with a wide variety of treatment programs, including residential care. As prison overcrowding has grown worse, more than half the states have taken some measures to change their probation guidelines to help reduce the prison population.[49]

Probation will continue to be the sentence of choice in both felony and misdemeanor cases because it holds the promise of great savings in cost at a time when many state budgets are being reduced. At least twenty-five states now impose some form of fee on probationers in order to defray the cost of community corrections. Massachusetts has initiated **day fees,** which are based on the probationer's wages (the usual fee is between one and three days' wages each month).[50] A recent analysis of the probation fee system found that it may actually improve the quality of services afforded clients.[51]

Probation is unquestionably undergoing dramatic changes. Almost a decade ago, some experts began to call for a reevaluation of probation services.[52] They argued that probation should become a central component of a series of **alternative sanctions** that could make community supervision available to all offenders, except for the most serious felons.[53] Probation could be supplemented with an increasingly restrictive series of controls and conditions tailored to match the dangerousness and criminality of the offenders.[54] Moving probation in this direction would be in opposition to the traditional view of probation as a provider of rehabilitative services for convicted offenders who have the capacity to accomplish positive change.[55]

In the past decade, probation has in fact been supplemented and used as a restrictive correctional alternative. Expanding the scope of probation has created a new term, *intermediate sanctions*, to signify penalties that fall between traditional community supervision and confinement in jail or prison. These new correctional services will be discussed in detail below.

Intermediate Sanctions

Community corrections traditionally emphasized offender rehabilitation. The probation officer was viewed as a caseworker or counselor whose primary job was to help the offender adjust to society. Offender surveillance and control seemed more appropriate for law enforcement, jails, and prisons, than for community corrections.[56]

Since 1980, a more conservative justice system has reoriented toward social control. While the rehabilitative ideals of probation have not been abandoned, new programs have been developed that add a control dimension to community corrections. These programs can be viewed as "probation plus," since they add restrictive penalties and/or conditions to community service orders. Being more punitive than probation, **intermediate sanctions** can be sold to conservatives, while they remain attractive to liberals as alternatives to incarceration.[57]

Intermediate sanctions include programs typically administered by probation departments: intensive probation supervision, house arrest, electronic monitoring, restitution orders, shock probation/split sentences, and residential community corrections.[58] Some experts also include high-impact shock incarceration, or "boot camp" experiences, within the definition of intermediate sanctions, but since these programs are typically operated by correctional departments, they are discussed separately in Chapter 16. Intermediate sanctions also involve sentences administered independently of probation staffs: fines and forfeiture, pretrial programs, and pre- and post-trial residential programs. Intermediate sanctions, therefore, range from the barely intrusive, such as restitution orders, to the highly restrictive, such as house arrest accompanied by electronic monitoring and a stay in a community correctional center (see Figure 15.2).

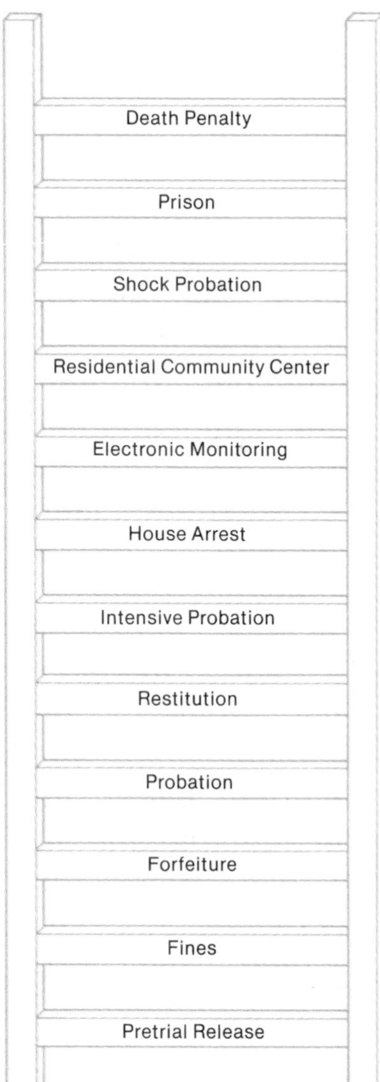

FIGURE 15.2
The Punishment Ladder

The Advantages of Intermediate Sanctions

What are the advantages of creating a system of intermediate sanctions? Primary is the need to develop alternatives to prisons and jails, which have proved to be costly, ineffective, and injurious. Research indicates that more than 60 percent of all prison inmates are rearrested and returned to prison, many within a short period after their release.[59] Little evidence exists that incapacitation is either a general deterrent to crime or a specific deterrent against future criminality. Some correctional systems have become innundated with new inmates. Even states that have extensively used alternative sanctions, such as Florida, have experienced rapid increases in their prison population. Florida courts sentenced twenty-five thousand inmates to alternative sanctions between 1984 and 1990; the pressure on the correctional system if all these defendants had been incarcerated is almost inconceivable.[60]

Intermediate sanctions can also save money. While they are more expensive than traditional community-release methods, they are far less costly than incarceration. If those given alternative sanctions would have otherwise been incarcerated, the extra cost would be significant. In addition, offenders given intermediate sanctions generate income, pay taxes, reimburse victims, perform community service, and provide other cost savings that would be nonexistent had they been incarcerated. Though it is unlikely that intermediate sanctions will pay an immediate "corrections dividend," since many correctional costs are fixed, they may curtail the need for future prison and jail construction.

Intermediate sanctions help meet the need for developing community sentences that are fair, equitable, and proportional.[61] It seems unfair to treat both a rapist and a shoplifter with the same type of community sentence, considering the differences in their crimes. Intermediate sanctions can form the successive steps of a meaningful "ladder" of scaled punishments outside of prison, thereby restoring fairness and equity to nonincarceration sentences.[62] For example, while forgers may be ordered to make restitution to their victims, rapists can be placed in a community correctional facility while they receive counseling at a local psychiatric center. This feature of intermediate sanctions allows judges to fit the punishment to the crime without resorting to a prison sentence. Intermediate sentences can be designed to increase in punishment for people whose serious and/or repeat crimes make a straight probation sentence inappropriate yet for whom a prison sentence would be unduly harsh and counterproductive.[63]

Target Populations

In the broadest sense, intermediate sanctions can serve the needs of a number of different offender groups. The most likely candidates are convicted criminals who would normally be sent to prison but pose either a low risk of recidivism or are of little threat to society (such as nonviolent property offenders). Used in this sense, intermediate sanctions are a viable solution to the critical problem of prison overcrowding.

Intermediate sanctions can also reduce overcrowding in jails by providing alternatives to incarceration for misdemeanants and also to cut the number of pretrial detainees who currently make up about 40 percent of the inmate population.[64] Some forms of bail already require conditions, such as supervision by court officers and periods of home confinement (conditional bail), that are a form of intermediate sanctions.

Intermediate sanctions also can potentially be used as "halfway back" strategies for probation and parole violators. Probationers who violate the conditions of their community release could be placed under increasingly more intensive supervision before actual incarceration is required. Parolees who pose the greatest risk of recidivism might receive conditions that require close monitoring or home confinement. Parole violators could be returned to a community correctional center, rather than to a walled institution.

In the following sections, the forms of intermediate sanctions now used are more thoroughly discussed.

Fines

Fines are monetary payments imposed on offenders as an intermediate punishment for their criminal acts. They are a direct offshoot of the early common law practice of requiring compensation be paid to the victim and the state (wergild) for criminal acts. Fines are still commonly used in Europe, where they are often the sole penalty even in cases involving chronic offenders who commit fairly serious crimes.[65]

In the United States, fines are most commonly used in cases involving misdemeanors and lesser offenses. Fines are also frequently used in felony cases where the offender benefited financially. Investor Ivan Boesky paid over $100 million for violating insider stock trading rules; the firm of Drexel Burnham Lambert paid a fine of $650 million in 1988 for securities violations.[66] A recent study sponsored by the federal government found that lower-court judges impose fines alone or in tandem with other penalties in 86 percent of their cases; superior-court judges imposed fines in 42 percent of their cases.[67]

Fines may be used as a sole sanction or combined with other punishments, such as probation or confinement. Quite commonly, judges levy other monetary sanctions along with fines, such as court costs, public defender fees, probation and treatment fees, and victim restitution, in order to increase the force of the financial punishment.[68] However, there is evidence that many offenders fail to pay fines and that courts are negligent in their efforts to collect unpaid fees; it has been estimated that defendants fail to pay upwards of $2 billion in fines each year![69]

Some jurisdictions, such as New York City, are experimenting with **day fines.**[70] A concept originated in Europe, day fines are geared to an offender's net daily income. In an effort to make them equitable and fairly distributed, fines are based on the severity of the crime weighted by a daily-income value taken from

This boat was forfeited by its owners when authorities found a small quantity of drugs on board.

a chart similar to an income-tax table; the number of the offender's dependents are also taken into account. Several demonstration programs have been set up recently in Bridgeport, Connecticut; Des Moines, Iowa; and Salem, Oregon, to determine the effectiveness of the day fine concept.[71]

Are Fines Effective?

In most jurisdictions, little guidance is given to the sentencing judge directing the imposition of the fine. Judges often have inadequate information on the offender's ability to pay, resulting in defaults and contempt charges. Because the standard sanction for nonpayment is incarceration, many offenders held in local jails are confined for nonpayment of criminal fines. Though the U.S. Supreme Court in *Tate v. Short* (1971) recognized that incarcerating a person who is financially unable to pay a fine discriminates against the poor, many judges continue to incarcerate offenders for noncompliance with financial orders.[72]

Recent research by Margaret Gordon and Daniel Glaser used Los Angeles County Probation Department data to determine the effectiveness of fines. They found that judges seemed to employ fines in a rational and fair manner: low-risk offenders were the ones most likely to receive fines instead of a jail sentence; and the more serious the crime, the higher the amount of the fine. Importantly, while controlling for personal factors and offense, Gordon and Glaser found that offenders who were fined were less likely to commit new crimes than those who received a jail sentence.[73] However, the way fines are calculated needs some fine-tuning. Judicial reliance on offense seriousness to fix the level of financial penalties may have a negative impact on success rates. The more serious the offense and the higher the fine, the greater the chances are of failure to pay the fine and risk probation revocation. The Gordon and Glaser research affirms the importance and effectiveness of fines in the criminal process.

Forfeiture

Another alternative sanction with a financial basis is criminal (*in personam*) and civil (*in rem*) **forfeiture.** Both involve the seizure of goods and instrumentalities related to the commission or outcome of a criminal act. For example, federal law provides that after arresting drug traffickers, the government may seize the boats they used to import the narcotics, the cars they used to carry the drugs overland, the warehouses in which the drugs were stored, and the homes paid for with the drug profits; upon conviction, the drug dealers lose permanent ownership of these "instrumentalities" of crime.

Forfeiture is not a new sanction. During the Middle Ages, "forfeiture of estate" was a mandatory result of most felony convictions. The crown could seize all of a felon's real and personal property. Forfeiture derived from the common law concept of "corruption of blood" or "attaint," which prohibited a felon's family from inheriting or receiving his or her property or estate. The common law mandated that descendants could not inherit property from a relative who may have attained the property illegally: "[T]he Corruption of Blood stops the Course of Regular Descent, as to Estates, over which the Criminal could have no Power, because he never enjoyed them."[74]

Forfeiture was reintroduced to U.S. law with the passage of the Racketeer Influenced and Corrupt Organizations and the Continuing Criminal Enterprises acts, both of which allow the seizure of any property derived from illegal enterprises or conspiracies. While these acts were designed to apply to ongoing criminal conspiracies, such as drug or pornography rings, they now are being applied to a far-ranging series of criminal acts, including white-collar crimes. Though law enforcement officials at first applauded the use of forfeiture as a hard-hitting way of seizing the illegal profits of drug law violators, the practice has been criticized because the government has often been overzealous in its application. For example, million-dollar yachts have been seized because someone aboard possessed a small amount of marijuana; this confiscatory practice is referred to as **zero tolerance.**

David Fried has criticized zero tolerance because it is often used capriciously, the penalty is sometimes disproportionate to the crime involved, and it makes the government "a . . . partner in crime." [75] Fried maintains that the originators of modern criminal forfeiture law originally viewed it as a way of preventing organized-crime figures from invading legitimate businesses, not as a means for the state to unfairly increase punishments and create a new class of "crime victim." He concludes that forfeiture:

> . . . leads to capricious and disproportionate punishments and is capable of dangerously discriminatory application.[76]

Despite these drawbacks, forfeiture likely will continue to be used as an alternative sanction against such selective targets as drug dealers and white-collar criminals.

Restitution

Another popular intermediate sanction is restitution, which can take the form of requiring offenders to either pay back the victims of crime (**monetary restitution**) or serve the community to compensate for their criminal acts (**community-service restitution**).[77] Restitution programs offer offenders a chance to avoid a jail or

prison sentence or a lengthier probationary period. It may help them develop a sense of allegiance to society, better work habits, and some degree of gratitude for being given a second chance. Restitution serves many other purposes, including giving the community something of value without asking it to foot the bill for an incarceration stay and helping victims regain lost property and income.[78] In their seventeen-state survey of probation, Langan and Cuniff found that financial restitution was ordered in about 29 percent of all probation cases and averaged thirty-four-hundred dollars per case; about 60 percent of all orders are paid in full within three years, and in another 11 percent at least something was paid.[79] If monetary restitution is called for, the probation department typically makes a determination of victim loss and develops a plan for paying fair compensation. To avoid the situation in which a well-heeled offender can fill a restitution order by merely writing a check, judges will sometimes order that compensation be paid out of income derived from a low-paid social service or public works job.

New York enacted a special form of restitution in which famous felons are required to turn over the profits from books or films based on their exploits to any victim who could obtain a civil judgment against them within a five-year period. The U.S. Supreme Court recently ruled (1991), however, that these so called "Son of Sam" laws (named after the famous serial killer whose potential earnings from books and films on his crimes prompted the law's passage) was a violation of the First Amendment right of free expression and therefore illegal.[80]

Community-service orders usually require duty in a public nursing home, shelter, hospital, drug treatment unit, or public work program; some young vandals may find that they must clean up the damage they caused to the school or the park. Judges sometimes have difficulty gauging the length of community-service orders. Norval Morris and Michael Tonry argue that the maximum order should be no more than 240 hours and that this should be considered the equivalent of a six-to-twelve-month jail term.[81] Whether these terms are truly equivalent remains a matter of personal opinion.

Judges and probation officers have embraced the concept of restitution because it appears to benefit the victim of crime, the offender, the criminal justice system, and society.[82] Financial restitution is inexpensive to administer, helps avoid stigma, and provides compensation for victims of crime. Offenders ordered to do community service work have been placed in schools, hospitals, and nursing homes. Helping them avoid a jail sentence can mean saving the public thousands of dollars that would have gone to maintaining them in a secure institution, frees up needed resources, and gives the community the feeling that equity has been returned to the justice system.

Does restitution work? Most reviews rate it as a qualified success. A national survey of juvenile restitution programs found that in a single year, some seventeen thousand orders were issued amounting to $2.6 million in monetary restitution, 340,000 hours of community service, and 5,300 hours of direct service (to victims) work.[83] It is estimated that almost 90 percent of the clients successfully completed their restitution orders and that 86 percent had no subsequent contact with the justice system. Other research indicates that those receiving restitution sentences have equal or lower recidivism rates compared to control groups that include those receiving incarceration sentences.[84] Malcolm Feeley and his associates evaluated community-service orders in a federal district court in northern California and found that groups of offenders receiving community service were no more likely to commit new crimes than equivalent groups who had suffered incarceration. The authors conclude that "community service does not hurt and may help—and is certainly cheaper than incarceration."[85]

The original enthusiasm for the restitution concept has been dampened somewhat by concern that it has not lived up to its promise of being an alternative to incarceration. Critics charge that restitution merely serves to "widen the net" and increase the proportion of persons whose behavior is regulated and controlled by the state.[86] Thus, restitution is believed to add to the burden of people who would ordinarily have been given a relatively lenient probation sentence instead of a prison term.[87]

Shock Probation and Split Sentencing

Split sentences and shock probation are alternative sanctions designed to allow judges to grant offenders community release only after they have sampled prison life. These sanctions are based on the premise that if offenders are given a taste of incarceration sufficient to shock them into law-abiding behavior, they will be reluctant to violate the rules of probation or commit another crime.

In a number of states and in the Federal Criminal Code, a jail term can actually be a condition of probation, known as **split sentencing.** Under current federal practices, about 15 percent of all convicted federal offenders receive some form of split sentence, including both prison and jail as a condition of probation; this number is expected to rise to 25 percent as tougher sentencing laws take effect.[88] Cuniff and his associates found that one half of all probationers received a jail term as a condition of probation. California and New York routinely included a jail term as a condition of probation, and in one California jurisdiction (Orange County), 100 percent of the felony probationers also received jail sentences.[89]

Another approach, known as **shock probation,** involves the resentencing of an offender to probation after a short prison stay. The shock comes because the offender originally receives a long maximum sentence but is then eligible for release to community supervision at the discretion of the judge (usually within ninety days of incarceration). About one third of all probationers in the fourteen states that use the program, including Ohio, Kentucky, Idaho, New Jersey, Tennessee, Utah, and Vermont, receive a period of confinement.[90] Evaluations of shock probation have indicated that it is between 78 percent and 91 percent effective.[91]

Some states have linked the short prison stay with a boot camp experience, referred to as shock incarceration, in which young inmates undergo a brief but intense period of military-like training and hard labor designed to impress them with the vigors of prison life.[92] Boot camp programs will be discussed in greater detail in Chapter 16.

Shock probation has been praised as a way to limit prison time, reintegrate the client quickly into the community, maintain family ties, and reduce prison populations and the costs of corrections.[93]

However, granting probation after a jail sentence is frowned on by experts who believe that even a brief period of incarceration can mitigate the purpose of probation, which is to provide the offender with nonstigmatizing community-based treatment. Split sentences defeat the core purpose of probation, which is the earliest possible reintegration of the offender into the community. Short-term commitment subjects probationers to the destructive effects of institutionalization, disrupts their life in the community, and stigmatizes them for having been in jail. Those who disagree with this view, however, argue that an initial jail sentence probably makes offenders more receptive to the conditions of probation, since it amply illustrates the problems they will face if probation is violated.

Intensive Probation Supervision

Intensive probation supervision (IPS) programs are another important form of intermediate sanctions (these programs are also referred to as intensive supervision programs, or ISP). IPS programs, which have been implemented in some form in about forty-five states and today include more than fifty-five thousand clients, involve small caseloads of fifteen to forty clients who are kept under close watch by probation officers.[94] The primary goal of IPS is **diversion:** without intensive supervision, clients would normally be sent to already overcrowded prisons or jails.[95] The second goal is **control:** high-risk offenders can be maintained in the community under much closer security than traditional probation efforts can provide. A third goal is **reintegration:** offenders can maintain community ties and be reoriented toward a more productive life while avoiding the pains of imprisonment.

In general, IPS programs rely on a great degree of client contact to achieve the goals of diversion, control, and reintegration.[96] Most programs have admissions criteria based on the nature of the offense and the offender's criminal background. Some programs, such as New Jersey's, exclude violent offenders; others will not consider substance abusers. In contrast, some jurisdictions, such as Massachusetts, do not exclude offenders based on their prior criminal history. About 60 percent of existing programs exclude offenders who have already violated probation orders or otherwise failed on probation.

IPS programs are used in several ways. In some states, IPS is a direct sentence imposed by a judge; in others, it is a postsentencing alternative used to divert offenders from the correctional system; a third practice is to use IPS as a case management tool to give the local probation staff flexibility in dealing with clients. Other jurisdictions, such as Georgia, use IPS in all three ways in addition to applying it to probation violators to bring them "half-way" back into the community without resorting to a prison term.

IPS in Practice

Numerous IPS programs operate around the United States. The most well-known is Georgia's, which serves as a model for many other states' efforts. Georgia's program includes such measures as:

- five face-to-face contacts per week;
- 132 hours of mandatory community service;
- mandatory curfew;
- mandatory employment;
- weekly check of local arrest records;
- automatic notification of arrest via the State Crime Information Network listing; and
- routine and unnanounced drug and alcohol testing.[97]

An evaluation of the Georgia program by Billie Erwin and Lawrence Bennett gave it generally high marks: it reached its target audience and resulted in a 10 percent reduction in the percent of felons who were incarcerated without a significant increase in the recidivism rate.[98] While IPS is more expensive than a straight probation sentence, it is far less costly than prison. IPS averages about sixteen dollars per day, while prison costs about sixty dollars; in addition, IPS clients are employed, which allows them to save the state additional revenues by paying taxes, making victim restitution, and supporting families.[99]

This youthful offender is performing community service restitution by helping maintain a social service center.

New Jersey's IPS has an active caseload of approximately four hundred nonviolent offenders.[100] It requires that clients be employed and uses a high number of field contacts, including random drug testing, to ensure compliance with rules. It also requires that participants spend a few months in an institution (shock incarceration), perform community service, and obey curfews. An evaluation of the New Jersey program by Frank Pearson shows that IPS works fairly well with felons who are neither dangerous nor habitual criminals. The program saves prison space and is cost-effective, and participants have slightly lower recidivsm rates than would be expected if they had been placed in the general prison population. The savings come to about eight thousand dollars per offender when compared with the cost of ordinary terms of incaceration and parole. The program is being expanded.[101]

How Effective Is IPS?

The New Jersey and Georgia programs are models for IPS programs around the United States. Evaluations indicate they are successful, deliver more services than would normally be received by probationers, are cost-effective, and produce recidivism rates equal to or better than those of offenders who have been confined.[102] However, evaluations have so far not been definitive, often ignoring such issues as whether the program met its stated goals, whether IPS is more attractive than other alternative sanctions, and which types of offenders are particularly suited for IPS. For example, James Byrne and Linda Kelly found in an evaluation of the Massachusetts IPS program that some courts did not fully implement their IPS programs. They also found that the client getting a good job while on IPS was a key to the program's success; clients who could not improve their employment were more likely to commit new crimes, indicating that program success may vary between offender types and groups.[103]

Indications also exist that the failure rate in IPS caseloads is quite high. Michael Agopian evaluated IPS programs in California and found that the failure rate in the IPS caseload was 50 percent.[104] Research conducted by Peter Jones in Kansas found that while IPS was successful in diverting inmates from the correctional system, failure rates were 45 percent within two years, compared to 32 percent for traditional probationers (former inmates committed new crimes at a higher rate, 52 percent).[105] And Langan and Cuniff's seventeen-state survey found that IPS clients had a higher rearrest rate (56 percent) than other probationers.

While these failure rates seem high, IPS programs are designed for clients who have more serious prior records and histories of drug abuse than regular probationers. However, in an important analysis of IPS in three California counties, Joan Petersilia and Susan Turner found that IPS clients were less dangerous than those sent to prison and just as likely to commit new crimes as clients in traditional probation caseloads.[106] IPS is a waste of taxpayers' money if it works no better than traditional probation and serves a similar clientele.

Though evidence that it can significantly reduce offending rates is still insufficient, IPS remains an attractive alternative to traditional correctional methods. However, it can succeed only if it is supported both within the probation organization and by the criminal justice system and the community.[107] While effective leadership is important, IPS can not survive in an atmosphere where people believe it is a device that allows dangerous offenders to remain in the community essentially unsupervised.

House Arrest

A number of states, including Florida, Oklahoma, Oregon, Kentucky, and California, have developed **house arrest** programs as an intermediate sanction. The house arrest concept requires convicted offenders to spend extended periods of time in their own home as an alternative to an incarceration sentence. For example, persons convicted on a drunk driving charge might be sentenced to spend between 6 P.M. Friday and 8 A.M. Monday and every weekday after 5:30 P.M. in their home for the next six months. Current estimates indicate that as many as ten thousand people are placed under house arrest yearly.[108]

As with IPS programs, there is a great deal of variation in house arrest initiatives: some are administered by probation departments, while others are simply judicial sentences monitored by **surveillance officers;** some check clients ten or more times a month, while others do only a few curfew checks; some use twenty-four-hour confinement, while others allow offenders to attend work or school. Regardless of the model used, house arrest programs are designed to be more punitive than IPS or any other community supervision alternative and are considered a "last chance" before prison.[109]

No definitive data exists yet indicating that house arrest is an effective crime deterrent, nor is there sufficient evidence to conclude that it has utility as a device to lower the recidivism rate. Nonetheless, considering its advantages in cost and the overcrowded status of prisons and jails, it is evident that house arrest will continue to grow in the 1990s.

Electronic Monitoring

In order for house arrest to work, sentencing authorities must be assured that arrestees are actually at home during their assigned times. Random calls and visits

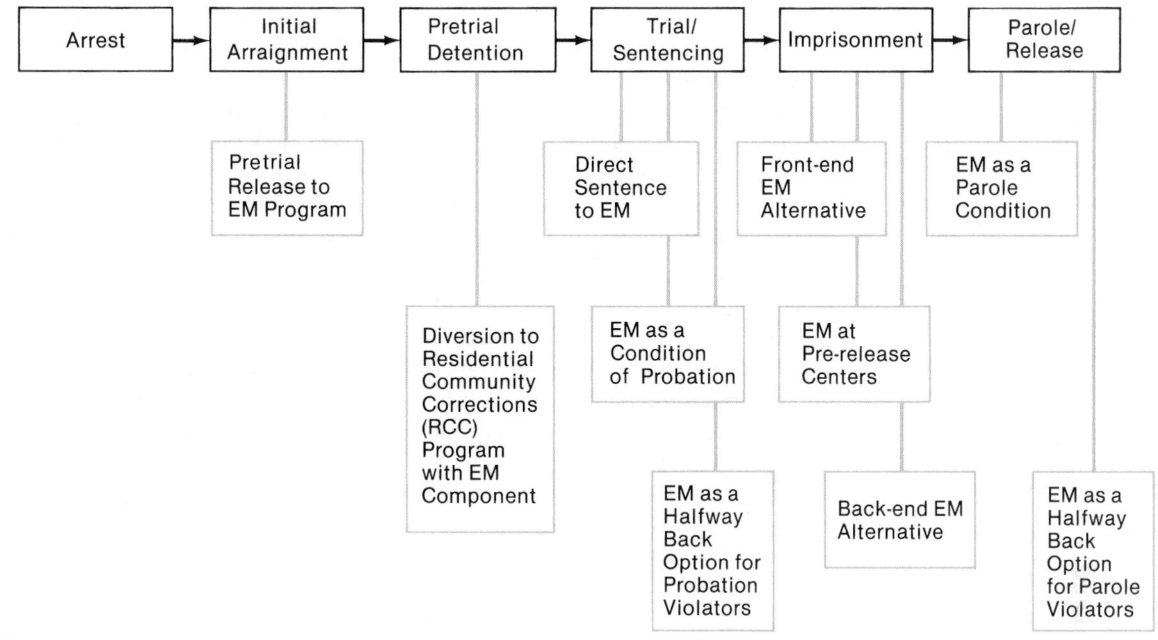

FIGURE 15.3

Key Decision Points Where Electronic Monitoring Programs Are Being Used

SOURCE: James Byrne, Arthur Lurigio, and Christopher Baird, *The Effectiveness of the New Intensive Supervision Programs,* Research in Corrections Series, vol. 2, no. 2 (preliminary unpublished draft; Washington, D.C.: National Institute of Corrections, 1989).

are one way to check on compliance with house arrest orders. However, one of the more interesting developments in the criminal justice system has been the introduction of **electronic monitoring** (EM) devices to manage offender obedience to home confinement orders. EM programs have been around since 1964, when Ralph Schwitzgabel of Harvard University experimented with linking offenders with a central monitoring station.[110] As Figure 15.3 shows, electronic monitoring can be used with offenders at a variety of points in the criminal justice system, ranging from pretrial release to parole. In 1990 there were about twelve to fourteen thousand probationers and an additional thirteen hundred parolees being supervised by electronic monitoring; today the number approaches forty thousand.[111] EM is also being used with pretrial detainess in the federal and state court systems.[112]

Electronically monitored offenders wear devices around their ankles, wrists, or necks that send signals back to a control office. Two basic types of systems are used: active and passive. Active systems constantly monitor offenders by continuously sending a signal back to the central office. If offenders leave their home at an unauthorized time, the signal is broken and the "failure" recorded. In some cases, the control officer is automatically notified electronically through a beeper.

In contrast, passive systems usually involve random phone calls generated by computers to which the offenders have to respond within a particular time (e.g., thirty seconds). Some passive systems require offenders to place their monitoring device into a verifier box that then sends a signal back to the control computer; another approach is to have the arrestee repeat words that are analyzed by a voice verifier and compared to tapes of the client's voice. Other systems employ radio transmitters that receive a signal from a device worn by the offenders and relay it back to the computer monitoring system via telephone lines.

Electronic monitoring combined with house arrest is being hailed as one of the most important developments in correctional policy.[113] Its supporters claim the EM has the benefits of relatively low cost and high security, while at the same time helping offenders avoid the pains of imprisonment in overcrowded, dangerous state facilities. Electronic monitoring is capital- rather than labor-intensive. Since offenders are monitored by computers, an initial investment in hardware rules out the need for hiring many more supervisory officers to handle large numbers of clients.

There are some indications that EM can be an effective addition to the galaxy of alternative sanctions, providing the judiciary with an enhanced supervision tool.[114] Program evaluations with pretrial, probation, and parole groups indicate that recidivism rates are no higher than in traditional programs, costs are lower, and system overcrowding is reduced.[115] Research by Terry Baumer and Robert Mendelsohn found that while almost half of all EM clients were cited for program violations, recidivism rates were quite low and clients found the program valuable and used the opportunity to obtain jobs and improve family relationships.[116]

The Limits of Electronic Monitoring

Electronic monitoring holds the promise of becoming a widely used intermediate sanction in the 1990s. Nevertheless, a few critics charge that the concept has drawbacks that can counterbalance the advantages gained from its provision of low-cost confinement.

First, current technology is limited.[117] Existing systems can be affected by faulty telephone equipment, radio beacons from powerful transmitters, such as those located at airports or radio stations, storms and weather disturbances, and even large concentrations of iron and steel, which can block signals or cause electromagnetic interference. Assessing what the proper response should be when tracking equipment reveals a breach of home confinement is difficult: can we incarcerate someone for what might be an equipment failure?

It may also be inaccurate to assume that electronic monitoring can provide secure confinement at a relatively low cost. In addition to the initial outlay for the cost of equipment, other expenses involved with electronic monitoring include overtime pay for control officers who must be on duty nights or weekends, the cost of training personnel to use the sophisticated equipment, and the cost of educating judges in the legality of home confinement; Joan Petersilia estimates the cost of home confinement with electronic monitoring to be four times greater than that of traditional probation.[118] Most electronic monitoring/house arrest programs do not provide for rehabilitation services, since the focus is on guaranteeing the secure incapacitation of offenders and not their treatment. Ultimately, it may lack the deterrent power of a prison sentence while containing little of the rehabilitative effects of traditional probation.

It is assumed that EM will be used as a cost-saving alternative to jail or prison. As Michael Tonry and Norval Morris point out, alternative sanctions are often directed at offenders who might have received more lenient sentences in the past, thereby "widening the net" of the criminal system of justice.[119] EM will not save money unless it eliminates the need for new jail and prison construction since it is unlikely that staff in existing institutions will be let go because offenders are being monitored in their homes.[120]

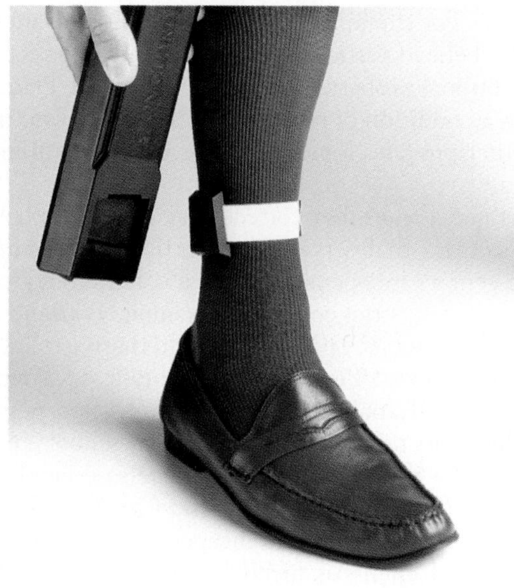

An electronic monitoring device.

Finally, electronic monitoring seems contrary to traditional U.S. values of privacy and liberty. It smacks of the ever-vigilant "big brother" centralized state authority that we deplore in totalitarian societies, such as Iran and China. Do we really want U.S. citizens watched over by a computer? What are the limits of electronic monitoring? Can it be used with mental patients? HIV virus carriers? Suicidal teenagers? Or those considered high-risk future offenders? Our democratic principles make us recoil at the prospect of having our behavior monitored by an all-powerful central government computer. While promising to reduce the correctional population, EM actually has the potential to substantially increase it by turning homes into prisons.[121]

While EM seems to hold great promise, both its effectiveness and its virtue are as yet undetermined. As Ronald Corbett and Gary Marx point out, it is not yet clear whether EM is a correctional savior or a temporary fad.[122]

Residential Community Corrections

The most secure intermediate sanction is a sentence to a residential community corrections (RCC) facility. These programs have been defined by the National Institute of Corrections as:

> a freestanding nonsecure building that is not part of a prison or jail and houses pre-trial and adjudicated adults. The residents regularly depart to work, to attend school, and/or participate in community corrections activities and programs.[123]

The traditional role of community corrections was the nonsecure "halfway house," designed to **reintegrate** soon-to-be-paroled prison inmates back into the community. Inmates spend the last few months in the halfway house acquiring suitable employment, building up cash reserves, obtaining an apartment, and developing a job-related wardrobe.

The traditional concept of community corrections has undergone a recent expansion. Today, the community correctional facility is a vehicle to provide intermediate sanctions as well as a prerelease center for those about to be paroled from the prison system. For example, RCC has been used as a direct sentencing option for judges who believe particular offenders need a correctional alternative halfway between traditional probation and a stay in prison. Placement in a RCC center can be used as a condition of probation for offenders who need a nonsecure community facility that provides a more structured treatment environment than traditional probation.

Probation departments and other correctional authorities have been charged with running RCC centers that serve as a preprison sentencing alternative. In addition, some RCC centers are operated by private, nonprofit groups who receive referrals from the county or district courts. For example, Portland House, a private residential center in Minneapolis, operates as an alternative to incarceration commitment for young adult felony offenders. The twenty-five residents receive group therapy and financial, vocational, educational, family, and personal counseling on a regular basis. Residents may work to earn a high-school equivalency degree. With funds withheld from their earnings at work-release employment, residents pay room and board, family and self support, and income taxes. Portland House appears to be successful. It is significantly cheaper to run than a state institution, and the recidivism rate of clients is much lower than that of those who have gone through traditional correctional programs.[124]

Nexus, in Onamia, Minnesota, accepts males ages thirteen to eighteen who have an intensive history of involvement in the criminal justice system. The Nexus program has a mixed population but provides primary treatment for young sex offenders. Services include treatment for chemical dependency as well as educational, financial, and vocational counseling. Each resident receives a comprehensive individual diagnosis of his treatment needs. The program philosophy stresses adoption of treatments that have a proven track record of success. Residents are often asked to make restitution to the victims of their crime. Nexus is currently expanding. A new residential program has been opened in Dupage County, Illinois, and the Nexus approach is being adapted to a nonresidential program developed in conjunction with social services, court services, mental health agencies and the schools in the Chicago suburbs.[125]

In addition to being a sole sentence and halfway houses, RCC facilities have also been residential pretrial release centers for offenders who are in immediate need of social services before their trial and as halfway-back alternatives for both parole and probation violators who might otherwise have to be imprisoned. In this capacity, RCC programs serve as a base from which offenders can be placed in outpatient psychiatric facilities, drug and alcohol treatment programs, job training, and so on.

Day Reporting Centers (DRC). One recent development has been the use of RCC facilities as **day reporting centers** (DRCs).[126] Day reporting centers provide a single location to which a variety of clients can report for supervision and treatment. Used in Massachusetts, Connecticut, Minnesota, and other locations, DRCs use existing RCC facilities to service nonresidential clients. DRCs can be used as a step-up for probationers who have failed in the community and a step-down in security for jail or prison inmates. For example, the Genesis II in Minneapolis, serves female clients with multiple problems who attend the program five days a week for up to six hours a day. The women have been involved in prostitution and child abuse and may be drug dependent. Genesis II operates a licensed day care center to both care for children while their mothers are in treatment and monitor the youngsters for signs of child abuse. DRCs report better success rates with inmates released from secure confinement (70 to 80 percent) and average success with probationers (50 percent). However, the former may be among the best risks in their groups, while the latter are generally program failures.

There are more than two thousand state-run community-based facilities in use today, serving more than fourteen thousand clients. In addition, up to twenty-five hundred private, nonprofit RCC programs operate in the United States. About half of these are traditional halfway houses, and the remainder are true intermediate sanctions, including about four hundred federally sponsored programs.[127]

Despite the thousands of traditional and innovative RCC programs in operation around the United States, relatively few efforts have been made to evaluate their effectiveness. One reason is that programs differ considerably with respect to target population, treatment alternatives, and goals. While some are rehabilitation-oriented and operate under loose security, others are control-oriented and use such security measures as random drug and alcohol testing.

The Future of Intermediate Sanctions

The rapid increase in the use of community corrections and the variety of alternative sanctions now available reflect the dual correctional concerns of economy and control. On the one hand, the public is concerned about the expensiveness of the criminal justice system. Existing facilities are overcrowded, and budget cutbacks in many states promise little chance of relief. On the other hand, the public wants to feel safe in their homes and protected from predatory criminals. Alternative, community-based sanctions hold the promise of satisfying both needs by being cost-effective crime control strategies without "widening the net" of the criminal justice system.[128] Richard Rosenfeld and Kimberly Kempf suggest that these sanctions fit well with their concept of a "sanctioning budget": a plan to reduce correctional spending by requiring judges to "spend" sanctions from a fixed schedule of sanction levels and types. Judges would not be able to "overdraw" their account without demonstrating exceptional needs and the legislature appropriating additional funds. "Budgeting" punishments would reduce overreliance on incarceration and exploding correctional construction costs.[129]

Alternative sanctions are likely to grow and evolve (though as the following Analyzing Criminal Justice suggests the number of eligible clients may be limited). One approach may be to meet offender needs with a market basket of community corrections. Already there are indications that intermediate sanctions can be made more effective if they are used collectively. For example, program evaluations indicate that electronic monitoring is highly successful when clients are also placed in treatment programs.[130] Annette Jolin and Brian Stipak's evaluation of a community-based drug treatment program for electronically monitored offenders in Oregon found that it was a highly successful alternative to incarceration. Electronic monitoring plus treatment helped lower recidivism rates for a client group that has typically resisted rehabilitation efforts.[131] Another effort in twenty-two Colorado jurisdictions combines electronic monitoring with intensive probation supervision. The program, which also features on-site drug testing, seems to be a successful alternative to prison at a reasonable cost ($2,938 per year).[132] Intensive probation is also being combined with intensive drug treatment programs so that it can be successfully used with high-risk substance abusers. A substance abuse program for probationers being tested in San Diego shows early promise of being a more successful strategy to produce a drug- and crime-free life-style than traditional probation.[133]

ANALYZING CRIMINAL JUSTICE ISSUES

Is There a Need for More Alternative Sanctions?

Though many criminal justice professionals welcome the use of intermediate sanctions as a practical alternative to prison, some experts are skeptical about the ability community sentences have to significantly reduce the correctional population. In a recent publication exploring "myths" about crime and punishment, John DiIulio and Charles Logan make the following argument about the capability of alternative sanctions:

> According to this myth, we could reduce prison crowding, avoid new construction, and cut our annual operating costs if we would just take greater advantage of intensive probation, fines, electronic monitoring, community service, boot camps, wilderness programs, and placement in nonsecure settings like halfway houses.
>
> It is important to distinguish the myth of a supposed need for "alternative" sanctions from the more valid assertion of a need for "intermediate" sanctions. Norval Morris and Michael Tonry, among others, argue that, for the sake of doing justice and achieving proportionality between crime and punishment, we need a greater variety of dispositions that are intermediate in punitivity between imprisonment and simple probation. Most people will find that argument perfectly sensible, even if they disagree about what crimes deserve which intermediate punishments.
>
> The myth that we need more sanctions to use as *alternatives* to imprisonment is based on the false premise that we do not already make the maximum feasible use of *existing* alternatives to imprisonment. Consider, however, the following figures for the most recent available years: (1990)
>
> | | |
> |---|---|
> | 2,356,486 (63%) | on probation |
> | 407,977 (11%) | on parole |
> | 771,243 (21%) | in state and federal prisons |
> | 195,661 (5%) | in jails, post-convicted |
> | 3,731,367 (100%) | Total |
>
> It is true that about two-thirds of convicted felons are sentenced to at least some period of incarceration. (A felony, by definition, is punishable by a year or more in prison.) However, at any time after sentencing and prior to final discharge from the criminal justice system, the great majority of those under correctional supervision (74 percent in the figures above) will be in the community and not incarcerated. In other words, they will be experiencing an "alternative sanction" for at least some part of their sentence.
>
> If one-third of convicted felons receive no incarceration at all, and three-quarters receive at least some time on probation or parole, how much room is left for expanding the use of alternatives to imprisonment? Some, perhaps, but probably not much, especially if you look at offender's prior records when searching for additional convicts to divert or remove from prison. Two-thirds of inmates currently in state prisons were given probation as an alternative sanction one or more times on prior convictions, and over 80 percent have had prior convictions resulting in either probation or incarceration. After how many failures for a given offender do we say that alternatives to imprisonment have been exhausted?
>
> In sum, the idea that we have not given alternatives to imprisonment a fair chance is a myth. Any day of the week you will find three times as many convicts under alternative supervision as you will find under the watchful eye of a warden. And most of those in the warden's custody probably are there at least partly because they did not do well under some prior alternative.

Critical Thinking Skills

1. DiIulio and Logan fail to consider that alternative sanctions seem to work as well as prison at a much lower cost. If non-violent offenders could be monitored in the community as effectively as they are in prison, would it not free up more cells to house dangerous predatory criminals for longer periods of time?

2. DiIulio and Logan use the fact that two-thirds of all inmates have already served probation sentences before their current incarceration as evidence that most inmates have failed in the community, and increasing the frequency of intermediate sanctions would be to no avail. It is unlikely that these inmates were placed in new alternative sanction programs, or were subject to a mix of community control and treatment. While probation has certainly been given a chance, the true value of intermediate sanctions has yet to be measured.

SOURCE: John DiIulio and Charles Logan, "The Ten Deadly Myths About Crime and Punishment in the U.S." Wisconsin Interest 1 (1992) 21–35.

SUMMARY

Probation can be traced to the common law practice of granting clemency to deserving offenders. The modern probation concept was developed by John Augustus of Boston, who personally sponsored two thousand convicted inmates over an eighteen-year period.

Today, probation is the community supervision of convicted offenders by order of the court. It is a sentence reserved for defendants whom the magistrate views as having potential for rehabilitation without needing to serve prison or jail terms. Probation is practiced in every state and by the federal government and includes both adult and juvenile offenders.

In the decision to grant probation, most judges are influenced by their personal views and the presentence reports of the probation staff. Once on probation, the offender must follow a set of rules or conditions, the violation of which may lead to revocation of probation and reinstatement of a prison sentence. These rules vary from state to state but usually involve such demands as refraining from using alcohol or drugs, obeying curfews, and terminating past criminal associations.

Probation officers are usually organized into countywide departments, although some agencies are statewide and others are combined parole-probation departments. Probation departments have instituted a number of innovative programs designed to bring better services to their clients. These include restitution and diversionary programs, intensive probation, and residential probation.

In recent years, the U.S. Supreme Court has granted probationers greater due process rights; today, when the state wishes to revoke probation, it must conduct a full hearing on the matter and provide the probationer with an attorney when that assistance is warranted.

To supplement probation, a whole new family of alternative sanctions has been developed. These range from pretrial diversion and end with residential community corrections. Other widely used alternative sanctions include fines and forfeiture, electronic monitoring by computers, house arrest, and intensive probation supervision. While it is too soon to determine whether these programs are successful, they provide the hope of being low-cost, high-security alternatives to traditional corrections.

QUESTIONS

1. What is the purpose of probation? Identify some conditions of probation, and discuss the responsibilities of the probation officer.
2. Discuss the procedures involved in probation revocation. What are the rights of the probationer?
3. Should probation be a privilege and not a right?
4. Should a convicted criminal make restitution to the victim? When is restitution inappropriate?
5. What are the pros and cons of electronic monitoring?
6. Does house arrest involve a violation of personal freedom?

NOTES

1. Allen Beck and Bernard Shipley, *Recidivism of Young Parolees* (Washington, D.C.: Bureau of Justice Statistics, 1987), p. 1.
2. Louis Jankowski, *Probation and Parole, 1990* (Washington, D.C.: Bureau of Justice Statistics, 1991), p. 1.
3. Ibid., p. 20.
4. David Rothman, *Conscience and Convenience* (Boston: Little, Brown & Co., 1980), pp. 82–117.
5. See, generally, Todd Clear and Vincent O'Leary, *Controlling the Offender in the Community* (Lexington, Mass.: Lexington Books, 1983).
6. Lawrence Greenfeld, *Probation and Parole, 1987* (Washington, D.C.: Bureau of Justice Statistics, 1988), p. 20.
7. Ibid.
8. Mark Cuniff, Dale Sechrest, and Robert Cushman, "Redefining Probation for the Coming Decade" (Paper presented at the annual meeting of the American Society of Criminology, San Francisco, November 1991), pp. 7–8.
9. American Law Institute, *Model Penal Code*, Proposed Official Draft, § 7.01. Copyright 1962 by the American Law Institute. Reprinted with the permission of the American Law Institute.
10. Mark Cuniff, *Sentencing Outcomes in Twenty-Eight Felony Courts, 1985* (Washington, D.C.: National Institute of Justice, 1987), p. 5.
11. *Higdon v. United States*, 627 F.2d 893 (9th Cir. 1980).
12. Ibid., at 897.
13. Jerome Weissman, "Constitutional Primer on Modern Probation Conditions," *New England Journal on Prison Law* 8 (1982):367–93.
14. Patrick Langan and Mark Cuniff, *Recidivism of Felons on Probation, 1986–1989* (Washington, D.C.: Bureau of Justice Statistics, 1992).
15. *Ramaker v. State*, 73 Wis.2d 563, 243 N.W.2d 534 (1976).

16. *United States v. Cothran*, 855 F.2d 749 (11th Cir. 1988).

17. *State v.* McCoy, 45 N.C.App. 686, 263 S.E.2d 801 (1980).

18. *United States v. Duff*, 831 F.2d 176 (9th Cir. 1987).

19. *United States v. Pierce*, 561 F.2d 735 (9th Cir. 1977), *cert. denied* 435 U.S. 923, 98 S.Ct.1486, 55 L.Ed.2d 516 (1978).

20. *United States v. Kahl*, 583 F.2d 1351 (5th Cir. 1978); see also Harvey Jaffe, "Probation with a Flair: A Look at Some Out-of-the-Ordinary Conditions," *Federal Probation* 33 (1979):29.

21. *People v. Johnson*, 175 Ill.App.3d 908, 125 Ill. Dec. 469, 530 N.E.2d 627 (1988).

22. *United States v. Williams*, 787 F.2d 1182 (7th Cir. 1986).

23. *United States v. Ofchinick*, 937 F.2d 892 (1991).

24. Ibid.

25. Patricia Harris, Todd Clear, and S. Christopher Baird, "Have Community Supervision Officers Changed Their Attitudes Toward Their Work?" *Justice Quarterly* 6 (1989):233–46.

26. John Rosencrance, Probation Supervision: Mission Impossible," *Federal Probation* 50 (1986):25–31.

27. "Drug Treatment Role Increasing for Probation, Parole Agencies," *Criminal Justice Newsletter* 49 (9 September 1988):6.

28. For example, see John Vandeusen, Joseph Yarbrough, and David Cornelson, "Short-Term System Therapy with Adult Probation Clients and Their Families," *Federal Probation* 49 (1985):21–26.

29. Richard Sluder and Rolando Del Carmen, "Are Probation and Parole Officers Liable for Injuries Caused by Probationers and Parolees?" *Federal Probation* 54 (1990):3–12.

30. *Turner v. Barry*, 856 F.2d 1539 (D.C. Cir. 1988).

31. Ibid., at 1538.

32. Cuniff, Sechrest, and Cushman, "Redefining Probation for the Coming Decade."

33. Peter Kratcoski, "The Functions of Classification Models in Probation and Parole: Control or Treatment-Rehabilitation," *Federal Probation* 49 (1985):49–56.

34. Clear and O'Leary, *Controlling the Offender in the Community*, pp. 11–29, 77–100.

35. Joan Petersilia, "An Evaluation of Intensive Probation in California," *Journal of Criminal Law and Criminology* 82 (1992): 610–58 at 648.

36. Greenfield, *Probation and Parole, 1987*.

37. Joan Petersilia, Susan Turner, James Kahan, and Joyce Peterson, *Granting Felons Probation: Public Risks and Alternatives* (Santa Monica, Calif.: Rand Corp., 1985).

38. Patrick Langan and Mark Cuniff, *Recidivism of Felons on Probation, 1986–1989* (Washington, D.C.: Bureau of Justice Statistics, 1992).

39. Cuniff, Sechrest, and Cushman, "Redefining Probation for the Coming Decade," pp. 7–8.

40. Langan and Cuniff, *Recidivism of Felons on Probation, 1986–1989*; Allen Beck and Bernard Shipley, *Recidivism of Prisoners Released in 1983* (Washington, D.C.: Bureau of Justice Statistics, 1989).

41. 465 U.S. 420, 104 S.Ct. 1136, 79 L.Ed.2d 409 (1984).

42. 483 U.S. 868, 107 S.Ct. 3164, 97 L.Ed.2d 709 (1987).

43. 389 U.S. 128, 88 S.Ct. 254, 19 L.Ed.2d 336 (1967).

44. 408 U.S. 471, 92 S.Ct. 2593, 33 L.Ed.2d 484 (1972).

45. 411 U.S. 778, 93 S.Ct. 1756, 36 L.Ed.2d 656 (1973).

46. *United States v. Carson*, 669 F.2d 216 (5th Cir. 1982).

47. 31 Cr.L. 2081 (1982).

48. Vincent O'Leary, "Probation: A System in Change," *Federal Probation* 51 (1987):8–11.

49. Peter Finn, "Prison Crowding: The Response of Probation and Parole," *Crime and Delinquency* 30 (1984):141–53.

50. "Law in Massachusetts Requires Probationers to Pay 'Day Fees'," *Criminal Justice Newsletter* 49 (15 September 1988):1.

51. Gerald Wheeler, Therese Macan, Rodney Hissong, and Morgan Slusher, "The Effects of Probation Service Fees on Case Management Strategy and Sanctions," *Journal of Criminal Justice* 17 (1989):15–24.

52. Patrick McAnany, Douglas Thomson, and David Fogel, eds., *Probation and Justice: Reconsideration of Mission* (Cambridge, Mass.: Oelgeschlager, Gunn and Hain, 1984).

53. Patrick McAnany, "Mission and Justice: Clarifying Probation's Legal Context," in *Probation and Justice: Reconsideration of Mission*, ed. Patrick McAnany, Douglas Thomson, and David Fogel (Cambridge, Mass.: Oelgeschlager, Gunn and Hain, 1984), pp. 39–63.

54. David Fogel, "The Emergence of Probation as a Profession in the Service of Public Safety: The Next Ten Years," in *Probation and Justice: Reconsideration of Mission*, ed. Patrick McAnany, Douglas Thomson and David Fogel (Cambridge, Mass.: Oelgeschlager, Gunn and Hain, 1984), pp. 65–99.

55. John Conrad, "The Redefinition of Probation: Drastic Proposals to Solve an Urgent Problem," in *Probation and Justice: Reconsideration of Mission*, ed. Patrick McAnany, Douglas Thomson, and David Fogel (Cambridge, Mass.: Oelgeschlager, Gunn and Hain, 1984), pp. 251–73.

56. Richard Lawrence, "Reexamining Community Corrections Models," *Crime and Delinquency* 37 (1991):449–64.

57. Todd Clear and Patricia Hardyman, "The New Intensive Supervision Movement," *Crime and Delinquency* 36 (1990):42–60.

58. For a thorough review of these programs, see James Byrne, Arthur Lurigio, and Joan Petersilia, eds., *Smart Sentencing: The Emergence of Intermediate Sanctions* (Newbury Park, Calif.: Sage Publications, in press). Hereinafter cited as *Smart Sentencing*.

59. Beck and Shipley, *Recidivism of Prisoners Released in 1983*.

60. S. Christopher Baird and Dennis Wagner, "Measuring Diversion: The Florida Community Control Program," *Crime and Delinquency* 36 (1990):112–25.

61. Norval Morris and Michael Tonry, *Between Prison and Probation* Intermediate Punishments in a Rational Sentencing System (New York: Oxford University Press, 1990).

62. Michael Tonry and Richard Will, *Intermediate Sanctions* (Washington, D.C.: National Institute of Justice, 1990).

63. Ibid., p. 8.

64. Michael Maxfield and Terry Baumer, "Home Detention with Electronic Monitoring: Comparing Pretrial and Postconviction Programs," *Crime and Delinquency* 36 (1990):521–56.

65. Sally Hillsman and Judith Greene, "Tailoring Fines to the Financial Means of Offenders," *Judicature* 72 (1988):38–45.

66. David Pauly and Carolyn Friday, "Drexel's Crumbling Defense," *Newsweek*, 19 December 1988, p. 44.

67. George Cole, Barry Mahoney, Marlene Thorton, and Roger Hanson, *The Practices and Attitudes of Trial Court Judges Regarding Fines as a Criminal Sanction* (Washington, D.C.: U.S. Government Printing Office, 1987).

68. Ibid.

69. George Cole, "Monetary Sanctions: The Problem of Compliance," in *Smart Sentencing*.

70. " 'Day Fines' Being Tested in a New York City Court," *Criminal Justice Newsletter* (1 September 1988):4–5.

71. Wade Lambert, "Three States, Seeking Alternatives to Jail, Will Test Fines Tied to Criminals' Income," *Wall Street Journal* 12 December 1991, p. 1B.

72. 401 U.S. 395, 91 S.Ct. 668, 28 L.Ed.2d 130 (1971).

73. Margaret Gordon and Daniel Glaser, "The Use and Effects of Financial Penalties in Municipal Courts," *Criminology* 29 (1991):651–76.

74. C. Yorke, "Some Consideration on the Law of Forfeiture for High Treason 2d ed. (1746), p. 26; cited in David Freid, "Rationalizing Criminal Forfeiture," *Journal of Criminal Law and Criminology* 79 (1988):328–436 at 329.

75. David Fried, "Rationalizing Criminal Forfeiture," *Journal of Criminal*

Law and Criminology 79 (1988):328–436, at 436.
76. Ibid., p. 436.
77. For a general review, see Burt Galaway and Joe Hudson, *Criminal Justice, Restitution, and Reconciliation* (New York: Criminal Justice Press, 1990); Robert Carter, Jay Cocks, and Daniel Glazer, "Community Service: A Review of the Basic Issues, *Federal Probation* 51 (1987):4–11.
78. Douglas McDonald, "Punishing Labor: Unpaid Community Service as a Criminal Sentence," in *Smart Sentencing*.
79. Langan and Cuniff, *Recidivism of Felons on Probation, 1986–1989*, p. 1.
80. *Simon and Schuster v. Members of New York State Crime Victims Board*, ___ U.S. ___, 112 S.Ct. 501, 116 L.Ed.2d 476 (1991).
81. Morris and Tonry, *Between Prison and Probation: Intermediate Punishments in a Rational Sentencing System*, pp. 171–75.
82. Frederick Allen and Harvey Treger, "Community Service Orders in Federal Probation: Perceptions of Probationers and Host Agencies," *Federal Probation* 54 (1990):8–14.
83. Peter Schneider, Anne Schneider, and William Griffith, *Monthly Report of the National Juvenile Restitution Evaluation Project V* (Eugene, Ore.: Institute for Policy Analysis, 1981).
84. Anne Schneider, "Restitution and Recidivism Rates of Juvenile Offenders: Four Experimental Studies," *Criminology* 24 (1986):533–52.
85. Malcolm Feeley, Richard Berk, and Alec Campbell, "Community Service Orders in the Northern District of California" (Paper presented at the annual meeting of the American Society of Criminology, San Francisco, November 1991).
86. James Austin and Barry Krisberg, "The Unmet Promise of Alternatives to Incarceration," *Crime and Delinquency* 28 (1982):374–409.
87. Alan Harland, "Court-Ordered Community Service in Criminal Law: The Continuing Tyranny of Benevolence," *Buffalo Law Review* (Summer 1980):425–86.
88. Michael Block and William Rhodes, *The Impact of Federal Sentencing Guidelines* (Washington, D.C.: National Institute of Justice, 1987).
89. Cuniff, Sechrest, and Cushman, "Redefining Probation for the Coming Decade," p. 6.
90. Jankowski, *Probation and Parole 1990* (Washington, D.C.: Bureau of Justice Statistics, 1991), p. 2.
91. Harry Allen, Chris Eskridge, Edward Latessa, and Gennaro Vito, *Probation and Parole in America* (New York: Free Press, 1985), p. 88.
92. Joan Petersilia, *The Influence of Criminal Justice Research* (Santa Monica, Calif.: Rand Corp., 1987).
93. Ibid.
94. James Byrne, Arthur Lurigio, and Christopher Baird, *The Effectiveness of the New Intensive Supervision Programs*, Research in Corrections Series, vol. 2, no. 2 (preliminary unpublished draft; Washington, D.C.: National Institute of Corrections, 1989), p. 16; Jankowski, *Probation and Parole, 1990*, p. 4.
95. Stephen Gettinger, "Intensive Supervision: Can It Rehabilitate Probation?" *Corrections Magazine* 9 (April 1983):7–18.
96. Byrne, Lurigio, and Baird, *The Effectiveness of the New Intensive Supervision Programs*.
97. Billie Erwin and Lawrence Bennett, *New Dimensions in Probation: Georgia's Experience with Intensive Probation Supervision (IPS)* (Washington, D.C.: National Institute of Justice, 1987).
98. Ibid.
99. Frank Pearson and Alice Glasel Harper, "Contingent Intermediate Sentences: New Jersey's Intensive Supervision Program," *Crime and Delinquency* 36 (1990):75–86.
100. Frank Pearson, "Evaluation of New Jersey's Intensive Supervision Program," *Crime and Delinquency* 34 (1988):437–48.
101. Pearson and Harper, "Contingent Intermediate Services: New Jersey's Intensive Supervision Program," pp. 83–85.
102. Edward Latessa and Gennaro Vito, "The Effects of Intensive Supervision on Shock Probationers," *Journal of Criminal Justice* 16 (1988):319–30.
103. James Byrne and Linda Kelly, *Restructuring Probation as an Intermediate Sanction: An Evaluation of the Massachusetts Intensive Probation Supervision Program* (Final Report to the National Institute of Justice, Research Program on the Punishment and Control of Offenders, Washington, D.C., 1989).
104. Michael Agopian, "The Impact of Intensive Supervision Probation on Gang-Drug Offenders," *Criminal Justice Policy Review* 4 (1990):214–22.
105. Peter Jones, "Expanding the Use of Noncustodial Sentencing Options: An Evaluation of the Kansas Community Corrections Act," *Howard Journal* 29 (1990):114–29.
106. Joan Petersilia, "Comparing Intensive and Regular Supervision for High-Risk Probationers: Early Results from Experiment in California," *Crime and Delinquency* 36 (1990):87–111.
107. Joan Petersilia, "Conditions That Permit Intensive Supervision Programs to Survive," *Crime and Delinquency* 36 (1990):126–45.
108. Ibid., p. 128.
109. Joan Petersilia, *Expanding Options for Criminal Sentencing* (Santa Monica, Calif.: Rand Corp., 1987), 32.
110. Marc Renzema, "Home Confinement Programs: Development, Implementation and Impact," in *Smart Sentencing*.
111. Jankowski, *Probation and Parole, 1990*, p. 4; Annesley Schmidt, "Electronic Monitors—Realistically, What Can Be Expected?" *Federal Probation* 55 (1991):47–53, Personal communication with Joseph Vaughn, Central Missouri State College, July 16, 1992.
112. Timothy Cadigan, "Electronic Monitoring in Federal Pretrial Release," *Federal Probation* 55 (1991):26–30.
113. Kenneth Moran and Charles Lindner, "Probation and the Hi-Technology Revolution: Is Reconceptualization of the Traditional Probation Officer Role Model Inevitable?" *Criminal Justice Review* 3 (1987):25–32.
114. Joseph Papy and Richard Nimer, "Electronic Monitoring in Florida," *Federal Probation* 55 (1991):31–33.
115. James Beck, Jody Klein-Saffran, and Harold Wooten, "Home Confinement and the Use of Electronic Monitoring with Federal Parolees," *Federal Probation* 54 (1990):22–31.
116. Terry Baumer and Robert Mendelsohn, "Electronically Monitored Home Confinement: Does It Work?" in *Smart Sentencing*.
117. Schmidt, "Electronic Monitors—Realistically, What Can Be Expected?"; James Byrne, Linda Kelly, and Susan Guarino-Ghezzi, "An Examination of the Use of Electronic Monitoring in the Criminal Justice System," *Perspectives* (Spring 1988):30–37.
118. Joan Petersilia, "Exploring the Option of House Arrest," *Federal Probation* (1986):50–55.
119. Morris and Tonry, *Between Prison and Probation*.
120. Schmidt, "Electronic Monitors—Realistically, What Can be Expected," p. 51.
121. Richard Rosenfeld, "The Scope and Purposes of Corrections: Exploring Alternative Responses to Crowding," *Crime and Delinquency* 37 (1991):500.
122. For a more complete analysis of the EM controversy, see Ronald Corbett and Gary Marx, "Critique: No Soul in the New Machine: Technofallacies in the Electronic Monitoring Movement," *Justice Quarterly* 8 (1991):399–414.
123. National Institute of Correction, 1987, p. 1.
124. Updated with personal correspondence with Jan Cartalucca, administrative assistant, and Tom Hayden, director, 8 January 1992.
125. Personal correspondence with Glen Just, Ph.D., executive director, Jan. 15, 1992.
126. Dale Parent, *Day Reporting Centers for Criminal Offenders—A Descriptive Analysis of Existing Programs* (Washington, D.C.: National Institute of Justice, 1990); Jack McDevitt and Robyn Miliano, "Day Reporting Cen-

ters: An Innovative Concept in Intermediate Sanctions," in *Smart Sentencing*.

127. For a description of these programs, see Edward Latessa and Lawrence Travis III, "Residential Community Correctional Programs," in *Smart Sentencing*; see also, Byrne and Kelly, *Restructuring Probation as an Intermediate Sanction: An Evaluation of the Massachusetts Intensive Probation Supervision Program*.

128. Peter R. Jones, "Community Corrections in Kansas: Extending Community-Based Corrections or Widening the Net?" *Journal of Research in Crime and Delinquemcy* 27 (1990):79–101.

129. Richard Rosenfeld and Kimberly Kempf, "The Scope and Purposes of Corrections: Exploring Alternative Responses to Crowding," *Crime and Delinquency* 37 (1991):481–505.

130. Joan Petersilia and Susan Turner, *Intensive Supervision for High-Risk Probationers* (Santa Monica, Calif.: Rand Corp., 1990).

131. Annette Jolin and Brian Stipak, "Drug Treatment and Electronically Monitored Home Confinement: An Evaluation of a Community-Based Sentencing Option" (Paper presented at the annual meeting of the American Society of Criminology, San Francisco, November 1991).

132. V. Fogg, "Expanding the Sanction Range of ISP Programs: A Report on Electronic Monitoring, *Journal of Offender Monitoring* 3 (1990):12–13, 16, 18.

Correctional History and Institutions

CHAPTER 16

OUTLINE

KEY TERMS

secure corrections
jails
reformatories
prisons
recidivism
hulks
John Howard
Walnut Street Jail
penitentiary house
tier system
congregate system
Auburn system
contract system
convict-lease system
Z. R. Brockway
Mutual Welfare League
medical model
reintegrated
maximum-security prisons
maxi-maxi prisons
medium-security prisons
minimum-security prisons
shock incarceration
boot camp
community corrections
halfway houses

When a person is convicted for a criminal offense, state and federal governments through their sentencing authority reserve the right to institutionally confine the offender for a period of time. The system of **secure corrections** comprises the entire range of treatment and/or punishment options available to the government, including community residential centers, **jails, reformatories,** and penal institutions (**prisons**).

Correctional treatment is currently practiced on federal, state, and local county levels of government. Felons may be placed in state or federal penitentiaries (prisons), which are usually isolated, fortress-like structures; misdemeanants are housed in county jails, sometimes called reformatories or houses of correction; and juvenile offenders have their own institutions, sometimes euphemistically called schools, camps, ranches, or homes. Typically, the latter are nonsecure facilities, often located in rural areas, that provide both confinement and rehabilitative services for young offenders.

Other types of correctional institutions include ranches and farms for adult offenders and community correctional settings, such as halfway houses, for inmates who are about to return to society. Today's correctional facilities encompass a wide range, from maximum security institutions, such as Cedar Junction Prison in Walpole, Massachusetts, to low-security camps that house white-collar criminals convicted of such crimes as insider trading and mail fraud.

One of the great tragedies of our time is that correctional institutions, whatever form they may take, do not seem to correct. They are, in most instances, overcrowded, understaffed, outdated warehouses for social outcasts. The overcrowding crisis is the most significant problem faced by the prison today: prisons now contain more than eight hundred thousand inmates. Prisons are more suited to control, punishment, and security than to rehabilitation and treatment. It is a sad but unfortunately accurate assessment that today's correctional institution has become a revolving door and that all too many of its residents return time and again. Although no completely accurate statement of the **recidivism** rate is available, it is estimated that about half of all inmates will be back in prison within six years of their release.[1]

Despite the apparent lack of success of penal institutions, great debate continues over the direction of their future operations. There are penal experts who maintain that prisons and jails are not really places for rehabilitation and treatment but should be used to keep dangerous offenders apart from society and give them the "just deserts" for their crimes.[2] In this sense, prison success would be measured by such factors as physical security, length of incapacitation, relationship between the crime rate and the number of incarcerated felons, and inmate perceptions that their treatment was fair and proportionate. The dominance of this correctional philosophy is illustrated by the facts that (1) presumptive and mandatory sentencing structures are now used in such traditionally progressive states as California, Massachusetts, and Illinois; (2) the number of people under lock and key has risen rapidly in the past few years; and (3) political candidates who are portrayed by their opponents as advocates of inmate rehabilitation soon find themselves on the defensive with voters.

While the conservative tide in corrections is self-evident, many penal experts still maintain that prisons can be useful places for offender rehabilitation.[3] Many examples of the treatment philosophy still flourish in prisons: educational programs allow inmates to get college credits; vocational training has become more sophisticated; counseling and substance abuse programs are almost universal; and every state maintains some type of early-release and community correctional programs.

In this chapter, we will explore the correctional system, beginning with the history and nature of correctional institutions. Then in Chapter 17, institutional life will be examined in some detail. Chapter 18 discusses how inmates leave the correctional system and the problems they face when they return to society.

History of Correctional Institutions

As you may recall, the original legal punishments were typically banishment or slavery, restitution (wergild), corporal punishment, and execution. The concept of incarcerating convicted offenders for long periods of time as a punishment for their misdeeds did not become the norm of corrections until the nineteenth century.[4]

While the use of incarceration as a routine punishment began much later, some very early European institutions were created specifically to detain and punish criminal offenders. Penal institutions were actually constructed in England during the tenth century to hold pretrial detainees and those waiting for their sentence to be carried out.[5] During the twelfth century, King Henry II of England constructed a series of county jails to hold thieves and vagrants prior to the disposition of their sentence. In 1557, the workhouse in Brideswell, England, was built to hold people convicted of relatively minor offenses who would work to pay off their debt to society; those committing more serious offenses were held there prior to their execution.

Le Stinche, a prison in Florence, Italy, was used to punish offenders as early as 1301.[6] Prisoners were enclosed in separate cells, classified on the basis of gender, age, mental state, and crime seriousness. Furloughs and conditional release were permitted, and perhaps for the first time, a period of incarceration replaced corporal punishment for some offenses. Though Le Stinche existed for five hundred years, relatively little is known about its administration or whether this early example of incarceration was unique to Florence.

The first penal institutions were foul places devoid of proper care, food, or medical treatment. The jailer, usually a shire reeve (sheriff), an official appointed by king or noble landholder as chief law enforcement official of a county, ran the jail under the "fee system." This required inmates to pay for their own food and services. Those who could not pay were fed scraps until they literally starved to death:

> In 1748 the admission to Southwark prison was eleven shillings and four pence. Having got in, the prisoner had to pay for having himself put in irons, for his

> bed, of whatever sort, for his room if he was able to afford a separate room. He had to pay for his food, and when he had paid his debts and was ready to go out, he had to pay for having his irons struck off, and a discharge fee . . . The gaolers [jailers] were usually "low bred, mercenary and oppressive, barbarous fellows, who think of nothing but enriching themselves by the most cruel extortion, and have less regard for the life of a poor prisoner than for the life of a brute."[7]

Jail conditions were deplorable because jailers ran them for personal gain; the fewer the services provided, the greater their profit. Early jails were catchall institutions that held not only criminal offenders awaiting trial but vagabonds, debtors, the mentally ill, and assorted others.

From 1776 to 1785, a growing inmate population that could not longer be transported to North America forced the English to house prisoners on **hulks,** abandoned ships anchored in harbors. The hulks became infamous for their degrading conditions and brutal punishments but were not totally abandoned until 1858.

The writings of **John Howard,** the reform-oriented sheriff of Bedfordshire, drew attention to the squalid conditions in British penal institutions. His famous book, *The State of Prisons,* published in 1777, condemned the lack of basic care given English inmates awaiting trial or serving sentences.[8] Howard's efforts to create humane standards in the British penal system resulted in the Penitentiary Act in which Parliament established a more orderly penal system, with periodic inspections, elimination of the fee system, and greater consideration for inmates.

American Developments

Though Europe had jails and a variety of other penal facilities, it was in the United States that correctional reform was first instituted. The first American jail was built in James City in the Virginia colonies in the early seventeenth century. However, the "modern" American correctional system had its origin in Pennsylvania under the leadership of William Penn.

At the end of the seventeenth century, Penn revised Pennsylvania's criminal code to forbid torture and the capricious use of mutilation and physical punishment. These penalties were replaced with imprisonment at hard labor, moderate flogging, fines, and forfeiture of property. All lands and goods belonging to felons were to be used to make restitution to the victims of crimes, with restitution being limited to twice the value of the damages. Felons who owned no property were required by law to work in the prison workhouse until the victim was compensated.

Penn ordered that a new type of institution be built to replace the widely used public forms of punishment—stocks, pillories, gallows, and branding iron. Each county was instructed to build a house of corrections similar to today's jails. County trustees or commissioners were responsible for raising money to build the jails and providing for their maintenance, though they were operated by the local sheriff.

Penn's reforms remained in effect until his death in 1718, when the criminal penal code was changed back to open public punishment and harsh brutality.

It is difficult to identify the first American prison. Alexis Durham has described the opening of the Newgate Prison of Connecticut in 1773 on the site of an abandoned copper mine. Newgate, which closed in the 1820s, is often ignored by correctional historians.[9] In 1785, Castle Island prison was opened in Massachusetts and operated for about fifteen years.

The origin of the modern correctional system is usually traced to eighteenth-century developments in Pennsylvania. In 1776, postrevolutionary Pennsylvania again adopted William Penn's code, and in 1787, a group of Quakers led by Dr. Benjamin Rush formed the Philadelphia Society for Alleviating the Miseries of Public Prisons. The aim of the Society was to bring some degree of humane and orderly treatment to the growing penal system. The Quakers' influence on the legislature resulted in limiting the use of the death penalty to cases involving treason, murder, rape, and arson. Their next step was to reform the institutional system so that the prison could serve as a suitable alternative to physical punishment.

The only models of custodial institutions at that time were the local county jails that Penn had established. These facilities were designed to detain offenders, to securely incarcerate convicts awaiting other punishment, or to hold offenders who were working off their crimes. The Pennsylvania jails placed men, women, and children of all ages indiscriminately in one room. Liquor was often freely sold.

Under pressure from the Quakers to improve these conditions, the Pennsylvania State Legislature in 1790 called for the renovation of the prison system. The ultimate result was the creation of a separate wing of Philadelphia's **Walnut Street Jail** to house convicted felons (except those sentenced to death). Prisoners were placed in solitary cells, where they remained in isolation and did not have the right to work.[10] Quarters that contained the solitary or separate cells were called the **penitentiary house**, as was already the custom in England.

The new Pennsylvania prison system took credit for a rapid decrease in the crime rate—from 131 convictions in 1789 to 45 in 1793.[11] The prison became known as a school for reform and a place for public labor. The Walnut Street Jail's equitable conditions were credited with reducing escapes to none in the first four years of its existence (except for fourteen on opening day).

However, the Walnut Street Jail was not a total success. Overcrowding undermined the goal of solitary confinement of serious offenders, and soon more than one inmate was placed in each cell. The isolation had a terrible psychological effect on inmates, and eventually inmates were given in-cell piecework on which they worked up to eight hours a day. Despite these difficulties, similar institutions were erected in New York (Newgate in 1791) and New Jersey (Trenton in 1798).

The Auburn System

As the nineteenth century got underway, both the Pennsylvania and the New York prison systems were experiencing difficulties maintaining the ever-increasing numbers of convicted criminals. Initially, administrators dealt with the problem by increasing the use of pardons, relaxing prison discipline, and limiting supervision.

In 1816, New York built a new prison at Auburn, hoping to alleviate some of the overcrowding at Newgate. The Auburn Prison design became known as the **tier system**, because cells were built vertically on five floors of the structure. It was also referred to as the **congregate system**, since most prisoners ate and worked in groups. Later, in 1819, construction was started on a wing of solitary cells to house unruly prisoners. Three classes of prisoners were then created: one group remained continually in solitary confinement as a result of breaches of prison discipline; the second group was allowed labor as an occasional form of recreation; and the third and largest class worked and ate together during the days and were separated only at night.

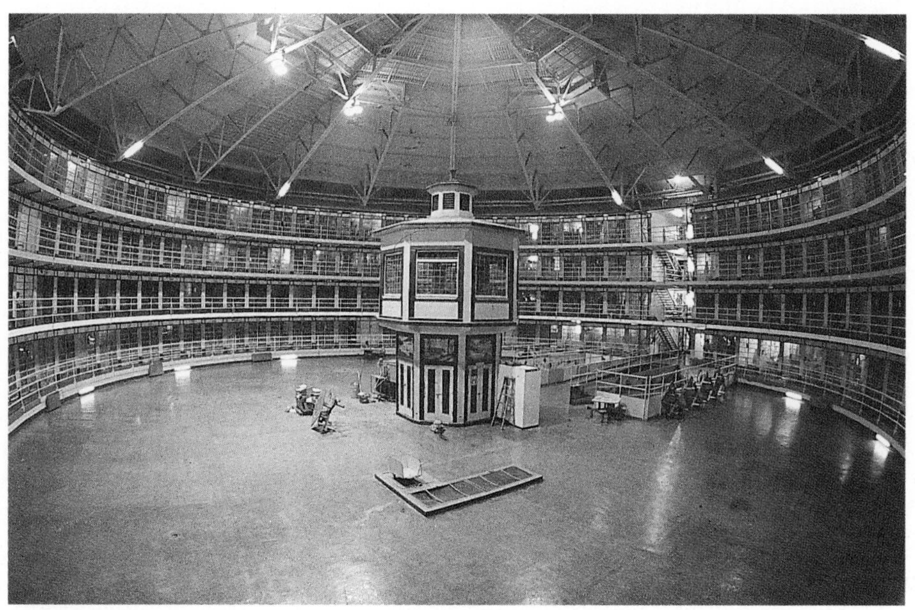

Auburn prison was the forerunner of today's large maximum security prisons. This is an interior view of the roundhouse in Statesville Prison in Joliet, Illinois.

The philosophy of the **Auburn system** was crime prevention through fear of punishment and silent confinement. The worst felons were to be cut off from all contact with other prisoners, and although they were treated and fed relatively well, they had no hope of pardon to relieve their solitude or isolation. For a time, some of the worst convicts were forced to remain totally alone and silent during the entire day; this practice caused many prisoners to have mental breakdowns, resulting in many suicides and self-mutilations. This practice was abolished in 1823.

The combination of silence and solitude as a method of punishment was not abandoned easily. Prison officials sought to overcome the side effects of total isolation while maintaining the penitentiary system. The solution adopted at Auburn was to keep convicts in separate cells at night but allow them to work together during the day under enforced silence. Hard work and silence became the foundation of the Auburn system wherever it was adopted. Silence was the key to prison discipline; it prohibited the formulation of escape plans, it prevented plots and riots, and it allowed prisoners to contemplate their infractions.

Why Prisons Developed

Why did prisons develop at this time? One reason, of course, was that during this period of "enlightenment," there was a concerted effort to alleviate the harsh punishments and torture that had been the norm. The interest of religious groups, such as the Quakers, in prison reform was prompted in part by humanitarian ideals. Another factor was the economic potential of prison industry, viewed as a valuable economic asset in times of a short labor supply.[12]

The concept of using harsh discipline and control to "retrain" the heart and soul of offenders has been the subject of an important book on penal philosophy—*Discipline and Punishment,* by French sociologist Michel Foucault.[13] Foucault's thesis is that as societies evolve and become more complex, they create increasingly more elaborate mechanisms to discipline their recalcitrant members and make them docile enough to obey social rules. In the seventeenth and eighteenth centuries, discipline was directed toward the human body itself, through torture. However, physical punishment and torture turned some condemned men into heroes and martyrs. Prisons presented the opportunity to rearrange, not diminish punishment, to make it more effective and regulated. In the development of the nineteenth-century prison, the object was to discipline the offender psychologically; "the expiation that once rained down on the body must be replaced by a punishment that acts in the depths of the heart."[14]

According to one historian, David Rothman, regimentation became the standard mode of prison life. Convicts did not simply walk from place to place; rather, they went in close order and single file, each looking over the shoulder of the preceding person, faces inclined to the right, feet moving in unison. The lockstep prison shuffle was developed at Auburn and is still employed in some institutions today.[15]

When discipline was breached in the Auburn system, punishment was applied in the form of a rawhide whip on the inmate's back. Immediate and effective, Auburn discipline was so successful that when a hundred inmates were used to build the famous Sing Sing Prison in 1825, not one dared to try to escape, although they were housed in an open field with only minimal supervision.[16]

The Pennsylvania System

In 1818, Pennsylvania took the radical step of establishing a prison that placed each inmate in a single cell for the duration of his sentence. Classifications were abolished, because each cell was intended as a miniature prison that would prevent the inmates from contaminating one another.

The new Pennsylvania state prison, called the Western Penitentiary, had an unusual architectural design. It was built in a semicircle, with the cells positioned along its circumference. Built back-to-back, some cells faced the boundary wall while others faced the internal area of the circle. Its inmates were kept in solitary confinement almost constantly, being allowed out for about an hour a day for exercise. In 1820, a second, similar penitentiary using the isolate system was built in Philadelphia and called the Eastern Penitentiary.

Supporters of the Pennsylvania system believed that the penitentiary was truly a place to do penance. By advocating totally removing the sinner from society and allowing the prisoner a period of isolation in which to reflect alone on the evils of crime, the supporters of the Eastern Penitentiary system reflected the influence of religion and religious philosophy on corrections. Solitary confinement (with in-cell labor) was believed to make work so attractive that upon release, the inmate would be well suited to resume a productive existence in society.

The Pennsylvania system eliminated the need for large numbers of guards or disciplinary measures. Isolated from one another, inmates could not plan escapes or collectively break rules. When discipline was a problem, however, the whip and the iron gag were used.

Many fiery debates occurred between advocates of the Pennsylvania system and the Auburn system. Those supporting the latter boasted of its supposed advantages; their system was the cheapest and most productive way to reform prisoners. They criticized the Pennsylvania system as cruel and inhumane, suggesting that solitary confinement was both physically and mentally damaging. The Pennsylvania system's devotees, on the other hand, argued that their system was quiet, efficient, humane, and well ordered and provided the ultimate correctional facility.[17] They chided the Auburn system for tempting inmates to talk by putting them together for meals and work and then punishing them when they did talk. Finally, the Auburn system was accused of becoming a breeding place for criminal associations by allowing inmates to get to know one another.

The Auburn system eventually prevailed and spread throughout the United States; many of its features are still used today. Its innovations included congregate working conditions, the use of solitary confinement to punish unruly inmates, military regimentation, and discipline. In Auburn-like institutions, prisoners were marched from place to place; their time was regulated by bells telling them to wake up, sleep, and work. The system was so like the military that many of its early administrators were recruited from the armed services.

Although the prison was viewed as an improvement over capital and corporal punishment, it quickly became the scene of depressed conditions; inmates were treated harshly and routinely whipped and tortured. As historian Samuel Walker notes:

> Prison brutality flourished. It was ironic that the prison had been devised as a more humane alternative to corporal and capital punishment. Instead, it simply moved corporal punishment indoors where, hidden from public view, it became even more savage.[18]

The Civil War Era

The prison of the late nineteenth century was remarkably similar to that of today. The congregate system was adopted in all states except Pennsylvania. Prisons were overcrowded, and the single-cell principle was often ignored. The prison, like the police department, became the scene of political intrigue and efforts by political administrators to control the hiring of personnel and dispensing of patronage.

Prison industry developed and became the predominant theme around which institutions were organized. Some prisons used the **contract system**, in which officials sold the labor of inmates to private businesses. Sometimes the contractor supervised the inmates inside the prison itself. Under the **convict-lease system**, the state leased its prisoners to a business for a fixed annual fee and gave up supervision and control. Finally, the state had prisoners produce goods in prison for its own use.[19]

The development of prison industry quickly led to the abuse of inmates, who were forced to work for almost no wages, and to profiteering by dishonest administrators and businessmen. During the Civil War era, prisons were major manufacturers of clothes, shoes, boots, furniture, and the like. Beginning in the 1870s, opposition by trade unions sparked restrictions on interstate commerce in prison goods.

Prison operations were also reformed. The National Congress of Penitentiary and Reformatory Discipline, held in Cincinnati in 1870, heralded a new era of prison reform. Organized by penologists Enoch Wines and Theodore Dwight, the congress provided a forum for corrections experts from around the nation to call for the treatment, education, and training of inmates.

One of the most famous people to attend the congress, **Z. R. Brockway**, warden at the Elmira Reformatory in New York, advocated individualized treatment, the indeterminate sentence, and parole. The reformatory program initiated by Brockway included elementary education for illiterates, designated library hours, lectures by faculty members of the local Elmira College, and a group of vocational training shops. From 1888 to 1920, Elmira administrators used military-like training to discipline the inmates and organize the institution. The military organization could be seen in every aspect of the institution: schooling, manual training, sports, supervision of inmates, and even parole decisions.[20] The cost to the state of the institution's operations was to be held to a minimum. Although Brockway proclaimed Elmira to be an ideal reformatory, his actual achievements were limited. The greatest significance of his contribution was the injection of a degree of humanitarianism into the industrial prisons of that day (though there were accusations that excessive corporal punishment was used and that Brockway personally administered whippings).[21] However, although many institutions were constructed across the nation and labeled reformatories based on the Elmira model, most of them continued to be industrially oriented.[22]

Reform Movements

The early twentieth century was a time of contrasts in the prison system of the United States.[23] At one extreme were those who advocated reform, such as the **Mutual Welfare League** led by Thomas Mott Osborne. Prison reform groups proposed better treatment for inmates, an end to harsh corporal punishment, the creation of meaningful prison industries, and educational programs. Reformers argued that prisoners should not be isolated from society, but that the best elements of society—education, religion, meaningful work, self-governance—should be brought to the prison. Osborne went so far as to spend one week in New York's notorious Sing Sing Prison in order to learn firsthand about its conditions.

Opposed to the reformers were conservative prison administrators and state officials who believed that stern disciplinary measures were needed to control dangerous prison inmates. They continued the time-honored system of regimentation and discipline. Although the whip and the lash were eventually abolished, solitary confinement in dark, bare cells became a common penal practice.

In time, some of the more rigid prison rules gave way to liberal reform. By the mid-1930s, few prisons required inmates to wear the red-and-white-striped convict suit and substituted nondescript gray uniforms. The code of silence ended, as did the lockstep shuffle. Prisoners were allowed "the freedom of the yard" to mingle and exercise an hour or two each day.[24] Movies and radio appeared in the 1930s. Visiting policies and mail privileges were liberalized.

A more important trend was the development of specialized prisons designed to treat particular types of offenders. For example, in New York, the prisons at Clinton and Auburn were viewed as industrial facilities for hard-core inmates, Great Meadow as an agricultural center to house nondangerous offenders, and Dannemora as a facility for the criminally insane. In California, San Quentin housed inmates considered salvageable by correctional authorities, while Folsom was reserved for hard-core offenders.[25]

Prison industry also evolved. Opposition by organized labor helped put an end to the convict-lease system and forced inmate labor. By 1900, a number of states had restricted the sale of prisoner-made goods on the open market. The world-wide depression that began in 1929 prompted industry and union leaders to further pressure state legislators to reduce competition from prison industries. A series of ever-more restrictive federal legislative initiatives led to the Sumners-Ashurst Act (1940), which made it a federal offense to transport in interstate commerce goods made in prison for private use, regardless of the laws of the state receiving the goods.[26] The restrictions imposed by the federal government helped to severely curtail prison industry for forty years. Private entrepreneurs shunned prison investments because they were no longer profitable; the result was inmate idleness and make-work jobs.[27]

Despite these changes and reforms, the prison in the mid-twentieth century remained a destructive total institution. Although some aspects of inmate life improved, severe discipline, harsh rules, and solitary confinement were the way of life in prison.

The Modern Era

The modern era has been a period of change and turmoil in the nation's correctional system. Three trends stand out. First, between 1960 and 1980, what is referred to as the prisoners' rights movement occurred. After many years of indifference, state and federal courts ruled in case after case that institutionalized inmates had rights to freedom of religion and speech, medical care, procedural due process, and proper living conditions. Inmates won rights unheard of in the early nineteenth- and twentieth-century prisons. Since 1980, however, an increasingly conservative judiciary has curtailed the growth of inmate rights.

Second, violence within the correctional system became a national concern. Well-publicized riots at New York's Attica Prison and the New Mexico State Penitentiary drew attention to the potential for death and destruction that lurks in every prison. One reaction has been to try to improve conditions and provide innovative programs that give inmates a voice in running the institution. Another reaction has been to tighten discipline and call for the building of new maximum-security prisons to control dangerous offenders.

Third, the view that traditional correctional rehabilitation efforts have failed has prompted many penologists to reconsider the purpose of incapacitating criminals. Between 1960 and 1980, correctional administrators commonly characterized their efforts as a "**medical model**" that would help rehabilitate people who were suffering from some social malady that prevented them from adjusting to society. In the 1970s, efforts were also made to help offenders become **reintegrated** into society by providing them with new career opportunities, work release, and furlough programs. However, during the past decade, prisons have come to be viewed as places for control, incapacitation, and punishment, rather than as sites for rehabilitation and reform. Nonetheless, efforts to use correctional institutions as treatment facilities have not ended, and such innovations as the development of private industries on prison grounds have kept the rehabilitative ideal alive.

The alleged failure of correctional treatment coupled with constantly increasing correctional costs has prompted the development of alternatives to incarceration, such as intensive probation supervision, house arrest, and electronic monitoring. What has arisen is a bifurcated correctional policy: keep as many nonviolent offenders out of the correctional system as possible by means of community-based programs; incarcerate dangerous, violent offenders for long periods of time.[28] These efforts have been compromised by a growing get-tough stance in judicial and legislative sentencing policy; despite the development of alternatives to incarceration, the number of people under lock and key has skyrocketed.

The following sections review the most prominent types of correctional facilities in use today.

Jails

The nation's jails are institutional facilities with five primary purposes: (1) they detain accused offenders who cannot make or are not eligible for bail prior to trial; (2) they hold convicted offenders awaiting sentence; (3) they serve as the principal institution of secure confinement for offenders convicted of misdemeanors; (4) they hold probationers and parolees picked up for violations and waiting for a hearing; and (5) they house felons when state prisons are overcrowded.

A number of different formats are used to jail offenders. About fifteen thousand local jurisdictions maintain short-term police or municipal lockups that house offenders for no more than forty-eight hours before a bail hearing can be held; thereafter, detainees are kept in the county jail. In some jurisdictions, such as New Hampshire and Massachusetts, a house of corrections holds convicted misdemeanants, while a county jail is used for pretrial detainees. According to the most recent statistics, about 42 percent of jailed inmates are unconvicted, awaiting formal charges (arraignment), bail, or trial. The remaining 57 percent are convicted offenders, serving time, awaiting parole or probation revocation hearings, or transferred from a state prison due to overcrowding.[29]

Unfortunately, jails are low-priority items in the criminal justice system. Since they are almost always administered on a county level, jail services have not been sufficiently regulated, nor has a unified national policy been developed to mandate what constitutes adequate jail conditions. Many jails have consequently developed into squalid, crumbling holding pens.

Jails are considered holding pens for the county's undesirables, rather than correctional institutions that provide meaningful treatment. They may house indigents who, looking for a respite from the winter's cold, commit a minor offense; the mentally ill who will eventually be hospitalized after a civil commitment hearing; and substance abusers who are suffering the first shocks of confinement. John Irwin found in his study of the county jail in San Francisco that the jail does not confine real "criminals," most of whom are able to make bail.[30] Instead, the jail holds the people considered detached from and disreputable in local society and who are frequently arrested because they are considered "offensive" by the local police. The purpose of the jail is to "manage" these persons and keep them separate from the rest of society. By intruding in their lives, jailing them actually increases their involvement with the law.

Jail Populations

There are about thirty-four hundred jails in the United States—twenty-nine hundred county facilities run by sheriffs, and six hundred municipal jails run by local corrections departments. Their average daily population is approximately four hundred thousand, more than double what it was in 1978; the jail population has risen more than 85 percent since 1983.[31] So, despite the popularity of ROR and other pretrial release programs, jail populations have increased significantly in the past decade, creating an overcrowding crisis in many jurisdictions.

Although some are repeat offenders who are incarcerated many times, large numbers of people are put in jail each year. The annual turnover is about 19 million, 9.7 million admissions and 9.5 discharges. While the great majority of these are adult males, more than 1 million women and sixty-five thousand juveniles are admitted annually. The housing of juvenile offenders within adult jails is especially troubling. Despite ongoing efforts to remove juveniles from adult jails, adolescents are held in adult facilities in some jurisdictions because simply no other facilities are available. In other jurisdictions, the age of criminal responsibility is as low as sixteen, resulting in the housing of youthful offenders with older, more experienced inmates. Approximately 1.5 percent of the daily jail population (about six thousand kids) is seventeen years old or less.[32]

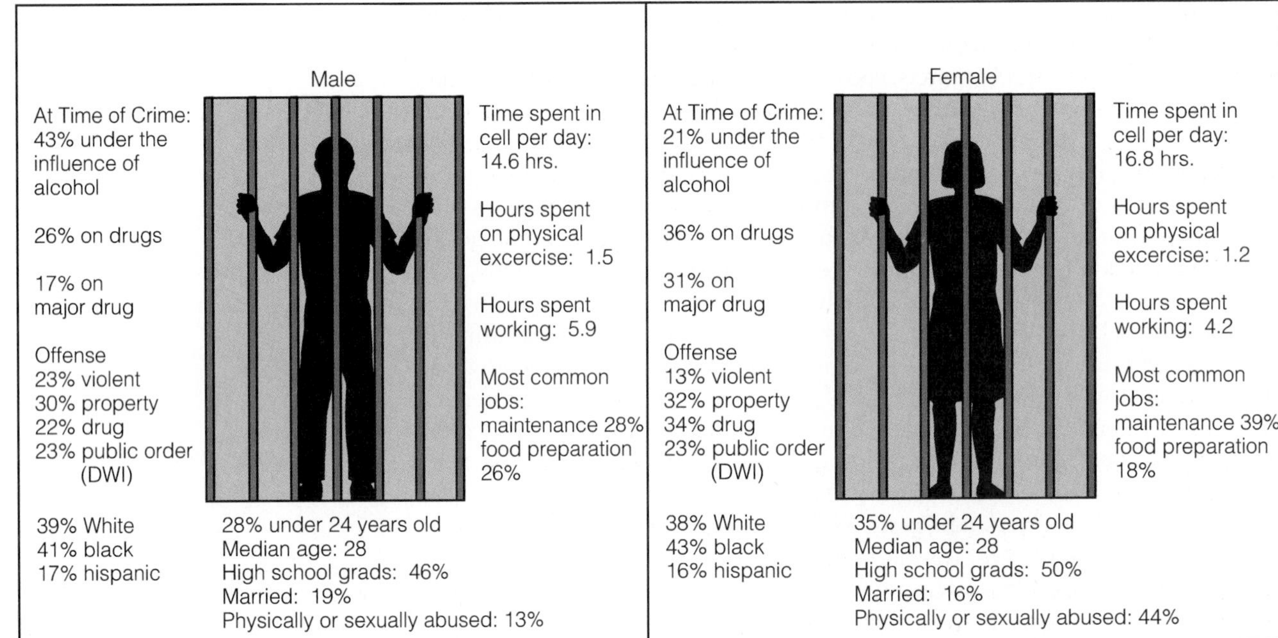

FIGURE 16.1
Profile of Jail Inmates

SOURCE: Tracy Snell, *Women in Jail, 1989* (Washington, D.C.: Bureau of Justice Statistics, 1992).

As might be expected, the personal profile of the jail inmate is similar to the typical arrestee (see Figure 16.1). Most are young (75 percent under thirty-five), male (90 percent), single (80 percent), and undereducated (54 percent did not graduate high school); minorities account for 57 percent of the jail population.[33]

Social trends are also distinct in the jail population. While the class-crime relationship is still debated, the life history of the typical jail inmate supports a relationship between poverty and crime. Less than half of the inmates reported an income over ten thousand dollars in the year before they were incarcerated; more than 26 percent earned less than three thousand dollars per year. Jail inmates were twice as likely as the general population to grow up in a single-parent household (39 percent versus 20 percent). More than 25 percent reported that their parents or guardians were substance abusers; 56 percent report being themselves under the influence of alcohol and/or drugs at the time of their offense.

Most inmates were either doing time or awaiting trial on property crime charges, such as burglary, larceny, or motor vehicle theft. However, the number of drug offenders has increased markedly. In 1983, about 9 percent of the total population was in jail for drug-related crimes; that number increased to 23 percent by 1989. The increase in drug offenders accounted for more than 40 percent of the total (160,000) increase in the jail population that occurred between 1983 and 1990.

Women in Jail. Since 1983, the number of women in jail has increased 138 percent, a percentage increase double that of male inmates.[34]

Female inmates suffer many of the social problems that plague U.S. society. Most are substance abusers: more than half had used drugs in the month prior to the current offense; about 40 percent were daily drug users; about one fifth report being under the influence of alcohol; about one quarter said they had committed crime to buy drugs. In 1983, about 15 percent of the female inmates had used cocaine or crack during the month preceding their arrest; by 1989, that number had increased to 39 percent. More women in jail are drug-involved than are men.

A strong association between child abuse and crime has long been assumed. Female inmates give evidence that this hypothesis is accurate. More than 44 percent report being physically or sexually abused at some time in their lives before their current incarceration; about one third had been abused before age eighteen. Abused women were more likely to be violent recidivists, affirming the view that "violence begets violence."

Jail Conditions

Jails are the oldest and most deteriorated institutions in the criminal justice system. Since they are usually run by the county government (and controlled by a sheriff), it is difficult to encourage taxpayers to appropriate money for improved facilities. In fact, jails are usually administered under the concept of "custodial convenience," which involves giving inmates minimum standards of treatment and benefits while controlling the cost of jail operations. Jail employees are often underpaid, ill-trained, and lacking in professional experience.

Some jails are practically run by violent inmate cliques that terrorize other prisoners; one former IBM executive who served time in jail for writing bad checks relates this story:

> I've seen people raped, especially young kids. You can get a kid as young as . . . 16. These young boys would come in and if they were fresh and young, the guys who run the tank and lived in the first cell, they would take the kid, forcibly hold him and someone would rape him. . . . Some of them go to pieces just right there and then, kids who can't hack it and are torn apart.[35]

A recent report on incarceration in the United States by the Human Rights Watch found that because they are short-term facilities, jails often lack basic programs and services. Because of insufficient data and record keeping, violence-prone inmates are held in the same cells as first offenders. The report cited the cases of an eighteen year old in California who committed suicide after being raped in a county jail and an AIDS-infected inmate who was denied a change of clothing, bedding, soap, towels, toothbrush, toilet paper, a Bible, or visitors; this inmate was left in a bare room and denied access to a telephone on the grounds that there was no disinfectant with which to clean the phone after he made a call.[36] About nine hundred people die in jail each year, and more than one-third of these are suicides.[37]

Well aware of these problems, some judges are reluctant to sentence offenders to a jail term. In one case, a New York judge refused to sentence a slightly built man to jail, even though he "deserved it." The judge stated in court: "He would be immediately subject to homosexual rape . . . and to brutalities from fellow prisoners such as make the imagination recoil in horror."[38]

Jails are also scenes of serious fires and other neglect-related tragedies. Similarly, the lack of screening and control procedures results in hundreds of in-jail suicides every year. About four hundred people, mostly white male detainees who were arrested on alcohol- or drug-related charges, kill themselves (usually by hanging) each year.[39] Some correctional officers may even take their job frustrations out on jail inmates. In 1991, correctional officers brutalized inmates at New York City's Rikers Island Jail during a disturbance that occurred in the midst of a hotly contested job action.[40]

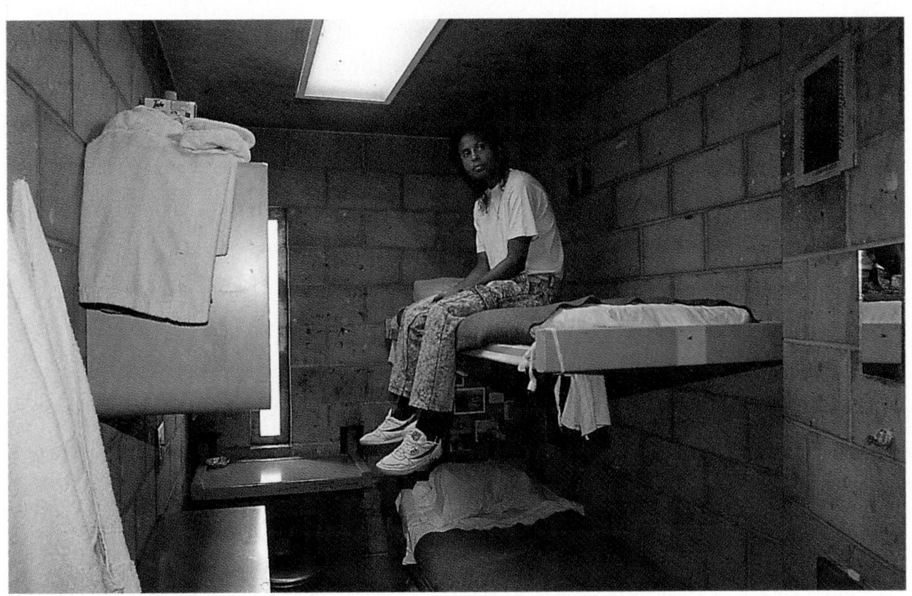

Since 1983, the number of women in jail has increased 138 percent.

Jail Overcrowding

One of the most critical problems of jails is overcrowding.[41] The one hundred largest jails—including the Los Angeles County Central Jail, Chicago's Cook County Jail, and New York's Correctional Institute for Men—hold about 40 percent of the total jail population in the United States. Los Angeles County jails hold an average of more than seventeen thousand inmates on any given day, and New York City jails hold over fourteen thousand. Due to overcrowding, 44 percent of the largest jurisdictions report that they had to hold inmates for other jurisdictions; prison inmates transferred to county jails because of overcrowded conditions in the correctional system made up 12 percent of the total jail population.

Considering these conditions, it is not surprising that 28 percent of the jurisdictions with large jail populations had at least one jail under court order to reduce the number of inmates. These court orders were based on judicial concerns about crowded living conditions, inadequate medical and recreational facilities, visitation policies, and inadequate food services.

Some jails are so overcrowded that they simply have no room to put people. A moratorium has been placed on new admissions to some city jails, and many detainees are given ROR who might ordinarily have been forced to put up cash bail.[42] In New York City, overcrowding prompted the city to purchase river barges to house the jail overflow.

Creating Overcrowded Jails

A number of factors lead to jail overcrowding. One is the concerted effort being made to reduce or control particular crime problems, including substance abuse, spousal abuse, and driving while intoxicated (DWI). For example, some jurisdictions have passed legislation requiring that people arrested on suspicion of domestic violence be held in confinement for a number of hours to "cool off" before becoming eligible for bail. Other jurisdictions have attempted to deter drunk driving by passing mandatory jail sentences for people convicted of DWI.

An evaluation of the mandatory jailing of drunk drivers in four jurisdictions (Seattle, Memphis, Minneapolis, and Cincinnati) found that such legislation can have a devastating effect on the justice system.[43] After a well-publicized campaign to alert the public about mandatory jail terms, arrests of drunk drivers began to increase, indicating that police departments were devoting greater resources and effort to controlling the DWI problem. Court caseloads also increased because more of the arrested violators contested their case, rather than face a jail term. The number of drunk drivers sent to jail increased dramatically. While before the legislation only 9 percent of convicted offenders went to jail in the four jurisdictions, the number climbed to 97 percent after the DWI laws took effect. Jailing DWI violators puts a tremendous strain on the correctional system. Since many drunk drivers did not have criminal histories, they were confined separately from the general jail population; many were entitled by law to special treatment and reform programs, creating additional costs and system overload. Some offenders had to wait six to seven months before serving their sentence due to overcrowding.

Prisons

The Federal Bureau of Prisons and every state government maintain closed correctional facilities, also called prisons, penitentiaries, or reformatories. Usually, prisons are organized or classified on three levels—maximum-, medium-, and minimum-security—and each has distinct characteristics.

1. Maximum-security prisons are probably the institutions most familiar to the public, since they house the most famous criminals and are often the subject of films and stories. Famous "max prisons" have included Sing Sing, Joliet, Attica, Walpole, and the most fearsome jail of all, the now-closed federal facility on Alcatraz Island known as The Rock.

A typical maximum-security facility is fortress-like, surrounded by stone walls with guard towers at strategic places. These walls may be twenty-five feet high, and sometimes inner and outer walls divide the prison into courtyards. Barbed wire or electrified fences are used to discourage escapes. High security, armed guards, and stone walls give the inmate the sense that the facility is impregnable and reassure the citizen outside that convicts will be completely incapacitated.

Inmates live in interior, metal-barred cells that contain their own plumbing and sanitary facilities and are locked securely either by key or electronic device. Cells are organized in sections called blocks, and in large prisons, a number of cell blocks comprise a wing. During the evening, each cell block is sealed off from the others, as is each wing. Thus, an inmate may be officially located in, for example, Block 3 of E Wing.

Every inmate is assigned a number and a uniform on entering the prison system. Unlike the striped, easily identifiable uniforms of old, the maximum-security inmate today wears khaki attire not unlike military fatigues. Dress codes may be strictly enforced in some institutions, but the closely cropped hair and other strict features are vestiges of the past.

During the day, the inmates engage in closely controlled activities: meals, workshops, education, and so on. Rule violators may be confined to their cells, and working and other shared recreational activities are viewed as privileges.

The byword of the maximum-security prison is security. Guards and other correctional workers are made aware that each inmate may be a dangerous criminal or violent and, as a result, the utmost in security must be maintained. In keeping with this philosophy, prisons are designed to eliminate hidden corners where people can congregate, and passages are constructed so that they can be easily blocked off to quell disturbances.

Some states have constructed **maxi-maxi prisons** to house the most predatory criminals. These high-security institutions can be independent correctional centers or locked wings of existing prisons. Maxi-maxi prisons are modeled on the federal penitentiary in Marion, Illinois, which is famous for its tight security and isolate conditions. Some maxi-maxi prisons lock inmates in their cells twenty-two to twenty-four hours a day, never allowing them out unless they are shackled. Threat of transfer to the maxi-maxi institution is used to deter inmate misbehavior in less restrictive institutions. Civil rights watch-dog groups charge that these maxi-maxi prisons violate the United Nations standards for the treatment of inmates.[44]

2. Medium-security prisons may be similar in appearance to the maximum-security prison; however, security and atmosphere are neither so tense nor so vigilant. Medium-security prisons are also surrounded by walls, but there may be fewer guard towers or other security precautions. For example, visitor privileges may be more extensive, and personal contact may be allowed; in a maximum-security prison, visitors may be separated from inmates by Plexiglas or other barriers (to prohibit the passing of contraband). While most prisoners are housed in cells, individual honor rooms in medium-security prisons are used to reward those who make exemplary rehabilitation efforts. Finally, medium-security prisons promote greater treatment efforts, and the relaxed atmosphere allows freedom of movement for rehabilitation workers and other therapeutic personnel.

3. Minimum-security prisons operate without armed guards or walls; usually, they are constructed in compounds surrounded by a Cyclone-type fence. Minimum-security prisons usually house the most trustworthy and least violent offenders; white-collar criminals may be their most common occupants. A great deal of personal freedom is allowed inmates. Instead of being marched to activities by guards, they are summoned by bells or loudspeaker announcements and assemble on their own. Work furloughs and educational releases are encouraged, and vocational training is of the highest level. Dress codes are lax, and inmates are allowed to grow beards or mustaches or demonstrate other individual characteristics.

Minimum-security facilities may have dormitories or small private rooms for inmates. Prisoners are allowed quite a bit of discretion in acquiring or owning personal possessions that might be deemed dangerous in a maximum-security prison, such as radios.

Minimum-security prisons have been scoffed at for being too much like country clubs; some federal facilities catering to white-collar criminals even have tennis courts and pools. Yet they remain prisons, and the isolation and loneliness of prison life deeply affects the inmates at these facilities.

Farms and Camps

In addition to closed institutions, prison farms and camps are used to detain offenders. This type of facility is found primarily in the South and the West. Today, about forty farms, forty forest camps, eighty road camps, and sixty-seven similar facilities (vocational training centers, ranches, etc.) exist in the nation.

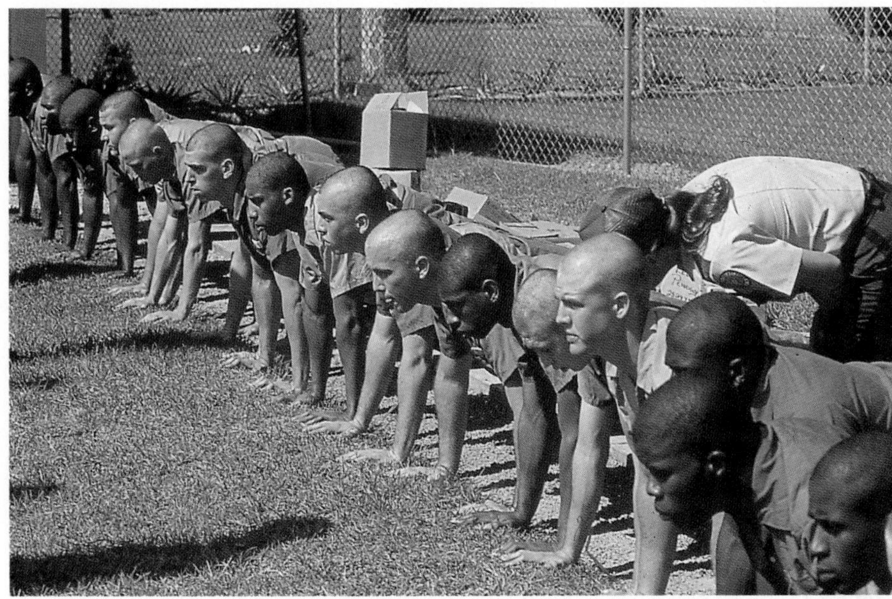

Inmates undergoing "shock incarceration" in a correctional boot camp.

Prisoners on farms produce dairy products, grain, and vegetable crops that are used in the state correctional system and other government facilities, such as hospitals and schools. Forestry camp inmates maintain state parks, fight forest fires, and do reforestation work. Ranches, primarily a western phenomenon, employ inmates in cattle raising and horse breeding, among other activities. Road gangs repair roads and state highways.

Boot Camps/Shock Incarceration

A recent approach to correctional care that is gaining popularity around the United States is **shock incarceration**. These programs typically include youthful, first-time offenders and feature military discipline and physical training. The concept is that short periods (90 to 180 days) of high-intensity exercise and work will "shock" the inmate into going straight. Tough physical training is designed to promote responsibility and improve decision-making skills, build self-confidence, and teach socialization skills. Inmates are treated with rough intensity by drill masters who may call them names and punish the entire group for the failure of one of its members. Most state programs also include educational and training components, counseling sessions, and treatment for inmates who have special needs. Examples of shock incarceration programs include the Regimented Inmate Discipline Programs in Mississippi, the About Face Program in Louisiana, and the shock incarceration program in Georgia. The U.S. Army has created a shock program, Specialized Treatment and Rehabilitation in Army Corrections, at its prison in Fort Riley, Kansas.[45] Four states have boot camp programs for women inmates—Oklahoma, Mississippi, South Carolina, and Louisiana.

Is shock incarceration a correctional panacea or another fad doomed to failure? The results so far are mixed. The costs of boot camps are no lower than traditional prisons, but because sentences are shorter, they do provide long-term savings. Some programs have high failure-to-complete rates, which make program evaluations difficult (even if "graduates" of the programs are successful, it is possible that the success rate is the result of troublesome cases dropping out and being placed in the general inmate population). What evaluations exist indicate that the recidivism rates of inmates released from shock programs are no lower than those released from traditional prisons.[46]

Some indications exist that shock incarceration programs can provide correctional benefits. New York houses inmates in these programs in separate institutions and provides most (but not all) "graduates" with extensive follow-up supervision. While recidivism rates for these programs in New York are similar to those of traditional prisons, there are indications that both inmates and staff view shock incarceration as a positive experience.[47] The New York program estimates that it has saved the public over $90 million in capital costs (because new long-term facilities did not have to be built) and $80 million in operating costs (because inmates had shorter institutional stays), for a total of over $170 million.

To date, no definitive evaluation has been made of the shock incarceration approach. It has the advantage of being a lower-cost alternative to overcrowded prisons since inmates are held in nonsecure facilities and sentences are of a short duration. Doris Layton Mackenzie reports that both staff and inmates seem excited by the programs, and even those who fail on parole report that they felt the shock incarceration was a valuable experience.[48]

Community Facilities

One of the goals of correctional treatment is to help reintegrate the offender back into society. By placing offenders in a prison, they are more likely to adapt an inmate life-style than to reassimilate conventional social norms. Because of this, the **community corrections** concept began to take off in the 1960s. State and federal correctional systems created community-based correctional models as an alternative to closed institutions. Today, there are hundreds of community-based facilities holding an estimated twelve thousand inmates.[49] Many are **halfway houses** to which inmates are transferred just before their release into the community. These facilities are designed to bridge the gap between institutional living and the community. Specialized treatment may be offered, and the resident uses the experience to cushion the shock of reentering society.

As you may recall, commitment to a community correctional center may also be used as an intermediate sanction and sole mode of treatment. An offender may be assigned to a community treatment center operated by the state department of corrections or probation. Or the corrections department can contract with a private community center. This practice is common in the treatment of drug addicts and other nonviolent offenders whose special needs can be met in a self-contained community setting that specializes in specific types of treatment.

Halfway houses and community correctional centers can look like residential homes and in many instances were originally residences; in urban centers, older apartment buildings can be adapted for the purpose. Usually, these facilities have a central treatment theme—such as group therapy or reality therapy—that is used to rehabilitate and reintegrate clients.

Another popular approach in community-based corrections is the use of ex-offenders as staff members. These individuals have made the transition between the closed institution and society and can be invaluable in helping residents overcome the many hurdles they face in proper readjustment.

Despite the encouraging philosophical concept presented by the halfway house, evaluation of specific programs has not led to a definite endorsement of this type of treatment.[50] One significant problem has been a lack of support from

On the "yard" in a modern American prison.

community residents, who fear the establishment of an institution housing "dangerous offenders" in their neighborhood. Court actions and zoning restrictions have been brought in some areas to foil efforts to create halfway houses.[51] As a result, many halfway houses are located in decrepit neighborhoods in the worst areas of town—certainly a condition that must influence the attitudes and behavior of inmates. Furthermore, the climate of control exercised in most halfway houses, where rule violation can be met with a quick return to the institution, may not be one that the average inmate can distinguish from his or her former high-security penal institution. Conflict theorist Andrew Scull suggests that community-based corrections are simply a way of managing offenders at a lower cost than in prison.[52] And John Hylton argues that they help "widen the net": "Persons who were not subjected to control previously," he charges, "may now be controlled under the guise of community treatment."[53]

Despite these problems, the promise held by community correctional centers coupled with their low cost of operations, has led to their continued use through the 1980s and into the 1990s. And some recent research efforts indicate that community correctional centers may produce lower recidivism rates than are found in the general prison population.[54]

Private Institutions

Correctional facilities are now being run by private firms as business enterprises.

The federal government has used private companies to run detention centers for illegal aliens who are being held for trial and/or deportation.[55] One private firm, the Corrections Corporation of America, runs a federal halfway house, two detention centers, and a 370-bed jail in Bay County, Florida. On January 6, 1986, the U.S. Corrections Corporation opened the first private state prison in Marion, Kentucky—a three-hundred-bed minimum-security facility for inmates who are within three years of parole. Today, more than twenty companies are trying to enter the private prison market, while three states have passed enabling legislation and more than ten others are considering doing so.

Though privately run institutions have been around for a few years, their increased use may present a number of problems. For example, will private providers be able to effectively evaluate programs, knowing that a negative evaluation might cause them to lose their contract? Will they skimp on services and programs in order to reduce costs? Might they not skim off the "easy" cases and leave the hard-core inmate to the state's care? And will the need to keep business booming require "widening the net" to fill empty cells? Must they maintain state-mandated liability insurance to cover inmate claims?[56]

Private corrections firms run also into opposition from existing state correctional staff and management who fear the loss of jobs and autonomy. Moreover, the public may be skeptical about an untested private concern's ability to provide security and protection.

There are also administrative problems in private corrections. How will program quality be controlled? In order to compete on price, a private facility may have to cut corners to beat out the competition. Determining accountability for problems and mishaps will be difficult when dealing with a corporation that is a legal fiction and protects its officers from personal responsibility for their actions. And legal problems can emerge very quickly: can privately employed guards patrol the perimeter and use deadly force to stop escape attempts?

The very fact that individuals can profit from running a prison may also prove unpalatable to large segments of the population. Should profit be made from human tragedy and suffering? However, is a private correctional facility really much different from a private hospital or mental health clinic that provides services to the public in competition with state-run institutions? The issue that determines the future of private corrections may be one of efficiency and cost effectiveness, not fairness and morality.

While a private correctional enterprise may be an attractive alternative to a costly correctional system, these legal, administrative, and cost issues need to be resolved before private prisons can become widespread.[57] A balance must be reached between the need for a private business to make a profit and the integrity of a prison administration that must be concerned with such complex issues as security, rehabilitation, and dealing with highly dangerous people in a closed environment.[58] While these issues remain to be settled, evaluations of existing private enterprises seem to suggest that they may provide better services at a lower cost than public facilities.[59]

Correctional Populations

The nation's vast system of penal institutions holds over 1 million people (counting jail and community correction center populations) and employs more than 250,000 to care for and guard them.

As Figure 16.2 indicates, the nation's prison population has had a number of cycles of growth and decline.[60] Between 1925 and 1939, it increased at about 5 percent a year, reflecting the nation's concern for the lawlessness of that time. The incarceration rate reached a high of 137 per 100,000 U.S. population in 1939. Then, during World War II, the prison population declined by 50,000, as potential offenders were drafted into the armed services. By 1956, the incarceration rate dropped to 99 per 100,000 U.S. population.

The postwar era saw a steady increase in the prison population until 1961, when 220,000 people were in custody, a rate of 119 per 100,000. During the Vietnam era (1961–1968), the prison population actually declined by 30,000.

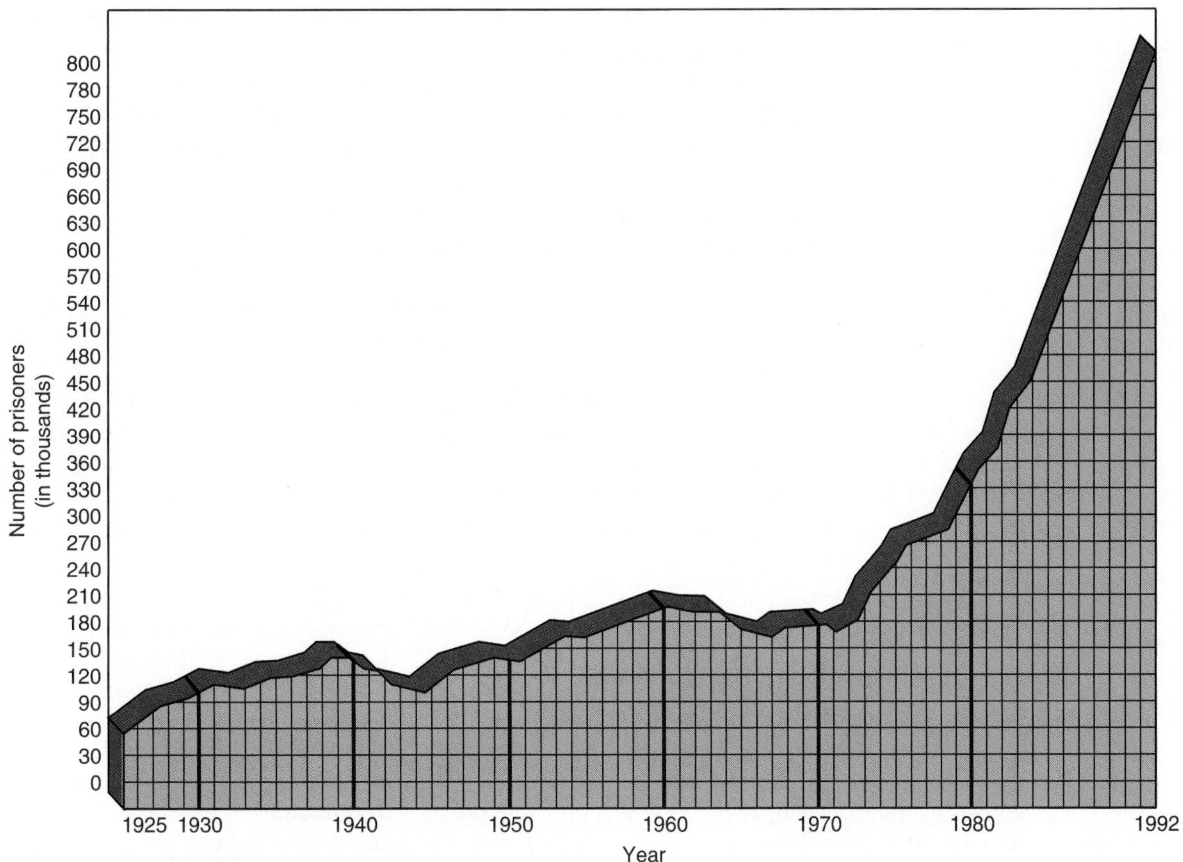

FIGURE 16.2
Number of Sentenced State and Federal Prisoners, Year-End, 1925–1992
SOURCE: Bureau of Justice Statistics, *Prisoners 1925–1981*. (Washington, D.C.: U.S. Government Printing Office, 1982), updated.

The incarceration rate remained rather stable until 1974, when the current dramatic rise began.

As Figure 16.2 shows, the number of inmates in state and federal prisons has more than doubled since 1980, when there were 329,821 inmates.[61] By 1992, the prison population exceeded 800,000, a rate of more than 293 per 100,000 population, the highest in history; about 400,000 people were in jail.[62] Considering these data, it is not surprising that some state correctional populations have grown tremendously. The number of prisoners in Colorado, New Hampshire, California, and Michigan increased by more than 90 percent between 1980 and 1990. California alone has about one hundred thousand prison inmates.

As the Analyzing Criminal Justice Issues in this chapter indicates, these trends place the United States first among all industrialized nations in its rate of incarceration.

The Growth of the Prison Population

How can this significant rise in the prison population be explained? Prison administrators have linked the growth of the correctional population to changes in

ANALYZING CRIMINAL JUSTICE ISSUES

International Incarceration Rates

How does the use of incarceration in the United States compare with that of other nations? The Sentencing Project, a nonprofit institution that promotes justice reform, has conducted two international surveys of incarceration rates in developed nations. The surveys found that, like it or not, the use of incarceration is one area in which the United States is a world leader. As figure A shows, the United States has by far the highest incarceration rate of all nations in the survey. While there are actually more people in prison in China (about 1.2 million), the rate of imprisonment per 100,000 is far lower there. What's more, the rate of increase in the United States has expanded, while in other nations, such as South Africa, the rate is decreasing. Table A shows incarceration rates for various nations studied by the Sentencing Project in 1989 and 1990/1991.

As you may recall, U.S. crime rates are far higher than in most other nations, and it should therefore come as no surprise that more of our citizens are in prison. However, the Sentencing Project's assistant director, Marc Mauer, is skeptical that increased incarceration has any effect on crime rates. Any benefits are more than made up by

TABLE A
Incarceration Rates for Selected Nations

1989 Nation	1989 Rate of Incarceration Per 100,000 Population	1990/1991 Nation	1990/1991 Rate of Incarceration Per 100,000 Population
United States	426	United States	455
South Africa	333	South Africa	311
Soviet Union	268	Venezuela	177
Hungary	196	Hungary	117
Malaysia	126	Canada	111
Northern Ireland	120	China	111
Hong Kong	118	Australia	79
Poland	106	Portugal	77
New Zealand	100	Czechoslovakia	72
United Kingdom	97	Denmark	71
Turkey	96	Albania	55
Portugal	83	Netherlands	46
France	81	Republic of Ireland	44
Austria	77	Sweden	44
Spain	76	Japan	42
Switzerland	73	India	34
Australia	72		
Denmark	68		
Italy	60		
Japan	45		
Netherlands	40		
Philippines	22		

(Note: 1989 data taken from *Americans Behind Bars: A Comparison of International Rates of Incarceration.* Incarceration rates for 1990/91 are for either 1990 or 1991, depending on the availability of data for each nation.)

public opinion, which has demanded a more punitive response to criminal offenders.[63] Public concern about drugs and violent crime has not been lost on state lawmakers. Mandatory and determinate sentencing laws have been implemented in such populous states as Pennsylvania, Michigan, Illinois, and California. These sentences both increase eligibility for incarceration and limit the availability for early release via parole. At the same time, arrests for drug and violent crimes, the target of this legislation, have increased significantly; the number of drug arrests have risen more than 70 percent between 1980 and 1990 and violent crime arrests are up 45 percent. In 1985, there were about 170,000 arrests for drug sales and manufacture, a number that grew to 400,000 in 1989.[64] Though probation and community sentences still predominate, structural changes in criminal codes and crime rates have helped produce an expanding correctional population.

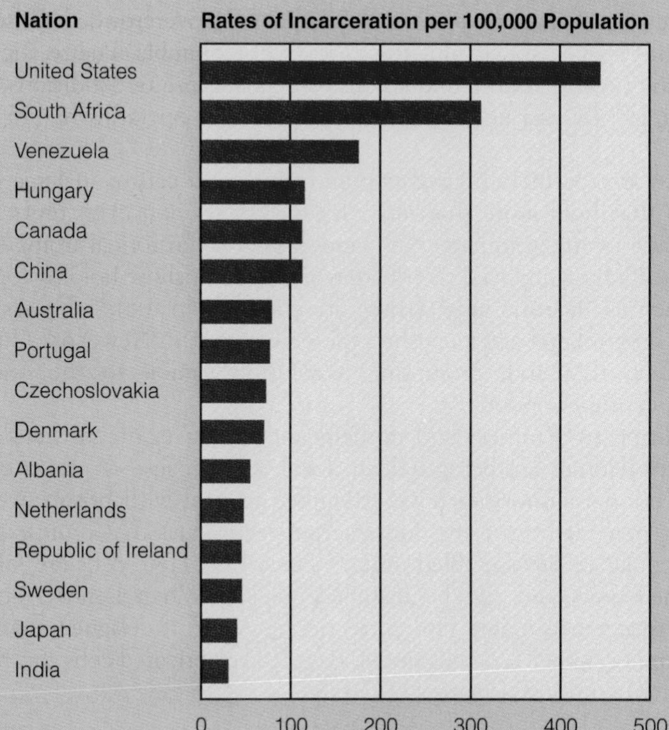

FIGURE A
Incarceration Rates for Selected Nations

the discrimination in sentencing that favors white defendants and targets African-Americans and Hispanics. Mauer points out that the incarceration for black males is 3,370 per 100,000 in the United States, compared to 681 per 100,000 in South Africa, a nation long vilified by the U.S. government for its racist policies.

Critical Thinking Skills

Mauer believes the government must reduce its reliance on prison to fight the "war on drugs" and get the crime rate down. He points to Great Britain and South Africa, which have made it a policy to reduce the use of prisons and rely more heavily on community supervision. He points out that medical experts do not suggest that the best method of treating cancer or AIDS is to build more hospitals but to discover methods of prevention or identify a cure.

Should the prison be deemphasized and replaced by alternative sanctions, or will these simply "widen the net"? Does the threat of prison have a useful purpose: deterring would-be criminals and convincing those who have already served time that "crime does not pay"?

SOURCES: Marc Mauer, *Americans Behind Bars: A Comparison of International Rates of Incarceration* (Washington, D.C.: The Sentencing Project, 1991); idem, *Americans Behind Bars: One Year Later* (Washington, D.C.: The Sentencing Project, 1992).

The nation's judges may also be increasing their use of incarceration sentences. In 1970, only twenty-three people were incarcerated for every 1000 reported index crimes. Commitment probability increased steadily throughout the 1980s, reaching 43 per 1,000 crimes by 1990, an increase of 72 percent between 1980 and 1990.[65] Similarly, while 196 of every 1,000 adults arrested for serious crimes were incarcerated in 1980, the rate rose to 392 per 1,000 by 1990. So while many convicted felons still receive community sentencing, a greater proportion are being sent to prisons.

It is also likely that the relatively high unemployment rate in some areas has influenced the incarcerated population. Though the evidence linking unemployment and crime is inconclusive, unemployed defendants have trouble making bail, increasing both their presence in the jail population and the likelihood they will receive a longer prison sentence upon conviction. At the back end of the system, declining employment opportunities make it difficult for incarcerated offenders to secure the jobs needed to make them eligible for parole.

Prison Overcrowding

As a result of such factors, prisons are desperately overcrowded. Prison systems in about thirty-seven states, plus the District of Columbia, Puerto Rico, and the Virgin Islands, are operating under court orders because of conditions relating to overcrowding.[66] By year end 1990, state prisons were operating at 115 percent of capacity.[67]

Inmates are routinely housed two and three to a cell or in large dormitory-like rooms that hold more than fifty. Military bases and even tents have been used to house overflow inmates. In a move of great historical irony, since 1989 New York City has employed river barges anchored offshore holding four hundred inmates each as "floating jails" (three are currently in use).[68] The skyrocketing number of drug-related arrests pushed the daily count in New York City's jails to over eighteen thousand, prompting a solution similar to the one used in eighteenth-century London.

In addition to detainees and misdemeants, about eighteen thousand people convicted of felonies are being held in local jails because of prison crowding.[69] State correctional authorities have attempted to deal with prison overcrowding by building new facilities using construction techniques that limit expenditures, such as modular or preassembled units.[70] Precast concrete cells are fabricated as fully finished units and can be installed quickly. When Pennsylvania needed additional space at its Camp Hill correctional center, it designed, manufactured, installed, and occupied 128 cells in 140 days.[71] Prefabricated cells can be installed in existing structures in a matter of days.

What the Future Holds

At the time of this writing, there is little evidence that the prison population and the incarceration rate will decrease soon. The violent crime rate has been increasing of late, and state legislators and judges are unlikely to suddenly become more liberal. A number of states have undertaken or are planning major correctional building projects. For example, Texas expects to spend between $600 million and $1.1 billion on new prison construction in the 1990s, increasing its existing system by up to thirty thousand beds.[72] The federal prison system received $2.4 billion in new funds for prison construction between 1988 and 1991; the Federal Bureau of Prisons, already operating at 59 percent over design capacity, expects the population to increase from sixty-two thousand in 1991 to about one hundred thousand in 1995 as mandatory drug laws take effect.[73]

Despite such ominous signs, the nation's prison population may be "maxing out." Budget cutbacks and belt-tightening may halt the expansion of prison construction and the housing of ever more prisoners in already crowded prison facilities. California, which has the nation's largest correctional system, reported that its prison population remained stable in 1991; Michigan's prison population, which grew by four thousand people in 1989 increased by only twenty-one in 1991.[74] While new modular construction techniques and double and triple bunking of inmates make existing prisons expandable, the secure population probably cannot expand endlessly.

In the final analysis, change in the correctional population may depend on the faith judges and legislators place on incarceration as a crime-control policy.

Between 1980 and 1989, the incarceration rate increased by almost 100 percent, while the overall rate of victimization declined by about 20 percent.[75] As long as policymakers believe that incarcerating predatory criminals can bring crime rates down, the likelihood of a significant decrease in the institutional population seems remote.

SUMMARY

Today's correctional institutions can trace their development from European origins. Punishment methods developed in Europe were modified and improved by American colonists, most notably William Penn. He replaced the whip and other methods of physical punishment with confinement in county institutions or penitentiaries.

Later, as needs grew, the newly formed states created their own large facilities. Discipline was harsh within them, and most enforced a code of total and absolute silence. The Auburn system of congregate working conditions during the day and isolation at night has been adopted in our present penal system.

The current correctional population has grown dramatically in the past few years. Although the number of inmates diminished in the late 1960s and early 1970s, it has since then hit an all-time high. This development may reflect a toughening of sentencing procedures nationwide.

A number of different institutions currently house convicted offenders. Jails are used for misdemeanants and minor felons. Since conditions are so poor in jails, they have become a major trouble spot for the criminal justice system.

Federal and state prisons—classified as minimum-, medium-, and maximum-security—house most of the nation's incarcerated felons. However, their poor track record of success has spurred the development of new correctional models, specifically the halfway house and the community correctional center. Nonetheless, the success of these institutions has been challenged by research efforts indicating that their recidivism rates are equal to those of state prisons. One recent development has been the privately run correctional institution. These are jails and prisons operated by private companies that receive a fee for their services. Used in a limited number of jurisdictions, they have been the center of some controversy: can a private company provide better management of what has traditionally been a public problem?

The greatest problem facing the correctional system today is overcrowding, which has reached a crisis level. To help deal with the problems of overcrowding, corrections departments have begun to experiment with modular prison construction and the use of alternative sanctions.

QUESTIONS

1. Would you allow a community correctional center to be built in your neighborhood?
2. Should pretrial detainees and convicted offenders be kept in the same institution?
3. What can be done to reduce correctional overcrowding?
4. Should private companies be allowed to run correctional institutions?
5. What are the drawbacks to shock incarceration?

NOTES

1. Allen Beck and Bernard Shipley, *Recidivism of Young Parolees* (Washington, D.C.: Bureau of Justice Statistics, 1987); see also, John Wallerstedt, *Returning to Prison*, (Washington, D.C.: Bureau of Justice Statistics, 1984).

2. See David Fogel, *We Are the Living Proof*, 2d ed. (Cincinnati: Anderson Publishing, 1978); Andrew von Hirsch, *Doing Justice: The Choice of Punishments* (New York: Hill and Wang, 1976); R. G. Singer, *Just Deserts—Sentencing Based on Equality and Desert* (Cambridge, Mass.: Ballinger Publishing, 1979).

3. Ted Palmer, *Correctional Intervention and Research* (Lexington, Mass.: Lexington Books, 1978); Michael Gottfredson, "The Social Scientist and Rehabilitative Crime Policy," *Criminology* 20 (1982): 29–42. The most widely cited source on the failure of rehabilitation is Robert Martinson; see

Robert Martinson, Douglas Lipton, and Judith Wilks, *The Effectiveness of Correctional Treatment* (New York: Praeger Publishers, 1975).

4. Among the most helpful sources in developing this section are David Duffee, *Corrections: Practice and Policy* (New York: Random House, 1989); Harry Allen and Clifford Simonsen, *Correction in America*, 5th ed. (New York: MacMillan, 1989); Benedict Alper, *Prisons Inside-Out* (Cambridge, Mass.: Ballinger Publishing, 1974); Harry Elmer Barnes, *The Story of Punishment*, 2d ed. (Montclair, N.J.: Patterson-Smith, 1972); Gustave de Beaumont and Alexis de Tocqueville, *On the Penitentiary System in the United States and Its Applications in France* (Carbondale: Southern Illinois University Press, 1964); Orlando Lewis, *The Development of American Prisons and Prison Customs, 1776–1845* (Montclair, N.J.: Patterson-Smith, 1967); Leonard Orland, ed., *Justice, Punishment, and Treatment* (New York: Free Press, 1973); J. Goebel, *Felony and Misdemeanor* (Philadelphia: University of Pennsylvania Press, 1976); Georg Rusche and Otto Kircheimer, *Punishment and Social Structure* (New York: Russell & Russell, 1939); Samuel Walker, *Popular Justice* (New York: Oxford University Press, 1980); Graeme Newman, *The Punishment Response* (Philadelphia: J. B. Lippincott, 1978); David Rothman, *Conscience and Convenience* (Boston: Little, Brown & Co., 1980).

5. F. Pollock and F. Maitland, *History of English Law* (London: Cambridge University Press, 1952).

6. Marvin Wolfgang, "Crime and Punishment in Renaissance Florence," *Journal of Criminal Law and Criminology* 81 (1990):567–84.

7. Margaret Wilson, *The Crime of Punishment*, Life and Letters Series, no. 64 (London: Johnathon Cape, 1934), p. 186.

8. John Howard, *The State of Prisons*, 4th ed. (1792; reprint ed., Montclair, N.J.: Patterson-Smith, 1973).

9. Alexis Durham III, "Newgate of Connecticut: Origins and Early Days of an Early American Prison," *Justice Quarterly* 6 (1989): 89–116.

10. Lewis, *Development of American Prisons and Prison Customs*, p. 17.

11. Ibid., p. 29.

12. Dario Melossi and Massimo Pavarini, *The Prison and the Factory: Origins of the Penitentiary System* (Totowa, N.J.: Barnes and Noble, 1981).

13. Michel Foucault, *Discipline and Punishment* (New York: Vintage Books, 1978).

14. Ibid., p. 16.

15. David Rothman, *The Discovery of the Asylum* (Boston: Little, Brown & Co., 1970).

16. Orland, *Justice, Punishment, and Treatment*, p. 143.

17. Ibid., p. 144.

18. Walker, *Popular Justice*, p. 70.

19. Ibid., p. 71.

20. Beverly Smith, "Military Training at New York's Elmira Reformatory, 1880–1920," *Federal Probation* 52: (1988):33–41.

21. Ibid.

22. See Z. R. Brockway, "The Ideal of a True Prison System for a State," in *Transactions of the National Congress on Penitentiary and Reformatory Discipline* (reprint ed., Washington, D.C.: American Correctional Association, 1970), pp. 38–65.

23. This section leans heavily on Rothman, *Conscience and Convenience*.

24. Ibid., p. 23.

25. Ibid., p. 133.

26. 18 U.S.C. § 1761.

27. Barbara Auerbach, George Sexton, Franlin Farrow, and Robert Lawson, *Work in American Prisons, The Private Sector Gets Involved* (Washington, D.C.: National Institute of Justice, 1988), p. 72.

28. See, generally, Jameson Doig, *Criminal Corrections: Ideals and Realities* (Lexington, Mass.: Lexington Books, 1983).

29. Allen Beck, *Profile of Jail Inmates, 1989* (Washington, D.C.: Bureau of Justice Statistics, 1991).

30. John Irwin, *The Jail: Managing the Underclass in American Society* (Berkeley: University of California Press, 1985).

31. Susan Kline, *Jail Inmates, 1989* (Washington, D.C.: Bureau of Justice Statistics, 1990).

32. Beck, *Profile of Jail Inmates*, p. 3.

33. Ibid.

34. Tracy Snell, *Women in Jail, 1989* (Washington, D.C.: Bureau of Justice Statistics, 1992).

35. Cited in Ben Bagdikan and Leon Dash, *The Shame of the Prisons* (New York: Pocket Books, 1972), p. 32.

36. Human Rights Watch, *Prison Conditions in the United States* (New York: Human Rights Watch, 1991).

37. Victor Kappeler, Michael Vaughn, and Rolando Del Carmen, "Death in Detention: An Analysis of Police Liability for Negligent Failure to Prevent Suicide," *Journal of Criminal Justice* 19 (1991):381–93.

38. "Judge Won't Subject Man to Jail 'Brutalities,' " *Omaha World Herald*, 10 April 1981, p. 21.

39. *National Study of Jail Suicides: Seven Years Later* (Alexandria, Va.: National Center on Institutions and Alternatives, 1988).

40. "2 Probes Yield Same Conclusion: Rikers Inmates Were Brutalized," *Criminal Justice Newsletter*, 22 (1 May 1991): 3.

41. Data in this section come from Kline, *Jail Inmates*, 1989.

42. "Philadelphia Frees Defendants to Meet Goal on Jail Crowding," *Criminal Justice Newsletter* 18 (15 June 1988).

43. Fred Heinzlemann, W. Robert Burkhart, Bernard Gropper, Cheryl Martorana, Lois Felson Mock, Maureen O'Connor, and Walter Philip Travers, *Jailing Drunk Drivers, Impact on the Criminal Justice System* (Washington, D.C.: National Institute of Justice, 1984).

44. Human Rights Watch, *Prison Conditions in the United States*.

45. Bascom Ratliff, "The Army Model, Boot Camp for Youthful Offenders," *Corrections Today* 50 (1988):98–102.

46. For a review, see Dale Sechrest, "Prison 'Boot Camps' Do Not Measure Up," *Federal Probation* 53 (1989):15–20.

47. "New York Correctional Groups Praises Boot Camp Programs," *Criminal Justice Newsletter* 22 (1 April 1991):4–5.

48. Doris Layton Mackenzie, "Boot Camp Prisons: Components, Evaluations, and Empirical Issues," *Federal Probation* 54 (1990):44–52; see, also, idem., "Boot Camp Programs Grow in Number and Scope," *NIJ Reports*, November/December 1990, pp. 6–8.

49. Bureau of Justice Statistics, *Prisons and Prisoners* (Washington, D.C.: U.S. Government Printing Office, 1982).

50. Correctional Research Associates, *Treating Youthful Offenders in the Community, An Evaluation Conducted by A. J. Reiss* (Washington, D.C.: Correctional Research Associates, 1966).

51. Kevin Krajick, "Not on My Block: Local Opposition Impedes the Search for Alternatives," *Corrections Magazine* 6 (1980):15–27.

52. Andrew Scull, *Decarceration: Community Treatment and the Deviant: A Radical View* (Englewood Cliffs, N.J.: Prentice-Hall, 1977); John Hylton, "Rhetoric and Reality: A Critical Appraisal of Community Correction Programs," *Crime and Delinquency* 28 (1982):341–73.

53. Ibid., p. 372.

54. "What Can We Learn from Recidivism Rates? Massachusetts Study Analyzes Trends, Patterns," *Corrections Digest* 16 (1985):5.

55. For a review, see John DiIulio, *Private Prisons* (Washington, D.C.: U.S. Government Printing Office, 1988); Joan Mullen, *Corrections and the Private Sector* (Washington, D.C.: National Institute of Justice, 1984).

56. Ira Robbins, *The Legal Dimensions of Private Incarceration* (Chicago: American Bar Foundation, 1988).

57. Lawrence Travis, Edward Latessa, and Gennaro Vito, "Private Enterprise and Institutional Corrections: A Call for Caution," *Federal Probation* 49 (1985):11–17.

58. Patrick Anderson, Charles Davoli, and Laura Moriarty, "Private Corrections: Feast or Fiasco," *Prison Journal* 65 (1985):32–41.
59. Charles Logan and Bill McGriff, "Comparing Costs of Public and Private Prisons: A Case Study," *NIJ Reports*, September-October 1989, pp. 2–8.
60. Data in this section come from Bureau of Justice Statistics, *Prisoners, 1925–1981* (Washington, D.C.: U.S. Government Printing Office, 1982).
61. Lawrence Greenfeld, *Prisoners in 1985* (Washington, D.C.: Bureau of Justice Statistics, 1986).
62. Bureau of Justice Statistics, National Update, January 1992 (Washington, D.C.: Bureau of Justice Statistics, 1992); Robyn Cohen, *Prisoners in 1990* (Washington, D.C.: Bureau of Justice Statistics, 1991), p. 2; Beck, *Profile of Jail Inmates, 1989*, p. 1.
63. George Cox and Susan Rhodes, "Managing Overcrowding: Corrections Administrators and the Prison Crisis," *Criminal Justice Policy Review* 4 (1990):115–43.
64. Cohen, *Prisoners in 1990*, p. 8.
65. Ibid.
66. *Status Report: The Courts and the Prisons*, (Washington, D.C.: National Prison Project, 1989).
67. Cohen, *Prisoners in 1990*, p. 6.
68. Celestine Bohlen, "Jail Influx Brings Plan for 2 Barges", *New York Times*, 3 March 1989, p. B1.
69. Cohen, *Prisoners in 1990*, p. 5.
70. Charles DeWitt, *New Construction Methods for Correctional Facilities* (Washington, D.C.: National Institute of Justice, 1986).
71. Steven Weirich, "Fully Equipped Precast Cells Offer Quality Construction Alternative," *Corrections Today* 53 (April 1991), p. 96.
72. "Texas Legislature Considered More Prisons and Alternatives," *Criminal Justice Newsletter* 22 (1 August 1991): 4.
73. "Congressional Report Questions Federal Prison Expansion Budget," *Criminal Justice Newsletter* (1991): 4.
74. Timothy Noah, "Prison Population Boom Sputters to Halt as States Lack Funds to House Criminals," *Wall Street Journal*, 3 February 1992, p. A7; Christopher Innes, *Profile of State Prison Inmates, 1986* (Washington, D.C.: Bureau of Justice Statistics, 1988). The survey of prison inmates is conducted by the Bureau of Justice Statistics every five to seven years.
75. Steven Dillingham and Lawrence Greenfeld, "An Overview of National Corrections Statistics," *Federal Probation* 55 (1991):27–33.

CHAPTER 17

Living in Prison

OUTLINE

KEY TERMS

total institutions
the hustle
niche
mature coping
inmate subculture
social code
argot
prisonization
importation model
Aryan Brotherhood
make-believe family
special-needs inmate
work-release
furlough
Free Venture
conjugal visit
coeducational prison
Fortune Society
self-governance
hands-off doctrine
substantive rights
jailhouse lawyer
exceptional circumstances doctrine
cruel and unusual punishment
double-bunked

To meet the needs of a growing inmate population, a vast and costly state and federal correctional system has developed. Today, there are approximately six hundred prison facilities in the United States.[1] A significant percentage of these are old, decrepit, archaic structures: 25 were built before 1875, 79 between 1875 and 1924, and 141 between 1925 and 1949. In fact, some of the first prisons ever constructed, such as New York's Auburn and Elmira facilities, are still in operation.

Although a majority of prisons are classified as medium-security, the more than half of all inmates are being held in large maximum-security institutions. Despite the continuous outcry by penologists against the use of fortress-like prisons, institutions holding a thousand or more inmates still predominate. Prison overcrowding is a significant problem. The prison system now holds over eight hundred thousand people. Some institutions are operating at two or three times their stated capacity. Recreation and workshop facilities have been turned into dormitories housing thirty or more inmates in a single room. While most prison experts agree that a minimum of sixty square feet is needed for each inmate, many prisons fail to reach this standard. In fact, surveys show that not one state has avoided crowding inmates in less than adequate space. It is estimated that 58 percent of all one-person cells, 90 percent of all two-person cells, and 20 percent of all larger living units (dormitories) are overcrowded.

This giant, overcrowded system designed to reform and rehabilitate offenders is instead undergoing a crisis of massive proportions. Institutions are so overcrowded that meaningful treatment efforts are often a matter of wishful thinking; recidivism rates are shockingly high. Inmates are resentful of the deteriorated conditions; correctional officers fear that the institution is ready to explode. This chapter presents a brief review of some of the most important issues confronting the nation's troubled correctional system.

Prison Inmates—A Profile

The Bureau of Justice Statistics conducts a survey of prison inmates every five to seven years.[2] The consistency of findings from prison surveys conducted during the past ten years suggest that the data collected represent a reasonably accurate portrait of today's prison inmate.

As might be expected, the personal characteristics of prison inmates reflect common traits of arrestees: inmates tend to be young, single, poorly educated,

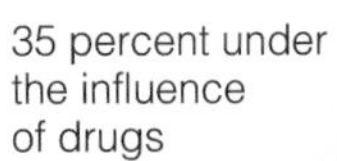

FIGURE 17.1
Characteristics of State Prison Inmates

SOURCE: Lawrence Greenfeld and Stephanie Minor-Harper, *Women in Prison* (Washington, D.C.: Bureau of Justice Statistics, 1991).

disproportionately male, and minority-group members (see Figure 17.1). About one third of all inmates report that they were not employed prior to their arrest and about one quarter had a yearly income of less than three thousand dollars. The picture that emerges is that prisons hold those people who face the toughest social obstacles in society. Only a few members of the educated middle-class wind up behind bars, and these people are usually held in low-security, "country club" institutions.

What did the inmates do to earn their present sentence? More than one half of all inmates are serving time for violent crimes. The percentage of drug offenders in the inmate population has increased by more than 50 percent since 1979, a reflection of either the increased emphasis on controlling the drug trade or greater offender involvement in drug trafficking. The most common offenses among the prison population were robbery (20.9 percent) and burglary (16.5 percent).

Gender differences in the prison population are considerable. Women are actually underrepresented in prison, and not solely because they commit less serious crimes. While the FBI reports that women generally are arrested for about 20 percent of all index crimes and 11 percent of all violent crimes, female inmates account for only 4 percent of the prison population. While the typical male inmate was a violent offender, female inmates committed property offenses.

Drug and Alcohol Abuse

The survey also found that many inmates had used drugs and alcohol throughout their life. More than half of all inmates report being under the influence of drugs, alcohol, or both when they committed their last offense. About 42 percent claim to have used a major drug, such as heroin, cocaine, PCP, or LSD, on a daily basis before their arrest, while 62 percent claim to be regular users.

These data support the view that a strong association exists between substance abuse and serious crime (unless one believes that only substance-abusing criminals are caught, convicted, and sent to prison). Considering the rampant drug and alcohol abuse, it is not surprising that crime-control strategies depending on general deterrence often fail to achieve their desired result: a majority of current inmates may have been incapable of appreciating both the severity of the punishments they faced and the certainty of their capture. Substance abuse may be the single greatest obstacle to creating a successful deterrence-based crime-control strategy.

In summary, the portrait of the prison inmate developed by the national survey is as follows: young, male, minority, poor, drug and/or alcohol abuser, undereducated, recidivist, violent.

Men Imprisoned

According to prevailing wisdom, prisons in the United States are **total institutions** (see the Analyzing Criminal Justice Issues on page 592 for an alternative view).

Inmates locked within their walls are segregated from the outside world, kept under constant scrutiny and surveillance, and forced to obey strict official rules to avoid facing formal sanctions. Their personal possessions are taken from them, and they must conform to institutional dress and personal appearance norms. Many human functions are strictly curtailed—heterosexual relationships and sex, friendships, family relationships, education, and participation in groups become past events. As prison expert Robert Johnson observes:

> Imprisonment is a disheartening and threatening experience for most men. The man in prison finds his career disrupted, his relationships suspended, his aspirations and dreams gone sour. Few prisoners have experienced comparable stress in the free world, or have developed coping strategies or perspectives that shield them from prison problems. Although prisoners differ from each other, and may feel the pressures of confinement somewhat differently, they concur on the extraordinarily stressful nature of life in maximum security penal institutions.[3]

Inmates quickly learn what the term *total institution* really means. When they arrive at the prison, they are stripped, searched, shorn, and assigned living quarters. Before they get there, though, their first experience occurs in a classification/reception center, where they are given a series of psychological and other tests and evaluated on the basis of their personality, background, offense history, and treatment needs. Based on the classification they are then given, they will be assigned to a permanent facility. Hard-core, repeat, and violent offenders will go to the maximum-security unit; offenders with learning disabilities may be assigned to an institution that specializes in educational services; mentally disordered offenders will be held in a facility that can provide psychiatric care, and so on.

Once they arrive at the long-term facility, inmates may be granted a short orientation period and then given a permanent cell assignment in the general population. Due to overcrowding, they may be sharing a cell designed for a single inmate with one or more others. All previous concepts of personal privacy and dignity are soon forgotten. Personal losses include the deprivation of liberty, goods, and services, heterosexual relationships, autonomy, and security.[4] Inmates may be subject to verbal and physical attack and threats with little chance of legal redress. While the criminal law applies to inmates as to any other citizen, it is rarely enforced within prison walls.[5] Therefore, part of living in prison includes learning to protect oneself, and developing survival instincts.

ANALYZING CRIMINAL JUSTICE ISSUES

Are Prisons "Total Institutions"?

The term *total institution* has been used to describe the prison experience in the United States ever since Erving Goffman published *Asylums* in 1961. In this classic work, Goffman described large places or residences where like-situated individuals live cut off from wider society. Total institutions were thought to be regimented and dehumanizing.

Sociologist Keith Farrington charges that applying the "total institution" concept to the prison experience may be misplaced; prisons might better be described as "not-so-total" institutions.

Farrington explains that modern prisons, even those located in remote areas, are never totally insulated from society. Most require a constant supply of goods, services, and materials from the outside world. The staff moves freely between the prison and the external world, carrying the prison into the community and vice versa. Similarly, inmates maintain aspects of their former lives, including gang memberships, while in prison. Many receive relatively short sentences and are sent back into the community, often without any real supervision.

The fact that prisons are not total institutions should come as no surprise since current prison reform efforts stress reintegration, rather than reform. It is common to reward good behavior with unsupervised family visits, furloughs, and other opportunities that further erode the total institution concept. It is in the nature of the American spirit to abhor isolation and encourage interdependence and socialization.

Farrington finds that the "total institution" concept is an enduring public myth. People still use such cliches as "lock them up and throw away the key" or send them "up the river" because most know relatively little about prison life and depend on films and TV for information; the result is an image of "wailing sirens, shot-gun wielding guards, and escaping inmates scaling the walls with ropes fashioned out of bed sheets." People cling to these images partly because it makes them feel safe and also because incarceration seems to be a fair and relatively humane method of treating felons: it provides offenders with an environment conducive to rehabilitation and is less severe than physical punishment or the death penalty.

The myth of the "total institution" is also cultivated by correctional administrators in order to smooth over challenges to prison sitings. Why worry about a prison in your backyard if it is a "total institution" from which nobody escapes or receives work furloughs; it is unlikely that the local town council members debating prison construction plans are informed of the number of inmates likely to remain in the community after they are paroled.

While the "total institution" myth may be comforting, it can have a negative influence on correctional policy. Prisons cannot hope to succeed in a fashion that would be expected from a total institution. Still, because the myth endures, laws have become harsher and more people are being sent to institutions that cannot hope to meet their stated goals of protection and rehabilitation.

Critical Thinking Skills

1. A plan has been developed to build an island prison, self-sufficient for all its needs and totally cut off from society. Inmates would serve their entire sentence on this island without outside interference or contact with families or friends. It would be safe, hygienic, and escape-proof. Do you approve of this plan, or are there some unforeseen consequences that might upset the applecart?

2. Research indicates that the most powerful predictor of recidivism is the amount of time spent in a maximum-security institution. Conversely, inmates placed in low-security camp-type institutions that offer family visitations, liberal furlough policies, and advanced educational opportunities have the lowest recidivism rates. How would you interpret this finding?

SOURCE: Keith Farrington, "The Modern Prison as Total Institution? Public Perception versus Objective Reality," *Crime and Delinquency* 38 (1992):6–26.

Inmates in large, inaccessible prisons may find themselves physically cut off from families, friends, and associates. Visitors may find it difficult to travel great distances to visit them; mail is censored and sometimes destroyed.

Inmates may go through a variety of attitude and behavior changes, or cycles, as their sentence unfolds. During the early part of their prison stay, inmates may become easily depressed while considering the long duration of the sentence and the loneliness and dangers of prison life. They must learn the ins and outs of survival in the institution: What persons can be befriended, what persons are best avoided? Who will grant favors, and for what repayment? Inmates may find that some prisoners have formed cliques or groups based on ethnic backgrounds or personal interests; Mafia-like or racial terror groups will soon be encountered and must be dealt with. Inmates may be the victim of homosexual attacks. They may find that power in the prison is being shared by terrified guards and inmate gangs; the only way to avoid being beaten and raped may be to learn how to beat and rape.[6] If they are weak and unable to defend themselves, new inmates may find that they are considered a "punk"; if they ask a guard for help, they are labeled a "snitch." After that, they may spend the rest of their sentence in protective custody, sacrificing the "freedom of the yard" and rehabilitation services for personal protection.[7]

Adjusting to Prison

Despite all these hardships, most inmates learn to adapt to the prison routine. Each prisoner has his own method of coping; he may stay alone, become friends with another inmate, join a group, or seek the advice of treatment personnel. New inmates must learn to deal with the guards and other correctional personnel; these relationships will determine whether the inmates do "hard time" or "easy time." Regardless of adaptation style, the first stage of the inmates' prison cycle is marked by a growing awareness that they can no longer depend on their traditional associates for help and support and that for better or worse, the institution is a new home to which they must adjust. Unfortunately for the goal of rehabilitation, the predominant emotion that inmates must confront is boredom. As Kevin Wright suggests:

> The unmitigated absence of anything constructive to do, the forced idleness, is what is so distracting, so frustrating, and often so damaging.[8]

Part of new inmates' early adjustment involves their becoming familiar with and perhaps participating in the black market, the hidden economy of the prison—**the hustle.** Hustling provides inmates with a source of steady income and the satisfaction that they are beating the system.[9] Hustling involves sales of such illegal commodities as drugs (uppers, downers, pot), alcohol, weapons, or illegally obtained food and supplies. When prison officials crack down on hustled goods, it merely serves to drive the price up—giving hustlers greater incentive to promote their black-market activities.[10]

Inmates must also learn to deal with the racial conflict that is a daily fact of life. Prisoners tend to segregate themselves, and if peace is to reign in the institution, they learn to stay out of each other's way. Often racial groupings are quite exact; for example, Hispanics will separate themselves according to their national origin (Mexico, Puerto Rico, Colombia, etc.). Since racial disparity in sentencing is common in many U.S. courts, prisons are one place where minorities often hold power; as sociologist James B. Jacobs observed, "Prison may be the one institution in American society that blacks control."[11]

Inmates may find that the social support of inmate peers can make incarceration somewhat less painful. They may begin to take stock of their situation and enter into education or vocational training programs, if they are available. They heed the inmate grapevine to determine what the parole board considers important in deciding to grant community release. They may become more politically aware due to the influence of other inmates, and the personal guilt they may

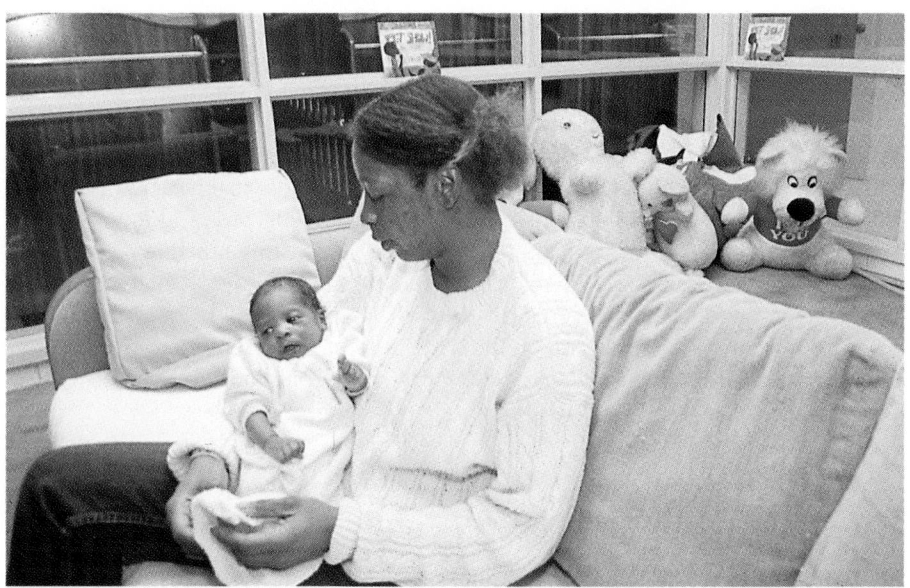

Women, many of whom have children, make up about 4 percent of the prison population. Authorities have attempted to provide facilities to keep infants with their mothers.

have felt may be shifted to society at large. Why should they be in prison when those equally guilty go free? They learn the importance of money and politics. Eventually, they may be called on by new arrivals to aid them in adapting to the system.

Coping Behavior

Even in the harsh prison environment, inmates may learn to find a **niche** for themselves. According to Hans Toch, inmates may be able to find a place, activity, or group in which they can feel comfortable and secure.[12] An inmate's niche is a kind of insulation from the pains of imprisonment, enabling him to cope and providing him with a sense of autonomy and freedom. As one prisoner says about his niche, a desirable work detail:

> Now I have to deal with one officer, and I work a very short period each day. The rest of the day is mine to do as I choose with, which gives me a great deal of time for myself . . . I don't have to lock in for some counts . . . I'm pretty much free here.[13]

Robert Johnson argues that inmates can adjust successfully to prison through a process of **mature coping.** This involves such tasks as:

> . . . dealing with problems . . . head-on, using all resources legitimately at one's disposal . . . addressing problems without resort to deception or violence, except where they are necessary for self-defense.
>
> . . . making an effort to empathize with and assist others in need, to act as though we are indeed members of a human community who can work together to create a more secure and gratifying existence.[14]

Mature coping strategies may be possible because, according to Johnson, many inmates reject the violent prison culture and are receptive to change. Even maximum-security prisons can provide the opportunity for mature change; "and they must do just that if they are to play a viable role in the correctional process."[15]

Of course, not all inmates learn to cope. Some inmates repeatedly violate institutional rules; 14 percent of all inmates have six or more such infractions yearly.[16] While it is difficult to predict who will become a institutional troublemaker, Leonore Simon found that rule-breaking behavior is associated with being a younger inmate with a low IQ possessing numerous juvenile convictions, being a repeat offender, and having victimized a stranger. Simon speculates that inmates who have limited intelligence and maintain low self-control may not be able to form adaptive coping mechanisms and manage the stress of being in prison.[17]

Inmate Society

For many years, criminal justice experts maintained that inmates formed their own world with a unique set of norms and rules known as the **inmate subculture.**[18] A significant aspect of the inmate subculture was a unique **social code,** unwritten guidelines that express the values, attitudes, and types of behavior that older inmates demand of young ones. Passed on from one generation of inmates to another, the inmate social code represents the values of interpersonal relations within the prison.

National attention was first drawn to the inmate social code and subculture by Donald Clemmer. In *The Prison Community,* Clemmer presented a detailed sociological study of life in a maximum-security prison.[19] Referring to thousands of conversations and interviews, as well as to inmate essays and biographies, Clemmer was able to identify a unique language **(argot)** that prisoners use. In addition, Clemmer found that prisoners tend to group themselves into cliques on the basis of such personal criteria as sexual preference, political beliefs, and offense history. He found complex sexual relationships in prison and concluded that many heterosexual men will turn to homosexual relationships when faced with long sentences and the loneliness of prison life.

Clemmer's most important contribution may have been his identification of the **prisonization** process. This he defined as the inmate's assimilation into the existing prison culture through acceptance of its language, sexual code, and norms of behavior. Those who become the most "prisonized" will be the least likely to reform on the outside.

Using Clemmer's work as a jumping-off point, a number of prominent sociologists have set out to explore more fully the various roles in the prison community. For example, in one important analysis entitled *The Society of Captives,* Gresham Sykes further defined prison argot and argued that the prison culture exists in response to the deprivations presented by the prison.[20] Later, writing with Sheldon Messinger, Sykes identified the following as the most important principles of the prison community:

> **1.** *Don't interfere with inmates' interests.* Within this area of the code are maxims concerning the serving of the least amount of time in the greatest possible comfort. For example, inmates are warned . . . never [to betray another] inmate to authorities; . . . [in other words,] grievances must be handled personally. Other aspects of the noninterference doctrine include "Don't be nosy," "Don't have a loose lip," "Keep off [the other inmates' backs]," and "Don't put [another inmate] on the spot."
> **2.** *Don't lose your head.* Inmates are also cautioned to refrain from arguing, [quarreling, or engaging in] other emotional displays with fellow inmates. The novice may hear such warnings as "Play it cool" and "Do your own time."
> **3.** *Don't exploit inmates.* Prisoners are warned not to take advantage of one another—"Don't steal from cons," "Don't welsh on a debt," "Be right."

4. *Inmates are cautioned to be tough and not lose their dignity.* While rule 2 forbids conflict, once it starts, an inmate must be prepared to deal with it effectively and [thoroughly]. Maxims include "Don't cop out," "Don't weaken," "Be tough; be a man."

5. *Don't be a sucker.* Inmates are cautioned not to make fools . . . of themselves and support the guards or prison administration over the interest of the inmates—"Be sharp."[21]

According to Sykes and Messinger, some inmates violate the code and exploit their peers, while the "right guy" is someone who personalizes the inmate social code as his personal behavior guide:

> A right guy is always loyal to his fellow prisoners. He never lets you down, no matter how rough things get. He keeps his promises. He's dependable and trustworthy. . . . The "right guy" never interferes with inmates who are conniving against the officials. He doesn't go around looking for a fight, but he never runs away from one when he is in the right . . . he acts like a man.[22]

The Importation Model

Not all prison experts believed that the prison culture reflected the harsh conditions existing in a total institution. In 1962, John Irwin and Donald Cressey published a paper in which they conceded that a prison culture exists but claimed that its principles are actually imported from the outside world.[23] In their **importation model,** Irwin and Cressey conclude that the inmate culture is affected as much by the values of newcomers as it is by traditional inmate values.[24] Irwin and Cressey found that the inmate world was actually divided into three groups, each corresponding to a role in the outside world. The thief subculture was made up of professional criminals who stick to themselves and always try to "do your own time." Members of the convict subculture try to obtain power in the prison and control others for their own needs. The conventional subculture is made up of inmates who try to retain legitimate elements of the outside world in their daily life (that is, they identify with neither of the deviant prison subcultures). Irwin and Cressey's research showed that the inmate culture could be influenced by outside events and that the values that inmates held on the outside could be imported into the prison.

The "New" Inmate Culture

While the "old" inmate subculture may have been harmful because its norms and values insulated the inmate from change efforts, it also helped create order within the institution and prevented violence among the inmates. People who violated the code and victimized others were sanctioned by their peers. An understanding developed between guards and inmate leaders: the guards would let the inmates have things their own way; the inmates would not let things get out of hand and draw the attention of the administration.

The old system may be dying or already dead in most institutions. The change seems to have been precipitated by the Black Power movement in the 1960s and 1970s. Black inmates were no longer content to fill a subservient role and challenged the power of established white inmates. As the Black Power movement gained prominence, racial tension in prisons created divisions that severely altered the inmate subculture. Older, respected inmates could no longer cross racial lines to mediate disputes. Predatory inmates could victimize others without fear of retaliation.[25] Consequently, more inmates than ever are now assigned to protective custody for their own safety.[26]

Sociologist James B. Jacobs is perhaps the most influential expert on the changing inmate subculture. His research has led him to conclude that the development of "black (and Latino) power" in the 1960s, spurred by the Black Power movement, significantly influenced the nature of prison life.[27]

According to Jacobs, African-American and Latin inmates are much more cohesively organized than whites. Their groups sometimes form out of religious or political affiliations, such as the Black Muslims; efforts to combat discrimination in prison, such as the Latin group La Familia; or street gangs, such as the Vice Lords, Disciples, or Blackstone Rangers in the Illinois prison system and the Crips in California. When white inmates have successfully organized, it is in the form of a neo-Nazi group called the **Aryan Brotherhood.** Racially homogenous gangs are so cohesive and powerful that they are able to supplant the original inmate code with one of their own. Consider the oath taken by new members of *Nuestra Familia* (Our Family), a Latin gang operating in California prisons: "If I go forward, follow me. If I hesitate, push me. If they kill me, avenge me. If I am a traitor, kill me."[28]

The racial polarity in today's prison system and its influence on the inmate culture have just begun to be explored in depth. Charles Stastny and Gabrielle Tyrnauer document the existence of racial cliques—the Black Prisoner's Forum Unlimited, the Confederated Indian Tribes, and United Chicanos—in the Washington state prison system. These groups not only provide protection to their members but also act as a bloc to make demands on prison administrators.[29] Although their members may adhere to principles of the traditional inmate code (e.g., "don't inform"), allegiance is always to members of one's own group.

Future research on prison culture will begin to evaluate the role race plays in prison life and how inmate racism influences the "traditional" prisoner culture. This research is particularly important when we consider that it has been estimated that just four California gangs—Nuestra Familia, the Mexican Mafia, the Aryan Brotherhood, and the Black Guerilla Family—have reportedly killed more than a hundred inmates and wounded scores of others.[30] In fact, the situation is so bad and tensions are so high that an authority as well-respected as James Jacobs has suggested that it may be humane and appropriate to segregate inmates along racial lines in order to maintain order and protect individual rights. Jacobs believes that in some prisons, administrators use integration as a threat to keep inmates in line; to be transferred to a racially mixed setting may mean beatings or death.[31]

Women Imprisoned

Before 1960, few women were in prison. Women's prisons were relatively rare and were usually an outgrowth of male institutions. Only four institutions for women were built between 1930 and 1950; in comparison, thirty-four women's prisons were constructed during the 1980s.

At the turn of the century, female inmates were viewed as morally depraved people who flaunted conventional rules of female behavior. The treatment of white and African-American women differed significantly. As Nicole Hahn Rafter points out, white women were placed in female-only reformatories designed to improve their deportment; black women were placed in male prisons, where they were subject to the chain gang and beatings.[32]

The place of women in the correctional system has changed rapidly. Today, approximately forty-five thousand women are in the state and federal systems, about 5.7 percent of the total inmate population.[33] Though still small compared to the male inmate population, the number of incarcerated women has grown at a faster pace since 1980, increasing more than 200 percent, compared to an increase of slightly more than 100 percent for males.

The female offender population has increased so rapidly for a number of reasons. Females have accelerated their crime rate at a faster pace than males. While the number of male index crime arrests increased 15 percent between 1981 and 1990, the number of female arrests increased 34 percent.[34] The female inmate population also increased because a greater percentage of convicted female offenders are being sent to prison: in 1980, for every 1,000 women arrested for serious crimes, 136 were incarcerated; by 1989, that number had grown to 272 per 1,000 serious arrests.[35] The "get tough" policies that produced mandatory and determinate sentencing statutes also helped reduce the judicial discretion that has traditionally benefited women. As Meda Chesney-Lind points out, women are swept up in the get-tough movement and no longer receive the benefits of male chivalry. The use of sentencing guidelines means that such factors as family ties and employment record, two elements that usually benefit women during sentencing, can no longer be considered by judges.[36] Chesney-Lind notes that judges seem willing once again to view female offenders as "depraved" and outside the ranks of "true womanhood."

Female Institutions

State jurisdictions have been responding to the influx of female offenders into the correctional system by expanding the facilities for housing and treating them. New construction efforts include a 132-bed facility opened in Minnesota (1986), a 300-bed prison in Michigan (1985), and a 400-bed institution in California (1987); California also has begun construction on a 2,200-bed facility.[37] Other states, such as New York, Georgia, Washington, and Florida, have geared home confinement, restitution, and other alternative programs specifically toward women in an effort to relieve overcrowding.[38]

A number of research efforts have described women's prisons.[39] Women's prisons tend to be smaller than those housing male inmates. Most are generally not high-security institutions, such are commonly used for male inmates. Although some female institutions are strictly penal, with steel bars, concrete floors, and other security measures, the majority are nonsecure institutions similar to college dormitories and group homes in the community. Women's facilities, especially those in the community, commonly offer a great deal of autonomy to inmates and allow them to make decisions affecting their daily life in the institution.

Women's prisons also suffer from the same lack of adequate training, health, treatment, and educational facilities as those that house male inmates. Psychological counseling often takes the form of group sessions conducted by lay people, such as correctional officers. Most trained psychologists and psychiatrists restrict themselves to such activities as intake classification, court-ordered examinations, and prescribing mood-controlling medication.

The Female Inmate

What are the characteristics of incarcerated women?[40] Like their male counterparts, female inmates are young (72 percent are under thirty-four years old), minority-group members (60 percent), unmarried (80 percent), undereducated (56 percent are not high school graduates), and underemployed (63 percent worked part-time or were unemployed prior to their arrest; of these, 31 percent were not even looking for work).

The family life of incarcerated women also appears troubled. Significant numbers were "at risk" children, products of "broken homes" and the welfare system; over half had received welfare sometime during their adult lives. They experienced a pattern of harsh discipline and physical abuse. About 41 percent claim to have been physically and/or sexually abused sometime in their life.[41] This pattern continued in their adult life: many female inmates had been the victim and perpetrator of domestic violence.

A serious problem of women in prison is the disruption of their families. More than 76 percent of the women in prison had children; of these, 80 percent were living with their children before arrest. Who takes care of the children while their mothers are incarcerated? Children of incarcerated women apparently are not bound over to foster parents. Some 90 percent are placed with their father, grandparent, other relative, or family friend. About 10 percent wind up in foster homes or state agencies.

A significant number of female inmates report having substance abuse problems. An estimated 72 percent of the women in state prisons had used drugs at some time in their lives, with 52 percent reporting using major drugs, such as cocaine, heroin, or PCP. There was little difference in major drug use among male and female offenders when measured over the lifespan or at the time of their current arrest. About 22 percent of female inmates report being on a major drug at the time of their arrest (compared to 18 percent of the men).

The picture that emerges of the female inmate is troubling. After a lifetime of emotional turmoil, physical and sexual abuse, and drug use, it seems improbable that overcrowded, underfunded correctional institutions can forge a dramatic turnaround in the behavior of the "at risk" female populations.

The Culture of the Female Prisoner

Daily life in the women's prison differs somewhat from that in male institutions. For one thing, unlike male inmates, women usually do not present an immediate, violent physical danger to staff and fellow inmates. A recent survey of female inmates in Minnesota by Candace Kruttschnitt and Sharon Krmpotich found that less than 25 percent engaged in violent behavior and that incidents of sexual aggression were virtually nonexistent.[42]

Nor does there exist the rigid antiauthority inmate social code found in many male institutions.[43] Confinement for women, however, may produce severe anxiety and anger, due to separation from families and loved ones and the inability to function in normal female roles. Unlike men, who direct their anger outward, female prisoners may revert to more self-destructive acts in order to cope with their problems. Female inmates are more likely than males to mutilate their own bodies and attempt suicide. For example, one common practice of female inmates is self-mutilation or "carving." This ranges from simple scratches, to carving the name of their boyfriend on their body or even complex statements or sentences ("To mother, with hate").[44]

Another form of adaptation to prison employed by women is the **make-believe family.** This group contains masculine and feminine figures acting as fathers and mothers; some even act as children and take on the role of either brother or sister. Formalized marriages and divorces may be conducted. Sometimes multiple roles are held by one inmate, so that a "sister" in one family may "marry" and become the "wife" of another inmate. In a highly detailed study of sex roles among young female inmates, Alice Propper found that about half were currently members of make-believe families (which she labels "quasi-kinship" groups).[45]

The primary female roles were sister-sister and mother-daughter; homosexual marriages were relatively rare, and most women did not wish to take on masculine roles. Nor were make-believe families unique to the female prisoners; when males were introduced into the institutions, they were included in the kinship groups.

Why do make-believe families exist? According to Propper and other experts, they provide the warm, stable relationships otherwise unobtainable in the prison environment:

> People in and out of prison have needs for security, companionship, affection, attention, status, prestige, and acceptance that can only be filled by having primary group relationships. Friends fill many of these needs, but the family better represents our ideal or desire for these things in a stable relationship.[46]

Institutional Treatment Programs

Almost every prison facility employs some mode of treatment for inmates.[47] This may come in the form of individual or group therapy programs or educational or vocational training.

Despite good intentions, rehabilitative treatment within prison walls is extremely difficult to achieve. Trained professional treatment personnel usually command high salaries, and most institutions do not have sufficient budgets to adequately staff therapeutic programs. Usually, a large facility may have a single staff psychiatrist and/or a few social workers. A second problem revolves around the philosophy of *less eligibility*, which has been interpreted to mean that prisoners should always be treated less well than the most underprivileged law-abiding citizen. Translated into today's terms, less eligibility usually involves the question "Why should correctional system inmates be treated to expensive programs denied to the average honest citizen?" Enterprising state legislators use this argument to block expenditures for prison budgets, and some prison administrators may actually agree with them.

Finally, correctional treatment is hampered by the ignorance surrounding the practical effectiveness of one type of treatment program over another. What constitutes proper treatment has not yet been determined, and studies evaluating treatment effectiveness have suggested that few, if any, of the programs currently employed in prisons actually produce significant numbers of rehabilitated offenders.

This section discusses a selected number of therapeutic methods that have been employed nationally in correctional settings and identifies some of their more salient features.

Counseling Programs

The most common type of institutional treatment is counseling, which is done through a wide variety of programs. The number of clinically trained mental health professionals on a corrections department's payroll is typically inadequate to carry out treatment requirements. Consequently, counseling programs commonly use nonclinical treatment personnel as group leaders.[48] Some are conducted under contract by private, nonprofit agencies that send counselors into the institution.[49]

In general, the goals of counseling therapy are:

1. To help prisoners adjust to the frustrations that are an unalterable part of life in an institution and in society.
2. To enable prisoners to recognize the role of emotional conflicts in their criminal behavior.
3. To provide inmates with the opportunity to learn from their peers about the social aspects of their personality.
4. To make possible a better understanding by inmates of how costly inappropriate behavioral responses can be to them.
5. To improve the emotional climate of the institution.[50]

Group counseling does not depend on or attempt to make fundamental changes in the inmate's personality but instead makes use of the group to stimulate his or her self-awareness and ability to deal with everyday problems within the institution. Inmates may use the group to learn to understand how others view them and how they view themselves. Group counseling can also be directed toward helping inmates solve perplexing personal problems that they are incapable of dealing with alone; for example, by helping them to end deviant or violent sexual behaviors.[51]

Many correctional systems employ a variety of more intensive individual and group techniques: behavior modification, aversive therapy, milieu therapy, reality therapy, transactional analysis, and responsibility therapy, among others.[52]

New therapy techniques are always being tried within the prison system. The Joseph Harp Correctional Center in Lexington, Oklahoma, has instituted "pet therapy" in the institution's mental health unit. Caring for and becoming affectionate with puppies have helped lift the spirits of violent inmates and reduced their aggression.[53] A new approach being used in Canadian prisons employs audiovisual aids, games, puzzles, and reasoning exercises with small groups of inmates to sharpen their cognitive skills and improve their reasoning power. The "Living Skills" program is designed to help inmates improve interpersonal skills in such areas as parenting, anger management, budgeting, work, and personal health care. Evaluations show that inmates who successfully complete the program have a recidivism rate of only 20 percent.[54]

While counseling is a major component of correctional treatment policy, the personnel and resources needed to carry out effective programs is often lacking. Many institutions maintain a unit for the emotionally disturbed and offer psychological services tied in with state hospitals and mental health services.[55] Yet the number of trained mental health professionals employed in the correctional system is far less than what is actually needed. This problem becomes even more acute when we consider that an estimated 10 percent of the prison population may be suffering from acute mental problems such as schizophrenia, that an additional 10 to 50 percent may suffer from adaption problems marked by nervousness, sleeplessness, and depression, and that another 30 percent or more suffer from what are termed as character disorders or antisocial behavior.[56]

Treating the Special-Needs Inmate

One of the challenges of correctional treatment is to care for the so-called **special-needs inmate.**[57] These individuals can have a variety of social problems. Some are mentally ill but have been assigned to prison because the state has toughened its insanity laws. Others suffer mental problems developed during their imprisonment. It is estimated that about 10 percent of all inmates suffer from acute

Pet therapy programs allow inmates to care for animals in an effort to lift spirits and reduce aggression.

mental disorders.[58] An additional 1 to 6 percent of the inmate population is mentally retarded.[59] Treating the mentally ill inmate has required the development and use of new therapies in the prison environment. While some critics warn of the overuse of "chemical straitjackets"—psychotropic medications—to keep disturbed inmates docile, recent research by Ira Sommers and Deborah Baskin found that the treatment of the mentally ill inmates is actually based on their treatment needs and not institutional security requirements.[60]

Restrictive crime-control policies have also produced another special-needs group, elderly inmates who require health care, diets, and work and recreational opportunities that are quite different from those of the general population. Some correctional systems have responded to the growing number of elderly inmates by creating facilities tailored to their needs. The State Park Correctional Institution in South Carolina houses a special 120-bed unit for geriatric and handicapped patients that can provide the special work opportunities and medical care they require.[61]

The Drug-Dependent Inmate. Another special-needs group in prison are drug-dependent inmates. Though most institutions attempt to provide drug and alcohol treatment, these efforts are often inadequate. A recent government survey found that an estimated half a million state inmates are in need of drug treatment, but due to lack of funding and inadequate security measures, only one hundred thousand receive adequate treatment.[62]

Because of this demand, a number of jurisdictions have implemented intensive drug treatment efforts. The federal prison system has started comprehensive drug abuse treatment programs in its facilities. Designed to handle around one hundred offenders at a time, the units feature the following components:

1. Unit-based programs;
2. Treatment staff-to-inmate ratio of 1 to 24;
3. Program participation of nine months and five hundred program hours, minimum;
4. Individualized treatment plans based on comprehensive assessment;

5. A prerequisite of forty hours of drug education;
6. Between three and four hours of drug treatment programming per day;
7. Comprehensive assessment;
8. Two hundred eighty hours of core group/individual treatment;
9. One hundred hours of wellness life-style training;
10. Forty hours of transitional living issues;
11. Full team reviews every ninety days;
12. Treatment team review every thirty days; and
13. Increased frequency of random urinalysis surveillance.[63]

While the ideal drug treatment has yet to be identified, experimental efforts around the country use counseling sessions, instruction in coping strategies, employment counseling, and strict security measures featuring random urinalysis.

The AIDS-Infected Inmate. The AIDS-infected prisoner is another acute special-needs inmate. Two groups of people at high risk of contracting the HIV virus are intravenous drug users who share needles and males who engage in homosexual sex, two life-styles common in prison. Though the numbers are constantly changing, more than seven thousand inmates have been diagnosed as having AIDS (1990 figures), and the incidence is increasing daily.[64] While an estimated 17 people in every 100,000 of the U.S. population may be infected with the AIDS virus, the rate in prison is much higher, ranging up to 1,047 per 100,000, depending on the prison system.[65]

Correctional administrators have found it difficult to arrive at effective policies to confront AIDS. While all state and federal jurisdictions do some AIDS testing, only fifteen states and the Federal Bureau of Prisons conduct mass screenings of all inmates. Most states test inmates only if there are significant indications that they are HIV-positive.

Most correctional systems are now conducting educational training sessions for staff. Educational programs for inmates are often inadequate because administrators are reluctant to give them information on the proper cleaning of drug paraphernalia and safe sex (since both drug-taking and homosexual sex are forbidden in prison).

Many questions remain about the proper treatment of AIDS-infected inmates. Should they be given the full range of treatment, including expensive medications such as AZT? While most jurisdictions report that they provide this care, many fail to provide treatment to *all* infected inmates. Should AIDS-infected inmates be excluded from the general population and held in restricted areas? While about 30 percent of the correctional systems have some type of segregation policy, most mainstream inmates with AIDS in the general inmate population. Cases challenging segregation policies have been filed, and in an important California case, *Gates v. Deukmejian*, a court ordered a one-year experimental program in which twenty to thirty HIV-infected inmates would live in a closed unit but be mainstreamed with the general population in all programs and activities.[66] Prison administrators have been sued over incidents in which staff or inmates were bitten or spit upon by HIV-infected inmates. So far, no cases have been reported of someone becoming infected as a result of such an incident.

What steps should be taken to limit the risk to inmates and staff of HIV infection? A majority of institutions now provide AIDS information and education to both groups. Most encourage the proper handling of inmates to reduce risk of infection. Controversy exists over whether condoms should be provided

These AIDS-infected inmates are being crowded into a facility designed to hold HIV-positive prisoners.

to inmates. Only five correctional systems currently take that step; the majority of officials believe condom distribution encourages and condones behavior that is illegal and—some feel—immoral.

Despite efforts at prevention and treatment, AIDS likely will continue to be a major problem for prison administrators, straining budgets and increasing tension within the institutions.

Educational and Vocational Programs

In addition to treatment programs stressing personal growth through individual analysis or group process, inmate rehabilitation is also pursued through vocational and educational training. While these two kinds of training sometimes differ in style and content, they can also overlap when, for example, education involves practical, job-related study.

The first prison treatment programs were in fact educational in nature. A prison school was opened at the Walnut Street Jail in 1784. Elementary courses were offered in New York's prison system in 1801 and in Pennsylvania's in 1844. An actual school system was established in Detroit's House of Corrections in 1870, and Elmira Reformatory opened a vocational trade school in 1876.[67]

Today, most institutions provide some type of educational program. At some prisons, inmates can obtain a high school diploma or a general educational development (GED) certificate through equivalency exams. Other institutions provide an actual classroom education, usually staffed by certified teachers employed full-time at the prison or by part-time teachers who also teach full-time at nearby public schools. The number of hours devoted to educational programs and the quality and intensity of these efforts vary greatly. Some are full-time programs employing highly qualified and concerned educators, while others are part-time programs without any real goals or objectives.[68]

While worthwhile attempts are being made, prison education programs often suffer from inadequate funding and administration. The picture is not totally bleak, however. In some institutions, programs have been designed to circumvent the difficulties inherent in the prison structure. They encourage volunteers from the community and local schools to tutor willing and motivated inmates. Some prison administrators have arranged flexible schedules for inmate students and actively encourage their participation in these programs. In several states, such as Texas, Connecticut, and Illinois, statewide school districts serving prisons have been created.[69] Forming such districts can make available better qualified staff and provide the materials and resources necessary for meaningful educational programs.

Every state correctional system also has some job-related services for inmates. Some have elaborate training programs within the institution, while others have instituted pre- and postrelease employment services. Inmates who hope to obtain parole need to participate in prison industry. Documenting a history of stable employment in prison is essential if parole agents are to convince prospective employers that the ex-offender is a good risk; postrelease employment is usually required for parole eligibility.[70]

A few of the more important work-related services are discussed below.

Basic Prison Industries. Prisoners are normally expected to work within the institution as part of their treatment program. Aside from saving money for the institution, prison work programs are supposed to help inmates develop good habits and skills. Most prominent among traditional prison industries are those designed to help maintain and run the institution and provide services for other public or state facilities, such as mental hospitals. These include:

1. *Food services*. Inmates are expected to prepare and supply food for the prisoners and the staff. These duties include baking bread, preparing meat and vegetables, and cleaning and maintaining kitchen facilities.
2. *Maintenance*. The buildings and grounds of most prisons are cared for by the inmates. Electrical work, masonry, plumbing, and painting are all inmate activities. Of a less skilled nature are such duties as garbage collection, gardening, and cleaning.
3. *Laundry*. Most prisons have their own inmate-run laundries. Quite often, prison laundries will also furnish services to other state institutions.
4. *Agriculture*. In western and southern states, many prisons farm their own land. Dairy herds, crops, and poultry all are managed by inmates. The products are used in the prison and in other state institutions.

Vocational Training. Most institutions also provide vocational training programs. In New York, for example, more than forty-two different trade and technical courses are provided in organized training shops under qualified civilian instructors. Some of these courses not only benefit the inmate but also provide services for the institution.[71] For example, New York has trained inmates to become dental laboratory technicians; this program provides dentures for inmates and saves the state money. Another New York program trains inmates to become optical technicians and has the added benefit of providing eyeglasses for inmates. Other New York correctional training programs include barber training, computer programming, auto mechanics, auto body work, and radio and television repair. The products of most of these programs save the taxpayers money while the programs provide the inmates with practical experience. Many other states offer this type of vocational programming.[72]

Despite the promising aspects of such programs, they have also been seriously criticized: inmates often have trouble finding skill-related, high-paying jobs on their release; equipment in prisons is often second-hand, obsolete, and hard to come by; some programs are thinly disguised excuses for prison upkeep and maintenance; and unions and other groups resent the intrusion of prison labor into their markets.[73]

There is little question that these programs should be expanded and improved. Research by Kathleen Maguire in New York found that inmates' prison industry participation has a positive impact on their behavior and adjustment to prison; the effect was most pronounced with the most troubled inmates.[74]

Work Release. To supplement programs stressing rehabilitation via in-house job training or education, more than forty-four states have attempted to implement **work-release** or **furlough** programs. These allow deserving inmates to leave the institution and hold regular jobs in the community.

Inmates enrolled in work release may live at the institutions at night while working in the community during the day. However, security problems (e.g., contraband may be brought in) and the usual remoteness of prisons often make this arrangement difficult. More typical is the extended work release, where prisoners are allowed to remain in the community for significant periods of time. To help inmates adjust, some states such as South Carolina operate community-based prerelease centers where inmates live while working. Some inmates may work at their previous jobs, while others seek new employment.

Like other programs, work release has its good and bad points. Inmates are sometimes reluctantly received in the community and find that certain areas of employment are closed to them. Citizens are often concerned about prisoners "stealing" jobs or working for lower than normal wages; consequently, such practices are prohibited by Federal Public Law 89–176, which controls the federal work-release program.[75] Some question also exists of whether inmates placed in furlough programs are any more successful upon release than nonfurloughed inmates. An analysis of forty work-release programs by Johnathan Katz and Scott Decker found that they were ineffective in reducing recidivism and providing other social benefits.[76]

On the other hand, inmates gain many benefits from work release, including the ability to maintain work-related skills, to maintain community ties, and to make an easier transition from prison to the outside world. For those who have learned a skill in the institution, work release offers an excellent opportunity to test out a new occupation. For others, the job may be a training situation in which new skills are acquired.[77] Similarly, a number of states have reported that few work-release inmates absconded while in the community.[78]

The Willie Horton Case, which became a cause célèbre during the 1988 presidential campaign has halted the growth of work-release programs. Horton was the Massachusetts inmate serving a life term who absconded while on furlough and brutalized a young couple in Maryland. The Horton case was used during the 1988 presidential campaign by Vice President George Bush as an example of Democratic candidate and Massachusetts Governor Michael Dukakis's ineffective policies, calling it "weekend passes for first-degree murderers." A number of state jurisdictions have altered their furlough programs since the 1988 election. A national survey found that thirteen states have eliminated furloughs for life-term inmates; other jurisdictions have shortened furloughs and eliminated eligibility for sex offenders.[79] Not surprisingly, two of the jurisdictions that sharply curtailed their furlough programs were Massachusetts, whose release levels went from 5,857 in 1987 to 1,423 in 1990, and the federal government, which authorized 17,860 furloughs in 1987 and 5,245 in 1990.

Helping Female Offenders. Critics have charged that educational and vocational programs are especially deficient in female institutions, which typically offered only remedial-level education or occasional junior college classes. Women were not being provided with the tools needed to succeed on the outside because the only vocational training available stressed what was considered traditional "women's work": cosmetology, secretarial work, and food services.

A recent survey by the American Correctional Association found that correctional authorities are now beginning to recognize the education and training shortfall in female institutions.[80] All but three states have instituted some sort of vocational training programs for women; the other three provide supplemental services for their few female inmates. While the traditional vocation of sewing was the most common industrial program, sixteen states taught data processing, and female inmates were involved in such other industries as farming, printing, telemarketing, and furniture repair. Thirty-six states said they were planning to expand programming, while fourteen indicated that their activities were influenced by litigation filed by female inmates charging that male inmates had more programming opportunities than women did. Clearly greater efforts are needed to improve the quality of work experiences for female inmates.

Private Prison Enterprise. While opposition from organized labor ended the profitability of commercial prison industries, a number of interesting efforts have been made to vary the type and productivity of prison labor.[81] The impetus for the development came from former Chief Justice Warren Burger, who long argued that prisons should be turned into "factories within walls" that could teach inmates marketable skills, allow them to earn money, and reduce idleness and boredom. The federal government helped put Burger's idea into operation when it approved the Free Venture program in 1976.[82] Seven states, including Connecticut, South Carolina, and Minnesota, were given grants to implement private industries within prison walls. This successful program led to the Percy Amendment (1979), federal legislation that allowed prison-made goods to be sold across state lines if the projects complied with strict rules, such as making sure unions were consulted and preventing manufacturers from undercutting the existing wage structure.[83] The new law authorized a number of Prison Industry Enhancement pilot projects. These were certified as meeting the Percy Amendment operating rules and were therefore free to ship goods out of state; by 1987, fifteen projects had been certified.[84]

Today, private prison industries have used a number of different models. One approach is to make the correctional system a supplier of goods and services that serves state-run institutions. New York has long been a leader in creating productive prison industries. Today, there are about three thousand inmates (8 percent of the population who earn an average of fifty cents per hour) in various manufacturing jobs.[85] The New York Department of Corrections has actually created a brand name (Corcraft) for its product line and grosses over $30 million a year. Corcraft products range from wire-mesh garbage cans to chairs, eyeglasses, clothing, mattresses, pillows, and auto body work.[86]

Other states have developed various types of partnerships with private industry that today employ about two thousand inmates in fifty-five different projects.[87] For example, La Pen, Inc., is a garment factory set up in a former gymnasium in the Nebraska State Penitentiary that employs eighty men.[88] Other models call for private companies to set up manufacturing units on prison grounds and/or purchase goods made by inmates in shops owned and operated by the corrections department.

Despite widespread publicity, the partnership between private enterprise and the prison community has been limited to a few experimental programs. However, it is likely to grow in the future.

Postrelease Programs. A final element of job-related programming involves helping inmates obtain jobs before they are released and keep them once they are on the outside. A number of correctional departments have set up employment services designed to ease the transition between institution and community. Employment program staff assess inmates' backgrounds to determine their abilities, interests, goals, and capabilities. They also help them create job plans essential to receiving early release (parole) and successfully reintegrating into the community. Some programs maintain community correctional placements in sheltered environments that help inmates bridge the gap between institutions and the outside world. Services include job placement, skill development, family counseling, and legal and medical assistance.

Not all employment service programs show positive results, however. In a project conducted within the Pennsylvania correctional system, clients were as likely to be employed on release as those in a noncounseled control group. Moreover, job counseling neither helped releasees obtain more prestigious jobs nor lowered their recidivism rates (one-third of the clients were rearrested within one year.[89] An evaluation of nine ex-offender vocational programs found that while the programs served thousands of clients (fourteen thousand in one year), many of whom had little education or skills, and were generally successful in placing them in jobs, none reduced recidivism.[90]

Maintaining Conventional Life-styles

Research studies generally agree that inmates who are able to maintain family ties have a better chance to succeed on the outside after they have been released.[91]

A few correctional systems have developed programs that help inmates maintain their emotional stability by having closer ties with their families and living in an environment that is more "normal" than that provided in the typical correctional facility. For example, some women's prisons now allow inmates who give birth in prison to keep their child in a nursery in the institution for up to a year, followed by liberal visitation rights with the child after that point. Others allow male and female inmates home visitation privileges if they show examplary behavior in the institution. Some programs provide direct support to families; for example, by involving them in self-help groups, providing counseling, helping them obtain transportation to the prison, and finding them overnight lodging.[92] Two other well-known programs, conjugal visits and coed prisons, are discussed below.

Conjugal (Family) Visits. The **conjugal** (or family) **visit** is a mode of treatment that has received renewed emphasis from correctional administrators. During conjugal visits, prisoners are able to have completely private meetings with their spouse and family on a regular basis. The explicit purpose of the program is to grant inmates access to normal family and sexual outlets and thereby counteract the pains of imprisonment.

Conjugal visitation is more frequently used in Latin America and Europe than in the United States. However, Mississippi has had such a program since 1900, and California began a program of family visits at its Tehachapi facility in 1971.[93] The New York prison system maintains a Family Reunion Program in seven of its facilities but restricts participation to well-adjusted prisoners without histories of disciplinary problems. Correctional administrators recently rescinded an order that barred HIV-infected inmates from having conjugal visits for fear of spreading the virus. Prison officials now realize that prohibiting HIV-infected inmates from family visits deters inmates from agreeing to being tested for AIDS because they fear losing conjugal privileges.[94]

In 1980, Connecticut adopted a family visitation program at its Somers and Enfield facilities. Similar programs have been created in Washington, South Carolina, California, and Minnesota.[95]

Women's facilities have made special efforts to provide for family visitations in order to maintain inmates' ties to their children and family. The Dwight Correctional Center in Illinois has even set up a special on-grounds overnight camping facility where inmates can stay with their families.[96]

Those who favor family visitation argue that, if properly administered, it could provide a number of important benefits: inmate frustration levels would diminish, family ties would be strengthened, and normal sexual patterns would be continued. Problems associated with conjugal visitation include:

1. Such visits can serve only the minority of inmates who are married; there is a question of fairness.
2. Appropriate facilities are almost universally lacking.
3. Administrative problems abound: security, staff abuses of power, jealousy.
4. Administrative support is lacking.
5. Spouses may feel embarrassment at openly sexual visits.
6. Children may be born to parents who cannot support them.[97]

After a careful analysis of conjugal visit programs, Anne Goetting found that there is "no solid research support for the contentions that such programs reduce homosexuality, enhance social control, normalize prison life style, increase post-release success or stabilize marriages."[98]

Coed Prisons. One recent trend, though one with strong historical roots, has been the **coeducational prison.** Since 1973, prisons housing both men and women have proliferated throughout the United States. How popular are coed prisons? A recent survey by Contact, Inc., a nonprofit correctional information center, found that thirty-five institutions were operating as coed centers around the country.[99] While most were minimum-security institutions, coed prisons were also found at the medium- and maximum-security levels, and some institutions operated with a mix of security levels. Officials reported that inmates commonly share food services, recreation, educational programs, and jobs. The typical coed prison is a small, low-security institution, predominantly of one sex (either mostly male or mostly female), and populated by nonviolent, carefully screened offenders. In most instances, males and females live in physically separate housing—either in different buildings or in separate cottages—but they participate jointly in most institution activities, such as work, recreation, and vocational and educational programs.[100]

The survey found that the benefits of coed prisons include the ease and cost effectiveness of a joint operation, the more normal environment produced by heterosexual contact, expanded programs available to women because of joint participation, greater flexibility in staffing, alleviated overcrowding at male institutions, and the fact that some inmates could be housed closer to home.

Coed prisons were not without their drawbacks. The greatest problems listed by administrators were illicit relationships, supervisory and disciplinary problems, negative staff attitudes, developing similar and equal programs without joint participation, and security.

Inmate Self-Help

Recognizing that the probability of failure on the outside is acute, inmates have attempted to organize self-help groups to provide the psychological tools needed to prevent recidivism.[101] Some are chapters of common national organizations, such as Alcoholics Anonymous. Membership in these programs is designed to improve inmates' self-esteem and help them cope with common problems, such as alcoholism, narcotics abuse, or depression. Special-needs inmates at the Kentucky State Reformatory outside of Louisville have taken the unusual step of forming a Boy Scout Troop within prison walls to serve as a vehicle for self-help and group solidarity.[102]

Other groups are organized along racial and ethnic lines. For example, there are chapters of the Chicanos Organizados Pintos Aztlan, the Afro-American Coalition, and the Native American Brotherhood in prisons stretching from California to Massachusetts. These groups try to establish a sense of brotherhood in order to work together for individual betterment. Members hold literacy, language, and religious classes, as well as offering counseling, legal advice, and prerelease support. Ethnic groups seek ties with outside minority organizations, such as the National Association for the Advancement of Colored People (NAACP), the Urban League, La Raza, and the American Indian Movement, as well as the religious and university communities.

A third type of self-help group are those developed specifically to help inmates find the strength to make it on the outside. The most well-known are the Fortune Society, which claims thirty thousand members, and the Seventh Step organization, which was developed by ex-offender Bill Sands. These groups try to raise inmate self-esteem. Another group, the Self-Development Group (SDG), was founded in the 1960s by LSD advocate Timothy Leary. A number of groups have followed in the footsteps of SDG, including Inward Bound, Church of the New Sing, Ring of Keys, Human Potential Seminars, Wake Up, and Discovery.

Administrators usually embrace self-help groups that do not challenge authority. For example, the Ring of Keys group, whose goal is the "betterment of the individual through finding keys that will open many doors for a brighter and happier future," and Discovery, which tries to "challenge inmates to explore alternative decision-making and life styles," have been formally recognized by prison authorities in some jurisdictions. In a similar vein, corrections officials anxious to help inmates build the capacity for positive change have provided funding for EST training programs developed by Werner Erhard.

Self-help programs that embrace religious principles, that do not engage in activities contrary to the corrections operation, and that cultivate strong administrative and outside support continue to flourish in modern prisons.

Can Rehabilitation Work?

Despite the variety and number of treatment programs in operation, questions remain about their effectiveness. In their oft-cited research, Robert Martinson and his associates found that a majority of treatment programs were failures.[103] Martinson found in a national study that, with few exceptions, rehabilitative efforts seemed to have no appreciable effect on recidivism; his research produced a "nothing works" view of correctional treatment.

Martinson's work was followed by efforts that found that some high-risk offenders were more likely to commit crimes after they had been placed in treatment programs than before the onset of rehabilitation efforts.[104] Even California's highly touted community treatment program, which matched youthful offenders and counselors on the basis of their psychological profiles, was found by Paul Lerman to exert negligible influence on its clients.[105] As recently as 1988, a review published by Steven Lab and John Whitehead found that correctional treatment efforts aimed at youthful offenders provide little evidence that rehabilitation can occur within correctional settings.[106] There is also scant evidence that general treatment efforts, which include vocational, educational, and mental health services, can consistently lower recidivism rates.[107]

The so-called failure of correctional treatment has helped promote a conservative view of corrections, in which prisons are considered places of incapacitation and punishment, not treatment centers.[108] Current policies stress eliminating the nonserious offender from the correctional system but at the same time increase the probability that serious, violent offenders will be incarcerated and serve longer sentences. This view supports the utility of mandatory and determinate sentences for serious offenders and the simultaneous utilization of intermediate sanctions, such as house arrest, restitution, and diversion, to limit the nonserious offender's involvement within the system.

While the concept of correctional rehabilitation is facing serious challenges, many experts still believe strongly in the rehabilitative ideal. Some, such as Elliott Currie, believe that rehabilitation has just not been given a realistic chance because of inadequate budgets and programs.[109] Others have shown through careful analysis that while not all programs are successful for all inmates, many treatment programs are effective and that participants, especially younger clients, have a better chance of success on the outside than those who forego treatment.[110] In an important review of this literature, Ted Palmer found that correctional treatment can work if administered properly and geared toward offender needs.[111] Palmer maintains that the "get tough" policies of the 1980s, which detonated an explosion in the prison population, have not produced a dramatic decrease in the violent crime rate. It is possible that the "get tough" approach, a costly and ineffective method of crime control, will soon fall out of favor in much the same fashion as the treatment doctrine did more than a decade ago.

Guarding the Institution

Control of a prison is a very complex task. On the one hand, a tough, high-security environment may meet the goals of punishment and control but fail to reinforce positive behavior changes. On the other hand, too liberal an administrative stance can lower staff morale and place inmates in charge of the institution.[112]

Caught up in the complexities of prison life is the guard staff. Over 120,000 correctional officers are now working in the nation's state prison facilities, an increase of about 25 percent since 1986.[113] Correctional officers are generally low paid: the average starting salary is about eighteen thousand dollars. About 85 percent are male and 15 percent female, a ratio that has remained stable since 1986.

Most states require that candidates for correctional officer positions meet an age requirement (usually eighteen or twenty-one) and have a high school education. Other common criteria are a "clean" criminal record, a driver's license, be drug free, and in good physical condition. Some states such as Oregon and Pennsylvania require either oral or written testing. After selection, most correctional officer candidates will have between one and six weeks of training; Pennsylvania requires a two-year apprenticeship program including four weeks of academy training. About twenty-six states provide forty hours a week of in-service training for correctional officers.[114] Surveys indicate that about two-thirds of all state correctional agencies have established independent training academies; however, as of 1991, correctional officers averaged only 116 hours of preservice training (compared to more than 1,000 for police officers).[115]

For many years, prison guards were viewed as ruthless people who enjoyed their positions of power over inmates, fought rehabilitation efforts, were racists, and had a "lock psychosis" developed from years of counting, numbering, and checking on inmates. This view has changed in recent years. Pioneering research by Lucien X. Lombardo and others has painted a picture of prison guards as people who are seeking the security and financial rewards of a civil service position.[116] Most are in favor of rehabilitation efforts and do not hold any particular animosity toward the inmates. The prison guard has been characterized by Lombardo as a "people worker" who must be prepared to deal with the problems of inmates on a personal level. The guard is also a member of a complex bureaucracy who must be able to cope with its demands.

Corrections officers play a number of roles within the institution. They supervise cell houses, dining areas, shops, and other facilities, as well as perch up on the walls armed with rifles to oversee the yard and prevent escapes. Corrections officers also sit on disciplinary boards and escort inmates to hospitals and court appearances.

The greatest problem faced by prison guards is the duality of their role: maintainer of order and security and advocate of treatment and rehabilitation. Added to this basic dilemma is the changing inmate role. Where before corrections officers could count on inmate leaders to help them maintain order, they are now faced with a racially charged atmosphere in which violence is a way of life. Today, correctional work is filled with danger, tension, boredom, and little evidence that efforts to help inmates lead to success. And, unlike police officers, correctional workers apparently do not form a close-knit subculture with unique values and a sense of intergroup loyalty. Correctional officers experience alienation and isolation from the inmates, the administration, and each other.[117] Interestingly, this sense of alienation seems greatest in younger officers; evidence exists that later in their careers, officers enjoy a revival of interest in their work and take great pride in providing human services to inmates.[118]

Many state prison authorities have developed training programs to prepare guards for the difficulties of prison work. Guard unions have also commonly been formed to negotiate wages and working conditions with the corrections department.

Female Correctional Officers

The issue of female correctional officers in male institutions comes up repeatedly. Today, an estimate of five thousand women are assigned to all-male institutions (out of a total of seventy-seven thousand correctional officers).[119] The employment of women as guards in close contact with male inmates has spurred many questions of privacy and safety and a number of legal cases. In one important case, *Dothard v. Rawlinson* (1977), the Supreme Court upheld Alabama's refusal to hire female correctional officers on the grounds that it would put them in significant danger from the male inmates.[120] Despite such setbacks, women now work side by side with male guards in almost every state, performing the same duties. Research indicates that discipline has not suffered because of the inclusion of women in the guard force. Sexual assaults have been rare, and more negative attitudes have been expressed by their male peers than by inmates.[121] Most commentators believe that the presence of female guards can have an important beneficial effect on the self-image of inmates and improve the guard-inmate working relationship.[122] Interestingly, little research has been conducted on male correctional officers in female prisons. David Duffee reports that male officers are generally well received. There was little evidence of sexual exploitation or privacy violations, and female inmates felt that the presence of male correctional officers helped to create a more natural environment and reduce tension.[123]

Prison Rules and Discipline

Every penal institution—jail, prison, or reformatory—has a specific set of official rules that guide prisoners' lives and dictate what they can and cannot do. These rules are of great significance; a violation may result in a loss of good time, which can lengthen the inmate's stay in prison. Violation of prison rules may also result in harsh disciplinary measures, such as solitary confinement, suspension of privileges, or transfer to a more secure facility.

Today, rules are more lenient than those in the past. Conversation is no longer prohibited, and rigid, military-like discipline is rare. Yet most institutions still have lengthy sets of rules.

Any violation of prison rules may result in disciplinary action against the inmate. Usually, a disciplinary board will meet to hear cases referred by administrative staff. Typically, the board will consist of members of the custodial, treatment, and administrative staffs. Punishment when deemed necessary is meted out by these individuals, and it affects good time, privileges, and parole.

Prison Conflict

Conflict, violence, and brutality are sad but ever-present facts of institutional life. Violence can involve individual conflict: inmate versus inmate, inmate versus staff, staff versus inmate. One common threat is homosexual rape. Research has shown that prison rapes usually involve a victim viewed as weak and submissive and a group of aggressive rapists who can dominate the victim through their collective strength. Sexual harassment leads to fights, social isolation, fear, anxiety, and crisis.[124] Nonsexual assaults may stem from an aggressor's desire to shake down the victim for money and personal favors, may be motivated by racial conflict, or may simply be used as a device to establish power within the institution.[125]

Violence can also involve large groups of inmates, such as the famous Attica riot in 1971, which claimed thirty-nine lives, or the New Mexico State Prison riot of February 1980, in which the death toll was thirty-three. More than three hundred prison riots have occurred since the first one in 1774; 90 percent of these have taken place since 1952.[126]

A number of factors can spark these damaging incidents. According to criminologist Edith Flynn, they include poor staff-inmate communications, destructive ecological conditions, faulty classification, and promised but undelivered reforms.[127] The 1980 New Mexico State Penitentiary riot drew national attention to the problem of prison riots. The prison was designed for 800 but actually held 1,136 prisoners; conditions of overcrowding, squalor, poor food, and lack of medical treatment abounded.[128] The state government, which had been called on to improve guard training, physical plant quality, and relief from overcrowding, was reluctant to spend the necessary money.

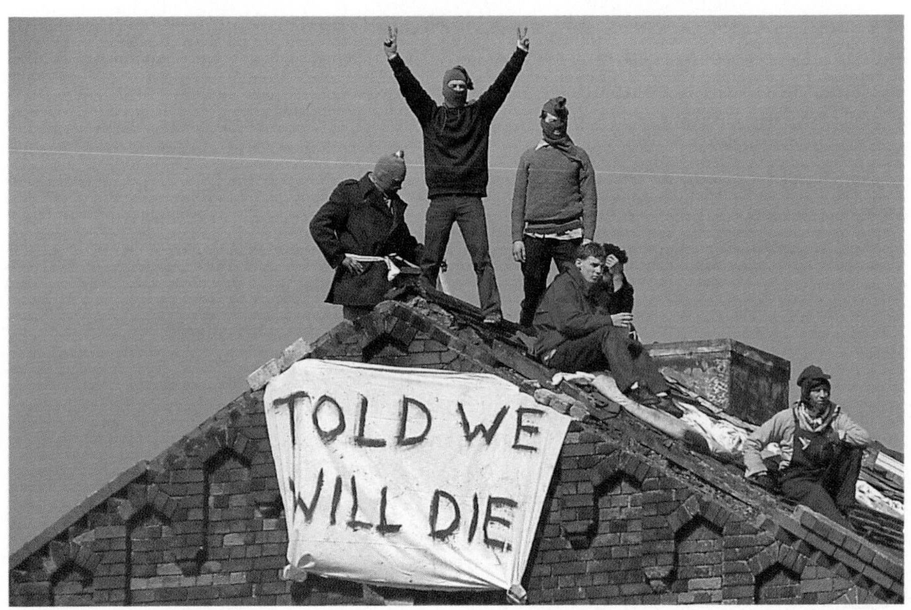

Prison violence is not unique to the U.S. This photo was taken at the Strangeways prison in Manchester, England.

The riot started when a guard attempted to confiscate some home-brewed liquor from an inmate. With only twenty-two guards on duty, inmates quickly seized control of the entire prison. After taking the guards hostage, the inmates seized the infirmary and made free use of the drugs. Rather than taking all their anger out on the hostage guards (though some guards were seriously injured), rioting inmates broke into Cell Block 4, in which "snitches" (informers) were held in protective custody and executed, by means so brutal that they defy imagination. While inmates were demanding better conditions from prison authorities, the widespread bloodletting soon caused many inmates, fearful for their lives, to try to escape into the hands of authorities. After almost totally destroying the institution, the remaining inmates peacefully surrendered to police units without a shot being fired. The inmates' "code of silence" and fear of reprisals make prosecution of the riot's worst offenders problematic.

Although revulsion over the violent riots in New Mexico and the earlier riot in New York's Attica prison led to calls for prison reform, prison violence has continued unabated.[129] About 100 inmates are killed by their peers each year in U.S. prisons, about six or seven staff members are murdered, and about 120 suicides are recorded.[130]

The Causes of Prison Violence

What are the causes of prison violence?[131] While there is no single explanation for either collective or individualistic violence, a number of theories abound. One position holds that inmates themselves are often violence-prone individuals who have always used force to get their own way. In the crowded, dehumanizing world of the prison, it is not surprising that some inmates resort to force to exert their dominance over others.[132]

A second view is that prisons convert people to violence by their inhuman conditions, including overcrowding, depersonalization, and the threat of homosexual rape.[133] Even in the most humane prisons, life is a constant put-down, and prison conditions are a threat to the inmates' sense of self-worth; violence is an expected consequence of these conditions.[134]

Prison violence may also be caused by prison mismanagement, lack of strong security, and inadequate control by prison officials.[135] Poor management may inhibit conflict management and set the stage for violence. Repressive administrations give inmates the feeling that nothing will ever change, that they have nothing to lose, and that violence is the only means for change.

Few prisons have effective grievance procedures for inmate complaints against either prison officials or other inmates. Prisoners who complain about other inmates are viewed as "rats" or "snitches" and are marked for death by their enemies. Similarly, complaints or lawsuits filed against the prison administration may result in the inmate being placed in solitary confinement—"the hole." The lack of communication is heightened by the diverse ethnic and racial backgrounds of the guards and inmates. The typical inmate at Attica prison at the time of the riot was a twenty-five-year-old black male from New York City, while the typical guard was a middle-aged white male from upstate rural New York. The frustration caused by living in a prison with a climate that promotes violence—that is, one that lacks physical security and adequate mechanisms for resolving complaints and where the "code of silence" protects violators—is believed to promote both collective and individual violence by inmates who might otherwise be controlled.[136]

Overcrowding and Violence

Overcrowding caused by the rapid increases in the prison population has been linked to prison violence. Data from Texas indicate that a large increase in the prison population, unmatched by the creation of new space, was associated with increases in suicide, violent death, and disciplinary action rates.[137] In 1991, inmates at the maxi-maxi security Southport prison in New York rioted and took three correctional officers hostage; fourteen officers and forty-four inmates were injured in a May 25, 1991, riot at the Correctional Institution at Hagerstown, Maryland. Both incidents were linked by correctional officials to overcrowding and understaffing.[138]

One explanation of the crowding-violence association is that a large population in an institution exerts a negative influence that is associated with violence. Feelings of crowding and blood pressure rates have been found to increase in cells occupied by more than one person.[139] Crowding has been associated with increased disciplinary infractions.[140]

As the prison population continues to climb, unmatched by expanded correctional capacity, prison violence may increase. Although judges in a number of states have ordered the mandatory release of prisoners because of overcrowded conditions, overcrowding may become even more acute in future years. Consequently, prison administrators have attempted to reduce tension levels by creating inmate councils to help govern the institution **(self-governance)** and grievance mechanisms so that inmates' complaints will be heard. Such measures have been effective in some institutions.

Managing Violence

Can prison violence be controlled, despite the fact that the inmate populations will not undergo significant decline or become less aggressive and hostile? In his book *Governing Prisons*, John DiIulio suggests that reform of prison management can help alter the violent institutional climate.[141] After studying prisons in three states, DiIulio finds that management can be classified into three types. The "consensual model," practiced in California, is based on the notion that prison government rests on the consent of the governed, the inmates. This model fails to provide a coherent basis of dealing with violence because it allows inmates a say in the management process.

In Michigan, the "responsibility model" is used. Here, inmates' rehabilitation is keyed to their participation in prison operations, and the staff is required to be facilitators in the process. The responsibility model has also failed because it offers weak controls on inmate behavior and produces disillusionment and alienation among the staff.

DiIulio finds that the "control model" used in the Texas prison system has more promise for reducing violence. The Texas system stresses clearly defined rules of behavior, inmate conformity with rules and regulations, and strong, independent top-down leadership.

DiIulio believes that the bureaucratic organization that works in large private corporations and government agencies can save prisons. In this approach, he relies on prison administrators acting in a caring yet efficient manner without prejudice and bias. His prescription for success is to have experienced correctional leaders create and enforce clear and fair rules. While this system may seem logical, what is known about the operations of criminal justice agencies indicates that "informal" rules and behaviors often dominate at the expense of the formal system and that leaders may be more self-serving than selfless.[142] The Texas prison system that DiIulio so admires was the location of overcrowding and brutality until subject to court-ordered reform. Even then, prison officials were reluctant to change and attempted to undermine reform efforts. While the "control model" may seem appealing to some experts, whether it can work in the "real world" remains to be seen.

Prisoner's Rights

Prior to the early 1960s, it was accepted that upon conviction, an individual forfeited all rights not expressly granted by statutory law or correctional policy; inmates were "civilly dead." The Supreme Court held that convicted offenders should expect to be penalized for their misdeeds and part of their punishment was the loss of freedoms free citizens take for granted.[143]

One reason that inmates lacked rights was because state and federal courts were reluctant to intervene in the administration of prisons unless the circumstances of a case clearly indicated a serious breach of the Eighth Amendment's protection against cruel and unusual punishment. This judicial policy is referred to as the **hands-off doctrine.** The courts used three basic justifications for their neglect of prison conditions:

1. Correctional administration was a technical matter best left to experts, rather than to courts ill-equipped to make appropriate evaluations.
2. Society as a whole was apathetic to what went on in prisons, and most individuals preferred not to associate with or know about the offender.
3. Prisoners' complaints involved privileges, rather than rights. Prisoners were considered to have fewer constitutional rights than other members of society.[144]

As the 1960s drew to a close, the hands-off doctrine was eroded. Federal district courts began seriously considering prisoners' claims concerning conditions in the various state and federal institutions and used their power to intervene on behalf of the inmates. In some ways, this concern reflected the spirit of the times, which saw the onset of the civil rights movement, and subsequently was paralleled in such areas as student rights, public welfare, mental institutions, juvenile court systems, and military justice.

Beginning in the late 1960s, such activist groups as the NAACP Legal Defense Fund and the American Civil Liberties Union's National Prison Project began to search for appropriate legal vehicles to bring prisoners' complaints before state and federal courts. The most widely used device was the Federal Civil Rights Act, 42 U.S.C. § 1983:

> Every person who, under color of any statute, ordinance, regulation, custom, or usage of any State or Territory subjects, or causes to be subjected, any citizen of the United States or other person within the jurisdiction thereof to the deprivation of any rights, privileges, or immunities secured by the Constitution and laws shall be liable to the party injured in an action at law, suit in equity, or other proper proceeding for redress.

The legal argument went that as U.S. citizens, prison inmates could sue state officials if their civil rights were violated; for example, if they were the victims of racial or religious discrimination.

The Supreme Court first recognized the right of prisoners to sue for civil rights violations in cases involving religious freedom brought by the Black Muslims. This well-organized group had been frustrated by prison administrators who feared its growing power and desired to place limits on its recruitment activities. In the 1964 case of *Cooper v. Pate*, however, the Supreme Court ruled that inmates who were being denied the right to practice their religion were entitled to legal redress under 42 U.S.C. § 1983.[145] Although *Cooper* applied to the narrow issue of religious freedom, it opened the door to providing other rights for inmates. As James B. Jacobs states:

> It was not the breadth of the decision that mattered, but the Supreme Court's determination that prisoners have constitutional rights; prison officials were not free to do with prisoners as they pleased. And the federal courts were permitted, indeed obligated, to provide a forum where prisoners could challenge and confront prison officials.[146]

The subsequent prisoners' rights crusade, stretching from 1960 to 1980, paralleled the civil rights and women's movements. Battle lines were drawn between prison officials hoping to maintain their power and resenting interference by the courts and inmate groups and their sympathizers, who used state and federal courts as a forum for demanding better living conditions and personal rights. Each decision handed down by the courts was viewed as a victory for one side or the other; this battle continues today.

Substantive Rights of Inmates

Through a slow process of legal review, the courts have granted inmates a number of **substantive rights** that have significantly influenced the entire correctional system. The most important of these rights are discussed below.

Access to Courts, Legal Services, and Materials. Without the ability to seek judicial review of conditions causing discomfort or violating constitutional rights, the inmate must depend solely on the slow and often insensitive administrative mechanism of relief within the prison system. Therefore, the right of easy access to the courts gives the inmates hope that their rights will be protected during incarceration within the institution.

In 1941, the U.S. Supreme Court, in the case of *Ex Parte Cleus Hull*, declared that access to the courts for an inmate was a basic constitutional right.[147] Although *Hull* granted inmates access to the courts, it was not uncommon for prison officials to take disciplinary action against inmates seeking legal remedies through court action. Most prisons lacked legal services, and in many situations, the use of a **jailhouse lawyer** (an inmate possessing some legal skills who offers legal advice to other inmates) was restricted. Most prisoners, therefore, found it virtually impossible to seek relief through the courts.

To resolve this problem, the Supreme Court in the case of *Johnson v. Avery* held that unless the state could provide some reasonable alternative to inmates in the preparation of petitions for postconviction relief, a jailhouse lawyer must be permitted to aid illiterate inmates in filing habeas corpus petitions.[148] Federal courts have expanded this right to include virtually all inmates with various legal problems, as the following cases show:

1. *DeMallory v. Cullen* (1988): An untrained inmate paralegal is not a constitutionally acceptable alternative to law library access.[149]

2. *Lindquist v. Idaho State Board of Corrections* (1985): Seven inmate law clerks for a prison population of 950 were sufficient legal representation since they had a great deal of experience.[150]

3. *Smith v. Wade* (1983): An inmate who has been raped can have access to the state court in order to sue a guard for failing to protect the inmate from aggressive inmates.[151]

4. *Bounds v. Smith* (1977): State correctional systems are obligated to provide inmates either with adequate law libraries or with the help of people trained in the law.[152]

Freedom of the Press and of Expression. Correctional administrators traditionally placed severe limitations on prisoners' speech and expression. For example, they have read and censored inmate mail and restricted their reading material. With the lifting of the hands-off doctrine, courts have consistently ruled that only when a compelling state interest exists can prisoners' First Amendment rights be modified; correctional authorities must justify the limiting of free speech by showing that granting it would threaten institutional security. The following list of cases related to prisoners' freedom of speech rights indicates current policy on the subject:

1. *Turner v. Safley* (1987): Prisoners do not have a right to receive mail from one another. Inmate-to-inmate mail can be banned if the reason is "related to legitimate penological interests."[153] Unless it presents a threat to security, prisoners retain the right to marry.

2. *Gregory v. Auger* (1985): Prison officials can restrict mail to those in temporary disciplinary detention as a means of increasing the deterrent value of this type of punishment.[154]

3. *Ramos v. Lamm* (1980): The institutional policy of refusing to deliver mail in a language other than English is unconstitutional.[155]

4. *Procunier v. Martinez* (1974): Censorship of a prisoner's mail is justified only when (1) there exists substantial government interest in maintaining the censorship in order to further prison security, order, and rehabilitation and (2) when the restrictions are not greater or more stringent than is demanded by security precautions.[156]

5. *Nolan v. Fitzpatrick* (1971): Prisoners may correspond with newspapers unless their letters discuss escape plans or contain contraband or otherwise objectionable material.[157]

6. *Saxbe v. Washington Post Co.* (1974): A federal prison rule forbidding individual press interviews with specific inmates was justified because there is no constitutional right to interview specific people; individual interviews would enhance the reputation of particular inmates and jeopardize the prison authorities' desire to treat everyone equally.[158]

Freedom of Religion. Freedom of religion is a fundamental right guaranteed by the Constitution's First Amendment. The religious freedom clause has a dual purpose: (1) It protects one's rights to freely practice one's religion, and (2) it prohibits the government from being partial to any particular religious group. In light of these two purposes, several issues pertaining to religious freedom within the context of the correctional setting have been raised and brought to the attention of the courts. These include (1) religious discrimination, (2) the right to hold religious services, (3) access to ministers, (4) the right to correspond with religious leaders, and (5) the right to wear religious medals. In general, the courts have ruled that inmates have the right to assemble and pray in the religion of their choice but the religious symbols and practices that interfere with institutional security can be restricted. Administrators can draw the line if religious needs become cumbersome or impossible to carry out for reason of cost or security. Granting special privileges can also be denied on the grounds that they will cause other groups to make similar demands.

Some of the issues surrounding religious practices in prison and a brief examination of how some courts have handled cases concerning religious freedom are outlined below:

1. *Mumin v. Phelps* (1988): If there is a legitimate penological interest, inmates can be denied special privileges to attend religious services.[159]
2. *O'Lone v. Estate of Shabazz* (1987): Prison officials can assign inmates work schedules that make it impossible for them to attend religious services as long as no reasonable alternative exists.[160]
3. *Rahman v. Stephenson* (1986): A prisoner's rights are not violated if the administration refuses to use the prisoner's religious name on official records.[161]
4. *Abdullah v. Kinnison* (1985): Muslim inmates do not have the right to wear white prayer robes in their cells if doing so interferes with prison security.[162]
5. *Cruz v. Beto* (1972): It would be discriminatory for a Buddhist prisoner to be denied a reasonable opportunity to pursue his or her faith while other inmates are allowed to participate in more conventional religious practices.[163]
6. *Kahane v. Carlson* (1975): An orthodox Jewish inmate has the right to a diet that can sustain him or her in good health without violating his or her religion, unless the government can show cause why it cannot be provided.[164]
7. *Chapman v. Pickett* (1978): A Black Muslim's placement in segregation for refusing to handle pork while on work detail was a violation of his right to religious freedom.[165]
8. *Gallahan v. Hollyfield* (1981): A Cherokee Indian has the right to have long hair if it is a requirement of his sincere religious beliefs.[166]

Medical Rights. Until recently, the courts restricted inmates' right to medical treatment through the creation of the **exceptional circumstances doctrine.** Using this policy, the courts would hear only those cases in which the circumstances totally disregarded human dignity, while denying hearings to other less serious cases. The cases that were allowed access to the courts usually represented a situation of total denial of medical care.

To gain their medical rights, prisoners have resorted to class actions (i.e., suits brought on behalf of all individuals affected by similar circumstances, in this case, poor medical attention). In the most significant case, *Newman v. Alabama* (1972), the entire Alabama prison system's medical facilities were declared inadequate.[167] The court cited the following factors as contributing to inadequate care: insufficient physician and nurse resources; reliance on untrained inmates for paramedical work; intentional failure in treating the sick and injured; and failure to conform to proper medical standards.

It was not until 1976, in *Estelle v. Gamble,* that the Supreme Court clearly mandated an inmate's right to have medical care:

> [The] principles [behind the guarantee against cruel and unusual punishment] establish the government's obligation to provide medical care for those whom it is punishing by incarceration. An inmate must rely on prison authorities to treat his medical needs; if the authorities fail to do so, those needs will not be met.[168]

Gamble had hurt his back in a Texas prison and filed suit because he contested the type of treatment he received and also questioned the lack of interest prison guards had shown in his case. The Supreme Court laid down the following standard for judging future complaints:

> Deliberate indifference to serious medical needs of prisoners constitutes the "unnecessary and wanton infliction of pain," . . . proscribed by the Eighth Amendment. This is true whether the indifference is manifested by prison doctors in their response to the prisoner's needs or by prison guards in intentionally denying or delaying access to medical care or intentionally interfering with the treatment once prescribed.[169]

Lower courts will now decide, on a case-by-case basis, whether "deliberate indifference" actually occurred.

Cruel and Unusual Punishment. The concept of **cruel and unusual punishment** is founded in the Eighth Amendment of the U.S. Constitution. The term itself has not been specifically defined by the Supreme Court, but the Court has held that treatment constitutes cruel and unusual punishment when it

1. Degrades the dignity of human beings.[170]
2. Is more severe than the offense for which it has been given.[171]
3. Shocks the general conscience and is fundamentally unfair.[172]

State and federal courts have placed strict limits on disciplinary methods that may be considered inhumane. Corporal punishment all but ended after the practice was condemned by then-Eighth Circuit Court of Appeals Judge Harry Blackmun in *Jackson v. Bishop* (1968).[173] Although the solitary confinement of disruptive inmates continues, its prolonged use under barbaric conditions has been held to be in violation of the Eighth Amendment. Courts have found that inmates placed in solitary have the right to adequate personal hygiene, exercise, mattresses, ventilation, and rules specifying how they can earn their release.

One issue relating to cruel and unusual punishment concerns overall prison conditions. In 1970, the district court of Arkansas in the case of *Holt v. Sarver* looked closely at the Arkansas prison system and found the conditions so deplorable that they were constitutionally unacceptable:

> For the ordinary convict a sentence to the Arkansas Penitentiary today amounts to a banishment from civilized society to a dark and evil world completely alien

to the free world, a world that is administered by criminals under unwritten rules and customs completely foreign to free world culture.[174]

Despite the court's demand for reform, little was done to improve conditions in the Arkansas prison system. More than seven years after the *Holt v. Sarver* decision, a federal court concluded that the inhumane conditions had not been fully improved.

Recent cases show the willingness of the Supreme Court to allow inmates to sue if correctional officers beat or abuse them; for example, the Court has allowed inmates to collect monetary damages in legal suits without requiring that they attempt to settle the case through prison administrative channels.[175]

Overall Prison Conditions. Prisoners have long had the right to the minimal conditions necessary for human survival, such as the necessary food, clothing, shelter, and medical care to sustain human life.[176] A number of attempts have been made to articulate reasonable standards of prison care and make sure they are carried out. Courts have held that while people are sent to prison for punishment, it does not mean that prison should be a punishing experience.[177] Inmates are entitled to reasonable care, protection, and shelter.

While inmates retain the right to reasonable care, if there is a legitimate purpose for the use of government restrictions, they may be considered constitutional. For example, it might be possible to restrict reading material, allow strip searches, and prohibit inmates from receiving packages from the outside if the restrictions are legitimate security measures.[178] If overcrowded conditions require it, inmates may be **double-bunked** in cells designed for a single inmate. In *Rhodes v. Chapman* (1981), the Supreme Court upheld the use of placing more than one inmate in a single cell to deal with overcrowding.[179]

Courts have also reviewed entire correctional systems in order to determine whether practices are unfair to inmates. In a critical case, *Estelle v. Ruiz*, the Texas Department of Corrections was ordered to provide new facilities to alleviate overcrowding; to abolish the practice of inmate trustees; to lower the staff-to-inmate ratio; to improve treatment services, such as medical, mental health, and occupational rehabilitation programs; and to adhere to the principles of procedural due process in dealing with inmates.[180] A court-ordered master was appointed to oversee change and served from 1981 to 1990, when the state was deemed in compliance with the most critical of the court-ordered changes.[181]

Ruiz illustrates the problems of achieving prison reform through court order. The case was filed in 1972 and the trial did not actually begin until 1978; the final court order took effect in 1981. Even with the final court decree, changes were slow in coming. Geoffrey Alpert, Ben Crouch, and C. Ronald Huff report that the final *Ruiz* decision created a crisis of control within the Texas Department of Corrections.[182] While prisoner expectations rose, staff uncertainty also increased. A period of tension and violence followed the decision, which may be partially explained by the fact that the staff and the administration felt that the court had undermined their authority. It took more then eighteen years for the case to be settled.

It is likely that the overcrowding crisis will prompt additional litigation requesting overall prison relief. At the time of this writing, correctional institutions in four states are under court order to reduce prison populations. In nine states, the entire correctional department is under court order to improve conditions and reduce the inmate population.[183] The Supreme Court has recently ruled (1992) that jurisdictions that voluntarily enter into pacts to reduce overcrowding can modify aspects of the agreement if unforseen circumstances, such as an upsurge in the inmate population, make satisfaction of the conditions impossible.[184]

Prisoners' Rights Today

Since 1980, a more conservative Supreme Court has curtailed the substantive right of prisoners to more freedom and greater privileges. For example, in *Daniels v. Williams*, the Court ruled that inmates do not have a constitutional right to collect damages if they are injured by another inmate due to a guard's negligence in protecting them from harm.[185] To receive damages, the inmates must show that they were intentionally harmed by a correctional official. So, for example, if inmates report that another prisoner threatened them and a correctional officer does nothing about the threat, the inmates have no legal recourse if the threat is carried out and they are seriously injured.[186] In *Wilson v. Seiter*, the Court ruled that to collect damages, inmates must prove not only that a prison condition caused them harm but that the behavior was a result of "deliberate indifference" of prison officials.[187] While these cases make it difficult for inmates to be compensated for injuries sustained in prison, it should be noted that the Court recently (1992) upheld the right of inmates to sue for damages after being beaten by guards, even though they did not sustain significant injuries.[188]

Limitations have also been placed on inmates' right to privacy. In *Hudson v. Palmer*, the Court ruled that inmates do not have a Fourth Amendment right to privacy over material contained in their cells.[189] Other rulings have denied inmates the right to contest their transfer to a more punitive institution[190] or to question their ineligibility for classification and rehabilitative programs.[191] The Court has also made it easier to punish inmates by relaxing the administrative procedures needed to place an inmate in segregation[192] and reducing the level of evidence required before an official can take away a prisoner's "good time" credit because of disciplinary violations.[193] The Court also allowed prison officials the right to use deadly force to put down a prison uprising as long as it was used in a "good faith" effort to maintain order and restore discipline.[194] In two 1989 cases, the Court ruled that it is not a violation of inmates' due process rights if correctional authorities restrict visitors whom they consider to be a "security threat" or prevent inmates from receiving publications if such a ban is related to reasonable penological interests, such as maintaining institutional security.[195]

In sum, the Court has recently reverted to a "hands-off" approach to handling prisoners' rights cases. Inmates must now make a powerful case to overcome the opinions of correctional authorities and their claim that restrictive conditions further prison security. Moreover, the *Turner* and *O'Lone* decisions, discussed earlier, indicate that even First Amendment rights, such as the right to attend religious services and to use the mails, are no longer immune to control.

SUMMARY

On entering a prison, offenders must make tremendous adjustments in order to survive. Usual behavior patterns or life-styles are radically changed. Opportunities for personal satisfaction are reduced. Passing through a number of adjustment stages or cycles, inmates learn to cope with the new environment.

Inmates also learn to obey the inmate social code, which dictates proper behavior and attitudes. If inmates break the code, they may be unfavorably labeled.

Once outside the institution, new inmates can avail themselves of a large number of treatment devices designed to help them readjust to the community. These include educational programs on the basic, high school, and even college levels, as well as vocational training programs. In addition, a number of treatment programs have offered inmates individualized and group psychological counseling; work furloughs, coed prisons, and conjugal visits have also been employed.

Despite such measures, prisons remain forbidding structures that house desperate men and women. Violence is a byword in prisons. Women often turn their hatred inward and hurt themselves, while male inmates engage in collective and individual violence against others. The Attica and New Mexico riots are examples of the most serious collective prison violence.

In years past, society paid little attention to the incarcerated offender. The majority of inmates confined in jails and prisons were basically deprived of the rights guaranteed them under the Constitution. Today, however, the judicial system is actively involved in the administration of correctional institutions. Inmates can now take their grievances to courts and seek due process and equal protection under the law. The courts have recognized that persons confined in correctional institutions have rights—which include access to the courts and legal counsel, the exercise of religion, the rights to correspondence and visitation, and the right to adequate medical treatment.

QUESTIONS

1. How might the prison experience be likened to living on a large university campus?
2. What steps could be taken to make prisons a more pleasant environment? Should these steps be taken?
3. What are the benefits and drawbacks of coed prisons? Of conjugal visits?
4. Should women be allowed to work as guards in male prisons? What about male guards in female prisons?
5. Should prison inmates be allowed a free college education while noncriminals are forced to pay tuition? Do you believe in less eligibility for prisoners?
6. Do double bunking and other conditions of overcrowded prisons represent violations of inmates' constitutional rights?

NOTES

1. The data in this section are from Bureau of Justice Statistics, *Prisons and Prisoners* (Washington, D.C.: U.S. Government Printing Office, 1992).
2. Christopher Innes, *Profile of State Prison Inmates, 1986* (Washington, D.C.: Bureau of Justice Statistics, 1988).
3. Robert Johnson, *Culture and Crisis in Confinement* (Lexington, Mass.: Lexington Books, 1976), pp. 1–2.
4. Gresham Sykes, *The Society of Captives* (Princeton, N.J.: Princeton University Press, 1958).
5. David Eichenthal and James Jacobs, "Enforcing the Criminal Law in State Prisons," *Justice Quarterly* 8 (1991):283–303.
6. David Anderson, *Crimes of Justice: Improving the Police, Courts, and Prison* (New York: Times Books, 1988).
7. Robert Johnson, *Hard Time, Understanding and Reforming the Prison* (Monterey, Calif.: Brooks Cole, 1987), p. 115.
8. Kevin Wright, *The Great American Crime Myth* (Westport, Conn.: Greenwood Press, 1985), p. 167.
9. Sandra Gleason, "Hustling: The 'Inside' Economy of a Prison," *Federal Probation* 42 (1978):32–39.
10. Ibid., p. 39.
11. *Newsweek*, 18 February 1980, p. 75.
12. Hans Toch, *Living in Prison* (New York: Free Press, 1977), pp. 179–205.
13. Ibid., p. 192.
14. Johnson, *Hard Time*, pp. 55–60.
15. Ibid., p. 70.
16. J. Stephan, *Prison Rule Violators* (Washington, D.C.: Bureau of Justice Statistics, 1989).
17. Leonore Simon, "Prison Behavior and Victim-Offender Relationships among Violent Offenders" (Paper presented at the annual meeting of the American Society of Criminology, San Francisco, November 1991).
18. John Irwin, "Adaptation to Being Corrected: Corrections from the Convict's Perspective," in *Handbook of Criminology*, ed. Daniel Glazer (Chicago: Rand McNally, 1974), pp. 971–93.
19. Donald Clemmer, *The Prison Community* (New York: Holt, Rinehart, and Winston, 1958).
20. Sykes, *The Society of Captives*.
21. Gresham Sykes and Sheldon Messinger, "The Inmate Social Code," in *The Sociology of Punishment and Corrections*, ed. Norman Johnston et al. (New York: John Wiley & Sons, 1970), pp. 401–8.
22. Ibid., p. 404.
23. John Irwin and Donald Cressey, "Thieves, Convicts, and the Inmate Culture," *Social Problems* 10 (1962):142–55.
24. Ibid., p. 145.
25. See, generally, Wright, *The Great American Crime Myth*, p. 167.
26. Paul Gendreau, Marie-Claude Tellier, and J. Stephen Wormith, "Protective Custody: The Emerging Crisis Within Our Prisons," *Federal Probation* 69 (1985):55–64.
27. James B. Jacobs, ed. *New Perspectives on Prisons and Imprisonment* (Ithaca, N.Y.: Cornell University Press, 1983); idem, "Street Gangs Behind Bars," *Social Problems* 21:(1974):395–409; idem, "Race Relations and the Prison Subculture," in *Crime and Justice*, Vol. 1, ed. Norval Morris and Michael Tonry (Chicago: University of Chicago Press, 1979), pp. 1–28.
28. Stanley Penn, "Prison Gangs Formed by Racial Groups Pose Big Problem in West," *Wall Street Journal*, 11 May 1983, p. A1.

29. Charles Stastny and Gabrielle Tyrnauer, *Who Rules the Joint?* (Lexington, Mass.: Lexington Books, 1982), pp. 143–145.

30. Penn, "Prisons Gangs Formed by Racial Groups Pose Big Problems in West."

31. Jacobs, *New Perspectives on Prisons and Imprisonment*, pp. 97–98.

32. Nicole Hahn Rafter, *Partial Justice* (New Brunswick, N.J.: Transaction Books, 1990), pp. 181–82.

33. Estimate based on Robyn Cohen, *Prisoners in 1990* (Washington, D.C.: Bureau of Justice Statistics, 1991).

34. Federal Bureau of Investigation *Crime in the United States, 1990* (Washington, D.C.: U.S. Government Printing Office, 1991), p. 179.

35. Lawrence Greenfeld and Stephanie Minor-Harper, *Women in Prison* (Washington, D.C.: Bureau of Justice Statistics, 1991).

36. Meda Chesney-Lind, "Patriarchy, Prisons and Jails: A Critical Look at Trends in Women's Incarceration" (Paper presented at the International Feminist Conference on Women, Law and Social Control, Mont Gabriel, Quebec, July 1991).

37. Elaine DeCostanzo and Helen Scholes, "Women Behind Bars, Their Numbers Increase," *Corrections Today* 50: (1988):104–6.

38. Ibid., p. 106.

39. This section synthesizes the findings of a number of surveys of female inmates, including DeCostanzo and Scholes, "Women Behind Bars, Their Numbers Increase"; Ruth Glick and Virginia Neto, *National Study of Women's Correctional Programs* (Washington, D.C.: U.S. Government Printing Office, 1977); Ann Goetting and Roy Michael Howsen, "Women in Prison: A Profile," *The Prison Journal* 63 (1983):27–46; Meda Chesney-Lind and Noelie Rodrigues, "Women under Lock and Key: A View from Inside," *Prison Journal* 63 (1983):47–65; Contact, Inc., "Women Offenders," *Corrections Compendium* 7 (1982):6–11.

40. Data in this section come from Greenfield and Minor-Harper, *Women in Prison;* other information comes from DeCostanzo and Scholes, "Women Behind Bars, Their Numbers Increase"; Goetting and Howsen, "Women in Prison: A Profile"; Chesney-Lind and Rodrigues, "Women under Lock and Key: A View from Inside."

41. Greenfeld and Minor-Harper, *Women in Prison*, p. 6.

42. Candace Kruttschnitt and Sharon Krmpotich, "Aggressive Behavior among Female Inmates: An Exploratory Study" *Justice Quarterly* 7 (1990):370–89.

43. Edna Erez, "The Myth of the New Female Offender: Some Evidence from Attitudes Toward Law and Justice," *Journal of Criminal Justice* 16 (1988):499–509.

44. Robert Ross and Hugh McKay, *Self-mutilation* (Lexington, Mass.: Lexington Books, 1979).

45. Alice Propper, *Prison Homosexuality* (Lexington, Mass.: Lexington Books, 1981).

46. Ibid.; see also Alice Propper, "Make-Believe Families and Homosexuality among Imprisoned Girls," *Criminology* 20 (1983):127–39.

47. For a review of rehabilitation techniques, see Ted Riggar and Jerome Lorenz, *Readings in Rehabilitation Administration* (New York: State University of New York Press, 1985).

48. Charles Tarr, "Group Counseling," *Corrections Today* 48 (1986):72–75.

49. Roger Crist, "Therapeutic Community Helps Change Inmates for the Better at Rincon," *Corrections Today* 53 (1991):96–100.

50. Gene Kassebaum, David Ward, and Daniel Wilner, "Group Counseling," in *Legal Process and Corrections*, ed. N. Johnston and D. Savitz (New York: John Wiley & Sons, 1982), p. 256.

51. Marie Clark, "Missouri's Sexual Offender Program," *Corrections Today* 48 (1986):84–89.

52. See, generally, William Glasser, *Reality Therapy* (New York: Harper & Row, 1965); Eric Berne, *Transactional Analysis in Psychotherapy* (New York: Grove Press, 1961).

53. Marcia Haynes, "Program Lifts Spirits, Reduces Violence in Institution's Mental Health Unit," *Corrections Today* 53 (1991):120–22.

54. Elizabeth Fabiano, Frank Porporino, and David Robinson, "Canada's Cognitive Skills Program Corrects Offenders' Faulty Thinking," *Corrections Today* 53 (1991):102–8.

55. Rafael Otero, Donna McNally, and Robert Powitzky, "Mental Health Services in Adult Correctional Systems," *Corrections Today* 43 (1981):8–18.

56. Max Mobley, "Mental Health Services Inmates in Need," *Corrections Today* 48 (1986):12–14; Edward Guy, Jerome Platt, Israel Swerling, and Samuel Bullock, "Mental Health Status of Prisoners in an Urban Jail," *Criminal Justice and Behavior* 12 (1985):17–29.

57. Richard Austin and Albert Duncan, "Handle with Care, Special Inmates, Special Needs," *Corrections Today* 50 (1988):116–20.

58. Glenn Walters, Millard Mann, Melvin Miller, Leslie Hemphill, and Michael Chlumsky, "Emotional Disorder among Offenders," *Criminal Justice and Behavior* 15 (1988):433–53.

59. Jean Spruill and Jack May, "The Mentally Retarded Offender," *Criminal Justice and Behavior* 15 (1988):484–91.

60. Ira Sommers and Deborah Baskin, "The Prescription of Psychiatric Medication in Prison: Psychiatric versus Labeling Perspectives," *Justice Quarterly* 7 (1990):739–55.

61. Judy Anderson and R. Daniel McGehee, "South Carolina Strives to Treat Elderly and Disabled Offenders," *Corrections Today* 53 (1991): 124–27.

62. "Few Inmates Get Drug Treatment, But Most Need It, GAO Finds," *Criminal Justice Newsletter*, 22 (November 1, 1991), p. 2.

63. Donald Murray, "New Initiatives in Drug Treatment in the Federal Bureau of Prisons," *Federal Probation* 55 (1991):35–40.

64. Theodore Hammett and Saira Moini, *Update on AIDS in Prisons and Jails* (Washington, D.C.: National Institute of Justice, 1990).

65. Theodore Hamett and Andrea Daugherty, *AIDS in Correctional Facilities: Issues and Options* (draft; Cambridge, Mass.: Abt Associates, 1991).

66. *Gates v. Deukmejian* (U.S.D.C., E.D. Cal.) CIVS 87–1636 (1990).

67. Alper, *Prisons Inside-Out*, pp. 43–94.

68. Sylvia McCollum, "New Designs for Correctional Education and Training Programs," *Federal Probation* 37 (1973):6–8.

69. Ibid., p. 8.

70. Howard Skolnik and John Slansky, "A First Step in Helping Inmates Get Good Jobs after Release," *Corrections Today* 53 (1991):92.

71. Albert Roberts, ed, *Readings in Prison Education* (Springfield, Ill.: Charles C. Thomas, 1973), p. 88.

72. Robert Walton, "New Jersey Places over 350 Trained Cooks, Bakers, and Meatcutters on Jobs During First 30 Months of Food Training," *American Journal of Corrections* 7 (1976):8–12.

73. Cited in Phyllis McCreary and John McCreary, *Job Training and Placement for Offenders and Ex-offenders* (Washington, D.C.: U.S. Government Printing Office, 1975), p. 10.

74. Kathleen Maguire, "Prison Industry and Inmate Behavior: An Examination of High-Rate Infractors" (Paper presented at the annual meeting of the American Society of Criminology, San Francisco, November 1991).

75. Ibid., p. 13.

76. Johnathon Katz and Scott Decker, "An Analysis of Work Release: The Institutionalization of Unsubstantiated Reforms," *Criminal Justice and Behavior* 9 (1982):229–50.

77. Ibid.

78. Paul Hahn, "Residential Alternatives to Incarceration," in *Order under Law*, ed, R. Culbertson and M. Tezak (Prospect Heights, Ill.: Waveland Press, 1981), pp. 244–60.

79. *Prison Furlough Survey* (Lincoln, Neb.: Corrections Compendium, 1991).

80. Donna Duncan, "ACA Survey Examines Industry Programs for

Women Offenders," *Corrections Today* 54 (1992):114.

81. This section leans heavily on Barbara Auerbach, George Sexton, Franklin Farrow, and Robert Lawson, *Work in American Prisons, The Private Sector Gets Involved* (Washington, D.C.: National Institute of Justice, 1988).

82. U.S. Department of Justice, *Impact of Free Venture Prison Industries upon Correctional Industries* (Philadelphia, Pa.: U.S. Department of Justice, 1981).

83. Public Law 96–157, § 827, codified as 18 U.S.C. § 1761(c).

84. Auerbach, et al. *Work in American Prisons*, p. 11.

85. Leslie Boellstorff, "Private Industry Goes to Prison," *Corrections Compendium* 13 (1988):1–8

86. *Correctional Services News* 8 (1983):1–8.

87. Figures cited are as of November 1988, Boellstorf, "Private Industry Goes to Prison," p. 5.

88. Ibid.

89. Pennsylvania Prison Society, "Employment Research Project," *Prison Journal* 60 (1980):1–67.

90. Cicero Wilson, Kenneth Lenihan, and Gail Gookasian, *Employment Services for Ex-offenders* (Washington, D.C.: U.S. Government Printing Office, 1981).

91. Barbara Bloom, "Families of Prisoners: A Valuable Resource" (Paper presented at the annual meeting of the Academy of Criminal Justice Sciences, St. Louis, March 1987); Daniel Leclair, "Home Furlough Program Effects on Rates of Recidivism," *Criminal Justice and Behavior* 5 (1978): 249–59.

92. Creasie Finney Hairston, "Family Ties During Imprisonment: Do They Influence Future Criminal Activity?" *Federal Probation* 52 (1988): 48–53.

93. Anne Goetting, "Conjugal Association in Prison: Issues and Perspectives," *Crime and Delinquency* 24 (1982):52–71.

94. "New York Allows Conjugal Visits for Inmates with AIDS Virus," *Criminal Justice Newsletter* 22 (Dec. 1991):6.

95. Ibid.

96. Norma Stumbo and Sandra Little, "Campground Offers Relaxed Setting for Children's Visitation Program," *Corrections Today* 53 (1991): 136–44.

97. Donald Johns, "Alternatives to Conjugal Visits," *Federal Probation* 35 (1971):48–50.

98. Anne Goetting, "Conjugal Association in Prison," p. 70.

99. "Coed Prisons," *Corrections Compendium* 10 (1986):7, 14–15.

100. Ibid.

101. This section leans heavily on Mark Hamm, "Current Perspectives on the Prisoner Self-Help Movement," *Federal Probation* 52 (1988):49–56.

102. Al Parke, "Bringing the Boy Scouts of America into Prison," *Corrections Today* 53 (1991):154–57.

103. D. Lipton, R. Martinson, and J. Wilks, *The Effectiveness of Correctional Treatment: A Survey of Treatment Evaluation Studies* (New York: Praeger, 1975).

104. Charles Murray and Louis Cox, *Beyond Probation: Juvenile Corrections and the Chronic Delinquent* (Beverly Hills, Calif.: Sage Publications, 1979).

105. Paul Lerman, *Community Treatment and Social Control* (Chicago: University of Chicago Press, 1975).

106. Steven Lab and John Whitehead, "An Analysis of Juvenile Correctional Treatment," *Crime and Delinquency* 34 (1988):60–83.

107. Kathleen Maguire, Timothy Flanagan, Terence Thornberry, "Prison Labor and Recidivism," *Journal of Quantitative Criminology* 4 (1988):3–18.

108. See, generally, James Q. Wilson, " 'What Works?' Revisited: New Findings on Criminal Rehabilitation," in *Legal Process and Corrections*, ed. N. Johnston and L. Savitz (New York: John Wiley & Sons, 1982).

109. Elliott Currie, *Confronting Crime: An American Challenge* (New York: Pantheon, 1985).

110. Mark Lipsey, *Juvenile Delinquency Treatment: A Meta-Analytic Inquiry into the Viability of Effects* (New York: Russell Sage Foundation, 1991).

111. Ted Palmer, "The Effectiveness of Intervention: Recent Trends and Current Issues," *Crime and Delinquency* 37 (1991):330–46.

112. Paul Keve, *Prison Life and Human Worth* (Minneapolis: University of Minnesota Press, 1974).

113. Emily Herrick, "Number of COs Up 25 Percent in Two Years," *Corrections Compendium* 13 (1988):9–21.

114. Ibid., p. 9.

115. Diane Carter, "The Status of Education and Training in Corrections," *Federal Probation* 55 (1991):17–22.

116. Lucien X. Lombardo, *Guards Imprisoned* (New York: Elsevier, 1981); James Jacobs and Norma Crotty, "The Guard's World," in James Jacobs, *New Perspectives on Prisons and Imprisonment* (Ithaca, N.Y.: Cornell University Press, 1983), pp. 133–41.

117. David Duffee, *Corrections: Practice and Policy* (New York: Random House, 1989), p. 401.

118. John Klofas and Hans Toch, "The Guard Subculture Myth," *Journal of Research in Crime and Delinquency* 19 (1982):238–54.

119. Peter Horne, "Female Correction Officers," *Federal Probation* 49 (1985):46–55

120. 433 U.S. 321, 97 S.Ct. 2720, 53 L.Ed.2d 786 (1977).

121. Horne, "Female Correction Officers," p. 53.

122. Robert Wicks, *Guard! Society's Professional Prisoner* (Houston: Gulf Publishing, 1980).

123. Duffee, *Corrections: Practice and Policy*, p. 305.

124. Daniel Lockwood, *Prison Sexual Violence* (New York: Elsevier Books, 1980).

125. Lee Bowker, *Prison Victimization* (New York: Elsevier Books, 1980).

126. Randy Martin and Sherwood Zimmerman, "A Typology of the Causes of Prison Riots and an Analytical Extension to the 1986 West Virginia Riot," *Justice Quarterly* 7 (1990):711–37.

127. Edith Flynn, "From Conflict Theory to Conflict Resolution: Controlling Collective Violence in Prison," *American Behavioral Scientist* 23 (1980):745–76.

128. Michael Serrill and Peter Katel, "The Anatomy of a Riot: The Facts Behind New Mexico's Bloody Ordeal," *Corrections Magazine* 6 (1980):6–24.

129. "Reported Riots/Disturbances," *Corrections Compendium* 10 (1986):13.

130. "Prison Violence Survey," *Corrections Compendium* 10 (1986):11.

131. For a detailed analysis of this issue, see Martin and Zimmerman, "A Typology of the Causes of Prison Riots and an Analytical Extension to the 1986 West Virginia Riot."

132. For a series of papers on the position, see A. Cohen, G. Cole, and R. Baily, eds., *Prison Violence* (Lexington, Mass.: Lexington Books, 1976).

133. See Hans Toch, "Social Climate and Prison Violence," *Federal Probation* 42 (1978):21–23.

134. Charles Silberman, *Criminal Violence, Criminal Justice* (New York: Vintage Books, 1978).

135. Toch, "Social Climate and Prison Violence," p. 21.

136. Ibid., p. 23.

137. Cited in G. McCain, V. Cox, and P. Paulus, *The Effect of Prison Crowding on Inmate Behavior* (Washington, D.C.: U.S. Government Printing Office, 1981), p. vi.

138. "Maryland and New York Prisons Suffer Serious Disturbances," *Criminal Justice Newsletter* 22 (1991):5.

139. Paul Paulus, V. Cox, G. McCain, and J. Chandler, "Some Effects of Crowding in a Prison Environment," *Journal of Applied Social Psychology* 5 (1975):86–91.

140. E. I. Megargee, "The Association of Population Density, Reduced Space, and Uncomfortable Temperatures with Misconduct in a Prison Community," *American Journal of Community Psychology* 5 (1977):289–98.

141. John DiIulio, *Governing Prison: A Comparative Study of Correctional*

Management (New York: Free Press, 1987).
142. Ben Crouch and James Marquart, *An Appeal to Justice* (Austin: University of Texas Press, 1989).
143. *Price v. Johnston*, 334 U.S. 266, 68 S.Ct. 1049, 92 L.Ed. 1356 (1948).
144. National Advisory Commission on Criminal Justice Standards and Goals, *Corrections* (Washington, D.C.: U.S. Government Printing Office, 1973), p. 18.
145. 378 U.S. 546, 84 S.Ct. 1733, 12 L.Ed.2d 1030 (1964).
146. James B. Jacobs, "The Prisoner's Rights Movement and Its Impacts, 1960–1980," in *Crime and Justice*, vol. 2, ed. Norval Morris and Michael Tonry (Chicago: University of Chicago Press, 1980), p. 434.
147. 312 U.S. 546, 61 S.Ct. 640, 85 L.Ed. 1034 (1941).
148. 393 U.S. 483, 89 S.Ct. 747, 21 L.Ed.2d 718 (1969).
149. 855 F.2d 442 (7th Cir. 1988).
150. 776 F.2d 851 (9th Cir. 1985).
151. 461 U.S. 30, 103 S.Ct. 1625, 75 L.Ed.2d 632 (1983).
152. 430 U.S. 817, 97 S.Ct. 1491, 52 L.Ed.2d 72 (1977).
153. 482 U.S. 78, 107 S.Ct. 2254, 2261, 96 L.Ed.2d 64 (1987).
154. 768 F.2d 287 (8th Cir. 1985).
155. 639 F.2d 559 (10th Cir. 1980).
156. 416 U.S. 396, 94 S.Ct. 1800, 40 L.Ed.2d 224 (1974).
157. 451 F.2d 545 (1st Cir. 1971); see also, *Washington Post Co. v. Kleindienst*, 494 F.2d 994 (D.C. Cir. 1974).
158. 417 U.S. 843, 94 S.Ct. 2811, 41 L.Ed.2d 514 (1974); see also, *Pell v. Procunier*, 417 U.S. 817, 94 S.Ct. 2800, 41 L.Ed.2d 495 (1974).
159. 857 F.2d 1055 (5th Cir. 1988).
160. 482 U.S. 342, 107 S.Ct. 2400, 96 L.Ed.2d 282 (1987).
161. 626 F.Supp. 886 (W.D. Tenn. 1986).
162. 769 F.2d 345 (6th Cir. 1985).
163. 405 U.S. 319, 92 S.Ct. 1079, 31 L.Ed.2d 263 (1972).
164. 527 F.2d 492 (2d Cir. 1975).
165. 586 F.2d 22 (7th Cir. 1978).
166. 516 F.Supp. 1004 (E.D. Va. 1981).
167. 349 F.Supp. 278 (M.D. Ala. 1972).
168. 429 U.S. 97, 97 S.Ct. 285, 50 L.Ed.2d 251 (1976).
169. 429 U.S. at 104, 97 S.Ct. at 291.
170. *Trop v. Dulles*, 356 U.S. 86, 78 S.Ct. 590, 2 L.Ed.2d 630 (1958); see also *Furman v. Georgia*, 408 U.S. 238, 92 S.Ct. 2726, 33 L.Ed.2d 346 (1972).
171. *Weems v. United States*, 217 U.S. 349, 30 S.Ct. 544, 54 L.Ed. 793 (1910).
172. *Lee v. Tahash*, 352 F.2d 970 (8th Cir. 1965).
173. 404 F.2d 571 (8th Cir. 1968).
174. 309 F.Supp. 362 (E.D. Ark. 1970), *affirmed*, 442 F.2d 304 (8th Cir. 1971).
175. *McCarthy v. Madigan*, ___ U.S. ___, 112 S.Ct. 1081, 117 L.Ed.2d 291 (1992).
176. Fred Cohen, "The Law of Prisoners' Rights: An Overview," *Criminal Law Bulletin* 24 (1988):321–50, at 322.
177. *Battle v. Anderson*, 447 F.Supp. 516 (1977); see also, *Pugh v. Locke*, 406 F.Supp. 318 (M.D. Ala. 1976); *Palmigiano v. Garrahy*, 443 F.Supp. 956 (D. R.I. 1977); *Jones v. Wittenberg*, 73 F.R.D. 82 (N.D. Ohio 1976).
178. *Bell v. Wolfish*, 441 U.S. 520, 99 S.Ct. 1861, 1873–1974, 60 L.Ed.2d 447 (1979).
179. 452 U.S. 337, 101 S.Ct. 2392, 69 L.Ed.2d 59 (1981). For further analysis of *Rhodes*, See Randall Pooler, "Prison Overcrowding and the Eighth Amendment: The *Rhodes* Not Taken," *New England Journal on Criminal and Civil Confinement* 8 (1983):1–28.
180. *Estelle v. Ruiz*, 74–329 (E.D. Tex. 1980).
181. "Ruiz Case in Texas Winds Down: Special Master to Close Office," *Criminal Justice Newsletter* 21 (1990):1.
182. Geoffrey Alpert, Ben Crouch, C. Ronald Huff, "Prison Reform by Judicial Decree: The Unintended Consequences of *Ruiz v. Estelle*," *Justice System Journal* 9 (1984):291–305.
183. American Correctional Association, *1991 Directory of Juvenile and Adult Correctional Departments, Institutions, Agencies and Paroling Authorities* (Laurel, Md.: American Correctional Association, 1991) p. 20.
184. *Rufo v. Inmates of Suffolk County Jail*, ___ U.S. ___, 112 S.Ct. 748, 116 L.Ed.2d 867 (1992).
185. 474 U.S. 327, 106 S.Ct. 662, 88 L.Ed.2d 662 (1986).
186. *Davidson v. Cannon*, 474 U.S. 344, 106 S.Ct. 668, 88 L.Ed.2d 677 (1986).
187. *Wilson v. Seiter*, ___ U.S. ___, 111 S.Ct. 2321, 115 L.Ed.2d 271 (1991).
188. *Hudson v. McMillian*, ___ U.S. ___, 112 S.Ct. 995, 117 L.Ed.2d 156 (1992).
189. 468 U.S. 517, 104 S.Ct. 3194, 82 L.Ed.2d 393 (1984).
190. *Meachum v. Fano*, 427 U.S. 215, 96 S.Ct. 2532, 49 L.Ed.2d 451 (1976).
191. *Moody v. Daggett*, 429 U.S. 78, 97 S.Ct. 274, 50 L.Ed.2d 236 (1976).
192. *Hewitt v. Helms*, 459 U.S. 460, 103 S.Ct. 864, 74 L.Ed.2d 675 (1983).
193. *Superintendant v. Hill*, 472 U.S. 445, 105 S.Ct. 2768, 86 L.Ed.2d 356 (1985).
194. *Whitley v. Albers*, 475 U.S. 312, 106 S.Ct. 1078, 89 L.Ed.2d 251 (1986).
195. *Kentucky Dept. of Corrections v. Thompson*, 490 U.S. 454, 109 S.Ct. 1904, 104 L.Ed.2d 506 (1989); *Thornburgh v. Abbott*, 490 U.S. 401, 109 S.Ct. 1874, 104 L.Ed.2d 459 (1989).

Returning to Society

CHAPTER 18

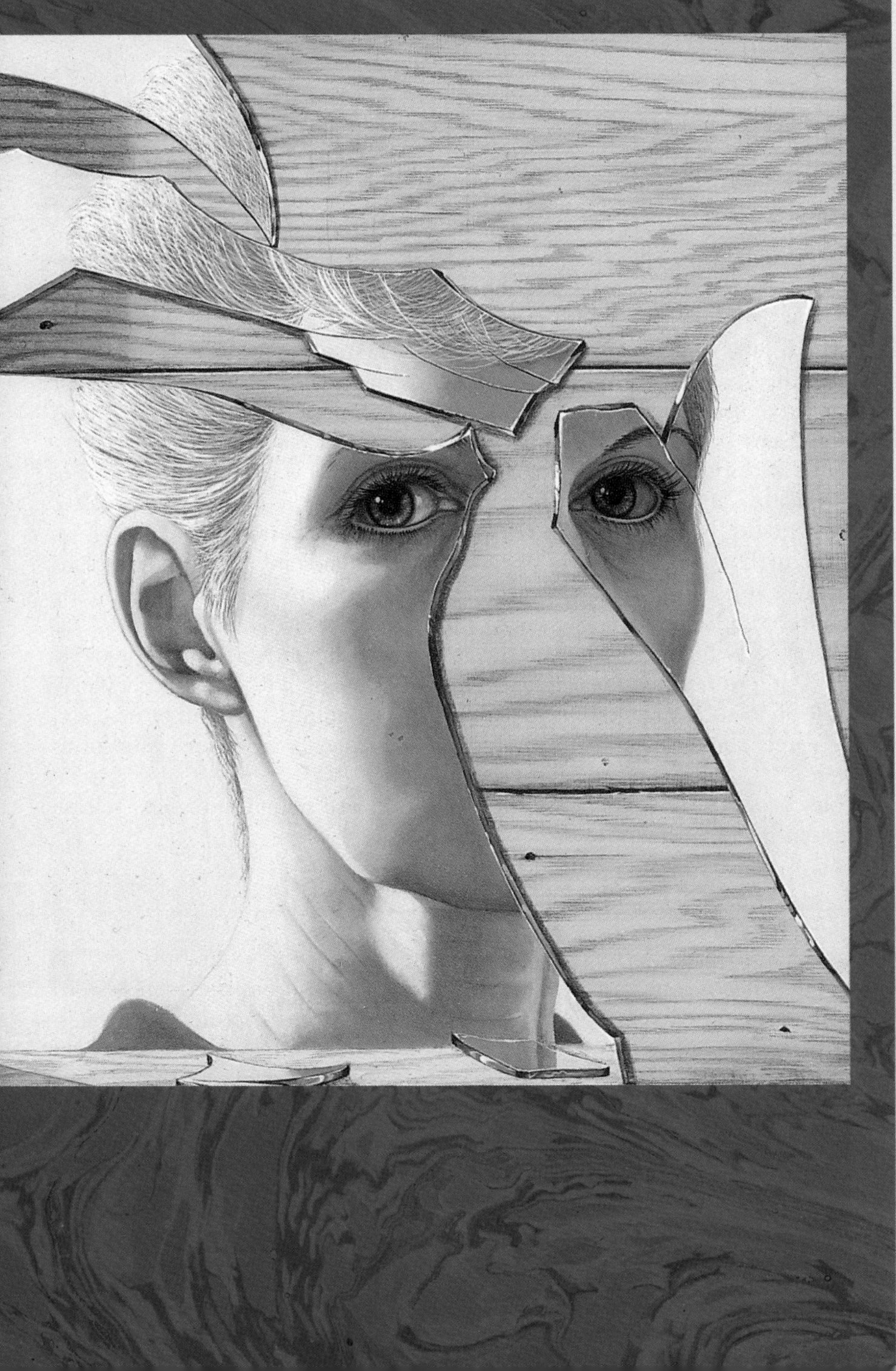

OUTLINE

KEY TERMS

parole
property in service
indentured servant
Alexander Maconochie
ticket of leave
good-time credit
procedural rights
Wolff v. McDonnell
technical parole violation
parole grant hearing
Emergency Powers Act (EPA)
parole guidelines
presumptive parole dates
parole rules
parole plan
salient factor score
intensive supervision probation (ISP)
parole revocation
Morrissey v. Brewer
"civil death"

At the expiration of their prison term, most inmates return to society and try to resume their life in the outside world. For some inmates, their reintegration into society comes by way of **parole,** the planned community release and supervision of incarcerated offenders prior to the actual expiration of their prison sentences. In states where determinate sentencing statutes have eliminated discretionary parole, offenders are released after having served their determinate sentence less time off for good behavior and other credits designed to reduce the term of incarceration. Their release may involve supervision in the community, and rule violations can result in return to prison for the balance of their unexpired sentence.[1] In a few instances, inmates are released after their sentence has been commuted by a board of pardons or directly by a state governor or even the president of the United States. About 15 percent of prison inmates are released after serving their entire maximum sentence without any time excused or forgiven.[2] And despite the efforts of correctional authorities, about seven thousand inmates escape every year from state and federal prisons (the number of escapes is actually declining due in part to better officer training and more sophisticated security measures).[3]

Regardless of the method of their release, former inmates face the formidable task of having to readjust to society. This means regaining legal rights they may have lost upon their conviction, reestablishing community and family ties, and finding employment. After being in prison, these goals are often difficult to achieve.

This chapter reviews this final stage of the justice system, including release from prison and adjustment to society.

History of Prison Release

The practice of releasing inmates from prison prior to the expiration of their sentence has had a long history. The term *parole* comes from the French word meaning "to promise," referring to the practice of releasing captured enemy soldiers if they promised not to fight again, along with the threat that they would be executed if recaptured.[4] However, the roots of early prison release can be most directly traced to one of the shifts in the history of punishment that occurred with the colonization efforts of the seventeenth century. Before that time, torture, mutilation, and death were the standard forms of punishment for offenders convicted of a felony.[5] In the seventeenth century, however, it became common for English judges to spare the lives of offenders by banishing them to the new overseas colonies. In 1617, the Privy Counsel of the British Parliament standardized this practice by passing an order granting reprieves and stays of execution to convicts willing to be transported to the colonies. Transportation was viewed as an answer to labor shortages caused by war, disease, and the opening of new commercial markets.

By 1665, transportation orders were modified to include specific conditions of employment and to provide for reconsideration of punishment if the conditions were not met (for example, if the offender returned to England before the expiration of the sentence).

In 1717, the British Parliament passed legislation creating the concept of **property in service.** Under this doctrine, control of prisoners was transferred to a contractor or shipmaster until the expiration of their sentences. When the prisoners arrived in the colonies, their services could be sold to the highest bidder. After the sale, their status changed from convict to **indentured servant.** Transportation quickly became the most common sentence for theft offenders.

The concept of early release and pardon underwent a series of transformations during the eighteenth century. In the American colonies, property in service was abandoned after the Revolution. It was replaced in the North by European immigrant labor and a greater reliance on machinery and in the South by the African slave system, which provided a long-term labor force and promised greater profits. Thereafter, Australia, claimed as a British colony in 1770, became the destination for most transported felons. From 1815 to 1850, large numbers of inmates were shipped to Australia to serve as indentured servants working on plantations, in mines, or on sheep stations.

In England, opposition to penal servitude and the deprivations associated with transportation produced such organizations as the Society for the Improvement of Prison Discipline. This group asked the famous reformer **Alexander Maconochie** to investigate conditions in Australia. Maconochie condemned transportation and eventually helped end the practice. Later, when appointed director of the infamous Australian prison on Norfolk Island, Maconochie instituted reforms, such as classification and rehabilitation programs, that became models for the treatment of convicted offenders.

After Maconochie was recalled from Australia to England, his efforts there led to the English Penal Servitude Act of 1853, which all but ended transportation and substituted imprisonment as a punishment. Part of the act made possible the granting of a **ticket of leave** to those who had served a sufficient portion of their prison sentence. This form of conditional release permitted former prisoners to be at large in specified areas. The conditions of their release were written on a license that they were required to carry with them at all times. Although the conditions of release usually required sobriety, lawful behavior, and hard work, many violated their leave provisions, prompting criticism of the system. Eventually, in response, prisoner aid society members helped supervise and care for releasees.

In Ireland, Sir Walter Crofton, a disciple of Maconochie's reforms, liberalized Irish prisons. He instituted a mark system in which inmates could earn their ticket of leave by accumulating credits for good conduct and hard work. Crofton also established a system in which private volunteers or police agents could monitor ticket-of-leave offenders in the community. The work of Crofton was considered an early form of parole.

U.S. Developments

In the United States, the concept of releasing inmates into the community before the expiration of their sentence can be traced to the first "good-time laws," developed in New York in 1817. Today, all states have statutes that enable prisoners to reduce their sentences through evidence of good behavior in prison.

In 1822, volunteers from the Philadelphia-based Society for Alleviating the Miseries of Public Prisons began to help offenders once they were released from prison. In 1851, the society appointed two agents to work with inmates discharged from Pennsylvania penal institutions. Massachusetts appointed an agent in 1845 to help released inmates obtain jobs, clothing, and transportation.

The real impetus for early release developed in the late nineteenth century, when prison reformers, such as Z. R. Brockway, lobbied for passage of indeterminate sentences and advocated the rehabilitation of prisoners. Brockway became warden of the Elmira Reformatory in 1876 and succeeded in having New York pass the first true indeterminate sentencing laws for adults. Using a carefully weighted screening procedure, Brockway selected the "rehabilitated" offenders for early release under supervision of citizen volunteers known as guardians. The guardians met with the parolees at least once a month and submitted written reports on their progress.

The parole concept spread rapidly. Ohio created the first parole agency in 1884. By 1901, as many as twenty states had created some type of parole agency. By 1927, only three states, Florida, Mississippi, and Virginia, had not established some sort of parole release. Parole had become institutionalized as the primary method of release for prison inmates, and half of all inmates released in the United States were paroled.

Early Release Today

The practice of releasing inmates from prison before the expiration of their sentence still continues. Most inmates do not serve their entire sentence before returning to society. In fact, the average stay is usually less than half of the original sentence.

A number of attempts have been made to determine the actual time served in prison. A survey of sentencing practices both nationally and in the seventy-five largest U.S. counties found that inmates served about 41 percent of their original sentence behind bars. As Table 18.1 shows, those convicted of drug trafficking served the smallest percentage of their sentence (32 percent), while rapists did the most time behind bars (44 percent). The relationship between the original sentence and the actual time served can be startling: murderers who were originally sentenced to about eighteen years in prison do only about seven years. These data tell us that despite years of "get tough" rhetoric from advocates of the crime-control model of justice, the average offender is back on the street in two years, violent offenders in three. While a greater percentage of convicted offenders are going to prison today, fewer are serving their entire sentence.

Inmates serve only a fraction of their sentence because prisons simply cannot maintain a continuously increasing inmate population. While legislators may be motivated by political expediency to produce tough determinate and mandatory sentencing laws, the result has been a rapidly expanding prison population. In 1850, the incarceration rate was 29 people per 100,000 (there were 6,737 inmates); today, the incarceration rate is about 275 per 100,000, with over 800,000 people in prison.[6] It would be impossible to maintain these inmates for their entire sentence without a massive correctional building program. Barring such an unlikely scenario, correctional administrators have relied on parole and other early-release mechanisms to reduce the inmate population and maintain order within the institutions.

TABLE 18.1
Average Time Served in Prison

Most Serious Conviction Offense	Percentage of Sentence Served in Prison	United States		75 Largest Countries	
		Mean Prison Sentence	Estimated Time to Be Served in Prison	Mean Prison Sentence	Estimated Time to Be Served in Prison
All	41%	81 mos.	33 mos.	75 mos.	31 mos.
Murder	39	221	86	220	86
Rape	44	151	66	164	72
Robbery	41	139	57	109	45
Aggravated assault	42	97	41	80	34
Burglary	41	75	31	60	25
Larceny	44	46	20	40	18
Drug trafficking	32	69	22	62	20
Other felonies	42	56	24	50	21

SOURCE: Patrick Lamgan, *Felony Sentences in State Courts* (Washington, D.C.: Bureau of Justice Statistics, 1989), p. 6.

The following sections review the administrative practices under which most inmates return to society before the completion of their prison sentence.

Time-Off for Good Behavior: "Good Time"

Most inmates do not serve their full sentence because they are awarded time off for good behavior, or "good time." An inmate can accumulate **good-time credit** today in both the state and federal prison systems by obeying prison rules and/or by performing meritorious service, such as volunteering for medical experiments, donating blood, or attending academic and/or vocational training programs.

The first good-time laws were passed in New York in 1817 to reduce the overcrowding at Newgate prison. Good-time laws permitted a reduction of up to 25 percent of inmates' sentence if they were first-time offenders who worked hard and had accumulated at least fifteen dollars while in prison.[7] The concept was spread by prison administrators who believed that rewards would control an inmate's behavior more effectively than punishments. In addition, their use represents an early effort by reformers throughout the nineteenth and early twentieth centuries to rehabilitate and reintegrate offenders into the community prior to the completion of their sentence.

Each correctional jurisdiction controls its own method of dispensing good time. Good-time credits may be deducted from both the minimum and maximum terms; some jurisdictions deduct credit from the maximum term only, while others deduct it from the minimum only. No matter what method is used, good time reduces the time inmates must serve before becoming eligible for release. If an inmate receives a determinate sentence of ten years, good-time credits might halve the time actually served. In an indeterminate-sentencing state that deducts good time from the minimum sentence, a prison term of two to twenty years might be served in less than one year.

The amount of good time granted an inmate also varies among jurisdictions. Some states allow good time on a flat basis per month or per year. For example, North Dakota grants inmates ten days per month served. Other states grant

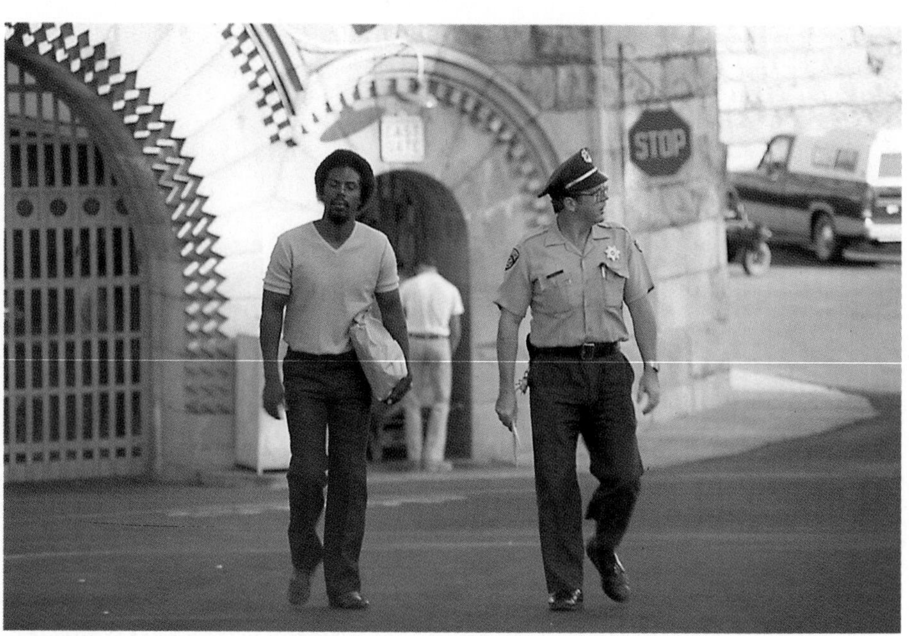

Most inmates leave prison via some form of parole or early release prior to the expiration of their sentence.

earned increases in good time for meritorious behavior. New Mexico allows inmates to earn up to thirty days of good time per month served. And some states provide both statutory and earned good time: Connecticut gives inmates twelve days off per month and allows one day per week of work credit; Maine grants ten days per month statutory good time and allows inmates to earn an additional five days per month.[8] Because of prison crowding, some jurisdictions have recently boosted good-time allowances in order to reduce the prison population. For example, in an effort to relieve its correctional system, which has a capacity of 24,000 and a population of twenty-nine thousand, Illinois recently instituted a program that gives inmates a ninety-day good-time bonus at the end of their sentence.[9]

In most jurisdictions, the good-time allowance is granted only while the inmate is incarcerated in a penal institution. In many cases, inmates do not receive credit for time spent in jail awaiting trial, in mental institutions pending psychiatric examinations, or while incarcerated pending an appeal. In the case of *McGinnis v. Royster* (1973), the U.S. Supreme Court upheld the constitutionality of a New York correctional law that did not require including jail detention time in good-time credit calculations when the inmate was transferred to a state prison.[10]

Losing Good-Time Credits

Once good-time credit is gained, an inmate can still forfeit it. State and federal statutes that allow for good-time credits include provisions governing the amounts of time that may be lost and by what methods. Ordinarily, the warden or superintendent of the institution, in conjunction with other prison officials, administers good-time credit programs. For minor prison infractions, the inmate may lose a month of good time; for serious violations of rules, such as an attempted escape, an inmate may lose all accumulated credit.

If correctional authorities decide to reduce good time because of misconduct, they must grant inmates the right to defend themselves against the charges. The

procedural rights granted inmates have varied from case to case and jurisdiction to jurisdiction; the following are some of the principal rights:

1. The right to notice of the nature of the complaint;
2. The right to a fair hearing before an impartial official or panel;
3. The right to an administrative review of the decision;
4. The right to confront witnesses; and
5. The right to counsel or counsel substitute.

In some cases, prisoners have been granted rights beyond these; in others, the courts have taken a more restrictive view.

In 1974, the Supreme Court in the case of ***Wolff v. McDonnell*** established the precise constitutional safeguards required at a disciplinary proceeding.[11] This case is highlighted in the Law in Review on page 634.

Wolff is a landmark case because it recognizes that inmates suffer a significant loss when their good time is eliminated and that they maintain the right to defend against the loss of their release-time benefits.

Parole

Most correctional administrations allow inmates to become eligible for parole after completing their minimum sentence less good time.[12] Parole is considered a way of completing a prison sentence in the community under the supervision of the correctional authorities. It is not the same as a pardon; paroled offenders can be legally recalled to serve the remainder of their sentence in an institution if the parole authorities deem the offenders' adjustment inadequate because they fail to obey the conditions of their release or commit another crime while on parole.

The decision to parole is determined by statutory requirement and usually occurs upon completion of a minimum sentence less any good-time or special release credits. In about 40 percent of all prison-release decisions, parole is granted by a parole board, a duly constituted body of men and women who review inmate cases and determine whether offenders have reached a rehabilitative level sufficient to deal with the outside world. The board also dictates what specific parole rules parolees must obey.

Once released into the community, the offender is supervised by a trained staff of parole officers who help the offender search for employment and monitor the parolee's behavior and activities to ensure that the conditions of parole are met.

Parolees are subject to strict rules, standardized and/or personalized, that guide their behavior and set limits on their activities. If these rules are violated, they can be returned to the institution to serve the remainder of their sentence; this is known as a **technical parole violation.** Parole can also be revoked by the offender committing a second offense while in the community. The offender may even be tried and sentenced for this subsequent crime.

Parole is generally viewed as a privilege granted to deserving inmates on the basis of their good behavior while in prison. Parole has two conflicting sides, however. On one hand, the paroled offender is allowed to serve part of the sentence in the community, an obvious benefit for the deserving offender. On the other hand, since parole is a "privilege and not a right," the parolee is viewed as a dangerous criminal who must be carefully watched and supervised. The conflict between the treatment and enforcement aspects of parole has not been reconciled by the criminal justice system, and the parole process still contains elements of both.

LAW IN REVIEW

Wolff v. McDonnell (1974)

Facts

In July 1970, Robert McDonnell, on behalf of himself and other inmates of the Nebraska Penal and Correctional Complex in Lincoln, filed a complaint in the form of a civil rights action under 42 U.S.C. § 1983 challenging as unconstitutional several of the practices in effect at the complex. In particular, McDonnell claimed that disciplinary proceedings did not comply with the due process clause of the U.S. Constitution, that the inmate legal assistance program did not meet constitutional standards, and that the regulations governing the inspection of inmates' mail to and from attorneys were unconstitutionally restrictive.

The U.S. Supreme Court granted the petition for a writ of certiorari because the case involved important issues dealing with the management of a state prison.

McDonnell requested relief in the form of the restoration of good-time credits, the development of a plan by the prison for a hearing procedure in connection with good time, and damages for the deprivation of civil rights.

Decision

In a 6-to-3 decision, the Supreme Court held that the due process clause of the Fourteenth Amendment provides inmates with procedural protections if they are facing a loss of good time or confinement because of an institutional disciplinary action. The Court ruled that a prisoner is not completely stripped of constitutional safeguards in prison. Even though prison disciplinary proceedings do not necessitate the full range of rights due a defendant in a criminal trial, such proceedings must be governed by an accommodation between prison needs and constitutional rights. Since prisoners under Nebraska law can only lose good-time credits if they are guilty of serious misconduct, the procedure for determining when this should occur requires due process of law.

In accommodating the interests of the state of Nebraska with those of the inmate, the Court concluded that due process requires the following in prison disciplinary proceedings for serious violations of conduct:

1. Advance written notice of the charges must be given to the inmate no less than twenty-four hours before the prisoner's appearance at the disciplinary committee hearing.
2. There must be a written statement by the factfinders listing the evidence relied on and the reasons for the disciplinary action.
3. The inmate should be allowed to call witnesses and present documentary evidence in his or her defense if this will not jeopardize institutional control.
4. The inmate has no constitutional right to confrontation and cross-examination in prison discipline proceedings.
5. Inmates have no right to retained or appointed counsel, although substitute counsel, such as a staff member or another inmate, may be provided in certain cases.
6. The record in this case did not show if the Adjustment Committee in the Nebraska Complex was impartial, but the inmate has the right to have an impartial group conduct disciplinary hearings.
7. In regard to regulations governing inmate mail, the Court held that the state may require that mail from an attorney to a prisoner be identified as such and that the attorney's name and address appear on the communication. In addition, as a protection against contraband, prison authorities may open mail in the inmate's presence.

In its decision, the Supreme Court rejected the state of Nebraska's assertion that disciplinary action against inmates is a matter of policy that raises no constitutional issues. At the same time, the Court did not adopt the prisoner's view that the full range of due process procedures should apply to disciplinary actions within an institutional setting. Instead, the Court addressed itself to the range of procedures applicable to a correctional institution.

Significance of the Case

Although the Court was faced with three major issues in this case (the adequacy of legal assistance, the confidentiality of the mail, and the loss of good time or confinement for prison infractions), primary emphasis was placed on the issue of procedural due process for prison misconduct. It represented a major breakthrough in the establishment of due process guidelines in prison disciplinary proceedings that affect the practices of state and federal prison systems. The Court recognized the violent nature of the prison setting and did not want to restrict the ability of correctional administrators to ensure the safety of their prisons. Thus, the Court sought a formula that maintained both prison security and provided constitutional safeguards. As a result, disciplinary action against an inmate for a serious infraction resulting in loss of good-time credits or confinement must be accompanied by due process of law.

In recent years, the nation's parole system has come under increasing criticism from those who believe that it is inherently unfair to inmates and fails to protect the public. It is unfair to the inmate because the decision to release is based on the discretion of parole board members who are forced to make predictions about the inmate's future behavior, an uncertain activity at best. It fails to protect the public because predatory criminals released before the expiration of their sentence are free to once again attack innocent victims. The movement toward determinate and mandatory sentences has limited the availability of parole and restricted the discretion of parole boards.

According to the most recent statistics, approximately 531,000 adults are on parole at any one time in the United States.[13] About 358,000 are released on parole each year and 284,000 complete their term.

The number of people on parole in a state is usually a function of the size of the state's prison population. For example, Texas, which has a relatively high prison population, has 90 people on parole per 10,000 population, while New Hampshire, with a relatively low prison population, places only 6 per 10,000 population on parole.

Mandatory Parole Release

In addition to the 40 percent of inmates released at the discretion of correctional authorities, another 30 percent are mandatory parole releasees—inmates whose discharge was a requirement of determinate sentencing statutes or good-time reductions but whose release was supervised by parole authorities. Mandatory release begins when the unserved portion of the maximum prison term equals the inmate's earned good time (less time served in jail awaiting trial). In some states, determinate sentences can be reduced by more than half with a combination of statutory and earned good time. If the conditions of their release are violated, mandatory releasees can have their good time revoked and be returned to the institution to serve the remainder of their unexpired term. The remaining 30 percent of inmates were released for a variety of reasons, including expiration of their term, commutation of their sentence, and court orders to relieve overcrowded prisons.

The movement to create mandatory and determinate sentencing statutes has significantly affected parole. As Figure 18.1 shows, the number of people leaving prison via discretionary parole has declined substantially in the past few years. While at one time more than 70 percent of releasees were paroled, that number has declined to 40 percent; conversely, mandatory releases have increased from about 6 percent in the late '70s to 30 percent today.

Almost all the mandatory parole releasees are in jurisdictions that rely heavily on determinate sentences, such as Illinois, Indiana, and Minnesota. The gap between the two forms of release has remained stable since 1985 because the rush to adopt determinate sentencing has also slowed.

The Parole Board

The authority to grant discretionary parole is usually vested in the parole board. The American Correctional Association has suggested that state parole boards have four primary functions:

1. To select and place prisoners on parole;

FIGURE 18.1
Method of prison release, 1977–1990

SOURCE: Louis Jankowski, *Probation and Parole, 1990* (Washington, D.C.: Bureau of Justice Statistics, 1991), p. 6.

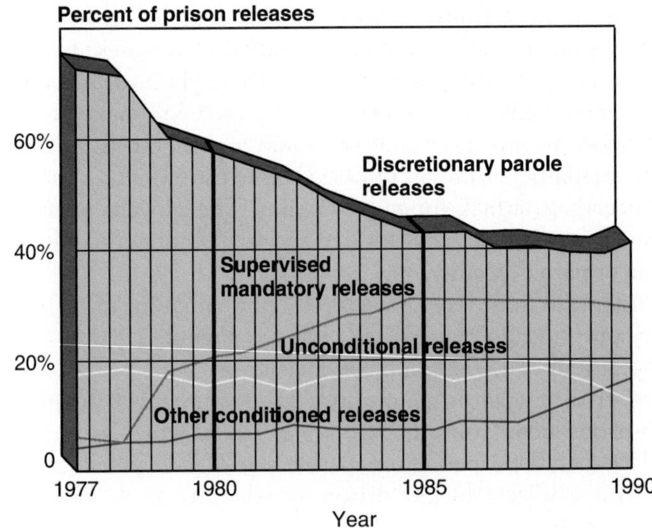

2. To aid, supervise, and provide continuing control of parolees in the community;
3. To determine when the parole function is completed and to discharge from parole; and
4. If violations of conditions occur, to determine whether parole revocation should take place.[14]

Most parole authorities are independent agencies with their own staff and administration, while a few parole boards (e.g., in Ohio and Maryland), are part of the state department of corrections.[15] Arguments for keeping the board within a corrections department usually include the improved communication and availability of more intimate knowledge about offenders.

Most boards are relatively small, usually numbering less than ten members. Their size, coupled with their large caseloads and the varied activities they are expected to perform, can prevent board members from becoming as well acquainted with the individual inmate as might be desired.

How parole board members are appointed differs from state to state. In most jurisdictions that use parole, the governor is the appointing authority; in a few others, parole board members are chosen from civil service lists; and in the remaining jurisdictions, they are appointed by a mayor (Washington, D.C.), the commissioner of corrections, or the governor and governor's cabinet from a prepared list. Terms of appointment also tend to vary; depending on the jurisdiction, they range from a life term (four states) to two years (one state); the average terms is six years (sixteen states).

Parole Hearings

The actual (discretionary) parole decision is made at a **parole grant hearing.** At this hearing, the full board or a selected subcommittee reviews information, may meet with the offender, and then decides whether the parole applicant has a reasonable probability of succeeding outside prison.

Each parole board has its own way of reviewing cases. In some, the full board meets with the applicant; in others, only a few members do that. In a number of jurisdictions, a single board member can conduct a personal investigation and submit the findings to the full board for a decision.

At the hearing, parole board members consider such information as police reports of the crime; the presentence investigation; psychological testing and scores developed by prison mental health professionals; and institutional reports of disciplinary actions, treatment, and adjustment. Letters may be solicited from the inmate's friends and family members. In some jurisdictions, victims may appear and make statements of the losses they suffered.

No specific national policy exists to determine the way in which inmates are informed of the board's decision. The inmate may be informed in writing by the board, or the parole board may confront the offender with its decision immediately after the hearing. It is believed that this latter method can promote in the offender a sense of participation in the correctional process and may also increase the offender's perceptions of its fairness. By speaking directly to the applicant, the board can also promote and emphasize the specific types of behavior and behavior changes it expects to see if the inmate is to eventually qualify for or effectively serve parole.[16]

The inmate's specific rights at a parole grant hearing also vary from jurisdiction to jurisdiction. In about half of the parol-granting jurisdictions, inmates are permitted counsel or allowed to present witnesses on their behalf; other jurisdictions do not permit these privileges. Because the federal courts have declared that the parole applicant is not entitled to any form of legal representation, the individual inmate may have to pay for legal services where this privilege is allowed.

In almost all parole-granting jurisdictions, the reasons for the parole decision must be given in writing, while in about half of the jurisdictions, a verbatim record of the hearing is made.

Due Process at Parole Grant Hearings. As noted previously, the due process rights of inmates vary widely at parole grant hearings. Some jurisdictions provide for counsel, allow witnesses and personal appearances, give reasons for decisions in writing, and allow appeals, while others provide none or only a few of these privileges.

The U.S. Supreme Court has reviewed the rights of inmates to secure due process at parole grant hearings in two important cases, *Greenholtz v. Inmates of the Nebraska Penal and Correctional Complex* (1979)[17] and *Connecticut Board of Pardons v. Dumschat* (1981).[18] In *Greenholtz*, the Court held that early release on parole was a privilege and not a right and that this act of "grace" did not entitle inmates to receive a full complement of due process rights (under the Fifth and Fourteenth Amendments) at a parole hearing (e.g., to have counsel or to call witnesses).

Thus, the Court suggested that the right to due process is not created merely because a state provides a possibility of parole. This is only a "mere hope" and is therefore distinguishable from revocation of parole (discussed later in this chapter). However, if the language of a particular state statute creates an "expectancy" of release, for example, by ordering parole for all inmates except those who violated prison rules, then inmates in that state have the right to due process at parole grant hearings.[19]

In *Dumschat*, the U.S. Supreme Court considered whether the granting of 75 percent of applications to the Connecticut Board of Pardons for commutation of life sentences created a "liberty interest" that entitled inmates to written reasons if their request for an early parole date was turned down. The Court ruled that inmates have only a "mere hope" of parole or pardon and therefore should not expect due process rights. The Court went on to state:

> No matter how frequently a particular form of clemency has been granted, the statistical probabilities standing alone generate no constitutional protections; a contrary conclusion would trivialize the Constitution. The ground for a constitutional claim, if any, must be found in statutes or other rules defining the obligations of the authority charged with exercising clemency.[20]

Thus, the Supreme Court has limited the inmate's right to due process at parole grant hearings.

Parole Board Discretion

In states that retain discretionary parole, the decision to release an inmate into the community is a function of parole board discretion. In deciding whether to grant parole, the board must take into account many important factors, some of which are discussed below.

Of primary concern to the board is whether the inmate can make an adequate adjustment to the community and refrain from further criminal activity. For example, the board must decide if it is the proper time to release the offender or whether continued confinement will be beneficial. Those parole board members concerned with protecting the community might argue that longer prison sentences help deter crime through incapacitation and at the same time increase the offender's awareness that the parole agency is a no-nonsense organization whose wishes must be respected. Other board members may be more concerned with the potential harm that continuation of a prison sentence might cause the inmate; this type of member believes that prolonging the release of the offender may cause further damage from the pains of imprisonment. Regardless of their orientation, most parole board members realize that the consequences of their decision can jeopardize the state's parole program if a too-hasty release turns out to have disastrous results for the community.[21]

Parole board members may also be concerned with the inherent justice and morality of their decision: Has the offender paid the debt to society? Should consideration be given to the victims of crimes (or potential victims)? Should revenge be a motive for denying parole? Board members may also ponder the fairness of releasing one inmate into the community while retaining another who has committed the same crime and has served the same amount of time.

Another consideration influencing the board's decision may be the condition and welfare of the prisoner's family. A family left alone while the breadwinner is imprisoned may become wards of the state, receive public welfare, and have children placed in foster homes. As a result, the offender's incarceration becomes a triple financial burden on the state and includes (1) the cost of imprisonment, (2) the cost of welfare and child support for the family, and (3) the lost tax dollars and revenue that would be acquired were the inmate productively employed while on parole. Furthermore, the economic, social, and psychological burdens of having a family member incarcerated may help push other members of the family into crime. Such considerations may work against the offender who has no dependents; again, the issue of fairness comes up.

Parole board members also base their decision on their perceptions of the values and attitudes of correctional personnel and other administrators of the criminal justice system. For example, if the parole board plans to release an inmate who has received a negative disciplinary report from prison authorities, its action

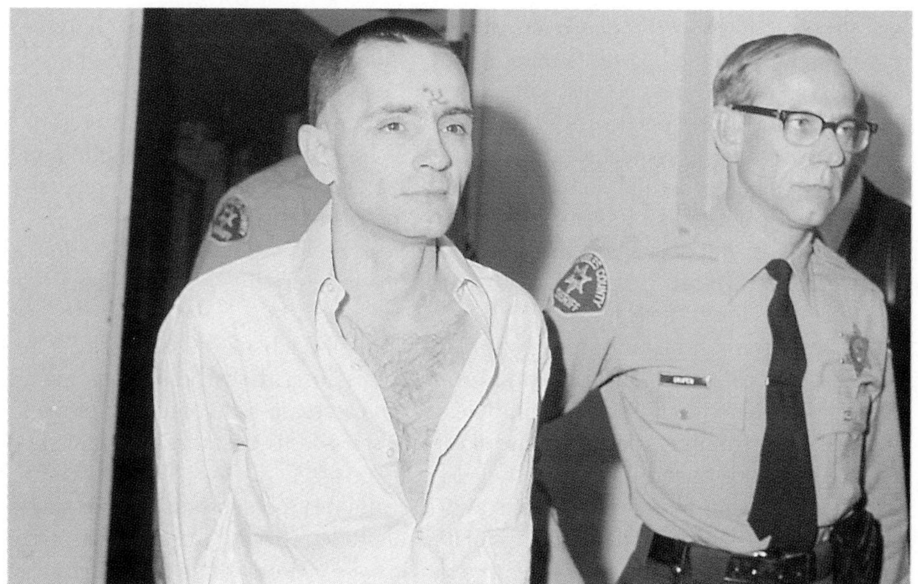

Some inmates, such as Charles Manson, are considered so dangerous that they are consistently rejected for parole release.

may serve to notify other inmates that prison rules need not be taken seriously. A decision to parole a particular inmate must thus be balanced with the need to maintain a cordial working relationship with prison and correctional authorities. Early parole decisions may also be viewed with disappointment by judicial authorities within the state. If parole board and judicial attitudes are not similar, some judges may counteract the policies of the parole board by setting high minimum sentences where the statutory law allows them that discretion. Consideration of the responses of criminal justice system personnel may influence the parole board members' decision to grant or deny parole or set specialized and stringent conditions on parolees.[22]

The public's response to a parole grant may also influence the board's decision making. If, for example, a particularly well-known criminal, such as Charles Manson or Sirhan Sirhan, is up for parole, a positive finding on the offender's behalf will receive widespread media coverage and possibly generate irate responses from the public. Conversely, in the case of offenders with well-defined sympathetic followings, such as battered women who kill their abusive spouses, the board may be swayed in a more lenient direction.

Discretion and the Correctional System

In many jurisdictions, the parole board is administratively part of the state's department of corrections; in other jurisdictions, the board may be historically and functionally tied to the prison system. Because of this connection, parole boards can be influenced by conditions within the prisons and may also affect these conditions themselves.

Input from correctional authorities can influence the board in a number of ways. Board members may be unwilling to contradict or disregard the disciplinary reports of prison administrators. Administrative bonds between parole boards and the correctional system can only help to make board members aware of the expanding variety of programs available to prisoners both inside and outside the institution. Parole may be granted because board members believe that the single most effective treatment method rests in the outside community (e.g., in a halfway house). If good treatment programs can be found in the prison, however, parole may be denied so that inmates can avail themselves of these programs.

Prison conditions can also affect parole decision making in other ways. If riots or disturbances occur, the board can systematically deny parole to present a more authoritative stance to the inmates. When inmates return to their cell blocks after being denied community release, the word may quickly spread that things are not going to be easy if violent or negative behavior continues.

Of utmost importance to inmates is their early release. This factor, combined with control of early release by the parole board, has the greatest impact on inmate behavior.

The inmate grapevine quickly spreads word of each parole decision. If the board seems to stress education and group counseling, then these programs are likely to be heavily attended by inmates eager to create a favorable impression; if vocational training and economic skills are stressed, then these programs may become oversubscribed.

The outcome of board decisions and the inmates' perceptions of those decisions have a significant effect on inmates' attitudes toward the fairness of the correctional system. If minority-group members see a trend of whites being given earlier release, the repercussions may be felt throughout the prison community. All these factors must be observed by board members if equilibrium is to be maintained within the prison system.

Overcrowding and Parole. Where prisons are overcrowded, parole may be viewed as a desirable, cost-effective alternative that can ease the pressure. The parole board can be informed either formally or informally that the state prison population is over capacity and that early release is needed to manage the population and conform to court-ordered capacity standards.

In some instances, overcrowding has forced states to take the discretion out of the parole board's hands and make release mandatory. More than twenty states have passed an **Emergency Powers Act (EPA)** to reduce the inmate population.[23] In general, these acts allow the governor to declare an emergency if state institutions become crowded. The governor can order the parole board to advance either the parole dates of inmates serving indeterminate sentences or, in states with determinate sentencing, the mandatory release date of inmates. EPAs place parole boards under a lot of stress as inmates are considered for release who otherwise would be kept in the institution.

For example, in Texas, the *Ruiz* case (see Chapter 17) prompted the state to enact the Prison Management Act of 1983, which allowed the governor to order inmates released if the correctional population exceeded 95 percent of rated capacity. In 1983, the Texas parole board selected about one thousand nonviolent offenders for early release. Between 1987 and 1989, overcrowding in the Texas prison system triggered an EPA release of inmates who were awarded twenty-one months' credit on their sentence.[24] Despite a massive prison construction effort, the board has continually been under pressure to release inmates. In 1981, about 34 percent of eligible inmates were granted parole; today, 70 percent of inmates initially eligible for parole are released.[25]

Parole Guidelines

About half of all parole-granting jurisdictions use some form of **parole guidelines** to limit parole board discretion. These employ a series of behavior and experience categories, including history of drug use, prior record, type of crime, and age at conviction, to classify inmates and structure the release decision.[26]

Inmates who have positive profiles are considered better risks and are more likely to be recommended for early release.[27] For example, Colorado has established parole guidelines that set out aggravating circumstances, such as whether the offenders were on probation or parole at the time they committed the crime or if they have numerous and~or escalating juvenile and adult convictions.[28]

In some jurisdictions, grids similar to those in sentencing guideline models are used to calculate the term to be served. Points are awarded for positive factors and subtracted for negative ones. Inmates are categorized by crime severity, and their score determines the average time they should serve. For example, Georgia's parole guideline grid suggests a sentence of 60 months for armed robbers with good prognosis and 102 months for those who score poorly as parole risks.[29]

Guidelines are discretionary and do not bind parole decision making. Boards may depart from the guidelines if they believe that there are aggravating circumstances that require the inmates spend more time in prison or mitigating factors that prompt their early release.

Limiting Parole Discretion

Other mechanisms are now being used to guide parole decision making. Some jurisdictions use **presumptive parole dates** to control release eligibility.[30] Under this procedure, offenders are notified of their presumed release date, based on a realistic expectation of their expected minimum sentence, shortly after the start of their prison term. Their term may be extended for serious disciplinary infractions, such as escape attempts. Similarly, parole release can be moved up if they show evidence of a superior record in prison rehabilitation programs. Presumptive parole dates allow inmates more control over their prison stay because they control their own release date.

Another effort to limit parole board discretion is the implementation of statutory changes that reduce the parole eligibility of some offenders, such as chronic offenders. For example, in Virginia, a first-time felon is eligible for parole after serving one-quarter of the sentence imposed, or twelve years, whichever is shorter; a second-time felon is eligible for parole after serving a third of the sentence, or thirteen years; three-time felons must serve half their sentence, or fourteen years; those people who have been convicted of four or more prior offenses must serve three-fourths of their sentence, or fifteen years.[31] Nevada requires the parole board to establish and enforce parole standards that "limit the release of persons with a history of repetitive criminal conduct."[32]

Habitual offender statutes also severely restrict parole eligibility. For example, New Jersey prohibits multiple-crime sex offenders from obtaining parole for at least five years. New Jersey also gives almost half of all defendants a stipulated initial parole minimum release date that requires that they serve a certain amount of time before the parole board can consider their release.

Suing the Parole Board

The parole board may also be influenced by its concern for the behavior of inmates in the outside world. Individual board members could be sued if an inmate they release injures someone. Traditionally, courts have ruled that parole board members are immune from liability for the actions of people they release. For example, in one Virginia case, a sixteen-year-old youth was released after eight months in an institution, though he could have been incarcerated for another five years. Three months after his release, he killed a robbery victim. The

Virginia Supreme Court ruled that in their decision to discharge him, the correctional employees were (1) performing judicial functions, (2) within their jurisdiction, and (3) acting in good faith. After weighing the interests of the parolee and the state, the court concluded that the decision to release the offender was a discretionary function and that the officials were immune from a lawsuit.[33]

However, the traditional immunity of parole boards is eroding. In an important case, *Tarter v. State of New York,* the New York Supreme Court ruled that the parole board could be sued if it failed to consider certain factors and criteria mandated in the New York parole guidelines. The court ruled that the decisions of the parole board amounted to carrying out government rules and standards in a prescribed manner not allowing for personal discretion. In the case at hand, a person was rendered a paraplegic after being shot by a parolee who had been released after serving the minimum time for a crime identical to another for which he had been imprisoned four years earlier. The court ruled that the victim could challenge in court whether rules and standards had been applied properly. With no discretion involved, there was no immunity from a lawsuit. The New York case lifted the mantle of immunity from a parole board and made it liable for the outcome of its decisions.[34]

While the Supreme Court has yet to rule on the issue of parole board and parole officer liability, lower courts have rendered a number of judgments granting damages to people injured because of the negligence of parole boards. Parole boards are at risk if they fail to carry out state directives for granting parole or neglect to impose special conditions where they are required. Because the board has the power to control behavior via special conditions, it can be held liable if it fails in its duty to impose proper restrictions.[35]

Parole Rules

Before release into the community, a parolee is given a standard set of rules and conditions that must be obeyed and conformed to. As with probation (see Chapter 15), the offender who violates these rules may have parole revoked and be sent back to the institution to serve the remainder of the sentence.

Parole rules may curtail or prohibit certain types of behavior while encouraging or demanding others. Some rules tend to be so moralistic or technical in nature that they severely inhibit the parolee's ability to adjust to society. By making life unnecessarily unpleasant without contributing to rehabilitation, such parole rules reflect the punitive side of community supervision. Rules such as these can prohibit marriage, ban the use of motor vehicles, or forbid the borrowing of money. Parolees must often check in and ask permission when leaving their residences, and they may find that the rules bar them from associating with friends with criminal records, which, in some cases, severely limits their social life.

The way in which parole rules are stated, the kinds of things they forbid or encourage, and their flexibility vary between jurisdictions. Some states expressly forbid a certain type of behavior, while others will require permission to engage in it.

Each item in the parole conditions must be obeyed lest the offender's parole be revoked for a technical violation. In addition, the parole board can impose specific conditions for a particular offender, such as demanding that the parolee receive psychiatric treatment.

A number of commentators have argued that parole rules are sometimes so vague and restrictive that they interfere with the rehabilitation of the offender.[36]

Gray Cavender found that while rehabilitation is cited as the official goal of parole rules, operationally, the control of the offender seems more important.[37]

Parole rules must be modernized and standardized if they are to conform with the rehabilitative or due process framework of justice desired by the majority of criminal justice experts. As they exist today, parole rules are often vestiges of prior attempts to demean and shackle offenders, both within and outside the institution. One controversial effort to reform standard rules has been made in Virginia, where a "no read, no parole" rule is in effect. The question of whether inmates can be denied parole because they are illiterate will most likely be settled in the courts.

Parole Supervision

Once released in the community, the offender normally comes under the control of a parole agent, who enforces parole rules, helps the inmate gain employment, and meets regularly with the parolee for reasons of treatment and rehabilitation. Parole officers and their supervisors may be under the administrative control of the parole board or, more commonly, an autonomous branch of the department of corrections. In about thirty states and in the federal parole service, supervision officers have combined caseloads of probation and parole clients.

Supervision in probation and parole is quite similar in some respects. In both, supervision attempts to help clients attain meaningful relationships in the community and uses similar enforcement, counseling, and treatment skills to gain that end. However, some major differences exist.

First, parole officers deal with more difficult cases. The parolee has been institutionalized for an extended period of time; to be successful on parole, the former inmate must adjust to the community, which at first can seem a strange and often hostile environment. The parolee's family life has been disrupted, and the person may find it difficult to resume employment. The paroled offender may have already been classified by probation officers (in a presentence report) as dangerous or as a poor risk for community adjustment. Furthermore, a prison sentence probably does little to improve the offender's chances for rehabilitation. To overcome these roadblocks to success, the parole officer may have to play a much greater role in directing and supervising clients' lives than the probation officer. Moreover, the parole officer may have to be less flexible in accepting rule violations and need to hold the parolee on a tighter rein. Richard McCleary argues that the typical parole officer is more concerned with the agency he or she works for and with improving his or her own career than with the welfare of clients.[38] McCleary believes that parole officer decision making is usually based on the desire to remove from the community any offender who might be an embarrassment to the parole department. Consequently, more parolees are sent to prison for technical rule violations than for actually breaking the law.

Second, the stigma of the "ex-con" label and former-inmate status follows the parolee everywhere. The presumed dangerousness of the ex-inmate, coupled with the limitations of strict parole rules, make parole supervision more of an enforcement function than probation supervision seems to be. The parole officer is aware of the consequences if the client commits a subsequent felony offense while on parole. Such violations hurt the chances of others to gain parole and jeopardize the whole parole concept. For example, some neighborhoods have petitioned their legislative representatives to pass zoning ordinances barring halfway houses and other types of aftercare centers for parolees from their communities because they fear their clients. Parole officers sensitive to these conditions may tend to put the needs of the community ahead of the needs of the client and evolve a supervisory stance that stresses control and enforcement, rather than treatment and rehabilitation.

A final difference between the two types of supervision is that in some jurisdictions, parole officers may be called on to personally arrest and take into custody parole violators; probation departments seek court orders, which are enforced by police agencies, when probation is to be revoked.

Parole supervision often begins in the prison when institutionally based agents help the inmate create a **parole plan.** This plan can include such activities as securing a promise of employment for the inmate, arranging for a residence, and developing community contacts. Often, the parole plan will require the inmate to spend time in a residential community treatment program, such as a halfway house. The adequacy of the parole plan is an important element in the board's decision to grant community release.

Once the inmate is paroled, a supervision program may be developed in any number of ways. The parole officer can meet individually or in group sessions with clients. Meetings can be weekly, biweekly, or monthly. The parole officer may check regularly with others who are in personal contact with the parolee, such as employers, teachers, neighbors, or family. Some agents may make unannounced spot checks to determine whether their clients are keeping regular hours, working steadily, and otherwise conforming to the parole contract.

Intensive Supervision Parole

To aid supervision, some jurisdictions are implementing systems that classify offenders on the basis of their supervision needs. Typically, a point or guideline system (sometimes called a **salient factor score**) based on prior record and prison adjustment divides parolees into three groups: (1) those who require intensive surveillance; (2) those who require social service, rather than surveillance; and (3) those who require limited supervision.

In some jurisdictions, parolees in need of closer surveillance are placed on **intensive supervision probation (ISP)**. These programs use limited caseload sizes, treatment facilities, the matching of parolee and supervisor by personality, and shock parole (which involves immediate short-term incarcerations for parole violators to impress them with the seriousness of a violation).

ISP clients are supervised in smaller caseloads and are required to attend more office and home visits than routine parolees. ISP also may require frequent drug testing, a term in a community correctional center, and electronic monitoring in the home. Today, about seventeen thousand parolees are under intensive supervision, and of these, fourteen hundred are monitored electronically by computer.[39]

While ISP seems like an ideal way of limiting already overcrowded prison populations, there is little evidence that these programs are effective; in fact, they may produce a higher violation rate than traditional parole supervision. Limiting caseload size allows parole officers to supervise their clients more closely and spot infractions more easily. A recent analysis of the Texas ISP program supports this. Susan Turner and Joan Petersilia were able to randomly assign inmates into traditional and ISP caseloads. At the end of one year, 30 percent of the ISP clients were in prison, while only 18 percent of those in the routine supervision caseload had been returned to the institution; ISP was also 1.7 times more expensive than routine parole.[40] Turner and Petersilia conclude that while ISP is truly an inter-

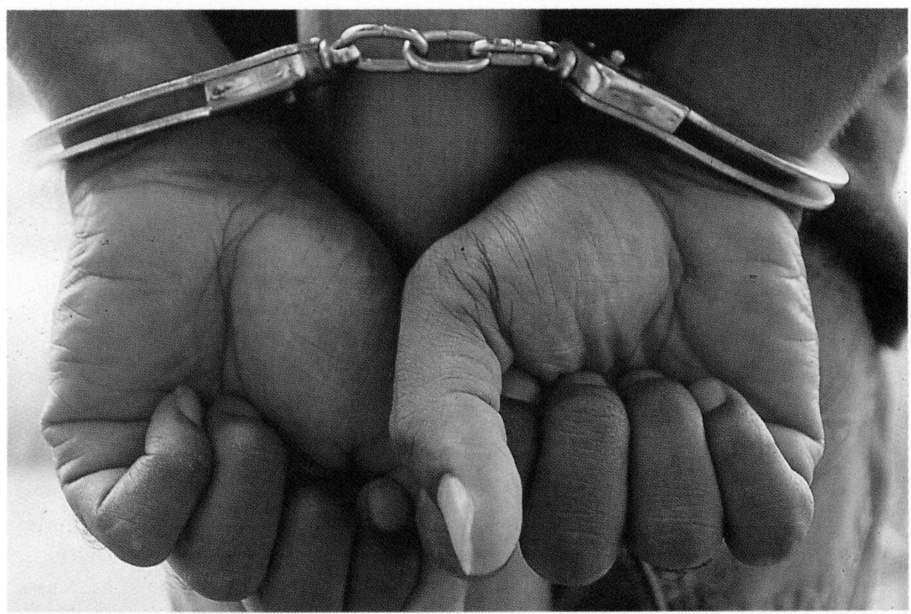

A majority of all inmates released on parole recidivate. The more prior offenses an inmate has, the greater the chance of his arrest, conviction, and return to prison.

mediate sanction (being more intrusive than routine supervision but less than prison), it may not provide dramatic improvement in correctional services.

Returning to Prison: The Effectiveness of Parole

Disagreement exists over the effectiveness of parole. It is popularly believed that recidivism rates are very high—approaching 70 percent.[41] Research efforts designed to study systematically the effectiveness of parole have produced a variety of results. For example, in one early study, the National Council on Crime and Delinquency (NCCD) collected data from every adult parole authority and found that parole is actually more effective than had been believed. Its research on a sample of over 104,000 parolees indicated that success was quite high, ranging from 90.1 percent of homicide offenders to 64.9 percent of motor vehicle theft violators.[42] Another NCCD survey of inmates released on parole found that after three years, 12.8 percent had been returned to prison as technical violators and 12.3 percent were sent back for committing a new offense, a total failure rate of about 25 percent.[43] In both NCCD surveys, the relationship between commitment offense and parole success was remarkably similar. Offenders who had committed the most serious offenses were most likely to be successful on parole. Similarly, those with poor conviction records were more likely to violate parole than first offenders.

However, not all research studies have found parole to be so successful. Howard Sacks and Charles Logan compared parolees with inmates who were discharged outright from prison and found that after two years, the recidivism rate for the parolees was 70 percent, and after three years, it was 77 percent.[44] Of those simply discharged from prison, 82 percent committed new crimes after two years and 85 percent after three years. Parolees who were recidivists did manage to remain in the community longer (an average of 12.8 months) than those who were discharged without supervision (8.3 months). Sacks and Logan conclude that parole supervision neither has long-term influence on the behavior of clients nor appears to have much worth as a rehabilitation tool.

A federal study of 108,580 men and women released in 11 states in 1983 found that 63 percent had been rearrested for a felony or serious misdemeanor, 47 percent had been convicted of a new crime, and 41 percent had been sent back to prison.[45]

The spectre of recidivism is especially frustrating to the U.S. public: it is so difficult to apprehend and successfully prosecute criminal offenders that it seems foolish to grant them early release so they can prey upon more victims. This problem is exacerbated when the parolee can be classified as a chronic offender who has engaged in frequent and repeat criminal acts (see the Analyzing Criminal Justice Issues entitled "Releasing the Chronic Offender").

Technical Violations

Many parolees return to prison because they violated the rules of parole, such as failing to stay in the jurisdiction or failing to keep a job. A federal survey found that a significant number of returning parolees actually committed no new offense but were incarcerated for technical violations of parole. In some jurisdictions, over 30 percent of the returnees had technical violations, and in one state, more than half of the returnees were technical violators.[46] These data are supported by a study conducted by the National Center on Institutions and Alternatives.[47] It surveyed ten states, including California, Florida, and Ohio, and found that 15,400 people were incarcerated for technical parole violations. Technical violators amounted to 7 percent of the prison population; in some states, technical violators made up 20 percent of the prison population.

Many parolees are in fact returned to prison for technical violations. It is therefore likely that one of the reasons for prison overcrowding is the large number of technical violators who are returned within three years of their release. If overcrowding is to be successfully addressed, a more realistic parole violation policy may have to be developed.

Legal Issues in Parole Revocation

Revocation proceedings in parole are similar to those in probation. When offenders violate a condition of probation or commit a new crime, the court may revoke probation and impose a sentence of incarceration. Similarly, when parolees violate their community status, the parole board has the authority to return them to prison.

The **parole revocation** process is almost always started by the parole officer who believes that the parolee has violated a parole condition or when the parolee has been charged with a new crime. In the past, the statutory requirements and practices of parole agencies that applied once the parole officer initiated this process varied greatly. Some states provided informal hearings to determine if there was reason to believe that the parolee had violated a condition, while others held more formal revocation hearings. Few states had any minimum due process requirements. Parolees were often taken into custody and even returned to prison before any hearing was held on the violation of parole. This practice was not only unfair but resulted in undue hardship for parolees and their families.

In 1972, the U.S. Supreme Court caused an uproar among parole agencies throughout the nation by handing down the landmark parole decision of ***Morrissey v. Brewer.*** This case held that the Fourteenth Amendment requirement of due process of law actually applied to the parole revocation process. The Court's decision established specific due process guidelines that parole boards must follow before revoking an offender's parole.

Since the *Morrissey* decision, appellate courts have upheld the Supreme Court's basic requirement for fairness and impartiality in the revocation hearing process. For example, in *Drayton v. McCall* (1978),[48] the Second Circuit Court of Appeals found that the due process clause mandates that certain procedural safeguards must be afforded to parolees before their community release may be rescinded. In reaffirming the *Morrissey* decision, the appellate court confirmed a parolee's right to a hearing before a detached and neutral hearing board, advance written notice of changes, and the right to call witnesses on behalf of the parolee. The court expressed distress over the U.S. Parole Board's refusal of parolee Drayton's request for a lawyer to represent him at the hearing.[49] The rights outlined in *Morrissey* have served as guidelines in subsequent parole-decision cases.[50]

Making It on the Outside

Why do so many released inmates end up back behind prison walls? For one thing, the social, psychological, and economic reasons that led them to crime probably have not been eliminated by a stay in prison. Despite rehabilitation efforts, the typical ex-convict is still the same undereducated, unemployed, substance-abusing lower-class male he was when arrested. Being separated from friends and family, not sharing in conventional society, associating with dangerous people, and adapting to a volatile life-style probably has done little to improve the offenders' personality or behavior. And when they return to society, it may be to the same destructive neighborhood and social groups that prompted their original law-violating behavior. Some ex-inmates may have to prove that the prison experience has not changed them: taking drugs or being sexually aggressive may show friends that they have not lost their "heart."

Ex-inmates may find their home life torn and disrupted. Laura Fishman has described the problems faced by prisoners' wives, who she describes as "doing time on the outside." These women must face the shame and stigmatization of having an incarcerated spouse while at the same time withstanding a barrage of calls from the "inside" made by jealous husbands who monitor their behavior and try to control their lives. Even family visitations become traumatic and strain interpersonal relationships because they often involve strip searches and other invasions of privacy.[51] Sensitive to these problems, some states have instituted support groups designed to help inmate families adjust to their loneliness and despair. Welcome House, operated on the grounds of California's Folsom prison, not only sponsors family visitation programs within the walls but also helps inmate wives' adjust with once-a-month potluck dinners that give the women a chance to visit and support each other on the outside.[52]

Ex-inmates may also find that going straight is an economic impossibility. Many employers are reluctant to hire people who have served time. Even if a criminal record does not automatically prohibit all chance of employment, why would an employer hire an "ex-con" when other applicants are available? If they lie about their prison experience and are later found out, ex-offenders will be dismissed for misrepresentation. "The wonder," claims Harry Allen and Clifford Simonsen, "is not that so many ex-offenders recidivate but that more do not."[53]

Losing Rights

One reason that ex-inmates find it so difficult to make it on the outside is the legal restrictions they are forced to endure. These may include bars on certain

ANALYZING CRIMINAL JUSTICE ISSUES

Releasing the Chronic Offenders

A federally sponsored study of parole recidivism by Allen Beck and Bernard Shipley sheds some light on chronic offenders and the contribution they make to the overall crime problem. The researchers followed the offending careers of 108,850 inmates released in 11 states during 1983. While their results are similar to other recidivism studies (62 percent of the parolees were rearrested within three years and 41 percent returned to prison), they also developed data that help us understand the particular problems faced by chronic offenders as they attempt to readjust to society.

Table A shows the total number of arrest charges among the 108,850 inmates released in 1983. About 26 percent of the inmates had been arrested twenty or more times, and they accounted for almost 60 percent of all arrests of the parolees. About 5 percent of the released inmates had been arrested 45 or more times in their lives. As Table B shows, the total sample of inmates had been arrested *1,333,293* times before their current incarceration and *326,746* times after their release; the 1.7 million charges came to an average of *15.3* per offender since the first adult arrest.

It might seem startling to some people that inmates who have been arrested more than fifteen times are still eligible for early release. How did they do once they were on the outside? Eighty-two percent of the inmates who had sixteen or more prior arrests were rearrested within three years of their release. A survey found that within the first six months, released prisoners with eleven or more prior arrests were nearly four times more likely than those with one prior arrest and more than twice as likely as those with two or three prior arrests to have been arrested for a new offense.

Other findings strongly support the conclusion that chronic offenders are not deterred by the threat or experience of punishment: Those who began their offending career at a younger age (under seventeen) were significantly more likely to be rearrested (72 percent) than those who were first arrested after they reached their thirtieth birthday (27 percent). In addition, those offenders who had started their career early and had eleven or more prior offenses had a 83 per-

TABLE A
Total Number of Arrest Charges Among State Prisoners Released in 1983

Total Number of Arrest Charges	Percentage of All Released Prisoners	Cumulative Percentage of All Released Prisoners	Cumulative Percentage of All Arrest Charges
45 or more	5.0%	5.0%	19.4%
35–44	4.4	9.4	30.5
25–34	9.2	18.6	47.8
20–24	7.7	26.3	58.8
15–19	11.7	38.0	71.6
10–14	17.1	55.1	84.9
5–9	26.2	81.3	96.7
1–4	18.9	100.0	100.0

SOURCE: Allen Beck and Bernard Shipley, *Recidivism of Prisoners Released in 1983* (Washington, D.C.: Bureau of Justice Statistics, 1989).

kinds of employment, limits on obtaining licenses, and restrictions on their freedom of movement.

The practice of penalizing people even after they have served their sentence is grounded in the common law. In England during the Middle Ages, under the common law of attainder, convicted felons forfeited their land, possessions, and civil rights and suffered "corruption of blood," preventing them from willing their land to heirs.[54] Although Article 1, Section 9, of the U.S. Constitution expressly forbids "bills of attainder," convicted felons still find that many of their activities are restricted once they are released from prison.

The degree to which these rights are lost varies from state to state and depends mainly on the judicial decisions of a particular jurisdiction. A list of rights that are now or were once lost to the convicted offender follows.[55]

TABLE B
Rearrest Rates of State Prisoners Released in 1983, by Number of Prior Adult Arrests

		Percent of Releasees Who Were Arrested	
Number of Adult Arrests Prior to Release	Percent of All Releases	Within 3 years	Within 1 year
All released prisoners	100.0%	62.5%	39.3%
1 prior arrest	9.1	38.1	19.0
2	10.8	48.2	25.5
3	10.8	54.7	30.1
4	9.7	58.1	35.5
5	8.0	59.3	33.4
6	7.0	64.8	38.2
7–10	18.8	67.7	42.0
11–15	11.9	74.9	53.3
16 or more	14.0	82.2	61.5

SOURCE: Allen Beck and Bernard Shipley, *Recidivism of Prisoners Released in 1983* (Washington, D.C.: Bureau of Justice Statistics, 1989).

cent chance of being rearrested, higher than any other age and offending group (in contrast, forty year olds with one prior offense had a 12 percent rearrest rate).

Beck and Shipley provide the following picture of the offender most likely to be rearrested after a prison experience: released at age twenty-four or younger; more than seven prior arrests; prior escape or revocation experience; committed robbery, burglary, or property offenses; was first arrested at a relatively young age; and had a prior drug and violent crime arrest.

Critical Thinking Skills

Should parole eligibility be cut off after a certain number of prior arrests and convictions? Is it futile to release offenders who consistently violate the law? Should people be punished for their past behavior, rather than their current offense? Determinate sentencing statutes do increase the time served by chronic offenders, but do they go far enough? Should early release and good-time credit be eliminated for habitual offenders?

SOURCE: Alen Beck and Bernard Shipley, *Recidivism of Prisoners Released in 1983* (Washington, D.C.: Bureau of Justice Statistics, 1989).

1. *The right to vote.* This right was denied on the grounds of compelling state interest. It was believed that the purity of the voting process must be protected against immoral and dishonest elements of society. This thinking, however, has changed, and today, the restrictions on voting rights have been eliminated.
2. *The right to hold public office.* Denial of this right is based on the philosophy that the public must be protected.
3. *The right to public employment.* This restriction is gradually being lifted. It is generally believed now that the offense must be directly related to a job in order for employment to be denied.
4. *The right to an occupational license.* More than fifteen hundred different licenses contain the requirement of "good moral character," which, according to many licensing boards, automatically bars ex-convicts from those fields.

5. *The right to serve on a jury*. Most states maintain that the "good character" qualification excludes a convicted offender from jury duty.
6. *The right to be a witness*. In most cases, convicted individuals can serve as a witness; however, their criminal record can be used to discredit the testimony.
7. *The right to life and automobile insurance*. Obtaining insurance is often difficult, if not impossible, when one has a criminal record.
8. *The right to adopt children*. In most jurisdictions, a record disqualifies an individual from adopting children.

A recent survey by Velmer Burton, Frank Cullen, and Lawrence Travis found that a significant number of states still restrict the activities of former felons.[56] Among their findings:

1. Nineteen states prevent convicted felons from holding public office.
2. Almost every state prevents ex-convicts from owning guns.
3. Twenty-eight states allow spouses to obtain a divorce on the basis of conviction and/or imprisonment for a felony.
4. Sixteen states allow courts to terminate parental rights because of a felony conviction and/or imprisonment.
5. About thirty states bar ex-offenders from public employment.

Courts have considered individual requests by convicted felons to have their rights restored. It is common for courts to look at such issues as how recently the criminal offense took place and its relationship to the particular right before deciding whether to restore it. For example, in *Carr v. Thompson*, a federal court ruled that a person could not be barred from a civil service job because of convictions on minor criminal charges occurring more than ten years earlier.[57] However, in *Pordum v. New York Board of Regents*, a federal appellate court upheld the right of school officials to refuse to rehire a teacher who had been convicted and had served time for bribery of public officials.[58]

A number of experts and national commissions have condemned the loss of rights of convicted offenders as a significant cause of recidivism. Consequently, courts have generally moved to eliminate the most restrictive elements of post-conviction restrictions. Most important, when the remaining **"civil death"** statutes have been challenged, state and federal courts have ruled they are denial of due process and equal protection rights. Such states as Idaho, New York, and Montana have eliminated "civil death" statutes.[59]

In sum, it is both emotionally and legally difficult for the ex-inmate to make it on the outside. The problems of recidivism and self-destruction have prompted inmates to form self-help groups to aid their adjustment.

SUMMARY

Most inmates return to society before the completion of their prison sentence. The majority earn early release through time off for good behavior or other sentence-reducing mechanisms.

In addition, about 40 percent of all inmates are paroled before the completion of their maximum term. Parole is the release of an offender into the community prior to the expiration of a prison sentence. Most state jurisdictions maintain an independent parole board whose members make the actual decisions to grant parole. Their decision making is extremely discretionary and is based on many factors, such as the perception of the needs of society, the correctional system, and the client.

Once paroled, the client is subject to control by parole officers who ensure that the conditions set by the board (the parole rules) are maintained. These officers employ individual styles in their operations. For example, one may stress community protection and view parole as a law enforcement function, while another may believe in the social welfare aspects of parole and view the role as that of a treatment agent.

Parole can be revoked if the offender violates the rules of parole or commits a new crime. In the past, revocation was purely an administrative function; however, recent Supreme Court decisions have granted procedural due process rights to offenders at parole revocation hearings, the most notable of which is the right to representation by an attorney.

Inmates have a tough time adjusting on the outside, and the recidivism rate is disturbingly high. Inmates have formed self-groups to aid in their adjustment.

QUESTIONS

1. Define parole, including its purposes and objectives. How does it differ from probation?
2. What is the role of the parole board?
3. Identify the procedures involved in parole revocation. What are the rights of the parolee?
4. Should a former prisoner have all the civil rights afforded the average citizen? Should people be further penalized after they have paid their debt to society?

NOTES

1. Louis Jankowski, *Probation and Parole, 1990* (Washington, D.C.: Bureau of Justice Statistics, 1991), p. 5.
2. Stephanie Minor-Harper and Christopher Innes, *Time Served in Prison and on Parole, 1984* (Washington, D.C.: Bureau of Justice Statistics, 1987), p. 2.
3. *Prison Escape Survey* (Lincoln, Neb.: Corrections Compendium, 1991).
4. David Duffee, *Corrections: Practice and Policy* (New York: Random House, 1989), p. 111.
5. These sections depend heavily on William Parker, *Parole: Origins, Development, Current Practices, and Statutes* (College Park, Md.: American Correctional Association, 1972); Gray Cavender, *Parole: A Critical Analysis* (Port Washington, N.Y.: Kennikat Press, 1982); Samuel Walker, *Popular Justice* (New York: Oxford University Press, 1980).
6. James Austin and Aaron McVey, *The NCCD Prison Population Forecast: The Growing Imprisonment of America* (San Francisco: National Council on Crime and Delinquency, 1988).
7. New York State Coalition for Criminal Justice, Albany, New York, 1982, p. 51.
8. Corrections Compendium, "Good Time Credits for Prison Inmates," reprinted in *Sourcebook of Criminal Justice Statistics, 1990*, Kathleen Maguire and Timothy Flanagan (Washington, D.C.: U.S. Government Printing Office, 1991), p. 111.
9. "Illinois 'Good Time' Law Eased Prison Crowding, Study Finds," *Criminal Justice Newsletter* 22 (3 June 1991): 5.
10. 410 U.S. 263, 93 S.Ct. 1055, 35 L.Ed.2d 282 (1973).
11. 418 U.S. 539, 94 S.Ct. 2963, 41 L.Ed.2d 935 (1974).
12. These sections make extensive use of Edward Rhine, William Smith, Ronald Jackson, Peggy Burke, and Roger Labelle, *Paroling Authorities, Recent History and Current Practice* (Laurel, Md.: American Correctional Association, 1991). Herein cited as *Paroling Authorities*.
13. Jankowski, *Probation and Parole, 1990*, p. 1.
14. Parker, *Parole*, p. 26.
15. American Correctional Association, *Directory of Juvenile and Adult Correctional Departments, Institutions, Agencies, and Paroling Authorities* (College Park, Md.: American Correctional Association, 1991).
16. Vincent O'Leary and Joan Nuffield, *The Organization of Parole Systems in the United States* (Hackensack, N.J.: National Council of Crime and Delinquency, 1972), p. xxix.
17. 442 U.S. 1, 99 S.Ct. 2100, 60 L.Ed.2d 668 (1979).
18. 452 U.S. 458, 101 S.Ct. 2460, 69 L.Ed.2d 158 (1981).
19. 442 U.S. at 12, 99 S.Ct. at 2106.
20. 452 U.S. at 464, 101 S.Ct. at 2464.
21. National Parole Institutes, "Selection for Parole," *Parole Resource Book—Part II* (April 1966), p. 168.
22. Franklin Zimring, "Making the Punishment Fit the Crime," in *Order Under Law*, ed. R. Culbertson and M. Tezak (Prospect Heights, Ill.: Waveland Press, 1981), pp. 180–90.
23. Edward Rhine, William Smith, Ronald Jackson, and Lloyd Rupp, "Parole: Issues and Prospects for the 1990's," *Corrections Today* 51 (1989): 78–83.
24. *Paroling Authorities*, p. 28.
25. Ibid., p. 95.
26. Todd Clear and George Cole, *American Corrections* (Monterey, Calif.: Brooks Cole (1986).
27. Peter Hoffman and Barbara Stone-Meierhoefer, "Post-Release Arrest Experiences of Federal Prisoners: A Six Year Follow-up," *Journal of Criminal Justice* 7 (1979): 193–216.
28. Colorado Criminal Code, 17–22.5–303.5.
29. *Paroling Authorities*, pp. 70–71.
30. Barbara Stone-Meierhoefer and Peter Hoffman, "Presumptive Parole Dates: The Federal Approach," *Federal Probation* 46 (1982): 41–56.
31. Paul Woodard, *Statutes Requiring the Use of Criminal History Record Information* (Washington, D.C.: Bureau of Justice Statistics, 1991), p. 55.
32. Ibid.
33. *Harlow v. Clatterbuck*, 230 Va. 490, 339 S.E.2d 181 (1986).
34. *Tarter v. State of New York*, 68 N.Y.2d 511, 510 N.Y.S.2d 528, 503 N.E.2d 84 (1986).
35. Richard Sluder and Rolando Del Carmen, "Are Probation and Parole Officers Liable for Injuries Caused by Probationers and Parolees?" *Federal Probation* 54 (1990): 3–12.

36. President's Commission on Law Enforcement and the Administration of Justice, *Task Force Report: Corrections* (Washington, D.C.: U.S. Government Printing Office, 1967), p. 86.

37. Cavender, *Parole: A Critical Analysis*, p. 55.

38. Richard McCleary, *Dangerous Men: The Sociology of Parole* (Beverly Hills, Calif.: Sage Publications, 1976).

39. Jankowski, *Probation and Parole, 1990*, p. 4.

40. Susan Turner and Joan Petersilia, "Focusing on High-Risk Parolees: An Experiment to Reduce Commitments to the Texas Department of Corrections," *Journal of Research in Crime and Delinquency* 29 (1992): 34–61.

41. "American Justice," *Newsweek*, 1 November 1982, p. 47.

42. Donald Gottfredson, M. G. Neithercutt, Joan Juffield, and Vincent O'Leary, *Four Thousand Lifetimes: A Study of Time Served and Parole Outcome* (Hackensack, N.J.: National Council on Crime and Delinquency, 1973).

43. National Council on Crime and Delinquency, *Characteristics of the Parole Population* (Hackensack, N.J.: National Council on Crime and Delinquency, 1982).

44. Howard Sacks and Charles Logan, *Parole: Crime Prevention or Crime Postponement?* (Storrs, Conn.: University of Connecticut School of Law Press, 1980).

45. Allen Beck and Bernard Shipley, *Recidivism of Prisoners Released in 1983* (Washington, D.C.: Bureau of Justice Statistics, 1989).

46. John Wallerstedt, *Returning to Prison* (Washington, D.C.: Bureau of Justice Statistics, 1984).

47. "Study Finds Many in Prison for Technical Parole Violation," *Criminal Justice Newsletter* 16 (16 January 1986):5.

48. 584 F.2d 1208 (2d Cir. 1978).

49. See also *Baldwin v. Benson*, 584 F.2d 953 (10th Cir. 1978).

50. *Harris v. Day*, 649 F.2d 755 (10th Cir. 1981).

51. Laura Fishman, *Women at the Wall: A Study of Prisoners' Wives Doing Time on the Outside* (New York: State University of New York Press, 1990).

52. Leslee Goodman Hornick, "Volunteer Program Helps Make Inmates' Families Feel Welcome," *Corrections Today* 53 (1991): 184–86.

53. Harry Allen and Clifford Simonsen, *Corrections in America*, 5th ed. (New York: Macmillan, 1989), p. 333.

54. See Sol Rubin, *United States Prison Law* (Dobbs Ferry, N.Y.: Oceana Publications, 1977), p. 1.

55. George Killinger, *Probation and Parole in the Criminal Justice System* (St. Paul: West Publishing, 1976), pp. 126–44.

56. Velmer Burton, Francis Cullen, and Lawrence Travis, "The Collateral Consequences of a Felony Conviction: A National Study of State Statutes," *Federal Probation* 51 (1987): 52–60.

57. *Carr v. Thompson*, 384 F.Supp. 544 (W.D.N.Y. 1974).

58. *Pordum v. N.Y. Board of Regents*, 491 F.2d 1281 (2d Cir. 1974).

59. See, for example, *Bush v. Reid*, 516 P.2d 1215 (Alaska 1973); *Thompson v. Bond*, 421 F.Supp. 878 (W.D. Mo. 1976); *Delorne v. Pierce Freightlines Co.*, 353 F.Supp. 258 (D.Or. 1973); *Beyer v. Werner*, 299 F.Supp. 967 (E.D. N.Y. 1969).

PART FIVE

THE NATURE AND HISTORY OF THE JUVENILE JUSTICE PROCESS

CHAPTER 19

Juvenile Justice

OUTLINE

KEY TERMS

juvenile justice system
parens patriae
poor laws
apprenticeship
chancery courts
child-saving movement
child savers
House of Refuge
Children's Aid Society
Illinois Juvenile Court Act
status offenders
transfer
waiver
Fare v. Michael C.
California v. Prysock
intake
detention
Schall v. Martin
Hendrickson v. Griggs
Kent v. United States
Breed v. Jones
In re Gault
In re Winship
balanced probation
Inmates v. Affleck
Morales v. Turman
Nelson v. Heyne
Ralston v. Robinson

Independent of yet interrelated with the adult criminal justice system, the **juvenile justice system** is primarily responsible for dealing with juvenile and youth crime, as well as with incorrigible and truant children and runaways. When the juvenile court was originally conceived at the turn of the century, its philosophy was based on the idea of ***parens patriae*:** the state was to act on behalf of the parent in the interests of the child. In the 1960s, however, the theme changed when the U.S. Supreme Court began ensuring that juveniles would be granted legal rights. Today, the emphasis of the juvenile justice system has shifted to controlling chronically delinquent youths.

The nation's juvenile justice system is in the midst of reexamining its fundamental operations and institutions. Although almost an entire century has passed since the first independent juvenile court was established, a comprehensive and comprehensible statement of its goals and purposes has yet to be developed. On the one hand, some authorities still hold to the original social welfare principles of the juvenile justice system. They argue that the juvenile court is primarily a treatment agency that acts as a wise parent, dispensing personalized, individual justice to needy children who seek guidance and understanding. On the other hand, those with a law enforcement orientation suggest that the juvenile court's *parens patriae* philosophy has neglected the victims of delinquency and that serious offenders should be punished and disciplined, rather than treated and rehabilitated. A third approach to juvenile justice takes the position that court processing has a potentially adverse effect on children, who are denied some of the constitutional rights afforded adult offenders. Advocates of this position believe that juvenile courts should dispense impartial justice and increase the due process rights of children who, depending on the outcome of their trial, may be subjected to extended periods of confinement.

Ideologically, supporters of each of these positions appear unwilling to yield to the others. The concept of *parens patriae* is deeply rooted in the U.S. system of juvenile justice and involves discretion, intervention, and treatment. Some experts believe that the principles underlying this concept have not been abandoned, despite the new legal procedures.[1] Those arguing for an increase in the due process rights of juveniles maintain that the substantive intent of the law implies a mandate based on duty and morality and that the full protection of the U.S. Constitution should be applied to any person who comes before the nation's tribunals at any time. To do otherwise, they contend, would abrogate the principle of equality under the law. Conflict over the proper role of the juvenile courts and the suspected negative impact of the stigma and delinquency labeling that follow a juvenile court appearance have also led some critics to advocate the total abolition of the juvenile court in favor of diversionary modes of justice.

These differing perspectives on juvenile court policy were reflected in the U.S. Supreme Court's reluctance to enter forcefully into the juvenile justice sphere until well into the 1960s. Since then, the Warren, Burger, and Rehnquist Courts have taken a due process approach to juvenile law. This chapter reviews the history of juvenile justice and discusses the justice system's processing of youthful offenders.

History of Juvenile Justice

Originally, adults and juveniles who violated the law were subject to the same punishments—whipping, mutilation, banishment, and death.[2] Although a judge would sometimes treat a youth with leniency, there was no basis in law for clemency.

Foundations of the Juvenile Court

The modern practice of legally separating adult and juvenile offenders can be traced to two developments in English customs and law: the chancery court and the development of the poor laws. Both were designed to allow the state to take control of the lives of needy, but not necessarily criminal, children.

Poor Laws. As early as 1535, the English passed statutes known as **poor laws.** These laws provided for the appointment of overseers to indenture destitute or neglected children as servants. Such children were forced to work during their minority for families who trained them in agricultural, trade, or domestic services. The Elizabethan poor laws of 1601 became a model for dealing with poor children for more than two hundred years. These laws created a system of church wardens and overseers who, with the consent of the justices of the peace, identified vagrant, delinquent, and neglected children and took measures to put them to work. Often this meant placing them in poorhouses or workhouses or, more commonly, apprenticing them to masters. **Apprenticeship** in England actually existed through almost the entire history of the country. Under this practice, children were placed in the care of adults who taught them a trade. Parents or guardians who wished to secure training for their children put them into voluntary apprenticeships. Involuntary apprentices were compelled to serve by the authorities until they were twenty-one or older. The master-apprentice relationship was similar to the parent-child relationship in that the master had complete responsibility for and authority over the apprentice. If an apprentice was unruly, the master could complain to the authorities, and the apprentice could be punished. Even at this early stage, the conviction was growing that the criminal law and its enforcement should be applied differently to children.

Chancery Courts. Chancery courts existed throughout the Middle Ages. They were concerned primarily with protecting property rights, although their authority extended to the welfare of children in general. The major issues that came before the medieval chancery courts involved guardianship, the uses and

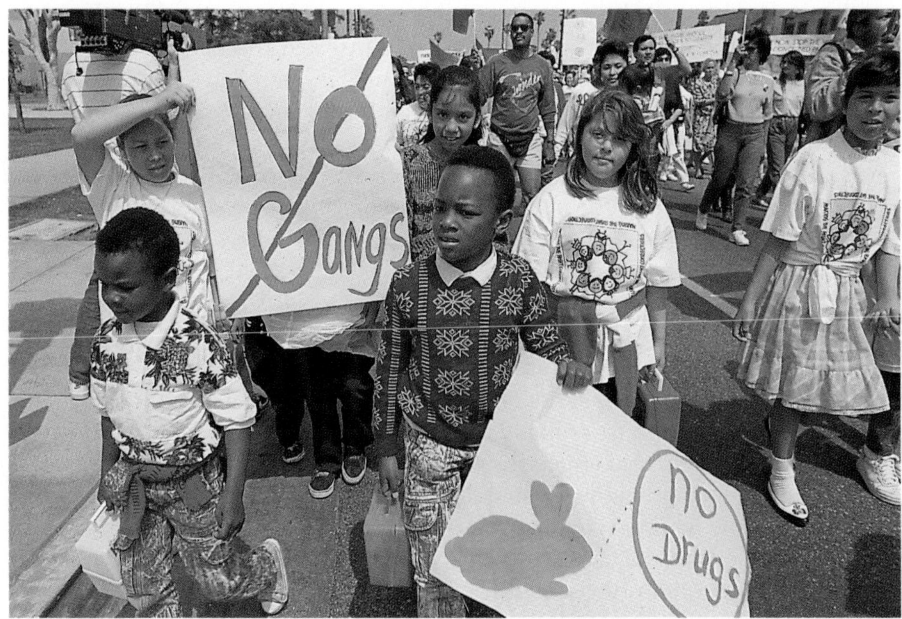

The juvenile justice system has struggled to control juvenile delinquency. At a Los Angeles neighborhood rally, kids protest against drug use and delinquency which continues to plague their neighborhood.

control of property, and the relationship of the people to the monarchy. These courts were founded on the proposition that children and other incompetents were under the protective control of the king. Thus, the Latin phrase *parens patriae* referred to the role of the king as the father of his country. As Douglas Besharov states, "The concept apparently was first used by English kings to justify their intervention in the lives of the children of their vassals—children whose position and property were of direct concern to the monarch."[3] In the famous English case *Wellesley v. Wellesley*, a duke's children were taken from him in the name of *parens patriae* because of his scandalous behavior.[4] Thus, the concept of *parens patriae* became the theoretical basis for the chancery courts acting on behalf of the crown.

As time passed, the crown increasingly used *parens patriae* to justify its intervention into the lives of families and children on the grounds of its interest in their general welfare. However, as Douglas Rendleman points out, "The idea of *parens patriae* was actually used to maintain the power of the crown and the structure of control over families known as feudalism."[5] The chancery courts dealt with the property and custody problems of the wealthier classes. They never had jurisdiction over children charged with criminal conduct. Juveniles who violated the law were handled within the regular criminal court system. Nevertheless, the concept of *parens patriae* came to refer primarily to the responsibility of the courts and the state to act in the best interests of the child. The idea that the state—and particularly the juvenile court—should act to protect the young, the incompetent, the neglected, and the delinquent subsequently became a major influence on the development of the U.S. juvenile justice system in the twentieth century.

Care of Children in Early America

The forced apprenticeship system and the poor laws were brought from England to colonial America. Poor laws were passed in Virginia in 1646 and in Connecticut and Massachusetts in 1678. Forced apprenticeship of poor and destitute youths continued until the early nineteenth century. However, youths who committed serious criminal offenses continued to be treated the same as adults.

By the beginning of the nineteenth century, the factory system was eliminating the apprenticeship system. Yet the problems of how to deal effectively with growing numbers of dependent youths continued to increase. Early American settlers were firm believers in hard work, strict discipline, and education. These principles were viewed as the only reliable way to salvation and became the basis for the treatment of youths.

To accommodate dependent and destitute youths, local jurisdictions developed almshouses, poorhouses, and workhouses. Crowded and unhealthy, these accepted the poor, the insane, the diseased, and vagrant and destitute children.

In addition, increased urbanization and industrialization led to the belief that certain segments of the population, namely youths in urban areas and immigrants, were particularly prone to criminal deviance and immorality. The children of these classes were regarded as persons who might be "saved" by state intervention. Such intervention, primarily by middle-class organizations and groups, became the basis of the **child-saving movement.** Wealthy, civic-minded citizens attempted to alleviate the burdens of the unfortunate urban classes and the immigrants through sponsoring shelter care for youths, educational and social activities, and the development of settlement houses. Their main focus, however, was on extending government control over a whole range of youthful activities that had previously been left to private or family control, including idleness, drinking, vagrancy, and delinquency.

Prominent among those interested in the problems of unfortunate children were penologist Enoch Wines, Judge Richard Tuthill, Lucy Flowers of the Chicago Women's Association, Sara Cooper of the National Conference of Charities and Corrections, and Sophia Minton of the New York Committee on Children.[6] These and other individuals became known as **child savers.** They believed that poor children presented a threat to the moral fabric of U.S. society and should be controlled because their behavior could lead to the destruction of the nation's economic system. Thus, as a result of industrialization and immigration, shortcomings in the criminal justice system, and the child-saving movement, special institutions for children emerged and eventually, the states began to expand their jurisdiction over children.

The Child-Saving Movement

While various legislatures enacted laws giving courts the power to commit children who were runaways, committed criminal acts, or were out of the control of their parents, specialized institutional programs were also created. One of the most concrete examples was the **House of Refuge** in New York in 1825.[7] Its aim was to protect youths by taking potential criminals off the streets and reforming them in a familylike environment.

When the House of Refuge opened, the majority of children were admitted because of vagrancy or neglect. The institution was run more like a prison, however, with work and study schedules, strict discipline, and absolute separation of the sexes. So many children ran away because of this harsh program that the House of Refuge was forced to adopt a more lenient approach. Children were placed in the house by court order, sometimes over parental objections, for vagrancy or delinquency. Their stay depended on their needs, age, and work skills. While there, they were required to do piecework provided by local manufacturers or to work part of the day in the community.

Despite criticisms, the concept enjoyed widespread popularity. In 1826, the Boston City Council founded the House of Reformation for juvenile offenders. Similar reform schools were opened in Massachusetts and New York in 1847.[8] To these schools, which were both privately and publicly funded, the courts committed children found guilty of criminal violations, as well as those beyond the control of their parents. Because the child-saving movement viewed convicted offenders and parents of delinquent children in the same light, they sought to have the reform schools establish control over the children. Robert Mennel argues that by training destitute and delinquent children and by separating them from their natural parents and adult criminals, refuge managers believed they were preventing poverty and crime.[9]

The child savers influenced state and local governments to create institutions, called reform schools, exclusively devoted to the care of vagrant and criminal youths. State institutions opened in Westboro, Massachusetts, in 1848 and in Rochester, New York, in 1849.[10] Other states soon followed suit—Ohio in 1850 and Maine, Rhode Island, and Michigan in 1860.[11] Children lived in congregate conditions and spent their days working at institutional jobs, learning a trade where possible, and receiving some basic education. They were racially and sexually segregated, discipline was harsh and often involved whipping and isolation, and the physical care was of poor quality.

Some viewed houses of refuge and reform schools as humanitarian answers to poorhouses and prisons for vagrant, neglected, and delinquent youths, but many opposed such programs. For example, as an alternative, New York philanthropist Charles Brace helped develop the **Children's Aid Society** in 1853. Brace's formula for dealing with neglected and delinquent youths was to rescue them from the harsh environment of the city and provide them with temporary shelter and care. He then sought to place them in private homes throughout the nation. This program was very similar to today's foster home programs.

Establishment of the Illinois Juvenile Court: 1899

Although the child reformers provided services for children, they could not stop juvenile delinquency. Most reform schools were unable to hold youthful law violators and reform them. Institutional life was hard. The large numbers of children needing placement burdened the public coffers. Thus, as state control over vagrant, delinquent, and neglected children became more widespread after the Civil War, it also grew more controversial. As the nation expanded, it became evident that private charities and public organizations were not caring adequately for the growing number of troubled youths.

The influence of the child savers prompted the development of the first comprehensive juvenile court in Illinois in 1899. The **Illinois Juvenile Court Act** set up an independent court to handle criminal law violations by children under sixteen years of age, as well as to care for neglected, dependent, and wayward youths. The act also created a probation department to monitor youths in the community and to direct juvenile court judges to place serious offenders in secure schools for boys and industrial schools for girls. The ostensible purpose of the act was to separate juveniles from adult offenders and provide a legal framework in which juveniles could get adequate care and custody. By 1925, most states had developed juvenile courts.

Although the efforts of the child savers were originally viewed as liberal reforms, modern scholars commonly view them as attempts to control and punish. Justice historians such as Anthony Platt have suggested that the reform move-

The juvenile court is a specialized court for children. Urban problems and adolescent conflict has heightened the need for special services for at-risk youth.

ment actually expressed the vested interests of a particular group. According to Platt:

> The child savers should not be considered humanists: (1) Their reforms did not herald a new system of justice but rather expedited traditional policies which had been informally developed during the nineteenth century; (2) they implicitly assumed the natural dependence of adolescents and created a special court to impose sanctions on premature independents and behavior unbecoming to youth; (3) their attitudes toward delinquent youth were largely paternalistic and romantic but their commands were backed up by force; (4) they promoted correctional programs requiring longer terms of imprisonment, longer hours of labor, and militaristic discipline, and the inculcation of middle class values and lower class skills.[12]

Thus, according to this revisionist approach, the reformers applied the concept of *parens patriae* for their own purposes, including the continuance of middle- and upper-class values, the control of the political system, and the furtherance of a child labor system consisting of lower-class workers with marginal skills.

Juvenile Justice Then and Now

The juvenile court movement quickly spread across the United States. In its early form, it provided youths with quasi-legal, quasi-therapeutic, personalized justice. The main concern was the "best interests of the child," not strict adherence to legal doctrine, constitutional rights, or due process of law. The court was paternalistic, rather than adversarial.

For example, attorneys were not required. Hearsay evidence, inadmissible in criminal trials, was admissible in the adjudication of juvenile offenders. Verdicts were based on a "preponderance of the evidence," instead of being "beyond a reasonable doubt," and children were often denied the right to appeal their convictions. These characteristics allowed the juvenile court to function in a nonlegal manner and to provide various social services to children in need.

The major functions of the juvenile justice system were to prevent juvenile crime and to rehabilitate juvenile offenders. The roles of the two most important parts of the system, the juvenile court judge and the probation staff, were to diagnose the child's condition and to prescribe programs to alleviate it. Until 1967, judgments about children's actions and consideration for their constitutional rights were secondary.

Juvenile corrections also underwent considerable change. Early reform schools were generally punitive and based on the concept of rehabilitation or reform through hard work and discipline. In the second half of the nineteenth century, the emphasis shifted from massive industrial schools to the cottage system. Juvenile offenders were housed in a series of small cottages in a compound, each one holding twenty to forty children. Each cottage was run by "cottage parents," who attempted to create a homelike atmosphere. It was felt that this would be more conducive to rehabilitation than the rigid bureaucratic organization of massive institutions. The first cottage system was established in Massachusetts, the second in Ohio. The system was generally applauded for being a great improvement over the industrial training schools. The general movement was away from punitiveness and toward rehabilitation: "By attending to the needs of the individual and by implementing complex programs of diagnosis and treatment, known offenders could not only be rehabilitated, but crime among dependent and unruly children could be prevented."[13]

By the 1950s, the influence of such therapists as Karen Horney and Carl Rogers promoted the introduction of psychological treatment in juvenile corrections. Group counseling techniques, such as guided interaction, became standard procedure in most juvenile institutions.

In the 1960s and 1970s, the U.S. Supreme Court radically altered the juvenile justice system when it issued a series of decisions that established the right of juveniles to receive due process of law: *Kent v. United States* (1966), *In re Gault* (1967), *In re Winship* (1970), and *Breed v. Jones* (1975).[14] These cases will be discussed later in this chapter.

The 1970s also saw an alarming rise in juvenile crime and revealed obvious inequities in the juvenile justice system. In addition to the legal revolution brought about by the Supreme Court, Congress passed the Juvenile Justice and Delinquency Prevention Act of 1974 (JJDP Act) and established the federal Office of Juvenile Justice and Delinquency Prevention (OJJDP).[15] This legislation was enacted to identify the needs of youth and fund programs in the juvenile justice system. As its centerpiece, the JJDP Act had two key compliance provisions:

1. Deinstitutionalization of status offenders, and
2. Separation and removal of juveniles from adult facilities.[16]

After the "due process revolution," juvenile justice began to take on many of the characteristics of adult criminal justice. The provision of defense counsel for almost every juvenile offender signaled the end of the informal, nonadversarial juvenile justice system.

Today, the distinctions between the adult and juvenile justice systems continue to blur. OJJDP has led the fight (through its ability to grant federal funds) to liberalize the system and diffuse its impact on young offenders. However, in the 1980s, the OJJDP has grown increasingly conservative and is now more concerned with the hard-core chronic offender than with aiding noncriminal youths;

TABLE 19.1
A Typical Status Offense Statute

Ohio Unruly Child Statute 2151.022 Unruly Child Defined
As used in sections 2151.01 to 2151.54, inclusive of the Revised Code, "Unruly child" includes any child:
Who does not subject himself to the reasonable control of his parents, teachers, guardian, or custodian, by reason of being wayward or habitually disobedient;
Who is an habitual truant from home or school;
Who so deports himself as to injure or endanger the health or morals of himself or others;
Who attempts to enter the marriage relation in any state without the consent of his parents, custodian, legal guardian, or other legal authority;
Who is found in a disreputable place, visits or patronizes a place prohibited by law, or associates with vagrant, vicious, criminal, notorious, or immoral persons;
Who engages in an occupation prohibited by law, or is in a situation dangerous to life or limb or injurious to the health or morals of himself or others;
Who has violated a law applicable only to a child.

SOURCE: *Ohio Rev. Code Ann.*, sec. 2151.022.

the role, and even the continued existence, of the OJJDP has been the subject of much debate in recent years.

The position of the federal government has not been lost on the states. Concern over serious juvenile crime has prompted a number of states to toughen their juvenile sentencing policies. Juvenile courts also commonly waive jurisdiction over serious cases, allowing youths to be tried in adult courts. Yet the rehabilitation ideal still lives in juvenile justice, and community treatment and reducing the number of incarcerated youths still remain top priorities.

Juvenile Court Jurisdiction

The modern juvenile court is a specialized court for children. It may be organized as an independent statewide court system, as a special session of a lower court, or even as part of a broader family court. Juvenile courts are normally established by state legislation and exercise jurisdiction over two distinct categories of juvenile offenders—delinquents and status offenders.[17] Delinquent children are those who fall under a jurisdictional age limit, which varies from state to state, and who commit an act in violation of the penal code. **Status offenders,** on the other hand, include truants and habitually disobedient and ungovernable children. They are commonly characterized in state statutes as persons or children in need of supervision (PINS or CHINS), and their proscribed actions are in the nature of status offenses (see Table 19.1). Most states distinguish such behavior from delinquent conduct to lessen the effect of any stigma on children as a result of their involvement with the juvenile court. In addition, juvenile courts generally have jurisdiction over situations involving conduct directed at (rather than committed by) juveniles, such as parental neglect, deprivation, abandonment, and abuse.

Today's juvenile court system embodies both rehabilitative and legalistic orientations; although the purpose of the court is therapeutic, rather than punitive, children under its jurisdiction must be accorded their constitutional rights. The administrative structure of the court revolves around a diverse group of actors—a juvenile court judge, the probation staff, social workers, prosecutors, and defense attorneys. Thus, the juvenile court functions sociolegally. It seeks to promote the rehabilitation of the child within a framework of procedural due process.

Juvenile court jurisdiction is established by state statute and based on several factors, the first of which is age. The states have set different maximum ages below which children fall under the jurisdiction of the juvenile court. Many states include all children under eighteen, others set the upper limit at seventeen, and still others include children under sixteen.[18]

Juvenile court jurisdiction is also based on the nature of a child's actions. If an action committed by a child is a crime, this conduct normally falls into the category of delinquency. Definitions of delinquency vary from state to state, but most are based on the common element that delinquency is an intentional violation of the criminal law. The juvenile courts also have jurisdiction over status offenders, or children whose offenses involve some lack of parental supervision and are not the types of activity for which adults could be similarly prosecuted. Statutes attempting to define such conduct are marked by a vagueness that would most likely be impermissible in an adult criminal code. For example, statutes of this kind commonly include such designations as "unmanageable," "unruly," and "in danger of leading an idle, dissolute, lewd, or immoral life." Understandably, statutory formulations such as these have been challenged as being unconstitutionally vague and indefinite.[19] However, most courts that have addressed this issue have upheld the breadth of the statutes in view of their overall concern for the welfare of the child.[20]

A juvenile court's jurisdiction is also affected by state statutes that exclude certain offenses from its consideration. Based on the premise that the rehabilitative resources and protective processes of the juvenile court are not appropriate in cases of serious criminal conduct, various states have excluded capital offenses, offenses punishable by death or life imprisonment, and certain other offenses from the juvenile court's jurisdiction. A more common exclusionary scheme involves **transfer** provisions, by means of which juvenile courts waive jurisdictions to the criminal court (waiver is discussed later in this chapter). Having once obtained jurisdiction of a child, the juvenile court ordinarily retains it until the child reaches a specified age, usually the age of majority. Court jurisdiction terminates in most states when the child is placed in a public child-care agency. Figure 19.1 depicts the basic juvenile justice system.

Police Processing of the Juvenile Offender

For the past several years, about 1.5 million youths under eighteen years of age have been arrested each year.[21] When a juvenile is found to have engaged in delinquent or incorrigible behavior, police agencies are charged with the decision to release or to detain the child and refer him or her to juvenile court.[22] This discretionary decision—to release or to detain—has been found to be based not only on the nature of the offense but also on police attitudes and the child's social and personal conditions at the time of the arrest.[23] The following is a partial list of factors believed to be significant in police decision making regarding juvenile offenders:

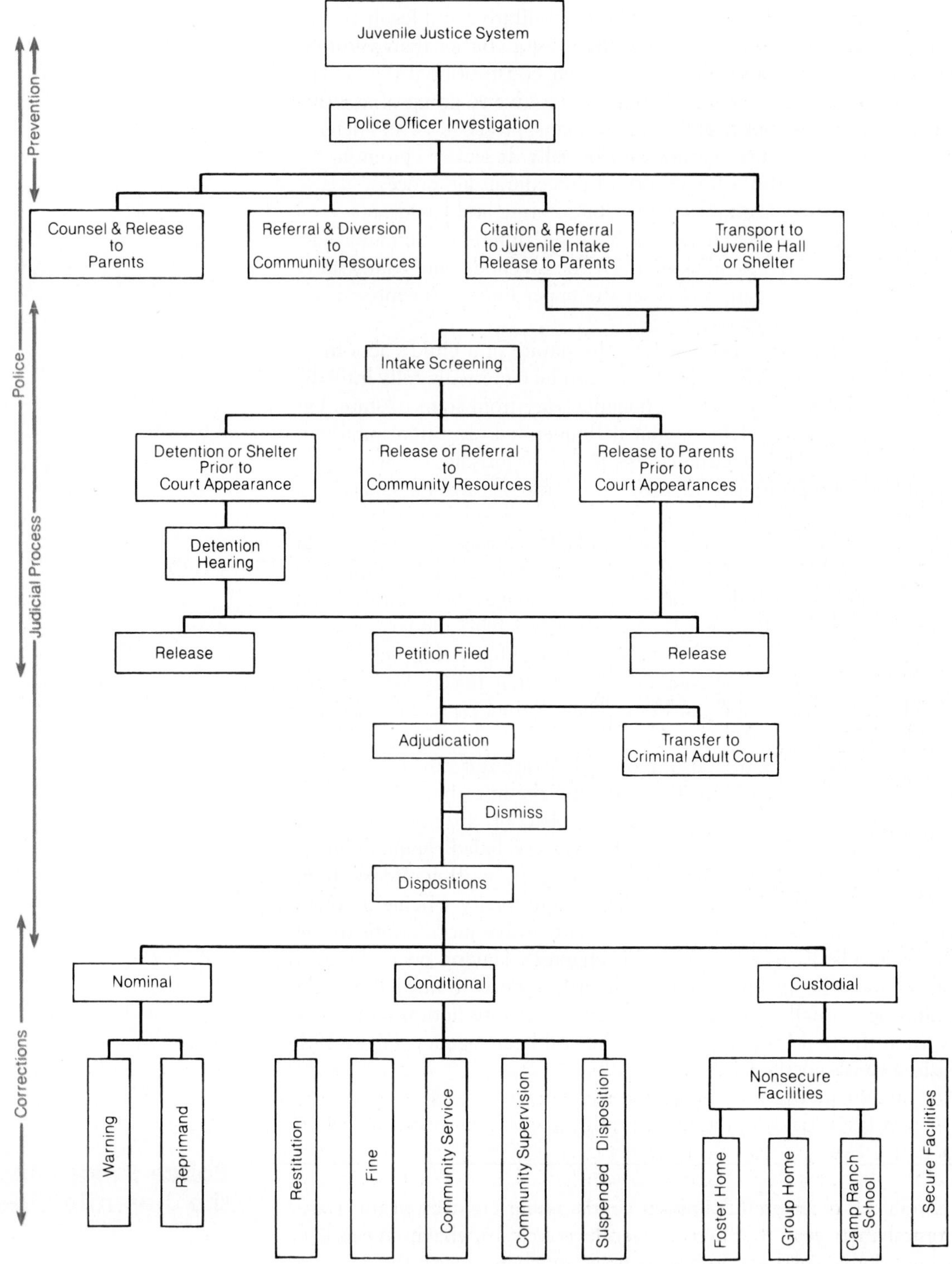

FIGURE 19.1

Juvenile Justice System

SOURCE: National Advisory Commission on Criminal Justice Standards and Goals, *Report of the Task Force on Juvenile Justice and Delinquency Prevention* (Washington, D.C.: Law Enforcement Assistance Administration, 1976), p. 9.

1. The type and seriousness of the child's offense.
2. The ability of the parents to be of assistance in disciplining the child.
3. The child's past contacts with police.
4. The degree of cooperation obtained from the child and parents and their demeanor, attitude, and personal characteristics.
5. Whether the child denies the allegations in the petition and insists on a court hearing.

The police may adjust a case by simply releasing the child at the point of contact on the street, giving an official warning and releasing the offender to the parents at the station house or the child's home, or referring the child to a social services program. Generally, cases involving violence and victims or serious property offenses are most often referred to court. On the other hand, police often attempt to divert from court action minor disputes between juveniles, school and neighborhood complaints, petty shoplifting cases, runaways, and ungovernable children.

When the police take a child into custody, the law of arrest requires that the police officer make a determination that probable cause exists that a crime has been committed and that the child may have committed it. Most states do not have specific statutory provisions distinguishing the arrest process for children from that for adults. Some jurisdictions, however, give broad arrest powers to the police in juvenile cases by authorizing the officer to make an arrest whenever it is believed that the child's behavior falls within the jurisdiction of the juvenile court.[24] Similarly, many states give the police authority to take a child into custody if the child's welfare requires it. Because of the state's interest in the child, the police generally have more discretion in the investigatory and arrest stages of the juvenile process than they do when dealing with adult offenders. Although most juvenile arrests are warrantless, the requirements for the issuance of an arrest warrant for a juvenile are generally similar to requirements in adult cases.

Once a juvenile has been taken into custody, the child has the same Fourth Amendment right to be free from unreasonable searches and seizures as an adult does. The most common legal procedure used to exclude any incriminating evidence is for the child's attorney to make a pretrial motion to suppress inadmissible evidence, barring its use in subsequent hearings.

School Searches

School officials often assume quasi-police powers over children. They may search students to determine whether they are in possession of contraband, such as drugs or weapons, search their lockers and desks, and question them about illegal activities. Such actions are comparable to the acts of the regular police. In *New Jersey v. T.L.O.* (1985), the U.S. Supreme Court held that a school official had the authority to search the purse of a student, even though no warrant was issued nor was there probable cause that a crime had been committed; there was only the suspicion that T.L.O. had violated school rules.[25]

This important case involved an assistant principal's search of the purse of a fourteen-year-old student observed smoking a cigarette in a school lavatory. The search was prompted when the principal found cigarette rolling papers as the pack of cigarettes was removed from the purse. A further search revealed marijuana and several items indicating marijuana selling; as a result, T.L.O. was adjudicated as a delinquent. The Supreme Court held that the Fourth Amendment protections against unreasonable searches and seizures apply to students but said that the need to maintain an orderly educational environment modified the usual Fourth Amendment requirements of warrants and probable cause. Thus, the Court relaxed the usual probable cause standard and found the search to be reasonable.[26] It declared that the school's right to maintain discipline on school grounds allowed it to search students and their possessions as a safety precaution. Thus the Court, which had guarded the warrant requirement and its exceptions in the past, now permits warrantless searches in school, based on the lesser standard of "reasonable suspicion." This landmark decision did not deal with other thorny issues, however, such as the search and seizure of contraband from a student's locker or desk.

Faced with increased crime by students in public schools, particularly illicit drug use, school administrators today are prone to enforce drug control statutes and administrative rules.[27] Some urban schools are using breathalyzers, drug-sniffing dogs, hidden video cameras, and routine searches of students' pockets, purses, lockers, and cars.[28] In general, courts consider such searches permissible when they are not overly offensive and where there are reasonable grounds to suspect that the student may have violated the law.[29] School administrators are walking a tightrope between a student's constitutional right to privacy and school safety. Some schools have developed risk assessment models to evaluate the probable legality of a search-and-seizure situation.[30] These models consider the interaction of the focus, purpose, and degree of risk associated with conducting an illegal search. However, it remains for future court decisions to indicate how far the state may go in curbing school crime before privacy rights are violated.

Juveniles and the *Miranda* Decision

Another issue related to the exclusion of evidence in juvenile matters is the use of statements made by juvenile offenders to police officers. In years past, police often questioned juveniles in the absence of their parents or an attorney. Any incriminatory statements or confessions made by juveniles could be placed in evidence at their trials. As mentioned in Chapter 9, the U.S. Supreme Court in *Miranda v. Arizona* (1966) placed constitutional limitations on police interrogation procedures regarding adult offenders.[31] The *Miranda* warning, which lists the adult defendant's Fifth Amendment rights against self-incrimination, has been made applicable to children. The *In re Gault* decision—which gave juveniles procedural safeguards similar to those awarded adults at trial proceedings, including the right to counsel, the right to confront witnesses, and the privilege against self-incrimination—has indirectly influenced and reinforced juvenile *Miranda* rights. In other words, adjudicatory rights seem to require that the *Miranda* warning be given to all juvenile offenders who are questioned in custody if the police intend to admit their statements in subsequent proceedings. Most states have incorporated the *Miranda* decision into their juvenile statutes, and today, a child's parents are usually contacted immediately after the child is taken into custody.

One of the most difficult problems involving self-incrimination is whether juveniles can waive their *Miranda* rights. This issue has resulted in considerable litigation. Some courts have concluded that it is not essential for the parent or the attorney to be present for the child to effectively waive his or her rights. The validity of the waiver in this respect is based on the totality of the circumstances of a given case. This means that the court must determine whether the child is able to make a knowing, intelligent, and voluntary waiver. On the other hand, some jurisdictions will not accept a waiver of the juvenile's *Miranda* rights unless it is made in the presence of the child's parents or attorney.

The Supreme Court has clarified the rights of juveniles in two cases, ***Fare v. Michael C.*** and ***California v. Prysock.***[32] In *Fare v. Michael C.* (1979), a young boy was arrested by police on suspicion of murder. After the *Miranda* warning was given, Michael requested to speak to his probation officer. This request was denied.

Michael then confessed to the crime and later appealed his conviction, charging that the police should have allowed him to speak to his probation officer. The Supreme Court found that the police were justified in refusing Michael's request and that, considering the "totality of the circumstances," they had made a reasonable attempt to inform the suspect of his rights.

In *California v. Prysock* (1981), the Court was asked to rule on the adequacy of a *Miranda* warning given Randall Prysock, a youthful murder suspect. In upholding Prysock's conviction, the Court ruled that even though the *Miranda* warning was not given in the precise manner as outlined in the case decision, its meaning was plain and easily understandable, even to a juvenile. In light of these problematic cases, some legal experts believe that *Miranda* warnings used in juvenile settings should be modified to ensure that they are comprehensible to the suspect. Waiver of *Miranda* rights by a juvenile is probably the most perplexing legal problem that has confronted the courts in recent years.

Today, almost as much procedural protection is generally given to children in the juvenile justice system as to adults tried in criminal court. Table 19.2 describes the basic similarities and differences between the juvenile and adult justice systems, while Table 19.3 points out how the language used in the juvenile court differs from that used in the adult system.

The Pretrial Stage of Juvenile Justice

After arrest and before trial, the juvenile defendant is processed through a number of important stages of the juvenile justice system. These may include intake, detention, bail, waiver hearing, and diversion programs. Each of these stages and processes is discussed in the following sections.

The Intake Process

As previously described, juveniles coming into contact with the police and juvenile courts generally may be categorized into two major groups: those accused of committing crimes that result in juvenile delinquency and those accused of committing acts of noncriminal behavior. Police officers who confront children committing a crime or behaving in a manner that could be dangerous to themselves or others must decide whether the situation warrants court attention or not. Thus, the police exercise a certain amount of discretion in dealing with children. If the police officer does not initiate court action, he or she may provide the child with a warning, advise the parents to refer the child to a welfare agency, or refer the child's case to a social agency.

When the police department believes the child needs a court referral, the police become involved in the **intake** division of the court. The term *intake* refers to the screening of cases by the juvenile court system. Intake probation officers review and initially screen the child and the family to determine if the child needs to be handled by the juvenile court. The intake stage is when the child can receive treatment in a most efficient and timely manner. It represents an

TABLE 19.2
Similarities and Differences between the Juvenile and Adult Justice Systems

Similarities

1. Discretion in decision making is used by police officers, judges, and correctional personnel in both adult and juvenile systems.
2. Search and seizure law and the Fourth Amendment apply to juvenile and adult offenders.
3. The right to receive the *Miranda* warning applies to juveniles as well as to adults.
4. Juveniles are protected, as are adults, from prejudicial lineups or other identification procedures.
5. Procedural safeguards similar to those of adults protect juveniles when they make an admission of guilt.
6. Prosecutors and defense attorneys play an equally critical role in juvenile and adult advocacy.
7. Juveniles, like adults, have the right to counsel at most key stages of the court process.
8. Pretrial motions are available in juvenile and criminal court proceedings.
9. Negotiations and plea bargaining are used with juvenile and adult offenders.
10. Children and adults have a right to a trial and appeal.
11. The standard of evidence in juvenile delinquency adjudications, as in adult criminal trials, is that of proof beyond a reasonable doubt.
12. Like adults, children waived from the juvenile court can receive the death penalty.

Differences

1. The primary purpose of juvenile procedures is protection and treatment; with adults, the aim is punishment of the guilty.
2. The jurisdiction of the juvenile court is determined chiefly by age; in the adult system, jurisdiction is determined primarily by the nature of the offense.
3. Juveniles can be held responsible for acts that would not be criminal if they were committed by an adult (status offenses).
4. Juvenile proceedings are not considered criminal, whereas adult proceedings are.
5. Juvenile court procedures are generally informal and private; those of adult courts are more formal and open to the public.
6. Courts cannot release identifying information to the press concerning a juvenile but must do so in cases involving adults.
7. Parents are highly involved in the juvenile process; with adults, this would not be the case.
8. The standard of arrest is more stringent for adults than for juveniles.
9. As a practical matter, juveniles are released into parental custody, whereas adults are generally given the opportunity for bail.
10. Plea bargaining is used in most adult cases, whereas most juvenile cases are settled by open admission of guilt.
11. Juveniles have no constitutional right to a jury trial; adults do have this right.
12. Juvenile dispositional decisions are ordinarily based on indeterminate terms, whereas adult sentences include proportionality and definiteness.
13. The procedural rights of juveniles are based on the concept of "fundamental fairness"; those of adults are based on the constitutional right to due process under the Bill of Rights and the Fourteenth Amendment.
14. Juveniles have the right to treatment under the Fourteenth Amendment; adult offenders have no such recognized right.
15. A juvenile's record is sealed when the age of majority is reached; the record of an adult is permanent.

opportunity to place a child in informal programs both within the court and in the community. The intake process also is critically important because more than half the referrals to the juvenile courts never go beyond this stage.

Juvenile court intake—which seeks to screen out cases not within the court's jurisdiction or not serious enough for court intervention—is now provided for by statute in the majority of states.[34] Virtually all the model acts and standards in juvenile justice suggest the development of juvenile court intake proceedings.[35]

Intake procedures in the juvenile court are desirable for a number of reasons, including: (1) filing a complaint against the child in a court may do more harm than good, since rehabilitation has often failed in the juvenile court system;

TABLE 19.3
Comparison of Terms Used in Adult and Juvenile Justice Systems

	Juvenile Terms	Adult Terms
The person and the act	Delinquent child	Criminal
	Delinquent act	Crime
Pre-adjudicatory stage	Take into custody	Arrest
	Petition	Indictment
	Agree to a finding	Plead guilty
	Deny the petition	Plead not guilty
	Adjustment	Plea-bargain
	Detention facility, child-care shelter	Jail
Adjudicatory stage	Substitution	Reduction of charges
	Adjudicatory or fact-finding hearing	Trial
	Adjudication	Conviction
Post-adjudicatory stage	Dispositional hearing	Sentencing hearing
	Disposition	Sentence
	Commitment	Incarceration
	Youth development center, treatment center, training school	Prison
	Residential child-care facility	Halfway house
	Aftercare	Parole

(2) processing a child in the juvenile court stigmatizes and labels the child a delinquent and may reinforce antisocial behavior; (3) nonjudicial handling gives the child and the family a second chance and an opportunity to work with a voluntary social service agency; and (4) screening helps conserve resources in already overburdened juvenile court systems. In addition, intake screening provides for a wide range of nonjudicial decisions regarding the child, including the use of nonjudicial or informal probation, the provision of services by the intake department of the juvenile court, the dismissal of a complaint, and the referral to a community social service agency. Finally, intake screening allows juvenile courts to enter into a consent decree with the juvenile without the filing of a petition or formal adjudication. The consent decree is basically a court order authorizing the disposition of the case without a formal finding of delinquency, based on an agreement between the intake department of the court and the juvenile who is the subject of the complaint.

Despite its advantages, intake does present some problems. Less than 50 percent of all juveniles who are arrested and brought to court actually proceed to trial. As a result, intake sections are constantly pressured to provide services for the large group of children not handled by the court. In addition to linking court and community services, intake programs need to be provided twenty-four hours a day in many urban courts, so that dispositions can be resolved quickly on the day the child is referred to the court. Furthermore, the key to good intake service is the quality of the intake staff. Poorly qualified personnel in intake is a serious flaw in many court systems. A variety of legal problems are also associated with the intake process, including whether the child has a right to counsel and a privilege against self-incrimination at this stage and to what degree the child needs to consent to nonjudicial disposition as recommended by the intake probation officer.

In some respects, juvenile intake can be compared to the adult plea-bargaining process. Both stages involve questions of due process, informal negotiations, discretionary justice, and issues of voluntarism.[36] Cases are generally resolved by making a deal and reaching a settlement, rather than by making a formal determination of guilt or innocence.

Detention

After a juvenile is formally taken into custody, either as a delinquent or as a status offender, a decision is usually made whether to release the child to the parent or guardian or detain the child in a shelter pending trial. In the past, far too many children were routinely placed in **detention** while awaiting court appearances. Detention facilities were inadequate—in many parts of the country, county jails were used to detain juvenile offenders. The emphasis in recent years has been on reducing the number of children placed in detention, although the practice continues.

The child is usually released to the parent or guardian. Most state statutes ordinarily require a hearing on the appropriateness of detention if the initial decision is to keep the child in custody. At this hearing, the child has a right to counsel and may be given other procedural due process safeguards, notably the privilege against self-incrimination and the right to confront and cross-examine witnesses.

Most state juvenile court acts provide criteria to support a decision to detain the child. These include (1) the need to protect the child, (2) whether the child presents a serious danger to the public, and (3) the likelihood that the juvenile will return to court for adjudication. Whereas in adult cases the sole criterion for pretrial release may be the offender's availability for trial, juveniles may be detained for other reasons, including their own protection. Normally, the finding of the judge that the child should be detained must be supported by factual evidence. When a valid reason for a child's detention has not appeared on the records, courts have mandated release from temporary custody. In the 1984 case of *Schall v. Martin*, the U.S. Supreme Court upheld the right of the states to detain a child before trial in order to protect his or her welfare and the public safety.[37]

Issues in Juvenile Detention. The use of juvenile detention involves three important issues. The first has been the mostly successful effort to remove status offenders from lockups containing delinquents. After a decade of effort, almost all states have passed laws requiring that status offenders be placed in shelters, rather than detention facilities. An analysis of this effort found that one problem of deinstitutionalizing status offenders was that many had prior delinquent records; in addition, the recidivism rate was not improved by their removal from secure lockups.[38]

Another serious problem is the detention of youths in adult jails. This practice is quite common in rural areas, where there are relatively few separate facilities for young offenders.

Although the federal government, through the OJJDP, has actively supported removing detained youths from adult jails, the practice still continues. In fact, under the JJDP Act, states obtaining federal funds were compelled to revise their jail practices and separate juveniles from adults.[39] By 1980, amendments to the act mandating the absolute removal of juveniles from jails had been adopted. Despite such efforts, more than half the states are not complying with the removal provisions, and some experts estimate that over one hundred thousand youths are annually detained in adult jails.[40] Whatever the actual number jailed today, placing young offenders in adult jails continues to be a significant problem in the juvenile justice system.

Juveniles detained in adult jails often live in squalid conditions and are subjected to physical and sexual abuse. A federally sponsored study found that children confined in adult institutions were eight times as likely to commit suicide as those placed in detention centers exclusively for juveniles and were 4.5 percent more likely to kill themselves as children in the general population.[41]

The OJJDP has given millions of dollars in aid to encourage the removal of juveniles from adult lockups.[42] These grants have helped many jurisdictions develop intake screening procedures, specific release or detention criteria, and alternative residential and nonresidential programs for juveniles awaiting trial.

Nevertheless, eliminating the confinement of juveniles in adult institutions remains a difficult task. In a recent comprehensive study of the jailing of juveniles in Minnesota, Ira Schwartz found that even in a state recognized nationally for juvenile justice reform, the rate of admission of juveniles to adult jails remains high.[43] His research also revealed that the rate of admission is not related to the seriousness of the offense and that minority juveniles are spending greater amounts of time in jail than white offenders for the same offenses.[44]

In his report, Schwartz suggests (1) that government enact legislation prohibiting the confinement of juveniles in jail; (2) that appropriate juvenile detention facilities be established; (3) that funds be allocated for such programs; (4) that racial disparity in detention be examined; and (5) that responsibility for monitoring conditions of confinement be fixed by statutes and court decisions.[45] California, for example, passed legislation ensuring that no minor under juvenile court jurisdiction can be incarcerated in any jail after July 1, 1989.[46] And in the recent landmark federal court case, ***Hendrickson v. Griggs,*** the court found that the state of Iowa had not complied with the juvenile jail removal mandate of the JJDP Act and ordered local officials to develop a plan for bringing the state into conformity with the law.[47] As a result, states will face increasing legal pressure to meet jail removal requirements in the future.

Since 1985, the number of youth held in short-term detention facilities has increased by about 15 percent, or over seventeen thousand children! In addition, the number of minority-group children (African-Americans and Hispanics) held in detention facilities has risen more than 30 percent, which has caused considerable concern to juvenile justice practitioners (see Figure 19.2).

Experts believe the steady increase in detention use may result from (1) a rise in serious crime by juveniles; (2) a growing link between juveniles and drug-related crimes; and (3) the involvement of younger children in the juvenile justice system. Detention of youth continues to be a major issue in the juvenile justice system and reducing its use has not been an easy task.

Bail

If a child is not detained, the question of bail arises. Federal courts have not found it necessary to rule on the issue of a constitutional right to bail since liberal

FIGURE 19.2

Increase in the Number of Minority-Group Juveniles in Detention, 1985–1987

SOURCE: "Growth in Minority Detentions Attributed to Drug Law Violators," *Juvenile and Family Court Newsletter,* vol. 20 (Reno, Nev.: National Court of Juvenile and Family Court Judges, 1990).

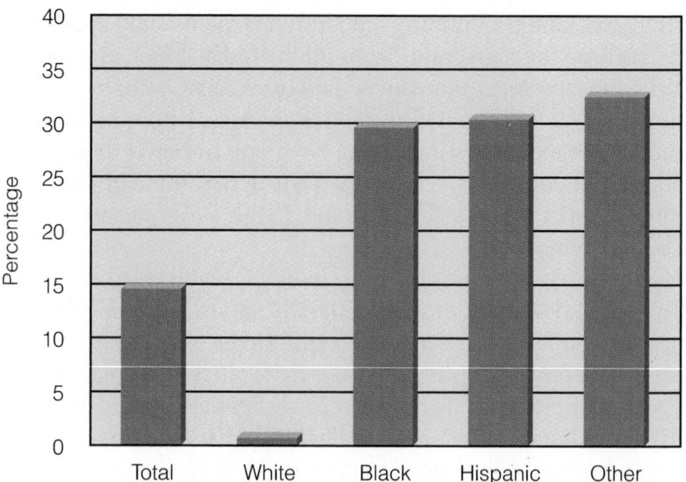

statutory release provisions act as appropriate alternatives. Although only a few state statutes allow release on money bail, many others have juvenile code provisions that emphasize the release of the child to the parents as an acceptable substitute. A constitutional right to bail that on its face seems to benefit a child may have unforeseen results. For example, money bail might impose a serious economic strain on the child's family while simultaneously conflicting with the protective and social concerns of the juvenile court. Considerations of economic liabilities and other procedural inequities have influenced the majority of courts confronting this question to hold that juveniles do not have a right to bail.

Plea Bargaining

A child may plead guilty or not guilty to a petition alleging delinquency. Today, states tend to minimize the stigma associated with the use of adult criminal standards by using other terminology, such as "agree to a finding" or "deny the petition." When the child makes an admission, juvenile court laws and rules of procedure in numerous jurisdictions require the following procedural safeguards: (1) that the child know of the right to a trial, (2) that the plea or admission be made voluntarily, and (3) that the child understand the charges and consequences of the plea. The same requirements for adult offenders have been established in a series of decisions by the U.S. Supreme Court.[48] Although such standards have not been established by constitutional law for juveniles, they carry equal weight in juvenile cases because the guilty plea constitutes a waiver of the juvenile's Fifth Amendment privilege against self-incrimination.

Open admission, as opposed to plea bargaining, seems to be the reason that the majority of juvenile court cases are not adjudicated. Unlike the adult system, where 70 to 90 percent of all charged offenders are involved in some plea bargaining, little plea bargaining apparently exists in the juvenile court. Most juvenile court legislation and rules of procedure do not provide rules governing the plea-bargaining process. The *parens patriae* philosophy of the juvenile court, the general availability of pretrial social services, and flexibility in the disposition of cases discourage the use of plea bargaining.

Plea bargaining in the juvenile court occurs practically when the government—represented by the prosecutor, police officer, or probation officer—negotiates a guilty plea from the defense attorney in exchange for a disposition generally involving community supervision. Both parties may seek the judge's guidance in reaching an agreement and obtain judicial consent to the bargain. Efficient disposition of the case after plea bargaining is also an essential element of the process because it reduces the juvenile court caseload and enhances the child's rehabilitative prospects.

The Waiver of Jurisdiction

Prior to the development of the first modern juvenile court in Illinois in 1899, juveniles were tried for violations of the law in adult criminal courts. The consequences were devastating; many children were treated as criminal offenders and often sentenced to adult prisons. Although the subsequent passage of state legislation creating juvenile courts eliminated this problem, the juvenile justice system did recognize that certain forms of conduct require that children be tried as adults. Today, most jurisdictions provide by statute for waiver, or transfer, of juvenile offenders to the criminal courts.

The transfer of a juvenile to the criminal court is often based on statutory criteria established by the state's juvenile court act, and waiver provisions vary considerably among jurisdictions. The two major criteria for waiver are the age of the child and the type of offense alleged in the petition. For example, some jurisdictions require that the child be over a certain age and be charged with a felony before being tried as an adult, while others permit waiver of jurisdiction to the criminal court if the child is above a certain age, regardless of the offense. Still other states permit waiver under any conditions.[49]

Because of the nature of the waiver decision and its effect on the child in terms of status and disposition, the U.S. Supreme Court has imposed procedural protections for juveniles in the waiver process. ***Kent v. United States*** (1966), the first major case before the Court on this issue, challenged the provisions of the District of Columbia code, which stated that the juvenile court could waive jurisdiction after a full investigation.[50] The Supreme Court in *Kent* held that the waiver proceeding is a critically important stage in the juvenile justice process and that juveniles must be afforded minimum requirements of due process of law at such proceedings.

In reaching this decision, Justice Abe Fortas declared:

> The Juvenile Court is theoretically engaged in determining the needs of the child and of society rather than adjudicating criminal conduct. The objectives are to provide measures of guidance and rehabilitation for the child and protection for society, not to fix criminal responsibility, guilt and punishment. The State is *parens patriae* rather than prosecuting attorney and judge. But the admonition to function in a "parental" relationship is not an invitation to procedural arbitrariness.[51]

In ***Breed v. Jones*** (1975), another significant decision on juvenile waiver proceedings, the Supreme Court held that the prosecution of a juvenile as an adult in the California Superior Court, following an adjudicatory proceeding in juvenile court, violated the double jeopardy clause of the Fifth Amendment as applied to the states through the Fourteenth Amendment.[52] The Court concluded that jeopardy attaches when the juvenile court begins to hear evidence at the adjudicatory hearing; this requires that the waiver hearing take place prior to any adjudication.

Youths in Adult Courts

Under certain circumstances, juveniles may be tried in criminal courts. The age at which the criminal court takes jurisdiction ranges from sixteen to nineteen.

The problem of youths processed in adult courts is a serious one. An important federally sponsored survey found that in a single year, nine thousand juveniles were waived to adult courts, two thousand were prosecuted as adults because of concurrent jurisdiction, and thirteen hundred were prosecuted as adults because the offenses they committed were excluded from juvenile court jurisdiction.[53] In addition, since twelve states have low maximum ages for juvenile courts, about 250,000 youths aged sixteen and seventeen are handled by adult courts each year. Among the other significant findings of the study were:

1. Most waived youths were not charged with violent crimes but with property and public-order (drug, alcohol) crimes.
2. Most of the youths tried in adult courts were convicted or pleaded guilty.
3. Youths were more likely to receive a probation sentence than confinement. However, 46 percent of the youths judicially waived were sent to adult correctional facilities.
4. Youths convicted as adults and sentenced to confinement did more time than they would have under juvenile court disposition.

Although the report did not recommend the abolition of waiver, it suggested that juveniles should always be kept out of adult correctional facilities and should be treated as juveniles for as long as possible.

Today, all states allow juveniles to be tried as adults in criminal courts in one of three ways:

1. *Concurrent jurisdiction*. The prosecutor has the discretion of filing charges for certain offenses in either juvenile or criminal court.
2. *Excluded offenses*. The legislature excludes from juvenile court jurisdiction certain offenses that are either very minor, such as traffic or fishing violations, or very serious, such as murder or rape.
3. *Judicial waiver*. The juvenile court waives its jurisdiction and transfers the case to criminal court (the procedure is also known as "binding over" or "certifying" juvenile cases to criminal court).

Today, twelve states authorize prosecutors to bring cases in the juvenile or adult criminal court at their discretion; thirty-six states exclude certain offenses from juvenile court jurisdiction; and forty-eight states, the District of Columbia, and the federal government have judicial waiver provisions.[54]

Barry Feld suggests that waiver to adult court should be mandatory for juveniles committing serious crimes.[55] He argues that mandatory waiver would jibe with the currently popular "just desert" sentencing policy and eliminate potential bias and disparity in judicial decision making.

In a recent extensive study of legislative changes in juvenile statutes, Feld found that most states rely on the seriousness of the current offense in deciding whether to waive a youth to adult court. However, as Feld points out, youths transferred under excluded offenses statutes may not be as criminally responsible as their adult counterparts.[56]

Another recent trend has been to enact statutes giving original jurisdiction for juvenile crimes to the adult courts and then allowing judges to waive deserving cases back to the juvenile authorities. The most well-known of these statutes is

New York's 1978 Omnibus Crime Act, which gives the adult courts jurisdiction over thirteen-year-olds accused of murder and fourteen- and fifteen-year-olds accused of serious crimes, such as murder, rape, and robbery.[57] The adult court judge is entitled to transfer these youths to juvenile court, but not vice versa. However, youths cannot be placed in adult correctional facilities until they reach age sixteen. New York's law has been criticized on several grounds:

1. Some 70 percent of the children arraigned in adult court are waived to juvenile court, wasting both time and money.
2. Some 40 percent of the juveniles tried in adult court are sentenced to probation.
3. Only 3 percent of the juvenile offenders tried in adult court received longer sentences than they would have if they had been tried in juvenile court.

The Effect of Waiver. The key question is what is accomplished by treating juveniles like adults. Studies of the impact of the recent waiver statutes have yielded inconclusive results.[58] Some juveniles whose cases are waived to criminal court are sentenced more leniently than they would have been in juvenile court. In many states, even when juveniles are tried in criminal court and convicted on the charges, they may still be sentenced to a juvenile or youthful offender institution, rather than to an adult prison. The laws may allow them to be transferred to an adult prison when they have reached a certain age. Some studies show that only a small percentage of juveniles tried as adults are incarcerated for periods longer than the terms served by offenders convicted on the same crime in the juvenile court. Moreover, judges tend to sentence sixteen-year-olds appearing in adult court to probation, rather than prison. In the end, what began as a "get tough" measure has had the opposite effect while costing taxpayers more money.

Critics view these new methods of dealing with juvenile offenders as inefficient, ineffective, and philosophically out of step with the original concept of the juvenile court. Supporters view the waiver process as a sound method of getting the most serious juvenile offenders off the streets while ensuring that rehabilitation plays a less critical role in the juvenile justice system.

The Juvenile Trial

Juvenile courts dispose of an estimated 1.3 million delinquency cases a year. The number of juvenile cases getting to court has stabilized in recent years, reflecting a downward trend in juvenile crime rates and the growth of alternative programs.[59]

During the adjudicatory or trial process, often called the fact-finding hearing in juvenile proceedings, the court hears evidence on the allegations stated in the delinquency petition. In its early development, the juvenile court did not emphasize judicial rule making similar to that of the criminal trial process. Absent were such basic requirements as the standard of proof, rules of evidence, and similar adjudicatory formalities.

Traditionally, the juvenile system was designed to diagnose and rehabilitate children appearing before the court. This was consistent with the view that the court should be social service-oriented. Proceedings were to be nonadversarial, informal, and noncriminal. Gradually, however, the juvenile court movement became the subject of much criticism. This growing dissatisfaction was based primarily on the inability of the court to rehabilitate juvenile offenders, while at

The criminalization of the juvenile justice process was prompted by the realization that youth are committing more serious crime than ever before, including gang delinquency. This is a Los Angeles female gang.

the same time failing to safeguard their constitutional rights. Juvenile courts were punishing many children under the guise of being social service agencies, arguing that constitutional protections were not necessary because the juveniles were being helped in the name of the state. Under the *parens patriae* philosophy, the adjudicatory proceeding, as well as subsequent dispositions, was seen as being in the child's best interests. Thus, the philosophy of the juvenile court saw no need for legal rules and procedures, as in the criminal process, nor for the introduction of prosecutors or defense attorneys. These views and practices have been changed by the U.S. Supreme Court. In 1966 with *Kent v. United States*, the Court began to consider the constitutional validity of juvenile court proceedings. This process culminated in the landmark case of ***In re Gault*** (1967).[60] In *Gault*, the Court ruled that the concept of fundamental fairness is applicable to juvenile delinquency proceedings.

Gerald Gault, a fifteen-year-old boy on probation, was arrested as the result of a complaint that he had made lewd telephone calls. After hearings before a juvenile court judge, Gault was ordered committed to the state industrial school as a juvenile delinquent until he reached his majority. The family brought a habeas corpus action in the state courts to challenge the constitutionality of the Arizona Juvenile Code on the ground that the boy was denied his procedural due process rights. The Court decided that the due process clause of the Fourteenth Amendment required that certain procedural guarantees were essential to the adjudication of delinquency cases. Justice Abe Fortas addressed this issue in the following manner:

> Due process of law is the primary and indispensable foundation of individual freedom. It is the basic and essential term in the social compact which defines the rights of the individual and delimits the powers which the state may exercise.[61]

The Court then specified the precise nature of due process by indicating that a juvenile who has violated a criminal statute and who may be committed to an institution is entitled to (1) fair notice of the charges, (2) the right to representation by counsel, (3) the right to confrontation by and cross-examination of witnesses, and (4) the privilege against self-incrimination.

Gault did not hold that the juvenile offender is entitled to all procedural guarantees applicable in the case of an adult charged with a crime. The Supreme Court did not rule, for instance, on whether the juvenile has the right to a transcript of the proceedings or the right to appellate review. Nor was it clear to what extent nondelinquent children have the right to counsel. *Gault* specifically ruled that a juvenile is entitled to counsel in delinquency actions that may result in institutionalization. In this regard, many states have gone beyond *Gault* to provide juveniles with a right to counsel in all stages of court proceedings. However, the question of which juveniles have a right to guarantees under *Gault* has not been completely settled. Some jurisdictions specify that the right to counsel is applicable only in delinquency and status offenses, while other states go beyond *Gault* and provide counsel in neglect and dependency proceedings as well.

The *Gault* decision, particularly as it applies to the constitutional right of a juvenile to the assistance of counsel, has completely altered the juvenile justice system. Instead of dealing with children in a benign and paternalistic fashion, the court must process juvenile offenders within the framework of appropriate constitutional procedures. Although *Gault* was technically limited to the adjudicatory stage, it has spurred further legal reform throughout the juvenile system. Today, the right to counsel, the privilege against self-incrimination, the right to treatment in detention and correctional facilities, and other constitutional protections are applied at all stages of the juvenile process, from investigation through adjudication to parole. Because of the significance of the *Gault* case, it is further described in the Law in Review on page 678.

After *Gault*, the Supreme Court continued its trend toward legalizing and formalizing the juvenile trial process with the decision in ***In re Winship*** (1970).[62] Relying on the "preponderance of the evidence" standard required by the New York Family Court Act, a judge found Winship, a twelve-year-old boy, guilty of the crime of larceny. In *Winship*, however, the Supreme Court held that the standard of proof beyond a reasonable doubt, which is required in a criminal prosecution, is also required in the adjudication of a delinquency petition. The *Winship* decision did not settle whether this burden of proof is also applicable to nondelinquent forms of conduct. As a result, some state statutes require proof beyond a reasonable doubt only in delinquency matters. In these jurisdictions, such standards of proof as clear and convicting evidence or a preponderance of the evidence are used for incorrigibility, neglect, or dependency cases. Other jurisdictions, however, apply the reasonable doubt standard in all types of juvenile actions. In spite of these various statutory differences, *Winship* does impose the constitutional requirement of proof beyond a reasonable doubt during the adjudicatory stage of a delinquency proceeding.

Although the traditional juvenile court was severely altered by *Kent*, *Gault*, and *Winship*, the trend for increased rights for juveniles was somewhat curtailed by the Supreme Court's decision in *McKeiver v. Pennsylvania* (1971).[63] In *McKeiver*, the Court held that trial by jury in a juvenile court's adjudicative stage is not a constitutional requirement. This decision, however, does not prevent the various states from giving the juvenile a trial by jury as a state constitutional right or by state statute. In the majority of states, a child has no such right.

Once an adjudicatory hearing has been completed, the court is normally required to enter a judgment against the child. This may take the form of declaring the child delinquent or a ward of the court or possibly even suspending judgment to avoid the stigma of a juvenile record. Following the entering of a

LAW IN REVIEW

In re Gault (1967)

Facts

Gerald Gault, fifteen years of age, was taken into custody by the sheriff of Gila County, Arizona. His arrest was based on the complaint of a woman who said that he and another boy had made an obscene telephone call to her. Gerald was then under a six-month probation for stealing a wallet. Because of the verbal complaint, Gerald was taken to the children's home. His parents were not informed that he was being taken into custody. His mother appeared in the evening and was told by the superintendent of detention that a hearing would be held in the juvenile court the following day. On the day in question, the police officer who had taken Gerald into custody filed a petition alleging his delinquency. Gerald, his mother, and the police officer appeared before the judge in his chambers. The complainant was not at the hearing. Gerald was questioned about the telephone calls and was sent back to the detention home and then subsequently released a few days later.

On the day of Gerald's release, Gault's mother received a letter indicating that a hearing would be held on Gerald's delinquency a few days later. A hearing was held, and the complainant was not present. No transcript or recording was made of the proceedings, and the juvenile officer stated that Gerald had admitted making the lewd telephone calls. Neither the boy nor his parents were advised of any right to remain silent or to be represented by counsel or of any other constitutional rights. At the conclusion of the hearing, the juvenile court committed Gerald as a juvenile delinquent to the state industrial school in Arizona for the period of his minority.

This meant that Gerald at the age of fifteen was being sent to a period of incarceration in the state school until age twenty-one, or unless discharged sooner, whereas an adult charged with the same crime would have received a maximum punishment of no more than a fifty dollar fine or two months in prison.

Decision

Gerald's attorneys filed a habeas corpus writ, which was denied by the superior court of the state of Arizona; that decision was subsequently affirmed by the Arizona Supreme Court. On appeal to the U.S. Supreme Court, Gerald's counsel argued that the juvenile code of Arizona under which Gerald was found delinquent was invalid because it was contrary to the due process clause of the Fourteenth Amendment. In addition, the attorney argued Gerald had been denied the following basic due process rights: (1) notice of charges with regard to the timeliness and specificity of the charges, (2) right to counsel, (3) right to confrontation and cross-examination, (4) privilege against self-incrimination, (5) right to a transcript of the trial record, and (6) right to appellate review. In deciding the case, the Supreme Court had to decide whether procedural due process of law within the context of fundamental fairness under the Fourteenth Amendment applied to juvenile delinquency proceedings in which a child is committed to a state industrial school.

The Court, in a far-reaching opinion written by Justice Abe Fortas, agreed that Gerald's constitutional rights were violated. Notice of charges is an essential ingredient of due process of law, as is right to counsel, right to cross-examine and to confront witnesses, and the privilege against self-incrimination. The questions of whether a juvenile has a right to appellate review and a right to a transcript were not answered by the Court in this decision.

Significance of the Case

The *Gault* case established that a child has procedural due process constitutional rights as listed above in delinquency adjudication proceedings based on alleged misconduct where the consequences are that the child may be committed to a state institution. The case was confined to rulings at the adjudication stage of the juvenile process.

However, this decision was significant not only because of the procedural reforms, such as the right to counsel, but also because of its far-reaching impact throughout the entire juvenile justice process. *Gault* led to the development of due process standards at the pretrial, trial, and posttrial stages of the juvenile process. While recognizing the history and the development of the juvenile court, it sought to accommodate the motives of rehabilitation and treatment with children's rights. It recognized the principles of fundamental fairness of the law, for children as well as for adults. Judged in the context of today's juvenile justice system, *Gault* redefined the relationship between the juvenile, the parents, and the state. It remains the single most significant constitutional case in the area of juvenile justice.

judgment, the court can begin its determination of possible dispositions for the child.

Disposition and Treatment

At the dispositional hearing, the juvenile court judge imposes a sentence on the juvenile offender in light of his or her offense, prior record, and family background. Normally, the judge has broad discretionary power to issue a range of dispositions from dismissal to institutional commitment. In theory, the dispositional decision is an effort by the court to serve the best interests of the child, the family, and the community. In many respects, this postadjudicative process is the most important stage in the juvenile court system because it represents the last opportunity for the court to influence the child and control his or her behavior.

Most jurisdictions have statutes that require the court to proceed with disposition following adjudication of the child as a delinquent or status offender. This is done as part of the adjudicatory process or at a separate dispositional hearing.

Statutory provisions that use a two-part hearing process are preferred, since different evidentiary rules apply at each hearing. The basic purpose of having two separate hearings is to ensure that only evidence appropriate to determining whether the child committed the alleged offense is considered by the court. If evidence relating to the presentence report of the child is used in the adjudicatory hearing, it would normally result in a reversal of the court's delinquency finding. On the other hand, the social history report is essential for court use in the dispositional hearing. Thus, the two-part hearing process seeks to ensure that the adjudicatory hearing is used solely to determine the merits of the allegations, while the dispositional hearing determines whether the child is in need of rehabilitation.

In theory, the juvenile court seeks to provide a disposition that represents an individualized treatment plan for the child. This decision is normally based on the presentence investigation of the probation department, reports from social agencies, and possibly a psychiatric evaluation. The judge generally has broad discretion in dispositional matters but is limited by the provisions of the state's juvenile court act. The prevailing statutory model provides for the following types of alternative dispositions:

1. Dismissal of the petition
2. Suspended judgment
3. Probation
4. Placement in a community treatment program
5. Commitment to the state agency responsible for juvenile institutional care

In addition, the court may place the child with parents or relatives, make dispositional arrangements with private youth-serving agencies, order the child committed to a mental institution.

One of the most complex problems in the juvenile system has been the limited number of alternative dispositions available for various types of juvenile offenders. Dismissal of the case only provides the court with legal authority to relinquish control over a juvenile. This occurs if allegations in the petition have not been sustained or where the court does not want to stigmatize the child with a juvenile court record. Similar to dismissal is suspended judgment, where the court will continue the case without any formal finding of adjudication. In some instances, the child may also be placed under court supervision for a stipulated period of time. If the child responds well to treatment, the charges are generally dismissed. On the other hand, if the delinquent or incorrigible conduct continues, the court may impose greater supervision.

Juvenile Sentencing

The juvenile court's traditional goal and philosophy have been the rehabilitation and treatment of the juvenile offender at disposition. The juvenile justice system operated to provide care for children "in their best interest" but often subjected them to harsh penalties without due process of law. In the mid-1960s, due process rights were granted to children, but the ideal of rehabilitation remained unfulfilled.

To achieve this goal, juvenile court dispositional orders were based on totally indeterminate sentencing terms for juvenile offenders. The indeterminate sentence is often defined as a term of incarceration with a stated minimum and maximum period, or with no minimum. For instance, a sentence to prison for three to ten years would constitute an indeterminate sentence. Based on the traditional belief that the disposition should fit the child's needs, such sentencing provisions allow for flexibility and individualized programs of treatment. In some jurisdictions, the juvenile court judge could sentence the juvenile for an indeterminate period to a particular type of program. In other jurisdictions, the judge was required to send a child to an agency, such as a division of youth services, that would be responsible for the child's placement and treatment.

Over the past few years, juvenile justice experts and the general public have become aroused about the serious juvenile crime rate in general and about violent acts committed by children in particular. As a result, reformers, especially law enforcement officials and legislators, have demanded that the juvenile justice system take a more serious stand with dangerous juvenile offenders. Some state legislatures have responded by amending their juvenile codes and passing harsh laws. For instance, in New York, children as young as thirteen accused of murder may be tried in adult courts and sentenced to life terms.[64] California has lowered the age to sixteen for transferring juvenile offenders to the adult court system.[65] Washington has passed a determinate sentencing statute that is discussed in detail later in this section. Other jurisdictions, including the District of Columbia, Colorado, Delaware, Florida, and Virginia, have passed mandatory or determinate prison sentences for juveniles convicted of serious felonies. The "get tough" approach even allows the use of the death penalty in juvenile cases. Not all experts agree with this approach. Victor Streib, in *Death Penalty for Juveniles*, the most comprehensive text on the subject, concludes that the Supreme Court should find a constitutional prohibition against such executions.[66] But the U.S. Supreme Court disagrees. (See Analyzing Criminal Justice Issues: Death Row Children on page 682).

A second recent reform movement involves status offenders. This approach suggests that status offenders and other minor juvenile offenders be removed from the juvenile justice system and kept out of institutional programs. Because of the development of numerous diversion programs, many children who are involved in truancy and incorrigible behavior and ordinarily would have been sent to a closed institution are now being placed in community programs.

A third reform effort especially focuses on sentencing and emanates from the American Bar Association's development of standards for the juvenile justice system on dispositions, dispositional procedures, juvenile delinquency and sanctions, and corrections administration. Stanley Fisher suggests that these standards point to a shift in juvenile court philosophy from traditional rehabilitation to the concept of "just desert."[67] In other words, the standards recommend that juveniles be given determinate or "flat" sentences without the possibility of parole, rather than indeterminate sentences. The standards further recommend that punishment be classified into three major categories: nominal, conditional, and custodial sanctions. Nominal sanctions consist of reprimands, warnings, or other minor actions that do not affect the child's personal liberty. Conditional sanctions include probation, restitution, and counseling programs. Custodial sanctions, the most extreme, remove juveniles from their homes into nonsecure or secure institutions. The National Advisory Commission on Criminal Justice Standards and Goals also recommended in 1976 that the dispositions available to the court for juveniles adjudicated delinquent include nominal, conditional, and custodial categories.[68]

Washington has already adopted a determinate sentencing law for juvenile offenders.[69] All children convicted of juvenile delinquency are evaluated on the basis of a point system based on their age, prior juvenile record, type of crime committed, and other factors. Minor offenders are handled in the community. Those committing more serious offenses are placed on probation. Children who commit the most serious offenses are subject to institutional penalties. Institutional officials, who had total discretion in the past for releasing children, now have limited discretion. As a result, juvenile offenders who commit such crimes as rape or armed robbery are being sentenced to institutionalization for two, three, and four years. This approach is different from the indeterminate sentencing under which children who had committed a serious crime might be released from institutions in less than a year. Thus, the use of presumptive sentencing provisions or proportionality in sentencing has become a factor in juvenile justice dispositional procedures.

Most jurisdictions, however, continue to be preoccupied with rehabilitation as a primary dispositional goal. Joseph Goldstein, Anna Freud, and Albert Solnit, in their classic work *Beyond the Best Interests of the Child*, indicate that placements should be based on the "least detrimental alternative" philosophy in order to safeguard the children's growth and development.[70] This goal applies to children involved in both delinquent behavior and noncriminal behavior and to those who may be neglected, abandoned, or abused. In reality today, most states apply custodial restrictions or institutionalization only to children who commit the most serious offenses.

In sum, rehabilitation and treatment remain the most realistic dispositional goals. Proportionality in juvenile sentencing is being recognized and implemented by some jurisdictions. Whether the philosophy of "just desert" is the answer to juvenile criminality remains unclear. Some critics suggest that the bar association's standards would "destroy the nation's juvenile court system and replace it with a junior criminal justice system."[71] There is no question that fitting the penalty to the child's behavior would effect a radical change in current juvenile justice sentencing philosophy. And the practical consequences can be tremendous—witness the increase in the number of institutionalized youth after a number of years of decline. The movement to toughen juvenile sentencing, like its adult counterpart, has produced an increased correctional population.

Juvenile Probation

Probation is the most commonly used formal sentence for juvenile offenders, and many states require that a youth fail on probation before being sent to an insti-

ANALYZING CRIMINAL JUSTICE ISSUES

Death Row Children

In more than half of the thirty-six states that provide for capital punishment, children who commit murder and who have been transferred to the adult court can be given the death penalty. In fact, more than thirty youths reside on death row today; some youths have been executed (though they were executed when they were in their twenties, after they had spent many years on death row).

The U.S. Supreme Court has ruled on this highly emotional issue. Two previous attempts to decide the issue left the justices closely divided. Bare majorities of the Court reversed the death sentences of both Monty Lee Eddings and William Wayne Thompson, but the justices could not agree on the fundamental question of whether it is "cruel and unusual" punishment to exact the penalty of death for murders committed by juveniles.[1]

However, the Court reviewed this issue in *Wilkins v. Missouri* and *Stanford v. Kentucky* in 1989.[2] Wilkins was sixteen when he committed murder, and Stanford was seventeen. The constitutional question raised by these two cases was basically the same as the Court considered before: At what age does the Eighth Amendment ban the death penalty as punishment, no matter what the crime? Critics of the death penalty believe that there is a consensus against executing young people in the United States. Supporters of capital punishment argue that juveniles after age sixteen should be held fully responsible for murder. The Supreme Court concluded that states are free to impose the death penalty for murderers who committed their crimes while age sixteen or seventeen. According to the majority opinion written by Justice Antonin Scalia, society has not formed a consensus that such executions constitute a cruel and unusual punishment in violation of the Eighth Amendment.

Kenneth Gewerth and Clifford Dorne suggest that the primary test of constitutionality of subjecting juvenile offenders to capital punishment may be based on standards of contemporary society, rather than on the Eighth Amendment, as was the case in *Stanford* and *Wilkins.* In their recent legal analysis, the authors point out that in using sixteen as the age for purpose of execution, the Supreme Court seems to have no clear method for determining the extent of any national consensus on executing such juveniles. The authors also indicate that the Supreme Court has chosen to ignore the weight of international opposition to the juvenile death penalty. In addition, the conclusion exists that juveniles under sixteen are too immature to be held accountable for their actions. Finally, the *Stanford* and *Wilkins* cases leave uncertain how punishment should be judged. Sentences are ordinarily unconstitutional if the punishment serves no purpose and is excessive under the Eighth Amendment. The authors indicate, however, that the Eighth Amendment may require that any punishment, particularly capital punishment involving children, be acceptable to contemporary society.

Critical Thinking Skills

1. Does it appear from this analysis that the U.S. Supreme Court has ruled correctly on this highly controversial issue? Should an "enlightened" society resort to the use of the death penalty for juvenile murderers?

2. In adult capital punishment cases, judges and jurors are often presented with information involving the aggravating and mitigating circumstances of the crime. Should such issues as mental retardation or education be factored into the sentencing decision?

[1] *Eddings v. Oklahoma,* 455 U.S. 104, S.Ct., L.Ed.2d (1982) and *Thompson v. Oklahoma,* 487 U.S. 815, 108 S.Ct. 2687, L.Ed.2d (1988).

[2] *Stanford v. Kentucky* and *Wilkins v. Missouri,* 492 U.S. 361, 109 S.Ct. 2969 (1989).

SOURCES: "Capital Punishment, 1985," *BJS Bulletin* (November 1986); Bureau of Justice Statistics (Washington, D.C.: U.S. Government Printing Office, 1988), p. 99; also, Kenneth Gewerth and Clifford Dorne, "Imposing the Death Penalty on Juvenile Murderers: A Constitutional Assessment," *Judicature* 75 (1991): 6.

tution (unless the criminal act is quite serious). Probation involves placing the child under the supervision of the juvenile probation department for the purpose of community treatment. Conditions of probation are normally imposed on the child by either statute or court order. General conditions, such as those that require the child to stay away from other delinquents or to obey the law, are often vague, but they have been upheld by the courts. More specific conditions of probation include requiring the child to participate in a vocational training

program, to attend school regularly, to obtain treatment at a child guidance clinic, or to make restitution. Restitution can be in the form of community service—for example, a youth found in possession of marijuana might be required to work fifty hours in a home for the elderly. Monetary restitution requires delinquents to pay back the victims of their crimes. Restitution programs have proven quite successful and have been adopted around the country.[72]

In recent years, some jurisdictions have turned to a **balanced probation** approach in an effort to enhance the success of probation.[73] Probation systems that integrate community protection, the accountability of the juvenile offender, competency, and individualization incorporate the treatment values of this balanced approach. Some of these juvenile protection programs offer renewed promise for community treatment.

Once placed on probation, the child is ordinarily required to meet regularly with the probation officer for counseling and supervision and to adhere to the conditions of probation established by the court. This plan may continue for possibly six months to two years, depending on the duration of probation as established by the statutory law. Most states allow early release from probation if the child is making a good adjustment or an extension of the probationary period if he or she is not. If the child complies with the court order, probation is terminated. Proceedings to revoke probation occur if the child commits a new offense. Most states provide that the child be given notice, a hearing, the right to counsel, and other due process safeguards similar to those given adult offenders at such proceedings.

Institutionalization

Outside of the death penalty, the most severe of the statutory dispositions available to the juvenile court involves committing the child to an institution. The committed child may be sent to a state training school or private residential treatment facility. These are usually minimum-security facilities with small populations and an emphasis on treatment and education. Some states, however, maintain facilities with populations over one thousand.

Most state statutes vary when determining the length of the child's commitment. Traditionally, many jurisdictions would commit the child up to majority, which usually meant twenty-one years of age. This normally deprived the child of freedom for an extensive period of time—sometimes longer than an adult sentenced for the same offense would be confined. As a result, some states have passed legislation under which children are committed for periods ranging from one to three years.

Profile of Incarcerated Youth

At last count, approximately 56,123 youths were in public custody facilities, and 37,000 were in private facilities (see Figure 19.3).[74] Most of the recent increase in population is accounted for by the growth in the number of delinquents held in public facilities, from about forty-nine thousand in 1979 to about fifty-five thousand in 1987. This number has grown 5 percent over the past two years and 14 percent over the past four years. The number of status offenders in public facilities has remained stable since 1979, at about nine thousand.

According to a census of children in custody in 1989, of the more than fifty-six thousand juveniles held in public facilities, about 86 percent were male, and 82 percent were between fourteen and seventeen years of age.[75] Minority-group

FIGURE 19.3
Rate for Incarcerated Children, 1975 to 1991.

SOURCE: Bureau of Justice Statistics, *Children in Custody 1975–85* and *Fact Sheet 1987–1989* (Washington, D.C.: U.S. Department of Justice, 1991).

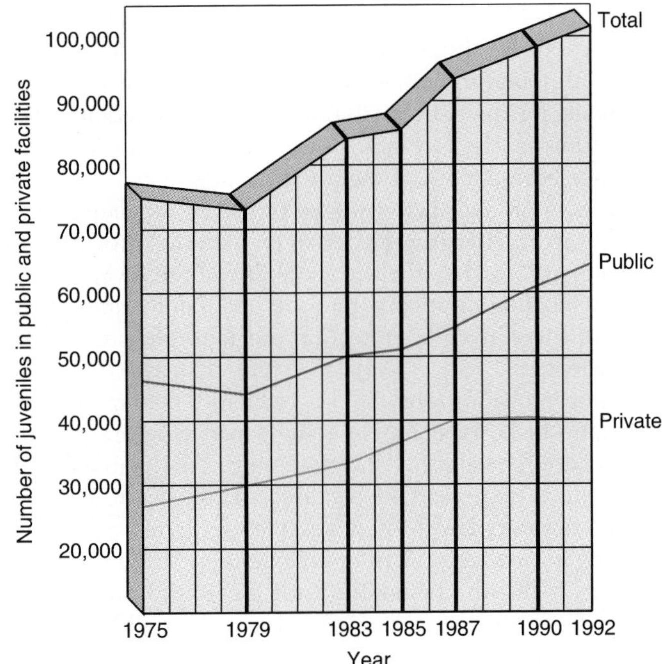

youths comprised more than half the juveniles in public facilities, and their number has risen in recent years. The number of white juveniles held in public facilities decreased slightly between 1985 and 1987, while the number of black and Hispanic juveniles increased 15 percent and 20 percent, respectively.[76]

The disproportionate number of minority youths incarcerated may mean that blacks, Hispanics, and other minorities are more likely to be arrested and charged with serious crimes than white youths.[77] However, some researchers, such as Barry Krisberg, question whether the seriousness of the offense alone can explain the differences in incarceration rates among racial groups.[78] With minority youths being incarcerated at a rate four times greater than their representation in the general population, it is appropriate to ask if we have a racist juvenile justice system.

Nine out of ten (94 percent) incarcerated juveniles were held for delinquent offenses—offenses that would be crimes if committed by adults. Twenty-five percent were held for person-oriented offenses, about 20 percent for alcohol, drug, and public order offenses, and over 40 percent for property crimes.[79] (See Figure 19.4.) Just over 5 percent were confined for a juvenile status offense, such as truancy, running away, or incorrigibility. The efforts made in the 1970s and 1980s to keep status offenders out of institutions seem to have paid off.

Over 43 percent of incarcerated juveniles have been arrested more than five times, and over 80 percent have been on probation previously. Over 97 percent of all incarcerated juveniles have committed prior violent offenses, and more than 80 percent have previously used illegal drugs.[80]

In summary, during the mid-1980s and early 1990s, despite the growth of incarceration alternatives, such as treatment, diversion, and restitution, the number of delinquents under secure supervision has increased. Like their adult counterparts, more juvenile offenders have been receiving incarceration sentences than before. In addition, nearly half of the juvenile offenders in custody were being held for violent crimes, and a very significant percentage (more than 60 percent)

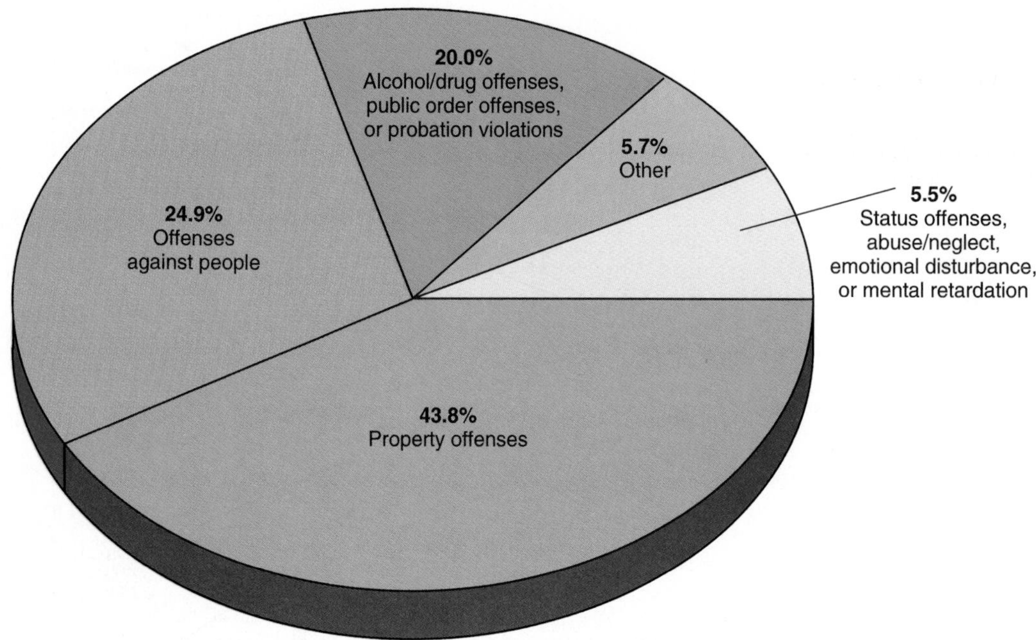

FIGURE 19.4
Types of Offenses and Other Reasons for Which Juvenile Offenders Were Held in Public Juvenile Facilities, 1987
SOURCE: Barbara Allen-Hagen, "Children in Custody," *Juvenile Justice Bulletin* (October 1988): 3.

used drugs regularly. Actually, the number of youths being held for drug-related and violent crimes has risen at a faster pace than that of the general juvenile correctional population. These percentages tend to explain why the juvenile justice system has become more formalized, restrictive, and punishment-oriented in recent years—in spite of stabilized arrest rates. (See Figure 19.5 for the various placement alternatives used for adjudicated youth.)

Deinstitutionalization

Some experts in delinquency and juvenile law question the policy of institutionalizing juvenile offenders. Many believe that large institutions are too costly to operate and only produce more sophisticated criminals. Michigan, for example, projects a need for two thousand more beds, at an annual cost of sixty thousand dollars per juvenile offender, in the next decade. This dilemma has produced a number of efforts to remove youth from juvenile facilities and replace large institutions with smaller community-based facilities. For example, led by its former corrections commissioner, Jerome Miller, a staunch opponent of incarcerating most youth, Massachusetts closed all its state training schools over a decade ago (subsequently, however, public pressure caused a few secure facilities to be reopened). Many other states have established small residential facilities operated by juvenile-care agencies to replace larger units.

Despite the daily rhetoric on crime, public support of community-based programs for juveniles still exists. Although such programs are not panaceas, a recent survey in California, for instance, found that a majority of those surveyed supported more treatment and less incarceration for juvenile offenders. Utah, Mary-

FIGURE 19.5
Placement Options for Adjudicated Youth

SOURCE: Robert Pierce, Criminal Justice Paper #4, National Conference of State Legislatures. "Juvenile Justice Reform: State Experiences," 1989.

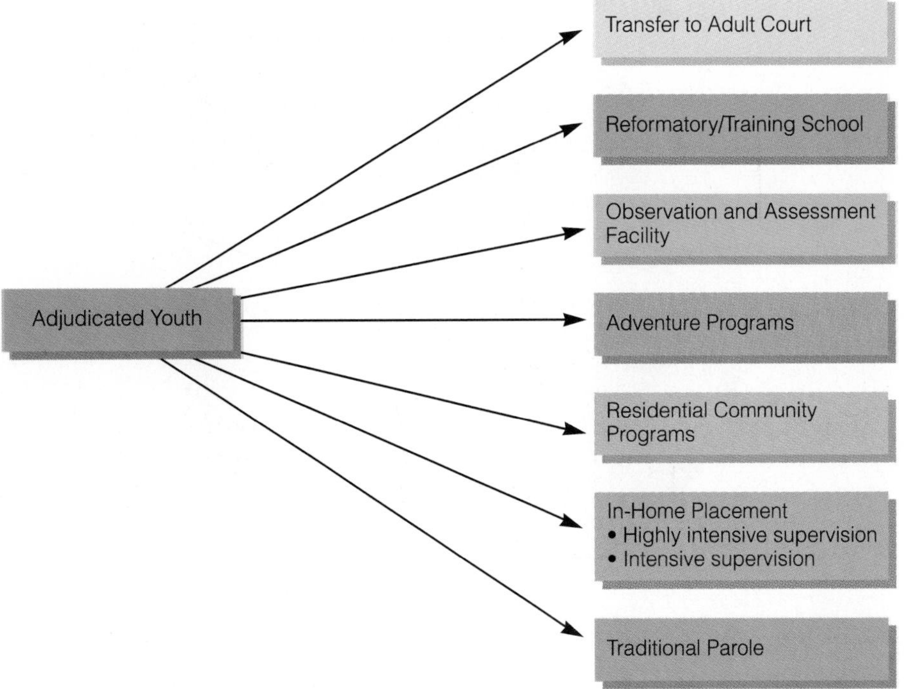

land, Vermont, and Pennsylvania, for example, have dramatically reduced their reform school populations while setting up a wide range of intensive treatment programs for juveniles. Many large, impersonal, and expensive state institutions with unqualified staff and ineffective treatment programs have been eliminated.

Susan Guarino-Ghezzi and Edward Loughran believe the "get-tough" response of the 1980s to juvenile offenders has waned. Their recent research suggests that the deinstitutionalization movement appears to be gaining momentum again.[81] Although a significant number of major jurisdictions still have large-scale institutional systems (New York, California, and Texas), many other states are shifting toward community programs. In addition to the states mentioned above, Ghezzi and Loughran point out in 1991 that New Hampshire has expanded its community placements, Delaware is implementing a community-based plan, North Dakota has created a new Youth Services Division, and a new round of reform is under way in Montana and Florida. Will community placement continue to expand into the 1990s? Is reducing the proportion of institutionalized youth the alternative society desires? The answer to these questions remains unclear.

What To Do with Status Offenders. It has been almost 25 years since the movement to deinstitutionalize status offenders (DSO) began.[82] Since its inception, the DSO approach has been hotly debated. Some have argued that early intervention is society's best hope of forestalling future delinquent behavior and reducing victimization. Others have argued that legal control over status offenders is a violation of youth's rights. Still others have viewed status-offending behavior as a symptom of some larger trauma or problem that requires attention. These diverse opinions still exist today.

Millions of federal, state, and local dollars have been spent on the DSO movement under the Juvenile Justice and Delinquency Prevention Act of 1974.

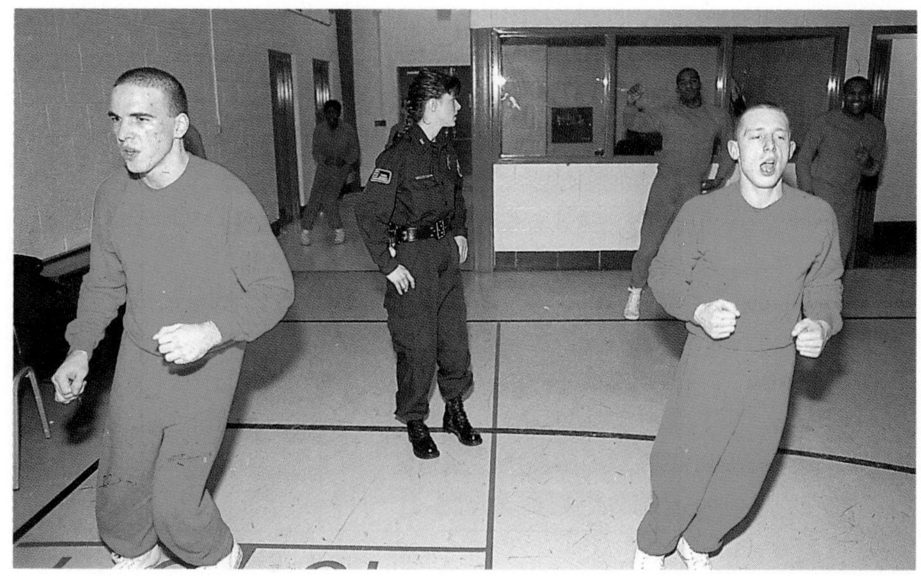

The number of youths being held in secure treatment facilities has grown despite an emphasis on community based corrections.

Vast numbers of programs have been created around the country to reduce the number of juveniles in secure confinement.

The twin concepts of "treatment" and "normalization" form the framework for the DSO approach. Since Congress passed the JJDP Act in 1974, fifty states have complied with some aspect of the deinstitutionalization mandate. What remains to be done, however, is to study the effect DSO has had on juveniles and the justice system. Previous research has focused on specific programs. Now DSO needs to be assessed as a reform movement of twenty-five years.

Treating the Chronic Offender

Chronic juvenile offenders are youths who are most likely to continue their law-violating behavior. One of the top priorities of recent years has been treating hard-core chronic delinquents while removing nonviolent and noncriminal youths from the juvenile correctional system.

Juvenile courts currently concentrate their resources on youths who have appeared in court five or six times and are truly chronic offenders. A recent study of court careers of juvenile offenders has shed new light on this issue, however.[83] The study's major finding—that youths who were referred to juvenile court for a second time before age sixteen were likely to continue their law-violating behavior—indicates that juveniles with two offenses may, in fact, be identified as chronic offenders (see Figure 19.6). This study argues that these juveniles should be treated the same as chronic offenders who have committed five or six offenses.

Thus, the study suggests that juvenile courts have the opportunity to intervene in the lives of a large number of youths at a time when problems first become apparent. In addition, the study implies that courts should not wait until the youth has returned for the fourth or fifth time before taking strong remedial action.[84]

Programs around the country have attempted to use swift prosecution, high-security incapacitation, and intensive treatment to reduce serious juvenile crime. One such program, the Habitual Serious and Violent Juvenile Offender Program, allowed prosecutors to target youths defined as chronic, serious, and violent of-

FIGURE 19.6

Court Cases of Juvenile Offenders

SOURCE: U.S. Department of Justice, Office of Juvenile Justice and Delinquency Prevention, *Juvenile Justice Bulletin* (August 1988): 3.

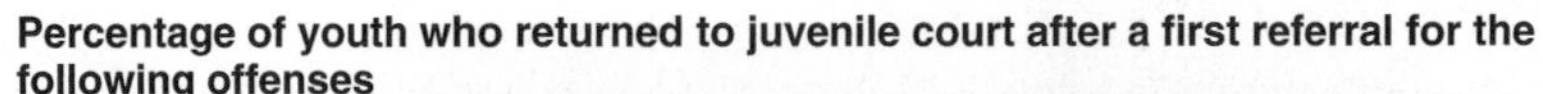

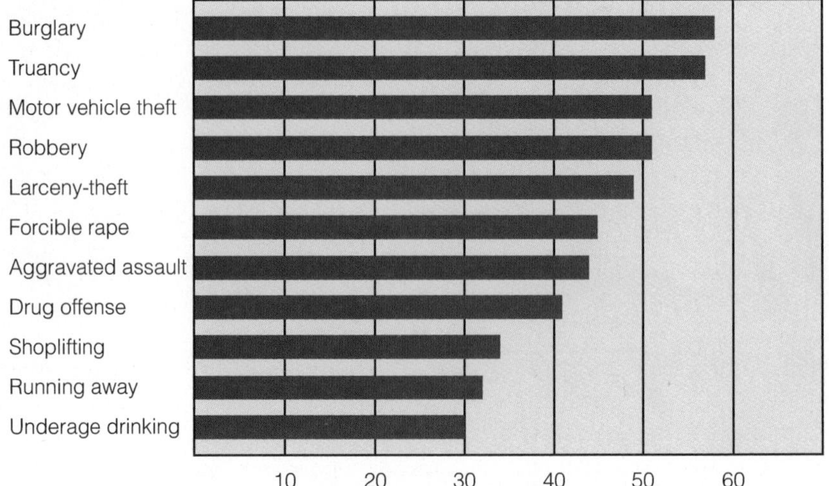

fenders.[85] Undertaken in thirteen locations nationwide from 1985 to 1987, the program resulted in speedier outcomes, more findings of guilt, more correctional commitments, and reduced plea-bargaining dispositions. The program thus revealed that special targeting and prosecution of serious and habitual juvenile offenders may prove successful.

Related to the problem of the chronic offender is the juvenile court's response to violent youth crime. Violent crime represents a relatively small though significant part of a juvenile court's total delinquency caseload. In a recent twelve-state sample, 6 percent of the youths referred to juvenile court for a criminal law violation were charged with a violent offense.[86] With such offenses as criminal homicides, violent sexual assaults, robberies, and aggravated assaults, the juvenile court detains larger numbers of youths before trial, has more adjudicatory hearings, initiates more transfer petitions to adult courts, and orders significantly more serious dispositions.

A greater percentage of young people are arrested for violent crimes today than thirty years ago and adolescents fifteen years old and younger are involved in more violent behavior than ever before. Much of the increase in youth violence has been linked to drug and gang activities, which are discussed later in this chapter.

Chronic and violent juvenile offenders represent a small proportion of the nation's juvenile population but commit a disproportionate amount of juvenile crime. Gun violence, for instance, is on the rise in many areas of the country. More dispositional alternatives aimed at this target population can only increase the effectiveness of the juvenile court system.

Postdisposition: The Right to Treatment

The postdisposition stage of the juvenile justice process normally involves aftercare and provisions for appeal of cases disposed of in the juvenile court. The question has been raised as to whether children committed to juvenile institutions have a constitutional or statutory right to treatment; advocates of this right claim that the state must provide treatment for the juvenile offender if it intends to exercise control over the offender.

A juvenile may be released from an institution to serve the rest of the sentence in aftercare, which usually involves parole. A juvenile parole officer provides the child with counseling, school referral, vocational training, and other services. Children who violate the conditions of parole may have their parole revoked and be returned to the institution. Unlike the adult postconviction process, where the U.S. Supreme Court has imposed procedural protections in probation and parole revocations, juveniles do not have such due process rights. State courts have also been reluctant to grant juvenile rights in this area, and those that have generally refuse to require the whole array of rights available to adult offenders. Since the *Gault* decision, however, many states have adopted administrative regulations requiring juvenile agencies to incorporate due process, such as proper notice of the hearing and the right to counsel in postconviction proceedings.

Finally, there is the question of whether juveniles who are committed to institutions have a right to treatment. Because the system of dealing with juvenile offenders is similar to the system of commitment for the mentally ill in that both are based on the *parens patriae* philosophy, juveniles have sought a right to treatment. In light of this similarity, the case of *Martarella v. Kelly* (1972) established that when juveniles judged to be "persons in need of supervision" are not furnished with adequate treatment, the failure to provide such treatment violates the Eighth and Fourteenth Amendments.[87] In ***Inmates v. Affleck*** (1972), the federal court recognized the right to treatment on statutory grounds and also required that minimum standards of treatment be implemented for juvenile offenders under institutional care.[88] The *Inmates v. Affleck* case illustrated the horrible conditions that exist in many juvenile institutions. Consider the following excerpt from the appellate court record in this case:

> Located on the floor above Annex C is a series of small, dimly lit, steel barred cells used for solitary confinement. Each cell is approximately eight feet by four feet, containing a metal slab bed and mattress, sink, and toilet. Boys confined there are released only to take showers, about twice a week. They get no exercise. The inmate's attorney, but not his family, is allowed to visit him there. Because windows on the wall opposite the cellblock are broken, the cells are cold. There is a small hole in the bars, through which meals, sometimes cold, are passed.[89]

Similar to *Affleck* was ***Morales v. Turman*** (1973), where the federal court specifically found that juveniles at a training school in Texas have a statutory right to treatment.[90] In accordance with these holdings, the Seventh U.S. Circuit Court of Appeals in ***Nelson v. Heyne*** (1974) upheld a constitutional right to treatment for institutionalized juveniles under the Fourteenth Amendment.[91] Supporting this position, the court said:

> Because children differ in their need for rehabilitation, individual need for treatment will differ. When a state assumes the place of a juvenile's parents, it assumes as well the parental duties, and its treatment of its juveniles should, so far as can be reasonably required, be what proper parental care would provide. . . . Without a program of individual treatment, the result may be that the juvenile "will not be rehabilitated, but warehoused. . . ."[92]

The *Nelson* case is significant because it was the first federal appellate court decision to affirm a constitutional right to treatment. Although the U.S. Supreme Court has not yet declared that juveniles do have such a right, these early decisions seem to indicate that juveniles do have a right, be it statutory or constitutional, to receive treatment and to be assured of a minimum standard of physical care if committed to an institution.

In recent years, however, progress in the movement for a legal right to treatment seems to have been curtailed. For example, in ***Ralston v. Robinson*** (1981), the Supreme Court held that a judge may modify the essential terms of treatment if he or she finds that such treatment was not consistent with the defendant's behavior.[93] Robinson, a seventeen-year-old who had pleaded guilty to a second-degree murder, was sentenced to ten years' imprisonment under the federal Youth Corrections Act (YCA). Subsequently, while incarcerated, he was found guilty of assaulting a federal officer, and the U.S. District Court, finding that he would not benefit from treatment under the YCA, imposed an adult sentence to be served consecutively with the YCA sentence. Strongly endorsing the judge's discretionary power, the Supreme Court concluded that a trial court may convert a rehabilitative disposition into a more severe punitive sentence when it becomes apparent that the initial treatment decision will not help the offender.

In 1987, the federal courts considered a class action case dealing with minimum standards of care for adolescents in the McClaren School for Boys in Oregon (*Gary H. v. Hegstrom*).[94] A federal appellate court ordered due process hearings prior to confinement in excess of twenty-four hours and minimum sanitary, health, educational, and medical resources for inmates, but it found that the wholesale adoption of various professional association concepts for model institutions was not constitutionally mandated. The court also held that it is not proper to order dispositions that are so expensive that other children may be deprived of services.

The future of the right to treatment for juveniles remains uncertain. Minimum standards of care and treatment have been mandated on a case-by-case basis, but some courts have limited the constitutional protections regarding the right to treatment. In light of the current hard-line approach to juvenile crime, the courts probably will not be persuaded to expand this constitutional theory further.

The termination of aftercare marks the final stage of the formal juvenile justice process.

Future Directions in Juvenile Justice

What does the future hold for the juvenile justice system? The following figures indicate the magnitude of the problem. Over 1.5 million youths under eighteen are arrested each year; juvenile courts order over 1.3 million delinquency dispositions and hear almost 1 million status offense cases and four hundred thousand child abuse cases; drug abuse is a significant factor in from 60 to 90 percent of all cases referred to juvenile courts; and alcohol is the major substance abuse of youth throughout the country.[95]

These statistics present a disturbing picture of U.S. youths who are not participating in traditional family, education, and community activities. Instead, many children are involved in disruptive behavior. Unfortunately, over the years, few effective prevention and rehabilitation programs have been available for juvenile offenders.

In the 1980s, the juvenile justice system was torn between two concerns: one is the noncriminal youths who can be salvaged during the early stages of their delinquent careers and status offenders who may be in court to cover up the sexual and physical abuse inflicted on them by their parents, and the other is hard-core delinquents who are a threat to society and to themselves.

After many years in which attention was directed at such liberal reforms as removing status offenders from detention facilities and from institutions that housed delinquents, U.S. society is now experiencing a period when the number of juveniles under lock and key is rising (although the number who are being arrested is declining). The supremacy of the crime-control perspective is affecting the juvenile justice system. Yet considering the fact that so many adult offenders have juvenile records, there is little to indicate that incarcerating youthful offenders is an answer to their criminal behavior.

The time is ripe for an attack on these problems. For years, the juvenile justice system has operated with ambiguous goals and limited resources. One suggestion is that we should develop a national commitment to children. Such a policy would seek to deter children from antisocial behavior early in their lives. Creating stronger family units, establishing better schools, and improving living conditions are all examples of sound delinquency prevention policies. Another recommendation is that the federal government should continue to focus on the problem of the serious, violent, and chronic offender, as it has done since 1986. This requires (1) prosecuting serious juvenile offenders more effectively; (2) preventing the victimization of children; and (3) maintaining the concept of responsibility in the juvenile justice system. Third, state and local jurisdictions need to see that juvenile justice agencies are well organized and efficiently managed. This involves ensuring (1) that all children processed through the juvenile justice system are treated fairly and in accordance with due process of law; (2) that programs based on empirical data are developed to control chronic offenders; and (3) that diversion and the removal of status offenders from juvenile court jurisdiction are given further consideration.

Today, no single ideology dominates the juvenile justice system. As the liberal program of the 1970s has faltered, more restrictive sanctions have been imposed. Both the old and the new juvenile justice agendas will probably dominate the 1990s. However, as Supreme Court Justice Harry A. Blackmun stated in *McKeiver v. Pennsylvania:*

> The juvenile concept held high promise. We are reluctant to say that, despite disappointment of so grave dimensions, it still does not hold promise, and we are particularly reluctant to say, as to the Pennsylvania petitions here, that the system cannot accomplish its rehabilitative goals. So much depends on the availability of resources, on the interest and commitment of the public, on willingness to learn, and on understanding as to cause and effect and cure. In this field, as in so many others, one perhaps learns best by doing.[96]

SUMMARY

The juvenile justice system is concerned with delinquent children, as well as with those who are beyond the care and protection of their parents. Juveniles involved in antisocial behavior come under the jurisdiction of juvenile or family court systems. These courts belong to a system of juvenile-justice agencies, including law enforcement, child care, and institutional services.

When a child is brought to the juvenile court, the proceedings are generally nonadversarial and informal. Representatives from different disciplines, such as lawyers, social workers, and psychiatrists, all play major roles in the judicial process.

In recent years, the juvenile court system has become more legalistic by virtue of the U.S. Supreme Court decisions that have granted children procedural safeguards. However, neither rehabilitation programs nor the application of due process rights has stemmed the growing tide of juvenile antisocial behavior. Perhaps the answer lies outside the courthouse, in the form of job opportunities for juveniles, improved family relationships, and more effective school systems. How to cope with the needs of children in trouble remains one of the most controversial and frustrating issues in the justice system.

QUESTIONS

1. Should status offenders be treated by the juvenile court? Should they be placed in confinement for running away or cutting school?
2. Should a juvenile ever be waived to adult court at the risk that the child will be incarcerated with adult felons?
3. Do you support the death penalty for children?
4. Should juveniles be given mandatory incarceration sentences for serious crimes, as adults are?
5. Is it fair to deny juveniles a jury trial?
6. Do you think the trend toward treating juveniles like adult offenders is desirable?
7. What programs should communities develop to prevent juvenile drug abuse?

NOTES

1. Ralph Weisheit and Diane Alexander, "Juvenile Justice Philosophy and Demise of *Parens Patriae,*" *Federal Probation* (December 1988):56.

2. Material in this section depends heavily on Sanford J. Fox, "Juvenile Justice Reform: A Historical Perspective," *Stanford Law Review* 22 (1970):1187–1205; Lawrence Stone, *The Family, Sex, and Marriage in England: 1500–1800* (New York: Harper & Row, 1977); Philipe Aries, *Century of Childhood: A Social History of Family Life* (New York: Vintage Press, 1962); Douglas R. Rendleman, "*Parens Patriae:* From Chancer to the Juvenile Court," *South Carolina Law Review* 23 (1971): 205–29; Wiley B. Sanders, *Some Early Beginnings of the Children's Court Movement in England,* National Probation Association Yearbook (New York: National Council on Crime and Delinquency, 1945); Anthony Platt, "The Rise of the Child Saving Movement: A Study in Social Policy and Correctional Reform," *Annals of the American Academy of Political and Social Science* 381 (1979):21–38; Anthony M. Platt, *The Child Savers: The Intervention of Delinquency* (Chicago: University of Chicago Press, 1969); Robert S. Pickett, *House of Refuge: Origins of Juvenile Reform in New York State, 1815–1857* (Syracuse, N.Y.: Syracuse University Press, 1969).

3. Douglas Besharov, *Juvenile Justice Advocacy: Practice in a Unique Court* (New York: Practicing Law Institute, 1974), p. 2.

4. 4 Eng. Rep. 1078 (1827).

5. Rendleman, "*Parens Patriae,*" p. 209.

6. Platt, *The Child Savers,* pp. 11–38.

7. Fox, "Juvenile Justice Reform," p. 1188.

8. Pickett, *House of Refuge.*

9. Robert Mennel, *Thorns and Thistles* (Hanover, N.H.: University Press of New England, 1973).

10. See U.S. Department of Justice, Juvenile Justice and Delinquency Prevention, *Two Hundred Years of American Criminal Justice: An LEAA Bicentennial Study* (Washington, D.C.: Law Enforcement Assistance Administration, 1976).

11. Ibid., pp. 62–74.

12. Platt, *The Child Savers,* p. 116.

13. LaMar T. Empey, *American Delinquency: Its Meaning and Construction* (Homewood, Ill.: Dorsey Press, 1978), p. 515.

14. *Kent v. United States,* 383 U.S. 541, 86 S.Ct. 1045, 16 L.Ed.2d 84 (1966): juveniles are entitled to minimum procedural safeguards in the waiver proceeding. *In re Gault,* 387 U.S. 1, 87 S.Ct. 1428, 18 L.Ed.2d 527 (1967): juveniles have the right to notice, counsel, confrontation, cross-examination, and the privilege against self-incrimination in juvenile court proceedings. *In re Winship,* 397 U.S. 358, 90 S.Ct. 1068, 25 L.Ed.2d 368 (1970): proof beyond a reasonable doubt is necessary for conviction in juvenile proceedings. *Breed v. Jones,* 421 U.S. 519, 95 S.Ct. 1779, 44 L.Ed.2d 346 (1975): jeopardy attaches in a juvenile court adjudicatory hearing, thus barring subsequent prosecution for the same offense as an adult.

15. Public Law 93-415.

16. Ibid.

17. For a comprehensive view of juvenile law, see, generally, Joseph J. Senna and Larry J. Siegel, *Juvenile Law: Cases and Comments* (St. Paul: West Publishing, 1976).

18. *Lamb v. Brown,* 456 F.2d 18 (10th Cir. 1972): states cannot distinguish between males and females with respect to juvenile court age limits.

19. The effort to remove status offenders was pioneered by the nonprofit National Council on Crime and Delinquency.

20. See, for example, *District of Columbia v. B.J.R.,* 332 A.2d 58 (D.C. App. 1975).

21. Federal Bureau of Investigation, *Crime in the United States, 1988* (Washington, D.C.: U.S. Government Printing Office, 1989), p. 188.

22. *In re Gault,* 387 U.S. 1, 87 S.Ct. 1428, 18 L.Ed.2d 527 (1967).

23. See Dennis Sullivan and Larry Siegel, "How Police Use Information to Make Decisions," *Crime and Delinquency* 23 (1972):253–62 for a discussion of the factors involved in police decision making.

24. See, generally, Donald Black and Albert Reis, "Police Control of Juveniles," *American Sociological Review* 35 (1960):63.

25. 469 U.S. 325, 105 S.Ct. 733, 83 L.Ed.2d 720 (1985).

26. See D. A. Walls, "*New Jersey v. T.L.O.*: The Fourth Amendment Applied to School Searches," *Oklahoma University Law Review* 11 (1986):225–41.

27. K. A. Bucker, "School Drug Tests: A Fourth Amendment Perspective," *University of Illinois Law Review* 5 (1987):275.

28. See J. Hogan and M. Schwartz, "Search and Seizure in the Public Schools," *Case and Comment* 90 (1985):28–32; see also M. Meyers, "T.L.O. *v. New Jersey*—Officially Conducted School Searches and a New Balancing Test," *Juvenile Family Journal* 37 (1986):27–37.

29. For an interesting article suggesting that school officials should not be permitted to search students without suspicion that each student searched has violated the drug or weapons law, see J. Braverman, "Public School Drug Searches," *Fordham Urban Law Journal* 14 (1986):629–84.

30. C. Avery and R. D. Simpson, "Search and Seizure: A Risk Assessment Model for Public School Officials," *Journal of Law and Education* 16 (1987):403–34.

31. 384 U.S. 436, 86 S.Ct. 1602, 16 L.Ed.2d 694 (1966). *Miranda* held that accused individuals in police custody must be given the following warning: (1) that they have a right to remain silent; (2) that any statements made can be used against them; (3) that they have a right to counsel; and (4) that if they cannot afford counsel, one will be furnished at public expense.

32. 442 U.S. 707, 99 S.Ct. 2560, 61 L.Ed.2d 197 (1979); 453 U.S. 355, 101 S.Ct. 2806, 69 L.Ed.2d 696 (1981).

33. Larry Holtz, "*Miranda* in a Juvenile Setting: A Child's Right to Silence," *Journal of Criminal Law and Criminology* 78 (1987):552.

34. American Bar Association, *Standards Relating to Juvenile Probation Function* (Cambridge, Mass.: Ballinger Press, 1977), p. 23.

35. See, generally, National Council on Crime and Delinquency, *Standard Family Court Act* (New York: National Council on Crime and Delinquency, 1965); National Conference of Commissioners on Uniform State Laws, *Uniform Juvenile Court Act* (Philadelphia: American Law Institute, 1968), sec. 9; William Sheridan, *Model Acts for Family Courts* (Washington, D.C.: U.S. Department of Health, Education, and Welfare, 1975), sec. 13.

36. Joyce Dougherty, "A Comparison of Adult Plea Bargaining and Juvenile Intake," *Federal Probation* (June 1988):72–79.

37. *Schall v. Martin*, 467 U.S. 253, 104 S.Ct. 2403, 81 L.Ed.2d 207 (1984).

38. Solomon Kobrin and Malcolm Klein, *National Evaluation of the Deinstitutionalization of Status Offenders Programs, Executive Summary* (Washington, D.C.: U.S. Government Printing Office, 1982).

39. See Juvenile Delinquency and Prevention Act of 1974, 42 U.S.C. § 5633.

40. Phyllis Jo Baunach and Melissa Sickmund, *Jail Inmates, 1984* (Washington, D.C.: Bureau of Justice Statistics, 1986).

41. Office of Juvenile Justice and Delinquency Prevention, News Release, 4 January 1981.

42. "$3.8 Million Awarded to Remove Juveniles from Adult Jails, Lockups," *Justice Assistance News* 3 (May 1982):5.

43. Ira Schwartz, Linda Harris, and Laurie Levi, "The Jailing of Juveniles in Minnesota," *Crime and Delinquency* 34 (1988):131.

44. See, generally, Ira Schwartz, ed., "Children in Jails," *Crime and Delinquency* 34 (1988):131–228.

45. See Schwartz, Harris, and Levi, "The Jailing of Juveniles in Minnesota," p. 134.

46. David Steinhart, "California Legislation Ends Jailing of Children—The Story of a Policy Reversal," *Crime and Delinquency* 34 (1988):150.

47. See Henry Swanger, "*Hendrickson v. Griggs*—A Review of Legal and Policy Implications for Juvenile Justice Policymakers," *Crime and Delinquency* 34 (1988):209.

48. See Chapter 9.

49. See Bureau of Justice Statistics, *Report to the Nation on Crime and Justice* (Washington, D.C.: U.S. Government Printing Office, 1988), p. 79.

50. 383 U.S. 541, 86 S.Ct. 1045, 16 L.Ed.2d 84 (1966).

51. Ibid., at 554–555, 86 S.Ct. at 1053–1054.

52. 421 U.S. 519, 528, 95 S.Ct. 1779, 1785, 44 L.Ed.2d 346 (1975).

53. Donna Hamparian et al., *Major Issues in Juvenile Justice Information and Training, Youth in Adult Courts: Between Two Worlds* (Rockville, Md.: National Criminal Justice Reference Service, 1982; see also Paul Marcotte, "Criminal Kids," *American Bar Association Jounral* 76 (1990):60–66.

54. Bureau of Justice Statistics, *Report to the Nation on Crime and Justice*, p. 79.

55. Barry Feld, "Delinquent Careers and Criminal Policy," *Criminology* 21 (1983):195–212.

56. Barry Feld, "The Juvenile Court Meets the Principle of the Offense: Legislative Changes in Juvenile Waiver Statutes," *Journal of Criminal Law and Criminology* 78 (1987):471–533. See also John Kramer, Henry Sontheimer, and John Lemmon, "Pennsylvania Waiver to Adult Court" (Paper presented at the annual meeting of the American Society of Criminology, San Francisco, November 1991): authors confirm that juveniles tried in adult courts are generally male, age seventeen or older, and disproportionally minorities.

57. Richard Allinson and Joan Potter, "Is New York's Tough Juvenile Law a 'Charade'?" *Corrections* 9 (February 1983): 40–45.

58. Peter Greenwood, *Juvenile Offenders* (Washington, D.C.: National Institute of Justice, 1986), p. 3.

59. Howard Snyder, Terrence A. Finnegan, Ellen Nimick, Melissa Sickmund, Dennis Sullivan, and Nancy Tierney, *Juvenile Court Statistics, 1984* (Pittsburgh: National Center of Juvenile Justice, 1987).

60. 387 U.S. 1, 87 S.Ct. 1428, 18 L.Ed.2d 527 (1967).

61. Ibid., at 20, 87 S.Ct. at 1439.

62. 397 U.S. 358, 90 S.Ct. 1068, 25 L.Ed.2d 368 (1970).

63. 403 U.S. 528, 91 S.Ct. 1976, 29 L.Ed.2d 647 (1971).

64. See the earlier discussion of New York's Omnibus Crime Act; see also S. Singer and C. Ewing, "Juvenile Justice Reform in New York State—The Juvenile Offender Law," *Law and Policy* 8 (1986):463.

65. "Justice, Treating Kids Like Adults," *Newsweek*, 27 June 1979, p. 54; see also B. Benda and D. Waite, "Proposed Determinate Sentencing Model in Virginia," *Juvenile and Family Court Journal* 39 (1988):55.

66. Victor Streib, *Death Penalty for Juveniles* (Bloomington: Indiana University Press, 1987); see also Paul Reidinger, "The Death Row Kids," *American Bar Association Journal* 70 (April 1989): 78; also Note, "The Death Penalty and 8th Amendment, An Analysis of *Stanford v. Kentucky*," *Yale Law Review* 35 (1990):641.

67. Stanley Fisher, "The Dispositional Process under the Juvenile Justice Standards Project," *Boston University Law Review* 57 (1977):732.

68. National Advisory Commission on Criminal Justice Standards and Goals, *Task Force Report on Juvenile Justice and Delinquency Prevention* (Washington, D.C.: Law Enforcement Assistance Administration, 1976), pp. 452–59.

69. See Michael Serrill, "Police Write a New Law on Juvenile Crime," *Police Magazine* (September 1979): 47; see also A. Schneider and D. Schram, *Assessment of Juvenile Justice Reform in Washington State*, vols. 1–4 (Washington, D.C.: U.S. Department of Justice, Institute of Policy Analysis, 1983); T. Castellano, "Justice Model in the Juvenile Justice System—Washington State's Experience," *Law and Policy* 8 (1986):479.

70. See Joseph Goldstein, Anna Freud, and Albert Solnit, *Beyond the Best Interest of the Child* (New York: Free Press, 1973).

71. Fisher, "The Dispositional Process," p. 732; also Martin Forst and Martha-Elin Blomquist, "Punishment, Accountability and The New Juvenile Justice," *Juvenile and Family Court* 43 (1992):1.

72. Anne Schneider, *Guide to Juvenile Restitution* (Washington, D.C.: U.S. Department of Justice, 1985).

73. Dennis Mahoney, Dennis Romig, and Troy Armstrong, "Juvenile Probation: The Balanced Approach," *Juvenile and Family Court Journal* 39 (1988): 26; see also Ted Pallmer and Robert Wedge, "California's Juvenile Probation Camps—Findings and Implications," *Crime and Delinquency* 35 (1989): 234; also National Council on Crime and Delinquency, *Juvenile Intensive Probation Programs: The State of the Art* (San Francisco: National Council on Crime and Delinquency, 1991).

74. Barbara Allen-Hagen, *Children in Custody, 1989* (Washington, D.C.: Bureau of Justice Statistics, 1991).

75. Office of Juvenile Justice and Delinquency Prevention, *Children in Custody, 1989* (Washington, D.C.: U.S. Government Printing Office, 1991).

76. Ibid.

77. See Barry Krisberg, ed., "Minority Youth Incarceration and Crime," *Crime and Delinquency*, Special Issue 33 (1987).

78. See Barry Krisberg, Ira Schwartz, Gideon Fishman, Zvi Eisikovits, and Edna Guttman, *The Incarceration of Minority Youth* (Minneapolis: University of Minnesota, 1986).

79. See *Children in Custody—Public Juvenile Facilities, Juvenile Justice Bul-*

letin (Washington, D.C.: U.S. Department of Justice, 1988), p. 3.

80. Bureau of Justice Statistics, *Survey of Youth in Custody, 1987* (Washington, D.C.: U.S. Department of Justice, 1988).

81. I. Bakal, *Closing Correctional Institutions: New Strategies for Youth Services* (Lexington, Mass.: Lexington Books, 1973); see also Daniel Curran, "Destructuring, Prevailization, the Promise of Juvenile Diversion: Compromising Community-Based Corrections," *Crime and Delinquency* 34 (1988):363; see also Susan Guarino-Ghezzi and Edward Loughran, "Deinstitutionalization in Juvenile Justice—Recent Trends" (Paper presented at the annual meeting of the American Society of Criminology, San Francisco, November 1991).

82. Office of Juvenile Justice and Delinquency Prevention, *Assessing the Effects of DSO* (Washington, D.C.: U.S. Department of Justice, 1989).

83. Howard Snyder, *Court Careers of Juvenile Offenders* (Washington, D.C.: U.S. Department of Justice, Office of Juvenile Justice and Delinquency Prevention, March 1988).

84. Office of Juvenile Justice and Delinquency Prevention, "Study Sheds New Light on Court Careers of Juvenile Offenders," *Juvenile Justice Bulletin* (August 1988); also Grant Grissom, "Dispositional Authority and Future of the Juvenile Justice System," *Juvenile and Family Court Journal* 42 (1991):25.

85. American Institute for Research, *Evaluation of the Habitual Serious and Violent Juvenile Offender Program* (Washington, D.C.: U.S. Department of Justice, Office of Juvenile Justice and Delinquency Prevention, January 1988); see also U.S. Department of Justice, Office of Juvenile Justice and Delinquency Prevention, "Targeting Serious Juvenile Offenders Can Make a Difference," *Juvenile Justice Bulletin* (December 1988).

86. Office of Juvenile Justice and Delinquency Prevention, "Juvenile Courts Respond to Violent Crime," *Juvenile Justice Bulletin* (January 1989); also Larry Siegel, *Criminal Justice Update* (West Publishing, 1991), p. 5; "Kids and Guns," 9 March 1992.

87. 349 F.Supp. 575 (S.D.N.Y. 1972).

88. 346 F.Supp. 1354 (D.R.I. 1972).

89. Ibid., at 1361.

90. 364 F.Supp. 166 (E.D. Tex. 1973).

91. 491 F.2d 352 (7th Cir. 1974).

92. Ibid., at 360.

93. 454 U.S. 201, 102 S.Ct. 233, 70 L.Ed.2d 345 (1981).

94. 831 F.2d 1430 (9th Cir. 1987).

95. National Council on Juvenile Court Judges, *Metropolitan Court Judges Committee Report*, p. 1.

96. 403 U.S. 528, 547, 91 S.Ct. 1976, 1987, 29 L.Ed. 647 (1971); see also Seymour Gelber, "Juvenile Justice System: Vision for the Future," *Juvenile and Family Court Journal* 41 (1990):15.

GLOSSARY

Absolute deterrent a legal control measure designed to totally eliminate a particular criminal act.

Academy of Criminal Justice Sciences the society that serves to further the development of the criminal justice profession and whose membership includes academics and practitioners involved in criminal justice.

Access control a crime prevention technique that stresses target hardening through security measures, such as alarm systems, that make it more difficult for criminals to attack a target.

Accountability system a way of dealing with police corruption by making superiors responsible for the behavior of their subordinates.

Actus reus an illegal act. The *actus reus* can be an affirmative act, such as taking money or shooting someone, or a failure to act, such as failing to take proper precautions while driving a car.

Adjudication the determination of guilt or innocence; a judgment concerning criminal charges. The majority of offenders charged plead guilty; of the remainder, some cases are adjudicated by a judge and a jury, some by a judge without a jury, and others are dismissed.

Adversary system the procedure used to determine truth in the adjudication of guilt or innocence in which the defense (advocate for the accused) is pitted against the prosecution (advocate for the state), with the judge acting as arbiter of the legal rules. Under the adversary system, the burden is on the state to prove the charges beyond a reasonable doubt. This system of having the two parties publicly debate has proved to be the most effective method of achieving the truth regarding a set of circumstances. (Under the accusatory, or inquisitorial, system, which is used in continental Europe, the charge is evidence of guilt that the accused must disprove; the judge takes an active part in the proceedings.)

Aging out the process in which the crime rate declines with the perpetrators' age.

Aggressive preventive patrol a patrol technique designed to suppress crime before it occurs.

Alien conspiracy theory the view that organized crime was imported by Europeans and that crime cartels restrict their membership to people of their own ethnic background.

Alternative sanctions the group of punishments falling between probation and prison; "probation plus." Community-based sanctions, including house arrest and intensive supervision, serve as an alternative to incarceration.

American Society of Criminology the professional society of criminology which is devoted to enhancing the status of the discipline.

Anger rape a rape incident motivated by the rapist's desire to release pent-up anger and rage.

Anomie a condition produced by normlessness. Because of rapidly shifting moral values, a person has few guides to what is socially acceptable behavior.

Appeal a review of lower-court proceedings by a higher court. There is no constitutional right to appeal. However, the right to appeal is established by statute in some states and by custom in others. All states set conditions as to the type of case or grounds for appeal, which appellate courts may review. Appellate courts do not retry the case under review. Rather, the transcript of the lower-court case is read by the judges, and the lawyers for the defendant and for the state argue about the merits of the appeal—that is, the legality of lower-court proceedings, rather than the original testimony. Appeal is more a process for controlling police, court, and correctional practices than for rescuing innocent defendants. When appellate courts do reverse lower-court judgments, it is usually because of "prejudicial error" (deprivation of rights), and the case is remanded for retrial.

Appellate courts courts that reconsider a case that has already been tried in order to determine whether the measures used complied with accepted rules of criminal procedure and were in line with constitutional doctrines.

Arbitrage the practice of buying large blocks of stock in companies that are believed to be the target of corporate buyouts or takeovers.

Argot the unique language that influences the prison culture.

Arraignment the step at which the accused are read the charges against them and are asked how they plead. In addition, the accused are advised of their rights. Possible pleas are guilty, not guilty, *nolo contendere*, and not guilty by reason of insanity.

Arrest the taking of a person into the custody of the law, the legal purpose of which is to restrain the accused until he or she can be held accountable for the offense at court proceedings. The legal requirement for an arrest is probable cause. Arrests for investigation, suspicion, or harassment are improper and of doubtful legality. The police have the responsibility to use only the reasonable physical force necessary to make an arrest. The summons has been used as a substitute for arrest.

Aryan Brotherhood a white supremacist prison gang.

Assembly-line justice the view that the justice process resembles an endless production line that handles most cases in a routine and perfunctory fashion.

Atavistic traits according to Lombroso, the physical characteristics that distinguish born criminals from the general population and are throwbacks to animals or primitive people.

Attainder the loss of all civil rights due to a conviction for a felony offense.

Attorney general the senior U.S. prosecutor and cabinet member who heads the Justice Department.

Auburn system the prison system developed in New York during the nineteenth century that stressed congregate working conditions.

Augustus, John the individual credited with pioneering the concept of probation.

Authoritarian a person whose personality revolves around blind obedience to authority.

Bail the monetary amount for or condition of pretrial release, normally set by a judge at the initial appearance. The purpose of bail is to ensure the return of the accused at subsequent proceedings. If the accused is unable to make bail, he or she is detained in jail. The Eighth Amendment provides that excessive bail shall not be required.

Bail bonding the business of providing bail to needy offenders, usually at an exorbitant rate of interest.

Bail Reform Act of 1984 Federal legislation that provides for both greater emphasis on release on recognizance for nondangerous offenders and preventive detention for those who present a menace to the community.

Base penalty the modal sentence in a structured sentencing state, which can be enhanced or diminished to reflect aggravating or mitigating circumstances.

Beccaria, Cesare an eighteenth-century Italian philosopher who argued that crime could be controlled by punishments only severe enough to counterbalance the pleasure obtained from them.

Behaviorism the branch of psychology concerned with the study of observable behavior, rather than unconscious motives. It focuses on the relationship between the particular stimuli and people's responses to them.

Bill of indictment a document submitted to a grand jury by the prosecutor asking it to take action and indict a suspect.

Bill of Rights the first ten amendments to the U.S. Constitution.

Blameworthiness the amount of culpability or guilt a person maintains for participating in a particular criminal offense.

Blue curtain according to William Westly, the secretive, insulated police culture that isolates the officer from the rest of society.

Booking the administrative record of an arrest listing the offender's name, address, physical description, date of birth, and employer, the time of arrest, offense, and name of arresting officer. Photographing and fingerprinting of the offender are also part of booking.

Boot camp a short-term militaristic correctional facility in which inmates undergo intensive physical conditioning and discipline.

Bot under Anglo-Saxon law, the restitution paid for killing someone in an open fight.

Bourgeoisie in Marxist theory, the owners of the means of production; the capitalist ruling class.

Broken windows the term used to describe the role of the police as maintainers of community order and safety.

Brutalization effect the belief that capital punishment creates an atmosphere of brutality that enhances, rather than deters, the level of violence in society. The death penalty reinforces the view that violence is an appropriate response to provocations.

Burglary breaking into and entering a home or structure for the purposes of committing a felony.

Capital punishment the use of the death penalty to punish transgressors.

Career criminal a person who repeatedly violates the law and organizes his or her life-style around criminality.

Carriers case a fifteenth-century case that defined the law of theft and reformulated the concept of taking the possessions of another.

Challenge for cause removing a juror because he or she is biased, has prior knowledge about a case, or for other reasons that demonstrate the individual's inability to render a fair and impartial judgment in a case.

Chancery court a court created in fifteenth-century England to oversee the lives of high-born minors who were orphaned or otherwise could not care for themselves.

Charge in a criminal case, the specific crime the defendant is accused of committing.

Chicago Crime Commission a citizen action group set up in Chicago to investigate problems in the criminal justice system and explore avenues for positive change. The forerunner of many such groups around the country.

Child abuse any physical, emotional, or sexual trauma to a child for which no reasonable explanation, such as an accident, can be found. Child abuse can also be a function of neglecting to give proper care and attention to a young child.

Chronic offender according to Wolfgang, a delinquent offender who is arrested five or more times before he or she is 18 and who stands a good chance of becoming an adult criminal; these offenders are responsible for more than half of all serious crimes.

Christopher Commission an investigatory group led by Warren Christopher that investigated the Los Angeles Police Department in the wake of the Rodney King beating.

Civil death the custom of terminating the civil rights of convicted felons, for example, forbidding them the right to vote or marry. No state uses civil death today.

Civil law all law that is not criminal, including torts (personal wrongs), contract, property, maritime, and commercial law.

Civil Rights Division that part of the U.S. Justice Department that handles cases involving violations of civil rights guaranteed by the Constitution and federal law.

Classification the procedure in which prisoners are categorized on the basis of their personal characteristics and criminal history and then assigned to an appropriate institution.

Classical theory the theoretical perspective suggesting that: (1) people have free will to choose criminal or conventional behaviors; (2) people choose to commit crime for reasons of greed or personal need; and (3) crime can be controlled only by the fear of criminal sanctions.

Code of Hammurabi the first written criminal code developed in Babylonia about 2000 B.C.

Coeducational prison an institution that houses both male and female inmates who share work and recreational facilities.

Cognitive theory the study of the perception of reality; the mental processes required to understand the world we live in.

Cohort study a study utilizing a sample whose behavior is followed over a period of time.

Common law early English law, developed by judges, which incorporated Anglo-Saxon tribal custom, feudal rules and practices, and the everyday rules of behavior of local villages. Common law became the standardized law of the land in England and eventually formed the basis of the criminal law in the United States.

Community treatment the actions of correctional agencies that attempt to maintain the convicted offender in the community, instead of a secure facility; includes probation, parole, and residential programs.

Community policing a police strategy that emphasizes fear reduction, community organization, and order maintenance, rather than crime fighting.

Community service restitution an alternative sanction that requires an offender to work in the community at such tasks as cleaning public parks or working with handicapped children in lieu of a incarceration sentence.

Compensation financial aid awarded to the victims of crime to repay them for their loss and injuries.

Complaint a sworn allegation made in writing to a court or judge that an individual is guilty of some designated (complained of) offense. This is often the first legal document filed regarding a criminal offense. The complaint can be "taken out" by the victim, the police officer, the district attorney, or other interested party. Although the complaint charges an offense, an indictment or information may be the formal charging document.

Concurrent sentence prison sentences for two or more criminal acts that are served simultaneously, or run together.

Conduct norms behaviors expected of social groups members. If group norms conflict with those of the general culture, members of the group may find themselves described as outcasts or criminals.

Conflict view the view that human behavior is shaped by interpersonal conflict and that those who maintain social power will use it to further their own needs.

Conjugal visit a prison program that allows inmates to receive private visits from their spouses for the purpose of maintaining normal interpersonal relationships.

Consecutive sentence prison sentences for two or more

criminal acts that are served one after the other, or follow one another.

Consensus view of crime the belief that the majority of citizens in a society share common ideals and work toward a common good and that crimes are acts that are outlawed because they conflict with the rules of the majority and are harmful to society.

Constable the peacekeeper in early English towns. The constable organized citizens to protect his territory and supervised the night watch.

Constructive intent the finding of criminal liability for an unintentional act that is the result of negligence or recklessness.

Constructive possession in the crime of larceny, willingly giving up temporary physical possession of property but retaining legal ownership.

Continuance a judicial order to continue a case without a finding in order to gather more information, allow the defendant to begin a community-based treatment program, etc.

Contract system (attorney) providing counsel to indigent offenders by having an attorney(s) under contract to the county to handle all (or some) such cases.

Contract system (convict) the system used earlier in the century by which inmates were leased out to private industry to work.

Convict subculture the separate culture that exists in the prison, which has its own set of rewards and behaviors. The traditional culture is now being replaced by a violent gang culture.

Conviction a judgment of guilt; a verdict by a jury, a plea by a defendant, or a judgment by a court that the accused is guilty as charged.

Corporal punishment the use of physical chastisement, such as whipping or electroshock, to punish criminals.

Corporate crime white-collar crime involving a legal violation by a corporate entity, such as price fixing, restraint of trade, or waste dumping.

Corpus dilecti the body of the crime made up of the *actus reus* and *mens rea.*

Corrections the agencies of justice that take custody of offenders after their conviction and are entrusted with their treatment and control.

Court administrator the individual who controls the operations of the courts system in a particular jurisdiction; he or she may be in charge of scheduling, juries, judicial assignment, and so on.

Court of last resort a court that handles the final appeal on a matter. The U.S. Supreme Court is the official court of last resort for criminal matters.

Courtroom work group the phrase used to denote that all parties in the adversary process work together in a cooperative effort to settle cases with the least amount of effort and conflict.

Courts of limited jurisdiction courts that handle misdemeanors and minor civil complaints.

Crackdown concentrating police resources on a particular problem area, such as street-level drug dealing, in order to eradicate or displace criminal activity.

Crime a violation of societal rules of behavior as interpreted and expressed by a criminal legal code created by people holding social and political power. Individuals who violate these rules are subject to sanctions by state authority, social stigma, and loss of status.

Crime control a model of criminal justice that emphasizes the control of dangerous offenders and the protection of society. Its advocates call for harsh punishments as a deterrent to crime, such as the death penalty.

Crime fighter the police style that stresses dealing with hard crimes and arresting dangerous criminals.

Criminal Division the branch of the U.S. Justice Department that prosecutes federal criminal violations.

Criminal justice process the decision-making points from the initial investigation or arrest by police to the eventual release of the offender and his or her reentry into society; the various sequential criminal justice stages through which the offender passes.

Criminal law the body of rules that define crimes, set their punishments out, and mandate the procedures in carrying out the criminal justice process.

Criminal sanction the right of the state to punish people if they violate the rules set down in the criminal code; the punishment connected to commission of a specific crime.

Criminology the scientific approach to the study of the nature, extent, cause, and control of criminal behavior.

Cross-examination the process in which the defense and the prosecution interrogate witnesses during a trial.

Cruel and unusual punishment physical punishment or punishment that is far in excess of that given to people under similar circumstances and is therefore banned by the Eighth Amendment. The death penalty has so far not been considered cruel and unusual if it is administered in a fair and nondiscriminatory fashion.

Cultural transmission the concept that conduct norms are passed down from one generation to the next so that they become stable within the boundaries of a culture. Cultural transmission guarantees that group life-style and behavior are stable and predictable.

Culture conflict According to Sellin, a condition brought about when the rules and norms of an individual's subcultural affiliation conflict with the role demands of conventional society.

Culture of poverty the view that people in lower-class society form a separate culture with its own values and norms that are in conflict with conventional society; the culture is self-maintaining and ongoing.

Curtilage the fields attached to a house.

Custodial convenience the principle of giving jailed inmates the minimum comforts required by law in order to contain the costs of incarceration.

Cynicism the belief that most peoples' actions are motivated solely by personal needs and selfishness.

DARE the acronym for Drug Abuse Resistance Education, a school-based antidrug program initiated by the Los Angeles police and now adopted around the United States.

Day fines fines geared to the average daily income of the convicted offender in an effort to bring equity to the sentencing process.

Day reporting centers nonresidential community-based treatment programs.

Deadly force the ability of the police to kill suspects if they resist arrest or present a danger to the officer or the community. The police cannot use deadly force against an unarmed fleeing felon.

Decriminalize to reduce the penalty for a criminal act but not actually legalize it.

Defeminization the process by which policewomen become enculturated into the police profession at the expense of their feminine identity.

Defendant the accused in criminal proceedings; he or she has the right to be present at each stage of the criminal justice process, except grand jury proceedings.

Defense attorney the counsel for the defendant in a criminal trial who represents the individual from arrest to final appeal.

Degenerate anomalies according to Lombroso, the primitive physical characteristics that make criminals animalistic and savage.

Deinstitutionalization the movement to remove as many offenders as possible from secure confinement and treat them in the community.

Demeanor the way in which a person outwardly manifests his or her personality.

Demystify the process by which Marxists unmask the true purpose of the capitalist system's rules and laws.

Desert-based sentences sentences in which the length is based on the seriousness of the criminal act and not the personal characteristics of the defendant or the deterrent impact of the law. Punishment based on what people have done and not on what others may do or what they themselves may do in the future.

Desistance the process in which crime rate declines with age, synonymous with the aging-out process.

Detention holding an offender in secure confinement before trial.

Determinate sentences fixed terms of incarceration, such as three years' imprisonment. Determinate sentences are felt by many to be too restrictive for rehabilitative purposes; the advantage is that offenders know how much time they have to serve, that is, when they will be released.

Detective the police agency assigned to investigate crimes after they have been reported, gather evidence, and identify the perpetrator.

Deterrence the act of preventing crime before it occurs by means of the threat of criminal sanctions.

Deviance behavior that departs from the social norm.

Discretion the use of personal decision making and choice in carrying out operations in the criminal justice system. For example, police discretion can involve the decision to make an arrest, while prosecutorial discretion can involve the decision to accept a plea bargain.

Differential association according to Edwin Sutherland, the principle that criminal acts are related to a person's exposure to an excess amount of antisocial attitudes and values.

Direct examination the questioning of one's own (prosecution or defense) witness during a trial.

Directed verdict the right of judge to direct a jury to acquit a defendant because the state has not proven the elements of the crime or otherwise has not established guilt according to law.

Disposition for juvenile offenders, the equivalent of sentencing for adult offenders. The theory is that disposition is more rehabilitative than retributive. Possible dispositions may be to dismiss the case, release the youth to the custody of his or her parents, place the offender on probation, or send him or her to an institution or state correctional institution.

District attorney the county prosecutor who is charged with bringing offenders to justice and enforcing the laws of the state.

Diversion a noncriminal alternative to trial usually featuring counseling, job training, and educational opportunities.

DNA profiling the identification of criminal suspects by matching DNA samples taken from their person with specimens found at crime scenes.

Double bunking the practice of holding two or more inmates in a single cell because of prison overcrowding; upheld in *Rhodes v. Chapman*.

Double marginality according to Alex, the social burden African-American police officers carry by being both minority-group members and law enforcement officers.

Drift according to Matza, the view that youths move in and out of delinquency and that their life-styles can embrace both conventional and deviant values.

Drug courier profile a way of identifying drug runners based on their personal characteristics; police may stop and question individuals based on the way they fit the characteristics contained in the profile.

Drug Enforcement Administration (DEA) the federal agency that enforces federal drug control laws.

Due process the basic constitutional principle based on the concept of the primacy of the individual and the complementary concept of limitation on governmental power; a safeguard against arbitrary and unfair state procedures in judicial or administrative proceedings. Embodied in the due process concept are the basic rights of a defendant in criminal proceedings and the requisites for a fair trial. These rights and requirements have been expanded by appellate court decisions and include (1) timely notice of a hearing or trial that informs the accused of the charges against him or her; (2) the opportunity to confront accusers and to present evidence on one's own behalf before an impartial jury or judge; (3) the presumption of innocence under which guilt must be proven by legally obtained evidence and the verdict must be supported by the evidence presented; (4) the right of an accused to be warned of constitutional rights at the earliest stage of the criminal process; (5) protection against self-incrimination; (6) assistance of counsel at every critical stage of the criminal process; and (7) the guarantee that an individual will not be tried more than once for the same offense (double jeopardy).

Durham rule a definition of insanity used in New Hampshire that required that the crime be excused if it was a *product* of a mental illness.

Economic crime an act in violation of the criminal law that is designed to bring financial gain to the offender.

Economism the policy of controlling white-collar crime through monetary incentives and sanctions.

Electroencephalogram (EEG) a device that can record the electronic impulses given off by the brain, commonly called brain waves.

Embezzlement a type of larceny that involves taking the possessions of another (fraudulent conversion) that have been placed in the thief's lawful possession for safekeeping; for example, a bank teller misappropriating deposits or a stockbroker making off with a customer's account.

Entrapment a criminal defense that maintains the police originated the criminal idea or initiated the criminal action.

Enterprise syndicate an organized crime group that profits from the sale of illegal goods and services, such as narcotics, pornography, and prostitution.

Equity the action or practice of awarding each his or her just due; sanctions based on equity seek to compensate individual victims and the general society for their losses due to crime.

Exceptional circumstances doctrine under this policy, courts would hear only those cases brought by inmates in which the circumstances indicated a total disregard for human dignity, while denying hearings to less serious crimes. Cases allowed access to the courts usually involved a situation of total denial of medical care.

Exclusionary rule the principle that prohibits using evidence illegally obtained in a trial. Based on the Fourth Amendment "right of the people to be secure in their persons, houses, papers, and effects, against unreasonable searches and seizures," the rule is not a bar to prosecution, as legally obtained evidence may be available that may be used in a trial.

Expressive crime a crime that has no purpose except to accomplish the behavior at hand, for example, shooting someone, as opposed to creating monetary gain.

Excuse a defense to a criminal charge in which the accused maintains he or she lacked the intent to commit the crime (*mens rea*).

***Ex post facto* laws** laws that make criminal an act after it was committed or retroactively increase the penalty for a crime. For example, an *ex post facto* law could change shoplifting from a misdemeanor to a felony and penalize people with a prison term even though they had been apprehended six months before; these laws are unconstitutional.

False pretenses illegally obtaining money, goods, or merchandise from another by fraud or misrepresentation.

Federal Bureau of Investigation (FBI) the arm of the U.S. Justice Department that investigates violations of federal law, gathers crime statistics, runs a comprehensive crime laboratory, and helps train local law enforcement officers.

Felony a more serious offense that carries a penalty of incarceration in a state prison, usually for one year or more. Persons convicted of felony offenses lose such rights as the right to vote, to hold elective office, or to maintain certain licenses.

Fence a buyer and seller of stolen merchandise.

Field training officer a senior police officer who trains recruits in the field, overseeing their on-the-job training.

Fixed time rule a policy in which people must be tried within a stated period after their arrest; overruled by *Barker v. Wingo,* which created a balancing test.

Flat or fixed sentencing a sentencing model that mandates that all people who are convicted of a specific offense and who are sent to prison must receive the same length of incarceration.

Focal concerns according to Walter Miller, the value orientations of lower-class cultures whose features include the need for excitement, trouble, smartness, fate, and personal autonomy.

Folkways generally followed customs that do not have moral values attached to them, such as not interrupting people when they are speaking.

Foot patrol police patrols that take officers out of cars and put them on a walking beat in order to strengthen ties with the community.

Forfeiture the seizure of personal property by the state as a civil or criminal penalty.

Fraud the taking of the possessions of another through deception or cheating, such as selling a person a desk that is represented as an antique but is known to be a copy.

Free venture privately run industries in a prison setting in which the inmates work for wages and the goods are sold for profit.

Functionalism the sociological perspective that suggests that each part of society makes a contribution to the maintenance of the whole. Functionalism stresses social cooperation and consensus of values and beliefs among a majority of society's members.

Furlough a correctional policy that allows inmates to leave the institution for vocational or educational training, for employment, or to maintain family ties.

General deterrence a crime-control policy that depends on the fear of criminal penalties. General deterrence measures, such as long prison sentences for violent crimes, are aimed at convincing the potential law violator that the pains associated with crime outweigh its benefits.

General intent actions that on their face indicate a criminal purpose, for example, breaking into a locked building or trespassing on someone's property.

Gentrification a process of reclaiming and reconditioning deteriorated neighborhoods by refurbishing depressed real estate and then renting or selling the properties to upper-middle-class professionals.

Good faith exception the principle of law that holds that evidence may be used in a criminal trial even though the search warrant used to obtain it is technically faulty, if the police acted in good faith and to the best of their ability when they sought to obtain it from a judge.

Good-time credit time taken off a prison sentence in exchange for good behavior within the institution; for example, ten days per month. A device used to limit disciplinary problems within the prison.

Grand jury a group (usually comprised of twenty-three citizens) chosen to hear testimony in secret and to issue formal criminal accusations (indictments). It also serves an investigatory function.

Grass eaters a term used for police officers who accept payoffs when their everyday duties place them in a position to be solicited by the public.

Greenmail the process by which an arbitrager buys large blocks of a company's stock and threatens to take over the company and replace the current management. To ward off the threat to their positions, members of management use company funds to repurchase the shares at a much higher price, creating huge profits for the corporate raiders.

Guardian *ad litem* a court-appointed attorney who protects the interests of a child in cases involving the child's welfare.

Habeas corpus see **writ of habeas corpus.**

Habitual criminal statutes laws that require long-term or life sentences for offenders who have multiple felony convictions.

Halfway house a community-based correctional facility that houses inmates before their outright release so that they can become gradually acclimated to conventional society.

Hallcrest Report a government-sponsored national survey of the private security industry conducted by the Hallcrest Corporation.

Hands-off doctrine the judicial policy of not interfering in the administrative affairs of a prison.

Hearsay evidence testimony that is not firsthand but relates information told by a second party.

Hot spots of crime according to Sherman, a significant portion of all police calls originate from only a few locations. These hot spots include taverns and housing projects.

House of correction a county correctional institution generally used for the incarceration of more serious misdemeanants, whose sentences are usually less than one year.

Howard, John an eighteenth century British penal reformer who wrote *The State of Prisons*.

Hue and cry in medieval England, the policy of self-help used in villages demanded that everyone respond if a citizen raised a hue and cry to get their aid.

Hulks mothballed ships that were used to house prisoners in eighteenth-century England.

Hundred in medieval England, a group of one hundred families that had the responsibility to maintain the order and try minor offenses.

Hustle the underground prison economy.

Importation model the view that the violent prison culture reflects the criminal culture of the outside world and is neither developed in nor unique to prisons.

Incapacitation the policy of keeping dangerous criminals in confinement to eliminate the risk of their repeating their offense in society.

Indentured servant prior to the eighteenth century, a debtor or convicted offender who would work off his or her debt by being assigned a term of servitude to a master who purchased the services from the state.

Indeterminate sentence a term of incarceration with a stated minimum and maximum length; for example, a sentence to prison for a period of from three to ten years. The prisoner would be eligible for parole after the minimum sentence had been served. Based on the belief that sentences should fit the criminal, indeterminate sentences allow individualized sentences and provide for sentencing flexibility. Judges can set a high minimum to override the purpose of the indeterminate sentence.

Inevitable discovery a rule of law that states that evidence that almost assuredly would be independently discovered can be used in a court of law even though it was obtained in violation of legal rules and practices.

Index crimes the eight crimes that, because of their seriousness and frequency, the FBI reports the incidence of in the annual Uniform Crime Reports. Index crimes include murder, rape, assault, robbery, burglary, arson, larceny, and motor vehicle theft.

Indictment a written accusation returned by a grand jury charging an individual with a specified crime after determination of probable cause; the prosecutor presents enough evidence (a *prima facie* case) to establish probable cause.

Information like the indictment, a formal charging document. The prosecuting attorney makes out the information and files it in court. Probable cause is determined at the preliminary hearing, which, unlike grand jury proceedings, is public and attended by the accused and his or her attorney.

Initial appearance the stage in the justice process during which the suspect is brought before a magistrate for consideration of bail. The suspect must be taken for initial appearance within a "reasonable time" after arrest. For petty offenses, this step often serves as the final criminal proceeding, either by adjudication by a judge or the offering of a guilty plea.

Inmate social code the informal set of rules that govern inmates.

Inmate subculture the loosely defined culture that pervades prisons and has its own norms, rules, and language.

Insanity a legal defense that maintains that a defendant was incapable of forming criminal intent because he or she suffered from a defect of reason or mental illness.

Insider trading the illegal buying of stock in a company based on information provided by another who has a fiduciary interest in the company, such as an employee or an outside attorney or accountant hired by the firm. Federal laws and the rules of the Security and Exchange Commission require that all profits from such trading be returned and provide for both fines and a prison sentence.

Instrumental Marxist theory the view that capitalist institutions, such as the criminal justice system, have as their main purpose the control of the poor in order to maintain the hegemony of the wealthy.

Intensive probation supervision a type of intermediate sanction involving small probation caseloads and strict monitoring on a daily or weekly basis.

Interactionist perspective the view that one's perception of reality is significantly influenced by one's interpretations of the reactions of others to similar events and stimuli.

Interrogation the method of accumulating evidence in the form of information or confessions from suspects by police; questioning, which has been restricted because of concern about the use of brutal and coercive methods and interest in protecting against self-incrimination.

Investigation an inquiry concerning suspected criminal behavior for the purpose of identifying offenders or gathering further evidence to assist the prosecution of apprehended offenders.

Jail a place to detain people awaiting trial, to serve as a lockup for drunks and disorderly individuals, and to confine convicted misdemeanants serving sentences of less than one year.

Jail house lawyer an inmate trained in law or otherwise educated who helps other inmates prepare legal briefs and appeals.

Just desert the philosophy of justice that asserts that those who violate the rights of others deserve to be punished. The severity of punishment should be commensurate with the seriousness of the crime.

Justice model a philosophy of corrections that stresses determinant sentences, abolition of parole, and the view that prisons are places of punishment and not rehabilitation.

Justification a defense to a criminal charge in which the accused maintains that his or her actions were justified by the circumstances and therefore he or she should not be held criminally liable.

Juvenile delinquency participation in illegal behavior by a minor who falls under a statutory age limit.

Juvenile justice process court proceedings for youths within the juvenile age group that differ from the adult criminal process. Originally, under the paternal (*parens patriae*) philosophy, juvenile procedures are informal and nonadversary, invoked *for* the juvenile offender, rather than *against* him or her; a petition instead of a complaint is filed; courts make findings of involvement or adjudication of delinquency, instead of convictions; and juvenile offenders receive dispositions, instead of sentences. Recent court decisions (*In re Kent* and *In re Gault*) have increased the adversary nature of juvenile court proceedings. However, the philosophy remains one of diminishing the stigma of delinquency and providing for the youth's well-being and rehabilitation, rather than seeking retribution.

Kansas City study an experimental program that evaluated the effectiveness of patrol. The Kansas City study found that the presence of patrol officers had little deterrent effect.

Knapp Commission a public body that led the investigation into police corruption in New York and uncovered a widespread network of payoffs and bribes.

Labeling the process by which a person becomes fixed with a negative identity, such as "criminal" or "ex-con," and is forced to suffer the consequences of outcast status.

Landmark decision a decision handed down by the Supreme Court that becomes the law of the land and serves as precedence for similar legal issues.

Legalization the removal of all criminal penalties from a previously outlawed act.

Life history a research method that uses the experiences of an individual as the unit of analysis, for example, using the life experience of an individual gang member to understand the natural history of gang membership.

Longitudinal cohort study research that tracks the development of a group of subjects over time.

Lower courts a generic term referring to those courts that have jurisdiction over misdemeanors and conduct preliminary investigations of felony charges.

Make-believe families peer units formed by women in prison to compensate for the loss of family and loved ones that contain mother and father figures.

***Mala in se* crimes** acts that are outlawed because they violate basic moral values, such as rape, murder, assault, and robbery.

***Mala prohibitum* crimes** acts that are outlawed by statute because they clash with current norms and public opinion, for example, tax, traffic, and drug laws.

Mandamus see **writ of mandamus.**

Manhattan Bail Project the innovative experiment in bail reform that introduced and successfully tested the concept of release on recognizance.

Mandatory sentence a statutory requirement that a certain penalty shall be set and carried out in all cases on conviction for a specified offense or series of offenses.

Marital exemption the practice in some states of prohibiting the prosecution of husbands for the rape of their wives.

Masculinity hypothesis the view that women who commit crimes have biological and psychological traits similar to those of men.

Mass murder the killing of a large number of people in a single incident by an offender who typically does not seek concealment or escape.

Matricide the murder of one's mother.

Maximum security prisons correctional institutions that house dangerous felons and maintain strict security measures, high walls, and limited contact with the outside world.

Maxi-maxi prisons high-security prisons, based on the federal prison in Marion, Illinois, that house the most dangerous inmates in around-the-clock solitary confinement.

Meat eaters a term used to describe police officers who actively solicit bribes and vigorously engage in corrupt practices.

Medical model a view of corrections that holds that convicted offenders are victims of their environment who need care and treatment to transform them into valuable members of society.

Medium-security prisons less secure institutions that house nonviolent offenders and provide more opportunities for contact with the outside world.

Mens rea guilty mind. The mental element of a crime or the intent to commit a criminal act.

Methadone a synthetic narcotic that is used as a substitute for heroin in drug-control efforts.

Middle-class measuring rods according to Cohen, the standards by which teachers and other representatives of state authority evaluate lower-class youths. Because they cannot live up to middle-class standards, lower-class youths are bound for failure, which gives rise to frustration and anger at conventional society.

Minimum-security prisons the least secure institutions that house white-collar and nonviolent offenders, maintain few security measures, and have liberal furlough and visitation policies.

***Miranda* warning** the result of two U.S. Supreme Court decisions (*Escobedo v. Illinois* [378 U.S. 478] and *Miranda v. Arizona* [384 U.S. 436]) that require that police officers inform individuals under arrest of their constitutional right to remain silent, to know that their statements can later be used against them in court, that they can have an attorney present to help them, and that the state will pay for an attorney if they cannot afford to hire one. Although aimed at protecting an individual during in-custody interrogation, the warning must also be given when the investigation shifts from the investigatory to the accusatory state, that is, when suspicion begins to focus on an individual.

Misdemeanor a minor crime usually punished by less than one year's imprisonment in a local institution, such as a county jail.

Missouri Plan a way of picking judges through nonpartisan elections as a means of ensuring judicial performance standards.

Monetary restitution a sanction that requires that convicted offenders compensate crime victims by reimbursing them for out-of-pocket losses caused by the crime. Losses can include property damage, lost wages, and medical costs.

Moonlighting the practice of police officers holding after-hours jobs in private security or other related professions.

Moral entrepreneurs people who use their influence to shape the legal process in ways they see fit.

Motion an oral or written request asking the court to make a specified finding, decision, or order.

Murder transaction the concept that murder is usually a result of behavior interactions between the victim and the offender.

National Crime Survey the ongoing victimization study conducted jointly by the Justice Department and the U.S. Census Bureau that surveys victims about their experiences with law violation.

Neighborhood policing a style of police management that emphasizes community-level crime-fighting programs and initiatives.

Neurotics people who fear that their primitive id impulses will dominate their personality.

Niche a way of adapting to the prison community that stresses finding one's place in the system, rather than fighting for one's individual rights.

No bill a decision by a grand jury not to indict a criminal suspect.

Nolo contendere no contest. An admission of guilt in a criminal case with the condition that the finding cannot be used against the defendant in any subsequent civil cases.

Nolle prosequi the term used when a prosecutor decides to drop a case after a complaint has been formally made. Reasons for a *nolle prosequi* include evidence insufficiency, reluctance of witnesses to testify, police error, and office policy.

Nonintervention a justice philosophy that emphasizes the least intrusive treatment possible. Among its central policies are decarceration, diversion, and decriminalization. Less is better.

Obscenity according to current legal theory, sexually explicit material that lacks a serious purpose and appeals solely to the prurient interest of the viewer. While nudity per se is not usually considered obscene, open sex behavior, masturbation, and exhibition of the genitals is banned in many communities.

Official crime criminal behavior that has been recorded by the police.

Opportunist robber someone who steals small amounts when a vulnerable target presents itself.

Parole the early release of a prisoner from imprisonment subject to conditions set by a parole board. Depending on the jurisdiction, inmates must serve a certain proportion of their sentences before becoming eligible for parole. If the inmate is granted parole, the conditions of which may require him or her to report regularly to a parole officer, to refrain from criminal conduct, to maintain and support his or her family, to avoid contact with other convicted criminals, to abstain from using alcohol and drugs, to remain within the jurisdiction, and so on. Violations of the conditions of parole may result in revocation of parole, in which case the individual will be returned to prison. The concept behind parole is to allow the release of the offender to community supervision, where rehabilitation and readjustment will be facilitated.

Parricide the killing of a close relative by a child.

Partial deterrent a legal measure designed to restrict or control, rather than eliminate, an undesirable act.

Particularity the requirement that a search warrant state precisely where the search is to take place and what items are to be seized.

Paternalism male domination. A paternalistic family, for instance, is one in which the father is the dominant authority figure.

Patriarchy a male-dominated system. The patriarchal family is one dominated by the father.

Patricide the murder of a father.

Pennsylvania system the prison system developed during the nineteenth century that stressed total isolation and individual penitence as a means of reform.

Peremptory challenge the dismissal of a potential juror by either the prosecution or the defense for unexplained, discretionary reasons.

Persisters those criminals who do not age out of crime; chronic delinquents who continue offending into their adulthood.

Plain view evidence that is in plain view to police officers may be seized without a search warrant.

Plea an answer to formal charges by an accused. Possible pleas are guilty, not guilty, *nolo contendere*, and not guilty by reason of insanity. A guilty plea is a confession of the offense as charged. A not guilty plea is a denial of the charge and places the burden on the prosecution to prove the elements of the offense.

Plea-bargaining the discussion between the defense counsel and the prosecution by which the accused agrees to plead guilty for certain considerations. The advantage to the defendant may be a reduction of the charges, a lenient sentence, or (in the case of multiple charges) dropped charges. The advantage to the prosecution is that a conviction is obtained without the time and expense of lengthy trial proceedings.

Pledge system an early method of law enforcement that relied on self-help and mutual aid.

Police discretion the ability of police officers to enforce the law selectively. Police officers in the field have great latitude to use their discretion in deciding whether to invoke their arrest powers.

Police officer style the belief that the bulk of police officers can be classified into ideal personality types. Popular style types include: supercops, who desire to enforce only serious crimes, such as robbery and rape; professionals, who use a broad definition of police work; service-oriented, who see their job as that of a helping profession; and avoiders, who do as little as possible. The actual existence of ideal police officer types has been much debated.

Poor laws seventeenth-century laws that bound out vagrants and abandoned children to masters as indentured servants.

Population all people who share a particular personal characteristic, for example, all high school students or all police officers.

Positivism the branch of social science that uses the scientific method of the natural sciences and that suggests that human behavior is a product of social, biological, psychological, or economic forces.

Power groups criminal organizations that do not provide services or illegal goods but trade exclusively in violence and extortion.

Power rape a rape motivated by the need for sexual conquest.

Power syndicates organized crime groups that use force and violence to exhort money from legitimate businesses and other criminal groups engaged in illegal business enterprises.

Praxis the application of theory in action; in Marxist criminology, applying theory to promote revolution.

Preliminary hearings the step at which criminal charges initiated by an information are tested for probable cause; the prosecution presents enough evidence to establish probable cause, that is, a *prima facie* case. The hearing is public and may be attended by the accused and his or her attorney.

Preponderance of the evidence the level of proof in civil cases; more than half the evidence supports the allegations of one side.

Presentence report an investigation performed by a probation officer attached to a trial court after the conviction of a defendant. The report contains information about the defendant's background, education, previous employment, and family; his or her own statement concerning the offense; prior criminal record; interviews with neighbors or acquaintances; and his or her mental and physical condition (i.e., information that would not be made record in the case of a guilty plea or that would be inadmissible as evidence at a trial but could be influential and important at the sentencing stage). After conviction, a judge sets a date for sentencing (usually ten days to two weeks from the date of conviction), during which time the presentence report is made. The report is required in felony cases in federal courts and in many states, is optional with the judge in some states, and in others is mandatory before convicted offenders can be placed on probation. In the case of juvenile offenders, the presentence report is also known as a social history report.

Presumptive sentences sentencing structures that provide an average sentence that should be served along with the option of extending or decreasing punishments because of aggravating or mitigating circumstances.

Preventive detention the practice of holding dangerous suspects before trial without bail.

Prison a state or federal correctional institution for incarceration of felony offenders for terms of one year or more.

Probability sample a randomly drawn sample in which each member of the population tapped has an equal chance of being selected.

Probable cause the evidentiary criterion necessary to sustain an arrest or the issuance of an arrest or search warrant; less than absolute certainty or "beyond a reasonable doubt" but greater than mere suspicion or "hunch." A set of facts, information, circumstances, or conditions that would lead a reasonable person to believe that an offense was committed and that the accused committed that offense. An arrest made without probable cause may be susceptible to prosecution as an illegal arrest under "false imprisonment" statutes.

Probation a sentence entailing the conditional release of a convicted offender into the community under the supervision of the court (in the form of a probation officer), subject to certain conditions for a specified time. The conditions are usually similar to those of parole. (*Note:* Probation is a sentence, an alternative to incarceration; parole is administrative release from incarceration.) Violation of the conditions of probation may result in revocation of probation.

Problem-oriented policing a style of police operations that stresses proactive problem solving, rather than reactive crime fighting.

Pro bono the practice by private attorneys of taking without fee the cases of indigent offenders as a service to the profession and the community.

Procedural law the rules that define the operation of criminal proceedings. Procedural law describes the methods that must be followed in obtaining warrants, investigating offenses, affecting lawful arrests, using force, conducting trials, introducing evidence, sentencing convicted offenders, and reviewing cases by appellate courts (in general, legislatures have ignored postsentencing procedures). While the substantive law defines criminal offenses, procedural law delineates how the substantive offenses are to be enforced.

Progressives early twentieth-century reformers who believed that state action could relieve human ills.

Proof beyond a reasonable doubt the standard of proof needed to convict in a criminal case. The evidence offered in court does not have to amount to absolute certainty, but it should leave no reasonable doubt that the defendant committed the alleged crime.

Property in service the eighteenth-century practice of selling control of inmates to shipmasters who would then transport them to colonies for sale as indentured servants.

Proximity hypothesis the view that people become crime victims because they live or work in areas with large criminal populations.

Psychopath a person whose personality is characterized by a lack of warmth and feeling, inappropriate behavior responses, and an inability to learn from experience. While some psychologists view psychopathy as a result of childhood trauma, others see it as a result of biological abnormality.

Psychotics people whose id has broken free and now dominates their personality. Psychotics suffer from delusions and experience hallucinations and sudden mood shifts.

Racketeer Influenced and Corrupt Organizations Act (RICO) Federal legislation that enables prosecutors to bring additional criminal or civil charges against people whose multiple criminal acts constitute a conspiracy. RICO features monetary penalties that allow the government to confiscate all profits derived from criminal activities. Originally intended to be used against organized criminals, RICO also has been employed against white-collar crime.

Random sample a sample selected on the basis of chance so that each person in the population has an equal opportunity to be selected.

Rationale choice the view that crime is a function of a decision-making process in which the potential offender weighs the potential costs and benefits of an illegal act.

Reasonable competence the standard by which legal representation is judged: did the defendant receive a reasonable level of legal aid?

Reasonable doubt a jury cannot find the defendant guilty if a reasonable doubt exists that he or she committed the crime.

Recoupment forcing indigents to repay the state for at least part of their legal costs.

Reintegration the correctional philosophy that stresses reintroducing the inmate back into the community.

Release on recognizance a nonmonetary condition for the pretrial release of an accused individual; an alternative to monetary bail that is granted after the court determines that the accused has ties in the community, has no prior record of default, and is likely to appear at subsequent proceedings.

Relative deprivation the condition that exists when people of wealth and poverty live in close proximity to one another. Some criminologists attribute crime-rate differentials to relative deprivation.

Restitution a condition of probation in which the offender repays society or the victim of crime for the trouble the offender caused. Monetary restitution involves a direct payment to the victim as a form of compensation. Community-service restitution may be used in victimless crimes and involves work in the community in lieu of more severe criminal penalties.

Routine activities the view that crime is a "normal" function of the routine activities of modern living. Offenses can be expected if there is a suitable target that is not protected by capable guardians.

Sadistic rape a rape motivated by the offender's desire to torment and abuse the victim.

Sample a limited number of persons selected for study from a population.

Schizophrenia a type of psychosis often marked by bizarre behavior, hallucinations, loss of thought control, and inappropriate emotional responses. There are different types of schizophrenia: catatonic, which characteristically involves impairment of motor activity; paranoid, which is characterized by delusions of persecution; and hebephrenic, which is characterized by immature behavior and giddiness.

Search and seizure the legal term, contained in the Fourth Amendment to the U.S. Constitution, that refers to the searching for and carrying away of evidence by police during a criminal investigation.

Secondary deviance according to Lemert, the accepting of deviant labels as a personal identity.

Selective incapacitation the policy of creating enhanced prison sentences for the small group of dangerous chronic offenders.

Self-report study a research approach that requires subjects reveal their own participation in delinquent or criminal acts.

Sentence the criminal sanction imposed by the court on a convicted defendant, usually in the form of a fine, incarceration, or probation. Sentencing may be carried out by a judge, jury, or sentencing council (panel or judges), depending on the statutes of the jurisdiction.

Sequester the insulation of jurors from the outside world so that their decision making cannot be influenced or affected by extralegal events.

Serial murder the killing of a large number of people over time by an offender who seeks to escape detection.

Sherman Report the national review of law enforcement education programs that found that a liberal arts-related curriculum was the most appropriate one for training police officers.

Sheriff the chief law enforcement officer in a county.

Shield laws laws designed to protect rape victims by prohibiting the defense attorney from inquiring about their previous sexual relationships.

Shire reeve in early England, the senior law enforcement figure in a county, the forerunner of today's sheriff.

Shock incarceration a short prison sentence served in boot camp-type facilities.

Shock probation a sentence in which offenders serve a short prison term to impress them with the pains of imprisonment before they begin probation.

Short-run hedonism according to Cohen, the desire of lower-class gang youths to engage in behavior that will give them immediate gratification and excitement but in the long run will be dysfunctional and negativistic.

Sir Robert Peel the British home secretary who in 1829 organized the London Metropolitan Police, the first local police force.

Social control the ability of society and its institutions to control, manage, restrain, or direct human behavior.

Social disorganization a neighborhood or area marked by culture conflict, lack of cohesiveness, transient population, insufficient social organizations, and anomie.

Special (specific) deterrence a crime-control policy that suggests that punishment should be severe enough to convince convicted offenders never to repeat their criminal activity.

Specific intent the intent to accomplish a specific purpose as an element of crime, for example, breaking into someone's house for the express purpose of stealing jewels.

Stare decisis to stand by decided cases. The legal principle by which the decision or holding in an earlier case becomes the standard by which subsequent similar cases are judged.

Statutory law laws created by legislative bodies to meet changing social conditions, public opinion, and custom.

Sting an undercover police operation in which police pose as criminals to trap law violators.

Stoopers petty criminals who earn their living by retrieving winning tickets that are accidentally discarded by race track patrons.

Stop and frisk the situation where police officers who are suspicious of an individual run their hands lightly over the suspect's outer garments to determine if the person is carrying a concealed weapon. Also called a "patdown" or "threshold inquiry," a stop and frisk is intended to stop short of any activity that could be considered a violation of Fourth Amendment rights.

Stradom formations according to the Schwendingers, adolescent social networks whose members have distinct dress, grooming, and linguistic behaviors.

Strain the emotional turmoil and conflict caused when people believe they cannot achieve their desires and goals through legitimate means.

Street crime illegal acts designed to prey on the public through theft, damage, and violence.

Strict-liability crimes illegal acts whose elements do not contain the need for intent or *mens rea;* usually acts that endanger the public welfare, such as illegal dumping of toxic wastes.

Structural Marxist theory the view that the law and the justice system are designed to maintain the capitalist system and that members of both the owner and worker classes whose behavior threatens the stability of the system will be sanctioned.

Subculture a group that is loosely part of the dominant culture but maintains a unique set of values, beliefs, and traditions.

Subpoena a court order requiring the recipient to appear in court on an indicated time and date.

Substantive criminal laws a body of specific rules that declare what conduct is criminal and prescribe the punishment to be imposed for such conduct.

Summons an alternative to arrest usually used for petty or traffic offenses; a written order notifying an individual that he or she has been charged with an offense. A summons directs the person to appear in court to answer the charge. It is used primarily in instances of low risk, where the person will not be required to appear at a later date. The summons is advantageous to police officers in that they are freed from having to spend time on arrest and booking procedures; it is advantageous to the accused in that he or she is spared time in jail.

Sureties during the Middle Ages, people who made themselves responsible for the behavior of offenders released in their care.

Surplus value the Marxist view that the laboring classes produce wealth that far exceeds their wages and goes to the capitalist class as profits.

Surrebuttal introducing witnesses during a criminal trial in order to disprove damaging testimony by other witnesses.

Suspended sentence a prison term that is delayed while the defendant undergoes a period of community treatment. If the treatment is successful, the prison sentence is terminated.

Team policing an experimental police technique in which groups of officers are assigned to a particular area of the city on a twenty-four-hour basis.

Technical parole violation revocation of parole because conditions set by correctional authorities have been violated.

Technique of neutralization according to neutralization theory, the ability of delinquent youth to neutralize moral constraints so they may drift into criminal acts.

Thanatos according to Freud, the instinctual drive towards aggression and violence.

Threshold inquiry a term used to describe a stop and frisk.

Tort the law of personal wrongs and damage. Tort-type actions include negligence, libel, slander, assault, and trespass.

Totality of the circumstances a legal doctrine that mandates that a decision maker consider all the issues and circumstances of a case before judging the outcome. For example, before concluding whether a suspect understood a *Miranda* warning, a judge must consider the totality of the circumstances under which the warning was given. The suspect's age, intelligence, and competency may influence his or her understanding and judgment.

Transferred intent if an illegal yet unintended act results from the intent to commit a crime, that act is also considered illegal.

Transitional neighborhood an area undergoing a shift in population and structure, usually from middle-class residential to lower-class mixed use.

Type I offenses another term for index crimes.

Type II offenses all crimes other than index and minor traffic offenses. The FBI records annual arrest information for Type II offenses.

Venire the group called for jury duty from which jury panels are selected.

Vice squad police officers assigned to enforce morally tinged laws, such as those on prostitution, gambling, and pornography.

Victimology the study of the victim's role in criminal transactions.

Victimization survey a crime-measurement technique that surveys citizens in order to measure their experiences as victims of crime.

Victim-precipitated describes a crime in which the victim's behavior was the spark that ignited the subsequent offense, for example, the victim abused the offender verbally or physically.

Voir dire the process in which a potential jury panel is questioned by the prosecution and the defense in order to select jurors who are unbiased and objective.

Waiver the act of voluntarily relinquishing a right or advantage; often used in the context of waiving one's right to counsel (e.g., *Miranda* warning) or waiving certain steps in the criminal justice process (e.g., the preliminary hearing). Essential to waiver is the voluntary consent of the individual.

Warrant a written court order issued by a magistrate authorizing and directing that an individual be taken into custody to answer criminal charges.

Watch system during the Middle Ages in England, men were organized in church parishes to guard at night against disturbances and breaches of the peace under the direction of the local constable.

Watchman a style of policing that stresses reacting to calls for service, rather than aggressively pursuing crime.

Wergild under medieval law, the money paid by the offender to compensate the victim and the state for a criminal offense.

White-collar crime illegal acts that capitalize on a person's place in the marketplace. White-collar crimes can involve theft, embezzlement, fraud, market manipulation, restraint of trade, and false advertising.

Wickersham Commission created in 1931 by President Herbert Hoover to investigate the state of the nation's police forces. The commission found that police training was inadequate and that the average officer was incapable of effectively carrying out his duties.

Widen the net the charge that programs designed to divert offenders from the justice system actually enmesh them further in the process by substituting more intrusive treatment programs for less intrusive punishment-oriented outcomes.

Wite the portion of the wergild that went to the victim's family.

Work furlough a prison treatment program that allows inmates to be released during the day to work in the community and returned to prison at night.

Writ of certiorari an order of a superior court requesting that the record of an inferior court (or administrative body) be brought forward for review or inspection.

Writ of habeas corpus a judicial order requesting that a person detaining another produce the body of the prisoner and give reasons for his or her capture and detention. Habeas corpus is a legal device used to request that a judicial body review the reasons for a person's confinement and the conditions of confinement. Habeas corpus is known as "the great writ."

Writ of mandamus an order of a superior court commanding that a lower court, administrative body, or executive body perform a specific function. It is commonly used to restore rights and privileges lost to a defendant through illegal means.

CONSTITUTION OF THE UNITED STATES

Preamble

We the People of the United States, in Order to form a more perfect Union, establish Justice, insure domestic Tranquility, provide for the common defence, promote the general Welfare, and secure the Blessings of Liberty to ourselves and our Posterity, do ordain and establish this Constitution for the United States of America.

Article I

Section 1. All legislative Powers herein granted shall be vested in a Congress of the United States, which shall consist of a Senate and House of Representatives.

Section 2. The House of Representatives shall be composed of Members chosen every second Year by the People of the several States, and the Electors in each State shall have the Qualifications requisite for Electors of the most numerous Branch of the State Legislature.

No Person shall be a Representative who shall not have attained to the Age of twenty five Years, and been seven Years a Citizen of the United States, and who shall not, when elected, be an Inhabitant of that State in which he shall be chosen.

Representatives and direct Taxes shall be apportioned among the several States which may be included within this Union, according to their respective Numbers, which shall be determined by adding to the whole Number of free Persons, including those bound to Service for a Term of Years, and excluding Indians not taxed, three fifths of all other Persons. The actual Enumeration shall be made within three Years after the first Meeting of the Congress of the United States, and within every subsequent Term of ten Years, in such Manner as they shall by Law direct. The Number of Representatives shall not exceed one for every thirty Thousand, but each State shall have at Least one Representative; and until such enumeration shall be made, the State of New Hampshire shall be entitled to choose three, Massachusetts eight, Rhode Island and Providence Plantations one, Connecticut five, New York six, New Jersey four, Pennsylvania eight, Delaware one, Maryland six, Virginia ten, North Carolina five, South Carolina five, and Georgia three.

When vacancies happen in the Representation from any State, the Executive Authority thereof shall issue Writs of Election to fill such Vacancies.

The House of Representatives shall choose their Speaker and other Officers; and shall have the sole Power of Impeachment.

Section 3. The Senate of the United States shall be composed of two Senators from each State, chosen by the Legislature thereof, for six Years; and each Senator shall have one Vote.

Immediately after they shall be assembled in Consequence of the first Election, they shall be divided as equally as may be into three Classes. The Seats of the Senators of the first Class shall be vacated at the Expiration of the second Year, of the second Class at the Expiration of the fourth Year, and of the third Class at the Expiration of the sixth Year, so that one third may be chosen every second Year; and if Vacancies happen by Resignation, or otherwise, during the Recess of the Legislature of any State, the Executive thereof may make temporary Appointments until the next Meeting of the Legislature, which shall then fill such Vacancies.

No Person shall be a Senator who shall not have attained to the Age of thirty Years, and been nine Years a Citizen of the United States, and who shall not, when elected, be an Inhabitant of that State for which he shall be chosen.

The Vice President of the United States shall be President of the Senate, but shall have no Vote, unless they be equally divided.

The Senate shall choose their other Officers, and also a President pro tempore, in the Absence of the Vice President, or when he shall exercise the Office of President of the United States.

The Senate shall have the sole Power to try all Impeachments. When sitting for that Purpose, they shall be on Oath or Affirmation. When the President of the

United States is tried, the Chief Justice shall preside: And no Person shall be convicted without the Concurrence of two thirds of the Members present.

Judgment in Cases of Impeachment shall not extend further than to removal from Office, and disqualification to hold and enjoy any Office of honor, Trust, or Profit under the United States: but the Party convicted shall nevertheless be liable and subject to Indictment, Trial, Judgment, and Punishment, according to Law.

Section 4. The Times, Places and Manner of holding Elections for Senators and Representatives, shall be prescribed in each State by the Legislature thereof; but the Congress may at any time by Law make or alter such Regulations, except as to the Places of choosing Senators.

The Congress shall assemble at least once in every Year, and such Meeting shall be on the first Monday in December, unless they shall by Law appoint a different Day.

Section 5. Each House shall be the Judge of the Elections, Returns, and Qualifications of its own Members, and a Majority of each shall constitute a Quorum to do Business; but a smaller Number may adjourn from day to day, and may be authorized to compel the Attendance of absent Members, in such Manner, and under such Penalties as each House may provide.

Each House may determine the Rules of its Proceedings, punish its Members for disorderly Behavior, and, with the Concurrence of two thirds, expel a Member.

Each House shall keep a Journal of its Proceedings, and from time to time publish the same, excepting such Parts as may in their Judgment require Secrecy; and the Yeas and Nays of the Members of either House on any question shall, at the Desire of one fifth of those Present, be entered on the Journal.

Neither House, during the Session of Congress, shall, without the Consent of the other, adjourn for more than three days, nor to any other Place than that in which the two Houses shall be sitting.

Section 6. The Senators and Representatives shall receive a Compensation for their Services, to be ascertained by Law, and paid out of the Treasury of the United States. They shall in all Cases, except Treason, Felony and Breach of the Peace, be privileged from Arrest during their Attendance at the Session of their respective Houses, and in going to and returning from the same; and for any Speech or Debate in either House, they shall not be questioned in any other Place.

No Senator or Representative shall, during the Time for which he was elected, be appointed to any civil Office under the Authority of the United States, which shall have been created, or the Emoluments whereof shall have been increased during such time; and no Person holding any Office under the United States, shall be a Member of either House during his Continuance in Office.

Section 7. All Bills for raising Revenue shall originate in the House of Representatives; but the Senate may propose or concur with Amendments as on other Bills.

Every Bill which shall have passed the House of Representatives and the Senate, shall, before it become a Law, be presented to the President of the United States; If he approve he shall sign it, but if not he shall return it, with his Objections to the House in which it shall have originated, who shall enter the Objections at large on their Journal, and proceed to reconsider it. If after such Reconsideration two thirds of that House shall agree to pass the Bill, it shall be sent together with the Objections, to the other House, by which it shall likewise be reconsidered, and if approved by two thirds of that House, it shall become a Law. But in all such Cases the Votes of both Houses shall be determined by Yeas and Nays, and the Names of the Persons voting for and against the Bill shall be entered on the Journal of each House respectively. If any Bill shall not be returned by the President within ten Days (Sundays excepted) after it shall have been presented to him, the Same shall be a Law, in like Manner as if he had signed it, unless the Congress by their Adjournment prevent its Return in which Case it shall not be a Law.

Every Order, Resolution, or Vote, to which the Concurrence of the Senate and House of Representatives may be necessary (except on a question of Adjournment) shall be presented to the President of the United States; and before the Same shall take Effect, shall be approved by him, or being disapproved by him, shall be repassed by two thirds of the Senate and House of Representatives, according to the Rules and Limitations prescribed in the Case of a Bill.

Section 8. The Congress shall have Power To lay and collect Taxes, Duties, Imposts and Excises, to pay the Debts and provide for the common Defence and general Welfare of the United States; but all Duties, Imposts and Excises shall be uniform throughout the United States;

To borrow Money on the credit of the United States;

To regulate Commerce with foreign Nations, and among the several States, and with the Indian Tribes;

To establish an uniform Rule of Naturalization, and uniform Laws on the subject of Bankruptcies throughout the United States;

To coin Money, regulate the Value thereof, and of foreign Coin, and fix the Standard of Weights and Measures;

To provide for the Punishment of counterfeiting the Securities and current Coin of the United States;

To establish Post Offices and post Roads;

To promote the Progress of Science and useful Arts, by securing for limited Times to Authors and Inventors the exclusive Right to their respective Writings and Discoveries;

To constitute Tribunals inferior to the supreme Court;

To define and punish Piracies and Felonies committed on the high Seas, and Offenses against the Law of Nations;

To declare War, grant Letters of Marque and Reprisal, and make Rules concerning Captures on Land and Water;

To raise and support Armies, but no Appropriation of Money to that Use shall be for a longer Term than two Years;

To provide and maintain a Navy;

To make Rules for the Government and Regulation of the land and naval Forces;

To provide for calling forth the Militia to execute the Laws of the Union, suppress Insurrections and repel Invasions;

To provide for organizing, arming, and disciplining, the Militia, and for governing such Part of them as may be employed in the Service of the United States, reserving to the States respectively, the Appointment of the Officers, and the Authority of training the Militia according to the discipline prescribed by Congress;

To exercise exclusive Legislation in all Cases whatsoever, over such District (not exceeding ten Miles square) as may, by Cession of particular States, and the Acceptance of Congress, become the Seat of the Government of the United States, and to exercise like Authority over all Places purchased by the Consent of the Legislature of the State in which the Same shall be, for the Erection of Forts, Magazines, Arsenals, dock-Yards, and other needful Buildings;—And

To make all Laws which shall be necessary and proper for carrying into Execution the foregoing Powers, and all other Powers vested by this Constitution in the Government of the United States, or in any Department or Officer thereof.

Section 9. The Migration or Importation of such Persons as any of the States now existing shall think proper to admit, shall not be prohibited by the Congress prior to the Year one thousand eight hundred and eight, but a Tax or duty may be imposed on such Importation, not exceeding ten dollars for each Person.

The privilege of the Writ of Habeas Corpus shall not be suspended, unless when in Cases of Rebellion or Invasion the public Safety may require it.

No Bill of Attainder or ex post facto Law shall be passed.

No Capitation, or other direct, Tax shall be laid, unless in Proportion to the Census or Enumeration herein before directed to be taken.

No Tax or Duty shall be laid on Articles exported from any State.

No Preference shall be given by any Regulation of Commerce or Revenue to the Ports of one State over those of another: nor shall Vessels bound to, or from, one State be obliged to enter, clear, or pay Duties in another.

No Money shall be drawn from the Treasury, but in Consequence of Appropriations made by Law; and a regular Statement and Account of the Receipts and Expenditures of all public Money shall be published from time to time.

No Title of Nobility shall be granted by the United States: And no Person holding any Office of Profit or Trust under them, shall, without the Consent of the Congress, accept of any present, Emolument, Office, or Title, of any kind whatever, from any King, Prince, or foreign State.

Section 10. No State shall enter into any Treaty, Alliance, or Confederation; grant Letters of Marque and Reprisal; coin Money; emit Bills of Credit; make any Thing but gold and silver Coin a Tender in Payment of Debts; pass any Bill of Attainder, ex post facto Law, or Law impairing the Obligation of Contracts, or grant any Title of Nobility.

No State shall, without the Consent of the Congress, lay any Imposts or Duties on Imports or Exports, except what may be absolutely necessary for executing it's inspection Laws: and the net Produce of all Duties and Imposts, laid by any State on Imports or Exports, shall be for the Use of the Treasury of the United States; and all such Laws shall be subject to the Revision and Control of the Congress.

No State shall, without the Consent of Congress, lay any Duty of Tonnage, keep Troops, or Ships of War in time of Peace, enter into any Agreement or Compact with another State, or with a foreign Power, or engage in War, unless actually invaded, or in such imminent Danger as will not admit of delay.

Article II

Section 1. The executive Power shall be vested in a President of the United States of America. He shall hold his Office during the Term of four Years, and, together with the Vice President, chosen for the same Term, be elected, as follows:

Each State shall appoint, in such Manner as the Legislature thereof may direct, a Number of Electors, equal to the whole Number of Senators and Representatives to which the State may be entitled in the Congress; but no

Senator or Representative, or Person holding an Office of Trust or Profit under the United States, shall be appointed an Elector.

The Electors shall meet in their respective States, and vote by Ballot for two Persons, of whom one at least shall not be an Inhabitant of the same State with themselves. And they shall make a List of all the Persons voted for, and of the Number of Votes for each; which List they shall sign and certify, and transmit sealed to the Seat of the Government of the United States, directed to the President of the Senate. The President of the Senate shall, in the Presence of the Senate and House of Representatives, open all the Certificates, and the Votes shall then be counted. The Person having the greatest Number of Votes shall be the President, if such Number be a Majority of the whole Number of Electors appointed; and if there be more than one who have such Majority, and have an equal Number of Votes, then the House of Representatives shall immediately choose by Ballot one of them for President; and if no Person have a Majority, then from the five highest on the List the said House shall in like Manner choose the President. But in choosing the President, the Votes shall be taken by States, the Representation from each State having one Vote; A quorum for this Purpose shall consist of a Member or Members from two thirds of the States, and a Majority of all the States shall be necessary to a Choice. In every Case, after the Choice of the President, the Person having the greater Number of Votes of the Electors shall be the Vice President. But if there should remain two or more who have equal Votes, the Senate shall choose from them by Ballot the Vice President.

The Congress may determine the Time of choosing the Electors, and the Day on which they shall give their Votes; which Day shall be the same throughout the United States.

No person except a natural born Citizen, or a Citizen of the United States, at the time of the Adoption of this Constitution, shall be eligible to the Office of President; neither shall any Person be eligible to that Office who shall not have attained to the Age of thirty five Years, and been fourteen Years a Resident within the United States.

In Case of the Removal of the President from Office, or of his Death, Resignation or Inability to discharge the Powers and Duties of the said Office, the same shall devolve on the Vice President, and the Congress may by Law provide for the Case of Removal, Death, Resignation or Inability, both of the President and Vice President, declaring what Officer shall then act as President, and such Officer shall act accordingly, until the Disability be removed, or a President shall be elected.

The President shall, at stated Times, receive for his Services, a Compensation, which shall neither be increased nor diminished during the Period for which he shall have been elected, and he shall not receive within that Period any other Emolument from the United States, or any of them.

Before he enter on the Execution of his Office, he shall take the following Oath or Affirmation: "I do solemnly swear (or affirm) that I will faithfully execute the Office of President of the United States, and will to the best of my Ability, preserve, protect and defend the Constitution of the United States."

Section 2. The President shall be Commander in Chief of the Army and Navy of the United States, and of the Militia of the several States, when called into the actual Service of the United States; he may require the Opinion, in writing, of the principal Officer in each of the executive Departments, upon any Subject relating to the Duties of their respective Offices, and he shall have Power to grant Reprieves and Pardons for Offenses against the United States, except in Cases of Impeachment.

He shall have Power, by and with the Advice and Consent of the Senate to make Treaties, provided two thirds of the Senators present concur; and he shall nominate, and by and with the Advice and Consent of the Senate, shall appoint Ambassadors, other public Ministers and Consuls, Judges of the supreme Court, and all other Officers of the United States, whose Appointments are not herein otherwise provided for, and which shall be established by Law; but the Congress may by Law vest the Appointment of such inferior Officers, as they think proper, in the President alone, in the Courts of Law, or in the Heads of Departments.

The President shall have Power to fill up all Vacancies that may happen during the Recess of the Senate, by granting Commissions which shall expire at the End of their next Session.

Section 3. He shall from time to time give to the Congress Information of the State of the Union, and recommend to their Consideration such Measures as he shall judge necessary and expedient; he may, on extraordinary Occasions, convene both Houses, or either of them, and in Case of Disagreement between them, with Respect to the Time of Adjournment, he may adjourn them to such Time as he shall think proper; he shall receive Ambassadors and other public Ministers; he shall take Care that the Laws be faithfully executed, and shall Commission all the Officers of the United States.

Section 4. The President, Vice President and all civil Officers of the United States, shall be removed from Office on Impeachment for, and Conviction of, Treason, Bribery, or other high Crimes and Misdemeanors.

Article III

Section 1. The judicial Power of the United States, shall be vested in one supreme Court, and in such inferior Courts as the Congress may from time to time ordain and establish. The Judges, both of the supreme and inferior Courts, shall hold their Offices during good Behavior, and shall, at stated Times, receive for their Services a Compensation, which shall not be diminished during their Continuance in Office.

Section 2. The judicial Power shall extend to all Cases, in Law and Equity, arising under this Constitution, the Laws of the United States, and Treaties made, or which shall be made, under their Authority;—to all Cases affecting Ambassadors, other public Ministers and Consuls;—to all Cases of admiralty and maritime Jurisdiction;—to Controversies to which the United States shall be a Party;—to Controversies between two or more States;—between a State and Citizens of another State;—between Citizens of different States;—between Citizens of the same State claiming Lands under Grants of different States, and between a State, or the Citizens thereof, and foreign States, Citizens or Subjects.

In all Cases affecting Ambassadors, other public Ministers and Consuls, and those in which a State shall be a Party, the supreme Court shall have original Jurisdiction. In all the other Cases before mentioned, the supreme Court shall have appellate Jurisdiction, both as to Law and Fact, with such Exceptions, and under such Regulations as the Congress shall make.

The Trial of all Crimes, except in Cases of Impeachment, shall be by Jury; and such Trial shall be held in the State where the said Crimes shall have been committed; but when not committed within any State, the Trial shall be at such Place or Places as the Congress may by Law have directed.

Section 3. Treason against the United States, shall consist only in levying War against them, or, in adhering to their Enemies, giving them Aid and Comfort. No Person shall be convicted of Treason unless on the Testimony of two Witnesses to the same overt Act, or on Confession in open Court.

The Congress shall have Power to declare the Punishment of Treason, but no Attainder of Treason shall work Corruption of Blood, or Forfeiture except during the Life of the Person attainted.

Article IV

Section 1. Full Faith and Credit shall be given in each State to the public Acts, Records, and judicial Proceedings of every other State. And the Congress may by general Laws prescribe the Manner in which such Acts, Records and Proceedings shall be proved, and the Effect thereof.

Section 2. The Citizens of each State shall be entitled to all Privileges and Immunities of Citizens in the several States.

A Person charged in any State with Treason, Felony, or other Crime, who shall flee from Justice, and be found in another State, shall on Demand of the executive Authority of the State from which he fled, be delivered up, to be removed to the State having Jurisdiction of the Crime.

No Person held to Service or Labour in one State, under the Laws thereof, escaping into another, shall, in Consequence of any Law or Regulation therein, be discharged from such Service or Labor, but shall be delivered up on Claim of the Party to whom such Service or Labor may be due.

Section 3. New States may be admitted by the Congress into this Union; but no new State shall be formed or erected within the Jurisdiction of any other State; nor any State be formed by the Junction of two or more States, or Parts of States, without the Consent of the Legislatures of the States concerned as well as of the Congress.

The Congress shall have Power to dispose of and make all needful Rules and Regulations respecting the Territory or other Property belonging to the United States; and nothing in this Constitution shall be so construed as to Prejudice any Claims of the United States, or of any particular State.

Section 4. The United States shall guarantee to every State in this Union a Republican Form of Government, and shall protect each of them against Invasion; and on Application of the Legislature, or of the Executive (when the Legislature cannot be convened) against domestic Violence.

Article V

The Congress, whenever two thirds of both Houses shall deem it necessary, shall propose Amendments to this Constitution, or, on the Application of the Legislatures of two thirds of the several States, shall call a Convention for proposing Amendments, which, in either Case, shall be valid to all Intents and Purposes, as part of this Constitution, when ratified by the Legislatures of three fourths of the several States, or by Conventions in three fourths thereof, as the one or the other Mode of Ratification may be proposed by the Congress; Provided that no Amendment which may be made prior to the Year One thousand eight hundred and eight shall in any Manner affect the first and fourth Clauses in the Ninth Section of the first Article; and that no State, without its Consent, shall be deprived of its equal Suffrage in the Senate.

Article VI

All Debts contracted and Engagements entered into, before the Adoption of this Constitution shall be as valid against the United States under this Constitution, as under the Confederation.

This Constitution, and the Laws of the United States which shall be made in Pursuance thereof; and all Treaties made, or which shall be made, under the Authority of the United States, shall be the supreme Law of the Land; and the Judges in every State shall be bound thereby, any Thing in the Constitution or Laws of any State to the Contrary notwithstanding.

The Senators and Representatives before mentioned, and the Members of the several State Legislatures, and all executive and judicial Officers, both of the United States and of the several States, shall be bound by Oath or Affirmation, to support this Constitution; but no religious Test shall ever be required as a Qualification to any Office or public Trust under the United States.

Article VII

The Ratification of the Conventions of nine States shall be sufficient for the Establishment of this Constitution between the States so ratifying the Same.

Amendment I [1791]

Congress shall make no law respecting an establishment of religion, or prohibiting the free exercise thereof; or abridging the freedom of speech, or of the press; or the right of the people peaceably to assembly, and to petition the Government for a redress of grievances.

Amendment II [1791]

A well regulated Militia, being necessary to the security of a free State, the right of the people to keep and bear Arms, shall not be infringed.

Amendment III [1791]

No Soldier shall, in time of peace be quartered in any house, without the consent of the Owner, nor in time of war, but in a manner to be prescribed by law.

Amendment IV [1791]

The right of the people to be secure in their persons, houses, papers, and effects, against unreasonable searches and seizures, shall not be violated, and no Warrants shall issue, but upon probable cause, supported by Oath or affirmation, and particularly describing the place to be searched, and the persons or things to be seized.

Amendment V [1791]

No person shall be held to answer for a capital, or otherwise infamous crime, unless on a presentment or indictment of a Grand Jury, except in cases arising in the land or naval forces, or in the Militia, when in actual service in time of War or public danger; nor shall any person be subject for the same offence to be twice put in jeopardy of life or limb; nor shall be compelled in any criminal case to be a witness against himself, nor be deprived of life, liberty, or property, without due process of law; nor shall private property be taken for public use, without just compensation.

Amendment VI [1791]

In all criminal prosecutions, the accused shall enjoy the right to a speedy and public trial, by an impartial jury of the State and district wherein the crime shall have been committed, which district shall have been previously ascertained by law, and to be informed of the nature and cause of the accusation; to be confronted with the witnesses against him; to have compulsory process for obtaining witnesses in his favor, and to have the Assistance of Counsel for his defence.

Amendment VII [1791]

In Suits at common law, where the value in controversy shall exceed twenty dollars, the right of trial by jury shall be preserved, and no fact tried by jury, shall be otherwise re-examined in any Court of the United States, than according to the rules of the common law.

Amendment VIII [1791]

Excessive bail shall not be required, nor excessive fines imposed, nor cruel and unusual punishments inflicted.

Amendment IX [1791]

The enumeration in the Constitution, of certain rights, shall not be construed to deny or disparage others retained by the people.

Amendment X [1791]

The powers not delegated to the United States by the Constitution, nor prohibited by it to the States, are reserved to the States respectively, or to the people.

Amendment XI [1798]

The Judicial power of the United States shall not be construed to extend to any suit in law or equity, commenced or prosecuted against one of the United States by Citizens of another State, or by Citizens or Subjects of any Foreign State.

Amendment XII [1804]

The Electors shall meet in their respective states, and vote by ballot for President and Vice-President, one of whom, at least, shall not be an inhabitant of the same state with themselves; they shall name in their ballots the person voted for as President, and in distinct ballots the person voted for as Vice-President, and they shall make distinct lists of all persons voted for as President, and of all persons voted for as Vice-President, and of the number of votes for each, which lists they shall sign and certify, and transmit sealed to the seat of the government of the United States, directed to the President of the Senate;—The President of the Senate shall, in the presence of the Senate and House of Representatives, open all the certificates and the votes shall then be counted;—The person having the greatest number of votes for President, shall be the President, if such number be a majority of the whole number of Electors appointed; and if no person have such majority, then from the persons having the highest numbers not exceeding three on the list of those voted for as President, the House of Representatives shall choose immediately, by ballot, the President. But in choosing the President, the votes shall be taken by states, the representation from each state having one vote; a quorum for this purpose shall consist of a member or members from two-thirds of the states, and a majority of all states shall be necessary to a choice. And if the House of Representatives shall not choose a President whenever the right of choice shall devolve upon them, before the fourth day of March next following, then the Vice-President shall act as President, as in the case of the death or other constitutional disability of the President.—The person having the greatest number of votes as Vice-President, shall be the Vice-President, if such number be a majority of the whole number of Electors appointed, and if no person have a majority, then from the two highest numbers on the list, the Senate shall choose the Vice-President; a quorum for the purpose shall consist of two-thirds of the whole number of Senators, and a majority of the whole number shall be necessary to a choice. But no person constitutionally ineligible to the office of President shall be eligible to that of Vice-President of the United States.

Amendment XIII [1865]

Section 1. Neither slavery nor involuntary servitude, except as a punishment for crime whereof the party shall have been duly convicted, shall exist within the United States, or any place subject to their jurisdiction.

Section 2. Congress shall have power to enforce this article by appropriate legislation.

Amendment XIV [1868]

Section 1. All persons born or naturalized in the United States, and subject to the jurisdiction thereof, are citizens of the United States and of the State wherein they reside. No State shall make or enforce any law which shall abridge the privileges or immunities of citizens of the United States; nor shall any State deprive any person of life, liberty, or property, without due process of law; nor deny to any person within its jurisdiction the equal protection of the laws.

Section 2. Representatives shall be apportioned among the several States according to their respective numbers, counting the whole number of persons in each State, excluding Indians not taxed. But when the right to vote at any election for the choice of electors for President and Vice President of the United States, Representatives in Congress, the Executive and Judicial officers of a State, or the members of the Legislature thereof, is denied to any of the male inhabitants of such State, being twenty-one years of age, and citizens of the United States, or in any way abridged, except for participation in rebellion, or other crime, the basis of representation therein shall be reduced in the proportion which the number of such male citizens shall bear to the whole number of male citizens twenty-one years of age in such State.

Section 3. No person shall be a Senator or Representative in Congress, or elector of President and Vice President, or hold any office, civil or military, under the United States, or under any State, who having previously taken an oath, as a member of Congress, or as an officer of the United States, or as a member of any State legislature, or as an executive or judicial officer of any State, to support the Constitution of the United States, shall have engaged in insurrection or rebellion against the same, or given aid or comfort to the enemies thereof. But Congress may by a vote of two-thirds of each House, remove such disability.

Section 4. The validity of the public debt of the United States, authorized by law, including debts incurred for payment of pensions and bounties for services in suppressing insurrection or rebellion, shall not be questioned. But neither the United States nor any State shall assume or pay any debt or obligation incurred in aid of insurrection or rebellion against the United States, or any claim for the loss or emancipation of any slave; but all such debts, obligations and claims shall be held illegal and void.

Section 5. The Congress shall have power to enforce, by appropriate legislation, the provisions of this article.

Amendment XV [1870]

Section 1. The right of citizens of the United States to vote shall not be denied or abridged by the United States or by any State on account of race, color, or previous condition of servitude.

Section 2. The Congress shall have power to enforce this article by appropriate legislation.

Amendment XVI [1913]

The Congress shall have power to lay and collect taxes on incomes, from whatever source derived, without apportionment among the several States, and without regard to any census or enumeration.

Amendment XVII [1913]

Section 1. The Senate of the United States shall be composed of two Senators from each State, elected by the people thereof, for six years; and each Senator shall have one vote. The electors in each State shall have the qualifications requisite for electors of the most numerous branch of the State legislatures.

Section 2. When vacancies happen in the representation of any State in the Senate, the executive authority of such State shall issue writs of election to fill such vacancies: Provided, That the legislature of any State may empower the executive thereof to make temporary appointments until the people fill the vacancies by election as the legislature may direct.

Section 3. This amendment shall not be so construed as to affect the election or term of any Senator chosen before it becomes valid as part of the Constitution.

Amendment XVIII [1919]

Section 1. After one year from the ratification of this article the manufacture, sale, or transportation of intoxicating liquors within, the importation thereof into, or the exportation thereof from the United States and all territory subject to the jurisdiction thereof for beverage purposes is hereby prohibited.

Section 2. The Congress and the several States shall have concurrent power to enforce this article by appropriate legislation.

Section 3. This article shall be inoperative unless it shall have been ratified as an amendment to the Constitution by the legislatures of the several States, as provided in the Constitution, within seven years from the date of the submission hereof to the States by the Congress.

Amendment XIX [1920]

Section 1. The right of citizens of the United States to vote shall not be denied or abridged by the United States or by any State on account of sex.

Section 2. Congress shall have power to enforce this article by appropriate legislation.

Amendment XX [1933]

Section 1. The terms of the President and Vice President shall end at noon on the 20th day of January, and the terms of Senators and Representatives at noon on the 3d day of January, of the years in which such terms would have ended if this article had not been ratified; and the terms of their successors shall then begin.

Section 2. The Congress shall assemble at least once in every year, and such meeting shall begin at noon on the 3d day of January, unless they shall by law appoint a different day.

Section 3. If, at the time fixed for the beginning of the term of the President, the President elect shall have died, the Vice President elect shall become President. If the President shall not have been chosen before the time fixed for the beginning of his term, or if the President elect shall have failed to qualify, then the Vice President elect shall act as President until a President shall have qualified; and the Congress may by law provide for the case wherein neither a President elect nor a Vice President elect shall have qualified, declaring who shall then act as President, or the manner in which one who is to act shall be selected, and such person shall act accordingly until a President or Vice President shall have qualified.

Section 4. The Congress may by law provide for the case of the death of any of the persons from whom the House of Representatives may choose a President whenever the right of choice shall have devolved upon them, and for the case of the death of any of the persons from whom the Senate may choose a Vice President whenever the right of choice shall have devolved upon them.

Section 5. Sections 1 and 2 shall take effect on the 15th day of October following the ratification of this article.

Section 6. This article shall be inoperative unless it shall have been ratified as an amendment to the Constitution by the legislatures of three-fourths of the several States within seven years from the date of its submission.

Amendment XXI [1933]

Section 1. The eighteenth article of amendment to the Constitution of the United States is hereby repealed.

Section 2. The transportation or importation into any State, Territory, or possession of the United States for delivery or use therein of intoxicating liquors, in violation of the laws thereof, is hereby prohibited.

Section 3. This article shall be inoperative unless it shall have been ratified as an amendment to the Constitution by conventions in the several States, as provided in the Constitution, within seven years from the date of the submission hereof to the States by the Congress.

Amendment XXII [1951]

Section 1. No person shall be elected to the office of the President more than twice, and no person who has held the office of President, or acted as President, for more than two years of a term to which some other person was elected President shall be elected to the office of President more than once. But this Article shall not apply to any person holding the office of President when this Article was proposed by the Congress, and shall not prevent any person who may be holding the office of President, or acting as President, during the term within which this Article becomes operative from holding the office of President or acting as President during the remainder of such term.

Section 2. This article shall be inoperative unless it shall have been ratified as an amendment to the Constitution by the legislatures of three-fourths of the several States within seven years from the date of its submission to the States by the Congress.

Amendment XXIII [1961]

Section 1. The District constituting the seat of Government of the United States shall appoint in such manner as the Congress may direct:

A number of electors of President and Vice President equal to the whole number of Senators and Representatives in Congress to which the District would be entitled if it were a State, but in no event more than the least populous state; they shall be in addition to those appointed by the states, but they shall be considered, for the purposes of the election of President and Vice President, to be electors appointed by a state; and they shall meet in the District and perform such duties as provided by the twelfth article of amendment.

Section 2. The Congress shall have power to enforce this article by appropriate legislation.

Amendment XXIV [1964]

Section 1. The right of citizens of the United States to vote in any primary or other election for President or Vice President, for electors for President or Vice President, or for Senator or Representative in Congress, shall not be denied or abridged by the United States, or any State by reason of failure to pay any poll tax or other tax.

Section 2. The Congress shall have power to enforce this article by appropriate legislation.

Amendment XXV [1967]

Section 1. In case of the removal of the President from office or of his death or resignation, the Vice President shall become President.

Section 2. Whenever there is a vacancy in the office of the Vice President, the President shall nominate a Vice President who shall take office upon confirmation by a majority vote of both Houses of Congress.

Section 3. Whenever the President transmits to the President pro tempore of the Senate and the Speaker of the House of Representatives his written declaration that he is unable to discharge the powers and duties of his office, and until he transmits to them a written declaration to the contrary, such powers and duties shall be discharged by the Vice President as Acting President.

Section 4. Whenever the Vice President and a majority of either the principal officers of the executive departments or of such other body as Congress may by law provide, transmit to the President pro tempore of the Senate and the Speaker of the House of Representatives their written declaration that the President is unable to discharge the powers and duties of his office, the Vice President shall immediately assume the powers and duties of the office as Acting President.

Thereafter, when the President transmits to the President pro tempore of the Senate and the Speaker of the House of Representatives his written declaration that no inability exists, he shall resume the powers and duties of his office unless the Vice President and a majority of either the principal officers of the executive department or of such other body as Congress may by law provide, transmit within four days to the President pro tempore of the Senate and the Speaker of the House of Representatives their written declaration and the President is unable to discharge the powers and duties of his office. Thereupon Congress shall decide the issue, assembling within forty-eight hours for that purpose if not in session. If the Congress, within twenty-one days after receipt of the latter written declaration, or, if Congress is not in session, within twenty-one days after Congress is required to assemble, determines by two-thirds vote of both Houses that the President is unable to discharge the powers and duties of his office, the Vice President shall continue to discharge the same as Acting President; otherwise, the President shall resume the powers and duties of his office.

Amendment XXVI [1971]

Section 1. The right of citizens of the United States, who are eighteen years of age or older, to vote shall not be denied or abridged by the United States or by any State on account of age.

Section 2. The Congress shall have power to enforce this article by appropriate legislation.

TABLE OF CASES

NAME INDEX

SUBJECT INDEX

Photos; **465** Bob Daemmrich/Stock, Boston; **466** AP/Wide World Photos; **474** ©Stacy Dick/Stock, Boston; **476** Library of Congress; **483** Curt Frankenstein, *Judicial Wheel of Fortune*, ©1980 West Publishing Company; **489** UPI/Bettmann Newsphotos; **496** AP/Wide World Photos; **502** Gamma/Liaison; **509** AP/Wide World Photos; **526** Charles Houseman, *Driver*, ©1980 West Publishing Company; **534** ©Harry Gustafson; **544** AP/Wide World Photos; **549** J. P. Laffont/Sygma; **553** photo courtesy of Digital Products Corporation; **561** Louis Bertrand *Tribunal French Guiana*, © 1981 West Publishing Company; **566** AP/Wide World Photos; **574** ©1990 Lester Sloan/Woodfin Camp & Associates, Inc.; **577** ©Steve Starr/Picture Group; **579** ©Harry Gustafson; **588** Jerry Rudquist, *Captive/Captor*, ©1986 West Publishing Company; **594** AP/Wide World Photos; **602** AP/Wide World Photos; **604** ©Scott Thode/JB Pictures; **614** ©Tom Stoddart/Woodfin Camp & Associates, Inc.; **627** Barbara Dixon Drewa, *Pools of Memory*, ©1989 West Publishing Company; **632** ©Harry Gustafson; **639** Bettmann Archive; **645** ©Wayne Miles/Liaison; **654** Daniel O'Sullivan, *Playing Knuckles*, ©1989 West Publishing Company; **657** ©1990 Doug Burrows, Gamma Liaison; **660** ©Barbara Alper/Stock, Boston; **676** ©Deborah Copaken/Gamma Liaison; **687** ©Brent Jones 1991.

DATE			